CRIMINOLOGY

CRIMINOLOGY

Seventh Edition

Freda Adler
University of Pennsylvania

Gerhard O. W. Mueller
Rutgers University

William S. Laufer
University of Pennsylvania

The McGraw·Hill Companies

Connect
Learn
Succeed™

Published by McGraw-Hill, an imprint of The McGraw-Hill Companies, Inc., 1221 Avenue of the Americas, New York, NY 10020. Copyright © 2010, 2007, 2004, 2001, 1998, 1995, 1991. All rights reserved. No part of this publication may be reproduced or distributed in any form or by any means, or stored in a database or retrieval system, without the prior written consent of The McGraw-Hill Companies, Inc., including, but not limited to, in any network or other electronic storage or transmission, or broadcast for distance learning.

This book is printed on acid-free paper.

2 3 4 5 6 7 8 9 0 DOW/DOW 0

ISBN: 978-0-07-340158-4
MHID: 0-07-340158-7

Editor in Chief: *Michael Ryan*
Sponsoring Editor: *Katie Stevens*
Marketing Manager: *Leslie Oberhuber*
Developmental Editor: *Kate Scheinman*
Production Editor: *Holly Paulsen*
Manuscript Editor: *Mary Roybal*
Design Manager: *Allister Fein*
Text Designer: *Linda M. Robertson*
Cover Designer: *Allister Fein*
Photo Research: *Pamela Carley*
Production Supervisor: *Louis Swaim*
Media Project Manager: *Vivek Iyer*
Composition: *9.5/11 Palatino by Laserwords*
Printing: *45# New Era Thin, RR Donnelley*

Cover: © Andre Burian/SuperStock

Credits: The credits section for this book begins on page C-1 and is considered an extension of the copyright page.

Library of Congress Cataloging-in-Publication Data has been applied for.

The Internet addresses listed in the text were accurate at the time of publication. The inclusion of a Web site does not indicate an endorsement by the authors or McGraw-Hill, and McGraw-Hill does not guarantee the accuracy of the information presented at these sites.

www.mhhe.com

About the Authors

FREDA ADLER is Visiting Professor and Director, Master of Science Program in Criminology, University of Pennsylvania, and Emeritus Distinguished Professor of Criminal Justice at Rutgers University, School of Criminal Justice. She received her B.A. in sociology, her M.A. in criminology, and her Ph.D. in sociology from the University of Pennsylvania. Dr. Adler began her career in criminal justice as an evaluator of drug and alcohol treatment programs for federal and state governments. She has been teaching since 1968; her subjects include criminal justice, criminology, comparative criminal justice systems, statistics, and research methods. She has served as criminal justice advisor to the United Nations, as well as to federal, state, and foreign governments. Dr. Adler's published works include 15 books as author or coauthor, 10 books as editor or coeditor, and over 80 journal articles. She has served on the editorial boards of the *Journal of Criminal Justice, Criminology,* and the *Journal of Research on Crime and Delinquency.* Dr. Adler is editorial consultant to the *Journal of Criminal Law and Criminology* and is coeditor of *Advances in Criminological Theory.* She has also served as president of the American Society of Criminology (1994–1995).

GERHARD O. W. MUELLER is the late Distinguished Professor of Criminal Justice at Rutgers University, School of Criminal Justice. After earning his J.D. degree from the University of Chicago, he went on to receive a master of laws degree from Columbia University. He was awarded the degree of Dr. Jur. h. c. by the University of Uppsala, Sweden. His career in criminal justice began in 1945, when he served as a chief petty officer in the British Military government Water Police, where he commanded a Coast Guard cutter. His teaching in criminal justice, begun in 1953, was partially interrupted between 1974 and 1982 when, as Chief of the United Nations Crime Prevention and Criminal Justice Branch, he was responsible for all of the United Nations' programs dealing with problems of crime and justice worldwide. He continued his service to the United Nations as chair ad interim of the Board of the International Scientific and Professional Advisory Council of the United Nations Crime Prevention and Criminal Justice Programme. Professor Mueller was a member of the faculties of law at the University of Washington, West Virginia University, New York University, and the National Judicial College, with visiting appointments and lectureships at universities and institutes in the Americas, western and eastern Europe, Africa, Asia, and Australia. He was the author of some 50 authored or edited books and 270 scholarly articles.

WILLIAM S. LAUFER is the Julian Aresty Professor at the Wharton School of the University of Pennsylvania, where he is Professor of Legal Studies and Business Ethics, Sociology, and Criminology. Dr. Laufer, graduate chair of the Department of Criminology at Penn, received his B.A. in social and behavioral sciences at Johns Hopkins University, his J.D. at Northeastern University School of Law, and his Ph.D. at Rutgers University, School of Criminal Justice. Dr. Laufer's research has appeared in law reviews and a wide range of criminal justice, legal, and psychology journals, including *Journal of Research in Crime and Delinquency, American Journal of Criminal Law, Law and Human Behavior, Journal of Personality and Social Psychology,* and *Business Ethics Quarterly.* His most recent book is *Corporate Bodies and Guilty Minds: The Failure of Corporate Criminal Liability* (University of Chicago Press). Dr. Laufer is coeditor of the *Handbook of Psychology and Law; Personality, Moral Development and Criminal Behavior;* and *Crime, Values and Religion.* He is series coeditor with Freda Adler of *Advances in Criminological Theory.*

To: *David S., Daniel A., Julia A., Noah A., Zoe A., Hannah M., Nicolai A., John J., Lauren E., Stephen W., Anna L., Erik D., Johann D., Sasha K., Misha K.*

Brief Contents

List of Boxes   xix

Preface   xx

PART I Understanding Criminology   1

1 The Changing Boundaries of Criminology   3

2 Counting Crime and Measuring Criminal Behavior   21

3 Schools of Thought throughout History   52

PART II Explanations of Crime and Criminal Behavior   71

4 Biological and Psychological Perspectives   73

5 Strain and Cultural Deviance Theories   102

6 The Formation of Subcultures   128

7 Social Control Theory   153

8 Labeling, Conflict, and Radical Theories   173

9 Environmental Theory   194

PART III Types of Crimes   217

10 Violent Crimes   219

11 Crimes against Property   267

12 White-Collar and Corporate Crime   296

13 Public Order Crimes   327

14 International and Comparative Criminology   356

PART IV* A Criminological Approach to the Criminal Justice System

15 Processes and Decisions

16 Enforcing the Law: Practice and Research

17 The Nature and Functioning of Courts

18 A Research Focus on Corrections

Notes   N-1

Glossary   G-1

Credits   C-1

Indexes   I-1

---

*Part IV, Chapters 15–18, are available only at the Instructor Edition of the Online Learning Center: **www.mhhe.com/adlercrim7e.**

Contents

List of Boxes   xix
Preface   xx

PART I Understanding Criminology   1

1 The Changing Boundaries of Criminology   3

The Changing Boundaries of Criminology   4
   Terrorism   4
   Illicit Drug Trafficking   5
   Money Laundering   5
   Infiltration of Legal Business   6
   Computer Crime   7
   Illicit Arms Trafficking   7
   Trafficking in Persons   7
   Destruction of Cultural Property   8
   The Reach of Criminology   8

What Is Criminology?   10

The Making of Laws   11
   Deviance   11
   The Concept of Crime   12
   The Consensus and Conflict Views of Law and Crime   14

The Breaking of Laws   15

Society's Reaction to the Breaking of Laws   16
   Criminology and the Criminal Justice System   17
   The Global Approach to the Breaking of Laws   18

Research Informs Policy   19

BOXES
   World News: *In the Words of Al Qaeda: What Else Is There to Say about September 11?*   6
   Window to the World: *Terrorism and the Fear of Terrorism*   12
   Debatable Issues: *Fame and Crime*   16

Review   19
Criminology & Public Policy   20
You Be the Criminologist   20
Key Terms   20

2 Counting Crime and Measuring Criminal Behavior   21

The Ingredients of Crime   22
   The Act Requirement   22
   The Legality Requirement   23
   The Harm Requirement   23
   The Causation Requirement   24
   Mens Rea: The "Guilty Mind" Requirement   24
   The Concurrence Requirement   25
   The Punishment Requirement   25

The Defenses 25

Typologies of Crime 26

Measuring Crime 26
    Methods of Collecting Data 27
    Ethics and the Researcher 31

The Nature and Extent of Crime 32
    Police Statistics 32
    Victimization Surveys 34
    Self-Report Surveys 35

Measuring Characteristics of Crime 37
    Crime Trends 37
    Locations and Times of Criminal Acts 38
    Severity of Crime 40

Measuring Characteristics of Criminals 40
    Age and Crime 41
    Gender and Crime 46
    Social Class and Crime 48
    Race and Crime 49

BOXES
    World News: *Statistics Watchdog Chief Accuses Home Office of Abusing Crime Statistics* 34
    Debatable Issues: *Murder Spike Poses Quandary* 40
    Window to the World: *Victims around the World* 44

Review 50
Criminology & Public Policy 50
You Be the Criminologist 51
Key Terms 51

3 Schools of Thought throughout History 52

Classical Criminology 53
    The Historical Context 53
    Cesare Beccaria 55
    Jeremy Bentham's Utilitarianism 57
    The Classical School: An Evaluation 57

Positivist Criminology 58

Biological Determinism: The Search for Criminal Traits 59
    Lombroso, Ferri, Garofalo: The Italian School 60
    A Return to Biological Determinism 63

Psychological Determinism 65
    Pioneers in Criminal Psychology 65
    Psychological Studies of Criminals 65

Sociological Determinism 65
    Adolphe Quételet and André Michel Guerry 65
    Gabriel Tarde 66
    Émile Durkheim 67

Historical and Contemporary Criminology: A Time Line 68

The Future of Our History 68

BOXES
    Window to the World: *Stone Age Crime and Social Control* 54
    Debatable Issues: *Utilitarianism Gone Astray* 58
    World News: *Who's Responsible?* 66

Review 70
Criminology & Public Policy 70
You Be the Criminologist 70
Key Terms 70

PART II Explanations of Crime and Criminal Behavior 71

4 Biological and Psychological Perspectives 73

Biology and Criminality 75
  Modern Biocriminology 75
  Genetics and Criminality 75
  The Controversy over Violence and Genes 77
  The IQ Debate 78
  Biochemical Factors 79
  Neurocriminology 81

Crime and Human Nature 83
  Criticisms of Biocriminology 83

Psychology and Criminality 86
  Psychological Development 86
  Moral Development 87
  Maternal Deprivation and Attachment Theory 89
  Learning Aggression and Violence 90
  Personality 95

Mental Disorders and Crime 97
  Psychological Causation 98
  An Integrated Theory 99

BOXES
  Debatable Issues: *Brain Overclaim Syndrome* 84
  Criminological Concerns: *Who Is Responsible for the Crime of Parricide?* 92
  World News: *China Launches Campaign to Crack Down on Web Porn* 94

Review 100
Criminology & Public Policy 100
You Be the Criminologist 100
Key Terms 101

5 Strain and Cultural Deviance Theories 102

The Interconnectedness of Sociological Theories 104

Anomie: Émile Durkheim 104
  The Structural-Functionalist Perspective 105
  Anomie and Suicide 105

Strain Theory 105
  Merton's Theory of Anomie 106
  Modes of Adaptation 106
  Tests of Merton's Theory 109
  Evaluation: Merton's Theory 110
  Institutional Imbalance and Crime 111
  General Strain Theory 111

Theory Informs Policy 113

Cultural Deviance Theories 115
  The Nature of Cultural Deviance 115
  Social Disorganization Theory 116
  Tests of Social Disorganization Theory 118
  Evaluation: Social Disorganization Theory 119

Theory Informs Policy 120
  Differential Association Theory 121
  Tests of Differential Association Theory 122
  Evaluation: Differential Association Theory 122

Theory Informs Policy 123
  Culture Conflict Theory 123

BOXES
    Window to the World: *A Social System Breaks Down* 107
    Debatable Issues: *Cults—Culture Conflict—Crime* 124

Review 126
Criminology & Public Policy 126
You Be the Criminologist 127
Key Terms 127

6 The Formation of Subcultures 128

The Function of Subcultures 130

Subcultural Theories of Delinquency and Crime 130
    The Middle-Class Measuring Rod 131
    Corner Boy, College Boy, Delinquent Boy 131
    Tests of Cohen's Theory 131
    Evaluation: Cohen's Theory 133

Delinquency and Opportunity 133
    Tests of Opportunity Theory 135
    Evaluation: Differential Opportunity Theory 136

The Subculture of Violence 136
    Tests of the Subculture of Violence 137
    Evaluation: The Subculture of Violence Theory 138

Focal Concerns: Miller's Theory 138
    Tests of Miller's Theory 139
    Evaluation: Miller's Theory 140

Gangs at the Turn of the Twenty-First Century 142
    Guns and Gangs 143

Female Delinquent Subcultures 144
    Early Research 144
    Recent Studies 144

Middle-Class Delinquency 146
    Explanations 148

Theory Informs Policy 149
    Getting Out: Gang Banging or the Morgue 150

BOXES
    Debatable Issues: *Cohen vs. Miller* 140
    Criminological Concerns: *The Girls in the Gang* 146
    Window to the World: *Gangs Terrorize Nigeria's Vital Oil Region* 150

Review 152
Criminology & Public Policy 152
You Be the Criminologist 152
Key Terms 152

7 Social Control Theory 153

What Is Social Control? 154

Theories of Social Control 155
    The Microsociological Perspective: Hirschi 155
    Social Bonds 155
    Empirical Tests of Hirschi's Theory 157
    Evaluation: Hirschi's Social Control Theory 158

Social Control and Drift 160

Personal and Social Control 161
    Failure of Control Mechanisms 161
    Stake in Conformity 161

Containment Theory   161
    Empirical Tests of Containment Theory   164
    Evaluation: Containment Theory   165
Theoretical Explorations   165
    Developmental/Life Course Theory   165
    Integrated Theory   168
    General Theories   169
Theory Informs Policy   170
BOXES
    Criminological Concerns: *Defying Convention and Control: "In Your Face"*   162
    Debatable Issues: *Are Human Beings Inherently Bad?*   163
    Window to the World: *Nations with Low Crime Rates*   168

Review   171
Criminology & Public Policy   172
You Be the Criminologist   172
Key Terms   172

8   **Labeling, Conflict, and Radical Theories**   173

Labeling Theory   174
    The Origins of Labeling Theory   175
    Basic Assumptions of Labeling Theory   175
    Labeling in the 1960s   176
    Labeling Theory in Action   177
    Empirical Evidence for Labeling Theory   177
    Evaluation: Labeling Theory   180

Conflict Theory   181
    The Consensus Model   182
    The Conflict Model   182
    Conflict Theory and Criminology   183
    Empirical Evidence for the Conflict Model   184

Radical Theory   184
    The Intellectual Heritage of Marxist Criminology   184
    Engels and Marx   185
    Willem Adriaan Bonger   185
    Georg Rusche and Otto Kirchheimer   185
    Radical Criminology since the 1970s   186
    Evaluation: Marxist Criminological Theory   187
    Emerging Explanations   190

BOXES
    Debatable Issues: *Racial Profiling—Labeling before the Fact*   178
    Criminological Concerns: *Labeling Countries "Corrupt": A Perverse Outcome?*   180
    Window to the World: *The Forgotten Criminology of Genocide*   188

Review   192
Criminology & Public Policy   192
You Be the Criminologist   193
Key Terms   193

9   **Environmental Theory**   194

Situational Theories of Crime   196
    Environmental Criminology   196
    Rational-Choice Perspective   197
    Routine-Activity Approach   198
    Practical Applications of Situational Theories of Crime   199

Theories of Victimization   201
    Lifestyle Theories   202
    Victim-Offender Interaction   203

Repeat Victimization 203
Hot Spots of Crime 204
Geography of Crime 204
Interrelatedness of Theories 204

Preventing Crimes against Places, People, and Valuable Goods 207
Situational Crime Prevention 210
Situational Crime Prevention—Pros and Cons 213
Displacement 214

Theory Informs Policy 215

BOXES
Criminological Concerns: *Unraveling Al-Qaida's Target
Selection Calculus* 206
Debatable Issues: *Maximum-Security Schools?* 208
World News: *Pakistan Is World Leader in Stolen Cars* 212

Review 216
Criminology & Public Policy 216
You Be the Criminologist 216
Key Terms 216

PART III Types of Crimes 217

10 Violent Crimes 219

Homicide 220
Murder 220
Manslaughter 221
The Extent of Homicide 222
The Nature of Homicide 224
A Cross-National Comparison of Homicide Rates 228

Assault 230

Family-Related Crimes 231
Spouse Abuse 232
Child Abuse 234
Abuse of the Elderly 235

Rape and Sexual Assault 235
Characteristics of the Rape Event 236
Who Are the Rapists? 236
Rape and the Legal System 237
Community Response 238

Kidnapping 238

Robbery 238
Characteristics of Robbers 239
The Consequences of Robbery 240

Organized Crime 240
The History of Organized Crime 241
The Structure and Impact of Organized Crime 242
The New Ethnic Diversity in Organized Crime 245

Emerging Problems 248
Terrorism 248
Hate Crimes 254
Militias 254
Violence in Schools 255

Violence and Gun Control 259
The Extent of Firearm-Related Offenses 259
Youths and Guns 259
Controlling Handgun Use 261
The Gun-Control Debate 264

BOXES
> **World News:** *Random Murders Set Record in 2008* 221
> **Window to the World:** *The Big Business of Organized Crime in Mexico* 246
> **Debatable Issues:** *Does the Brady Law Work?* 262

Review 265
Criminology & Public Policy 265
You Be the Criminologist 266
Key Terms 266

11 Crimes against Property 267

Larceny 268
   The Elements of Larceny 268
   The Extent of Larceny 268
   Who Are the Thieves? 269
   Shoplifting 270
   Art Theft 272
   Motor Vehicle Theft 274
   Boat Theft 276

Fraud 277
   Obtaining Property by False Pretenses 277
   Confidence Games and Frauds 280
   Check Forgery 280
   Credit Card Crimes 281
   Insurance Fraud 282

High-Tech Crimes: Concerns for Today and Tomorrow 284
   Characteristics of High-Tech Crimes 285
   Computers and the Internet: Types of Crimes 285
   Characteristics of the High-Tech Criminal 291
   The Criminal Justice Problem 292

Burglary 292

Fencing: Receiving Stolen Property 293

Arson 294

Comparative Crime Rates 294

BOXES
> **Debatable Issues:** *Piracy Emerges as a Major Worldwide Problem: How Can It Be Controlled?* 276
> **Criminological Concerns:** *Mortgage Fraud* 278
> **Criminological Concerns:** *Insurance Fraud* 283

Review 295
Criminology & Public Policy 295
You Be the Criminologist 295
Key Terms 295

12 White-Collar and Corporate Crime 296

Defining White-Collar Crime 298
   Crimes Committed by Individuals 299
   Types of White-Collar Crimes 301

Corporate Crime 309
   Frequency and Problems of Definition 309
   Phases of Corporate Criminal Law 309
   Theories of Corporate Liability 315
   Models of Corporate Culpability 316
   Governmental Control of Corporations 317
   Investigating Corporate Crime 318
   Environmental Crimes 319
   Curbing Corporate Crime 323
   The Future of White-Collar and Corporate Crime 323

BOXES
   Window to the World: *Al Qaeda's Battle Is Economic, Not Military*   304
   Debatable Issues: *How Much Corporate Power Is Too Much?*   310
   Criminological Concerns: *Corporate Fraud*   320

Review   325
Criminology & Public Policy   325
You Be the Criminologist   326
Key Terms   326

13 Public Order Crimes 327

Drug Abuse and Crime   328
  The History of Drug Abuse   328
  The Extent of Drug Abuse   331
  Patterns of Drug Abuse   331
  Crime-Related Activities   334
  Drug Control   337

Alcohol and Crime   340
  The History of Legalization   340
  Crime-Related Activities   340

Sexual Morality Offenses   342
  Deviate Sexual Intercourse by Force or Imposition   343
  Prostitution   343
  Pornography   345

BOXES
   Window to the World: *Global Sexual Slavery: Women and Children*   346
   Debatable Issues: *Cyberporn: Where Do We (Should We) Draw the Line?*   348
   World News: *Preventing Child Pornography*   351

Review   353
Criminology & Public Policy   354
You Be the Criminologist   354
Key Terms   355

14 International and Comparative Criminology 356

What Is Comparative Criminology?   357
  The Definition of Comparative Criminology   357
  The History of Comparative Criminology   358
  The Goals of Comparative Research   359

Engaging in Comparative Criminological Research   359
  Comparative Research   361
  Comparative Research Tools and Resources   361
  The Special Problems of Empirical Research   361

Theory Testing   362
  Validation of Major Theories   363
  The Socioeconomic Development Perspective   363

Practical Goals   363
  Learning from Others' Experiences   363
  Developing International Strategies   364
  Globalization versus Ethnic Fragmentation   372

BOXES
   Criminological Concerns: *The Motives and Intentions of
    Terrorist Organizations*   364
   Debatable Issues: *What Should Be Done to Prevent International
    Corporate Fraud?*   366

Review   373
Criminology & Public Policy   374
You Be the Criminologist   374
Key Terms   374

PART IV* A Criminological Approach to the Criminal Justice System

15 Processes and Decisions

The Stages of the Criminal Justice Process
    Entry into the System
    Prosecution and Pretrial Services
    Adjudication Decisions
    Sentencing Decisions
    Corrections Decisions
    Diversion out of the System

Juvenile Justice
    The Development of the Juvenile Justice System
    The Juvenile Justice Process

Victims and Criminal Justice
    Victims' Rights
    The Victim's Role in the Criminal Justice Process

BOXES
    Debatable Issues: *From Carlos the Jackal to Osama bin Laden: How Far Should We Go?*
    Criminological Concerns: In re Gault: *The Demise of Parens Patriae*

Review
Criminology & Public Policy
You Be the Criminologist
Key Terms

16 Enforcing the Law: Practice and Research

The History of Policing
    The English Heritage
    Policing in the United States

Law Enforcement Agencies
    Federal Law Enforcement
    Department of Homeland Security
    State Police
    County Police
    Municipal Police
    Special-Purpose Police
    Private Police

Command Structure
    Operations Bureau: Patrol
    Operations Bureau: Investigation
    Specialized Units
    Nonline Functions

Police Functions
    Law Enforcement
    Order Maintenance
    Community Service

The Police and the Community
    Community Policing
    Police-Community Relations Programs

The Rule of Law in Law Enforcement
    Constitutional Due Process
    Civil Rights
    Use of Deadly Force and Police Brutality

*Part IV, Chapters 15–18, are available only at the Instructor Edition of the Online Learning Center:
www.mhhe.com/adlercrim7e.

Abuse of Discretion
Corruption
Police Officers and Their Lifestyle
Qualifications
Changing Composition of the Police Force
The Police Subculture

BOXES
Window to the World: *Interpol: The International Criminal Police Organization*
Criminological Concerns: *Fear of Crime Decreases—Fear of Police Increases*
World News: *Delhi Cops Are Ten-ted!*

Review
Criminology & Public Policy
You Be the Criminologist
Key Terms

17 The Nature and Functioning of Courts

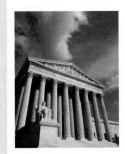

The Origins of Courts
The U.S. Court System
State Courts
Federal Courts
Interaction between State Courts and Federal Courts
Lawyers in the Court System
The Role of the Trial Judge
Arraignment
Pretrial Motions
Release Decisions
Plea Bargaining

The Trial
Selecting the Jury: Voir Dire
The Proceedings
Jury Decision Making
Sentencing: Today and Tomorrow
Incapacitation
Deterrence
Retribution
Rehabilitation
Model Penal Code Sentencing Goals
Just Deserts
Restorative Justice
Sentencing Limits and Guidelines
Capital Punishment
The Deterrence Argument
The Discrimination Argument
Other Arguments
Trends in American Capital Punishment

BOXES
Window to the World: *Judging at the World Level*
Criminological Concerns: *A New Crime: Hate;*
   A New Punishment: Sentence Enhancement
Debatable Issues: *Life or Death?*

Review
Criminology & Public Policy
You Be the Criminologist
Key Terms

18 A Research Focus on Corrections

Punishment and Corrections: A Historical Overview
From Antiquity to the Eighteenth Century
Punishment in the New World
The Reformatory Movement
The Medical Treatment Model
Community Involvement
The Prisoners' Rights Movement

Corrections Today
Types of Incarceration
The Size and Cost of the Correctional Enterprise
The Problem of Overcrowding
Prison Culture and Society
Correctional Officers
Programs in Penal Institutions
Evaluation of Rehabilitation
Medical Problems: AIDS, TB, and Mental Illness
The Elderly Inmate
Women in Prison
Privatization of Corrections

Community Alternatives
Probation
Parole
The Search for Cost-Beneficial Alternatives
Evaluation of Community Alternatives

BOXES
Window to the World: *Nigeria's Prison System Fails Its People*
Debatable Issues: *Beyond the Conjugal Visit?*
Criminological Concerns: *Boot Camp: A Military Option for Corrections*

Review
Criminology & Public Policy
You Be the Criminologist
Key Terms

Notes   N-1
Glossary   G-1
Credits   C-1
Indexes   I-1

List of Boxes

CRIMINOLOGICAL CONCERNS

Who Is Responsible for the Crime of
Parricide? 92
The Girls in the Gang 146
Defying Convention and Control: "In Your
Face" 162
Labeling Countries "Corrupt": A Perverse
Outcome? 180
Unraveling Al-Qaida's Target Selection
Calculus 206
Mortgage Fraud 278
Insurance Fraud 283
Corporate Fraud 320
The Motives and Intentions of Terrorist
Organizations 364

In re Gault: The Demise of Parens Patriae
Fear of Crime Decreases—Fear of Police
Increases
A New Crime: Hate; A New Punishment:
Sentence Enhancement
Boot Camp: A Military Option for
Corrections

DEBATABLE ISSUES

Fame and Crime 16
Murder Spike Poses Quandary 40
Utilitarianism Gone Astray 58
Brain Overclaim Syndrome 84
Cults—Culture Conflict—Crime 124
Cohen vs. Miller 140
Are Human Beings Inherently Bad? 163
Racial Profiling—Labeling before the Fact 178
Maximum-Security Schools? 208
Does the Brady Law Work? 262
Piracy Emerges as a Major Worldwide Problem:
How Can It Be Controlled? 276
How Much Corporate Power Is Too Much? 310
Cyberporn: Where Do We (Should We) Draw the
Line? 348
What Should Be Done to Prevent International
Corporate Fraud? 366

From Carlos the Jackal to Osama Bin Laden:
How Far Should We Go?
Life or Death?
Beyond the Conjugal Visit?

WINDOW TO THE WORLD

Terrorism and the Fear of Terrorism 12
Victims around the World 44
Stone Age Crime and Social Control 54
A Social System Breaks Down 107
Gangs Terrorize Nigeria's Vital Oil Region 150
Nations with Low Crime Rates 168
The Forgotten Criminology of Genocide 188
The Big Business of Organized Crime in
Mexico 246
Al Qaeda's Battle Is Economic, Not Military 304
Global Sexual Slavery: Women and
Children 346

Interpol: The International Criminal Police
Organization
Judging at the World Level
Nigeria's Prison System Fails Its People

WORLD NEWS

In the Words of Al Qaeda: What Else Is There to
Say about September 11? 6
Statistics Watchdog Chief Accuses Home Office
of Abusing Crime Statistics 34
Who's Responsible? 66
China Launches Campaign to Crack Down on
Web Porn 94
Pakistan is World Leader in Stolen Cars 212
Random Murders Set Record in 2008 221
Preventing Child Pornography 351

Delhi Cops Are Ten-ted!

Preface

Criminology is a young discipline—in fact, the term "criminology" is only a little over a century old. But in this brief time, criminology has emerged as an important social and behavioral science devoted to the study of crime as a social phenomenon. Criminology fosters theoretical debates, contributes ideas, and suggests solutions to a crime problem that many consider intolerable. Problems as vital and urgent as those addressed in this book are challenging, exciting, and, at the same time, disturbing and tragic. Moreover, these problems are immediately relevant to students' lives. This is especially true today, when crime rates in inner cities remain high, threats of additional terrorist attacks against the United States are regularly discussed, and revelations of corporate scandals appear daily.

Our goal with this book has been, and remains, to discuss these problems, their origins, and their possible solutions in a clear, practical, straightforward fashion that brings the material to life for students. We invite teachers and students alike to join us in traveling along criminology's path, exploring its expanding domain and mapping out its future.

THE SEVENTH EDITION

In the six preceding editions of this text, we prepared students of criminology to understand the contemporary problems with which criminology is concerned and to anticipate those problems society would have to face in the twenty-first century. We have now firmly entered that century. It is time to face the new century's problems as we simultaneously continue to work on solutions to old problems. Because of the forward-looking orientation of previous editions of *Criminology* and the wide respect and acceptance those editions have enjoyed, we have maintained the book's established structure and approach with modest but important changes.

In the prior edition, we gave the crime of terrorism center stage in Chapter 1. No single crime was ever poised to shape and reshape the field of criminology like the crime of terrorism. It is far from clear that this has happened. There can be no doubt, however, that terrorism will continue to be studied intensely by criminologists around the globe and that such research will result in practical, policy-relevant proposals. To that end, we continue to incorporate the latest findings from criminological research into terrorist organizations, and we include original Al Qaeda communiqués.

The emergence of a new age of corporate malfeasance represents another potential milestone in our field. We have expanded our coverage of white-collar and corporate crimes, including expansion of our coverage of mortgage fraud, one antecedent of the credit crisis. Like the crime of terrorism, white-collar and corporate offenses have been on the periphery of the field of criminology—but not for much longer.

As in prior revisions, we have vigorously researched, refined, and updated every chapter of the text—not only to maintain the book's scholarly integrity, but also to ensure its relevance for today's students. In addition to updating every chapter's research base and statistical information, we have expanded coverage of the most critical issues facing the field of criminology.

Inasmuch as developments in criminology influence and are influenced by media reports of national significance, students will find discussion and analysis of recent major current events.

As in previous editions, we have endeavored not only to reflect developments and changes, but also to anticipate them on the basis of the latest criminological data. After all, those who study criminology with our text today must be ready to address and resolve new criminological problems tomorrow, when they are decision makers, researchers, teachers, and planners. The aim, however, remains constant: to arrive at a future as free from crime as possible.

ORGANIZATION

This seventh edition represents a change in the format of our book. The printed book contains Chapters 1–14, covering criminology. The remaining criminal justice chapters (Chapters 15–18) are available solely at the Instructor Edtion of our book-specific Online Learning Center (www.mhhe.com/adlercrim7e). For schools that retain the traditional criminology course, which includes criminological coverage of criminal justice, our text and the online chapters provide the ideal resource.

Part I, "Understanding Criminology," presents an overview of criminology—now made more exciting with integrated coverage of terrorism and related crimes—and describes the vast horizon of this science. It explains what crime is and techniques for measuring the amount and characteristics of crime and criminals. It also traces the history of criminological thought through the era that witnessed the formation of the major schools of criminology: classicism and positivism (eighteenth and nineteenth centuries).

Part II, "Explanations of Crime and Criminal Behavior," includes explanations of crime and criminal behavior based on the various theories developed in the twentieth century. Among the subjects covered are theories that offer biological, neurocriminological, psychological, sociological, sociopolitical, and integrated explanations. Coverage of research by radical, socialist, and feminist criminologists has been updated. Theories that discuss why offenders choose to commit one offense rather than another at a given time and place are also covered in Part II.

Part III, "Types of Crimes," covers the various types of crimes from a legal and sociological perspective. The familiar street crimes, such as homicide and robbery, are assessed, as are criminal activities such as white-collar and corporate crime—so much in the spotlight these days—as well as technology-dependent crimes that have been highlighted by researchers only in recent years.

Part IV, "A Criminological Approach to the Criminal Justice System" (available only online), includes an explanation of the component parts and functioning of the system. It explains contemporary criminological research on how the people who run the criminal justice system operate it, the decision-making processes of all participants, and the interaction of all the system components.

PEDAGOGICAL AIDS

Working together, the authors and the editors have developed a format for the text that supports the goal of achieving a readable, practical, and attractive text. In addition to the changes already mentioned, we include plentiful, current photographs to make the book even more approachable. Redesigned and carefully updated tables and figures highlight and amplify the text coverage. Chapter outlines, lists of key terms, chapter review sections, and a comprehensive end-of-book glossary all help students master the material. Always striving to help students see the relevance of criminology in their lives, we also include a number of unique, innovative features in this edition:

- **New *Theory Connects* marginal inserts.** These notes in the text margins correlate the intensely applied material in Part III of the text ("Types of Crimes") with the heavily theoretical material in Part II ("Explanations of Crime"), giving students much-needed cross-reference material and posing critical-thinking questions that will help them truly process what they are reading.

- **New *Criminology & Public Policy* exercises.** These end-of-chapter activities challenge students to explore policy issues related to criminology.

- *Crime Surfing.* These particularly interesting web addresses accompanied by mini-exercises allow students to explore chapter topics further.

- *Did You Know?* These surprising factual realities provide eye-opening information about chapter topics.

- *Theory Informs Policy.* These brief sections in theory chapters demonstrate how problems identified by criminologists have led to practical solutions.

Our "box" program continues to be updated and improved. In the boxes, we highlight significant criminological issues that deserve special discussion. Every chapter has new boxes.

- *Debatable Issues* boxes highlight current controversies that challenge us to arrive at a resolution.

- *Criminological Concerns* boxes highlight problems "of the moment," due to their technological nature or human implications that challenge us to come up with specific effective responses right now. For example, in light of our experience with hate-motivated crimes, are harsher laws called for?

- *Window to the World* boxes examine developments abroad that affect America's crime situation. For example, now that ethnic gangs have emerged around the world and are, among other things, forcibly transporting women and young girls to be sex slaves, how can nations deal with the problem?

- *World News* boxes discuss current issues and problems reported in media coverage around the world. Our field is increasingly feeling the full force of globalization. Considering the media coverage of crime around the world is essential to both researchers and policy makers.

SUPPLEMENTS PACKAGE

Visit our Online Learning Center at www.mhhe.com/adlercrim7e for robust student and instructor resources.

For the Student

Our book-specific Online Learning Center features unique Interactive Modules that allow students to explore some of the hottest topics in criminal justice today, including terrorism, white-collar crime, and the drug trade. Multiple-choice quizzes and Internet exercises allow students to delve deeper into topics within each chapter.

For the Instructor

The password-protected instructor portion of the Online Learning Center includes Chapters 15–18 on the criminal justice system. These chapters can be distributed to your students. The site also includes the instructor's manual, a comprehensive computerized test bank, and PowerPoint lecture slides. Other dynamic instructor resources include the following:

 With the CourseSmart eTextbook version of this title, students can save up to 50% off the cost of a print book, reduce their impact on the environment, and access powerful web tools for learning. Faculty can also review and compare the full text online without having to wait for a print desk copy. CourseSmart is an online eTextbook, which means users need to be connected to the Internet in order to access it. Students can also print sections of the book for maximum portability. For futher details contact your sales representative or go to www.coursesmart.com.

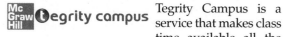 Tegrity Campus is a service that makes class time available all the time by automatically capturing every lecture in a searchable format for students to review when they study and complete assignments. With a simple one-click start-and-stop process, you can capture all computer screens and corresponding audio. Students can replay any part of any class with easy-to-use browser-based viewing on a PC or Mac.

Educators know that the more students can see, hear, and experience class resources, the better they learn. With Tegrity Campus, students quickly recall key moments by using Tegrity Campus's unique search feature, which helps students efficiently find what they need when they need it across an entire semester of class recordings. Help turn all your students' study time into learning moments immediately supported by your lectures.

To learn more about Tegrity Campus, watch a 2-minute Flash demo at http://tegritycampus.mhhe.com.

- McGraw-Hill's online courses provide interactive digital content and activities aligned with learning objectives that work with most learning management systems. Designed to be used in conjunction with a textbook, McGraw-Hill's online course tools combine visual, auditory, and interactive elements to encourage all types of learners to connect with and retain knowledge. Course content includes animation, graphics, streaming video, and interactive activities to enliven the content and motivate the learner. Specifically, for the area of criminal justice, the McGraw-Hill online course content tools were developed around content areas that have been established by the Academy of Criminal Justice Sciences' Minimum Standards of Criminal Justice Education. Preview the criminal justice course content and more at www.OnlineLearning.com.

- *NBC News Lecture Launcher DVD.* This unique video features several brief clips from *NBC News* that can be used to jump-start lectures in the most exciting, relevant ways.

- *Full-Length Videotapes.* A wide variety of videotapes from the Films for the Humanities and Social Sciences series is available to adopters of the text.

- *Course Management Systems.* Whether you use WebCT, Blackboard, e-College, or another course management system, McGraw-Hill will provide you with a *Criminology* cartridge that enables you either to conduct your course entirely online or to supplement your lectures with online material.

- *Primis Online.* This unique database publishing system allows instructors to create their own custom text from material in *Criminology* or elsewhere and deliver that text to students electronically as an e-book or in print format via the bookstore.

Please contact your local McGraw-Hill representative for more information on any of the above supplements.

IN APPRECIATION

We greatly acknowledge the assistance and support of a number of dedicated professionals. At Rutgers University, the librarian of the N.C.C.D. Criminal Justice Collection, Phyllis Schultze, has been most helpful in patiently tracking and tracing sources. We thank Professor Sesha Kethineni (Illinois State University) for her tireless assistance on the first edition, Deborah Leiter-Walker for her help on the second, Kerry Dalip and Nhung Tran (University of Pennsylvania) for their assistance on the fourth, Reagan Daly and Ashish Jatia (University of Pennsylvania) for their work on the sixth edition, and Melissa Meltzer (University of Pennsylvania) for her work on this current edition. Gratitude is also owed to the many former and current Rutgers University students who have valiantly contributed their labors to all editions. They include Susanna Cornett, Dory Dickman, Lisa Maher, Susan Plant, Mangai Natarajan, Dana Nurge, Sharon Chamard, Marina Myhre, Diane Cicchetti, Emmanuel Barthe, Illya Lichtenberg, Peter Heidt, Vanja Steniius, Christine Tartaro, Megan McNally, Danielle Gunther, Jennifer Lanterman, Smita Jain, and Kim Roberts. Thanks also to Maria Shields for revising the supplements to accompany the seventh edition of this text.

Many academic reviewers offered invaluable help in planning and drafting chapters. We thank them for their time and thoughtfulness and for the experience they brought from their teaching and research:

Jay Albanese, *Virginia Commonwealth University*

Thomas E. Allen, Jr., *University of South Dakota*

W. Azul La Luz, *University of New Mexico*

Tony A. Barringer, *Florida Gulf Coast University*

Stephen Brodt, *Ball State University*

Daniel Burgel, *Vincennes University*

David A. Camp, *Culver-Stockton College*

Daniel D. Cervi, *University of New Hampshire*

Bernard Cohen, *Queens College, New York*

Cavit Cooley, *Truman State University*

Roger Cunningham, *Eastern Illinois University*

Richard P. Davin, *Riverside Community College*

Julius Debro, *University of Hartford*

Albert Dichiara, *Eastern Illinois University*

Sandra Emory, *University of New Mexico*

Edna Erez, *Kent State University*

Raymond A. Eve, *University of Texas, Arlington*

The late Franco Ferracuti, *University of Rome, Italy*

Edith Flynn, *Northeastern University*

Harold A. Frossard, *Moraine Valley Community College*

Karen Gilbert, *University of Georgia*

Ronald J. Graham, *Fresno City College*

Clayton Hartjen, *Rutgers University*

Marie Henry, *Sullivan County Community College*

John Hill, *Salt Lake Community College*

Matrice Hurrah, *Southwest Tennessee Community College*

Randy Jacobs, *Baylor University*

Joseph Jacoby, *Bowling Green State University*

Debra L. Johnson, *Lindenwood University*

Deborah Kelly, *Longwood College*

Dennis Kenney, *John Jay College of Criminal Justice*

James Kenny, *Fairleigh Dickinson University*

Nicholas Kittrie, *American University*

James J. Lauria, *Pittsburgh Technical Institute*

Matthew T. Lee, *University of Akron*

Anna C. Leggett, *Miami Dade Community College*

Linda Lengyel, *The College of New Jersey*

Michael A. Long, *Colorado State University*

Joel Maatman, *Lansing Community College*

Coramae Mann, *Indiana University, Bloomington*

Harry L. Marsh, *Indiana State University*

Robert McCormack, *The College of New Jersey*

P. J. McGann, *University of Michigan*

Jean Marie McGloin, *University of Maryland*

Sharon S. Oselin, *University of California, Irvine*

Jesenia Pizarro, *Michigan State University*

Lydia Rosner, *John Jay College of Criminal Justice*

Lee E. Ross, *University of Wisconsin*

Harjit Sandhu, *Oklahoma State University*

Jennifer L. Schulenberg, *Sam Houston State University*

Clayton Steenberg, *Arkansas State University*

Richard Steinhaus, *New Mexico Junior College*

Melvina Sumter, *Old Dominion University*

Austin T. Turk, *University of California, Riverside*

Prabha Unnithan, *Colorado State University*

James Vrettos, *John Jay College of Criminal Justice*

Charles Wellford, *University of Maryland at College Park*

Frank Williams, *California State University, San Bernardino*

The late Marvin E. Wolfgang, *University of Pennsylvania*

We thank our colleagues overseas who have prepared translations of *Criminology* to help familiarize students of foreign cultures with criminological problems that are now global, with our theories, and with efforts to deal with the persistent problem of crime in the future:

The Arabic translation:
    Dr. Mohammed Zeid, Cairo, Egypt, and Rome, Italy

The Japanese translation:
    Dr. Toyoji Saito, Kobe, Japan, and his colleagues

The Hungarian translation:
    Dr. Miklos Levai, Miskolc, Hungary, and his colleagues

The Georgian translation:
    Dr. Georgi Glonti, Tbilisi, Georgia

Finally, we owe a special debt to the team at McGraw-Hill: to executive editor Katie Stevens for her leadership, vision, encouragement, and support, and to Kate Scheinman for her expert and timeless editorial work.

A combined total of over a hundred years of teaching criminology and related subjects provides the basis for the writing of *Criminology, Seventh Edition.* We hope the result is a text that is intellectually provocative, factually rigorous, and scientifically sound and that offers a stimulating learning experience for the student.

Freda Adler
William S. Laufer

A Guided Tour

Up-to-the-Minute Coverage

The expansion of white-collar and corporate crime, the effects of the current global economic downturn, and a new look at the connection between biology and criminology are among the cutting-edge topics discussed in this Seventh Edition.

hypoglycemia. According to a sheriff's spokesman, "he had virtually no thought process."[45]

Hypoglycemia is a condition that occurs when the level of sugar in the blood falls below an acceptable range. The brain is particularly vulnerable to hypoglycemia, and such a condition can impair its function. Symptoms of hypoglycemia include anxiety, headache, confusion, fatigue, and even aggressive behavior. As early as 1943, researchers linked the condition with violent crime, including murder, rape, and assault. Subsequent studies found that violent and impulsive male offenders had a higher rate of hypoglycemia than noncriminal controls.

Consider the work of Matti Virkkunen, who has conducted a series of studies of habitually violent and psychopathic offenders in Finland. In one such study done in the 1980s, he examined the results of a glucose tolerance test (used to determine whether hypoglycemia is present) administered to 37 habitually violent offenders with antisocial personalities, 31 habitually violent offenders with intermittent explosive disorders, and 20 controls. The offenders were found to be significantly more hypoglycemic than the controls.[46]

Hormones

Experiments have shown that male animals typically are more aggressive than females. Male aggression is directly linked to male hormones. If an aggressive male mouse is injected with female hormones, he will stop fighting.[47] Likewise, the administration of male hormones to pregnant monkeys results in female offspring who, even 3 years after birth, are more aggressive than the daughters of non-injected mothers.[48]

While it would be misleading to equate male hormones with aggression and female hormones with nonaggression, there is some evidence that abnormal levels of male hormones in humans may

▓ Andrea Yates, convicted of drowning her children in a bathtub, was sentenced to life in prison in March 2002. Yates pleaded not guilty by reason of insanity—claiming postpartum psychosis and postpartum depression.

evidence of a brain tumor, which, he argued, resulted in uncontrollable rage and violence. A jury acquitted him on the grounds that the brain tumor had deprived him of any control over and knowledge of the act he was committing.[52] Brain

▓ Bernard ("Bernie") Madoff, former chairman of the NASDAQ stock exchange and a large securities firm, has been convicted of carrying out the largest Ponzi scheme in U.S. history—perhaps world history—with losses to investors that might exceed $100 billion. He is serving a 150-year sentence in prison.

- Protects the objectivity and independence of securities analysts
- Increases Securities and Exchange Commission resources

Perhaps most noteworthy, CEOs and chief financial officers must personally vouch for the truth and fairness of their company's disclosures.

Prosecutors, regulators, and legislators are carefully considering the consequences of the most recent credit crisis and the resulting recession. They are asking: Were crimes committed by large and small financial firms? In what ways did regulators and regulations fail? What role should the criminal law play in policing the very behaviors that resulted in one of the worst series of economic failures in our nation's history?

For those who think that the problem of white-collar and corporate crime is young, consider that in ancient Greece, public officials reportedly violated the law by purchasing land slated for government acquisition. Much of what we today define as white-collar crime, however, is the result of laws passed within the last century. For example, the Sherman Antitrust Act, passed by Congress in 1890, authorized the criminal prosecution of corporations engaged in monopolistic practices.[3] Federal laws regulating the issuance and sale of stocks and other securities were passed in 1933 and 1934. In 1940, Edwin H. Sutherland provided criminologists with the first scholarly account of

white-collar crime. He defined it as crime "committed by a person of respectability and high social status in the course of his occupation."[4]

The 2002 conviction of Arthur Andersen, LLP, for obstruction of justice (overturned in 2005 by the U.S. Supreme Court) demonstrates that Sutherland's definition is not entirely satisfactory: White-collar crime can be committed by a corporation as well as by an individual. As Gilbert Geis has noted, Sutherland's work is limited by his own definition. He has a "striking inability to differentiate between the corporations themselves and their executive management personnel."[5] Other criminologists have suggested that the term "white-collar crime" not be used at all; we should speak instead of "corporate crime" and "occupational crime."[6] Generally, however, **white-collar crime** is defined as a violation of the law committed by a person or group of persons in the course of an otherwise respected and legitimate occupation or business enterprise[7] (Table 12.1).

Just as white-collar and corporate offenses include a heterogeneous mix of corporate and individual crimes, from fraud, deception, and corruption to pollution of the environment, victims of white-collar crime range from the savvy investor to the unsuspecting consumer. No one person or group is immune[8] (Table 12.2). The Vatican lost millions of dollars in a fraudulent stock scheme; fraudulent charities have swindled fortunes from unsuspecting investors; and many banks have been forced into bankruptcy by losses due to deception and fraud.[9] Perhaps just as important, public perceptions of the legitimacy of financial institutions and markets have been undermined, at least in part, by allegations of corporate abuses.

Crimes Committed by Individuals

As we have noted, white-collar crime occurs during the course of a legitimate occupation or business enterprise. Over time, socioeconomic developments have increasingly changed the dimensions of such crimes.[10] Once, people needed only a few business relationships to make their way through life. They dealt with an employer or with employees. They dealt on a basis of trust and confidence with the local shoemaker and grocer. They had virtually no dealings with government.

This way of life has changed significantly and very rapidly during the past decades. People have become dependent on large bureaucratic structures; they are manipulated by agents and officials with whom they have no personal relationship. This situation creates a basis for potential abuses in four sets of relations:

- Employees of large entities may abuse their authority for private gain by making their services to members of the public contingent on a

> **THEORY CONNECTS**
>
> **Crimes Committed by Individuals (White-Collar Crime)**
>
> To what extent does Robert Merton's strain theory (page 105) offer an explanation for white-collar crimes such as embezzlement and tax fraud?

Chapter Openers

Each chapter opens with an outline of key topics, followed by a lively excerpt highlighting concepts from the field of criminology.

8 Labeling, Conflict, and Radical Theories

Labeling Theory
The Origins of Labeling Theory
Basic Assumptions of Labeling Theory
Labeling in the 1960s
Labeling Theory in Action
Empirical Evidence for Labeling Theory
Evaluation: Labeling Theory
Conflict Theory
The Consensus Model
The Conflict Model
Conflict Theory and Criminology
Empirical Evidence for the Conflict Model
Radical Theory
The Intellectual Heritage of Marxist Criminology
Engels and Marx
Willem Adriaan Bonger
Georg Rusche and Otto Kirchheimer
Radical Criminology since the 1970s
Evaluation: Marxist Criminological Theory
Emerging Explanations
Review
Criminology & Public Policy
You Be the Criminologist
Key Terms

▓ On November 30, 1999, Seattle police clashed with demonstrators at the opening ceremony of the World Trade Organization, using tear gas and rubber bullets to disperse the crowds.

Each era of social and political turmoil has produced profound changes in people's lives. Perhaps no such era was as significant for criminology as the 1960s. A society with conservative values was shaken out of its complacency when young people, blacks, women, and other disadvantaged groups demanded a part in the shaping of national policy. They saw the gaps between philosophical political... Rebellion broke out, and some criminologists joined the revolution.

These criminologists turned away from theories that explained crime by characteristics of the offender or of the social structure. They set out to demonstrate that individuals become criminals because of what people with power, especially those in the criminal justice system, do. Their explanations largely reject the consensus

9 Environmental Theory

Situational Theories of Crime
Environmental Criminology
Rational-Choice Perspective
Routine-Activity Approach
Practical Applications of Situational Theories of Crime
Theories of Victimization
Lifestyle Theories
Victim-Offender Interaction
Repeat Victimization
Hot Spots of Crime
Geography of Crime
Interrelatedness of Theories
Preventing Crimes against Places, People, and Valuable Goods
Situational Crime Prevention
Situational Crime Prevention—Pros and Cons
Displacement
THEORY INFORMS POLICY
Review
Criminology & Public Policy
You Be the Criminologist
Key Terms

▓ At the New York Stock Exchange, barriers have been erected to help protect the building and the workers inside. How do criminals choose their targets? What conditions invite crime? Alternatively, what measures can prevent crime?

New York: A Diamond District jeweler was busted yesterday for allegedly orchestrating the hijacking of a FedEx truck in a bungled attempt to steal millions of dollars worth of gems—and then planning to try it again. Brian Greenwald, president of Doppelt & Greenwald, is also suspected of being 11th Avenue at 47th Street on Dec. 20, 2007, according to a Manhattan federal court complaint. They got the truck, but the hapless thieves had to abandon it—its contents intact—when they couldn't figure out how to offload the baubles, which were in containers locked to the floor.[1]

NEW! World News Boxes

Part of our acclaimed thematic box program, World News boxes feature current issues and problems reported from across the globe.

■ WORLD NEWS ■

China Launches Campaign to Crack Down on Web Porn

The Ministry of Public Security (MPS), along with nine other government departments, announced the launching of a campaign yesterday to restrict the spread of pornography on the Internet in China.

"The boom of pornographic content on the Internet has contaminated cyberspace and perverted China's young minds," said Zhang Xinfeng, vice minister of MPS.

In the next six months, Zhang said, the ministries will crack down on illegal on-line activities such as distributing pornographic materials and organizing cyber strip shows, and purge the web of sexually-explicit images, stories, and audio and video clips.

The campaign will also target on illegal on-line lotteries and contraband trade, fraud, and "content that spreads rumors and is of a slanderous nature," said Zhang.

In Nov. 2006, Chinese police cracked the largest pornographic website in the country and arrested the creator Chen Hui, who was later sentenced to life imprisonment.

The website Chen started contained more than nine million pornographic images and articles and it had attracted more than 600,000 registered users.

"The inflow of pornographic materials from abroad and lax domestic control are to blame for the existing problems in China's cyberspace," Zhang said.

China has roughly 123 million Internet users, most of whom are young people. The Chinese government believes they need to be protected from negative on-line influences.

A report by the Beijing Reformatory for Juvenile Delinquents said 33.5 percent of its detainees were influenced by violent on-line games or erotic websites when they committed crimes such as robbery and rape.

Questions for Discussion
1. How successful will China be in restricting or limiting Web content?
2. Is China's attempt to restrict or limit Web content justifiable? How does it differ, if at all, from such attempts in the United States?

SOURCE: Xinhua, "China Launches Campaign to Crack Down on Web Porn," April 13, 2007. http://news.xinhuanet.com/english/2007-04/12/content_5968968.htm.

Window to the World Boxes

Drawing on criminology's increased emphasis on global factors, Window to the World boxes examine developments abroad that affect America's crime situation.

WINDOW TO THE WORLD

Nations with Low Crime Rates

Most criminologists devote their efforts to learning why people commit crime and why there is so much crime. A few have looked at the question from the opposite perspective: In places with little crime, what accounts for the low crime rate? Using the United Nations' first World Crime Survey (1970–1975), Freda Adler studied the two countries with the lowest crime rates in each of five general cultural regions of the world:(1)

Western Europe: Switzerland and the Republic of Ireland

Eastern Europe: the former German Democratic Republic (East Germany) and Bulgaria

Arab countries: Saudi Arabia and Algeria

Asia: Japan and Nepal

Latin America: Costa Rica and Peru (2)

This is an odd assortment of countries. They seem to have little in common. Some are democratic, others authoritarian. Some are republics, others monarchies. Some are ruled by dictators, others by communal councils. Some are rural, others highly urbanized. Some are remote and isolated; others are in the political mainstream. Some are highly religious, some largely atheistic. Some have a very high standard of living, others a very low one.

■ Workers in Japan showing solidarity in an early morning exercise ritual.

What explains their common characteristic of low crime rates?

Investigations slowly revealed a common factor in all 10 countries: Each appeared to have an intact social control system, quite apart from whatever formal control system (law enforcement) it had. Here are brief descriptions of the types of social control systems identified:

Western Europe: Switzerland fostered a strong sense of belonging to and participating in the local community. (3)

which served as continuing social centers.

Arab countries: Islam continued to be strong as a way of life and exercised a powerful influence on daily activities, especially in Saudi Arabia. Algeria had, in addition, a powerful commitment to socialism in its postindependence era, involving the citizens in all kinds of commonly shared development activities.

Asia: Nepal retained its strong family and clan ties, augmented by councils of elders that oversaw the community and resolved problems. Highly industrialized Japan had lost some of the social controls of family and kinship, but it found a substitute family in the industrial community, to which most Japanese belonged: Mitsubishi might now be the family that guides one's every step.

Latin America: Costa Rica spent all the funds that other governments devoted to the military on social services and social development, caring for and strengthening its families. Peru went through a process of urbanization in stages: Village and family cohesion marked the lives of people in the countryside, and this cohesion remained with the people as they migrated from Andean villages to smaller towns and then to the big city, where they

The family was still strong in the Republic of Ireland, and it was strengthened by shared religious values.

Eastern Europe: The former German Democratic Republic involved all youths in communal activities, organized by groups and aimed at having young people excel for the glory of self and country. In Bulgaria, industrialization focused on regional industry centers so that the workers would not be dislodged from their hometowns,

were received by and lived surrounded by others from their own hometowns.

The study concluded that **synnomie,** a term derived from the Greek *syn* meaning "with" and *nomos* meaning "norms," marked societies with low crime rates.

In an update of Adler's original low-crime-rate study, Janet Stamatel wrote:

The capacity for societies to maintain social control can change over time in response to other changes in social conditions. This means that countries labeled as either "low crime" or "high crime" at one point in time may experience changes in their crime status as social control mechanisms change over time. For example, in a study examining how crime rates in the ten countries that Adler identified as low crime in the late 1970s have changed as of 2000, Stamatel analyzed crime statistics from the United Nations and the World Health Organization to find that several of these countries (e.g., Algeria, Japan, Nepal, Saudi Arabia, and Switzerland) have remarkably been able to maintain low crimes rates for several decades. In contrast, a couple of these countries, namely Bulgaria and Peru, were not able to maintain their "low crime" status as dramatic political and economic changes severely disrupted their social control systems. Not

only can we learn a lot about how to control crime from countries with consistently low crime rates, but we can also learn much about what happens to crime rates when social control mechanisms are no longer able to function as intended by studying changing crime rates over time.(4)

Sources
1. United Nations, *Report of the Secretary General on Crime Prevention and Control,* A/32/199 (popularly known as the First U.N. World Crime Survey) (New York: United Nations, 1977).
2. Freda Adler, *Nations Not Obsessed with Crime* (Littleton, Colo.: Fred B. Rothman, 1983).
3. Marshall B. Clinard, *Cities with Little Crime: The Case of Switzerland* (Cambridge, Mass.: Cambridge University Press, 1978).
4. Janet P. Stamatel, "Revisiting Nations Not Obsessed with Crime" (working paper, December 2008).

Questions for Discussion
1. People in the United States work in factories, live in family groups, go to church, and join youth groups. Why do these institutions not function effectively as forms of social control to keep the crime rate low?
2. How could government or community decision makers use the information presented by this study to help solve crime problems in the United States?

Debatable Issues Boxes

These boxes highlight controversies requiring real-world resolutions.

DEBATABLE ISSUES

Maximum-Security Schools?

The 2005 Indicators of School Crime and Safety report places the problem of school violence in some perspective:

> In the 2002–03 school year, an estimated 54.2 million students in prekindergarten through grade 12 were enrolled in about 125,000 U.S. elementary or secondary schools. Preliminary data on fatal victimizations show youth ages 5–19 were victims of 22 school-associated violent deaths from July 1, 2001, through June 30, 2002 (17 homicides and 5 suicides) (*Indicator 1*). In 2003, students ages 12–18 were victims of about 1.9 million nonfatal crimes at school, including about 1.2 million thefts and 740,000 violent crimes (simple assault and serious violent crime)—150,000 of which were serious violent crimes (rape, sexual assault, robbery, and aggravated assault) (*Indicator 2*). These figures represent victimization rates of 45 thefts and 28 violent crimes, including 6 serious violent crimes, per 1,000 students at school in 2003. Students were more likely to be victims of serious violence or a homicide away from school. In 2003, students ages 12–18 reported being victims of serious violence at a rate of 12 crimes per 1,000 students away from school and 6 crimes per 1,000 students at school. Similarly, in each school year from July 1, 1992, through June 30, 2002, youth ages 5–19 were over 70 times more likely to be murdered away from school than at school.
>
> For several measures, data show trends in student victimization decreasing over the last decade. The nonfatal victimization rate for students ages 12–18 at school generally declined between 1992 and 2003; this was true for the total crime rate and for thefts, violent crimes, and serious violent crimes (*Indicator 2*). However, when looking at the most recent years, no differences were detected between 2002 and 2003 in the rates of total victimization, violent victimization, or theft at school. For fatal victimization, between July 1, 1992, and June 30, 2002, the number of homicides of school-age youth at school declined as well (*Indicator 1*). Specifically, between the 1998–99 and 1999–2000 school years, the number of homicides of school-age youth at school declined from 33 to 14 homicides. Since then, there have been between 12 and 17 homicides in each school year through 2001–02.(1)

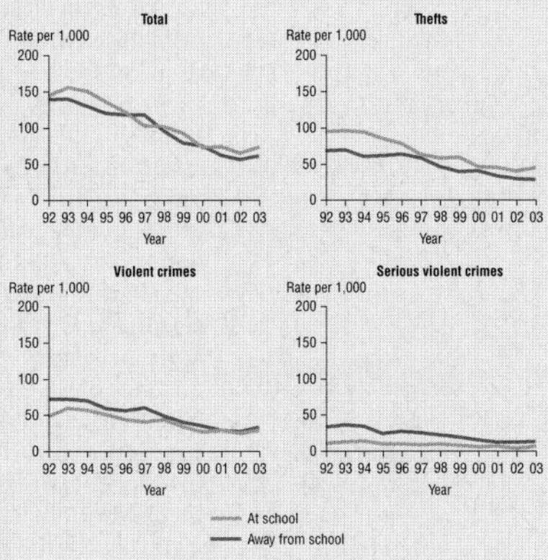

Rate of student-reported nonfatal crimes against students ages 12–18 per 1,000 students, by type of crime and location: 1992–2003.

Note: Serious violent crimes include rape, sexual assault, robbery, and aggravated assault. Violent crimes include serious violent crimes and simple assault. Total crimes include violent crimes and theft. "At school" includes inside the school building, on school property, or on the way to or from school.

Source: U.S. Department of Justice, Bureau of Justice Statistics, *National Crime Victimization Survey (NCVS)*, 1992–2003.

Although you would not know it, given all the media coverage surrounding school-shooting incidents, as well as experts' premonitions of doom and gloom, we are actually in the midst of a decline in violent crime in American schools.

In some inner-city schools, security measures rival those used in prison: metal detectors, drug-sniffing dogs, frequent searches for weapons, and surveillance cameras that monitor the movement of students in and out of classrooms.

Target hardening and situational crime prevention in schools are taken quite seriously. Schools in certain parts of some cities have had metal detectors, doors with alarms, and locker searches for years. Then there are the other schools in towns few have heard of: places like Paducah, Conyers, and Littleton. The image of these suburban schools as safe havens has been shattered. Although the likelihood of a shooting in any particular school is small, officials are not taking any chances. Interestingly, the prevention measures listed below fall squarely into Clarke and Homel's situational-crime-prevention model (see Table 9.4).

Access control

- Intercom systems are being used at locked doors to buzz in visitors.(2)
- Students have to flash or swipe computerized identification cards to get into school buildings.
- Perimeter fences delineate school property and secure cars after hours.

Controlling facilitators

- Students in Deltona, Florida, get an extra set of books to leave at home. The schools have banned backpacks and dismantled lockers to eliminate places to stash weapons. Other school districts are encouraging see-through lockers and backpacks.
- After the Littleton, Colorado, incident, school boards across the country banned trench coats and other oversize garments, apparently to prevent students from hiding weapons on their bodies or in their clothing.

Entry/exit screening

- Handheld and walk-through metal detectors keep anyone with a weapon from entering schools.

Formal surveillance

- Uniformed police officers and private security guards, some of them armed, patrol school halls.
- Schools are installing surveillance cameras in hallways and on school buses.

Surveillance by employees (or, in this case, students)

- Students are carrying small notebooks so that they can log and then report overheard threats.

Identifying property

- Tiny microfilm is hidden inside expensive school property so that it can be identified if stolen.

On the face of it, these measures seem to make good sense. They can prevent people from bringing weapons into schools and keep unauthorized people out. They increase the ability of school officials to detect crime, identify evildoers, and prevent criminal incidents from happening. But have school officials and others gone too far? Diana Philip is the director of the American Civil Liberties Union of Texas for the northern region, which has filed several lawsuits against schools. She observes that "over the summer, we have had school boards putting together the most restrictive policies we have ever seen. A lot of them are in clear violation of the Fourth Amendment, which guarantees freedom from unreasonable searches."(3)

Chicago Tribune columnist Steve Chapman argues that schools treat students as "dangerous, incorrigible, undeserving of respect" or privacy. He asks, "What's the difference between school and prison? At school, you don't get cable TV."(4)

Sources

1. J. F. DeVoe, K. Peter, M. Noonan, T. D. Snyder, and K. Baum, *Indicators of School Crime and Safety: 2005* (Washington, D.C.: Department of Justice, 2005).
2. Jacques Steinberg, "Barricading the School Door," *New York Times*, Aug. 22, 1999, New York section, p. 5.
3. S. C. Gwynne, "Is Anyplace Safe?" *Time*, Aug. 23, 1999.
4. Walter Olson, "Dial 'O' for Outrage: The Sequel—Tales from an Overlawyered America," *Reason*, Nov. 1999, pp. 54–56.

Questions for Discussion

1. Do you think there would be as much concern over school violence if these shooting incidents had happened in urban schools? Why are people more upset when crime happens in places they perceive to be safe (such as in the suburbs)?
2. Does your high school or college campus have any security measures in place? If so, how do they fit into Clarke and Homel's 16 techniques of situational prevention?
3. Is there a point at which security measures in schools become so extreme that they can no longer be justified? Have we reached that point yet?

Criminological Concerns Boxes

These boxes focus on problems that challenge us to come up with effective responses right now.

CRIMINOLOGICAL CONCERNS

The Girls in the Gang

Psychologist Anne Campbell studied female gangs in New York City and published her findings in her 1984 book, *The Girls in the Gang*. She summarizes some of her observations here:

A portrait of Hispanic teen female members of the Pico Rivera gang, with one member holding her child.

> All the girls in the gang come from families that are poor. Many have never known their fathers. Most are immigrants from Puerto Rico. As children the girls moved from apartment to apartment as they were evicted or burned out by arsonists. Unable to keep any friends they managed to make and alienated from their mothers, whose lack of English restricted their ability to control or understand their daughters' lives, the girls dropped out of school early and grew up on the streets. In the company of older kids and street-corner men, they graduated early into the adult world. They began to use drugs and by puberty had been initiated into sexual activity. By fifteen many were pregnant. Shocked, their mothers tried to pull them off the streets. Some sent their daughters back to relatives in Puerto Rico while they had their babies. Abortion was out of the question in this Catholic world.
>
> Those who stayed had "spoiled their identity" as good girls. Their reputations were marred before they ever reached adulthood. On the streets, among the gang members, the girls found a convenient identity in the female gang. Often they had friends or distant relatives who introduced them as "prospects." After a trial period, they could undertake the initiation rite: they had to fight an established member nominated by the godmother. What was at issue was not winning or losing but demonstrating "heart," or courage. Gangs do not welcome members who join only to gain protection. The loyalty of other gang members has to be won by a clear demonstration of willingness to "get down," or fight.
>
> Paradoxically, the female gang goes to considerable lengths to control the sexual behavior of its members. Although the neighborhood may believe they are fast women, the girls themselves do not tolerate members who sleep around. A promiscuous girl is a threat to the other members' relationships with their boyfriends. Members can take a boyfriend from among the male gang members (indeed, they are forbidden to take one from any other gang) but they are required to be monogamous. A shout of "Whore!" is the most frequent cause of fistfights among the female members.
>
> On the positive side, the gang provides a strong sense of belonging and sisterhood. After the terrible isolation of their lives, the girls acquire a ready-made circle of friends who have shared many of their experiences and who are always willing to support them against hostile words or deeds by outsiders. Fighting together generates a strong sense of camaraderie and as a bonus earns them the reputation of being "crazy." This reputation is extremely useful in the tough neighborhoods where they live. Their reputation for carrying knives and for solidarity effectively deters outsiders from challenging them. They work hard at fostering their tough "rep" not only in their deeds but in their social talk. They spend hours recounting and embroidering stories of fights they have been in. Behind all this bravado it is easy to sense the fear they work so hard to deny. Terrified of being victims (as many of them have already been in their families and as newcomers in their schools), they make much of their own "craziness"—the violent unpredictability that frightens away anyone who might try to harm them.(1)

Campbell demonstrates the commonality of violence in the lives of female gang members in the early 1980s. Today there is growing concern over the increasing prevalence and severity of violence in some areas of the country.(2) The number of female gang members and the extent of changes in the use of violence are, however, still debated among researchers.(3)

Sources

1. Written by Anne Campbell. Adapted from Anne Campbell, *The Girls in the Gang* (New York: Basil Blackwell, 1984).
2. John M. Hagedorn, "Gang Violence in the Postindustrial Era," in *Youth Violence, Crime and Justice: A Review of Research*, vol. 24, eds. Michael Tonry and Mark H. Moore (Chicago: University of Chicago Press, 1998), pp. 365–419.
3. Margaret O'Brien, "At Least 16,000 Girls in Chicago's Gangs More Violent than Some Believe, Report Says," *Chicago Tribune*, Sept. 17, 1999, p. 5.

Questions for Discussion

1. How similar are Campbell's female gangs to the male gangs described in this chapter? Are there any significant differences?
2. Would you expect female gangs to become as involved in criminal activity as male gangs? Why or why not?

Crime Surfing Features

Internet references accompanied by mini-exercises allow students to further explore chapter topics.

Did You Know? Facts

Intriguing, little-known facts related to specific chapter topics engage students' natural curiosity about criminology.

Crime Surfing WWW

www.ncjrs.org

Maternal deprivation can be related to delinquent behavior. What happens to deprived (often abused and neglected) children? Is there a cycle of violence?

DID YOU KNOW?

... that, while evidence is lacking that deprivation directly causes delinquency, research on the impact of family-based crime prevention programs is promising? Programs that target family risk factors in multiple settings (ecological contexts) have achieved success (Table 4.2).

Family Atmosphere and Delinquency

Criminologists also have examined the effects of the mother's absence, whether because of death, divorce, or abandonment. Does her absence cause delinquency? Empirical research is equivocal. Perhaps the most persuasive evidence comes from longitudinal research conducted by Joan McCord, who has investigated the relationship between family atmosphere (such as parental self-confidence, deviance, and affection) and delinquency.

In one study, she collected data on the childhood homes of 201 men and their subsequent court records in order to identify family-related variables that would predict criminal activity. Variables such as inadequate maternal affection and supervision, parental conflict, the mother's lack of self-confidence, and the father's deviance were significantly related to the commission of crimes against persons and/or property. The father's absence by itself was not correlated with criminal behavior. Heather Juby and David Farrington also provide support for the importance of maternal presence. Using data from the Cambridge Study in Delinquent Development, they examined the impact of family structure on juvenile and adult crime and found that delinquency rates are lower among boys who live with their mother postseparation compared to those who live with their father. They also found that delinquency rates are very similar in disrupted families and high-conflict intact families.[79]

Other studies, such as those by Sheldon and Eleanor Glueck and the more recent studies by Lee

---

federal definition of elder abuse, neglect, and exploitation. The definition is used only as a guideline and not for enforcement purposes. State laws provide their own definitions of elder abuse, and these definitions vary across state jurisdictions. Nevertheless, three basic categories of elder abuse emerged: domestic elder abuse, institutional elder abuse, and self-neglect or self-abuse. Domestic elder abuse results when an older person is maltreated by a person who has a special relationship with the elder, such as a spouse, sibling, child, or friend. Institutional elder abuse occurs in the context of a residential facility, such as a nursing home, in which paid caregivers or other staff are the perpetrators. Self-neglect or self-abuse occurs when elderly persons threaten their own health or safety by, for example, failing to provide themselves with proper amounts of food, clothing, shelter, or medication.[96]

Abuse of the elderly has become an area of special concern to social scientists. The population group that is considered to be elderly is variously defined. The majority of researchers consider 65 the age at which an individual falls into the category "elderly." As health care in the United States has improved, longevity has

RAPE AND SEXUAL ASSAULT

The common law defined **rape** as an act of enforced intercourse by a man of a woman (other than the attacker's wife) without her consent. Intercourse includes any sexual penetration, however slight. The exclusion of wives from the crime of rape rested on several outdated legal fictions, among them the propositions that the marriage vows grant implicit permanent rights of sexual access and that spouses cannot testify against each other. The Hale Doctrine, written in the seventeenth century and recognized judicially in 1857 by the United States, stated specifically that "the husband cannot be guilty of a rape committed by himself upon his lawful wife, for by their mutual matrimonial consent and a contract the wife hath given up herself in this kind unto her husband which she cannot retract."[100] Older laws universally classify rape as a sex crime. But rape has always been much more than that. It is inherently a crime of violence, an exercise of power.

Oddly, as Susan Brownmiller forcefully argues, it really started as a property crime. Men as archetypal aggressors (the penis as a weapon) subju-

THEORY CONNECTS

Rape and Sexual Assault

What theories of crime causation explain rape and sexual assault? Why do you suppose most of the theories discussed in Chapters 4 through 8 are generally unhelpful? Is the crime of rape or sexual assault that different from homicide, robbery, or even assault?

Theory Connects Features

These marginal notes correlate the applied material in Part III of the text ("Types of Crimes") with the theoretical material in Part II ("Explanations of Crime"), giving students much needed cross-reference material and posing critical-thinking questions.

vast body of research for which they laid the groundwork.

Theorists of the Chicago school were the first social scientists to suggest that most crime is committed by normal people responding in expected ways to their immediate surroundings, rather than by abnormal individuals acting out individual pathologies. If social disorganization is at the root of the problem, crime control must involve social organization. The community, not individuals, needs treatment. Helping the community, then, should lower its crime rate.

The Chicago Area Project

Social disorganization theory was translated into practice in 1934 with the establishment of the Chicago Area Project (CAP), an experiment in neighborhood reorganization. The project was initiated by the Institute for Juvenile Research, at which Clifford Shaw and Henry McKay were working. It coordinated the existing community support groups—local schools, churches, labor unions, clubs, and merchants. Special efforts were made to control delinquency through recreational facilities, summer camps, better law enforcement, and the upgrading of neighborhood schools, sanitation, and general appearance.

In 1994, this first community-based delinquency-prevention program could boast 60 years of achievement. South Chicago remains an area of poverty and urban marginalization, dotted with boarded-up buildings and signs of urban decay, though the pollution from the nearby steel mills is under control. But the Chicago Area Project initiated by Shaw and McKay is as vibrant as ever, with its three-pronged attack on delinquency: direct service, advocacy, and community involvement. Residents, from clergy to gang members, are working with CAP to keep kids out of trouble, to help those in trouble, and to clean up the neighborhoods. "In fact, in those communities where area projects have been in operation for a number of years, incidents of crime and delinquency have decreased (Figure 5.6)."[64]

Operation Weed and Seed and Others

Operation Weed and Seed is a federal, state, and local effort to improve the quality of life in targeted high-crime urban areas across the country. The strategy is to "weed" out negative influences (drugs, crime) and to "seed" the neighborhoods with prevention and intervention.

When the program began in 1991, there were three target areas—Kansas City, Missouri; Trenton, New Jersey; and Omaha, Nebraska. By 1999, the number of target areas had increased to 200 sites. An

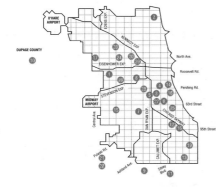

FIGURE 5.6 CAP affiliates now dot the Chicago landscape, from (1) Agape Youth Development/Family Services at 320 South Spaulding (East Garfield), and (2) Alternatives, Inc., at 1126 West Granville Avenue (Rogers Park—Uptown) to (28) Wentworth Residents United for Survival at 3752 South Wells (Wentworth Gardens) and (29) Youth Service Committee of the WestSide at 1832 West Washington (Henry Horner Homes).

Source: www.chicagoareaproject.org/map.html.

Theory Informs Policy

These brief sections in theory chapters demonstrate how problems identified by criminologists have led to practical solutions.

REVIEW In the history of criminology from ancient times to the early twentieth century, its many themes at times have clashed and at times have supported one another. There is no straight-line evolutionary track that we can follow from the inception of the first "criminological" thought to modern theories. Some scholars concentrated on criminal law and procedure, others on criminal behavior. Some took the biological route, others the psychological, and still others the sociological. And the work of some investigators has encompassed a combination of factors. Toward the end of the nineteenth century, a discipline began to emerge.

Tracing the major developments back in time helps us understand how criminology grew into the discipline we know today. Many of the issues that appear on the intellectual battlefields early in the twenty-first century are the same issues our academic ancestors grappled with for hundreds, indeed thousands, of years. With each new clash, some old concepts died, while others were incorporated within competing doctrinal boundaries, there to remain until the next challenge. The controversies of one era become the foundations of knowledge for the next. As societies develop and are subjected to new technologies, the crime problem becomes ever more complex. So do the questions it raises. In Part II we will see how twentieth-century theorists have dealt with those questions.

CRIMINOLOGY & PUBLIC POLICY The execution methods debate is played out by legislative decision-makers, who oftentimes turn a blind eye to the concerns of those who actually have to kill. In turn, a considerable portion of doctors, nurses, and other medical personnel willingly participate in executions. Prison officials face the worst of both worlds: They have limited political clout by which to make their choices known and minimal guidance provided by those who make the choices for them. The process is made all the more perplexing because those who report the problems with the system—media witnesses—have questionable credibility when experts attempt to use their accounts in court. "As a result," in Foucault's words, "justice no longer takes public responsibility for the violence that is bound up with its practice." The system becomes literally and symbolically unobservable. In the context of applying execution methods, when justice becomes unobservable, it ceases to exist. (Source: From Deborah W. Denno, "When Legislatures Delegate Death: The Troubling Paradox behind State Uses of Electrocution and Lethal Injection and What

It Says about Us," *Ohio State Law Journal*, **63**, [2002]: 63. Reprinted by permission of *Ohio State Law Journal* and the author.)

Questions for Discussion Beccaria voiced concerns over bad laws (see the section "Cesare Beccaria" earlier in this chapter). He made an inspired call for an end to medieval barbarism. Punishment should be prompt and effective. Capital punishment should be abolished—and so, too, should the use of torture. Debate over the death penalty in recent years has turned on concerns over executing innocents, the mentally ill, and the insane. Much has been written about the racial application of the death penalty as well. Professor Denno raises a very different concern: Are the methods we use to execute inmates justifiable? Interestingly, Professor Denno raises this concern about the use of lethal injection—considered to be the most humane of the methods of execution. If you agree with her reasoning, do you then conclude that all methods of execution should be abolished?

YOU BE THE CRIMINOLOGIST A historical society has invited you to represent criminology in a discussion group made up of experts from various disciplines. The topic is:

How do the foundations of your discipline help us understand contemporary developments in the field? What would you discuss?

KEY TERMS *The numbers next to the terms refer to the pages on which the terms are defined.*

anomie (68)
atavistic stigmata (61)
born criminal (61)
classical school (53)
eugenics (64)

laws of imitation (67)
phrenology (60)
physiognomy (60)
positivist school (53)
somatotype school (63)
utilitarianism (57)

End-of-Chapter Features

Every chapter concludes with a Review, Criminology & Public Policy exercise, You Be the Criminologist exercise, and a listing of chapter-specific Key Terms. These tools help students reinforce and expand the chapter content.

Online Learning Center, Including Additional Chapters

Visit our Online Learning Center at www.mhhe.com/adlercrim7e for robust student and instructor resources. Also included on the password-protected instructor portion of the site are Chapters 15–18, covering the Criminal Justice system.

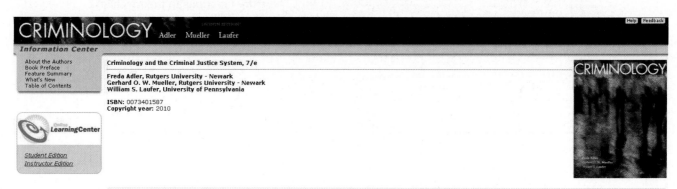

Understanding Criminology

Criminology is the scientific study of the making of laws, the breaking of laws, and society's reaction to the breaking of laws. Sometimes these laws are arrived at by the consensus of most members of a community; sometimes they are imposed by those in power. Communities have grown in size, from village to world, and the threats to communities have grown accordingly. World-level threats, or at least perceptions of threats, necessitated that criminological research and crime prevention strategies become globalized. Nationally and internationally, criminological research has become influential in policy making, and criminologists seek greater influence (Chapter 1).

Criminologists have adopted methods of study from all the social and behavioral sciences. Like all other scientists, criminologists measure. They assess crime over time and place, and they measure the characteristics of criminals and crimes. Like other social scientists, criminologists pose research questions, state hypotheses, and test the validity of these hypotheses. (Chapter 2).

Throughout history, thinkers and rulers have written about crime and criminals and the control of crime. Yet the term *criminology* is little more than a century old, and the subject has been of scientific interest for only two centuries. Two schools of thought contributed to modern criminology: the classical school, associated predominantly with Cesare Beccaria (eighteenth century), which focused on crime, and the positivist school, associated with Cesare Lombroso, Enrico Ferri, and Raffaele Garofalo (nineteenth and early twentieth centuries), which focused on criminals (Chapter 3). Contemporary American criminology owes much to these European roots.

The Changing Boundaries of Criminology

The Changing Boundaries of Criminology
Terrorism
Illicit Drug Trafficking
Money Laundering
Infiltration of Legal Business
Computer Crime
Illicit Arms Trafficking
Trafficking in Persons
Destruction of Cultural Property
The Reach of Criminology
What Is Criminology?
The Making of Laws
Deviance
The Concept of Crime
The Consensus and Conflict Views of Law
  and Crime
The Breaking of Laws
Society's Reaction to the Breaking of Laws
Criminology and the Criminal Justice System
The Global Approach to the Breaking of Laws
Research Informs Policy
Review
Criminology & Public Policy
You Be the Criminologist
Key Terms

■ *"A Louisiana State Police tactical unit patrols the streets following Hurricane Katrina. In the wake of such a disaster, police are often called on to help protect the people and prevent crimes such as looting and violence. But at the same time the officials in charge are often unprepared for the types of crimes they will face and the disaster's full impact on the community."*

August 26, 2005. It is a Friday. People all along America's Gulf Coast are going about their business and pleasure. Letter carriers deliver the mail. Tourists flock to New Orleans's fabled French Quarter to enjoy the incomparable jazz that only this city can offer. Shoppers make their weekend purchases in the supermarkets of Baton Rouge and hundreds of other towns, and gamblers play the slot machines of Biloxi's floating gambling casinos. Out in the Gulf of Mexico, a monstrous tropical storm is developing, dubbed Katrina. Its winds blow at category 5, the most severe type of storm. As a precaution, the governor of Louisiana and the mayor of New Orleans declare a state of emergency, requesting federal assistance.

People in New Orleans begin boarding up their homes and shops. The hurricane makes a broad landfall early in the morning of August 29, with devastating consequences. Roofs are blown off houses; houses are blown away; all power is severed; 80 percent of the city is under water, and thousands of residents huddle on rooftops waiting to be rescued. Normal social life ceases to exist. Looters take over the city, forcing the mayor to order 1,500 police officers on search-and-rescue duty to return to the streets to rein them in.

By now you may well be asking, What does this have to do with criminology? A great deal. Criminologists who study disasters have found that different types of crimes (including looting, violence, and fraud) can be expected at each stage of a disaster.[1] Why, then, are officials in charge of emergencies so totally unprepared to deal with the crimes and their impact on communities, which cause losses of life, destruction of property, and exploitation of the population? One answer, both self-serving and apparently true, is that those most responsible for failed leadership before, during, and after a disaster are not as acquainted as they should be with criminological research.

The first lesson of this book, then, is that criminology is not simply an abstract, theoretical science. Rather, it is a science that has much to offer policy—specifically, policy aimed at protecting the community from the most significant of all harms, criminal harm. There is a second lesson in the Hurricane Katrina story. Criminology is not concerned only with street crimes such as robbery or assault. Much of what happens on Earth has criminological significance. Indeed, we may well (and prematurely) suggest that there is not one criminology but many criminologies, such as a criminology of white-collar and corporate crimes (Chapter 12) and a criminology of terrorism (Chapters 1 and 10), among others. Many criminologies are yet to be discovered. And this is where our story begins.

THE CHANGING BOUNDARIES OF CRIMINOLOGY

911 is the number Americans call when they need police protection from a criminal attack or similar emergency. In a very real sense, then, 911 starts the process of criminal justice and its inquiry about perpetrators and victims, causes and motivations, offenses and defenses. 911, therefore, is a good symbol with which to start a course—or

a book—dedicated to criminology. In 2001, 911 took on yet another meaning, not only to the worldwide public, in general, but to criminologists, in particular.

It was in the morning hours of September 11, 2001, that four airliners were diverted in flight by perpetrators who had subdued or killed the crews. Two of the jets crashed into the New York World Trade Center. A third plane smashed into the Pentagon, in Washington, D.C. The fourth plane, apparently headed toward Washington, D.C., crashed into a field in Pennsylvania, allegedly as a result of passengers trying to overpower the hijackers.

The World Trade Center collapsed within the hour; the Pentagon was in flames; all passengers and crews of the airplanes died in fiery crashes. The death toll was nearly three thousand. It was the worst criminally caused catastrophe in American history. To this day, neither the American economy nor the American psyche has fully recovered from this act of terrorism.

In this post-9/11 world, the threat of another domestic terrorist attack—no matter how inevitable or likely—is used to support legislation and criminal justice policies that affect our civil rights and liberties. Criminologists have been slow to respond to reforms justified by concerns over homeland security with systematic research, and even slower to tackle the criminology of terrorism. However, criminologists have much to say. After all, terrorism is a crime!

Terrorism

The federal and state penal codes contain a number of crimes referring to terrorism. The federal criminal code has listed several new crimes regarding terrorism, including "acts of terrorism transcending national boundaries," "use of certain weapons of mass destruction," and "financial transactions" to finance terrorism. Several states have adopted similar legislation, many of which are based on global United Nations conventions.[2] Few of these laws define terrorism as such. Most incorporate crimes that terrorists are likely to commit in furtherance of their objective, such as murder, arson, kidnapping, and so on. While there is no universally agreed-upon definition of the term "terrorism" Title 22 of the United States Code, Section 2656f(d), defines it as "premeditated, politically motivated violence perpetrated against noncombatant targets by subnational groups or clandestine agents, usually intended to influence an audience."[3] Most definitions imply the use of violence or other significant forms of criminality to achieve the perpetrators' purpose. We are proposing our own definition: "The use or threat of violence directed at people or governments to punish them for past action and/or to bring about a change of policy that is consistent with the terrorists' objectives." This concept

FIGURE 1.1 Wheel of terrorism.

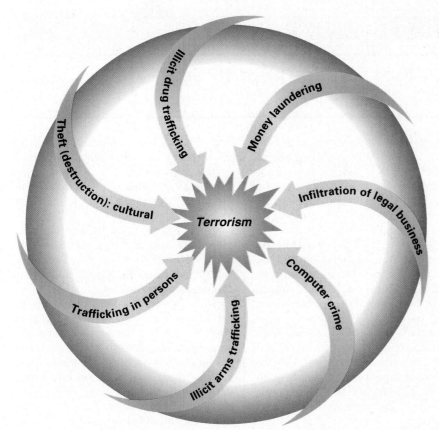

incorporates many forms of criminal conduct and is therefore of prime significance to criminologists.

There is a second and equally important reason for criminologists to study terrorism: It is at the center of many forms of criminality that feed or are fed by terrorism. This can best be demonstrated by a wheel, the hub of which is terrorism. The seven spokes of the wheel are the seven forms of transnational criminality (see Chapter 14) that are directly relevant to terrorism, either because they support it or because they are a consequence or by-product of it. Let us continue our search for the reach of criminology by examining these seven categories (Figure 1.1).

Illicit Drug Trafficking

Terrorists need money for their operations. The drug trade provides easy access to large funds. The Taliban financed their terrorist activities from the vast opium production of Afghanistan. Terrorists in Colombia derive their funds from the coca trade of Latin America. And that holds true for just about every other terrorist group around the world. Globally, it has been estimated that approximately $1 trillion in "dirty money" is available for financing illegal activities, including terrorism. Approximately $500 billion comes into the West from transitional and emerging economies, much of it from the illegal drug trade. While the "war on drugs" had received widespread

attention in the media and on the part of government officials and criminologists, the "war against terrorism" has virtually replaced the prior emphasis. This is particularly disturbing when it is becoming ever more clear that the drug trade nurtures terrorism and fosters the growth of international criminal organizations.[4]

Money Laundering

"Dirty" (illegally obtained) money cannot be spent freely. While there is evidence that terrorist weapons have been obtained by direct exchange for drugs, or for dirty money, most expenditures by terrorists are for goods or services obtained on the free market, which demands clean cash. Hence, much of the dirty money must be laundered in a vast criminal enterprise called "money laundering." Of course, it is not just drug money that requires laundering. All illegally obtained funds (for example, from bribery, black-market activities, corruption, extortion, and embezzlement) require laundering. Thus, money laundering is an activity aimed at making illegally obtained and, therefore, untaxed funds appear legitimate. Usually this is done by depositing such funds in numbered but unnamed (secret) accounts in banks of a number of countries where that is still possible. From there the funds are rapidly transferred elsewhere, and yet again, until it becomes impossible to trace

In the Words of Al Qaeda: What Else Is There to Say about September 11?

AKHU MAN TA`A ALLAH

Since September 11th America has been spending billions of dollars to protect its infrastructure and interests around the world.

The attacker determines the timing of the strike. He will carry a concentrated strike one time at a weak point and then sit in ambush again. So the enemy will look for a gap and close it, this is not necessarily where he was hit but all other similar targets. So striking the American embassies in Kenya and Tanzania means protecting every American embassy in the world. Striking the [U.S.S.] Cole at sea means protecting all American assets in the seas. Diversifying targets means protecting all American things in every land that may have terrorists!!

So if the strategic goal is defense, this does not mean that the tactic should also be defense, the best method of defense is offense. Here we choose guerilla warfare that relies on the principle of (defense strategy in an offensive tactic) in which you withdraw from every position of defense and take an offensive posture everywhere and strike the enemy where he does not expect it.

If the enemy is situated within the [Muslim] nation, then he should be struck everywhere he is present to show the [Muslim] population, and to have the Muslim nation participate in fighting its enemy. If the enemy possesses agents and collaborators, then we should strike the enemy by targeting these agents and collaborators, to expose to the people his agents who will find it necessary to declare their collaboration and defend their master to the death.

If the enemy places his armies away from his soil to get internal peace of mind for the attacks on the military will occur away from home, then we should sneak deep into enemy territory and strike him in the heart. This is what we mean by using guerrilla warfare in urban areas which is also named city warfare. It is when you are close to the enemy and you strike him so he does not recover, with god's per-mission.

If the enemy used his economy to rule the world and hire collaborators, then we need to strike this economy with harsh attacks to bring it down on the heads of its owners.

If the enemy has built his economy on the basis of open markets and free trade by getting the monies of investors, then we have to prove to these investors that the enemy's land is not safe for them, that his economy is not capable of guarding their monies, so they would abandon him to suffer alone the fall of his economy.

If the enemy like everyone else has points of strength and points of weakness, we should surpass his points of strength and attack his points of weakness to collapse his strength.

■ *Money laundering allows crime to pay by permitting criminals to hide and legitimize proceeds derived from illegal activities. According to one recent estimate, worldwide money-laundering activity amounts to roughly $1 trillion a year.*

Source: U.S. State Department, "The Fight against Money Laundering," *Economic Perspectives,* **6**(2), May 2001, http://usinfo.state .gov/journals/ites/0501/ ijee0501.htm.

them to the criminal activity that created them.[5] Despite increased international cooperation to curb money laundering, it appears that terrorism has benefited greatly from this criminal activity.

Infiltration of Legal Business

Dirty money, once laundered, can be used freely (for example, to buy or establish a legitimate business). By way of example, police in Hamburg, Germany, discovered that the innocent-looking import-export firms Tatari Design and Tatex Trading GmbH were not so innocent at all. They had been established as fronts for terrorist operatives to smuggle money, agents, and supplies.[6] Of course, it is often the case that laundered funds, rather than directly financing terrorist enterprises, will be invested in businesses controlled by organized crime, such as trash hauling, construction, seafood, or investment banking.[7]

If the enemy terrorizes us by killing civilians, then we should strike at his civilians which god allows us to kill, and to not decrease our strikes on the military which the enemy accepts their deaths, for this is the nature of military.

If the enemy has build his country on the principles of institutions and democracy where people rule, then we should make the people take our side not the side of the enemy, by proving to the people that the policies of their government bring forth more and more attacks against them. This is what we saw in the attacks in Spain which in turn fired its dictator (Aznar).

This is about Jihad against the crusader enemy, so what about the September 11th operation?

Hijacking planes is a well known tactic, which was used by various fighters and freedom fighters, so what's new about this operation?

People used to hijack planes and consider them a target, but those who are willing to put in the extra effort turned these planes into a method only, a projectile shot into the heart of the enemy.

The hijackers used to pressure the pilot to do what they wish, but would the pilot be receptive if you order him to kill himself and his passengers and destroy his infidel country with his plane? Of course not. So the planes are going to be flown by young men you surrendered their lives to god, this is what happened when the hijackers became pilots who mastered flying.

The enemy used to protect his external interests and has spent exuberant sums for this protection, so he was surprised when he was struck inside his borders. The enemy used to protect a thousand interests outside his county, now he has to protect a million interests inside his country that need continuing protection!!

The attack on the [World] Trade Center forced America since that day to spend billions to protect the huge economic infrastructure that runs the American economy.

Using planes in this attack has forced America to spend billions to protect the planes and airports in all possible ways. This protection is not limited to the hundreds of American airports but also to every airport in the world. Anyone related to the aviation industry is spending excessive amounts to guard air travel; the matter has reached protecting the skies.

Has anyone throughout history ever heard of protecting the skies?

America is conducting patrols, not with cars like Ford and Lumina, but rather patrols with F-16s that circle the skies of New York since September 11th and up to today. Now they are debating reducing these patrols.

This is how America was transformed after one strike, protecting all that can be struck, as they guard all that can be used to strike with!! This is related to armed protection. As for surveillance, now America monitors everything, it even needed to change its laws and to give up on what it used to pride itself of civil rights and personal freedoms. It has violated all previous taboos searching for terrorists.

Questions for Discussion

1. Some scholars arque that Al Qaeda is a "rational" organization. After reading this excerpt, do you agree?
2. Based on this excerpt alone, how significant a threat is Al Qaeda?

SOURCE: Akhu Man Ta`a Allah, "What Else Is There to Say about September 11?" *Sawt al-Jihad* (Voice Of Jihad magazine—Al Qaeda's official publication in Saudi Arabia), vol. 26, pp. 35–42.

Computer Crime

Cyberspace is there for everyone to use—or to abuse. And the abuses are increasingly being discovered and, indeed, legislated as crime. Above all, there is the abuse of cyberspace for money laundering, ultimately to support terrorist groups.[8] Beyond that, there is the potential of cyberattacks on the national security and technology infrastructure of the United States. The security community generally expects terrorists to launch major strikes through networks in the intermediate, if not immediate, future.[9] Al Qaeda is deemed to possess the capacity for these major cyber-attacks.[10]

Illicit Arms Trafficking

The wars of the past have provided terrorists of the past—and the present—with surplus and remnant arms and munitions to fight for their causes. The market in small arms is vast and mostly clandestine. What is new, however, is the market for weapons of mass destruction: nuclear, biological, and chemical. There is considerable evidence that nuclear materials have been diverted from now-defunct former Soviet installations. During both the Clinton and the Bush administrations, fears were expressed that rogue states that have traditionally supported terrorism sought these materials for the creation of weapons of mass destruction. The United States finds itself at war with this justification as its premise. One of the pretexts for the U.S.-Iraq war was the issue of United Nations inspections of suspected Iraqi nuclear arms facilities. As history has demonstrated, no weapons of mass destruction were found by UN inspectors or U.S. military personnel.

Trafficking in Persons

Smuggling would-be illegal migrants from less-desirable homelands to more promising lands of opportunity has become a huge criminal enterprise involving millions of human beings, billions

■ The perils of illegal immigration are vast. Many risk not only arrest and deportation but their lives for the hope of a better life in the United States.

in funds paid to smugglers, and the loss of a great number of innocent lives. Many of the countries of destination fear the growth of immigrant communities that might be terrorist havens, like the refugee camps of Palestine. Even greater is the fear that terrorist organizations deliberately infiltrate their members into immigrant populations. To their dismay, for example, Italian law enforcement authorities have learned that among the waves of illegal immigrants washing ashore in Sicily are increasing numbers of persons linked to terrorist organizations.[11] There are also masses of illegal aliens who have moved from Iran, Iraq, and Turkey—across the Aegean Sea—into Northern Africa, where they become vulnerable recruits for terrorist activities. The problem of illegal immigration is now a major political issue in the United States, raising concerns about border security, civil liberties, and the rights of citizenship.

Destruction of Cultural Property

Lenin's terrorists became infamous for their efforts to destroy the evidence of a culture past: Christian churches were destroyed. Hitler's terrorists burned down the synagogues of Germany and every other cultural symbol, especially literature, art, and music, deemed inconsistent with the new "culture" they wanted to impose. The Taliban took delight in firing artillery shells into two ancient statues of Buddha—the largest in the world—reducing them to rubble. And when the 9/11 terrorists destroyed the World Trade Center, they not only eradicated a symbol of American trade leadership, but also destroyed a beautiful, unique structure of American architecture. Terrorists, especially those with millennial goals or of religious or political extremism, seek to destroy past cultures and to impose their own vision of culture.

The Reach of Criminology

We have completed our examination of the hub and the seven spokes of our criminological wheel. These represent terrorism and seven other forms of criminality that support or are the product of terrorism. These eight forms of criminality are part of a group of 18 that the United Nations has defined as "transnational criminality." Not crimes by themselves but rather a mixture of other crimes, they all have in common the fact that they transcend national boundaries and affect several nations and therefore are hard for just one nation to deal with. (We shall return to transnational criminality in Chapter 14, where we discuss the remaining 10 forms.)

Our effort to demonstrate the reach of criminology is not yet complete. As any exposure to today's media will tell you, there is a competition for attention among those who deem terrorism to be the principal national problem and those who point to our lagging economy. Why? Democrats and Republicans might give you different answers, but all agree that the compromise of our credit markets by a wide range of lending and financial institutions (known generally as the "subprime crisis") lies at the root of the markets' most recent decline. It remains to be seen just how much criminal fraud was involved in lending practices and whether criminal prosecutions will follow the government's bailout of some key lending institutions (e.g., Fannie Mae). Preliminary evidence suggests that significant fraud and related crimes occurred in a number of housing markets that today are suffering from extremely high home foreclosure rates, such as Florida.

In 2001 to 2005, investor confidence was shaken by a sudden and staggering series of corporate governance failures involving Enron, WorldCom, Adelphi, Chevron Texaco, Tyco, and a host of

A gaping hole in the mountain is all that is left of Buddhism's most prized religious symbols: the colossal Buddhas of Afghanistan—purposefully destroyed by Taliban artillery.

Sailors of a Spanish naval vessel—part of an international armada—boarding an unflagged ship, the Sosan, 600 miles off the coast of East Africa, after the captain refused to identify the vessel. Initially, the North Korean master of the vessel claimed she was carrying cement. The Spanish search revealed 15 missiles and other sophisticated weaponry.

other corporate giants. Allegations of fraud and financial mismanagement led to the collapse of many leading companies, including a top-five accounting firm with a long and very distinguished history—Arthur Andersen, L.L.C. Across a wide range of corporations from a host of industries, billions of dollars were mismanaged, embezzled, stolen, illegally transferred, and withheld from tax authorities.[12] You will find out more about this in Chapter 12.

By this time, you may be asking, Is there no limit to the reach of criminological inquiry? There is not, because every human activity is capable of deviance that produces significant harm, thus requiring criminological scrutiny. Not even the ocean is the limit. It is the oceans, covering nearly three-quarters of the world's surface, that make life on Earth possible. Yet the oceans are being threatened by many types of criminality, of which the most deadly is pollution. In earlier editions of this book, we discussed the case of the supertanker *Exxon Valdez*, which negligently had ruptured her hull in Alaska waters, spilling 11 million gallons of crude oil. This caused the greatest environmental disaster North America had yet known. At the time we expressed our hope that this criminally caused disaster would lead to greater efforts to prevent recurrences. But no. Oil spill disasters that should have been prevented have occurred with heightening regularity off the coasts of China, South Africa, the Galápagos Islands, the United States, American Samoa, Denmark, Thailand, Brazil, Finland, Germany, the Netherlands, and Vietnam, among other areas.[13] This criminality, destroying the environment, is called "ecocide." It presents yet another task for criminologists.

As far as the reach of criminology is concerned, do not be deceived by the media and their symbiotic relationship with legislatures. Today's focus of the media on a given crime problem is no indication of the extent of criminology's tasks. In the 1960s, the emphasis was on juvenile delinquency; in the 1970s, attention turned to street crime in general and drugs in particular, which led, in the 1980s, to a focus on prison overcrowding, on one hand, and target hardening, on the other. Then, in the 1990s, more attention was being paid to foreign influences on our crime rates, in the wake of globalization. Domestic (school shootings) and foreign violence, along with terrorism, dictated the market for ideas, with competing attention focused on computer, white-collar, and corporate criminality. Today, entering the second decade of the twenty-first century, it is clear that these problems demand more of criminology than it is capable of delivering as yet. The principal crime problems of today are totally globalized. Criminology has to become equally globalized.

Seemingly we have neglected street crimes and delinquency in this survey of the reach of criminology. These topics are, and will remain, a major focus of criminologists—in competition with all the other forms of criminality to which we have alluded. Now that you are acquainted with the changing boundaries of criminology, we next introduce you to what this discipline is all about.

WHAT IS CRIMINOLOGY?

In the Middle Ages, human learning was commonly divided into four areas: law, medicine, theology, and philosophy. Universities typically had four faculties, one for each of these fields. Imagine a young person in the year 1392—100 years before Columbus came ashore in America—knocking at the portal of a great university with this request: "I would like to study criminology. Where do I sign up?" A stare of disbelief would have greeted the student, because the word had not yet been coined. Cautiously the student would explain: "Well, I'm interested in what crime is, and how the law deals with criminals." The university official might smile and say, "The right place for you to go is the law faculty. They will teach you everything there is to know about the law."

The student might feel discouraged. "That's a lot more than I want to know about the law. I really don't care about inheritance laws and the law of contracts. I just want to study all about crime and criminality. For example, why are certain actions considered wrong or evil in the first place, and—" The official would interrupt: "Then you must go to the faculty of theology. They know all there is to know about good and evil, heaven and hell." The student might persist: "But could they teach me what it is about the human body and mind that could cause some people and not others to commit crime?" "Oh, I see," the official would say. "You really should study medicine." "But, sir, medicine probably is only part of what I need to know, and really only part of medicine seems relevant. I want to know all there is to know about—" And then would come the official's last attempt to steer the student in the right direction: "Go and study philosophy. They'll teach you all there is to know!"

For centuries, all the knowledge the universities recognized continued to be taught in these four faculties. It was not until the eighteenth and nineteenth centuries that the natural and social sciences became full-fledged disciplines. In fact, the science of criminology has been known as such for only a little more than a century.

In 1885, the Italian law professor Raffaele Garofalo coined the term "criminology" (in Italian, *criminologia*).[14] The French anthropologist Paul Topinard used it for the first time in French (*criminologie*) in 1887.[15] "Criminology" aptly described and encompassed the scientific concern with the phenomenon of crime. The term immediately gained acceptance all over the world, and criminology became a subject taught at universities. Unlike their predecessors in 1392—or even in 1892—today's entering students will find that teaching and learning are distributed among 20 or 30 disciplines and departments. And criminology or criminal justice is likely to be one of them.

Criminology is a science, an empirical science. More particularly, it is one of the social, or behavioral, sciences. It has been defined in various ways by its scholars. The definition provided in 1934 by Edwin H. Sutherland, one of the founding scholars of American criminology, is widely accepted:

> **Criminology** is the body of knowledge regarding crime as a social phenomenon. It includes within its scope the process of making laws, of breaking laws, and of reacting toward the breaking of laws. . . . The objective of criminology is the development of a body of general and verified principles and of other types of knowledge regarding this process of law, crime, and treatment or prevention.[16]

This definition suggests that the field of criminology is narrowly focused on crime yet broad in scope. By stating as the objective of criminology the "development of a body of general and verified principles," Sutherland mandates that **criminologists,** like all other scientists, collect information for study and analysis in accordance with the research methods of modern science. As we shall see in Chapter 3, it was in the eighteenth century that serious investigations into criminal behavior were first conducted. The investigators, however, were not engaged in empirical research, although they based their conclusions on factual information. Only in the nineteenth century did criminologists begin to systematically gather facts about crime and criminals and evaluate their data in a scientific manner.

Among the first researchers to analyze empirical data (facts, statistics, and other observable information) in a search for the causes of crime was Cesare Lombroso (1835–1909) of Italy (Chapter 3). His biologically oriented theories influenced American criminology at the turn of the twentieth century. At that time, the causes of crime were thought to rest within the individual: Criminal behavior was attributed to feeblemindedness and "moral insanity." From then on, psychologists and psychiatrists played an important role in the study of crime and criminals.

By the 1920s, other scholars attributed the cause of crime to the influx of immigrants and their alien behaviors. The search then moved on to cultural and social interpretations. Crime was explained not only in terms of the offender but also in terms of social, political, and economic problems.

In increasing numbers, sociologists, political scientists, legal scholars, and economists have entered the arena of criminology. Architects, too, have joined the ranks of criminologists in an effort to design housing units that will be relatively free from crime. Engineers are working to design cars that are virtually theft-proof. Pharmacologists play a role in alleviating the problem of drug addiction. Satellites put into space by astrophysicists can help control the drug trade. Specialists in public administration work to improve the functioning of the criminal justice system. Educators have been enlisted to prepare children for a life as free from delinquency as possible. Economists and social workers are needed to help break the cycle of poverty and crime. Biologists neuroscientists and endocrinologists have expanded our understanding of the relationship between biology, the brain, and deviant behavior. Clearly, criminology is a discipline composed of the accumulated knowledge of many other disciplines. Criminologists acknowledge their indebtedness to all contributing disciplines and concede that

the most powerful explanations of crime and criminality likely will come from interdisciplinary scholarship.

In explaining what is meant by Sutherland's definition—"making laws," "breaking laws," and "reacting toward the breaking of laws"—we will use a contemporary as well as a historical perspective on these processes, and a global as well as a local focus.

THE MAKING OF LAWS

Conjure up a picture of a crowded supermarket just after working hours, when most people are eager to get home after a busy day. The checkout counters have long lines of carts overflowing with groceries. One counter—an express line—takes 10 items only. You have 15, but you get in line anyway. People behind you in the line stare. Your behavior is not acceptable. You are a nonconformist, a deviant.

Deviance

Criminologists use the term **deviance** to describe behavior that violates **social norms,** including laws. The customary ways of doing everyday things (like not exceeding the posted limit of items at supermarket express lines) are governed by norms other than laws. More serious deviant behavior, like taking someone else's property, is governed by laws. Criminologists are interested in all social norms and in how society reacts to success or failure of compliance.[17] They are interested in what society does when customary ways of doing things no longer prove effective in controlling conduct perceived as undesirable. New Yorkers concerned over the problem of dog droppings provide an example.

Disciplined city dwellers had always observed the custom of curbing their dogs. Street signs warned them to do this. But as more and more dog owners failed to comply, New Yorkers decided that the cleanliness of the sidewalks was an important issue. Laws were enacted making it an offense not to clean up after one's dog. In Beijing, China, and Reykjavik, Iceland, dogs have been severely restricted or banned from the city altogether.

The difference between crime and other forms of deviance is subject to constant change and may vary from one state or country to another and from one time to another. What yesterday was only distasteful or morally repugnant may today be illegal. Criminologists are therefore interested in all norms that regulate conduct. Making something that is distasteful into a crime

Crime Surfing

http://www.ussc .gov/moneylau/ monisum.htm

One of the components of Sutherland's definition of criminology focuses on the making of laws. For example, Congress created the offense of money laundering in 1986. How did Congress define this crime?

Terrorism and the Fear of Terrorism

Since it opened in 1903, The Taj Mahal Palace & Tower, Mumbai, has created its own unique history. From Maharajas and Princes to various Kings, Presidents, CEOs and entertainers, the Taj has played the perfect host, supportive of their every need.

Built in 1903, the hotel is an architectural marvel and brings together Moorish, Oriental and Florentine styles. Offering panoramic views of the Arabian Sea and the Gateway of India, the hotel is a gracious landmark of the city of Mumbai, showcasing contemporary Indian influences along with beautiful vaulted alabaster ceilings, onyx columns, graceful archways, hand-woven silk carpets, crystal chandeliers, a magnificent art collection, an eclectic collection of furniture, and a dramatic cantilever stairway.

Over the past century, The Taj Mahal Palace & Tower, Mumbai, has amassed a diverse collection of paintings and works of art and is a veritable showcase of artifacts and art of the era. From Belgian chandeliers to Goan Christian artifacts, the hotel incorporates a myriad of artistic styles and tastes.(1)

■ The Taj Mahal Palace & Tower, Mumbai.

Voted "The World's Best Overseas Business Hotel" by readers of Condé Nast Traveller UK in 2008, the Taj Mahal Palace & Tower is nothing short of a hotel icon. It stands as India's most famous and most luxurious hotel. In November 2008, it was also the primary site of an extremely well-coordinated terror plot that, along with separate attacks in nine other locations in this capital city of India, resulted in the death of more than 180 people.(2) More than 240 people were injured.

may be counterproductive and detrimental to the social order. If everything deviant (inconsistent with the majority's norms) were to be made criminal, society would become very rigid. The more rigid a society, the more that behavior defined as violating social norms is prohibited by law.

Jack D. Douglas and Frances C. Waksler have presented the continuum of deviance as a funnel (Figure 1.2). This funnel consists of definitions ranging from the broadest (a "feeling that something is vaguely wrong, strange, peculiar") to the narrowest (a "judgment that something is absolutely evil"). Somewhere between these two extremes, deviant behavior becomes criminal behavior. The criminologist's interest in understanding the process begins at the earliest point— when a behavior is first labeled "deviant."[18]

Although criminologists are interested in all deviant behavior—even that of no interest to the law—their primary interest is in criminal behavior, behavior that violates the law.

The Concept of Crime

A **crime** is any human conduct that violates a criminal law and is subject to punishment. What leads a society to designate some deviant behavior a crime and leave other wrongs to be settled by private or civil remedies? For centuries, natural-law philosophers, believing in the universal rightness and wrongness of certain human behavior, held the view that some forms of behavior are innately criminal and that all societies condemn them equally. Homicide and theft were thought to be among these.

The hotel had prior warning that an attack might take place. Staff heeded the warning, but to no avail. Even with additional security, the attack was not easily prevented. According to Ratan Tata, chairman of the Tata Group that owns the hotel, "[The terrorists] knew what they were doing, and they did not go through the front. All of our [security] arrangements are in the front," he said. "They planned everything. I believe the first thing they did, they shot a sniffer dog and his handler. They went through the kitchen." To make matters worse, according to Tata, Mumbai's emergency response infrastructure was inadequate.

There is an emerging consensus about the lessons learned from this attack, lessons that complement Ratan Tata's critical view:

- *The public expects and deserves competent law enforcement responses.* Law enforcement's response in Mumbai was underwhelming.
- *Low-tech, highly synchronized attacks can exact a significant toll.* The only weapons it takes for a successful terrorist attack are automatic rifles and hand grenades.
- *Terrorists can influence elections.* Major terrorist incidents tend to congregate around election time.

Bloodshed in Mumbai: Tourists and police targeted in 10 attacks.

Madrid, Iraq, and Pakistan are far from coincidences.
- *Despite promises of prompt reform, don't expect much.* In the past year, India has experienced a dramatic upsurge in terrorism, even though such attacks are far from new.

As you read this book, consider how a criminologist might best be deployed in order to strengthen homeland security for all the obvious and less-than-obvious targets.

Sources
1. www.tajhotels.com/Palace/The%20 Taj%20Mahal%20Palace%20 &%20Tower,MUMBAI/default.htm.
2. "Bloodshed in Mumbai: Tourists and Police Targeted in 10 Attacks," Associated Press, Nov. 28, 2008.

Questions for Discussion
1. What are the most likely targets of terrorist groups?
2. How would you go about developing a counterterrorist strategy?

Most inclusive
  I. Feeling that something is vaguely wrong, strange, peculiar
  II. Feelings of dislike, repugnance
  III. Feeling that something violates values or rules
  IV. Feeling that something violates moral values or moral rules
  V. Judgment that something violates values or rules
  VI. Judgment that something violates moral values or moral rules
  VII. Judgment that something violates morally legitimate misdemeanor laws
  VIII. Judgment that something violates morally legitimate felony laws
  IX. Judgment that something violates moral human nature
  X. Judgment that something is absolutely evil

Least inclusive

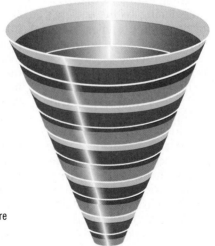

FIGURE 1.2 The funnel of deviance.

Source: Adapted from Jack D. Douglas and Frances Chaput Waksler, *The Sociology of Deviance* (Boston: Little, Brown, 1982), Figure 1.1, p. 11. Copyright © 1982 by Jack D. Douglas and Frances Chaput Waksler. Reprinted by permission of the authors.

This notion is no longer supported. Raffaele Garofalo, who gave our discipline its name, defended the concept of natural crime, by which he meant behavior that offends basic moral sentiments, such as respect for the property of others and revulsion against the infliction of suffering. Nevertheless, he admitted that although we might think such crimes as murder and robbery would be recognized by all existing legal systems, "a slight investigation seems to dispel this idea."[19]

Garofalo was right. The earliest codes, including the Babylonian Code of Hammurabi (about 1750 B.C.) and the Roman Law of the Twelve Tables (451–450 B.C.), do not list homicide or ordinary theft as crimes. Problems like these were settled without resorting to punishment. But all early societies imposed punishment for acts detrimental to their own existence: acts of treason. Other crimes depended on socioeconomic needs (destroying a bridge was a crime among the Incas; stealing a beehive was a crime among the ancient Germanic tribes; stealing a horse or a blanket was a crime among American Plains Indians).

The question arises: Who in a society decides—and when and under what circumstances—which acts that are already considered deviant in that society should be elevated to the level of gross deviance or crime, subject to punishment?

The Consensus and Conflict Views of Law and Crime

In the traditional interpretation of the historical development of legal systems, and of criminal justice in particular, lawmaking is an accommodation of interests in a society, whether that society is composed of equals (as in a democracy) or of rulers and ruled (as in absolute monarchies), so as to produce a system of law and enforcement to which everybody basically subscribes. This is the **consensus model.** According to this view, certain acts are deemed so threatening to the society's survival that they are designated crimes. If the vast majority of a group shares this view, we can say the group has acted by consensus.

The model assumes that members of a society by and large agree on what is right and wrong and that codification of social values becomes law, with a mechanism of control that settles disputes that arise when some individuals stray too far from what is considered acceptable behavior. In the words of the famous French sociologist Émile Durkheim, "we can . . . say that an act is criminal when it offends strong and defined states of the collective conscience."[20] Consensus theorists view society as a stable entity in which laws are created for the general good. Laws function to reconcile and to harmonize most of the interests that most of us accept, with the least amount of sacrifice.

■ *The Code of Hammurabi, king of ancient Babylonia, is the oldest complete legal code in existence (about 1750 B.C.). The 8.2-foot carving, found in Iraq in 1902, is now on display in the Louvre in Paris. The only exact replica is at the United Nations building in New York.*

Some criminologists view the making of laws in a society from a different theoretical perspective. In their interpretation, known as the **conflict model,** the criminal law expresses the values of the ruling class in a society, and the criminal justice system is a means of controlling the classes that have no power. Conflict theorists claim that a struggle for power is a far more basic feature of human existence than is consensus. It is through power struggles that various interest groups manage to control lawmaking and law enforcement. Accordingly, the appropriate object of criminological investigation is not the violation of laws but the conflicts within society.

Traditional historians of crime and criminal justice do not deny that throughout history there have been conflicts that needed resolution. Traditionalists claim that differences have been resolved by consensus, while conflict theorists claim that the dominant group has ended the conflicts by imposing its will. This difference in perspective marks one of the major criminological debates today, as we shall see in Chapter 8. It also permeates criminological discussion of who breaks the criminal laws and why.

THE BREAKING OF LAWS

Sutherland's definition of criminology includes within its scope investigating and explaining the process of breaking laws. This may seem simple if viewed from a purely legal perspective. A prosecutor is not interested in the fact that hundreds of people are walking on Main Street. But if one of those hundreds grabs a woman's purse and runs away with it, the prosecutor is interested, provided the police have brought the incident to the prosecutor's attention. What alerts the prosecutor is the fact that a law has been broken, that one of those hundreds of people on Main Street has turned from a law-abiding citizen into a lawbreaker. This event, if detected, sets in motion a legal process that ultimately will determine whether someone is indeed a lawbreaker.

Sutherland, in saying that criminologists have to study the process of lawbreaking, had much more in mind than determining whether someone has violated the criminal law. He was referring to the process of breaking laws. That process encompasses a series of events, perhaps starting at birth or even earlier, that results in the commission of crime by some individuals and not by others.

Let us analyze the following rather typical scenario: In the maximum-security unit of a Midwestern penitentiary is an inmate we will call Jeff. He is one of three robbers who held up a check-cashing establishment. During the robbery, another of the robbers killed the clerk. Jeff has been sentenced to life imprisonment.

Born in an inner-city ghetto, Jeff was the third child of an unwed mother. He had a succession of temporary "fathers." By age 12, he had run away from home for the first time, only to be brought back to his mother, who really did not care much whether he returned. He rarely went to school because, he said, "all the guys were bigger." At age 16, after failing two grades, Jeff dropped out of school completely and hung around the streets of his deteriorated, crime-ridden neighborhood. He had no job. He had no reason to go home, because usually no one was there.

One night he was beaten up by members of a local gang. He joined a rival gang for protection and soon began to feel proud of his membership in one of the toughest gangs in the neighborhood. Caught on one occasion tampering with parking meters and on another trying to steal a car navigation system, he was sentenced to two months in a county correctional institution for boys. By the age of 18, he had moved from petty theft to armed robbery.

Many people reading the story of Jeff would conclude that he deserves what is coming to him and that his fate should serve as a warning to others. Other people would say that with his background, Jeff did not have a chance. Some may even marvel at Jeff's ability to survive at all in a very tough world.

To the criminologist, popular interpretations of Jeff's story do not explain the process of breaking laws in Sutherland's terms. Nor do these interpretations explain why people in general break a certain law. Sutherland demanded scientific rigor in researching and explaining the process of breaking laws. As we will see later in the book (Parts II and III), scientists have thoroughly explored Jeff's story and the stories of other lawbreakers. They ask, Why are some people prone to commit crime and others are not? There is no agreement on the answer as yet. Researchers have approached the question from different perspectives. Some have examined delinquents (juvenile offenders) and criminals from a biological perspective in order to determine whether some human beings are constitutionally more prone to yield to opportunities to commit criminal acts. Are genes to blame? Hormones? Diet? Neuroanatomical differences? Others have explored the role played by moral development and personality. Is there a criminal personality? (These questions are discussed in Chapter 4.)

Most contemporary criminologists look to factors such as economic and social conditions, which can produce strain among social groups and lead to lawbreaking (Chapter 5). Others point to subcultures committed to violent or illegal activities (Chapter 6). Yet another argument is that the motivation to commit crime is simply part of human nature. So some criminologists examine the ability of social groups and institutions to make their rules effective (Chapter 7).

The findings of other scholars tend to show that lawbreaking depends less on what the offender does than on what society, including the criminal justice system, does to the offender (Chapter 8). This is the perspective of the labeling, conflict, and radical theorists, who have had great influence on criminological thinking since the 1970s.

Scholars have also researched the question of why people who are inclined to break laws engage in particular acts at particular times. They have demonstrated that opportunity plays a large role in the decision to commit a crime. Opportunities are suitable targets inadequately protected. In these circumstances, all that is required for a crime to be committed is a person motivated to offend. These claims are made by criminologists who explain crime in terms of two perspectives: routine activities and rational choice (Chapter 9).

Fame and Crime

- Lindsay Lohan was arrested on December 11, 2006, on DUI charges after witnesses saw her driving the wrong way on the Burbank freeway in her black Mercedes-Benz sport utility vehicle. In a deal with prosecutors, Lohan pleaded guilty to a misdemeanor DUI charge, to avoid a longer jail term since it was her second DUI conviction.

  On November 15, 2007, Lohan reported to the Los Angeles County women's detention center in Lynwood where she was searched and fingerprinted, then stayed in a holding cell and released in just 84 minutes.

- On November 25, 2008, Michael Vick submitted a guilty plea to a single Virginia felony charge for dog fighting. He received a three year prison sentence and was fined $2500. [The accompanying photo of Vick was taken at the court-house.]

- In January 2004, [James] Brown was arrested on a domestic violence charge after his 33-year-old wife, Tomi Rea Brown, called police to report that Brown pushed her onto the ground during an argument. She suffered scratches and bruises on her arm and hip. Brown ended up pleading no contest and paid $1,087 as punishment.

- On October 9th, 2007, [Kiefer] Sutherland pled no contest to a DUI charge and received a 48-day jail sentence. This mug shot was taken on December 6, 2007, when he surrendered to the Glendale Police Department to begin his jail term.

- On July 28, 2006, actor, director, and producer Mel Gibson was arrested on suspicion of driving under the influence while speeding (87 miles per hour in a 45-mph zone) in Malibu, California.

  The intoxicated Gibson became belligerent with police during his arrest and according to L.A. County Sheriff's Deputy James Mee's report, Gibson used bad language, threatened the arresting officer, repeatedly banged himself against the police car interior and made anti-Semitic statements, including telling the policeman that, "The Jews are responsible for all the wars in the world."

  On August 18, Gibson pleaded no contest to one count of driving with blood alcohol content above .08%. The other charges were dropped, and he was sentenced to three years probation, 90-day alcohol-abuse program, 12 months of Alcoholics Anonymous meetings and fined $1,300 with a 90-day license restriction. Gibson volunteered to do public-service announcements on hazards of drinking and driving, and to enter rehab.

- In July 1994, [O.J.] Simpson was arrested in Los Angeles, and charged with the murder of his wife, Nicole Simpson and her friend Ron Goldman. He was found not guilty in a highly publicized trial. He was later found liable for damages in the murders during a civil trial.

  Five years before the murder of Nicole and Goldman, Simpson was arrested for beating his wife, paid a fine and did 200 hours of community service.

  Nicole and Goldman were viciously attacked and butchered outside of Nicole's home. No one else was ever charged for the murders.

- R. Kelly was charged with 14 counts of child pornography and illegally engaging in sexual acts with a minor [occurring sometime] between November 1997 and February 2002.(1)

The stories never seem to end. One star after another faces arrest. The mug shots of famous musicians, sports heroes, actors, comedians, business tycoons, and public officials make their way to tabloid websites, magazines, and newspapers. Their dramatic fall from grace is amazing, exciting, and tragic all at the same time.

Criminologists look at these arrests and think about a wide range of explanations, from failures of self-control and social control (Chapter 7) to the strain of celebrity (Chapter 5), from drug

SOCIETY'S REACTION TO THE BREAKING OF LAWS

Criminologists' interest in understanding the process of breaking a law (or any other social norm) is tied to understanding society's reaction to deviance. The study of reactions to lawbreaking demonstrates that society has always tried to control or prevent norm-breaking.

In the Middle Ages, the wayfarer entering a city had to pass the gallows, on which the bodies of criminals swung in the wind. Wayfarers had to enter through gates in thick walls, and the drawbridges were lowered only during the daylight hours; at nightfall the gates were closed. In front of the town hall, stocks and pillory warned dishonest vendors and pickpockets. Times have changed, but perhaps less than we think. Today penitentiaries and jails dot the countryside. Teams of work-release convicts work along highways under guard. Signs proclaim "Drug-Free School Zone," and decals on doors announce "Neighborhood Crime Watch." Police patrol cars are as visible as they are audible.

These overt signs of concern about crime provide us with only a surface view of the apparatus society has created to deal with lawbreaking; they tell us little of the research and policy making that have gone into the creation of the apparatus. Criminologists have done much of the research on society's reaction to the breaking of laws, and the results have influenced policy making and legislation aimed at crime control. The research has also revealed that society's reaction to lawbreaking has often been irrational, arbitrary, emotional, politically motivated, and counterproductive.

abuse and dependence (Chapter 13) to rational-choice and routine-activity theories (Chapter 9). Criminologists think about how representative these cases are relative to the street crimes of inner-city youth. They wonder how the criminal justice system accommodates privilege, wealth, celebrity, and fame. Do police, prosecutors, and judges deal differently with such cases? Should they?

To a large extent, the images of Lindsay Lohan, Michael Vick, James Brown, Kiefer Sutherland, Mel Gibson, O.J. Simpson, and R. Kelly frame our perceptions about deviance. Their arrests are remarkable for so many fascinating and disturbing reasons. They have wealth and fame. They are at the top of their game and have so much to lose. We idolize them, admire their talent and boundless success, and think about what life might be like as a world famous rapper, actor, or sports star.

Source

1. Charles Montaldo, "Celebrity Mug Shots: Celebrities at Their Worst," at http://crime.about.com/od/famousdiduno/ig/celebrity_mugshots.

Questions for Discussion

1. What can we learn from the celebrities' arrests about why people, in general, commit crime, about who commits crime, and about how society should respond to crime?

Lindsay Lohan

Michael Vick

James Brown

Kiefer Sutherland

Mel Gibson

O. J. Simpson

R. Kelly

2. To what extent are celebrities victimized by their own fame and thus less blameworthy for acts of deviance? (See, e.g., Ruth Penfold, "The Star's Image, Victimization and Celebrity Culture," *Punishment & Society*, 6, [**3**], [2004]: 289–302.)

Research on society's reaction to the breaking of laws is more recent than research on the causes of crime. It is also more controversial. For some criminologists, the function of their research is to assist government in the prevention or repression of crime. Others insist that such a use of science only supports existing power structures that may be corrupt. The position of most criminologists is somewhere in between. Researchers often discover inhumane and arbitrary practices and provide the database and the ideas for a humane, effective, and efficient **criminal justice system.**

Criminology and the Criminal Justice System

The term "criminal justice system" is relatively new. It became popular only in 1967, with the publication of the report of the President's Commission on Law Enforcement and Administration of Justice, *The Challenge of Crime in a Free Society.* The discovery that various ways of dealing with lawbreaking form a system was itself the result of criminological research. Research into the functioning of the system and its component parts, as well as into the work of functionaries within the system, has provided many insights over the last few decades.

Scientists who study the criminal justice system are frequently referred to as "criminal justice specialists." This term suggests a separation between criminology and criminal justice. In fact, the two fields are closely interwoven. Scholars of both disciplines use the same scientific research methods. They have received the same rigorous education, and they pursue the same goals. Both

In Placentia, California, residents clamor for protection of children from convicted and released child molesters. Public protests have led to a flood of local laws regarding the identification of where these ex-offenders are residing.

fields rely on the cooperation of many other disciplines, including sociology, psychology, political science, law, economics, management, and education. Their origins, however, differ. Criminology has its roots in European scholarship, although it has undergone refinements, largely under the influence of American sociology. Criminal justice is a recent American innovation.

The two fields are also distinguished by a difference in focus. Criminology generally focuses on scientific studies of crime and criminality, whereas criminal justice focuses on scientific studies of decision-making processes, operations, and justice-related concerns such as the efficiency of police, courts, and corrections systems; the just treatment of offenders; the needs of victims; and the effects of changes in sentencing philosophy.

The United States has well over 50 criminal justice systems—those of the 50 states and of the federal government, the District of Columbia, Puerto Rico, Guam, the U.S. Virgin Islands, American Samoa, the Commonwealth of the Northern Mariana Islands, Palau, and the military. They are very similar: All are based on constitutional principles and on the heritage of the common law, and all were designed to cope with the problem of crime within their territories on the assumption that crime is basically a local event calling for a local response. Crimes that have an interstate or international aspect are under the jurisdiction of federal authorities, and such offenses are prosecuted under the federal criminal code.

The Global Approach to the Breaking of Laws

Until fairly recently, there was rarely any need to cooperate with foreign governments, because crime had few international connections. This situation has changed drastically. Crime, like life itself, has become globalized, and responses to lawbreaking have inevitably extended beyond local and national borders. In the first three and a half decades after World War II, from 1945 until the late 1970s, the countries of the world gradually became more interdependent. Commercial relations among countries increased. Modern commercial aviation (the "jet age") brought a huge increase in international travel and transport. Satellite communications facilitated intense and continuous public and private relationships. The Internet added the final touch to globalization.

Beginning in the 1980s, the internationalization of national economies accelerated sharply, and with the collapse of Marxism in Eastern Europe in the 1990s, a global economy is being created. These developments, which turned the world into what has been called a "global village," have also had considerable negative consequences. As everything else in life became globalized, so did crime. Transnational crimes, with which we began this chapter, suddenly boomed. Then there are the truly international crimes—those that are proscribed by international law—such as crimes against the peace and security of mankind, genocide, and war crimes. But even many apparently purely local crimes, whether local drug crime or handgun violence, now have international dimensions. In view of the rapid globalization of crime, we devote an entire chapter (Chapter 14) to the international dimensions of criminology. In addition, "Window to the World" boxes explore the international implications of crime and criminology.

The importance of a global approach to criminology is beyond controversy. However, developing the cross-national dialogue and collaboration necessary to build a robust field remains a challenge. This challenge will gain significance as the effects of globalization reveal just how connected we are to the economic and social development of emerging and transitional countries. It will be affected as well by global threats not typically considered by criminologists, such as climate change. Even the most conservative scenarios by leading nongovernmental organizations (for example, the Intergovernmental Panel on Climate Change) suggest massive displacement and shifts in population in some of the poorest of the poor nations. The consequences of these movements, along with the changing landscape of countries already experiencing dramatic social and economic crises, will likely keep criminologists busy for many years to come.

RESEARCH INFORMS POLICY

Skeptics often ask: With so many criminologists at work in the United States, and so many studies conducted over the last half century, why do we have so much crime, why is some of it increasing, and why do new forms of crime emerge constantly? There are several answers. Crime rates go up and down. Through the 1990s crime decreased, and then in the first decade of the new century it increased. The perception that the crime problem is increasing or decreasing rests on a fear of crime that is fueled by media portrayals. Sensational reports often sell newspapers and TV programs. Politicians, in turn, seek security in office by catering to public perceptions of crime

rather than to its reality. They therefore propose and enact measures that respond to popular demands and that often are more symbolic than result-oriented. At the moment, this means ever harsher and more punitive measures for dealing with the crime problem.

Few criminologists believe that enough research exists at present to justify such an approach. In fact, some criminological research demonstrates the futility of escalating punishments and often points to measures of quite a different nature as more promising, more humane, and more cost-beneficial. So why do criminologists not make themselves heard? The answer is that criminologists are social scientists, not politicians. Criminologists are not voted into Congress or to the presidency or a governorship. Criminologists have served on virtually every federal and state commission dealing with problems of crime or criminal justice, but just as the Pentagon cannot declare war, criminologists cannot dictate national or state crime-control policies. They can, however, provide pertinent research findings that inform national policy making.[21] In the past, the attorney general of the United States asked criminologists to formulate policy recommendations based on their research findings in areas such as delinquency prevention, drug control, global crime, youth violence, and violence against women.[22] More collaboration is being sought in order to bring the field of criminology to those responsible for setting criminal justice policy.

Very little happens on Earth that does not concern criminology. Yet criminology as a science is only a century old. Edwin H. Sutherland provided the most widely accepted definition: "The body of knowledge regarding crime as a social phenomenon. It includes within its scope the process of making laws, of breaking laws, and of reacting toward the breaking of laws."

Criminologists study behavior that violates all social norms, including laws. They distinguish between two conflicting views of the history of criminal law: the consensus view, which regards lawmaking as the result of communal agreement about what is to be prohibited, and the conflict view, according to which laws are imposed by those with power over those without power.

The breaking of laws (the subject to which much of this book is devoted) is not merely a formal act that may lead to arrest and prosecution, but an intricate process by which some people violate some laws under some circumstances. Many disciplines contribute to understanding the process of breaking laws or other norms, but as

yet there is no consensus on why people become criminals. Society has always reacted to lawbreaking, although the scientific study of lawbreaking is of very recent origin. Today criminologists analyze the methods and procedures society uses in reacting to crime; they evaluate the success or failure of such methods; and on the basis of their research, they propose more effective and humane ways of controlling crime.

Criminologists have discovered that the various agencies society has created to deal with lawbreaking constitute a system that, like any other system, can be made more efficient. Research on the system depends on the availability of a variety of data, especially statistics. The gathering and analysis of statistics on crime and criminal justice are among the primary tasks of criminologists. The effectiveness of their work depends on reliable data.

The province of criminology today is the entire world: Every aspect of life, including crime, has become increasingly globalized in recent years as a result of both rapid advances in technology and economic integration.

Criminology is a politically sensitive discipline. Its findings inform public policy. While criminologists cannot dictate what the branches of government—the legislative, the judicial, and the executive—should do about crime, their research findings are being used increasingly in making governmental decisions.

CRIMINOLOGY & PUBLIC POLICY

Crime waves always carry with them calls for more law enforcement authority. What happened on September 11, 2001, was, among other things, a crime wave—that one day caused the number of homicides in America in 2001 to be 20 percent higher than the year before. It is no surprise, then, that even before the fires in the rubble that was the World Trade Center burned themselves out, some politicians were calling for broader powers for law enforcement and greater restrictions on citizens, all in the effort to fight this particular crime wave.

That is not a bad thing. Law enforcement authority naturally varies with the nature and size of the crime problems police must combat. A glance at the recent history of criminal procedure shows as much. Most legal restrictions on policing date from the criminal procedure revolution of the 1960s, which itself can be seen as a consequence of the low-crime 1950s. Higher crime rates led to cutbacks in those legal protections in the 1970s and 1980s, just as lower crime rates have led to some expansion in the past few years. In short, Fourth and Fifth Amendment rights have varied with crime before, and they will probably do so in the future, as they must if the law is to reflect a sensible balance between the social need for order and individuals' desire for privacy and liberty. The terrorist attacks on New York and Washington raised the demands on law enforcement. Those increased demands have already led to some increases in law enforcers' legal authority, and that trend will—and probably should—continue, at least for a while. (Source: William J. Stuntz, "Local Policing after Terror." Reprinted by permission of The Yale Law Journal Company, Inc., from *The Yale Law Journal*, vol. 111, p. 2137 [2002]).

Questions for Discussion Sutherland's broad definition of criminology (see p. 10) includes a critical examination of the criminal justice response to crimes. Following the spirit of his definition, how should we fashion and refashion our criminal justice system in response to the threat of terrorism in the United States? Should we increasingly delegate the responsibility for investigating and combating terrorism to local law enforcement agencies? How, then, do we control the flow of intelligence data?

One of the most significant questions concerns the extent to which our response to 9/11 will jeopardize the constitutional rights of U.S. citizens. How much freedom are you willing to give up in the name of law enforcement?

YOU BE THE CRIMINOLOGIST

How would you teach the ideal course on criminology? (Don't answer until you have completed the course!)

KEY TERMS

The numbers next to the terms refer to the pages on which the terms are defined.

conflict model (14)

consensus model (14)

crime (12)

criminal justice system (17)

criminologists (11)

criminology (10)

deviance (11)

social norms (11)

Counting Crime and Measuring Criminal Behavior

2

The Ingredients of Crime
The Act Requirement
The Legality Requirement
The Harm Requirement
The Causation Requirement
Mens Rea: The "Guilty Mind" Requirement
The Concurrence Requirement
The Punishment Requirement
The Defenses
Typologies of Crime
Measuring Crime
Methods of Collecting Data
Ethics and the Researcher
The Nature and Extent of Crime
Police Statistics
Victimization Surveys
Self-Report Surveys
Measuring Characteristics of Crime
Crime Trends
Locations and Times of Criminal Acts
Severity of Crime
Measuring Characteristics of Criminals
Age and Crime
Gender and Crime
Social Class and Crime
Race and Crime
Review
Criminology & Public Policy
You Be the Criminologist
Key Terms

Many large police departments conduct weekly crime-control strategy sessions or COMPSTAT (Computerized Statistics) meetings to increase the flow of information between police executives and the commanders of operational units.

In 1978, inmates of Rahway maximum-security prison in New Jersey started a program for young "delinquent" teens called Scared Straight. The premise of the program was simple: Take juvenile delinquents into a rough prison environment, have inmates expose them to what it means to live a life of crime and to the horrors of incarceration, and literally scare them straight. If these at-risk teens understood the path they were on and the brutality of prison life, most if not all would reconsider their deviant ways. At least this was the hypothesis behind Scared Straight.

Early evidence of the success of Scared Straight was hyped in a 1979 documentary, in which viewers were told of a 94 percent success rate for juveniles over a 3-month period; that is, only 6 percent of those "scared straight" were arrested. The program now had both intuitive appeal and some (apparent) empirical evidence of its success in deterring youth from a life of adult crime. Moreover, at times when the public urges politicians to get tough on crime, programs such as Scared Straight fit the bill—literally. The cost of Scored Straight was estimated to be no more than $1 per participant.

Three years after the start of the program, Jim Finckenauer conducted a simple experiment to test, far more rigorously, just how successful Scared Straight was.[1] Using a randomized controlled trial—much in the same way drug companies ensure the efficacy of a new pain reliever—Finckenauer compared the arrest rates of the participants of Scared Straight (treatment group) with a no-treatment control group of at-risk juveniles.

Finckenauer's results were remarkable, for a host of reasons. First, the Scared Straight program was not deterring at-risk youth. Second, arrest rates were actually higher in the treatment group than in the controls. Perhaps as important, Finckenauer's work suggested the importance of moving beyond politically expedient, ideologically consistent, and intuitively pleasing juvenile justice programs to those shown by empirical (experimental) evidence to work. In other words, programs designed to deter juveniles must be evidenced-based. A systematic review of randomized experimental research on Scared Straight programs over the past 25 years recently concluded, as Finckenauer did, that Scared Straight was actually more harmful to juveniles than doing nothing at all.[2]

The field of criminology has increasingly embraced systematic, empirically rigorous tests of criminal justice programs and initiatives. The trend in recent years is to subject our evaluation of such programs and initiatives to randomized controlled trials, a trend captured by the emergence of an evidence-based approach to criminology called "experimental criminology."

Questions about how crime is measured and what those measurements reveal about the nature and extent of crime are among the most important issues in contemporary criminology. Researchers, theorists, and practitioners need information in order to explain and prevent crime, to evaluate the success of programs like Scared Straight, and to operate agencies that deal with problems of crime and justice.

We begin this chapter with an explanation of the ingredients that all crimes share. We then look at the objectives and methods of collecting information on specific types of crimes. Next, we consider the limitations of the information sources criminologists most frequently use to estimate the nature and extent of crime in the United States. We then explore measurement of the characteristics of crimes and criminals.

THE INGREDIENTS OF CRIME

Before we begin to measure specific crimes, we will examine the part of criminal law that deals with the common legal ingredients, or elements, found in all crimes. Generally speaking, if any one of these elements is not present, no crime has been committed. All the defenses available to a person charged with a crime allege that at least one of these elements is not present.

American criminal law scholar Jerome Hall has developed the theory that a human event, in order to qualify as a crime, must meet seven basic requirements:[3]

1. The act requirement

2. The legality requirement

3. The harm requirement

4. The causation requirement

5. The mens rea requirement

6. The concurrence requirement

7. The punishment requirement[4]

The Act Requirement

Legal scholars have long agreed that one fundamental ingredient of every crime is a human act. In this context, what is an "act"? Suppose a sleepwalker, in a trance, grabs a stone and hurls it at a passerby, subsequently killing him. The law does not consider this event to be an act. Before any human behavior can qualify as an act, there must be a conscious interaction between mind and body, a physical movement that results from the determination or effort of the actor. Thus, a reflex or convulsion, a bodily movement that occurs during unconsciousness or sleep, conduct that occurs during hypnosis or results from hypnotic suggestion, or a bodily movement that is not determined by the actor—as when somebody is pushed by another person—is a behavior that is not considered a voluntary act.[5] It is only when choices are overpoweringly influenced by forces beyond our control that the law will consider behavior irrational and beyond its reach.

Act versus Status

The criminal law, in principle, does not penalize anyone for a status or condition. Suppose the law made it a crime to be more than 6 feet tall or to have red hair. Or suppose the law made it a crime to be a member of the family of an army deserter or to be of a given religion or ethnic background. That was exactly the situation in the Soviet Union under Stalin's penal code, which made it a crime to be related to a deserter from the Red Army.[6]

There is thus more to the act requirement than the issue of a behavior's being voluntary and rational: There is the problem of distinguishing between act and status. A California law made it a criminal offense, subject to a jail term, to be a drug addict. In *Robinson v. California*, the U.S. Supreme Court held that statute to be unconstitutional. By making a status or condition a crime, the statute violated the Eighth Amendment to the U.S. Constitution, which prohibits "cruel and unusual punishments." Addiction, the Court noted, is a condition, an illness, much like leprosy or venereal disease.[7]

Failure to Act

The act requirement has yet another aspect. An act requires the interaction of mind and body. If only the mind is active and the body does not move, we do not have an act: Simply thinking about punching someone in the nose is not a crime (Figure 2.1). We are free to think. But if we carry a thought into physical action, we commit an act, which may be a crime.

Then there is the problem of omission, or failure to act. If the law requires that convicted sex offenders register with the police, and such a person decides not to fill out the registration form, that person is guilty of a crime by omission. But he has acted! He told his hand not to pick up that pen, not to fill out the form. Inaction may be action when the law clearly spells out what one has to do and one decides not to do it.

The law in most U.S. states imposes no duty to be a Good Samaritan, to offer help to another person in distress. The law requires action only if one has a legal duty to act. Lifeguards, for example, are contractually obligated to save bathers from drowning; parents are obligated by law to protect their children; law enforcement officers and firefighters are required to rescue people in distress.

The Legality Requirement

Marion Palendrano was charged with, among other things, being a "common scold" because she disturbed "the peace of the neighborhood

FIGURE 2.1 Can you see all seven requirements? When is a crime committed?

Source: © 1962 *The Saturday Evening Post.* Reprinted by permission of *The Saturday Evening Post.*

and of all good and quiet people of this State."[8] Mrs. Palendrano moved that the charge be dismissed, and the Superior Court of New Jersey agreed with her, reasoning:

1. Such a crime cannot be found anywhere in the New Jersey statute books. Hence there is no such crime, although, long ago, the common law of England may have recognized such a crime.

2. "Being a common scold" is so vague a concept that to punish somebody for it would violate constitutional due process: "We insist that laws give the person of ordinary intelligence a reasonable opportunity to know what is prohibited, so that he may act accordingly," ruled the court.[9]

If we want a person to adhere to a standard, the person has to know what that standard is. Thus, we have the ancient proposition that only conduct that has been made criminal by law before an act is committed can be a crime. Police, prosecutors, and courts are not interested in the billions of acts human beings engage in unless such acts have previously been defined by law as criminal. The law is interested only in an act (*actus*) that is guilty, evil, and prohibited (*reus*).

The Harm Requirement

Every crime has been created to prevent something bad (a given harm) from happening.

■ *The posting of "pooper-scooper" regulations has had its effect. Most inner-city residents consider the failure to "pick up" to be a sign of disrespect and a violation of custom.*

Murder is prohibited because we don't want people to be killed. This detrimental consequence that we are trying to avoid is called "harm." If the specified harm has not been created by the defendant's act, the crime is not complete. Just think of would-be assassin John W. Hinckley Jr., who tried to kill President Reagan. He shot Reagan, but the president did not die. The harm envisioned by the law against murder had not been accomplished. (Hinckley could have been found guilty of attempted murder, but he was acquitted by reason of insanity; see Chapter 4.)

From a criminological perspective, most crimes are grouped by the harm that each entails. Offenses against the person involve harm to an individual, and offenses against property involve damage to property or loss of its possession.

The Causation Requirement

What is the act of hitting a home run? Of course, it is a hit that allows a batter to run to first, second, and third base, and then back to home plate.

Actually, it is much more complicated than that. It starts with the decision to swing a bat, at a certain angle, with a particular intensity, in a specific direction, in order to cause a home run. Suppose that at a San Diego Padres home game, the batter hits a ball unusually high into the air. A passing pelican picks it up, flies off with it, and then drops it into the bleachers. Has the batter hit a home run? We doubt it.

It's the same in crime. Causation requires that the actor achieve the result (the harm) through his or her own effort. Suppose that A, in an effort to kill B, wounds him and that B actually dies when the ambulance carrying him to the hospital collides with another vehicle. Despite B's death, A did not succeed in her personal attempt to kill B. Thus, the act of murder is incomplete, although A may be guilty of an attempt to kill. The causation requirement, then, holds that a crime is not complete unless the actor's conduct necessarily caused the harm without interference by somebody else and that it is the proximate cause of the act.[10]

Mens Rea: The "Guilty Mind" Requirement

Every crime, according to tradition, requires **mens rea, a** "guilty mind." Let us examine the case of Ms. Lambert. She was convicted in Los Angeles of an offense created by city ordinance: having lived in the city without registering with the police as a person previously convicted of a crime. Ms. Lambert had no idea that Los Angeles had such a registration requirement. Nor could she possibly have known that she was required to register. She appealed all the way to the U.S. Supreme Court, and she won. Said the Court: "Where a person did not know [of the prohibition] (s)he may not be convicted consistent with due process."[11]

Of course, to blame Ms. Lambert for violating the Los Angeles city ordinance would make no sense. Ms. Lambert had no notion that she was doing something wrong by living in Los Angeles and not registering herself as a convicted person. With Ms. Lambert's case, we have reached a fundamental point: No one can be guilty of a crime unless he or she acted with the knowledge of doing something wrong. This principle always has existed. It is implicit in the concept of crime that the perpetrator know the wrongfulness of the act. It is not required that the perpetrator know the penal code or have personal feelings of guilt. It is enough that the perpetrator knows that he or she had no right to do what he or she did and decided to do it anyway.[12]

Anyone who violently attacks another person, takes another's property, invades another's home, forces intercourse, or forges a signature on someone else's check knows rather well that he or she is doing something wrong. All these examples of mens rea entail an intention to achieve harm or a knowledge that the prohibited harm will result. For some crimes, however, less than a definite intention suffices: reckless actions by which the actors consciously risk causing a prohibited harm (for example, the driver who races down a rain-slicked highway or the employer who sends his employees to work without safety equipment, knowing full well that lives are thereby being endangered).

Strict liability is an exception to the mens rea requirement. There is a class of offenses for which legislatures or courts require no showing of criminal intent or mens rea. For these offenses, the fact that the actor makes an innocent mistake and proceeds in good faith does not affect criminal liability. Strict-liability offenses range all the way from possessing a firearm to distributing adulterated food to running a red light. Typically, these offenses are subject to small penalties only, but in a few cases substantial punishments can be and have been imposed.

The Concurrence Requirement

The concurrence requirement states that the criminal act must be accompanied by an equally criminal mind. Suppose a striker throws a stone at an office window in order to shatter it, and a broken piece of glass pierces the throat of a secretary, who bleeds to death. Wanting to damage property deserves condemnation, but of a far lesser degree than wanting to kill. Act and intent did not concur in this case, and the striker should not be found guilty of murder. The law has created many exceptions to the concurrence requirement, one of which, the felony murder rule, we discuss in Chapter 10.

The Punishment Requirement

The last ingredient needed to constitute a crime is that of punishment. An illegal act coupled with an evil mind (criminal intent or mens rea) still does not constitute a crime unless the law subjects it to a punishment. If a sign posted in the park states "Do not step on the grass" and you do it anyway, have you committed a criminal offense? Not unless there is a law that subjects that act to punishment. Otherwise it is simply an improper or inconsiderate act.

The punishment requirement, more than any of the others, helps us differentiate between crimes (which are subject to punishments) and **torts,** civil wrongs for which the law does not prescribe punishment but merely grants the injured party the right to recover damages.

The nature and severity of punishments also help us differentiate between grades of crime. Most penal codes recognize three degrees of severity: **Felonies** are severe crimes, subject to punishments of a year or more in prison or to capital punishment. **Misdemeanors** are less-severe crimes, subject to a maximum of 1 year in jail. (For crimes of both grades, fines can also be imposed as punishments.) **Violations** are minor offenses, normally subject only to fines.

THE DEFENSES

You will soon see that we measure the amount of crime at various stages of the criminal process. For example: How many crimes are reported to the police? For how many of these crimes have convictions been obtained? There is a huge discrepancy. Far fewer convictions have been obtained than crimes reported or even prosecuted. There are several reasons for this discrepancy. One of the principal reasons is that not all elements of the crime charged could be proved in court. Why not? Because frequently the defendant has offered one of a number of defenses to the offense charged. Each of these defenses simply negates the existence of one (or more) of the elements of the offense charged.

Let us take the insanity defense as an example. When the defendant pleads the existence of a mental disease or defect (a psychiatric question), he claims that he could not have acted (did not appreciate the nature and quality of the act—consequently, no *actus reus*) or he could not form the requisite mens rea (did not appreciate the wrongfulness of the act).[13]

The defense of infancy could have been worked out similarly. But instead, it was decided at common law that nobody under age 7 should be deemed capable of acting rationally or to have the requisite mens rea. At age 14, all youngsters are deemed to have that capacity. The defense of infancy varies widely among the states.

Let us look at the defense of mistake of fact. Here the defendant claims that by reason of a factual error (e.g., taking someone else's coat believing it to be one's own), she did not, and could not, realize that she did something wrong. Hence, there was no mens rea (or sometimes not even the requisite *actus reus*).

In some situations, the defendant's defense is that the element of wrongfulness was lacking (the legality requirement). Normally, touching another person without consent amounts to assault and battery. The police officer's defense is that the law requires that he touch others without consent. Therefore, what is normally illegal has become legal (the defense of public duty). Other defenses, such as duress, necessity, self-defense, and defense of property, all work pretty much on the same principle—they negate an essential element of the offense charged.

TYPOLOGIES OF CRIME

The general term "crimes" covers a wide variety of types of crimes, with their own distinct features. Murder and arson, for example, both are crimes. They have the same seven general elements, including a criminal intent (mens rea) and a harm element. But these elements take different forms in different crimes. In murder, the criminal intent takes the form of intending to kill another human being wrongfully, while in arson the intent is that of wrongfully burning the property of another. Lawyers and criminologists have searched for a system of grouping the many types of crimes into coherent, rational categories, for ease of understanding, of learning, and of finding them in the law books and for purposes of studying them from both a legal and a criminological perspective. Such categorizations are called "typologies."

Here are some examples: The ancient Romans classified their crimes as those against the gods and those against other human beings. As late as the eighteenth century, some English lawyers simply listed crimes alphabetically. The French of the early nineteenth century created a typology with three categories: serious crimes (which we would call "felonies"), medium-serious crimes (which we would call "misdemeanors"), and crimes of a petty character (which we would call "violations"). The more serious crimes were grouped into categories based on the harm those crimes entailed, such as harm against life, against physical integrity, against honor, against property, and so on.

Nowadays the French categorization is generally accepted worldwide, although lawyers and criminologists may differ on the desirability of lumping various crime types together into categories. Lawyers, after all, may be much more interested in the procedural consequences that flow from the categorizations, while criminologists may be much more concerned with criminological implications for studying different types of perpetrators and devising schemes of crime prevention.

There are also political considerations in devising a typology. For example, the criminal codes of the former communist countries had large categories of political crimes, which were given the most prominent place in those codes. They included many crimes that in Western democracies are grouped in other categories, such as property crimes or crimes against the person, or that may have no counterpart at all.

The typology we have chosen for this book seeks to accommodate both the established legal typology—for example, that used in the Model Penal Code—and the criminological objectives that are so important for the study of crime from a sociological and behavioral perspective. These categories are:

- Violent crimes
- Crimes against property
- White-collar and corporate crime
- Drug-, alcohol-, and sex-related crimes

We discuss these categories in Part III.

MEASURING CRIME

There are three major reasons for measuring characteristics of crimes and criminals. First, researchers need to collect and analyze information in order to test theories about why people commit crime. One criminologist might record the kinds of offenses committed by people of different ages; another might count the number of crimes committed at different times of the year. But without ordering these observations in some purposeful way, without a **theory,** a systematic set of principles that explain how two or more phenomena are related, scientists would be limited in their ability to make predictions from the data they collect.

The types of data that are collected and the way they are collected are crucial to the research process. Criminologists analyze these data and use their findings to support or refute theories. In Part II, we examine several theories (including the one outlined briefly here) that explain why people commit crime, and we will see how these theories have been tested.

One theory of crime causation, for example, is that high crime rates result from the wide disparity between people's goals and the means available to them for reaching those goals. Those who lack legitimate opportunities to achieve their goals (primarily, people in the lower class) try to reach them through criminal means. To test this theory, researchers might begin with the **hypothesis** (a testable proposition that describes how two or more factors are related) that lower-class individuals engage in more serious crimes and do so more frequently than middle-class individuals. (See "Social Class and Crime" later in this chapter.) Next they would collect facts, observations, and other pertinent information—called **data**—on the criminal behavior of both lower-class and middle-class individuals. A finding that lower-class persons commit more crimes would support the theory that people commit crimes because they do not have legitimate means to reach their goals.

The second objective of measurement is to enhance our knowledge of the characteristics of various types of offenses. Why are some offenses more likely to be committed than others? What situational factors, such as time of day or type of place, influence the commission of crime? Experts have argued that this information is needed if we are to prevent crime and develop strategies to control it (Chapter 9 deals with this subject).

Measurement has a third major objective: Criminal justice agencies depend on certain kinds of information to facilitate daily operations and to anticipate future needs. How many persons flow through county jails? How many will receive prison sentences? Besides the questions that deal with the day-to-day functioning of the system (number of beds, distribution and hiring of personnel), other questions affect legislative and policy decisions. For instance, what effect does a change in law have on the amount of crime committed? Consider legislation on the death penalty. Some people claim that homicides decrease when a death penalty is instituted. Others claim that capital punishment laws make no difference. Does fear of crime go down if we put more police officers in a neighborhood? Does drug smuggling move to another entry point if old access routes are cut off? These and other potential changes need to be evaluated—and evaluations require measurement.

Methods of Collecting Data

Given the importance of data for research, policy making, and the daily operation and planning of the criminal justice system, criminologists have continued to refine data-collection techniques. Through the years, these methods have become increasingly sophisticated.

Depending on what questions they are asking, criminologists collect their data in a variety of ways: through survey research, experiments, observation, and case studies. One of the most widely used methods is survey research, which is a cost-effective method of measuring characteristics of groups. Experimental studies are difficult and costly to conduct, and for that reason they are used infrequently. But they have been, and still are, an important means of collecting data on crime. Participant observation involves the direct participation of the researcher in the activities of the people who are the subjects of the research. A variation of this technique is nonparticipant observation, in which the researcher collects data without joining in the activity. Another way to collect information about crime, and especially about criminal careers, is to examine biographical and autobiographical accounts of individual offenders (the case-study method).

Data can be found in a wide variety of sources, but the most frequently used sources are statistics compiled by government agencies, private foundations, and businesses. Familiarity with the sources of data and the methods used to gather data will help in understanding the studies we discuss throughout this book. The facts and observations researchers gather for the purpose of a particular study are called **primary data.** Those they find in government sources, or data that were previously collected for a different investigation, are called **secondary data.**

Surveys

Most of us are familiar with surveys—in public-opinion polls, marketing research, and election-prediction studies. Criminologists use surveys to

■ The year 2000 census started when Harold Johnson visited the Eskimo village of Unalkleet, Alaska, on January 19, 2000. The U.S. Census provides information on all Americans and their lifestyles and problems, including, through random survey done in cooperation with the Bureau of Justice Statistics, data on crime victimization.

obtain quantitative data. A **survey** is the systematic collection of respondents' answers to questions asked in questionnaires or interviews; interviews may be conducted face-to-face or by telephone. Generally, surveys are used to gather information about the attitudes, characteristics, or behavior of a large group of persons, who are called the **population** of the survey. Surveys conducted by criminologists measure, for example, the amount of crime, attitudes toward police or toward the sentencing of dangerous offenders, assessment of drug abuse, and fear of crime.

Instead of interviewing the total population under study, most researchers interview a representative subset of that population—a **sample.** If a sample is carefully drawn, researchers can generalize the results from the sample to the population. A sample determined by random selection, whereby each person in the population to be studied has an equal chance of being selected, is called a **random sample.**

Surveys are a cost-effective method, but they have limitations. If a study of drug use by high school students were done one time only, the finding of a relationship between drug use and poor grades would not tell us whether drug use caused bad grades, whether students with bad grades turned to drugs, or whether bad grades and drug taking resulted from some other factor, such as lack of a stable family. Panel studies, which repeatedly survey the same sample at various points in time, address this problem. Not surprisingly, they are more costly than cross-sectional studies.

DID YOU KNOW?

. . . that some treatment programs for offenders based on cognitive behavioral therapy work? See "Experiments in Criminology" later in this chapter.

Experiments

The **experiment** is a technique used in the physical, biological, and social sciences. An investigator introduces a change into a process and makes measurements or observations in order to evaluate the effects of the change. Through experimentation, scientists test hypotheses about how two or more **variables** (factors that may change) are related. The basic model for an experiment involves changing one variable, keeping all other factors the same (controlling them, or holding them constant), and observing the effect of that change on another variable. If you change one variable while keeping all other factors constant and then find that another variable changes as well, you may safely assume that the change in the second variable was caused by the change in the first.

Most experiments are done in laboratories, but it is possible to do them in real-world, or field, settings (hence the name **field experiment**), as we see with the Scared Straight program evaluation.

Evidence that criminologists are embracing experimental methods is seen in the creation of the Academy of Experimental Criminology (AEC). The AEC seeks to promote the use of randomized trials in crime and justice research and to recognize criminologists who have successfully led randomized field experiments. David Weisburd and his colleagues explain, in simple terms, why such research is important:

> Random allocation thus allows the researcher to assume that the only logical explanation for any systematic differences between the treatment and comparison groups are due to the treatments or interventions applied. When the study is complete, the researcher can argue with confidence that if a difference has been observed between treatment and comparison groups, it is likely the result of the treatment itself (since randomization has isolated the treatment effect from other possible causes). In non-randomized studies, it is much more difficult to make this claim because of the difficulty of controlling for both measured and unmeasured factors or influences. For this reason, randomized experiments have often been described as the "gold standard" for evaluation research.[14]

The requirements for experiments using randomized controlled trials (RCT) are threefold:

1. Program participants and nonparticipants can be randomly assigned to two or more groups large enough to comprise a statistically valid sample.

2. Each group can be administered a distinct intervention (or nonintervention, which would be the control condition).

3. For each group, the program can measure the outcomes that the intervention is designed to improve.[15]

■ Despite experimental evidence that the Scared Straight experience may be counterproductive, the program (now called the Juvenile Awareness Program) continues at East Jersey State Prison (formerly Rahway State Prison). Here, a member of the Lifer's group appears in a 1999 Scared Straight! video. The film is an update of the original Scared Straight! video that shows how inmates give young people in trouble a taste of prison life.

Experiments employing RCT have been used to test the effectiveness of substance-abuse treatment, child-care and preschool interventions, police strategies in inner-city high-crime areas, prosecutorial and sentencing strategies, prison reentry programs, and sales tax compliance strategies.[16] According to Lawrence Sherman, its application to critically important questions in criminology cannot be underestimated. We can now ask and answer, with definitive evidence, questions such as these: How much crime does prison prevent—or cause—for different kinds of offenders? Does visible police patrol prevent crime everywhere or just in certain locations? What is the best way for societies to prevent crime from an early age? How can murder be prevented among high-risk groups of young men?

Research employing RCT has some limitations, however. The Coalition for Evidence-Based Policy noted some general characteristics of research that lends itself to experiments using RCT:

- There must be a possibility of selecting randomized intervention and control groups.

- There must be sufficient discretion in the administration of the program to permit random assignment of groups that will receive a program intervention and groups that will not (or that will receive a different intervention).

- Subjects should not be excluded from an intervention that provides a public good (for example, clean air or homeland security), as this would likely raise ethical—if not legal—issues.[17]

The coalition also offered some concrete examples of research that defies the use of RCTs:

- One cannot carry out an RCT to evaluate whether reducing carbon emissions will prevent global warming, because there is only one planet Earth. (However, it may be possible to randomize industrial sites in order to evaluate the effectiveness and cost of various methods of reducing carbon emissions.)

- One cannot carry out an RCT to evaluate the effectiveness of manned space flight, because we can only afford to carry out one such program.

- One cannot carry out an RCT to evaluate military assistance to NATO countries because of the political impossibility of randomizing countries as well as the lack of sufficient numbers of countries to allow valid statistical groupings.

- One cannot choose a random sample of military operations in which to use particular operational strategies, because once a particular operation is approved, any tool or strategy that might help under changing conditions must be available for use.[18]

Experiments in Criminology: The Importance of Evidence-Based Crime and Justice Policy

1. **Do certain community-based treatment programs work? Yes.**

J. McGuire and colleagues report the outcome of a 17-month follow-up of three different community-based, offense-focused intervention programs in England created to decrease the rate of reconviction of offenders receiving probation supervision. The study included three treatment groups (215 male offenders who had completed programs, 181 male offenders who had not completed programs, and 339 male offenders who had not started programs) compared to a control group of 339 male offenders who were not assigned to treatment programs. The authors first evaluated the groups by comparing the three experimental groups to the comparison (control) group and found that individuals in the comparison group were not more likely to be reconvicted. McGuire and colleagues also compared all four groups separately. They found that those offenders who had completed programs were significantly less likely to be reconvicted than were offenders in the other three groups.[19]

2. **Do "closed-circuit television" monitoring efforts decrease crime rates? Yes.**

D. S. Farrington and his colleagues conducted an analysis of 14 closed-circuit television (CCTV) projects in several different areas in England, including city and town centers, a hospital, parking areas, and residential areas. The question they asked was, What are the effects of CCTV on crime? They reviewed CCTV police and victimization data in the above-noted areas before and after CCTV was installed. They found that CCTV was useful in decreasing crime in parking areas of train stations and also seemed to be effective in decreasing vehicle crimes but was not effective in city or town centers. CCTV intervention was most effective when coverage was high and when other interventions, such as improved lighting, were included.[20]

3. **Do written warnings threatening an investigation for insurance fraud deter fraud claims? Yes.**

E. Blais and J. L. Bacher designed a randomized field experiment to evaluate the effects of a written threat in the form of a deterrent letter, which reminded the insured individual of punishment for insurance fraud. They wanted to evaluate if there would be a difference between those receiving the written warning and those subject to the usual standard of practice in the insurance company (control) with regard to claim-padding behaviors for individuals filing claims for residential theft. They performed this experiment at four insurance companies. The authors found that individuals in the experimental group (those receiving a written warning) were less likely to pad their claims than those in the control group, independent of how the letter was delivered. The authors concluded that having a written threat at the time of this criminal opportunity seems to be effective in preventing this type of economic crime.[21]

4. Do boot camps decrease recidivism? Not sure.

D. L. MacKenzie and colleagues' study evaluated 234 adult male inmates entering prison who were randomly assigned to a program in a correctional boot camp or a large, traditional prison in the Maryland state correctional system. They wanted to look at the impact of boot camp on recidivism. They had three main areas of focus: comparing the recidivism between the two groups, the impact of the two programs on participants' criminogenic attitudes and impulses, and whether changes in these attitudes and impulses could explain the differences in recidivism. The authors found that participation in boot camp was associated with a marginally significant lower recidivism compared to those who entered the traditional correctional facility. The boot camp program had little effect on criminogenic characteristics noted by pre- and posttest self-report surveys, except for a lowering of self-control. On the other hand, inmates in the traditional correctional facility became more antisocial, had lower self-control, were worse at anger management, and self-reported more criminal tendencies by the end of their prison stay. The authors noted that these findings suggested that differences in criminal behavior were due to negative changes in the controls, rather than to changes in the boot camp participants.[22]

Participant and Nonparticipant Observation

Researchers who engage in participant and nonparticipant observation use methods that provide detailed descriptions of life as it actually is lived—in prisons, gangs, and other settings.

Observation is the most direct means of studying behavior. Investigators may play a variety of roles in observing social situations. When they engage in **nonparticipant observation,** they do not join in the activities of the groups they are studying; they simply observe the activities in everyday settings and record what they see. Investigators who engage in **participant observation** take part in many of the activities of the groups in order to gain acceptance, but they generally make clear the purpose of their participation. Anne Campbell, a criminologist who spent 2

years as a participant observer of the lifestyles of girl gang members, explains:

> My efforts to meet female gang members began with an introduction through the New York City Police Department's Gang Crimes Unit. Through one of their plain-clothes gang liaison officers, John Galea, I was introduced first to the male gang members of a number of Brooklyn gangs. On being reassured that I "only" wanted to talk to the female members, the male leaders gave their OK and I made arrangements to meet with the girls' leaders or "godmothers." At first they were guarded in their disclosures to me. They asked a lot about my life, my background and my reasons for wanting to hang out with them. Like most of us, however, they enjoyed talking about themselves and over the period of six months that I spent with each of three female gangs they opened up a good deal—sitting in their kitchens, standing on the stoops in the evenings or socializing at parties with allied gangs.[23]

Observations of groups in their natural setting afford the researcher insights into behavior and attitudes that cannot be obtained through techniques such as surveys and experiments.

Case Studies

A **case study** is an analysis of all pertinent aspects of one unit of study, such as an individual, an institution, a group, or a community. The sources of information are documents such as life histories, biographies, diaries, journals, letters, and other records. A classic demonstration of criminologists' use of the case-study method is found in Edwin Sutherland's *The Professional Thief,* which is based on interviews with a professional thief.

Sutherland learned about the relationship between amateur and professional thieves, how thieves communicate, how they determine whether to trust each other, and how they network. From discussions with the thief and an analysis of his writings on topics selected by the researcher, Sutherland was able to draw several conclusions that other techniques would not have yielded. For instance, a person is not a professional thief unless he is recognized as such by other professional thieves. Training by professional thieves is necessary for the development of the skills, attitudes, and connections required in the "profession."[24] One of the drawbacks of the case-study method is that the information given by the subject may be biased or wrong and by its nature is limited. For these reasons it is difficult to generalize from one person's story—in this instance—to all professional thieves.

Using Available Data in Research

Besides collecting their own data, researchers often utilize secondary data collected by private and public organizations. The police, the courts, and corrections officials, for example, need to know the number of persons passing through the criminal justice system at various points in order to carry out day-to-day administrative tasks and to engage in long-range planning. It is not always feasible to collect new data for a research project, nor is it necessary to do so when such vast amounts of relevant information are already available.

To study the relationship between crime and variables such as average income or single-parent households, one might make use of the Uniform Crime Reports (see "Police Statistics" later in this chapter), together with information found in the reports of the Bureau of the Census. Various other agencies, among them the Federal Bureau of Prisons, the Drug Enforcement Agency, the Treasury Department, and the Labor Department, are also excellent sources of statistics useful to criminologists. At the international level, UN world crime surveys contain information on crime, criminals, and criminal justice systems in countries on all continents.

Researchers who use available data can save a great deal of time and expense. However, they have to exercise caution in fitting data not collected for the purpose of a particular study into their research. Many official records are incomplete, or the data have been collected in such a way as to make them inadequate for the research. It is also frequently difficult to gain permission to use agency data that are not available to the public because of a concern about confidentiality.

Ethics and the Researcher

In the course of their research, criminologists encounter many ethical issues. Chief among such issues is confidentiality. Consider the dilemma faced by a group of researchers in the late 1960s. In interviewing a sample of 9,945 boys born in 1945, the team collected extensive self-reported criminal histories of offenses the boys had committed before and after they turned 18. Among the findings were four unreported homicides and 75 rapes. The researchers were naturally excited about capturing such interesting data. More important, the researchers had feelings of grave concern. How should they handle their findings?

Should the results of these interviews be published?

Could the failure of the research staff to disclose names be considered the crime of obstructing justice?

Does an obligation to society as a whole to release the names of the offenders transcend a researcher's obligation to safeguard a subject's confidentiality?

What is the best response to a demand by the police, a district attorney, or a court for the researchers' files containing the subjects' names?

Should criminologists be immune to prosecution for their failure to disclose the names of their subjects?

Is it possible to develop a technique that can ensure against the identification of a subject in a research file?[25]

Such questions have few clear-cut answers. When researchers encounter these problems, however, they can rely on standards for ethical human experimentation. Institutional review boards (IRBs), also referred to as independent ethics committees (IECs) or ethical review boards (ERBs), exist in all government agencies and nearly all universities to ensure the protection of human subjects. The committee is responsible for approving the initial research proposal to certify that the project has scientific merit, the risks to subjects are balanced by the potential benefits to society, and, most important, informed consent is adequately addressed. Study participants must be fully notified about all the potential risks associated with the study, alternatives to participation, and the extent to which the researchers can protect participants' confidentiality. Researchers must obtain informed consent in writing for all study participants.

Because of heightened awareness of the ethical issues involved in human experimentation—particularly in correctional institutions, where coercion is difficult to avoid—the field of criminology and criminal justice is in the process of adopting formal codes of ethics. The guidelines include fully reporting experimental findings, honoring commitments made to respondents, not misleading respondents, and protecting respondents' confidentiality. Special provisions for what are called "vulnerable populations" (e.g., the illiterate, the mentally ill, children, those with low social status, and those under judicial or penal supervision) include taking appropriate steps to secure informed consent and to avoid invasions of privacy.[26] In the end, however, as Seth Bloomberg and Leslie Wilkins have noted, "the responsibility for safeguarding human subjects ultimately rests with the researcher. . . . A code of ethics may provide useful guidelines, but it will not relieve the scientist of moral choice."[27]

Crime Surfing

www.jrsainfo.org/
ibrrc/index.html

The Justice Research and Statistics Association (JRSA) is a national nonprofit group of state-level statistical analysis centers. The group gathers data from across the country, conducts studies on criminal justice issues, and helps people find information on topics related to criminal justice programs and research. The JRSA website discusses the National Incident-Based Reporting System (NIBRS).

THE NATURE AND EXTENT OF CRIME

As we have seen, criminologists gather their information in many ways. The methods they choose depend on the questions they want answered. To estimate the nature and extent of crime in the United States, researchers rely primarily on the Uniform Crime Reports, data compiled by the police; on the National Crime Victimization Survey, which measures crime through reports by victims; and on various self-report surveys, which ask individuals about criminal acts they have committed, whether or not these acts have come to the attention of the authorities.

Official statistics gathered from law enforcement agencies provide information available on the crimes actually investigated and reported by these agencies. But not all crimes appear in police statistics. In order for a criminal act to be "known to the police," the act first must be *perceived* by an individual (the car is not in the garage where it was left). It must then be *defined*, or classified, as something that places it within the purview of the criminal justice system (a theft has taken place), and it must be *reported* to the police. Once the police are notified, they classify the act and often *redefine* what may have taken place before *recording* the act as a crime known to the police (Figure 2.2). Information about criminal acts may be lost at any point along this processing route, and many crimes are never discovered to begin with.

Police Statistics

In 1924, the director of the Bureau of Investigation, J. Edgar Hoover, initiated a campaign to make the bureau responsible for gathering national statistics. With support from the American Bar Association (ABA) and the International Association of Chiefs of Police (IACP), the House of Representatives in 1930 passed a bill authorizing the bureau (later renamed the Federal Bureau of Investigation, or FBI) to collect data on crimes known to the police. These data are compiled into reports called the Uniform Crime Reports (UCR). At present, approximately 17,000 city, county, and state law enforcement agencies, which cover 95 percent of the total population, voluntarily contribute information on crimes brought to their attention. These agencies represent over 254 million U.S. inhabitants, with higher representation in large urban areas (97 percent) than in smaller cities (90 percent) or rural areas (87 percent). If the police verify that a crime has been committed, that crime goes into the report, whether or not an arrest has been made. Each month, reporting agencies provide data on offenses in 29 categories.

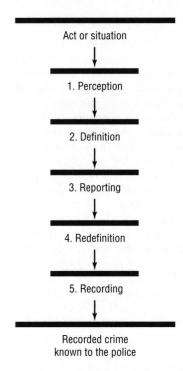

FIGURE 2.2 The process of bringing crime to the attention of police.

Source: R. F. Sparks, H. G. Genn, and D. J. Dodd, *Surveying Victims: A Study of the Measurement of Criminal Victimization, Perceptions of Crime, and Attitudes to Criminal Justice* (Chichester, Eng.: Wiley, 1977), p. 6. Copyright © 1977 by John Wiley & Sons Ltd. Reproduced with permission.

Part I and Part II Offenses

The UCR divide offenses into two major categories: Part I and Part II. Part I offenses include eight crimes, which are aggregated as **crimes against the person** (criminal homicide, forcible rape, robbery, and aggravated assault) and **crimes against property** (burglary, larceny-theft, motor vehicle theft, and arson). Collectively, Part I offenses are called **Index crimes.** Because they are serious, these crimes tend to be reported to the police more reliably than others and therefore can be used in combination as an index, or indicator, of changes over time. All other offenses, except traffic violations, are Part II crimes. These 21 crimes include fraud, embezzlement, weapons offenses, vandalism, and simple assaults.

Crime Rates

To analyze crime data, experts frequently present them as crime rates. Crime rates are computed by the following formula:

$$\text{Crime rate} = \frac{\text{number of reported crimes}}{\text{total population}} \times 100{,}000$$

One offense   Six offenses

FIGURE 2.3 Counting crime in the Uniform Crime Reports.

Crime rates may be computed for groups of offenses (such as the Index crimes or crimes against the person) or for specific offenses (such as homicide). If we say, for example, that the homicide rate is 10.2, we mean that there were 10.2 homicides for every 100,000 persons in the population under consideration (total U.S. population, say, or all males in the United States). Expressing the amount of crime in terms of rates over time shows whether an increase or a decrease in crime results from a change in the population or a change in the amount of crime committed.

In addition to data on reported crimes, the UCR include the number of offenses cleared by arrest. Crimes may be cleared in one of two ways: by the arrest, charging, and turning over to the courts of at least one person for prosecution; or by disposition of a case when an arrest is not possible, as when the suspect has died or has fled the jurisdiction. Besides reported crimes and crimes cleared by arrest, the reports contain data on characteristics of crimes (such as geographical location, time, and place), characteristics of criminals (such as gender, age, and race), and distribution of law enforcement personnel. We shall look at what these statistics reveal about the characteristics of crime and criminals in more detail later, but first we must recognize their limitations.

Limitations of the Uniform Crime Reports

Despite the fact that the UCR are among the main sources of crime statistics, their research value has been questioned. The criticisms deal with methodological problems and reporting practices. Some scholars argue, for example, that figures on reported crime are of little use in categories such as larceny, in which a majority of crime is not reported. The statistics present the amount of crime known to law enforcement agencies, but they do not reveal how many crimes have actually been committed. Another serious limitation is the fact that when several crimes are committed in one event, only the most serious offense is included in the UCR; the others go unreported. At the same time, when certain other crimes are committed, each individual act is counted as a separate offense. If a person robs a group of six people, for example, the UCR list one robbery (Figure 2.3). But if a person assaults six people, the UCR list six assaults. UCR data are further obscured by the fact that they do not differentiate between completed acts and attempted acts.

Police reports to the FBI are voluntary and vary in accuracy. In a study conducted on behalf of the Police Foundation, Lawrence Sherman and Barry Glick found that while the UCR require that arrests be recorded even if a suspect is released without a formal charge, all 196 departments surveyed recorded an arrest only after a formal booking procedure.[28] In addition, police departments may want to improve their image by showing that their crime rate has either declined (meaning the streets are safer) or risen (justifying a crackdown on, say, prostitution).[29] New record-keeping

Crime Surfing

http://www.jrsainfo
.org/ibrrc/background
-status/nibrs_states
.shtml

As of September 2007, 6,235 agencies in 31 states had been certified to submit official NIBRS data to the FBI. Eight states are currently in the testing phase of NIBRS, and seven states are in the developmental stages of implementation.

Statistics Watchdog Chief Accuses Home Office of Abusing Crime Statistics

RICHARD FORD

The Home Office is at the centre of another row over crime figures after the head of the UK Statistics Authority accused it of issuing "selective" statistics on knife offending.

Sir Michael Scholar, head of the Authority, said the release of details on an initiative to tackle knife attacks by both the Home Office and 10 Downing Street had been "premature."

The rebuke, which oversees the Office for National Statistics, is highly damaging, particularly as it follows disputes over the way the Home Office has dealt with release of crime and immigration and asylum figures.

Sir Michael said that the release of stabbing data was "premature, irregular and selective."

The figures were handed to the BBC which used them in its lead story during early morning bulletins on Radio 4.

Sir Michael wrote to Jeremy Heywood, permanent secretary at 10 Downing Street, and said that figures on hospital admissions for stabbing injuries had not been properly checked and putting them out early was "corrosive of public trust."

He said in his letter that he had been told that officials or advisors in Number 10 had "caused" the Home Office to issue the release.

The statisticians who produced the figures attempted to block their release

on the grounds it was in breach of the National Statistics Code of Practice.

Sir Michael said: "These statistics were not due for publication for some time and had not therefore been through the regular process of checking and quality assurance.

"The statisticians who produced them, together with the National Statistician, tried unsuccessfully to prevent their premature, irregular and selective release.

"I hope you will agree that the publication of prematurely released and unchecked statistics is corrosive of public trust in official statistics and incompatible with the high standards which we are all seeking to establish.

---

procedures can also create significant changes (the New York robbery rate appeared to increase 400 percent in 1 year).[30] Many fluctuations in crime rates may therefore be attributable to events other than changes in the actual numbers of crimes committed.

Finally, the UCR data suffer from several omissions. Many arsons go unreported because not all fire departments report to the UCR.[31] Federal cases go unlisted. Most white-collar offenses are omitted because they are reported not to the police but to regulatory authorities, such as the Securities and Exchange Commission and the Federal Trade Commission.

In 1986, The International Association of Chiefs of Police, the National Sheriffs' Association, and state-level UCR programs joined forces with the FBI to develop an incident-based reporting system to address the limitations associated with the UCR data.[32] The National Incident-Based Reporting System (NIBRS) provides data on each single crime occurrence and arrest from local, state, and federal automated records systems. Reporting to the NIBRS is voluntary and coexists with the UCR. The NIBRS is a major attempt to improve the collection of crime data. But it deals only with crimes that come to the attention of the police. What about crimes that remain unreported? For what is called the "dark figure of crime," we have to rely on victimization data and self-report studies.

Victimization Surveys

Victimization surveys measure the extent of crime by interviewing individuals about their experiences as victims. The Bureau of the Census, in cooperation with the Bureau of Justice Statistics, collects information annually about persons and households that have been victimized. The report is called the "National Crime Victimization Survey" (NCVS). Researchers for the NCVS estimate the total number of crimes committed by asking respondents from a national sample of approximately 43,000 households, representing 80,000 persons over the age of 12 (parental permission is needed for those under 14 years old), about their experiences as victims during a specific time period. Interviewers visit (or sometimes telephone) the homes selected for the sample. Each housing unit remains in the sample for 3 years. Every 6 months, 10,000 households are rotated out of the sample and replaced by a new group.

The NCVS measures the extent of victimization by rape, robbery, assault, larceny, burglary, personal theft, and motor vehicle theft. Note that two of the UCR Part I offenses—criminal homicide and arson—are not included (Table 2.1, page 36).[33] Homicide is omitted because the NCVS covers only crimes whose victims can be interviewed. The designers of the survey also decided to omit arson, a relative newcomer to the UCR, because

"I would be grateful for your comments and for your assurance that there will be no repetition of this breach of the National Statistics Code of Practice."

In the press release Jacqui Smith, the Home Secretary, said there had been an overall fall in the number of people caught carrying knives and claimed that those found guilty of possessing knives were receiving longer sentences.

But the Home Office was unable to provide the statistics to support the claims saying they were "interim findings."

A Home Office fact sheet claimed hospital admissions were down 27 per cent since the crackdown on knife crime in ten areas began in July and stated there had been 18 per cent fewer victims under 20 in London between April and September 2008 than in the same period in 2007.

Sources at the authority said Sir Michael was "furious" over the breach of the rules.

Sir Michael's intervention follows concern in the Office for National Statistics at the way in which the Home Office has dealt with figures in politically sensitive areas such as crime and asylum and immigration.

It is the second time in recent months that the Home Office has been criticised over its use of statistics.

Professor David Hand, head of the Royal Statistical Society, highlighted "serious" bad practices during the release of immigration figures in August.

The latest row over is damaging for the Government as it once again casts doubt on whether people can believe official statistics on crime—an area where ministers are struggling to convince the public that offending is falling.

In October the Home Office was forced to admit that serious violent crime is much worse than they had been claiming because police forces had been failing to record offences properly.

Dominic Grieve, the shadow Home Secretary, said: "The knife crime epidemic is a tragedy that has claimed too many young lives.

"If government ministers have sanctioned the selective and manipulative spinning of these statistics, it is reckless and irresponsible.

"Labour should immediately publish the full figures so that we can see the truth."

Questions for Discussion

1. How vulnerable are crime statistics to political pressure?
2. What are the limitations of "official" statistics, that is, those statistics issued by the government?

SOURCE: Richard Ford, "Statistics Watchdog Chief Accuses Home Office of Abusing Crime Statistics." © Richard Ford/NI Syndication Limited, December 12, 2008.

measuring it with some validity by means of a victimization survey was deemed to be too difficult. Part II offenses have been excluded altogether because many of them are considered victimless (prostitution, vagrancy, drug abuse, drunkenness) or because victims are willing participants (gambling, con games) or do not know they have been victimized (forgery, fraud).

The survey covers characteristics of crimes such as time and place of occurrence, number of offenders, use of weapons, economic loss, and time lost from work; characteristics of victims, such as gender, age, race, ethnicity, marital status, household composition, and educational attainment; perceived characteristics of offenders, such as age, gender, and race; circumstances surrounding the offenses and their effects, such as financial loss and injury; and patterns of police reporting, such as rates of reporting and reasons for reporting and for not reporting. Some questions also encourage interviewees to discuss family violence.

Limitations of Victimization Surveys

While victimization surveys give us information about crimes that are not reported to the police, these data, too, have significant limitations. The NCVS covers crimes in a more limited way than the UCR; the NCVS includes only 7 offenses, whereas there are 8 offenses in Part I of the UCR and an additional 21 in Part II. Although the NCVS

is conducted by trained interviewers, some individual variations in interviewing and recording style are inevitable, and, as a result, the information recorded may vary as well.

Because the NCVS is based on personal reporting, it also suffers from the fact that memories may fade over time, so some facts are forgotten while others are exaggerated. Moreover, some interviewees may try to please the interviewer by fabricating crime incidents.[34] Respondents also have a tendency to telescope events—that is, to move events that took place in an earlier time period into the time period under study. Like the UCR, the NCVS records only the most serious offense committed during an event in which several crimes are perpetrated.

Self-Report Surveys

Another way to determine the amount and types of crime actually committed is to ask people to report their own criminal acts in a confidential interview or, more commonly, on an anonymous questionnaire. These investigations are called **self-report surveys.**

Findings of Self-Report Surveys

Self-reports of delinquent and criminal behavior have produced several important findings since their development in the 1940s. For one thing,

TABLE 2.1 How Do the Uniform Crime Reports and the National Crime Victimization Survey Differ?

	Uniform Crime Reports	National Crime Victimization Survey
Offenses measured	Homicide	
	Rape	Rape
	Robbery (personal and commercial)	Robbery (personal)
	Assault (aggravated)	Assault (aggravated and simple)
	Burglary (commercial and household)	Household burglary
	Larceny (commercial and household)	Larceny
	Motor vehicle theft	Personal theft
	Arson	Motor vehicle theft
Scope	Crimes reported to the police in most jurisdictions; considerable flexibility in developing small-area data	Crimes both reported and not reported to police; all data are for the nation as a whole; some data are available for a few large geographical areas
Collection method	Police department reports to FBI	Survey interviews; periodically measures the total number of crimes committed by asking a national sample of 42,000* households representing 76,000* persons over the age of 12 about their experiences as victims of crime during a specified period
Kinds of information	In addition to offense counts, provides information on crime clearances, persons arrested, persons charged, law enforcement officers killed and assaulted, and characteristics of homicide victims	Provides details about victims (such as age, race, sex, education, and income, and whether the victim and offender were related to each other) and about crimes (such as time and place of occurrence, whether reported to police, use of weapons, occurrence of injury, and economic consequences)
Sponsor	Department of Justice, Federal Bureau of Investigation	Department of Justice, Bureau of Justice Statistics

*Figures have been updated.

SOURCES: Adapted from U.S. Department of Justice, Bureau of Justice Statistics, *Report to the Nation on Crime and Justice*, 2d ed. (Washington, D.C.: U.S. Government Printing Office, 1988), p. 11; U.S. Department of Justice, Bureau of Justice Statistics, *Criminal Victimization 1997* (Washington, D.C.: U.S. Government Printing Office, December 1998), pp. 1–2.

they quickly refuted the conventional wisdom that only a small percentage of the general population commits crimes. The use of these measures over the last several decades has demonstrated very high rates of law-violating behavior by seemingly law-abiding people. Almost everyone, at some point in time, has broken a law.

In 1947, James S. Wallerstein and Clement J. Wyle questioned a group of 1,698 individuals on whether they had committed any of 49 offenses that were serious enough to require a maximum sentence of not less than 1 year. They found that over 80 percent of the men reported committing malicious mischief, disorderly conduct, and larceny. More than 50 percent admitted a history of crimes, including reckless driving and driving while intoxicated, indecency, gambling, fraud, and tax evasion. The authors acknowledged the lack of scientific rigor of their study. No attempt was made to ensure a balanced or representative cross section of the individuals surveyed.[35] However, these findings do suggest that the distinction between criminals and noncriminals may be more apparent than real.

Studies conducted since the 1940s have provided a great deal more information. These studies suggest that a wide discrepancy exists between official and self-report data with regard to the age, race, and gender of offenders.[36] Unrecorded offenders commit a wide variety of offenses, rather than specializing in one type of offense.[37] It also appears that only one-quarter of all serious, chronic juvenile offenders are apprehended by the police. Moreover, an estimated 90 percent of all youths commit delinquent or criminal acts, primarily truancy, use of false identification, alcohol abuse, larceny, fighting, and marijuana use.[38]

From 1991 to 1993, the first International Self-Report Delinquency (ISRD) study was conducted in Finland, Great Britain, the Netherlands, Belgium, Germany, Switzerland, Portugal, Spain, Italy, Greece, the United States, and New Zealand. Each country used the same questionnaire, which had been translated into the respective languages. The studies used various sampling techniques, so the results from each country are not strictly comparable. Nonetheless, the findings support much of what is found in the self-report literature. Boys commit about twice as many offenses as girls. The peak age of offending in the participating countries is 16 to 17 years. Violence is strongly related to lower educational levels. No relationship was found between socioeconomic status and delinquency. Drug use seems related to truancy and unemployment. School failure is related to violent offenses.[39]

Limitations of Self-Report Surveys

Self-report surveys have taught us a great deal about criminality. But, like the other methods of data collection, they have drawbacks. The questionnaires are often limited to petty acts, such as truancy, and therefore do not represent the range of criminal acts that people may commit. Michael Hindelang, Travis Hirschi, and Joseph Weis argue that researchers who find discrepancies with respect to gender, race, and class between the results produced by official statistics and those collected by self-report methods are in fact measuring different kinds of behavior rather than different amounts of the same behavior. They suggest that if you take into account the fact that persons who are arrested tend to have committed more serious offenses and to have prior records (criteria that affect decisions to arrest), then the two types of statistics are quite comparable.[40]

Another drawback of self-reports is that most of them are administered to high school or college students, so the information they yield applies only to young people attending school. And who can say that respondents always tell the truth? The information obtained by repeated administration of the same questionnaire to the same individuals might yield different results. Many self-report measures lack validity; the data obtained do not correspond with some other criterion (such as school records) that measures the same behavior. Finally, samples may be biased. People who choose not to participate in the studies may have good reason for not wanting to discuss their criminal activities.

Each of the three commonly used sources of data—police reports, victim surveys, and self-report surveys—adds a different dimension to our knowledge of crime. All of them are useful in our search for the characteristics of crimes, criminals, and victims.

MEASURING CHARACTERISTICS OF CRIME

Streets in Charlotte, North Carolina, with tranquil names—Peaceful Glen, Soft Wind, Gentle Breeze—were killing lanes.[41] The city that had hoped to displace Atlanta as the "Queen City of the South" had 115 homicides in 1992, more than double the number it had had 6 years earlier. It seemed that the city was out of control. Experts pointed to drugs and to a growing number of swap shops and flea markets that served as unregulated outlets for buying guns as the reasons for the high number of homicides. Most of the killings took place in a 26-square-mile area inhabited primarily by low-income African-American families. Fortunately, within 8 years, the situation reversed itself. In 2003, the number of homicides in Charlotte was reduced to 66.[42] This information not only gives us general insights into the crime problem in Charlotte, but also enables us to examine the changes in the homicide rate over time, the high-risk areas, and the racial and economic composition of those areas in order to provide a full picture of the crime history.

Criminologists use these kinds of data about crimes in their research. Some investigators, for example, may want to compare drug use to crime in major cities. Others may want to explain a decrease or an increase in the crime rate in a single city (Charlotte), in a single neighborhood (the impoverished inner city), or perhaps in the nation as a whole.

Crime Trends

One of the most important characteristics of any crime is how often it is committed. From such data we can determine crime trends, the increases and decreases of crime over time. The UCR show that about 11.2 million Index crimes (excluding arson) were reported to the police in 2007 (Figure 2.4b). Of the total number of Index crimes, violent crimes make up a small portion—12 percent—with a murder rate of 5.6 per 100,000. Most Index crimes are property offenses (88 percent), and two-thirds of property crimes in 2007 were larceny thefts.[43]

The 2007 NCVS presents a somewhat different picture (Figure 2.4a). Although the data presented in the NCVS and the UCR are not entirely comparable because the categories differ, the number of crimes reported to the police and the number reported in the victimization survey clearly are far apart. According to the NCVS, there were

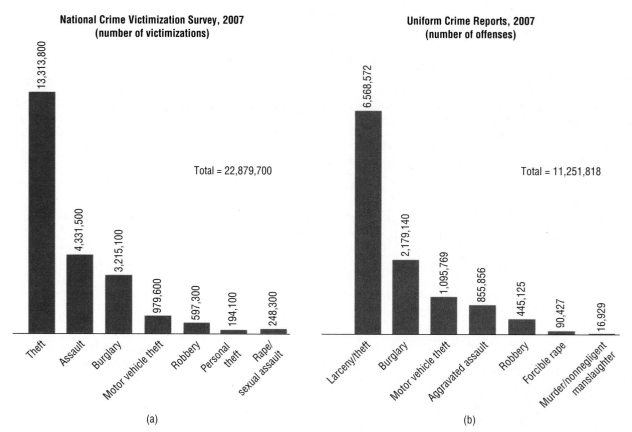

National Crime Victimization Survey, 2007
(number of victimizations)

13,313,800

Total = 22,879,700

4,331,500
3,215,100
979,600
597,300
194,100
248,300

Theft | Assault | Burglary | Motor vehicle theft | Robbery | Personal theft | Rape/ sexual assault

(a)

Uniform Crime Reports, 2007
(number of offenses)

6,568,572

Total = 11,251,818

2,179,140
1,095,769
855,856
445,125
90,427
16,929

Larceny/theft | Burglary | Motor vehicle theft | Aggravated assault | Robbery | Forcible rape | Murder/nonnegligent manslaughter

(b)

FIGURE 2.4 National Crime Victimization Survey and Uniform Crime Reports: a comparison of number of crimes reported. (a) National Crime Victimization Survey: total number of victimizations, 2007. (b) Uniform Crime Reports: Total number of Index offenses, 2007.

Sources: (a) Michael R. Rand, *National Crime Victimization Survey: Criminal Victimization, 2007* (Washington, D.C.: Bureau of Justice Statistics, 2008), p. 1. (b) Adapted from U.S. Department of Justice, Federal Bureau of Investigation, *Crime in the United States, 2007* (Washington, D.C., Federal Bureau of Investigation, 2008). Retrieved Feb. 1, 2009, from http://www.fbi.gov/ucr.

almost 23 million victimizations. Indeed, the NCVS reports more thefts than the total number of UCR Index offenses.[44]

According to UCR data, the crime rate increased slowly between 1930 and 1960. After 1960, it began to rise much more quickly. This trend continued until 1980 (Figure 2.5), when the crime rate rose to 5,950 per 100,000. From that peak, the rate steadily dropped until 1984, when there were 5,031.3 crimes per 100,000. After that year, the rate rose again until 1991. Since then, it has decreased every year, to 3,803.0 in 2006, the lowest rate since 1969.[45] The NCVS also shows that the victimization rate peaked from 1979 to 1981, but that in the 5-year span from 1993 to 1998, the victimization rates for all crimes dropped.[46] This trend continued through 2007.

The gradual decline in the crime rate after 1980 is an important phenomenon that requires a bit more analysis. One important factor is the age distribution of the population. Given the fact that young people tend to have the highest crime rate, the age distribution of the population has a major effect on crime trends. After World War II, the birthrate increased sharply in what is known as the "baby boom." The baby-boom generation reached its crime-prone years in the 1960s, and the crime rate duly rose. As the generation grew older, the crime rate became more stable and in the 1980s began to decline. Some researchers claim that the children of the baby boomers may very well expand the ranks of the crime-prone ages once again and that crime will again increase.

During the period when the baby-boom generation outgrew criminal behavior, U.S. society was undergoing other changes. We adopted a get-tough crime-control policy, which may have deterred some people from committing crimes. Mandatory prison terms meant judges had less discretion in sentencing, and fewer convicted felons were paroled. In addition, crime prevention programs, such as Neighborhood Watch groups, became popular. These and other factors have been suggested to explain why the crime rate dropped, but we have no definitive answers.

Locations and Times of Criminal Acts

Statistics on the characteristics of crimes are important not only to criminologists who seek to know why crime occurs but also to those who

Crime Surfing

http://www.albany .edu/sourcebook

The "Sourcebook of Criminal Justice Statistics" is an excellent place to look for official data on all parts of the criminal justice system. Go to this website to find the most recent arrest data for the area in which you live. Which three offenses have the most arrests?

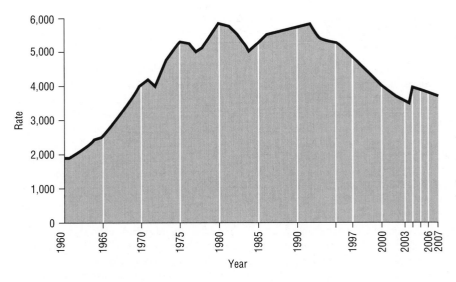

FIGURE 2.5 Uniform Crime Reports: rate of all Index crimes per 100,000 people, 1960–2007.

Sources: U.S. Department of Justice, Federal Bureau of Investigation, *Crime in the United States, 1975; 1980; 1992; 1994; 1997; 2000; 2003; 2004; 2005; 2006; 2007* (Washington D.C.: U.S. Government Printing Office, 1976, 1981, 1993, 1995, 1998, 2001, 2004, 2005, 2006, 2007, 2008).

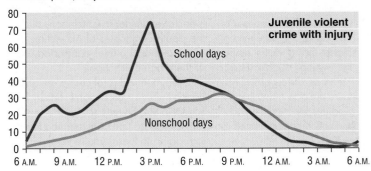

FIGURE 2.6 Serious juvenile violent crime with injury by time of day. On school days, violent crimes with injury cluster in the hours immediately after the close of school. On school days, violent crime with injury by juveniles peaks at 3:00 P.M., markedly decreasing in the evening hours. On nonschool days, the temporal pattern of juvenile violence with injury is similar to the overall pattern for adults: Juvenile violence occurs throughout the day and peaks between 7:00 P.M. and 9:00 P.M.

Note: Violent crimes include murder, violent sexual assault, robbery, aggravated assault, and simple assault.

Source: H. Snyder and M. Sickmund, *Juvenile Offenders and Victims: 2006 National Report* (Washington, D.C.: Office of Juvenile Justice and Delinquency Prevention, 2006), ch. 3. Retrieved June 4, 2008 from *OJJDP Statistical Briefing Book*, available at http://ojjdp.ncjrs.gov/ojstatbb/offenders/qa03304 .asp?qaDate=2001.

want to know how to prevent it (Chapter 9). Two statistics of use in prevention efforts are those on *where* crimes are committed and *when* they are committed.

Most crimes are committed in large urban areas rather than in small cities, suburbs, or rural areas. This pattern can be attributed to a variety of factors that might include population, economic conditions, and the quality of law enforcement. The statistics for Charlotte, North Carolina, for example, show that most arrests took place in the poverty-ridden ghetto areas. The fact that the majority of those arrests were made in neighborhoods where drug dealers were visibly present on the streets fits the national picture.

According to NCVS data, the safest place to be is at home; however, we are most likely to be victimized when we are in familiar territory, In 2005, one-quarter of violent crimes took place at or near the victim's home, and nearly three-quarters of violent crimes occurred within 5 miles of the home. Common locations for violent crimes are streets other than those near the victim's home (15 percent), at school (14 percent), or at a commercial establishment (8 percent).[47]

NCVS data further reveal that more than half of violent crimes take place between 6:00 A.M. and 6:00 P.M., but nearly two-thirds of sexual assaults take place at night. Household crimes follow the same pattern: Of crimes committed within a known period, 70 percent of household larcenies and 75 percent of motor vehicle thefts are committed at night. Most personal thefts, however, are committed during the day. For juveniles, 20 percent of violent crimes occur in the 4 hours (3:00 P.M. to 7:00 P.M.) immediately after the close of school (Figure 2.6).[48]

Nationwide crime rates also vary by season. Personal and household crimes are more likely to be committed during the warmer months of the year, perhaps because in summer people spend more time outdoors, where they are more vulnerable to crime.[49] People also often leave doors and windows open when they go out in warm weather.

Murder Spike Poses Quandary

Edward Bedenbaugh III was about to start a job as a youth-violence counselor working in inner-city schools, mediating disputes before they escalated into lethal exchanges. He was celebrating his appointment at a nightspot in an upscale part of the nation's capital when he was shot in the back five times. The 29-year-old man died the next morning, April 17, two days before his oldest daughter's 10th birthday.

He was one of 14 people, all African-Americans, to die in a 13-day spasm of violence. That surge was enough to help make this April, with 18 murders, 20% deadlier than April 2007.

The grim run hasn't been limited to Washington. Several cities around the country, including Chicago and Philadelphia, endured similar mini murder waves during the same period, leading criminologists to worry whether this signifies the beginning of a trend—or evidence of an unnoticed one.

What is most troubling to people who study crime is that there is no simple explanation for this rise. There are the usual reasons—the economy, poverty, gangs and crews, and the availability of firearms, but there is one that has been little explored: the migration of the prison culture back to the streets. As nearly 700,000 convicts a year return home, some may be bringing prison culture with them.

"This is part of the price we're paying for 20 years of mass incarceration," said David Kennedy, director of the Center for Crime Prevention and Control at New York City's John Jay College of Criminal Justice.

While he acknowledges that the economy and demographics might have a role in some cases, they don't explain the current spate of crime, which he calls "God-awful serious."

He said the violence also turns on a central currency within prisons: respect. Disrespect can lead to lethal responses at the slightest provocation. In one recent case, police suspect that a victim simply strayed into the wrong neighborhood, which can be seen as disrespectful. Mr. Kennedy said there are now many people on the streets who live by a prison code, as the prison population has ballooned to 2.2 million from 330,000 in 1980.

The cycle of violent retribution can be seen at the funerals of the younger victims, where, in some cases, the families of the slain beseech the attendees to refrain from revenge.

The result is that while the overall murder rate has dropped for years, it has been inching up in the black community in recent years. African-Americans make up only 13% of the nation's population, but more are killed in the U.S. than any other racial group, accounting for 49% of all murder victims, according to Federal Bureau of Investigation statistics.

A county medical examiner who has analyzed all the available data on his murder victims thinks that education—or the lack of it—is a vital component. O'dell Owens, the Hamilton County medical examiner in Cincinnati, studied the death certificates of his victims and found that over a five-year period, 60% of them had quit school.

"The homicides occur in neighborhoods where folks don't finish high school," Mr. Owens said. "If you can't make the transition from learning to read to reading to learn, you're done."

Severity of Crime

We have seen that crime rates vary by time and place. They also vary in people's perception of their severity. To some extent, legislation sets a standard of severity by the punishments it attaches to various crimes. But let us take a critical look at such judgments.

Do you believe that skyjacking an airplane is a more serious offense than smuggling heroin? Is forcible rape more serious than kidnapping? Is breaking into a home and stealing $1,000 more serious than using force to rob a person of $10? A yes answer to all three questions conforms to the findings of the National Survey of Crime Severity, which in 1977 measured public perceptions of the seriousness of 204 events, from planting a bomb that killed 20 people to playing hooky from school.[50]

The survey, conducted by Marvin E. Wolfgang and his colleagues, found that individuals generally agree about the relative seriousness of specific crimes (Table 2.2). In ranking severity, people seem to base their decisions on such factors as the ability of victims to protect themselves, the amount of injury and loss suffered, the type of business or organization from which property is stolen, the relationship between offender and victim, and (for drug offenses) the types of drugs involved. Respondents generally agreed that violent crime is more serious than property crime. They also considered white-collar crimes, such as engaging in consumer fraud, cheating on income taxes, polluting, and accepting bribes, to be as serious as many violent and property crimes.

MEASURING CHARACTERISTICS OF CRIMINALS

Information on the characteristics of crimes is not the only sort of data analyzed by criminologists. They also want to know the characteristics of the people who commit those crimes.

Behind each crime is a criminal or several criminals. Criminals can be differentiated by age, ethnicity, gender, socioeconomic level, and other criteria. These characteristics enable researchers to group criminals into categories, and it is these categories that researchers find useful. They study the various offender groups to determine why some people are more likely than others to commit crimes

Jack Levin, head of Northeastern University's Brudnick Center on Violence and Conflict, believes the troubled economy indirectly affects crime levels. In tough economic times, "one of the first things to go are policies and programs for fighting crimes," he said. Combine that with rising desperation and frustration, especially in the less affluent areas of society, and violence is the outcome.

Police also blame a rise in gang violence, as well as domestic incidents. But some, like James Pasco, executive director of the Fraternal Order of Police, said the surge is also the result of changing age demographics, particularly the 18-to-25-year-old group. "That is the adult age group most prone to violence," and it's growing, he said. But "it remains to be seen if the uptick will continue."

Mr. Bedenbaugh was going to be one of the counselors who tried to slow the violence. The father of two had been a basketball coach and youth volunteer at LifeStarts Youth and Community Services while also working with his father in a landscaping business.

His boss at LifeStarts, Curtis Watkins, said Mr. Bedenbaugh was known for his ability to reach even the hard-core teen-agers in the neighborhood. "You have to have people who can relate to these kids, who can give them a vision beyond their neighborhood and the 'hood," said Mr. Watkins, whose own son's 2006 murder has never been solved. "Ed could do that. He had that magic."

What sparked the argument is unclear. According to court papers, Mr. Bedenbaugh tried to defuse the situation by refusing to go outside with the would-be gunman to continue the argument. The gunman had hidden in an alley nearby and had to wait for an hour, pacing back and forth, according to witnesses. When Mr. Bedenbaugh finally came out, he shot him in the back.

An arrest has been made, but that is of little consolation for the family, said his sister, Latia Davis, 27. She works a half-block from where her brother was fatally wounded, and her daughter was born this year in the hospital where he died. "He wasn't some guy out there selling drugs or on the streets," she says. "This guy doesn't know what he took." The evidence, she said, is in the hundreds of people who came to pay their respects at his services.

Mr. Bedenbaugh was killed in an area better known for lawyers and lobbyists. Albert Herring, the executive assistant U.S. attorney for the District of Columbia, says the location holds a lesson for those who think that violent crime is confined to certain neighborhoods. "The problem that affects everybody, whether they appreciate it or not, is this: Crime migrates," he said.

Source

Gary Fields, "Murder Spike Poses Quandary," *Wall Street Journal*, May 6, 2008, p. A16. Copyright 2008 by Dow Jones & Company, Inc. Reproduced with permission of Dow Jones & Company, Inc. in the format Textbook via Copyright Clearance Center.

Questions for Discussion

1. What is your best guess as to why a murder rate might significantly increase or decrease?
2. To what extent can police be effective, or at least have an impact, in reducing a murder rate?
3. What role do race, class, and gender play in violent crime rates?

---

or particular types of crimes. It has been estimated that 14.4 million arrests were made in 2006 for all criminal offenses except traffic violations. Figure 2.7 (page 43) shows how these arrests were distributed among the offenses. During the 9 years between 1997 and 2006, the number of arrests for Index offenses fell 12.2 percent and 24.5 percent for violent crimes and property crimes, respectively.[51]

Age and Crime

Six armed men who have been called the "over-the-hill gang" were arrested trying to rob an elegant bridge and backgammon club in midtown New York City. The robbery began at 10:25 P.M. when the men, wearing rubber gloves and ski masks and armed with two revolvers, a shotgun, and a rifle, forced the customers and employees to lie down in a back room while they loaded a nylon bag with wallets, players' money, and the club's cash box. A club worker slipped out a side door to alert police, who arrived within minutes. They surprised and disarmed one member of the gang, a 48-year-old, whom they found clutching a .22-caliber revolver. They took a .38-caliber revolver from another gang member, 41 years old.

During the scuffle with the officers, one suspect tried to escape, fell, and broke his nose. The officers then found and arrested a 40-year-old man standing in the hallway with a 12-gauge Winchester shotgun. Meanwhile, the other gang members abandoned their gloves and masks and lay down among the people they had robbed. One of the suspects, age 72, who wore a back brace, complained of chest and back pain as police locked handcuffs on him. He was immediately hospitalized.[52]

In another case, 94-year-old career criminal Wesley (Pop) Honeywood, from Jacksonville, Florida, was sentenced to 7 years after he pointed an unloaded gun at another man who warned him not to eat grapes growing in the man's yard. Mr. Honeywood was given the option of going to a nursing home instead of prison, but he resisted, saying, "If I go to jail, I may be out in a couple of years. If I go to a nursing home, I may be there the rest of my life."[53]

These cases are extraordinary for at least two reasons. First, in any given year, approximately half of all arrests are of individuals under age 25; second, gang membership is ordinarily confined to the young. Though juveniles (people under age 18)

Crime Surfing

www.unodc.org

The United Nations Office on Drugs and Crime (UNODC) is a resource for investigating international crimes such as corruption, human trafficking and migrant smuggling, illicit drugs, money laundering, and organized crime. The URL above will take you to information and reported crime data for several countries. Check this data to compare the crime patterns in other countries to those in the United States.

TABLE 2.2 How Do People Rank the Severity of Crime?

Severity Score	Ten Most Serious Offenses	Severity Score	Ten Least Serious Offenses
72.1	Planting a bomb in a public building. The bomb explodes and 20 people are killed.	1.3	Two persons willingly engage in a homosexual act.
52.8	A man forcibly rapes a woman. As a result of physical injuries, she dies.	1.1	Disturbing the neighborhood with loud, noisy behavior.
43.2	Robbing a victim at gunpoint. The victim struggles and is shot to death.	1.1	Taking bets on the numbers.
39.2	A man stabs his wife. As a result, she dies.	1.1	A group continues to hang around a corner after being told to break up by a police officer.
35.7	Stabbing a victim to death.	0.9	A youngster under 16 years old runs away from home.
35.6	Intentionally injuring a victim. As a result, the victim dies.	0.8	Being drunk in public.
33.8	Running a narcotics ring.	0.7	A youngster under 16 years old breaks a curfew law by being out on the street after the hour permitted by law.
27.9	A woman stabs her husband. As a result, he dies.	0.6	Trespassing in the backyard of a private home.
26.3	An armed person skyjacks an airplane and demands to be flown to another country.	0.3	A person is a vagrant. That is, he has no home and no visible means of support.
25.8	A man forcibly rapes a woman. No other physical injury occurs.	0.2	A youngster under 16 years old plays hooky from school.

SOURCE: Adapted from Marvin E. Wolfgang, Robert Figlio, Paul E. Tracey, and Simon I. Singer, *National Survey of Crime Severity* (Washington, D.C.: U.S. Government Printing Office, 1985).

■ *Two very old inmates in the geriatric unit at Estelle Prison, Huntsville, Texas: an increasing burden for custodial care.*

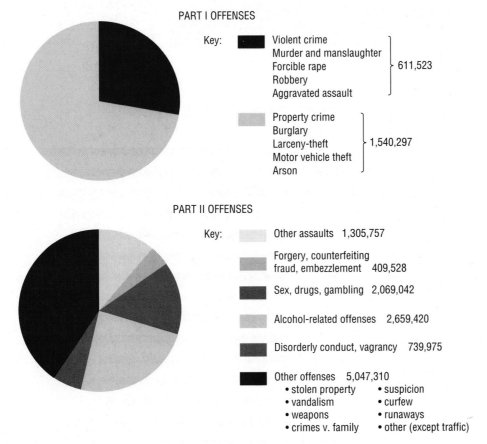

PART I OFFENSES

Key:
■ Violent crime
Murder and manslaughter
Forcible rape
Robbery
Aggravated assault
} 611,523

▨ Property crime
Burglary
Larceny-theft
Motor vehicle theft
Arson
} 1,540,297

PART II OFFENSES

Key:
▨ Other assaults   1,305,757

▨ Forgery, counterfeiting
fraud, embezzlement   409,528

▨ Sex, drugs, gambling   2,069,042

▨ Alcohol-related offenses   2,659,420

▨ Disorderly conduct, vagrancy   739,975

■ Other offenses   5,047,310
• stolen property   • suspicion
• vandalism   • curfew
• weapons   • runaways
• crimes v. family   • other (except traffic)

FIGURE 2.7   Distribution of total number of arrests, 2006 (estimated).

Source: U.S. Department of Justice, Federal Bureau of Investigation, *Crime in the United States, 2006.* Retrieved June 5, 2008, from http://www.fbi.gov/ucr/cius2006/data/table_29.html.

constitute about 8 percent of the population, they account for 15 percent of arrests for Index crimes in 2006. One-quarter of all larceny-theft offenses involved juveniles, and juveniles comprised half of all arson arrests (Figure 2.8).[54] While people age 65 and over constitute 12.4 percent of the population, they account for less than 1 percent of all arrests.[55] This **aging-out phenomenon**—or decline in criminal activities with age—have sparked a lively scientific debate. Michael Gottfredson and Travis Hirschi contend there is a certain inclination to commit crimes that peaks in the middle or late teens and then declines throughout life. This relationship between crime and age does not change, "regardless of sex, race, country, time, or offense."[56]

Crime decreases with age, the researchers add, even among people who commit frequent offenses. Thus, differences in crime rates found among young people of various groups, such as males and females or lower class and middle class, will be maintained throughout the life cycle. If lower-class youths are three times more likely to commit crimes than middle-class youths, for instance, then 60-year-old lower-class persons will be three times more likely to commit crimes than 60-year-old middle-class persons, though crimes committed

by both lower-class and middle-class groups will constantly decline.[57] According to this argument, all offenders commit fewer crimes as they grow older because they have less strength, less mobility, and so on.

James Q. Wilson and Richard Herrnstein support the view that the aging-out phenomenon is a natural part of the life cycle.[58] Teenagers may become increasingly independent of their parents yet lack the resources to support themselves; they band together with other young people who are equally frustrated in their search for legitimate ways to get money, sex, alcohol, and status. Together they find illegitimate sources. With adulthood, the small gains from criminal behavior no longer seem so attractive. Legitimate means open up. They marry. Their peers no longer endorse lawbreaking. They learn to delay gratification. Petty crime is no longer adventurous. It is at this time that the aging-out process begins for most individuals. Even those who continue to commit offenses will eventually slow down with increasing age.

The opposing side in this debate, sometimes called the "life-course perspective," argues that the decrease in crime rates after adolescence does

Victims around the World

The International Crime Victim Survey (comparable to our National Crime Victimization Survey) became operational in 1989. The main object of ICVS is to advance international and comparative criminological research without the obvious limitations of officially recorded crime data.

ICVS surveys were administered in 1992, 1996, and 2000. The survey's fifth administration was in 2005. Within the past 15 years, a total of more than 300,000 people from 78 countries have been interviewed about their victimization.

As the graph in this box reveals, the top 15 countries by victimization rate include very affluent parts of the world. Some comparative criminologists, in response, ask whether there is still any truth to the conventional wisdom that poverty is the "dominant root cause of common crime."

Source

J. van Dijk, J. van Kerteren, and P. Smit, *Criminal Victimisation in International Perspective: Key Findings from the 2004–2005 ICVS and EU ICS* (The Hague: Boom Legal Publishers, 2007).

Questions for Discussion

1. Why are the victimization rates so high in affluent countries?
2. Are you surprised by how the United States ranks relative to other countries? Why or why not?

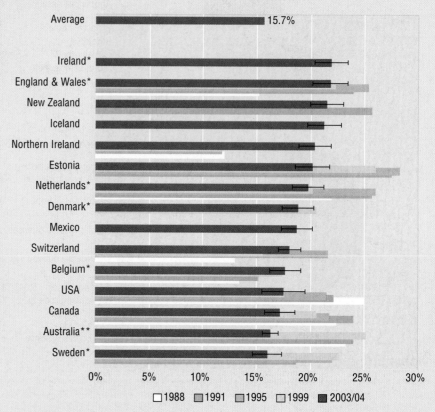

* Source: J. J. M. van Dijk, R. Manchin, J. N. van Kesteren, and G. Hideg, *The Burden of Crime in the EU. Research Report: A Comparative Analysis of the European Crime and Safety Survey (EU ICS)* 2005. (Brussels: Gallup Europe, 2007), p.19.

** The Australian victimization rate is based on nine crimes because the question about victimization by sexual offenses was omitted; if data on sexual victimization were included, the overall victimization rate would be a percentage point higher (est. 16.5 percent).

Overall victimization for 10 crimes; 1-year prevalence rates in 2003/04 of the top 15 countries and results from earlier surveys (1989–2005 ICVS and 2005 EU ICS).

---

not imply that the number of crimes committed by all individual offenders declines. In other words, the frequency of offending may go down for most offenders, but some chronic active offenders may continue to commit the same amount of crime over time. Why might this be so? Because the factors that influence any individual's entrance into criminal activity vary, the number and types of offenses committed vary, and the factors that eventually induce the individual to give up criminal activity vary.[59]

According to this argument, the frequency of criminal involvement, then, depends on such social factors as economic situation, peer pressure, and lifestyle, and it is these social factors that explain the aging-out phenomenon. A teenager's unemployment, for example, may have very little to do with the onset of criminal activity because the youngster is not yet in the labor force and still lives at home. Unemployment may increase an adult's rate of offending, however, because an adult requires income to support various responsibilities. Thus, the relationship between age and crime is not the same for all offenders. Various conditions during the life cycle affect individuals' behavior in different ways.[60]

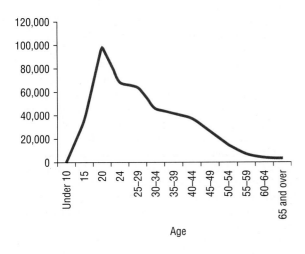

FIGURE 2.8 Violent crime Index arrests by age, 2006.

Source: U.S. Department of Justice, Federal Bureau of Investigation, *Crime in the United States 2006,* (Released Sept. 2007). Retrieved June 6, 2008, from http://www.fbi.gov/ucr/cius2006/data/table_38.html.

To learn how the causes of crime vary at different ages, Alfred Blumstein and his colleagues suggest that we study **criminal careers,** a concept that describes the onset of criminal activity, the types and amount of crime committed, and the termination of such activity.[61] **Longitudinal studies** of a particular group of people over time should enable researchers to uncover the factors that distinguish criminals from noncriminals and those that differentiate criminals in regard to the number and kinds of offenses they commit.

Those involved in research on criminal careers assume that offenders who commit 10 crimes may differ from those who commit 1 or 15. They ask: Are the factors that cause the second offense the same ones that cause the fourth or the fifth? Do different factors move one offender from theft to rape or from assault to shoplifting? How many persons in a **birth cohort** (a group of people born in the same year) will become criminals? Of those, how many will become career criminals (chronic offenders)?

In the 1960s, researchers at the Sellin Center of the University of Pennsylvania began a search for answers. Their earliest publication, in 1972, detailed the criminal careers of 9,945 boys (a cohort) born in Philadelphia in 1945. Marvin Wolfgang, Robert Figlio, and Thorsten Sellin obtained their data from school records and official police reports. Their major findings were that 35 percent of the boys had had contact with the police before reaching their 18th birthday; of those boys, 46 percent were one-time offenders and 54 percent were repeat offenders. Of those with police contact, 18 percent had committed five or more offenses; they represented 6 percent of the total. The "chronic 6 percent," as they are now called,

were responsible for more than half of all the offenses committed, including 71 percent of the homicides, 73 percent of the rapes, 82 percent of the robberies, and 69 percent of the assaults.[62]

Research continued on 10 percent of the boys in the original cohort until they reached the age of 30. This sample was divided into three groups: those who had records of offenses only as juveniles, those who had records only as adults, and those who were persistent offenders with both juvenile and adult records. Though they made up only 15 percent of the follow-up group, those who had been chronic juvenile offenders made up 74 percent of all the arrests. Thus, chronic juvenile offenders do indeed continue to break laws as adults.[63]

The boys in the original cohort were born in 1945. Researchers questioned whether the same behavior patterns would continue over the years. Criminologist Paul Tracy and his associates found the answer in a second study, which examined a cohort of 13,160 males born in 1958. The two studies show similar results. In the second cohort, 33 percent had had contact with the police before reaching their 18th birthday, 42 percent were one-time offenders, and 58 percent were repeat offenders. Chronic delinquents were found in both cohorts. The chronic delinquents in the second cohort, however, accounted for a greater percentage of the cohort—7.5 percent. They also were involved in more serious and injurious acts than the previous group.

The 1945 cohort study did not contain females, so no overall comparisons can be made over time. But comparing females and males in the 1958 cohort, we see significant gender differences. Of the 14,000 females in the cohort, 14 percent had had contact with the police before age 18. Among the female delinquents, 60 percent were one-time offenders, 33 percent were repeat offenders, and 7 percent were chronic offenders. Overall, female delinquency was less frequent and less likely to involve serious charges.[64]

In another longitudinal study, researchers followed about 4,000 youngsters in Denver, Pittsburgh, and Rochester, New York, for 5 years, 1988 through 1992. By age 16, over half the youngsters admitted to committing violent criminal acts. According to Terence P. Thornberry, the principal investigator in Rochester, chronic offenders also accounted for a high percentage of all violent offenses: 15 percent of the youths in the sample were responsible for 75 percent of the criminal acts.[65]

The policy implications of such findings are clear. If a very small group of offenders is committing a large percentage of all crime, the crime rate should go down if we incarcerate those offenders for long periods of time. Many jurisdictions around the country are developing sentencing policies to do just that, but such policies are quite controversial.

DID YOU KNOW?

. . . that one in every three delinquents with a history of violent offenses has a juvenile court record before reaching age 14?

Gender and Crime

Except for such crimes as prostitution, shoplifting, and welfare fraud, males traditionally commit more crimes than females at all ages. According to the UCR for 2007, the arrest ratio is more than 3 male offenders to 1 female offender.[66] The NCVS reports a wider gap: For personal crimes of violence involving a single offender, 82 percent of victims perceived the gender of the offender as male.[67]

Since the 1960s, however, there have been some interesting developments in regard to gender and crime data. In 1960, females accounted for 11 percent of the total number of arrests across the country. They now account for about 23 percent. And while the female arrest rate is still much lower than that of males, the rate of increase for women has risen faster than the rate for men (Figure 2.9 shows juvenile rates).[68]

Self-report surveys, which show more similarities in male and female criminal activity than official reports do, find that males commit more offenses than females. However, several of these studies suggest that gender differences in crime may be narrowing. They demonstrate that the patterns and causes of male and female delinquent activity are becoming more alike.[69] John Hagan and his associates agree, but only with respect to girls raised in middle-class egalitarian families in which husband and wife share similar positions of power at home and in the workplace. They argue that girls raised in lower-class, father-dominated households grow up in a cult of domesticity that reduces their freedom and thus the likelihood of their delinquency.[70] Researchers Merry Morash and Meda Chesney-Lind disagree. In a study of 1,427 adolescents and their caretakers, they found gender differences in delinquency between girls and boys regardless of the type of family in which the youngsters were raised.[71]

Because women traditionally have had such low crime rates, the scientific community and the mass media have generally ignored the subject of female criminality. Both have tended to view female offenders as misguided children who are an embarrassment rather than a threat to society. Only a handful of the world's criminologists have deemed the subject worthy of independent study. Foremost among them was Cesare Lombroso (whom we shall meet again in Chapter 3). His book *The Female Offender* (coauthored by William Ferrero), which appeared in 1895, detailed the physical abnormalities that would predestine some girls to be criminal from birth.[72] Lombroso's findings on male criminals, however, have not stood the test of later scientific research, and his portrayal of the female criminal has been found to be similarly inaccurate.

A little over a generation later, in the 1930s, Sheldon and Eleanor Glueck launched a massive research project on the biological and environmental causes of crime, with a separate inquiry into female offenders. Their conclusions were decidedly sociological. They said, in essence, that in order to change the incidence of female criminality, there would have to be a change in the social circumstances in which females grow up.[73]

Otto Pollack shared the Gluecks' views on sociological determinants. In 1952, he proposed that female crime has a "masked character" that keeps it from being properly recorded or otherwise noted in statistical reports. Protective attitudes toward women make police officers less willing to arrest them, victims less eager to report their offenses, district attorneys less enthusiastic about prosecuting them, and juries less likely to find them guilty. Moreover, Pollack noted that women's social roles as homemakers, child rearers, and shoppers furnish them with opportunities for concealed criminal activity and with victims who are the least likely to complain to and/or cooperate with the police. He also argued that female crime was limited by the various psychological and physiological characteristics inherent in the female anatomy.[74]

A quarter-century after Pollack's work, two researchers, working independently, took a fresh look at female crime in light of women's new roles in society. In 1975, Freda Adler posited that as social and economic roles of women changed in the legitimate world, their participation in crime would also change. According to this argument, the temptations, challenges, stresses, and strains to which women have been increasingly subjected in recent years cause them to act or react in the same manner in which men have consistently reacted to the same stimuli. In other words, equalization of social and economic roles leads to similar behavior patterns, both legal and illegal, on the part of both men and women. To steal a car, for example, one needs to know how to drive. To embezzle, one needs to be in a position of trust and in control of funds. To get into a bar fight, one needs to go to a bar. To be an inside trader on Wall Street, one needs to be on the inside.[75]

Rita Simon has taken a similar position. She, too, has argued that female criminality has undergone changes. But these changes, according to Simon, have occurred only in regard to certain property crimes, such as larceny/theft and fraud/embezzlement. Women are becoming more involved in these crimes because they have more opportunities to commit them. Simon hypothesizes that since the propensity of men and women to commit crime is not basically different, as more women enter the labor force and work in a much broader range of jobs, their property crime rate will continue to go up.[76]

Robbery

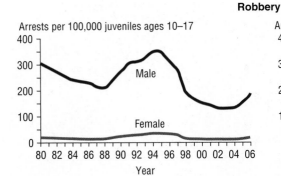

Arrests per 100,000 juveniles ages 10–17

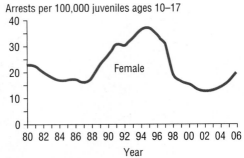

Arrests per 100,000 juveniles ages 10–17

FIGURE 2.9 Juvenile male and female arrest trends, 1980–2006. Trends were similar for robbery and drug law violations but differed for aggravated and simple assault.

Source: Howard N. Snyder, *Juvenile Arrests 2006* (Washington, D.C.: Office of Juvenile Justice and Delinquency Prevention, 2008), p. 8.

Aggravated assault

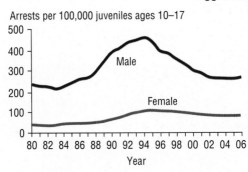

Arrests per 100,000 juveniles ages 10–17

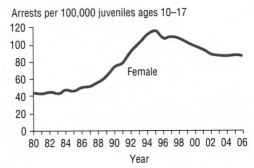

Arrests per 100,000 juveniles ages 10–17

Other (simple) assault

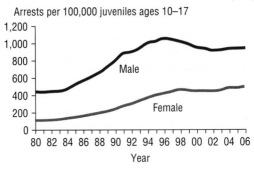

Arrests per 100,000 juveniles ages 10–17

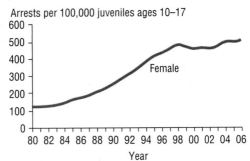

Arrests per 100,000 juveniles ages 10–17

Drug abuse violations

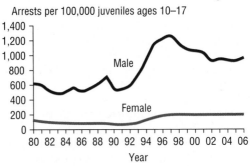

Arrests per 100,000 juveniles ages 10–17

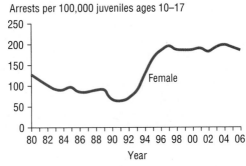

Arrests per 100,000 juveniles ages 10–17

◆ A similar growth and subsequent decline in juvenile male and female robbery arrest rates between 1980 and 2006 left each below their 1980s levels (36% and 12%, respectively). Over the period, juvenile male and female drug arrest rates both increased by half (55% and 47%, respectively).

◆ Unlike robbery, the juvenile female arrest rate for aggravated assault did not decline after its 1990s peak as much as did the male rate. As a result, in 2006, the juvenile male arrest rate was just 13% above its 1980 level, while the female rate was almost double its 1980 rate (up 94%). Similarly, while the male arrest rate for simple assault over the 1980–2006 period doubled, the female rate quadrupled.

Data source: Analysis of arrest data from the FBI and population data from the U.S. Census Bureau and the National Center for Health Statistics.

Lisa Marie Nowak, U.S. Naval Officer and former NASA astronaut (left), was charged in February 2007 with attempted kidnapping, burglary with assault, and misdemeanor battery (right). Nowak had a 2-year affair with fellow astronaut William Oefelein before he ended the relationship with Nowak to date U.S. Air Force Captain Colleen Shipman. Nowak drove from Houston to Orlando with latex gloves, a pistol and ammunition, pepper spray, a trench coat, a hammer drill, plastic bags, and an 8-inch knife to kidnap Shipman.

Some criminologists have challenged the views of Adler and Simon. Many questions have been asked about the so-called new female criminal. Does she exist? If so, does she commit more crimes than the former female criminal did? What types of crimes? Is she still involved primarily in offenses against property, or has she turned to more violent offenses? Researchers differ on the answers. Some contend that the extent of female criminality has not changed through the years but that crimes committed by women are more often making their way into official statistics simply because they are more often reported and prosecuted. In other words, the days of chivalry in the criminal justice system are over.[77]

Others argue that female crime has indeed increased, but they attribute the increase to nonviolent, petty property offenses that continue to reflect traditional female gender roles.[78] Moreover, some investigators claim, the increased involvement in these petty property offenses suggests that women are still economically disadvantaged, still suffering sexism in the legitimate marketplace.[79] Other researchers support the contention of Adler and Simon that female roles have changed and that these changes have indeed led women to commit the same kinds of crimes as men—violent as well as property offenses.[80]

Though scholars disagree on the form and extent of female crime, they do seem to agree that the crimes women commit are closely associated with their socioeconomic position in society. The controversy has to do with whether that position has changed. In any case, the association between gender and crime has become a recognized area of concern in the growing body of research dealing with contemporary criminological issues.[81]

Social Class and Crime

Researchers agree on the importance of age and gender as factors related to crime, but they disagree strongly about whether social class is related to crime. First of all, the term "class" can have many meanings. If "lower class" is defined by income, then the category might include graduate students, unemployed stockbrokers, pensioners, welfare mothers, prison inmates, and many others who have little in common except low income. Furthermore, "lower class" is often defined by the low prestige associated with blue-collar occupations. Some delinquency studies determine the class of young people by the class of their fathers, even though the young people may have jobs quite different from those of their fathers.

Another dispute focuses on the source of statistics used by investigators. Many researchers attribute the relatively strong association between class and crime found in arrest statistics to class bias on the part of the police. If the police are more likely to arrest a lower-class suspect than a middle-class suspect, they say, arrest data will show more involvement of lower-class people in criminality whether or not they are actually committing more crimes. When Charles Tittle, Wayne Villemez, and Douglas Smith analyzed 35 studies of the relationship between social class and crime rates in 1978, they found little support for the claim that crime is primarily a lower-class phenomenon. An update of that work, which evaluates studies done between 1978 and 1990, again found no pervasive relationship.[82]

Many scholars have challenged such conclusions. They claim that when self-report studies are used for analysis, the results show few class differences because the studies ask only about trivial offenses. Delbert Elliott and Suzanne Ageton, for example, looked at serious crimes among a national sample of 1,726 young people ages 11 to 17. According to the youths' responses to a self-report questionnaire, lower-class young people were much more likely than middle-class young people to commit serious crimes such as burglary, robbery, assault, and sexual assault.[83] A follow-up study concluded that middle-class and lower-class youths differed significantly in both the nature and the number of serious crimes they committed.[84]

Controversies remain about the social class of people who commit crimes. There is no controversy, however, about the social class of people in prison. The probability that a person such as Martha Stewart—chief executive officer of Martha Stewart Omnimedia, who was convicted of lying to the government—would face prison time is usually extremely low. Stewart does not fit the typical profile of the hundreds of thousands of inmates of our nation's jails and prisons. She is educated. Only 28 percent of prison inmates have completed high school.[85] Her income is that of a high-ranking corporate officer. The average yearly income of jail inmates who work is $5,600. She has a white-collar job. Eighty-five percent of prison inmates are blue-collar workers. She committed a white-collar offense. Only 18 percent of those convicted of such offenses go to prison for more than 1 year, whereas 39 percent of the violent offenders and 26 percent of the property offenders go to prison.[86] Finally, Martha Stewart is white in a criminal justice system where blacks are disproportionately represented.

Race and Crime

Statistics on race and crime show that while African Americans constitute 12 percent of the population, they account for 31.3 percent of all arrests for Index crimes.[87] Other statistics confirm their disproportionate representation in the criminal justice system. Fifty percent of black urban males are arrested for an Index crime at least once during their lives, compared with 14 percent of white males. The likelihood that any man will serve time in jail or prison is estimated to be 18 percent for blacks and 3 percent for whites. Moreover, the leading cause of death among young black men is murder.[88]

These statistics raise many questions. Do blacks actually commit more crimes, or are they simply arrested more often? Are black neighborhoods under more police surveillance than white neighborhoods? Do blacks receive differential treatment in the criminal justice system? If blacks commit more crimes than whites, why?

Some data support the argument that there are more African Americans in the criminal justice system because bias operates from the time of arrest through incarceration. Other data support the argument that racial disparities in official statistics reflect an actual difference in criminal behavior. Much of the evidence comes from the statistics of the NCVS, which are very similar to the statistics on race found in arrest data. When interviewers asked victims about the race of offenders in violent crimes, 21.3 percent identified the assailants as black.[89] Similarly, while self-report data demonstrate that less-serious juvenile offenses are about equally prevalent among black and white youngsters, more serious ones are not: Black youngsters report having committed many more Index crimes than do whites of comparable ages.[90]

If the disparity in criminal behavior suggested by official data, victimization studies, and self-reports actually exists, and if we are to explain it, we have to try to discover why people commit crimes. A history of hundreds of years of abuse, neglect, and discrimination against black Americans has left its mark in the form of high unemployment, residence in socially disorganized areas, one-parent households, and negative self-images.

In 1968, in the aftermath of the worst riots in modern American history, the National Advisory Commission on Civil Disorders alluded to the reasons blacks had not achieved the successes accomplished by other minority groups that at one time or another also were discriminated against. European immigrants provided unskilled labor needed by industry. By the time blacks migrated from rural areas to cities, the U.S. economy was changing and soon there was no longer much demand for unskilled labor. Immigrant groups had also received economic advantages by working for local political organizations. By the time blacks moved to the cities, the political machines no longer had the power to offer help in return for votes. Though both immigrants and blacks arrived in cities with little money, all but the very youngest members of the cohesive immigrant family contributed to the family's income. As slaves, however, black persons had been forbidden to marry, and the unions they formed were subject to disruption at the owner's convenience and therefore tended to be unstable. We will have more to say about the causal factors associated with high crime rates and race in Chapters 5 and 6.

CHAPTER 2

REVIEW

Researchers have three main objectives in measuring crime and criminal behavior patterns. They need (1) to collect and analyze data to test theories about why people commit crime, (2) to learn the situational characteristics of crimes in order to develop prevention strategies, and (3) to determine the needs of the criminal justice system on a daily basis. Data are collected by surveys, experiments, nonparticipant and participant observation, and case studies. It is often cost-effective for researchers to use repositories of information gathered by public and private organizations for their own purposes. The three main sources of data for measuring crime are the Uniform Crime Reports, the National Crime Victimization Survey, and self-report questionnaires. Though each source is useful for some purposes, all three have limitations.

By measuring the characteristics of crime and criminals, we can identify crime trends, the places and times at which crimes are most likely to be committed, and the public's evaluation of the seriousness of offenses. Current controversies concerning offenders focus on the relationship between crime and age throughout the life cycle, the changing role of women in crime, and the effects of social class and race on the response of the criminal justice system. Crime is an activity disproportionately engaged in by young people, males, and minorities.

CRIMINOLOGY & PUBLIC POLICY

Police defend their racially disparate practices by saying that, generally, minorities commit more crimes than whites. They also hold that enforcement of criminal laws that are violated by whites and minorities in roughly even numbers (for example, narcotics violations) is disproportionate because the location and social impact of the same types of crimes justifies a more aggressive response in minority communities. They argue that current practices work: Aggressive policing and targeting of minority communities have led to significant seizures of contraband, weapons, and fugitives—and a reduction in crime.

In the wake of September 11 events, advocates of racial and ethnic profiling point to the need for heightened suspicion regarding the activities of young Arabic men. The arrests and detention of hundreds of people after the terrorist attacks has created considerable controversy—many of these people would not have been subject to this treatment were it not for ethnic characteristics, and the government has not yet provided evidence linking them to terrorist activities. Furthermore, it is not likely that ethnic profiling will be any more useful or constitutional than racial profiling. In the area in which racial profiling has been most controversial—narcotics enforcement—proponents' arguments do not withstand empirical and legal scrutiny. For example, the data do not indicate a minority-dominated drug trade. National drug abuse studies show that minorities possess and use drugs only slightly more frequently than whites do. "The typical cocaine user is white, male, a high school graduate employed full-time, and living in a small metropolitan area or suburb," former drug czar William Bennett has said.

Arrest statistics are also misleading. New Jersey's attorney general pointed out that these statistics are "a self-fulfilling prophecy where law enforcement agencies rely on arrest data that they themselves generated as a result of the discretionary allocation of resources and targeted drug enforcement efforts." Empirical evidence from reviews of car stops and searches supports this view. On the New Jersey Turnpike, 10.5 percent of contraband seized during traffic stops came from white drivers and 13.5 percent from African American drivers. In Maryland, searches on I-95 resulted in "find rates" that were roughly equal by race. In both states, mostly small amounts of drugs were seized, indicating possession for personal use. Millions of drivers use these highways each day, yet so few stops or searches of motorists—black or white—result in contraband seizures that it's hard to justify stopping large numbers of African Americans so the police can make the occasional seizure. The logic behind racial profiling is faulty, as Ira Glasser, former executive director of the American Civil Liberties Union, has said:

Even if most of the drug dealers in the Northeast corridor or in any particular neighborhood or city are black or Latino, it does not follow that most blacks and Latinos are drug dealers. . . . Think about it for a minute. Most players in the NBA are black. But if you were trying to get a team together, you wouldn't go out in the street and round up random African-Americans.

It's a very simple, logical fallacy. The fact that most drug dealers are X does not mean that most X are drug dealers.

In policing, as in many areas of contemporary American life, race matters—and it matters a lot. The substantial racial disparities documented in stop, frisk, and search practices cannot be fully explained or rationalized by crime patterns, police deployment, or policing tactics. (SOURCE: David Rudovsky, "Breaking the Pattern of Racial Profiling," *Trial*, August 2002. © 2002, Association of Trial Lawyers of America. Reprinted with permission.)

Questions for Discussion Crime data are often discussed in racial terms. As we note in the "Race and Crime" section of this chapter, these data raise a host of questions, including, as Professor Rudovsky notes, the way people of color are treated by police. Is racial profiling justifiable? Ever? If the answer is yes, how effective must the profiling be to remain justified? If the answer is no, do the events of 9/11 suggest a justification for other forms of ethnic profiling?

YOU BE THE CRIMINOLOGIST

Your agency has been asked by the mayor's office to develop a program to reduce youth violence. Of course, you must first determine the extent of youth violence before going out into the field to talk to people. You plan to use information that is publicly available. What specifically will you measure, and what data will you use?

KEY TERMS

The numbers next to the terms refer to the pages on which the terms are defined.

aging-out phenomenon (43)

birth cohort (45)

case study (30)

crimes against property (32)

crimes against the person (32)

criminal careers (45)

data (26)

experiment (28)

felonies (25)

field experiment (28)

hypothesis (26)

Index crimes (32)

longitudinal studies (45)

mens rea (24)

misdemeanors (25)

nonparticipant observation (30)

participant observation (30)

population (27)

primary data (27)

random sample (27)

sample (27)

secondary data (27)

self-report surveys (35)

strict liability (25)

survey (27)

theory (26)

torts (25)

variables (28)

victimization surveys (34)

violations (25)

3 Schools of Thought throughout History

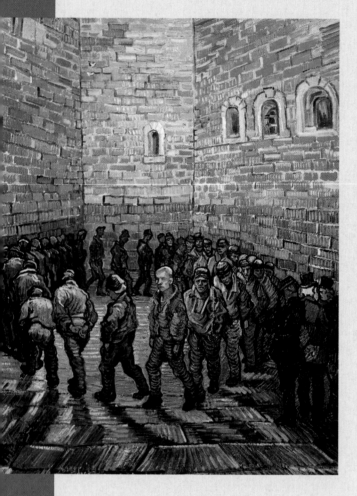

Classical Criminology
The Historical Context
Cesare Beccaria
Jeremy Bentham's Utilitarianism
The Classical School: An Evaluation
Positivist Criminology
Biological Determinism: The Search for Criminal Traits
Lombroso, Ferri, Garofalo: The Italian School
A Return to Biological Determinism
Psychological Determinism
Pioneers in Criminal Psychology
Psychological Studies of Criminals
Sociological Determinism
Adolphe Quételet and André Michel Guerry
Gabriel Tarde
Émile Durkheim
Historical and Contemporary Criminology: A Time Line
The Future of Our History
Review
Criminology & Public Policy
You Be the Criminologist
Key Terms

◼ *Painter Vincent van Gogh portrayed himself among the inmates in* The Prison Courtyard, *1890. Oil on canvas. The Pushkin Museum of Fine Art, Moscow, Russia.*

Criminologists traditionally consider that their field has its origins as a science in the eighteenth century, when Cesare Beccaria established what came to be known as the "classical school of criminology." But when we look at what some much earlier thinkers had to say about crime, we may have to reconsider this assumption. Take a look at this quotation: "Children now love luxury. They have bad manners, contempt for authority. They show disrespect for elders. They contradict their parents, chatter before company, cross their legs and tyrannize their teachers."[1] This may appear to be a modern description of delinquent youth, but Socrates made this observation over 2,300 years ago.

Scholars, philosophers, and poets have speculated about the causes of crime and possible remedies since ancient times, and modern criminology owes much to the wisdom the ancient philosophers displayed. The philosophical approach culminated in the middle of the eighteenth century in the **classical school** of criminology. It is based on the assumption that individuals choose to commit crimes after weighing the consequences of their actions. According to classical criminologists, individuals have free will. They can choose legal or illegal means to get what they want, fear of punishment can deter them from committing crime, and society can control behavior by making the pain of punishment greater than the pleasure of the criminal gains.

The classical school did not remain unchallenged for long. In the early nineteenth century, great advances were made in the natural sciences and in medicine. Physicians in France, Germany, and England undertook systematic studies of crimes and criminals. Crime statistics became available in several European countries. There emerged an opposing school of criminology, the **positivist school**. This school posits that human behavior is determined by forces beyond individual control and that it is possible to measure those forces. Unlike classical criminologists, who claim that people rationally choose to commit crime, positivist criminologists view criminal behavior as stemming from biological, psychological, and social factors.

The earliest positivist theories centered on biological factors, and studies of those factors dominated criminology during the last half of the nineteenth century. In the twentieth century, biological explanations were ignored (and even targeted as racist after World War II). They did not surface again until the 1970s, when scientific advances in psychology shifted the emphasis from defects in criminals' bodies to defects in their minds. Throughout the twentieth century, psychologists and psychiatrists have played a major role in the study of crime causation. A third area of positivist criminology focuses on the relation of social factors to crime. Sociological theories, developed in the second half of the nineteenth century and advanced throughout the twentieth, continue to dominate the field of criminology today.

An understanding of the foundations of modern criminology helps us understand contemporary developments in the field. Let us begin with the developments that led to the emergence of the classical school.

CLASSICAL CRIMINOLOGY

In the late eighteenth to the mid-nineteenth centuries, during what is now called the "neoclassical period," the classical culture of the ancient Mediterranean was rediscovered. This was also a period of scientific discoveries and the founding of new scholarly disciplines. One of these disciplines was criminology, which developed as an attempt to apply rationality and the rule of law to brutal and arbitrary criminal justice processes. The work of criminology's founders—scholars like Cesare Beccaria and Jeremy Bentham— became known as "classical criminology."

The Historical Context

Classical criminology grew out of a reaction against the barbaric system of law, punishment, and justice that existed before the French Revolution of 1789.

▨ Public punishment: Painting depicts beheading of the French king's wife, Marie Antoinette, at the guillotine, October 16, 1793.

Stone Age Crime and Social Control

On a fine Thursday afternoon in September 1991, vacationers from Germany, on an alpine hiking trip, spotted a head protruding from the glacial ice. They hurried to a nearby guesthouse and reported their find to the innkeeper, who promptly called both the Italian and the Austrian police. It became immediately apparent that this corpse was no ordinary mountain casualty. Rather, this was an ancient mountain casualty. Experts were brought in from Austrian universities, and the body was freed from its icy embrace. It was dubbed "Oetzi" after the Oetztal Alps, site of the discovery.

Oetzi is 5,300 years old, a robust young man, 25 to 30 years old at the time of his death. Completely mummified, he was found in the position in which he had placed himself, in a crevice, probably to escape a snowstorm. He was fully dressed, in an unlined fur robe. Originally fashioned with great skill, the robe was badly repaired with

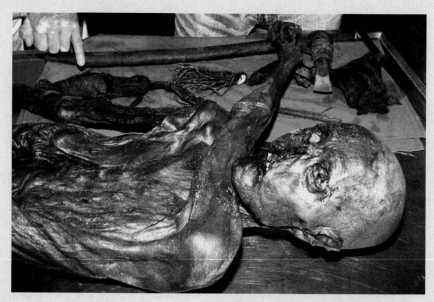

Oetzi, who was preserved in the glacial crevice in which he died 5,000 years ago.

sinew and plant fiber, suggesting that he could not have relied on the services of his wife or the village seam-

stress for some time. Oetzi had placed his equipment by his side, most of it of the best Stone Age craftsmanship. What

---

Until that time, there was no real system of criminal justice in Europe. There were crimes against the state, against the church, and against the crown. Some of these crimes were specified; some were not. Judges had discretionary power to convict a person for an act not even legally defined as criminal.[2] Monarchs often issued what were called in French *lettres de cachet,* under which an individual could be imprisoned for almost any reason (disobedience to one's father, for example) or for no reason at all.

Many criminal laws were unwritten, and those that had been drafted, by and large, did not specify the kind or amount of punishment associated with various crimes. Arbitrary and often cruel sentences were imposed by judges who had unbounded discretion to decide questions of guilt and innocence and to mete out punishment. Due process in the modern sense did not exist. While there was some official consensus on what constituted crime, there was no real limit to the amount and type of legal sanction a court could command. Punishments included branding, burning, flogging, mutilating, drowning, banishing, and beheading.[3] In England, a person might receive the death penalty for any of more than 200 offenses, including what we today call "petty theft."

Public punishments were popular events. When Robert-François Damiens was scheduled to be executed on March 2, 1757, for the attempted murder of Louis XV, so many people wanted to attend the spectacle that window seats overlooking the execution site were rented for high prices. Torture to elicit confessions was common. A criminal defendant in France might be subjected to the *peine forte et dure,* which consisted of stretching him on his back and placing over him an iron weight as heavy as he could bear. He was left that way until he died or spoke. A man would suffer these torments and lose his life in order to avoid trial—and therefore conviction—so that his lands and goods would not be confiscated and would be preserved for his family. This proceeding was not abolished until 1772.[4]

Even as Europe grew increasingly modern, industrial, and urban in the eighteenth century, it still clung to its medieval penal practices. With prosperity came an increasing gulf between the haves and the have-nots. Just before the French Revolution, for example, a Parisian worker paid 97 percent of his daily earnings for a 4-pound loaf of bread.[5] Hordes of unemployed people begged by day and found shelter under bridges by night. One is surprising is that he did not carry with him a ready-to-shoot bow.

Investigators determined that Oetzi was an outdoor type, a shepherd who sought refuge in the crevice, froze to death, and was preserved for 5 millennia by permafrost and glacial ice. But what was Oetzi doing at 3,210 meters (nearly 10,000 feet) above sea level on a fall day? Obviously, he was not a herder because he was far above the grazing range of a herd. Nor was he a trader trying to cross the Alps in the fall. So what was he doing up there, where nothing grows and where it is hard to breathe? One answer, based on all the evidence available so far, is that Oetzi may have been an outlaw.

Oetzi was a Late Stone Age (Neolithic) man, likely to have come from a herding community of, at most, 200 persons. Robert Carneiro of the American Museum of Natural History has figured out that a community of 200 produces 20,000 one-on-one disagreement possibilities. Oetzi may have had such interpersonal problems.

The tasks of social control even within such a small community stagger the imagination. Fighting could have erupted within the community. Jealousy could be engendered about who deserves more respect as the best hunter, the best storyteller, the best healer, or the wisest person. A dispute could have happened over the distribution of food or the sharing of tools.

The evidence about Neolithic society permits us to conclude that these societies had no institution that we could compare with modern criminal justice, although they had problems that today might be referred to a criminal justice system. How were such problems solved? Minor problems were dealt with by the use of shaming, by dispute resolution, by compensation, and by sacrifices. Major unforgivable offenses led to casting out the wrongdoers: They would be declared outlaws. They had to leave camp instantly, without gathering weapons or tools, and flee to the wilderness. Oetzi fits the description of such an outlaw, literally, a person cast outside the protection of the laws, the customs, and his group, to take to the wilderness and perhaps to die there. If Oetzi was a criminal banished from his village, the punishment clearly was effec-

tive. In 2007, a team from the Institute of Anatomy at the University of Zurich, Switzerland, discovered a lesion caused by an arrowhead near Oetzi's shoulder. At first they concluded that Oetzi died within minutes of being shot, bleeding to death. CAT scans, however, revealed that he died from a blow to the head, not by arrow wound. The mystery continues.

Source

Adapted from Gerhard O. W. Mueller and Freda Adler, "The Emergence of Criminal Justice: Tracing the Route to Neolithic Times," in *Festskrift till Jacob W. F. Sundberg*, eds. Erik Nerep and Wiweka Warnling Nerep (Stockholm: Jurisförlaget, 1993), pp. 151–170.

Questions for Discussion

1. For purposes of improving modern crime-control techniques, can we learn anything from Stone Age societies?
2. What crimes do you think might result in the banishment of one of the members of such a community?

---

of the few ways in which the established upper class could protect itself was through ruthless oppression of those beneath it, but ruthless oppression created more problems. Social unrest grew. And as crime rates rose, so did the brutality of punishment. Both church and state became increasingly tyrannical, using violence to conquer violence.

The growing educated classes began to see the inconsistency in these policies. If terrible tortures were designed to deter crime, why were people committing even more crimes? Something must be wrong with the underlying reasoning. By the mid-eighteenth century, social reformers were beginning to suggest a more rational approach to crime and punishment. One of them, Cesare Beccaria, laid the foundation for the first school of criminology—the classical school.

Cesare Beccaria

Cesare Bonesana, Marchese di Beccaria (1738–1794), was rather undistinguished as a student. After graduating with a law degree from the University of Pavia, he returned home to Milan and joined a group of articulate and radical intellectuals. Disenchanted with contemporary European society,

they organized themselves into the Academy of Fists, one of many young men's clubs that flourished in Italy at the time. Their purpose was to discover what reforms would be needed to modernize Italian society.

In March 1763, Beccaria was assigned to prepare a report on the prison system. Pietro Verri, the head of the Academy of Fists, encouraged him to read the works of English and French philosophers—David Hume (1711–1776), John Locke (1632–1704), Claude Adrien Helvétius (1715–1771), Voltaire (1694–1778), Montesquieu (1689–1755), and Jean-Jacques Rousseau (1712–1778). Another member of the academy, the protector of prisons, revealed to him the inhumanities that were possible under the guise of social control. Beccaria learned well. He read, observed, and made notes on small scraps of paper. These notes, Harry Elmer Barnes has observed, were destined to "assure to its author immortality and would work a revolution in the moral world" upon their publication in July 1764 under the title *Dei delitti e delle pene* (*On Crimes and Punishment*).[6] Beccaria presented a coherent, comprehensive design for an enlightened criminal justice system that was to serve the people rather than the monarchy.

■ *Cesare Beccaria, the young Italian nobleman-dissident who became the father of modern criminology with his monograph* On Crimes and Punishment.

The climate was right. With the publication of this small book, Cesare Beccaria became the "father of modern criminology." The controversy between the rule of men and the rule of law was at its most heated. Some people defended the old order, under which judges and administrators made arbitrary or whimsical decisions. Others fought for the rule of law, under which the decision making of judges and administrators would be confined by legal limitations. Beccaria's words provided the spark that ultimately ended medieval barbarism.

According to Beccaria, the crime problem could be traced not to bad people but to bad laws. A modern criminal justice system should guarantee all people equal treatment before the law. Beccaria's book supplied the blueprint. That blueprint was based on the assumption that people freely choose what they do and are responsible for the consequences of their behavior. Beccaria proposed the following principles:

- *Laws should be used to maintain the social contract.* "Laws are the conditions under which men, naturally independent, united themselves in society. Weary of living in a continual state of war, and of enjoying a liberty, which became of little value, from the uncertainty of its duration, they sacrificed one part of it, to enjoy the rest in peace and security."

- *Only legislators should create laws.* "The authority of making penal laws can only reside with the legislator, who represents the whole society united by the social compact."

- *Judges should impose punishment only in accordance with the law.* "[N]o magistrate then, (as he is

one of the society), can, with justice inflict on any other member of the same society punishment that is not ordained by the laws."

- *Judges should not interpret the laws.* "Judges, in criminal cases, have no right to interpret the penal laws, because they are not legislators. . . . Every man hath his own particular point of view, and, at different times, sees the same objects in very different lights. The spirit of the laws will then be the result of the good or bad logic of the judge; and this will depend on his good or bad digestion."

- *Punishment should be based on the pleasure/pain principle.* "Pleasure and pain are the only springs of actions in beings endowed with sensibility. . . . If an equal punishment be ordained for two crimes that injure society in different degrees, there is nothing to deter men from committing the greater as often as it is attended with greater advantage."

- *Punishment should be based on the act, not on the actor.* "Crimes are only to be measured by the injuries done to the society. They err, therefore, who imagine that a crime is greater or less according to the intention of the person by whom it is committed."

- *The punishment should be determined by the crime.* "If mathematical calculation could be applied to the obscure and infinite combinations of human actions, there might be a corresponding scale of punishments descending from the greatest to the least."

- *Punishment should be prompt and effective.* "The more immediate after the commission of a crime a punishment is inflicted, the more just and useful it will be. . . . An immediate punishment is more useful; because the smaller the interval of time between the punishment and the crime, the stronger and more lasting will be the association of the two ideas of crime and punishment."

- *All people should be treated equally.* "I assert that the punishment of a nobleman should in no wise differ from that of the lowest member of society."

- *Capital punishment should be abolished.* "The punishment of death is not authorized by any right; for . . . no such right exists. . . . The terrors of death make so slight an impression, that it has not force enough to withstand the forgetfulness natural to mankind."

- *The use of torture to gain confessions should be abolished.* "It is confounding all relations to expect . . . that pain should be the test of truth, as if truth resided in the muscles and fibres of a wretch in torture. By this method the robust will escape, and the feeble be condemned."

- *It is better to prevent crimes than to punish them.* "Would you prevent crimes? Let the laws be clear and simple, let the entire force of the nation be united in their defence, let them be intended rather to favour every individual than any particular classes. . . . Finally, the most certain method of preventing crime is to perfect the system of education."[7]

Perhaps no other book in the history of criminology has had so great an impact. Beccaria's ideas were so advanced that Voltaire, the great French philosopher of the time, who wrote the commentary for the French version, referred to Beccaria as "brother."[8] The English version appeared in 1767; by that time, 3 years after the book's publication, it had already gone through six Italian editions and several French editions.

After the French Revolution, Beccaria's basic tenets served as a guide for the drafting of the French penal code, which was adopted in 1791. In Russia, Empress Catherine II (the Great) convened a commission to prepare a new code and issued instructions, written in her own hand, to translate Beccaria's ideas into action. The Prussian King Friedrich II (the Great) devoted his reign to revising the Prussian laws according to Beccaria's principles. Emperor Joseph II had a new code drafted for Austria-Hungary in 1787—the first code to abolish capital punishment. The impact of Beccaria's treatise spread across the Atlantic as well: It influenced the first 10 amendments to the U.S. Constitution (the Bill of Rights).

Jeremy Bentham's Utilitarianism

Legal scholars and reformers throughout Europe proclaimed their indebtedness to Beccaria, but none owed more to him than the English legal philosopher Jeremy Bentham (1748–1832). Bentham had a long and productive career. He inspired many of his contemporaries, as well as criminologists of future generations, with his approach to rational crime control.

Bentham devoted his life to developing a scientific approach to the making and breaking of laws. Like Beccaria, he was concerned with achieving "the greatest happiness of the greatest number."[9] His work was governed by utilitarian principles. **Utilitarianism** assumes that all human actions are calculated in accordance with their likelihood of bringing happiness (pleasure) or unhappiness (pain). People weigh the probabilities of present and future pleasures against those of present and future pain.

Bentham proposed a precise pseudomathematical formula for this process, which he called "felicific calculus." According to his reasoning, individuals are "human calculators" who put all the factors into an equation in order to decide whether a particular crime is worth committing. This notion may seem rather whimsical today, but at a time when there were over 200 capital offenses, it provided a rationale for reform of the legal system.[10] Bentham reasoned that if prevention was the purpose of punishment, and if punishment became too costly by creating more harm than good, then penalties needed to be set just a bit in excess of the pleasure one might derive from committing a crime, and no higher. The law exists in order to create happiness for the community. Because punishment creates unhappiness, it can be justified only if it prevents greater evil than it produces. Thus, Bentham suggested, if hanging a man's effigy produced the same preventive effect as hanging the man himself, there would be no reason to hang the man.

Sir Samuel Romilly, a member of Parliament, met Jeremy Bentham at the home of a mutual friend. He became interested in Bentham's idea that the certainty of punishment outweighs its severity as a deterrent against crime. On February 9, 1810, in a speech before Parliament, he advocated Benthamite ideas:

> So evident is the truth of that maxim that if it were possible that punishment, as the consequence of guilt, could be reduced to an absolute certainty, a very slight penalty would be sufficient to prevent almost every species of crime.[11]

Although conservatives prevented any major changes during Romilly's lifetime, the program of legislative pressure he began was continued by his followers and culminated in the complete reform of English criminal law between 1820 and 1861. During that period, the number of capital offenses was reduced from 222 to 3: murder, treason, and piracy. Gradually, from the ideals of the philosophers of the Age of Enlightenment and the principles outlined by the scholars of the classical school, a new social order was created, an order that affirmed a commitment to equal treatment of all people before the law.

The Classical School: An Evaluation

Classical criminology had an immediate and profound impact on jurisprudence and legislation. The rule of law spread rapidly through Europe and the United States. Of no less significance was the influence of the classical school on penal and correctional policy. The classical principle that punishment must be appropriate to the crime was universally accepted during the nineteenth and early twentieth centuries. Yet the classical approach had weaknesses. Critics attacked the simplicity of its argument: The responsibility of the criminal justice system was simply to enforce the law with

Crime Surfing

www.utm.edu/
research/iep/b/
beccaria.htm

If Beccaria were alive today, what arguments would he use in a debate on capital punishment?

Utilitarianism Gone Astray

Few people can be credited for their contribution to Anglo-American criminal law philosophy as much as Jeremy Bentham (1748–1832), the foremost spokesperson for the utilitarian approach to the management of people in general and criminals and potential criminals in particular. Above all, he is remembered for his proposition that the purpose of all legislation is to achieve "the greatest happiness of the greatest number." Punishments, he argued, should be no greater (or less) than necessary to achieve government's purpose to control crime.(1)

According to Princeton University professor Peter Singer, utilitarianism—the greatest good of the greatest number— implies that a child born with incurable birth defects should be killed, as its life would impose a far greater emotional and financial burden on its family and the community than its death.(2) Thus, Singer argues that "some infanticide is not even as important as, say, killing a happy cat."(3) Among his principal examples for justifiable infanticide are babies born with Down syndrome. Singer's argument fails to take into account the many adults with Down syndrome who take a bus to work every day, earn a salary, and pay taxes on their earnings.(2)

Demonstrators picket Princeton University over its appointment of a controversial bioethics professor, Peter Singer, in Princeton, New Jersey, April 1999.

Putting aside the difficulty of making a prognosis about a baby's chances of having a productive and content life, how would society determine where to put the limit on legalizing infanticide? Justice Holmes ruled in *Buck v. Bell* that

swiftness and certainty and to treat all people in like fashion, whether the accused were paupers or nobles; government was to be run by the rule of law rather than at the discretion of its officials. In other words, the punishment was to fit the crime, not the criminal. The proposition that human beings had the capacity to choose freely between good and evil was accepted without question. There was no need to ask why people behave as they do, to seek a motive, or to ask about the specific circumstances surrounding criminal acts.

During the last half of the nineteenth century, scholars began to challenge these ideas. Influenced by the expanding search for scientific explanations of behavior in place of philosophical ones, criminologists shifted their attention from the act to the actor. They argued that people did not choose of their own free will to commit crime; rather, factors beyond their control were responsible for criminal behavior.

POSITIVIST CRIMINOLOGY

During the late eighteenth century, significant advances in knowledge of both the physical and the social world influenced thinking about crime. Auguste Comte (1798–1857), a French sociologist, applied the modern methods of the physical sciences to the social sciences in his six-volume *Cours de philosophie positive* (*Course in Positive Philosophy*), published between 1830 and 1842. He argued that there could be no real knowledge of social phenomena unless it was based on a positivist (scientific) approach. Positivism alone, however, was not sufficient to bring about a fundamental change in criminological thinking. Not until Charles Darwin (1809–1882) challenged the doctrine of creation with his theory of the evolution of species did the next generation of criminologists have the tools with which to challenge classicism.

"three generations of imbeciles are enough" in upholding a state statute that mandated the sterilization of "imbeciles" with a family record of imbecility. (4) By those utilitarian standards, killing *all* imbecile babies would be even more cost-beneficial. Should a similar mandate apply to three generations of criminals, as determined by convictions? And would society not be better off (in terms of cost-benefit calculations) if it were to get rid of *all* troublemakers? Would Professor Singer go that far?

Bentham had nothing of that sort in mind when he set forth his utilitarian principles. In fact, he was not even an advocate of capital punishment, considering it to be "unfrugal" and "irremissible."(1)

To demonstrate his utilitarianism, Jeremy Bentham decreed that upon his death (June 6, 1832) his body be dissected in the presence of his friends and the skeleton be reconstructed, supplied with a wax head to replace the original (to be mummified), dressed in his own clothes, and placed upright in a glass case so that he, himself, could be useful as a reminder of his principles. Until recently, once a year at meetings of the Bentham Society in London, Bentham's body was wheeled out and celebrated with a feast.

François de la Rochefoucauld once wrote, "Intellectual blemishes, like facial ones, grow more prominent with age." To refute this wonderful maxim with,

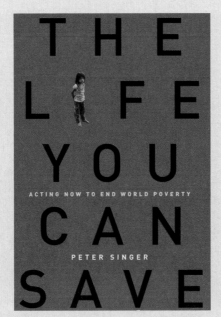

albeit, a single case example, Singer's most recent intellectual efforts stand in very sharp contrast to his earlier work on infanticide. He is now, apparently, both altruistic and strategically philanthropic. Evidence of this profound change may be found in Singer's most recent book, *The Life You Can Save: Acting Now to End World Poverty*.(5) This work suggests that we need to reconsider what it means to say that we are living an ethical life. Singer argues in favor of a life defined by personal philanthropy, local activism, and political awareness.

Sources

1. Jeremy Bentham, *An Introduction to the Principles of Morals and Legislation* (1789; New York: Haffner Library of Classics, 1948), esp. pp. 197, 200.
2. Peter Singer, *Rethinking Life and Death: The Collapse of Our Traditional Ethics* (New York: St. Martin's Press, 1996); *How Are We to Live? Ethics in an Age of Self-Interest* (New York: Prometheus Books, 1995).
3. George F. Will, "Life and Death at Princeton," *Newsweek*, Sept. 13, 1999, pp. 80–81.
4. *Buck v. Bell*, 274 U.S. 200, 207 (1927).
5. Peter Singer, *The Life You Can Save: Acting Now to End World Poverty* (New York: Random House, 2009).

Questions for Discussion

1. According to utilitarian principles, is capital punishment preferable to a life sentence?
2. Should abortion be legalized when a baby can be profiled (by family history) as at high risk for a life in crime?
3. Can you think of a way to use utilitarian principles to reduce the use and duration of imprisonment?

The turning point was the publication in 1859 of Darwin's *Origin of Species.* Darwin's theory was that God did not make all the various species of animals in 2 days, as proclaimed in Genesis 1:20–26, but rather that the species had evolved through a process of adaptive mutation and natural selection. The process was based on the survival of the fittest in the struggle for existence. This radical theory seriously challenged traditional theological teaching. It was not until 1871, however, that Darwin publicly took the logical next step and traced human origins to an animal of the anthropoid group—the ape.[12] He thus posed an even more serious challenge to a religious tradition that maintained that God created the first human in his own image (Genesis 1:27).

The scientific world would never be the same again. The theory of evolution made it possible to ask new questions and to search in new ways for the answers to old ones. New biological theories replaced older ones. Old ideas that demons and animal spirits could explain human behavior were replaced by knowledge based on new scientific principles. The social sciences were born.

The nineteenth-century forces of positivism and evolution moved the field of criminology from a philosophical to a scientific perspective. But there were even earlier intellectual underpinnings of the scientific criminology that emerged in the second half of the nineteenth century.

BIOLOGICAL DETERMINISM: THE SEARCH FOR CRIMINAL TRAITS

Throughout history, a variety of physical characteristics and disfigurements have been said to characterize individuals of "evil" disposition. In the earliest pursuit of the relationship between

A criminological examination according to an 1890 caricature.

biological traits and behavior, a Greek scientist who examined Socrates found his skull and facial features to be those of a person inclined toward alcoholism and brutality.[13] The ancient Greeks and Romans so distrusted red hair that actors portraying evil persons wore red wigs. Through the ages, cripples, hunchbacks, people with long hair, and a multitude of others were viewed with suspicion. Indeed, in the Middle Ages, laws indicated that if two people were suspected of a crime, the uglier was the more likely to be guilty.[14]

The belief that criminals are born, not made, and that they can be identified by various physical irregularities is reflected not only in scientific writing but in literature as well. Shakespeare's Julius Caesar states:

> Let me have men about me that are fat; Sleek-headed men, and such as sleep o' nights.
> Yond Cassius has a lean and hungry look; He thinks too much: such men are dangerous.

Although its roots can be traced to ancient times, it was not until the sixteenth century that Italian physician Giambattista della Porta (1535–1615) founded the school of human **physiognomy**, the study of facial features and their relation to human behavior. According to Porta, a thief had large lips and sharp vision. Two centuries later, Porta's efforts were revived by Swiss theologian Johann Kaspar Lavater (1741–1801).[15] They were elaborated on by the German physicians Franz Joseph Gall (1758–1828) and Johann Kaspar Spurzheim (1776–1832), whose science of **phrenology** posited that bumps on the head were indications of psychological propensities.[16] In the United States, these views were supported by physician Charles Caldwell (1772–1853), who searched for evidence that brain tissue and cells regulate human

action.[17] By the nineteenth century, the sciences of physiognomy and phrenology had introduced specific biological factors into the study of crime causation.

Lombroso, Ferri, Garofalo: The Italian School

Cesare Lombroso (1835–1909) integrated Comte's positivism, Darwin's evolutionism, and the many pioneering studies of the relation of crime to the body. In 1876, with the publication of *L'uomo delinquente* (*The Criminal Man*), criminology was permanently transformed from an abstract philosophy of crime control through legislation to a modern science of investigation into causes. Lombroso's work replaced the concept of free will, which had reigned for over a century as the principle that explained criminal behavior, with that of determinism. Together with his followers, the Italian legal scholars Enrico Ferri and Raffaele Garofalo, Lombroso developed a new orientation: the Italian, or positivist, school of criminology, which seeks explanations for criminal behavior through scientific experimentation and research.

Cesare Lombroso

After completing his medical studies, Cesare Lombroso served as an army physician, became a professor of psychiatry at the University of Turin, and later in life accepted an appointment as professor of criminal anthropology. His theory of the "born criminal" states that criminals are a lower form of life, nearer to their apelike ancestors than noncriminals in traits and dispositions. They are distinguishable from noncriminals by various

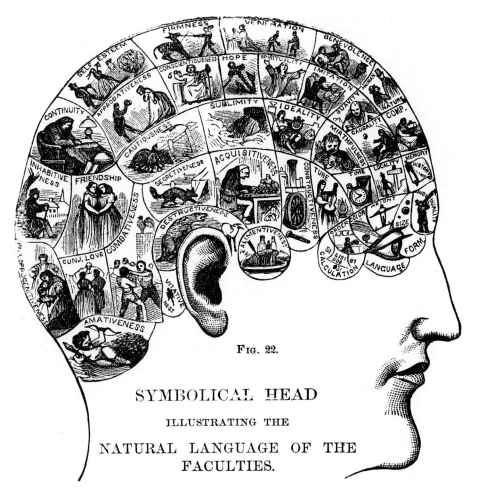

FIG. 22.

SYMBOLICAL HEAD

ILLUSTRATING THE

NATURAL LANGUAGE OF THE FACULTIES.

atavistic stigmata—physical features of creatures at an earlier stage of development, before they became fully human.

He argued that criminals frequently have huge jaws and strong canine teeth, characteristics common to carnivores who tear and devour meat raw. The arm span of criminals is often greater than their height, just like that of apes, who use their forearms to propel themselves along the ground. An individual born with any five of the stigmata is a **born criminal.** This category accounts for about a third of all offenders.

The theory became clear to Lombroso "one cold grey November morning" while he pored over the bones of a notorious outlaw who had died in an Italian prison:

This man possessed such extraordinary agility, that he had been known to scale steep mountain heights bearing a sheep on his shoulders. His cynical effrontery was such that he openly boasted of his crimes. On his death . . . I was deputed to make the postmortem, and on laying open the skull I found . . . a distinct depression . . . as in inferior animals.

Lombroso was delighted by his findings:

This was not merely an idea, but a revelation. At the sight of that skull, I seemed to see all of a sudden, lighted up as a vast plain under a flaming sky the problem of the nature of the criminal—an atavistic being who reproduces in his person the ferocious instincts of primitive humanity.[18]

Criminal women, according to Lombroso, are different from criminal men. It is the prostitute who represents the born criminal among them:

We also saw that women have many traits in common with children; that their moral sense is different; they are revengeful, jealous, inclined to vengeance of a refined cruelty. . . . When a morbid activity of the psychical centres intensifies the bad qualities of women . . . it is clear that the innocuous semi-criminal present in normal women must be transformed into a born criminal more terrible than any man. . . . The criminal woman is consequently a monster. Her normal sister is kept in the paths of virtue by many causes, such as maternity, piety, weakness, and when these

■ *Dr. Cesare Lombroso (1835–1909), professor of criminal anthropology at Turin University and founder of the positivist school of criminology.*

DID YOU KNOW?

... that certain Nazi anthropologists and physicians made use of Lombroso's ideas about born criminals? They proposed "scientific" classification of Aryans and non-Aryans (and ultimately death or denial of civil rights to non-Aryans) on the basis of skull measurements.

counter influences fail, and a woman commits a crime, we may conclude that her wickedness must have been enormous before it could triumph over so many obstacles.[19]

To the born criminal, Lombroso added two other categories: insane criminals and criminoloids. "Insane criminals" are not criminal from birth; they become criminal as a result of some change in their brains that interferes with their ability to distinguish between right and wrong.[20] "Criminoloids" make up an ambiguous group that includes habitual criminals, criminals by passion, and other diverse types.

Most scientists who followed Lombroso did not share his enthusiasm or his viewpoint. As happens so often in history, his work has been kept alive more by criticism than by agreement. The theory that criminals were lodged on the lower rungs of the evolutionary ladder did not stand up to scientific scrutiny. But the fact that Lombroso measured thousands of live and dead prisoners and compared these measurements with those obtained from control groups (however imperfectly derived) in his search for determinants of crime changed the nature of the questions asked by the generations of scholars who came after him.

His influence continues in contemporary European research; American scientists, as criminologist Marvin Wolfgang says, use him "as a straw man for attack on biological analyses of criminal behavior."[21] Thorsten Sellin has noted: "Any scholar who succeeds in driving hundreds of fellow-students to search for the truth, and whose ideas after half a century possess vitality, merits an honorable place in the history of thought."[22] At his death, true to his lifetime pursuits, Lombroso willed his body to the laboratory of legal medicine and his brain to the Institute of Anatomy at the University of Turin, where for so many years the father of empirical criminology had espoused biological determinism.[23]

Enrico Ferri

The best known of Lombroso's associates was Enrico Ferri (1856–1929). Member of Parliament, accomplished public lecturer, brilliant lawyer, editor of a newspaper, and esteemed scholar, Ferri had published his first major book by the time he was 21. By age 25, he was a university professor. Although Ferri agreed with Lombroso on the biological bases of criminal behavior, his interest in socialism led him to recognize the importance of social, economic, and political determinants.

Ferri was a prolific writer on a vast number of criminological topics. His greatest contribution was his attack on the classical doctrine of free will, which argued that criminals should be held morally responsible for their crimes because they must have made a rational decision to commit these acts. Ferri believed criminals could not be held morally responsible because they did not choose to commit crimes but, rather, were driven to commit them by conditions in their lives. He did, however, stress that society needed protection against criminal acts and that it was the purpose of the criminal law and penal policy to provide that protection.

Although he advocated conventional punishments and even the death penalty for individuals he assumed would never be fit to live in society, he was more interested in controlling crime through preventive measures—state control of the manufacture of weapons, inexpensive housing, better street lighting, and so forth.

Ferri claimed that strict adherence to preventive measures based on scientific methods would eventually reduce crime and allow people to live together in society with less dependence on the penal system. Toward the end of his life, he proudly admitted that he was an idealist, a statement with which generations of scholars have agreed. Though his prescription for crime reduction was overly optimistic, Ferri's importance to the development of modern criminology is undisputed. "When Enrico Ferri died on April 12, 1929," wrote Thorsten Sellin, "one of the most colorful, influential figures in the history of criminology disappeared."[24]

Raffaele Garofalo

Another follower of Lombroso was the Italian nobleman, magistrate, senator, and professor of law Raffaele Garofalo (1851–1934). Like Lombroso and Ferri, Garofalo rejected the doctrine of free will and supported the position that the only way to understand crime was to study it by scientific methods. Influenced by Lombroso's theory of atavistic stigmata, in which he found many shortcomings, Garofalo traced the roots of criminal behavior not to physical features but to their psychological equivalents, which he called "moral anomalies." According to this theory, natural crimes are found in all human societies, regardless of the views of lawmakers, and no civilized society can afford to disregard them.[25]

Natural crimes, according to Garofalo, are those that offend the basic moral sentiments of probity (respect for the property of others) and piety (revulsion against the infliction of suffering on others). An individual who has an organic deficiency in these moral sentiments has no moral constraints against committing such crimes. Garofalo argued that these individuals could not be held responsible for their actions. But, like Ferri, he also emphasized that society needed protection and that penal policy should be designed to prevent criminals from inflicting harm.[26]

Influenced by Darwinian theory, Garofalo suggested that the death penalty could rid society of its maladapted members, just as the natural selection process eliminated maladapted organisms. For less-serious offenders, capable of adapting themselves to society in some measure, other types of punishments were preferable: transportation to remote lands, loss of privileges, institutionalization in farm colonies, or perhaps simply reparation. Clearly, Garofalo was much more interested in protecting society than in defending the individual rights of offenders.

Challenges to Lombrosian Theory

Although Lombroso, Ferri, and Garofalo did not always agree on the causes of criminal behavior or on the way society should respond to it, their combined efforts marked a turning point in the development of the scientific study of crime. These three were responsible for developing the positivist approach to criminality, which influences criminology to the present day. Nevertheless, they had their critics. By using the scientific method to explore crime causation, they paved the way for criminologists to support or refute the theories they had devised. The major challenge to Lombrosian theory came from the work of Charles Buckman Goring.

From 1901 until 1913, Charles Buckman Goring (1870–1919), a medical officer at Parkhurst Prison in England, collected data on 96 traits of more than 3,000 convicts and a large control group of Oxford and Cambridge university students, hospital patients, and soldiers. Among his research assistants was a famous statistician, Karl Pearson. When Goring had completed his examinations, he was armed with enough data to refute Lombroso's theory of the anthropological criminal type. Goring's report to the scientific community proclaimed:

> From a knowledge only of an undergraduate's cephalic [head] measurement, a better judgment could be given as to whether he were studying at an English or Scottish university than a prediction could be made as to

whether he would eventually become a university professor or a convicted felon.[27]

This evaluation still stands as the most cogent critical analysis of Lombroso's theory of the born criminal. Although Goring rejected the claim that specific stigmata identify the criminal, he was convinced that poor physical condition plus a defective state of mind were determining factors in the criminal personality.

A Return to Biological Determinism

After Goring's challenge, Lombrosian theory lost its academic popularity for about a quarter century. Then, in 1939, Ernest Hooten (1887–1954), a physical anthropologist, reawakened an interest in biologically determined criminality with the publication of a massive study comparing American prisoners with a noncriminal control group. He concluded:

> [I]n every population there are hereditary inferiors in mind and in body as well as physical and mental deficients. . . . Our information definitely proves that it is from the physically inferior element of the population that native born criminals from native parentage are mainly derived.[28]

Like his positivist predecessors, Hooten argued for the segregation of those he referred to as the "criminal stock," and he recommended their sterilization as well.[29]

The Somatotype School

In the search for the source of criminality, other scientists, too, looked for the elusive link between physical characteristics and crime. The **somatotype school** of criminology, which related body build to behavior, became popular during the first half of the twentieth century. It originated with the work of a German psychiatrist, Ernst Kretschmer (1888–1964), who distinguished three principal types of physiques: (1) the asthenic—lean, slightly built, narrow shoulders; (2) the athletic—medium to tall, strong, muscular, coarse bones; and (3) the pyknic—medium height, rounded figure, massive neck, broad face. He then related these physical types to various psychiatric disorders: pyknics to manic depression, asthenics and athletics to schizophrenia, and so on.[30]

Kretschmer's work was brought to the United States by William Sheldon (1898–1977), who formulated his own group of somatotypes: the "endomorph," the "mesomorph," and the "ectomorph." Sheldon's father was a dog breeder who used a point system to judge animals in competition, and Sheldon worked out a point system of his own for judging humans. Thus, one could actually measure on a scale from 1 to 7 the relative dominance of each body type in any given individual. People with predominantly mesomorph traits (physically powerful, aggressive, athletic physiques), he argued, tend more than others to be involved in illegal behavior.[31] This finding was later supported by Sheldon Glueck (1896–1980) and Eleanor Glueck (1898–1972), who based their studies of delinquents on William Sheldon's somatotypes.[32]

By and large, studies based on somatotyping have been sharply criticized for methodological flaws, including nonrepresentative selection of their samples (bias), failure to account for cultural stereotyping (our expectations of how muscular, physically active people should react), and poor statistical analyses. An anthropologist summed up the negative response of the scientific community by suggesting that somatotyping was "a New Phrenology in which the bumps on the buttocks take the place of the bumps on the skulls."[33] After World War II, somatotyping seemed too close to **eugenics** (the science of controlled reproduction to improve hereditary qualities), and the approach fell into disfavor. During the 1960s, however, the discovery of an extra sex chromosome in some criminal samples (see Chapter 4) revived interest in this theory.

Inherited Criminality

During the period when some researchers were measuring skulls and bodies of criminals in their search for the physical determinants of crime, others were arguing that criminality was an inherited trait passed on in the genes. To support this theory, they traced family histories. Richard Dugdale (1841–1883), for example, studied the lives of more than a thousand members of the family he called "Jukes." His interest in the family began when he found six related people in a jail in upstate New York. Following one branch of the family, the descendants of Ada Jukes, whom he referred to as the "mother of criminals," Dugdale found among the thousand of descendants 280 paupers, 60 thieves, 7 murderers, 40 other criminals, 40 persons with venereal disease, and 50 prostitutes.

His findings indicated, Dugdale claimed, that since some families produce generations of criminals, they must be transmitting a degenerate trait down the line.[34] A similar conclusion was reached by Henry Goddard (1866–1957). In a study of the family tree of a Revolutionary War soldier, Martin Kallikak, Goddard found many more criminals among the descendants of Kallikak's illegitimate son than among the descendants of his son by a later marriage with "a woman of his own quality."[35]

These early studies have been discredited primarily on the grounds that genetic and environmental influences could not be separated. But in the early twentieth century, they were taken quite seriously. On the assumption that crime could be controlled if criminals could be prevented from transmitting their traits to the next generation, some states permitted the sterilization of habitual offenders. Sterilization laws were held constitutional by the U.S. Supreme Court in a 1927 opinion written by Justice Oliver Wendell Holmes Jr., which included the following well-known pronouncement:

> It is better for all the world, if instead of waiting to execute degenerate offspring for crime, or to let them starve for their imbecility, society can prevent those who are manifestly unfit from continuing their kind. . . . Three generations of imbeciles are enough.[36]

Clearly, the early positivists, with their focus on physical characteristics, exerted great influence. They were destined to be overshadowed, though, by investigators who focused on psychological characteristics.

■ Dugdale and others identified the Jukes clan as determined by heredity to be criminals, imbeciles, and paupers. Research since then has shown that the methodology was flawed and many conclusions were fabricated.

PSYCHOLOGICAL DETERMINISM

On the whole, scholars who investigated criminal behavior in the nineteenth and early twentieth centuries were far more interested in the human body than in the human mind. During that period, however, several contributions were made in the area of psychological explanations of crime. Some of the earliest contributions came from physicians interested primarily in the legal responsibility of the criminally insane. Later, psychologists entered the field and applied their new testing techniques to the study of offenders (see Chapter 4).

Pioneers in Criminal Psychology

Isaac Ray (1807–1881), acknowledged as America's first forensic psychiatrist, was interested throughout his life in the application of psychiatric principles to the law. He is best known as the author of *The Medical Jurisprudence of Insanity*, a treatise on criminal responsibility that was widely quoted and influential.[37] In it he defended the concept of moral insanity, a disorder first described in 1806 by the French humanitarian and psychiatrist Philippe Pinel (1745–1826).[38] "Moral insanity" was a term used to describe persons who were normal in all respects except that something was wrong with the part of the brain that regulates affective responses. Ray questioned whether we could hold people legally responsible for their acts if they had such an impairment, because such people committed their crimes without an intent to do so.

Born in the same year as Lombroso, Henry Maudsley (1835–1918), a brilliant English medical professor, shared Ray's concerns about criminal responsibility. According to Maudsley, some people may be considered either "insane or criminal according to the standpoint from which they are looked at." He believed that for many persons, crime is an "outlet in which their unsound tendencies are discharged; they would go mad if they were not criminals."[39] Most of Maudsley's attention focused on the line between insanity and crime.

Psychological Studies of Criminals

Around the turn of the twentieth century, psychologists used their new measurement techniques to study offenders. The administering of intelligence tests to inmates of jails, prisons, and other public institutions was especially popular at that time, because it was a period of major controversy over the relation of mental deficiency to criminal behavior. The new technique seemed to provide an objective basis for differentiating criminals from noncriminals.

In 1914, Henry H. Goddard, research director of the Vineland, New Jersey, Training School for the Retarded, examined some intelligence tests that had been given to inmates and concluded that 25 to 50 percent of the people in prison had intellectual defects that made them incapable of managing their own affairs.[40] This idea remained dominant until it was challenged by the results of intelligence tests administered to World War I draftees, whose scores were found to be lower than those of prisoners in the federal penitentiary at Leavenworth. As a result of this study and others like it, intelligence quotient (IQ) measures largely disappeared as a basis for explaining criminal behavior.

SOCIOLOGICAL DETERMINISM

During the nineteenth and early twentieth centuries, some scholars began to search for the social determinants of criminal behavior. The approach had its roots in Europe in the 1830s, the time between Beccaria's *On Crimes and Punishment* and Lombroso's *The Criminal Man*.

Adolphe Quételet and André Michel Guerry

Belgian mathematician Adolphe Quételet (1796–1874) and French lawyer André-Michel Guerry (1802–1866) were among the first scholars to repudiate the classicists' free-will doctrine. Working independently on the relation of crime statistics to factors such as poverty, age, sex, race, and climate, both scholars concluded that society, not the decisions of individual offenders, was responsible for criminal behavior.

The first modern criminal statistics were published in France in 1827. Guerry used those statistics to demonstrate that crime rates varied with social factors. He found, for example, that the wealthiest region of France had the highest rate of property crime but only half the national rate of violent crime. He concluded that the main factor in property crime was opportunity: There was much more to steal in the richer provinces.

Quételet did an elaborate analysis of crime in France, Belgium, and Holland. After analyzing criminal statistics, which he called "moral statistics," he concluded that if we look at overall patterns of behavior of groups across a whole society, we find a startling regularity of rates of various behaviors. According to Quételet:

> We can enumerate in advance how many individuals will soil their hands in the blood of their fellows, how many will be frauds, how many prisoners; almost as one can enumerate in advance the births and deaths that will take place.[41]

Who's Responsible?

For more than two centuries, scholars, psychologists, and criminologists have been debating the question of whether people with mental deficiencies should be held fully responsible for their crimes, especially when the death penalty is involved. In June 2002, the U.S. Supreme Court barred the execution of mentally retarded inmates, stating that "today our society views mentally retarded offenders as categorically less culpable than the average criminal."

The decision was based on the case of a Virginia man, Daryl Atkins, with an IQ of 59, who was convicted of committing a murder and robbery at the age of 18. The generally accepted definition of mental retardation is an IQ of approximately 70, accompanied by limitations on abilities like communication or caring for oneself. Fifteen countries of the European Union filed a brief on behalf of Mr. Atkins, and a group of American diplomats told the Court that executing the retarded was out of step with the rest of the world. Amnesty International reported that since 1995, only three countries had executed mentally retarded people: Kyrgyzstan, Japan, and the United States.

The Court made its ruling based on the majority's view that a "national consensus" now rejected such executions as cruel and unusual punishment, as put forward in the Eighth Amendment of the Constitution.

In another case, decided in November 2002, the Supreme Court granted a last-minute reprieve to a death-row inmate who suffers from severe mental illness, halting his execution at 5:59 P.M., one minute before the inmate was scheduled to be led to the death chamber. In 1994, James Blake Colburn raped and murdered a woman he knew. Although he had a history of psychiatric problems, including chronic paranoid schizophrenia and 15 suicide attempts, the jury sentenced him to death. The Court granted the stay "pending the timely filing and disposition of a petition for writ of certiorari," or a request for the Court to review the case. That means they did not ban the execution of the mentally ill; instead they gave Mr. Colburn's attorneys more time to prove that he had not been given a fair trial or an appropriate sentence.

Questions for Discussion

1. Where do we draw the line on who is responsible for his or her own behavior and who is not? Should this be determined on a case-by-case basis, or can laws cover such instances "across the board"?

2. The U.S. Supreme Court banned the execution of retarded offenders, not because it found the practice morally or legally wrong, but because it found a "national consensus" that such executions were excessive and inappropriate. Can you think of ways such a method of determination might have both positive and negative effects?

3. James Blake Colburn was executed on March 26, 2003. Do you believe that inmates with serious mental illness should be put to death?

SOURCES: Linda Greenhouse, "The Supreme Court: The Death Penalty; Citing 'National Consensus,' Justices Bar Death Penalty for Retarded Defendants," *New York Times*, June 21, 2002; Jim Yardley, "Court Stays Execution of Mentally Ill Texan," *New York Times*, Nov. 7, 2002.

By focusing on groups rather than individuals, Quételet discovered that behavior is indeed predictable, regular, and understandable. Just as the physical world is governed by the laws of nature, human behavior is governed by forces external to the individual. The more we learn about those forces, the easier it becomes to predict behavior. A major goal of criminological research, according to Quételet, should be to identify factors related to crime and assign to them their "proper degree of influence."[42] Though neither he nor Guerry offered a theory of criminal behavior, the fact that both studied social factors scientifically, using quantitative research methods, made them key figures in the subsequent development of sociological theories of crime causation.

Gabriel Tarde

One of the earliest sociological theories of criminal behavior was formulated by Gabriel Tarde (1843–1904), who served 15 years as a provincial judge and then was placed in charge of France's national statistics. After an extensive analysis of these statistics, he came to the following conclusion:

The majority of murderers and notorious thieves began as children who had been abandoned, and the true seminary of crime must be sought for upon each public square or each crossroad of our towns, whether they be small or large, in those flocks of pillaging street urchins who, like bands of sparrows, associate together, at first for marauding, and then for theft, because of a lack of education and food in their homes.[43]

Tarde rejected the Lombrosian theory of biological abnormality, which was popular in his time, arguing that criminals were normal people who learned crime just as others learned legitimate trades. He formulated his theory in terms of **laws of imitation**—principles that governed the process by which people became criminals. According to Tarde's thesis, individuals emulate behavior patterns in much the same way they copy styles of dress. Moreover, there is a pattern to the way such emulation takes place: (1) Individuals imitate others in proportion to the intensity and frequency of their contacts; (2) inferiors imitate superiors—that is, trends flow from town to country and from upper to lower classes; and (3) when two behavior patterns clash, one may take the place of the other, as when guns largely replaced knives as murder weapons.[44] Tarde's work served as the basis for Edwin Sutherland's theory of differential association, which we will examine in Chapter 5.

Émile Durkheim

Modern criminologists take two major approaches to the study of the social factors associated with crime. Tarde's approach asks how individuals become criminal. What is the process? How are behavior patterns learned and transmitted? The second major approach looks at the social structure and its institutions. It asks how crime arises in the first place and how it is related to the functioning of a society. For answers to these questions, scholars begin with the work of Émile Durkheim (1858–1917).

Of all nineteenth-century writers on the relationship between crime and social factors, none has more powerfully influenced contemporary criminology than Durkheim, who is universally acknowledged as one of the founders of sociology. On October 12, 1870, when Durkheim was 12 years old, the German army invaded and occupied his hometown, Epinal, in eastern France. Thus, at a very early age, he witnessed social chaos and the effects of rapid change, topics with which he remained preoccupied throughout his life. At the age of 24, he became a professor of philosophy, and at 29 he joined the faculty of the University of Bordeaux. There he taught the first course in sociology ever to be offered by a French university.

By 1902, he had moved to the University of Paris, where he completed his doctoral studies. His *Division of Labor* became a landmark work on the organization of societies. According to Durkheim, crime is as normal a part of society as birth and death. Theoretically, crime could disappear altogether only if all members of society had the same values, and such standardization is

Émile Durkheim (1858–1917), one of the founders of sociology.

neither possible nor desirable. Furthermore, some crime is in fact necessary if a society is to progress:

> The opportunity for the genius to carry out his work affords the criminal his originality at a lower level. . . . According to Athenian law, Socrates was a criminal, and his condemnation was no more than just. However, his crime, namely, the independence of his thought, rendered a service not only to humanity but to his country.[45]

Durkheim further pointed out that all societies have not only crime but also sanctions. The rationale for the sanctions varies in accordance with the structure of the society. In a strongly cohesive society, punishment of members who deviate is used to reinforce the value system—to remind people of what is right and what is wrong—thereby preserving the pool of common belief and the solidarity of the society. Punishment must be harsh to serve these ends. In a large, urbanized, heterogeneous society, on the other hand, punishment is used not to preserve solidarity but rather to right the wrong done to a victim. Punishment thus is evaluated in accordance with the harm done, with the goal of restitution and reinstatement of order as quickly as possible.

 Crime Surfing

http://durkheim.itgo
.com/religion.html

According to Durkheim, what role does religion play in society?

The offense is not considered a threat to social cohesion, primarily because in a large, complex society, criminal events do not even come to the attention of most people.

The most important of Durkheim's many contributions to contemporary sociology is his concept of **anomie,** a breakdown of social order as a result of a loss of standards and values. In a society plagued by anomie (see Chapter 5), disintegration and chaos replace social cohesion.

HISTORICAL AND CONTEMPORARY CRIMINOLOGY: A TIME LINE

Classical criminologists thought the problem of crime might be solved through limitations on governmental power, the abolition of brutality, and the creation of a more equitable system of justice. They argued that the punishment should fit the crime. For over a century, this perspective dominated criminology. Later on, positivist criminologists influenced judges to give greater consideration to the offender than to the gravity of the crime when imposing sentences. The current era marks a return to the classical demand that the punishment correspond to the seriousness of the crime and the guilt of the offender. Table 3.1 presents a chronology of all the pioneers in criminology we have discussed.

As modern science discovered more and more about cause and effect in the physical and social universes, the theory that individuals commit crimes of their own free will began to lose favor. The positivists searched for determinants of crime in biological, psychological, and social factors. Biologically based theories were popular in the late nineteenth century, fell out of favor in the early part of the twentieth century, and emerged again in the 1970s (see Chapter 4) with studies of hormone imbalances, diet, environmental contaminants, and so forth. Since the studies of criminal responsibility in the nineteenth century centering on the insanity defense and of intelligence levels in the twentieth century, psychiatrists and psychologists have continued to play a major role in the search for the causes of crime, especially after Sigmund Freud developed his well-known theory of human personality (Chapter 4). The sociological perspective became popular in the 1920s and has remained the predominant approach of criminological studies. (We will examine contemporary theories in Chapters 5 through 9.)

THE FUTURE OF OUR HISTORY

All the social sciences appear to follow alternating patterns of tradition-bound periods, such as periods of prevailing classical, deterministic and neoclassical thought. Emerging ideas and paradigms that mark these periods often reflect the maturity of scientific growth—from preparadigmatic immature science, to normal science, and finally to a series of intellectual milestones that effectively upset tradition, prompting the establishment of new paradigms. Prior generations of criminological thought discussed earlier in this chapter were, for much of the time, characteristically preparadigmatic. By the 1960s, however, the academic subject matter of criminology was bordering on what some have called "normal science" or "research firmly based upon one or more past scientific achievements, achievements that some particular community acknowledges for a time as supplying the foundation for its further practice."[46] By the late 1960s and early 1970s, a new generation of criminologists upset the accepted paradigms, repeatedly calling into question the value of "normal science."

To the extent that the history of criminology is fluid, it is only fair to ponder its future—the future of our history. First it is notable that some old but emergent themes are returning. For example, as we will see in Chapter 4, advances in the neurosciences are allowing a glimpse inside the neuroanatomy of the brain that reframes the old field of biological determinism and opens the door to new inquiry. A new specialty—neurocriminology—marks the progress of our field. Second, evidence-based research and the priority given to randomized controlled experiments encourage a new emphasis on criminology as a cutting-edge scientific discipline. As noted briefly in Chapter 2, the experimental method allows for definitive answers to some of the most important policy questions of our time. Finally, the somewhat provincial and often bounded view of American criminology is slowly giving way to the realization that research on crime and criminality outside the United States has much unrealized value.

In his 2006 presidential address to the American Society of Criminology, Gary LaFree argued in favor of expanding the domain of the field. This may be accomplished by exploring ways criminological research can nurture democratic, non-authoritarian societies. "Although the most recent wave of democratization produced a record number of democratic regimes," LaFree writes, "we are observing ominous challenges to fundamental democratic rights from around the world. As criminologists, we have a vested interest in supporting the democratic, nonauthoritarian societies in which our craft has thrived."[47]

TABLE 3.1   Pioneers in Criminology: A Chronology   **69**

Classical Criminology

FREE WILL

Cesare Beccaria (1738–1794). Devised the first design for a comprehensive, enlightened criminal justice system based on law

Jeremy Bentham (1748–1832). Developed utilitarian principles of punishment

Positivist Criminology

BIOLOGICAL DETERMINISM

Giambattista della Porta (1535–1615). Was the founder of the school of physiognomy, which is the study of facial features and their relation to human behaviors

Johann Kaspar Lavater (1741–1801). Espoused a biological approach to crime causation; developed phrenology

Franz Joseph Gall (1758–1828). Espoused a biological approach to crime causation; further developed phrenology

Charles Caldwell (1772–1853). Was a physician who searched for evidence that brain tissue and cells regulate human behavior

Johann Kaspar Spurzheim (1776–1832). Espoused a biological approach; continued studies of phrenology

Charles Darwin (1809–1882). Formulated theory of evolution, which changed explanations of human behavior

Cesare Lombroso (1835–1909). Saw determinism as explanatory factor in criminal behavior; posited the "born criminal"; father of modern criminology

Richard Dugdale (1841–1883). Related criminal behavior to inherited traits (Jukes family)

Raffaele Garofalo (1851–1934). Traced roots of criminal behavior to "moral anomalies" rather than physical characteristics

Enrico Ferri (1856–1929). Produced first penal code based on positivist principles; replaced moral responsibility with social accountability

Ernest Hooten (1887–1954). Related criminality to hereditary inferiority

Ernst Kretschmer (1888–1964). Introduced the somatotype school of criminology

William Sheldon (1898–1977). Related body types to illegal behavior

PSYCHOLOGICAL DETERMINISM

Isaac Ray (1807–1881). Questioned whether those who were "morally insane" could be held legally responsible for their acts

Henry Maudsley (1835–1918). Pioneered criteria for legal responsibility

Henry H. Goddard (1866–1957). Related criminal behavior to intelligence (Kallikak family)

SOCIOLOGICAL DETERMINISM

Adolphe Quételet (1796–1874). Was one of the first to repudiate classical free-will doctrine; studied social determinants of behavior

Auguste Comte (1798–1857). Brought modern scientific methods from physical to social sciences

André-Michel Guerry (1802–1866). Was one of the first to repudiate free-will doctrine; related crime statistics to social factors

Gabriel Tarde (1843–1904). Explained crime as learned behavior

Émile Durkheim (1858–1917). Was one of the founders of sociology; developed theory of anomie and idea that crime is normal in all societies

Charles Buckman Goring (1870–1919). Used empirical research to refute Lombroso's theory of criminal types

Sheldon Glueck (1896–1980) and Eleanor Glueck (1898–1972). Espoused primarily social causes of delinquency, but also psychological and biological explanations

CHAPTER 3

REVIEW

In the history of criminology from ancient times to the early twentieth century, its many themes at times have clashed and at times have supported one another. There is no straight-line evolutionary track that we can follow from the inception of the first "criminological" thought to modern theories. Some scholars concentrated on criminal law and procedure, others on criminal behavior. Some took the biological route, others the psychological, and still others the sociological. And the work of some investigators has encompassed a combination of factors. Toward the end of the nineteenth century, a discipline began to emerge.

Tracing the major developments back in time helps us understand how criminology grew into the discipline we know today. Many of the issues that appear on the intellectual battlefields early in the twenty-first century are the same issues our academic ancestors grappled with for hundreds, indeed thousands, of years. With each new clash, some old concepts died, while others were incorporated within competing doctrinal boundaries, there to remain until the next challenge. The controversies of one era become the foundations of knowledge for the next. As societies develop and are subjected to new technologies, the crime problem becomes ever more complex. So do the questions it raises. In Part II we will see how twentieth-century theorists have dealt with those questions.

CRIMINOLOGY & PUBLIC POLICY

The execution methods debate is played out by legislative decision-makers, who oftentimes turn a blind eye to the concerns of those who actually have to kill. In turn, a considerable portion of doctors, nurses, and other medical personnel willingly participate in executions. Prison officials face the worst of both worlds: They have limited political clout by which to make their choices known and minimal guidance provided by those who make the choices for them. The process is made all the more perplexing because those who report the problems with the system— media witnesses—have questionable credibility when experts attempt to use their accounts in court. "As a result," in Foucault's words, "justice no longer takes public responsibility for the violence that is bound up with its practice." The system becomes literally and symbolically unobservable. In the context of applying execution methods, when justice becomes unobservable, it ceases to exist. (SOURCE: From Deborah W. Denno, "When Legislatures Delegate Death: The Troubling Paradox behind State Uses of Electrocution and Lethal Injection and What It Says about Us," *Ohio State Law Journal,* **63,** [2002]: 63. Reprinted by permission of *Ohio State Law Journal* and the author.)

Questions for Discussion Beccaria voiced concerns over bad laws (see the section "Cesare Beccaria" earlier in this chapter). He made an inspired call for an end to medieval barbarism. Punishment should be prompt and effective. Capital punishment should be abolished—and so, too, should the use of torture. Debate over the death penalty in recent years has turned on concerns over executing innocents, the mentally ill, and the insane. Much has been written about the racial application of the death penalty as well. Professor Denno raises a very different concern: Are the methods we use to execute inmates justifiable? Interestingly, Professor Denno raises this concern about the use of lethal injection— considered to be the most humane of the methods of execution. If you agree with her reasoning, do you then conclude that all methods of execution should be abolished?

YOU BE THE CRIMINOLOGIST

A historical society has invited you to represent criminology in a discussion group made up of experts from various disciplines. The topic is: How do the foundations of your discipline help us understand contemporary developments in the field? What would you discuss?

KEY TERMS

The numbers next to the terms refer to the pages on which the terms are defined.

anomie (68)

atavistic stigmata (61)

born criminal (61)

classical school (53)

eugenics (64)

laws of imitation (67)

phrenology (60)

physiognomy (60)

positivist school (53)

somatotype school (63)

utilitarianism (57)

PART II

Explanations of Crime and Criminal Behavior

Having explored the history of criminology, the early explanations of criminal behavior, and the scientific methods used by criminologists, we turn now to contemporary theories and research. Current explanations of criminal behavior focus on biological, psychological, social, and economic factors. Biological and psychological theories assume that criminal behavior results from underlying physical or mental conditions that distinguish criminals from noncriminals (Chapter 4). These theories and related research yield insight into individual cases, but they do not explain why crime rates vary from place to place and from one situation to another.

Sociological theories seek to explain criminal behavior in terms of the environment. Chapter 5 examines strain and cultural deviance theories, which focus on the social forces that cause people to engage in criminal behavior. Both theories assume that social class and criminal behavior are related. Strain theorists argue that people commit crimes because they are frustrated by not being able to achieve their goals through legitimate means. Cultural deviance theorists claim that crime is learned in socially disorganized neighborhoods where criminal norms are transmitted from one generation to the next. In Chapter 6, we examine subcultures that have their own norms, beliefs, and values, which differ significantly from those of the dominant culture. Chapter 7 explains how people remain committed to conventional behavior in the face of frustration, poor living conditions, and other criminogenic factors. In Chapter 8, we discuss three theoretical perspectives that focus on society's role in creating criminals and defining them as such. Finally, in Chapter 9, we explain why offenders choose to commit one offense rather than another at a given time and place.

Biological and Psychological Perspectives

Biology and Criminality
Modern Biocriminology
Genetics and Criminality
The Controversy over Violence
   and Genes
The IQ Debate
Biochemical Factors
Neurocriminology
Crime and Human Nature
Criticisms of Biocriminology
Psychology and Criminality
Psychological Development
Moral Development
Maternal Deprivation and
   Attachment Theory
Learning Aggression and Violence
Personality
Mental Disorders and Crime
Psychological Causation
An Integrated Theory
Review
Criminology & Public Policy
You Be the Criminologist
Key Terms

■ *Bind, Torture, and Kill (BTK) killer Dennis Lynn Rader, a now-infamous serial murderer, may be responsible for at least 10 deaths in and around Wichita, Kansas, between 1974 and 1991. Rader wrote letters to the police and local newspapers right after the killings, boasting of the crimes and revealing details about them.*

On June 27, 2005, nearly three decades after his first killing, Dennis Rader, or the BTK killer as he is more commonly known, pleaded guilty in front of a Wichita, Kansas, courtroom to killing 10 people between 1974 and 1991. He described calmly and in great detail how he committed each murder.

Rader broke into the Otero home and tied up Julie, Joseph, and two of their children. He told them he just needed a car and food, and even put a pillow under Joseph's head so that he would be more comfortable. Then he realized that the family could identify him. "I didn't have a mask on or anything . . . [so] I made a decision to go ahead and put 'em down, I guess, or strangle them. . . . I had never strangled anyone before, so I really didn't know how much pressure you had to put on a person."[1]

Rader recounted how he selected several victims, or "projects," at a time and stalked them until one came to fruition. He chose them to fulfill sexual fantasies. He came to each crime with a "hit kit" and "hit clothes," which he later destroyed. Rader often took pictures of his victims in lewd poses after he killed them.

Jeff Davis, whose mother, Dolores, was

Rader's final victim in 1991, called the killer a "classic, textbook sociopath" with "no conscience, just a black hole inside the shell of a human being." He compared Rader's rendition of the killing to the reading of a recipe out of a cookbook.[2] Rader was sentenced to 10 consecutive life sentences and is serving these sentences in the Special Management Unit (solitary confinement) of the El Dorado Correctional Facility in El Dorado, Kansas. He remains in his cell for 23 hours a day, with an hour exercise time.

In the United States, explanations of criminal behavior have been dominated by sociological theories. These theories focus on lack of opportunity and the breakdown of the conventional value system in urban ghettos, the formation of subcultures whose norms deviate from those of the middle class, the disconnect between culturally prescribed goals and the means to attain those goals, and the increasing inability of social institutions to exercise control over behavior. Criminological texts treat biological and psychological theories as peripheral, perhaps because criminology's disciplinary allegiance is to sociology. Biological explanations have always raised a wide range of concerns, from intractable ethical questions to practical questions such as how data from genetic, biochemical, or neuroanatomical research might be used in the criminal justice system. When psychological theories were first advanced to explain criminal behavior, their emphasis was largely psychoanalytic, so they may have seemed not quantitative or scientific enough to some criminologists.[3] Others may have considered the early work of Lombroso, Goring, and Hooten too scientifically naive to be taken seriously. Over the past two decades, psychological research on crime and criminality has enjoyed a renaissance.

Sociological theories focus on crime rates of groups that experience frustration in their efforts to achieve accepted goals, not on the particular individual who remains law-abiding or becomes a criminal. Sociological theories cannot explain how one person can be born in a slum, be exposed to family discord and abuse, never attend school, have friends who are delinquents, and yet resist opportunities for crime, while another person can grow up in an affluent suburban neighborhood in a two-parent home, attend the finest schools, have every financial need met, and end up firing a gun at the president. In other words, sociologists do not address individual differences.[4] Instead, biologists and psychologists are interested in finding out what may account for individual differences.

It is clear that biological, psychological, and sociological explanations are not competing to answer the same specific questions. Rather, all three disciplines are searching for answers to different questions, even though they study the same act, status, or characteristic. We can understand crime in a society only if we view criminality from more than one level of analysis: why a certain individual commits a crime (biological and psychological explanations) and why some groups of individuals commit more or different criminal acts than other groups (sociological explanations).

Sociological theory and empirical research often ignore factors such as genetics and personality, almost as if they were irrelevant. And biological and psychological theories often focus on the individual, with little regard for the fact that while each one of us comes into the world with certain genetic predispositions, characteristics, and traits, from the moment we are born we interact with others in a complex social world that influences our behavior.

■ *Serial killers stop murdering when they are caught or killed.*

BIOLOGY AND CRIMINALITY

Within the last three decades, biologists have followed in the tradition of Cesare Lombroso, Raffaele Garofalo, and Charles Goring in their search for answers to questions about human behavior. Geneticists, for example, have argued that the predisposition to act violently or aggressively in certain situations may be inherited. In other words, while criminals are not born criminal, the predisposition to be violent or to commit crime may be present at birth.

To demonstrate that certain traits are inherited, geneticists have studied children born of criminals but reared from birth by noncriminal adoptive parents. They have wanted to know whether the behavior of the adoptive children was more similar to that of their biological parents than to that of their adoptive parents. Their findings play an important role in the debate on heredity versus environment. Other biologists, sometimes called "biocriminologists" or "neurocriminologists," take a different approach. Some ask whether the brain's anatomy, brain damage, or inadequate nutrition results in criminal behavior. Others are interested in the influence of hormones, chromosomal abnormalities, and allergies. They investigate complex interactions between brain and behavior and between diet and behavior.

Modern Biocriminology

Biocriminology is the study of the physical aspects of psychological disorders.[5] It has been known for some time that adults who suffer from depression show abnormalities in brain waves during sleep, experience disturbed nervous system functioning, and display biochemical abnormalities. Research on depressed children reveals the same physical problems; furthermore, their adult relatives show high rates of depression as well. In fact, children whose parents suffer from depression are more than four times more likely than the average child to experience a similar illness.[6] Some researchers believe depression is an inherited condition that manifests itself in psychological and physical disturbances. The important point is that until only recently, physicians may have been missing the mark in their assessment and treatment of depressed children and adults by ignoring the physiological aspects.

Criminologists who study sociology and psychology to the exclusion of the biological sciences may also be missing the mark in their efforts to discover the causes of crime. Recent research has demonstrated that crime does indeed have psychobiological aspects similar to those found in studies of depression: biochemical abnormalities, abnormal brain waves, nervous system dysfunction. There is also evidence that strongly suggests a genetic predisposition to criminality.[7]

The resurgence of interest in integrating modern biological advances, theories, and principles into mainstream criminology began over three decades ago. The sociobiological work of Edward Wilson on the interrelationship of biology, genetics, and social behavior was pivotal.[8] So were the contributions of C. Ray Jeffery, who argued that a biosocial interdisciplinary model should become the major theoretical framework for studying criminal behavior.[9]

Criminologists once again began to consider the possibility that there are indeed traits that predispose a person to criminality and that these traits may be passed from parent to child through the genes. Other questions arose as well. Is it possible, for instance, that internal biochemical imbalances or deficiencies cause antisocial behavior? Could too much or too little sugar in the bloodstream increase the potential for aggression? Or could a vitamin deficiency or some hormonal problem be responsible? We will explore the evidence for a genetic predisposition to criminal behavior, the relationship between biochemical factors and criminality, and neurophysiological factors that result in criminal behavior. We will also briefly explore the emergence of a new specialty in criminology, neurocriminology. Advances in brain imaging allow some criminologists to make fascinating connections between the neuroanatomy of the brain and criminal behavior. The possibilities and boundaries of neurocriminology are still undefined, but the prospect for path-breaking research seems quite likely.

Genetics and Criminality

Today the proposition that human beings are products of an interaction between environmental and genetic factors is all but universally accepted.[10] We can stop asking, then, whether nature or nurture is more important in shaping us; we are the products of both. But what does the interaction between the two look like? And what concerns are raised by reliance on genetics to the exclusion of environmental factors? Consider the example of the XYY syndrome.

The XYY Syndrome

Chromosomes are the basic structures that contain our genes—the biological material that makes each of us unique. Each human being has 23 pairs of inherited chromosomes. One pair determines gender. A female receives an X chromosome from both mother and father; a male receives an X chromosome from his mother and a Y from his father. Sometimes a defect in the production of sperm or egg results in genetic abnormalities. One type of abnormality is the XYY chromosomal male. The XYY male receives two Y chromosomes from his father rather than one. Approximately 1 in 1,000 newborn males in the general population has this genetic composition.[11] Initial studies done in the 1960s found the frequency of XYY chromosomes to be about 20 times greater than normal XY chromosomes among inmates in maximum-security state hospitals.[12] The XYY inmates tended to be tall, physically aggressive, and, frequently, violent.

Supporters of these data claimed to have uncovered the mystery of violent criminality. Critics voiced concern over the fact that these studies were done on small and unrepresentative samples. The XYY syndrome, as this condition became known, received much public attention because of the case of Richard Speck. Speck, who in 1966 murdered eight nurses in Chicago, initially was diagnosed as an XYY chromosomal male. However, the diagnosis later turned out to be wrong. Nevertheless, public concern was aroused: Were all XYY males potential killers?

Studies undertaken since that time have discounted the relation between the extra Y chromosome and criminality.[13] Although convincing evidence in support of the XYY hypothesis appears to be slight, it is nevertheless possible that aggressive and violent behavior is at least partly determined by genetic factors. The problem is how to investigate this possibility. One difficulty is separating the external or environmental factors, such as family structure, culture, socioeconomic status, and peer influences, from the genetic predispositions with which they begin to interact at birth.

A particular individual may have a genetic predisposition to be violent but be born into a wealthy, well-educated, loving, and calm familial environment. He may never commit a violent act. Another person may have a genetic predisposition to be rule-abiding and nonaggressive yet be born into a poor, uneducated, physically abusive, and unloving family. He may commit violent criminal acts. How, then, can we determine the extent to which behavior is genetically influenced? Researchers have turned to twin studies and adoption studies in the quest for an answer.

Twin Studies

To discover whether crime is genetically predetermined, researchers have compared identical and fraternal twins. Identical twins, or **monozygotic (MZ) twins,** develop from a single fertilized egg that divides into two embryos. These twins share all their genes. Fraternal twins, or **dizygotic (DZ) twins,** develop from two separate eggs, both fertilized at the same time. They share about half their genes. Since the prenatal and postnatal family environments are, by and large, the same, greater behavioral similarity between identical twins than between fraternal twins would support an argument for genetic predisposition.

In the 1920s, a German physician, Johannes Lange, found 30 pairs of same-sex twins—13 identical and 17 fraternal pairs. One member of each pair was a known criminal. Lange found that in 10 of the 13 pairs of identical twins, both twins were criminal; in 2 of the 17 pairs of fraternal twins, both were criminal.[14] The research techniques of the time were limited, but Lange's results were nevertheless impressive.

Many similar studies have followed. The largest was a study by Karl Christiansen and Sarnoff A. Mednick that included all twins born between 1881 and 1910 in a region of Denmark, a total of 3,586 pairs. Reviewing serious offenses only, Christiansen and Mednick found that the chance of there being a criminal twin when the other twin was a criminal was 50 percent for identical twins and 20 percent for same-sex fraternal twins.[15] Such findings lend support to the hypothesis that some genetic influences increase the risk of criminality.[16] A more recent American study conducted by David C. Rowe and D. Wayne Osgood reached a similar conclusion.[17]

While the evidence from these and other twin studies looks persuasive, we should keep in mind the weakness of such research. It may not be valid to assume a common environment for all twins who grow up in the same house at the same time. If the upbringing of identical twins is much more similar than that of fraternal twins, as it well may be, that circumstance could help explain their different rates of criminality.

Adoption Studies

One way to separate the influence of inherited traits from that of environmental conditions would be to study infants separated at birth from their natural parents and placed randomly in foster homes. In such cases, we could determine whether the behavior of the adopted child resembled that of the natural parents or that of the adoptive parents, and by how much. Children, however, are adopted at various ages and are not placed randomly in foster homes. Most such children are matched to their foster or adoptive parents by racial and religious criteria. And couples who adopt children may differ in some important ways from other couples. Despite such shortcomings, adoption studies do help us expand our knowledge of genetic influences on human variation.

The largest adoption study conducted so far was based on a sample of 14,427 male and female adoptions in Denmark between 1924 and 1947. The hypothesis was that criminality in the biological parents would be associated with an increased risk of criminal behavior in the child. The parents were considered criminal if either the mother or the father had been convicted of a felony. The researchers had sufficient information on more than 4,000 of the male children to assess whether both the biological and the adoptive parents had criminal records. Mednick and his associates reported the following findings:

- Of boys whose adoptive and biological parents had no criminal record, 13.5 percent were convicted of crimes.
- Of boys who had criminal adoptive parents and noncriminal biological parents, 14.7 percent were convicted of crimes.
- Of boys who had noncriminal adoptive parents and criminal biological parents, 20 percent were convicted of crimes.
- Of boys who had both criminal adoptive parents and criminal biological parents, 24.5 percent were convicted of crimes.[18]

These findings support the claim that the criminality of the biological parents has more influence on the child than does that of the adoptive parents. Other research on adopted children has reached similar conclusions. A major Swedish study examined 862 adopted males and 913 adopted females. The researchers found a genetic predisposition to criminality in both sexes, but an even stronger one in females. An American study of children who were put up for adoption by a group of convicted mothers supports the Danish and Swedish findings on the significance of genetic factors.[19]

Results of adoption studies have been characterized as "highly suggestive" or "supportive" of a genetic link to criminality. But how solid is this link? There are significant problems with adoption studies. One is that little can be done to ensure the similarity of adopted children's environments. Of even greater concern to criminologists, however, is the distinct possibility of mistaking correlation for causation. In other words, there appears to be a significant correlation between the criminality of biological parents and adopted children in the research we have reviewed, but this correlation does not prove that the genetic legacy passed on by a criminal parent causes an offspring to commit a crime.

So far, research has failed to shed any light on the nature of the biological link that results in the association between the criminality of parents and that of their children. Furthermore, even if we could identify children with a higher-than-average probability of committing offenses as adults on the basis of their parents' behavior, it is unclear what we could do to prevent these children from following the parental model.

The Controversy over Violence and Genes

At the same time that advances in research on the biological bases of violence shed new light on crime, attacks on such research are calling its usefulness into question. Government-sponsored research plans have been called racist, a conference on genetics and crime was canceled after protests, and a session on violence and heredity at a recent American Association for the Advancement of Science meeting became "a politically correct critique of the research."[20]

Few involved in such research expect to find a "violence gene"; rather, researchers are looking for a biological basis for some of the behaviors associated with violence. As one explanation put it:

Scientists are . . . trying to find inborn personality traits that might make people more physically aggressive. The tendency to be a thrill seeker may be one such characteristic. So might "a restless impulsiveness, an inability to defer gratification." A high threshold for anxiety or fear may be another key trait. . . . Such people tend to have a "special biology," with lower-than-average heart rates and blood pressure.[21]

No one yet has found any direct link between genes and violence. In fact, Sarnoff Mednick, the psychologist who conducted adoption studies of criminal behavior in Denmark, found no evidence for the inheritance of violence. "If there were any genetic effect for violent crimes, we would have picked it up," says Mednick, whose study included 14,427 men.

The controversy over a genetic basis for violent behavior seems to deal less with actual research findings than with the implications of such findings. For example, Harvard psychologist Jerome Kagan predicts that in 25 years, biological and genetic tests will make it possible to identify the 15 children in every 1,000 who may have violent tendencies. Of those 15, only 1 will actually become violent. The ethical question, then, is what to do with this knowledge. "Do we tell the mothers of all 15 that their kids might be violent?" he asks. "How are the mothers then going to react to their children if we do that?"[22]

A National Academy of Science (NAS) report on violence recommended finding better ways to intervene in the development of children who could become violent, and it listed risk factors statistically linked to violence: hyperactivity, poor early grades, low IQ, fearlessness, and an inability to defer gratification, for example. A report released by the Office of Juvenile Justice and Delinquency Prevention's Study Group on Serious and Violent Juvenile Offenders identifies a number of behavioral precursors to juvenile violence, including difficult temperament, hyperactivity, impulsivity, aggression, lying, and risk-taking behavior.[23]

What frightens those opposed to biological and genetic research into the causes of violence is the thought of how such research could be used by policy makers. If a violent personality can be shown to be genetically determined, crime-prevention strategies might try to identify "potential criminals" and to intervene before their criminal careers begin and before anyone knows if they would ever have become criminals. "Should genetic markers one day be found for tendencies . . . that are loosely linked to crime," explains one researcher, "they would probably have little specificity, sensitivity or explanatory power: most people with the markers will not be criminals and most criminals will not have the markers."[24] On the other hand, when environment—poverty, broken homes, and other problems—is seen as the major cause of violence, crime prevention takes the shape of improving social conditions rather than labeling individuals.

A middle-of-the-road approach is proposed by those who see biological research as a key to helping criminals change their behavior. "Once you find a biological basis for a behavior, you can try to find out how to help people cope," says one such scholar. "Suppose the link is impulsivity, an inability to defer gratification. It might be you could design education programs to teach criminals to readjust their time horizon."[25]

The IQ Debate

A discussion of the association between genes and criminality would be incomplete without paying at least some attention to the debate over IQ and crime. Is an inferior intelligence inherited, and, if so, how do we account for the strong relationship between IQ and criminality?

The Research Background

Nearly a century ago, scientists began to search for measures to determine people's intelligence, which they believed to be genetically determined. The first test to gain acceptance was developed by a French psychologist, Alfred Binet. Binet's test measured the capacity of individual children to perform tasks or solve problems in relation to the average capacity of their peers.

Between 1888 and 1915, several researchers administered intelligence tests to incarcerated criminals and to boys in reform schools. Initial studies of the relationship between IQ and crime revealed some surprising results. Psychologist Hugo Munsterberg estimated that 68 percent of the criminals he tested were of low IQ. Using the Binet scale, Henry H. Goddard found that between 25 and 50 percent of criminals had low IQs.[26] What could account for such different results?

Edwin Sutherland observed that the tests were poor and there were too many variations among the many versions administered. He reasoned that social and environmental factors caused delinquency, not low IQ.[27] In the 1950s, psychologist Robert H. Gault added to Sutherland's criticism. He noted particularly that it was "strange that it did not occur immediately to the pioneers that they had examined only a small sample of caught and convicted offenders."[28]

For more than a generation, the question about the relationship between IQ and criminal behavior was not studied, and the early inconsistencies remained unresolved. Then, in the late 1970s, the debate resumed.[29] Supporters of the view that inheritance determines intelligence once again began to present their arguments. Psychologist Arthur Jensen suggested that race was a key factor in IQ differences; Richard J. Herrnstein, a geneticist, pointed to social class as a factor.[30] Both positions spurred a heated debate in which criminologists soon became involved. In 1977, Travis Hirschi and Michael Hindelang evaluated the existing literature on IQ and crime.[31] They cited the following three studies as especially important:

- Travis Hirschi, on the basis of a study of 3,600 California students, demonstrated that the effect of a low IQ on delinquent behavior is more significant than that of the father's education.[32]
- Marvin Wolfgang and associates, after studying 8,700 Philadelphia boys, found a strong relationship between low IQ and delinquency, independent of social class.[33]
- Albert Reiss and Albert L. Rhodes, after an examination of the juvenile court records of 9,200 white Tennessee schoolboys, found IQ to be more closely related to delinquency than is social class.[34]

Hirschi and Hindelang concluded that IQ is an even more important factor in predicting crime than is either race or social class. They found significant differences in intelligence between criminal and noncriminal populations within like racial and socioeconomic groups. A lower IQ increases the potential for crime within each group. Furthermore, they found that IQ is related to school performance. A low IQ ultimately results in a youngster's associating with similar nonperformers, dropping out of school, and committing delinquent acts. Hirschi and Hindelang's findings were confirmed by James Q. Wilson and Richard Herrnstein but rejected by criminologist Deborah Denno, who conducted a prospective investigation of 800 children from birth to age 17. Her results failed to confirm a direct relationship between IQ and delinquency. A recent review of research on IQ and delinquency suggests an indirect link as well, mediated by academic competence.[35]

The Debate: Genetics or Environment?

The debate over the relationship between IQ and crime has its roots in the controversy over whether intelligence is genetically or environmentally determined. IQ tests, many people believe, measure cultural factors rather than the innate biological makeup of an individual.[36] Studies by psychologists Sandra Scarr and Richard Weinberg of black and white adopted children confirmed that environment plays a significant role in IQ development. They found that both black and white children adopted by white parents had comparable IQs and performed similarly.[37] With evidence of cultural bias and environmental influence, why not abandon the use of intelligence tests? The answer is simple: They do predict performance in school and so have significant utility. It appears that this debate will be with us for a long time to come.

Biochemical Factors

Biocriminologists' primary focus has been on the relationship between criminality and biochemical and neurophysiological factors. Biochemical factors include food allergies, diet, hypoglycemia, and hormones. Neurophysiological factors include brain lesions, brain wave abnormalities, and minimal brain dysfunction.

Food Allergies

In 1993, by the time Rachel was 2 years old, she displayed a pattern of behavior that went way beyond the "terrible twos." Without warning, her eyes would glaze over, her speech would develop a lisp, and she'd kick and hit and thrash about wildly until her mother swaddled her tightly and she fell asleep, exhausted. She even developed a "kitty-cat" routine, complete with meowing, stalking, and growling, that often went on for hours.

When Rachel's sister Emma was born later that year, she nursed poorly and never slept through the night. After their mother introduced baby corn into her diet, Emma experienced severe intestinal distress, for which she was hospitalized. After a battery of medical tests proved inconclusive, she was sent home, but the symptoms continued intermittently, without apparent reason.

The following year, in desperation, their mother had Rachel and Emma, then 3 years and 15 months, tested for food allergies. Both showed marked sensitivity to corn, wheat, sugar, preservatives, and dairy products. After those foods were eliminated, Emma's health and well-being improved, and Rachel's perplexing and worrisome behavior all but disappeared.[38]

Over the last two decades, researchers have investigated the relation between food allergies and aggression and antisocial behavior. In fact, since 1908 there have been numerous medical reports indicating that various foods cause reactions such as irritability, hyperactivity, seizures, agitation, and behavior that is "out of character."[39] Investigators have identified the following food components as substances that may result in severe allergic reactions:

Phenylethylamine (found in chocolate)
Tyramine (found in aged cheese and wine)
Monosodium glutamate (used as a flavor enhancer in many foods)
Aspartame (found in artificial sweeteners)
Xanthines (found in caffeine)

Each of these food components has been associated with behavioral disorders, including criminality.

Diet

- Susan had been charged with 16 offenses, including criminal damage, solvent abuse, and vehicle theft, by the time she was 13. She had no friends, showed no affection toward her parents, and frequently hit her mother. Her schoolwork deteriorated, and she played truant most days. After 6 months on a changed diet, which excluded burgers, bananas, and chocolate, the number of her offenses dropped to zero. And for the first time since she was a young child, Susan gave her mother a hug.

- Craig, 15, vandalized his home several times and committed numerous petty crimes. He was a bully and was virtually impossible to teach. And his 8-year-old brother was beginning to follow in his footsteps. Both were put on a special diet, cutting out fizzy drinks and sweets and including more green vegetables and fresh fruit. Within months, says their mother, both were more pleasant and easier to deal with. But Craig has since quit the diet and has reoffended. The bullying and the violence have started again.

- Graham, an 11-year-old, turned from an uncontrollable delinquent into a normal, pleasant boy when pizzas, baked beans, and chocolate in his diet were replaced by fresh vegetables, coconut milk, and carrots. He became less aggressive and argumentative and, reportedly, was "happy" for the first time in his life. Graham's schoolwork improved, and he began to make friends.

Anecdotal reports, in addition to more scientific investigations, link criminality to diets high in sugar and carbohydrates, to vitamin deficiency or dependency, and to excessive food additives.

Criminologist Stephen Schoenthaler conducted a series of studies on the relation between sugar and the behavior of institutionalized offenders. In these investigations, inmates were placed on a modified diet that included very little sugar. They received fruit juice in place of soda and vegetables instead of candy. Schoenthaler found fewer disciplinary actions and a significant drop in aggressive behavior in the experimental group.[40] Some individuals charged with crimes have used this finding to build a defense like that of Dan White.

In 1979, San Francisco city supervisor Dan White was on trial for the murder of his fellow supervisor, Harvey Milk, and Mayor George Moscone—as depicted in the recent movie *Milk*. White defended himself with testimony on the impact of sugar on his behavior. The testimony

showed that when White was depressed, he departed from his normal, healthy diet and resorted to high-sugar junk food, including Twinkies, Coca-Cola, and chocolates. Thereafter, his behavior became less and less controllable. The jury found White guilty of manslaughter, rather than murder, due to diminished capacity. White served 5 years in prison and committed suicide after his release. His defense was promptly dubbed the "junk-food defense," "Dan White's defense," or the "Twinkie defense."

Most subsequent attempts to use the junk-food defense have failed. In a 1989 Ohio case, it was ruled that the defense may not be used to establish diminished capacity. In 1990, a Cape Cod man was unsuccessful when he defended himself on a charge of stealing (and eating) 300 candy bars. Nor did this defense (Twinkie and soda pop) succeed in a murder case in Ohio. But in a 1987 Florida case, a defendant was acquitted of drunk-driving charges on evidence that consumption of chocolate mousse after half a glass of sherry caused an unusual blood-sugar reaction.

Other researchers have looked for the causes of crime in vitamin deficiencies. One such study found that 70 percent of criminals charged with serious offenses in one Canadian jurisdiction had a greater-than-normal need for vitamin B_6.[41] Other studies have noted deficiencies of vitamins B_3 and B_6 in criminal population samples.

Some investigators have examined the effects of food additives and food dyes on behavior. Benjamin Feingold has argued that between 30 and 60 percent of all hyperactivity in children may be attributable to reactions to food coloring.[42] There is additional support for this hypothesis.[43] Some studies have suggested that a diet deficient in protein may be responsible for violent aggression.

Let us look at the association between the consumption of tryptophan, an amino acid (a protein building block), and crime rates. Tryptophan is a normal component of many foods. Low levels of it have been associated with aggression and, in criminal studies, an increased sensitivity to electric shock. Anthony R. Mawson and K. W. Jacobs reasoned that diets low in tryptophan would be likely to result in higher levels of violent crime, particularly violent offenses such as homicide.

They hypothesized that because corn-based diets are deficient in tryptophan, a cross-national comparison of countries should reveal a positive relationship between corn consumption and homicide rates. Mawson and Jacobs obtained homicide data from the United Nations and the mean per capita corn intake rates of 53 foreign countries from the U.S. Department of Agriculture. They discovered that countries whose per capita rates of corn consumption were above the median had significantly higher homicide rates than countries whose diets were based on wheat or rice.[44]

Hypoglycemia

What prompted an otherwise loving father to throw his 20-month-old daughter into a nearby lake? Neighbors knew that something was amiss when they noticed 22-year-old Joe Holt climb on the roof of his duplex in a quiet Orlando suburb. Joe then proceeded to dance, touching power lines in the course of his pantomime. No one sounded the alarm, however, until he disappeared into his lakeside apartment, returning momentarily with his daughter Ashley in his arms. The police arrived on the scene to find Joe in a state of agitation and Ashley facedown in Lake Apopka. Seated in the back of a squad car, handcuffed, the bewildered Joe had no recollection of the preceding events. When his blood was tested, he had a glucose level of 20 milligrams per deciliter of blood. The average is 80 to 120 milligrams. Joe was suffering from severe hypoglycemia. According to a sheriff's spokesman, "he had virtually no thought process."[45]

Hypoglycemia is a condition that occurs when the level of sugar in the blood falls below an acceptable range. The brain is particularly vulnerable to hypoglycemia, and such a condition can impair its function. Symptoms of hypoglycemia include anxiety, headache, confusion, fatigue, and even aggressive behavior. As early as 1943, researchers linked the condition with violent crime, including murder, rape, and assault. Subsequent studies found that violent and impulsive male offenders had a higher rate of hypoglycemia than noncriminal controls.

Consider the work of Matti Virkkunen, who has conducted a series of studies of habitually violent and psychopathic offenders in Finland. In one such study done in the 1980s, he examined the results of a glucose tolerance test (used to determine whether hypoglycemia is present) administered to 37 habitually violent offenders with antisocial personalities, 31 habitually violent offenders with intermittent explosive disorders, and 20 controls. The offenders were found to be significantly more hypoglycemic than the controls.[46]

Hormones

Experiments have shown that male animals typically are more aggressive than females. Male aggression is directly linked to male hormones. If an aggressive male mouse is injected with female hormones, he will stop fighting.[47] Likewise, the administration of male hormones to pregnant monkeys results in female offspring who, even 3 years after birth, are more aggressive than the daughters of non-injected mothers.[48]

While it would be misleading to equate male hormones with aggression and female hormones with nonaggression, there is some evidence that abnormal levels of male hormones in humans may prompt criminal behavior. Several investigators have found higher levels of testosterone (the male hormone) in the blood of individuals who have committed violent offenses.[49] Some studies also relate premenstrual syndrome (PMS) to delinquency and conclude that women are at greater risk of aggressive and suicidal behavior before and during the menstrual period. After studying 156 newly admitted adult female prisoners, Katharina Dalton concluded that 49 percent of all their crimes were committed either in the premenstrual period or during menstruation.[50] More recently, however, critics have challenged the association between menstrual distress and female crime.[51]

Neurocriminology

In England in the mid-1950s, a father hit his son with a mallet and then threw him out of a window, killing him instantly. Instead of pleading insanity, as many people expected him to do, he presented

Andrea Yates, convicted of drowning her children in a bathtub, was sentenced to life in prison in March 2002. Yates pleaded not guilty by reason of insanity—claiming postpartum psychosis and postpartum depression.

evidence of a brain tumor, which, he argued, resulted in uncontrollable rage and violence. A jury acquitted him on the grounds that the brain tumor had deprived him of any control over and knowledge of the act he was committing.[52] Brain lesions or brain tumors have led to violent outbursts in many similar cases. Neurocriminological studies, however, have not focused exclusively on brain tumors; they have included a wide range of investigations: studies of cerebral structure, brain wave studies, clinical reports of minimal brain dysfunction, and theoretical explorations into the relationship between the limbic system and criminality.[53]

Recent advances in brain imaging made accessible by functional magnetic resonance imaging (fMRI) and other imaging technologies (for example, positron emission tomography, or PET scan) offer dramatic new insights into the brains of criminals. With well over a hundred brain imaging studies, evidence is steadily emerging that the brain functioning of murderers, psychopaths, and aggressive criminals simply is different.

In combination with the previously mentioned twin and adoption studies, Adrian Raine and others make the case that there are prefrontal

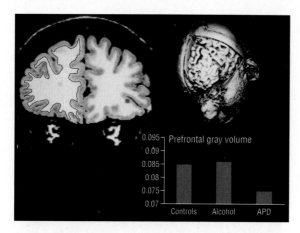

FIGURE 4.1 Differences in brain volume between alcoholic offenders and those with anti-personality disorder (APD).

Source: Adrian Raine, "Neurocriminology and Neuroethics: Brain Systems That Predispose to Violence, and Societal Implications" (lecture, National Taiwan University, Taiwan, October 12, 2007).

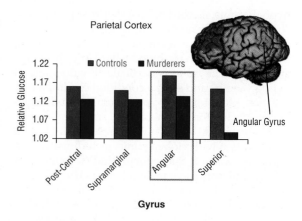

FIGURE 4.2 Differences in the volume of that part of the brain responsible for language and cognition between murderers and matched controls.

Source: A. Raine, M. S. Buchsbaum, and L. La Casse, "Brain Abnormalities in Murderers Indicated by Position Emission Tomography," *Biological Psychiatry,* **42** (1997): 495–508.

structural and functional deficits strongly associated with delinquency. They maintain that empirical research and neurological case studies confirm the importance of the prefrontal and frontal lobes in a person's ability to organize, execute, and inhibit prosocial behavior. Thus, disruptions of these lobes are associated with antisocial and aggressive behavior.

Even more significant, the neuroanatomy of the brains of criminals seems to differ in prefrontal cortex volume. Overall, criminals appear to have an 11 percent reduction in gray matter relative to matched controls. Research reveals differences in the anatomy of mass murderers versus murderers and matched controls;[54] affective versus predatory murderers and matched controls;[55] and alcoholics versus offenders with anti-personality disorder[56] (Figure 4.1).

Additional research focuses on specific parts of the brain of criminals, identifying differences in cranial volume that are consistent, given our knowledge of brain function, with behavioral research. For example, Raine and his colleagues found significant differences in the volume of the angular and superior gyrus in murderers, parts of the brain responsible for language and cognition[57] (Figure 4.2). Most recently, Raine and his colleagues report brain volume differences in self-reported offenders across a wide range of anatomies[58] (Figure 4.3).

The implications of these studies are dramatic and, at the same time, concerning. What should be done if violent offenders have the anatomical capacity to regulate behavior? Assuming that subsequent studies confirm and add to this line of research, what policy ramifications flow from it? In what ways can this research assist in crime prevention efforts? Can you anticipate ethical concerns that

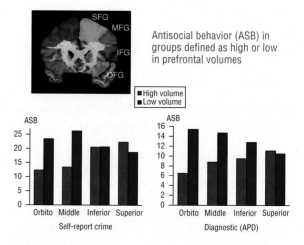

FIGURE 4.3 Differences in brain volume across a wide range of anatomies.

Source: A. Raine and Y. Yang, "The Neuroanatomical Bases of Psychopathy: A Review of Brain Imaging Findings," in *Handbook of Psychopathy,* ed. C. J. Patrick (New York: Guilford Press, 2006), pp. 278–295.

may be raised? What, if anything, does this research tell us about the importance of the work discussed in later chapters, which links concentrated poverty or the absence of social resources, for example, with the very same kind of behavior? As neurocriminological research continues, these questions remain largely unanswered.

In many ways, these are new questions. The neurophysiological factors criminologists once were exclusively concerned with—for example, EEG abnormalities and minimal brain dysfunction—raised fewer concerns.

EEG Abnormalities

Sam recalled that his wife, Janet, looked slightly different and that the house smelled funny, and he felt out of sorts. During an intimate moment in bed, Janet made a funny remark, after which Sam flew into a rage, choked her, and slashed her throat. When he came to his senses, he immediately went to the police and admitted to the crime, although he had little memory of his violent acts. Can EEG (electroencephalogram) tracings explain the behavior of this young U.S. Marine who had returned home on leave? Subsequent tracings were found to be abnormal—indicative of an "intermittent explosive disorder." After reviewing this evidence, the court reduced Sam's charges from first-degree murder to manslaughter.

The EEG is a tracing made by an instrument that measures cerebral functioning by recording brain wave activity with electrodes placed on the scalp. Numerous studies that have examined the brain activity of violent prisoners reveal significant differences between the EEGs of criminals and those of noncriminals. Other findings relate significantly slow brain wave activity to young offenders and adult murderers.[59] When Sarnoff A. Mednick and his colleagues examined the criminal records and EEGs of 265 children in a birth cohort in Denmark, they found that certain types of brain wave activity, as measured by the EEG, enabled investigators to predict whether convicted thieves would steal again.[60]

When Jan Volavka compared the EEGs of juvenile delinquents with those of comparable nondelinquents, he found a slowing of brain waves in the delinquent sample, most prominently in those children convicted of theft. He concluded that thievery "is more likely to develop in persons who have a slowing of alpha frequency than in persons who do not."[61]

Using positron emission tomography (PET) brain imaging, Adrian Raine, Monte Buchsbaum, and Lori LaCasse examined cortical and subcortical brain functioning in a matched sample of 41 murderers pleading not guilty by reason of insanity and 41 controls. Findings indicate that the murderers had abnormal brain functioning, including reduced glucose metabolism and abnormal asymmetries of activity.

Minimal Brain Dysfunction

Minimal brain dysfunction (MBD) is classified as "attention deficit hyperactivity disorder."[62] MBD produces asocial behavioral patterns such as impulsivity, hyperactivity, aggressiveness, low self-esteem, and temper outbursts. The syndrome is noteworthy for at least two reasons. First, MBD may explain criminality when social theories fail to do so—that is, when neighborhood, peer, and familial associations do not suggest a high risk of delinquency. Second, MBD is an easily overlooked

diagnosis. Parents, teachers, and clinicians tend to focus more on the symptoms of a child's psychopathology than on the possibility of brain dysfunction, even though investigators have repeatedly found high rates of brain dysfunction in samples of suicidal adolescents and youthful offenders.[63]

CRIME AND HUMAN NATURE

Criminologist Edward Sagarin has written:

> In criminology, it appears that a number of views . . . have become increasingly delicate and sensitive, as if all those who espouse them were inherently evil, or at least stupidly insensitive to the consequences of their research. . . . In the study of crime, the examples of unpopular orientations are many. Foremost is the link of crime to the factors of genes, biology, race, ethnicity, and religion.[64]

Criticisms of Biocriminology

What is it about linking biology and criminality that makes the subject delicate and sensitive? Why is the concept so offensive to so many people? One reason is that biocriminologists often deny the existence of individual free will. The idea of predisposition to commit crimes fosters a sense of hopelessness. But this criticism seems to have little merit. As Diana H. Fishbein has aptly noted, the idea of a "conditioned free will" is frequently advocated.[65] This view suggests that individuals make choices in regard to a particular action within a range of possibilities that is "preset" yet flexible. When conditions permit rational thought, one is fully accountable and responsible for one's actions. It is only when conditions are somehow disturbed that free choice is constricted. The child of middle-class parents who has a low IQ might avoid delinquent behavior. But if that child's circumstances changed so that he lived in a lower-class, single-parent environment, he might find the delinquent lifestyle of the children in the new neighborhood too tempting to resist.

Critics have other concerns as well. Some see a racist undertone to biocriminological research. If there is a genetic predisposition to commit crime and if minorities account for a disproportionate share of criminal activity, are minorities then predisposed to commit crime? In Chapter 2, we learned that self-reports reveal that most people have engaged in delinquent or criminal behavior. How, then, do biocriminologists justify their claim that certain groups are more prone than others to criminal behavior? Could it be that the subjects of their investigations are only criminals who have been caught and incarcerated? And is the attention of the police disproportionately drawn to members of minority groups?

Brain Overclaim Syndrome

The field of neurocriminology is both new and exciting. It encourages significant speculation about connections between the brain and misbehavior. Increasingly, thoughtful commentators, from ethicists to legal scholars, ask that we receive neuroscientific research carefully, especially when we use such evidence to address questions about culpable, blameworthy behavior.

Over the years, Stephen J. Morse has urged caution in overstating and/or misstating the place of "scientific" evidence in excusing criminal behavior committed by those who have the general capacity for rationality. He now urges caution in receiving neurocriminological evidence. In "Brain Overclaim Syndrome," Morse reflects on the efforts of attorneys representing a death row inmate, Christopher Simmons, to consider neurological evidence. Simmons was 17 years old and a junior in high school when he brutally killed Shirley Crook. The U.S. Supreme Court granted certiorari to determine whether the imposition of the death penalty on a juvenile is cruel and unusual punishment and therefore barred by the Eighth and Fourteenth Amendments.

In Morse's own words:

Brains do not commit crimes; people commit crimes. This conclusion should be self-evident, but, infected and inflamed by stunning advances in our understanding of the brain, advocates all too often make moral and legal claims that the new neuroscience does not entail and cannot sustain. Particular brain findings are thought to lead inevitably to moral or legal conclusions. Brains are blamed for offenses; agency and responsibility disappear from the legal landscape. For example, in Roper v. Simmons, advocates for abolition of the death penalty for adolescents who committed murder when they were sixteen or seventeen years old argued that the demonstrated lack of

complete myelination of the cortical neurons of the adolescent brain was reason to believe that sixteen and seventeen year old murderers were insufficiently responsible to deserve capital punishment. These types of responses, I claim, are the signs of a disorder that I have preliminarily entitled Brain Overclaim Syndrome [BOS]. . . .

The criteria for responsibility are behavioral and normative, not empirically demonstrable states of the brain. Even if there were a perfect correlation between brain states and the behavioral criteria for responsibility, the brain states would be nothing more than evidence of the behavioral states. Such a correlation is a fantasy based on present knowledge and probably always will be when we are considering complex human actions. If the person meets the behavioral criteria for responsibility, the person should be held responsible, whatever the brain evidence may indicate, such as the presence of an abnormality. If the person does not meet the behavioral criteria, the person should be held not responsible, however normal the brain may look. Brains are not held responsible. Acting people are. To believe that brain evidence has more than simple evidentiary value for assessing responsibility is to misconceive the criteria for responsibility. . . .

What was striking and new about the argument in Roper, however, was that advocates of abolition used newly discovered neuroscientific evidence concerning the adolescent brain to bolster their argument that sixteen and seventeen year old killers do not deserve to die. Editorial pages encouraged the High Court to consider the neuroscientific evidence to help it reach its decision. Although neuroscience evidence had been adduced in earlier, high profile cases, such as the 1982 prosecution of John Hinckley, Jr., for the attempted assassination of President Reagan and others, Roper

has been the most important case to propose use of the new neuroscience to affect responsibility questions generally. Indeed, the American Medical Association, the American Bar Association, the American Psychiatric Association, and the American Psychological Association, among others, all filed or subscribed to amicus briefs urging abolition based in part on the neuroscience findings. The real question was whether and how the new neuroscience was relevant to responsibility ascriptions and just punishment for adolescent offenders (or anyone else).

Here is the opening of the summary of the amicus brief filed by, inter alia, the American Medical Association, the American Psychiatric Association, the American Academy of Child and Adolescent Psychiatry, and the American Academy of Psychiatry and the Law: "The adolescent's mind works differently from ours. Parents know it. This Court [the United States Supreme Court] has said it. Legislatures have presumed it for decades or more."

Precisely. The brief points to evidence concerning impulsivity, poor short term risk and long term benefit estimations, emotional volatility, and susceptibility to stress among adolescents compared to adults. These are common sense, "fireside" conclusions that parents and others have drawn in one form or another since time immemorial. In recent years, common sense has been bolstered by methodologically rigorous behavioral investigations that have confirmed ordinary wisdom. Most important, all these behavioral characteristics are clearly relevant to responsibility because they all bear on the adolescent's capacity for rationality. Without any further scientific evidence, advocates of abolition would have an entirely ample factual basis to support the types of moral and constitutional claims they made.

The Roper briefs were filled with discussion of new neuroscientific evidence that confirms that adolescent brains are different from adult brains in ways consistent with the observed behavioral differences that alone bear on culpability and responsibility. Assuming the validity of the neuroscientific evidence, what does it add? The rigorous behavioral studies already confirm the behavioral differences. No one thinks that these data are invalid because adolescent subjects are faking or for some other reason. The moral and constitutional implications of the data may be controversial, but the data are not. At most, the neuroscientific evidence provides a partial causal explanation of why the observed behavioral differences exist and thus some further evidence of the validity of the behavioral differences. It is only of limited and indirect relevance to responsibility assessment, which is based on behavioral criteria.

Advocates claimed, however, that the neuroscience confirmed that adolescents are insufficiently responsible to be executed, thus confusing the positive and the normative. The neuroscience evidence in no way independently confirms that adolescents are less responsible. If the behavioral differences between adolescents and adults were slight, it would not matter if their brains are quite different. Similarly, if the behavioral differences were sufficient for moral and constitutional differential treatment, then it would not matter if the brains were essentially indistinguishable.

Decisions regarding whether the mean differences are large enough and whether the overlap between the two populations is small enough to warrant treating adolescents differently categorically as a class rather than trying to individuate responsibility are normative, moral, political, social, and ultimately legal constitutional questions about which behavioral and neuroscience must finally fall silent. Even if there were virtually no behavioral or brain overlaps between, say, sixteen and seventeen year olds on the one hand and eighteen and nineteen year olds on the other, it

would still not entail that we must categorize rather than individuate. After all, because there is overlap—indeed, substantial overlap in the groups just mentioned—we know that some sixteen and seventeen years olds will be behaviorally and neurologically indistinguishable from many eighteen and nineteen year olds. Finally, even if there were no behavioral or brain overlap whatsoever, it would still not entail that abolition was constitutionally mandated. As a normative matter, the Court could decide that sixteen and seventeen year olds are responsible enough to be executed despite all of them being less responsible than older murderers. Assuming the validity of the findings of behavioral and biological difference, the size of that difference entails no necessary moral or constitutional conclusions.

In the event, the Roper majority cited many reasons for its decision, including the abundant common sense and behavioral science evidence that adolescents differ from adults. This evidence demonstrates, said the Court, "that juvenile offenders cannot with reliability be classified among the worst offenders," for whom capital punishment is reserved. The Court cited three differences: adolescents have "[a] lack of maturity and an underdeveloped sense of responsibility;" adolescents are more "vulnerable or susceptible to negative influences and outside pressures, including peer pressure," a difference in part explained by the adolescent's weaker control or experience of control over his or her own environment; adolescents do not have fully formed characters. As a result of these factors—all of which, we may note, are behavioral and all of which can be confirmed with behavioral evidence alone—juvenile culpability is diminished and the penological justifications for capital punishment apply to adolescents with "lesser force." The Court's opinion thus reflects two conclusions: the group difference between the rationality of late adolescents and of adults is constitutionally significant

for Eighth Amendment purposes and it is large enough to justify abandoning individualized decision-making concerning responsibility for the former.

Characteristically, the Court did not cite much evidence for the empirical propositions that supported its diminished culpability argument. What is notable, however, is that the Court did not cite any of the neuroscience evidence concerning myelination and pruning that the amici and others had urged them to rely on. It did cite six behavioral sources, five of which were high quality behavioral science. Perhaps the neuroscience evidence actually played a role in the decision, as many advocates for the use of neuroscience would like to believe, but there is no evidence in the opinion to support this speculation.

As this note has argued, the behavioral science was crucial to proper resolution of the case and furnished completely adequate resources to decide the issue. The neuroscience was largely irrelevant. The reasoning of the case is consistent with this argument and the opinion showed no signs of Brain Overclaim Syndrome. In my view, Roper properly disregarded the neuroscience evidence and thus did not provide unwarranted legitimation for the use of such evidence to decide culpability questions generally.

Source

Stephen J. Morse, "Brain Overclaim Syndrome and Criminal Responsibility: A Diagnostic Note," *Ohio State Journal of Criminal Law*, 3(2006): 397, 405, 408–410. Reprinted by permission of the author.

Questions for Discussion

1. How should neurocriminological evidence be used in courts, if at all?
2. Is Morse right in dismissing the normative value of brain-behavior associations?
3. What are the central ethical questions raised by neuocriminological research?

How do biocriminologists account for the fact that most criminologists see the structure of our society, the decay of our neighborhoods, and the subcultures of certain areas as determinants of criminality? Are biocriminologists unfairly deemphasizing social and economic factors? (In Chapters 5 through 9, we review theories that attribute criminality to group and environmental forces.)

These issues raise a further question that is at the core of all social and behavioral science: Is human behavior the product of nature (genetics) or nurture (environment)? The consensus among social and behavioral scientists today is that the interaction of nature and nurture is so pervasive that the two should not be viewed in isolation without appropriate caveats.

Supporters of biocriminology also maintain that recognizing a predisposition to crime is not inconsistent with considering environmental factors. In fact, some believe that predispositions are triggered by environmental factors. Even if we agree that some people are predisposed to commit crime, we know that the crime rate will be higher in areas that provide more triggers. In sum, while some people may be predisposed to certain kinds of behavior, most scientists agree that both psychological and environmental factors shape the final forms of those behaviors.

PSYCHOLOGY AND CRIMINALITY

Psychologists have considered a variety of possibilities to account for individual differences—defective conscience, emotional immaturity, inadequate childhood socialization, maternal deprivation, and poor moral development. They study how aggression is learned, which situations promote violent or delinquent reactions, how crime is related to personality factors, and how various mental disorders are associated with criminality.

Psychological Development

The **psychoanalytic theory** of criminality attributes delinquent and criminal behavior to at least three possible causes:

- A conscience so overbearing that it arouses feelings of guilt
- A conscience so weak that it cannot control the individual's impulses
- The need for immediate gratification

Consider the case of Richard. Richard was 6 when he committed his first delinquent act: He stole a comic book from the corner drugstore. Three months before the incident, his father, an alcoholic, had been killed in an automobile accident, and his mother, unable to care for the family, had abandoned the children.

For the next 10 years, the county welfare agency moved Richard in and out of foster homes. During this time, he actively pursued a life of crime, breaking into houses during daylight hours and stealing cars at night. By age 20, while serving a 10-year prison sentence for armed robbery, he had voluntarily entered psychoanalysis. After 2 years, Richard's analyst suggested three reasons for his criminality:

1. Being caught and punished for stealing made him feel less guilty about hating both his father for dying and thus abandoning him as well as his mother for deliberately abandoning him.

2. Stealing did not violate his moral and ethical principles.

3. Stealing resulted in immediate gratification and pleasure, both of which Richard had great difficulty resisting.

Sigmund Freud (1856–1939), the founder of psychoanalysis, suggested that an individual's psychological well-being is dependent on a healthy interaction among the id, ego, and superego—the three basic components of the human psyche. The **id** consists of powerful urges and drives for gratification and satisfaction. The **ego** is the executive of the personality, acting as a moderator between the superego and id. The **superego** acts as a moral code or conscience. Freud proposed that criminality may result from an overactive superego or conscience. In

■ "The first human who hurled an insult instead of a stone was the founder of civilization."

Sigmund Freud

treating patients, he noticed that those who were suffering from unbearable guilt committed crimes in order to be apprehended and punished.[66] Once they had been punished, their feelings of guilt were relieved. Richard's psychoanalyst suggested that Richard's anger over his father's death and his mother's abandonment created unconscious feelings of guilt, which he sought to relieve by committing a crime and being punished for it.

The psychoanalyst also offered an alternative explanation for Richard's persistent criminal activities: His conscience was perhaps not too strong, but too weak. The conscience, or superego, was so weak or defective that he was unable to control the impulses of the id. Because the superego is essentially an internalized parental image, developed when the child assumes the parents' attitudes and moral values, it follows that the absence of such an image may lead to an unrestrained id and thus to delinquency.[67]

Psychoanalytic theory suggests yet another explanation for Richard's behavior: an insatiable need for immediate reward and gratification. A defect in the character formation of delinquents drives them to satisfy their desires at once, regardless of the consequences.[68] This urge, which psychoanalysts attribute to the id, is so strong that relationships with people are important only so long as they help satisfy it. Most analysts view delinquents as children unable to give up their desires for instant pleasure.

The psychoanalytic approach is still one of the most prominent explanations for both normal and asocial functioning. Despite criticism,[69] three basic principles appeal to psychologists who study criminality:

1. The actions and behavior of an adult are understood in terms of childhood development.

2. Behavior and unconscious motives are intertwined, and their interaction must be unraveled if we are to understand criminality.

3. Criminality is essentially a representation of psychological conflict.

In spite of their appeal, psychoanalytic treatment techniques devised to address these principles have been controversial since their introduction by Freud and his disciples. The controversy has involved questions about improvement following treatment and, perhaps more important, the validity of the hypothetical conflicts the treatment presupposes.

Moral Development

Consider the following moral dilemma:

> In Europe, a woman is near death from a special kind of cancer. There is one drug that the doctors think might save her. It is a form of radium that a druggist in the same town has recently discovered. The drug is expensive to make, and the druggist is charging ten times that cost. He paid $200 for the radium and is charging $2,000 for a small dose of the drug. The sick woman's husband, Heinz, goes to everyone he knows to borrow the money, but he can get together only $1,000. He tells the druggist that his wife is dying and asks him to sell the drug more cheaply or to let him pay later. The druggist says, "No, I discovered the drug and I'm going to make money from it." Heinz is desperate and considers breaking into the man's store to steal the drug for his wife.[70]

This classic dilemma sets up complex moral issues. While you may know that it is wrong to steal, you may believe that this is a situation in which the law should be circumvented. Or is it always wrong to steal, no matter what the circumstances? Regardless of what you decide, the way you reach the decision about whether to steal reveals much about your moral development.

Psychologist Lawrence Kohlberg, who pioneered moral developmental theory, has found that moral reasoning develops in three phases.[71] In the first, the preconventional level, children's moral rules and moral values consist of dos and don'ts to avoid punishment. A desire to avoid punishment and a belief in the superior power of authorities are the two central reasons for doing what is right. According to the theory, until the ages of 9 to 11, children usually reason at this level. They think, in effect, "If I steal, what are my chances of getting caught and being punished?"

Adolescents typically reason at the conventional level. Here individuals believe in and have adopted the values and rules of society. Moreover, they seek to uphold these rules. They think, in effect, "It is illegal to steal and therefore I should not steal, under any circumstances." Finally, at the postconventional level, individuals examine customs and social rules according to their own sense of universal human rights, moral principles, and duties. They think, in effect, "One must live within the law, but certain universal ethical principles, such as respect for human rights and for the dignity of human life, supersede the written law when the two conflict." This level of moral reasoning is generally seen in adults after the age of 20 (Table 4.1).

According to Kohlberg and his colleagues, most delinquents and criminals reason at the preconventional level. Low moral development or preconventional reasoning alone, however, does not result in criminality. Other factors, such as the presence or the absence of significant social bonds, may play a part. Kohlberg has argued that basic moral principles and social norms are learned through social interaction and

TABLE 4.1 Kohlberg's Sequence of Moral Reasoning

Level	Stage	Sample Moral Reasoning	
		In Favor of Stealing	**Against Stealing**
Level 1: Preconventional morality. At this level, the concrete interests of the individual are considered in terms of rewards and punishments.	*Stage 1: Obedience and punishment orientation.* At this stage, people stick to rules in order to avoid punishment, and there is obedience for its own sake.	If you let your wife die, you will get in trouble. You'll be blamed for not spending the money to save her, and there'll be an investigation of you and the druggist for your wife's death.	You shouldn't steal the drug because you'll be caught and sent to jail if you do. If you do get away, your conscience will bother you, thinking how the police will catch up with you at any minute.
	Stage 2: Reward orientation. At this stage, rules are followed only for one's own benefit. Obedience occurs because of rewards that are received.	If you do happen to get caught, you could give the drug back and you wouldn't get much of a sentence. It wouldn't bother you much to serve a little jail term, if you have your wife when you get out.	You may not get much of a jail term if you steal the drug, but your wife will probably die before you get out, so it won't do much good. If your wife dies, you shouldn't blame yourself; it wasn't your fault she had cancer.
Level 2: Conventional morality. At this level, moral problems are approached by an individual as a member of society. People are interested in pleasing others by acting as good members of society.	*Stage 3: "Good boy" morality.* Individuals at this stage show an interest in maintaining the respect of others and doing what is expected of them.	No one will think you're bad if you steal the drug, but your family will think you're an inhuman husband if you don't. If you let your wife die, you'll never be able to look anybody in the face again.	It isn't just the druggist who will think you're a criminal; everyone else will too. After you steal it, you'll feel bad, thinking how you've brought dishonor on your family and yourself; you won't be able to face anyone again.
	Stage 4: Authority and social-order-maintaining morality. People at this stage conform to society's rules and consider that "right" is what society defines as right.	If you have any sense of honor, you won't let your wife die just because you're afraid to do the only thing that will save her. You'll always feel guilty that you caused her death if you don't do your duty to her.	You're desperate and you may not know you're doing wrong when you steal the drug. But you'll know you did wrong after you're sent to jail. You'll always feel guilty for your dishonesty and lawbreaking.
Level 3: Postconventional morality. People at this level use moral principles that are seen as broader than those of any particular society.	*Stage 5: Morality of contract, individual rights, and democratically accepted law.* People at this stage do what is right because of a sense of obligation to laws that are agreed upon within society. They perceive that laws can be modified as part of changes in an implicit social contract.	You'll lose other people's respect, not gain it, if you don't steal. If you let your wife die, it will be out of fear, not out of reasoning. So you'll just lose self-respect and probably the respect of others too.	You'll lose your standing and respect in the community and violate the law. You'll lose respect for yourself if you're carried away by emotion and forget the long-range point of view.
	Stage 6: Morality of individual principles and conscience. At this final stage, a person follows laws because they are based on universal ethical principles. Laws that violate the principles are disobeyed.	If you don't steal the drug, if you let your wife die, you'll always condemn yourself for it afterward. You won't be blamed and you'll have lived up to the outside rule of the law, but you won't have lived up to your own standards of conscience.	If you steal the drug, you won't be blamed by other people, but you'll condemn yourself because you won't have lived up to your own conscience and standards of honesty.

SOURCE: Adapted from Robert S. Feldman, *Understanding Psychology*, p. 378. Copyright © 1987 by The McGraw-Hill Companies, Inc. Reprinted by permission of The McGraw-Hill Companies, Inc.

role-playing. In essence, children learn how to be moral by reasoning with others who are at a higher level of moral development.[72]

Students of Kohlberg have looked at practical applications of his theory. Joseph Hickey, William Jennings, and their associates designed programs for Connecticut and Florida prisons and applied them in school systems throughout the United States. The "just-community intervention" approach involves a structured educational curriculum stressing democracy, fairness, and a sense of community. A series of evaluations of just-community programs has revealed significant improvement in moral development. A more recent review examines the impact of two other rehabilitation programs on recidivism. The first, Moral Reconation Therapy, aims to improve the moral reasoning of offenders, while the second, Reasoning and Rehabilitation, attempts to alter underlying criminal attitudes. Reviewers concluded that both programs reduce recidivism.[73]

Maternal Deprivation and Attachment Theory

In a well-known psychological experiment, infant monkeys were provided with the choice between two wire "monkeys." One, made of uncovered cage wire, dispensed milk. The other, made of cage wire covered with soft fabric, did not give milk. The infant monkeys in the experiment gravitated to the warm cloth monkey, which provided comfort and security even though it did not provide food. What does this have to do with criminality? Research has demonstrated that a phenomenon important to social development takes place shortly after the birth of any mammal: the construction of an emotional bond between the infant and its mother. The strength of this emotional bond, or **attachment,** will determine, or at least materially affect, a child's ability to form attachments in the future. In order to form a successful attachment, a child needs a warm, loving, and interactive caretaker.

Studies of Attachment

British psychiatrist John Bowlby has studied both the need for warmth and affection from birth onward and the consequences of not having it. He has proposed a theory of attachment with seven important features:

- *Specificity.* Attachments are selective, usually directed to one or more individuals in some order of preference.
- *Duration.* Attachments endure and persist, sometimes throughout the life cycle.
- *Engagement of emotion.* Some of the most intense emotions are associated with attachment relationships.

▩ *Experiments with young monkeys and surrogate mothers reveal the power of attachment in behavioral development. Here, a frightened baby rhesus monkey holds on to a terry-cloth mother.*

- *Ontogeny (course of development).* Children form an attachment to one primary figure in the first 9 months of life. That principal attachment figure is the person who supplies the most social interaction of a satisfying kind.
- *Learning.* Though learning plays a role in the development of attachment, Bowlby finds that attachments are the products not of rewards or reinforcements, but of basic social interaction.
- *Organization.* Attachment behavior follows cognitive development and interpersonal maturation from birth onward.
- *Biological function.* Attachment behavior has a biological function—survival. It is found in almost all species of mammals and in birds.[74]

Bowlby contends that a child needs to experience a warm, intimate, and continuous relationship with either a mother or a mother substitute in order to be securely attached. When a child is separated from the mother or is rejected by her, anxious attachment results. Anxious attachment affects the capacity to be affectionate and to develop intimate relationships with others. Habitual criminals, it is claimed, typically have an inability to form bonds of affection.[75]

Considerable research supports the relationship between anxious attachment and subsequent behavioral problems:

- In a study of 113 middle-class children observed at 1 year of age and again at 6 years, researchers noted a significant relationship between behavior at age 6 and attachment at age 1.[76]

- In a study of 40 children seen when they were 1 year old and again at 18 months, it was noted that anxiously attached children were less empathetic, independent, compliant, and confident than securely attached children.[77]

- Researchers have noted that the quality of one's attachment correlates significantly with asocial preschool behavior—being aggressive, leaving the group, and the like.[78]

Family Atmosphere and Delinquency

Criminologists also have examined the effects of the mother's absence, whether because of death, divorce, or abandonment. Does her absence cause delinquency? Empirical research is equivocal. Perhaps the most persuasive evidence comes from longitudinal research conducted by Joan McCord, who has investigated the relationship between family atmosphere (such as parental self-confidence, deviance, and affection) and delinquency.

In one study, she collected data on the childhood homes of 201 men and their subsequent court records in order to identify family-related variables that would predict criminal activity. Variables such as inadequate maternal affection and supervision, parental conflict, the mother's lack of self-confidence, and the father's deviance were significantly related to the commission of crimes against persons and/or property. The father's absence by itself was not correlated with criminal behavior. Heather Juby and David Farrington also provide support for the importance of maternal presence. Using data from the Cambridge Study in Delinquent Development, they examined the impact of family structure on juvenile and adult crime and found that delinquency rates are lower among boys who live with their mother postseparation compared to those who live with their father. They also found that delinquency rates are very similar in disrupted families and high-conflict intact families.[79]

Other studies, such as those by Sheldon and Eleanor Glueck and the more recent studies by Lee N. Robins, which were carried out in schools, juvenile courts, and psychiatric hospitals, suggest a moderate to strong relation between crime and childhood deprivation.[80] However, evidence that deprivation directly causes delinquency is lacking.[81]

So far we have considered psychological theories that attribute the causes of delinquency or criminality to unconscious problems and failures in moral development. Not all psychologists agree with these explanations of criminal behavior. Some argue that human behavior develops through learning. They say that we learn by observing others and by watching the responses to other people's behavior (on television or in the movies, for instance) and to our own. Social learning theorists reject the notion that internal functioning alone makes us prone to act aggressively or violently.

Learning Aggression and Violence

Social learning theory maintains that delinquent behavior is learned through the same psychological processes as any other behavior. Behavior is learned when it is reinforced or rewarded; it is not learned when it is not reinforced. We learn behavior in various ways: observation, direct experience, and differential reinforcement.

Observational Learning

Albert Bandura, a leading proponent of social learning theory, argues that individuals learn violence and aggression through **behavioral modeling:** Children learn how to behave by fashioning their behavior after that of others. Behavior is socially transmitted through examples, which come primarily from the family, the subculture, and the mass media.[82]

Psychologists have been studying the effects of family violence (Chapter 10) on children. They have found that parents who try to resolve family controversies by violence teach their children to use similar tactics. Thus, a cycle of violence may be perpetuated through generations. Observing a healthy and happy family environment tends to result in constructive and positive modeling.

To understand the influence of the social environment outside the home, social learning theorists have studied gangs, which often provide excellent models of observational learning of violence and aggression. They have found, in fact, that violence is very much a norm shared by some people in a community or gang. The highest incidence of aggressive behavior occurs where aggressiveness is a desired characteristic, as it is in some subcultures.

Observational learning takes place in front of the television set and at the movies as well. Children who have seen others being rewarded for violent acts often believe that violence and aggression are acceptable behaviors.[83] And today children can see a lot of violence. Psychologist Leonard Eron has argued that the "single best predictor of how aggressive a young man would be when he was 19 years old was the violence of

Crime Surfing

www.ncjrs.org

Maternal deprivation can be related to delinquent behavior. What happens to deprived (often abused and neglected) children? Is there a cycle of violence?

DID YOU KNOW?

... that, while evidence is lacking that deprivation directly causes delinquency, research on the impact of family-based crime prevention programs is promising? Programs that target family risk factors in multiple settings (ecological contexts) have achieved success (Table 4.2).

TABLE 4.2 Family-Based Crime Prevention by Ecological Context

Ecological Context	Program	Prevention Agent
Home	Regular visits for emotional, informational, instrumental, and educational support for parents of preschool (or older) children	Nurses, teachers, paraprofessionals, preschool teachers
	Foster care outplacement for the prevention of physical and sexual abuse or neglect	Family services, social workers
	Family preservation of families at risk of outplacement of child	Private family-preservation teams
	Personal alarm for victims of serious domestic violence	Police
	In-home proactive counseling for domestic violence	Police, social workers
Preschool	Involvement of mothers in parent groups, job training, parent training	Preschool teachers
School	Parent training	Psychologists, teachers
	Simultaneous parent and child training	Psychologists, child-care workers, social workers
Clinics	Family therapy	Psychologists, psychiatrists, social workers
	Medication—psychostimulants for treatment of hyperactivity and other childhood conduct disorders	Psychiatrists, psychologists, pediatricians
Hospitals	Domestic violence counseling	Nurses, social workers
	Low-birthweight baby mothers' counseling and support	Nurses, social workers
Courts	Prosecution of batterers	Police, prosecutors
	Warrants for unarrested batterers	Police, prosecutors
	Restraining orders or "stay away" order of protection	Police, prosecutors, judges, victims' advocates
	Hotline notification of victim about release of incarcerated domestic batterer	Probation, victim's advocates
Battered-women's shelters	Safe refuge during high-risk 2 to 7 days' aftermath of domestic assault; counseling; hotlines	Volunteers, staff

the television programs he preferred when he was 8 years old."[84]

Results from the 3-year landmark *National Television Violence Study* initiated in 1994 suggest that the problem is one not only of violence, but also of the portrayal of violence—the absence of consequences for violent acts and the glamorization of violence.[85]

More recently, the Parents Television Council examined TV violence on the six major broadcast networks (ABC, CBS, NBC, Fox, UPN, and the WB) during prime time. With reference to earlier surveys conducted during the 1998, 2000, and 2002 television seasons, PTC examined trends over the past 8 years. PTC captured more than 1,180 programming hours combined.

Over the course of 8 years (from 1998 to 2006):

- Violence increased in every time slot:
    During the 8:00 P.M. Family Hour by 45 percent
    During the 9:00 P.M. hour by 92 percent
    During the 10:00 P.M. hour by 167 percent

Who Is Responsible for the Crime of Parricide?

Mark Martone was 16 when he shot his father to death. [He] remembers abuse back to age five, when he told his dad he was scared of the dark. "Oh, Jesus Christ," said the parent in disgust. Then he led the terrified boy down to the cellar, handcuffed his arms over a rafter, turned off the light and shut the door. Mark dangled in silence for hours. When Mark was nine, his father held the boy's hand over a red-hot burner as punishment for moving a book of matches on a bureau. And when he was 15, his dad, angered by a long-distance phone bill, stuck a gun in his son's mouth and "told me he was going to blow my brains out."(1)

Sylvester Hobbs III, a 20-year-old, said to be depressed and withdrawn, stabbed and killed his stepfather and wounded his mother.(2)

Eleven-year-old identical twins were charged with murdering their father and attempting to kill their mother and 16-year-old sister in their house.(3)

James Brian Hill, 28, said he was defending his own life when he killed his father, who had previously assaulted his mother.(2)

Carlton Akee Turner Jr., 19, killed his parents because his father was said to be abusive.(2)

An estimated 5.7 million children in the United States are physically, mentally, and sexually abused by their parents annually, and the problem is not lessening. Of those millions of children, maybe a few hundred each year fight back with the ultimate weapon: They kill the abusive parent. In the past, such children were regarded as particularly evil, and the law reserved the most terrible forms of capital punishment for parricides. With the growing understanding of the horrors of child abuse, however, these youths are being treated with increasing sympathy. "They know what they're doing is wrong," comments a psychologist at the University of Virginia. "But they are desperate and helpless, and they don't see alternatives."(1)

The typical case involves a 16- to 18-year-old from a white middle-class family. Sons are more likely than daughters to commit murder, and the victim is more likely to be a father than a mother. While children who kill nonabusive parents usually display some sign of mental disorder, the killers of abusive parents generally are seen as well adjusted.(1)

The increasing sympathy for these teenagers has led to verdicts of not guilty by reason of self-defense or guilty of reduced charges (for example, manslaughter instead of first-degree murder). A battered-child-syndrome defense sometimes is successful, but the killings do not usually fit the typical idea of self-defense: Most happen when the parent is in a vulnerable position instead of in the middle of an attack on the child. But mental health experts think that treatment is more appropriate than punishment for children who kill their abusive parents. "These kids don't need to be locked up for our protection," says one attorney and psychologist. "Some may benefit in the sense that they've been able to atone and overcome some guilt. But beyond that, it's really Draconian."(1)

Even with an increased "sympathy" for battered and abused children, some think that the problem of child abuse needs to be reconceived. According to Jennifer M. Collins, "There is a striking contrast in this regard between the development of our approach to crimes committed against women versus crimes committed against children. Efforts to protect children from family violence

- ABC experienced the biggest increase in violent content overall. In 1998, ABC averaged 0.93 instance of violence per hour during prime time. By 2006, ABC was averaging 3.80 instances of violence per hour—an increase of 309 percent.

- Fox, the second-most-violent network in 1998, experienced the smallest increase. Fox averaged 3.43 instances of violence per hour in 1998 and 3.84 instances of violence per hour by 2006—an increase of only 12 percent.

- Violent scenes increasingly include a sexual element. Rapists, sexual predators, and fetishists are cropping up with increasing frequency on prime-time programs like *Law and Order: SVU, CSI, CSI: Miami, CSI: New York, Medium, Crossing Jordan, Prison Break, ER,* and *House.*

On an hour-by-hour basis:

- Every network experienced an increase in violence during the 9:00 P.M. and 10:00 P.M. hours between 1998 and the 2005–2006 television season.

- During the Family Hour, ABC experienced the biggest increase in violent content. In 1998, ABC was the least-violent network, averaging only 0.13 instance of violence per hour. By 2006, ABC was averaging 2.23 instances of violence per hour, an increase of 1,615.4 percent.

- UPN and Fox were the only networks to feature less violence during the Family Hour in 2005–2006 than in 1998: Violence decreased on Fox by 18 percent, and on UPN by 83 percent.

primarily have emphasized a therapeutic approach, while efforts to curb violence against women have been far more likely in recent years to emphasize a criminal approach."(5) Quite obviously, Collins is not arguing that less should be done to protect the rights of women.

Collins argues persuasively that we are all guilty of romanticizing the parent-child relationship to the point that we are unwilling to conceive of a role for the criminal law. "One of the most striking ways in which our romanticization of the parent-child relationship victimizes children," according to Collins, "is the treatment of sexual abuse committed against children by family members. We persist in viewing intrafamilial sexual abuse as less noteworthy and, indeed, as less blameworthy than sexual abuse perpetrated by strangers."(5)

CHARACTERISTICS ASSOCIATED WITH ADOLESCENT PARRICIDE OFFENDERS

1. Patterns of family violence exist (parental brutality and cruelty toward child and/or toward one another).
2. Adolescent's attempts to get help from others fail.
3. Adolescent's efforts to escape family situation fail (e.g., running away, thoughts of suicide, suicide attempts).

4. Adolescent is isolated from others/fewer outlets.
5. Family situation becomes increasingly intolerable.
6. Adolescent feels increasingly helpless, trapped.
7. Adolescent's inability to cope leads to loss of control.
8. Prior criminal behavior is minimal or nonexistent.
9. Gun is available.
10. Homicide victim is alcoholic.
11. Evidence to suggest dissociative state in some cases.
12. Victim's death perceived as relief to offender/family; initial absence of remorse.(4)

Sources

1. Hannah Bloch and Jeanne McDowell, "When Kids Kill Abusive Parents," *Time*, Nov. 23, 1992, p. 60.
2. Nancy Calaway, "Spotlight Intensifies on Children Who Murder Parents; Recent Focus on Crime Doesn't Mean It's Increasing, Analyst Says," *Dallas Morning News*, Aug. 30, 1999, p. 1A.
3. Anne Saker, "Twin Boys Face Trial in Father's Killing" (Raleigh, N.C.), *News and Observer*, Aug. 1, 1999, p. A1.
4. Kathleen M. Heide, *Why Kids Kill Parents* (Columbus: Ohio State University Press, 1992), pp. 40–41, Table 3.1.

5. Jennifer M. Collins, "Lady Madonna, Children at Your Feet: The Criminal Justice System's Romanticization of the Parent-Child Relationship," *Iowa Law Review*, **93**(2007): 131, 132, 134.

Questions for Discussion

1. If you were on a jury, would you be willing to consider that what appears to be cold-blooded murder might have been a form of self-defense for a battered child?
2. An attorney specializing in parricide feels that such cases "open a window on our understanding of child abuse." How would you go about determining which of millions of child abuse cases are likely to lead to parricide for which a standard defense should be recognized?

- During the 9:00 P.M. hour, ABC experienced the biggest increase in violent content, jumping from 0.31 instance per hour in 1998 to 5.71 instances per hour during the 2005–2006 season—an increase of 1,742 percent.

- During the 10:00 P.M. hour, NBC experienced the biggest increase in violent content—635 percent—from 2 instances of violence per hour in 1998 to nearly 15 instances of violence per hour in 2005–2006.[86]

Direct Experience

What we learn by observation is determined by the behavior of others. What we learn from direct experience is determined by what we ourselves do and what happens to us. We remember the past and use its lessons to avoid future mistakes. Thus, we learn through trial and error. According to social learning theorists, after engaging in a given behavior, most of us examine the responses to our actions and modify our behavior as necessary to obtain favorable responses. If we are praised or rewarded for a behavior, we are likely to repeat it. If we are subjected to verbal or physical punishment, we are likely to refrain from such behavior. Our behavior in the first instance and our restraint in the second are said to be "reinforced" by the rewards and punishments we receive.

Psychologist Gerald Patterson and his colleagues examined how aggression is learned by direct experience. They observed that some passive children at play were repeatedly victimized by other children but were occasionally successful in curbing the attacks by counteraggression. Over time, these children learned defensive fighting, and eventually

China Launches Campaign to Crack Down on Web Porn

The Ministry of Public Security (MPS), along with nine other government departments, announced the launching of a campaign yesterday to restrict the spread of pornography on the Internet in China.

"The boom of pornographic content on the Internet has contaminated cyberspace and perverted China's young minds," said Zhang Xinfeng, vice minister of MPS.

In the next six months, Zhang said, the ministries will crack down on illegal on-line activities such as distributing pornographic materials and organizing cyber strip shows, and purge the web of sexually-explicit images, stories, and audio and video clips.

The campaign will also target on illegal on-line lotteries and contraband trade, fraud, and "content that spreads rumors and is of a slanderous nature," said Zhang.

In Nov. 2006, Chinese police cracked the largest pornographic website in the country and arrested the creator Chen Hui, who was later sentenced to life imprisonment.

The website Chen started contained more than nine million pornographic images and articles and it had attracted more than 600,000 registered users.

"The inflow of pornographic materials from abroad and lax domestic control are to blame for the existing problems in China's cyberspace," Zhang said.

China has roughly 123 million Internet users, most of whom are young people. The Chinese government believes they need to be protected from negative on-line influences.

A report by the Beijing Reformatory for Juvenile Delinquents said 33.5 percent of its detainees were influenced by violent on-line games or erotic websites when they committed crimes such as robbery and rape.

Questions for Discussion

1. How successful will China be in restricting or limiting Web content?
2. Is China's attempt to restrict or limit Web content justifiable? How does it differ, if at all, from such attempts in the United States?

SOURCE: Xinhua, "China Launches Campaign to Crack Down on Web Porn," April 13, 2007. http://news.xinhuanet.com/english/2007-04/12/content_5968968.htm.

---

they initiated fights. Other passive children, who were rarely observed to be victimized, remained submissive.[87] Thus, children, like adults, can learn to be aggressive and even violent by trial and error.

While violence and aggression are learned behaviors, they are not necessarily expressed until they are elicited in one of several ways. Albert Bandura describes the factors that elicit behavioral responses as "instigators." Thus, social learning theory describes not only how aggression is acquired but also how it is instigated. Consider the following instigators of aggression:

- *Aversive instigators.* Physical assaults, verbal threats, and insults; adverse reductions in conditions of life (such as impoverishment) and the thwarting of goal-directed behavior

- *Incentive instigators.* Rewards, such as money and praise

- *Modeling instigators.* Violent or aggressive behaviors observed in others

- *Instructional instigators.* Observations of people carrying out instructions to engage in violence or aggression

- *Delusional instigators.* Unfounded or bizarre beliefs that violence is necessary or justified[88]

Differential Reinforcement

In 1965, criminologist C. Ray Jeffery suggested that learning theory could be used to explain criminality.[89] Within one year, Ernest Burgess and Ronald Akers combined Bandura's psychologically based learning theory with Edwin Sutherland's sociologically based differential association theory (Chapter 5) to produce the theory of **differential association-reinforcement.** This theory suggests that (1) the persistence of criminal behavior depends on whether or not it is rewarded or punished and (2) the most meaningful rewards and punishments are those given by groups that are important in an individual's life—the peer group, the family, teachers in school, and so forth. In other words, people respond more readily to the reactions of the most significant people in their lives. If criminal behavior elicits more positive reinforcement or rewards than punishment, such behavior will persist.[90]

Social learning theory helps us understand why some individuals who engage in violent and aggressive behavior do so: They learn to behave that way. But perhaps something within the personality of a criminal creates a susceptibility to aggressive or violent models in the first place. For example, perhaps criminals are more extroverted, irresponsible, or unsocialized than noncriminals. Or perhaps criminals are more intolerant and impulsive or have lower self-esteem.

■ Thomas Junta, a 6-foot, 270-pound truck driver, demonstrates how he shook the coach of his son's hockey team, Michael Costin, after practice. A resulting fight led to Costin's death. Junta was convicted of involuntary manslaughter on January 25, 2002, and sentenced to 6 to 10 years in prison.

Personality

Four distinct lines of psychological research have examined the relationship between personality and criminality.[91] First, investigators have looked at the differences between the personality structures of criminals and noncriminals. Most of this work has been carried out in state and federal prisons, where psychologists have administered personality questionnaires such as the Minnesota Multiphasic Personality Inventory (MMPI) and the California Psychological Inventory (CPI) to inmates. The evidence from these studies shows that inmates typically are more impulsive, hostile, self-centered, and immature than noncriminals.[92]

Second, a vast amount of literature is devoted to the prediction of behavior. Criminologists want to determine how an individual will respond to prison discipline and whether he or she will avoid crime after release. The results are equivocal. At best, personality characteristics seem to be modest predictors of future criminality.[93] Yet when they are combined with variables such as personal history, they tend to increase the power of prediction significantly.[94]

Third, many studies examine the degree to which normal personality dynamics operate in criminals. Findings from these studies suggest that the personality dynamics of criminals are often quite similar to those of noncriminals. Social criminals (those who act in concert with others), for example, are found to be more sociable, affiliative, outgoing, and self-confident than solitary criminals.[95]

Finally, some researchers have attempted to quantify individual differences between types and groups of offenders. Several studies have compared the personality characteristics of first-time offenders with those of repeat or habitual criminals. Other investigators have compared violent offenders with nonviolent offenders, and murderers with drug offenders. In addition, prison inmates have been classified according to personality type.[96]

In general, research on criminals' personality characteristics has revealed some important associations. However, criminologists have been skeptical of the strength of the relationship of personality to criminality. A review of research on that relationship published in 1942 by Milton Metfessel and Constance Lovell dismissed personality as an important causal factor in criminal behavior.[97] In 1950, Karl Schuessler and Donald Cressey reached the same conclusion.[98] Twenty-seven years later, Daniel Tennenbaum's updated review agreed with earlier assessments. He found that "the data do not reveal any significant differences between criminal and noncriminal psychology. . . . Personality testing has not differentiated criminals from noncriminals."[99]

Despite these conclusions, whether or not criminals share personality characteristics continues to be debated. Are criminals in fact more aggressive, dominant, and manipulative than noncriminals? Are they more irresponsible? Clearly, many criminals are aggressive; many have manipulated a variety of situations; many assume no responsibility for their acts. But are such characteristics common to all criminals? Samuel Yochelson and Stanton Samenow addressed these questions. In *The Criminal Personality*, this psychiatrist-psychologist team described their growing disillusion with traditional explanations of criminality.

From their experience in treating criminals in the Forensic Division of St. Elizabeth's Hospital in Washington, D.C., they refuted psychoanalysts' claims that crime is caused by inner conflict. Rather, they said, criminals share abnormal thinking patterns that lead to decisions to commit crimes. Yochelson and Samenow identified as many as 52 patterns of thinking common to the criminals they studied. They argued that criminals

■ *With 15,577 fans watching, rookie Joe Thornton took on the 6-foot-2-inch, 217-pound Canucks forward Dave Scatchard, who had just run him into the boards near the penalty box after some words were exchanged. What was the reaction of the fans? Violent fights are the highlight of hockey games. Fans, young and old, cheered Thornton for standing up to Scatchard.*

are angry people who feel a sense of superiority, expect not to be held accountable for their acts, and have a highly inflated self-image. Any perceived attack on their glorified self-image elicits a strong reaction, often a violent one.[100]

Other researchers have used different methods to study the association between criminality and personality. For example, criminologists have reviewed the findings of a large sample of studies that use the California Psychological Inventory. Their research has revealed a common personality profile: the criminals tested showed remarkable similarity in their deficient self-control, intolerance, and lack of responsibility.[101]

Though studies dealing with personality correlates of criminals are important, some psychologists are concerned that by focusing on the personalities of criminals in their search for explanations of criminal behavior, investigators may overlook other important factors, such as the complex social environment in which a crime is committed.[102] A homicide that began as a barroom argument between two intoxicated patrons who backed different teams to win the Super Bowl, for example, is very likely to hinge on situational factors that interact with the participants' personalities.

Eysenck's Conditioning Theory

For over 30 years, Hans J. Eysenck has been developing and refining a theory of the relationship between personality and criminality that considers more than just individual characteristics.[103] His theory has two parts. First, Eysenck claims that all human personality may be seen in three dimensions—psychoticism, extroversion, and neuroticism. Individuals who score high on measures of **psychoticism** are aggressive, egocentric, and impulsive. Those who score

high on measures of **extroversion** are sensation-seeking, dominant, and assertive. High scorers on scales assessing **neuroticism** may be described as having low self-esteem, excessive anxiety, and wide mood swings. Eysenck has found that when criminals respond to items on the Eysenck Personality Questionnaire (EPQ), they uniformly score higher on each of these dimensions than do noncriminals.

The second part of Eysenck's theory suggests that humans develop a conscience through **conditioning.** From birth, we are rewarded for social behavior and punished for asocial behavior. Eysenck likens this conditioning to training a dog. Puppies are not born house trained. You have to teach a puppy that it is good to urinate and defecate outside your apartment or house by pairing kind words and perhaps some tangible reward (such as a dog treat) with successful outings. A loud, angry voice will convey disapproval and disappointment when mistakes are made inside.

In time, most dogs learn and, according to Eysenck, develop a conscience. But as Eysenck also has noted, some dogs learn faster than others. German shepherds acquire good "bathroom habits" faster than basenjis, who are most difficult to train. It is argued that the same is true of humans; there are important individual differences. Criminals become conditioned slowly and appear to care little whether their asocial actions bring disapproval.

Eysenck has identified two additional aspects of a criminal's poor conditionability. First, he has found that extroverts are much more difficult to condition than introverts and thus have greater difficulty in developing a conscience. Youthful offenders tend to score highest on measures of extroversion. Second, differences in conditionability are dependent on certain physiological

Crime Surfing WWW

http://www.trutv .com/library/crime/ criminal_mind/ psychology/ insanity/1.html

Are you interested in the insanity defense? Go to Court TV's Crime Library site to read all about it.

factors, the most important of which is **cortical arousal,** or activation of the cerebral cortex.

The cortex of the brain is responsible for higher intellectual functioning, information processing, and decision making. Eysenck found that individuals who are easily conditionable and develop a conscience have a high level of cortical arousal; they do not need intense external stimulation to become aroused. A low level of cortical arousal is associated with poor conditionability, difficulty in developing a conscience, and need for external stimulation.

MENTAL DISORDERS AND CRIME

It has been difficult for psychiatrists to derive criteria that would help them decide which offenders are mentally ill. According to psychiatrist Seymour L. Halleck, the problem lies in the evolving conceptualization of mental illness. Traditionally, the medical profession viewed mental illness as an absolute condition or status—either you are afflicted with **psychosis** or you are not. Should such a view concern us? Halleck suggests that it should. "Although this kind of thinking is not compatible with current psychiatric knowledge," he writes, "it continues to exert considerable influence upon psychiatric practice. . . . As applied to the criminal, it also leads to rigid dichotomies between the 'sick criminal' and the 'normal criminal.'"[104]

Halleck and other psychiatrists, such as Karl Menninger, conceptualize mental functioning as a process.[105] Mental illness should not be considered apart from mental health—the two exist on the same continuum. At various times in each of our lives, we move along the continuum from health toward illness.[106] For this reason, a diagnosis of "criminal" or "mentally ill" may overlook potentially important gradations in mental health and mental illness. This issue is perhaps no more apparent than in the insanity defense, which calls for proof of sanity or insanity and generally does not allow for gradations in mental functioning (see Chapter 2).

Estimates vary, but between 20 and 60 percent of state correctional populations suffer from a type of mental disorder that in the nineteenth century was described by the French physician Philippe Pinel as *manie sans délire* ("madness without confusion"), by the English physician James C. Prichard as "moral insanity," and by Gina Lombroso Ferrero as "irresistible atavistic impulses." Today such mental illness is called **psychopathy,** sociopathy, or antisocial personality—a personality characterized by the inability to learn from experience, lack of warmth, and absence of guilt.

Psychiatrist Hervey Cleckley views psychopathy as a serious illness even though patients may not appear to be ill. According to Cleckley, psychopaths appear to enjoy excellent mental health, but what we see is only a "mask of sanity." Initially, they seem free of any kind of mental disorder and appear to be reliable and honest. After some time, however, it becomes clear that they have no sense of responsibility whatsoever. They show a disregard for truth; are insincere; and feel no sense of shame, guilt, or humiliation. Psychopaths lie and cheat without hesitation and engage in verbal as well as physical abuse without any thought. Cleckley describes the following case:

> A sixteen-year-old boy was sent to jail for stealing a valuable watch. Though apparently . . . untouched by his situation, after a few questions were asked he began to seem more like a child who feels the unpleasantness of his position. He confessed that he had worried much about masturbation, saying he had been threatened and punished severely for it and told that it would cause him to become "insane."
>
> He admitted having broken into his mother's jewelry box and stolen a watch valued at $150.00. He calmly related that he exchanged the watch for 15 cents' worth of ice cream and seemed entirely satisfied with what he had done. He readily admitted that his act was wrong, used the proper words to express his intention to cause no further trouble, and, when asked, said that he would like very much to get out of jail.
>
> He stated that he loved his mother devotedly. "I just kiss her and kiss her ten or twelve times when she comes to see me!" he exclaimed with shallow zeal. These manifestations of affection were so artificial, and, one would even say, unconsciously artificial, that few laymen would be convinced that any feeling, in the ordinary sense, lay in them. Nor was his mother convinced.
>
> A few weeks before this boy was sent to jail he displayed to his mother some rifle cartridges. When asked what he wanted with them he explained that they would fit the rifle in a nearby closet. "I've tried them," he announced. And in a lively tone added, "Why, I could put them in the gun and shoot you. You would fall right over!" He laughed and his eyes shone with a small but real impulse.[107]

Psychologists also have found that psychopaths, like Hans Eysenck's extroverts, have a low internal arousal level; thus, psychopaths constantly seek external stimulation, are less susceptible to learning by direct experience (they do not modify their behavior after they are punished), are more impulsive, and experience far less anxiety than nonpsychopaths about any adverse consequences of their acts.[108] Some psychiatrists consider "psychopathy" to be an artificial label for an antisocial personality.[109] To Eysenck and others, it is a major behavioral category that presents significant challenges. Eysenck sums up this view by writing that the psychopath poses the riddle of delinquency. If we could solve the riddle, then we would have a powerful weapon to fight the problem of delinquency.[110]

TABLE 4.3 Defenses Sometimes Attempted by Defense Lawyers

Defense	Description of Defense
The Twinkie defense (hypoglycemia)	Because he lost his job as a San Francisco supervisor, Dan White gorged on junk food—Twinkies, Coca-Cola, candy. Depressed, he sneaked a gun into city hall. After killing Mayor Moscone, he killed a leader of the gay community, Supervisor Milk, in 1978.
Defendants or victims with multiple personalities	Many psychiatric experts agree that the disorder exists but disagree on how common it is. If a woman with multiple personalities complains of rape, the defendant might argue that consent to sex was given by one of the personalities. A defendant with multiple personalities might argue that he or she could not control the bad personality.
Sleepwalking and other forms of automatism (unconsciousness)	Automatism is a state in which a person is capable of action but is not conscious of what he or she is doing. This defense is statutorized in some states, including California, and held to be an affirmative defense separate from the insanity defense. *Fulcher v. State*, 633 P.2d 142, 29 CrL 2556 (Wyo. 1981).
Cultural disorientation	Some immigrants to the United States bring with them cultural practices that are in conflict with our criminal codes. For example, some continue the ancient traditions of the medicinal use of opium, the practice of capturing young brides, and the ritual slaughtering of animals. In 1985, when a young Japanese mother of two children learned that her husband was having an affair with another woman, she walked into the Pacific Ocean with her children to commit suicide (*oy ako shinju*). She was saved but the children drowned.
Premenstrual syndrome (PMS) and tension	PMS, a form of emotional and physical stress, afflicts some women before their monthly periods. In certain cases, such stress is so severe that it seriously disrupts the women's lives. In 1982, a British Appeal Court held that PMS could not be used as a defense to a criminal charge but could be used in mitigation to lessen sentences.
Television intoxication	In the 1978 case of *Zamora v. State*, 361 So.2d 776 (Fla. 1978), the defendant was convicted after arguing temporary insanity from "involuntary subliminal television intoxication."
XYY chromosome defense	Everyone has chromosomes. Some have either too few or too many, causing abnormalities. Some scientists believe that the abnormality of the supermale, or XYY in males, can cause such men to exhibit antisocial or criminal conduct. The XYY syndrome is not recognized as a defense unless the requirements of the insanity test of the state are met.

SOURCE: Adapted from Thomas J. Gardner and Terry M. Anderson, *Criminal Law*, 7th ed., pp. 100–101. © 2000 Wadsworth, a part of Cengage Learning, Inc. Reproduced by permission. www.cengage.com/permissions.

Psychological Causation

With all this discussion of possible psychological correlates of criminal behavior, it is easy to make what Stephen Morse calls the **fundamental psycholegal error**. This error in thinking or mistaken belief occurs when we identify a cause for criminal behavior and then assume that it naturally follows that any behavior resulting from that "cause" must be excused by law. Think about the kinds of defenses to criminal charges raised by lawyers and ask yourself whether Professor Morse is correct (Table 4.3).

Consider, for example, the likelihood of psycholegal error in cases where lawyers have raised an insanity defense. Park Dietz, a highly regarded forensic psychiatrist, was interviewed recently and revealed just how easy it is to confuse the cause of criminal behavior with an appropriate and legally justifiable defense.

Interviewer: . . . Many defense attorneys argue that sick deeds are born in sick minds, and you have difficulty with that.

PD [Park Dietz]: With rare exceptions, people are responsible for what they do. Killers seldom meet the legal standard for insanity, which is quite different from the way most people use the word every day. Killers may be *disturbed*, but that doesn't necessarily mean that they can't tell right from wrong or are compelled to maim or murder.

Interviewer: But what about someone like Jeffrey Dahmer? People say, "If he wasn't crazy, who is?"

PD: He was certainly *disturbed*, but he knew what he was doing was wrong. He tried to conceal his victims' bodies. He also wore a condom while having sex with the corpses, which indicates that the intensity of his sexual urge was less than many teenagers experience in backseats with their girlfriends.

John Dupont, heir to the Dupont fortune who imagined himself to be the Christ child, the Dalai Lama, and the crown prince of Russia, killed the Olympic wrestler he had hired as a coach. Dupont was found guilty but mentally ill at trial and was sentenced to 13 to 30 years in prison.

Interviewer: Still, doesn't that elude the bigger issue, his frame of reference? If I believe that little green men are descending from outer space and the only way to get rid of them is to sprinkle blue cheese on the lawn, and I go out and sprinkle cheese, that would be logical rational behavior given my overarching belief.

PD: And if that were a *crime,* you'd be insane for it.

Interviewer: But Dahmer doesn't fall into that category? It seems to me that while his separate actions may seem rational, he's operating under the idea that he can turn strangers into companions by killing and eating them. Why isn't that insane?

PD: If Dahmer had had the delusion that he'd have companions for life if he killed them and ate them, and that that was somehow a good thing and not *criminal,* that would make him insane. But those weren't the facts at all. Even the defense experts agreed that Dahmer knew it was wrong. In fact, Dahmer was so offended by the idea of killing that he had to get himself drunk to overcome his aversion to doing the killing. It's that point that proves that he did not have an irresistible impulse to kill.[111]

An Integrated Theory

In recent years, the debate over the explanation of criminal behavior has found a new forum in integrated biocriminological theories, such as the one

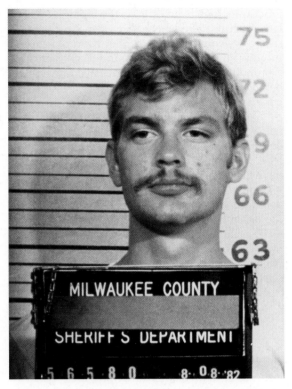

Jeffrey Dahmer murdered more than 17 boys and men before his capture. He was beaten to death by a fellow inmate on November 28, 1994.

proposed by James Q. Wilson and Richard Herrnstein. These scholars explain predatory street crime by showing how human nature develops from the interplay of psychological, biological, and social factors. It is the interaction of genes with environment that in some individuals forms the kind of personality likely to commit crimes. The argument takes into account factors such as IQ, body build, genetic makeup, impulsiveness, ability to delay gratification, aggressiveness, and even the drinking and smoking habits of pregnant mothers.

According to Wilson and Herrnstein, the choice between crime and conventional behavior is closely linked to individual biological and psychological traits and to social factors such as family and school experiences. Their conclusion is that "the offender offends not just because of immediate needs and circumstances, but also because of enduring personal characteristics, some of whose traces can be found in his behavior from early childhood on."[112] In essence, they argue that behavior results from a person's perception of the potential rewards and/or punishments that go along with a criminal act. If the potential reward (such as money) is greater than the expected punishment (say, a small fine), the chance that a crime will be committed increases.

CHAPTER 4

REVIEW

Biocriminologists investigate the biological correlates of criminality, including a genetic predisposition to commit crime. The XYY syndrome, though now generally discounted as a cause of criminality, suggests that aggressive and violent behavior may be at least partly determined by genetic factors. Studies of the behavior of identical and fraternal twins and of the rates of criminality among adopted children with both criminal and noncriminal biological and adoptive parents tend to support this hypothesis. Investigators have also found a strong correlation between low IQ and delinquency. Criminologists are still debating what public policy issues are raised by the possible role of genetics in crime.

Biocriminologists' most recent and perhaps most important discovery is the relation of criminal behavior to brain anatomy and function. Most scientists agree that if some people are biologically predisposed to certain behaviors, both psychological and environmental factors shape the forms of those behaviors.

When psychologists have attempted to explain criminality, they have taken four general approaches. First, they have focused on failures in psychological development—an overbearing or weak conscience, inner conflict, insufficient moral development, and maternal deprivation, with its concomitant failure of attachment. Second, they have investigated the ways aggression and violence are learned through modeling and direct experience. Third, they have investigated the personality characteristics of criminals and found that criminals tend to be more impulsive, intolerant, and irresponsible than noncriminals. Fourth, psychologists have investigated the relationship of criminality to mental disorders such as psychosis and psychopathy.

CRIMINOLOGY & PUBLIC POLICY

Sexual predators fall into the gap between criminal and civil confinement. They are routinely held fully responsible and blameworthy for their behavior because they almost always retain substantial capacity for rationality, they remain entirely in touch with reality, and they know the applicable moral and legal rules. Consequently, even if their sexual violence is in part caused by a mental abnormality, they do not meet the usual standards for an insanity defense. For the same reason, they do not meet the usual nonresponsibility standards for civil commitment and retain the competence to make rational decisions about treatment. Moreover, in most cases in which civil commitment is justified, most states no longer maintain routine, indefinite, involuntary civil commitment but instead tend to limit the permissible length of commitment.

To fill the gap, Kansas and a substantial minority of other states have adopted a form of indefinite, involuntary civil commitment that applies to "sexually violent predators who have a mental abnormality or personality disorder." The Kansas definition of a sexually violent predator, which is similar to those that other states have adopted, is "any person who has been convicted of or charged with a sexually violent offense and who suffers from a mental abnormality or personality disorder which makes the person likely to engage in repeat acts of sexual violence." The state may impose this form of civil commitment not only when a person has been charged with or convicted of a sexual offense but also after an alleged predator has completed a prison term for precisely that type of sexually violent conduct. Commitment is for an indefinite period, and thus potentially for life, although an annual review of the validity of the commitment is required. (SOURCE: From Stephen J. Morse, "Uncontrollable Urges and Irrational People," *Virginia Law Review*, **88**, [2002]: 1025. Copyright 2002 by Virginia Law Review. Reproduced with permission of Virginia Law Review in the format Textbook via Copyright Clearance Center.)

Questions for Discussion How should criminologists view the commitment of "sexual predators" to mental institutions for an indefinite term after serving time in prison? Does this commitment amount to a second round of punishment? If not, and little treatment takes place, how is this additional term of incapacitation justified? Should sexual predators be diverted from the criminal justice system in the first place? All these questions raise serious concerns over the problem of mentally ill offenders in the criminal justice system.

YOU BE THE CRIMINOLOGIST

For many years, psychologists searched for the criminal personality, a common set of personality characteristics associated with criminals. If you were asked to assist in this effort, what methods would you use to capture the criminal personality? Would you use objective personality inventories? If you were successful, what would you do with your findings? How could this common personality profile be used in the criminal justice system?

The numbers next to the terms refer to the pages on which the terms are defined.

attachment (89)

behavioral modeling (90)

biocriminology (75)

chromosomes (75)

conditioning (96)

cortical arousal (97)

differential association-reinforcement (94)

dizygotic (DZ) twins (76)

ego (86)

extroversion (96)

fundamental psycholegal error (98)

hypoglycemia (81)

id (86)

minimal brain dysfunction (MBD) (83)

monozygotic (MZ) twins (76)

neuroticism (96)

psychoanalytic theory (86)

psychopathy (97)

psychosis (97)

psychoticism (96)

social learning theory (90)

superego (86)

5 Strain and Cultural Deviance Theories

Jamal Malik, the main character in Slumdog Millionaire (portrayed here by Ayush Mahesh Khedekar) went from living on the streets of Mumbai to millionaire and national hero. For those not as fortunate as Jamal, how do they respond to their circumstances?

The Interconnectedness of Sociological Theories
Anomie: Émile Durkheim
The Structural-Functionalist Perspective
Anomie and Suicide
Strain Theory
Merton's Theory of Anomie
Modes of Adaptation
Tests of Merton's Theory
Evaluation: Merton's Theory
Institutional Imbalance and Crime
General Strain Theory
THEORY INFORMS POLICY
Cultural Deviance Theories
The Nature of Cultural Deviance
Social Disorganization Theory
Tests of Social Disorganization Theory
Evaluation: Social Disorganization Theory
THEORY INFORMS POLICY
Differential Association Theory
Tests of Differential Association Theory
Evaluation: Differential Association Theory
THEORY INFORMS POLICY
Culture Conflict Theory
Review
Criminology & Public Policy
You Be the Criminologist
Key Terms

Danny Boyle's "Slumdog Millionaire" hits the ground running. This is a breathless, exciting story, heartbreaking and exhilarating at the same time, about a Mumbai orphan who rises from rags to riches on the strength of his lively intelligence. The film's universal appeal will present the real India to millions of moviegoers for the first time.

The real India, supercharged with a plot as reliable and eternal as the hills. The film's surface is so dazzling that you hardly realize how traditional it is underneath. But it's the buried structure that pulls us through the story like a big engine on a short train.

By the real India, I don't mean an unblinking documentary like Louis Malle's "Calcutta" or the recent "Born Into Brothels." I mean the real India of social levels that seem to be separated by centuries. What do people think of when they think of India? On the one hand, Mother Teresa, "Salaam Bombay!" and the wretched of the earth. On the other, the "Masterpiece Theater"-style images of "A Passage to India," "Gandhi" and "The Jewel in the Crown."

The India of Mother Teresa still exists. Because it is side-by-side with the new India, it is easily seen. People living in the streets. A woman crawling from a cardboard box.

Men bathing at a fire hydrant. Men relieving themselves by the roadside. You stand on one side of the Hooghly River, a branch of the Ganges that runs through Kolkuta, and your friend tells you, "On the other bank millions of people live without a single sewer line."

On the other hand, the world's largest middle class, mostly lower-middle, but all the more admirable. The India of "Monsoon Wedding." Millionaires. Mercedes-Benzes and Audis. Traffic like Demo Derby. Luxury condos. Exploding education. A booming computer segment. A fountain of medical professionals. Some of the most exciting modern English literature. A Bollywood to rival Hollywood. "Slumdog Millionaire" bridges these two Indias by cutting between a world of poverty and the Indian version of "Who Wants to be a Millionaire." It tells the story of an orphan from the slums of Mumbai who is born into a brutal existence. A petty thief, impostor and survivor, mired in dire poverty, he improvises his way up through the world and remembers everything he has learned.

His name is Jamel (played as a teenager by Dev Patel). He is Oliver Twist. High-spirited and defiant in the worst of times, he survives. He scrapes out a living at the Taj Mahal, which he did not know about but discovers by being thrown off a train. He pretends to be a guide, invents "facts" out of thin air, advises tourists to remove their shoes and then steals them. He finds a bit part in the Mumbai underworld, and even falls in idealized romantic love, that most elusive of conditions for a slumdog.

His life until he's 20 is told in flashbacks intercut with his appearance as a quiz show contestant. Pitched as a slumdog, he supplies the correct answer to question after question and becomes a national hero. The flashbacks show why he knows the answers. He doesn't volunteer this information. It is beaten out of him by the show's security staff. They are sure he must be cheating.

The film uses dazzling cinematography, breathless editing, driving music and head-long momentum to explode with narrative force, stirring in a romance at the same time. For Danny Boyle, it is a personal triumph. He combines the suspense of a game show with the vision and energy of "City of God" and never stops sprinting.

When I saw "Slumdog Millionaire" at Toronto, I was witnessing a phenomenon: dramatic proof that a movie is about how it tells itself. I walked out of the theater and flatly predicted it would win the Audience Award. Seven days later, it did. And that it could land a best picture Oscar nomination. We will see. [In fact, it won not only a nomination, but also the Oscar.] It is one of those miraculous entertainments that achieves its immediate goals and keeps climbing toward a higher summit.[1] (Taken from the ROGER EBERT column by Roger Ebert © 2008 The Ebert Company. Dist. by UNIVERSAL PRESS SYNDICATE. Reprinted with permission. All rights reserved.)

Stories about the triumph of sheer will over class are more than stirring. They are truly inspiring. The scripts do everything to convince us that the impossible is possible, that aspiration and inspiration trump centuries of deeply encoded class differences that are apparent by appearance, speech, and one's last name. If only life were better at imitating art! If so, we would be nonplussed by the plot of *Slumdog Millionaire.* There would also be no need for a chapter that explores the effects of aspirations that meet frustration and strain where the means to obtain one's goals simply are not there. There would be no need for a chapter that considers theories of norms and values that, we are told, distinguish persons of different social and economic classes.

For all those who do not make it to a millionaire game show, who do not win the multistate lottery, or who do not grow up to be the next greatest sports hero, there are, of course, ways to adapt to the strain and frustration of not meeting aspirations. One way, as we shall see, is to reject the more conventional path to success when this path is unavailable or appears as if it is. And this takes us to the beginning of Chapter 5, to the early decades of the twentieth century that brought major changes to American society. One of the most significant was the change in the composition of the populations of cities. Between 1840 and 1924, 45 million people—Irish, Swedes, Germans, Italians, Poles, Armenians, Bohemians, Russians—left the Old World; two-thirds of them were bound for the United States.[2] At the same time, increased mechanization in this country deprived many American farmworkers of their jobs and forced them to join the ranks of the foreign-born and the black laborers who had migrated from the South to northern and midwestern industrial centers. During the 1920s, large U.S. cities swelled with 5 million new arrivals.[3]

Chicago's expansion was particularly remarkable: Its population doubled in 20 years. Many of the new arrivals brought nothing with them except what they could carry. The city offered them only meager wages, 12-hour working days in conditions that jeopardized their health, and tenement housing in deteriorating areas. Chicago had other problems as well. In the late 1920s and early 1930s, it was the home of major organized crime groups, which fought over the profits from the illegal production and sale of liquor during Prohibition (as we shall see in Chapter 10).

Teeming with newcomers looking for work, corrupt politicians trying to buy their votes, and bootleggers growing more influential through sheer firepower and the political strength they controlled, Chicago also had a rapidly rising crime rate. The city soon became an inviting urban laboratory for criminologists, who began to challenge the then-predominant theories of crime causation, which were based on biological and psychological factors. Many of these criminologists were associated with the University of Chicago, which has the oldest sociology program in the United States (begun in 1892). By the 1920s, these criminologists began to measure scientifically the amount of criminal behavior and its relation to the social turmoil Chicago was experiencing. Since that time, sociological theories have remained at the forefront of the scientific investigation of crime causation.

THE INTERCONNECTEDNESS OF SOCIOLOGICAL THEORIES

The biological and psychological theories of criminal behavior (Chapter 4) share the assumption that such behavior is caused by some underlying physical or mental condition that separates the criminal from the noncriminal. They seek to identify the kind of person who becomes a criminal and to find the factors that caused the person to engage in criminal behavior. Biological and psychological theories offer insight into individual cases, but they do not explain why crime rates vary from one neighborhood to the next, from group to group, within large urban areas, or within groups of individuals. Sociological theories seek the reasons for differences in crime rates in the social environment. These theories can be grouped into three general categories: strain, cultural deviance, and social control.[4]

The strain and cultural deviance theories formulated between 1925 and 1940 are still popular today and focus on the social forces that cause people to engage in criminal activity. These theories laid the foundation for the subcultural theories we discuss in Chapter 6. Social control theories (Chapter 7) take a different approach: They are based on the assumption that the motivation to commit crime is part of human nature. Consequently, social control theories seek to discover why people do not commit crime. They examine the ability of social groups and institutions to make their rules effective.

Strain and cultural deviance theories both assume that social class and criminal behavior are related, but they differ about the nature of the relationship. **Strain theory** argues that all members of society subscribe to one set of cultural values—that of the middle class. One of the most important middle-class values is economic success. Because lower-class persons do not have legitimate means to reach this goal, they turn to illegitimate means in desperation. **Cultural deviance theories** claim that lower-class people have a different set of values, which tend to conflict with the values of the middle class. Consequently, when lower-class persons conform to their own value system, they may be violating conventional or middle-class norms.

ANOMIE: ÉMILE DURKHEIM

Imagine a clock with all its parts finely synchronized. It functions with precision. It keeps perfect time. But if one tiny weight or small spring breaks down, the whole mechanism will not function properly. One way of studying a society is to look at its component parts in an effort to find out how they relate to one another. In other words, we look at the structure of a society to see how it functions. If the society is stable, its parts operating smoothly, the social arrangements are functional. Such a society is marked by cohesion, cooperation, and consensus. But if the component parts are arranged in such a way as to threaten the social order, the arrangements are said to be dysfunctional. In a class-oriented society, for example, the classes tend to be in conflict.

The Structural-Functionalist Perspective

The structural-functionalist perspective was developed by Émile Durkheim (1858–1917) before the end of the nineteenth century.[5] At the time, positivist biological theories, which relied on the search for individual differences between criminals and noncriminals, were dominant. So at a time when science was searching for the abnormality of the criminal, Durkheim was writing about the normality of crime in society. To him, the explanation of human conduct, and indeed human misconduct, lies not in the individual but in the group and the social organization. It is in this context that he introduced the term "anomie," the breakdown of social order as a result of the loss of standards and values.[6]

Throughout his career, Durkheim was preoccupied with the effects of social change. He believed that when a simple society develops into a modern, urbanized one, the intimacy needed to sustain a common set of norms declines. Groups become fragmented, and in the absence of a common set of rules, the actions and expectations of people in one sector may clash with those of people in another. As behavior becomes unpredictable, the system gradually breaks down, and the society is in a state of anomie.

Anomie and Suicide

Durkheim illustrated his concept of anomie in a discussion not of crime, but of suicide.[7] He suggested several reasons why suicide was more common in some groups than in others. For our purposes, we are interested in the particular form of suicide he called "anomic suicide." When he analyzed statistical data, he found that suicide rates increased during times of sudden economic change, whether that change was major depression or unexpected prosperity. In periods of rapid change, people are abruptly thrown into unfamiliar situations. Rules that once guided behavior no longer hold.

Consider the events of the 1920s. Wealth came easily to many people in those heady, prosperous years. Toward the end, through July, August, and September of 1929, the New York stock market soared to new heights. Enormous profits were made from speculation. But on October 24, 1929, a day history records as Black Thursday, the stock market crashed. Thirteen million shares of stock were sold. As more and more shares were offered for sale, their value plummeted. In the wake of the crash, a severe depression overtook the country and then the world. Banks failed. Mortgages were foreclosed. Businesses went bankrupt. People lost their jobs. Lifestyles changed overnight. Many people were driven to sell apples on street corners to survive, and they had to stand in mile-long breadlines to get food to feed their families. Suddenly the norms by which people lived were no longer relevant. People became disoriented and confused. Suicide rates rose.

It is not difficult to understand rising suicide rates in such circumstances, but why would rates also rise at a time of sudden prosperity? According to Durkheim, the same factors are at work in both situations. What causes the problems is not the amount of money available but the sudden change. Durkheim believed that human desires are boundless, an "insatiable and bottomless abyss."[8] Because nature does not set such strict biological limits on the capabilities of humans as it does on those of other animals, he argued, we have developed social rules that put a realistic cap on our aspirations. These regulations are incorporated into the individual conscience and thus make it possible for people to feel fulfilled.

But with a sudden burst of prosperity, expectations change. When the old rules no longer determine how rewards are distributed among members of society, there is no longer any restraint on what people want. Once again the system breaks down. Thus, whether sudden change causes great prosperity or great depression, the result is the same—anomie.

STRAIN THEORY

A few generations after Durkheim, American sociologist Robert Merton (1910–2003) also related the crime problem to anomie. But his conception differs somewhat from Durkheim's. The real problem, Merton argued, is created not by sudden social change but by a social structure that holds out the same goals to all its members without giving them equal means to achieve them. This lack of integration between what the culture calls for and what the structure permits, the former encouraging success and the latter preventing it, can cause norms to break down because they no longer are effective guides to behavior.

Merton borrowed the term "anomie" from Durkheim to describe this breakdown of the normative system. According to Merton,

> it is only when a system of cultural values extols, virtually above all else, certain common

symbols of success for the population at large while its social structure rigorously restricts or completely eliminates access to approved modes of acquiring these symbols for a considerable part of the same population, that antisocial behavior ensues on a considerable scale.[9]

From this perspective, the social structure is the root of the crime problem (hence, the approach Merton takes is sometimes called a "structural explanation"). "Strain theory," the name given by contemporary criminologists to Merton's explanation of criminal behavior, assumes that people are law-abiding but when under great pressure will resort to crime. Disparity between goals and means provides that pressure.

Merton's Theory of Anomie

Merton argued that in a class-oriented society, opportunities to get to the top are not equally distributed. Very few members of the lower class ever get there. His anomie theory emphasizes the importance of two elements in any society: (1) cultural aspirations, or goals that people believe are worth striving for, and (2) institutionalized means or accepted ways to attain the desired ends. If a society is to be stable, these two elements must be reasonably well integrated; in other words, there should be means for individuals to reach the goals that are important to them. Disparity between goals and means fosters frustration, which leads to strain.

Merton's theory explains crime in the United States in terms of the wide disparities in income among the various classes. Statistics clearly demonstrate that such disparities exist. American families had a median income of $48,201 in 2006. While 11 percent of all families had incomes above $100,000, 12 percent had incomes below the poverty level—$ 20,614 for a family of four: Nine percent of whites, 23 percent of blacks, and 20 percent of Hispanics were living below the poverty level, and nearly 18 percent of the poor were children.[10]

It is not, however, solely wealth or income that determines people's position on a social ladder that ranges from the homeless to the very, very rich who live on great estates. In 1966, Oscar Lewis described the "culture of poverty" that exists in inner-city slums. It is characterized by helplessness, apathy, cynicism, and distrust of social institutions such as schools and the police.[11] A few years later, Gunnar Myrdal argued that there is a worldwide "underclass, whose members lack the education and skills necessary to compete with the rest of society."[12] And in 1987, William Julius Wilson depicted the ranks of the underclass as the "truly disadvantaged." This group of urban inner-city dwellers is at the bottom of the ladder. Basic institutions such as the school and the family have deteriorated. There is little community cohesion.

The people remain isolated—steeped in their own ghetto culture and the anger and aggression that accompany their marginal existence.[13]

In our society, opportunities to move up the social ladder exist, but they are not equally distributed. A child born to a single, uneducated, 13-year-old girl living in a slum has practically no chance to move up, whereas the child of a middle-class family has a better-than-average chance of reaching a professional or business position. Yet all people in our society share the same goals. And those goals are shaped by billions of advertising dollars spent each year to spread the message that everyone can tote around MacBook Air, drive an Aston Martin, and vacation in Santorini.

The mystique is reinforced by instant lottery millionaires, the earnings of superstar athletes, and rags-to-riches stories of people such as Ray Kroc. Kroc, a high school dropout, believed that a 15-cent hamburger with a 10-cent bag of French fries could make dining out affordable for low-income families; his idea spread quickly through the United States—and to 116 other countries with 24,500 McDonald's restaurants and their golden arches all over the world. Superstar athletes are another example of American icons. Consider Michael Jordan. At age 21 he had a rookie contract worth $6 million over 7 years, which increased to the $25 million salary range per season with the NBA plus $40 million in commercial endorsements. And now in retirement he has yet another multimillion-dollar venture—the famous Michael Jordan's Restaurants in Chicago and in New York, where guests can dine and buy an array of memorabilia in his bustling boutiques. In like manner, record-setting home-run hitter Sammy Sosa was making over $9 million in salary and $8 million in endorsements at the height of his career. Sosa, now in his 40s, worked as a shoeshine boy in the Dominican Republic to help support his fatherless family. Although Merton argued that lack of legitimate means for everyone to reach material goals like these does create problems, he also made it clear that the high rate of deviant behavior in the United States cannot be explained solely on the basis of lack of means.[14]

Modes of Adaptation

To be sure, not everyone who is denied access to a society's goals becomes deviant. Merton outlined five ways in which people adapt to society's goals and means. Individuals' responses (modes of adaptation) depend on their attitudes toward the cultural goals and the institutional means of attaining those goals. The options are conformity, innovation, ritualism, retreatism, and rebellion (Table 5.1).

Merton does not tell us how any one individual chooses to become a drug pusher, for example, and another chooses to work on an assembly

A Social System Breaks Down

American anthropologist Kenneth Good committed—for anthropologists—the unpardonable sin of marrying a young woman of the tribe he studied, the Yanomami. The young bride returned with her husband to suburban Pennsylvania in 1988, and there they raised their children.(1) But in 1993, the Yanomami wife slipped back into the Amazon jungle to live among her own people.

Who are the Yanomami?

When another anthropologist, Robert Carneiro, went to the Amazon jungle in 1975 to study the Yanomami, he found them to be a remote, Stone Age people dedicated to frequent intervillage warfare.(2)

Indeed, the Yanomami are the last major remaining Stone Age people on Earth, living their lives in harmony with nature but also engaging in tribal warfare, according to their customs.

But all went awry in the 1980s, when gold was discovered in the Yanomami territory.(3) As many as 40,000 prospectors had invaded by 1987, clearing the jungle for airstrips, bringing diseases—venereal and others—against which the Yanomami had no immunity, importing modern weapons to replace Stone Age clubs, and raising the homicide rate.(4) What once was a nation of 100,000 was reduced to 22,000 (9,400 in Brazil; 12,600 in Venezuela). A severe drought in the late 1990s added to the suffering of the Yanomami, who use ancient incantations to bring rain as well as to quench forest fires and to drive out invaders.(2)

Help is under way and more is promised. The United Nations sent an emergency team of firefighters to deal with the forest fires. The Brazilian government clamped down on encroachments

A Yanomami man with the trappings of modern civilization.

by rogue miners. The U.S. Congress made some assistance available to protect the rain forests but did not designate preservation of the Yanomami territory and lifestyle a priority.

Too little, too late? The Yanomami's traditional way of life has broken down. The chances that they can withstand the attack of the Western culture invasion are slim. The large deposits of gold, diamonds, tin, and other minerals in the soil of their land will continue to attract invaders, with their attack on the traditional culture. Yanomami are dying faster than ever before, hunting and fishing are increasingly difficult, alcohol and prostitution are taking their toll, firearms are escalating the death

rate, and infant mortality is 24 times that of the United States.(5)

What are we to do about the Yanomami? It does not seem possible to transplant Yanomami into suburbia. Forcing modern capitalism on them is even more destructive.

Should we just build a fence around the Yanomami territory and allow them to live their accustomed lifestyle? The specter of an entrepreneur flying in tourists in jumbo jets and charging admission to view "unspoiled," Stone Aged Yanomami is just too daunting.

Are we witnessing a genocide in the making?

Sources

1. Kenneth Good with David Chernoff, *Into the Heart* (New York: Simon and Schuster, 1991).
2. Robert L. Carneiro, "War and Peace: Alternating Realities in Human History," in *Studying War—Anthropological Perspectives,* eds. S. P. Reyna and R. E. Downs (Langhorn, Pa.: Gordon and Breach, 1994), pp. 3–27.
3. Lynne Wallis, "Quiet Genocide: Miners Seeking Precious Metals Are Causing Deaths of the Yanomami," *Ottawa Citizen,* June 28, 1993, p. A6.
4. "Aid for an Ancient Tribe," *Newsweek,* Apr. 9, 1990, p. 34.
5. "Genocide in the Amazon," *Newsweek,* Aug. 30, 1993, p. 61.

Questions for Discussion

1. As the Yanomami culture is being destroyed, how would you expect the tribe's traditional ways of dealing with crime to be affected? Explain.
2. What measures might be effective in protecting indigenous peoples in all parts of the world from suffering a fate similar to that of the Yanomami?

---

line. Instead, he explains why crime rates are high in some groups and low in others.

Conformity

Conformity is the most common mode of adjustment. Individuals accept both the culturally defined goals and the prescribed means for achieving those goals. They work, save, go to school, and follow the legitimate paths. Look around you in the classroom. You will see many children of decent, hardworking parents. After college they will find legitimate jobs. Some will excel. Some will walk the economic middle path. But all those who are conformists will accept (though not necessarily achieve)

■ *Sammy Sosa takes a few minutes before a game in Seattle (June 2000) to greet Cubs fans, Kerry and Sammy Lepse. Kerry, left, was named after the Cubs' Kerry Wood, and Sammy, middle, was named after Sosa.*

TABLE 5.1 A Typology of Modes of Individual Adaptation		
Mode of Adaptation	**Culture Goals***	**Institutionalized Means***
Conformity	+	+
Innovation	+	−
Ritualism	−	+
Retreatism	−	−
Rebellion	±	±

*+ = acceptance; − = rejection; ± = rejection and substitution

SOURCE: Reprinted with the permission of The Free Press, a Division of Simon & Schuster, Inc., from *Social Theory and Social Structure* by Robert K. Merton, p. 140. Copyright © 1957 by The Free Press. Copyright renewed © 1985 by Robert K. Merton. All rights reserved.

the goals of our society and the means it approves for achieving them.

Innovation

Individuals who choose the adaptation of innovation accept society's goals, but because they have few legitimate means of achieving them, they design their own means for getting ahead. The means may be burglary, robbery, embezzlement, or a host of other crimes. Youngsters who have no parental attention, no encouragement in school, no way to the top—no future—may scrawl their signatures on subway cars and buildings and park benches in order to achieve recognition of a sort. Such illegitimate forms of innovation are certainly not restricted to the lower classes, as evidenced by crimes such as stock manipulation, sale of defective products, and income tax evasion.

Ritualism

People who adapt by ritualism abandon the goals they once believed to be within reach and resign themselves to their present lifestyles. They play by the rules; they work on assembly lines, hold middle-management jobs, or follow some other safe routine. Many workers have been catching a bus at the same street corner at the same hour every day for 20 years or more. They have long forgotten why, except that their jobs are where their paychecks come from. Their great relief is a 2-week vacation in the summer.

Retreatism

Retreatism is the adaptation of people who give up both the goals (can't make it) and the means (why try?) and retreat into the world of drug addiction or alcoholism. They have internalized the value system and therefore are under internal pressure not to innovate. The retreatist mode allows an escape into a nonproductive, nonstriving lifestyle. Some members of the antiwar movement of the 1960s opted to drop out entirely. The pressure was too great; the opportunities were unacceptable. They became addicts or followers of occult religions.

Rebellion

Rebellion occurs when both the cultural goals and the legitimate means are rejected. Many individuals substitute their own goals (get rid of the establishment) and their own means (protest). They have an alternative scheme for a new social structure, however ill-defined. Many of the so-called militias operating in America today, ranging in size from two to several hundred persons, have lost faith in the legitimacy of the U.S. government and are trying to establish their own alternative quasi-governmental structures.

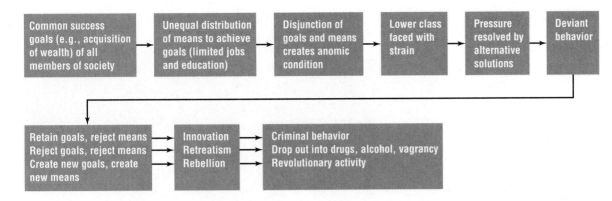

FIGURE 5.1 Modes of deviant behavior.

Merton's theory of how the social structure produces strain that may lead to deviant behavior is illustrated in Figure 5.1. His theory has challenged researchers for over half a century.

Tests of Merton's Theory

Merton and his followers (Chapter 6) predict that the greatest proportion of crime will be found in the lower classes because lower-class people have the least opportunity to reach their goals legitimately. Many research studies designed to test the various propositions of strain theory focus on the association between social class and delinquency (an association that evokes considerable controversy). Some studies report a strong inverse relationship: As class goes up, crime rates go down. Others find no association at all between these two variables (Chapter 2).

Social Class and Crime

The controversy over the relationship between social class and crime began when researchers, using self-report questionnaires, found more serious and more frequent delinquency among lower-class boys than among those of higher classes.[15] In Chapter 2, we saw that other researchers seriously questioned those findings.[16] When Charles Tittle and his colleagues attempted to clarify the relationship by analyzing 35 empirical studies, they concluded that "class is not now and has not been related to criminality in the recent past."[17] Summarizing the research literature on social class and crime, Gary Jensen and Kevin Thompson wrote, "The safest conclusion concerning class structure and delinquency is the same one that has been proposed for several decades: Class, no matter how defined, contributes little to explaining variation in self-reports of common delinquency."[18]

Once again there was a critical reaction. A summary of more than 100 projects concluded that "lower-class people do commit those direct interpersonal types of crime which are normally handled by the police at a higher rate than middle-class people."[19] But if low social status creates frustration that pushes people to commit crime, why don't all the people in the lowest class commit crimes, or drop out into the drug world, or become revolutionaries? They clearly do not, so there must be some limitations to the causal relationship between crime and social class.

Nikos Passas answers the question by pointing out that not all those persons exposed to the same problems respond in the same way. In fact, not all people perceive the same situation as a problem. He explains that anomie theorists base their arguments on rates of crime, rather than on individual behavior.[20]

Terence Thornberry and Margaret Farnsworth argue that there is no simple connection between class and crime. The relationship, they say, is highly complex; it involves race, seriousness of the offense, education of family and offender, and many other factors.[21] Some evidence shows that class interacts with race to affect adult criminality. Individuals who are racial minorities and come from disadvantaged class positions are at an increased risk for crime.[22] Other researchers have found that low social status promoted delinquency by increasing individuals' strain and by decreasing educational and occupational aspirations, whereas high social status promoted individuals' delinquency by increasing risk taking and decreasing conventional values.[23]

According to a number of studies, we may be able to learn more about the relationship between social class and crime if we look closely at specific types of offenses rather than at aggregate crime (or delinquency) rates. Take homicide, for example: In a study of 190 U.S. cities with populations of 100,000 or more, it was found that both income inequality and poverty are related to homicide rates. The researchers argue that the relationship can be explained "through the legitimate desires of impoverished persons to reduce deprivation and through their decreased ability to compete for legitimate employment."[24] In two large cross-national studies, two teams of Canadian researchers explored the relationship between income inequality and national homicide rates.[25] Both teams reported results that support strain theory. When opportunities or means for success are not

■ *At a Los Angeles welfare agency, masses of adults and children just sit and wait.*

provided equally to all members of society (as indicated by crime rates), pressure is exerted on some members of that society to engage in deviant behavior (in this case, homicide). Further analyses by one of the teams showed that the effects of inequality on homicide may be even more pronounced in more democratic societies. The researchers commented, "Income inequality might be more likely to generate violent behavior in more democratic societies because of the coexistence of high material inequality and an egalitarian value system."[26]

David Brownfield also related social class to specific offenses, in this instance to fistfights and brawls among teenagers.[27] His information came from two sources: the Richmond Youth Study, conducted at the University of California at Berkeley, and the Community Tolerance Study, done by a team of researchers at the University of Arizona. Brownfield's analysis of questionnaires completed by 1,500 white male students in California and 1,300 white male students in Arizona suggests a very strong relation between poverty—as measured by unemployment and welfare assistance—and violent behavior. He concluded that the general public expresses much hostility against the "disreputable poor," a term used by David Matza to describe people who remain unemployed for a long time, even during periods of full employment.[28]

John Hagan argues that youngsters who grow up in a culture where friends are delinquent, parents are criminals, and drug abuse is common, and where early experiences with delinquent activities are widespread, become "embedded" in behaviors that result in later adult unemployment. They are excluded from employment by events that begin early in life. Of course, youngsters can become equally "embedded" in a culture of middle-class values, economic stability, and early work experiences—the foundation for job stability and career success.[29]

Race and Crime

Yet another question that relates to strain theory concerns the relationship between racial inequality and violent crime. Judith and Peter Blau studied data from 125 metropolitan areas in the United States.[30] Their primary finding was that racial inequality—as measured by the difference in socioeconomic status between whites and nonwhites—is associated with the total rate of violent crime. The conclusion fits well with Merton's theory.

The Blaus argued that in a democratic society that stresses equal opportunities for individual achievement but in reality distributes resources on the basis of race, there is bound to be conflict. The most disadvantaged are precisely those who cannot change their situation through political action. In such circumstances, the frustrations created by racial inequalities tend to be expressed in various forms of aggression, such as violent crime. Several researchers have supported these findings. But not all researchers are in agreement.

John Braithwaite examined Uniform Crime Report statistics for a sample of 175 American cities. He compared the rates of violent crime with racial inequality, as measured by the incomes of black families and the incomes of all other families in his sample cities. He concluded that racial inequality does not cause specific crime problems.[31] Perhaps the crucial point is not whether one actually has an equal chance to be successful but rather how one perceives one's chances. According to this reasoning, people who feel the most strain are those who have not only high goals but also low expectations of reaching them. So far, however, research has not supported this contention.

Evaluation: Merton's Theory

The strain perspective developed by Merton and his followers has influenced both research and theoretical developments in criminology.[32] Yet, as popular as this theory remains, it has been questioned on a variety of grounds.[33] By concentrating on crime at the lower levels of the socioeconomic hierarchy, for example, it neglects crime committed by middle- and upper-class people. Radical criminologists (see Chapter 8), in fact, claim that strain theory "stands accused of predicting too little bourgeois criminality and too much proletarian criminality."[34]

Other critics question whether a society as heterogeneous as ours really does have goals on which everyone agrees. Some theorists argue that American subcultures have their own value systems (Chapter 6). If that is the case, we cannot account for deviant behavior on the basis of Merton's cultural goals. Other questions are asked about the theory. If we have an agreed-upon set of goals, is material gain the dominant one? If crime is a means to an end, why is there so much useless, destructive behavior, especially among teenagers?

No matter how it is structured, each society defines goals for its members. The United States is far from being the only society in which people strive for wealth and prestige. Yet, while some people in other cultures have limited means for achieving these goals, not all these societies have high crime rates. Two such societies—Japan and Switzerland—are among the most developed and industrialized in the world. Although the United States has quite a bit in common with them, it does not share their very low crime rates.[35]

Despite the many critical assessments, strain theory, as represented primarily by Merton's formulation of anomie, has had a major impact on contemporary criminology. It dominated the delinquency research of the 1950s and 1960s. During the 1970s, the theory lost its dominant position as criminologists paid increasing attention to how crime and delinquency were related to individuals' loss of attachment to their social institutions—the family, the school, or the government (see Chapter 7). Then, in the mid-1980s and continuing unabated into the 2000s, there was a resurgence of interest in empirical research and theorizing based on strain concepts.

Institutional Imbalance and Crime

In their book *Crime and the American Dream,* Steven Messner and Richard Rosenfeld agree with Merton that the material success goal is pervasive in American culture. In essence, the American dream is quite clear—succeed by any means necessary, even if those means are illegitimate.[36] The American dream, then, encourages high crime rates. Messner and Rosenfeld expand on Merton's ideas on the relationships among culture, social structure, anomie, and crime rates (Figure 5.2). High crime rates, they contend, are more than a result of striving for monetary gains. They also result from the fact that our major social institutions

do not have the capacity to control behavior. These institutions fail to counterbalance the ethos of the American dream. The dominance of economic institutions manifests itself in three ways: devaluation of other institutions, the accommodation of other institutions to economic needs, and the penetration of economic norms.

- *The devaluation of noneconomic roles and functions.* Performance in the economic world takes precedence over performance in other institutional settings: Noneconomic functions are devalued. Education is important, for example, only because it promises economic gains. Learning for its own sake is relatively unimportant. In the context of the family, the home owner is more important than the homemaker. In politics, too, there is a devaluation: If a citizen does not vote, there may be mild disapproval; if an adult citizen does not work, he or she loses status.

- *The accommodation of other institutions to economic needs.* In situations where institutions compete, noneconomic ones **accommodate.** Family life is generally dominated by work schedules. Individuals go to school primarily to get a "good" job. Once out of school, those who return usually do so to get a better job. In political accommodation, government strives to maintain an environment hospitable to business.

- *The penetration of economic norms.* Penetration of economic norms into those of other institutions is widespread. Spouses become partners in "managing" the home, business people/politicians campaign for public office claiming they will "run the country like a corporation," and economic terms such as "accountability" are adopted by educators.

Messner and Rosenfeld contend that as long as there is a disproportionate emphasis on monetary rewards, the crime problem will increase. In fact, if economic opportunities increase, there may be an increase in the preoccupation with material success. Crime will decrease only when noneconomic institutions have the capacity to control behavior.[37]

Freda Adler's study of 10 countries with low crime rates supports this argument. She demonstrates that where economic concerns have not devalued informal social control institutions such as family, community, or religion, crime rates are relatively low and stable. This finding held for nonindustrialized *and* highly industrialized societies.[38]

General Strain Theory

Sociologist Robert Agnew substantially revised Merton's theory in order to provide a broader explanation of criminal behavior.[39] The reformulation is

FIGURE 5.2 Comparing Merton's anomie (strain) theory with Messner and Rosenfeld's institutional anomie (strain) theory.

Source: Eric P. Baumer and Regan Gustafson; "Social Organization and Instrumental Crime: Assessing the Empirical Validity of Classic and Contemporary Anomie Theories," *Criminology,* **45** (2007): 617–663.

A. Merton's Anomie Theory

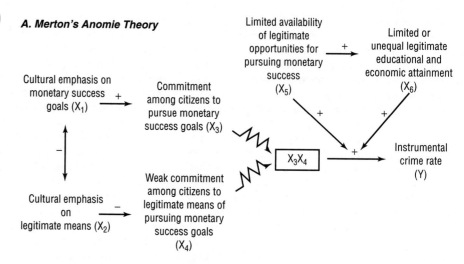

B. Messner and Rosenfeld's Institutional Anomie Theory

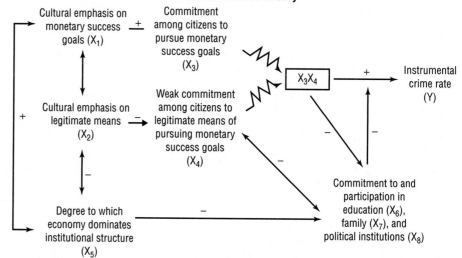

called **general strain theory.** Agnew argues that failure to achieve material goals (the focal point of Merton's theory) is not the only reason for committing crime. Criminal behavior may also be related to the anger and frustration that result when an individual is treated in a way he or she does not want to be treated in a social relationship. General strain theory explains the range of strain-producing events:

• *Strain caused by failure to achieve positively valued goals.* This type of strain is based on Merton's view that lower-class individuals are often prevented from achieving monetary success goals through legitimate channels. When people do not have the money to get what they want, some of them turn to illegitimate means to get it.

• *Stress caused by the removal of positively valued stimuli from the individual.* This type of strain results from the actual or anticipated loss of something or someone important in one's life: death of a loved one, breakup with a boyfriend/girlfriend, divorce of parents, move to a new school. Criminal behavior results when individuals seek revenge

against those responsible, try to prevent the loss, or escape through illicit drug use.

• *Strain caused by the presentation of negative stimuli.* The third major source of strain involves stressful life situations. Adverse situations and events may include child abuse, criminal victimization, bad experiences with peers, school problems, or verbal threats. Criminal behavior in these situations may result when an individual tries to run away from the situation, end the problem, or seek revenge.[40]

According to Agnew, each type of strain increases an individual's feelings of anger, fear, or depression. The most critical reaction for general strain theory is anger, an emotion that increases the desire for revenge, helps justify aggressive behavior, and stimulates individuals to act.

General strain theory acknowledges that not all persons who experience strain become criminals. Many are equipped to cope with their frustration and anger. Some come up with rationalizations ("don't really need it anyway"), others use techniques for physical relief (a good workout at the gym), and still others walk away from the condition causing stress (get out of the house). The capacity to deal with strain depends on personal experience throughout life. It involves the influence of peers, temperament, attitudes, and, in the case of pressing financial problems, economic resources. Recent empirical tests show preliminary support for general strain theory.[41] By broadening Merton's concepts, general strain theory has the potential to explain a wide range of criminal and delinquent behavior, including aggressive acts, drug abuse, and property offenses, among individuals from all social classes.

THEORY INFORMS POLICY

Strain theory has helped us develop a crime-prevention strategy. If, as the theory tells us, frustration builds up in people who have few means for reaching their goals, it makes sense to design programs that give lower-class people a bigger stake in society.

Head Start

It was in the 1960s that President Lyndon Johnson inaugurated the Head Start program as part of a major antipoverty campaign. The goal of Head Start is to make children of low-income families more socially competent, better able to deal with their present environment and their later responsibilities. The youngsters get a boost (or a head start) in a 1-year preschool developmental program that is intended to prevent them from dropping out of society. Program components include community and parental involvement, an 8-to-1 child-staff ratio, and daily evaluation and involvement of all the children in the planning of and responsibility for their own activities.

Because a 1-year program could not be expected to affect the remainder of a child's life, Project Follow Through was developed in an effort to provide the same opportunities for Head Start youngsters during elementary school. What began as a modest summer experience for half a million preschool children has expanded into a year-round program that provides educational and social services to millions of young people and their families. Head Start is a poignant example of a program intended to lower stress in the group most likely to develop criminal behavior.

A 2005 evaluation of Head Start programs sought evidence of the impact of Head Start on children's school readiness and on parental practices that support children's development. The study also examined the conditions under which Head Start achieves its greatest impact and for which children. Data from the four domains studied revealed, at best, small to moderate associations between the program objectives and results.[42]

- *Parenting practices domain.* The key findings in this domain, consisting of three constructs, are these:

  For children who entered the program as 3-year-olds, there are small statistically significant impacts in two of the three parenting constructs, including a higher use of educational activities and a lower use of physical discipline by parents of Head Start children. There were no significant impacts for safety practices.

  For children who entered the program as 4-year-olds, there are small statistically significant impacts on parents' use of educational activities. No significant impacts were found for discipline or safety practices.

- *Cognitive domain.* The cognitive domain consists of six constructs, each comprising one or more measures. The key findings in this domain are these:

  There are small to moderate statistically significant positive impacts for both 3- and 4-year-old children on several measures across four of the six cognitive constructs, including pre-reading, pre-writing, vocabulary, and parent reports of children's literacy skills.

  No significant impacts were found for the constructs oral comprehension and phonological awareness or early mathematics skills for either age group.

- *Social-emotional domain.* The social-emotional domain consists of three constructs, each comprising one or more parent-reported measures. The key findings in this domain are these:

  For children who entered the study as 3-year-olds, there is a small statistically significant impact in one of the three social-emotional constructs—problem behaviors.

  There were no statistically significant impacts on social skills and approaches to learning or on social competencies for 3-year-olds.

  No significant impacts were found for children entering the program as 4-year-olds.

- *Health domain.* The key findings in this domain, consisting of two constructs, are these:

  For 3-year-olds, there are small to moderate statistically significant impacts in both constructs: higher parent reports of children's access to health care and reportedly better health status for children enrolled in Head Start.

FIGURE 5.3 Major findings of the High/Scope Perry Preschool Project for participants followed up at age 27.

Source: High/Scope Educational Research Foundation, *High-Quality Preschool Program Found to Improve Adult Status,* (Ypsilanti, Mich.: High/Scope Educational Research Foundation, 1999). Retrieved March 13, 2000, from www.highscope.org/research/Perry%20fact%20sheet.htm. Reprinted with the permission of the High/Scope Educational Research Foundation.

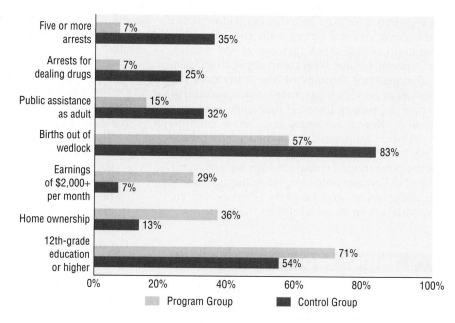

Perry Preschool Project

Another program that tried to ameliorate the disparity between goals and means in society was the Perry Preschool Project, begun in 1962 on the south side of Ypsilanti, Michigan. Its purpose was to develop skills that would give youngsters the means of getting ahead at school and in the workplace, thereby reducing the amount and seriousness of delinquent behavior. Overall, 123 black children 3 and 4 years old participated for 2 years, 5 days a week, 2½ hours a day. The program provided a teacher for every five children, weekly visits by a teacher to a child's home, and a follow-up of every child annually until age 11 and thereafter at ages 14, 15, and 19.

There is little doubt about the effectiveness of the project. The participants did better in several areas than a group that had not participated:

- Employment rates doubled.
- Rates of postsecondary education doubled.
- Teenage pregnancy was cut in half.
- The high school graduation rate was higher.
- Arrest rates were significantly lower (Figure 5.3).[43]

Job Corps

Yet another survivor of President Johnson's War on Poverty is the federal Job Corps program. It aims at "the worst of the worst," as Senator Orrin Hatch of Utah said.[44] The program enables neglected teenagers—otherwise headed for juvenile detention or jail—to master work habits that they did not learn at home. In 2007, 62,000 young people were serving in the Job Corps. Most of them had enlisted on the basis of recruitment posters, like those distributed by the armed forces. The average length of stay in the corps is just short of a year, at an annual cost of $18,831. That sounds expensive, but juvenile detention costs $29,600 a year—and residential drug-treatment centers cost $19,000. Since its inception in 1964, the program has served over 1.8 million people.[45]

Over two-thirds of former Job Corps members find jobs, and 17 percent go on to higher education. Research has shown that the Job Corps returns $1.46 for every dollar spent, because of increased tax revenue and decreased cost of welfare, crime, and incarceration. Over two-thirds of Job Corps members are members of minority groups; over 80 percent are high school dropouts. A recent advisory committee evaluation of Job Corps revealed some promising placement rates.

In a report to the United States Congress on which programs prevent crime, researchers at the University of Maryland classified the Job Corps program as "promising." Its potential for success includes the resocialization of youth through prosocial role models, a residential requirement that reduces contact with antisocial groups, and its vocational focus and attachment to the job market (Table 5.2.).[46]

For children who entered the program as 4-year-olds, there are moderate statistically significant impacts on access to health care, but no significant impacts on health status.

TABLE 5.2 Job Corps Common Measures—Performance and Results, Program Years 2004–2006.*

Performance Goal 1.1B: Improve the educational achievements of Job Corps students and increase participation of Job Corps graduates in employment and education

Indicator	2004[†]		2005		2006	
	Target	Result	Target	Result	Target	Result
1. *Placement:* The percent of participants who will enter employment or enroll in postsecondary education or training/occupational skills training in the first quarter after exit	85%	84%	85%	80%	87%	75%
2. *Certificate Attainment:* The percent of students who will attain a GED, high school diploma, or certificate while enrolled in the program	64%	64%	64%	60%	65%	56%
3. *Literacy/Numeracy:* The percent of students who will achieve literacy or numeracy gains of one Adult Basic Education (ABE) level, equivalent to two grade levels	45%	47%	45%	58%	58%	56%

*2006 data through 3/31/07.

[†]Placement (for 2004 and 2005) was defined as the percent of Job Corps graduates (within one year of program exit) and former enrollees (within 90 days of program exit) who will enter employment or enroll in postsecondary education or advanced training/occupational skills training.

SOURCE: *Advisory Committee on Job Corps: Report and Recommendations to the Secretary of Labor.* Washington, DC: U.S. Department of Labor, April 2008, p. 34. Available at http://www.docstoc.com/docs/841778/Advisory-Committee-on-Job-Corps-Report.

CULTURAL DEVIANCE THEORIES

The programs that emanate from strain theory attempt to give underprivileged children ways to achieve middle-class goals. Programs based on cultural deviance theories concentrate on teaching middle-class values.

Strain theory attributes criminal behavior in the United States to the striving of all citizens to conform with the conventional values of the middle class, primarily financial success. Cultural deviance theories, on the other hand, attribute crime to a set of values that exist in disadvantaged neighborhoods. Conformity with the lower-class value system, which determines behavior in slum areas, causes conflict with society's laws. Both strain and cultural deviance theories locate the causes of crime in the marginalized position of those at the lowest stratum in a class-based society.

Scholars who view crime as resulting from cultural values that permit, or even demand, behavior in violation of the law are called "cultural deviance theorists." The three major cultural deviance theories are social disorganization, differential association, and culture conflict. **Social disorganization theory** focuses on the development of high-crime areas in which there is a disintegration of conventional values caused by rapid industrialization, increased immigration, and urbanization. **Differential association theory** maintains that people learn to commit crime as a result of contact with antisocial values, attitudes, and criminal behavior patterns. **Culture conflict theory** states that different groups learn different conduct norms (rules governing behavior) and that the conduct norms of some groups may clash with conventional middle-class rules.

All three theories contend that criminals and delinquents do in fact conform—but to norms that deviate from those of the dominant middle class. Before we examine the specific theories that share the cultural deviance perspective, we need to explore the nature of cultural deviance.

The Nature of Cultural Deviance

When you drive through rural Lancaster County in Pennsylvania or through Holmes County in Ohio or through Elkhart and Lagrange Counties in Indiana, in the midst of fertile fields and well-tended orchards, you will find isolated villages with prosperous and well-maintained farmhouses but no electricity. You will see the farmers and their families traveling in horse-drawn buggies, dressed in homespun clothes, and wearing brimmed hats. These people are Amish. Their ancestors came to this country from the German-speaking Rhineland region as early as 1683 to escape persecution for their fundamentalist Christian beliefs. Shunning motors, electricity, jewelry, and affiliation with political parties, they are a *nonconformist* community within a highly materialistic culture.

Motorcycle gangs made their appearance shortly after World War II. The Hell's Angels was the first of many gangs to be established in slum areas of cities across the country. To become a member of this gang, initiates are subjected to grueling and revolting degradations. They are conditioned to have allegiance only to the gang. Contacts with middle-class society are usually antagonistic and criminal. Motorcycle gangs finance their operations through illegal activities, such as dealing drugs, running massage parlors and gambling operations, and selling stolen goods. The members' code of loyalty to one another and to their national and local groups makes the gangs extremely effective criminal organizations.

The normative systems of the Amish and the bikers are at odds with the conventional norms of the society in which they live. Both deviate from middle-class standards. Sociologists define **deviance** as any behavior that members of a social group define as violating their norms. As we can see, the concept of deviance can be applied to noncriminal acts that members of a group view as peculiar or unusual (the lifestyle of the Amish) or to criminal acts (behavior that society has made illegal). The Hell's Angels fit the expected stereotype of deviance as negative; the Amish culture demonstrates that deviance is not necessarily bad, just different.

Cultural deviance theorists argue that our society is made up of various groups and subgroups, each with its own standards of right and wrong. Behavior considered normal in one group may be considered deviant by another. As a result, those who conform to the standards of cultures considered deviant are behaving in accordance with their own norms but may be breaking the law—the norms of the dominant culture.

You may wonder whether the Hell's Angels are outcasts in the slum neighborhoods where they live. They are not. They may even be looked up to by younger boys in places where toughness and violence are not only acceptable but also appropriate. Indeed, groups such as the Hell's Angels may meet the needs of youngsters who are looking for a way to be important in a disorganized ghetto that offers few opportunities to gain status.

A man with a Hitler tattoo on his back sells white-power T-shirts at a Ku Klux Klan cross-burning rally in Hico, Texas. Deviant hate groups such as these exist throughout the United States and in many foreign countries.

Social Disorganization Theory

Scholars associated with the University of Chicago in the 1920s became interested in socially disorganized Chicago neighborhoods where criminal values and traditions replaced conventional values and were transmitted from one generation to the next. In their classic work *The Polish Peasant in Europe and America*, W. I. Thomas and Florian Znaniecki described the difficulties Polish peasants experienced when they left their rural life in Europe to settle in an industrialized city in America.[47] The scholars compared the conditions the immigrants had left in Poland with those they found in Chicago. They also investigated the immigrants' assimilation.

Older immigrants, they found, were not greatly affected by the move because they managed, even within the urban slums, to continue living as they had lived in Poland. But the second generation did not grow up on Polish farms; these people were city dwellers, and they were American. They had few of the old Polish traditions but were not yet assimilated into the new ones. The norms of the stable, homogeneous folk society were not transferable to the anonymous, materially oriented urban settings. Rates of crime and delinquency rose. Thomas and Znaniecki attributed this result to *social disorganization*—the breakdown of effective social bonds, family and

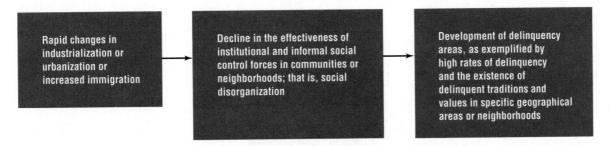

FIGURE 5.4 Social disorganization.

Source: Donald J. Shoemaker, *Theories of Delinquency: An Examination of Explanations of Delinquent Behavior,* 4th ed. (2000), Figure 4 (p. 79). By permission of Oxford University Press, Inc. www.oup.com

neighborhood associations, and social controls in neighborhoods and communities (Figure 5.4).

The Park and Burgess Model

Thomas and Znaniecki's study greatly influenced other scholars at the University of Chicago. Among them were Robert Park and Ernest Burgess, who advanced the study of social disorganization by introducing ecological analysis into the study of human society.[48] Ecology is the study of plants and animals in relation to each other and to their natural habitat, the place where they live and grow. Ecologists study these interrelationships, how the balance of nature continues, and how organisms survive. Much the same approach is used by social ecologists, scholars who study the interrelationships of people and their environment.

In their study of social disorganization, Park and Burgess examined area characteristics instead of criminals for explanations of high crime rates. They developed the idea of natural urban areas, consisting of concentric zones extending out from the downtown central business district to the commuter zone at the fringes of the city. Each zone had its own structure and organization, its own cultural characteristics and unique inhabitants (Figure 5.5). Zone I, at the center—called the "Loop" because the downtown business district of Chicago is demarcated by a loop of the elevated train system—was occupied by commercial headquarters, law offices, retail establishments, and some commercial recreation. Zone II was the zone in transition, where the city's poor, unskilled, and disadvantaged lived in dilapidated tenements next to old factories. Zone III housed the working class, people whose jobs enabled them to enjoy some of the comforts the city had to offer at its fringes. The middle class—professionals, small-business owners, and the managerial class—lived in Zone IV. Zone V was the commuter zone of satellite towns and suburbs.

Shaw and McKay's Work

Clifford Shaw and Henry McKay, two researchers at Chicago's Institute for Juvenile Research, were particularly interested in the model Park and Burgess had created to demonstrate how people were distributed spatially in the process of urban growth. They decided to use the model to investigate the relationship between crime rates and the various zones of Chicago. Their data, found in 55,998 juvenile court records covering a period of 33 years, from 1900 to 1933, indicated the following:

- Crime rates were differentially distributed throughout the city, and areas of high crime rates had high rates of other community problems, such as truancy, mental disorders, and infant mortality.

- Most delinquency occurred in the areas nearest the central business district and decreased with distance from the center.

- Some areas consistently suffered high delinquency rates, regardless of the ethnic makeup of the population.

- High-delinquency areas were characterized by a high percentage of immigrants, nonwhites, and low-income families and a low percentage of home ownership.

- In high-delinquency areas, there was a general acceptance of nonconventional norms, but these norms competed with conventional ones held by some of the inhabitants.[49]

Shaw and McKay demonstrated that the highest rates of delinquency persisted in the same areas of Chicago over the extended period from 1900 to 1933, even though the ethnic composition changed (German, Irish, and English at the turn of the century; Polish and Italian in the 1920s; an increasing number of blacks in the 1930s). This finding led to the conclusion that the crucial factor was not ethnicity but, rather, the position of the group in terms of economic status and cultural values. Finally, through their study of three sets of Cook County juvenile court records—1900 to 1906, 1917 to 1923, and 1927 to

FIGURE 5.5 Park and Burgess's conception of the "natural urban areas" of Chicago.

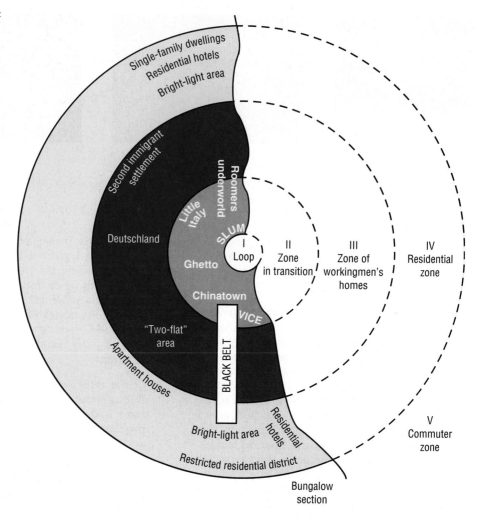

1933—they learned that older boys were associated with younger boys in various offenses and that the same techniques for committing delinquent acts had been passed on through the years. The evidence clearly indicated to them that delinquency was socially learned behavior, transmitted from one generation to the next in disorganized urban areas.[50] This phenomenon is called **cultural transmission.**

Tests of Social Disorganization Theory

Social disorganization, like early strain theory, was overshadowed in the 1970s by social control theorists who turned to explanations of why people do *not* break laws in the face of poor social environments with few means of becoming successful. While these explanations still have widespread impact on the scholarly community, the 1980s and 1990s saw a major resurgence of interest in how neighborhoods affect people's lives. Modern-day social ecologists have once again begun to focus on the interrelationship of individuals and their environment. What are the consequences of rising crime rates in a neighborhood? Ralph Taylor suggests separating these consequences into three categories: psychological and social, behavioral, and economic.[51]

Psychological and Social Effects

Life in physically deteriorated neighborhoods, with their rat-infested buildings, graffiti-ridden streets, trash-strewn vacant lots, boarded-up windows, and openly conducted drug selling, takes its psychological toll on residents.[52] They feel less emotional investment in their communities, mistrust their neighbors, and harbor increasing desires to "get out." Frustration mounts because they are unable to do so. Many parents are so worried about violence on their streets that they confine their youngsters to the home except for school attendance. Young people refer to this confinement as "lockdown" (a term used to describe the locking of prison cells for security reasons). This desperate move to protect children from getting hurt physically has had harmful psychological effects. According to one professor of developmental psychology, in a world where a simple altercation can end as an assault or even a murder,[53] these "protected" children are at a disadvantage. When they eventually go back on the streets, they don't know how to survive.

Researchers are questioning whether people living in socially disorganized neighborhoods become more fearful. The answer is, they usually do.[54] When word of victimization begins to spread, fear can reach epidemic proportions. Residents begin to stay off the streets, abandoning them to the gangs, drug dealers, and others involved in illicit activities. Fear becomes greatest in communities undergoing rapid age and racial-composition changes.[55]

Fear increases when there is a perception that the police care little about a neighborhood. Douglas Smith looked at police behavior and characteristics of 60 neighborhoods in three large U.S. cities (Rochester, New York; St. Louis, Missouri; Tampa/St. Petersburg, Florida). His major findings suggest that police officers are less likely to file reports of crime incidents in high-crime areas than in low-crime areas and that they are more likely to assist residents and initiate contacts with suspicious-looking people in low-crime neighborhoods.[56]

Dina Rose and Todd Clear link social disorganization to high incarceration rates. They suggest that when large numbers of males are removed from the community through incarceration, local social, political, and economic systems in already disorganized communities become even weaker. In these areas, children are more likely to experience lack of supervision, more single-parent families, and few effective guardians. The researchers do not advocate policies that allow those who threaten the personal safety of residents to be on the streets. But, they argue, there are many offenders who can be regulated in the community through various neighborhood-based approaches monitored by collaborative efforts of the police, probation and parole officers, and local groups, leaders, and residents. This crime-control strategy, one that ties the offender to the community, could then strengthen, rather than weaken, already socially disorganized neighborhoods.[57]

Behavioral Effects

A 1999 report on an ongoing research project that focuses on 343 urban neighborhoods in Chicago shows that residents overall consider substance abuse and fistfighting "very wrong" to "extremely wrong." Broken down by racial and ethnic groups, minority-group members were more intolerant of deviance than were whites.[58] Regardless of the level of residents' intolerance, however, widespread deviance in a community generally tends to make people limit their participation in efforts to "clean up" the neighborhood. There are, however, communities that fight back with community patrols, anti-crime programs, and various activities to protect

children. Many people would prefer to move away, but few do. Factors besides crime come into play: low income, stage of life cycle, an affordable place to live, and location of employment.[59] Those moving in usually do so because it is the only place they can find an affordable place to live.[60]

Economic Effects

Crime problems in a community influence assessments of property values by realtors and lenders. Research in Boston suggests that a 5 percent decrease in crime could bring in $7 million to $30 million in increased tax revenue.[61] In another investigation, researchers asked about the impact of Atlantic City casinos and the related increased crime rate on real estate in three southern New Jersey counties.[62] They found a sizable drop in house values. Those communities most accessible to Atlantic City suffered the worst economic consequences.

Middle- and working-class people tend to escape the urban ghetto, leaving behind the most disadvantaged. When you add to those disadvantaged the people moving in from outside who are also severely disadvantaged, over time these areas become places of concentrated poverty, isolated from the mainstream.

Some social ecologists argue that communities, like people, go through life cycles. Neighborhood deterioration precedes rising crime rates. When crime begins to rise, neighborhoods go from owner-occupied to renter-occupied housing, with a significant decline in the socioeconomic status of residents and an increase in population density. Later in the community life cycle, there is a renewed interest on the part of investors in buying up the cheap real estate with the idea of renovating it and making a profit (gentrification).[63]

Evaluation: Social Disorganization Theory

Although their work has had a significant impact, social ecologists have not been immune to challenges. Their work has been criticized for its focus on how crime patterns are transmitted, rather than on how they start in the first place. The approach has also been faulted for failing to explain why delinquents stop committing crime as they grow older, why most people in socially disorganized areas do not commit criminal acts, and why some bad neighborhoods seem to be insulated from crime. Finally, critics claim that this approach does not come to grips with middle-class delinquency.

Clearly, however, modern criminology owes a debt to social disorganization theorists, particularly to Shaw and McKay, who in the 1920s began to look at the characteristics of people and places and to relate both to crime. There is now a

Crime Surfing

www.ojp.usdoj.gov/bjs

Is the association between victimization levels and neighborhoods supported by recent survey data?

vast body of research for which they laid the groundwork.

THEORY INFORMS POLICY

Theorists of the Chicago school were the first social scientists to suggest that most crime is committed by normal people responding in expected ways to their immediate surroundings, rather than by abnormal individuals acting out individual pathologies. If social disorganization is at the root of the problem, crime control must involve social organization. The community, not individuals, needs treatment. Helping the community, then, should lower its crime rate.

The Chicago Area Project

Social disorganization theory was translated into practice in 1934 with the establishment of the Chicago Area Project (CAP), an experiment in neighborhood reorganization. The project was initiated by the Institute for Juvenile Research, at which Clifford Shaw and Henry McKay were working. It coordinated the existing community support groups—local schools, churches, labor unions, clubs, and merchants. Special efforts were made to control delinquency through recreational facilities, summer camps, better law enforcement, and the upgrading of neighborhood schools, sanitation, and general appearance.

In 1994, this first community-based delinquency-prevention program could boast 60 years of achievement. South Chicago remains an area of poverty and urban marginalization, dotted with boarded-up buildings and signs of urban decay, though the pollution from the nearby steel mills is under control. But the Chicago Area Project initiated by Shaw and McKay is as vibrant as ever, with its three-pronged attack on delinquency: direct service, advocacy, and community involvement. Residents, from clergy to gang members, are working with CAP to keep kids out of trouble, to help those in trouble, and to clean up the neighborhoods. "In fact, in those communities where area projects have been in operation for a number of years, incidents of crime and delinquency have decreased (Figure 5.6)."[64]

Operation Weed and Seed and Others

Operation Weed and Seed is a federal, state, and local effort to improve the quality of life in targeted high-crime urban areas across the country. The strategy is to "weed" out negative influences (drugs, crime) and to "seed" the neighborhoods with prevention and intervention.

When the program began in 1991, there were three target areas—Kansas City, Missouri; Trenton, New Jersey; and Omaha, Nebraska. By 1999, the number of target areas had increased to 200 sites. An

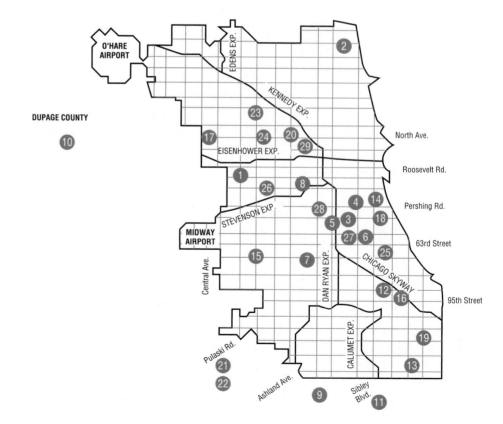

FIGURE 5.6 CAP affiliates now dot the Chicago landscape, from (1) Agape Youth Development/Family Services at 320 South Spaulding (East Garfield), and (2) Alternatives, Inc., at 1126 West Granville Avenue (Rogers Park—Uptown) to (28) Wentworth Residents United for Survival at 3752 South Wells (Wentworth Gardens) and (29) Youth Service Committee of the WestSide at 1832 West Washington (Henry Horner Homes).

Source: www.chicagoareaproject.org/map.html.

eight-state evaluation showed that the effectiveness of Operation Weed and Seed varied by the original severity of the crime problems, the strength of the established network of community organizations, early seeding with constant weeding, active leadership of key community members, and the formation of partnerships among local organizations.[65]

Another community action project has concentrated on revitalizing a Puerto Rican slum community. Sister Isolina Ferre worked for 10 years in the violent Navy Yard section of Brooklyn, New York. In 1969, she returned to Ponce Plaza, a poverty-stricken area in Ponce, Puerto Rico, infested with disease, crime, and unemployment. The area's 16,000 people had no doctors, nurses, dentists, or social agencies. The project began with a handful of missionaries, university professors, dedicated citizens, and community members who were willing to become advocates for their neighborhood. Among the programs begun were a large community health center, Big Brother/Big Sister programs for juveniles sent from the courts, volunteer tutoring, and recreational activities to take young people off the streets. Young photographers of Ponce Plaza, supplied with a few cameras donated by friends at Kodak, mounted an exhibit at the Metropolitan Museum of Art in New York. Regular fiestas have given community members a chance to celebrate their own achievements as well.[66]

Programs based on social disorganization theory attempt to bring conventional social values to disorganized communities. They provide an opportunity for young people to learn norms other than those of delinquent peer groups. Let us see how such learning takes place.

Differential Association Theory

What we eat, what we say, what we believe—in fact, the way we respond to any situation— depends on the culture in which we have been reared. In other words, to a very large extent, the social influences that people encounter determine their behavior. Whether a person becomes law-abiding or criminal, then, depends on contacts with criminal values, attitudes, definitions, and behavior patterns. This proposition underlies one of the most important theories of crime causation in American criminology—differential association.

Sutherland's Theory

In 1939, Edwin Sutherland introduced differential association theory in his textbook *Principles of Criminology*. Since then, scholars have read, tested, reexamined, and sometimes ridiculed this theory, which claimed to explain the development of all criminal behavior. The theory states that crime is learned through social interaction. People come into constant contact with "definitions favorable to violations of law" and "definitions unfavorable to violations of law." The ratio of these definitions— criminal to noncriminal—determines whether a person will engage in criminal behavior.[67] In formulating this theory, Sutherland relied heavily on Shaw and McKay's findings that delinquent values are transmitted within a community or group from one generation to the next.

Sutherland's Nine Propositions

Nine propositions explained the process by which this transmission of values takes place:

1. Criminal behavior is learned.

2. Criminal behavior is learned in interaction with other persons in a process of communication. A person does not become a criminal simply by living in a criminal environment. Crime is learned by participation with others in verbal and nonverbal communications.

A Latin Kings gang member teaches gang hand symbols to a child. Social interactions like these are learned and then transmitted from one generation to the next.

3. The principal part of the learning of criminal behavior occurs within intimate personal groups. Families and friends have the most influence on the learning of deviant behavior. Their communications far outweigh those of the mass media.

4. When criminal behavior is learned, the learning includes (a) techniques of committing the crime, which are sometimes very complicated, sometimes very simple, and (b) the specific direction of motives, drives, rationalizations, and attitudes. Young delinquents learn not only how to shoplift, crack a safe, pick a lock, or roll a joint but also how to rationalize and defend their actions. One safecracker accompanied another safecracker for 1 year before he cracked his first safe.[68] In other words, criminals, too, learn skills and gain experience.

5. The specific direction of motives and drives is learned from definitions of the legal codes as favorable or unfavorable. In some societies, an individual is surrounded by persons who invariably define the legal codes as rules to be observed, while in others he or she is surrounded by persons whose definitions are favorable to the violation of the legal codes. Not everyone in our society agrees that the laws should be obeyed; some people define them as unimportant. In American society, where definitions are mixed, we have a culture conflict in relation to legal codes.

6. A person becomes delinquent because of an excess of definitions favorable to violation of law over definitions unfavorable to violation of law. This is the key principle of differential association. In other words, learning criminal behavior is not simply a matter of associating with bad companions. Rather, learning criminal behavior depends on how many definitions we learn that are favorable to law violation as opposed to those that are unfavorable to law violation.

7. Differential associations may vary in frequency, duration, priority, and intensity. The extent to which associations and definitions will result in criminality is related to the frequency of contacts, their duration, and their meaning to the individual.

8. The process of learning criminal behavior by association with criminal and anticriminal patterns involves all the mechanisms that are involved in any other learning. Learning criminal behavior patterns is very much like learning conventional behavior patterns and is not simply a matter of observation and imitation.

9. While criminal behavior is an expression of general needs and values, it is not explained by those general needs and values, since noncriminal behavior is an expression of the same needs and values. Shoplifters steal to get what they want. Others work to get money to buy what they want. The motives—frustration, desire to accumulate goods or social status, low self-concept, and the like—cannot logically be the same because they explain both lawful and criminal behavior.

Tests of Differential Association Theory

Since Sutherland presented his theory 70 years ago, researchers have tried to determine whether his principles lend themselves to empirical measurement. James Short tested a sample of 126 boys and 50 girls at a training school and reported a consistent relationship between delinquent behavior and frequency, duration, priority, and intensity of interactions with delinquent peers.[69] Similarly, Travis Hirschi demonstrated that boys with delinquent friends are more likely to become delinquent.[70] Research on seventh- and eighth-grade students attending Rochester, New York, public schools in the late 1980s and early 1990s shows that gang membership is strongly associated with peer delinquency and the amount of delinquency and drug use.[71] Mark Warr demonstrated that while the duration of delinquent friendships over a long period of time has a greater effect than exposure over a short period, it is recent friendships rather than early friendships that have the greatest effect on delinquency.[72]

Adults have also been the subjects of differential association studies. Two thousand residents of New Jersey, Oregon, and Iowa were asked questions such as how many people they knew personally had engaged in deviant acts and how many were frequently in trouble. They were also asked how often they attended church (assumed to be related to definitions unfavorable to the violation of law). This differential association scale correlated significantly with crimes such as illegal gambling, income tax cheating, and theft.[73]

Evaluation: Differential Association Theory

Many researchers have attempted to validate Sutherland's differential association theory. Others have criticized it. Much of the criticism stems from errors in interpretation. Perhaps this type of error is best demonstrated by the critics who ask why it is that not everyone in heavy, prolonged contact with criminal behavior patterns becomes a criminal. Take, for argument's sake, corrections officers, who come into constant contact with more criminal associations than noncriminal ones. How do they escape learning to be law violators themselves?

The answer, of course, is that Sutherland does not tell us that individuals become criminal by associating with criminals or even by association with criminal behavior patterns. He tells us, rather, that a person becomes delinquent because of an "excess of definitions favorable to violation of law over definitions unfavorable to violation of law." The key word is "definitions." Furthermore, unfavorable definitions may be communicated by persons who are not robbers or murderers or tax evaders. They may, for example, be law-abiding parents who, over time, define certain situations in such a way that their children get verbal or nonverbal messages to the effect that antisocial behavior is acceptable.

Several scholars have asked whether the principles of differential association really explain all types of crime. They might explain theft, but what about homicide resulting from a jealous rage?[74] Why do some people who learn criminal behavior patterns not engage in criminal acts? Why is no account taken of nonsocial variables, such as a desperate need for money? Furthermore, while the principles may explain how criminal behavior is transmitted, they do not account for the origin of criminal techniques and definitions. In other words, the theory does not tell us how the first criminal became a criminal.

Differential association theory suggests that there is an inevitability about the process of becoming a criminal. Once you reach the point where your definitions favorable to law violation exceed your definitions unfavorable to law violation, have you crossed an imaginary line into the criminal world? Even if we could add up the definitions encountered in a lifetime, could scientists measure the frequency, priority, duration, and intensity of differential associations?

Despite these criticisms, the theory has had a profound influence on criminology.[75] Generations of scholars have tested it empirically, modified it to incorporate psychologically based learning theory (see Chapter 4), and used it as a foundation for their own theorizing (Chapter 6). The theory has also had many policy implications.

THEORY INFORMS POLICY

If, according to differential association theory, a person can become criminal by learning definitions favorable to violating laws, it follows that programs that expose young people to definitions favorable to conventional behavior should reduce criminality. Educational efforts such as Head Start and the Perry Preschool Project have attempted to do just that. The same theory underlies many of the treatment programs for young school dropouts and pregnant teenagers.

An innovative Ohio program is trying to break the vicious cycle between poverty–welfare–school dropout–drugs–delinquency and teenage pregnancy. This program, LEAP (for learning, earning, and parenting), provides financial rewards for teenage single parents to stay in, or return to, school and deductions from the welfare checks of those who do not participate in education. A 1993 evaluation found that the program, which costs the state very little, has

been moderately successful. Success appears to increase with increased counseling and aid services. Several states (for example, Virginia, Florida, Maryland, and Oklahoma) have instituted similar "learnfare" programs, while others are considering this option.[76]

Recently, schools in Chicago, New York, Boston, Los Angeles, Tucson, and Washington have introduced conflict resolution into the curriculum. These programs zero in on teaching youngsters to deal with problems nonviolently. For example, by role-playing situations, children practice how to respond when someone insults or challenges them. In the Chicago area alone, 5,000 students are going through this antiviolence program, which is supported by the National Institute of Mental Health.[77]

Culture Conflict Theory

Differential association theory is based on the learning of criminal (or deviant) norms or attitudes. Culture conflict theory focuses on the

■ MOVE members and neighbors watch their houses burn after aerial and ground attacks by the Philadelphia police, in May 1985. Over the next 11 years the city paid more than $30 million to rebuild homes and settle lawsuits filed by cult members and their families.

Cults—Culture Conflict—Crime

As the Hale-Bopp comet streaked through the sky over California on March 26, 1997, 39 members of the computer-related cult Heaven's Gate committed suicide at their luxurious Rancho Santa Fe, California, estate. The victims, males between 18 and 24 years old, fully expected to be conveyed to heaven by a waiting spacecraft.(1)

Heaven's Gate is but one of many unusual cults that attract media coverage. In fact, in a ranking of the Top Ten cults, it places only third. Consider the beliefs and practices of the following "cults":

10. *Raëlians:* If you believe UFOs spawned most religions, mind transfer is possible, and cloning can lead to reincarnation, then you might be a candidate for the Raëlian Church, started in France in the 1970s. A Raëlian follower made headlines in 2003 when she claimed to have conceived the first cloned human, but the event was later called a hoax.

9. *Cargo Cults:* If you're an island native isolated from modern society, encountering an AM/FM radio —or a boat full of symbol-clad soldiers—can be quite a shock. Many societies form a cult-like obsession with the technologically advanced "cargo." Some South Pacific islanders reportedly tote wooden guns and paint "USA" on their chests in rituals to attract more of the mysterious objects.

8. *Villa Baviera:* Also known as "Colonia Dignidad" (Dignidad Colony in English), Villa Baviera is a commune of German immigrants that was founded in 1961 by Paul Schäfer Schneider, a former Nazi party member. Human rights groups argue that Chile's secret police used the compound to torture and interrogate subjects, and former members have since issued apologies for molesting children.

7. *Order of the Solar Temple:* Luc Jouret, a Belgian religious leader and neo-Nazi, reportedly started the group in 1984 under Christian guises, namely the second coming of Christ and the Knights Templar. Jouret and other leaders in a Swiss village allegedly sacrificed a child they thought to be the Antichrist in 1994, days later committing suicide with dozens of followers. The French consider the organization to be criminal today.

6. *Bhagwan Shree Rajneesh's Communities:* Indian mystic Bhagwan Shree Rajneesh founded several cultist towns in Oregon through the 1980s—strangely, communities chock-full of Rolls Royce cars. Shree allegedly poisoned hundreds in The Dalles, Oregon, with salmonella bacteria in 1984 to rig local elections in his cult's favor. It's considered the first bioterrorist attack in the United States.

5. *Branch Davidians:* Considered to be a major split from the Seventh-Day Adventist Church, the Branch Davidians are famous for a 1993 FBI raid on their Waco, Texas, compound that left 76 dead. The event more or less resulted in the disappearance of what many consider to be a cult, whose members believed in an imminent apocalypse.

4. *Manson Family:* Charles Manson, who learned to play guitar in prison, formed his infamous "Family" of criminals in 1968. Manson thought an apocalyptic race war between whites and blacks would occur in 1969, after which the commune would rule the new world. When this didn't happen, he sent his followers on a string of murders to "show blacks how to do it," but the victims Manson selected were those who had not helped him with his music career.

3. *Heaven's Gate:* Followers of the Heaven's Gate cult, led primarily by Marshall Applewhite, thought Earth and everything on it were about to be "recycled" to a clean slate and believed that hitching a ride on comet Hale-Bopp in March 1997 could allow them to survive. Thirty-nine members (including Applewhite) poisoned themselves in shifts in a California mansion wearing Nike sneakers and armbands that read "Heaven's Gate Away Team."

2. *Aum Shinrikyo:* Founded some time in the mid-1980s, Aum Shinrikyo is famous for attacking Tokyo's subway system with Sarin gas in 1995, killing 12 and injuring more than 5,000. The cult's beliefs are often described

source of these criminal norms and attitudes. According to Thorsten Sellin, **conduct norms**—norms that regulate our daily lives—are rules that reflect the attitudes of the groups to which each of us belongs.[78] Their purpose is to define what is considered appropriate or normal behavior and what is inappropriate or abnormal behavior.

Sellin argues that different groups have different conduct norms and that the conduct norms of one group may conflict with those of another. Individuals may commit crimes by conforming to the norms of their own group if that group's norms conflict with those of the dominant society. According to this rationale, the main difference between a criminal and a noncriminal is that each is responding to different sets of conduct norms.

Examples of groups with values significantly deviating from those of the surrounding majority include MOVE, an African American group concerned with issues like police brutality, animal rights, and African heritage. MOVE, located in a as a hodgepodge of destructive aspects of various religions, and while many followers thought they would develop supernatural powers, others relished the chance to fight Japanese materialism.

1. *Peoples Temple:* Reverend Jim Jones started the Peoples Temple to help homeless, jobless, and sick people of all races, but former members claimed widespread abuse within the group. To remove his group from further scrutiny, Jones started a colony in the jungles of Guyana, where he hoped to build a tropical utopia. When a congressman visited the commune with three journalists to investigate the abuse claims, they were shot and killed when trying to leave. After the shootings, 913 commune members—including hundreds of children—drank poisoned Flavor Aid in a mass suicide.(2)

A cult is defined as "a great devotion to a person, idea, object, [or] movement; . . . a usually small group of people characterized by such devotion" (*Merriam Webster's Collegiate®* Dictionary, Tenth Edition). Most cults are marked by

- a dynamic leader;
- the willingness of members to surrender their worldly possessions;
- strict obedience to the leader;
- a communal social structure, with its own set of norms and values that are in conflict with those of conventional societies.

Experts estimate that there are 1,000 to 2,000 cults in America with as many as 4 to 6 million members.

Shoko Asahara, leader of the Japanese cult Aum Shinrikyo.

Criminologists are interested primarily in destructive cults such as those in the Top Ten. There are other destructive cults of lesser rank. They exist worldwide. An Indian cult, for example, has its devotees "marry" their little daughters to a goddess. Upon reaching puberty, the little girls are sold into prostitution for about $200 each.(3)

A number of governments (China, Germany, and Russia) have outlawed cults. The Vatican has issued a strong report exhorting the church to fulfill the spiritual needs of the people to keep them from seeking salvation in cults.(4) The debate in America centers on First Amendment religious freedom. What governments, theologians, and criminologists have in common is their determination to bring alienated members of society into the mainstream to keep them out of destructive cults. But what is a destructive cult? Where should we draw the line between the freedom to exercise one's religious beliefs and the government's legitimate interest in protecting its citizens from coercive, destructive, and often violent religious groups?

Sources

1. Shirley Levung, "Deaths May Be Work of Religious Cult, Expert Says," *Boston Globe,* Mar. 27, 1997, p. A15.
2. LiveScience, Top 10 Crazy Cults, http://www.livescience.com/strangenews/top-10-crazy-cults-1.html. Reprinted by permission of Imaginova Corp.
3. "India Sex Cult's 'Handmaidens' Join Tribute to Hindu Goddess, Secret Society Forces Girls Who 'Marry' Yelamma into Prostitution," *Toronto Star,* Jan. 23, 1997, p. A16.
4. E. J. Dionne, "Vatican, Taking Some Blame, Cites Threat of Cults," *New York Times,* May 4, 1986, p. A10.

Questions for Discussion

1. Where and how can we draw the line between those cults that engage in violations of the criminal law (such as murder, arson, incitation to suicide, rape, child abuse, and prostitution) and those that have not (yet) committed any criminal act and therefore enjoy First Amendment privileges?
2. Both theologians and criminologists advocate narrowing the gap between conduct norms of deviant cultures (cults, sects) and the rules of mainstream society. How could either group practically accomplish that goal?

house on Osage Street in Philadelphia, alienated its neighbors by broadcasting loud and profanitylaced loudspeaker messages. Mutual animosity escalated. Some MOVE members armed themselves. A police officer was killed. Ultimately, the police, armed with arrest warrants for some members, entered the area. The group did not surrender. The police attacked: 10,000 rounds of ammunition were fired, and a bomb was dropped from a police helicopter. All but two of the MOVE members died, and all the houses on the street went up in flames.

The last chapter in the MOVE drama was not written until February 1997, when the City of Philadelphia agreed to pay more than $500,000 each to the estates of MOVE founders John Africa and Frank James—after having spent over $30 million to rebuild the houses destroyed by the police bombing and to settle lawsuits filed by the estates of nine other MOVE members who had perished.

Another example—far more criminal—was the Solar Temple, founded by a former Gestapo officer, which flourished in Switzerland and

Canada. This mystic cult attracted wealthy members who "donated" all their property to the cult, perhaps $93 million in all; much of it was spent for the personal benefit of two cult leaders. Cult members were heavily armed (and engaged in arms trading) in anticipation of the end of the world. Their end of the world came in the fall of 1994, when the two cult leaders murdered nearly all their followers and then committed suicide.

Sellin distinguishes between primary and secondary conflicts. "Primary conflict" occurs when norms of two cultures clash. A clash may occur at the border between neighboring cultural areas; a clash may occur when the law of one cultural group is extended to cover the territory of another; or it may occur when members of one group migrate to another culture. In a widening gap between cultural norms and generations, Southeast Asian immigrant children are running away from home in increasing numbers. They often run to an informal nationwide network of "safe houses." No one knows how many runaways there are, but it is estimated that at least one-third of all refugee families have had at least one child vanish for days, months, or even longer.

"Secondary conflict" arises when a single culture evolves into a variety of cultures, each with its own set of conduct norms. This type of conflict occurs when the homogeneous societies of simpler cultures become complex societies in which the number of social groupings multiplies constantly and norms are often at odds. Your college may make dormitory living mandatory for all freshmen, for example, but to follow the informal code of your peer group, you may seek the freedom of off-campus housing. Or you may have to choose whether to violate work rules by leaving your job half an hour early to make a mandatory class or to violate school rules by walking into class half an hour late. Life situations are frequently controlled by conflicting norms, so no matter how people act, they may be violating some rule, often without being aware that they are doing so.

In the next chapter, which deals with the formation and operation of subcultures, we will expand the discussion of the conflict of norms. We will also examine the empirical research that seeks to discover whether there is indeed a multitude of value systems in our society and, if so, whether and how they conflict.

CHAPTER 5

REVIEW

Criminologists tend to divide the sociological explanation of crime into three categories: strain, cultural deviance, and social control. The strain and cultural deviance perspectives, described in this chapter, focus on the social forces that cause people to engage in deviant behavior. They assume that there is a relationship between social class and criminal behavior. Strain theorists argue that all people in society share one set of cultural values and that because lower-class persons often do not have legitimate means to attain society's goals, they may "innovate" by turning to illegitimate means instead. General strain theory, a revision of Merton's theory, relates criminal behavior to the anger that results when an individual is treated in a way he or she does not want to be treated in a social relationship. Cultural deviance theorists maintain that the lower class has a distinctive set of values and that these values often conflict with those of the middle class.

Cultural deviance theories—social disorganization, differential association, and culture conflict—relate criminal behavior to the learning of criminal values and norms. Social disorganization theory focuses on the breakdown of social institutions as a precondition for the establishment of criminal norms. Differential association theory concentrates on the processes by which criminal behavior is taught and learned. Culture conflict theory focuses on the specifics of how the conduct norms of some groups may clash with those of the dominant culture.

CRIMINOLOGY & PUBLIC POLICY

"In American society, personal worth tends to be evaluated on the basis of what people have achieved rather than who they are or how they relate to others in social networks. 'Success' is to a large extent the ultimate measure of social worth. Quite understandably, then, there are pervasive cultural pressures to achieve at any cost. A strong achievement orientation, at the level of basic cultural values, thus cultivates and sustains a mentality that 'it's not how you play the game; it's whether you win or lose.'" (Source: Richard Rosenfeld and Steven F. Messner, "Crime and the American Dream: An Institutional Analysis," in *The Legacy of Anomie: Advances in Criminological Theory*, eds. F. Adler and W. S. Laufer, [New Brunswick, N.J.: Transaction, 1999].)

Questions for Discussion Robert Merton's notion of strain may be traced to the same values on which the American Dream rests, in particular, a strong achievement orientation. What are the ramifications of such a theoretical premise? What kind of social programs address this orientation? Do programs grounded in this success orientation promote an unrealistic and unattainable goal?

A major funding agency has given a large grant for changing the quality of life in a high-crime inner-city neighborhood where residents are afraid to let their children play outside. You are the project director. Whom would you hire as consultants? Would you work with law enforcement? Finally, what would be your goals, and how would you reach them?

The numbers next to the terms refer to the pages on which the terms are defined.

accommodate (111)
conduct norms (124)
cultural deviance theories (104)
cultural transmission (118)
culture conflict theory (115)
deviance (116)
differential association theory (115)
general strain theory (112)
social disorganization theory (115)
strain theory (104)

6 The Formation of Subcultures

One increasingly prevalent subculture is that of gangs, such as the Mara Salvatrucha, or MS-13, whose members can be found throughout the country, and who are responsible for a variety of criminal acts.

The Function of Subcultures
Subcultural Theories of Delinquency and Crime
The Middle-Class Measuring Rod
Corner Boy, College Boy, Delinquent Boy
Tests of Cohen's Theory
Evaluation: Cohen's Theory
Delinquency and Opportunity
Tests of Opportunity Theory
Evaluation: Differential Opportunity Theory
The Subculture of Violence
Tests of the Subculture of Violence
Evaluation: The Subculture of Violence Theory
Focal Concerns: Miller's Theory
Tests of Miller's Theory
Evaluation: Miller's Theory
Gangs at the Turn of the Twenty-First Century
Guns and Gangs
Female Delinquent Subcultures
Early Research
Recent Studies
Middle-Class Delinquency
Explanations
THEORY INFORMS POLICY
Getting Out: Gang Banging or the Morgue
Review
Criminology & Public Policy
You Be the Criminologist
Key Terms

They perpetrate violence—from assaults to homicides, using firearms, machetes, or blunt objects—to intimidate rival gangs, law enforcement, and the general public. They often target middle and high school students for recruitment. And they form tenuous alliances . . . and sometimes vicious rivalries . . . with other criminal groups, depending on their needs at the time.

Who are they? Members of Mara Salvatrucha, better known as MS-13, who are mostly Salvadoran nationals or first generation Salvadoran-Americans, but also Hondurans, Guatemalans, Mexicans, and other Central and South American immigrants. And according to our recent national threat assessment of this growing, mobile street gang, they could be operating in your community . . . now or in the near future.

Based on information from our own investigations, from our state and local law enforcement partners, and from community organizations, we've concluded that while the threat posed by MS-13 to the U.S. as a whole is at the "medium" level, membership in parts of the country is so concentrated that we've labeled the threat level there "high."

Here are some other highlights from our threat assessment:

MS-13 operates in at least 42 states and the District of Columbia and has about 6,000–10,000 members nationwide. Currently, the threat is highest in the western and northeastern parts of the country, which coincides with elevated Salvadoran immigrant populations in those areas. In the southeast and central regions, the current threat is moderate to low, but recently, we've seen an influx of MS-13 members into the southeast, causing an increase in violent crimes there.

MS-13 members engage in a wide range of criminal activity, including drug distribution, murder, rape, prostitution, robbery, home invasions, immigration offenses, kidnapping, carjackings/auto thefts, and vandalism. Most of these crimes, you'll notice, have one thing in common—they are exceedingly violent. And while most of the violence is directed toward other MS-13 members or rival street gangs, innocent citizens often get caught in the crossfire.

MS-13 is expanding its membership at a "moderate" rate through recruitment and migration. Some MS-13 members move to get jobs or to be near family members—currently, the southeast and the northeast are seeing the largest increases in membership. MS-13 often recruits new members by glorifying the gang lifestyle (often on the Internet, complete with pictures and videos) and by absorbing smaller gangs.

Speaking of employment, MS-13 members typically work for legitimate businesses by presenting false documentation. They primarily pick employers that don't scrutinize employment documents, especially in the construction, restaurant, delivery service, and landscaping industries.

Right now, MS-13 has no official national leadership structure. MS-13 originated in Los Angeles, but when members migrated eastward, they began forming cliques that for the most part operated independently. These cliques, though, often maintain regular contact with members in other regions to coordinate recruitment/criminal activities and to prevent conflicts. We do believe that Los Angeles gang members have an elevated status among their MS-13 counterparts across the country, a system of respect that could potentially evolve into a more organized national leadership structure.

One final word about MS-13: The FBI, through its MS-13 National Joint Task Force and field investigations, remains committed to working with our local, state, national, and international partners to disrupt and dismantle this violent gang.[1]

There is a sense of urgency and concern underpinning this bulletin from the Federal Bureau of Investigation. Before dismissing both, it is worth considering these somber conclusions of the 2005 National Gang Threat Assessment from the United States Department of Justice:

- Gangs remain the primary distributors of drugs throughout the United States.

- Gangs are associating with organized crime entities such as Mexican drug organizations, Asian criminal groups, and Russian organized crime groups. These groups often turn to gangs to conduct low-level criminal activities, protect territories, and facilitate drug-trafficking activities. Financial gain is the primary goal of any association between these groups.

- Gang members are becoming more sophisticated in their use of computers and technology. These new tools are used to communicate, to facilitate criminal activity, and to avoid detection by law enforcement.

- Prison gangs pose a unique threat to law enforcement and communities. The incarceration of gang members often does little to disrupt their activities. High-ranking gang members often are able to exert their influence on the street from within prison.

- Hispanic gang membership is on the rise. These gangs are migrating and expanding their jurisdictions throughout the country. Identification and differentiation of these gangs pose new obstacles for law enforcement, especially in rural communities.

- Migration of California-style gang culture remains a particular threat. The migration spreads the reach of gangs into new neighborhoods and promotes a flourishing gang subculture.

- While the number of all-female gangs remains low, the role of women in gangs is evolving. Women are taking more active roles, such as assisting in the movement of drugs and weapons and gathering intelligence from other gangs.

- Indian country is increasingly reporting escalating levels of gang activity and gang-related crime and drug trafficking. The remote nature of many reservations and a thriving gang subculture make youth in these environments particularly vulnerable to gangs.

- Outlaw motorcycle gangs (OMGs) are expanding their territory and forming new clubs, as reflected in increased violence among OMGs battling over territories.

- Approximately 31 percent of survey respondents indicated that their communities refused to acknowledge the gang problem. Several communities began to address gang issues only when high-profile gang-related incidents occurred.

- Forming multiagency task forces and joint community groups is an effective way to combat the problem of gangs. However, decreases in funding and staffing for many task forces have created new challenges for communities.[2]

How did gangs get started in American society? What keeps them going? And, just as important, how do criminological theories account for gang behavior?

THE FUNCTION OF SUBCULTURES

Strain theorists explain criminal behavior as a result of the frustrations suffered by lower-class individuals deprived of legitimate means to reach their goals. Cultural deviance theorists assume that individuals become criminal by learning the criminal values of the groups to which they belong. In conforming to their own group standards, these people break the laws of the dominant culture. These two perspectives are the foundation for subcultural theory, which emerged in the mid-1950s.

A **subculture** is a subdivision within the dominant culture that has its own norms, beliefs, and values. Subcultures typically emerge when people in similar circumstances find themselves isolated from the mainstream and band together for mutual support. Subcultures may form among members of racial and ethnic minorities, among prisoners, among occupational groups, and among ghetto dwellers. Subcultures exist within a larger society, not apart from it. They therefore share some of its values. Nevertheless, the lifestyles of their members are significantly different from those of individuals in the dominant culture.

SUBCULTURAL THEORIES OF DELINQUENCY AND CRIME

Subcultural theories in criminology were developed to account for delinquency among lower-class males, especially for one of its most important expressions—the teenage gang. According to subcultural theorists, delinquent subcultures, like all subcultures, emerge in response to special problems that members of the dominant culture do not face. Theories developed by Albert Cohen and by Richard Cloward and Lloyd Ohlin are extensions of the strain, social disorganization, and differential association theories. They explain why delinquent subcultures emerge in the first place (strain), why they take a particular form (social disorganization), and how they are passed on from one generation to the next (differential association).

The explanations of delinquency developed by Marvin Wolfgang and Franco Ferracuti and by Walter Miller are somewhat different from those previously mentioned. These theorists do not suggest that delinquency begins with failure to reach middle-class goals. Their explanations are rooted in culture conflict theory. The subculture of violence thesis argues that the value systems of some subcultures demand the use of violence in certain social situations. This norm, which affects daily behavior, conflicts with conventional middle-class norms. Along the same lines, Miller suggests that the characteristics of lower-class delinquency reflect the value system of the lower-class culture and that the lower-class values and norms conflict with those of the dominant culture.

Although Miller contends that the lower-class culture as a whole—not a subculture within it—is responsible for criminal behavior in urban slums, his theory is appropriate to our discussion because it demonstrates how the needs of young urban males are met by membership in a street gang. Miller's street gangs, like those of Cohen and of Cloward and Ohlin, condone violent criminal activity as one of the few means of attaining status in a slum.

The Middle-Class Measuring Rod

Albert Cohen was a student of Robert Merton and of Edwin Sutherland, both of whom had made convincing arguments about the causes of delinquency. Sutherland persuaded Cohen that differential association and the cultural transmission of criminal norms led to criminal behavior. From Merton he learned about structurally induced strain. Cohen combined and expanded these perspectives to explain how the delinquent subculture arises, where it is found within the social structure, and why it has the particular characteristics that it does.[3]

According to Cohen, delinquent subcultures emerge in the slum areas of large American cities. They are rooted in class differentials in parental aspirations, child-rearing practices, and classroom standards. The relative position of a youngster's family in the social structure determines the problems the child will have to face throughout life.

Lower-class families who have never known a middle-class lifestyle, for example, cannot socialize their children in a way that prepares them to enter the middle class. The children grow up with poor communication skills, a lack of commitment to education, and an inability to delay gratification. Schools present a particular problem. There lower-class children are evaluated by middle-class teachers on the basis of a middle-class measuring rod. The measures are based on middle-class values such as self-reliance, good manners, respect for property, and long-range planning. By such measures, lower-class children fall far short of the standards they must meet if they are to compete successfully with middle-class children. Cohen argues that they experience status frustration and strain, to which they respond by adopting one of three roles: corner boy, college boy, or delinquent boy.

Corner Boy, College Boy, Delinquent Boy

"Corner boys" try to make the best of bad situations. The corner boy hangs out in the neighborhood with his peer group, spending the day in some group activity, such as gambling or athletic competition. He receives support from his peers and is very loyal to them. Most lower-class boys become corner boys. Eventually, they get menial jobs and live a conventional lifestyle.

There are very few "college boys." These boys continually strive to live up to middle-class standards, but their chances for success are limited because of academic and social hardships.

"Delinquent boys" band together to form a subculture in which they can define status in ways that to them seem attainable. Cohen claims that even though these lower-class youths set up their own norms, they have internalized the norms of the dominant class and feel anxious when they go against those norms. To deal with this conflict, they resort to **reaction formation,** a mechanism that relieves anxiety through the process of rejecting with abnormal intensity what one wants but cannot obtain. These boys turn the middle-class norms upside down, thereby making conduct right in their subculture precisely because it is wrong by the norms of the larger culture (Figure 6.1).

Consequently, their delinquent acts serve no useful purpose. They do not steal things to eat them, wear them, or sell them. In fact, they often discard or destroy what they have stolen. They appear to delight in the discomfort of others and in breaking taboos. Their acts are directed against people and property at random, unlike the goal-oriented activities of many adult criminal groups. The subculture typically is characterized by short-run hedonism, pure pleasure seeking, with no planning or deliberation about what to do or where or when to do it. The delinquents hang out on the street corner until someone gets an idea; then they act impulsively, without considering the consequences. The group's autonomy is all-important. Its members are loyal to each other and resist any attempts on the part of family, school, or community to restrain their behavior.

Tests of Cohen's Theory

Criminological researchers generally agree that Cohen's theory is responsible for major advances in research on delinquency.[4] Among them are researchers who have found a relationship between delinquency and social status in our society (Chapter 5). Much evidence also supports Cohen's assumption that lower-class children perform more poorly in school than middle-class children.[5] Teachers often expect them to perform less ably than their middle-class students, and this expectation is one of the components of poor performance.

Researchers have demonstrated that poor performance in school is related to delinquency. When Travis Hirschi studied more than 4,000 California schoolchildren, he found that youths

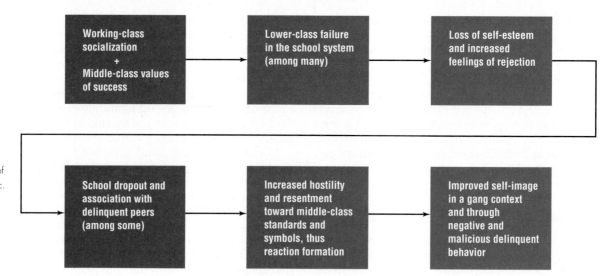

FIGURE 6.1 The process of reaction formation among delinquent boys.

Source: Donald J. Shoemaker, *Theories of Delinquency: An Examination of Explanations of Delinquent Behavior,* 4th ed. (2000), Figure 7 (p. 109). By permission of Oxford University Press, Inc. www.oup.com

Boredom in class, as demonstrated by this ninth-grade student, may lead to dropout and delinquency.

who were academically incompetent and performed poorly in school came to dislike school. Disliking it, they rejected its authority; rejecting its authority, they committed delinquent acts (Chapter 7).[6] Delbert Elliott and Harwin Voss also investigated the relationship between school and delinquency. They analyzed annual school performance and delinquency records of 2,000 students in California from ninth grade to 1 year after the expected graduation date. Their findings indicated that those who dropped out of school had higher rates of delinquency than those who graduated. They also found that academic achievement and alienation from school were closely related to dropping out of school.[7]

From analysis of the dropout-delinquency relationship among over 5,000 persons nationwide, G. Roger Jarjoura concluded that while dropouts were more likely than graduates to engage in delinquent acts, the reason was not always simply the fact that they had dropped out. Dropping out because of a dislike for school, poor grades, or

financial reasons was related to future involvement in delinquency; dropping out because of problems at home was not. Dropping out for personal reasons such as marriage or pregnancy was significantly related to subsequent violent offending.[8] All these findings support Cohen's theory. Other findings, however, do not.

In a study of 12,524 students in Davidson County, Tennessee, Albert Reiss and Albert Rhodes found only a slight relationship between delinquency and status deprivation.[9] This conclusion was supported by the research of Marvin Krohn and his associates.[10] Furthermore, several criminologists have challenged Cohen's claim that delinquent behavior is purposeless.[11] They contend that much delinquent behavior is serious and calculated and often engaged in for profit.[12] Others have also questioned the consistency of the theory: Cohen argues that the behavior of delinquent boys is a deliberate response to middle-class opinion, yet he also argues that the boys do not care about the opinions of middle-class people.[13]

Evaluation: Cohen's Theory

Researchers have both praised and criticized Cohen's work. Cohen's theory answers a number of questions left unresolved by the strain and cultural deviance theories. It explains the origin of delinquent behavior and why some youths raised in the same neighborhoods and attending the same schools do not become involved in delinquent subcultures. His concepts of status deprivation and the middle-class measuring rod have been useful to researchers. Yet his theory does not explain why most delinquents eventually become law-abiding even though their position in the class structure remains relatively fixed. Some criminologists also question whether youths are driven by some serious motivating force or are simply out on the streets looking for fun.[14] Moreover, if delinquent subcultures result from the practice of measuring lower-class boys by a middle-class measuring rod, how do we account for the growing number of middle-class gangs?

Other questions concern the difficulty of trying to test the concepts of reaction formation, internalization of middle-class values, and status deprivation, among others. To answer some of his critics, Cohen, with his colleague James Short, expanded the idea of delinquent subcultures to include not only lower-class delinquent behavior but also variants such as middle-class delinquent subcultures and female delinquents.[15] Cohen took Merton's strain theory a step further by elaborating on the development of delinquent behavior. He described how strain actually creates frustration and status deprivation, which in turn fosters the development of an alternative set of values that give lower-class boys a chance to achieve recognition. Since the mid-1950s, Cohen's theory has stimulated not only research but also the formulation of new theories.

DELINQUENCY AND OPPORTUNITY

Like Cohen's theory, the theory of differential opportunity developed by Richard Cloward and Lloyd Ohlin combines strain, differential association, and social disorganization concepts.[16] Both theories begin with the assumption that conventional means to conventional success are not equally distributed among the socioeconomic classes, that lack of means causes frustration for lower-class youths, and that criminal behavior is learned and culturally transmitted. Both theories also agree that the common solution to shared problems leads to the formation of delinquent subcultures. They disagree, however, on the content of these subcultures. As we have noted, norms in Cohen's delinquent subcultures are right precisely because

■ Multicultural advertisements appeal to young males concerned with showing toughness through masculinity. This billboard suggests that Converse sneakers are not for kids' playgrounds.

they are wrong in the dominant culture. Delinquent acts are negative and nonutilitarian. Cloward and Ohlin disagree; they suggest that lower-class delinquents remain goal-oriented. The kind of delinquent behavior they engage in depends on the illegitimate opportunities available to them.

According to Cloward and Ohlin's **differential opportunity theory,** delinquent subcultures flourish in lower-class areas and take the particular forms they do because opportunities for illegitimate success are no more equitably distributed than those for conventional success. Just as means—opportunities—are unequally distributed in the conventional world, opportunities to reach one's goals are unequally distributed in the criminal world. A person cannot simply decide to join a theft-oriented gang or, for that matter, a violence-oriented one. Cloward and Ohlin maintain that the types of subcultures and the juvenile gangs that flourish within them depend on the types of neighborhoods in which they develop (Figure 6.2).

In areas where conventional and illegitimate values and behavior are integrated by a close connection of illegitimate and legitimate businesses, "criminal gangs" emerge. Older criminals serve

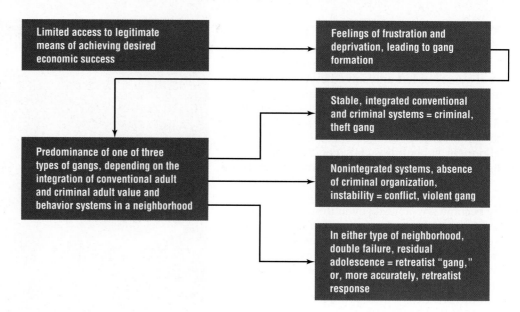

FIGURE 6.2 Factors leading to the development of three types of delinquent gangs.

Source: Donald J. Shoemaker, *Theories of Delinquency: An Examination of Explanations of Delinquent Behavior,* 4th ed. (2000), Figure 8 (p.117). By permission of Oxford University Press, Inc. www.oup.com

as role models. They teach youngsters the kinds of people to exploit, the necessary criminal skills, the importance of loyal relationships with criminal associates, and the way to make the right connections with shady lawyers, bail bondsmen, crooked politicians, and corrupt police officers. Adolescent members of criminal gangs, like adult criminals in the neighborhood, are involved in extortion, fraud, theft, and other activities that yield illegal income.

This type of neighborhood was described by one of its members in a classic work published in 1930:

> Stealing in the neighborhood was a common practice among the children and approved by the parents. Whenever the boys got together they talked about robbing and made more plans for stealing. I hardly knew any boys who did not go robbing. The little fellows went in for petty stealing, breaking into freight cars, and stealing junk. The older guys did big jobs like stickups, burglary, and stealing autos. The little fellows admired the "big shots" and longed for the day when they could get into the big racket. Fellows who had "done time" were the big shots and looked up to and gave the little fellows tips on how to get by and pull off big jobs.[17]

Neighborhoods characterized by transience and instability, Cloward and Ohlin argue, offer few opportunities to get ahead in organized criminal activities. This world gives rise to "conflict gangs," whose goal is to gain a reputation for toughness and destructive violence. Thus "one particular biker would catch a bird and then bite off its head, allowing the blood to trickle from his mouth as he yelled 'all right!' "[18] It is the world of the warrior: Fight, show courage against all odds, defend and maintain the honor of the group. Above all, never show fear.

Violence is the means used to gain status in conflict gangs. Conventional society's recognition of the "worst" gangs becomes a mark of prestige, perpetuating the high standards of their members. Conflict gangs emerge in lower-class areas where neither criminal nor conventional adult role models exercise much control over youngsters.

A third subcultural response to differential opportunities is the formation of "retreatist gangs." Cloward and Ohlin describe members of retreatist gangs as double failures because they have not been successful in the legitimate world and have been equally unsuccessful in the illegitimate worlds of organized criminal activity and violence-oriented gangs. This subculture is characterized by a continuous search for getting high through alcohol, atypical sexual experiences, marijuana, hard drugs, or a combination of these.

The retreatist hides in a world of sensual adventure, borrowing, begging, or stealing to support his habit, whatever it may be. He may peddle drugs or work as a pimp or look for some other deviant income-producing activity. But the income is not a primary concern; he is interested only in the next high. Belonging to a retreatist gang offers a sense of superiority and well-being that is otherwise beyond the reach of these least-successful dropouts.

Not all lower-class youngsters who are unable to reach society's goals become members of criminal, conflict, or retreatist gangs. Many choose to accept their situation and to live within its constraints. These law-abiding youngsters are Cohen's corner boys.

Tests of Opportunity Theory

Cloward and Ohlin's differential opportunity theory presented many new ideas, and a variety of studies emerged to test it empirically.

The first of Cloward and Ohlin's assumptions—that blocked opportunities are related to delinquency—has had mixed support. Travis Hirschi, for example, demonstrated that "the greater one's acceptance of conventional (or even quasi-conventional) success goals, the less likely one is to be delinquent, regardless of the likelihood these goals will someday be attained."[19] In other words, the youngsters who stick to hard work and education to get ahead in society are the least likely to become delinquent, no matter what their real chances are of reaching their goals. John Hagedorn disagrees. In late 1992 and early 1993, he conducted interviews with 101 founding members of 18 gangs in Milwaukee. His conclusion: "Most of those we were trying to track appeared to be on an economic merry-go-round, with continual movement in and out of the secondary labor market. Although their average income from drug sales far surpassed their income from legal employment, most Milwaukee male gang members apparently kept trying to find licit work."[20] There is also evidence that both gang and nongang boys believe the middle-class values of hard work and scholastic achievement to be important. Gang boys, however, are more ready to approve of a wide range of behaviors, including aggressive acts and drug use.[21]

The second assumption of differential opportunity theory—that the type of lower-class gang depends on the type of neighborhood in which it emerges—has also drawn the attention of criminologists. Empirical evidence suggests that gang behavior is more versatile and involves a wider range of criminal and noncriminal acts than the patterns outlined by Cloward and Ohlin. Ko-lin Chin's research on New York gangs in 1993 demonstrates that Chinese gangs are engaged in extortion, alien smuggling, heroin trafficking, and the running of gambling establishments and houses of prostitution.[22] A report from the Denver Youth Survey showed that while the most frequent form of illegal activity is fighting with other gangs, gang members are also involved in robberies, joyriding, assaults, stealing, and drug sales.[23]

Research does, however, support Cloward and Ohlin's argument that criminal gangs emerge in areas where conventional and illegitimate behavior have a close connection with illegitimate and legitimate businesses. Chinatowns in America, for example, are social, economic, political, and cultural units.[24] All types of organizations, including those that dominate illegal activities, play an important role in the maintenance of order in the community. The illegitimate social order has control of territorial rights, gambling places, heroin trafficking, alien smuggling, and loan-sharking. The illegal order defines who is in control of particular restaurants, retail shops, garment factories, and the like. Business owners pay a "membership fee" for protection. Adult criminals maintain control of youth gang members by threatening to exclude them from work that pays well. They also resolve conflicts, provide recreational facilities, lend money, and give the young gang members a chance to climb the illegitimate career ladder within the criminal organization. Gang activities are closely supervised by their

leaders, who work with the adult crime groups. Elaborate initiation rites are conducted by an adult the youngsters call "uncle"—the link between the gang and the adult sponsoring organization.

Gang members (1,015) from California, Illinois, Iowa, Michigan, and Ohio also reported having a variety of legal and illegal income sources, collective gang "treasuries," and mostly adult leaders.[25] Their businesses included dance clubs; billiard halls; and stereo, liquor, jewelry, grocery, cellular phone/beeper, and auto repair shops. They also sold illegal goods: $268 for a 9-mm Glock semiautomatic pistol, $42 for a box of cartridges, $882 for 1 ounce of cocaine, and $155 for a stolen 12-gauge shotgun.[26] Such gangs operate somewhat like a union for the underground economy. Members attend meetings, pay dues, follow rules, have their own language, and make collective expenditures (for guns, funerals, attorneys).

Evaluation: Differential Opportunity Theory

For three decades, criminologists have reviewed, examined, and revised the work of Cloward and Ohlin.[27] One of the main criticisms is that their theory is class-oriented. If, as Cloward and Ohlin claim, delinquency is a response to blocked opportunities, how can we explain middle-class delinquency? Another question arises from contradictory statements. How can delinquent groups be nonutilitarian, negativistic, and malicious (Cohen)—and also goal-oriented and utilitarian? Despite its shortcomings, however, differential opportunity theory has identified some of the reasons lower-class youngsters may become alienated. Cloward and Ohlin's work has also challenged researchers to study the nature of the subcultures in our society. Marvin

Wolfgang and Franco Ferracuti have concentrated on one of them—the subculture of violence.

THE SUBCULTURE OF VIOLENCE

Like Cohen, and like Cloward and Ohlin, Marvin Wolfgang and Franco Ferracuti turned to subcultural theory to explain criminal behavior among lower-class young urban males. All three theories developed by these five researchers assume the existence of subcultures made up of people who share a value system that differs from that of the dominant culture. And they assume that each subculture has its own rules or conduct norms that dictate how individuals should act under varying circumstances. The three theories also agree that these values and norms persist over time because they are learned by successive generations. The theories differ, however, in their focus.

Cohen and Cloward and Ohlin focus on the origin of the subculture, specifically, culturally induced strain. The thrust of Wolfgang and Ferracuti's work is culture conflict. Furthermore, the earlier theories encompass all types of delinquency and crime; Wolfgang and Ferracuti concentrate on violent crime. They argue that in some subcultures, behavior norms are dictated by a value system that demands the use of force or violence.[28] Subcultures that adhere to conduct norms conducive to violence are referred to as **subcultures of violence.**

Violence is not used in all situations, but it is frequently an expected response. The appearance of a weapon, a slight shove or push, a derogatory remark, or the opportunity to wield power undetected may very well evoke an aggressive reaction that seems uncalled for to middle-class

TABLE 6.1 Moderate and High Gang Involvement in Distribution (percent, by region)

Drug Type	Northeast	South	Midwest	West	Total
Powdered cocaine	52.9%	38.7%	37.5%	32.9%	38.2%
Crack cocaine	52.9	45.7	60.2	39.2	47.3
Heroin	45.1	17.9	25.0	35.7	27.9
Marijuana	56.9	54.3	67.0	79.0	64.8
Methamphetamine	17.6	24.9	23.9	73.4	39.1
MDMA	31.4	19.1	18.1	30.1	23.7

SOURCE: *The 2005 National Gang Threat Assessment* (Washington, D.C.: Bureau of Justice Assistance, 2006), p. vi; available at www.nagia.org/PDFs/2005_national_gang_threat_assessment.pdf.

people. Fists rather than words settle disputes. Knives or guns are readily available, so confrontations can quickly escalate. Violence is a pervasive part of everyday life. Childrearing practices (hitting), gang activities (street wars), domestic quarrels (battering), and social events (drunken brawls) are all permeated by violence.

Violence is not considered antisocial. Members of this subculture feel no guilt about their aggression. In fact, individuals who do not resort to violence may be reprimanded. The value system is transmitted from generation to generation, long after the original reason for the violence has disappeared. The pattern is very hard to eradicate.

When Wolfgang and Ferracuti described population groups that are likely to respond violently to stress, they posed a powerful question to the criminal justice system: How does one go about changing a subcultural norm? This question becomes increasingly significant with the merging of the drug subculture and the subculture of violence.

Tests of the Subculture of Violence

Howard Erlanger, using nationwide data collected for the President's Commission on the Causes and Prevention of Violence, found no major differences in attitudes toward violence by class or race. Erlanger concluded that though members of the lower class show no greater approval of violence than middle-class persons do, they lack the sophistication necessary to settle grievances by other means. Not all studies support this idea, however. In *Code of the Street,* Elijah Anderson presents ethnographic evidence that violence is part of a complex street culture in impoverished communities that develops in response to structural obstacles. Other quantitative and review studies provide mixed evidence on the race/class/subculture of violence hypothesis.[29]

The subculture of violence thesis has also generated a line of empirical research that looks at regional differences in levels of violent crime.

The South (as you will see in Chapter 10) has the highest homicide rate in the country. Some researchers have attributed this high rate to subcultural values.[30] They argue that the Southern subculture of violence has its historical roots in an exaggerated defense of honor by Southern gentlemen, mob violence (especially lynching), a military tradition, the acceptance of personal vengeance, and the widespread availability and use of handguns.[31]

The problem with many of these studies is that it is difficult to separate the effects of economic and social factors from those of cultural values. Several researchers have sought to solve this problem. Colin Loftin and Robert Hill, for example, using a sophisticated measure of poverty, found that economic factors, not cultural ones, explained regional variation in homicide rates.[32] Similarly, others suggest that high homicide rates and gun ownership may have a great deal to do with socioeconomic conditions, especially racial inequality in the South.[33]

Researchers who support the subculture of violence thesis point to statistics on characteristics of homicide offenders and victims: Lower-class, inner-city black males are disproportionately represented in the FBI's Uniform Crime Reports.[34]

Furthermore, in a study of 556 males interviewed at age 26, 19 percent of the respondents, all inner-city males, reported having been shot or stabbed. These victimizations were found to be highly correlated with both self-reported offenses and official arrest statistics. In fact, the best single predictor of committing a violent act was found to be whether the individual had been a victim of a violent crime. Though most people in the dominant society who are shot or stabbed do not commit a criminal act in response, it appears that many inner-city males alternate the roles of victim and offender in a way that maintains the values and attitudes of a violent subculture.[35]

DID YOU KNOW?

. . . the extent of gang involvement in drug distribution across all regions of the United States (Table 6.1)?

Evaluation: The Subculture of Violence Theory

Though empirical evidence remains inconclusive, the subculture of violence theory is supported by the distribution of violent crime in American society.[36] The number of gangs and the violence associated with their activities is growing.[37] Jeffrey Fagan noted that "drug use is widespread and normative" among gangs.[38] Gang warfare, which takes the lives of innocent bystanders in ghetto areas, is a part of life in most of the impoverished, densely populated neighborhoods in major cities such as Los Angeles, New York, Chicago, Miami, Washington, D.C., and Atlanta, as well as in smaller disintegrating urban centers. For example, over the 3 years between 1985 and 1988, Jamaican "posses"—gangs transplanted from Kingston, Jamaica, to the United States—were involved in 1,400 homicides.[39]

Though not all persons in these subcultures follow the norm of violence, it appears that a dismaying number of them attach less and less importance to the value of human life and turn increasingly to violence to resolve immediate problems and frustrations. (We return to this issue later in the chapter.)

FOCAL CONCERNS: MILLER'S THEORY

All the theorists we have examined thus far explain criminal and delinquent behavior in terms of subcultural values that emerge and are perpetuated from one generation to the next in lower-class urban slums. Walter Miller reasons differently. According to Miller,

> in the case of "gang" delinquency, the cultural system which exerts the most direct influence on behavior is that of the lower-class community itself—a long-established, distinctively patterned tradition with an integrity of its own—rather than a so-called "delinquent subculture" which has arisen through conflict with middle-class culture and is oriented to the deliberate violation of middle-class norms.[40]

To Miller, juvenile delinquency is not rooted in the rejection of middle-class values; rather, it stems from lower-class culture, which has its own value system. This value system has evolved as a response to living in disadvantaged neighborhoods characterized by single-parent households (Table 6.2). Gang norms are simply the adolescent expression of the lower-class culture in which the boys have grown up. This lower-class culture exists apart from the middle-class culture, and it has done so for generations. The value system, not the gang norms, generates delinquent acts.

Miller has identified six focal concerns, or areas, to which lower-class males give persistent

TABLE 6.2 Percentage of Children Living in Poverty or with No Working Parent

Many children live in poverty, often residing in single-parent households where the head of household does not have a job.

Living Arrangement	No Working Parent	Living in Poverty
Both parents	14%	10%
Single parent	34	43
Mother	37	47
Father	19	22

SOURCE: *Juvenile Offenders and Victims: 1999 National Report* (Washington, D.C.: Office of Juvenile Justice and Delinquency Prevention, 1999), pp. 6, 8.

Rapper 50 Cent, pictured here in February 2003, expressed his values with his debut record, *Get Rich or Die Tryin'*, which sold 892,000 copies in 4 days. His follow-up record, *Massacre*, sold 771,000 copies in its first full week of release.

attention: trouble, toughness, smartness, excitement, luck, and autonomy. Concern over trouble is a major feature of lower-class life. Staying out of trouble and getting into trouble are daily preoccupations. Trouble can get a person into the hands of the authorities, or it can result in prestige among

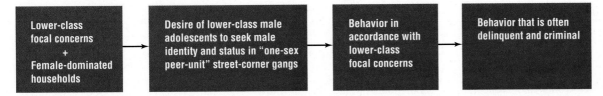

FIGURE 6.3 The relationship between delinquency and lower-class focal concerns.

Source: Donald J. Shoemaker, *Theories of Delinquency: An Examination of Explanations of Delinquent Behavior,* 4th ed. (2000), Figure 9 (p. 125). By permission of Oxford University Press, Inc. www.oup.com

peers. Lower-class individuals are often evaluated by the extent of their involvement in activities such as fighting, drinking, and sexual misbehaving. In this case, the greater the involvement or the more extreme the performance, the greater the prestige or "respect" the person commands.

These young men are almost obsessively concerned with "toughness"; the code requires a show of masculinity, a denial of sentimentality, and a display of physical strength. Miller argues that this concern with toughness is related to the fact that a large proportion of lower-class males grow up in female-dominated households and have no male figure from whom to learn the male role. They join street gangs in order to find males with whom they can identify.

Claude Brown's classic 1965 autobiography, *Manchild in the Promised Land,* illustrates the concerns about trouble and toughness among adolescents growing up in an urban slum:

> My friends were all daring like me, tough like me, dirty like me, ragged like me, cursed like me, and had a great love for trouble like me. We took pride in being able to hitch rides on trolleys, buses, taxicabs and in knowing how to steal and fight. We knew that we were the only kids in the neighborhood who usually had more than ten dollars in their pockets. . . . Somebody was always trying to shake us down or rob us. This was usually done by the older hustlers in the neighborhood or by storekeepers or cops. . . . We accepted this as a way of life.[41]

Another focal concern is "smartness"—the ability to gain something by outsmarting, outwitting, or conning another person. In lower-class neighborhoods, youngsters practice outsmarting each other in card games, exchanges of insults, and other trials. Prestige is awarded to those who demonstrate smartness.

Many aspects of lower-class life are related to another focal concern, the search for "excitement." Youngsters alternate between hanging out with peers and looking for excitement, which can be found in fighting, getting drunk, and using drugs. Risks, danger, and thrills break up the monotony of their existence.

Fate, particularly "luck," plays an important role in lower-class life. Many individuals believe that their lives are subject to forces over which they have little control. If they get lucky, a rather drab life could change quickly. Common discussions center on whether lucky numbers come up, cards are right, or dice are good. Brown recalls:

> After a while [Mama] settled down, and we stopped talking about her feelings, then somebody came upstairs and told her she had hit the numbers. We just forgot all about her feelings. I forgot about her feelings. Mama forgot about her feelings. Everybody did. She started concentrating on the number. This was the first time she'd had a hit in a long time. They bought some liquor. Mama and Dad started drinking: everyone started making a lot of noise and playing records.[42]

Miller's final focal concern, "autonomy," stems from the lower-class person's resentment of external controls, whether parents, teachers, or police. This desire for personal freedom is expressed often in terms such as "No one can push me around" and "I don't need nobody."[43]

According to Miller, status in every class is associated with the possession of qualities that are valued. In the lower class, the six focal concerns define status. It is apparent that by engaging in behavior that affords status by these criteria, many people will be breaking the laws of the dominant society (Figure 6.3).

Tests of Miller's Theory

An obvious question is whether in our urban, heterogeneous, secular, technologically based society any isolated pockets of culture are still to be found. The pervasiveness of mass advertising, mass transit, and mass communication makes it seem unlikely that an entire class of people could be unaware of the dominant value system. Empirical research on opportunity theory has found that lower-class boys share the conventional success goals of the dominant culture. This finding suggests that the idea of isolation from the dominant system does not fit with reality. Empirical research has also found, however, that while gang boys may support middle-class values,

Cohen vs. Miller

Both Albert Cohen and Walter Miller argue that deviant subcultures develop among disadvantaged segments of society. Their theories diverge, however, when it comes to the association of these subcultures with the values of mainstream society. According to Cohen, delinquent subcultures are formed when disadvantaged youths cannot adhere to the same middle-class standards as their more-advantaged peers. In other words, deviant subculture develops in response to mainstream culture. Miller, on the other hand, hypothesizes that the subculture of violence develops in isolation from mainstream society. It is part of a more general culture that exists among the lower class, but it is not formed as a symbolic rejection of middle-class values and goals.

Overall, a comparison of Cohen and Miller's theories raises the question of whether it is disadvantage itself that leads to the formation of deviant subcultures or disadvantage *relative* to other segments of society.

In general, U.S. census data on poverty favors Cohen's theory. The United States has one of the highest violent-crime rates in the world, and it is also characterized by a mix of wealthy and impoverished segments of society. In 2006, 9.8 percent of families and 13.3 percent of individuals were living below the poverty line. At the same time, 19.1 percent of households were earning an annual income of $100,000 or more. The United States scored a 45 on the Gini index of income inequality.(1) When we con-

sider concentrated poverty, however, the implications are less clear. Concentrated poverty, or the proportion of individuals living in high-poverty areas, declined between 1990 and 2000, but in 2000 it was still substantial at 10 percent and varied considerably depending on the region (see figure).(2) This can be interpreted as support for Miller or Cohen, depending on your perspective. On one hand, it indicates that a significant proportion of the United States is covered by clusters of impoverished communities where lower-class culture is likely to flourish in isolation from mainstream culture. On the other hand, the clustering of these communities together in space may make inhabitants more aware of the gap between themselves and the middle class.

International data are equally contradictory. Some international data support Cohen's theory. Between 1998 and 2001, South Africa had an average yearly homicide rate of 55.86 per 100,000 individuals, which is more than 10 times higher than that of the United States during roughly the same time period.(3) South Africa also has one of the largest wealth gaps in the world as measured by the Gini index of income inequality.(4) Other countries, such as China, have high income inequality but low crime rates.(5, 6) It appears that the direction of the relationship between inequality and crime varies by nation.

Aside from the international evidence, which provides no clear conclusions, one may ask which theory makes

more intuitive sense. Does it seem possible for disadvantaged segments of society not only to be indifferent to mainstream culture, but also to be completely unaware of it? On the other hand, doesn't rejection of middle-class values suggest that disadvantaged youths have internalized them to some degree? In other words, if they do not care about mainstream values at all, wouldn't they retreat from them without hostility?

One may also point out that Cohen and Miller focus on the development of different types of subcultures—Cohen's theory explains delinquent subcultures, while Miller's explains violent subcultures. However, neither scholar offers any insight into why the two types of subcultures may develop differently from each other. Is this difference enough to reconcile the disparities between the two lines of thinking? Why might violent subcultures develop solely from lower-class culture and delinquent subcultures develop in response to middle-class standards?

If, according to Cohen, it is the inadequacy felt by disadvantaged youths when they are measured against the middle class that leads to delinquency, then why is this mentality limited to those individuals? Why does it not extend to middle-class youths when they compare themselves to upper-class peers, for example, or to upper-class youths when they compare themselves to celebrity children? Cohen would argue that the expectations of society are grounded in middle-class rather than upper-class standards and that it is the expectations

they are willing to deviate from them. If an opportunity arises to gain prestige in a fight, gang boys are willing to take the chance that their act will not result in punishment.

Most empirical tests of values question young people on their attachment to middle-class values. Stephen Cernovich expanded this type of research by investigating attachment to lower-class focal concerns.[44] He found that toughness, excitement, trouble, and pleasure-seeking were related to self-reported delinquency in all classes. His findings

also showed that boys of all classes were committed to delayed gratification, hard work, and education. Cernovich concluded that it is values, rather than class, that are associated with delinquency.

Evaluation: Miller's Theory

Criminologists have been disturbed by Miller's assumption that the lower-class lifestyle is generally focused on illegal activity. In making such an assumption, they say, Miller disregards the fact that

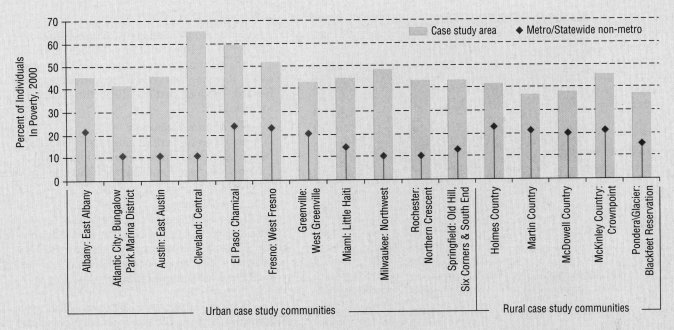

Poverty rates in the case study communities and their comparison areas. (Comparison areas are metropolitan areas for urban case study communities, and statewide nonmetropolitan areas for rural case study communities).

Sources: U.S. Census Bureau, Census 2000; Berube, A. Concentrated poverty in America: An overview. In D. Erickson, et al., eds. *The Enduring Challenge of Concentrated Poverty in America: Case studies from Communities across the U.S.*, p. 6, Figure 1A. © 2008 The Federal Reserve System and The Brookings Institution. Reprinted with permission. www.brookings.edu/metro

of society rather than those of the individual that influence subculture formation. Does this mean that awareness of an even higher standard has no influence? In other words, is it only expectations that matter, or do individual desires play a role as well? According to Miller, the question is irrelevant because deviant subculture is a product of membership in the lower class and thus does not apply to other individuals, regardless of their aspirations.

Sources

1. United States Census, 2008.
2. Paul Jargowsky, "Stunning Progress, Hidden Problems: The Dramatic Decline of Concentrated Poverty in the 1990s," *Living Cities Census Series,* Center on Urban and Metropolitan Studies (Washington, D.C.: Brookings Institute, 2003).
3. Gordon Barclay and Cynthia Tavares, "International Comparisons of Criminal Justice Statistics 2001," Home Office and Council of Europe, October 24, 2003.
4. Jens Martins, "A Compendium of Inequality: The Human Development Report 2005," FES briefing paper, October 2005.
5. Michael Yates, "Poverty and Inequality in the Global Economy," *Monthly Review* **55**(9), February, 2004, www.monthlyreview.org/0204yates.htm.
6. Yuri Andrienko, "Crime, Wealth, and Inequality: Evidence from International Crime Victim Surveys," Economics Education and Research Consortium, Moscow, November 2002.

Questions for Discussion

1. What is your position on the Cohen versus Miller debate? Explain.
2. What are the possible effects of attributing a "subculture of violence" to the lower class?

most people in the lower class do conform to conventional norms. Moreover, some criminologists ask, if lower-class boys are conforming to their own value system, why would they suffer guilt or shame when they commit delinquent acts?[45]

Perhaps the best support for Miller's ideas is found in qualitative, rather than quantitative, accounts of life in a lower-class slum. In our discussion of cultural deviance and subcultural theories, we noted that the values and norms that define behavior in these areas do not change much over time or from place to place. Successive generations have to deal with the same problems. They typically demonstrate similar responses. Angela D'Arpa-Calandra, a former probation officer who now directs a Juvenile Intensive Supervision program, says she recently walked into a New York courtroom and "saw a mother and grandmother sitting with the 14-year-old offender. 'I had the grandmother in criminal court in 1963,' D'Arpa-Calandra says. 'We didn't stop it there. The grandmother was 14 when she was arrested. The mother

■ *"Migrant Mother and Children," 1936. Dorothea Lange's photographic portrayal of the plight of a poor Southern family.*

had this child when she was 14. It's like a cycle we must relive.' "[46]

By and large, descriptions of life in poverty-stricken areas, whether written by people who have lived in them or by people who have studied them, reveal dreary routine, boredom, constant trouble, and incessant problems with drugs, alcohol, and crime. As the father tells his son in Eugene O'Neill's autobiographical play *Long Day's Journey into Night,* "There was no damned romance in our poverty."[47] O'Neill's words were captured by photographer Dorothea Lange, who startled and moved the world with images of the poor, destitute, and displaced during the Great Depression (1930–1939). The photograph above, in particular, inspired Steinbeck in *The Grapes of Wrath*—and millions of others—to consider the plight shown of the so very disadvantaged.[48]

GANGS AT THE TURN OF THE TWENTY-FIRST CENTURY

In Los Angeles:
A 7-year-old boy was slain and his 10-month-old brother seriously injured by stray bullets as members of the Crips gang opened fire in a parking lot to avenge shootings that had occurred two hours earlier.[49]

In New York:
An 11-year-old boy was killed as two gang members bicycled up to a crowded playground and opened fire. The goal was to kill a member of a rival gang.[50]

In Washington, D.C.:
An 18-year-old pleaded guilty to first-degree murder of a 12-year-old boy. He beat and shot the victim whom he had warned to stay out of the gang war. When the warning was not heeded, he concluded that the victim "wanted to be dead."[51]

In Santa Monica, California:
Within a 2-week period, gang wars left five people dead and three seriously injured. In the previous year Santa Monica had one homicide.[52]

In Houston, Texas:
A 16-year-old girl and member of the Hispanic gang Crazy Crew plunged a double-bladed knife with serrated edges into the heart of a 15-year-old boy and member of the rival gang MS-13, killing him.[53]

The new subculture that emerged in the 1980s and continues into the new century combines violence, which has become more vicious than in earlier years, with big business in drug trafficking. Many gangs have transitioned from turf-oriented to profit-driven organizations. Highly sophisticated gangs, such as the Latin Kings, Gangster Disciples, and Vice Lords, have forged relationships with Colombian and Dominican drug-trafficking organizations (DTOs) and are heavily involved in nearly every aspect of the retail drug trade, including smuggling, transportation, and the wholesale distribution of drugs nationwide.[54] The Latin Kings and Mara Salvatrucha (MS-13), for example, smuggle multikilogram-quantities of methamphetamine into the Southwest and transport the drug to previously untapped methamphetamine markets throughout the United States.[55] Meanwhile, it is estimated that one gang alone, the Eight Trey Gangster Crips, has distributed hundreds of kilos of crack and powdered cocaine worth over $10 million on the streets of Los Angeles and five other cities, as far east as Atlanta. The FBI reports that there are hundreds of similar drug networks operating across the country.

Gangs continue to control a significant portion of the illicit drug market in urban areas, as well as in rural and suburban areas. In fact, gangs are the principal distributors of illicit drugs in the United States, and drug trafficking is their primary source of financial equity. (See Tables 6.3 and 6.4.) Research continues to demonstrate that as gangs become more entrenched in the drug market, the likelihood of criminal offending increases.[56] Movies like *Colors, American Me, Belly,* and *Baby Boy* capture the realities of life in a gang and, in some cases, provide models for gang activities.

Crime Surfing WWW

www.ncjrs.gov/ spotlight/gangs/ summary.html

Would you like to find out more about the prevalence of gangs in various areas?

TABLE 6.3 Level of Street Gang Involvement in Distribution (percentage by region)

	Northeast	South	Midwest	West	Total
			STREET SALES		
High	39.2%	24.3%	29.5%	39.2%*	31.6%
Moderate	21.6	28.9	22.7	34.3	28.6
Low	17.6	23.1	27.3	16.1	21.1
None/unknown	21.6	23.7	20.5	10.5	18.7
			WHOLESALE		
High	15.7	14.5*	22.7	20.3*	18.0
Moderate	25.5	19.7	20.5	24.5	22.0
Low	25.5	32.4	31.8	28.7	30.3
None/unknown	33.3	33.5	25.0	26.6	29.7

*Table columns do not sum to 100% due to rounding.

SOURCE: *2005 National Gang Threat Assessment* (Washington, D.C.: Department of Justice and National Alliance of Gang Investigators Associations, 2005), p. 1. Retrieved July 1, 2008, from www.ojp.usdoj.gov/BJA/what/2005_threat_assesment.pdf.

TABLE 6.4 Level of Gang Involvement in Drug Distribution (by drug type)

Level of Gang Involvement	High (%)	Moderate (%)	Low (%)	None/ Unknown (%)
Street sales	39.2	34.3	16.1	10.5
Wholesale	20.3	24.5	28.7	26.6
Marijuana	54.5	24.5	9.8	11.2
Methamphetamine	45.5	28.0	15.4	11.2
Crack cocaine	28.0	11.2	35.7	25.2
Heroin	12.6	23.1	39.2	25.2
Powdered cocaine	12.6	20.3	41.3	25.9
MDMA	11.2	18.9	34.3	35.7

SOURCE: *2005 National Gang Threat Assessment* (Washington, D.C.: Department of Justice and National Alliance of Gang Investigators Associations, 2005), p. 33. Retrieved July 1, 2008, from www.ojp.usdoj.gov/BJA/what/2005_threat_assesment.pdf.

Guns and Gangs

It is estimated that between 50 and 70 percent of gang members own or have access to weapons. In fact, gangs often judge each other by their firepower. Their arsenal of weapons includes sawed-off rifles and shotguns, semiautomatic weapons like the Uzi and the AK-47, all types of handguns, body armor, and explosives.[57] Gangs have "treasuries" to buy the sophisticated weapons that are now used on the street for resolving conflicts, for demonstrating bravery, for self-defense, and for protecting turf.[58]

Use of guns rather than knives and clubs turns violent events into life-and-death situations; gangs battle gangs in a kind of street guerrilla warfare. Drive-by shootings, in particular, have become a favored method of operation. A "drive-by" involves members of one gang driving into a rival gang's turf to shoot at someone, followed by a high-speed escape. Gang members take great pride in this hit-and-run technique. Often these

■ *Violence and police raids are part of everyday life in many inner-city housing projects.*

encounters occur spontaneously, but they easily spiral into planned events. The sequence may reflect the following:

Crime Surfing

www.nagia.org/
Home/tabid/36/
Default.aspx

Find out more about the gangs in your state.

> A gang member shoots a rival gang member during an argument. The surviving rival or his friends get a gun and conduct a drive-by on the initial instigator or members of his gang at their home(s). During this retaliatory strike, a friend, family member or gang member is killed or seriously wounded. The original instigatory gang now views itself as the "passive victim" and sets out to get back at the new aggressor. This spiral which, in real time, can result in several drive-by shootings or other murders within a few hours, can and often does lead to protracted gang wars.[59]

Some drive-bys are for "fun," some for defending gang honor, some for initiation purposes, and others for eliminating competition in the drug business.

FEMALE DELINQUENT SUBCULTURES

Traditionally, gang membership has been limited primarily to young, inner-city males. Theoretical and empirical studies in this area therefore focused on that population. More recently, however, gang membership has been changing. There are increasing numbers of white participants, members younger than 14, members older than 18, and females (Table 6.5). Little was known about female subcultures until recently. Researchers are now focusing more attention on the two types of female gangs—those that are affiliates of male gangs and those that consist of all females.

Early Research

In one of the few early studies, done in 1958, Albert Cohen and James Short suggested that female delinquent subcultures, like their male counterparts, were composed of members who had been frustrated in their efforts to achieve conventional goals (respectability, marriage, status). The girls had drifted into a subculture that offered them substitute status, albeit outside legitimate society. Drug use and prostitution became all but inevitable. Because the research that led to this finding was conducted among mostly lower-class black females, Cohen and Short admitted that their findings probably could not be generalized to all female delinquent subcultures.[60]

Recent Studies

Twenty-six years after these tentative findings, Anne Campbell published the first major work on the lifestyle of female gang members in New York. She spent 2 years with three gangs: one Hispanic (the Sex Girls), one black (the Five Percent Nation), and one racially mixed (the Sandman Ladies). Campbell's findings demonstrate that girls, like boys, join gangs for mutual support, protection, and a sense of belonging. They, too, gain status by living up to the value system of their gang. Campbell also noted that these youngsters will probably end up, as their mothers have, living on welfare assistance in a ghetto apartment. Men will come and go in their lives, but after their gang days the women feel they have lost their support group and are constantly threatened by feelings of isolation.[61]

TABLE 6.5 Demographic Profile of Gang Members, 1995	
Total number	846,000
SEX	
Male	90%
Female	10
RACE-ETHNICITY	
Hispanic	44%
Black	35
White	14
Asian	5
Other	2
AGE	
14 or younger	16%
15–17	34
18–24	37
25 or older	13

SOURCE: *Juvenile Offenders and Victims: 1999 National Report* (Washington, D.C.: Office of Juvenile Justice and Delinquency Prevention, 1999).

Between 10 and 25 percent of gang members nationwide are female. In major cities the number is higher. Among 214 wards of the state of California in 1990, 32 percent were gang members, ages 14 to 21.[62] Among them they had 289 arrests. All but 3 of the women had been arrested for a violent crime—22 murders, 31 armed robberies, and 31 assaults with a deadly weapon.

Many of the female gangs are affiliates of male gangs, often offering support for the young men they refer to as their "homeboys." Initiation rites for "wannabes" or outsiders vary depending on the particular gang.

Some females are afforded the opportunity to select how they will "prove themselves," but most female initiates will be told. Female initiation methods are usually classified in one of four categories:

- "Violated" or "jumped in" refers to a physical beating endured by the initiate to confirm her toughness, commitment, and loyalty to the gang.

- The mission method refers to the girl's is committing a criminal act; this may require her to be in the car during a drive-by shooting, or she may be dropped off in another gang's territory and be forced to make it home alive.

- "Sexed in" occurs when the girl agrees to have sex with a gang member; contrary to stereotypes, this is not the most common initiation method. It is the method that is least respected and is frowned on by both sexes. It is usually reserved for girls with very low status.

- "Walked in" or "blessed in" is saved for girls who are at least second-generation gang members, who have an immediate family member in good gang standing, or who have grown up in their "hood" and have established themselves and proved their loyalty.[63]

Some female affiliate gangs, however, have their own initiation rites (which mimic male ceremonies but are usually much less violent) and their own gang colors.

A strong allegiance exists among gang members. For many of these youngsters, the gang takes the place of a family. Shorty, a member of Los Angeles's Tiny Diablas, had no family except a grandmother, who had given up on trying to control her. Shorty's mother, who had herself been a gang member, abandoned her at an early age. Her father overdosed on heroin and was identified by a tattoo of Shorty's name. Her aunt had a teardrop tattoo next to her eye, to signify 1 year in jail; her uncle had two teardrops. Such family ties are not unusual among gang members.[64]

Not all female gangs have male affiliates. In a study of crack sales and violence among gangs in San Francisco, researchers interviewed members of an all-female group, the Potrero Hill Posse (PHP).[65] This independent group was formed in the mid-1980s when the females realized that their gang-affiliated boyfriends were not distributing the profits and labor of their crack sales fairly. The young PHP women run "rock houses" (outlets for crack sales, lent by tenants who receive a small quantity of crack in return), procure other women to provide sex to male customers, and engage in a major shoplifting business that fills orders placed by people who do not want to pay retail prices.

Gang members rely on the gang for assistance ("Nobody will mess with me . . . because they know that I got back-up. I got back-up. I got my homegirls behind me. And whatever goes down with me, they are going to have to take up with them") and for status ("It [membership] means being bad, being tough, and being able to walk without . . . you know, everybody just respects me because they know I am one of the Potrero Hill Posse girls").[66]

Overall, according to gang research done as part of the Rochester Youth Development Study, the extent and nature of female participation in gangs has changed considerably over the last few

The Girls in the Gang

Psychologist Anne Campbell studied female gangs in New York City and published her findings in her 1984 book, *The Girls in the Gang*. She summarizes some of her observations here:

All the girls in the gang come from families that are poor. Many have never known their fathers. Most are immigrants from Puerto Rico. As children the girls moved from apartment to apartment as they were evicted or burned out by arsonists. Unable to keep any friends they managed to make and alienated from their mothers, whose lack of English restricted their ability to control or understand their daughters' lives, the girls dropped out of school early and grew up on the streets. In the company of older kids and street-corner men, they graduated early into the adult world. They began to use drugs and by puberty had been initiated into sexual activity. By fifteen many were pregnant. Shocked, their mothers tried to pull them off the streets. Some sent their daughters back to relatives in Puerto Rico

A portrait of Hispanic teen female members of the Pico Rivera gang, with one member holding her child.

while they had their babies. Abortion was out of the question in this Catholic world.

Those who stayed had "spoiled their identity" as good girls. Their reputations were marred before they ever reached adulthood. On the streets, among the gang members, the girls found a convenient identity in the female gang. Often they had friends or distant relatives who introduced them as "prospects." After a trial period, they could undertake the initiation rite:

decades. The findings show increased participation both in gangs (in this study, about equal to that of males) and in gang-related activities, including serious delinquent acts and drug abuse.[67]

MIDDLE-CLASS DELINQUENCY

In Tucson, Arizona, a white middle-class teenager wearing gang colors died, a victim of a drive-by shooting as he stood with black and Hispanic members of the Bloods gang.

At Antelope Valley High School in Lancaster, California, about 50 miles north of Los Angeles, 200 students threw stones at a policeman who had been called to help

enforce a ban on the gang outfits that have become a fad on some campuses. . . .

A member of the South Bay Family gang in Hermosa Beach, a 21-year-old surfer called Road Dog, who said his family owned a chain of pharmacies, put it this way: "This is the 90's, man. We're the type of people who don't take no for an answer. If your mom says no to a kid in the 90's, the kid's just going to laugh." He and his friends shouted in appreciation as another gang member lifted his long hair to reveal a tattoo on a bare shoulder: "Mama tried."[68]

Most people think of gangs as synonymous with inner-city slums, low-income housing projects, turf wars, and a membership that often comes into conflict with law enforcement. But now the they had to fight an established member nominated by the godmother. What was at issue was not winning or losing but demonstrating "heart," or courage. Gangs do not welcome members who join only to gain protection. The loyalty of other gang members has to be won by a clear demonstration of willingness to "get down," or fight.

Paradoxically, the female gang goes to considerable lengths to control the sexual behavior of its members. Although the neighborhood may believe they are fast women, the girls themselves do not tolerate members who sleep around. A promiscuous girl is a threat to the other members' relationships with their boyfriends. Members can take a boyfriend from among the male gang members (indeed, they are forbidden to take one from any other gang) but they are required to be monogamous. A shout of "Whore!" is the most frequent cause of fistfights among the female members.

On the positive side, the gang provides a strong sense of belonging and sisterhood. After the terrible isolation of their lives, the girls acquire a ready-made circle of friends who have shared many of their experiences and who are always willing to support them against hostile words or deeds by outsiders. Fighting together generates a strong sense of camaraderie and as a bonus earns them the reputation of being "crazy." This reputation is extremely useful in the tough neighborhoods where they live. Their reputation for carrying knives and for solidarity effectively deters outsiders from challenging them. They work hard at fostering their tough "rep" not only in their deeds but in their social talk. They spend hours recounting and embroidering stories of fights they have been in. Behind all this bravado it is easy to sense the fear they work so hard to deny. Terrified of being victims (as many of them have already been in their families and as newcomers in their schools), they make much of their own "craziness"—the violent unpredictability that frightens away anyone who might try to harm them.(1)

Campbell demonstrates the commonality of violence in the lives of female gang members in the early 1980s. Today there is growing concern over the increasing prevalence and severity of violence in some areas of the country.(2) The number of female gang members and the extent of changes in the use of violence are, however, still debated among researchers.(3)

Sources

1. Written by Anne Campbell. Adapted from Anne Campbell, *The Girls in the Gang* (New York: Basil Blackwell, 1984).
2. John M. Hagedorn, "Gang Violence in the Postindustrial Era," in *Youth Violence, Crime and Justice: A Review of Research*, vol. 24, eds. Michael Tonry and Mark H. Moore (Chicago: University of Chicago Press, 1998), pp. 365–419.
3. Margaret O'Brien, "At Least 16,000 Girls in Chicago's Gangs More Violent than Some Believe, Report Says," *Chicago Tribune*, Sept. 17, 1999, p. 5.

Questions for Discussion

1. How similar are Campbell's female gangs to the male gangs described in this chapter? Are there any significant differences?
2. Would you expect female gangs to become as involved in criminal activity as male gangs? Why or why not?

gang lifestyle is moving to suburbia (Figure 6.4).[69] Affluent youngsters are joining established gangs such as the Crips and the Bloods or forming their own gangs, sometimes referred to as "yuppie gangs."[70] Their activities can be as harmless as adherence to a particular dress code or as violent as a drive-by shooting. Experts have identified several types of suburban gangs.[71]

Delinquent Gangs

Delinquent gangs are similar to most inner-city gangs. Criminal activities include physical assaults, theft, burglary, and distribution of illegal drugs. The members seek money, peer recognition, the thrill of high-risk behavior, or even protection: "If you want to be able to walk the mall, you have to know you've got your boys behind you."[72] They typically adopt hand signals used by inner-city gangs.

Hate Gangs

These gangs, such as skinheads, attach themselves to an ideology that targets racial and ethnic groups. Vandalism, destruction of property, terrorist threats, physical assaults, and even murder are justified by their belief system. In 2003, three men and a pregnant woman, all members of the Tacoma Skinhead Movement, beat and kicked a homeless man to death to achieve status and earn the right to wear red bootlaces—signifying that they have attacked an enemy of the white race. The number of racist skinheads is growing at an alarming rate. In 1988, 1,000 to 1,500 skinheads were operating in

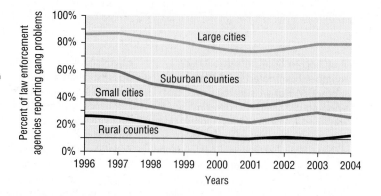

FIGURE 6.4 The number of law enforcement agencies reporting gang problems. The number appears to have stabilized.

Notes: Large cities have populations of 50,000 or more. Small cities have populations of 2,500 to 49,999. The observed changes in the percentage of agencies in small cities and rural counties reporting gang problems between 2000 and 2004 are within the range attributable to sample error and, thus, do not indicate actual change.

Source: Juvenile Offenders and Victims: 2006 National Report (Washington, D.C.: Office of Juvenile Justice and Delinquency Prevention, 2007), p. 82.

■ Hate is shown by the demeanor and facial expressions of Denver skinheads at a demonstration against Martin Luther King Day.

12 states. By June 1993, the number was close to 3,500 spread across 40 states.[73] In 2006, the Anti-Defamation League identified 110 racist skinhead groups operating in every state, with as many as 10,000 members.[74] According to the FBI, there were 7,722 hate-crime incidents and 9,652 victims of hate crimes in 2006. Racial bias motivated 51.8 percent of the incidents, 18.9 percent were motivated by religious bias, crimes perpetrated based on sexual orientation accounted for 15.5 percent, and 12.7 percent were based on the ethnicity of the victim. Sixty percent of the hate crimes reported in 2006 were classified as person offenses.[75] Because of the difficulties involved in gathering hate-crime statistics, these numbers most likely represent only a small percentage of the actual figure.[76]

Satanic Gangs

These groups are affiliated with the controversial satanic cults. Their practices include the worship of specific gods, desecration of graveyards, use of a Ouija board to predict the future, ritualistic drug consumption, animal sacrifice, various witchcraft and pagan rituals, and submission to sexual abuse or pain. The common element among these gangs

is heavy-metal music. Satanic gang members can be identified by their dress: metal-spiked wrist cuffs, belts, anti-Christian items, and T-shirts labeled with heavy-metal band names such as Iron Maiden, Venom, Judas Priest, and Dio.[77]

Explanations

Most explanations of middle-class delinquency are extensions of subcultural explanations of lower-class delinquency. Albert Cohen, for example, suggested that changes in the social structure have weakened the value traditionally associated with delay of gratification.[78] Some criminologists say that a growing number of middle-class youngsters no longer believe that the way to reach their goals is through hard work and delayed pleasure. They prefer reaping profits from quick drug sales or shoplifting goods that attract them. Behavior has become more hedonistic and more peer-oriented. While most of this youth subculture exhibits nondelinquent behavior, sometimes the pleasure-seeking activities have led to delinquent acts. Bored and restless, these youngsters seek to break the monotony with artificial excitement and conspicuous indulgence: fast cars, trendy clothes, alcohol, drugs, and sexual activity. Experts note that many affluent gang members come from broken, unstable, or extremely dysfunctional homes. Their problems stem from divorce, separation, child maltreatment (physical abuse, sexual abuse, emotional abuse, or neglect), a drug- or alcohol-addicted parent, a parent with a mental illness, limited parental supervision, or a lack of parental involvement.[79]

THEORY INFORMS POLICY

Subcultural theory assumes that individuals engage in delinquent or criminal behavior because (1) legitimate opportunities for success are blocked and (2) criminal values and norms are learned in lower-class slums. The theory was translated into action programs during the 1960s. Two presidents, John F. Kennedy and Lyndon Johnson, directed that huge sums of money be spent on programs to help move lower-class youths into the social mainstream.

MOBY

The best-known program, Mobilization for Youth (MOBY), was based on opportunity theory. It provided employment, social services, teacher training, legal aid, and other crime-prevention services to an area on New York's Lower East Side. The cost was over $12 million. MOBY ultimately became highly controversial. Many people accused it of being too radical, especially when neighborhood participants became involved in rent strikes, lawsuits charging discrimination, and public demonstrations. News of the conflict between supporters and opponents, and between the staff and the neighborhood it served, reached Congress, which made it clear that the point of the project was to reduce delinquency, not to reform society.

Little was done to evaluate the program's success. The project was eventually abandoned, and the commission that had established it ceased to exist. The political climate had changed, and federal money was no longer available for sweeping social programs. However, MOBY's failure does not disprove the opportunity theory on which it was based. In 1995, the Office of Juvenile Justice and Delinquency Prevention (OJJDP) launched the Comprehensive Gang Model, a pilot project based on the same principles as MOBY. Evaluations of the Comprehensive Gang Model reveal mixed results. The program has been shown to reduce arrests for serious violence and drugs in some sites. In others, however, it has had no significant effect on gang involvement or serious delinquency among participants compared to nonparticipants.[80]

Other Programs

Many other programs based on subcultural theory have attempted to change the attitudes and behavior of ghetto youngsters who have spent most of their lives learning unconventional street norms. Change is accomplished by setting up an extended-family environment for high-risk youths, one that provides positive role models, academic and vocational training, strict rules for behavior, drug treatment, health care, and other services. For many youths, these programs provide the first warm, caring living arrangement they have ever had.

One such program is the House of Umoja (a Swahili word for "unity") in Philadelphia. At any given time, about 25 black male teenage offenders live together as "sons" of the founder, Sister Fattah. Each resident signs a contract with Umoja obligating himself to help in the household, become an active part of the family group, study, and work in one of the program's businesses (a restaurant, a moving company, a painting shop) or elsewhere. By many measures this program is successful.

Programs similar to Umoja have spread throughout the country; they include Argus in New York's South Bronx; Violent Juvenile Offender Research and Development programs in Chicago, Dallas, New Orleans, Los Angeles, and San Diego; and Neighborhood Anticrime Self-Help programs in Baltimore, Newark, Cleveland, Boston, Miami, and Washington, D.C. All have the same mission: to provide a bridge from a delinquent subcultural value system to a conventional one.[81]

Other means have been used to break up delinquent subcultures. Street workers, many of them former gang members (called "OGs," for "original gangsters"), serve as a "street-smart diplomatic corps" in many of the poorest ghettos in the country.[82] In Los Angeles, where gang members control many streets, the OGs work for the Community Youth Gang Service (a government-funded agency). Five nights a week, more than 50 of these street workers cover the city, trying to settle disputes between rival gangs and to discourage nonmembers from joining them. They look for alternatives to violence, in baseball games, fairs, and written peace treaties. During a typical evening, the street workers may try to head off a gang fight:

> *Parton [street worker]:* Hey, you guys, Lennox is going to be rollin' by here....
>
> *Ms. Diaz [street worker]:* You with your back to the street, homeboy. They goin' to be lookin' for this car, some burgundy car.

Gangs Terrorize Nigeria's Vital Oil Region

Rosemary Douglas has no connection to the oil business that pumps more than two million barrels of crude a day from beneath the swampy Niger Delta. But the violence surrounding it pierced her home in September anyway, when a bullet shattered her upper left arm as she napped with her 2-year-old daughter.

"I don't know why this happened to me," she said, grimacing in pain as she gave a bewildered account of the gunplay that has engulfed her neighborhood and much of this oil-drenched city. "I mind my own business."

The violence that has rocked the Niger Delta in recent years has been aimed largely at foreign oil companies, their expatriate workers and the police officers and soldiers whose job it is to protect them. Hundreds of kidnappings, pipeline bombings and attacks on flow stations and army barracks have occurred in the past two years alone.

But these days the guns have turned inward, and open battles have erupted with terrifying frequency on the pothole-riddled streets of this ramshackle city. The origins of the violence are as murky and convoluted as the mangrove swamps that snake across the delta, one of the poorest places on earth. But they lie principally in the rivalry among gangs, known locally as cults, that have ties to political leaders who used them as private militias during state and federal elections in April, according to human rights advocates, former gang members and aid workers in the region.

"What is happening now cannot be separated from politics," said Anyakwee Nsirimovu of the Institute for Human Rights and Humanitarian Law in Port Harcourt. "The cults are part and parcel of our politics. They have become part of the system, and we are paying in blood for it."

The cults go by names that veer from the chilling to the improbable—like the Black Axe, the Klansmen, the Icelanders, the Outlaws and the Niger Delta Vigilante. Separate but not entirely distinct from the militant groups that have attacked the oil industry in the past, they represent a new, worrisome phase in a region that has been convulsed by conflict since oil was discovered here in 1956.

Since democracy returned to Nigeria in 1999, politicians across the country have used cults to intimidate opponents and rig votes. A Human Rights Watch report published in October concluded that the political system was so corroded by corruption and violence that, in some places, it resembled more a criminal enterprise than a system of government. The April elections were so brazenly rigged in some areas and so badly marred by violence that international observers said the results were not credible.

Nowhere is political violence more severe than here in the Niger Delta, where control over state government means access to billions of dollars in oil revenues and control of enough patronage for an army.

According to former gang members and human rights workers, the governing People's Democratic Party and some opposition parties employed cult members in the delta during the election, as they had in the two previous ones, which led to landslide victories for the governing party.

One powerful gang leader, Soboma George, was given the lion's share of patronage, they contend. Mr. George displayed his prowess in the months before the election by having his foot soldiers break him out of a city jail in a brazen assault. He then demonstrated his impunity by driving through the streets of Port Harcourt, the capital of Rivers State, in flashy cars, seemingly fearless of arrest.

The other gangs resented the growing influence and control Mr. George had over lucrative security contracts, and a war between them has turned increasingly bloody. Caught in the middle have been all kinds of civilians; no one is off limits to the violence.

Boy: If they want to find me, they know where I'm at.

Ms. Diaz: I'm tellin' you to be afraid of them. There are some girls here. You better tell them to move down the street. . . . We are goin' back over there to try to keep them there. Don't get lazy or drunk and not know what you're doin'. I know you don't think it's serious, but if one of your friends gets killed tonight, you will.

Boy: It's serious, I know.

Ms. Diaz: We're goin' to keep them in their 'hood, you just stay in yours for a while.

Boy: All right.[83]

After 2 hours of negotiation, the fight was called off. There was plenty of work left for the team. They would continue the next day to help the gang members find jobs.

Getting Out: Gang Banging or the Morgue

The most difficult problem that counselors and street workers face is the power gangs have over their members. Gangs, through loyalty and terror, make it almost impossible for members to quit. Many gang members would gladly get out, but

The elderly mother of the newly elected state governor was kidnapped and held for ransom in the spring. Toddlers related to senior government officials and business leaders have been seized to extract ransom payments or settle political disputes.

The violence reached such a pitch that at Teme Hospital here, surgeons from the aid group Doctors Without Borders struggled to keep up with a flood of 71 gunshot victims in just two weeks in August, and more than a month later they were still treating many people recovering from shattered bones and flesh wounds from the fighting.

Ibinabo Bob-Manuel, a 25-year-old college student, said she was at home with her aunt and 6-year-old sister, Lolo, on Aug. 16 when shooting broke out between soldiers and a gang that had occupied the area.

Four bullets pierced the fleshy part of her thigh, and one remained lodged inside. She lost so much blood that she passed out. The top half of a toe was blown off. Her sister was shot through her hands as she pressed her palms in prayer in the hail of bullets, Ms. Bob-Manuel said.

"We were bleeding and crying," she said. "My auntie shouted, 'You killed my family!' I thought I would die."

The government says it is cracking down on gangs, and it has sent an elite army unit into Port Harcourt and the surrounding areas to impose law and halt the violence. The gunplay in the city streets has since died down, but it is a tense, uneasy calm.

Many residents worry that rivalries may soon heat up again. On Oct. 25 a judicial panel removed the new governor of Rivers State, Celestine Omehia, ruling that he had not been an eligible candidate because he did not win his party's primary. The winner of the primary, Rotimi Amaechi, was sworn in as governor, and many worry that violent clashes will ensue between their supporters.

The bloodshed has reached beyond the cities, deep into the creekside communities of the delta. In Ogbogoro the fights between rival gangs were so intense in August that the council of traditional rulers felt compelled to act. Two cults, the Debam and the Dewell, were fighting over political turf, oil and contracts for security work with oil services companies, according to local officials.

"No one could sleep in the town," said Chief Clement Chuku, one of the traditional rulers of Ogbogoro. "Bullets were flying all night."

The chiefs met to announce an ultimatum: all cult members had to leave or risk being arrested by vigilante youths from the community. The vigilantes rounded up a few members as examples, Mr. Chuku said, and were planning to turn them over to the military.

But just as a community meeting got under way in the town hall in early September, dozens of young men on motorbikes, carrying machine guns and grenade launchers, overran the meeting. Two traditional rulers were shot dead and their bodies were dumped on a weedy riverbank.

George Ogan, a retired doctor and church leader who has been trying to stem gang violence farther down the delta in his hometown, Okrika, where some of the most fearsome cults are based, said that such violence was completely bound up with politics.

"Our politicians cannot stand on their own, so they find those who will stand with guns for them," Dr. Ogan said.

Source

Questions for Discussion

1. How universal is the problem with gangs?
2. To what extent do gangs in Nigeria share common elements with gangs in the United States and Europe?
3. Are the causes of gangs and gang violence similar in Africa and in countries in the West?

any move to leave leads to gang banging or the morgue. Second Chance Grace, a nonprofit organization in Meridian, Idaho, works with at-risk youth and young adults immersed in drugs, gangs, and other criminal activities. The organization has developed a program that offers laser tattoo removal free or at reduced cost to ex-gang members and former drug addicts.[84] A Wichita, Kansas, group, the church-sponsored Project Freedom, has created an "underground railroad," a network of local contacts that leads families with gang members to anonymity and freedom out of state.[85]

Gangs, once a local problem, have become a national concern. The federal antigang budget goes primarily to police and prosecution. In 1992, the Department of Justice spent $500 million on law enforcement. Crime has decreased over all in the last several years, yet gang-related crime continues to rise.[86] In 2007, Deputy U.S. Marshals and their task-force partners apprehended nearly 2,500 fugitives who were affiliated with gangs.[87] Despite this upward trend in gang activity, the Department of Justice was allocated $418,376 in antigang funds in 2008, and President Bush budgeted $386,713 for 2009.[88] Experts agree that unless we put more money into educational and socioeconomic programs, there is little likelihood that America's gang problems will lessen in the near future.

CHAPTER 6

REVIEW

In the decade between the mid-1950s and mid-1960s, criminologists began to theorize about the development and content of youth subcultures and the gangs that flourish within them. Some suggested that lower-class males, frustrated by their inability to meet middle-class standards, set up their own norms by which they could gain status. Often these norms clashed with those of the dominant culture. Other investigators have refuted the idea that delinquent behavior stems from a rejection of middle-class values. They claim that lower-class values are separate and distinct from middle-class values and that it is the lower-class value system that generates delinquent behavior.

Gangs in the twenty-first century show increasing violence and reliance on guns, as is the case with MS-13. They are involved in large profit-making activities such as drug distribution. The number of homicides is rising.

Explanations of female delinquent subcultures and middle-class delinquency are an extension of subcultural explanations of lower-class delinquency. While the theories of reaction formation, the subculture of violence, and differential opportunity differ in some respects, they all share one basic assumption—that delinquent and criminal behaviors are linked to the values and norms of the areas where youngsters grow up.

CRIMINOLOGY & PUBLIC POLICY

"Many aspects of female gang functioning and the lives of female gang members remain a mystery because relatively few researchers have considered female gangs worthy of study. In addition, researchers face serious obstacles to the study of female gangs and, because of these obstacles, they often settle for unrepresentative samples. Gangs are highly suspicious of researchers and cooperate with them only under unusual circumstances. Female gang members, in particular, have been averse to talking about sexual abuse, whether it occurred at home or within the gang. . . . Unfortunately, female gang members have received little programmatic attention." (SOURCE: Joan Moore and John Hagedorn, *Female Gangs: A Focus on Research* [Washington, D.C.: OJJDP, 2001].)

Questions for Discussion   Can you conceive of other reasons why female gangs have been overlooked? After reviewing the work of Professor Anne Campbell (See the box "Criminological Concerns: The Girls in the Gang"), what kinds of programs do you suppose would help female gang members make a transition to prosocial activities and lifestyles? In what ways must these programs differ from those proposed for male gang members?

YOU BE THE CRIMINOLOGIST

You are a consultant called in to address the rise in female gang activity and violence. On what theory or theories would you base your intervention? Are the theories based on male delinquency sufficient? Are gender-based theories necessary?

KEY TERMS

The numbers next to the terms refer to the pages on which the terms are defined.

differential opportunity theory (133)

reaction formation (131)

subculture (130)

subcultures of violence (136)

Social Control Theory

What Is Social Control?
Theories of Social Control
The Microsociological Perspective: Hirschi
Social Bonds
Empirical Tests of Hirschi's Theory
Evaluation: Hirschi's Social Control Theory
Social Control and Drift
Personal and Social Control
Failure of Control Mechanisms
Stake in Conformity
Containment Theory
Empirical Tests of Containment Theory
Evaluation: Containment Theory
Theoretical Explorations
Developmental/Life Course Theory
Integrated Theory
General Theories
THEORY INFORMS POLICY
Review
Criminology & Public Policy
You Be the Criminologist
Key Terms

North Korean Communist Party in May Day Stadium as 100,000 spectators witness a 25,000-person display of political might.

Obedience, respect for authority, shared goals and values, commitment to and investment in custom and convention—this is the glue that makes a successful sports team, no less a powerful social order.

In William Golding's novel *Lord of the Flies,* a group of boys is stranded on an island far from civilization. Deprived of any superior authority—their teacher, their parents, all the grown-ups who have until now determined their lives—and likewise deprived of a government, they begin to decide on a structure of government for themselves. Ralph declares:

"We can't have everybody talking at once. We'll have to have 'Hands up'

like at school . . . . Then I'll give him the conch."

"Conch?"

"That's what this shell is called. I'll give the conch to the next person to speak. He can hold it when he's speaking!" . . . .

Jack was on his feet.

"We'll have rules!" he cried excitedly. "Lots of rules!"[1]

But do rules alone guarantee the peaceful existence of the group? Who and what ensure compliance with the rules? Social control theorists study these questions.

■ *Learning to play by the rules: The Harlem Little League team was challenged at the Little League World Series at Williamsport, Pennsylvania, August 2002, for having outside players on their team.*

Strain theories, as we noted, study the question of why some people violate norms—for example, by committing crimes. Social control theorists are interested in learning why people conform to norms. Control theorists take it for granted that drugs can tempt even the youngest schoolchildren; that truancy can lure otherwise good children onto a path of academic failure and lifetime unemployment; that petty fighting, petty theft, and recreational drinking are attractive features of adolescence. They ask why people conform in the face of so much temptation and peer pressure. The answer, according to social control theory, is that juveniles and adults conform to the law in response to certain controlling forces in their lives. They become criminals when the controlling forces are weak or absent.

WHAT IS SOCIAL CONTROL?

What are those controlling forces? Think about the time and energy you have invested in your education, your job, your extracurricular activities. Think about how your academic or vocational ambition would be jeopardized by persistent delinquency. Consider how the responsibility of homework has weighed on you, restricting your free time. Reflect on the quality of your relationships with your family, friends, and acquaintances and on how your attachment to them has encouraged you to do right and discouraged you from doing wrong.

Social control theory focuses on techniques and strategies that regulate human behavior and lead to conformity, or obedience to society's rules—the influences of family and school, religious beliefs, moral values, friends, and even beliefs about government. The more involved and committed a person is to conventional activities and values and the greater the attachment to parents, loved ones, and friends, the less likely that person is to violate society's rules and to jeopardize relationships and aspirations.

The concept of social control emerged in the early 1900s in a volume by E. A. Ross, one of the founders of American sociology. According to Ross, belief systems, rather than specific laws, guide what people do and universally serve to control behavior. Since that time, the concept has taken on a wide variety of meanings. Social control has been conceptualized as representing practically any phenomenon that leads to conformity. The term is found in studies of laws, customs, mores, ideologies, and folkways describing a host of controlling forces.[2]

Is there danger in defining social control so broadly? It depends on your perspective. To some sociologists, the vagueness of the term—its tendency to encompass almost the entire field of sociology—has significantly decreased its value as a concept.[3] To others, the value of social control lies in its representation of a mechanism by which society regulates its members. According to this view, social control defines what is considered deviant behavior, what is right or wrong, and what is a violation of the law.

Theorists who have adopted this orientation consider laws, norms, customs, mores, ethics, and etiquette to be forms of social control. Donald Black, a sociologist of law, noted that "social control is found whenever people hold each other to standards, explicitly or implicitly, consciously or not: on the street, in prison, at home, at a party."[4]

Consider that as recently as 20 years ago, there were no legal restrictions, norms, or customs regulating the smoking of cigarettes in public places. The surgeon general's declaration in 1972 that secondhand smoke poses a health hazard ushered in two decades of controls over behavior that not too long ago was considered sociable—even sophisticated and suave.

At present, 24 states and the District of Columbia have banned smoking in all public places; seven states have banned smoking in nonhospitality workplaces and restaurants; one state (South Dakota) has banned smoking in nonhospitality workplaces only; one state (New Hampshire) has banned smoking in restaurants and bars; two states (Georgia and Idaho) have banned smoking in restaurants only; and 15 states have no laws banning smoking. The U.S. Supreme Court followed this emerging convention, holding that it is "cruel and unusual punishment" to expose prison inmates to levels of tobacco smoke that place their health at risk. The Federal Bureau of Prisons, along with 27 states, has made prison facilities 100 percent smoke-free in indoor areas. Arkansas currently is the only state where smoking is prohibited both indoors and outdoors in its prisons. All correctional facilities in both Michigan and Iowa will be smoke-free as of 2009.[5]

THEORIES OF SOCIAL CONTROL

Why is social control conceptualized in such different ways? Perhaps because social control has been examined from both a macrosociological and a microsociological perspective. **Macrosociological studies** explore formal systems for the control of groups:

- The legal system, laws, and particularly law enforcement

- Powerful groups in society

- Social and economic directives of governmental or private groups

These types of control can be either positive—that is, they inhibit rule-breaking behavior by a type of social guidance—or negative—that is, they foster oppressive, restrictive, or corrupt practices by those in power.[6]

The microsociological perspective is similar to the macrosociological approach in that it, too, explains why people conform. **Microsociological studies**, however, focus on informal systems. Researchers collect data from individuals (usually by self-report methods), are often guided by hypotheses that apply to individuals as well as to groups, and frequently make reference to or examine a person's internal control system.

The Microsociological Perspective: Hirschi

Travis Hirschi has been the spokesperson of the microsociological perspective since the publication of his *Causes of Delinquency* in 1969. He is not, however, the first scholar to examine the extent of individual social control and its relationship to delinquency. In 1957, Jackson Toby introduced the notion of individual "commitment" as a powerful determining force in the social control of behavior.[7] Scott Briar and Irving Piliavin extended Toby's thesis by advancing the view that the extent of individual commitment and conformity plays a role in decreasing the likelihood of deviance. They noted that the degree of an adolescent's commitment is reflected in relationships with adult authority figures and with friends and is determined in part by "belief in God, affection for conventionally behaving peers, occupational aspirations, ties to parents, desire to perform well at school, and fear of material deprivations and punishments associated with arrest."[8]

Briar and Piliavin were not entirely satisfied with control dimensions alone, however, and added another factor: individual motivation to be delinquent. This motivation may stem from a person's wish to "obtain valued goods, to portray courage in the presence of, or to belong to, peers, to strike out at someone who is disliked, or simply to get his kicks."[9]

Hirschi was less interested in the source of an individual's motivation to commit delinquent acts than in the reasons people do not commit such acts. He claimed that social control theory explains conformity and adherence to rules, not deviance. It is thus not a crime-causation theory in a strict sense but a theory of prosocial behavior used by criminologists to explain deviance.

Social Bonds

Hirschi posited four social bonds that promote socialization and conformity: attachment, commitment, involvement, and belief. The stronger these bonds, he claimed, the less likelihood of delinquency.[10] To test this hypothesis, he administered a self-report questionnaire to 4,077 junior and senior high school students in California (see Table 7.1). The survey measured both involvement in delinquency and the strength of the four social bonds. Hirschi found that weakness in any of the bonds was associated with delinquent behavior.

Attachment

The first bond, **attachment**, takes three forms: attachment to parents, to school (teachers), and to peers. According to Hirschi, youths who have formed a significant attachment to a parent refrain from delinquency because the consequences of such an act might jeopardize that relationship. The bond of affection between a parent and a child thus becomes a primary deterrent to criminal activities.[11] Its strength depends on the depth and quality of parent-child interaction. The parent-child bond forms a path through which conventional ideals and expectations can pass. This bond is bolstered by:

- The amount of time the child spends with parents, particularly the presence of a parent at times when the child is tempted to engage in criminal activity

DID YOU KNOW?

. . . that death row inmates in Florida are exempt from the nonsmoking policy? They are the only people allowed to smoke on prison grounds.

TABLE 7.1 Items from Travis Hirschi's Measure of Social Control

1. In general, do you like or dislike school?
   A. Like it
   B. Like it and dislike it about equally
   C. Dislike it

2. How important is getting good grades to you personally?
   A. Very important
   B. Somewhat important
   C. Fairly important
   D. Completely unimportant

3. Do you care what teachers think of you?
   A. I care a lot
   B. I care some
   C. I don't care much

4. Would you like to be the kind of person your father is?
   A. In every way
   B. In most ways
   C. In some ways
   D. In just a few ways
   E. Not at all

5. Did your mother read to you when you were little?
   A. No
   B. Once or twice
   C. Several times
   D. Many times, but not regularly
   E. Many times, and regularly
   F. I don't remember

6. Do you ever feel that "there's nothing to do"?
   A. Often
   B. Sometimes
   C. Rarely
   D. Never

SOURCE: Travis Hirschi, *Causes of Delinquency.* Copyright © 2002 by Transaction Publishers. Reprinted by permission of the publisher.

- The intimacy of communication between parent and child

- The affectional identification between parent and child[12]

Next Hirschi considered the importance of the school. As we saw in Chapter 6, Hirschi linked inability to function well in school to delinquency through the following chain of events: Academic incompetence leads to poor school performance; poor school performance results in a dislike of school; dislike of school leads to rejection of teachers and administrators as authorities. The result is delinquency. Thus, attachment to school depends on a youngster's appreciation for the institution, perception of how he or she is received by teachers and peers, and level of achievement in class.

Hirschi found that attachment to parents and school overshadows the bond formed with peers:

> As was true for parents and teachers, those most closely attached to or respectful of their friends are least likely to have committed delinquent acts. The relation does not appear to be as strong as was the case for parents and teachers, but the ideas that delinquents are unusually dependent upon their peers, that loyalty and solidarity are characteristic of delinquent groups, that attachment to adolescent peers fosters nonconventional behavior, and that the delinquent is unusually likely to sacrifice his personal advantage to the "requirements of the group" are simply not supported by the data.[13]

Commitment

Hirschi's second group of bonds consists of **commitment** to or investment in conventional lines of action—that is, support of and participation in social activities that tie the individual to the society's moral or ethical code. Hirschi identified a number of stakes in conformity or commitments: vocational aspirations, educational expectations, educational aspirations.

Many programs and institutions currently strive to nurture and encourage such aspirations. Research has consistently demonstrated that youth who participate in after-school programs and activities have better attendance, achieve higher grades, perform better on standardized tests, exhibit fewer behavioral problems, and are more confident and better equipped to handle conflicts.[14] After School Matters (ASM) is a Chicago-based organization dedicated to providing out-of-school opportunities for Chicago teens. ASM partners with the City of Chicago, the Parks District, the Department of Children and Youth Services, the Police Department, the Public Library, the Department of Cultural Affairs, and more than a hundred community-based organizations to provide Chicago high school students with a safe place in which to take part in "activities that offer positive relationships, skills that translate into the workplace, and exposure to career and educational opportunities throughout the city."[15] In 2007, ASM offered nearly 900 programs available to more than 58 high schools in Chicago.

Though Hirschi's theory is at odds with the competing theories of Albert Cohen and Richard Cloward and Lloyd Ohlin (Chapter 6), Hirschi provided empirical support for the notion that the greater the aspiration and expectation, the more unlikely delinquency becomes. Also, "students who smoke, those who drink, and those who date are more likely to commit delinquent acts; . . . the more the boy is involved in adult activities, the greater his involvement in delinquency."[16]

Involvement

Hirschi's third bond is **involvement**, or preoccupation with activities that promote the interests of society. This bond is derived from involvement in school-related activities (such as homework) rather than in working-class adult activities (such as smoking and drinking). A person who is busy doing conventional things has little time for deviant activities.

With this premise in mind, a number of regional schools now follow the example set by Parrot Middle School in southwest Florida. Parrot Middle School offers an after-school program that provides counseling and tutoring services and gives students the opportunity to participate in a diverse range of recreational courses, including martial arts, gymnastics, and computer basics. The program is designed to provide constructive pastimes for youths formerly left unsupervised during the time between the end of the school day and the end of the typical workday. A similar initiative began in Philadelphia in 2002. After-School Activities Partnerships offers a variety of clubs, ranging from chess to dance, to school-age children during after-school hours. The goals of this program are to supervise children during the hours of the day when they are likely to be on their own and to keep them involved in productive activities.[17]

Belief

"This type of prejudice insults me as an individual, but I am helpless because I can't vote. Then again, it's not as if any of the new legislation is affecting me, right? Why should I have any say in my own life? After all, I'm just a teen."

Jeff Lofvers's sentiments reflect much of Florida's teenage population. As of July 1, 1996, the state of Florida enacted a curfew restricting late-night driving for all licensed drivers under the age of 18. Between the hours of 11:00 P.M. and 6:00 A.M., 16-year-olds cannot legally drive unless accompanied by a licensed driver at least 21 years old. The same applies to 17-year-olds between 1:00 A.M. and 6:00 A.M. "It amazes me that my friends and I can walk around town as late as we want, yet we're not allowed to be safely locked in our cars past 11:00 P.M.," protested one angry teen. And another's defiant response when asked to comment on the anticipated effectiveness of this law? "[I]f they (legislators) are trying to trap us in our homes, it won't work."[18]

The last of the bonds, **belief**, consists of assent to the society's value system. The value system of any society entails respect for its laws and for the people and institutions that enforce them. The results of Hirschi's survey lead to the conclusion that if young people no longer believe laws are fair, their bond to society weakens, and the probability that they will commit delinquent acts increases.

Empirical Tests of Hirschi's Theory

Hirschi's work has inspired a vast number of studies. We can examine only a small selection of some of the more significant research.

Michael Hindelang studied rural boys and girls in grades 6 through 12 on the East Coast. His self-report delinquency measure and questionnaire items were very similar to those devised by Hirschi. Hindelang found few differences between his results and those of Hirschi. Two of those differences, however, were significant. First, he found no relationship between attachment to mother and attachment to peers. Hirschi had observed a positive relationship (the stronger the attachment to the mother, the stronger the attachment to peers). Second, involvement in delinquency was positively

■ A group of teenagers work together at a car wash illustrating attachment to peers, one of Hirschi's ways to fight delinquency.

Crime Surfing

www.street-soldiers.org/

Hirschi identified four social bonds that promote socialization: attachment, commitment, involvement, and belief. How do the programs and resources of the Omega Boys Club promote a commitment to conventional lines of action?

related to attachment to peers.[19] Hirschi had found an inverse relationship (the stronger the attachment to peers, the less the involvement in delinquency).

In another study, criminologists administered a self-report questionnaire to 3,056 male and female students in three Midwestern states. The researchers were critical of Hirschi's conceptualization of both commitment and involvement, finding it difficult to understand how he separated the two. Serious involvement, they argued, is quite unlikely without commitment. They combined commitment and involvement items and ended up with only three bonds: attachment, commitment, and belief.[20]

The study related these bonds to alcohol and marijuana use, use of strong drugs, minor delinquent behavior, and serious delinquent behavior. The results suggested that strong social bonds were more highly correlated with less-serious deviance than with delinquent acts such as motor vehicle theft and assault. Also, the social bonds were more predictive of deviance in girls than in boys. Moreover, criminologists who conducted this study noticed that the commitment bond (now joined with involvement) was more significantly correlated with delinquent behavior than were attachment and belief.

Other researchers administered questionnaires to 2,213 10th-grade boys at 86 schools, seeking to answer three questions: First, are Hirschi's four bonds distinct entities? Second, why did Hirschi name only four bonds? Third, why were some factors that are related to educational and occupational aspiration (such as ability and family socioeconomic status) omitted from his questionnaire? The researchers constructed new scales for measuring attachment, commitment, involvement, and belief. They then used a self-report measure to assess delinquency. These researchers found little that is independent or distinctive about any of the bonds.[21]

Robert Agnew provided the first longitudinal test of Hirschi's theory by using data on 1,886 boys in the 10th and 11th grades. Eight social control scales (parental attachment, grades, dating index, school attachment, involvement, commitment, peer attachment, and belief) were examined at two periods in relation to two self-report scales (one measuring total delinquency and the other measuring seriousness of delinquency). Agnew found the eight control scales to be strongly correlated with the self-reported delinquency, but the social control measures did little to predict the extent of future delinquency reported at the second testing. Agnew concluded that the importance of Hirschi's control theory has probably been exaggerated.[22]

Most of the recent empirical work on Hirschi's theory explores the relationship between social bonds and other, competing theories.[23] Researchers have discovered that the explanatory power of social control theory is enhanced dramatically when it is joined with other structural and process theories.

Evaluation: Hirschi's Social Control Theory

While social control theory has held a prominent position in criminology for several decades, it is not without weaknesses. For example, social control theory seeks to explain delinquency, not adult crime. It concerns attitudes, beliefs, desires, and behaviors that, though deviant, are often characteristic of adolescents. This is unfortunate, because there has long been evidence that social bonds are also significant explanatory factors in postadolescent behavior.[24]

Questions also have been raised about the bonds. Hirschi claims that antisocial acts result from a lack of affective values, beliefs, norms, and attitudes that inhibit delinquency. But these terms are never clearly defined.[25] Critics have also faulted Hirschi's work for other reasons:

- Having too few questionnaire items that measure social bonds

- Failing to describe the chain of events that results in defective or inadequate bonds

- Creating an artificial division of socialized versus unsocialized youths

- Suggesting that social control theory explains why delinquency occurs, when in fact it typically explains no more than 50 percent of delinquent behavior and only 1 to 2 percent of the variance in future delinquency[26]

Despite the criticisms, Hirschi's work has made a major contribution to criminology. The mere fact that almost a half-century of scholars have tried to validate and replicate it testifies to its importance.

Furthermore, research using and extending Hirschi's constructs has become increasingly sophisticated. Research from the Rochester Youth Development Study, for example, has considered not only the role of weakened bonds to family and school in promoting delinquency but also the role of delinquent behavior in attenuating the strength of those very bonds. Criminologists have refined Hirschi's constructs so that the effects of social control on delinquency, as well as the effects of delinquency on social control, are considered.[27]

Finally, Hirschi's conception of social bonds has complemented competing explanations of group-level criminality such as gang behavior (see discussion of subcultural theories in Chapter 6). Social control is now discussed in relation to community, family, school, peer group, and individual factors (Table 7.2).

TABLE 7.2 Risk Factors for Youth Gang Membership

How powerful is social control theory? Consider the premise of this theory in relation to the risk factors for gang membership.

Domain	Risk Factors
Community	Social disorganization, including poverty and residential mobility
	Organized lower-class communities
	Underclass communities
	Presence of gangs in the neighborhood
	Availability of drugs in the neighborhood
	Availability of firearms
	Barriers to and lack of social and economic opportunities
	Lack of social capital
	Cultural norms supporting gang behavior
	Feeling unsafe in neighborhood; high crime
	Conflict with social control institutions
Family	Family disorganization, including broken homes and parental drug/alcohol abuse
	Troubled families, including incest, family violence, and drug addiction
	Family members in a gang
	Lack of adult male role models
	Lack of parental role models
	Low socioeconomic status
	Extreme economic deprivation, family management problems, parents with violent attitudes, sibling antisocial behavior
School	Academic failure
	Low educational aspirations, especially among females
	Negative labeling by teachers
	Trouble at school
	Few teacher role models
	Educational frustration
	Low commitment to school, low school attachment, high levels of antisocial behavior in school, low achievement test scores, and identification as being learning disabled
Peer group	High commitment to delinquent peers
	Low commitment to positive peers
	Street socialization
	Gang members in class
	Friends who use drugs or who are gang members
	Friends who are drug distributors
	Interaction with delinquent peers

(continues)

TABLE 7.2 (continued)

Domain	Risk Factors
Individual	Prior delinquency
	Deviant attitudes
	Street smartness; toughness
	Defiant and individualistic character
	Fatalistic view of the world
	Aggression
	Proclivity for excitement and trouble
	Locura (acting in a daring, courageous, and especially crazy fashion in the face of adversity)
	Higher levels of normlessness in the context of family, peer group, and school
	Social disabilities
	Illegal gun ownership
	Early or precocious sexual activity, especially among females
	Alcohol and drug use
	Drug trafficking
	Desire for group rewards, such as status, identity, self-esteem, companionship, and protection
	Problem behaviors, hyperactivity, externalizing behaviors, drinking, lack of refusal skills, and early sexual activity
	Victimization

SOURCE: James C. Howell, *Youth Gangs: An Overview* (Washington, D.C.: U.S. Department of Justice, 1998).

SOCIAL CONTROL AND DRIFT

In the 1960s, David Matza developed a different perspective on social control that explains why some adolescents drift in and out of delinquency. According to Matza, juveniles sense a moral obligation to be bound by the law. A "bind" between a person and the law, something that creates responsibility and control, remains in place most of the time. When it is not in place, the youth may enter into a state of **drift**, or a period when he or she exists in limbo between convention and crime, responding in turn to the demands of each, flirting now with one, now with the other, but postponing commitment, evading decision. Thus, the person drifts between criminal and conventional actions.[28]

If adolescents are indeed bound by the social order, how do they justify their delinquent acts? The answer is that they develop techniques to rationalize their actions. These techniques are defense mechanisms that release the youth from the constraints of the moral order:

- Denial of responsibility ("It wasn't my fault; I was a victim of circumstances.")

- Denial of injury ("No one was hurt, and they have insurance, so what's the problem?")

- Denial of the victim ("Anybody would have done the same thing in my position—I did what I had to do given the situation.")

- Condemnation of the condemner ("I bet the judge and everyone on the jury has done much worse than what I was arrested for.")

- Appeal to higher loyalties ("My friends were depending on me and I see them every day—what was I supposed to do?")[29]

Empirical support for drift theory has not been clear. Some studies show that delinquents consider these rationalizations valid,[30] while other research suggests that they do not. Later investigations also demonstrate that delinquents do not share the moral code or values of nondelinquents.[31]

PERSONAL AND SOCIAL CONTROL

Over the last 50 years, support has increased for the idea that both social (external) and personal (internal) control systems are important forces in keeping individuals from committing crimes. In other words, Hirschi's social bonds and Matza's drift paradigm may not be enough by themselves to explain why people do not commit crimes.

Failure of Control Mechanisms

Albert J. Reiss, a sociologist, was one of the first researchers to isolate a group of personal and social control factors. According to Reiss, delinquency is the result of (1) a failure to internalize socially accepted and prescribed norms of behavior; (2) a breakdown of internal controls; and (3) a lack of social rules that prescribe behavior in the family, the school, and other important social groups.

To test these notions, Reiss collected control-related data on 1,110 juvenile delinquents placed on probation in Cook County (Chicago), Illinois. He examined three sources of information: (1) a diverse set of data on such variables as family economic status and moral ideals and/or techniques of control by parents during childhood; (2) community and institutional information bearing on control, such as residence in a delinquency area and home ownership; and (3) personal control information, such as ego or superego controls, from clinical judgments of social workers and written psychiatric reports. Reiss concluded that measures of both personal and social control seem "to yield more efficient prediction of delinquent recidivism than items which are measures of the strength of social control."[32]

Stake in Conformity

Imagine that your earliest childhood memory conjures up the sound of splintering wood as the police break down your front door and the image of your grandmother being led away in handcuffs. You are 4 years old. What impact would such an image have on you? What if your formative years were spent in an impoverished urban environment where your mother and grandmother sold heroin out of your living room; your closest friends were high school dropouts with criminal records; and your adolescent confrontations did not involve the school bully demanding your lunch money, but rather the neighborhood drug dealer stopping by to settle overdue debts? Where would you be today?

Six years after the publication of Reiss's study, Jackson Toby proposed a different personal and social control model. Toby discussed the complementary role of neighborhood social disorganization and an individual's own stake in conformity. He agreed that the social disorganization of the slums explains why some communities have high crime rates while others do not: In slums, both the community and the family are powerless to control members' behavior. Thieves and hoodlums usually come from such neighborhoods. But a great many law-abiding youngsters come from slums as well. Toby questioned how a theory that explained group behavior could account for individual differences in response to a poor environment. In other words, how can the theory of social disorganization explain why only a few among so many slum youths actually commit crimes?[33]

According to Toby, the social disorganization approach can explain why one neighborhood has a much higher crime rate than another, but not why one particular individual becomes a hoodlum while another does not. What accounts for the difference is a differing stake in **conformity**, or correspondence of behavior to society's patterns, norms, or standards. One person may respond to conditions in a "bad" neighborhood by becoming hostile to conventional values, perhaps because he or she knows that the chances for legitimate success are poor. Another person in the same neighborhood may maintain his or her stake in conformity and remain committed to abiding by the law. Toby reminds us that when we try to account for crime in general, we should look at both group-level explanations (social disorganization) and individual-level explanations (stake in conformity).

CONTAINMENT THEORY

A broad analysis of the relationship between personal and social controls is found in Walter Reckless's presentation of containment theory.[34] **Containment theory** assumes that for every individual, there exists a containing external structure and a protective internal structure, both of which provide defense, protection, or insulation against delinquency.

According to Reckless, "outer containment," or the structural buffer that holds the person in bounds, can be found in the following components:

- A role that provides a guide for a person's activities

- A set of reasonable limits and responsibilities

- An opportunity for the individual to achieve status

- Cohesion among members of a group, including joint activity and togetherness

Defying Convention and Control: "In Your Face"

The Lambeau Leap, the Ickey Shuffle, the Fun Bunch, and the Sack Dance. Perhaps you were fortunate enough to watch "Monday Night Football" and see a Green Bay Packer leap into a row of Cheesehead fans. Or maybe you joined others in amazement as Ickey Woods shuffled across the artificial turf, moving side to side, as he passed the football back and forth—to himself. Who could forget the celebratory moves of the Washington Redskins' wide receivers after a touchdown—a collective and well-choreographed high five.(1) What could be worse (or better) than Terrell Owens celebrating on the Dallas Cowboys' midfield star as a player for the San Francisco 49ers? The answer is the cutthroat.

The cutthroat, also known as the "slash," is a simple and less-elegant move—just run your hand across your throat in a symbolic gesture that, to Brett Favre, Ricky Watters, Akili Smith, and Keyshawn Johnson, meant nothing more than "you cannot stop me" and "in your face." To the National Football League (NFL), however, it meant more. The gesture was nothing less than a taunt that crossed the line. This is the line drawn between aggression, confidence, pride, celebration, and sportsmanship on one side—all necessary and important characteristics of the game—and a clear breach of contract between the offending players and fans on the other side. Football players, like their brothers in baseball and hockey, are expected to fight hard to win, to be brutal when necessary, to break bones and teeth when given no other choice, but all within a game that has a set of conventional rules—rules that reflect agreed-upon values that include a strong and intractable commitment to the fans, who pay to watch, admire, and fantasize about playing in a game that is uniquely American. This is a familiar pact.

This pact reflects the very social bonds that promote and sustain our conventional life. That is why all of these violations of convention are so very easy to spot, even when referees fail to throw down their penalty flags. One commentator noted with wonderful sarcasm that there is a reason we do not do the same as Brett, Ricky, Akili, and Keyshawn in "real life." Just imagine:

> There is nothing too mundane to lord over a co-worker today. Start with hanging your coat. Turn this nonevent into an in-your-face "gotcha." Scream "This is my house." Let everybody know that you cannot and will not be stopped from putting your coat on that hanger.
>
> If you work in retail—let's say the jewelry counter at a department store—slam the register shut after a transaction, stare at the lady in housewares and menacingly trace a dollar sign in the air. . . .
>
> If you work in an airport control tower, punctuate every safe landing by throwing off your headset so everybody can see your face more clearly. Point up in the sky. Thump your chest.
>
> If you're a surgeon, heckle the patient for needing anesthesia. Don't just remove the tonsils. Say, "I got your tonsils right here." Then spike them.(2)

None of this is done, of course, because places of work reflect our relational attachments, our commitment to convention, a valued involvement in being productive, and our contribution to a shared belief system. With all the effort it takes to succeed—along with the good fortune—few want to lose out on their investment. Few knowingly violate a shared and agreed-to set of values—especially one that has a national time-honored tradition.

After the NFL (known in some circles as the "No Fun League") warned

Brett Favre challenging custom and convention by completing the cutthroat gesture.

team owners that large fines and significant game penalties would follow the cutthroat, would Brett, Ricky, Akili, and Keyshawn conform? Social control theorists would have said yes—not only for fear of fines, but for fear of breaching custom and violating convention, and for fear of losing the admiration of the fans. So far, at least in the case of the "cutthroat," this prediction seems to have been right, as very few fines for the gesture have been doled out in the 10 years since the ban.

Sources

1. Harriet Barovick et al., "Banned Zone," *Time*, Dec. 6, 1999, p. 37.
2. Bud Shaw, "For Many Pro Athletes, Showtime Is All about Me," (New Orleans) *Times-Picayune*, Dec. 12, 1999, p. 7c.

Questions for Discussion

1. As NFL commissioner, would you impose strict rules on this kind of behavior?
2. Can you think of a sport where custom and convention allow for even more significant demonstrations of individual pride?

Are Human Beings Inherently Bad?

One of the most notable distinctions between Hirschi's social control theory and other criminological theories that explain delinquency is the assumption made about human nature. It is most apparent when we compare social control theory to Merton's theory of anomie. Merton argues that individuals commit crimes when they experience strain as a result of their inability to meet society's goals with the resources available to them. Merton thus assumes that humans do not have a natural tendency to engage in offending behavior, but that it is strain that causes them to do so. Social control theory, on the other hand, makes the opposite assumption. Hirschi argues that individuals will engage in crime and delinquency unless they are bonded to society in four ways: attachment to family, peers, and school; commitment to conventional goals; involvement in conventional activities; and belief in the legitimacy of society's laws and norms. In other words, human beings are inherently criminal. Social control theory thus explains what prevents individuals from committing crimes rather than what causes them to commit crimes.

Although research provides support for the idea that individuals with strong social bonds are less likely to engage in crime and delinquency,[1] it is impossible to test Hirschi's underlying assumption about human nature because we cannot examine human behavior in a vacuum, removed from all social and environmental influences. The best we can do is speculate on the question based on knowledge about patterns of juvenile delinquency and criminal offending.

The most convincing argument in support of Hirschi's assumption is one that is often used to criticize other theories of delinquency. This argument points out that not all individuals who experience "causes" of crime, such as economic stress or educational failure, engage in delinquency. Some individuals who are exposed to risk factors commit crimes, while others do not. A good theory of crime must explain why this happens. Social control theory is consistent with this line of thinking because it is based on the idea that there are no causes of crime—that all humans will commit crime unless they are adequately bonded to society. Thus, the behavior of individuals who are exposed to the "causes" alleged by other scholars but do not commit crimes can be explained by stronger social bonds among these individuals.

On the other hand, a similar type of argument can be made against Hirschi's assumption about human nature. If all human beings will commit crimes without social bonds, then why don't all juveniles with weak bonds engage in delinquency? And why do some juveniles with strong bonds engage in delinquency? Studies show that college students engage in illegal behaviors.[2] How can this be explained? Arguably, these students have relatively strong social bonds. The fact that they are in college suggests that they at least have a commitment to conventional aspirations. We could also ask why some offenders engage in some types of criminal activities but refrain from others. Evidence indicates that although juvenile offenders tend to engage in a variety of offenses, offense specialization increases with age.[3] Offense specialization is inconsistent with Hirschi's assumption about human nature. If humans have an inherent predisposition toward criminal behavior, then offenders should not be selective about their criminal endeavors. In contrast, they should have a natural tendency toward all types of crime.

Sources

1. Stephen Demuth and Susan L. Brown, "Family Structure, Family Processes, and Adolescent Delinquency: The Significance of Parental Absence versus Parental Gender," *Journal of Research in Crime and Delinquency,* **41**(1) (2004): 58–81; Wendy D. Manning and Kathleen A. Lamb, "Adolescent Well-Being in Cohabiting, Married, and Single-Parent Families," *Journal of Marriage and Family,* **65** (2003): 876–893.
2. R. Tewksbury and E. E. Mustaine, "Lifestyles of the Wheelers and Dealers: Drug Dealing Among Ameri-can College Students," *Journal of Crime and Justice,* **21**(2) (1998): 37–56.
3. Alex Piquero, Raymond Paternoster, Paul Mazerolle, Robert Brame, and Charles W. Dean, "Onset Age and Offense Specialization," *Journal of Research in Crime and Delinquency,* **36**(3) (1999): 275–299.

Questions for Discussion

1. Do you think humans have an inherent inclination to commit crimes? Explain why or why not.
2. What are the implications of your perspective for crime prevention initiatives and laws? What is the best way to reduce crime?

- A sense of belonging (identification with the group)

- Identification with one or more persons within the group

- Provisions for supplying alternative ways and means of satisfaction (when one or more ways are closed)[35]

"Inner containment," or personal control, is ensured by:

- A good self-concept

- Self-control

- A strong ego

- A well-developed conscience

TABLE 7.3 The Probability of Deviance as Indicated by Inner and Outer Containment*

Outer Containment (Social Control)	Inner Containment (Personal Control)	
	Strong	Weak
Strong	+ +	+ −
Weak	+ −	− −

* + + = very low; + − = average; − − = very high

SOURCE: Adapted from Walter C. Reckless, "A Non-Causal Explanation: Containment Theory," *Excerpta Criminologia*, **2** (1962): 131–132.

- A high frustration tolerance

- A high sense of responsibility

Reckless suggests that the probability of deviance is directly related to the extent to which internal pushes (such as a need for immediate gratification, restlessness, and hostility), external pressures (such as poverty, unemployment, and blocked opportunities), and external pulls are controlled by one's inner and outer containment. The primary containment factor is found in self-concept, or the way one views oneself in relation to others and to the world. A strong self-concept, coupled with some additional inner controls (such as a strong conscience and sense of responsibility) plus outer controls, makes delinquency highly unlikely.

Table 7.3 shows how the probability of deviance changes as an individual's inner and outer containment weakens. But why is it important to examine inner and outer controls simultaneously? Consider John, a college freshman, who had extensive community ties and strong family attachments and was valedictorian of his high school class. He also was a dealer in cocaine. All efforts to explain John's drug selling would prove disappointing if measures of social control were used alone. In other words, according to Hirschi's social control theory, John should be a conformist—he should focus his efforts on becoming a pharmacist or a teacher. Containment theory, on the other hand, would be sensitive to the fact that John, while socially controlled and bonded by external forces, had a poorly developed self-concept, had an immature or undeveloped conscience, and was extremely impulsive. In short, he was driven to selling drugs as a result of a poor set of inner controls.

The idea that both internal and external factors are involved in controlling behavior has interested a number of scholars. Francis Ivan Nye, for example, developed the notion that multiple control factors determine human behavior.

He argued that **internalized control**, or self-regulation, was a product of guilt aroused in the conscience when norms have been internalized. **Indirect control** comes from an individual's identification with noncriminals and a desire not to embarrass parents and friends by acting against their expectations.

Nye believes that social control involves "needs satisfaction," by which he means that control depends on how well a family can prepare the child for success at school, with peers, and in the workplace. Finally, **direct control**, a purely external control, depends on rules, restrictions, and punishments.[36]

Other researchers have looked at direct controls in different ways. Parental control, for example, may depend on factors such as a broken home, the mother's employment, and the number of children in the family; such factors indicate some loss of direct control. Once again we find mixed results. Some studies indicate very little relationship between a broken home and delinquency, except for minor offenses such as truancy and running away.[37] The same can be said about the consequences of a mother's employment and of family size.[38] Other studies, however, have shown that direct control is a mediating factor between family structure and delinquency. Recent research on family structure and social control indicates that the relationship between social control and delinquency is complex—it varies by the type of control being measured as well as the type of delinquency.[39]

Empirical Tests of Containment Theory

Not when you're 15 and live in a crowded apartment with seven siblings, all younger than 6. Not when your mom has no job, is coming off drugs and belongs to the same gang as you, your drug-addicted dad, and all your relatives belong to. Not when you have to dress so carefully for the trip to class each day, because one mistake could kill. Does Calvin Klein know his logo means 'Crips Killer' in Southeast L.A.? Green means you deal drugs. The wrong belt buckle or shoelace knot is big trouble if you meet rival gangs on your way.[40]

How can a child living in this neighborhood grow up to be a good, law-abiding citizen? How is he or she protected from the crime-producing influences lurking around each corner? To answer these questions, Reckless and his associates had high school teachers in a high-crime neighborhood nominate boys they believed would neither commit delinquent acts nor come into contact with police and juvenile court.

The 125 "good boys" scored high on a social responsibility test and low on a delinquency-proneness test. These boys avoided trouble, had

At a wilderness camp in Florida, adolescent probationers learn positive values at a program characterized by its rules and restrictions.

good relations with parents and teachers, and had a good self-concept. They thought of themselves as obedient. Reckless concluded that nondelinquent boys follow conventional values even in bad neighborhoods if they maintain a positive self-image. It is this positive self-image that protects them. In a follow-up study, the research team compared good boys with those nominated by teachers as "bad boys" (those they believed were headed for trouble). The good boys scored better on parental relation, self-image, and social responsibility tests. Far more of the bad boys had acquired police and juvenile court records.[41]

Evaluation: Containment Theory

Containment theory, like Hirschi's social control theory, has received significant criticism.[42] The most damaging has come from Clarence Schrag, who contends that the terminology used is vague and poorly defined, that the theory is difficult to test empirically, and that the theory fails to consider why some poorly contained youths commit violent crimes while others commit property crimes.[43] These criticisms are not easy to answer. And because little empirical research has been done to test the findings of Reckless and his colleagues in nearly 50 years, there is little evidence of the validity of containment theory.

THEORETICAL EXPLORATIONS

Over the past several years, a number of attempts have been made to reconceptualize social control by joining, merging, integrating, and testing different theoretical hypotheses and propositions.[44]

As Table 7.4 reveals, theoretical criminologists have relied on social control theory to propose developmental, integrated, and general theories of crime.

Developmental/Life Course Theory

All developmental theories have one thing in common: explanations for why offending starts (onset), why it continues (continuance), why it becomes more frequent or more serious (escalation), why it de-escalates (de-escalation), and why, inevitably, it stops (desistance). Most theories are static, focusing exclusively on childhood, adolescence, young adulthood, or adulthood, and fail to capture the different developmental pathways to delinquency and future offending. Developmental theories, on the other hand, consider each phase in relation to the life span of an offender.

Life course theory was first introduced in the 1980s as the study of criminal careers, or "the longitudinal sequence of crimes committed by an individual offender."[45] Examining criminal careers allowed researchers to consider the mechanisms by which criminal offending behaviors develop. Nearly a decade later, Robert Sampson and John Laub reintroduced the notion of criminal careers and formally named it life course perspective. The life course perspective has gained considerable attention in the twenty-first century.

Central to research over the life course are the underlying devices and procedures that lead to desistance from deviant behaviors and whether these shift over time. Research must develop further to address how the predictors and processes differ by race, ethnicity, structural context, and

DID YOU KNOW?

. . . that most criminologists favor social control theory as an explanation of criminal behavior?

TABLE 7.4 Examples of Recent Theoretical Explanations

LIFE COURSE/DEVELOPMENTAL THEORY	
Farrington	A combination of multiple personal (e.g., impulsivity), social (e.g., poor parental supervision), and environmental (e.g., low income) factors are associated with crime over the course of a lifetime.
Thornberry	Crime is a function of a dynamic social process that is determined by learning variables (e.g., association with delinquent peers) and boundary variables (e.g., attachment and commitment to conventional activities), as well as social class, race, and gender.
Moffitt	Life-course-persistent offending is explained by faulty interactions between children and their parents, resulting in poor self-control and impulsivity. Adolescent-limited offending is traced to social mimicry, antisocial reinforcements, and models.
LeBlanc	An integrative, multilayered control theory that borrows heavily from competing perspectives explains criminality, the criminal, and the criminal event in both static and developmental terms.
Laub and Sampson	Crime causation must be viewed developmentally—in the context of the turning points in a criminal career.
INTEGRATED THEORY	
Weis	Crime results from an interaction between diminished social controls and influences from delinquent peers.
Elliott	Delinquency is traced to strain, weak social bonds, and deviant subcultures.
GENERAL THEORY	
Hirschi and Gottfredson	Individual differences in crime commission can be attributed to levels of self-control.
Agnew	Individual differences in offending behavior can be explained by interactions between five clusters of causes (self, family, peer group, work, and school).

maltreatment type. Another seminal study of continuity and change in criminal offending across the life span was conducted in 1950 by Sheldon and Eleanor Glueck. In their *Unraveling Juvenile Delinquency* study, a sample of 500 delinquents and 500 nondelinquents was examined to determine which factors distinguish boys reared in poverty-ridden neighborhoods who later become serious delinquents from boys raised in the same locality who did not exhibit problem behaviors.[46] The sample was reassessed at age 25 and again at age 32.[47] Upon their retirement in 1972, Sheldon and Eleanor Glueck donated their data to the Harvard Law School.[48]

In 1987, more than a decade after the Gluecks made their donation, John Laub happened upon the data. Within a year, he and Robert Sampson recoded, computerized, and reanalyzed the data. In 1994, Laub and Sampson pioneered a follow-up study of the original sample. At the time of reinterview, the subjects were between 62 and 70 years of age, and criminal and death records were collected at the state and national level.[49] Sampson and Laub produced the only criminological study in the world that contains data from birth to age 70 for such a large collection of juvenile offenders.[50]

Research over the life course embodies the fundamental questions inherent in the study of resilience and desistance while also contemplating the stability of criminal offending over the life span. In an extension of Hirschi's theory to the "life course," for example, Robert J. Sampson and John H. Laub found that family, school, and peer attachments were most strongly associated with delinquency from childhood to adolescence (through age 17).[51] From the transition to young adulthood through the transition to middle adulthood, attachment to work (job stability) and family (marriage) appear most strongly related to crime causation. Sampson and Laub found evidence that these positive personal and professional relationships build a "social capital" in otherwise vulnerable

individuals that significantly inhibits deviance over time.

Another life course theory combines control theory with social learning theory (Chapter 4). Terence Thornberry argues that the potential for delinquency begins with the weakening of a person's bonds to the conventional world (parents, school, and accepted values). For this potential to be realized, there must be a social setting in which to learn delinquent values. In this setting, delinquents seek each other out and form common belief systems. There is nothing static about this kind of learning. Criminality, according to Thornberry, is a function of a dynamic social process that changes over time.[52]

David Farrington's work with the data from the Cambridge Study of Delinquent Development reveals different explanations for the general tendency to engage in crime (long-term variables) over time, as well as the influences that prompt an individual, at any given time, to engage in crime (short-term variables) (Table 7.4). The former include impulsivity, low empathy, and belief systems favorable to law violation. The latter consider momentary opportunities and situationally induced motivating factors, such as alcohol consumption and boredom.[53]

In one of the most elegant developmental theories to date, Marc LeBlanc employs social control theory to provide both static (pertaining to a particular time and place) and dynamic (occurring over time) explanations of criminality (the total number of infractions), the criminal (personal

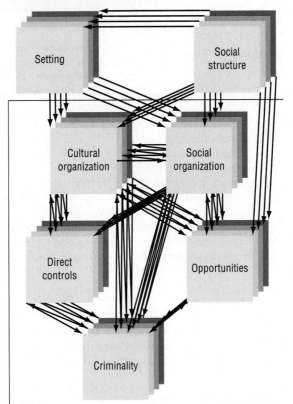

FIGURE 7.1 Control theory at the level of criminality.

Source: Marc LeBlanc, "A Generic Control Theory of the Criminal Phenomenon: The Structural and Dynamic Statements of an Integrative Multilayered Control Theory," in *Developmental Theories of Crime and Delinquency: Advances in Criminological Theory*, vol. 7, T. P. Thornberry, ed. (New Brunswick, N.J.: Transaction, 1997), p.238. Copyright © 1997 by Transaction Publishers. Reprinted by permission of the publisher.

Nations with Low Crime Rates

Most criminologists devote their efforts to learning why people commit crime and why there is so much crime. A few have looked at the question from the opposite perspective: In places with little crime, what accounts for the low crime rate? Using the United Nations' first World Crime Survey (1970–1975), Freda Adler studied the two countries with the lowest crime rates in each of five general cultural regions of the world:(1)

Western Europe: Switzerland and the Republic of Ireland

Eastern Europe: the former German Democratic Republic (East Germany) and Bulgaria

Arab countries: Saudi Arabia and Algeria

Asia: Japan and Nepal

Latin America: Costa Rica and Peru (2)

This is an odd assortment of countries. They seem to have little in common. Some are democratic, others authoritarian. Some are republics, others monarchies. Some are ruled by dictators, others by communal councils. Some are rural, others highly urbanized. Some are remote and isolated; others are in the political mainstream. Some are highly religious, some largely atheistic. Some have a very high standard of living, others a very low one.

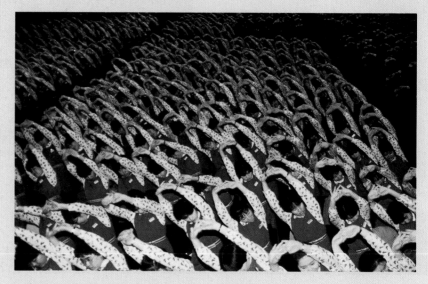

■ *Workers in Japan showing solidarity in an early morning exercise ritual.*

What explains their common characteristic of low crime rates?

Investigations slowly revealed a common factor in all 10 countries: Each appeared to have an intact social control system, quite apart from whatever formal control system (law enforcement) it had. Here are brief descriptions of the types of social control systems identified:

Western Europe: Switzerland fostered a strong sense of belonging to and participating in the local community. (3)

The family was still strong in the Republic of Ireland, and it was strengthened by shared religious values.

Eastern Europe: The former German Democratic Republic involved all youths in communal activities, organized by groups and aimed at having young people excel for the glory of self and country. In Bulgaria, industrialization focused on regional industry centers so that the workers would not be dislodged from their hometowns,

---

characteristics of an offender), and the crime (the criminal event). To construct his models, LeBlanc borrows from a host of disciplines (Figure 7.1).

Integrated Theory

Integrated theory combines a criminological theory, such as differential association, with a number of social controls. Delbert Elliott and his colleagues have integrated the social bonds of Hirschi's theory of social control with strain theories. These researchers suggest that limited or blocked opportunities and a subsequent failure to achieve cultural goals would weaken or even destroy bonds

to the conventional or social order. In other words, even if someone establishes strong bonds in childhood, a series of negative experiences in school, in the community, and at home, along with blocked access to opportunity, would be likely to lead to a weakening of those social bonds. As strain weakens social bonds, the chance of delinquency increases.[54]

Joseph Weis has proposed a social development model of crime that is an elegant integration of social control and social learning theory. He proposes that delinquency is minimized when youths who are at risk to commit crime have the opportunity to engage in conforming activities and which served as continuing social centers.

Arab countries: Islam continued to be strong as a way of life and exercised a powerful influence on daily activities, especially in Saudi Arabia. Algeria had, in addition, a powerful commitment to socialism in its postindependence era, involving the citizens in all kinds of commonly shared development activities.

Asia: Nepal retained its strong family and clan ties, augmented by councils of elders that oversaw the community and resolved problems. Highly industrialized Japan had lost some of the social controls of family and kinship, but it found a substitute family in the industrial community, to which most Japanese belonged: Mitsubishi might now be the family that guides one's every step.

Latin America: Costa Rica spent all the funds that other governments devoted to the military on social services and social development, caring for and strengthening its families. Peru went through a process of urbanization in stages: Village and family cohesion marked the lives of people in the countryside, and this cohesion remained with the people as they migrated from Andean villages to smaller towns and then to the big city, where they

were received by and lived surrounded by others from their own hometowns.

The study concluded that **synnomie**, a term derived from the Greek *syn* meaning "with" and *nomos* meaning "norms," marked societies with low crime rates.

In an update of Adler's original low-crime-rate study, Janet Stamatel wrote:

The capacity for societies to maintain social control can change over time in response to other changes in social conditions. This means that countries labeled as either "low crime" or "high crime" at one point in time may experience changes in their crime status as social control mechanisms change over time. For example, in a study examining how crime rates in the ten countries that Adler identified as low crime in the late 1970s have changed as of 2000, Stamatel analyzed crime statistics from the United Nations and the World Health Organization to find that several of these countries (e.g., Algeria, Japan, Nepal, Saudi Arabia, and Switzerland) have remarkably been able to maintain low crimes rates for several decades. In contrast, a couple of these countries, namely Bulgaria and Peru, were not able to maintain their "low crime" status as dramatic political and economic changes severely disrupted their social control systems. Not

only can we learn a lot about how to control crime from countries with consistently low crime rates, but we can also learn much about what happens to crime rates when social control mechanisms are no longer able to function as intended by studying changing crime rates over time.(4)

Sources

1. United Nations, *Report of the Secretary General on Crime Prevention and Control,* A/32/199 (popularly known as the First U.N. World Crime Survey) (New York: United Nations, 1977).
2. Freda Adler, *Nations Not Obsessed with Crime* (Littleton, Colo.: Fred B. Rothman, 1983).
3. Marshall B. Clinard, *Cities with Little Crime: The Case of Switzerland* (Cambridge, Mass.: Cambridge University Press, 1978).
4. Janet P. Stamatel, "Revisiting Nations Not Obsessed with Crime" (working paper, December 2008).

Questions for Discussion

1. People in the United States work in factories, live in family groups, go to church, and join youth groups. Why do these institutions not function effectively as forms of social control to keep the crime rate low?
2. How could government or community decision makers use the information presented by this study to help solve crime problems in the United States?

---

are rewarded for doing so. Consistent reinforcement maximizes the social bonds, which, in turn, diminish associations with delinquent peers and reduce crime.[55]

General Theories

In *A General Theory of Crime,* Travis Hirschi and Michael Gottfredson propose a model of personal and social control designed to explain an individual's propensity to commit crime.[56] Hirschi and Gottfredson claim that their model, unlike earlier conceptualizations, explains the tendency to commit all crimes, from crimes of violence such as

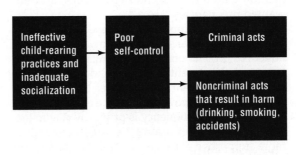

FIGURE 7.2 The Hirschi-Gottfredson self-control model. Hirschi and Gottfredson's model assumes that poor self-control is an intervening variable that explains all crime, as well as differences in crime rates by age, gender, and race.

TABLE 7.5 Violence-Prevention Programs in Boston (listed by start date)

1982
Boston City Hospital Violence Prevention
Program

1985
Friends for Life—PSA Campaign Ad
Council of Boston
WEATOC Teen Theatre Group Adds
Violence Prevention to Its Repertoire

1986
South Boston Boys and Girls Club—Friends
for Life Clubs and Violence Prevention
Programs

1987
Violence Prevention Curriculum for
Adolescents Published for Distribution

1989
Gang Peace

1990
Mayor's Safe Neighborhood Initiative
Teens against Gang Violence
Citizens for Safety

1992
WBZ-TV Stop the Violence Campaign Ten-Point Coalition

1994
Louis D. Brown Peace Curriculum
Community Policing in Boston
Adolescent Wellness Program

1995
Ceasefire

1996
Strike Force

2005
B-SMART (Boston Strategic Multi-Agency Response Teams)

SOURCE: Boston Police Department, as cited in *What Can the Federal Government Do to Decrease Crime and Revitalize Communities?* (Washington, D.C.: National Institute of Justice, 1998), p. 60 (updated).

robbery and sexual assault to white-collar offenses such as mail fraud and federal securities violations.[57]

This "general theory" of propensity to commit crimes, shown in Figure 7.2, assumes that offenders have little control over their own behavior and desires. When the need for momentary pleasure and immediate gratification outweighs long-term interests, crime occurs. In short, crime is a function of poor self-control.

What leads to poor self-control? Inadequate socialization and poor child-rearing practices, coupled with poor attachment, increase the probability of impulsive and uncontrolled acts. According to Hirschi and Gottfredson, individuals with low self-control also tend to be involved in noncriminal events that result in harm, such as drinking, smoking, and most types of accidents, including auto crashes, household fires, and unwanted pregnancies.

Evidence in support of this theory is mixed. Recent studies have shown that low self-control is linked to violent offending, homicide victimization, and delinquent behavior and that the link holds across different genders, races, and cultures.[58] One study found, however, that the effect of parental efficacy on delinquency is primarily due to factors other than self-control.[59] Overall, research is more supportive of the second link of Gottfredson and Hirschi's theory than the first one.

Robert Agnew has recently developed another general theory of crime. In his theory, Agnew combines the main arguments from social control, social learning, self-control, strain, labeling, social support, and biopsychological theories to explain the major parameters of criminal offending. The crux of his argument is that causes of crime can be grouped into five clusters (self, family, peer group, work, and school) that interact in complex ways to influence offending behavior.[60]

It is important to remember that all of these recent explanations of criminality share one common variable—the social bonds that are at the foundation of social control theory. The ingredients of social control theory have been used quite effectively over the last several decades as building blocks for these recent developments.

THEORY INFORMS POLICY

Social control theory tells us that people commit crimes when they have not developed adequate attachments, have not become involved in and committed to conventional activities, and have not internalized the rules of society (or do not care about them). Efforts to prevent crime must therefore include the teaching of conventional values. It is also necessary to find ways to strengthen individual bonds to society, commitment to the conventional order, and involvement in conventional activities. One way is to strengthen the institutions that socialize people and continue to regulate their behavior throughout life—the family, the school, and the workplace.[61]

Family

Experimental school-based parent-training programs are offered in many states. The major premise of these programs is that a child's bond to a family is crucial. To develop this bond, parents learn to provide opportunities that would help the child participate and succeed in a social unit such as the school (by demonstrating good study habits, for example) and to reinforce conformity or punish violations of the group's norms. Results suggest that these initiatives decrease children's aggressiveness and increase parenting skills.[62]

School

A program called PATHE (Positive Action Through Holistic Education) operates in middle schools and high schools around the United States. Its objective is to reduce delinquency by strengthening students' commitment to school and attachment to conforming members—in other words, by bonding young people to the conventional system.[63]

Neighborhood

Historically, church and family have helped protect and maintain the social order in neighborhoods and instill a sense of pride and comfort in residents. This is no longer the case in many areas. The neighborhood as an institution of informal social control has been very much weakened. Various agencies have tried to reverse this trend with programs to prevent juvenile crime that are implemented through neighborhood-based organizations, for example, in Chicago, Dallas, Los Angeles, New Orleans, New York, and San Diego. Federally funded programs seek to reduce crime by strengthening neighborhood cohesion. Programs assess the needs of residents and then set up crisis-intervention centers, mediation (between youngsters and school, family, or police and between warring gangs), youth training, supervision programs, and family support systems.

Program evaluations reveal that serious juvenile crime decreases.[64] Hundreds of such community crime-prevention projects around the country have been organized by government agencies, private persons, and religious groups.[65] They have made a local impact, but they have not been able to change the national crime rate. The most successful models, however, may offer a plan for crime prevention on a broader, perhaps even a national, scale.

As our understanding of control theory evolves, so will our appreciation of the effects of control interventions. If nothing else, it is fair to say that social control programs and interventions are proliferating and may be found in every state. Here are just a few examples:

Homebuilders (Tacoma, Washington). A family preservation program that seeks to keep at-risk children at home[66]

Families First (Michigan). A program that strengthens vulnerable families[67]

S.W.E.A.T. Team (Bridgeport, Connecticut). A project that employs teenagers to create new activities for children who may be tempted to join gangs or sell drugs[68]

Learnfare (Ohio, Virginia, Florida, Maryland, and Oklahoma). Programs that provide financial and social support for teenage welfare mothers who attend school[69]

Table 7.5 lists programs that Boston, Massachusetts, has initiated since 1982.

Crime-prevention programs like those initiated in Boston over the past decade have met with significant success. Most of these efforts are grounded in principles of social control.

REVIEW

The term "social control" has taken on a wide variety of meanings. In general, it describes any mechanism that leads to conformity to social norms. Mainstream studies of social control take one of two approaches. Macrosociological studies focus on formal systems of social control. Most contemporary criminological research takes the microsociological approach, which focuses on informal systems. Travis Hirschi's social control theory has had a long-lasting impact on the scholarly community. Hirschi identified four social bonds that promote adherence to society's values: attachment, commitment, involvement, and belief. The stronger these bonds, Hirschi claimed, the less the likelihood of delinquency.

According to the containment theory of Walter Reckless, every person has a containing external structure (a role in a social group with reasonable limits and responsibilities and alternative means of attaining satisfaction). In addition, each individual has a protective internal structure that depends on a good self-concept, self-control, a well-developed conscience, a tolerance for frustration, and a strong sense of responsibility.

Most investigators today believe that personal (inner) controls are as important as social (external) controls in keeping people from committing crimes. Albert Reiss found that personal controls reinforce social controls. Jackson Toby stressed the importance of a stake in conformity in keeping a person from responding to social disorganization with delinquent behavior. Recent efforts to integrate social control theories with other theories have resulted in developmental, integrated, and general theories of crime. All share one common variable—the social bonds that constitute social control theory. These efforts are notable, however, for their explanations of criminal behavior over the life course. More so than ever before, criminologists are examining the onset, continuance, desistance, and stability of criminal offending over the life course.

As part of an effort to reduce delinquency, a variety of programs at the local and regional levels help parents, schools, and neighborhood groups develop social controls.

CRIMINOLOGY & PUBLIC POLICY

In recent years, lawmakers at both the state and federal levels have passed legislation increasing penalties for criminal offenses, particularly violent crimes. These actions came in response to public concerns about crime and the belief that many serious offenders are released from prison too soon. Many such laws have come under the general label of "three strikes and you're out." The purpose of these laws is simple: Offenders convicted repeatedly of serious offenses should be removed from society for long periods of time, in many cases for life. For many years, most states have had provisions in their laws that included enhanced sentencing for repeat offenders. Yet between 1993 and 1995, 24 states and the federal government enacted new laws using the "three strikes" moniker, with similarly labeled bills introduced in a number of other states.

The rapid expansion of three-strikes laws, regardless of how they are defined, reflects the perception that existing laws did not adequately protect public safety in their application and/or outcome, that exceptional incidents had occurred that the new laws would address, or that the intent of current laws was being frustrated by other factors such as prison crowding. Whether the perception was accurate and what the impact of the new laws will be are questions that cannot yet be answered. (SOURCE: John Clark, James Austin, and D. Alan Henry, *Three Strikes and You're Out: A Review of State Legislation* [Washington, D.C.: NIJ, 1997].)

Questions for Discussion Three-strikes laws can be harsh. Offenders committing petty thefts as their third strike may in some jurisdictions, for example, receive 25 or more years in prison as courts and prosecutors take their prior record into consideration. Such sentences were upheld by the U.S. Supreme Court in 2003. What concerns with three-strikes laws are raised by recent extensions to Hirschi's notion of social control—life course theories of offending? If the fundamental rationale of three-strikes laws is to protect the community from habitual offenders, are life course theories supportive? If we know what best predicts future offending and if programs can be created to address these causal factors, why rely on long prison sentences?

YOU BE THE CRIMINOLOGIST

The desire for stability, involvement, belief, and conformity can have a dark side. Consider how mechanisms of social control, narrowly conceived, can support new religious, political, and psychosocial cults or sects. How does social control theory help explain the attraction to Heaven's Gate, the Aum Shinrikyo, the Order of the Solar Temple, or the Branch Davidians?

KEY TERMS

The numbers next to the terms refer to the pages on which the terms are defined.

attachment (155)

belief (157)

commitment (156)

conformity (161)

containment theory (161)

direct control (164)

drift (160)

indirect control (164)

internalized control (164)

involvement (157)

macrosociological studies (155)

microsociological studies (155)

social control theory (154)

synnomie (169)

Labeling, Conflict, and Radical Theories

Labeling Theory
The Origins of Labeling Theory
Basic Assumptions of Labeling Theory
Labeling in the 1960s
Labeling Theory in Action
Empirical Evidence for Labeling Theory
Evaluation: Labeling Theory
Conflict Theory
The Consensus Model
The Conflict Model
Conflict Theory and Criminology
Empirical Evidence for the Conflict Model
Radical Theory
The Intellectual Heritage of Marxist
  Criminology
Engels and Marx
Willem Adriaan Bonger
Georg Rusche and Otto Kirchheimer
Radical Criminology since the 1970s
Evaluation: Marxist Criminological Theory
Emerging Explanations
Review
Criminology & Public Policy
You Be the Criminologist
Key Terms

■ On November 30, 1999, Seattle police clashed with demonstrators at the opening ceremony of the World Trade Organization, using tear gas and rubber bullets to disperse the crowds.

Each era of social and political turmoil has produced profound changes in people's lives. Perhaps no such era was as significant for criminology as the 1960s. A society with conservative values was shaken out of its complacency when young people, blacks, women, and other disadvantaged groups demanded a part in the shaping of national policy. They saw the gaps between philosophical political demands and reality: Blacks had little opportunity to advance; women were kept in an inferior status; old politicians made wars in which the young had to die.

Rebellion broke out, and some criminologists joined the revolution.

These criminologists turned away from theories that explained crime by characteristics of the offender or of the social structure. They set out to demonstrate that individuals become criminals because of what people with power, especially those in the criminal justice system, do. Their explanations largely reject the consensus model of crime, on which all earlier theories rested. Their theories not only question the traditional explanations of the creation and enforcement of criminal law

173

but also blame that law for the making of criminals (Table 8.1).

It may not sound so radical to assert that unless an act is made criminal by law, no person who performs that act can be adjudicated a criminal. The exponents of contemporary alternative explanations of crime grant that much. But—justifiably—they also ask, Who makes these laws in the first place? And why? Is breaking such laws the most important criterion for being a criminal? Are all people who break these laws criminals? Do all members of society agree that those singled out by the criminal law to be called "criminals" are criminals and that others are not?

LABELING THEORY

The 1950s were a period of general prosperity and pride for Americans. Yet some social scientists, uneasy about the complacency they saw, turned their attention to the social order. They noted that some of the ideals the United States had fought for in World War II had not been achieved at home. Human rights existed on paper but were often lacking in practice. It was clear that blacks continued to live as second-class citizens. Even though the Fourteenth Amendment to the Constitution guaranteed blacks equal rights, neither the law of the country nor the socioeconomic system provided them with equal opportunities.

Nowhere was this fact more apparent than in the criminal justice system. Social scientists and liberal lawyers pressed for change, and the Supreme Court, under Chief Justice Earl Warren, responded. In case after case, the Court found a pervasive influence of rules and customs that violated the concepts of **due process,** under which a person cannot be deprived of life, liberty, or property without lawful procedures; and **equal protection,** under which no one can be denied the safeguards of the law. The result of hundreds of Supreme Court decisions was that both black and white citizens now were guaranteed the right to counsel in all criminal cases, freedom from self-incrimination, and other rights enumerated in the first 10 amendments to the Constitution. Nevertheless, a great deal of social injustice remained.

In this social climate, a small group of social scientists, known as "labeling theorists," began to explore how and why certain acts were defined as criminal or, more broadly, as deviant behavior and others were not, and how and why certain people were defined as criminal or deviant. These theorists viewed criminals not as inherently evil

Perspective	Origin of Criminal Law	Causes of Criminal Behavior	Focus of Study
TABLE 8.1 Comparison of Four Criminological Perspectives			
Traditional/consensus	Laws reflect shared values.	Psychological, biological, or sociological factors.	Biological and psychological factors (Chap. 4); unequal opportunity (Chap. 5); learning criminal behavior in disorganized neighborhoods (Chap. 5); subculture values (Chap. 6); social control (Chap. 7).
Labeling	Those in power create the laws, decide who will be the rule breakers.	The process that defines (or labels) certain persons as criminals.	Effects of stigmatizing by the label "criminal"; sociopolitical factors behind reform legislation; origin of laws; deviant behavior (Chap. 8).
Conflict	Powerful groups use laws to support their interests.	Interests of one group do not coincide with needs of another.	Bias and discrimination in criminal justice system; differential crime rates of powerful and powerless; development of criminal laws by those in power; relationship between rulers and ruled (Chap. 8).
Radical (Marxist)	Laws serve interests of the ruling class.	Class struggle over distribution of resources in a capitalist system.	Relationship between crime and economics; ways in which state serves capitalist interests; solution to crime problem based on collapse of capitalism (Chap. 8).

persons engaged in inherently wrong acts but rather as individuals who had had criminal status conferred upon them by both the criminal justice system and the community at large.

Viewed from this perspective, criminal acts themselves are not particularly significant; the social reaction to them, however, is. Deviance and its control involve a process of social definition in which the response of others to an individual's behavior is the key influence on subsequent behavior and on individuals' views of themselves. Sociologist Howard S. Becker has written:

> Deviance is not a quality of the act the person commits, but rather a consequence of the application by others of rules and sanctions to an "offender." The deviant is one to whom that label has successfully been applied; deviant behavior is behavior that people so label.[1]

In focusing on the ways in which social interactions create deviance, **labeling theory** declares that the reactions of other people and the subsequent effects of those reactions create deviance. Once it becomes known that a person has engaged in deviant acts, he or she is segregated from conventional society, and a label ("thief," "whore," "junkie") is attached to the transgressor. This process of segregation creates "outsiders" (as Becker called them), or outcasts from society, who begin to associate with others like themselves.[2]

As more people begin to think of these people as deviants and to respond to them accordingly, the deviants react to the response by continuing to engage in the behavior society now expects of them. Through this process, their self-images gradually change as well. So the key factor is the label that is attached to an individual: "If men define situations as real, they are real in their consequences."[3]

The Origins of Labeling Theory

The intellectual roots of labeling theory can be traced to the post–World War I work of Charles Horton Cooley, William I. Thomas, and George Herbert Mead. These scholars, who viewed the human self as formed through a process of social interaction, were called **social interactionists.** In 1918, Mead compared the impact of social labeling to "the angel with the fiery sword at the gate who can cut one off from the world to which he belongs."[4]

Labeling separates the good from the bad, the conventional from the deviant. Mead's interest in deviance focused on the social interactions by which an individual becomes a deviant. The person is not just a fixed structure whose action is the result of certain factors acting upon it. Rather, social behavior develops in a continuous process of action and reaction.[5] The way we perceive ourselves, our self-concept, is built not only on what we think of ourselves but also on what others think of us.

Somewhat later, historian Frank Tannenbaum (1893–1969) used the same argument in his study of the causes of criminal behavior. He described the creation of a criminal as a process: Breaking windows, climbing onto roofs, and playing truant are all normal parts of the adolescent search for excitement and adventure. Local merchants and others who experience these activities may consider them a nuisance or perhaps even evil. This conflict is the beginning of the process by which the evil act transforms the transgressor into an evil individual. From that point on, the evil individuals are separated from those in conventional society. Given a criminal label, they gradually begin to think of themselves as they have been officially defined.

Tannenbaum maintained that it is the process of labeling, or the "dramatization of evil," that locks a mischievous boy into a delinquent role ("the person becomes the thing he is described as being"). Accordingly, "the entire process of dealing with young delinquents is mischievous insofar as it identifies him to himself and to the environment as a delinquent person."[6] The system starts out with a child in trouble and ends up with a juvenile delinquent.

Basic Assumptions of Labeling Theory

In the 1940s, sociologist Edwin Lemert elaborated on Tannenbaum's discussion by formulating the basic assumptions of labeling theory.[7] He reminded us that people are constantly involved in behavior that runs the risk of being labeled delinquent or criminal. But although many run that risk, only a few are so labeled. The reason, Lemert contended, is that there are two kinds of deviant acts: primary and secondary.[8]

"Primary deviations" are the initial deviant acts that bring on the first social response. These acts do not affect the individual's self-concept. It is the "secondary deviations," the acts that follow the societal response to the primary deviation, that are of major concern. These are the acts that result from the change in self-concept brought about by the labeling process.[9] The scenario goes somewhat like this:

1. An individual commits a simple deviant act (primary deviation)—throwing a stone at a neighbor's car, for instance.

2. There is an informal social reaction: The neighbor gets angry.

3. The individual continues to break rules (primary deviations)—he lets the neighbor's dog out of the yard.

4. There is increased, but still primary, social reaction: The neighbor tells the youth's parents.

5. The individual commits a more serious deviant act—he is caught shoplifting (still primary deviation).

6. There is a formal reaction: The youth is adjudicated a "juvenile delinquent" in juvenile court.

7. The youth is now labeled "delinquent" by the court and "bad" by the neighborhood, by his conventional peers, and by others.

8. The youth begins to think of himself as "delinquent"; he joins other unconventional youths.

9. The individual commits another, yet more serious, deviant act (secondary deviation)—he robs a local grocery store with members of a gang.

10. The individual is returned to juvenile court, has more offenses added to his record, is cast out further from conventional society, and takes on a completely deviant lifestyle.

According to Lemert, secondary deviance sets in after the community has become aware of a primary deviance. Individuals experience "a continuing sense of injustice, which [is] reinforced by job rejections, police cognizance, and strained interaction with normals."[10] In short, deviant individuals have to bear the stigma of the "delinquent" label, just as English and American convicts, as late as the eighteenth century, bore stigmas, in the form of an "M" for murderer or a "T" for thief, burned or cut into their bodies to designate them as persons to be shunned.[11] Once such a label is attached to a person, a deviant or criminal career has been set in motion. The full significance of labeling theory was not recognized, either in Europe or in the United States, until political events provided the opportunity.[12]

Labeling in the 1960s

The 1960s witnessed a movement among students and professors to join advocacy groups and become activists in the social causes that were rapidly gaining popularity on college campuses across the nation, such as equal rights for minorities, liberation for women, and peace for humankind. The protests took many forms—demonstrations and rallies, sit-ins and teach-ins, beards and long hair, rock music and marijuana, dropping out of school, burning draft cards.

Arrests of middle-class youths increased rapidly; crime was no longer confined to the ghettos. People asked whether arrests were being made for behavior that was not really criminal. Were the real criminals the legislators and policy makers who pursued a criminal war in Vietnam while creating the artificial crime of draft card burning at home? Were the real criminals the National Guardsmen who shot and killed campus demonstrators at Kent State University? Labeling theorists made their

■ A Kent State University protestor grieving over the body of a fellow student shot and killed by National Guardsmen, Ohio, 1970.

appearance and provided answers. Sociologist Kai Erickson has put it well:

> Deviance is not a property inherent in certain forms of behavior; it is a property conferred upon these forms by audiences which directly or indirectly witness them. The critical variable in the study of deviance, then, is the social audience rather than the individual actor, since it is the audience which eventually determines whether or not any episode or behavior or any class of episodes is labeled deviant.[13]

Edwin Schur, a leading labeling theorist of the 1960s, elaborated on Erickson's explanation:

> Human behavior is deviant to the extent that it comes to be viewed as involving a personally discreditable departure from a group's normative expectation, and it elicits interpersonal and collective reactions that serve to "isolate," "treat," "correct," or "punish" individuals engaged in such behavior.[14]

Schur also expanded on Lemert's secondary deviance with his own concept of "secondary elaboration," by which he meant that the effects of the labeling process become so significant that individuals who want to escape from their deviant groups and return to the conventional world find it difficult to do so. Schur points to members of the gay and drug cultures.[15] The strength of the label, once acquired, tends to exclude such people permanently from the mainstream culture.[16] Schur found that involvement in activities that are disapproved of may very well lead to more participation in deviance than one had originally planned, and so increase the social distance between the person labeled "deviant" and the conventional world.[17]

The labeling theorists then asked, Who makes the rules that define deviant behavior, including crime? According to Howard Becker, it is the "moral entrepreneurs"—the people whose high social position gives them the power to make and enforce the social rules by which members of society have to live. By making the rules that define the criminal, Becker argues, certain members of society create outsiders.

The whole process thus becomes a political one, pitting the rule makers against the rule breakers. Becker goes even further, suggesting that people can be labeled simply by being falsely accused. As long as others believe that someone has participated in a given deviant behavior, that individual will experience negative social reaction. People can also suffer the effects of labeling when they have committed a deviant act that has not been discovered. Because most people know how they would be labeled if they were caught, these secret deviants may experience the same labeling effects as those who have been caught.[18]

Labeling Theory in Action

Specialist Osvaldo Hernandez, a 25-year-old paratrooper in the 82nd Airborne Division, knows firsthand the detrimental effects of a label and its subsequent implications. It was 2003, and Hernandez—who at the time was not even old enough to legally buy alcohol and was living in a dangerous neighborhood in Queens, New York—was pulled over by plainclothes officers and arrested for possessing a semiautomatic .380 pistol, which officers found under the seat of the car.

Hernandez, who had never been arrested before, pleaded guilty to third-degree criminal possession of a weapon and served 1 year in jail. Hernandez was determined to turn his life around, and one day after being released from jail he applied to the U.S. Army. The army was struggling to recruit enough people to populate the ranks and granted him an enlistment waiver. Hernandez served a 15-month combat tour in Afghanistan and was honorably discharged. Armed with stellar recommendations from his supervisors, Hernandez applied to become a New York City police officer. However, his felony conviction precluded him from being considered for a position with the New York Police Department (NYPD). The majority of felons are prohibited by law from carrying a firearm, which excludes all individuals with a felony conviction from serving as a police officer.

Specialist Hernandez continues to serve as a member of the army and legally carries an M4 assault rifle and a machine gun. The U.S. Army has provided him with additional training in other, more advanced weapon systems used by enemy forces.[19]

Empirical Evidence for Labeling Theory

Empirical investigations of labeling theory have been carried out by researchers in many disciplines using a variety of methodologies. One group of investigators arranged to have eight sane volunteers apply for admission to various mental hospitals. In order to get themselves admitted, the subjects claimed to be hearing voices, a symptom of schizophrenia. Once admitted to the hospital, however, they behaved normally. The experiences of these pseudopatients clearly reveal the effects of labeling.

Doctors, nurses, and assistants treated them as schizophrenic patients. They interpreted the normal everyday behavior of the pseudopatients as manifestations of illness. An early arrival at the lunchroom, for example, was described as exhibiting "oral aggressive" behavior; a patient seen writing something was referred to as a "compulsive note-taker." Interestingly enough, none of the other patients believed the pseudopatients were

Racial Profiling—Labeling before the Fact

New York Times, April 20, 2002:(1)

It's one thing to be labeled a criminal after you've broken the law, but what happens when you're targeted for arrest before you've done anything? For years, blacks and Latinos have complained that they were being stopped and searched for no reason except the color of their skin. After September 11th racial profiling became an even stronger subject of debate.

In fact, racial profiling has been a controversial subject in law enforcement for many years. It came into the national spotlight in April 1998, when four black and Latino men were shot in New Jersey during a traffic stop—an incident that raised public awareness of allegations that state police officers pulled people over simply because of their race.

Four years later, New Jersey state prosecutors decided to dismiss criminal charges in 86 cases involving people who said that state troopers singled them out because of the color of their skin. All of the dismissed cases were related to charges involving drugs, weapons, or other forms of contraband. The dismissals were welcomed by lawyers representing those who said they were singled out because of racial profiling. There were also many critics of the decision, including Kenneth J. McClelland, president of the state troopers' fraternal association. According to McClelland, "The state is going to put drug dealers and thugs who were found to be breaking the law back on the streets, based on nothing but political correctness."

Since September 11, racial profiling has extended to people of Middle Eastern descent as well. The most common example of this is on airplanes—many individuals claim they were kicked off flights after they had passed vigorous security checks just because another passenger or flight attendant felt uncomfortable with them on board. It is not limited to airline transportation, however. On September 19, 2005, five Muslim football fans were detained at a Giants game, at which President Bush was present, for praying.(2) According to the accounts, the men left their seats around halftime and went to pray near an air duct. They were soon approached by ten security guards and three state troopers for questioning. The fans believe they were victims of racial profiling. Sami Shaban, a law student at Seton Hall, said, "I'm as American as apple pie and I'm sitting there and now I'm made to feel like an outsider for no reason other than that I have a long beard and I prayed." FBI officials argue that the men were not stopped because of their behavior and background. According to Agent Steven Siegel, "You had 80,000 people there, Bush 41 was there, and you had a group of gentlemen gathering in an area not normally used by the public right near the main air intake duct for the stadium. . . . It was where they were, not what they were doing."

Bernard E. Harcourt wrestles with post-9/11 profiling by asking a simple question: Does such profiling work?

Racial profiling as a defensive counterterrorism measure necessarily

insane; they assumed they were researchers or journalists. When the subjects were discharged from the hospital, it was as "schizophrenics in remission."

The findings support criminological labeling theory. Once the sane individuals were labeled "schizophrenic," they were unable to eliminate the label by acting normally. Even when they supposedly had recovered, the label stayed with them in the form of "schizophrenia in remission," which implied that future episodes of the illness could be expected.[20]

Researchers have also looked at how labels affect people and groups with unconventional lifestyles, whether prohibited by law or not—"gays," "public drunks," "junkies," "strippers," "streetwalkers."[21] The results of research, no matter what the group, were largely in conformity: "Once a _____, always a _____." Labeling by adjudication may have lifelong consequences. Richard Schwartz and Jerome Skolnick, for example, found that employers were reluctant to hire anyone with a court record even when the person had been found not guilty.[22]

Criminologist Anthony Platt has investigated how certain individuals are singled out to receive labels. Focusing on the label "juvenile delinquent," he shows how the social reformers of the late nineteenth century helped create delinquency by establishing a special institution, the juvenile court, for the processing of troubled youths. The Chicago society women who lobbied for the establishment of juvenile courts may have had the best motives in trying to help immigrants' children who, by their standards, were out of control. But by getting the juvenile court established, they simply widened the net of state agencies empowered to label some children as deviant.

The state thus aggravated the official problem of juvenile delinquency, which until then had been a neighborhood nuisance handled by parents, neighbors, priests, the local grocer, or the police officer on the street. Juvenile delinquency, according to Platt, was invented. Through its labeling effect, it contributed to its own growth.[23]

Criminologist William Chambliss also studied the question of the way labels are distributed. Consider the following description:

implicates a rights trade-off: if effective, racial profiling limits the right of young Muslim men to be free from discrimination in order to promote the security and well-being of others. Proponents of racial profiling argue that it is based on simple statistical fact and represents "just smart law enforcement." Opponents of racial profiling, like New York City police commissioner Raymond Kelly, say that it is dangerous and "just nuts."

As a theoretical matter, both sides are partly right. Racial profiling in the context of counterterrorism measures may increase the detection of terrorist attacks *in the short term,* but create the possibility of dangerous substitutions *in the long run.* Defensive counterterrorism measures are notoriously tricky and can easily backfire. The installation of metal detectors in airports in 1973, for instance, produced a dramatic reduction in the number of airplane hijackings, but also resulted in a proportionally larger increase in bombings, assassinations, and hostage-taking incidents. Target hardening of U.S. embassies and missions abroad produced a transitory reduction in attacks on those sites, but an increase in assassinations. The evidence shows that some defensive counterterrorism measures do not work and others increase the likelihood of terrorist acts.

As a practical matter, then, both sides are essentially wrong: racial profiling is neither "just" smart, nor "just" nuts. The truth is, we simply have no idea whether racial profiling would be an effective counterterrorism measure or would lead instead to *more* terrorist attacks. There is absolutely no empirical evidence on its effectiveness, nor any solid theoretical reason why it would be effective overall. As a result, there is no good reason to make the rights trade-off implicated by a policy of racial profiling in the counterterrorism context.(3)

In the absence of empirical support of the efficacy of profiling, Harcourt's conclusion is an invitation to criminologists to engage in evidence-based research on all counterterrorism strategies.

Sources

1. Richard Lezin Jones, "New Jersey Prosecutors Cite Racial Profiling in Dismissal of 86 Criminal Cases," *New York Times,* April 20, 2002.
2. "FBI: Muslims Detained at Stadium Weren't Profiled," CNN.com., November 2, 2005.
3. Bernard E. Harcourt, "Muslim Profiles Post 9/11: Is Racial Profiling an Effective Counterterrorist Measure and Does It Violate the Right to Be Free from Discrimination?" Paper presented at the Oxford Colloquium on Security and Human Rights, Oxford University, March 17, 2006, p. 1.

Questions for Discussion

1. Are there any circumstances under which racial profiling is justified? If so, where do you draw the line?
2. Should offenders who have been detained as a result of racial profiling have their cases dismissed as a result?
3. What do you think is the best way to minimize racial profiling among criminal justice and law enforcement officials?
4. What do you think are the effects of racial profiling among those who are profiled? How do you think it influences their respect for the criminal justice system and the law?

Eight promising young men [the Saints]—children of good, stable, white upper-middle-class families, active in school affairs, good pre-college students—were some of the most delinquent boys at Hanibal High School. . . . The Saints were constantly occupied with truancy, drinking, wild driving, petty theft and vandalism. Yet not one was officially arrested for any misdeed during the two years I observed them.

This record was particularly surprising in light of my observations during the same two years of another gang of Hanibal High School students, six lower-class white boys known as the Roughnecks. The Roughnecks were constantly in trouble with police and community even though their rate of delinquency was about equal with that of the Saints.[24]

What accounts for the different responses to these two groups of boys? According to Chambliss, the crucial factor is the social class of the boys, which determined the community's reaction to their activities. The Roughnecks were poor, outspoken, openly hostile to authority, and highly visible because they could not afford cars to get out of town. The Saints, on the other hand, had reputations for being bright, they acted apologetic when authorities confronted them, they held school offices, they played on athletic teams, and they had cars to get them out of town. Their behavior went undiscovered, unprocessed, and unpunished.

Chambliss's research reveals what many believe is the inherent discrimination in the juvenile justice system that causes the police and courts to identify the behavior of some as delinquent more so than others. These criminologists state that young minority males are more likely to be arrested and officially processed. This is also true of members of the lower economic classes. Those with wealth or political power, on the other hand, are more likely to be given simply a warning. In this way, a Roughneck who spends all his time around other Roughnecks, but does not engage in criminal behavior, would be more likely to be arrested and processed than a Saint who was engaged in illegal activity. Research also seems to indicate that the level of seriousness of the crime committed and the prior record of the individual

Labeling Countries "Corrupt": A Perverse Outcome?

When we label countries "corrupt" in an effort to encourage necessary reforms, do we risk a perverse outcome? By ranking countries as more or less corrupt, based on aggregate perceptions of businesspeople, do such labels discourage private-sector and public investments, thereby perpetuating poverty and corruption?

Given the power of labels ("Haiti is a corrupt country and is too risky to invest in"), the answer to both questions may be yes.

Every year, Transparency International publishes a number of rankings that governments and businesses refer to regularly in thinking about the scourge of corruption. The Corruption Perceptions Index (CPI), ranking more than 150 countries, is its best-known survey. The table shows the five countries perceived to be least corrupt (Denmark, New Zealand, Sweden, Singapore, and Finland) and the five perceived to be most corrupt (Afghanistan, Haiti, Iraq, Myanmar, and Somalia) in 2008.

With Transparency International's release of this index came the following observations:

With countries such as Somalia and Iraq among those showing the highest levels of perceived corruption, Transparency International's (TI) 2008 Corruption Perceptions Index (CPI) . . . highlights the fatal link between poverty,

2008 Corruption Perceptions Index

Country Rank	Country	2008 CPI Score
1	Denmark	9,3
1	New Zealand	9,3
1	Sweden	9,3
4	Singapore	9,2
5	Finland	9,0
176	Afghanistan	1,5
177	Haiti	1,4
178	Iraq	1,3
178	Myanmar	1,3
180	Somalia	1,0

SOURCE: Reprinted from Transparency International 2008 Corruption Perceptions Index. Copyright 2008 Transparency International: the global coalition against corruption. Used with permission. For more information, visit http://www.transparency.org.

committing the crime have much influence on delinquency processing.

Up to this point, the contentions of labeling theorists and the evidence they present provide a persuasive argument for the validity of labeling theory. But despite supportive scientific evidence, labeling theory has been heavily criticized.

Evaluation: Labeling Theory

Critics ask, Why is it that individuals, knowing they might be labeled, get involved in socially disapproved behavior to begin with? Most labeled persons have indeed engaged in some act that is considered morally or legally wrong.[25] According to sociologist Ronald Akers, the impression is sometimes given that people are passive actors in a process by which the bad system bestows a derogatory label, thereby declaring them unacceptable or different or untouchable.[26] Critics suggest that the labels may identify real behavior rather than create it. After all, many delinquents

have in fact had a long history of deviant behavior, even though they have never been caught and stigmatized. These critics question the overly active role labeling theory has assigned to the community and its criminal justice system and the overly passive role it has assigned to offenders.

Some criminologists also question how labeling theory accounts for individuals who have gone through formal processing but do not continue deviant lifestyles. They suggest that punishment really does work as a deterrent.[27] The argument is that labeling theorists are so intent on the reaction to behavior that they completely neglect the fact that someone has defied the conventions of society.[28] Criminologist Charles Wellford reminds us that, by and large, offenders get into the hands of authorities because they have broken the law. Furthermore, the decisions made about them are heavily influenced by the seriousness of their offenses.[29]

While most critics believe that labeling theorists put too much emphasis on the system, others failed institutions and graft. But other notable backsliders in the 2008 CPI indicate that the strength of oversight mechanisms is also at risk among the wealthiest.

"In the poorest countries, corruption levels can mean the difference between life and death, when money for hospitals or clean water is in play," said Huguette Labelle, Chair of Transparency International. "The continuing high levels of corruption and poverty plaguing many of the world's societies amount to an ongoing humanitarian disaster and cannot be tolerated. But even in more privileged countries, with enforcement disturbingly uneven, a tougher approach to tackling corruption is needed."

Whether in high- or low-income countries, the challenge of reining in corruption requires functioning societal and governmental institutions. Poorer countries are often plagued by corrupt judiciaries and ineffective parliamentary oversight. Wealthy countries, on the other hand, show evidence of insufficient regulation of the private sector, in terms of ad-

dressing overseas bribery by their countries, and weak oversight of financial institutions and transactions.

"Stemming corruption requires strong oversight through parliaments, law enforcement, independent media and a vibrant civil society," said Labelle. "When these institutions are weak, corruption spirals out of control with horrendous consequences for ordinary people, and for justice and equality in societies more broadly."(1)

For the sake of discussion, assume the following facts:

1. Criminologists do not have valid and reliable data on the extent of corruption in countries around the world.
2. Perception data (like those presented above) persuade prospective investors of the risks of corruption.
3. The private sector is less likely to invest in countries perceived as most corrupt.
4. Multilateral institutions such as the World Bank and the International Monetary Fund (IMF) are less likely

to offer loans and grants to countries perceived to be corrupt.
5. Investments from both the private sector and multilaterals are the key to moving countries away from corrupt practices.

Source

1. Reprinted from http://www.transparency.org/news_room/latest_news/press_releases/2008/2008_09_23_cpi_2008_en. Copyright 2008 Transparency International: the global coalition against corruption. Used with permission. For more information, visit http://www.transparency.org.

Questions for Discussion

1. What role should corruption perception rankings play in, for example, the investment decisions of the World Bank?
2. Are you concerned with the labeling effects of perception rankings?

---

of a more radical or Marxist persuasion believe that labeling theorists have not gone far enough. They claim that the labeling approach concentrates too heavily on "nuts, sluts, and perverts," the exotic varieties of deviants who capture public imagination, rather than on "the unethical, illegal and destructive actions of powerful individuals, groups, and institutions of our society."[30] We will look at this argument more closely in a moment.

Empirical evidence that substantiates the claims of labeling theory has been modest. All the same, the theory has been instrumental in calling attention to some important questions, particularly about the way defendants are processed through the criminal justice system. Labeling theorists have carried out important scientific investigations of that system that complement the search of more traditional criminologists for the causes of crime and delinquency.

Some of the criticism of labeling theory can best be countered by one of its own proponents.

Howard Becker explains that labeling is intended not as a theory of causation but rather as a perspective, "a way of looking at a general area of human activity, which expands the traditional research to include the process of social control."[31] Labeling theory has provided this perspective; it has also spawned further inquiry into the causes of crime.

In a recent extension of labeling theory to a developmental control theory, Sampson and Laub conclude that some delinquency persists because of the reactions to their criminal behavior that offenders receive. Add significant socioeconomic disadvantage, and the result is often a breakdown in social control.[32]

CONFLICT THEORY

Labeling theorists are as well aware as other criminologists that some people make rules and some break them. Their primary concern is the

consequences of making and enforcing rules. One group of scholars has carried this idea further by questioning the rule-making process itself. They claim that a struggle for power is a basic feature of human existence and it is by means of such power struggles that various interest groups manage to control lawmaking and law enforcement.[33] To understand the theoretical approach of these conflict theorists, we must go back to the traditional approach, which views crime and criminal justice as arising from communal consensus.

The Consensus Model

Sometimes members of a society consider certain acts so threatening to community survival that they designate these acts as crimes. If the vast majority of a group's members share this view, the group has acted by consensus. This is the **consensus model** of criminal lawmaking. The model assumes that members of society by and large agree on what is right and wrong and that law is the codification of these agreed-upon social values. The law is a mechanism to settle disputes that arise when individuals stray too far from what the community considers acceptable.

In Durkheim's words, "We can . . . say that an act is criminal when it offends strong and defined states of the collective conscience."[34] Consensus

theorists view society as a stable entity in which laws are created for the general good. The laws' function is to reconcile and to harmonize most of the interests that most members of a community cherish, with the least amount of sacrifice.

Deviant acts not only are part of the normal functioning of society but in fact are necessary, because when the members of society unite against a deviant, they reaffirm their commitment to shared values.[35]

Societies in which citizens agree on right and wrong and the occasional deviant serves a useful purpose are scarce today. Such societies could be found among primitive peoples at the very beginning of social evolution. By and large, consensus theory recognizes that not everyone can agree on what is best for society. Yet consensus theory holds that conflicting interests can be reconciled by means of law.[36]

The Conflict Model

With this view of the consensus model, we can understand and evaluate the arguments of the conflict theorists. In the 1960s, while labeling theorists were questioning why some people were designated as criminals, another group of scholars began to ask who in society has the power to make and enforce the laws. Conflict theory, already well established in the field of sociology, thus became popular as an explanation of crime and justice as well.

Like labeling theory, **conflict theory** has its roots in rebellion and the questioning of values. But while labeling theorists and traditional criminologists focused on the crime and the criminal, including the labeling of the criminal by the system, conflict theorists questioned the system itself. The clash between traditional and labeling theorists, on one hand, and conflict theorists, on the other, became ideological.

Conflict theorists asked, If people agree on the value system, as consensus theorists suggest, why are so many people in rebellion, and why are there so many crimes, so many punitive threats, so many people in prison? Clearly, conflict is found everywhere in the world, between one country and another, between gay rights advocates and antigay groups, between people who view abortion as a right and others who view it as murder, between suspects and police, between family members, between neighbors. If the criminal law supports the collective communal interest, why do so many people deviate from it?

Conflict theorists argue that, contrary to consensus theory, laws do not exist for the collective good; rather, they represent the interests of specific groups that have the power to get them enacted.[37] The key concept in conflict theory is power. The people who have political control in

■ *Conflict: Pro-choice advocates confront right-to-life supporters over the explosive issue of abortion.*

any given society are those who are able to make things happen. They have power. Conflict theory holds that the people who possess the power work to keep the powerless at a disadvantage. The laws thus have their origin in the interests of the few; these few shape the values, and the values, in turn, shape the laws.[38]

It follows that the person who is defined as criminal and the behavior that is defined as crime at any given time and place mirror the society's power relationships. The definitions are subject to change as other interests gain power. The changing of definitions can be seen in those acts we now designate as "victimless" crimes. Possession of marijuana, prostitution, gambling, refusing to join the armed forces—all have been legal at some times, illegal at others. We may ask, then, whether any of these acts is inherently evil. The conflict theorist would answer that all are *made* evil when they are so designated by those in power and thus defined as crimes in legal codes.

The legal status of victimless crimes is subject to change. But what about murder, a crime considered evil in all contemporary societies? Many conflict theorists would respond that the definition of murder as a criminal offense is also rooted in the effort of some groups to guard their power. A political terrorist may very well become a national hero.

Conflict theorists emphasize the relativity of norms to time and place: Capital punishment is legal in some states, outlawed in others; alcohol consumption is illegal in Saudi Arabia but legal in the United States. Powerful groups maintain their interests by making illegal any behavior that might be a threat to them. Laws thus become a mechanism of control, or "a weapon in social conflict."[39]

Conflict Theory and Criminology

Sociologist George Vold (1896–1967) was the first theorist to relate conflict theory to criminology. He argued that individuals band together in groups because they are social animals with needs that are best served through collective action. If the group serves its members, it survives; if not, new groups form to take its place. Individuals constantly clash as they try to advance the interests of their particular group over those of all the others. The result is that society is in a constant state of conflict, "one of the principal and essential social processes upon which the continuing ongoing of society depends." For Vold, the entire process of lawmaking and crime control is a direct reflection of conflict between interest groups, all trying to get laws passed in their favor and to gain control of the police power.[40]

Sociologist Ralf Dahrendorf and criminologist Austin Turk are major contemporary contributors to the application of conflict theory to criminology. To Dahrendorf, the consensus model of society is utopian. He believes that enforced constraint, rather than cooperation, binds people together. Whether society is capitalist, socialist, or feudal, some people have the authority and others are subject to it. Society is made up of a large number of interest groups, and the interests of one group do not always coincide with the needs of another—unions and management, for instance.

Dahrendorf argues that social change is constant, social conflicts are ever-present, disintegration and change are ongoing, and all societies are characterized by the coercion of some people by others. The most important characteristics of class, he contends, are power and authority. The inequities remain for him the lasting determinant of social conflict. Conflict can be either destructive or constructive, depending on whether it leads to a breakdown of the social structure or to positive change in the social order.[41]

Austin Turk has continued and expanded this theoretical approach. "Criminality is not a biological, psychological, or even behavioral phenomenon," he says, "but a social status defined by the way in which an individual is perceived, evaluated, and treated by legal authorities." Criminal status is defined by those he calls the "authorities," the decision makers. Criminal status is imposed on the "subjects," the subordinate class. Turk explains that this process works so that both authorities and subjects learn to interact as performers in their dominant and submissive roles. There are "social norms of dominance" and "social norms of deference." Conflict arises when some people refuse to go along, and they challenge the authorities. "Law breaking, then, becomes a measure of the stability of the ruler/ruled relationship."[42]

People with authority use several forms of power to control society's goods and services: police or war power, economic power, political power, and ideological power (beliefs, values).[43] The laws made by the "ins" to condemn or condone various behaviors help shape all social institutions—indeed, the entire culture. Where education is mandatory, for example, the people in power are able to maintain the status quo by passing on their own value system from one generation to the next.[44]

History seems to demonstrate that primitive societies, in their earliest phases of development, tend to be homogeneous and to make laws by consensus. The more a society develops economically and politically, the more difficult it becomes to resolve conflict situations by consensus.[45]

Empirical Evidence for the Conflict Model

Researchers have tested several conflict theory hypotheses, including those pertaining to bias and discrimination in the criminal justice system, differential crime rates of powerful and powerless groups, and the intent behind the development of the criminal law. The findings offer mixed support for the theory.

Alan Lizotte studied 816 criminal cases in the Chicago courts over a 1-year period to test the assumption that the powerless receive harsher sentences. His analysis relating legal factors (such as the offense committed) and extralegal factors (such as the race and job of the defendant) to length of prison sentence pointed to significant sentencing inequalities related to race and occupation.[46] When Freda Adler studied the

importance of nonlegal factors in the decision making of juries, she found that the socioeconomic level of the defendants significantly influenced the juries' judgment.[47]

While these and similar studies tend to support conflict theory by demonstrating class or racial bias in the administration of criminal justice, others, unexpectedly, show an opposite bias.[48] When we evaluate the contribution of conflict theory to criminological thought, we must keep in mind Austin Turk's warning that conflict theory is often misunderstood. The theory does not, he points out, suggest that most criminals are innocent or that powerful persons engage in the same amount of deviant behavior as do powerless persons or that law enforcers typically discriminate against people without power. It does acknowledge, however, that behaviors common among society's more disadvantaged members have a greater likelihood of being called "crimes" than do those activities in which the more powerful typically participate.[49]

Conflict theory does not attempt to explain crime; it simply identifies social conflict as a basic fact of life and as a source of discriminatory treatment by the criminal justice system of groups and classes that lack the power and status of those who make and enforce the laws. Once we recognize this, we may find it possible to change the process of criminalizing people in order to provide greater justice. Conflict theorists anticipate a guided evolution, not a revolution, to improve the existing criminal justice system.

RADICAL THEORY

While labeling and conflict theorists were developing their perspectives, social and political conditions in the United States and Europe were changing rapidly and drastically. The youth of America were deeply disillusioned about a political and social structure that had brought about the assassinations of John F. Kennedy, Robert Kennedy, and Martin Luther King Jr.; the war in Vietnam; and the Watergate debacle. Many looked for radical solutions to social problems, and a number of young criminologists searched for answers to the nation's questions about crime and criminal justice. They found their answers in Marxism, a philosophy born in similar social turmoil a century earlier.

The Intellectual Heritage of Marxist Criminology

The major industrial centers of Europe suffered great hardships during the nineteenth century. The mechanization of industry and of agriculture, heavy population increases, and high rates of urbanization had created a massive labor surplus, high unemployment, and a burgeoning class of young urban migrants forced into the streets by poverty. London is said to have had at least 20,000 individuals who "rose every morning without knowing how they were to be supported through the day or where they were to lodge on the succeeding night, and cases of death from starvation appeared in the coroner's lists daily."[50] In other cities, conditions were even worse.

Engels and Marx

It was against this background that Friedrich Engels (1820–1895) addressed the effects of the Industrial Revolution. A partner in his father's industrial empire, Engels was himself a member of the class he attacked as "brutally selfish." After a 2-year stay in England, he documented the awful social conditions, the suffering, and the great increase in crime and arrests. All these problems he blamed on one factor—competition. In *The Condition of the Working Class in England,* published in 1845, he spelled out the association between crime and poverty as a political problem:

> The earliest, crudest, and least fruitful form of this rebellion was that of crime. The working man lived in poverty and want, and saw that others were better off than he. . . . Want conquered his inherited respect for the sacredness of property, and he stole.[51]

Though Karl Marx (1818–1883) paid little attention to crime specifically, he argued that all aspects of social life, including laws, are determined by economic organization. His philosophy reflects the economic despair that followed the Industrial Revolution. In his *Communist Manifesto* (1848), Marx viewed the history of all societies as a documentation of class struggles: "Freeman and slave, patrician and plebeian, lord and serf, guildmaster and journeyman, in a word, oppressor and oppressed, stood in constant opposition to one another."[52]

Marx went on to describe the most important relationship in industrial society as that between the capitalist bourgeoisie, who own the means of production, and the proletariat, or workers, who labor for them. Society, according to Marx, has always been organized in such a hierarchical fashion, with the state representing not the common interest but the interests of those who own the means of production. Capitalism breeds egocentricity, greed, and predatory behavior; but the worst crime of all is the exploitation of workers. Revolution, Marx concluded, is the only means to bring about change, and for that reason it is morally justifiable.

Many philosophers before Marx had noted the link between economic conditions and social problems, including crime. Among them were Plato, Aristotle, Virgil, Horace, Sir Thomas More, Cesare Beccaria, Jeremy Bentham, André Guerry, Adolphe Quételet, and Gabriel Tarde (several of whom we discussed in Chapter 3). But none of them had advocated revolutionary change. And none had constructed a coherent criminological theory that conformed with economic determinism. The cornerstone of the Marxist explanation is that people who are kept in a state of poverty will rebel by committing crimes. Not until 1905 can we speak of Marxist criminology.

Willem Adriaan Bonger

As a student at the University of Amsterdam, Willem Adriaan Bonger (1876–1940) entered a paper in a competition on the influence of economic factors on crime. His entry did not win, but its expanded version, *Criminality and Economic Conditions,* which appeared in French in 1905, was selected for translation by the American Institute of Criminal Law and Criminology. Bonger wrote in his preface, "[I am] convinced that my ideas about the etiology of crime will not be shared by a great many readers of the American edition."[53] He was right. Nevertheless, the book is considered a classic and is invaluable to students doing research on crime and economics.

Bonger explained that the social environment of primitive people was interwoven with the means of production. People helped each other. They used what they produced. When food was plentiful, everyone ate. When food was scarce, everyone was hungry. Whatever people had, they shared. People were subordinate to nature. In a modern capitalist society, people are much less altruistic. They concentrate on production for profit rather than for the needs of the community. Capitalism encourages criminal behavior by creating a climate that is less conducive to social responsibility. "We have a right," argued Bonger, "to say that the part played by economic conditions in criminality is predominant, even decisive."[54]

Willem Bonger died as he had lived, a fervent antagonist of the evils of the social order. An arch-enemy of Nazism and a prominent name on Hitler's list of people to be eliminated, he refused to emigrate even when the German army was at the border. On May 10, 1940, as the German invasion of Holland began, he wrote to his son: "I don't see any future for myself and I cannot bow to this scum which will now overmaster us."[55] He then took his own life. He left a powerful political and criminological legacy. Foremost among his followers were German socialist philosophers of the progressive school of Frankfurt.

Georg Rusche and Otto Kirchheimer

Georg Rusche and Otto Kirchheimer began to write their classic work at the University of Frankfurt. Driven out of Germany by Nazi persecution, they continued their research in exile in Paris and

Crime Surfing

http://critcrim.org/ perspectives

Do critical criminologists support the death penalty, or are they opposed?

completed it at Columbia University in New York in 1939. In *Punishment and the Social Structure*, they wrote that punishments had always been related to the modes of production and the availability of labor, rather than to the nature of the crimes themselves.

Consider galley slavery. Before the development of modern sailing techniques, oarsmen were needed to power merchant ships; as a result, galley slavery was a punishment in antiquity and in the Middle Ages. As sailing techniques were perfected, galley slavery was no longer necessary, and it lost favor as a sanction. By documenting the real purposes of punishments through the ages, Rusche and Kirchheimer made **penologists,** those who study the penal system, aware that severe and cruel treatment of offenders had more to do with the value of human life and the needs of the economy than with preventing crime.

The names Marx, Engels, Bonger, and Rusche and Kirchheimer were all but forgotten by mainstream criminologists of the 1940s and 1950s, perhaps because of America's relative prosperity and conservatism during those years. But when tranquillity turned to turmoil in the mid-1960s, the forgotten names provided the intellectual basis for American and European radical criminologists, who explicitly stated their commitment to Marxism.

Radical Criminology since the 1970s

Radical criminology (also called "critical," "new," and "Marxist criminology") made its first public appearance in 1968, when a group of British sociologists organized the National Deviancy Conference (NDC), a group of more than 300 intellectuals, social critics, deviants, and activists of various persuasions. What the group members had in common was a basic disillusionment with the criminological studies being done by the British Home Office, which they believed was system-serving and "practical." They were concerned with the way the system controlled people rather than with traditional sociological and psychological explanations of crime. They shared a respect for the interactionist and labeling theorists but believed that these theorists had become too traditional. Their answer was to form a new criminology based on Marxist principles.

The conference was followed by the publication in 1973 of *The New Criminology*, the first textual formulation of the new radical criminology. According to its authors, Ian Taylor, Paul Walton, and Jock Young, it is the underclass, the "labor forces of the industrial society," that is controlled through the criminal law and its enforcement, while "the owners of labor will be bound only by a civil law which regulates their competition between each other." The economic institution, then, is the source of all conflicts. Struggles between classes always relate to the distribution of resources and power, and only when capitalism is abolished will crime disappear.[56]

About the time that Marxist criminology was being formulated in England, it was also developing in the United States, particularly at the School of Criminology of the University of California at Berkeley, where Richard Quinney, Anthony Platt, Herman and Julia Schwendinger, William Chambliss, and Paul Takagi were at the forefront of the movement. These researchers were also influenced by interactionist and labeling theorists, as well as by the conflict theories of Vold, Dahrendorf, and Turk.

Though the radical criminologists share the central tenet of conflict theory—that laws are created by the powerful to protect their own interests—they disagree on the number of forces competing in the power struggle. For Marxist criminologists, there is only one dominating segment, the capitalist ruling class, which uses the criminal law to impose its will on the rest of the people in order to protect its property and to define as criminal any behavior that threatens the status quo.[57] The leading American spokesperson for radical criminology is Richard Quinney. His earliest Marxist publications appeared in 1973: "Crime Control in Capitalist Society" and "There's a Lot of Us Folks Grateful to the Lone Ranger."[58] The second of these essays describes how Quinney drifted away from capitalism, with its folklore myths embodied in individual heroes like the Lone Ranger.[59]

In *Class, State, and Crime*, Quinney proclaims that "the criminal justice movement is . . . a state-initiated and state-supported effort to rationalize mechanisms of social control. The larger purpose is to secure a capitalist order that is in grave crisis, likely in its final stage of development."[60] Quinney challenges criminologists to abandon traditional ways of thinking about causation, to study what could be rather than what is, to question the assumptions of the social order, and to "ultimately develop a Marxist perspective."[61]

Marxist theory also can be found in the writings of other scholars who have adopted the radical approach to criminology. William Chambliss and Robert Seidman present their version in *Law, Order, and Power*:

> Society is composed of groups that are in conflict with one another and . . . the law represents an institutionalized tool of those in power (ruling class) which functions to provide them with superior moral as well as coercive power in conflict.[62]

They comment that if, in the operation of the criminal justice system by the powerful, "justice or fairness happen to be served, it is sheer coincidence."[63]

To Barry Krisberg, crime is a function of privilege. The rich create crimes to distract attention from the injustices they inflict on the masses. Power determines which group holds the privilege, defined by Krisberg as that which is valued by a given social group in a given historical time.[64] Herman and Julia Schwendinger supported this idea in their summary of the causes of delinquency. They stated that legal relations secure a capitalistic mode of production, while laws are created to secure the labor force. The bourgeoisie are always in a state of being threatened by the proletariats; therefore, while some laws may secure lower-class interests, capitalist interests underlie the basic constitutional laws. Laws in general, according to the Schwendingers, contradict their stated purpose. The Schwendingers went even further in proposing that the state fails to control delinquency because lower-class deviants supply factories with a ready pool of low-wage laborers.[65]

Anthony Platt, in a forceful attack on traditional criminology, has even suggested that it would not be "too farfetched to characterize many criminologists as domestic war criminals" because they have "serviced domestic repression in the same way that economics, political science, and anthropology have greased the wheels and even manufactured some of the important parts of modern imperialism."[66]

He suggests that traditional criminology serves the state through research studies that purport to "investigate" the conditions of the lower class but in reality only prove, with their probes of family life, education, jobs, and so on, that the members of the lower class are in fact less intelligent and more criminal than the rest of us. Platt claims that these inquiries, based as they are on biased and inaccurate data, are merely tools of the middle-class oppressors.

A number of other areas have come under the scrutiny of Marxist criminologists.[67] They have studied:

- How informal means of settling disputes outside courts actually extend the control of the criminal justice system by adjudicating cases that are not serious enough for the courts

- How juvenile court dispositions are unfairly based on social class

- How sentencing reform has failed to benefit the lower class

- How police practices during the latter half of the nineteenth century were geared to control labor rather than crime

- How rape victims are made to feel guilty

- How penitentiary reform has benefited the ruling class by giving it more control over the lower class

- How capitalist interests are strengthened by private policing[68]

Evaluation: Marxist Criminological Theory

Critiques of Marxist criminology range from support for the attention the approach calls to the crimes of the powerful to accusations that it is nothing more than a revival of the Robin Hood myth, in which the poor steal from the rich in order to survive.[69] By far the most incisive criticism is that of sociologist Carl Klockars, who points out that the division of society into social classes may have a beneficial effect, contrary to Marxist thought. Standards, he argues, are created by some people to inspire the remainder of society. In present-day America, Klockars claims, poverty has lost some of its meaning because luxuries and benefits are spread out over classes. To him, ownership and control of industry are two different things. Anyone who buys a share of stock, for example, can be an owner, while control is handled by bureaucrats who may or may not be owners.[70]

Class Interests versus Interest Groups

Klockars attacks Marxists for focusing exclusively on class interests and ignoring the fact that society is made up of many interest groups. This Marxist bias has yielded results that are untrustworthy and predictable, ignore reality, explain issues that are self-evident (some businesspeople are greedy and corrupt), and do not explain issues that are relevant (why socialist states have crime).[71]

Not without a note of sympathy, Richard Sparks summed up the criticism:

> Marxist criminologists tend to be committed to praxis and the desire for radical social reform; but this commitment is not entailed by the scientific claims which Marxists make, and it has sometimes led to those claims being improperly suspect.[72]

Opposition to the new criminology follows many paths, but the most popular is concerned with its oversimplification of causation by the exclusive focus on capitalism.[73] Critics also attack Marxist criminologists for their assertion that even by studying crime empirically, criminologists are supporting the status quo. That puts Marxist criminologists on the defensive, because if they are not ideologically in a position to expose their theories to empirical research or are unwilling to do so, their assertions will remain just that—assertions with no proof.[74]

Collapse of the Economic Order

Even sharper criticism of Marxist theory can be anticipated in the wake of the collapse of the Marxist economic order in the Soviet Union, Poland,

WINDOW TO THE WORLD

The Forgotten Criminology of Genocide

Why has criminology forgotten the systematic decimation of 1.5 million Armenians by the Young Turks during World War I, as well as the systematic killing of 6 million Jews and the extermination of another 5 million, including Gypsies, political opponents, mentally ill, retarded, and other "inferior" peoples between 1941 and 1945? How could criminology have neglected an examination of the crimes against humanity that resulted in an estimated 7 million to 16 million deaths since World War II? You would think that criminology, an academic field concerned with violence, aggression, power, and victimization, would focus on the crime of genocide.

If not in the violence literature, one would expect to find this scholarship in the efforts of conflict, critical, and Marxist theorists in their explanations of organized, state-sanctioned violence and oppression. Criminologists whose life's work is crime prevention also must regularly discuss the causal factors that lead to acts of genocide. If you search through every issue of the journals *Criminology* and *Journal of Criminal Law and Criminology* since their inception, however, you will find only two articles on genocide, the most serious of all crimes, and one of these was written over 40 years ago.(1) So why is there no criminology of genocide? Our answers to this question, regrettably, are inadequate.

1. *Genocide is a political act reflecting the will of sovereignty.* Genocide, it has been said, is a political rather than criminal act, most often employed to enhance a country's solidarity and unification. Decisions to liquidate, exterminate, and cleanse a minority population are matters of political policy reflecting the will of sovereignty. The immorality of genocide is tempered by a moral generosity to a sovereign's motivation. The effect of shrouding genocide in a political cloth is to see the annihilation of certain populations as something less than or different from a crime.(2)
2. *Genocide is a breach of international norms and international law.*

Several years ago, two groups of victims and representatives of victims from Bosnia-Herzegovina brought an action in federal court under the Alien Tort Claims Act against the president and leader of the Bosnian Serb forces for aggravated sexual assault, forced prostitution and impregnation, various acts of extreme torture, and mass execution.(3) The case carried significant symbolic value. Are acts of genocide torts or crimes in violation of international norms or international law? The answers to these questions are far from simple.

3. *Genocide is committed by the state.* Of the many revelations over the past 50 years, criminologists seem to have the most difficulty with the notion that an organization or entity, whether a corporation or nation-state, may commit a crime. When crimes are imputed from an individual to an inanimate entity, the intellectual challenge becomes, Should an individual be blamed as well? The equivocation with bringing those responsible for ethnic cleansing and planned mass murder to justice may be explained, at least in part, by a resistance to the notion that individuals within a "guilty" collective are to blame.
4. *The magnitude of victimization in genocide defies belief.* The extent of victimization and harm in genocide strains any assessment of seriousness. Who appreciates differences in seriousness when the offense is, for example, 100,000, 250,000, or 500,000 butchered Hutus or Tutsis? Is there a difference in judgments of offense seriousness between the planned killing of 6 million versus 7 million people?
5. *Problems arise regarding both denying and admitting atrocity.* Two prominent themes that emerge from the literature on genocide capture an ambivalence hard felt by some survivors and refugees of genocide. This ambivalence is captured in the titles of two books on the Holocaust— Deborah Lipstadt's *Denying the*

Holocaust and Lawrence L. Langer's *Admitting the Holocaust.*(4) The problem of admission is with the casting of genocide as a historical problem requiring serious study; the effects of intellectualizing mass torture and death; the packaging of the Holocaust neatly into a social science; and the elevation of genocide to a respectable academic discipline of its own, with courses that fit a core curriculum and endow Holocaust professorships. The problem with denial comes from historical revisionists.

Many have commented that the field of criminology has matured. Unfortunately, it has done so without considering the most serious of all crimes.(5)

This crime is taking place right now, in ways that most of us simply cannot imagine. Consider the plight of those raped in Darfur. In the words of David Scheffer, the U.S. ambassador-at-large for war crimes issues from 1997 to 2001:

People hear the word "genocide" and think of 6 million Jews killed by the Nazis during the Holocaust or the estimated 800,000 mostly Tutsis slaughtered in Rwanda. They do not imagine that rape can be so well planned and done on such a mass scale as to wipe out much of an ethnic group just as thoroughly, if more slowly, than large-scale murder.

Sudan's president, Omar Hassan Ahmed Bashir, stands accused of— among other horrible crimes—masterminding the use of rape as a form of genocide against several ethnic groups in Darfur. In the coming weeks, three judges of the International Criminal Court in The Hague will decide whether that controversial charge will be included in the likely arrest warrant against him. Hanging in the balance is whether the heinous modern warfare strategy of mass rape will be condemned and prosecuted for what it truly is: genocide.

The court's prosecutor, Luis Moreno-Ocampo, has filed other charges as well, including war crimes, crimes against humanity and "mass murder as genocide." But the groundbreaking charge is rape as genocide, which relies on two lesser-known ways of destroying a people: "causing serious bodily or mental harm to members of the group" or "deliberately inflicting on the group conditions of life calculated to bring about its physical destruction in whole or in part."

Prosecuting the crime of rape under these particular formulations is unprecedented for the International Criminal Court. There were mass rapes in Rwanda in 1994, for instance, but many of the victims were quickly killed as part of the overall genocide. In Darfur, many rape victims survive, but they suffer grievous harm to their bodies, minds and ethnic identities that can lead to a genocidal result.

Despite rulings from earlier Rwanda and Bosnia war crimes tribunals that offer guidance, the relative novelty and complexity of rape-as-genocide cases may impel the judges to stick to more familiar war crimes terrain. But the judges only have to find reasonable grounds to include the rape-as-genocide charges on the Bashir warrant. They need not establish proof beyond a reasonable doubt, the standard applied at trial.

The evidence presented by Moreno-Ocampo appears compelling. The prosecutor's investigation reveals that, since 2003, Bashir's forces and agents have driven about 2.5 million Sudanese, including substantial numbers of the Fur, Massalit and Zaghawa ethnic groups, into camps of internally displaced persons. They then raped and inflicted other forms of severe sexual violence on thousands, and continue to do so. A common tactic is for the *janjaweed* militia and Sudan's armed forces and security agents to lie in wait outside the camps to rape—or often gang-rape—the women and girls who come out to collect firewood, grass or water in order to survive.

"Maybe around 20 men rape one woman," said one victim in a report cited by the prosecutor. "These things are normal for us here in Darfur. . . . They rape women in front of their mothers and fathers."

"*Janjaweed* babies" born of the rapes rarely have a future in the mother's ethnic group. Infanticide and abandonment are common. Another victim explained: "They kill our males and dilute our blood with rape. [They] . . . want to finish us as a people, end our history."

Imagine the collective horror if men and boys in these ethnic groups were raped and then castrated. Would any-

one doubt that genocidal impulses were at work by depriving men of their ability to father children? In Darfur, raped women and girls are similarly crippled.

In the 1990s, when I was the U.S. ambassador at large for war crimes issues, I met scores of women who had been raped during the atrocities in the Balkans, Sierra Leone, Uganda and the eastern Congo. In most cases, the experience was devastating to their character, their ethnic bonds and often to their physical health. Even if they were still physically able to bear children, these women typically were ostracized from their communities and could not marry their ethnic men. Confronted with these stories, I recognized that mass rape can destroy a substantial part of a group and thus constitute genocide.

Prosecuting the rapes in Darfur as a crime against humanity would get at the crime's seriousness. But genocide is another order of destruction altogether. Elevating the mass-rape charges to that level indicates that Bashir intended not only to terrorize women or force a population out of a particular region but to end—or substantially imperil—the very existence of the three ethnic groups that dared to challenge his power.

Between September 2003 and January 2005, Sudanese military and *janjaweed* militia slaughtered an estimated 35,000 civilians in Darfur. Since the onset of the violence, an additional 265,000 civilians have suffered slow deaths caused by injury, starvation, lack of water or other conditions of deprivation in the camps. The evidence shows a highly sophisticated strategy at work: scorched-earth assaults on ethnic villages followed by isolation in displacement camps where starvation, illness and rape take a gruesome toll.

Indeed, it would be easier for the court to focus on these almost undeniable crimes against humanity. But here the judges confront a harder task: to find reasonable grounds that Bashir had the "specific criminal intent" to use rape as a genocidal tool.

Genocide cases prosecuted before other war crimes tribunals have found that specific intent can be inferred from the factual circumstances of the crime. In Darfur, clearly, there is no shortage of actions, including repeated mass rapes, that point to Bashir's aim

to destroy substantial parts of the Fur, Massalit and Zaghawa ethnic groups.

The wild card remains the UN Security Council. Under the treaty that governs the International Criminal Court, the council can suspend any prosecution for a year. China, Russia and even the African Union are pressuring the council to invoke that right. They claim that Bashir will unleash hell on U.N. peacekeepers in Darfur if he is charged and destroy hope for any peace settlement in Sudan. So far, the United States has signaled it will oppose any such efforts to stall the case—as well it should.

The judges of the International Criminal Court must be afforded the opportunity to continue reviewing the evidence without interference by the Security Council. If they find reasonable grounds to charge Bashir with rape as genocide, thousands of women and girls attacked by rapists as a means of destroying their ethnic groups will share a small measure of justice and peace."(6)

Sources

1. John Hagen, Wenona Rymond-Richmond, and Patricia Parker, "The Criminology of Genocide: The Death and Rape of Darfur, *Criminology*, **43** (2005): 525–561.
2. Irving Louis Horowitz, *Taking Lives: Genocide and State Power* (New Brunswick, N.J.: Transaction, 1997).
3. *Kaic v. Karadzic*, 70 F.3d 232 (2d Cir. 1995).
4. Deborah Lipstadt, *Denying the Holocaust: The Growing Assault on Truth and Memory* (New York: Free Press, 1993); Lawrence L. Langer, *Admitting the Holocaust: Collected Essays* (New York: Oxford, 1996).
5. William S. Laufer, "The Forgotten Criminology of Genocide," *Advances in Criminological Theory*, **8** (1999): 45–58.
6. David Scheffer, "Rape as Genocide in Darfur: Sudan's President May Face Additional Charges," *Los Angeles Times*, Nov. 13, 2008. Reprinted by permission of David Scheffer.

Questions for Discussion

1. How satisfactory are the answers to why there is no criminology of genocide?
2. What could conflict and radical theorists contribute to this dialogue?

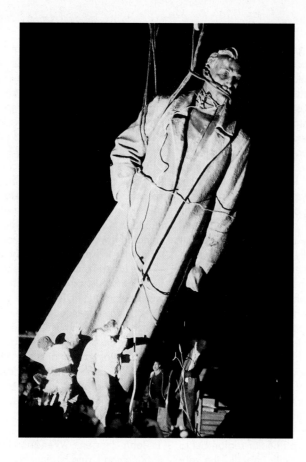

■ As the Marxist socioeconomic order was toppled, so was the statue of the founder of the KGB, Felix Dzerzhinsky, at the Moscow headquarters.

Czechoslovakia, Hungary, the German Democratic Republic, Bulgaria, Albania, and Romania, as well as in countries in Africa and Latin America.[75] Many Eastern European criminologists are no longer quoting Marx in their publications, which tend increasingly to focus on the classical rule-of-law concept. But Quinney has never seen the conditions in those countries as representative of Marxism. According to him, a true Marxist state has not yet been attained, but the ideal is worth pursuing.[76]

To the credit of radical criminologists, it must be said that they have encouraged their more traditional colleagues to look with a critical eye at all aspects of the criminal justice system, including the response of the system to both poor and rich offenders. Their concern is the exercise of power. They ask: Whose power? On whose behalf? For whose benefit? What is the legitimacy of that power? And who is excluded from the exercise of power, by whom, and why? Criminologists have had to address all these questions. Many may not have changed their answers, but the fact that the questions have been raised has ensured clearer answers than had been offered before.

Emerging Explanations

Over the last decade, a number of important critical perspectives have emerged that are worthy of attention. These perspectives include radical feminist theory, left realism, abolitionist and anarchist criminology, and peacemaking criminology.

Radical Feminist Theory

One significant limitation to critical and Marxist work is an almost exclusive focus on crime committed by males. This male-centered approach has been addressed only recently by both radical and socialist (Marxist) feminists. Radical criminologists find the cause of crime in women to be male aggression as well as men's attempts to control and subordinate women. Radical feminism has contributed to the study of child sexual abuse, domestic violence, and, in its most extreme form, prostitution. The application of radical feminist theory in the context of prostitution has earned considerable criticism given the "absolutist, doctrinaire and unscientific nature" of its adaptation.[77] Research on the most radical end of the spectrum posits that prostitution is perpetrated by sexual predators and "these men must be viewed as batterers rather than customers."[78] Margaret Farley claims that "johns are regularly murderous toward women"[79] and prostitution "must be exposed for what it really is—a particularly lethal form of male violence against women."[80] Unfortunately, few radical feminist claims about prostitution are amenable to either verification or falsification.[81]

Socialist feminists view female crime in terms of class, gender, and race oppression. In a rare study that took into account both Marxist and socialist feminist theories when predicting rape rates, research conducted by Kimberly Martin, Lynne Vieraitis, and Sarah Britto found that one of the strongest predictors of rape rates was women's absolute status. In cities populated by women with high incomes, a higher percentage of college degrees obtained, higher female employment rates, and high occupational status, rape rates were significantly lower. The study found that higher absolute status of women was associated with lower rape rates. The findings buttress the Marxist and socialist feminist hypotheses.[82]

Left Realism

Another branch of critical criminology is left realism.[83] This school of thought emerged over the last decade as a response to the perception that radical criminologists (called "radical idealists" by left realists) place far too much weight on the evils of elite deviance, largely ignoring the fact that the disenfranchised lower classes are persistently victimized by street crime. Left realists contend that radical criminologists are simply radical idealists and have developed only weak crime-control strategies, while the left realists recognize crime as an inevitable outcome of social and political deprivation. According to Jock Young, one of the most significant contributors to left realism, four elements must be considered when addressing

The organization *Witness for Peace*, a politically independent grassroots organization, recently demonstrated against U.S. policies and corporate practices that contribute to poverty and oppression.

crime: the victim, the offender, the state, and the general public (Table 8.2). Young believes that these elements are interrelated and form a "square of crime."[84] Unlike other theories, left realism includes society in explanations of crime.

Left realists seek a crime-control agenda, capable of being implemented in a capitalist system, that will protect the more vulnerable members of the lower classes from crime and the fear of crime. The latter, according to left realists, has given right-wing politicians a green light to promote a repressive law-and-order agenda.

Abolitionist and Anarchist Criminology

Both abolitionist and anarchist critical theories dispute the existing systems of supremacy. Abolitionism is very much like left realism in its rejection of state controls, as it focuses on the punitive response of segregative punishment. According to abolitionist theory, crime and punishment have a reciprocal effect on each other, with one causing the other. Abolitionist theory advocates the redistribution of power by returning it to communities and individuals, in order to fix the existing power differential. Similar to this is the anarchist theory of criminology, which also believes that the destruction of communities by the state is at the root of crime. Anarchists, however, reject the sensible and organized opposition to this condition led by abolitionists, opting instead to wage the struggle with chaos and disorder.

TABLE 8.2 Elements of Crime

Actors	Reactors
offender	state
victim	general public

SOURCE: Jock Young, "Ten Points of Realism," in *Rethinking Criminology: The Realist Debate*, J. Young, ed. (London: Sage, 1992), pp. 24–68.

Peacemaking Criminology

The most recently articulated critical perspective, peacemaking, promotes the idea of peace, justice, and equality in society. The current obsession with punishment and the war on crime suggests an orientation to criminology that only encourages violence. Peacemakers suggest that mutual aid, mediation, and conflict resolution, rather than coercive state control, are the best means to achieve a harmonious, peaceful society.[85] In short, peacemaking criminology advocates humanistic, nonviolent, and peaceful solutions to crime.

The peacemaking perspective is part of an intellectual and social movement toward restorative justice. What is restorative justice? According to Braithwaite, restorative justice "means restoring victims, a more victim centered criminal justice system, as well as restoring offenders and restoring community." This includes restoring the following elements:

- Property loss
- Sense of security
- Dignity
- Sense of empowerment
- Deliberative democracy
- Harmony based on a feeling that justice has been done
- Social support

Basing their study on anarchist, peacemaking, and cultural criminology, Bruce Arrigo and Yoshiko Takahashi examined the eight-stage model of recommunalizing the homeless in single-room-occupancy (SRO) units at the Wood Street Commons project, located in downtown Pittsburgh. The eight stages—alienation, powerlessness, disaffiliation, values of the community assumed, social structure perceived as open, performance, embracement, and role distance—reflect the processes the residents experience in order to "rediscover their identities, overcome their problems through collective efficacy and contribute to the building's dynamic culture."[86]

Using peacemaking and anarchist criminology to develop a successful single-room-occupancy program has proved successful with the homeless and holds promise for use with those caught in the justice system, including juveniles and those in drug treatment.

REVIEW

Labeling theory, conflict theory, and radical theory offer alternative explanations of crime, in the sense that they do not restrict their inquiry to individual characteristics or to social or communal processes. These three theories examine the impact of law-making and law enforcement processes on the creation of offenders. The labeling and conflict theories, as critical as they are of the existing system of criminal justice, envisage a system made more just and equitable by reform and democratic processes; radical theory demands revolutionary change. With long historical antecedents, all three theories gained prominence in the 1960s and early 1970s, during an era of rebellion against social, political, and economic inequities.

Labeling theory does not presume to explain all crime, but it does demonstrate that the criminal justice system is selective in determining who is to be labeled a criminal. It explains how labeling occurs, and it blames the criminal justice system for contributing to the labeling process and, therefore, to the crime problem.

Conflict theory goes a step beyond labeling theory in identifying the forces that selectively decide in the first place what conduct should be singled out for condemnation—usually, so it is claimed, to the detriment of the powerless and the benefit of the powerful.

Radical theory singles out the relationship between the owners of the means of production and the workers under capitalism as the root cause of crime and of all social inequities. Radical theory demands the overthrow of the existing order, which is said to perpetuate criminality by keeping the oppressed classes under the domination of the capitalist ruling class.

All three theories have adherents and opponents. Research to demonstrate the validity of the theories has produced mixed results. More important, these theories have challenged conventional criminologists to rethink their approaches and to provide answers to questions that had not been asked before.

CRIMINOLOGY & PUBLIC POLICY

The United States has a long history of denying convicted felons the right to vote. At common law, "when all felons were in principle subject to capital punishment," worrying about convicted felons' voting rights was almost nonsensical. Yet the expansion of the "concept of felony," accompanied by rising incarceration rates, has called into question the traditional practice of "disenfranchising" convicts for life. Today, one might be permanently disenfranchised for participating with others "in a course of disorderly conduct," "breaking a water pipe," "aiding or inducing another to engage in gambling," or aiding, abetting, or encouraging any "bull, bear, dog, or cock fight." Current estimates place the total number of disenfranchised felons and ex-felons at approximately 3.9 million voting-age citizens. Of this number, approximately 1.4 million have completed their sentences. Over one-third of the total disenfranchised population are black men.

Recently, felon disenfranchisement laws have received considerable attention from a variety of studies and in the popular press. Some commentators discuss felon disenfranchisement in terms of altered electoral outcomes; others emphasize

its effect on democratic representation. Still others focus on felon disenfranchisement's disparate impact, contending that such laws deny the vote to over 10 percent of the black voting-age population in 15 states.

No matter how one views the issue, it is difficult to deny that skyrocketing incarceration rates have raised the stakes of criminal disenfranchisement, altering the composition of the American electorate. Moreover, given this nation's history of voting discrimination, any process that disproportionately disenfranchises racial minorities should be cause for concern. (SOURCE: From "Developments in the Law: One Person, No Vote: The Laws of Felon Disenfranchisement." Reprinted by permission of the Harvard Law Review Association and William S. Hein Company from *The Harvard Law Review*, Vol. 115, page 1939.)

Questions for Discussion What is the justification for these laws? What do you suppose the effect is of taking away an ex-offender's voting rights? Does it unfairly contribute to the labeling of ex-offenders? What role does race play in the effect of these laws? Do you support law reform in this area? If so, what would you propose?

What kind of crime-prevention program is suggested by conflict, Marxist, and labeling theories?

How would you go about designing such a program? How would you evaluate its effectiveness?

The numbers next to the terms refer to the pages on which the terms are defined.

conflict theory (182)
consensus model (182)
due process (174)
equal protection (174)
labeling theory (175)
penologists (186)
radical criminology (186)
social interactionists (175)

9 Environmental Theory

Situational Theories of Crime
Environmental Criminology
Rational-Choice Perspective
Routine-Activity Approach
Practical Applications of Situational Theories of Crime
Theories of Victimization
Lifestyle Theories
Victim-Offender Interaction
Repeat Victimization
Hot Spots of Crime
Geography of Crime
Interrelatedness of Theories
Preventing Crimes against Places, People, and Valuable Goods
Situational Crime Prevention
Situational Crime Prevention—Pros and Cons
Displacement
THEORY INFORMS POLICY
Review
Criminology & Public Policy
You Be the Criminologist
Key Terms

■ *At the New York Stock Exchange, barriers have been erected to help protect the building and the workers inside. How do criminals choose their targets? What conditions invite crime? Alternatively, what measures can prevent crime?*

New York: A Diamond District jeweler was busted yesterday for allegedly orchestrating the hijacking of a FedEx truck in a bungled attempt to steal millions of dollars worth of gems—and then planning to try it again. Brian Greenwald, president of Doppelt & Greenwald, is also suspected of being in on the robbery of nearly $5 million worth of gems from his wholesale business in 2005. He led a dozen thugs who hijacked a FedEx truck at gunpoint on

11th Avenue at 47th Street on Dec. 20, 2007, according to a Manhattan federal court complaint. They got the truck, but the hapless thieves had to abandon it—its contents intact—when they couldn't figure out how to offload the baubles, which were in containers locked to the floor.[1]

Los Angeles: A 37-year-old mother was killed by gunfire from a passing car and her daughter and stepdaughter wounded Sunday evening as she was driving her family home in South Los Angeles, police said. Stephanie Smith, 37, was in her car with her 13-year-old daughter, 15-year-old stepdaughter and 21-year-old son when the vehicle came under fire about 8:30 P.M. in the 500 block of West 102nd street. According to Los Angeles Police Department detectives, Smith and her family were near their home when a vehicle that was behind them passed her car on the driver's side. As it went by, someone in the car fired multiple shots at Smith and her passengers, striking her and the two girls. The gunman's vehicle then fled east.[2]

Columbus, Ohio: The serial rapist who police say has been preying on the women of western Franklin County likely has struck again—the first assault after investigators went public with their suspicions. Police revealed yesterday that they think the man is responsible for a seventh sexual assault, this one on the Far West Side and not far from an earlier attack. The latest assault occurred about 1:15 A.M. on Nov. 2. Police said the man entered the Marlowe Court apartment of a woman in her 20s, who was alone with a young child. The apartment complex is near Sullivant Avenue and Norton Road, and in the same area of an Oct. 5 attack on White Cedar Court. The victim on Marlowe Court had been sleeping when the rapist entered her home, Sgt. David Pelphrey of the sexual-assault unit said.[3]

Here we have three different types of crime, committed in three different jurisdictions—New York, Los Angeles, and Columbus, Ohio—involving three different types of harm—the taking of property by force or violence, the taking of a life, and a series of violent, nonconsensual sexual acts. The prosecutors in these jurisdictions will know what to do. They will identify these crimes under their respective penal codes as armed robbery,

criminal homicide (murder or manslaughter, and related offenses), and sexual assault (also known as rape in some jurisdictions). But the criminologist, looking more deeply into these crime scenarios, will consider something in addition, something seemingly not of interest to the law—namely, that each of the three crimes occurs at a specific time, at a specific place. The presence of an offender is only one of the necessary components: Crimes require many conditions that are independent of the offender, such as the availability of a person to be assaulted or of goods to be stolen.

In other chapters, we have focused on factors explaining why individuals and groups engage in criminal behavior. Now we look at how, in recent years, some criminologists have focused on why offenders choose to commit one offense rather than another at a given time and place. They identify conditions under which those who are prone to commit crime will in fact do so. Criminological research reveals that both a small number of victims and a small number of places experience a large amount of all crime committed. Crimes are events. Criminals choose their targets. Certain places actually attract criminals. Think about the community you live in. Are there some places you hesitate to go to alone? If so, you recognize that some spaces are more dangerous than others. Are there areas that are safe during the day but not at night? Crime has temporal patterns—some crimes happen more often at night than during the day; others happen more often on the weekend than during the rest of the week. There are even what criminologists call "seasonal patterns." Certain lifestyles also increase people's chances of being victimized. For example, is a drunk person walking alone more likely to be attacked than a sober one? Although victims of crime rarely are to blame for their victimization, they frequently play a role in the crimes of which they are the target.

In this chapter, we discuss theories of crime and theories of victimization. We demonstrate how various environmental, opportunity, and victimization theories are interrelated. We also explore the prevention of crimes against people, places, and valuable goods, presenting current criminological research. In this discussion, we include situational crime prevention, diffusion of benefits, routine precautions, and the theoretical and practical implications of focusing on the victims and targets of crime.

SITUATIONAL THEORIES OF CRIME

Among those theories of crime that focus on the situation in which a crime occurs, three distinct approaches have been identified: environmental criminology, the rational-choice perspective, and the routine-activity approach. These theoretical approaches to crime are sometimes called "opportunity theories" because they analyze the various situations that provide opportunities for specific crimes to occur (Table 9.1).

TABLE 9.1 Ten Principles of Opportunity and Crime

1. Opportunities play a role in causing all crime.

2. Crime opportunities are highly specific.

3. Crime opportunities are concentrated in time and space.

4. Crime opportunities depend on everyday movements.

5. One crime produces opportunities for another.

6. Some products offer more tempting crime opportunities.

7. Social and technological changes produce new crime opportunities.

8. Opportunities for crime can be reduced.

9. Reducing opportunities does not usually displace crime.

10. Focused opportunity reduction can produce wider declines in crime.

SOURCE: Marcus Felson and Ronald V. Clarke, *Opportunity Makes the Thief: Practical Theory for Crime Prevention*, Police Research Series Paper 98 (London: Home Office, 1998), p. 9. © Crown Copyright 1998. Reprinted by permission of Her Majesty's Stationery Office.

Environmental Criminology

Environmental criminology examines the location of a specific crime and the context in which it occurred in order to understand and explain crime patterns. It asks: Where and when did the crime occur? What are the physical and social characteristics of the crime site? What movements bring offender and target together at the crime site? Environmental criminologists want to know how physical "location in time and space" interacts with the offender, the target/victim, and the law that makes the crime an illegal act.[4]

Contrary to the conventional criminological theories that explain criminal motivation, environmental criminology begins with the assumption that some people are criminally motivated. Through mapping crimes on global, country, state, county, city, or site-specific levels, such as a particular building or plot of land, environmental criminologists can see crime patterns. They then relate these crime patterns to the number of targets; to the offender population; to the location of routine activities, such as work, school, shopping, or recreation; to security; and to traffic flow.

Mapping crimes and analyzing spatial crime patterns is not new (Chapter 3). In the nineteenth century, Guerry examined the spatial patterning of crime through his comparison of conviction rates in various regions in France.[5] Quételet tried to establish links between seasonal differences and the probability of committing crime. He found, for instance, that property crimes increase in the winter months in France, whereas "the violence of the passions predominating in summer, excites to more frequent personal collisions" and a rise in crimes against persons.[6] Contemporary research takes a more focused, crime-specific approach, leveraging cutting-edge technologies.

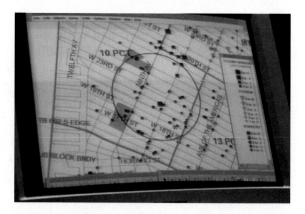

■ *New York Police Department COMPSTAT: Crime mapping is now a powerful tool in the fight against crime. Police departments around the country are developing sophisticated mapping programs to track crime trends, "hot spots," and the pattern of offending.*

Rational-Choice Perspective

The **rational-choice** perspective, developed by Ronald Clarke and Derek Cornish, is based on two main theoretical approaches.[7] The first of these—utilitarianism—was addressed in Chapter 3. It assumes that people make decisions with the goal of maximizing pleasure and minimizing pain. The second basis for the rational-choice perspective is traditional economic choice theory, which argues that people evaluate the options and choose what they believe will satisfy their needs. According to this perspective, a person decides to commit a particular crime after concluding that the benefits (the pleasure) outweigh the risks and the effort (the pain).[8]

The rational-choice perspective assumes that people make these decisions with a goal in mind and that they are made more or less intelligently and with free will. This contrasts with the theories of criminality whose underlying assumption is that people commit a crime when forces beyond their control drive them. Rational choice implies a limited sense of rationality. An offender does not know all the details of a situation; rather, he or she relies on cues in the environment or characteristics of targets. This means the offender may not be able to calculate the costs and benefits accurately, and in hindsight the decision may seem foolish. Further, an offender may have an impaired ability to make wise choices, perhaps because of intoxication due to drugs or alcohol.

According to the rational-choice perspective, most crime is neither extraordinary nor the product of a deranged mind. Most crime is quite ordinary and committed by reasoning individuals who decide that the chances of getting caught are low and the possibilities for a relatively good payoff are high. Since the rational-choice perspective treats each crime as a specific event and focuses on analyzing all its components, it looks at crime in terms of an offender's decision to commit a *specific* offense at a *particular* time and place.

A variety of factors (or characteristics) come into play when an offender decides to commit a crime. These factors are called "choice structuring properties." With the emphasis of rational-choice theory on analyzing each crime on a crime-specific basis, each particular type of crime has its own set of choice structuring properties (Figure 9.1). Those for sexual assault differ from those for computer crime, and those for burglary differ from those for theft. Nevertheless, these properties tend to fall into the same seven categories. Thus, a potential thief, before committing a theft, is likely to consider the following aspects (categories):

- The number of targets and their accessibility
- Familiarity with the chosen method (for example, fraud by credit card)

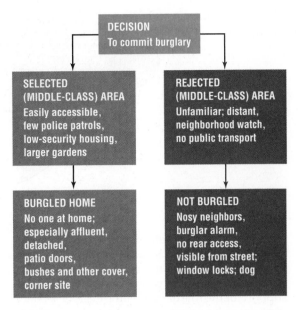

FIGURE 9.1 Event model (*example:* burglary in a middle-class suburb).

Source: Adapted from Ronald V. Clarke and Derek B. Cornish, "Modeling Offenders' Decisions: A Framework for Research and Policy," in *Crime and Justice*, vol. 6, eds. Michael Tonry and Norval Morris, p. 169. © 1985 by The University of Chicago. All rights reserved. Reprinted by permission of the University of Chicago Press.

- The monetary yield per crime
- The expertise needed
- The time required to commit the act
- The physical danger involved
- The risk of apprehension

Characteristics fall into two distinct sets: those of the offender and those of the offense. The offender's characteristics include specific needs, values, learning experiences, and so on. The characteristics of the offense include the location of the target and the potential yield. According to rational-choice theory, involvement in crime depends on a personal decision made after one has weighed available information.

Rational-choice theory is behind cutting-edge research on the deterrence effects of certain crime-control policies and, more generally, punishment. Research by David Weisburd and his colleagues, for example, found that probationers in New Jersey randomly selected to face an increased risk of prison for nonpayment of fines were significantly more likely than controls to pay their fines.[9] The threat of a violation of probation, in other words, works.

The rationality of offenders led Bradley Wright and his colleagues to look at the association of criminal propensity, perceived risks and costs of

FIGURE 9.2 Components of a criminal event: the model of the routine-activity approach.

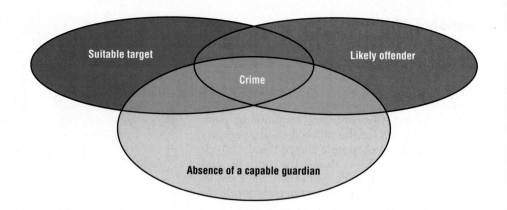

punishment, and criminal behavior. Wright examined more than a thousand individuals from the Dunedin (New Zealand) Study, a longitudinal study from birth through age 26, and found some support for the role of rationality. Results revealed that deterrence perceptions had their greatest impact on criminally prone study members.[10]

As criminologists continue to seek evidence that the rational decision making of offenders leads to calculated choices, it is worth heeding the sage counsel of Daniel Nagin: "Just like medications for treatment of disease have no single effect across type of medication and disease, we cannot expect that all sanctions will be equally effective."[11]

Rational-choice theory, unlike traditional theories, is not concerned with strategies of overall crime prevention. (It leaves those problems to others.) Rather, it is concerned with reducing the likelihood that any given offense will be committed by somebody "involved" in criminal activity. This theory, therefore, has its greatest potential in developing strategies to frustrate perpetrators and prevent them from committing a crime then and there. It has its greatest challenge in demonstrating that such prevention will not lead to the commission of the intended crime later on or to the commission of other crimes (displacement). We turn to both of these issues shortly.

Routine-Activity Approach

According to Lawrence Cohen and Marcus Felson, a crime can occur only if there is someone who intends to commit a crime (likely offender), something or someone to be victimized (a suitable target), and no other person present to prevent or observe the crime (the absence of a capable guardian) (Figure 9.2). Later revisions added a fourth element—no person to control the activities of the likely offender (personal handler). When a suitable target that is unguarded comes together in time and space with a likely offender who is not "handled," the potential for a crime is there.[12] This explanation is called the **routine-activity**

approach. It does not explore the factors that influence the offender's decision to commit a crime. Instead, Cohen and Felson focus on the routine or everyday activities of people, such as going to work, pursuing recreation, running errands, and the like. It is through routine activities that offenders come into contact with suitable victims and targets.

The routine-activity approach began with an analysis of crime rate increases in the post–World War II era (1947 to 1974), when socioeconomic conditions had improved in America. The increase was puzzling, since the general public (and some criminologists) expected crime rates to decrease with an increase in prosperity. But the authors of the routine-activity approach demonstrated that certain technological changes and alterations in the workforce create new crime opportunities. They referred to increases in female participation in the labor force, out-of-town travel, automobile usage, and technological advances as factors that account for higher risks of predatory victimization. Further advances in technology create further opportunities for the commission of crime. For example, as flat-screen televisions, DVD players, personal and laptop computers, and iPods have become more common and lighter to carry, they have become attractive targets for thieves and burglars. The chance that a piece of property will become the target of a theft is based on the value of the target and its weight.[13] One need only compare the theft of washing machines and of electronic goods. Although both washing machines and electronic goods (such as televisions and computers) are expensive, washing machines are so heavy that their value is estimated at $4 per pound, compared with roughly $400 per pound for a laptop computer. And, of course, cell phones have increasingly been subject to theft—for resale, for unauthorized telephone use, and for the facilitation of other crimes. Thus, cell phones, as useful as they are in helping potential crime victims feel more secure, are also used increasingly by criminals who seek to reduce the risk of having their calls traced.[14] It may be concluded that while technological developments help society run more smoothly, they also create new targets for theft, make old targets more suitable, or create new tools for criminals to use in committing their crimes. As people's daily work and leisure activities change with time, the location of property and personal targets also changes.

The logic of the routine-activity argument is straightforward: Routine patterns of work, play, and leisure time affect the convergence in time and place of motivated offenders who are not "handled," suitable targets, and the absence of guardians. If one component is missing, crime is not likely to be committed. And if all components are in place and one of them is strengthened, crime is likely to increase. Even if the proportions of motivated offenders and targets stay the same, changes in routine activities alone—for example, changes of the sort we have experienced since World War II—will raise the crime rate by multiplying the opportunities for crime. This approach has helped explain, among other things, rates of victimization for specific crimes, rates of urban homicide, and "hot spots"—areas that produce a disproportionate number of calls to police.[15]

Practical Applications of Situational Theories of Crime

The trio of approaches discussed here—environmental criminology, rational choice, and routine activities—often work together to explain why a person may commit a crime in a particular situation. We look now at how these theories of crime are used to explain specific varieties of crime, and how the ideas that arise from these theories have practical applications.

Burglars and Burglary

Criminologists are increasingly interested in the factors that go into a decision to burglarize: the location or setting of the building, the presence of guards or dogs, the type of burglar alarms and external lighting, and so forth. Does a car in the driveway or a radio playing music in the house have a significant impact on the choice of home to burglarize? George Rengert and John Wasilchick conducted extensive interviews with suburban burglars in an effort to understand their techniques. They found significant differences with respect to several factors:[16]

- *The amount of planning* that precedes a burglary. Professional burglars plan more than do amateurs.

- The extent to which a burglar engages in *systematic selection of a home.* Some burglars examine the obvious clues, such as presence

A male thief shoplifts from a store by slipping merchandise into his jacket.

of a burglar alarm, a watchdog, mail piled up in the mailbox, newspapers on a doorstep. More experienced burglars look for subtle clues—for example, closed windows coupled with air conditioners that are turned off.

- The extent to which a burglar pays *attention to situational cues.* Some burglars routinely choose a corner property because it offers more avenues of escape, has fewer adjoining properties, and offers visibility.

Rengert and Wasilchick have also examined the use of time and place in burglary (Figure 9.3). Time is a critical factor to burglars, for three reasons:

- They must minimize the time spent in targeted places so as not to reveal their intention to burglarize.

- Opportunities for burglary occur only when a dwelling is unguarded or unoccupied, that is, during daytime. (Many burglars would call in sick so often that they would be fired from their legitimate jobs; others simply quit their jobs because the jobs interfered with their burglaries.)

- Burglars have "working hours"; that is, they have time available only during a limited number of hours (if they have a legitimate job).

■ *Thomas Crown (portrayed by Pierce Brosnan) crafted an extremely clever and well-planned theft of a painting from a well-guarded museum. Of course, not all burglars are so affluent and calculative.*

Before committing their offenses, burglars take into account familiarity with the area, fear of recognition, concern over standing out as somebody who does not belong, and the possibility (following some successful burglaries) that a particular area is no longer cost-beneficial. Season, too, plays an important role. One experienced burglar stated that because neighborhoods are populated with children in the summer, he opted for winter months: "The best time to do crime out here is between 8:00 and 9:00 [A.M.]. All the mothers are taking the kids to school. I wait until I see the car leave. By the time she gets back, I've come and gone."[17]

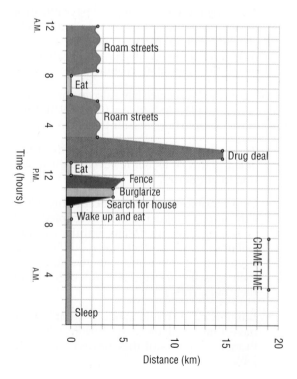

FIGURE 9.3 Crime day of burglar #26.

Source: From George Rengert and John Wasilchick, *Suburban Burglary: A Time and a Place for Everything,* 1985, p. 35. Courtesy of Charles C Thomas Publisher, Ltd., Springfield, Illinois.

Recent research demonstrates how important it is for burglars to have prior knowledge of their targets. They obtain such knowledge by knowing the occupants, by being tipped off about the occupants, or by observing the potential target. Some burglars even acquire jobs that afford them the opportunity to observe their potential victims' daily activities; others gain access to the interior of a house, search for valuable goods, and steal them at a later date. There are others, however, who come across burglary opportunities during the course of their daily routine instead of planning them. For these offenders, rational-choice decisions are made right before the criminal event.[18]

Robbers and Robberies

Richard Wright and Scott Decker conducted in-depth interviews with street robbers and found that they frequently victimize other street-involved individuals—drug dealers, drug users, and gang members—who, because they are criminals themselves, are unlikely to go to the police. These people are also targeted because they are believed to have a lot of money, jewelry, and other desirable items. Street robbers report that they sometimes specifically target people whom they do not like or people who have hurt or offended them in the past. When women are targeted, it is because robbers believe they will not resist and are not armed. On the other hand, women are not the desirable targets that men are because robbers think women do not carry as much money.[19]

Criminologists also study whether commercial robbers operate the same way as street robbers in their selection of targets. Robbers who target business establishments are interested in some of the same factors that concern burglars. Perpetrators carefully examine the location of the potential

■ This woman, walking alone in a dark, deserted area, demonstrates how a victim can play a significant part in a criminal event.

robbery, the potential gain, the capability of security personnel, the possibility of intervention by bystanders, and the presence of guards, cameras, and alarms.[20]

Criminologists have found that potential victims and establishments can do quite a bit to decrease the likelihood of being robbed. Following a series of convenience-store robberies in Gainesville, Florida, in 1985, a city ordinance required store owners to clear their windows of signs that obstructed the view of the interior, to position cash registers where they would be visible from the street, and to install approved electronic cameras. Within a little over a year, convenience-store robberies had decreased 64 percent.[21] We will return to this discussion later in this chapter.

Hot Products

Why do thieves decide to steal some things and not others? What makes targets attractive? We have examined how burglars select which homes to burglarize, but once they have broken into a residence, how do they decide what to steal? When robbers target victims, they do so believing their chances of making off with something valuable are greater than their chances of not being successful in the robbery attempt. But what is it about things that makes them valuable to robbers? Cohen and Felson argued that items are attractive if they are visible, easy to take away, valuable, and accessible.[22] Twenty years later, Ronald Clarke expanded this idea with his discussion of hot products—those consumer goods that are attractive to thieves (Table 9.2). Using an acronym (CRAVED) to organize this idea, Clarke claimed that goods are attractive if they are concealable, removable, available, valuable, enjoyable, and disposable (i.e., can be easily fenced). This approach takes into account what thieves do with goods after they are stolen, because that factor figures into their decisions about the attractiveness of items.[23]

College Campus Crime

Crime on college campuses follows patterns that routine-activity theorists would expect; that is, if you engage in a risky and deviant lifestyle, your risk is significantly increased. Students who party frequently and use recreational drugs regularly are at risk. You are more likely to be a victim of property crime if you are a male age 17 to 20. If you live in an all-female dorm, you are less likely to experience a theft. Not surprisingly, students who spend several nights per week on campus and full-time students are more vulnerable to property crime than part-time students or those who do not spend as many nights on campus. With respect to target attractiveness, people who spend large amounts of money on nonessential items have a higher risk of on-campus theft than those who spend less.[24]

THEORIES OF VICTIMIZATION

Although the victim is mentioned in many theories of crime, direct consideration of the role that victims play in the criminal event has been of secondary significance. As a result of the "missing victim" in basic criminology, **theories of victimization** have been developed for the purpose of understanding crime from the victim's perspective or with the victim in mind.

The history of victims in criminology can be traced to Hans von Hentig's first article on the subject of victims, in 1941, in which he postulated that crime was an "interaction of perpetrator and victim."[25] Von Hentig, a highly respected scientist, had been a victim of Nazi persecution. It was that experience that made him focus on the significance of the victim. By carefully gathering and

TABLE 9.2 Items Most Often Stolen by Apprehended Shoplifters, United States 1995

	Number of Chains	Number of Stores	Number of Apprehended Shoplifters	Most Stolen Items
Book shops	1	111	678	Cassette tapes; magazines
Department stores	12	641	10,995	Clothing; shirts; jeans; Hilfiger and Polo items
Discount stores	12	5,677	120,415	Clothing; undergarments; CDs
Drug stores/Pharmacies	16	1,517	3,060	Medicines; beauty aids; cigarettes; batteries; birth control
Fashion merchandise stores	13	2,216	3,120	Sneakers
General merchandise stores	8	2,447	300	"Costume" earrings
Groceries/Supermarkets/ Convenience stores	49	4,990	25,532	Medicines; beauty aids; cigarettes; video cassettes
Hardware/DIY stores	15	755	1,402	Hand tools
Recorded music shops	3	284	433	CDs
Sporting goods stores	4	241	4,047	Nike shoes
Theme park shops	8	152	1,881	Jewelry; key chains
Toy shops	3	408	603	Action figures; children's apparel

SOURCE: From Hayes, R., "Retail Theft: An Analysis of Apprehended Shoplifters," *Security Journal*, 8 (1997): 233–246. Reproduced with permission of Palgrave Macmillan.

analyzing information, he demonstrated that tourist resorts were attractive to criminals who wanted to prey on unsuspecting vacationers. Von Hentig, through his book *The Criminal and His Victim*, published in 1948, founded the criminological subdiscipline of victimology, which examines the role played by the victim in a criminal incident.[26] Nevertheless, it must be acknowledged that the term "victimology" is a year older than von Hentig's book. The term was coined in 1947 by the Romanian lawyer Beniamin Mendelsohn, in a lecture before the Romanian Psychiatric Association in Bucharest titled "New Bio-Psycho-Social Horizons: Victimology."[27] In 1948, Frederic Wertham, an American psychiatrist, first used the term "victimology" in America.[28]

According to Canadian criminologist Ezzat Fattah, "von Hentig insisted that many crime victims contribute to their own victimization be it by inciting or provoking the criminal or by creating or fostering a situation likely to lead to the commission of the crime."[29] Thus, the entire event is regarded as crucial, because criminal behavior involves both the action of the offender and interaction between offender and victim. Nor is it tenable to regard "criminals and victims . . . as different as night and day," because there is an undeniable link between offending and victimization.[30] Many offenders are victimized repeatedly, and victims are frequently offenders.

Such findings may be deemed highly controversial in a time when victims' rights groups have been active, and successful, in securing rights for victims of crimes. It must be understood, however, that *guilt* is not shared by offender and victim. Criminal guilt belongs to the perpetrator of a crime—and it must be proved at trial beyond a reasonable doubt. The victim is free of guilt. Victimology, however, can demonstrate how potential victims, by acting differently, can decrease the risk of being victimized.[31]

We turn now to a discussion of the dominant victimological theories.

Lifestyle Theories

A "lifestyle theory of victimization" was developed by Michael Hindelang, Michael Gottfredson, and James Garofalo in 1978. It argues that because of changing roles (working mother versus homemaker) and schedules (a child's school calendar), people lead different lifestyles (work and leisure activities). Variations in lifestyle affect the number of situations with high victimization risks that a person experiences.[32] The kinds of people someone associates with, such as coworkers, friends, and sexual partners, also affect victimization rates. For instance, someone who has a drug dealer or an insider trader as a friend has a greater chance of being victimized than a person who associates only with law-abiding people. (The similarity of the lifestyle theory of victimization and the routine-activities approach is quite apparent.)

The lifestyle theory of victimization centers on a number of specific propositions that outline the essence of the theory and signal directions for future research:[33]

Proposition 1: The probability of suffering a personal victimization is directly related to the amount of time that a person spends in public places (e.g., on the street, in parks), and particularly in public places at night.

Proposition 2: The probability of being in public places, particularly at night, varies as a function of lifestyle.

Proposition 3: Social contacts and interactions occur disproportionately among individuals who share similar lifestyles.

Proposition 4: An individual's chances of personal victimization are dependent upon the extent to which the individual shares demographic characteristics with offenders (such as young urban males).

Proposition 5: The proportion of time that an individual spends among nonfamily members varies as a function of lifestyle.

Proposition 6: The probability of personal victimization, particularly personal theft, increases as a function of the proportion of the time that an individual spends among nonfamily members (such as a young man who works a double shift at a factory versus a middle-aged woman who stays home to take care of an elderly parent).

Proposition 7: Variations in lifestyle are associated with variations in the ability of individuals to isolate themselves from persons with offender characteristics (being able to leave high-crime urban areas for sheltered suburbs).

Proposition 8: Variations in lifestyle are associated with variations in the convenience, the desirability, and the vincibility of the person as a target for a personal victimization (people who pass within the view of offenders, seem to have what the offender wants, appear unable to resist, or would probably not report the crime to the police).

Both the lifestyle theory of victimization and the routine-activity approach present some basic guidelines for reducing one's chances of victimization. And just as these theories themselves tend to embody common sense, so do the preventive measures derived from them. For instance, people in American society are told not to drive while intoxicated, not to smoke or abuse alcohol or drugs, and not to eat too much trans fat. All these messages are intended to reduce the risks of dying in a motor vehicle accident, or from lung or liver cancer, or from an overdose, or from a heart attack. Although public-service messages designed to protect health may not always be heeded, people do not see them as "blaming the victim." Similarly, messages to prevent criminal victimization, like not walking alone and not frequenting deserted or unfamiliar places late at night, should not be viewed as overly restrictive and intrusive or as blaming victims who did not heed the advice. The messages directed at preventing victimization are based on theory and research and merely promote living and acting responsibly to ensure a more crime-free existence.

Victim-Offender Interaction

Marvin Wolfgang, one of the preeminent criminologists of his time, studied homicides in Philadelphia during the 1950s. He found that many of the victims had actually brought upon themselves the attack that led to their murder (see Chapter 10 for further discussion of Wolfgang's work). He coined the term "victim precipitation" to refer to situations where victims initiate the confrontations that lead to their death. Wolfgang estimated that as many as one-quarter to one-half of intentional homicides are victim-precipitated.[34] James Tedeschi and Richard Felson put forward a theory of "coercive actions," which stresses that the way victims and offenders interact plays a large role in violent crime.[35] They argue that people commit violence purposefully. In other words, people don't just lose control. When they are violent, it is with a particular goal in mind. They make a decision to be violent (note the similarity between this theory and the rational-choice perspective) and tend to choose targets who are less powerful than themselves. In unarmed attacks, males are more likely to injure their opponents, while females are more likely to be injured. Gender is not the determinant so much as body size.[36] There are also victims who instigate attacks by irritating others. Schoolyard bullies are a good example.[37]

Repeat Victimization

Not unlike the lifestyle theory of victimization, theories of repeat victimization focus on the specific characteristics of situations in order to determine which factors account for the initial, as well as for repeat, victimization.[38] Theories of repeat victimization, also called "multiple victimization," dispel the myth that crime is uniformly distributed. Research shows that a small number of people and places account for a large number of the crimes committed. For example, an analysis of the British Crime Survey (a victimization survey) from 1982 to 1992 found that between 24 and 38 percent of all victims of property and personal crime experienced five or more such offenses in a little over a year.[39]

The research literature on repeat victimization is increasing rapidly. A study of police calls for service from 34 fast-food restaurants in San Antonio, Texas, from 1990 to 1992 found that fast-food restaurants had the greatest chance of repeat police calls for service within 1 week of the last call. Thereafter, the number of calls decreases as the time between calls increases.[40] Similar findings have been made in research on the repeat risks of burglary.[41] Risks of a repeat burglary are highest immediately after a previous burglary. In their analysis of repeat victimization for crimes ranging from the repeated physical and sexual abuse of children to repeated credit card fraud, researchers concluded that the rational-choice theory of offender decision making is useful in understanding repeat victimization. Offenders choose targets based on the knowledge they gained in the previous victimization about the risks and rewards of a particular offense.[42] A study also found that repeat burglary victimization is a bigger problem in disadvantaged areas than in well-off areas.[43]

Formulating strategies to deal with repeat victimizations would certainly be cost-beneficial. Resources could be concentrated on relatively few targets. Unfortunately, police recording systems are not designed to keep track of repeat victimizations. To overcome this problem, several innovative researchers have created their own databases, starting a line of research called "hot-spots" research.

Hot Spots of Crime

In 1989, Lawrence Sherman, Patrick Gartin, and Michael Buerger published the results of a study that immediately excited the profession. They had analyzed 911 calls for police assistance in Minneapolis, Minnesota, for the period between December 15, 1985, and December 15, 1986. After plotting the more than 320,000 calls on a map, they discovered that 3 percent of the addresses and intersections in the city were the subject of 50 percent of the calls received.[44]

They also found that certain types of crime were committed in specific places—for example, all auto thefts at 2 percent of all places. The researchers concluded that attempts to prevent victimization should be focused not on victims, but on the places themselves by making them less vulnerable to crime. Change places, not people! We should identify neighborhood hot spots (areas of concentrated crime), reduce social disorder and physical "incivilities," and promote housing-based neighborhood stabilization. Subsequent research provides support for this idea by showing the crime and disorder reduction effects of hot-spots policing.[45]

Criminologists have proposed a number of crime hot-spot theories, including place theories that explain why it is that crime occurs at any one specific location, street theories that consider why crimes are committed on particular inner-city streets or blocks, and neighborhood theories that explore why crimes are more frequent in one or more neighborhood areas (Table 9.3).

Geography of Crime

Research based on the idea of hot spots has matured in recent years. It is labeled "geography of crime" or "crime and place research." Researchers found that more crime occurs around high schools[46] and blocks with bars,[47] liquor stores,[48] the city center,[49] and abandoned buildings.[50] Higher crime in areas that border high schools and bars is readily explainable: High schools contain a highly crime-prone age group. Bars attract, among others, offenders.[51] In city centers, there are more opportunities to commit crime and generally fewer social controls in place. Abandoned buildings that are open and unsecured attract illegal users.

A study on the vulnerability of ports and marinas to vessel and equipment theft found that the proximity of a port or marina to a high-crime area is significant in predicting boat theft.[52] Research on drug markets in Jersey City, New Jersey, showed that areas with illicit drug markets account for a disproportionate amount of arrests and calls for police service.[53] In summary, the discovery that a large amount of crime occurs at a small number of places, and that such places have distinct characteristics, has led criminologists to explain crime in terms not only of who commits it, but also of where it is committed.[54]

Interrelatedness of Theories

Environmental criminology, the rational-choice perspective, and the routine-activity approach focus on the interactions among the victim (or target), the offender, and the place. There has been an integration of these theories of crime with theories of victimization.[55] For example, one study using the lifestyle theory of victimization and the routine-activity approach explores how drinking routines are linked with victimization.[56] It found that alcohol contributes to victimization by making potential victims less able to protect themselves (more suitable targets).

■ This graffiti-covered, seedy neighborhood in Manhattan, with its bars, walk-in hotels, and liquor stores, represents a prime "hot spot" for crime.

TABLE 9.3 Hot-Spot Concentrations, Evidence, Theory, and Causes

Concentration	Map Pattern	Geometric Dimension	Theories	Likely Causes	Examples
Place—at specific addresses, corners, or other places	Point concentration; a few places with many crimes and many places with few or no crimes. Repeat crime places or often concentrated.	Zero; concentration at points	Routine-activity theory; place management	Management of behavior at places	Bar fights, convenience store robberies, ATM patron robberies, drug-dealing locations
Among victims	Often confused with repeat crime places (above). Only visible on maps if victims are concentrated at places, on streets, or in areas.	Zero, one, or two; concentration at points, lines, and areas	Routine-activity theory; lifestyles	Victim routines and lifestyle choices	Domestic violence
Street—along a street or block face	Linear concentration along major thoroughfares; a few blocks with much crime and many blocks with little crime	One; concentration along lines	Offender search theory	Offender movement patterns and target concentrations	Outside street prostitution, street drug dealing, robberies of pedestrians
Area—neighborhood areas	Concentration covering multiblock areas	Two; concentration in areas	Disorganization theory and related ecologic theories of crime; opportunity theories	Low collective efficacy, social fragmentation, concentrations of youth, economic disinvestments; concentrations of crime targets	Residential burglary, gang violence

SOURCE: John E. Eck et al., *Mapping Crime: Understanding Hot Spots* (Washington, D.C.: U.S. Department of Justice, Office of Justice Programs, National Institute of Justice (2005), p. 5. http://www.ncjrs.gov/pdffiles1/nij/209393.pdf.

Unraveling Al-Qaida's Target Selection Calculus

The topic of al-Qaida's choice of targets has been the subject of much conjecture and speculation in open source literature. Some analysts state that al-Qaida's modus operandi is similar to traditional terrorism in that it is a form of "political theater" meant to bring attention to the group and its objectives by attacking targets of high importance. Others have diverged from this view, arguing that unlike traditional terror organizations, the al-Qaida network is more interested in the mass killing of Western civilians as revenge for perceived historical injustices against Muslims. In some cases, the debate concerning al-Qaida's target selection is based on the assumption that al-Qaida will target symbolic facilities within the United States to demonstrate its military prowess and long-reach capability. Others argue that al-Qaida attacks soft targets due to the difficulty of attacking military and security facilities in the West.

Yet an examination of primary al-Qaida operational manuals and open source published literature reveals a much different set of considerations in the group's target selection. Such analysis of what al-Qaida tells the world—and, most importantly, what it instructs its recruits and would-be cell members—indicates that al-Qaida's target selection calculus is motivated by a far more ambitious, sophisticated and sinister motive: to destroy the economy of the United States and other Western powers by striking economic targets in the West and in the Muslim world. This ambition includes the final objective of severing American and Muslim alliances and bringing about the removal of all Western influence from the Middle East, as well as the overthrow of current Muslim regimes.

To best understand al-Qaida's target selection calculus, it is important to keep in mind al-Qaida's foremost strategic objective, which is to "bleed" [exhaust] the United States economically and militarily by forcing the U.S. to spend exuberant amounts of money on protecting its numerous sectors and facilities. Al-Qaida's primary literature and manuals affirm that the United States draws its formidable military power and political influence from its superior economy. Therefore, if the American economy is derailed, then the United States will crumble and will not be able to sustain its military hegemony and presence overseas. One al-Qaida member stated that hindering Western economies is "the most dangerous and effective arena of Jihad, because we live in a materialistic world." Accordingly, al-Qaida cells are encouraged to attack targets that have a high economic value and will cause the United States severe economic losses.

The calculus of primarily attacking western targets of significant economic value is bluntly discussed in al-Qaida's political publications which aim to "educate" the Muslim world about al-Qaida's objectives and methods. These publications elaborate in sinister detail the network's intention to empower individual cell members with the training and skills required to sustain al-Qaida's global Jihad. The following excerpts from *Sawt al-Jihad* (Voice of Jihad), the official publication of al-Qaida in Saudi Arabia, illustrate the rationale behind al-Qaida's target selection:

What Else Is There to Say about September 11?

Since September 11th America has been spending billions of dollars to protect its infrastructure and interests around the world. . . . The attacker determines the timing of the strike. He will carry a concentrated strike one time at a weak point and then sit in ambush again. So the enemy will look for a gap and close it, this is not necessarily where he was hit but all other similar targets. So striking the American embassies in Kenya and Tanzania means protecting every American embassy in the world. Striking the [U.S.S.] Cole at sea means protecting all American assets in the seas. Diversifying targets means protecting all American things in every land that may have terrorists!!. . .

If the enemy used his economy to rule the world and hire

Motivated offenders also knew where to find their targets (in bars). Although the evidence on the relationships among alcohol, lifestyle, and increased risks of victimization is not conclusive, this research represents an important attempt to test the interaction of lifestyle and routine-activity theories.

A further study on the relationship of alcohol and risks of victimization focused specifically on the "suitable target" portion of routine-activity theory as it relates to sexual assault against women on college campuses.[57] It found that women who were sexually victimized went out more often and drank more when they were out than other women. Moreover, many of the women surveyed had experienced "uncomfortable advances in a bar or restaurant" or "on the street" or had "received obscene or threatening phone calls." To sum up, by successfully combining theories of crime, such as routine-activity theory, with lifestyle theory, situational factors (e.g., alcohol), and place considerations (e.g., bars and college settings) to examine victimization rates, criminological research has added a new dimension to efforts to explain crime.[58]

collaborators, then we need to strike this economy with harsh attacks to bring it down on the heads of its owners. If the enemy has built his economy on the basis of open markets and free trade by getting the monies of investors, then we have to prove to these investors that the enemy's land is not safe for them, that his economy is not capable of guarding their monies, so they would abandon him to suffer alone the fall of his economy. . . .

This is about Jihad against the crusader enemy, so what about the September 11th operation? Hijacking planes is a well known tactic, which was used by various fighters and freedom fighters, so what's new about this operation? People used to hijack planes and consider them a target, but those who are willing to put in the extra effort turned these planes into a method only, a projectile shot in the heart of the enemy. . . . The enemy used to protect his external interests and spend exuberant sums for this protection, so he was surprised when he was struck inside his borders. The enemy used to protect a thousand interests outside his country, now he has to protect a million interests inside his country that need continuing protection!! The attack on the Trade Center forced America since that day to spend billions to protect the huge economic infrastructure that runs the American economy. Using planes in this attack has forced America to spend billions to protect the planes and airports in all possible ways. This protection is not limited to the hundreds of American airports but also to every airport in the world. Anyone related to the aviation field is spending excessive amounts to guard air travel; the matter has reached protecting the skies. . . . This is how America was transformed after one strike, protecting all that can be struck, and they guard all that can be used to strike with!

Source

Sammy Salama and David Wheeler, "From the Horse's Mouth: Unraveling Al-Qaida's Target Selection Calculus." Reprinted by permission of James Martin Center for Nonproliferation Studies, Monterey Institute of International Studies.

Question for Discussion

1. If you were asked to report to the Joint Counter-Terrorism Task Force of the FBI on the likely locations of the next Al-Qaida terrorist attack, what would they be? In addition to your intuitions, and this essay on target selection, you have some excellent theoretical tools at your disposal, including the following material found in Chapter 9:

   - Situational theories of crime Environmental criminology Rational-choice perspectives Routine-activity approaches

- Theories of victimization Lifestyle theories Victim-offender interactions Repeat victimization Hot spots of crime Geography of crime
- Situational crime prevention CPTED (crime prevention through environmental design) Techniques of situational prevention

The targets that the FBI has asked you to consider include:

- Post offices and business mailrooms
- Large stadiums and concert auditoriums in municipal areas
- Shopping malls (of particular concern: the Mall of America in Minneapolis)
- Entertainment parks (of particular concern: Disneyland and Disney World)
- Nuclear power plants
- Chemical plants (approximately 15,000) and pipelines carrying hazardous liquids and natural gas (spread across approximately 490,000 miles)
- Airports (9 million commercial flights each year in the United States, carrying 600 million people)
- Skyscrapers
- Mass transit systems
- Computer networks
- Food supplies
- Water supplies

PREVENTING CRIMES AGAINST PLACES, PEOPLE, AND VALUABLE GOODS

Situational crime prevention seeks to protect places, people, and valuable goods from victimization. It is rooted in the 1971 work of C. Ray Jeffery's "crime prevention through environmental design" (CPTED)[59] and in Oscar Newman's concept of defensible space.[60] CPTED posits that environments can be altered, often at little expense, to decrease victimization. "Defensible space" refers to improved architectural designs, particularly of public housing, in order to provide increased security. Design can enhance surveillance, reduce offenders' escape possibilities, and give residents a feeling of ownership that encourages them to protect their own space.[61] CPTED and defensible space have converged with the rational-choice and routine-activity approaches to form a new approach called "situational crime prevention."

Maximum-Security Schools?

The 2005 Indicators of School Crime and Safety report places the problem of school violence in some perspective:

In the 2002–03 school year, an estimated 54.2 million students in prekindergarten through grade 12 were enrolled in about 125,000 U.S. elementary or secondary schools. Preliminary data on fatal victimizations show youth ages 5–19 were victims of 22 school-associated violent deaths from July 1, 2001, through June 30, 2002 (17 homicides and 5 suicides) (*Indicator 1*). In 2003, students ages 12–18 were victims of about 1.9 million nonfatal crimes at school, including about 1.2 million thefts and 740,000 violent crimes (simple assault and serious violent crime)—150,000 of which were serious violent crimes (rape, sexual assault, robbery, and aggravated assault) (*Indicator 2*). These figures represent victimization rates of 45 thefts and 28 violent crimes, including 6 serious violent crimes, per 1,000 students at school in 2003. Students were more likely to be victims of serious violence or a homicide away from school. In 2003, students ages 12–18 reported being victims of serious violence at a rate of 12 crimes per 1,000 students away from school and 6 crimes per 1,000 students at school. Similarly, in each school year from July 1, 1992, through June 30, 2002, youth ages 5–19 were over 70 times more likely to be murdered away from school than at school.

For several measures, data show trends in student victimization decreasing over the last decade. The nonfatal victimization rate for students ages 12–18 at school generally declined between 1992 and 2003; this was true for the total crime rate and for thefts, violent crimes, and serious violent crimes (*Indicator 2*). However, when looking at the most recent years, no differences were detected between 2002 and 2003 in the rates of total victimization, violent victimization, or theft at school. For fatal victimization, between July 1, 1992, and June 30, 2002, the number of homicides of school-age youth at school declined as well (*Indicator 1*).

Specifically, between the 1998–99 and 1999–2000 school years, the number of homicides of school-age youth at school declined from 33 to 14 homicides. Since then, there have been between 12 and 17 homicides in each school year through 2001–02.(1)

Although you would not know it, given all the media coverage surrounding school-shooting incidents, as well

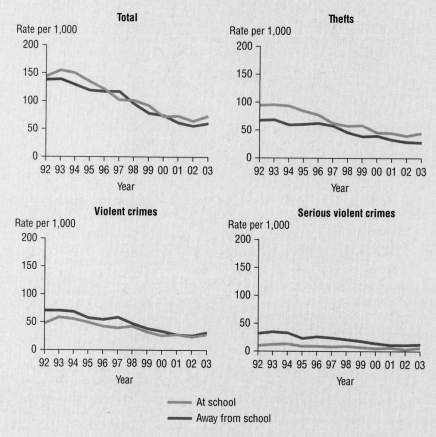

Rate of student-reported nonfatal crimes against students ages 12–18 per 1,000 students, by type of crime and location: 1992–2003.

Note: Serious violent crimes include rape, sexual assault, robbery, and aggravated assault. Violent crimes include serious violent crimes and simple assault. Total crimes include violent crimes and theft. "At school" includes inside the school building, on school property, or on the way to or from school.

Source: U.S. Department of Justice, Bureau of Justice Statistics, *National Crime Victimization Survey (NCVS)*, 1992–2003.

In some inner-city schools, security measures rival those used in prison: metal detectors, drug-sniffing dogs, frequent searches for weapons, and surveillance cameras that monitor the movement of students in and out of classrooms.

as experts' premonitions of doom and gloom, we are actually in the midst of a decline in violent crime in American schools.

Target hardening and situational crime prevention in schools are taken quite seriously. Schools in certain parts of some cities have had metal detectors, doors with alarms, and locker searches for years. Then there are the other schools in towns few have heard of: places like Paducah, Conyers, and Littleton. The image of these suburban schools as safe havens has been shattered. Although the likelihood of a shooting in any particular school is small, officials are not taking any chances. Interestingly, the prevention measures listed below fall squarely into Clarke and Homel's situational-crime-prevention model (see Table 9.4).

Access control

- Intercom systems are being used at locked doors to buzz in visitors.(2)

- Students have to flash or swipe computerized identification cards to get into school buildings.
- Perimeter fences delineate school property and secure cars after hours.

Controlling facilitators

- Students in Deltona, Florida, get an extra set of books to leave at home. The schools have banned backpacks and dismantled lockers to eliminate places to stash weapons. Other school districts are encouraging see-through lockers and backpacks.
- After the Littleton, Colorado, incident, school boards across the country banned trench coats and other oversize garments, apparently to prevent students from hiding weapons on their bodies or in their clothing.

Entry/exit screening

- Handheld and walk-through metal detectors keep anyone with a weapon from entering schools.

Formal surveillance

- Uniformed police officers and private security guards, some of them armed, patrol school halls.
- Schools are installing surveillance cameras in hallways and on school buses.

Surveillance by employees (or, in this case, students)

- Students are carrying small notebooks so that they can log and then report overheard threats.

Identifying property

- Tiny microfilm is hidden inside expensive school property so that it can be identified if stolen.

On the face of it, these measures seem to make good sense. They can prevent people from bringing weapons into schools and keep unauthorized people out. They increase the ability of school officials to detect crime, identify evildoers, and prevent criminal incidents from happening. But have school officials and others gone too far? Diana

Philip is the director of the American Civil Liberties Union of Texas for the northern region, which has filed several lawsuits against schools. She observes that "over the summer, we have had school boards putting together the most restrictive policies we have ever seen. A lot of them are in clear violation of the Fourth Amendment, which guarantees freedom from unreasonable searches."(3)

Chicago Tribune columnist Steve Chapman argues that schools treat students as "dangerous, incorrigible, undeserving of respect" or privacy. He asks, "What's the difference between school and prison? At school, you don't get cable TV."(4)

Sources

1. J. F. DeVoe, K. Peter, M. Noonan, T. D. Snyder, and K. Baum, *Indicators of School Crime and Safety: 2005* (Washington, D.C.: Department of Justice, 2005).
2. Jacques Steinberg, "Barricading the School Door," *New York Times*, Aug. 22, 1999, New York section, p. 5.
3. S. C. Gwynne, "Is Anyplace Safe?" *Time*, Aug. 23, 1999.
4. Walter Olson, "Dial 'O' for Outrage: The Sequel—Tales from an Overlawyered America," *Reason*, Nov. 1999, pp. 54–56.

Questions for Discussion

1. Do you think there would be as much concern over school violence if these shooting incidents had happened in urban schools? Why are people more upset when crime happens in places they perceive to be safe (such as in the suburbs)?
2. Does your high school or college campus have any security measures in place? If so, how do they fit into Clarke and Homel's 16 techniques of situational prevention?
3. Is there a point at which security measures in schools become so extreme that they can no longer be justified? Have we reached that point yet?

TABLE 9.4 Sixteen Techniques of Situational Crime Prevention

Increasing Perceived Effort	Increasing Perceived Risks	Reducing Anticipated Rewards	Inducing Guilt or Shame
1. *Target hardening:* Slug-rejector device Steering locks Bandit screens	5. *Entry/exit screening:* Automatic ticket gates Baggage screening Merchandise tags	9. *Target removal:* Removable car radio Women's refuges Phone card	13. *Rule setting:* Harassment codes Customs declaration Hotel registrations
2. *Access control:* Parking lot barriers Fenced yards Entry phones	6. *Formal surveillance:* Burglar alarms Speed cameras Security guards	10. *Identifying property:* Property marking Vehicle licensing Cattle branding	14. *Strengthening moral condemnation:* "Shoplifting is stealing" Roadside speedometers "Bloody idiots drink and drive"
3. *Deflecting offenders:* Bus stop placement Tavern location Street closures	7. *Surveillance by employees:* Pay phone location Park attendants CCTV systems	11. *Reducing temptation:* Gender-neutral phone lists Off-street parking	15. *Controlling disinhibitors:* Drinking-age laws Ignition interlock Server intervention
4. *Controlling facilitators:* Credit card photo Caller ID Gun controls	8. *Natural surveillance:* Defensible space Street lighting Cab driver ID	12. *Denying benefits:* Ink merchandise tags PIN for car radios Graffiti cleaning	16. *Facilitating compliance:* Improved library checkout Public lavatories Trash bins

SOURCE: Reprinted from Ronald V. Clarke and Ross Homel, "A Revised Classification of Situational Crime Prevention Techniques," in Steven P. Lab, ed., *Crime Prevention at a Crossroads*, p.24, with permission. Copyright 1997 Matthew Bender & Company, Inc., a member of the LexisNexis Group. All rights reserved.

Crime Surfing

http://www.ncjrs.gov/works/wholedoc.htm

John Eck, contributing to *Crime Prevention: What Works, What Doesn't, What's Promising*, compiled an extremely comprehensive literature review of research into the effectiveness of situational-crime-prevention strategies.

Situational Crime Prevention

Rational-choice theory provides the foundation for designing situational-crime-prevention techniques and their classification (Table 9.4). Situational crime prevention consists of the knowledge of how, where, and when to implement a specific measure that will alter a particular situation in order to prevent a crime from occurring. The routine-activity approach also aims at situational crime prevention by reducing the opportunities for likely offenders to commit crimes. Techniques include protecting suitable targets (making them less suitable) and increasing the presence of capable guardians. Measures such as steering-column locks, vandal-resistant construction, enhanced street lighting, and improved library checkout systems demonstrably decrease opportunities for crime. These are **target-hardening** techniques.

Rational-choice theorists have reviewed their situational-crime-prevention techniques and have added aspects of the offender's *perception* of a crime opportunity (Table 9.5) to the catalog of relevant factors, along with the element of guilt or shame.[62] The addition of the category of "perception" of opportunity was self-evident. After all, offenders act only in accordance with what they perceive. The addition of a category called "inducing guilt or shame," on the other hand, is a significant expansion of rational choice.[63] Techniques that induce guilt or shame include the installation of signs saying "shoplifting is stealing" or other measures calculated to prevent common crimes by increasing the personal and social cost in terms of shaming—especially after being caught in the act. For instance, if a high school student is leaving the school library with friends and the library checkout system detects a copy of *Rolling Stone* in his book bag (a magazine that is not allowed to leave the library), two things are expected to happen. First, the librarian will make the student surrender the magazine. Second, the student may be so embarrassed by having the librarian search his book bag while his friends stand by that he will not try to steal anything from the library again.

There are a number of successful examples of situational crime prevention. For example, situational-crime-prevention techniques have been successfully implemented to prevent crime at Disney World, to stop auto theft, to deter robberies at convenience stores, and to lessen crime in parking facilities.

The Phantom Crime Prevention at Disney World

Disney World, home of Donald Duck, Mickey and Minnie Mouse, Goofy, and their friends, provides us with an example of environmental/situational crime prevention. Illegal behavior is successfully controlled, yet in an environment that does not have the sterile, fortresslike appearance

TABLE 9.5 Ten Factors Considered by Commercial Burglars in Suburban Philadelphia

1. *Revenues generated by burglary:*
   Is there a high "payoff"?

2. *Chances of being caught:*
   Can I get away with it?

3. *Location of target:*
   Is the target near a major road or thoroughfare?
   Commercial burglars like remote targets.

4. *Corner lot:*
   Is the target at the corner?
   Corner properties are easier to get into and out of.

5. *Shopping mall:*
   Is the target in a mall?
   Malls and large retail stores are ideal targets.

6. *Concentration of businesses:*
   Are there other businesses around?
   The more commercial establishments around, the greater the likelihood of burglary.

7. *Burglar alarm:*
   Is there a visible alarm or alarm sign?

8. *Exterior lighting:*
   How dark is the area around the target?

9. *Length of time the establishment has been in business:*
   Is this a new store?
   New commercial establishments are prime targets.

10. *Retail store:*
    Is the target retail?
    Retail is preferred over wholesale.

SOURCE: Simon Hakim and Yochanan Shachmurove, "Spatial and Temporal Patterns of Commercial Burglaries: The Evidence Examined," *American Journal of Economics and Sociology*, **55,** (1996): 443–456.

■ *Even Goofy is part of the Disney crime prevention and control strategy, making Disneyland and Disney World two of the safest locations in the United States.*

Pakistan is World Leader in Stolen Cars

Islamabad: On an average, cars worth Rs 1 billion are stolen every month in Pakistan, said a report of the country's Interior Ministry, adding that cars worth Rs 18 billion were stolen in the past 18 months.

According to the report, 14,037 vehicles worth Rs 7 billion were stolen or snatched across the country during the first half of 2008, compared to 23,144 during 2007.

Thefts of vehicles are on the rise in the neigbouring country with clear indications that police and the vehicle registration offices are part of the mafia, reported The News.

A professional car lifter on condition of anonymity said that bigwigs in the police and the bureaucracy, besides top politicians, are directly involved in the lucrative business.

"I enjoy my job. I earn hundreds of thousands for a 3- to 4-minute effort. I can lift at least three vehicles in a day," the daring car lifter said.

He further said, "Toyota Corolla, Honda, Suzuki Mehran, Alto are the favourite vehicles to steal but we follow the demand of the receivers. Motorway is the safest way to take the stolen vehicles to Peshawar and Mardan."

According to him, Peshawar, Hazara and Mardan Divisions are havens for carjackers.

The mafia chiefs involved in this particular crime are known to the police, and so are their dens, mostly in the NWFP [North-West Frontier Province], but no one dares to take them to justice, added the paper.

According to the report, Punjab had the highest number of vehicle lifting incidents, as 7,432 vehicles were taken away in the first half of 2008.

A 49.07 percent increase of the crime was seen in Islamabad Capital Territory (ICT) as 401 vehicles were lifted during first two quarters of 2008 as compared to 269 during the same period in 2007.

Questions for Discussion

1. What, if anything, can Pakistan do to slow the rate of auto thefts?
2. How do the environmental conditions in Pakistan contribute to the auto theft problem in that country? How do these conditions differ from those in the United States?

SOURCE: ANI, "Pakistan is World Leader in Stolen Cars," *Mumbai Mirror*, August 19, 2008. Retrieved from http://www.mumbai mirror.com/index.aspx?Page=article&sect name=News%20-%20World&sectid=4&cont entid=20080819200808190020854153512d75c7, Dec. 28, 2008.

---

so often associated with security. How has this been accomplished?[64]

The intricate web of security and crowd control (not visible to the untrained eye) starts at the parking lot with advice to lock your car and remember that you have parked at a particular lot, for example, "Donald Duck 1." With friendly greetings of "have a good time," watchful eyes surround visitors on the rubber-wheeled train into never-never land. Crowd control is omnipresent yet unobtrusive. Signs guide you through the maze of monorails, rides, and attractions. Physical barriers prevent injury and regulate the movement of adults and children alike. Mickey Mouse and Goofy monitor movements. Flower gardens, pools, and fountains are pretty to look at; they also direct people toward particular locations. Yet with all these built-in control strategies, few visitors realize the extent to which their choices of movement and action are limited.

Situational Prevention: Auto Theft

Information provided by the National Insurance Crime Bureau indicates the most-targeted vehicles for theft throughout the nation (Tables 9.6 and 9.7). Situational-crime-prevention practitioners are trained to analyze the vehicles and the specific situational factors that lead to their being targeted for theft. They then devise measures to block the opportunities that give rise to the theft of these particular vehicles—for example, side window panels that are particularly vulnerable, or key codes in the gas tank compartment (the thief simply writes down the key code and gets a replacement of the "lost" car key).[65]

Devising situational prevention measures, however, is usually not as easy as suggesting to a car manufacturer that the key code be placed in a more secure place. It is important that a researcher also analyze the type of offenders who steal cars (Table 9.8).

Convenience Stores

One of the most successful crime-prevention studies was the Tallahassee Convenience Store Study. In fact, it launched the concept of crime prevention through environmental design. It had long been known that convenience stores, like the 7-Eleven shops, were prime robbery targets. Researchers studied the vulnerability of these stores in great detail, assessing risks as well as losses, in terms of lives and property. The researchers

TABLE 9.6 NICB's Top 10 Most Stolen Autos in 2006

1. 1995 Honda Civic
2. 1991 Honda Accord
3. 1989 Toyota Camry
4. 1997 Ford F150 Series
5. 2005 Dodge Ram P/UP
6. 1994 Chevy 1500 P/UP
7. 1994 Nissan Sentra
8. 1994 Dodge Caravan
9. 1994 Saturn SL
10. 1990 Acura Integra

SOURCE: National Insurance Crime Bureau, "Hot Wheels: Vehicle Theft Continuing to Decline; available at www.NICB.org.

TABLE 9.7 Top 10 Auto-Theft Cities in 2007

1. Modesto, California
2. Las Vegas, Nevada
3. San Diego/Carlsbad/San Marcos, California
4. Stockton, California
5. San Francisco/Oakland/Fremont, California
6. Laredo, Texas
7. Albuquerque, New Mexico
8. Phoenix/Mesa/Scottsdale, Arizona
9. Yakima, Washington
10. Tuscon, Arizona

Note: Ranked by the rate of vehicle thefts reported per 100,000 people based on the 2007 U.S. Census Population Estimates.

SOURCE: National Insurance Crime Bureau, "Where Does Your City Rank?" available at www.NICB.org.

recommended that stores have two or more clerks on duty, post "limited cash" signs, increase exterior lighting, and restrict escape routes and potential hiding places for robbers. The study led to the passage of the Florida Convenience Store Security Act (1990), which made certain security measures mandatory.[66] Convenience-store robberies in Florida have since dropped by two-thirds.

Parking Facilities[67]

Parking garages are said to be dangerous places: Individuals are alone in a large space, there are many hiding places, the amount of valuable property (cars and their contents) is high, they are open to the public, an offender's car can go unnoticed, and lighting is usually poor. Yet statistics indicate that because of the small amount of time and the relatively limited number of trips that each person takes to and from parking facilities, an individual's chances of being raped, robbed, or assaulted in a parking facility are very low. Nevertheless, the fear of victimization in these facilities is high. Efforts to improve conditions include better lighting, stairways and elevators that are open to the air or glass-enclosed, ticket-booth personnel monitoring drivers exiting and entering, color-coded signs designating parking areas, elimination or redesign of public restrooms, panic buttons and emergency phones, closed-circuit television, and uniformed security personnel.

Situational Crime Prevention—Pros and Cons

Despite the increasing popularity of situational crime prevention (SCP), the perspective has been the target of criticism by more traditional-minded criminologists. The debate on the merits of SCP techniques centers on a number of issues, including the following:

1. *SCP excludes "undesirables" from public places:*[68] For example, excluding would-be offenders from a mall by limiting shopping hours makes it more difficult for them to buy needed material goods.[69]

Response: The exclusion of "troublemakers" from public and semipublic places falls under order-maintenance duties of police officers, so it is not considered SCP.[70] "Deflecting offenders," which is one SCP technique identified by theorists, does have some exclusionary potential, but it is not meant to exclude undesirables; rather, the aim is to keep likely offenders away from suitable targets.

2. *SCP will only displace crime to new locations and times:* It may also lead to the escalation of crime to a more serious level, and the benefits of SCP are skewed toward more-advantaged classes who can afford security measures.[71]

Response: Behavior is influenced by situational factors, so there is no reason to assume that blocked crime at one location will lead to the commission of crime in a different situation. There will be different factors at play. Evidence also suggests that displacement is not as prevalent as critics claim, and the idea of escalation is inconsistent with many types of crime. For example, it is unlikely that reduced opportunities for shoplifting would lead offenders to start stealing shopping baskets from other customers.[72]

TABLE 9.8 Typologies of Frequent Auto Theft Offenders

ACTING-OUT JOYRIDER

- Most emotionally disturbed of the offenders—derives status from having his peers think he is crazy and unpredictable.

- Engages in outrageous driving stunts—dangerous to pursue—possesses a kamikaze attitude.

- Vents anger via car—responsible for large proportion of the totaled and burned cars.

- Least likely to be deterred—doesn't care what happens.

THRILL-SEEKER

- Heavily into drugs—doing crime is a way to finance the habit—entices others to feel the "rush" of doing crime.

- Engages in car stunts and willful damage to cars, but also steals them for transportation and to use in other crimes.

- Steals parts for sale in a loosely structured friendship network.

- Thrill-seeking behavior likely to be transferred to other activities and might be directed to legitimate outlets.

INSTRUMENTAL OFFENDER

- Doing auto theft for the money—most active of the offenders (five or more cars a week) but the smallest proportion of the sample—connected to organized theft operations.

- Rational, intelligent—does crimes with least risk—may get into auto theft from burglary—thinks about outcomes.

- Doing crime while young offender status affords them lenient treatment—indicate that they will quit crime at age 18.

SOURCE: Zachary Fleming, Patricia Brantingham, and Paul Brantingham, "Exploring Auto Theft in British Columbia," in *Crime Prevention Studies*, vol. 3, ed. Ronald V. Clarke (Monsey, N.Y.: Criminal Justice Press, 1994), p. 62. Reprinted by permission of the publisher.

3. *SCP inconveniences law-abiding citizens and infringes on their freedom:*[73] Crime-prevention efforts should focus on offenders—the burden should not be placed on law-abiding citizens.[74]

Response: Many SCP measures are unobtrusive, and human beings generally accept the need for implementing security measures in their own lives.[75]

4. *SCP treats the symptoms of the crime problem rather than the causes:*[76] Crime prevention should focus on the root causes of crime—unemployment, racial discrimination, and inadequate schooling, among others. Along the same lines, it is questionable whether the end (lower crime) justifies the means.[77] SCP is not necessarily the most appropriate way to deal with crime just because it is more efficient than other methods; it may not be if it prevents crime for the wrong reasons. For example, one way to reduce crime is by excluding everyone under the age of 21 from shopping malls because they are at highest risk for shoplifting. This measure reduces crime, but the means are questionable because they exclude these individuals from being able to shop freely.

Response: SCP avoids stigmatizing certain groups of individuals as likely criminals because it acknowledges that everyone is vulnerable to temptation.[78] Also, people change in response to their experiences, so SCP has the potential to minimize or promote particular social practices.[79]

Despite the criticism, Felson and Clarke argue that situational crime prevention meets the three goals of crime control required by democratic standards—to provide crime prevention equally to all social groups, to respect individual rights, and to share responsibility for crime prevention with all parts of society—better than other crime policies.[80]

Displacement

One important question concerning crime-prevention measures remains. What will happen, for example, if these measures do prevent a particular crime from being committed? Will the would-be offender simply look for another target? Crime-prevention strategists have demonstrated that **displacement**—the commission of a quantitatively similar crime at a different time or place—does not always follow. German motorcycle helmet legislation demonstrates the point. As a result of a large number of accidents, legislation that required motorcyclists to wear helmets was passed and strictly enforced. It worked: Head injuries decreased. But there were additional, unforeseen consequences. Motorcycle theft rates

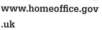
Crime Surfing

www.homeoffice.gov.uk

This crime-prevention guide by the Home Office in Britain includes details about how one can avoid becoming a crime victim. The Home Office and its staff conduct extensive research on the effectiveness of situational-crime-prevention strategies.

decreased dramatically. The risks of stealing a motorcycle became too high because a would-be offender could not drive it away without wearing a helmet. At this point, researchers expected to see a rise in the number of cars or bikes stolen. They did not. In other words, there was very little displacement. Studies of hot-spots policing provide mixed evidence of displacement.[81] The research reveals a wide variety of types. Marcus Felson and Ronald Clarke propose five different forms:

1. Crime can be moved from one location to another (geographical displacement).

2. Crime can be moved from one time to another (temporal displacement).

3. Crime can be directed away from one target to another (target displacement).

4. One method of committing crime can be substituted for another (tactical displacement).

5. One kind of crime can be substituted for another (crime type displacement).[82]

Rarely noted but worthy of consideration is the fact that displacement can have positive as well as negative effects. These effects can take several forms:

- *Positive.* A crime is displaced to a less serious type of crime or a crime with greater risk, with lower rewards or less serious damage. It represents a success because it produces a net gain.

- *Neutral.* A crime is displaced to one of the same seriousness, the same risk, and the same rewards and damage.

- *Even-handed.* Prevention is concentrated on those who are repeatedly victimized in order to achieve a more equitable distribution of crime.

- *Negative.* A crime is displaced to a more serious crime, a crime with greater reward, or a crime with greater social cost.

- *Attractive.* Activities and/or places attract crime from other areas or activities (e.g., "red light" districts attract customers, as well as other criminal activities, from other areas).[83]

THEORY INFORMS POLICY

The study of targets and victims is crucial to preventing crime. Understanding how offenders make decisions helps policy makers allocate resources efficiently. For example, if it is possible to significantly reduce convenience-store robbery

THE FAR SIDE® By GARY LARSON

Inconvenience stores

by relatively simple measures, isn't it better to spend time and money doing those things rather than trying to prevent crime by focusing exclusively on troubled people (who may or may not rob convenience stores anyway)? If we know that repeat victimization can be prevented by intervening with high-risk people and properties, isn't that the most cost-beneficial way to proceed?

We usually think of crime policy as being made by governments, for only they can control the police, courts, and corrections. Decisions about crime prevention, on the other hand, can be made by small communities, neighborhoods, schools, businesses, and individuals. We discussed how simple precautions lower the risk of convenience-store robbery. This knowledge not only encouraged governments to pass certain laws mandating that stores take those precautions, but led many in private industry to adopt the measures as well. Knowledge about crime prevention is especially valuable to all people because everyone can use these tools to reduce the chances of being a victim. Having discussed the application of theories of crime to conventional crime, we are left with the question of whether these theories are also applicable to unconventional crimes, such as terrorism.

CHAPTER 9

REVIEW

This chapter focuses on situational theories of crime. These theories, which assume that there are always people motivated to commit crime, try to explain why crimes are being committed by a particular offender against a particular target. They analyze opportunities and environmental factors that prompt a potential perpetrator to act.

We discussed the three most prominent situational approaches to crime: environmental criminology, the rational-choice perspective, and the routine-activity approach. We noted that they have merged somewhat, particularly insofar as all these approaches aim at preventing victimization by altering external conditions that are conducive to crime.

Theories of victimization view crime as the dynamic interaction of perpetrators and victims (at a given time and place). Here, too, the aim is to find ways for potential victims to protect themselves. Research into lifestyles, victim-offender interaction, repeat victimization, hot spots, and geography of crime has vast implications for crime control in entire cities or regions. Situational theories of crime and theories of victimization are interrelated. Most of the theories and perspectives in this chapter can be used to explain and possibly predict the decision making of criminal organizations, including terrorist organizations.

CRIMINOLOGY & PUBLIC POLICY

The kind of terrorism we are talking about is different in many respects from other crimes such as murder, rape, and robbery. The difference is that terrorism is generally more calculated, more premeditated, and more goal-oriented than impulsive crimes or crimes of passion. Criminal justice expert Philip Heymann has observed:

> As a crime, terrorism is different. Most crimes are the product of greed, anger, jealousy, or the desire for domination, respect, or position in a group, and not of any desire to "improve" the state of the world or of a particular nation. Most crimes do not involve—as part of the plan for accomplishing their objectives—trying to change the occupants of government positions, their actions, or the basic structures and ideology of a nation. Some would argue that violence carried out for political purpose is more altruistic; others would vigorously deny that. But all would agree that political violence is different from ordinary crime, in that it is planned to force changes in government actions, people, structure, or even ideology as a means to whatever ends the perpetrators are seeking with whatever motivations drive them towards those ends. It is in that sense that the U.S. State Department definition says that the violence is usually "perpetrated for political reasons."

Terrorism—at least of the kind described by Heymann—is thus more, not less, subject to disincentive and deterrence techniques than most ordinary crimes. To be sure, some acts of terrorism are revenge-driven and impulsive, but most are carefully calculated to achieve a goal. Sometimes the goal will be specific and immediate, while other times it may be more general, long term, and apocalyptic. But whatever the object, if it becomes clear that it will be disserved by terrorism—that the cause will be worse off—then it will be only a matter of time until co-supporters of the cause turn against those who resort to terrorism. Without widespread support from within the cause they are seeking to promote, terrorists cannot long thrive. Certainly if there is widespread opposition to terrorism within the cause, it will soon dry up. (SOURCE: Alan M. Dershowitz, *Why Terrorism Works* ([New Haven, CT: Yale University Press, 2002].)

Questions for Discussion What do rational-choice theorists have to contribute to the ongoing "war" against terrorism? Is terrorism rational? In what ways? What counterterrorist strategies can you think of that would be effective against terrorism committed against targets in the United States?

YOU BE THE CRIMINOLOGIST

Imagine that you are a security consultant working for a major department store chain. Recently, one of the stores, located in the downtown area of a large city, has experienced very high levels of shoplifting and employee theft. You must design a comprehensive program to protect merchandise from theft by customers and by people who work at the store. First, identify some of the store's most vulnerable areas (it may help to visit a local department store to observe how it operates). Then, using the 16 techniques of situational crime prevention as a model, prepare a list of prevention strategies.

KEY TERMS

The numbers next to the terms refer to the pages on which the terms are defined.

displacement (214)

environmental criminology (196)

rational choice (197)

routine activity (198)

target hardening (210)

theories of victimization (201)

PART 3

Types of Crimes

The word "crime" conjures up many images: mugging and murder, cheating on taxes, and selling crack. Penal codes define thousands of different crimes. These crimes are grouped into convenient and comprehensive categories for access and understanding.

In this part, we examine the specific categories of crimes. Violent crimes (Chapter 10) are crimes against the person, ranging from assault to homicide. Many of these crimes have been well established for centuries, although modern codes have transformed them, however slightly. Most of the crimes against property (Chapter 11) have also been well defined over the centuries. Yet recent developments in commerce and technology have prompted legislatures to define new forms of crimes against property. With a spate of corporate scandals, reports of white-collar and corporate crime (Chapter 12) fill the pages of newspapers and news magazines. In this chapter, we discuss how white-collar crime and corporate crime are defined and measured. The corporate criminal law is described in some detail, with a focus on corporate liability and corporate sanctions. In the next chapter (Chapter 13), we address the controversial types of crimes related to drug and alcohol trafficking and consumption, as well as those violating the sexual mores of the establishment. Finally, the occurrence of these various types of crime is discussed in comparison with their occurrence elsewhere in the world (Chapter 14). This chapter is concerned with comparative criminology and, inevitably, the emergence of transnational and international criminality.

Violent Crimes

10

Homicide
Murder
Manslaughter
The Extent of Homicide
The Nature of Homicide
A Cross-National Comparison of Homicide
   Rates
Assault
Family-Related Crimes
Spouse Abuse
Child Abuse
Abuse of the Elderly
Rape and Sexual Assault
Characteristics of the Rape Event
Who Are the Rapists?
Rape and the Legal System
Community Response
Kidnapping
Robbery
Characteristics of Robbers
The Consequences of Robbery
Organized Crime
The History of Organized Crime
The Structure and Impact of Organized Crime
The New Ethnic Diversity in Organized Crime
Emerging Problems
Terrorism
Hate Crimes
Militias
Violence in Schools
Violence and Gun Control
The Extent of Firearm-Related Offenses
Youths and Guns
Controlling Handgun Use
The Gun-Control Debate
Review
Criminology & Public Policy
You Be the Criminologist
Key Terms

■ *Mark of violence: one of the first shots in a sniper spree that numbed the Washington, D.C., area in October 2002.*

To millions of Americans, few things are more pervasive, more frightening, more real today than violent crime and the fear of being assaulted, mugged, robbed, or raped. The fear of being victimized by criminal attack has touched us all in some way. People are fleeing their residences in cities to the expected safety of suburban living. Residents of many areas will not go out on the street at night. Others have added bars and extra locks to windows and doors in their homes. Bus drivers in major cities do not carry cash because incidents of robbery have been so frequent. In some areas, local citizens patrol the streets at night to attain the safety they feel has not been provided. . . .

There are numerous conflicting definitions of criminal violence as a class of behavior. Police, prosecutors, jurists, federal agents, local detention officials, and behavioral scientists all hold somewhat different viewpoints as to what constitute acts of violence. All would probably agree, however—as the police reports make abundantly clear—that criminal violence involves the use of or the threat of force on a victim by an offender.[1]

The penal law defines types of violent crime, and each is distinguished by a particular set of elements. We concentrate on criminological characteristics: the frequency with which each type of violent crime is committed, the methods used in its commission, and its distribution through time and place. We also examine the people who commit the offense and those who are its victims. If we can determine when, where, and how a specific type of crime is likely to be committed, we will be in a better position to reduce the incidence of that crime by devising appropriate strategies to prevent it.

We begin with homicide, since the taking of life is the most serious harm one human being can inflict on another. Serious attacks that fall short of homicide are assaults of various kinds, including serious sexual assault (rape) and the forceful taking of property from another person (robbery). Other patterns of violence are not defined as such in the penal codes but are so important in practice as to require separate discussion. Family-related violence and terrorism, both of which encompass a variety of crimes, fall into this category.

HOMICIDE

Homicide is the killing of one human being by another. Some homicides are sanctioned by law. In this category of **justifiable homicide,** we find

Yolanda Manuel, mother of 7-year-old sexual assault and murder victim Sherrice Iverson, speaks at a rally on the U.C. Berkeley campus, 1998. The rally was staged to protest the presence on the Berkeley campus of sophomore David Cash, who watched and did nothing as a friend, Jeremy Strohmeyer, dragged Sherrice into a Las Vegas casino bathroom stall where he killed her.

homicides committed by law enforcement officers in the course of carrying out their duties, homicides committed by soldiers in combat, and homicides committed by a home owner who has no recourse other than to kill an intruder who threatens the lives of family members. Criminologists are most interested in *criminal homicides*—unlawful killings, without justification or excuse. Criminal homicides are subdivided into three separate categories: murder, manslaughter, and negligent homicide.

Murder

At common law, **murder** was defined as the intentional killing of another person with **malice aforethought.** Courts have struggled with an exact definition of "malice." To describe it, they have used terms such as "evil mind" and "abandoned and malignant heart." Actually, malice is a very simple concept. It is the defendant's awareness that he or she had no right to kill but intended to kill anyway.[2]

Originally the malice had to be "aforethought": The person had to have killed after some contemplation, rather than on the spur of the moment. The concept eventually became meaningless because

Random Murders Set Record in 2008

KYODO NEWS

2008 has seen 11 random murders and two attempted random murders up till November, passing last year's combined total of eight and hitting a record, according to a report released Thursday by the National Police Agency.

The figure is the highest since the NPA began to compile data in 1993 on so-called random crimes.

Among the 11 random slayings during the January–November period were the seven people killed in the June vehicle and stabbing rampage in the Akihabara district of Tokyo.

Police nationwide probed 1,674,773 criminal cases during the 11 months, down 4.9 percent from the same period last year, the report says.

Cases covered in the report include violations of the Penal Code, the antiviolence law and the antiorganized crime law, but not traffic violations.

Agency officials said they expect crimes for the whole of 2008, however, to stay below the 2007 level and decline for the sixth straight year. In 2007, police processed 1.9 million criminal cases.

The ratio of crimes solved to crimes probed in the 11 months dipped 0.2 percentage point from a year earlier to 32.0 percent, the report says.

The number of serious crimes—murder, robbery, arson and rape—came to 7,862, down 6.1 percent. Of the four categories, only murder rose, up 7.4 percent to 1,200 cases.

Thefts, which account for the bulk of all cases, totaled 1,262,670, down 4.1 percent.

Crimes including fraud and bribery fell 1.8 percent to 68,598, with 34,475 solved, up 9.1 percent.

Violent crimes, including infliction of injury and extortion, totaled 63,419, down 5.8 percent.

Perpetrators were arrested or rounded up without being arrested in 535,856 of all cases probed, down 5.5

percent. Those arrested or questioned came to 313,111, down 7.5 percent. Of these, people aged 19 or younger dropped 12.3 percent to 82,748.

Annual crimes set a record for seven years in a row between 1996 and 2002. In 2002, the figure reached about 2.85 million, the NPA said.

In 2007, it fell below 2 million for the first time in 10 years.

Questions for Discussion

1. Why do you think the number of murders in Japan rose in 2008 while the number of all other types of crimes fell?
2. How do murder rates in Japan compare to those in the United States? What might account for the difference?

SOURCE: Kyodo News, "Random Murders Set Record in '08," *Japan Times*, December 13, 2008. Reprinted by permission of Kyodo News.

---

some courts considered even a few seconds sufficient to establish forethought. The dividing line between planned and spur-of-the-moment killings disappeared. But many legislators believed contemplation was an appropriate concept, because it allowed us to distinguish the various types of murder. They reintroduced it, calling it "premeditation and deliberation." A premeditated, deliberate, intentional killing be-came murder in the first degree; an intentional killing without premeditation and deliberation became murder in the second degree.

States that had the death penalty reserved it for murder in the first degree. Some state statutes listed particular means of committing murder as indicative of premeditation and deliberation, such as killing by poison or by lying in wait. More recently, the charge of murder in the first degree has been reserved for the killing of a law enforcement officer or of a corrections officer and for the killing of any person by a prisoner serving a life sentence. Among the most serious forms of murder is *assassination*, the killing of a head of state or government or of an otherwise highly visible figure.

A special form of murder, **felony murder,** requires no intention to kill. It requires, instead, the intention to commit some other felony, such as robbery or rape, and the death of a person during the commission of or flight from that felony. Even accomplices are guilty of felony murder when one of their associates has caused a death. For example, while A and B are holding up a gas station attendant, A fires a warning shot, and the bullet ricochets and kills a passerby. Both A and B are guilty of felony murder. The rule originated in England centuries ago, when death sentences were imposed for all felonies, so it made no difference whether a perpetrator actually intended to kill or merely to rob. Most states today apply the felony murder rule only when the underlying felony is a life-endangering one, such as arson, rape, or robbery.

Manslaughter

Manslaughter is the unlawful killing of another person without malice. Manslaughter may be either voluntary or involuntary.

Voluntary Manslaughter

Voluntary manslaughter is a killing committed intentionally but without malice—for example, in the heat of passion or in response to strong provocation. Persons who kill under extreme provocation cannot make rational decisions about whether they have a right to kill. They therefore act without the necessary malice.[3]

Just as passion, fright, fear, or consternation may affect a person's capacity to act rationally, so may drugs or alcohol. In some states, a charge of murder may be reduced to voluntary manslaughter when the defendant was so grossly intoxicated as not to be fully aware of the implications of his or her actions. All voluntary-manslaughter cases have one thing in common: The defendant's awareness of the unlawfulness of the act was dulled or grossly reduced by shock, fright, consternation, or intoxication.

Involuntary Manslaughter

A crime is designated as **involuntary manslaughter** when a person has caused the death of another unintentionally but recklessly by consciously disregarding a substantial and unjustifiable risk that endangered another person's life. Many states have created an additional category, **negligent homicide,** to establish criminal liability for grossly negligent killing in situations where the offender assumed a lesser risk.

Manslaughter plays an increasingly prominent role in our society, with its high concentrations of population, high-tech risks, and chemical and even nuclear dangers. The reach of the crime of involuntary manslaughter was clearly demonstrated in the 1942 Coconut Grove disaster in Boston, in which 491 people perished because of a nightclub owner's negligence in creating fire hazards. The nightclub was overcrowded, it was furnished and decorated with highly flammable materials, and exits were blocked. The court ruled that a reasonable person would have recognized the risk. If the defendant is so "stupid" as not to have recognized the risk, he is nevertheless guilty of manslaughter.[4]

The Extent of Homicide

Social scientists who look at homicide have a different perspective from that of the legislators who define such crimes. Social scientists are concerned with rates and patterns of criminal activities. (For a rank ordering of violent crime rates, see Table 10.1.)

Homicide Rates in the United States Today

The American murder rate has always been high. It reached a peak in 1980 and has been declining erratically since then. In 2007, our population experienced 16,929 murders and nonnegligent

TABLE 10.1 Where Does Your State Rank According to Rates of Violent Crime (per 100,000 population)?

*1999 Violent Crime**

Rank	State	Rate
United States, total		524.7
1	District of Columbia	1,627.7
2	Florida	854.0
3	South Carolina	847.1
4	New Mexico	834.5
5	Maryland	743.4
6	Delaware	734.0
7	Louisiana	732.7
8	Illinois	732.5
9	Tennessee	694.9
10	Alaska	631.5
11	California	627.2
12	New York	588.8
13	Michigan	574.9
14	Nevada	570.0
15	Texas	560.3
16	Arizona	551.2
17	Massachusetts	551.0
18	North Carolina	542.1
19	Georgia	534.0
20	Oklahoma	508.2
21	Missouri	500.2
22	Alabama	490.2
23	Nebraska	430.2
24	Arkansas	425.2
25	Pennsylvania	420.5
26	New Jersey	411.9
27	Kansas	382.8
28	Washington	377.3
29	Oregon	374.9
30	Indiana	374.6
31	West Virginia	350.6
32	Mississippi	349.3
33	Connecticut	345.6
34	Colorado	340.5
35	Ohio	316.4
36	Virginia	314.7
37	Kentucky	300.6
38	Rhode Island	286.6
39	Iowa	280.0
40	Utah	275.5
41	Minnesota	274.0
42	Wisconsin	245.9
43	Idaho	244.9
44	Hawaii	235.0
45	Wyoming	232.3
46	Montana	206.5
47	South Dakota	167.4
48	Vermont	113.8
49	Maine	112.2
50	New Hampshire	96.5
51	North Dakota	66.9

*Note: Violent crime is defined as murder and nonnegligent manslaughter, robbery, aggravated assault, and forcible rape.

SOURCE: Adapted from *Sourcebook of Criminal Justice Statistics, 2000* (Albany, N.Y.: State University of New York at Albany, 2000), p. 290.

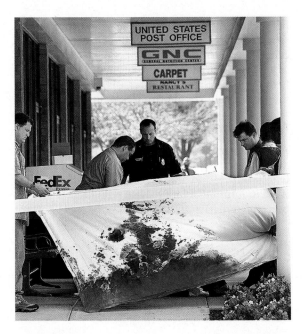

Yet another victim of the infamous Washington, D.C., area snipers. This scene of the 2002 murder rampage is the Silver Spring post office, located next to the Leisure World retirement community.

homicides (as reported to the police), or 5.6 per 100,000 population.[5] This is the second lowest the murder rate has been since 1967, when the murder rate was 7 murders per 100,000 population. This rate is not equally distributed over the whole country: Murder rates are higher in the southern and western states (7.0 and 5.3 per 100,000, respectively) than in the northeastern and midwestern states (4.1 and 4.9 per 100,000, respectively).[6]

Your chance of becoming a murder victim is much higher if you are male than if you are female: Of all murder victims, 78.3 percent are male, 21.7 percent female. Age plays a role—nearly half of all murder victims are between the ages of 20 and 34; so does race—46.8 percent of all murder victims are white, 49.3 percent are black, and the remaining 3.9 percent are of other ethnic origins.[7]

About 90 percent of the black murder victims were slain by black offenders, and about 85 percent of the white murder victims were killed by white offenders. Intentional criminal homicide apparently is an intraracial crime. But it is not an intragender crime. The data show that males were most often killed by males and virtually all female victims also were murdered by males.[8]

Homicide Rates over Time

Researchers have asked what happens to homicide rates over time when the composition of the population changes. Some scholars have found that changes in age and race structure play a modest role in explaining crime trends during the last several decades. According to James Fox, the age-race-sex structure accounted for about 10 percent of the 1990s decline in homicide rates, and Steven Levitt found that changes in the age distribution explain between 15 and 20 percent of variance in crime rates between 1960 and 1980 and between 1980 and 1995. Roland Chilton, using data on offenses committed in Chicago between 1960 and 1980 and census data for those years, found that about 20 percent of the total increase in homicide rates could be explained by increases in the nonwhite male population. The same correlation is found in most major cities in the United States. Chilton argues that the problem will remain because of the poverty and demoralization of the groups involved.[9]

In a 1996 article, "Work," sociologist William Julius Wilson explains why America's ghettos have descended into "ever-deeper poverty and misery." According to him,

> for the first time in the 20th century, a significant majority of adults in many inner-city neighborhoods are not working in a typical week. Inner cities have always featured high levels of poverty, but the current levels of joblessness in some neighborhoods are unprecedented. For example, in the famous black-belt neighborhood of Washington Park on Chicago's South Side, a majority of adults had jobs in 1950; by 1990, only 1 in 3 worked in a typical week. High neighborhood joblessness has a far more devastating effect than high neighborhood poverty. A neighborhood in which people are poor but employed is different from a neighborhood in which people are poor and jobless. Many of today's problems in the inner-city neighborhoods—crime, family dissolution, welfare—are fundamentally a consequence of the disappearance of work.[10]

Until conditions change, what has been poignantly referred to as "the subculture of exasperation" will continue to produce a high homicide rate among nonwhite inner-city males.[11] Coramae Mann has found that although black women make up about 11 percent of the female population in the United States, they are arrested for three-fourths of all homicides committed by females. She argues that given such a disproportionate involvement in violent crime, one has to question whether the subculture of exasperation alone is entirely responsible.[12] But so few studies have been done on the subject that we cannot reach any definitive conclusion. Other investigators agree that homicide rates cannot be explained solely by factors such as poverty; the rates are also significantly associated with cultural approval of a resort to violence.

The Nature of Homicide

Let us take a closer look at killers and their victims and see how they are related to each other. In the 1950s, Marvin Wolfgang studied homicide situations, perpetrators, and victims in the Philadelphia area. Victims and offenders were predominantly young black adults of low socioeconomic status. The offenses were committed in the inner city; they occurred primarily in the home of the victim or offender, on weekends, in the evening hours, and among friends or acquaintances.

Building on the pioneering work of Hans von Hentig,[13] Wolfgang found that many of the victims had actually initiated the social interaction that led to the homicidal response, in either a direct or subliminal way. He coined the term **victim precipitation** for such instances, which may account for as many as a quarter to a half of all intentional homicides. In such cases, it is the victim who, by insinuation, bodily movement, verbal incitement, or the actual use of physical force, initiates a series of events that results in his or her own death. For example:

> During an argument in which a male called a female many vile names, she tried to telephone the police. He grabbed the phone from her hands, knocked her down, kicked her, and hit her with a tire gauge. She ran to the kitchen, grabbed a butcher knife, and stabbed him in the stomach.[14]

A study by Richard Felson and Steven Messner found that victim precipitation is more often seen in cases where women kill their husbands as opposed to incidents in which men kill their wives. However, males tend to be more violent than females in their killing methods.[15]

Other studies have provided additional insight into the patterns of homicide. Robert Silverman and Leslie Kennedy demonstrated that gender relationships, age, means of commission of the act, and location vary with relational distance, ranging from closest relatives (lovers, spouses) to total strangers.[16]

Margaret Zahn and Philip Sagi have developed a model that distinguishes among homicides on the basis of characteristics of victims, offenders, location, method of attack, and presence of witnesses. They conclude that all these characteristics and variables serve to differentiate four categories of homicides: (1) those within the family, (2) those among friends and acquaintances, (3) stranger homicides associated with felonies, and (4) stranger homicides not associated with felonies.[17]

Stranger Homicides

The rate of **stranger homicide**—a killing in which killer and victim have had no known previous contact—was 13 percent in 2007.[18] Marc Riedel, however, found these stranger homicide rates to be considerably understated. The true figures, according to Riedel, ranged from 14 to 29 percent.[19] Furthermore, the impact of stranger homicides on the quality of urban life—especially the fear of crime they engender—is far greater than their relatively small numbers would suggest.[20]

Relatives and Acquaintances

A significant percentage of all homicides occurs among relatives and acquaintances (Table 10.2).[21] One study found that 44 percent of the victims were in intimate relationships with their killers, 26 percent were friends and acquaintances, 11 percent

TABLE 10.2 Murder by Relationship,* 2007

Relationship	Number of Murders
Husband	138
Wife	573
Mother	94
Father	107
Son	240
Daughter	235
Brother	93
Sister	26
Other family	264
Acquaintance	3,061
Friend	483
Boyfriend	150
Girlfriend	471
Neighbor	110
Employee	5
Employer	9
Stranger	1,924
Unknown	6,848
Total Murder Victims	14,831

*Relationship is that of victim to offender.

Note: The relationship categories of husband and wife include both common-law and ex-spouses. The categories of mother, father, sister, brother, son, and daughter include stepparents, stepchildren, and stepsiblings. The category of acquaintance includes homosexual relationships and the composite category of other known to victim.

SOURCE: U.S. Department of Justice—Federal Bureau of Investigation, *Crime in the United States, 2007;* available at http://www.fbi.gov/ucr/cius2007/offenses/expanded_information/data/shrtable_09.html.

were the offenders' own children, and only 7.5 percent were strangers. Of these homicides, those in which women killed their mates have received particular attention. Criminologists take special interest in the factors behind such crimes.[22] Researchers have found a high incidence of long-term abuse suffered by women who subsequently kill their mates.[23] They also suggest that mate homicides are the result of a husband's efforts to control his wife and the wife's efforts to retain her independence.[24]

Other recent trends are also noteworthy: One study found an increase in the number of women who kill in domestic encounters, more planned killings, and less acceptance of self-defense as a motive in such cases.[25] Children are also at risk of death at the hands of family members. Research suggests that as the age of the child victim increases, so does the level of violence used to fatally injure the child.[26] Also, the closer the family relationship to the victim (e.g., mother and child), the more passive the form of homicide (e.g., asphyxiation or abandonment), whereas the more distant a relative is from the victim, the more violent the method used (e.g., stabbing).[27] In most murders of a child under age 15, a family member killed the child, while murder victims ages 15 to 17 are more likely to be killed by an acquaintance of the victim or by someone unknown to the law enforcement authorities.[28] Whether killed by a family member or an acquaintance, boys are more often the victims of violent deaths than are girls.[29]

Young and Old Perpetrators

Not surprisingly, the very young and the elderly have low homicide rates. In 2007, 1,063 murder charges were placed against youngsters under 18, but this figure does not include the number of homicides in which the young killers were dealt with by juvenile courts or welfare agencies. The elderly, too, are underrepresented. People age 55 and older accounted for under 4 percent of all murders in 2007.[30]

Homicide without Apparent Motive

In most homicides, the killer has a motive or a reason for killing the victim. Popular fiction tells us that detectives tend to consider a case solved if they can establish the motive. But research shows that in a substantial number of murders, the motive remains unclear. The "unmotivated" murderers are a puzzle—and they constitute 25 percent of all homicide offenders.

Though in most respects the killers without motive are similar to those who kill for a reason, they are more likely to have "(1) no history of alcohol abuse; (2) a recent release from prison; (3) claims of amnesia for the crime; (4) denial of the crime; and (5) a tendency to exhibit psychotic behavior following the crime and to be assessed not guilty of the crime due to mental illness."[31]

Serial and Mass Murders

Criminological researchers have paid special attention to two types of murder that are particularly disturbing to the community: **serial murder,** the killing of several victims over a period of time, and **mass murder,** the killing of multiple victims in one event or in very quick succession. Between 1970 and 1993, U.S. police knew of approximately 125 cases of multiple homicides. The literature on the subject is enormous.[32] Some serial murderers have become infamous.

Theodore "Ted" Bundy, law student and former crime commission staff member, killed between 19 and 36 young women in the northwestern states and Florida. David Berkowitz, the "Son of Sam," killed 6 young women in New York. Douglas Clark, the "Sunset Strip killer," killed between 7 and 50 prostitutes in Hollywood. The "Green River killer" of Seattle may have killed more than 45 victims. In the Midwest, Jeffrey Dahmer preserved, and took Polaroid photographs of, the mutilated body parts of his 11 to 17 victims (Chapter 4); and on Long Island, Joel Rifkin collected souvenirs—a shoe, an earring, a driver's license—from the more than 13 streetwalkers he claimed as his victims.

In just one week in June 1996, two men, both suspected of being serial killers, were captured in New York City. Heriberto Seda, 28, lived a largely solitary life, except for those moments when he would emerge from the apartment he shared with his mother and sister. The self-proclaimed New York Zodiac Killer allegedly shot eight people, killing three, in two separate crime waves (in 1990, then again during 1992 and 1993). Larry Stevens, 31, who also lived with his mother, would allegedly trick elderly people into letting him into their homes. He would beat them or throw them down stairs, and then rob them. He is suspected of killing at least two elderly persons.[33]

Pedro Alonso Lopez, however, is considered the deadliest serial killer of all time, having killed over 300 people in Colombia, Peru, and Ecuador. Lopez has been dubbed the "Monster of the Andes."[34] In 1999, suspected serial killer Angel Leonicio Reyes Maturino Resendez was finally captured. Resendez was referred to as the "railroad killer" because all his slayings occurred near railroad tracks.[35]

Although the most notorious serial killers are men, female serial killers do exist. They are considered to be more difficult to apprehend and to have more complex motivations than their male counterparts.[36]

Throughout the 1990s, an unusual number of mass murders occurred. In 1991, an unemployed young man drove his pickup through the glass window of a Texas café and opened fire with a semiautomatic pistol, leaving 22 dead. James Huberty walked into a McDonald's in California

and killed 20 people. Colin Ferguson boarded a train where he killed 6 and wounded 17 in the Long Island massacre of 1993. In 1996, Thomas Hamilton entered a school in Dunblane, Scotland, shot and killed 16 kindergarten students and their teacher, and wounded 12 others.[37] In 1998, 5 of the 16 persons shot at a Jonesboro, Arkansas, middle school died. In 1999, there were 15 victims of a massacre at Columbine High School in Littleton, Colorado, and 7 victims of a mass shooting at a Baptist church in Fort Worth, Texas. Other 1999 incidents included 3 dead in Pelham, Alabama; 12 dead in Atlanta, Georgia; and 2 dead in Salt Lake City, Utah. In 2000, 7 masked gunmen entered a Philadelphia crack house and shot 10 people, killing 7. In 2001, unprecedented terror attacks on the World Trade Center in New York City killed thousands and sent shock waves throughout the world. In 2002, a New Jersey policeman went on a shooting rampage, killing 5 people before killing himself. Other incidents in 2002 included 18 killed in a school shooting in Erfurt, Germany; 5 children drowned in Texas; 5 killed in Los Angeles; 4 killed in San Bruno, California; and 3 killed in Long Beach, California. The two "Beltway" snipers, John Muhammed and John Lee Malvo, have been linked to 19 shootings and 13 deaths—in Washington, D.C., Maryland, Virginia, Louisiana, Georgia, and Alabama. Dennis Rader (aka the BTK Killer) has been linked to 10 murders committed between 1974 and 1991. Killing rampages seem to be on the rise. Over the past 50 years, there has been a nearly tenfold increase in the number of massacres, to between seven and eight annually.

Mass murders in the workplace are also far from rare (Table 10.3). From 1992 to 1996, more than 1,000 workplace homicides occurred annually. The number of workplace homicides has declined in recent years, however, from 860 in 1997 to 609 in 2002.[38]

TABLE 10.3 Workplace Homicides, 2006

Total	540	Police officers, detectives, investigators	45
VICTIM CHARACTERISTICS		Security guards	38
Employee status		Food preparation and serving	46
Wage and salary workers	409	Building and grounds maintenance	13
Self-employed	131	Personal care and service	13
Sex		Sales	151
Male	420	Office and administrative support	25
Female	120	Farming, forestry, and fishing	*
Age		Construction and extraction	15
Under 17 years	*	Installation, maintenance, repair	13
18 to 19 years	10	Production	11
20 to 24 years	34	Transportation and material moving	66
25 to 34 years	121	**MAJOR INDUSTRY**	
35 to 44 years	141	Agriculture, forestry, fishing, mining	*
45 to 54 years	117	Construction	19
55 to 64 years	82	Manufacturing	16
65 years and older	32	Trade, transportation, and utilities	187
Race, ethnicity		Taxi and limousine service	33
White, non-Hispanic	253	Retail trade	141
Black, non-Hispanic	120	Grocery, convenience stores	46
Asian or Pacific Islander	70	Gasoline service stations	40
American Indian, Eskimo, or Aleut	*	Finance, insurance, real estate	30
Other or unspecified	8	Professional and business services	34
Hispanic	83	Investigation, security, armored car services	14
TYPE OF EVENT		Education and health services	25
Shooting	436	Leisure, accommodation, food services	114
Stabbing	39	Other services, not public administration	31
Hitting, kicking, beating	33	Public administration	45
Other	30	Government	79
MAJOR OCCUPATION		State	12
Management	51	Local	54
Healthcare and technical	11		
Protective service	92		

*No data available.

SOURCE: *Sourcebook of Criminal Justice Statistics Online,* 2000, http://www.albany.edu/sourcebook/pdf/t31352006.pdf.

As of 2006, the number of workplace homicides declined to 540. San Franciscan failed businessman Gian Luigi Ferri, who blamed lawyers for his problems, burst into the 34th-floor law office where he had been a client and, with two pistols, killed 8 persons working in the firm. Disgruntled employee Paul Calder returned 8 months after being fired to kill 3 and wound 2 at a Tampa insurance company. In 1999, day trader Mark O. Barton, after losing over $100,000 in the stock market in almost 2 months, bludgeoned his wife and 2 children to death. He then drove to an office complex in the Buckhead district of Atlanta. There he opened fire inside two brokerage firms where he had been employed. Barton killed a total of 13 people before committing suicide as police were closing in on him.[39] The U.S. Postal Service, where 38 employees died violently between 1986 and 1993, continues to look into ways to reduce employer-employee tension, especially when layoffs are imminent.[40]

It is popularly believed that multiple murderers are mentally ill; their offenses, after all, are often quite bizarre. In many such cases, psychiatrists have found severe pathology.[41] Yet juries are reluctant to find these offenders not guilty by reason of insanity. Albert Fish, who cooked and ate the children he murdered, died in the electric chair.[42] Edmund Kemper, who killed hitchhikers as well as his own mother (he used her head as a dartboard), received a life term.[43]

Criminologists Jack Levin and James Fox do not agree with the hypothesis that all mass and serial murderers are mentally diseased (for example, psychotic) and therefore legally insane or incompetent. On the contrary, they say, serial killers are **sociopaths,** persons who lack internal controls, disregard common values, and have an intense desire to dominate others. But psychological characteristics alone cannot explain the actions of these people. They are also influenced by the social environment in which they function: the openness of our society, the ease of travel, the availability of firearms, the lack of external controls and supervision, and the general friendliness and trust of Americans in dealing with each other and with strangers.[44]

The American public is fascinated with the phenomena of mass and serial murder.[45] Levin and Fox suggest that the recent increase in mass and serial murders, despite a general decline in the murder rate, is to some extent attributable to the publicity given to mass murders and the resulting copycat phenomenon—the repetition of a crime as a result of the publicity it receives.[46] When one person killed at random by poisoning Tylenol capsules with cyanide, others copied the idea. This phenomenon has prompted experts to recommend that the media cooperate with the criminal justice system when the circumstances demand discretion.[47] Yet cooperation may be hard to achieve when media help is needed to alert the public to

a health hazard (as in the Tylenol cases). In any event, the First Amendment's guarantee of freedom of the press does not permit controls.

Gang Murder

Up to this point we have dealt largely with homicides committed by single offenders. But what about homicides by gangs of offenders? Are there any differences between the two types? On the basis of an analysis of data contained in 700 homicide investigation files, researchers found that "gang homicides differ both qualitatively and quantitatively from nongang homicides. Most distinctly, they differ with respect to ethnicity [more likely to be intraethnic], age [gang killers are five years younger], number of participants [2½ times as many participants], and relationship between the participants [gang killers are twice as likely not to know their victims]."[48] But similarities can also be seen. The causes of gang homicides, like those by single offenders, are often attributable to social disorganization, economic inequality, and deprivation.[49]

Since the 1950s, the nature of gang murder has changed dramatically. As we discuss in Chapter 6, besides the major increase in killings, gang homicides have also become more brutal. Drive-by and crossfire shootings of intended victims and innocent bystanders are no longer uncommon. From 1989 to 1993, there were 6,327 drive-by shootings, 9,053 people shot at, and 590 homicides; 47 percent of the people shot at and 23 percent of the homicide victims were innocent bystanders.[50] In Brooklyn, New York, all three brothers in one family fell victim to street violence. Motives also have changed through the years. Once, gang wars, with a few related homicides, took place over "turf," territory that members protected with knives, rocks, or metal chains as weapons. Now the wars are over drugs, and the weapons are assault rifles and semiautomatic guns.[51]

A Cross-National Comparison of Homicide Rates

The criminal homicides we have been discussing are those committed in the United States. By comparing homicide rates in this country with those of other countries, we can gain a broader understanding of that crime. In the World Crime Survey ending with the year 1995, the United Nations revealed that the average rate of intentional homicide was 7.2 per 100,000 for developed (industrialized Western) countries and 3.5 per 100,000 for developing countries.[52] The Survey figures demonstrate that with the decline in U.S. homicide rates to 5.6 per 100,000 in 2001 from 9 per 100,000 in 1994, the United States no longer has the highest rate among industrialized countries.[53] (Figure 10.1.) Data, however, show that the number of homicides per 100,000 children under age

Rank	Country	Number (per 1,000 people)		Rank	Country	Number (per 1,000 people)	
1	Colombia	0.617847	████████	32	Romania	0.0250784	▮
2	South Africa	0.496008	███████	33	Portugal	0.0233769	▮
3	Jamaica	0.324196	████	34	Malaysia	0.0230034	▮
4	Venezuela	0.316138	████	35	Macedonia, Former Yugoslav Republic of	0.0229829	▮
5	Russia	0.201534	███	36	Mauritius	0.021121	▮
6	Mexico	0.130213	██	37	Hungary	0.0204857	▮
7	Estonia	0.107277	█	38	Korea, South	0.0196336	▮
8	Latvia	0.10393	█	39	Slovenia	0.0179015	▮
9	Lithuania	0.102863	█	40	France	0.0173272	▮
10	Belarus	0.0983495	█	41	Czech Republic	0.0169905	▮
11	Ukraine	0.094006	█	42	Iceland	0.0168499	▮
12	Papua New Guinea	0.0838593	█	43	Australia	0.0150324	▮
13	Kyrgyzstan	0.0802565	█	44	Canada	0.0149063	▮
14	Thailand	0.0800798	█	45	Chile	0.014705	▮
15	Moldova	0.0781145	█	46	United Kingdom	0.0140633	▮
16	Zimbabwe	0.0749938	█	47	Italy	0.0128393	▮
17	Seychelles	0.0739025	█	48	Spain	0.0122456	▮
18	Zambia	0.070769	█	49	Germany	0.0116461	▮
19	Costa Rica	0.061006	█	50	Tunisia	0.0112159	▮
20	Poland	0.0562789	█	51	Netherlands	0.0111538	▮
21	Georgia	0.0511011	▮	52	New Zealand	0.0111524	▮
22	Uruguay	0.045082	▮	53	Denmark	0.0106775	▮
23	Bulgaria	0.0445638	▮	54	Norway	0.0106684	▮
24	United States	0.042802	▮	55	Ireland	0.00946215	▮
25	Armenia	0.0425746	▮	56	Switzerland	0.00921351	▮
26	India	0.0344083	▮	57	Indonesia	0.00910842	▮
27	Yemen	0.0336276	▮	58	Greece	0.0075928	▮
28	Dominica	0.0289733	▮	59	Hong Kong	0.00550804	▏
29	Azerbaijan	0.0285642	▮	60	Japan	0.00499933	▏
30	Finland	0.0283362	▮	61	Saudi Arabia	0.00397456	▏
31	Slovakia	0.0263303	▮	62	Qatar	0.00115868	▏

Weighted average: 0.1 per 1,000 people ▮

Definition: Total recorded intentional homicides, completed. Crime statistics are often better indicators of prevalence of law enforcement and willingness to report crime than of actual prevalence.

FIGURE 10.1 Murders (per capita) by country.

Source: NationMaster.com. Data source Seventh United Nations Survey of Crime Trends and Operations of Criminal Justice Systems, covering the period 1998–2000 (United Nations Office on Drugs and Crime, Centre for International Crime Prevention).

15 in the United States was 5 times the number in the other countries combined. And the number of murders committed by youths places the United States third in a ranking of 73 countries.[54]

One cross-national study found a moderate association between inequality of income and rate of homicide. It likewise revealed a relationship between a youthful population and the homicide rate. The analysis, the study concluded, "suggests that homicide rates are higher in poorer countries, in more culturally diverse countries, in countries which spend less on defense, in less-democratic societies, and in countries where fewer young people are enrolled in school."[55] Another researcher who compared the homicide rates in 76 countries with the rate in the United States found that when he took into consideration the differences in the age and sex distributions of the various populations, the United States had a higher rate than all but 15 countries,[56] most of which were experiencing civil war or internal strife.

A comparison of homicide rates with historical and socioeconomic data from 110 nations over a 5-year period led researchers to the following conclusions:

- Combatant nations experience an increase in homicides following cessation of hostilities (violence has come to be seen as a legitimate means of settling disputes).

- The largest cities have the highest homicide rates; the smallest have the lowest homicide rates; but, paradoxically, as a city grows, its homicide rate per capita does not.

- The availability of capital punishment does not result in fewer homicides and in fact often results in more; abolition of capital punishment decreases the homicide rate.[57]

We have seen that murder rates are not distributed equally among countries or within a single country, or even within neighborhoods. As noted earlier, in the United States, homicide rates tend to be higher in the West and the South.[58] A greater proportion of males, young people, and blacks are perpetrators and victims of homicide, which tends to be committed against someone the killer knows, at or near the home of at least one of the persons involved, in the evening or on a weekend. Gang murders are increasing dramatically. A number of experts have found that homicides are related to the everyday patterns of interactions in socially disorganized slum areas.[59]

ASSAULT

The crimes of homicide and serious assault share many characteristics. Both typically are committed by young males, and a disproportionate number of arrestees are members of minority groups. Assault victims, too, often know their attackers. Spatial and temporal distributions are also quite comparable. Assault rates, like those of homicide, are highest in urban areas, during the summer months, in the evening hours, and in the South.

Though the patterns are the same, the legal definitions are not. A murder is an act that causes the death of another person and that is intended to cause death. An **assault** is an attack on another person that is made with apparent ability to inflict injury and that is intended to frighten or to cause physical harm. (An attack that results in touching

Anger at street encounters may escalate to assault or even homicide.

or striking the victim is called a **battery.**) Modern statutes usually recognize two types of assault: A **simple assault** is one that inflicts little or no physical hurt; a felonious assault, or **aggravated assault,** is one in which the perpetrator inflicts serious harm on the victim or uses a deadly weapon.

Criminologists have looked closely at situations in which assaults are committed. One researcher identified six stages of a confrontational situation that leads to an assault:

1. One person insults another.

2. The insulted person perceives the significance of the insult, often by noting the reactions of others present, and becomes angry.

3. The insulted person contemplates a response: fight, flight, or conciliation. If the response chosen is a fight, the insultee assaults the insulter then and there. If another response is chosen, the situation advances to stage 4.

4. The original insulter, now reprimanded, shamed, or embarrassed, makes a countermove: fight or flight.

5. If the choice is a fight, the insulter assaults (and possibly kills) the insultee.

6. The "triumphant" party either flees or awaits the consequences (for example, police response).[60]

We can see that crucial decisions are made at all stages and that the nature of the decisions depends on the context in which they are made. At stage 1, nobody is likely to offer an insult in a peaceful group or situation. At stage 2, the witnesses to the scene could respond in a conciliatory manner. (Let us call this a conflict-resolution situation.) At stage 3, the insulted person could leave the scene with dignity. (A confrontational person would call it flight; a conflict-resolution-minded person would call it a dignified end to a confrontational situation.) Stage 4 is a critical stage, because it calls for a counterresponse. The original aggressor could see this as the last chance to avoid violence and withdraw with apologies. That would be the end of the matter. In a confrontational situation, however, the blows will be delivered now, if none have been dealt already.

A similar pattern was proposed by James Tedeschi and Richard Felson, who developed a theory of aggression as instrumental behavior— that is, goal-oriented behavior carried out intentionally with the purpose of obtaining something. This is a different way of thinking about aggression. For years, criminologists and psychologists have generally accepted that aggression (and the violence that often goes with it) happens when a person reaches a "breaking point." There is little premeditation or thought given to some aggressive or violent behavior. But for Tedeschi and Felson, all aggression occurs after the person has thought about it first, even though these thoughts may be disorganized or illogical and may last for just a fraction of a second.[61]

The National Crime Victimization Survey estimates that 3,776,559 simple assaults were committed in 2006. Assault is the most common of all violent crimes reported to the police. The number of aggravated assaults has risen in recent years, reaching 1,344,280 in 2006.[62] These figures, however, grossly underestimate the real incidence. Many people involved in an assault consider the event a private matter, particularly if the assault took place within the family or household. Consequently, until recently little was known about family-related violence. But the focus of recent research is changing that situation rapidly.

FAMILY-RELATED CRIMES

In 1962, five physicians exposed the gravity of the "battered child syndrome" in the *Journal of the American Medical Association*.[63] When they reviewed X-ray photographs of patients in the emergency rooms of 71 hospitals across the country over the course of a year, they found 300 cases of child abuse, of which 11 percent resulted in death and over 28 percent in permanent brain damage. Shortly thereafter, the women's movement rallied to the plight of the battered wife and, somewhat later, to the personal and legal problems of wives who were raped by their husbands.[64]

In the 1960s and 1970s, various organizations, fighting for the rights of women and children, exposed the harm that results from physical and psychological abuse in the home. They demanded public action and created public awareness of the extent of the problem. Psychologists, physicians, anthropologists, and social scientists, among others, increasingly focused attention on the various factors that enter into episodes of domestic violence. Such factors include the sources of conflict, arguments, physical attacks, injuries, and temporal and spatial elements.

Within three decades, family violence, the "well-kept secret," has come to be recognized as a major social problem.[65] Family violence shares some of the characteristics of other forms of violence, yet the intimacy of marital, cohabitational, or parent-child relationships sets family violence apart. The physical and emotional harm inflicted in violent episodes tends to be spread over longer periods of time and to have a more lasting impact on all members of the living unit. Moreover, such events tend to be self-perpetuating.

■ *A spectator holds up a sign offering advice to Boston Red Sox batter Wilfredo Cordero as he pinch-hits for Reggie Jefferson in a game with the Toronto Blue Jays. The fans at Fenway Park, Boston, greeted him with boos as he stepped up to the plate.*

Spouse Abuse

In May 1998, Motley Crüe drummer Tommy Lee was sentenced to 6 months in jail and 3 years probation for battering his wife, former *Baywatch* beauty Pamela Anderson. Lee was also ordered to perform 200 hours of community service and donate $5,000 to a battered women's shelter. He had been arrested in February 1998 after Anderson called 911 to report a domestic dispute in which Lee had kicked her in the back while she was holding 7-week-old Dylan Jagger. Lee was charged with spousal abuse, child abuse, and unlawful possession of a firearm. As the result of a plea agreement, all charges except the spousal abuse charge were dropped.

Media celebrity and former star athlete O. J. Simpson was convicted in 1989 of assaulting his wife, Nicole Brown Simpson. For this offense, he served no time in prison, nor was he required to undergo counseling. On June 13, 1994, Nicole Brown Simpson and her friend Ronald Goldman were found lying dead in pools of their own blood, victims of a vicious knife attack. O. J. Simpson was accused of their murder. Following a lengthy, highly publicized, and much-discussed trial, Simpson was found not guilty by a jury of his peers. The verdict had a wide-reaching impact on various aspects of the criminal justice system. It also made abused women fear for their lives. Concerned that a man who was a convicted batterer could be found not guilty of killing his ex-wife, despite what was perceived by many as convincing evidence, they wondered if they could eventually share the same fate as Nicole Brown Simpson.[66] O. J. Simpson was convicted of robbing two sports memorabilia dealers in 2008

and was sentenced to a minimum of 9 years in prison.

The Extent of Spouse Abuse

In a national sample of 6,002 households, Murray A. Straus and Richard J. Gelles found that about one of every six couples experiences at least one physical assault during the year.[67] While both husbands and wives perpetrate acts of violence, the consequences of their acts differ.[68] Men, who more often use guns, knives, or fists, inflict more pain and injury. About 60 percent of spousal assaults consist of minor shoving, slapping, and pushing; the other 40 percent are considered severe: punching, kicking, stabbing, choking.[69] According to the National Institute of Justice, partner violence is strongly linked to a variety of mental illnesses, a background of family adversity, dropping out of school, juvenile aggression, drug abuse, long-term unemployment, and cohabitation and/or parenthood at a young age. Research also suggests that women who have children by the age of 21 are two times more likely to be victims of domestic violence than are women who are not mothers, and that men who father children by age 21 are three times more likely to be perpetrators of abuse than are men who are not fathers.[70]

Researchers agree that assaultive behavior within the family is a highly underreported crime. Data from the National Crime Victimization Survey indicate:

- One-half of the incidents of domestic assault are not reported;

- The most common reason given for failure to report a domestic assault to the police was that the victim considered the incident a private matter.

- Victims who reported such incidents to the police did so to prevent future assaults.

- Although the police classified two-thirds of the reported incidents of domestic violence as simple assaults, half of them inflicted bodily injury as serious as, or more serious than, the injuries inflicted during rapes, robberies, and aggravated assaults.[71]

The Nature of Spouse Abuse

Before we can understand spouse abuse, we need information about abusers. Some experts have found that interpersonal violence is learned and transmitted from one generation to the next.[72] Studies demonstrate that children who are raised by aggressive parents tend to grow up to be aggressive adults.[73] Other researchers have demonstrated how stress, frustration, and severe psychopathology take their toll on family relationships.[74] A few researchers have also explored the role of body chemistry; one investigation ties abuse to the tendency of males to secrete adrenaline when they feel sexually threatened.[75]

The relationship between domestic violence and the use of alcohol and drugs has also been explored. Abusive men with severe drug and alcohol problems are more likely to abuse their wives or girlfriends when they are drunk or high and to inflict more injury.[76]

Several studies of other societies demonstrate cultural support for the abuse of women. Moroccan researcher Mohammed Ayat reported that of 160 battered women, about 25 percent believed that a man who does *not* beat his wife must be under some magic spell; 8 percent believed that such a man has a weak personality and is afraid of his wife; 2 percent believed that he must be abnormal; and another 2 percent believed that he doesn't love her or has little interest in her.[77] Wife beating, then, appears to be accepted as a norm by over one-third of the women studied—women who are themselves beaten. It even appears to be an expected behavior. In fact, in a study of 90 cultures, spouse beating was rare or nonexistent in only 15.[78]

Spouse abuse has often been attributed to the imbalance of power between male and female partners. According to some researchers, the historical view of wives as possessions of their husbands persists even today.[79] Until recently, spousal abuse was perceived as a problem more of social service than of criminal justice.[80] Police responding to domestic disturbance calls typically do not make an arrest unless the assailant is drunk, has caused serious injury, or has assaulted the officers. Take, for example, the case of *Thurman v. Torrington.* Tracey Thurman had repeatedly requested police

assistance because she feared her estranged husband. Even after he threatened to shoot her and her son, the police merely told her to get a restraining order. Eventually, the husband attacked Thurman, inflicting multiple stab wounds that caused paralysis from the neck down and permanent disfigurement. The police had delayed in responding to her call on that occasion, and the city of Torrington, Connecticut, was held liable for having failed to provide her with equal protection of the law. In the suit that followed, Ms. Thurman was awarded $2.3 million in damages.[81]

According to the U.S. Department of Justice, between 1998 and 2002:

- Of the almost 3.5 million violent crimes committed against family members, 49 percent were crimes against spouses.

- 84 percent of spouse abuse victims were female, and 86 percent of victims of dating partner abuse were female.

- Males made up 83 percent of spouse murderers and 75 percent of dating partner murderers.

- 50 percent of offenders in state prison for spousal abuse had killed their victims. Wives were more likely than husbands to be killed by their spouses: Wives comprised about half of all spouses in the population in 2002 but 81 percent of all persons killed by their spouse.[82]

The Thurman case is rare. The majority of assault incidents within the family either are unreported to the police or, if reported, are classified as simple assaults. By and large, the victims of family violence—those who are willing to look for help—have turned to crisis telephone lines and to shelters for battered women (safe havens that first appeared in the early 1970s to provide legal, social, and psychological services).

Whether informal interventions are as effective as the criminal justice system, however, is a matter of controversy.[83] In a study conducted some years ago, the Minneapolis Domestic Violence Experiment, three types of action were taken: (1) The batterer was arrested, (2) the partners were required to separate for a designated period of time, or (3) a mediator intervened between the partners. Over a 6-month period, the offenders who were arrested had the lowest recidivism rate (10 percent), those who were required to separate had the highest (24 percent), and those who submitted to mediation fell in between (19 percent).[84] More recently, a 1991 study revealed that neither short-custody arrests for domestic violence in inner-city areas nor longer-term arrests are effective in curbing domestic violence, especially in the long run.[85] Questions on the subject of spouse abuse still far outnumber answers. Personal, ethical, and moral concerns make the issue highly sensitive. Researchers, however, are seeking answers.

Child Abuse

Spouse abuse is closely related to child abuse. One-half to three-quarters of men who batter women also beat their children, and many sexually abuse them as well. Children are also injured as a result of reckless behavior on the part of their fathers while the latter are abusing their mothers. In fact, the majority of abused sons over 14 suffer injuries trying to protect their mothers.[86]

The Extent of Child Abuse

According to the U.S. Department of Health and Human Services, approximately 3.3 million reports of suspected child abuse or neglect were made to Child Protective Services (CPS) in 2006.[87] The reports concern an estimated 6.0 million children, and 61.7 percent of them led to an investigation. These investigations, in turn, found 30 percent of these children to be the victims of abuse or neglect. About 64 percent of victims experienced neglect, followed by 15 percent who experienced physical abuse. Sexual and emotional abuse were less prevalent, accounting for 9 and 7 percent of victims, respectively.[88] Furthermore, approximately 1,530 children died of abuse or neglect in the year 2006. It is still very difficult, however, to measure the extent of child abuse. Maltreatment usually takes place in the home, and the child victims rarely notify the police.[89]

The Nature of Child Abuse

When child abuse first began to be investigated in the early 1960s, the investigators were predominantly physicians, who looked at the psychopathology of the abusers. They discovered that a high proportion of abusers suffered from alcoholism, drug abuse, mental retardation, poor attachment, low self-esteem, or sadistic psychosis. Later the search for causes moved in other directions. Some researchers pointed out that abusive parents did not know how to discipline children or, for that matter, even how to provide for basic needs, such as nutrition and medical attention. Claims have been made that abusers have themselves been abused; to date, however, the evidence in regard to this hypothesis is mixed.[90]

The list of factors related to child abuse is long. We know, for example, that the rate of child abuse in lower-income families is high.[91] This finding is probably related to the fact that low-income parents have few resources for dealing with the stresses to which they are subjected, such as poor housing and financial problems. When they cannot cope with their responsibilities, they may become overwhelmed. Moreover, the risk of

Fatal child abuse cases attract media attention to the point of possible media exploitation. When is this line crossed?

abuse is twice as great for children living with single parents as for children living with both parents.[92] The rate of child abuse may also be related to the acceptance of physical responses to conflict situations in what has been termed the "subculture of violence" (Chapter 6). Moreover, because child abuse among poor families is likely to be handled by a public agency, these cases tend to appear in official statistics.

When child abuse is reported to the authorities, the case goes through the criminal justice system just like any other case. However, certain factors are associated with how, and to what extent, these types of cases are prosecuted. One study suggests that, particularly in the case of child sexual abuse, those offenders who are charged with abusing multiple victims are much more likely to be prosecuted than are offenders charged with abusing only one victim. Also, offenders who are strangers to the victim are more likely to be prosecuted than are offenders related to the victim. Cases in which serious abuse was involved and medical evidence of abuse existed were also more likely to be prosecuted.[93]

Some researchers have found that formal action—arrest and prosecution—is the most effective means for limiting repeat offenses in the case of battered wives. The situation seems to be different when children are involved. Several advocates for children oppose any involvement of the criminal justice system. They believe that the parent-child attachment remains crucial to the child's development, and they fear that punishment of parents can only be detrimental to the child's need for a stable family environment. Only in the most extreme cases would they separate children from parents and place them in shelters or in foster homes. The preference is to prevent child abuse by other means, such as self-help groups (Parents Anonymous), babysitting assistance, and crisis phone lines.

The results of various types of intervention are characterized by the title of a report on child maltreatment: "Half Full and Half Empty."[94] Rates of repeated abuse are high; yet some families have had positive results, and advances have been made in identifying the best treatment for various types of problems. Although our understanding of the problem has indeed increased, we need to know a great deal more about the offense before we can reduce its occurrence.[95]

Abuse of the Elderly

When the amendments to the Older Americans Act appeared in 1987, they brought with them a federal definition of elder abuse, neglect, and exploitation. The definition is used only as a guideline and not for enforcement purposes. State laws provide their own definitions of elder abuse, and these definitions vary across state jurisdictions. Nevertheless, three basic categories of elder abuse emerged: domestic elder abuse, institutional elder abuse, and self-neglect or self-abuse. Domestic elder abuse results when an older person is maltreated by a person who has a special relationship with the elder, such as a spouse, sibling, child, or friend. Institutional elder abuse occurs in the context of a residential facility, such as a nursing home, in which paid caregivers or other staff are the perpetrators. Self-neglect or self-abuse occurs when elderly persons threaten their own health or safety by, for example, failing to provide themselves with proper amounts of food, clothing, shelter, or medication.[96]

Abuse of the elderly has become an area of special concern to social scientists. The population group that is considered to be elderly is variously defined. The majority of researchers consider 65 the age at which an individual falls into the category "elderly." As health care in the United States has improved, longevity has increased. The population of elderly people has grown larger over the decades: from 4 percent of the total population in 1900 to 12 percent in 2006.[97] Every day 1,000 more people join the ranks.

Elderly persons who are being cared for by their adult children are at a certain risk of abuse. The extent of the problem, however, is still largely unknown. The abused elderly frequently do not talk about their abuse for fear of the embarrassment of public exposure and possible retaliation by the abuser. Congressional hearings on domestic abuse estimate that between 500,000 and 2.5 million elderly people are abused annually.[98] Among the causes of such abuse are caregivers who themselves grew up in homes where violence was a way of life, the stress of caregiving in a private home rather than an institution, generational conflicts, and frustration with gerontological (old-age) problems of the care receiver, such as illness and senility.[99]

We can see that criminologists share a growing concern about family-related violence. Child abuse

has received the attention of scholars for over three decades. Spousal abuse has been studied for over two decades. The abuse of the elderly has begun to receive attention much more recently. Family abuse is not new; our awareness of the size and seriousness of the problem is. The same could be said about yet another offense. It was not until the 1960s that women's advocates launched a national campaign on behalf of victims of rape. Since then, rape has become a major topic in criminological literature and research.

RAPE AND SEXUAL ASSAULT

The common law defined **rape** as an act of enforced intercourse by a man of a woman (other than the attacker's wife) without her consent. Intercourse includes any sexual penetration, however slight. The exclusion of wives from the crime of rape rested on several outdated legal fictions, among them the propositions that the marriage vows grant implicit permanent rights of sexual access and that spouses cannot testify against each other. The Hale Doctrine, written in the seventeenth century and recognized judicially in 1857 by the United States, stated specifically that "the husband cannot be guilty of a rape committed by himself upon his lawful wife, for by their mutual matrimonial consent and a contract the wife hath given up herself in this kind unto her husband which she cannot retract."[100] Older laws universally classify rape as a sex crime. But rape has always been much more than that. It is inherently a crime of violence, an exercise of power.

Oddly, as Susan Brownmiller forcefully argues, it really started as a property crime. Men as archetypal aggressors (the penis as a weapon) subjugated women by the persistent threat of rape. That threat forced each woman to submit to a man for protection and thus to become a wife, the property of a man. Rape then was made a crime to protect one man's property—his wife—from the sexual aggressions of other men.[101] But even that view regards rape as a violent crime against the person, one that destroys the freedom of a woman (and nowadays of a man as well) to decide whether, when, and with whom to enter into a sexual relationship.

Well over a thousand books, scholarly articles, and papers have been produced on the topic of rape and sexual assault since the 1960s. Much that was obscure and poorly understood has now been clarified by research generated largely by the initiatives of the feminist movement, the National Center for the Prevention and Control of Rape (NCPCR), and other governmental and private funding agencies. While most of the crimes in our penal codes have more or less retained their original form, the law on rape has

THEORY CONNECTS

Rape and Sexual Assault

What theories of crime causation explain rape and sexual assault? Why do you suppose most of the theories discussed in Chapters 4 through 8 are generally unhelpful? Is the crime of rape or sexual assault that different from homicide, robbery, or even assault?

FIGURE 10.2 Percent of crimes cleared by arrest or exceptional means, 2007.

Source: U.S. Department of Justice—Federal Bureau of Investigation, *Crime in the United States, 2007*; available at www.fbi.gov/ucr/cius2007/offenses/clearances/index.html.

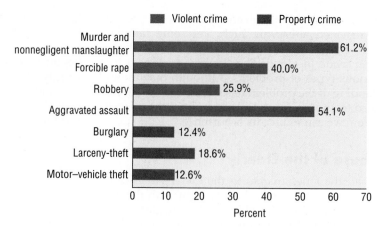

■ Violent crime   ■ Property crime

	Percent
Murder and nonnegligent manslaughter	61.2%
Forcible rape	40.0%
Robbery	25.9%
Aggravated assault	54.1%
Burglary	12.4%
Larceny-theft	18.6%
Motor-vehicle theft	12.6%

changed rapidly and drastically. The name of the crime, its definition, the rules of evidence and procedure, society's reaction to it—all have changed.[102] Nevertheless, Americans still regard rape as one of the most serious crimes.

Characteristics of the Rape Event

According to the Uniform Crime Reports, there were 90,427 forcible rapes in 2007.[103] The incidence of rape dropped 2.9 percent between 1998 and 2007. Of all those arrested for forcible rape, 45 percent were under age 25, and 63 percent were white.[104] Most rapes are committed in the summer, particularly in July and in marriages involving alcoholic husbands.[105] Several decades ago, Menachem Amir demonstrated that close to half of all rapes in Philadelphia from 1958 to 1965 were committed by a person known to or even friendly with the victim.[106] More recent victimization data show that the situation has not changed: 48 percent of rapes are committed by men who know their victims.[107] The offender may even be the husband, who in some states can now qualify as a rapist. Nevertheless, marital rape is still minimized by the law. We know little about it except that it often occurs in marriages that are characterized by other forms of violence.

Researchers have developed a three-category typology of rape. Stranger rape occurs when the victim has had little or no prior contact with the offender. Predatory rape involves a man who, using deception or force, intends and plans to rape his victim by pretending to engage in legitimate dating behavior. Date rape involves a legitimate dating situation turned bad, when force is eventually used to gain sex from a woman who is an unwilling participant.[108] In these situations, the offenders sometimes use the date-rape "drug of choice," Rohypnol, commonly referred to as "Roofies." Rohypnol falls into the same class of drugs as marijuana. It is a sedative that is said to be 10 times the strength of Valium. Twenty to 30

minutes after it is consumed—often after being dropped into a drink at a social gathering—this tasteless, odorless drug produces in its victim muscle relaxation, a slowing of psychomotor responses, and amnesia.[109] Some research indicates that as many as 25 percent of all female college students may have experienced rape.[110] Criminologists have difficulty estimating the frequency of date rape, but in all likelihood such rape has increased significantly. It is estimated that only one-tenth of the date rapes committed are reported to the police.

There is an arrest made for all types of forcible rape in about 40 percent of the cases (Figure 10.2).[111] Many stranger rapists remain at large because they commit their acts in ways that produce little tangible evidence as to their identities. They maintain a distance from the victim by not interacting with her before the attack. The serial rapist also attacks strangers, but because he finds his victims repeatedly in the same places, his behavior is more predictable and so leads to a better arrest rate.[112]

Who Are the Rapists?

Explanations of rape fall into two categories, psychological and sociocultural. While research in these areas has expanded over the last three decades, the causes of rape remain speculative.

Psychological Factors

Several experts view rapists as suffering from mental illness or personality disorders. They argue that some rapists are psychotic, sociopathic, or sadistic or feel deficient in masculinity. Most rapists show hostile feelings toward women, have histories of violence, and tend to attack strangers. They commit the offense because of anger, a drive for power (expressed as sexual conquest), or the enjoyment of maltreating a victim (sadism). Some rapists view women as sex objects whose role is to satisfy them.

Sociocultural Factors

Psychological explanations assume that men who rape are maladjusted in some way. But several studies done in the 1980s demonstrate that rapists are indistinguishable from other groups of offenders.[113] These studies generally conclude that rape is culturally related to societal norms that approve of aggression as a demonstration of masculinity (as we saw in Chapter 6) or that rape is the mechanism by which men maintain their power over women.

The social significance of rape has long been a part of anthropological literature. A cross-cultural study of 95 tribal societies found that 47 percent were rape-free, 35 percent intermediate, and 18 percent rape-prone. In the rape-prone societies, women had low status and little decision-making power, and they lived apart from men. The author of this study concluded: "Violence is socially, not biologically, programmed."[114]

Despite anthropologists' traditional interest in gender relationships, it was not until the feminist movement and radical criminology focused on the subject that the relationship of rape, gender inequality, and socioeconomic status was fully articulated. Writing from the Marxist perspective, which we explore in Chapter 8, Julia and Herman Schwendinger posited that "the impoverishment of the working class and the widening gap between rich and poor" create conditions for the prevalence of sexual violence.[115] A test of this hypothesis showed that while the incidence of sexual violence was not related to ethnic inequality, it was significantly related to general income inequality.[116]

A more recent study analyzed these findings and concluded that economic inequality was not the sole determinant of violent crime in our society. Forcible rape was found to be an added "cost" of many factors, including social disorganization.[117] In sum, many factors have been associated with the crime of rape: psychological problems, social factors, and even sociopolitical factors. Some experts suggest that boys are socialized to be aggressive and dominating, that the innate male sex drive leads to rape, and that pornography encourages men to rape by making sex objects of women, degrading women, and glamorizing violence against them. Rape has been explained in such a wide variety of ways that it is extremely difficult to plan preventive strategies and to formulate crime-control policy. Moreover, it has created major difficulties in the criminal justice system.

Rape and the Legal System

The difficulties of rape prosecutions have their roots in English common law. Sir Matthew Hale, a seventeenth-century jurist, explained in *Pleas of the Crown* (1685, 1736) how a jury was to be cautious in viewing evidence of rape: "[It] must be remembered . . . that it is an accusation easily to be made and hard to be proved, and harder to be defended, by the party accused, tho never so innocent."[118] This instruction, which so definitively protects the defendant, has until recently been a mandatory instruction to juries in the United States. Along with many other legal and policy changes, many jurisdictions have now cast it aside. The requirement of particularly stringent proof in rape cases had always been justified by the seriousness of the offense and the heavy penalties associated with it, plus the stigma attached to such a conviction.

Difficulties of Prosecution

Victims of rape have often been regarded with suspicion by the criminal justice system. The victim's testimony has not sufficed to convict the defendant, no matter how unimpeachable that testimony may have been. There had to be "corroborating evidence," such as semen, torn clothes, bruises, or eyewitness testimony.

Another major issue has been that of consent. Did the victim encourage, entice, or maybe even agree to the act? Was the attack forced? Did the victim resist? Martin Schwartz and Todd Clear sum up the reasons for such questions: "There is a widespread belief in our culture that women 'ask for it,' either individually or as a group." They compare rape victims to victims of other offenses: "Curiously, society does not censure the robbery victim for walking around with $10, or the burglary victim for keeping all of those nice things in his house, or the car theft victim for showing off his flashy new machine, just asking for someone to covet it."[119]

Because defendants in rape cases so often claim that the victim was in some way responsible for the attack, rape victims in the courtroom tend to become the "accused," required to defend their good reputations, their propriety, and their mental soundness. The severity of the assault, the injuries the victim sustains, whether or not the assailant was a stranger, and the victim's social support network all play a role in terms of the rape-reporting process.[120] Experts claim that as many as 60 percent of rapes are not reported.[121] In sum, so many burdens are placed on the victim that no one seriously wonders why so few rapes are reported and why so few men accused of rape are convicted.

Legislative Changes

The feminist movement has had a considerable impact on laws and attitudes concerning rape in our country. The state of Michigan was a leader in the movement to reform such laws by creating, in 1975, the new crime of "criminal sexual conduct" to replace the traditional rape laws. It distinguishes four degrees of assaultive sexual acts, differentiated by the amount of force used, the infliction of injury, and the age and mental condition of the victim.

The law is gender-neutral, in that it makes illegal any type of forcible sex, including homosexual rape. Other states have followed Michigan's lead. Schwartz and Clear have suggested that reform should go one step further. They argue that if rape were covered by the general assault laws rather than by a separate statute on sex crimes, the emphasis would be on the assault (the action of the offender) and not on the resistance (the action of the victim).

Some states have also removed many of the barriers women previously encountered as witnesses in the courtroom. Thus, in states with rape shield laws, women are no longer required to disclose their prior sexual activity, and corroboration requirements have been reduced or eliminated; as noted earlier, some states have reversed two centuries of legal tradition by striking down the "marital rape exemption" so that a wife may now charge her husband with rape.[122] But law reform has limits. Unfortunately, prejudices die hard.

Community Response

Women's advocates have taken an interest not only in legislative reform but also in the community's response to the victims of rape. In 1970, the first rape-specific support project, Bay Area Women Against Rape—a volunteer-staffed emergency phone information service—was established in Berkeley, California.[123] By 1973, similar projects had spread throughout the country. Run by small, unaffiliated groups, they handled crises, monitored agencies (hospitals, police, courts) that came in contact with victims, educated the public about the problems of victims, and even provided lessons in self-defense.

By the late 1970s, the number of these centers and their activities had increased dramatically. The mass media reported on their successes. Federal and, later, state and local support for such services rose. As the centers became more professional, they formed boards of directors, prepared detailed budgets to comply with the requirements of funding agencies, hired social workers and mental health personnel, and developed their political action component. But even with increased support, the demand for the services of rape crisis centers far outweighs the available resources.

KIDNAPPING

Kidnapping, as such, was not recognized as a felony under English common law; it was a misdemeanor. Some forms of kidnapping were later criminalized by statute. In the eighteenth century, the most frequent form of kidnapping, according to the great legal scholar Sir William Blackstone, was stealing children and sending them to servitude in the American colonies. Other forms of kidnapping were the "crimping," or shanghaiing, of persons for involuntary service aboard ships and the abduction of women for purposes of prostitution abroad.

All these offenses have elements in common, and together they define the crime of **kidnapping**: abduction and detention by force or fraud and transport beyond the authority of the place where the crime was committed. It was not until the kidnapping of Charles Lindbergh's infant son in 1932 that comprehensive kidnapping legislation was enacted in the United States. In passing the federal kidnapping statute—the so-called Lindbergh Act (now 18 U.S. Code [sec.] 1201)—Congress made it a felony to kidnap and transport a victim across a state or national border. The crime was subject to the death penalty, unless the victim was released unharmed.

In the United States, kidnapping often involves the abduction of a child from one parent by the other. One interesting case recently appeared in the news. In October 1979, Stephen Fagan kidnapped his two daughters, Lisa (age 2) and Rachael (age 5), from Massachusetts and then moved to Florida. He told his daughters that their mother had died. It was not until 1998 that an anonymous tip led to his arrest in Florida, where he was living the high life as a socialite under the name Dr. William Martin. Fagan claimed that he took his daughters away from his ex-wife, Barbara Kurth, who he believed was an unfit and alcoholic mother. Kurth vehemently denied the allegation. Fagan was charged with kidnapping his daughters even though the crime had occurred 20 years earlier. In a plea agreement, Fagan was spared jail time; instead, he was fined $100,000 and received a suspended 3- to 5-year prison sentence. He was also required to serve probation for 5 years. The two daughters stood by their father and decided not to reunite with their mother.[124]

ROBBERY

Robbery is the taking of property from a victim by force and violence or by the threat of violence. The Model Penal Code (Section 222.1) grades robbery as a felony of the second degree, commanding a prison term of up to 10 years. If the robber has intentionally inflicted serious physical injury or attempted to kill, the sentence may be as long as life. In reality, however, the average sentence upon conviction for one charge of robbery is 6 years.[125] In 2007, the number of robbery offenses was 445,125, or 147.6 robberies per 100,000 population.[126]

Offenders display weapons, mostly guns and knives, in about 50 percent of all robberies (Table 10.4). Since 22.2 percent of all robberies net the perpetrator less than $50, the overall reporting rate for robbery is only slightly higher than 60 percent. Robberies occur most frequently on the street and in the home[127] (Table 10.5).

Characteristics of Robbers

Criminologists have classified the characteristics of robbers as well as the characteristics of robberies. John Conklin detected four types of robbers:

- The *professional robber* carefully plans and executes a robbery, often with many accomplices; steals large sums of money; and has a long-term, deep commitment to robbery as a means of supporting a hedonistic lifestyle.

- The *opportunistic robber* (the most common) has no long-term commitment to robbery; targets victims for small amounts of money ($20 or less); victimizes elderly women, drunks, cab drivers, and other people who seem to be in no position to resist; and is young and generally inexperienced.

TABLE 10.4   Robbery, Types of Weapons Used: Percent Distribution by Region, 2007

Region	Total All Weapons*	Firearms	Knives or Cutting Instruments	Other Weapons	Strong-arm
Total	100.0	42.8	8.3	9.0	39.9
Northeast	100.0	34.6	10.5	8.3	46.6
Midwest	100.0	43.7	6.4	9.0	41.0
South	100.0	50.4	7.4	9.0	33.2
West	100.0	34.8	9.6	9.4	46.2

*Because of rounding, the percentages may not sum to 100.0.

SOURCE: U.S. Department of Justice, Federal Bureau of Investigation, *Crime in the United States, 2007* (September 2008); available at http://www.fbi.gov/ucr/cius2007/offenses/expanded_information/data/robberytable_03.html.

TABLE 10.5   Robbery, Location: Percent Distribution by Population Group, 2007

Type	Group I (61 cities, 250,000 and over; population 38,190,834)	Group II (162 cities, 100,000 to 249,999; population 24,273,026)	Group III (426 cities, 50,000 to 99,999; population 29,252,848)	Group IV (724 cities, 25,000 to 49,999; population 24,940,391)	Group V (1,599 cities, 10,000 to 24,999; population 25,356,536)	Group VI (6,425 cities, under 10,000; population 20,816,186)	County agencies (3,612 agencies; population 82,797,741)
Total*	100.0	100.0	100.0	100.0	100.0	100.0	100.0
Street/highway	52.5	44.8	39.5	37.1	30.1	25.5	33.8
Commercial house	11.9	14.7	15.6	14.8	16.7	13.1	16.2
Gas or service station	1.9	2.5	3.0	3.3	3.9	4.0	3.4
Convenience store	4.1	5.8	6.4	6.7	8.0	8.8	6.8
Residence	14.0	14.5	13.7	13.6	15.6	14.7	21.2
Bank	1.4	2.0	2.6	2.9	3.6	3.3	2.3
Miscellaneous	14.1	15.7	19.3	21.6	22.1	30.7	16.3

*Because of rounding, the percentages may not sum to 100.0

SOURCE: U.S. Department of Justice, Federal Bureau of Investigation, *Crime in the United States, 2007* (September 2008); available at http://www.fbi.gov/ucr/cius2007/offenses/expanded_information/data/robberytable_02.html.

- The *addict robber* is addicted to drugs, has a low level of commitment to robbery but a high level of commitment to theft, plans less than professional robbers but more than opportunistic robbers, wants just enough money for a fix, and may or may not carry a weapon.

- The *alcoholic robber* has no commitment to robbery as a way of life, has no commitment to theft, does not plan his or her robberies, usually robs people after first assaulting them, takes few precautions, and is apprehended more often than other robbers.[128]

According to the Uniform Crime Reports, nearly 90 percent of those arrested for robbery in 2007 were males. Approximately 60 percent of the arrestees were under 25 years of age. In terms of race, blacks accounted for more than 50 percent of all robbery arrests, whites accounted for 45 percent, and all other races constituted the remaining 1 percent of all robbery arrests.[129]

The Consequences of Robbery

Robbery is a property crime as well as a violent crime. It is the combination of the motive for economic gain and the violent nature of robbery that makes it so serious.[130] An estimated $588 million was lost as a result of robbery in 2007 alone. The value of stolen property per incident averaged $1,321.[131] Loss of money, however, is certainly not the only consequence of robbery. The million-odd robberies that take place each year leave psychological and physical trauma in their wake, not to mention the pervasive fear and anxiety that have contributed to the decay of inner cities.

Not all criminologists agree, however, that the high level of fear is warranted. After examining trends in robbery-homicide data from 52 of the largest cities in the United States, one researcher found "little support for the fears that there is a new breed of street criminals who cause more serious injuries and deaths in robberies. Very recent trends point in the other direction. Killing a robbery victim appears to be going out of fashion."[132]

ORGANIZED CRIME

It's enough to make John Gotti turn in his grave—the feds are administering the last rites to his once-powerful Gambino crime family.

Only five days after the godfather's funeral, FBI agents yesterday pounced on 14 alleged family members and associates wanted for murder and racketeering crimes stretching back to the late '80s—a time when the Gambinos ruled New York's gangland with iron fists.

"It's a whole different world than it was," U.S. Attorney Jim Comey said, pointing proudly to a pyramid chart of rubbed-out Gambino mobsters with black crosses stamped on their faces.

"'This thing of ours'—La Cosa Nostra—is very, very different today."

The freshest black cross was on the head of one of the late Dapper Don's longest serving capos, Louis "Big Louie" Vallario, who was one of four men indicted for the 1989 execution of Staten Island businessman Fred Weiss.

One of the Gambinos' rising stars, Michael "Mikey Scars" DiLeonardo, was also arrested for the execution-style slaying. It was allegedly carried out as a favor to Gotti, who feared Weiss was cooperating with the feds.

Comey said the three indictments unsealed yesterday represented a "further dismantling of the Gambino family's leadership" and sent a signal that the feds will prevent the family from re-establishing its "violent, extortionate grip" over New York.

New York FBI assistant director Kevin Donovan described the busts as the "latest chapter in the decade-long saga of the decline of the Gambinos."

"Making money the mob way has always meant instilling fear through intimidation and violence, and it is not true that the victims of mob violence are just other mobsters," Donovan said.

Since Gotti was put away for the last time in June 1992, the Gambinos' grip over legitimate industries, such as garbage carting and the waterfront, has been pried loose.

And the family's ability to rebuild was dealt a further blow this month, when Peter Gotti, who took over from his ailing brother this year, was arrested along with 16 other soldiers and associates.

As part of the indictments unsealed yesterday, the feds claim to have busted a large-scale theft racket centered on a vegetable store in The Bronx, called Top Tomato. It was owned by Salvatore Sciandra, brother of Gambino member Carmine Sciandra, the indictment says.

Sciandra's wife, Margaret, and her mother, Mildred Scarpati, are also facing up to five years in prison after being charged with conspiracy to defraud Allstate Insurance by filing a bogus car-loss claim.

Three Gambino associates were also charged with extorting two Manhattan garment businesses.[133]

Earlier we noted that all forms of organizational criminality have in common the use of business enterprises for illegal profit. We have recognized some significant problems not only with existing definitions and conceptualizations of white-collar and corporate crime but also with the criminal justice response to such offenses. Similar problems arise in efforts to deal with organized crime. It, too, depends on business enterprises. And, like corporate crime, organized crime comes in so many varieties that attempts to define it precisely lead to frustration.

The difficulty of gaining access to information on organized crime has also hindered attempts to conceptualize the problems posed by this kind of law violation. Finally, law enforcement efforts have been inadequate to control the influence of organized crime. As will be evident, a greater effort must be made to uncover the nature, pattern, and extent of organized crime.

The History of Organized Crime

Organized crime had its origin in the great wave of immigrants from southern Italy (especially from Sicily) to the United States between 1875 and 1920. These immigrants came from an environment that historically had been hostile to them. Suppressed by successive bands of invaders and alien rulers dating back some 800 years before Christ, Sicily was first coveted by the Greeks and Phoenicians as a strategic location between major Mediterranean trade routes. In later centuries, Roman, Byzantine, Arab, Norman, German, Spanish, Austrian, and French soldiers all laid siege and claim to Sicily. Exploited by mostly absentee landlords with their armies, Sicilians had learned to survive by relying on the strength of their own families. Indeed, these families had undergone little change since Greco-Roman times, two millennia earlier.

A traditional Sicilian family has been described as an extended family, or clan; it includes lineal relations (grandparents, parents, children, grandchildren) and lateral relations through the paternal line—uncles, aunts, and cousins as far as the bloodline can be traced. This *famiglia* is hierarchically organized and administered by the head of the family, the *capo di famiglia* (the Romans called him *pater familias*), to whom all members owe obedience and loyalty. Strangers, especially those in positions of power in state or church, are not to be trusted. The importance of the family is evident in the famous Sicilian proverb *"La legge é per l ricchi, La forca é per l poveri, E la giustizie é per l buffoni."* (The law is for the rich, the gallows are for the poor, and justice is for the fools.) For Sicilians, all problems are resolved within the family, which must be kept strong. Its prestige, honor, wealth, and power have to be defended and strengthened, sometimes through alliances with more distant kin.[134]

Throughout history, these strong families have served each other and Sicily. Upon migration to the United States, members of Sicilian families soon found that the social environment in their new country was as hostile as that of the old. Aspirations were encouraged, yet legitimate means to realize them were often not available. And the new country seemed already to have an established pattern for achieving wealth and power by unethical means. Many of America's great fortunes—those of the Astors, the Vanderbilts, the Goulds, the Sages, the Stanfords, the Rockefellers, the Carnegies, the Lords, the Harrimans—had been made by cunning, greed, and exploitation.

As time passed, new laws were enacted to address conspiracies in restraint of trade and other economic offenses. Yet by the time the last wave of Sicilian immigrants reached the United States, the names of the great robber barons were connected with major universities, foundations, and charitable institutions.[135] At the local level, the Sicilian immigrants found themselves involved in a system of politics in which patronage and protection were dispensed by corrupt politicians and petty hoodlums from earlier immigrant groups—German, Irish, and Jewish. The Sicilian family structure helped its members survive in this hostile environment. It also created the organizational basis that permitted them to respond to the opportunity created when, on January 16, 1920, the Eighteenth Amendment to the Constitution outlawed the manufacture, sale, and transportation of alcoholic beverages.

Howard Abadinsky explains what happened:

> Prohibition acted as a catalyst for the mobilization of criminal elements in an unprecedented manner. Pre-prohibition crime, insofar as it was organized, centered around corrupt political machines, vice entrepreneurs, and, at the bottom, gangs. Prohibition unleashed an unparalleled level of competitive criminal violence and changed the order—the gang leaders emerged on top.[136]

During the early years of Prohibition, the names of the most notorious bootleggers, mobsters, and gangsters sounded German, Irish, and Jewish: Arthur Flegenheimer (better known as "Dutch Schultz"), Otto Gass, Bo and George Weinberg, Arnold Rothstein, John T. Nolen (better known as "Legs Diamond"), Vincent "Mad Dog" Coll, Waxey Gordon, Owney Madden, and Joe Rock. By the time Prohibition was repealed, Al Capone, Salvatore Luciana (better known as "Lucky Luciano"), Frank Costello, Johnny Torrio, Vito Genovese, Guiseppe Doto (better known as "Joe Adonis"), and many other Sicilians were preeminent in the underworld. They had become folk heroes and role models for young boys in the Italian ghettos, many of whom were to seek their own places in this new society.

Sicilian families were every bit as ruthless in establishing their crime empires as the earlier

■ On St. Valentine's Day, 1929, while Al Capone vacationed in Florida, his mobsters machine-gunned their rivals in Chicago. The victims were lured to this garage (to buy prohibited liquor) where the hit men, dressed in stolen police uniforms and driving a stolen police car, "raided" the place, told the victims to line up against the wall, and then opened fire.

immigrant groups had been. They were so successful in their domination of organized crime that, especially after World War II, organized crime became virtually synonymous with the Sicilian Mafia.

The term "Mafia" appears to derive from an Arabic word denoting "place of refuge." The concept, which was adopted in Sicily during the era of Arab rule, gradually came to describe a mode of life and survival. Sicilians trace the word to a tale of revenge that took place on Easter Monday, 1282. On this day, a French soldier who was part of a band of marauding foreigners raped a Sicilian woman on her wedding day. Following the assault, bands of Sicilians went to the streets of Palermo to slaughter hundreds of Frenchmen, spurred on by the screams of the young girl's mother: *Ma fia, ma fia* ("My daughter, my daughter").[137]

Ultimately, the **Mafia** became the entirety of those Sicilian families that were loosely associated with one another in operating organized crime, both in America and in Sicily.[138] The first realistic depiction of the organization of the Mafia came with the testimony of Joseph Valachi before the Senate's McClellan Committee in 1963. Valachi, a disenchanted soldier in New York's Genovese crime family, was the first member of Italian organized crime to describe a quasi-military secret criminal syndicate. From that point on, the Mafia has also been referred to as *La Cosa Nostra,* literally translated as "this thing of ours."[139]

Despite Valachi's testimony and later revelations, some scholars still doubt the existence of a Sicilian-based American crime syndicate. To criminologist Jay Albanese, for instance,

> it is clear . . . that despite popular opinion which has for many years insisted on the existence of a secret criminal society called

"the Mafia," which somehow evolved from Italy, many separate historical investigations have found no evidence to support such a belief.[140]

The Structure and Impact of Organized Crime

Americans have felt the impact of organized crime, and they have followed the media coverage of the mob wars and their victims with fascination. But little was known about the Mafia's actual structure in the United States until a succession of government investigations began to unravel its mysteries. The major investigations were conducted by the Committee on Mercenary Crimes, in 1932; the Special Senate Committee to Investigate Organized Crime in Interstate Commerce (the Kefauver crime committee), from 1950 to 1951; the Senate Permanent Subcommittee on Investigations (the McClellan committee), from 1956 to 1963; President Lyndon Johnson's Commission on Law Enforcement and Administration of Justice (the Task Force on Organized Crime), from 1964 to 1967; and the President's Commission on Organized Crime, which reported to President Reagan in 1986 and 1987.[141]

The findings of these investigations established the magnitude of organized crime in the United States. It had become an empire almost beyond the reach of government, with vast resources derived from a virtual monopoly on gambling and loan-sharking; drug trafficking; pornography and prostitution; labor racketeering; murder for hire; the control of local crime activities; and the theft and fencing of securities, cars, jewels, and consumer goods of all sorts.[142] Above all, it was found that organized crime had

infiltrated a vast variety of legitimate businesses, such as stevedoring (the loading and unloading of ships), the fish and meat industries, the wholesale and retail liquor industry (including bars and taverns), the vending machine business, the securities and investment business, the waste disposal business, and the construction industry.[143]

Specific legislation and law enforcement programs have allowed governmental agencies to assert some measure of control over organized crime. Cases have been successfully prosecuted under the **Racketeer Influenced and Corrupt Organizations (RICO) Act** of 1970.[144] This statute attacks racketeering activities by prohibiting the investment of any funds derived from racketeering in any enterprise that is engaged in interstate commerce. In addition, the **Federal Witness Protection Program,** established under the Organized Crime Control Act of 1970 (also known as the Witness Security Program, or "Wit Sec"), has made it easier for witnesses to testify in court by guaranteeing them a new identity, thus protecting them against revenge.[145] More than 7,500 witnesses and close to 10,000 family members have sought the services of this flagship program within the United States Marshals Service.

The information provided by the governmental commissions, in combination with scholarly research, has established that the structure of an organized crime group is similar to that of a Sicilian family. Family members are joined by "adopted" members; the family is then aided at the functional level by nonmember auxiliaries.[146] The use of military designations such as *caporegima* ("lieutenant") and "soldier" does not alter the fact that a criminal organization is rather more like a closely knit family business enterprise than like an army.[147] On the basis of testimony presented by Joseph Valachi in 1963, the commission's

Task Force on Organized Crime was able to construct an organization chart of the typical Mafia, or Cosa Nostra, family (Figure 10.3).

Relations among the various families, which formerly were determined in ruthlessly fought gang wars, have more recently been facilitated by a loosely formed coordinating body called "the Commission." By agreement, the country has been divided into territorial areas of jurisdiction, influence, and operation. These arrangements are subject to revision from time to time, by mutual agreement. Likewise, rules of conduct have become subject to control or regulation by the heads of the various crime families. They consider, for example, to what extent each family

"I TAKE IT YOU'RE ALSO IN THE FEDERAL WITNESS-PROTECTION PROGRAM."

Sidney Harris. ScienceCartoonsPlus.com.

FIGURE 10.3 Organization chart of the typical Mafia family.

Source: President's Commission on Law Enforcement and Administration of Justice, *Task Force Report: Organized Crime* (Washington, D.C.: U.S. Government Printing Office, 1967), p. 9.

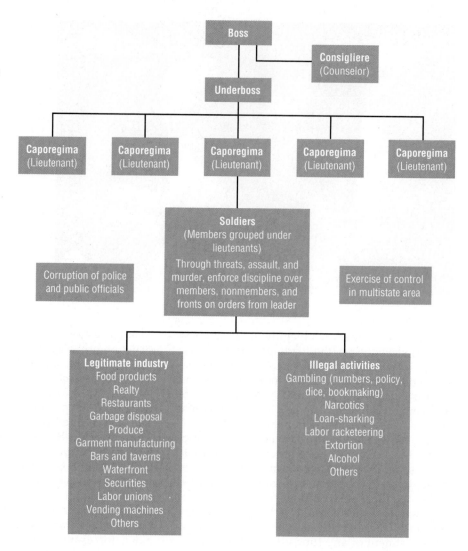

should enter the hard-drug market, how much violence should be used, and how each will deal with public officials and the police.[148]

Informants at the "convention" of the so-called Apalachin conspirators provided a rare opportunity to learn about the way crime families reach agreement on their operations. On November 14, 1957, 63 of the country's most notorious underworld figures were arrested in Apalachin, New York, at or near the home of Joseph M. Barbara, a well-known organized-crime figure. Participants included New York's Vito Genovese, Carlo Gambino, Paul Castellano, and Joe Bonanno. Also arrested were Florida's don, Santo Trafficante Jr.; Sam ("Momo") Giancana of Chicago; Detroit boss Joe Zerilli; and the boss of the Buffalo rackets, Stefano Magaddino. Apparently, they had congregated at Barbara's home to settle a dispute among the families, which 3 weeks earlier had resulted in the assassination of Mangano family boss Albert Anastasia (the Mangano family was predecessor to the largest contemporary crime family in the United States, the Gambino crime family) and the

attempted murder in May 1957 of Francesco Castiglia, better known as Frank Costello, by the current godfather of the Genovese crime family, Vincent "The Chin" Gigante.

The presence of so many out-of-state license plates on brand-new Cadillacs and Lincolns in this small upstate New York town caught the attention of New York State police sergeant Edgar Croswell, an amateur organized-crime buff. Croswell, already somewhat suspicious of the true nature of Barbara's business dealings, put in a call to federal authorities and arranged to have a roadblock set up to guard against any of the participants leaving without being questioned. The police presence didn't go unnoticed by the gangsters, who rushed to make a quick escape back to their fiefdoms.

The comical scene of men in silk suits and fedora hats running through the forest was enough for Croswell. He caught as many as he could and placed them under arrest. None of the conspirators, however, publicly revealed the true nature of their meeting. Some suggested that,

quite by coincidence, all had simply come to visit their sick friend Joe Barbara, who would die of a heart attack 2 years later. All were indicted and convicted for refusing to answer the grand jury's questions about the true purpose of the meeting. The convictions were subsequently reversed.[149]

Certain core business matters were decided at that meeting:

- Carlo Gambino was given the leadership of the New York crime family that still bears his name, a family made famous by the subsequent exploits of the late John Gotti.

- As a vote of confidence for Vito Genovese, Frank Costello was asked to go into semiretirement to pave the way for Genovese to take over the family that Lucky Luciano had started.

- A ban was placed on any "made man" trafficking in drugs. "If you deal, you die" was the slogan that resonated throughout organized crime as of the late 1950s. Although widely ignored, the ban still exists today.

The activities of the Mafia appear to have shifted from the once extremely violent bootlegging and street-crime operations to a far more sophisticated level of criminal activity.[150] Modern organized crime has assumed international dimensions.[151] It extends not only to international drug traffic, but also to legitimate enterprises such as real estate and trade in securities, as well as to many other lucrative business enterprises. This transition has been accomplished both by extortion and by entry with laundered money derived from illegitimate activity. It is tempting to wonder whether we may be witnessing the same kind of metamorphosis that occurred a century ago, when the robber barons became legitimate business tycoons and, ultimately, philanthropists.

The New Ethnic Diversity in Organized Crime

Organized crime is not necessarily synonymous with the Mafia. Other groups also operate in the United States. Foremost among them are the Colombian crime families, whose brutality is unrivaled by any other organized-crime group; and Bolivian, Peruvian, and Jamaican crime families, which since the 1970s have organized the production, transportation, and distribution within the United States of cocaine and marijuana.

Another form of organized crime, initiated by disillusioned veterans of the Korean War and reinforced by veterans of Vietnam, appears in the outlaw motorcycle gangs. Among them are the Hell's Angels, the Pagans, the Outlaws, the Sons of Silence, and the Bandidos. All are organized along military lines; all are devoted to violence; all are involved in the production and distribution of narcotics and other drugs. Many members are also involved in other criminal activities, including extortion and prostitution, trafficking in stolen motorcycles and parts, and dealing in automatic weapons and explosives.

Among other organized groups engaged in various criminal activities are Chinese gangs (Figure 10.4), the so-called Israeli Mafia, the recently emerging Russian-Jewish Mafia, Jamaican posses, and the "Tattooed Men" of Japan's Yakuza, whose Yamaguchi-Gumi family alone has over

The Big Business of Organized Crime in Mexico

Mexican President Felipe Calderon told a U.N. representative in Mexico City recently that the deployment of the Mexican military in counternarcotics operations is only a temporary solution, and that he plans to phase out the military's role in these efforts. In recent weeks, the military has launched a large-scale security operation in select cities along the U.S.-Mexico border, disarming local police forces and conducting sweeps and raids in an effort to strike back at the increasingly violent Mexican drug cartels.

Calderon's comments address a standing question on both sides of the border: What is the best way to deal with cartel activity? Germane to that question is defining just what it is that the security forces are up against.

The violence taking place in northern Mexico—and leaking across the border into the southern United States—is viewed by some as the result of the actions of narco-terrorists, while others call it an insurgency. But for the most part, those charged with countering the problem refer to it as criminality—more specifically, as organized crime. Defining the problem this way shapes the decisions regarding the tools and policies that are best suited to fighting it.

On both sides of the border, the primary forces tasked with dealing with the drug cartels and the spillover effects are law enforcement elements. In a law enforcement operation, as opposed to a counterinsurgency or counterterrorism operation, the ultimate goal is not only to stop the criminal behavior but also to detain the criminals and amass sufficient evidence to try them in court. The need for such evidence is not always as pressing in counterterrorism cases, in which the intelligence case can be made without having to reach the stricter threshold prosecution would require. Since taking office, Calderon has involved the military more than his predecessors in what traditionally has been the realm of law enforcement. This has had positive results against drug traffickers, at the expense of occa-

sional higher tensions between federal and local authorities.

Meanwhile, on the U.S. side of the border, the Bush administration's war on terrorism appears much more pressing and therefore receives many more resources than the fight against illegal drug activity and border violence. This does not mean the United States has not devoted modern technological resources to battle drug traffickers along the border. In fact, it has devoted significant intelligence assets to assist in tracking and cracking down on the drug cartels, from collecting signals and electronic intelligence to offering training and assistance to Mexican forces.

In viewing this as mainly a law enforcement issue, rather than a military one, several additional problems are being encountered on both sides of the border—not the least of which is a significant lack of coordination. On the Mexican side, local law enforcement often is infiltrated by the cartels and does not cooperate fully with essential government agencies—a phenomenon not unheard of north of the border as well. On the U.S. side, the various counties along the border like to run their own programs, and there are issues of federal American Indian land and private land to consider as well. A similar split between federal and local regulations and enforcement occurs on the Mexico side, where drug laws are all federal, so local officials can make arrests but must hand over suspects to the federal police. Further, while there is some level of coordination between the Mexican and the U.S. sides, frequently there is a lack of communication or significant miscommunication, such that an operation on one side of the border is not communicated to the other side.

These problems exist in many places, but they are particularly sensitive on the U.S.-Mexico border. A miscommunication between the United States and, say, the Colombian government does not have the immediate impact as a similar miscommunication along the U.S. border. Moves are under

way to increase the coordination of overall counterdrug efforts along the border, but the contentious issue of immigration adds a second layer to the problem. For the United States, while there apparently are similarities between what is happening in Mexico and previous counterdrug fights in Colombia—or even in Thailand and Afghanistan—the contiguous border consistently adds a layer of complexity to the problem.

The United States has experience shutting down major drug-trafficking routes. It significantly disrupted the Caribbean drug routes, using naval interdiction (though this shifted many of these routes to Mexico, accelerating the rise of the Mexican cartels). And there is plenty of global experience sealing borders. The Germans were quite effective at sealing the border after World War II, as were many of the Soviet bloc states. The problem, of course, with completely sealing a border is that it stops trade, something the United States is not willing to do. Therefore, if the United States cannot effectively seal the border without risking trade, it instead can channel the flow of traffic and migration across the border. But even by channeling the flow, it is extremely difficult to separate the illegal trade from the legal.

As we have mentioned before, there is a significant economic component to this trade, both legal and illegal. By some estimates, some $24 billion a year is transferred to Mexico as a result of the drug trade. This is essentially free money and needs to go somewhere, making it a substantial portion of the Mexican economy. While the Mexican government is keen to stop the violence along the border and among the cartels, in some ways it is less interested in stopping the flow of money. History has shown that countries with large-scale criminal enterprises—such as the United States in the 1920s and 1930s—get rich, given the tremendous pool of capital available for investment. This illicit money eventually works it way into the system through legal channels.

This is a fundamental aspect of the phenomenon we are seeing now. It is a classic case of organized crime. The Mexican drug cartels are, for the most part, organized crime groups. What distinguishes Mexican organized crime groups and others from revolutionaries, terrorists and hybrid organizations such as the Revolutionary Armed Forces of Colombia (FARC) is the underlying principle of making money.

In the global system, there is an economy of crime. It currently is built around drugs, but any item that is illegal in one place and legal in [an] other and has an artificially inflated price quickly can become the center of the system. Human trafficking, smuggling and counterfeiting are cases in point, as was alcohol during prohibition. Products move from where they are legal (or at least not well-controlled) to where they are in demand but illegal. The money, of course, moves in the opposite direction. That money eventually ends up in the normal banking system. Organized crime wants to make money and it might want to manipulate the system, but it does not seek to overthrow the system or transform society. Insurgencies and revolutions seek to transform.

In the end, organized crime is about making money. Endemic organized crime leads to corruption and collusion, and in the long term often burns itself out as the money earned through its activities eventually moves into the legal economic system. When organized crime groups become rich enough, they move their money into legitimate businesses in order to launder it or at least use it, eventually turning it into established money that has entered the realm of business. This can get more complicated when organized crime and insurgents/guerrillas overlap, as is the case with FARC.

The problems we are seeing in Mexico are similar to those we have seen in past cases, in which criminal elements become factionalized. In Mexico, these factions are fighting over control of drug routes and domain. The battles that are taking place are largely the result of fighting among the organized crime groups, rather than cartels fighting the Mexican government. In some ways, the Mexican military and security forces are a third party in this—not the focus. Ultimately, the cartels—not the government—control the level of violence and security in the country.

As new groups emerge and evolve, they frequently can be quite violent and in some sense anarchic. When a new group of drug dealers moves into a neighborhood, it might be flamboyant and excessively violent. It is the same on a much larger scale with these organized crime cartels. However, although cartel infighting is tolerated to some extent, the government is forced to react when the level of violence starts to get out of hand. This is what we are seeing in Mexico.

However, given that organized crime tends to become more conservative as it grows and becomes more established, the situation in Mexico could be reaching a tipping point. For example, during the summer of 2007, the Gulf and Sinaloa cartels declared a temporary truce as their rivalry began to impact their business operations. As the competition among the cartels settles, they could begin to draw back their forces and deal with those members who are excessively violent or out of control. This is simply a way of assuring their operations. The American Mafia followed a similar pattern, evolving into an organism with strong discipline and control.

There is a question now as to whether the Mexican cartels are following the American model or imitating the Colombian model, which is a hybrid of organized crime and an insurgency. In fact, they might be following both. Mexico, in some sense, is two countries. The North has a much higher standard of living than the rest of the country, especially the area south of Mexico City. In the North, we could ultimately see a move in the direction of the American Mafia, whereas in the South—the home of the domestic guerrilla groups Zapatista National Liberation Army and Popular Revolutionary Army—it could shift more toward the Colombian model.

While the situation is evolving, the main battle in Mexico continues to be waged among various cartel factions, rather than among the cartels and the Mexican government or security forces. The goal of organized crime, and the goal of many of these cartels, is to get rich within the system, with minor variations on how that is achieved. A revolutionary group, on the other hand, wants to overthrow and change the system. The cartels obviously are working outside the legal framework, but they are not putting forward an alternative—nor do they seem to want to. Rather, they can achieve their goals simply through payoffs and other forms of corruption.

The most likely outcome is not a merger between the cartels and the guerrilla groups, or even a shift in the cartels' priorities to include government overthrow. However, as the government turns up the pressure, the concern is that the cartels will adopt insurgent-style tactics.

Organized crime is not street crime; it is systemic geopolitical crime. It is a significant social force, bringing huge amounts of capital into a system. This flow of money can reshape the society. But this criminal supply chain runs parallel to, and in many cases intersects, the legitimate global supply chain. Whether through smuggling and money laundering or increased investment capital and higher consumption rates, the underground and aboveground economies intersect.

U.S. and Mexican counternarcotics operations have an instant impact on the supply chain. Such operations shift traffic patterns across the border, affect the level of stability in the border areas—where there is a significant amount of manufacturing and trade—and impact sensitive social and political issues between the two countries, particularly immigration. In this light, then, violence is only one small part of the total impact that cartel activities and government counternarcotics efforts are having on the border.

Source

Rodger Baker, "The Big Business of Organized Crime in Mexico," Feb. 13, 2008; available at http://www.stratfor.com/weekly/big_business_organized_crime_mexico. Copyright 2008 by Strategic Forecasting Inc. Reprinted with permission of Strategic Forecasting Inc. in the format Textbook via Copyright Clearance Center.

Questions for Discussion

1. To what extent does the problem of organized crime in the United States require an international or global solution?
2. Assuming that organized crime is a "systemic geopolitical crime," do we have the law-enforcement and regulatory resources necessary to combat it?

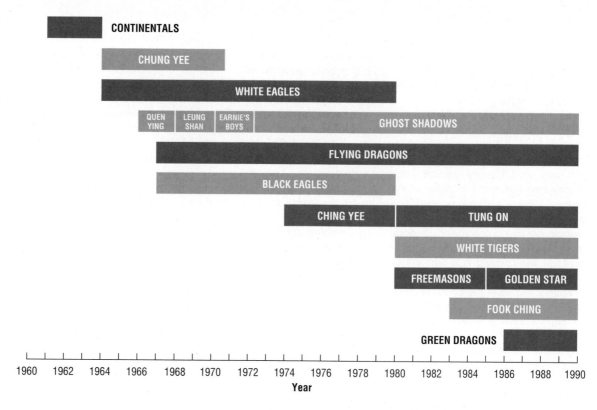

FIGURE 10.4 Time line of New York City's Chinese gangs, 1960–1990.

Source: From *Chinese Subculture and Criminality: Non-traditional Crime Groups in America* by Ko-lin Chin, p. 76. Copyright © 1990 by Ko-lin Chin. Reproduced with permission of Greenwood Publishing Group, Inc., Westport, CT.

56,000 members, or nearly 20 times the number of fully initiated Italian organized-crime members in all the crews of all the families in the United States. All these groups have demonstrated potential for great social disruption.[152]

EMERGING PROBLEMS

Some of the more pressing issues we face today include global terrorism, an increase in hate crimes nationwide, the spread of racist and anti-government militias, and deadly shootings in American schools. In recent years, largely as a result of media attention, these crimes have had a dramatic impact on the public's perception that violence has reached epidemic proportions. In reality, these crimes account for an extremely low proportion of all violent crimes, and rates for two of them (terrorism and violence in schools) have even gone down.

Terrorism

Many of those who worked in the South and North Towers of the World Trade Center arrived like clockwork—6:30 A.M., 7:00 A.M., 7:30 A.M., 8:00 A.M., and 8:30 A.M. They poured in from all over the tristate area (New York, New Jersey, and Connecticut) by car, rail, bus, ferry, and foot to ascend the two most visible symbols of New York.

Every day the mall on the ground floor was a teaming mass of blue- and white-collar workers—all marching toward one of two towers. It was no different on the morning of September 11, 2001. Secretaries were already checking e-mail at Nishi-Nippon Bank, Ltd., on the 102nd floor. Bond traders from Cantor Fitzgerald Securities were grabbing their morning coffee on the 105th floor. And waiters were setting the tables for a private function at the restaurant Windows on the World on the 107th floor.

Life was its usual fast pace for over 30,000 people working or visiting the World Trade Center—that is, until hijacked American Airlines Flight 11 crashed into the central core of the North Tower, raining a hail of debris over much of lower Manhattan. Witnesses said that the tall, sleek building literally swallowed the Boeing 767. Twenty-one minutes later, United Airlines Flight 175 collided with the South Tower, igniting a second fire that trapped helpless workers high above the New York City skyline. Desperate and with no means of escape, several hundred jumped to their tragic deaths.

At 10:00 A.M., the South Tower collapsed, the building imploding from the burning jet fuel and instantly killing thousands of workers, police, and firefighters. A thick and dark cloud enveloped Tribeca (the neighborhood in Manhattan represented by the *Tri*angle *Be*low *Ca*nal Street) like a fast-moving volcano. Thousands ran from lower Manhattan with an understandable mix of panic, fear, anger, confusion, and hysteria.

In a matter of seconds, everything and everybody left behind were covered in ash. It was, as some described it, like hell breaking loose or hell on Earth. After the thunderous crash of metal and concrete, the air had a strong and pungent smell of a chemical burn. The scene had all trappings of a movie set—a high-budget pyrotechnic war movie. Huge chunks of metal, tons of paper, and thick ash covered the deserted streets of a fallen city. Anyone approaching Liberty Street or West Street would see the unimaginable. Familiar landmarks were gone—buildings were no longer where they once were. Cars close to "Ground Zero" had literally melted to the ground from the heat of the fire and implosions.

People who had escaped from the North and South Towers, and those who emerged from adjoining buildings, were dazed. Some were in shock. Many were crying and consoling each other. Others were in desperate need of medical attention, with first- and second-degree burns. People who were bleeding from falling debris and choking from fumes rushed from lower Manhattan toward the Brooklyn Bridge, up Church Street and West Broadway. Many were crowded onto ferries to New Jersey. Everything that was typical, normal, and usual no longer was.

Emergency personnel from all five boroughs of New York City raced toward Tribeca and Ground Zero in a frenzied effort to put out the fire, to save and comfort the injured, to rescue the trapped, to evacuate the surrounding area, to set up roadblocks, and to pray for the dead. Twenty-nine minutes after the South Tower disappeared, the North Tower followed. Once again, the building incinerated its victims.

Within less than 2 hours after the first plane hit the North Tower, emergency and rescue workers set up a triage area. All hospitals with trauma centers were immediately instructed to make room for thousands of victims. Empty stretchers and gurneys were brought to the sidewalk in front of Saint Vincents Hospital to speed the receipt of a mass of casualties. Only 250 ambulances left the site of the World Trade Center.

Firefighters and rescue workers dotted the remnants of the Twin Towers, sifting through the sharp and twisted debris, hoping against hope for one miracle at a time. There were precious few. Families of the missing posted photos of lost loved ones. Maybe someone had seen them—perhaps they were unconscious in a hospital or still alive buried in the rubble.

Less than 1 hour after the World Trade Center was attacked, American Airlines Flight 77 crashed into the western facade of the Pentagon, setting off an enormous fireball that shot way up in the sky. Black smoke filled the air, along with the smell of jet fuel. It was pandemonium.

Soon thereafter, another hijacked plane, United Airlines Flight 93, crashed in a rural part of Pennsylvania. The United States, it appeared, was under attack. The White House was quickly evacuated. Thirty-thousand commercial airline flights were grounded. Incoming international flights were diverted.

As these events were unfolding, President George W. Bush was in Sarasota, Florida, about to address an elementary-school class about the importance of reading. President Bush addressed the nation that same evening, vowing to bring to justice those who committed these "despicable acts of terror."

The United States opted for a swift military response—called Operation Enduring Freedom. Both U.S. and British military operations using aircraft and cruise missiles commenced on October 7, 2001, against Afghanistan. Three carrier battle groups were promptly deployed, in addition to a sizable number of aircraft and special operations

The FBI list of Most Wanted Terrorists as of July, 2009.

Most Wanted Terrorists

Submit A Tip | **Wanted by the FBI** | **Counterterrorism** | **FBI Home Page**

The alleged terrorists on this list have been indicted by sitting Federal Grand Juries in various jurisdictions in the United States for the crimes reflected on their wanted posters. Evidence was gathered and presented to the Grand Juries, which led to their being charged. The indictments currently listed on the posters allow them to be arrested and brought to justice. Future indictments may be handed down as various investigations proceed in connection to other terrorist incidents, for example, the terrorist attacks on September 11, 2001.

The Rewards for Justice program, administered by the United States Department of State's Bureau of Diplomatic Security, offers rewards for information leading to the arrest of many of these terrorists.

It is also important to note that these individuals will remain wanted in connection with their alleged crimes until such time as the charges are dropped or when credible physical evidence is obtained, which proves with 100% accuracy, that they are deceased.

Usama Bin Laden

Adam Yahiye Gadahn

Daniel Andreas San Diego
En Espanol

Abdullah Ahmed Abdullah

Ayman Al-Zawahiri

Ali Atwa

Anas Al-Liby

Fazul Abdullah Mohammed

Hasan Izz-Al-Din

Ahmed Mohammed Hamed Ali

Jaber A. Elbaneh

Sheikh Ahmed Salim Swedan

Abdul Rahman Yasin

Fahid Mohammed Ally Msalam

Ahmad Ibrahim Al-Mughassil

Ali Saed Bin Ali El-Hoorie

Saif Al-Adel

Ibrahim Salih Mohammed
Al-Yacoub

Ramadan Abdullah Mohammad
Shallah

Abd Al Aziz Awda

Isnilon Totoni Hapilon

Mohammed Ali Hamadei

Jamel Ahmed Mohammed Ali
Al-Badawi

Abdelkarim Hussein Mohamed
Al-Nasser

forces. The objectives of Operation Enduring Freedom were the destruction of terrorist training camps in Afghanistan, the apprehension of Al Qaeda leaders, and the cessation of terrorist activities in Afghanistan. The history of this conflict is still being written, as U.S. forces continue to be drawn into armed conflict.

Terrorism is a resort to violence or a threat of violence on the part of a group seeking to accomplish a purpose against the opposition of constituted authority. Crucial to the terrorists' scheme is the exploitation of the media to attract attention to their cause. A series of coordinated terrorist attacks in Mumbai, India, in November 2008 captured the attention of the world's media outlets. The attackers killed more than 170 people and wounded hundreds more. Target selection—particularly the choice of the famed Taj Mahal Palace & Tower hotel—guaranteed notoriety.

Many clandestine organizations around the world have sought to draw attention to their causes—the Irish Republican Army (IRA), committed to the cause of uniting the British counties of Northern Ireland with the Republic of Ireland; Islamic fundamentalists committed to the protection of Islam in its purist form against any Western influence; various Palestinian factions opposed to Israeli occupation or to any Mideast peace settlement; radical groups all over the world seeking an end to capitalism or colonialism or the imposition of one or another form of totalitarian rule.

From the outset, the member states of the United Nations have been concerned about international terrorism because it endangers or takes innocent lives and jeopardizes fundamental freedoms, such as the freedom to travel and to congregate for public events. The UN effort to control international terrorism concentrates on removal of the underlying grievances that provoke people to sacrifice human lives, including their own, in an attempt to effect radical changes.[153] This approach to the control of terrorism is not concerned with the individual motivations of terrorists. Some of them may be highly motivated idealists; others are recruited for substantial rewards. The control effort is directed, rather, at the conditions that give rise to terrorism and at the removal of such conditions.

To the extent that some grievances have been reduced by political action, such as the granting of independence to colonies and the political accord reached in Northern Ireland in November 1999, terrorism has declined. But other problems remain, especially in the Balkans, India, Central America, Africa, and the West Bank and Gaza Strip occupied by Israel. Crimes of a terrorist nature occur virtually every day and are likely to continue wherever the underlying problems are not resolved. Terrorist activities include but are not restricted to assassinations, hostage taking, and interference with or destruction of ships, aircraft, or means of land transport. When funding by clandestine supporters is not forthcoming, terrorists have carried out robberies to finance their operations.

The 1998 bombings of the U.S. embassies in Kenya and Tanzania, as well as the October 2000 attack on the USS *Cole,* have increased American awareness of terrorist activities. The impact of the networking of international terrorist groups has become apparent.[154] Osama bin Laden, the reputed mastermind of the embassy bombings, is referred to as the "new model terrorist" and the "chief executive officer" of a network of terrorist groups. He is considered one of the most significant sponsors of Islamic extremist activities in the world today. In fact, bin Laden's so-called terrorist network is considered the most prominent threat to our national security in spite of the recent killing and capture of key Al Qaeda leaders and operatives. As of 2009, bin Laden remains a fugitive. His name is on the FBI's "Ten Most Wanted Fugitives" list, and the United States government has offered a reward of up to $25 million for his capture.[155]

In August 1999, a series of bombings began in Moscow.[156] Some researchers suggest that the 15 newly independent states of the former Soviet Union are replacing the Middle East as the primary generator of international terrorism. Of additional concern to the Russians is blood-feud terrorism, or acts of retaliation perpetrated solely on the basis of satisfying a vengeance code of a blood feud or clan vendetta, in ethnic communities and regions. More recently, in July 2005, the London public transportation system was the target of terrorist activities. On July 7, four bombs exploded within an hour of one another—three in the underground and one on a bus. The explosions killed 56 people and wounded an additional 700. Two weeks later, on July 21, another four explosions occurred, although the second time only the detonators exploded and not the bombs. In contrast to many other terrorist incidents, the main suspects in these attacks are British citizens.[157]

The Extent of Terrorism

The incidence of terrorism may seem slight in the light of overall national crime statistics. But the worldwide destructive impact of such acts is considerable and has the potential to increase significantly over time as the number and power of terrorist organizations grow (Table 10.6). Also considerable are the costs of increased security to combat terrorism. The airline industry alone spends an estimated $200 billion a year for security.[158] After the bombing of the U.S. embassy complex in Beirut, Lebanon, with the loss of the lives of 241 marines and sailors, the strengthening of U.S. embassy security all over the world cost well over $3 billion.

TABLE 10.6 Foreign Terrorist Organizations

Foreign Terrorist Organizations (FTOs) are foreign organizations that are designated by the Secretary of State in accordance with section 219 of the Immigration and Nationality Act (INA), as amended. FTO designations play a critical role in our fight against terrorism and are an effective means of curtailing support for terrorist activities and pressuring groups to get out of the terrorism business.

1. Abu Nidal Organization (ANO)
2. Abu Sayyaf Group
3. Al-Aqsa Martyrs Brigade
4. Al-Shabaab
5. Ansar al-Islam
6. Armed Islamic Group (GIA)
7. Asbat al-Ansar
8. Aum Shinrikyo
9. Basque Fatherland and Liberty (ETA)
10. Communist Party of the Philippines/New People's Army (CPP/NPA)
11. Continuity Irish Republican Army
12. Gama'a al-Islamiyya (Islamic Group)
13. HAMAS (Islamic Resistance Movement)
14. Harakat ul-Jihad-i-Islami/Bangladesh (HUJI-B)
15. Harakat ul-Mujahidin (HUM)
16. Hizballah (Party of God)
17. Islamic Jihad Group
18. Islamic Movement of Uzbekistan (IMU)
19. Jaish-e-Mohammed (JEM) (Army of Mohammed)
20. Jemaah Islamiya organization (JI)
21. al-Jihad (Egyptian Islamic Jihad)
22. Kahane Chai (Kach)
23. Kongra-Gel (KGK, formerly Kurdistan Workers' Party, PKK, KADEK)
24. Lashkar-e Tayyiba (LT) (Army of the Righteous)
25. Lashkar i Jhangvi
26. Liberation Tigers of Tamil Eelam (LTTE)
27. Libyan Islamic Fighting Group (LIFG)
28. Moroccan Islamic Combatant Group (GICM)
29. Mujahedin-e Khalq Organization (MEK)
30. National Liberation Army (ELN)
31. Palestine Liberation Front (PLF)
32. Palestinian Islamic Jihad (PIJ)
33. Popular Front for the Liberation of Palestine (PFLP)
34. PFLP-General Command (PFLP-GC)
35. Tanzim Qa'idat al-Jihad fi Bilad al-Rafidayn (QJBR) (al-Qaida in Iraq) (formerly Jama'at al-Tawhid wa'al-Jihad, JTJ, al-Zarqawi Network)
36. al-Qa'ida
37. al-Qaida in the Islamic Maghreb (formerly GSPC)
38. Real IRA
39. Revolutionary Armed Forces of Colombia (FARC)
40. Revolutionary Nuclei (formerly ELA)
41. Revolutionary Organization 17 November
42. Revolutionary People's Liberation Party/Front (DHKP/C)
43. Shining Path (Sendero Luminoso, SL)
44. United Self-Defense Forces of Colombia (AUC)

SOURCE: U.S. Department of State, Office of the Coordinator for Counterterrorism, "Fact Sheet," April 8, 2008; available at http://www.state.gov/s/ct/rls/fs/08/103392.htm.

International Efforts to Control Terrorism

The world community has agreed on several international conventions to combat terrorism:

1. Convention on Offenses and Certain Other Acts Committed on Board Aircraft, signed in Tokyo on September 14, 1963.
   Convention entered into force on December 4, 1969.
   Status: 183 parties.

2. Convention for the Suppression of Unlawful Seizure of Aircraft, signed in The Hague on December 16, 1970.
   Convention entered into force on October 14, 1971.
   Status: 182 parties.

3. Convention for the Suppression of Unlawful Acts against the Safety of Civil Aviation, signed in Montreal on September 23, 1971.
   Convention entered into force on January 26, 1973.
   Status: 185 parties.

4. Convention on the Prevention and Punishment of Crimes against Internationally Protected Persons, including Diplomatic Agents, adopted in New York on December 14, 1973.
   Convention entered into force on February 20, 1977.
   Status: 166 parties.

5. International Convention against the Taking of Hostages, adopted in New York on December 17, 1979.
   Convention entered into force on June 3, 1983.
   Status: 164 parties.

6. Convention on the Physical Protection of Nuclear Material, signed in Vienna on October 26, 1979.
   Convention entered into force on February 8, 1987.
   Status: 130 parties.

7. Protocol for the Suppression of Unlawful Acts of Violence at Airports Serving International Civil Aviation, Supplementary to the Convention for the Suppression of Unlawful Acts against the Safety of Civil Aviation, signed in Montreal on February 24, 1988.
   Protocol entered into force on August 6, 1989.
   Status: 161 parties.

8. Convention for the Suppression of Unlawful Acts against the Safety of Maritime Navigation, done in Rome on March 10, 1988.
   Convention entered into force on March 1, 1992.
   Status: 147 parties.

9. Protocol for the Suppression of Unlawful Acts against the Safety of Fixed Platforms Located on the Continental Shelf, done in Rome on March 10, 1988.
   Protocol entered into force on March 1, 1992.
   Status: 136 parties.

10. Convention on the Marking of Plastic Explosives for the Purpose of Detection, done in Montreal on March 1, 1991.
    Convention entered into force on June 21, 1998.
    Status: 137 parties.

11. International Convention for the Suppression of Terrorist Bombings, adopted in New York on December 15, 1997.
    Convention entered into force on May 23, 2001.
    Status: 153 parties.

12. International Convention for the Suppression of the Financing of Terrorism, adopted in New York on December 9, 1999.
    Convention entered into force on April 10, 2002.
    Status: 160 parties.

13. International Convention for the Suppression of Acts of Nuclear Terrorism, adopted in New York on April 13, 2005.
    Convention entered into force on July 7, 2007.
    Status: 115 parties.[159]

These conventions, which provide for widespread international cooperation, cover a wide range of terrorist acts across a host of jurisdictions.

It appears that by 1989 several governments that had been supporting "freedom fighters" (elsewhere called "terrorist groups") had grown disenchanted with the groups' exercise of arbitrary violence against uninvolved civilian targets, such as airplane passengers, and had ceased to support such groups. In addition, the end of the cold war and the breakup of the Soviet bloc have deprived many of these groups of funding; consequently, they are on the decline. Rising in their stead is a new type of terrorist group, more difficult to monitor and perhaps even more dangerous. The old-style politically motivated mayhem has been replaced with ethnically and religiously inspired violence.

More recently, cults have sprung up whose members believe that a catastrophic war or natural disaster will land the "chosen few" in paradise. These doomsday cults can turn inward, leading to mass suicide or the murder of the membership. Eighty-six of David Koresh's followers at the Branch Davidian compound in Waco, Texas, died a fiery death after a lengthy siege by the FBI. It is still unclear whether the Branch Davidians set fire to the compound themselves or if the FBI was responsible. Other groups direct their actions at outsiders. In Japan, the Aum Shinrikyo ("Supreme Truth") sect was implicated in the deadly sarin nerve gas attack on the Tokyo subway, which killed 10 and injured over 5,000. The leader of the sect, Shoko Asahara, preached about the end of the world and claimed that sarin would be a primary weapon in the "final world war."[160]

Hate Crimes

In June 1998, James Byrd Jr., an African American, was dragged to his death in Jasper, Texas. Byrd was hitchhiking on a Saturday night when John William King and two friends chained him to their truck and pulled him, alive, for over 2 miles. His head was finally severed from his body. King, who was sentenced to death in March 1999, and his two friends were Ku Klux Klan (KKK) members.

An equally barbaric hate crime occurred in October 1998. Russell Henderson and Aaron McKinney posed as homosexuals and lured gay college student Matthew Shepard out of a bar in Wyoming. They robbed, pistol-whipped, and burned him with cigarettes before leaving him tied to a fence in near-freezing temperatures. Shepard died 5 days later in a hospital. The murder trial of Henderson and McKinney incited further displays of hate, with antigay demonstrators shouting and waving signs that read "God Hates Fags."[161] Only a few months later, in Alabama, Steven Mullins and Charles Butler lured Billy Jack Gaither, another gay male, out of a bar into a secluded area where they beat him and then dumped him into the trunk of their car. They drove about 15 miles, took him out of the trunk, and killed him with an ax handle. Mullins and Butler then placed Gaither's body on top of two old tires that they had set on fire.[162]

In August 1999, Buford O. Furrow, a former member of the Aryan Nation, walked into the lobby of the North Valley Jewish Community Center in the Granada Hills area of Los Angeles, shooting and wounding a receptionist, a camp counselor, and three children. After leaving the scene, Furrow carjacked a person's vehicle, drove to the residential area of Chatsworth, and shot Joseph Ileto, a Filipino-American postman who was in the middle of making his rounds. Furrow later turned himself in.[163]

During 2006, the United States experienced some of the most gruesome displays of hate-crime violence. According to the Uniform Crime Reports, there were 7,722 incidents of hate crimes, which involved 9,080 separate offenses reported from

■ *Mary Nell Verrett remembers her brother, James Byrd Jr., who was brutally murdered in a hate crime in Jasper, Texas.*

over 12,000 law enforcement agencies to the FBI. Of the 7,722 incidents, 4,000 were racially motivated, 1,462 were religiously motivated, 1,195 targeted victims because of their sexual preferences, 982 were ethnically motivated, and 79 were disability motivated.[164] According to the Southern Poverty Law Center, the number of hate groups increased from 474 in 1997 to 926 in 2008 (Figure 10.5).[165] It also appears that groups are recruiting more violent members to carry out their messages of hate nationwide. One of the most recent tools used to attract these members is the Internet. Since 1995, over 160 online hate sites have been identified.[166]

Although hate crimes make up only a small percentage of overall criminality, the viciousness of the acts and their impact on broad population groups give them prominence in the media and pose extraordinary challenges to the criminal justice system. Presently, some police departments are forming bias-crime units to further the investigation of these crimes.

Militias

Militias have come to the attention of the American public only within the last decade. Most of them are groups whose memberships consist of white,

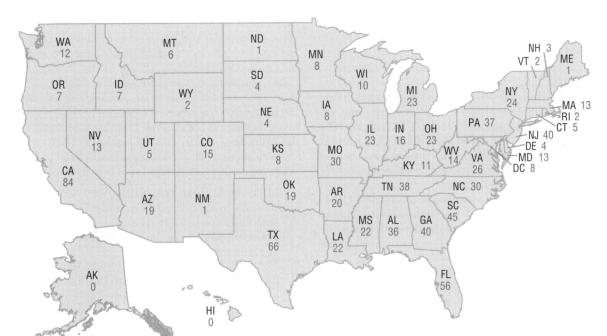

FIGURE 10.5
Active U.S. hate groups. The Southern Poverty Law Center counted 926 active hate groups in the United States in 2008. Only organizations and their chapters known to be active during 2008 are included.

Source: Southern Poverty Law Center. Reprinted with Permission.

Volunteers from the Minuteman Project militia group monitor the U.S.-Mexico border near Naco, Arizona, in April 2005. The Minuteman Project is a volunteer organization that watches the border and reports illegal border crossers to the United States Border Patrol.

Christian, working- and middle-class Americans whose fundamental belief is that their constitutional right to bear arms (protected under the Second Amendment) is threatened. Members tend to have apocalyptic, paranoid views of U.S. politics and the federal government. Their anti-government beliefs are intertwined with some forms of white supremacy. They believe leading Democratic politicians are "liberal elitists who betray traditional American values."[167] Members of these groups believe that the federal government is preparing for a war against its own citizens.[168] The movement is a collection of grassroots groups who call themselves Patriots, Militiamen,

Freemen, Common-Law Advocates, and Strict Constitutionalists. Although they are often labeled "right-wing," members' backgrounds touch all points on the political spectrum. The movement is so fragmented that membership estimates are unreliable. The Southern Poverty Law Center says that members can be found in all 50 states.[169] Some estimates are that as many as 100,000 Americans are involved.[170]

Most militia groups are nonviolent. Members have a fondness for wearing battle fatigues, participating in paramilitary maneuvers, and stockpiling firearms. Yet there are growing indications of involvement in illegal activities. The Michigan

Crime Surfing

www.splcenter.org

The Southern Poverty Law Center is a nonprofit organization that combats hate, intolerance, and discrimination through education and litigation. For more information, visit the center's website.

Militia Corps, for example, one of the nation's largest, with an estimated membership of 10,000 to 12,000, has alleged ties to Timothy McVeigh and Terry Nichols, both charged in the Oklahoma City bombing.[171]

Long before this bombing focused attention on the radical right, the FBI had insiders and informants tracking the Freemen of Montana. The Freemen, 13 of whom were indicted for counterfeiting and tax fraud, are reported to have posted $1 million rewards on the heads of local officials, threatened to hang local judges, and intimidated potential jurors in a case against a Freeman. Using bits of the Constitution, the Bible, and the Magna Carta, they put together a doctrine that says the federal government has illegally usurped the common law and power of localities. They also reject the American flag. In their own courts, the Freemen have filed multimillion-dollar "liens" against government officials and "subpoenaed" public officials to appear before their own grand juries.

For the Freemen, their 960-acre Cranfield County, Montana, farm is sovereign territory, with its own laws, courts, and officials. They also have an armory and a bank. According to federal indictments, the bank turned over $1.8 million in phony money orders and other financial instruments. These were used in fraudulent transactions with credit card companies, mail-order houses, and banks. In 1996, 26 of the antigovernment fanatics holed up in the Freemen's enclaves. Eighty-one days and millions of dollars later, they all left the compound. The standoff was one of the longest armed sieges in U.S. history.

Violence in Schools

In the nineteenth century, school violence was seen in the form of teachers' inflicting abuse on students, primarily by slapping a student's hand with a ruler. Parents and members of the community looked upon this "violence" as a way to remind students that they must respect authority.

The mid-twentieth century brought a new look to school violence. By the 1950s, students were viewed not as the victims but rather as the agents of violence. In response, schools with high levels of violence developed security plans.[172] While, overall, violence in schools has decreased, media accounts of school shootings have caused a nationwide panic, and many Americans have lost faith in the ability of the educational system to keep children safe.

Consider the following incidents: It was 12:35 P.M. on March 24, 1998, when the fire alarm bell sounded at Westside Middle School in Jonesboro, Arkansas. The children filed out of their classrooms—as in so many previous drills—and exited into an open area. Then the rifle shots rang out. By 12:39 P.M., 15 students and teachers lay in pools of blood; 4 students and 1 teacher did not survive. The shots were fired from the perimeter of the school grounds by two assailants dressed in army fatigues who had been hiding in the shrubbery. The assailants, 11-year-old Andrew Golden and his 13-year-old accomplice, had planned the attack well. They had arrived in a stolen van, armed with 10 rifles and handguns, plenty of ammunition, and survival gear.[173] That was America's seventh school massacre in little over a year. School massacre eight was not far behind.

> Littleton, Colorado (April 23, 1999)—"The school's in a panic, and I'm in the library," the teacher is desperately trying to explain to the police dispatcher as she begs for help. "I've got students down."
>
> "Under the table, kids!" she says now, directing her attention back to the students who, moments before, had been quietly studying in the library at Columbine High School. "Kids, under the table. Kids, stay on the floor. . . . Oh, God. Oh, God—kids, just stay down." The teacher's frantic voice, heard as gunfire reverberated in the background, was part of a tape recording released by the police today of some of the emergency calls placed on Tuesday as two students began their lethal rampage.[174]

This 911 call depicts the horror of April 20, 1999. Eric Harris, 18 years old, and Dylan Klebold, 17 years old, executed a massacre they had planned for a year, to occur on Hitler's birthday, at the Littleton, Colorado, Columbine High School. Harris and Klebold were members of a group who referred to themselves as the "Trench-coat Mafia," a group reportedly known to dislike athletes and minorities. Armed with four firearms and over 30 explosives, they killed 14 students, one teacher, and, last, themselves.

The media made much of the fact that schools had been turned into killing fields. Fear gripped students and parents all over the country. In fact, shortly after the Columbine shootings, copycat crimes and attempts occurred. In Alberta, Canada, a 14-year-old boy wearing a three-quarter-length parka walked into W. R. Myers High School, whipped out a .22 caliber rifle, killed a 17-year-old boy, and critically wounded another. In Brooklyn, New York, five students were arrested for bragging about plans to blow up the school on graduation day. It was also no surprise when schools in Hillsborough, New Jersey, closed for a day after students began receiving e-mail messages stating, "If you think what happened in Colorado was bad, wait until you see what happens in Hillsborough Middle School on Friday."[175] Yet another incident occurred on December 9, 1999, when a seventh-grade honor student opened fire on his classmates, wounding five, at the Fort Gibson Middle School in Fort Gibson, Oklahoma.

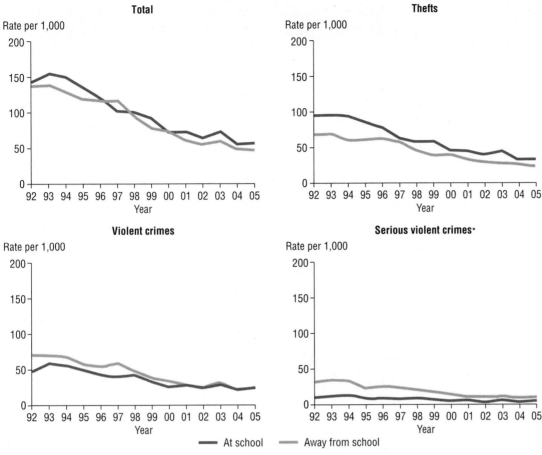

Total

Rate per 1,000

Thefts

Rate per 1,000

Violent crimes

Rate per 1,000

Serious violent crimes*

Rate per 1,000

—— At school —— Away from school

*Serious Violent crimes are also included in violent crimes.

FIGURE 10.6 Rate of student-reported nonfatal crimes against students ages 12–18 per 1,000 students, by type of crime and location, 1992–2005.

Note: Serious violent crimes include rape, sexual assault, robbery, and aggravated assault. Violent crimes include serious violent crimes and simple assault. Total crimes include violent crimes and theft. "At school" includes inside the school building, on school property, or on the way to or from school. Population sizes for students ages 12–18 are 23,740,000 in 1992; 24,558,000 in 1993; 25,327,000 in 1994; 25,715,000 in 1995; 26,151,000 in 1996; 26,548,000 in 1997; 26,806,000 in 1998; 27,013,000 in 1999; 27,169,000 in 2000; 27,380,000 in 2001; 27,367,000 in 2002; 26,386,000 in 2003; 26,372,000 in 2004; and 26,456,000 in 2005.

Source: U.S. Department of Justice, Bureau of Justice Statistics, *National Crime Victimization Survey (NCVS), 1992–2005;* available at http://nces .ed.gov/programs/crimeindicators/crimeindicators2007/figures/fig_02_1.asp?referrer=report.

Educators called for stricter security, and legislators responded to the media frenzy with proposals ranging from keeping students away from school during all but regular school hours to seeking the death penalty for 11-year-olds.

What is the reality? What do experts tell us? A National School Safety Center research report shows that the probability of being killed by lightning is twice as high as that of being killed at school.[176] And the 2007 Indicators of School Safety Report shows that school crime decreased between 1992 and 2007. According to the report, violent victimization rates at school dropped from 48 per 1,000 students in 1992 to 24 per 1,000 in 2005 (Figure 10.6 and Table 10.7).[177]

The public looks for scapegoats. Who did what wrong? And what happened to the days when throwing a spitball or an eraser got a student in big trouble? The answer must come from specialists in criminology. All too often, policy and legislation in matters of crime and criminal justice are the result of publicity given to emotion-charged media reports rather than of research data from scientific studies. Experts need to look into the causes of school violence. What do the events have in common? Some say that students are growing up with violence. One survey of inner-city children showed that 43 percent of 7- to 19-year-olds have witnessed a homicide.[178]

What can be done specifically, not only in the aftermath of such events, but also in terms of preventive measures? According to the 1994 Gun Free Schools Act, all schools that receive federal education funding must maintain policies mandating expulsion for any student caught bringing a

TABLE 10.7 Number of Student-Reported Nonfatal Crimes against Students Ages 12–18 and Rate of Crimes per 1,000 Students, by Location and Year, 1992–2005

	Number of Crimes				Rate of Crimes per 1,000 students			
Year	Total	Theft	Violent	Serious Violent*	Total	Theft	Violent	Serious Violent*
AT SCHOOL								
1992	3,409,200	2,260,500	1,148,600	245,400	144	95	48	10
1993	3,795,200	2,357,000	1,438,200	306,700	155	96	59	12
1994	3,795,500	2,371,500	1,424,000	322,400	150	94	56	13
1995	3,467,900	2,177,900	1,290,000	222,500	135	85	50	9
1996	3,163,000	2,028,700	1,134,400	225,400	121	78	43	9
1997	2,721,200	1,666,000	1,055,200	201,800	102	63	40	8
1998	2,715,600	1,562,300	1,153,200	252,700	101	58	43	9
1999	2,489,700	1,605,500	884,100	185,600	92	59	33	7
2000	1,946,400	1,246,600	699,800	128,400	72	46	26	5
2001	2,001,300	1,237,600	763,700	160,900	73	45	28	6
2002	1,753,600	1,095,000	658,600	88,100	64	40	24	3
2003	1,930,100	1,191,400	738,700	154,200	73	45	28	6
2004	1,445,800	863,000	582,800	107,400	55	33	22	4
2005	1,496,300	868,100	628,200	136,500	57	33	24	5
AWAY FROM SCHOOL								
1992	3,286,800	1,607,600	1,679,200	750,200	138	68	71	32
1993	3,419,700	1,691,800	1,728,000	849,500	139	69	70	35
1994	3,258,100	1,521,700	1,736,400	832,700	129	60	69	33
1995	3,058,300	1,561,800	1,496,500	599,000	119	61	58	23
1996	3,050,600	1,622,900	1,427,700	670,600	117	62	55	26
1997	3,107,300	1,551,600	1,555,800	635,900	117	58	59	24
1998	2,534,500	1,236,400	1,298,100	550,200	95	46	48	21
1999	2,106,600	1,048,200	1,058,300	476,400	78	39	39	18
2000	2,011,800	1,091,000	920,800	373,100	74	40	34	14
2001	1,670,500	912,900	757,500	290,300	61	33	28	11
2002	1,510,400	790,100	720,300	309,200	55	29	26	11
2003	1,592,600	746,200	846,400	325,000	60	28	32	12
2004	1,262,200	706,400	555,800	228,600	48	27	21	9
2005	1,241,100	610,100	630,900	267,800	47	23	24	10

*Serious violent crimes are also included in violent crimes.

Note: Serious violent crimes include rape, sexual assault, robbery, and aggravated assault. Violent crimes include serious violent crimes and simple assault. Total crimes include violent crimes and theft. "At school" includes inside the school building, on school property, or on the way to or from school. Population sizes for students ages 12–18 are 23,740,000 in 1992; 24,558,000 in 1993; 25,327,000 in 1994; 25,715,000 in 1995; 26,151,000 in 1996; 26,548,000 in 1997; 26,806,000 in 1998; 27,013,000 in 1999; 27,169,000 in 2000; 27,380,000 in 2001; 27,367,000 in 2002; 26,386,000 in 2003; 26,372,000 in 2004; and 26,456,000 in 2005. Detail may not sum to totals because of rounding. Estimates of number of crimes are rounded to the nearest 100.

SOURCE: U.S. Department of Justice, Bureau of Justice Statistics, *National Crime Victimization Survey (NCVS)*. *1992–2005;* available at http://nces.ed.gov/programs/crimeindicators/crimeindicators2007/tables/table_02_1.asp?referrer=report.

firearm to school.[179] In addition, individual schools are making major changes. Following the shootings at Columbine, new security measures were instituted, including the installation of 16 color TV cameras to monitor both indoor and outdoor activities, the issuance of identification badges, the restriction of access to locked entryways, and the addition of another uniformed guard to patrol the hallways.[180] Other schools are suggesting the use of computer-coded identification badges.[181] Any way the situation is viewed, there is a noticeable shift from general security in schools to crisis management. Schools are also becoming more militaristic. In some California schools, there are random checks with metal-detector wands. Policies requiring uniforms or, at a minimum, tucked-in shirts, are aimed at preventing the carrying of concealed weapons.[182] Still other responses to school violence include the implementation of lockdowns, detector dogs, and rent-a-cops. The entire situation begs the question: Is it truly necessary to turn schools into prisonlike structures? (See also "Debatable Issues" in Chapter 9.)

With the implementation of security measures comes an increase in safety, but at what cost? The level of trust between administrators and students dwindles. Innocent and normally well-behaved students feel they are being targeted and their privacy is being invaded. The result could be increased levels of alienation, which in some cases lies at the root of most violence. Zero-tolerance policies for weapons, including guns, switchblades, pocketknives, box cutters, razors, ice picks, blackjacks, and chains, are a necessity.[183] High-tech solutions are clearly not the only alternative. Also needed are efforts aimed at increasing communication and interpersonal skills, the availability of counseling, and guidance in relationship building. If there is one thing to learn from the reported school shootings, it is that no school is immune to violence. School violence is no longer a problem restricted to inner cities. It is a nationwide concern.

VIOLENCE AND GUN CONTROL

The tragedies of the recent school shootings have fueled the gun-control debate. Estimates indicate that in the wake of the school massacres, more than 80 percent of Americans support stricter gun laws.[184] In fact, following the Columbine High School shooting in Colorado, the National Rifle Association was politely asked by various officials and concerned citizens to cancel its national meeting that was to be held in Denver, Colorado, only weeks after the shootings.[185]

Violence in the United States is frequently attributed to historical conditioning (the need of frontier people to survive in a hostile environment), social factors (poverty, inequities, and other inner-city problems), and the laxity of the criminal justice system (failure to apprehend and convict enough criminals and to imprison long enough those who are convicted). Some researchers have focused on one common element in a large proportion of violent crime: the availability of firearms in the United States.

One of the hottest and longest political and scholarly debates in our history centers on this point: Should and can Americans drastically restrict the availability of firearms, and would such controls substantially reduce the rate and severity of violent crime?

The Extent of Firearm-Related Offenses

It is difficult to be certain how many guns there are in the United States. Before 1850, less than 10 percent of U.S. citizens were believed to own guns, and between 1800 and 1845, only about 15 percent of all violent deaths were caused by guns.[186] It is also unknown how many of the guns available in this country have been seized, destroyed, or lost, or do not work properly.[187] Law enforcement estimates that there are over 200 million firearms in circulation in the United States, including about 70 million handguns.[188] The rate of firearms crimes has dropped significantly over the past 30 years (Table 10.8). In 1973, the rate was 172.1 per 100,000 population. Thirty-three years later, the rate was 129.9.[189]

In any case, firearm-related crime is still more prevalent in the United States than in other developed Western nations. According to the Task Force on Firearms of the National Commission on the Causes and Prevention of Violence, the rate of homicide by gun is 40 times higher in the United States than in England and Wales, and our rate of robbery by gun is 60 times higher.

The financial cost of gunshot injury and death, in terms of medical costs, lost productivity, and pain, suffering, and reduced quality of life, has been estimated at over $60 billion each year. The Centers for Disease Control and Prevention estimated that approximately 96,000 persons in the United States sustained gunshot wounds in 1997.[190]

Youths and Guns

Three young thugs boarded a city bus in Queens yesterday, brandished guns like Wild West bandits and staged a frontier-style holdup. They strode up and down the aisle, fired shots into the roof, terrorized and robbed 22 passengers, struck a girl in the face with a gun butt and escaped with $300 in cash and fistfulls of jewelry.

The outlaws—one armed with a silver revolver and another with a pair of guns, while a third carried a book bag—made no

TABLE 10.8 Murders, Robberies, and Aggravated Assaults in Which Firearms Were Used, Numbers of Offenses and Rates per 100,000 Population, 1973–2006

Year	Total Firearm Crimes		Murders with Firearms		Robberies with Firearms		Aggravated Assaults with Firearms	
	Number	Rate	Number	Rate	Number	Rate	Number	Rate
1973	361,141	172.1	13,072	6.2	241,088	114.9	106,981	51.0
1974	326,235	154.3	13,987	6.6	197,257	93.3	114,991	54.4
1975	342,495	160.7	13,496	6.3	208,307	97.7	120,693	56.6
1976	307,252	143.1	11,982	5.6	179,430	83.6	115,841	54.0
1977	301,590	139.4	11,950	5.5	168,418	77.9	121,222	56.0
1978	307,603	141.1	12,437	5.7	170,152	78.0	125,015	57.3
1979	340,202	154.6	13,582	6.2	185,352	84.2	141,269	64.2
1980	392,083	174.0	14,377	6.4	221,170	98.1	156,535	69.5
1981	396,197	172.9	14,052	6.1	230,226	100.5	151,918	66.3
1982	372,477	160.9	12,648	5.5	214,219	92.5	145,609	62.9
1983	330,419	141.2	11,258	4.8	183,581	78.5	135,580	57.9
1984	329,232	139.4	10,990	4.7	173,634	73.5	144,609	61.2
1985	340,942	142.8	11,141	4.7	175,748	73.6	154,052	64.5
1986	376,064	156.0	12,181	5.1	186,174	77.2	177,710	73.7
1987	365,709	150.3	11,879	4.9	170,841	70.2	182,989	75.2
1988	385,934	157.0	12,553	5.1	181,352	73.8	192,029	78.1
1989	410,039	165.2	13,416	5.4	192,006	77.3	204,618	82.4
1990	492,671	198.1	15,025	6.0	233,973	94.1	243,673	98.0
1991	548,667	217.6	16,376	6.5	274,404	108.8	257,887	102.3
1992	565,575	221.7	16,204	6.4	271,009	106.2	278,362	109.1
1993	581,697	225.5	17,048	6.6	279,738	108.5	284,910	110.5
1994	542,529	208.4	16,314	6.3	257,428	98.9	268,788	103.2
1995	504,421	192.0	14,686	5.6	238,023	90.6	251,712	95.8
1996	458,458	172.8	13,319	5.0	218,579	82.4	226,559	85.4
1997	414,530	154.9	12,346	4.6	197,686	73.9	204,498	76.4
1998	364,776	135.0	10,977	4.1	170,611	63.1	183,188	67.8
1999	338,535	124.1	10,128	3.7	163,458	59.9	164,949	60.5
2000	341,831	121.5	10,179	3.6	166,807	59.3	164,845	58.6
2001	354,754	124.3	11,106	3.9	177,627	62.3	166,021	58.2
2002	357,822	124.3	10,808	3.8	177,088	61.5	169,926	59.0
2003	347,705	119.6	11,041	3.8	172,802	59.4	163,863	56.3
2004	338,587	115.3	10,650	3.6	162,938	55.5	164,998	56.2
2005	368,178	124.2	11,351	3.8	175,608	59.2	181,219	61.1
2006	388,897	129.9	11,566	3.9	188,804	63.1	188,527	63.0

Note: These numbers are estimates calculated from data from the FBI Uniform Crime Reports as published annually in *Crime in the United States.*

SOURCE: U.S. Department of Justice, Bureau of Justice Statistics; available at http://www.ojp.usdoj.gov/bjs/glance/tables/guncrimetab.htm.

effort to conceal their faces as they boarded the Q-85 bus at 8:30 A.M. at 140th Avenue and Edgewood Avenue in Springfield Gardens, a residential neighborhood just northeast of Kennedy International Airport.[191]

The "bandits" were three youths ages 15 to 19. In a growing number of incidents across the United States, young people are using guns for robberies, gang warfare, initiation rites (drive-by shootings by wanna-be gang members), random shootings (in fact, James Jordan, father of former basketball star Michael Jordan, fell victim), and protection from their peers.[192]

Concern is mounting over adolescent illegal gun ownership and use. In 1995, the National Institute of Justice interviewed a sample of arrested individuals in Denver, the District of Columbia, Indianapolis, Los Angeles, Phoenix, St. Louis, and San Diego. The study found that juveniles are more likely than arrestees overall to commit crime with a gun. Of the juveniles interviewed, 20 percent said they carried a gun most or all of the time, 25 percent had stolen a gun, and 33 percent who owned a gun had used one in a crime (the percentages were considerably higher for gang members). Eighteen percent of the juveniles agreed that it was appropriate to use a gun "to shoot someone who disrespected you."[193]

Another study, of inner-city high schools in California, Illinois, Louisiana, and New Jersey, found a connection between involvement in drugs and gun carrying.[194] The same study sampled female students as well; 1 in 10 female students owned a gun at some time, and roughly the same percentage carried a gun.[195]

Why have youths turned to guns? When asked, many of them respond the way three teenagers did: "You fire a gun and you can just *hear* the power. It's like *yeah!*" or "It became cool to say you could get a gun," or "Nobody messes with you if they think you may have a gun."[196] While there are many studies on adolescent violent behavior, there are few on adolescent illegal gun use. One of the few, a study of ninth- and tenth-grade boys, 14- and 15-year-olds, in Rochester, New York, found that most boys who owned illegal guns had friends who owned guns, over half of the illegal gun owners were gang members, and selling drugs was a prime motivation for carrying a gun. Moreover, illegal gun ownership, friends' gun ownership, gang membership, and drug use were closely related to gun crime, street crime, and minor delinquency.[197] Illegal firearms have traditionally been used by youths in low-income urban neighborhoods. The problem, like that of school shootings, has now spread to the suburbs.

Controlling Handgun Use

While most people agree that gun-related crime is a particularly serious part of our crime problem,

A powerful protest plea outside the Denver NRA convention in 1999.

there is little agreement on what to do about it. Some want prohibition. Others want comprehensive licensing and registrations.[198] Civic organizations and police associations call for more laws prescribing mandatory sentences for the illegal purchase, possession, or use of firearms. Close to 20,000 laws that regulate firearms already exist in the United States.

A variety of methods of controlling handgun use have been tried:

• In 1996 the Bureau of Alcohol, Tobacco and Firearms established the Youth Crime Gun Interdiction Initiative *to trace crime guns* (those illegally possessed or used in a crime) recovered by law enforcement. In its first year, 76,000 crime guns were traced. Almost half were recovered from persons under the age of 25.[199]

• A *prohibition against carrying guns* in public seemed to be related to a drop in gun crimes in Boston[200] and a leveling off of handgun violence in Detroit.[201]

• In Kansas City, Missouri, a *police gun-confiscation program* was implemented in gun-crime hot spots in the target area, which had a murder rate 20 times the national average. Gun seizures in the target area increased by over 65 percent, while gun crimes decreased by 49 percent. Homicides were also significantly reduced in the target area.[202]

THEORY CONNECTS

Youths and Guns

How do subculture theories of delinquency (Chapter 6) help explain gun ownership among the young? In particular, does the notion of reaction formation (p. 131) reveal why so many adolescents are drawn to the violence of gang life?

 Crime Surfing

www.atf.gov

The Bureau of Alcohol, Tobacco and Firearms provides information on firearms use, guns in circulation, and programs aimed at reducing the possession of illegal firearms.

Does the Brady Law Work?

When John Hinckley attempted to assassinate President Ronald Reagan in 1981, he wounded the president, along with two law enforcement officers and the White House press secretary, James Brady. Brady, who suffered a debilitating head wound, worked tirelessly for the next 12 years to institute gun control laws. In 1994, the Brady Law went into effect; it requires background checks and a 5-day waiting period for people who buy handguns from federally licensed firearms dealers. The question of the effectiveness of the Brady Law has been debated ever since.

In August 2000, a study published in the *Journal of the American Medical Association* concluded that there was no evidence that the Brady Law contributed to a reduction in homicide rates. The study's authors compared two sets of states: 32 states that installed the law in 1994, and 18 states plus the District of Columbia, all of which have had Brady-style restrictions for much longer. The authors said that based on their statistical analysis, the decline in handgun homicide in the states that recently installed the Brady Law would have been much more rapid if the law had really had an effect.

Advocates of gun control, however, say that the study is flawed. For instance, two studies done by Dr. Garen Wintemute, director of the Violence Prevention Research Program at the University of California at Davis, have found that California laws requiring background checks of convicted felons and criminals who committed violent misdemeanors reduced crimes committed with guns by 25 percent to 30 percent.

The National Rifle Association, which argues that laws don't stop criminals from getting guns, was delighted with the results of the 2000 study. However, even the study's authors acknowledge that a major reason the Brady Law may not have been effective is that the law does not go far enough.(1)

As part of the fifteenth anniversary of the passage of the Brady Law, the Brady Center to Prevent Gun Violence issued a news release recognizing the lives saved, the reduction in gun crime, and the work that still needs to be done. The debate over guns continues.

Washington, DC—Fifteen years ago today, President William Jefferson Clinton signed the Brady Bill into law, America's first critical step toward requiring criminal background checks for all firearm purchases in order to keep guns out of the hands of dangerous people.

A new Brady Center report, called Brady Background Checks: 15 Years of Saving Lives, details the Brady Law's long record of success, available here: http://www.bradycenter.org/xshare/pdf/reports/brady-law-15years.pdf. A true success story, the law has blocked 1.6 million bad sales to felons, fugitives, domestic abusers, dangerously mentally ill and other prohibited purchasers—but the nation still allows too many sales to go forward without a Brady background check.

"This is a happy anniversary, but a reminder that we need to do more," said Sarah Brady, Chair of the Brady Center to Prevent Gun Violence.

"Every day, Brady criminal background checks help save lives, reduce gun crime, and keep dangerous weapons out of the hands of dangerous people," said Paul Helmke, President of the Brady Center. "Though just one of a handful of federal gun laws on the books, Americans can take pride in the Brady Law as a prime example of how strong gun laws work to protect our communities and our families," Helmke said. "But while we celebrate the Brady Law's huge success, we also must remember that too many sales—from so-called 'private sellers' at gun shows, through classified ads and by word of mouth—still don't require background checks," Helmke said.

• Some states have passed what are referred to as *sentence-enhancement statutes:* The punishment for an offense is more severe if a person commits it under certain conditions, such as by using a gun. The Massachusetts law (1975) mandates a minimum sentence of 1 year's incarceration upon conviction for the illegal carrying of a firearm.[203] Michigan created a new offense—commission of a felony while possessing a firearm—and added a mandatory 2-year prison sentence to the sentence received for the commission of the felony itself. The state mounted a widespread publicity campaign: "One with a gun gets you two," read the billboards and bumper stickers.[204]

Sentence enhancement has been studied in six U.S. cities. Homicides committed with firearms decreased in all six after sentence-enhancement laws took effect, although the decline in homicides was large in some cities and small in others. Researchers studying sentence enhancement point out that its effectiveness is related to how closely judges follow the law. An additional 3 years in prison may deter criminals from using guns, while an additional month may not.

• Project Exile began in Richmond, Virginia, in 1997. This program specifies that any time a gun is found on a person, whether a drug dealer, drug user, convicted felon, or suspect in a crime, the case will be tried under federal statutes in federal court. By moving gun offenses into the federal system, offenders face mandatory sentences of 5 years without parole. Prison time is increased for repeat or aggravated offenses. This project is advertised all over the city on billboards that in bold letters say, "An Illegal Gun Gets You Five Years in Federal Prison." After implementation of this program, murders in Richmond dropped significantly, from 140 in 1997 to 94 in 1998 and 32 in the first 6 months of 1999. Project Exile also led to the recovery of

Many Americans are too young to remember the long struggle to get the Brady Law passed by the Brady Center (formerly known as Handgun Control, Inc.) said Sarah Brady, the Republican activist and wife of former Reagan Press Secretary Jim Brady, who was wounded in an assassination attempt on President Reagan in March of 1981. Though Sarah Brady had been profoundly impacted by her husband's shooting, what made her become an activist for sensible gun laws was finding an unattended handgun next to her young son in a pickup truck—the gun's owner was the father of one of Sarah's son's friends, and was dropping the boy off after a play date.

Years earlier, in 1968, Congress had passed, and President Lyndon Johnson signed, the 1968 Gun Control Act, establishing categories of individuals who would be prohibited from purchasing firearms. But from 1968 until the Brady Law was signed in late 1993 and took effect three months later, gun dealers were not required to check to see if a prospective buyer was a prohibited purchaser. The would-be Presidential assassin who shot President Reagan and Jim Brady would have been rejected from purchasing a gun if a background check system had been in place.

The 1.6 million prohibited purchasers blocked from buying guns from licensed gun dealers include an estimated 842,000 convicted felons, 236,000 domestic abusers and 68,000 fugitives

from justice. And in the 15 years since the Brady Law took effect, many types of gun crimes have dropped, including gun homicides. The total combined number of robberies and aggravated assaults committed with firearms decreased from 564,648 in 1993 to 377,331 in 2006, a decrease of 33 percent. And after the signing of the Brady Law, gun murders declined 32 percent, from 17,048 in 1993 to 11,566 in 2006.

Sarah Brady, who worked tirelessly for more than eight years to secure passage of the Brady Law, urged lawmakers to finish the job.

"Take it from Jim and me, this happy anniversary shows that background checks make a difference. But there is much more work to do," Mrs. Brady said. "Loopholes in the Brady Law mean about 40 percent of all gun sales in America take place without background checks. That means too many dangerous people are allowed to slip through the cracks and easily purchase firearms, fueling the illegal gun market and putting children and families at risk," Mrs. Brady said. "Jim and I urge the Obama Administration and the new Congress to take effective action to improve public safety by requiring Brady criminal background checks for all gun sales." . . .

The Brady Center to Prevent Gun Violence is a national non-profit organization working to reduce the tragic toll of gun violence in America, through education, research, and legal advo-

cacy. The programs of the Brady Center complement the legislative and grassroots mobilization of its sister organization, the Brady Campaign to Prevent Gun Violence with its dedicated network of Million Mom March Chapters.(2)

Sources

1. Adapted from Fox Butterfield, "Study Disputes Success of the Brady Law," New York Times, Aug. 2, 2000; and Fox Butterfield, "July 30–August 5; Questions on Brady Law," New York Times, Aug. 6, 2000.
2. News Release, Brady Law at Fifteen: 1.6 Million Dangerous Sales Blocked, But There's More Work to Do. November 30, 2008. http://www.bradycampaign.org/media/release.php?release=1086. Reprinted by permission of The Brady Center to Prevent Gun Violence.

Question for Discussion

1. The Brady Law requires background checks only for those who buy handguns from federally licensed firearms dealers. It does not cover the unregulated market involving an estimated 30 to 40 percent of all gun sales, such as gun shows and private transactions. Do you think the law should be extended to cover these venues? What would be your argument in its favor? What would be your argument against extending the scope of the law?

---

almost 500 illegal handguns, indictments against about 400 people on gun charges, and a conviction rate of 86 percent through trials and plea bargains.[205] This Virginia program is being mirrored in other cities as well, with anticipation of a similar effect.[206] The National Rifle Association supports this program, claiming that it is the best alternative to restrictive gun laws.[207]

• A *total ban on handguns* was tried in Washington, D.C., beginning in 1976. Both gun homicides and gun suicides dropped visibly after the ban took effect, while no change occurred in homicides and suicides not committed with guns.[208]

• Some communities have tried *buy-back programs.* St. Louis, San Francisco, Philadelphia, New York, and several other cities have embarked on such programs to reduce the number of handguns in circulation in the community. Police departments buy guns, no questions asked, for

$50 each. In October 1991, the St. Louis Police Department bought 5,371 guns from citizens in 10 days. The Philadelphia police received 1,044 guns within a 2-week period.

• *Federal legislation* has been passed in an attempt to prevent criminals from buying guns. The Brady Law, named after James Brady, the White House press secretary who was injured in the 1981 assassination attempt on President Ronald Reagan, went into effect on February 28, 1994. It calls for a 5-day waiting period and a background check before a handgun can be purchased. Further, the law prevents certain groups of people, including convicted felons, fugitives from justice, illegal aliens, juveniles, and the mentally ill, from buying guns. Between February 1994, when the Brady Law was first implemented, and the end of the interim period, November 1998, at which time the permanent provisions of the law became effective,[209] approximately 12.7 million background checks resulted in about 312,000 rejections, a rejection rate of 2.4 percent. The reasons for rejection varied: 63 percent of applicants were rejected as a result of prior felony convictions or current felony indictments; 10 percent of applicants were rejected as a result of domestic violence misdemeanor convictions; and 3 percent of applicants were rejected as a result of the presence of domestic violence protection orders. During the interim period, the U.S. Department of Justice established the National Instant Criminal Background Check System, which indexes and accesses criminal justice agency databases that are used in the background-check process. When the permanent provisions for the Brady act became effective, presale background checks were expanded to include not only handguns, but all other types of firearms as well.[210] Supporters of the Brady Law claim this shows that fewer felons are managing to obtain handguns. Others argue that felons can still obtain handguns through illegal channels. James Q. Wilson, for example, says the real test of the Brady Law is whether "felons have been stopped from buying guns and then killing people with them."

None of these methods resulted in drastic reductions in the number of handgun-related deaths, although some led to a small decrease. As two gun-control researchers point out, the important question to be answered with regard to gun control is this: How many deaths must be prevented by a gun-control method to justify its use? Very few of the millions of people who own guns commit crimes with them, and control policies affect legitimate owners as well as criminals. David McDowall and Alan Lizotte ask,

> Is the legitimate happiness of 10 million gun owners worth the lives of 10,000 murder victims? One murder victim? In another context, is a highly restrictive measure that would save 200 lives better than a less restrictive measure that would save 100? There is no obvious answer to these questions, and different people will draw the line in different places.[211]

Perhaps we can learn from the countries with low gun-related homicide rates. Many citizens of Switzerland and Israel, for example, have army-issue firearms at their constant disposal by virtue of citizen-army requirements, yet these weapons are rarely used for homicides. What factors control the use of handguns in these countries? Many European countries and Canada maintain strict national gun laws. These countries often require that guns be registered, that owners be licensed, and that guns be stored with the greatest security. In some countries, it is mandatory that a gun license applicant pass an examination on gun safety.[212] Even if comparative studies come up

with useful findings, some researchers believe the political problems surrounding gun control in the United States will probably continue to hinder the development of nationwide, or even statewide, gun-control policies for some time to come.

The Gun-Control Debate

The battle line on gun control appears to be clearly drawn between the opponents of regulation (including the 3 million members of the National Rifle Association, or NRA, and their supporters) on one hand and the advocates of control (including the 12 major law enforcement groups, the private organization Handgun Control, and three-quarters of the American public) on the other. The gun lobby likes to say that it is people who kill, not guns, so it is the people who use guns illegally who should be punished. To deter these people, gun enthusiasts say, we need to have stiffer penalties, including mandatory sentences that take these offenders off the streets.

Gun-control opponents often have bumper stickers that read "When guns are outlawed, only outlaws will have guns." Moreover, most gun owners claim that it is their right to own firearms to protect their homes, especially when they lose confidence in the police and courts.[213] And by controlling guns, they say, the government intrudes in their private affairs. They interpret the Second Amendment to the Constitution as giving them an individual right "to keep and bear arms." Furthermore, the gun lobby maintains, people may wish to enjoy their guns as collectors or for sport and hunting.

Another argument concerns what is called the "displacement effect": People who are deterred by gun-control legislation from using guns to commit offenses will use some other weapon to achieve their goals. Or perhaps even more violent offenses will be committed if offenders can rely on the fact that the consequences of a nonfirearm offense are less serious.

Finally, in the face of increasing random violence and a perceived inability of the police to safeguard citizens, more people are routinely carrying guns for self-protection. In many states, it is now becoming easier to do so, as more and more jurisdictions adopt "carrying-concealed-weapons" laws.[214]

Gun-control advocates compare our extremely high homicide rate to the much lower rates of other countries with tighter gun-control laws, including our neighbor Canada. They also argue that the availability of a gun makes homicide and suicide much more probable, because it is easier to produce death with a gun than with any other weapon. Moreover, they claim, better regulation or prohibition of gun ownership is a much faster way to lessen gun-related criminality than such long-term approaches as finding remedies for social problems. Researchers are testing the

claims, but thus far no definitive conclusions have been reached.

In a related aspect of the gun-control debate, the gun industry finds itself under pressure. Many lawsuits have been filed against the gun industry on the basis that gun manufacturers have neglected to incorporate safety devices into their products. Gun makers are also cited with allowing their products to be marketed in such ways that both criminals and juveniles can easily obtain them for illicit use.[215] As a response to these lawsuits, many gun makers are attempting to install various safety devices on their products, including trigger locks and cable locks.

REVIEW

Murder, assaults of various kinds, rape, robbery, kidnapping—all share the common element of violence, though they differ in many ways: in the harm they cause, the intention of the perpetrator, the punishment they warrant, and other legal criteria. Social scientists have been exploring the frequency with which these crimes are committed in our society and elsewhere, their distribution through time and place, and the role played by circumstances—including the environment and behavior patterns—in facilitating or preventing them.

Categories such as mass murder, serial murder, gang murder, and date rape are shorthand designations for frequently occurring crime patterns that have not been specifically identified in penal codes. Another pattern of crime that also is not defined as such in the penal codes has become so important that it may be considered in conjunction with the other crimes of violence: family-related crime. This pattern encompasses a variety of violent crimes including the abuse of spouses, children, and the elderly.

Some of the more pressing problems we face today are global terrorism, an increase in hate crimes nationwide, the spread of racist and anti-government militias, and deadly shootings in American schools. The media attention given to these crimes has had a dramatic effect on the public's perception that violence has reached epidemic proportions.

The gun-control controversy demonstrates that both the definitions of crimes and the social and environmental characteristics associated with them must be studied in order to develop control and prevention strategies. Our violence-prone society will have to make serious choices if it is to reach that level of peaceful living achieved by many other modern societies.

CRIMINOLOGY & PUBLIC POLICY

Just how far is too far? Consider the next step of possible privacy invasion that the Bush Administration had planned for us. With very little public fanfare, and insignificant media attention, the Pentagon's Information Awareness Office (IAO) designed a system called "Total Information Awareness" that was supposed to give the government access to an ultra-large-scale database of personal information from all communications (phone calls, e-mails, and Web searches) and to financial records, medical records, and travel history.

John Poindexter, former national security advisor (under President Ronald Reagan), was approved head of IAO and promoted the idea of a virtual centralized database that would serve as a central repository of information in our war against terrorism. (Source: http://www.darpa.MIL/iao/.)

Questions for Discussion Where should we draw the line when it is clear that "intelligence" is the best weapon against the next big terrorist attack on the United States? To what extent has the Obama Administration changed the priority given to aggressive domestic intelligence gathering, and is this a positive development? Do you believe that programs like Total Information Awareness contribute to the perception that the United States has lost moral legitimacy in its war against terrorism?

YOU BE THE CRIMINOLOGIST

You are the superintendent of schools for your district. Your schools have not experienced any violent incidents, but because of the media hype surrounding the school shootings throughout the country, you are under pressure to take preventive measures. What actions would you take and what programs would you develop to make your schools safe and gun-proof? How would you implement these preventive measures? What are their advantages and disadvantages? How would you target your audience? What are the likely positive and negative reactions to the preventive measures?

KEY TERMS

The numbers next to the terms refer to the pages on which the terms are defined.

aggravated assault (231)

assault (230)

battery (231)

Federal Witness Protection Program (243)

felony murder (221)

homicide (220)

involuntary manslaughter (222)

justifiable homicide (220)

kidnapping (238)

Mafia (242)

malice aforethought (220)

manslaughter (221)

mass murder (225)

murder (220)

negligent homicide (222)

Racketeer Influenced and Corrupt Organizations (RICO) Act (243)

rape (235)

robbery (238)

serial murder (225)

simple assault (231)

sociopaths (228)

stranger homicide (224)

terrorism (251)

victim precipitation (224)

voluntary manslaughter (222)

Crimes against Property

Larceny
The Elements of Larceny
The Extent of Larceny
Who Are the Thieves?
Shoplifting
Art Theft
Motor Vehicle Theft
Boat Theft
Fraud
Obtaining Property by False Pretenses
Confidence Games and Frauds
Check Forgery
Credit Card Crimes
Insurance Fraud
**High-Tech Crimes: Concerns for Today
  and Tomorrow**
Characteristics of High-Tech Crimes
Computers and the Internet: Types of Crimes
Characteristics of the High-Tech Criminal
The Criminal Justice Problem
Burglary
Fencing: Receiving Stolen Property
Arson
Comparative Crime Rates
Review
Criminology & Public Policy
You Be the Criminologist
Key Terms

■ In the film The Gods Must Be Crazy, the concept of property rights had a profound affect on the lives of the previously happy bushmen.

The motion picture *The Gods Must Be Crazy* introduces us to a tribe of happy bushmen living on the Kalahari desert of sub-Saharan Africa, remote from the hustle and bustle of modern life. The tribe members live well—they are content with their lot in life and peaceful. Such tools as they have are shared and can easily be replaced from an abundance of sticks and stones.

High up, a "noisy bird" passes over the camp of these happy people. The pilot of the noisy bird casually throws an empty Coke bottle out of the cockpit. It lands in the middle of the camp. The bushmen stare at this foreign object. They handle it

delicately and then discover what a useful object it is: It holds water; it can be used for rolling dough, for hammering, for many things. Everybody needs it and wants it. Fights ensue over who can have it. The peace and tranquillity of this tribe are shattered. They have discovered the concept of property.

The film has a happy ending. The bushmen finally get rid of the bottle, and life returns to normal. The importance of property in our society cannot be overstated. Property rights and interests bring corresponding challenges, as the film *The Gods Must be Crazy* reveals. These challenges include intentional violations of property

267

rights and interests (crimes against property), as described in this chapter.

We have just explored some of the patterns of social interaction and the routine activities of daily life that set the stage for offenders to commit violent crimes and for other people—family members, acquaintances, strangers, airplane passengers—to become victims. We know that if we are to develop effective policies to prevent and control violent crime, we must have a thorough understanding of the characteristics of specific offenses; we need to know where, when, and how they are committed, and which individuals are most likely to commit them. The same is true for property offenses. To develop crime-prevention strategies, we need to study the characteristics that differentiate the various types of offenses that deprive people of their property.

Do offenses such as pocket-picking (pickpocketing), shoplifting, check forgery, theft by use of stolen credit cards, car theft, computer crimes, and burglary have different payoffs and risks? What kinds of resources are needed (weapons, places to sell stolen property)? Are any specific skills needed to carry out these offenses? The opportunities to commit property crime are all but unlimited. Studies demonstrate that if these opportunities are reduced, the incidence of crime is reduced as well.

The traditional property crimes are larceny (theft, or stealing); obtaining property by fraud of various sorts, including false pretenses, confidence games, forgery, and unauthorized use of credit cards; burglary, which does not necessarily involve theft; and arson, which not only deprives the owner of property but also endangers lives. New crime types, such as software piracy, online frauds, and computer viruses, are associated with high-technology equipment. We defer until Chapter 12 discussion of the crimes by which criminals deprive people of their property through organizational manipulations—individual white-collar crimes and corporate crimes.

LARCENY

Larceny (theft, stealing) is the prototype of all property offenses. It is also the most prevalent crime in our society; it includes contemporary forms such as purse-snatching, pickpocketing, shoplifting, art theft, and vehicle theft. In the thirteenth century, when Henry de Bracton set out to collect from all parts of England what was common in law—and thus, common law—he learned to his surprise that there was no agreement on a concept of larceny. He found a confusing variety of ancient Germanic laws. So he did what he always did in such circumstances: He remembered what he had learned about Roman law from Professor Azo in Bologna and simply inserted it into his new text of English law. Thus, our common law definition of larceny is virtually identical with the concept in Roman law.[1]

The Elements of Larceny

Here are the elements of **larceny** (or theft, or stealing):

> A trespassory
> Taking and
> Carrying away of
> Personal property
> Belonging to another
> With the intent to deprive the owner of the property permanently

Each of these elements has a long history that gives it its meaning. The first element is perhaps the easiest. There must be a trespass. "Trespass," a Norman-French term, has a variety of meanings. In the law of larceny, however, it simply means any absence of authority or permission for the taking. Second, the property must be taken: The perpetrator must exert authority over the property, as by putting a hand on a piece of merchandise or getting into the driver's seat of the targeted car.

Third, the property must be carried away. The slightest removal suffices to fulfill this element: moving merchandise from a counter, however slightly; loosening the brakes of a car so that it starts rolling, even an inch. Fourth, the property in question, at common law, has to be personal property. (Real estate is not subject to larceny.) Fifth, the property has to belong to another, in the sense that the person has the right to possess that property. Sixth, the taker must intend to deprive the rightful owner permanently of the property. This element is present when the taker (thief) intends to deprive the rightful owner of the property forever. In many states, however, the law no longer requires proof that the thief intended to deprive the owner "permanently" of the property.

The Extent of Larceny

Larceny, except for the most petty varieties, was a capital offense in medieval England.[2] Courts interpreted all its elements quite strictly—that is, in

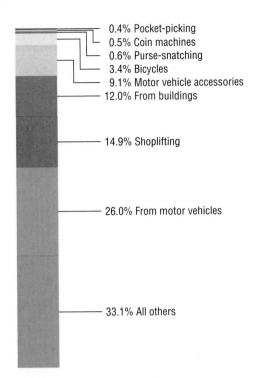

0.4% Pocket-picking
0.5% Coin machines
0.6% Purse-snatching
3.4% Bicycles
9.1% Motor vehicle accessories
12.0% From buildings

14.9% Shoplifting

26.0% From motor vehicles

33.1% All others

FIGURE 11.1 Distribution of larcenies known to police, 2007.

Source: Uniform Crime Reports, 2007.

favor of defendants—so as to limit the use of capital punishment. Only once did the courts expand the reach of larceny, when they ruled that a transporter who opens a box entrusted to him and takes out some items has committed larceny by "breaking bulk." For the other forms of deceptive acquisition of property, such as embezzling funds and obtaining property by false pretenses, Parliament had to enact separate legislation.

In the United States, the rate of larceny is extraordinarily high. The UCR reported 6.6 million thefts in 2007, or a rate of 2,177.8 for each 100,000 population.[3] The NCVS figure, 14.2 million, is more than two times the UCR number, and neither figure includes automobile thefts.[4] The vast majority of thefts are, and always have been, committed furtively and without personal contact with the victims. Thefts involving personal contact—pickpocketing, purse-snatching, and other varieties of larceny—lag behind. Figure 11.1 shows the distribution of all larcenies known to the police in 2007. The estimated dollar value of stolen goods to victims nationally was over $5.1 billion.[5]

Who Are the Thieves?

Nobody knows exactly how many of the total number of thefts are committed by amateurs who lead rather conventional lives and how many are the work of professionals. According to some criminologists, the two types differ considerably.[6]

The Amateur Thief

Amateur thieves are occasional offenders who tend to be opportunists. They take advantage of a chance to steal when little risk is involved. Typically, their acts are carried out with little skill, are unplanned, and result from some pressing situation, such as the need to pay the rent or a gambling debt.[7] In other words, amateurs resolve some immediate crisis by stealing. Most occasional offenders commit few crimes; some commit only one crime. Many are juveniles who do not go on to commit crimes in adulthood.

Amateur thieves do not think of themselves as professional criminals, nor are they recognized as such by those who do think of themselves as professionals. The lives of amateur thieves are quite conventional: Amateurs work, go to school, have conventional friends, and find little support or approval for their criminal behavior.

The Professional Thief

Professional thieves make a career of stealing. They take pride in their profession. They are imaginative and creative in their work and accept its risks. The most common crimes committed by professional thieves are pickpocketing, shoplifting, forgery, confidence swindling, and burglary. Professional thieves also are involved in art theft, motor vehicle theft, and fraud or theft by use of stolen or forged credit cards, among other crimes.

Thomas Bartholomew Moran, a professional thief who died in a Miami rescue mission in 1971, has been considered the best of American pickpockets. His career began in 1906, when, as a teenager, he started to pick women's purses. Under the careful guidance of Mary Kelly, a well-known pickpocket, he soon sharpened his skills until he could take wallets from pants, jeweled pins from clothing, and watches from vests without alerting the victims. He devoted his life to shoplifting, forgery, and other forms of theft. In 1912, he boarded the *Titanic,* with the intention of profiting handsomely from proximity to

> the more than 300 first-class passengers whose collective wealth exceeded $250 million. His immediate ambitions were dimmed, however, when the Titanic brushed an iceberg in the North Atlantic [and sank] only two hours and forty minutes later. But Moran was among the 705 passengers who managed to find space in one of the ship's twenty lifeboats, and his career in crime continued to flourish for the better part of the 59 remaining years of his life.[8]

The most influential study of professional thieves was conducted by Edwin Sutherland in 1937. Sutherland found that professional thieves share five characteristics:

THEORY CONNECTS

Who Are the Thieves?

Situational theories of crime, such as rational choice and routine-activities theories, suggest that offenders calculate the costs and benefits of committing crimes. In what ways do these theories explain the behavior of professional thieves?

TABLE 11.1 Shoplifting Apprehensions Survey

Hayes International's 20th Annual Retail Theft Survey reports on over 620,000 shoplifting apprehensions taking place in just 24 large retail companies representing 19,151 stores with combined 2007 annual sales in excess of $689 billion.

	Shoplifting		Difference	
	2006	**2007**	**Number/$**	**Percent**
Apprehensions	573,769	626,314	52,545	9.16%
Recoveries*	$77,299,608	$83,245,923	$5,946,315	7.69%
Average case value	$134.72	$132.91	($ 1.81)	(1.34%)
Hours per apprehension†	70.84	70.75		(0.13%)
Recoveries (no apprehensions made)‡	$26,528,990	$30,531,116	$4,002,126	15.09%

*For the 7th straight year, dollars recovered from shoplifting apprehensions increased.
†Eleven companies reporting.
‡For the 11th consecutive year, dollars recovered from shoplifters where no apprehension was made increased.
SOURCE: From "Theft Surveys." http://www.hayesinternational.com/thft_srvys.html.

1. They have well-developed technical skills for their particular mode of operation.

2. They enjoy status, accorded to them by their own subculture and by law enforcement.

3. They are bound by consensus, a sharing of values with their own peers.

4. Not only do they learn from each other, but they also protect each other.

5. They are organized, however loosely.[9]

Subsequent studies have tended to confirm Sutherland's findings.

Shoplifting

Shoplifting, the stealing of goods from retail merchants, is a very common crime; it constitutes about 15 percent of all larcenies. A survey in Spokane, Washington, revealed that every twelfth shopper is a shoplifter and that men and women are equally likely to be offenders.[10] Perhaps shoplifting is so frequent because it is a low-risk offense, with a detection rate of perhaps less than 1 percent.[11] Shoppers are extremely reluctant to report shoplifters to the store management.[12] According to one study, of those apprehended for shoplifting, approximately 45.5 percent are actually prosecuted. It is also estimated that men are slightly more likely than women to be shoplifters, and that 41 percent of offenders are white, 29 percent are black, and 16 percent are Hispanic. More than half of shoplifting events occur between the hours of 12:00 P.M. and 6:00 P.M.[13] Interviews with 740 shoplifters in 50 Minneapolis stores revealed that almost half of those who expressed motivation for stealing said that they stole the merchandise because they liked it and did not have enough money to pay for it.[14] A Hayes International Retail Theft Survey revealed significant increases in apprehensions and recoveries over the past years of reporting[15] (Table 11.1).

Mary Owen Cameron found that professional shoplifters largely conform to Sutherland's five characteristics but that amateurs do not. She estimates that of all shoplifters, only 10 percent are professionals—people who derive most of their income from the sale of stolen goods.[16] A broad range of motivations may lead to shoplifting. Among amateurs, need and greed as well as opportunity may precipitate the event.[17] Some researchers point to depression and other emotional disturbances and to the use of various prescription drugs.[18]

To most people, shoplifting is a rather insignificant offense. After all, how much can be stolen? On an individual basis, usually not very much: The average theft amount for each incident is roughly $133.[19] Taken together, however, all shoplifting incidents cost U.S. retail businesses over $25 billion every year.[20] In 2007, approximately $83 million worth of stolen merchandise was recovered. (See Table 11.2 for shoplifted items.)

As shoplifters decrease store profits, the price of goods goes up; stepped-up security adds even more to costs. Stores typically hire more and more security personnel, although it has been demonstrated that physical or electronic methods of securing merchandise are more cost effective than

TABLE 11.2 Most Frequently Shoplifted Items by Store Type

Type of Retailer	Merchandise
Auto parts	Hard parts
Bookstores	Electronics, CDs, cassettes, videos
Consumer electronics/computer stores	Portable CD players, car alarms, cordless phones
Department stores	Clothing: shirts
Discount stores	Clothing: undergarments, CDs
Drugstores/pharmacies	Cigarettes, batteries, over-the-counter remedies
Fashion merchandise stores	Sneakers
General merchandise stores	Earrings
Grocery stores/supermarkets	Over-the-counter remedies, health and beauty aids, cigarettes
Home centers/hardware stores	Assorted hand tools
Music stores	Compact discs
Shoe stores	Sneakers
Specialty apparel stores	Assorted clothes, shoes
Specialty stores	Bedsheets
Sporting goods stores	Nike shoes
Theme parks	Key chains, jewelry
Toy stores	Action figures
Video stores	Video games
Warehouse stores	Pens, movie videos

SOURCE: Read Hayes, *1996 Retail Theft Trends Report: An Analysis of Customer Theft in Stores* (Winter Park, Fla.: Loss Prevention Specialists, 1996). Reprinted by permission of the author.

■ At the upscale Beverly Hills Saks Fifth Avenue on December 12, 2001, actress Winona Ryder is seen on a security surveillance tape released by the Los Angeles County Courts. On November 6, 2002, a jury found the two-time Oscar nominee guilty of grand theft and felony vandalism for stealing designer clothes worth about $5,000.

the deployment of guards.[21] It is only the amateur shoplifter who is deterred by the presence of guards or store personnel, not the professional.[22]

Given the significantly high costs of shoplifting to retailers, what can be done to reclaim what has been stolen? One option, practiced quite often in the United Kingdom, is the use of civil recovery. Civil recovery is an administrative process that enables store owners to utilize the civil law in an attempt to collect restitution from shoplifters directly, whether the shoplifters are customers or store employees. This civil action operates parallel to the criminal process, meaning that stores can both report instances of shoplifting to the police and file separate civil complaints against the shoplifters to obtain restitution. Those apprehended for shoplifting can then either pay the civil penalty imposed upon them or appear before a civil court. Research has shown that for amateur shoplifters (as opposed to professionals), the use of civil recovery does not have a significant impact on their initial offense but does have an impact on preventing them from reoffending.[23]

Art Theft

At the high end of the larceny scale we find art theft. The public knows and seems to care little about art theft, yet it is as old as art itself. Looters have stolen priceless treasures from Egyptian tombs ever since they were built. As prices for antiques and modern art soar, the demand for stolen art soars. Mexico and other countries with a precious cultural heritage are in danger of losing their treasures to gangs of thieves who take what they can from archaeological sites and leave the rest in ruins.

One of the most grandiose art thefts occurred on May 21, 1986, when a gang of Irish thieves invaded an estate in Ireland with commando precision and made off with 11 paintings, among them a Goya, two Rubenses, a Gainsborough, and a Vermeer.

Art theft, particularly the illicit trade in objects of cultural heritage, has increased significantly worldwide in recent years. Art thieves use a variety of means, including forms of shoplifting, burglary, and robbery, to either steal individual works of art, illegally export pieces of art, or pillage archaeological sites.[24] Despite the widespread incidence of art theft, nobody knows the overall cost. Some paintings are worth $50, others $5,000, and others $50 million. Tens of thousands of paintings and other art objects are missing.[25]

In response to the increasing problem of art theft, the Federal Bureau of Investigation (FBI) has created the National Stolen Art File, which consists of a computerized index of stolen art and other forms of cultural property (Table 11.3). Once items are reported to either local law enforcement

agencies within the United States or law enforcement agencies abroad, the FBI is notified and then incorporates images and physical descriptions of the objects, as well as information specific to the investigation of the particular art theft, into the National Stolen Art File index. The database that is created is used as an analytical tool to investigate and recover these items. According to the FBI, for an object to be entered into the National Stolen Art File, three specific criteria must be met. First, the object must be of artistic or historic significance. This includes fine arts, ethnographic objects, archaeological material, coins, stamps, musical instruments, and the like. Second, the stolen object in question must have a value of $2,000 or more. However, if the object is worth less than $2,000 but is associated with a major crime, the stolen object will meet the necessary criteria. Finally, the request for inclusion in the National Stolen Art File must be made by a law enforcement agency. Included in the request must be a description of the object, a photograph of the object, and, if available, a police report and any other investigative information.[26]

Inasmuch as Hollywood movies are considered art, a new form of art theft has emerged—video piracy. Various video piracy rings exist throughout the country. They produce and sell bootleg tapes of films currently in movie theaters. Enforcement efforts have increased over the past few years. In 1999, a New York–based piracy ring operating one of the largest video piracy operations along the East Coast was dismantled, resulting in 11 arrests and the confiscation of approximately 30,000 videotapes. This particular ring earned roughly $50,000 a week after producing and selling bootleg tapes of first-run films. The bootleg tapes sold for between $5 and $10 on the street. Those arrested were charged with trademark counterfeiting and failure to disclose the origin of a recording.[27]

People who commit larceny aim for places and objects that seem to offer the highest and most secure rewards. Our open, mercantile society affords an abundance of opportunities. While shoplifters need little expertise and a low level of professional connection, art thieves must have sophisticated knowledge of art and its value as well as good connections in the art world if they are to dispose of the items they steal. Art thieves methodically select the gallery from which they plan to steal objects of art, paying particular attention to the area in which the gallery is located, the floor of the gallery in which the art is housed, the showrooms with and without closed-circuit television (CCTV), and the number of visitors at the gallery at a particular time.[28] Other types of larceny, such as theft of automobiles and boats, require a moderate degree of skill—but more and more members of the general public are acquiring such skills.

TABLE 11.3 FBI Top Ten Art Crimes

IRAQI LOOTED AND STOLEN ARTIFACTS

In March–April 2003, Iraqi cultural institutions and archaeological sites suffered major losses of priceless historical artifacts. Looting from archaeological sites continues on a massive scale. A number of artifacts stolen from the Iraq National Museum have been returned, but between 7,000 and 10,000 remain missing. Among the missing are the diorite statue of Entemena and almost 5,000 cylinder seals. In February 2005, the FBI recovered and repatriated 8 cylinder seals taken from archaeological sites in Iraq.

ISABELLA STEWART GARDNER MUSEUM THEFT

In March 1990, the Isabella Stewart Gardner Museum, Boston, was robbed by two unknown men. The thieves removed works of art whose value has been estimated as high as $300 million. These include: Vermeer, *The Concert;* Rembrandt, *A Lady and Gentleman in Black;* Rembrandt, *The Storm on the Sea of Galilee;* Rembrandt, *Self-Portrait;* Govaert Flinck, *Landscape with Obelisk;* Manet, *Chez Tortoni.*

THEFT OF CARAVAGGIO'S NATIVITY WITH SAN LORENZO AND SAN FRANCESCO

In October 1969, two thieves entered the Oratory of San Lorenzo, Palermo, Italy, and removed the Caravaggio *Nativity* from its frame. Experts estimate its value at $20 million.

THEFT OF THE DAVIDOFF-MORINI STRADIVARIUS

In October 1995, it was reported that a $3 million Stradivarius violin had been stolen from the New York City apartment of Erica Morini, a noted concert violinist. Made in 1727 by Antonio Stradivari, the violin is known as the Davidoff-Morini Stradivarius.

THE VAN GOGH MUSEUM ROBBERY

In December 2002, two thieves used a ladder to climb to the roof and break in to the Vincent Van Gogh Museum, Amsterdam, The Netherlands. In just a few minutes the thieves stole two paintings: Van Gogh's *View of the Sea at Scheveningen* and *Congregation Leaving the Reformed Church in Nuenen,* valued at $30 million. Dutch police convicted two men in December 2003 but did not recover the paintings.

THEFT OF CEZANNE'S VIEW OF AUVERS-SUR-OISE

On December 31, 1999, during the fireworks that accompanied the celebration of the millennium, a thief broke into the Ashmolean Museum, Oxford, England, to steal Cezanne's landscape painting *View of Auvers-sur-Oise.* Valued at £3 million, the painting has been described as an important work illustrating the transition from early to mature Cezanne painting.

THEFT OF THE GERTRUDE VANDERBILT WHITNEY MURALS, PANELS 3-A AND 3-B

In July 2002, two oil paintings by Maxfield Parrish were stolen during a burglary of a gallery in West Hollywood, California. The paintings are two panels from a series commissioned for Gertrude Vanderbilt Whitney's 5th Avenue mansion in New York. The paintings were cut from their frames during the theft. The value of the two paintings is estimated at $4 million.

THEFT FROM THE MUSEU CHACARA DO CÉU

On February 24, 2006, about 4:00 P.M., four works of art and other objects were stolen from the Museu Chacara do Céu, Rio de Janeiro, by four armed men. The value of the stolen items has not been estimated.

THEFT OF VAN MIERIS'S A CAVALIER

On June 10, 2007, *A Cavalier,* a self portrait in oil on wood panel by Dutch Master Frans Van Mieris, was stolen from the Art Gallery of New South Wales, Sydney, Australia. The piece was stolen while the gallery was open for public viewing. The relatively small portrait measures 20 × 16 cm. Its value is estimated at over $1 million.

THEFT FROM E. G. BÜHRLE COLLECTION, ZURICH

Four masterpieces were stolen in an armed robbery on February 10, 2008, from the E. G. Bührle Collection in Zurich, Switzerland. Two paintings were recovered.

SOURCE: Available at http://www.fbi.gov/hq/cid/arttheft/arttheft.htm.

Motor Vehicle Theft

Motor vehicle theft is the largest property crime in the United States. According to the Uniform Crime Reports, approximately 1.1 million motor vehicles were stolen in the United States in 2007.[29] The value of motor vehicles stolen in 2007 was roughly $7.4 million.[30]

In 2007, 73 percent of the vehicles stolen were passenger cars, 18.1 percent were trucks and buses, and 8.6 percent were other types of vehicles.[31] The clearance rate (by arrest), as distinguished from the recovery rate of vehicles, is low—about 12.6 percent. Many cars are stolen during July and August, when schools are not in session. Of car thieves, 26.5 percent are youngsters under 18. Most of their acts amount to "joyriding," a type of larceny that lacks the element of "intent to deprive the owner of the property permanently." The thieves simply take the vehicle for the momentary pleasure of transportation.

More recently, young car thieves have used stolen vehicles for racing, a show of status among peers, or for the "kick" of destroying them (Figure 11.2). At the other end of the spectrum are older, professional auto thieves who steal designated cars on consignment for resale in an altered condition (with identifying numbers changed) or for disposition in "chop shops," which strip the cars for the resale value of their parts.[32] Some estimate that a vehicle is worth three times its value when sold illegally for parts by professional car thieves.[33] In 2001 alone, more than 200,000 vehicles were illegally shipped abroad.[34] Table 11.4 describes the 10 areas in the United States with the highest vehicle theft rates in 2005. The types of vehicles

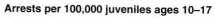

Arrests per 100,000 juveniles ages 10–17

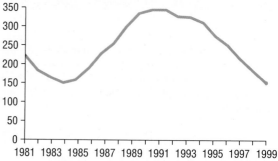

The juvenile arrest rate for motor vehicle theft increased 130 percent between 1983 and 1989. The decline in the 1990s resulted in a 1999 arrest rate that was about the same as the 1983 low point and equal to the 1980 rate.

FIGURE 11.2 Motor vehicle theft. Juvenile arrest rates for motor vehicle theft soared between 1984 and 1989, then decreased through the 1990s.

Source: Juvenile Offenders and Victims: 1999 National Report. Washington, D.C.: Office of Juvenile Justice and Delinquency Prevention, 1999, p.129.

stolen have changed over the years. It is interesting to note that sport utility vehicles and pickup trucks are becoming just as popular with thieves as they are with consumers. In fact, 1998 was the second year in a row in which these types of vehicles made the top 10 stolen vehicles category.

A variety of strategies are used to steal vehicles for financial gain. The "strip and run" occurs when a thief steals a car, strips it for its parts, and then abandons the vehicle. The frame of the car is all that is left. The "scissors job" occurs when scissors

Rank	Metropolitan Statistical Area	Vehicles Stolen	Rate*
1	Modesto, Calif.	7,071	1,418.80
2	Las Vegas/Paradise, Nev.	22,465	1,360.90
3	Stockton, Calif.	7,586	1,167.30
4	Phoenix/Mesa/Scottsdale, Ariz.	41,000	1,103.50
5	Visalia/Porterville, Calif.	4,257	1,060.20
6	Seattle/Tacoma/Bellevue, Wash.	33,494	1,057.60
7	Sacramento/Arden-Arcade/Roseville, Calif.	20,268	1,005.00
8	San Diego/Carlsbad/San Marcos, Calif.	28,845	983.90
9	Fresno, Calif.	8,478	978.11
10	Yakima, Wash.	2,212	965.54

TABLE 11.4 Motor Vehicle Theft, Top 10 U.S. Metropolitan Areas, 2005

*Ranked by the rate of vehicle thefts reported per 100,000 population based on the 2000 census.

SOURCE: National Insurance Crime Bureau, available at www.nicb.org.

■ *Philadelphia police officer John Logan carrying "chopped" parts of stolen cars from the city's East Frankford section.*

are jammed into certain ignition locks in mostly American-made cars, allowing the thief to easily start the car. A "valet theft" takes place when a thief dresses and poses as a valet attendant, opens the car door for the driver, takes the keys, and quickly drives away. Another strategy for vehicle theft is simply the "insurance fraud" scheme, in which a car owner reports his or her car stolen and hides the car for approximately 30 days. Once 30 days have passed without the car's being recovered, insurance claims are often paid without question. After the claim is paid, the cars are often miraculously "found" but are in very poor condition. The owner will then use the money from the insurance claim to purchase a newer car.[35]

Carjacking is considered a combination of motor vehicle theft and robbery. Not only is a car stolen, but it is stolen by use of force or threat of force. Carjacking has become quite a widespread occurrence over the past few years. During each year between 1993 and 2002, there was an average of about 38,000 completed or attempted nonfatal carjackings. In about half of the incidents, the offender was successful in taking the victim's automobile. Approximately 7 out of 10 completed carjackings involved the use of firearms, whereas about 2 out of 10 attempted carjackings involved the use of firearms. Surprisingly, most carjackings, whether they were completed or attempted, did not result in injury to the victim.[36]

The invention of the ignition key made it harder to steal cars. Manufacturers of automobiles have tried to make cars more theftproof. Steering-shaft locks, cutoff switches, better door locks, and alarm systems have increased the security of protected cars.

One of the most successful of the high-tech options for car protection may be electronic tracking systems, including the widely known and utilized Lo-Jack. A small electronic transmitter, installed in the car, is activated by police transmitters once a car is reported stolen. A homing signal allows tracking computers in police cruisers to determine the location of the stolen car. A direction finder and a signal-strength meter let the police know how close they are to the stolen car, thereby facilitating the search.[37] A newer type of antitheft device is called the "Unbreakable Autolock." This particular device, when in place, locks one of the strongest parts of the car, the steel brake pedal. Once the Autolock is in place, the brake pedal cannot be depressed. Most cars built after 1990 feature a component called the "brake pedal shift interlock," which requires that the brake pedal be depressed before the vehicle can be put into gear. Since the Autolock locks the brake, it cannot be depressed, and therefore the car cannot be driven, making theft impossible.[38] One other antitheft device is the "Silent Scorpion." Unlike many car alarm systems, this device does not emit any sounds upon activation. Instead, it actually prevents the car thief from driving the car more than a quarter mile. The system is activated automatically whenever the driver's door is opened and then closed while the engine is running. Once the Silent Scorpion is activated, the engine will run normally for about 4 seconds, at which time it will then begin to simulate engine failure. The engine will shudder and, after about 25 seconds, will shut off; the thief will be unable to restart the car.[39]

A development by the U.S. attorney general's office in response to the Motor Vehicle Theft Prevention Act of 1994 is the national "Watch Your Car" program. A car owner can voluntarily display a decal or a special customized license plate on his or her vehicle signifying one of two things: that the car normally is not driven between the hours of 1:00 A.M. and 5:00 A.M. or that the vehicle normally is not driven in the proximity of international land borders or ports. As a member of this program, the car owner consents to vehicle stops if the car is being driven under the conditions described above.[40]

Such efforts (as described in Chapter 9) are examples of target hardening—that is, designing the target (the car) in such a way that it is harder to steal. Other means of providing greater car protection include safer parking facilities. Ronald Clarke has demonstrated that parking lots with attendants experience far fewer motor vehicle thefts than do unattended lots.[41]

Crime Surfing

www.ncjrs.gov/
pdffiles/car.pdf

Check this website for more information on the Watch Your Car program.

Piracy Emerges as a Major Worldwide Problem: How Can It Be Controlled?

In December 2008, the European Union initiated a major naval operation (code-named Operation Atalanta) in the Gulf of Aden, off the coast of Somalia. The strategy came in response to outcries from ship owners and governments desperately trying to find countermeasures to end the rapidly increasing number of pirate attacks. In the Gulf of Aden, there were 102 ships attacked, 40 hijacked, and $50 million in ransom paid in 2008 alone.(1) Among these ships were:

- The Sirius Star, a Saudi-owned oil supertanker the size of an aircraft carrier loaded with $1 million worth of crude oil. The 25-person crew came from Britain, Croatia, the Philippines, and Saudi Arabia
- A Ukrainian vessel loaded, to the surprise of the pirates, with $30 million worth of grenade launchers, artillery, ammunition, and 33 battle tanks weighing 80,000 pounds each.
- An American cruise liner, the M/S Nautica, with 656 passengers and 399 crew members on a 32-day cruise from Rome to Singapore. When pirates began firing at the ship, the captain, over the loud speaker, ordered all passengers to remain in an interior space. He managed to outrun the attackers.

The northeastern coast of Africa is only one of the pirate-infested waters of the world. Another high-risk area is the Malacca Strait near Malaysia, a body of water that serves as a major shipping lane from the Middle East to the Far East. Many commodities are identified and sold even before the pirates capture the ship. Worldwide piracy is often referred to as an activity of the "Ocean Mafia." In many cities, it is easy to spot its members. In the capital of Somalia, for example, wealthy pirates live in luxury next to the tin shacks of their neighbors. In places where children are starving, they drive expensive cars and entertain lavishly.

Pirates are not selective when it comes to their targets. They will attack anything that will bring ransom money or goods to be sold: container ships, oil tankers, cruise ships, sailing yachts, or fishing trawlers.(2) They can afford fast boats for surprise attacks, expensive GPS equipment, the latest weaponry, and supplies that enable them to wait at sea for the right target.

The Scope of Crime on the Oceans

Piracy is only one of the crimes committed on the oceans. Following are examples of other crimes:

- Fraud in the marine shipping industry has caused severe damage to international trade and threatened the collapse of entire national economies.
- The international drug trade uses the oceans for about half its shipments from the points of origin or manufacture to the points of distribution.
- Currently over 30,000 American boats are listed in the FBI's Stolen Boat File as having been stolen and not recovered.

The Lack of Policing

Unfortunately, the world does not yet have an international marine enforcement agency to police the oceans. There is no one to spot a vessel dumping nuclear waste into the high seas or into an exclusive economic zone. Who can intercept arms or narcotics smugglers? Even powerful nations like the United States have trouble policing their own zones. The problems are much worse for small nations that cannot afford to maintain marine police forces of any size. Most regions affected by piracy and terrorism are in areas of notoriously underpoliced territorial waters.

Sources

1. Mark McDonald, "Array of Strategies Are Tried to Turn Back Pirates at Sea," New York Times, Dec. 10, 2008, p. A10.
2. G. O. W. Mueller and Freda Adler, Outlaws of the Ocean (New York: Hearst Marine Books, 1985), p. 150.

Questions for Discussion

1. How is crime on the high seas related to (or possibly related to) terrorist acts?
2. In your opinion, what is the best way to control and prevent crime on the oceans?

Boat Theft

It is not our purpose to classify all larceny by the type of property stolen. We have singled out automobile theft and art theft to demonstrate the socioeconomic significance of these types of larceny, their dependence on the economic situation, and the challenge of changing the situational conditions that encourage people to commit them. Another type of larceny, the theft of working and pleasure boats, of little fishing skiffs and rowboats, is similarly tied to socioeconomic conditions.

No statistics were kept on boat theft in the United States before 1970. Obviously, boat thefts have occurred ever since there have been boats, but such thefts did not attain high proportions until the 1970s and 1980s. The FBI's National Crime Information Center started a stolen-boat file in 1969. During the first few years, this service was little known, and the number of boats listed as stolen was initially small. But by the mid-1970s, law enforcement agencies all over the country had become familiar with this service and had begun reporting the number of stolen boats in

■ *U.S. Coast Guard law enforcement team boarding a vessel in American territorial waters.*

their jurisdictions. Between 1975 and 1990, the number of boats stolen and not recovered tripled, from 11,000 to over 30,000. That number does not include boats eliminated from the file after a given expiration period (of from 1 to 5 years). After 1990, the number of thefts declined, and approximately 10,000 boats are now stolen each year.

Most boat thefts, both in the water and on land, are linked to the vast increase in the number of boats in the United States. Increased boat ownership among all population groups goes hand in hand with a proliferation of skills in handling boats and outboard motors. The number of automobile thefts rose during the days when automobile ownership and driving skills increased rapidly. Now we are witnessing the same phenomenon with boats. Some of the same crime-specific approaches developed to render cars more theftproof are currently being tried to protect boats and boating equipment—registration, secret and indelible identification numbers, locking devices, alarm systems, marina guards, and protection campaigns for boat owners. Already there is some indication that the choices for boat thieves are becoming more limited and that the thieves are choosing their targets with increasing care.[42]

With the exception of some brazen pickpockets, people who commit larcenies tend to avoid personal contact with their victims. Other criminals seek such contact in order to deprive victims of their property by deception.

FRAUD

Fraud is the acquisition of the property of another person through cheating or deception. In England, such crimes owed their existence to the interaction of five circumstances: the advancement of trade and commerce, the inventiveness of swindlers in exploiting these economic advances, the demand of merchants for better protection, the unwillingness of the royal courts to expand the old concept of larceny, and the willingness of Parliament to designate new crimes in order to protect mercantile interests. In brief, medieval England developed a market economy that required the transport of goods by wagon trains across the country, from producer or importer to consumer. Later on, when the Crown sought to encourage settlement of colonies overseas, stock companies were created to raise money for such ventures. People with money to invest acquired part ownership in these companies in the expectation of profit.

Just as some dishonest transporters withheld some of the property entrusted to them for transport, some dishonest investment clerks used funds entrusted to them for their own purposes. Merchants suffered greatly from such losses, yet the royal courts refused to extend the definition of larceny to cover this new means of depriving owners of their property. But merchants demanded protection, and from time to time, as need arose, Parliament designated new, noncapital offenses so that the swindlers could be punished.

Obtaining Property by False Pretenses

The essence of the crime of **obtaining property by false pretenses** is that the victim is made to part with property voluntarily, as a result of the perpetrator's untrue statements regarding a supposed fact. Assume the doorbell rings. A gentleman greets you politely and identifies himself as a representative of a charitable organization, collecting money for disaster victims. On a typed list are the names of all the households in your building, with a dollar amount next to each name. Each household has supposedly contributed an average of $20. Not wanting to be considered cheap, you hand the gentleman a $20 bill. He promptly writes "$20" next to your name and thanks you.

Of course, the gentleman does not represent the charitable organization, there may not even be such a charity, there may not have been a disaster, and you may have been the first victim on his list. The man has obtained property from you by false pretenses. He has not committed a common law larceny because he did not engage in any "trespassory taking" of property.

Cheating was made a crime relatively late in history (in 1757 in England). Until that time, the

Mortgage Fraud

Of all the factors leading to the recession that started in 2007, mortgage fraud is the most frequently cited. After it became clear that fraud was involved in at least some of the more-questionable mortgage transactions, the Federal Bureau of Investigation increased the priority given to mortgage fraud investigations. In its most recent report on financial crimes, the FBI provides significant details of its accomplishments.

I. GENERAL OVERVIEW

The potential impact of mortgage fraud on financial institutions and the stock market is clear. If fraudulent practices become systemic within the mortgage industry and mortgage fraud is allowed to become unrestrained, it will ultimately place financial institutions at risk and have adverse effects on the stock market. Investors may lose faith and require higher returns from mortgage backed securities. This may result in higher interest rates and fees paid by borrowers and limit the amount of investment funds available for mortgage loans.

The increased reliance by both financial institutions and non-financial institution lenders on third-party brokers has created opportunities for organized fraud groups, particularly where mortgage industry professionals are involved.

Combating significant mortgage industry fraud is a priority, because mortgage lending and the housing market have a significant overall effect on the nation's economy. All retail mortgage fraud investigations are managed within the Economic Crimes Unit II.

Each mortgage fraud scheme contains some type of "material misstatement, misrepresentation, or omission relating to the property or potential mortgage relied on by an underwriter or lender to fund, purchase or insure a loan." The FBI compiles data on mortgage fraud through Suspicious Activity Reports (SARs) filed by federally-insured financial institutions and the Department of Housing and Urban Development—Office of Inspector General (HUD-OIG) reports. The FBI also receives complaints from the mortgage industry at large.

A significant portion of the mortgage industry is void of any mandatory fraud reporting. In addition, as initial mortgage products are repackaged and sold on secondary markets, the sale of the mortgages in many cases conceals or distorts the fraud, causing it not to be reported. Therefore, the true level of mortgage fraud is largely unknown. However, based on various industry reports and FBI analysis, mortgage fraud is pervasive and growing. For example, SARs in Fiscal Year 2005 were over 35,000; Fiscal Year 2006 were over 46,000; and the 1st Quarter of Fiscal Year 2007 were 14,916, which extrapolates to 60,000 [2007] SARs.

The FBI investigates mortgage fraud in two distinct areas: fraud for profit and fraud for housing. Fraud for profit is sometimes referred to as "Industry Insider Fraud," and the motive is to revolve equity, falsely inflate the value of the property, or issue loans based on fictitious properties. Based on existing investigations and mortgage fraud reporting, 80 percent of all reported fraud losses involve collaboration or collusion by industry insiders. Fraud for housing represents illegal actions perpetrated solely by the borrower. The simple motive behind this fraud is to acquire and maintain ownership of a house under false pretenses. This type of fraud is typified by a borrower who makes misrepresentations regarding his income or employment history to qualify for a loan.

The defrauding of mortgage lenders should not be compared to predatory lending practices that primarily affect borrowers. Predatory lending typically affects senior citizens, lower income, and challenged credit borrowers. Predatory lending forces borrowers to pay exorbitant loan origination/settlement fees, subprime or higher interest rates, and in some cases, unreasonable service fees. These practices often result in the borrower defaulting on his mortgage payment and undergoing foreclosure or forced refinancing.

Although there are many mortgage fraud schemes, the FBI is focusing its efforts on those perpetrated by industry insiders. The FBI is engaged with the mortgage industry primarily in identifying fraud trends and educating the public. Some of the current rising mortgage fraud trends include: equity skimming, property flipping, and mortgage related identity theft. Equity skimming is a tried and true method of committing mortgage fraud. Today's common equity skimming schemes involve the use of corporate shell companies, corporate identity theft, and the use or threat of bankruptcy/foreclosure to dupe homeowners and investors. Property flipping is nothing new; however, once again law enforcement is faced with an educated criminal element that is using identity theft, straw borrowers, shell companies, along with industry insiders, to conceal their methods and override lender controls.

Property flipping is best described as purchasing properties and artificially inflating their value through false appraisals. The artificially valued properties are then repurchased several times for a higher price by associates of the "flipper." After three or four sham sales, the properties are foreclosed on by victim lenders. Often flipped properties are ultimately repurchased for 50 to 100 percent of their original value.

Since 1999, the FBI has been actively investigating mortgage fraud in various cities across the U.S. The FBI also focuses on fostering relationships and partnerships with the mortgage industry to promote mortgage fraud awareness. To raise awareness of this issue and provide easy accessibility to investigative personnel, the FBI has provided points of contact to relevant groups including the Mortgage Bankers Association (MBA), the Mortgage Asset Research Institute (MARI), the Mortgage Insurance Companies of America, Fannie Mae, Freddie Mac, and others.

The FBI initiates many of its mortgage fraud cases through the review of SARs. In fact, due to the vast amounts of intelligence contained in SARs, the FBI has developed a number of new analytical tools to further exploit this intelligence. The benefits have not only enhanced the mortgage fraud program, but all other FBI investigative and intelligence programs as well. The FBI works closely with FinCEN [Financial Crimes Enforcement Network] in sharing analytical strategies and trend data that both agencies develop from SARs.

The FBI also works closely with individual lenders, as well as national associations such as the MBA, the Appraisal Institute, the National Association of Mortgage Brokers, and the National Notary Association, to define and combat the mortgage fraud problem. In addition, on a case-by-case basis, the FBI receives close cooperation from lenders. An example of this is the usage of Real Estate Owned properties from lender inventories to facilitate mortgage fraud undercover operations.

III. SIGNIFICANT CASES

RAYMOND JOSEPH COSTANZO, JR.(ATLANTA): From late 2004 to early 2006, Raymond Joseph Costanzo, Jr., an attorney, participated in closing millions of dollars in fraudulently inflated mortgage loans for unqualified straw borrowers. These straw borrowers were paid as much as $600,000 from fraudulently obtained loan proceeds through shell companies. Costanzo himself obtained mortgage loans totaling over $1.5 million by providing the lender with false qualifying information and falsified down payments. Costanzo received $250,000 in scheme proceeds from this transaction and arranged for disbursements of fraudulently obtained loan proceeds to co-conspirators from this and other loans. On February 1, 2008, Costanzo was sentenced to three years, five months in prison to be followed by four years supervised release and ordered to pay $7,843,184 in restitution. On October 17, 2006, Costanzo pleaded guilty to these charges and surrendered his license to practice law.

GHANDI BEN MORKA (DALLAS): Gandhi Ben Morka, a real estate appraiser who was convicted at trial of several offenses related to his involvement in a mortgage fraud scheme, was sentenced January 23, 2008, by U.S. District Court for the Northern District of Texas, to 60 months in prison and ordered to pay more than $2.3 million in restitution. Morka was arrested in May 2007 and indicted along with seven others for various offenses related to a mortgage fraud scheme to defraud Countrywide Home Loans, doing business as America Wholesale Lender (Countrywide). Morka conspired with co-defendants to defraud Countrywide by locating single family residences in and around the Dallas area and recruiting straw purchasers and borrowers to purchase the targeted residences. Morka would prepare appraisals on the properties, inflating the value to an amount far greater than the fair market value. Then he and co-conspirators prepared and submitted false and fraudulent loan applications in the names of the straw purchasers to secure mortgage loans from Countrywide in amounts substantially greater than the fair market value of the purchased property. Morka and the co-conspirators paid the original owners of the properties and distributed the remaining fraudulent proceeds obtained from the loan proceeds among themselves. The scheme resulted in millions of dollars of losses to Countrywide.

DARRYL L. COOPER (ATLANTA): On January, 11, 2008, Darryl L. Cooper of Decatur, Georgia, was sentenced to one year, six months in federal prison, followed by three years of supervised release, for a scheme to defraud mortgage lenders by creating fraudulent appraisals that reflected completed construction.

Cooper was recruited by builder/co-conspirator Jeffrey Allen Teague to prepare fraudulent appraisals reflecting photographs and $5 million in appraisal valuations for 15 completed houses in the Greenleaf Subdivision of Forsyth County, when Teague had not completed the construction of these homes. A California lender relied on Cooper's fraudulent appraisals that reflected completed construction to make $4.7 million in mortgage loans secured by these properties, which in fact had no value at all.

U.S. Attorney David E. Nahmias said of the case, "This case highlights the problems created by mortgage fraud in which the appraiser conspired with the builder to misrepresent that construction on homes was complete, compounded by out-of-state 'investors,' who sign for loans without inspecting the properties. The partially built houses in this case may be subject to condemnation, as the portions completed were not built to code, leaving mortgage lenders with little security for their loans, 'investors' with nothing to resell, and neighborhoods full of vacant and uninhabitable houses."

Cooper pleaded guilty to a one-count criminal information on November 7, 2007, on a charge of mortgage fraud conspiracy and has been ordered to pay $4,720,500 in restitution. Teague was sentenced on October 26, 2007, to 15 years, eight months in prison and ordered to pay $7,803,701 in restitution for his part in the fraud.

NELSON MILLER, FREEDOM FINANCIAL (LITTLE ROCK): The top ten executives of Freedom Financial and Absolute Abstract and Title, at one time the largest mortgage broker in the state of Arkansas, were charged criminally for their part in devising, implementing, and carrying out various fraud schemes that involved falsification of hundreds of loan files. The analysis of seized documents revealed employees of Freedom Financial had submitted Uniform Residential Loan Applications and supporting documents to lenders containing false and fraudulent information. This false information in all its variations was submitted by the employees of Freedom Financial to lenders to induce the lenders to fund loans or make loans in larger amounts than would normally be given if there had been truthful and complete disclosure. Seven of the nine defendants in this case entered guilty pleas, and two of the defendants were convicted on August 31, 2006, and January 28, 2008, respectively.

(continued)

CHRISTOPHER CRAIG (SACRAMENTO): In May 2007, Christopher Craig of Auburn, California, pled guilty to bank fraud charges related to a foreclosure scheme. Craig approached homeowners who were on the verge of foreclosure and promised to loan them money. Instead, he created documents deeding away their properties to straw buyers, then applied for home equity loans from Washington Mutual Bank. Washington Mutual disbursed $1.2 million in loan proceeds to Craig based on the false loan applications. Craig was sentenced in the Eastern District of California to five years in federal prison and ordered to pay $974,452 in restitution. Property and cash were also seized for asset forfeiture from Craig, including a 2007 GMC Hummer SUV.

Source

Federal Bureau of Investigation, Financial Crimes Report to the Public, Fiscal Year 2007 (October 1, 2006—September 30, 2007). Available at http://www.fbi.gov/publications/financial/fcs_report2007/financial_crime_2007.htm.

Questions for Discussion

1. What role should the criminal law play in policing the subprime crisis?
2. How much blame should consumers assume for their failure to live up to their financial responsibilities?

---

attitude was that people should look out for their own interests. Today obtaining property by false pretenses is a crime in all 50 states, and some states have included it in their general larceny statutes.

Confidence Games and Frauds

In an attempt to protect people from their own greed, a few fraud statutes have included a statutory offense called **confidence game.** In an effort to cover the enormous variety of confidence swindles, legislators have worded the statutory definitions somewhat vaguely. The essence of the offense is that the offender gains the confidence of the victim, induces in the victim the expectation of a future gain, and—by abusing the trust thus created—makes the victim part with some property. In a sense, confidence games are an aggravated form of obtaining property by false pretenses.

To illustrate: A woman (A) sees a shiny object lying on the sidewalk. As she stoops to pick it up, a man (B) grabs it. A dispute ensues over who should have the "lost diamond ring." A third person (C) comes by and offers to mediate. He happens to be a jeweler, he says. C takes a jeweler's loupe out of his pocket, examines the diamond ring, and pronounces it worth $500. At this point, B generously offers his share in the ring to A for a mere $100. A pays—and gets what turns out to be a worthless object. By the time she discovers this fact, B and C are long gone.

Frauds of this sort have been with us for centuries. But frauds change with commercial developments. Some of the more prevalent fraud schemes of today would have been unimaginable a few decades ago, simply because the commercial opportunities for their occurrence had not yet been invented.

Check Forgery

Those motivated to deprive others of their property have always exploited new opportunities to do so. The invention of "instant cash," or credit, by means of a check issued by a creditable, trustworthy person provided just such new opportunities. Ever since checks were invented, they have been abused. All jurisdictions make it a criminal offense to use a counterfeit or stolen check or to pass a check on a nonexistent account, or even on one with insufficient funds, with intent to defraud. The intent may be demonstrated by the defendant's inability or unwillingness to reimburse the payee within a specified time period.

Another fraud, called **check forging,** consists of altering a check with intent to defraud. Criminologist Edwin Lemert found that most check

Darlene Gillespie, former Mouseketeer, was convicted of fraud in a Los Angeles, California, federal court in 1999.

forgers—or "hot-check artists," as they are frequently called—are amateurs who act in times of financial need or stress, do not consider themselves criminals, and often believe that nobody really gets hurt.[43] With the increase in check forgeries over the past few decades, the primary means of dealing with the problem has been the introduction of identification requirements when either cashing a check at a financial institution or presenting a check for payment. The downside of this approach is the annoyance to check users of having to put up with increased restrictions.[44]

Some retailers have begun using Telecheck, by which a check presented for payment is run through a machine that verifies whether the funds presented as payment on the check are in fact available at the time of sale.

Credit Card Crimes

Just as the introduction of checks for payment for goods and services opened up opportunities for thieves to gain illegitimate financial advantage, so did the introduction of "plastic money." Many

---

United States Attorney's Office
Eastern District of Virginia

Alexandria   Newport News   Norfolk   Richmond

United States Attorney Chuck Rosenberg

FOR IMMEDIATE RELEASE
July 25, 2008

Jim Rybicki
Public Information Officer
Phone: (703) 842-4050 Fax: (703) 549-5202
Email: usavae.press@usdoj.gov

Further Information Contact:
Kim Williams
Phone: (703) 299-3700

Web Address: www.usdoj.gov/usao/vae

Ringleader of Credit Card and Mortgage Scam Sentenced to 212 Months in Prison, $5 Million in Forfeiture, and More Than $3 Million in Restitution

(Alexandria, Virginia)—Abdul Hameed, age 46, of Houston, Texas, was sentenced today to 212 months in prison following his conviction on May 5, 2008, on a 21-count superseding indictment charging him with conspiracy, engaging in a continuing financial crimes enterprise, mail fraud, aggravated identity theft, and credit card fraud. Chuck Rosenberg, United States Attorney for the Eastern District of Virginia, made the announcement following Hameed's sentencing before United States District Judge Leonie M. Brinkema.

The indictment alleged that Hameed and others conspired to devise a scheme to defraud in which the defendants used various fraudulent identities that they controlled to obtain numerous credit card accounts, personal and business bank accounts, and mortgage loan accounts. According to the indictment, the defendants also established multiple false businesses that were used to give the appearance that the false identities were employed by fabricating employment and salary documents for the false identities. The phony documents were then provided to credit card companies, leasing offices, mortgage companies, and financial institutions to obtain credit in the names of the false identities. Hameed and his co-conspirators also rented apartments and purchased properties using false identities. These locations were then used to receive mail from the lenders that was addressed to the false identities and false businesses. They also used these locations to receive shipments of goods purchased using credit cards in the names of the false identities. According to the indictment, Hameed organized, managed, and supervised a continuing financial crimes enterprise—that is, a series of violations of the mail fraud statute that affected a financial institution and was committed by at least four persons acting in concert—and received $5,000,000 or more in gross receipts from the criminal enterprise during a 24-month period from in or about May 2005 to May 2007. According to the indictment, hundreds of thousands of dollars obtained from the scheme were transferred by the defendants to accounts in Pakistan.

Hameed was also ordered to pay forfeiture of $5 million and more than $3 million in restitution to the victims.

The case was prosecuted by Assistant United States Attorneys James P. Gillis, Gordon D. Kromberg, and Karen L. Taylor, and was investigated by a team of law enforcement agents from the Federal Bureau of Investigation, the Fairfax County Police Department, and the U.S. Postal Inspection Service.

FIGURE 11.3 Press Release about a Credit Card and Mortgage Scam.

Source: The United States Attorney's Office for the Eastern District of Virginia; available at http://www.usdoj.gov/usao/vae.

U.S. Secret Service Director Mark Sullivan (left) and U.S. Attorney General Michael Mukasey (right) at a news conference on August 5, 2008, where charges were announced in a major credit card theft. The Department of Justice charged 11 people in connection with the hacking of nine major retailers, including Office Max and Boston Market, and the theft and sale of more than 40 million credit and debit card numbers.

believe that the widespread use of credit cards, debit cards, and charge cards—in combination with Internet-based payments—is quickly making ours a cashless society.[45] New risks accompany our cashless society, including credit card fraud. As of 2007, the FBI estimates the losses associated with credit card fraud to be near $60 billion annually. This may be a quite conservative estimate.[46]

Credit card fraud during the 1980s was associated primarily with counterfeiting and lost or stolen cards. Now many cards are stolen while in transit from the issuer to the cardholder or during cell phone transmissions of wireless refunds, or in large-scale thefts of retail store databases.[47] Other offenses are extremly elaborate (Figure 11.3).

The economic rewards of credit card fraud are quick and relatively easy. The risks are low. However, the banking industry has studied credit card schemes and has improved the electronic system with target-hardening responses. In 1971, Congress enacted legislation that limited the financial liability of owners of stolen credit cards to $50. Many states have enacted legislation making it a distinct offense to obtain property or services by means of a stolen or forged credit card, while others include this type of fraud under their larceny statutes.

Several fraud-prevention initiatives have been developed in response to the prevalence of credit card fraud. The use of laser-engraved photography and signatures on credit cards makes impersonation more difficult. Other initiatives are the use of increased authorization levels on credit card transactions, as well as reduced floor limits above which transactions must be authorized to be guaranteed. Better technology has been developed to quickly transmit data on cards that have been reported lost and stolen to retailers worldwide. Further, with the ever-increasing "card not present" situations, such as when a person is purchasing items over the Internet, additional methods are being developed to verify the identity of the cardholder.[48]

Insurance Fraud

Insurance fraud is a major problem in the United States. Auto insurance, in particular, has been the target of many dishonest schemes. About $60 billion is paid in auto insurance claims annually. It is estimated that 10 percent of those claims are fraudulent.[49] The National Automobile Theft Bureau holds manufacturers' records on 188 million vehicles (about 95 percent of U.S. cars); its theft and loss data indicate that 15 percent of all reported thefts are fraudulent.[50] Auto insurance schemes include:

- *Staged claims.* Parts of a car are removed, reported stolen, and later replaced by the owner.

- *Owner dumping.* The car is reported stolen; it is stripped by the owner, and the parts are sold.

- *Abandoned vehicles.* The car is left in a vulnerable spot for theft; then it is reported stolen.[51]

- *Staged accidents.* No collision occurs, but an "accident scene" is prepared with glass, blood, and so forth.

- *Intended accidents.* All parties to the "accident" are part of the scheme.

- *Caused accidents.* The perpetrator deliberately causes an innocent victim in a targeted car to crash into his or her car (often in the presence of "friendly" witnesses).[52]

There are many types of insurance fraud besides that involving automobiles. One rapidly

Insurance Fraud

The battle against insurance fraud is fought at the local, state, and federal levels. Increasingly, the Financial Crimes Section of the Federal Bureau of Investigation plays a central role. Its most recent fiscal year report (2007) appears here.

I. GENERAL OVERVIEW

Insurance fraud continues to be an investigative priority for the FBI's Financial Crimes Section, due in large part to the insurance industry's significant status in the U.S. economy. The U.S. insurance industry consists of thousands of companies and collects nearly one trillion dollars in premiums each year. The size of the industry, unfortunately, makes it a prime target for criminal activity; the Coalition Against Insurance Fraud (CAIF) estimates that the cost of fraud in the industry is as high as $80 billion each year. This cost is passed on to consumers in the form of higher premiums. In fact, the National Insurance Crime Bureau (NICB) calculates insurance fraud raises the yearly cost of premiums by $300 for the average household.

The FBI continues to identify the most prevalent schemes and the top echelon criminals defrauding the insurance industry in an effort to reduce this type of fraud. The FBI works closely with the National Association of Insurance Commissioners, NICB, CAIF, as well as state fraud bureaus, state insurance regulators, and other federal agencies to combat insurance fraud. In addition, the FBI is a member of the International Association of Insurance Fraud Agencies, an international non-profit organization, whose mission is to maintain an international presence to address insurance and insurance-related financial crimes on a global basis. Currently, the FBI is focusing a majority of its resources relating to insurance fraud on the following schemes:

Arson Fraud Related to Mortgage Industry Credit Crisis—Whether unable or unwilling to meet their mortgage obligations, it is believed that some number of distressed homeowners, property flippers, and/or other real estate investors have resorted to committing arson to avoid real estate foreclosure. The insurance policy holders for these properties are then able to extract otherwise unattainable proceeds/profits through the filing of false insurance claims. This inherently dangerous and illicit means of collecting insurance proceeds and avoiding loan delinquency is being prioritized as a focus of inquiry due to market forecasts calling for increasing numbers of real estate foreclosures.

Hurricane Katrina Insurance Fraud—In late August 2005, Hurricane Katrina made landfall along America's Gulf Coast, severely damaging the region and causing approximately $100 billion in damages. According to the CAIF, Katrina generated approximately 1.6 million insurance claims totaling $34.4 billion in insured losses. The destruction caused by the storm has resulted in a marked increase in insurance fraud in the area. Of the more than 80 billion government dollars appropriated for reconstruction efforts in the region, it is estimated insurance fraud accounts for between $4 and $6 billion. The Insurance Fraud Task Force (IFTF) was created to investigate the spike in insurance fraud related to Katrina.

Insurance-Related Corporate Fraud—Although corporate fraud is not unique to any particular industry, there has been a recent trend involving insurance companies caught in the web of these schemes. The temptations for fraud within the corporate industry can be greater during periods of financial downturns. Insurance companies hold customer premiums which are forbidden from operational use by the company. However, when funding is needed, unscrupulous executives invade the premium accounts in order to pay corporate expenses. This leads to financial statement fraud because the company is required to "cover its tracks" to conceal the improper utilization of customer premium funds.

Premium Diversion/Unauthorized Entities—The most common type of fraud involves insurance agents and brokers diverting policyholder premiums for their own benefit. Additionally, there is a growing number of unauthorized and unregistered entities engaged in the sale of insurance-related products. As the insurance industry becomes open to foreign players, regulation becomes more difficult. Additionally, exponentially rising insurance costs in certain areas (i.e., terrorism insurance, directors'/officers' insurance, and corporations), increases the possibility for this type of fraud.

Viatical Settlement Fraud—A viatical settlement is a discounted, pre-death sale of an existing life insurance policy on the life of a person known to have a terminal condition. The parties to a viatical settlement include the insured party, insurance agent/broker, insurance company, viatical company/broker, and the investor. Viatical settlement fraud occurs when misrepresentations are made on the insurance policy applications, in effect, hiding the fact that the party applying for a policy has already been diagnosed with a terminal condition. On the investor end, the fraud occurs when misrepresentations are made to the investors by the viatical companies about life expectancies of insured parties and guaranteed high rates of return.

Workers Compensation Fraud—The Professional Employer Organization (PEO) industry operates chiefly to provide workers compensation insurance coverage to small businesses by pooling businesses together to obtain reasonable rates. Workers compensation insurance accounts for as much as 46 percent of a small business owners' general operating expenses. Due to this, small business owners have an incentive to shop workers compensation insurance on a regular basis. This has made it ripe for entities who purport to provide workers compensation insurance to enter the marketplace, offer reduced
(continued)

premium rates, and misappropriate funds without providing insurance. The focus of these investigations is on allegations that numerous entities within the PEO industry are selling unauthorized and non-admitted workers compensation coverage to businesses across the United States. This insurance fraud scheme has left injured and deceased victims without workers compensation coverage to pay their medical bills.

With the cooperation of the insurance industry, through referrals from industry liaison and other law enforcement agencies, the FBI continues to target the individuals and organizations committing insurance fraud. The FBI continues to initiate and conduct traditional investigations as well as utilize sophisticated techniques, to include undercover investigations, to apprehend the fraudsters.

II. OVERALL ACCOMPLISHMENTS

During Fiscal Year 2007, 209 cases investigated by the FBI resulted in 39 indictments and 47 convictions of insurance fraud criminals. The number of cases and subsequent arrest and conviction statistics will likely rise in the near future as more fraud is uncovered in the wake of Hurricane Katrina. The Jackson Division has hosted the IFTF that continues to investigate insurance fraud related to Katrina. The following notable statistical accomplishments reflect Fiscal Year 2007 for insurance fraud: $27.2 million in restitutions and $427,000 in fines.

Source

Federal Bureau of Investigation, Financial Crimes Report to the Public, Fiscal Year 2007 (October 1, 2006—September 30, 2007). Available at http://www.fbi.gov/publications/financial/fcs_report2007/financial_crime_2007.htm.

Questions for Discussion

1. What type of punishment is appropriate for an insurance fraud offender?
2. What other types of laws and policies could be created in an attempt to prevent insurance fraud?

---

growing type involves filing fraudulent health insurance claims. Various terms have been created to describe the schemes that are used in medical fraud. "Overutilization" involves billing for superfluous and unnecessary tests and other services.[53] "Ping-Ponging" occurs when physicians refer patients to several practitioners when symptoms do not warrant such referrals. "Family ganging" takes place when a doctor extends several unnecessary services to all members of a patient's family. "Steering" is a practice in which doctors direct patients to the clinic's pharmacy to fill unneeded prescriptions. Finally, "upgrading" occurs when a patient is billed for services more extensive than those that were actually performed.[54]

Credit card crimes and insurance schemes are comparatively recent types of fraud, but they are not the last opportunities for swindlers to deprive others of their property. Computer crime, for example, is a growing concern, and technological advances continue to offer new possibilities for theft. Opportunities will always challenge the imagination of entrepreneurs—illegitimate as well as legitimate.

Crime Surfing WWW

www.cybercrime.gov

The Computer Crime & Intellectual Property Section of the U.S. Department of Justice prevents, investigates, and prosecutes computer crimes.

HIGH-TECH CRIMES: CONCERNS FOR TODAY AND TOMORROW

Orange County, California (September 15, 1999). Six Southern California telemarketers have been charged in connection with an Internet gaming scam. Federal prosecutors say the scam took in almost $5 million from more than 500 investors. The six worked for Gecko Holdings. They offered investors stock in Gecko, telling them it was an on-line gambling business about to go public. Investors were promised that their shares, priced at two dollars, would double or triple the value in a few months. But the stock never went public. Instead, prosecutors say, the owners took off with the money. The six are charged with 26 counts each of mail and wire fraud.[55]

Crimes evolve with the environments we live in. The rise of computers and other high-technology equipment has paved the way for the genesis of new crime types. These present yet another set of challenges for potential victims, law enforcement personnel, criminologists, and other criminal justice professionals.

What exactly is high-technology crime? While there may be debates over its definition, it is generally agreed that **high-tech crime** involves an attempt to pursue illegal activities through the use of advanced electronic media. We define "high technology" as "a form of sophisticated electronic device—computer, cell phone, or other digital communication—that is in common use today."[56] The new waves of computer crime are perhaps the most illustrative examples of high-technology crime, although sophisticated credit card fraud schemes and cell phone scams are also modern problems. In this section, we will refer to crimes relying on modern electronic technology as "high-tech crimes."

Characteristics of High-Tech Crimes

High-tech crimes have affected the nature of property crimes by taking on a few distinct characteristics.

Role of Victims, Type of Property

Criminals engaging in high-tech crimes no longer need actual direct contact with their victims; computers equipped with modems have unlimited range, enabling offenders to victimize people thousands of miles away. The reach of motivated offenders has been considerably extended. Physical movement has been replaced by virtual travel, especially with the recognition that computers are global networks.

The type of property that is stolen or affected is also very different in nature. While other property crimes (arson, vandalism, theft, larceny, burglary) victimize concrete targets, high-tech crimes involve less-visible and less-tangible kinds of property, such as information, data, and computer networks. In addition, many victims of high-tech crime realize they have been victimized only long after the crime has taken place. In most other property crimes, there is often little time between the actual crime and the realization that a crime has taken place (as in cases of burglary or arson, for example).

Profits of Crime

The profits from high-tech crimes are vast. The rise in the incidence of computer crime, for example, is a testament to its efficacy and the profit to be made. The British Banking Association in London estimates the cost of computer fraud worldwide to be about $8 billion a year.[57] With the increasing sophistication of equipment, computer hackers are able to steal greater amounts with greater ease, and sometimes a single act can victimize multiple people or places at once.

Detection

High-tech crime is also attractive to some individuals because they find evading detection and prosecution relatively easy. Few law enforcement agencies are equipped to detect the high-tech crimes occurring within their jurisdictions. Furthermore, because the nature of high-tech crime allows perpetrators to carry out their illegal activities without any geographic limitations, tracing high-tech criminal activity to the responsible individual is very difficult. Identifying the crime location becomes harder as street corners and physical space are replaced by airwaves, cyberspace, and other electronic media. Often, by the time illegal activity has been detected, the criminals have already moved on to a new target.

Degree of Criminal Complexity

Another important aspect of high-technology crimes involves the complicated nature of the crimes being committed. Every day, new crimes are being developed and refined by highly skilled computer users. Traditional law enforcement techniques are not designed to deal with such novel and complex crimes. High-tech criminals are, in a sense, sophisticated criminals. Stealing credit card numbers from the Internet for illicit purposes requires a certain degree of proficiency in Internet navigation, knowledge of how to break into the system to commit the thefts, and, finally, experience in using the stolen credit card numbers for criminal gain—all the while avoiding detection.

International Component

Phone companies and computer network systems often advertise that using their services will allow individuals to communicate with people located at the other side of the globe. Such ease of electronic travel is appealing to high-tech criminals, who now participate in a modern phenomenon: global criminality. High-tech crimes can easily go beyond national boundaries, making them transnational crimes—a criminal activity of serious concern for targeted countries. Using a computer, a high-tech criminal can make illegal international money transfers, steal information from a computer located in another country, or diffuse illicit information (such as child pornography or terrorist propaganda) worldwide. The ability to detect and successfully deal with such criminal activities is a major challenge for law enforcement agencies around the world.

Computers and the Internet: Types of Crimes

High-tech criminals have also created their own crime types. While some seek the same ends as more traditional property offenders (financial gain), modern technology allows for novel and totally new crimes.[58]

There are three main categories of computer crimes. First, the computer can be used as a storage or communication device whereby information can be created, stored, manipulated, and communicated electronically. In this instance, the computer is incidental, since it is not required for the crime itself but is used in some way that is connected to the criminal activity. An example is financial records kept on a drug dealer's computer.

Second, the computer can be used as an instrument or a tool of crime. In this case, the computer is used to commit traditional offenses, such as the creation of counterfeit money or official documents, or newer computer crime offenses, such as the distribution of child pornography, confidence schemes, and illegal gambling networks on the Internet.

FIGURE 11.4 *2007 top 10 IC3 complaint categories.*

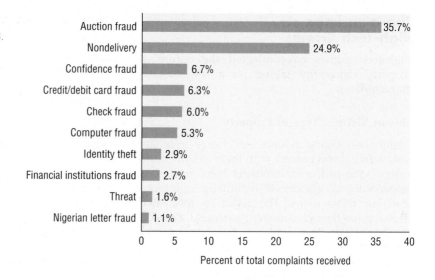

Percent of total complaints received

Finally, a computer can be used as a weapon to commit attacks on the confidentiality, integrity, and availability of information, including theft of information, theft of services, and damage to computer systems.[59] This type of computer crime involves the widespread problem of viruses and other forms of siege attacks, such as those referred to as "denial of service" attacks. The purpose of a denial-of-service attack is to prevent the normal operation of a digital system. It is often committed by "cyber vandals." An increasing number of electronic siege attacks employing some form of denial of service have been initiated against organizations worldwide.[60]

The Internet Crime Complaint Center (IC3) received nearly 210,000 fraud complaints in 2007.[61] A wide range of frauds is reported regularly (Figure 11.4).

Computer Network Break-Ins

There are two types of computer network break-ins. The first is commonly known as "hacking." It is not practiced for criminal gain and therefore can be considered more mischievous than malicious. Nevertheless, network intrusions have been made illegal by the U.S. federal government. A hacker's reward is being able to tell peers that he or she has managed to break into a network, demonstrating superior computing ability, especially the ability to bypass security measures. Hackers, for the most part, seek entry into a computer system and "snoop around," often leaving no sign of entry. It can be likened to an individual's stealthily gaining entry into another person's house, going through a few personal belongings, and carefully leaving without taking anything.

The second type of break-in is that done for illegal purposes. A criminal might break into a large credit card company's database to steal card numbers or into a network to steal data or sensitive information. Other criminal acts include computer vandalism, whereby individuals break into a system, alter its operating structure, delete important files, change passwords, or plant viruses that can destroy operating systems, software programs, and data.

Industrial Espionage

In an age where information can create power, it should not be surprising that competing industries are very curious to know what the others are doing. "Cyber spies" can be hired to break into a competitor's computer system and gather secret information, often leaving no trace of the intrusion. Once again, these spies have such powerful technology at their disposal that they are able to target computers and information that may be thousands of miles away, making detection even more difficult.

In response to the growing problem of industrial and economic espionage, Congress passed the Industrial Espionage Act of 1996. This law makes the theft, unauthorized appropriation, or other misuse of **proprietary economic information** a federal crime.

Proprietary economic information means all forms and types of financial, business, scientific, technical, economic, or engineering information, including data, plans, tools, mechanisms, compounds, formulas, designs, prototypes, processes, procedures, programs, codes, or commercial strategies, whether tangible or intangible, and whether stored, compiled, or memorialized physically, electronically, graphically, photographically, or in writing, that—

(A) the owner thereof has taken reasonable measures to keep such information confidential; and (B) the information derives independent economic value, actual or potential, from not being generally known to and

DID YOU KNOW?

. . . that online auctions were named the number-one Internet fraud problem in 1998?

not being readily ascertainable, acquired, or developed by legal means by the public.

Penalties for violations of this law include fines of up to $500,000 per offense ($10 million for organizations) and imprisonment of up to 15 years for individuals.[62]

Congress deliberated long and hard about the need for this legislation and concluded that in a world where a nation's power is now determined as much by economic strength as by armed might, we cannot afford to neglect to protect our intellectual property. Today, a piece of information can be as valuable as a factory is to a business. The theft of that information can do more harm than if an arsonist torched that factory. But our Federal criminal laws do not recognize this and do not punish the information thief. This is an unacceptable oversight. The Industrial Espionage Act is an effort to remedy the problem."[63]

As of January 2009, there have been three indictments under the act, with only one conviction. In June 2008, Xiaodong Sheldon Meng, a Canadian engineer employed by Quantum 3D, a technology house based in San Jose, was convicted and sentenced to 2 years in federal prison after admitting that he had attempted to sell fighter-pilot-training software to the Chinese navy.

Software Piracy

It is estimated by the U.S. Software-Publisher's Association that approximately $7.5 billion worth of American software is illegally copied and distributed annually worldwide. Software piracy ranges from friends sharing and occasionally copying software to international fraudulent schemes whereby software is replicated and passed on as the original product, sometimes at a lower price. Recent research indicates that employees contribute significantly to the presence of illegal software in the workplace, either by bringing software from home (40 percent), downloading unauthorized copies from the Internet (24 percent), or sharing programs with other employees (24 percent).[64] The duplication process is relatively simple, and, once it is mastered, any software can be pirated and copies sold worldwide. Software developers are constantly trying to stay ahead of the pirates by attempting to render their software resistant to such duplication. The advent of the compact disc and digital video disc unfortunately makes casual software piracy relatively easy.

Efforts to estimate the extent and costs of software piracy around the world must be viewed with some caution. That said, the data are nevertheless important and, for many, shocking. Perhaps the most-cited effort to track global software piracy is underwritten by the Business Software Association (BSA). In collaboration with IDC, a leading information technology market research

and forecasting firm, BSA produces an annual Global Software Piracy Study that covers piracy of all PC software. Here are some excerpts from the 2007 study:[65]

China's piracy rate stayed at 82% for a second consecutive year after dropping by ten points over the previous three years. Despite appearances, this does not signify that the declining trend has halted. In late 2007, IDC found that PCs sold by local assemblers (also known as "white box" vendors) were higher than previously counted, which raised the overall estimate of the PC market by more than 25% and, hence, the 2007 piracy rate. Without this new information, IDC believes the 2007 rate would have been closer to 80%. Thus, China is demonstrating progress in fighting PC software piracy. Indeed, PC software piracy in the government and large enterprises in China is decreasing and piracy in the consumer and small business markets, which accounted for two-thirds of the country's PC market last year, is also beginning to drop. The results have been aided by a legal requirement for PC manufacturers to ship legal operating systems with new PCs. Nonetheless, it is important to keep in mind that there is still much more work to do in addressing the use of pirated and unlicensed PC software applications by state-owned and other enterprises in China. It is also important for the government to ensure that it remains in compliance going forward with its own legalization and legally licensed operating system pre-install directives. . . .

India's piracy rate dropped two percentage points to 69% as a result of government and industry education and enforcement efforts, software vendor activation controls, and an increase in PC market share by multinational vendors. Dealing with software piracy in emerging markets is still a challenge. Rapid growth in first-time users from the high piracy consumer and small-business sectors affects country averages even when piracy drops in other areas. The increase in Internet access, especially broadband access, increases the supply of pirated software. Sprawling geographies and weak institutional infrastructure make education and enforcement all the more difficult. In some cases, even culture is involved, where societies see intellectual creation as a common good and not the property of its creator. . . .

There was notable progress in the battle against PC software piracy in 2007. Of the 108 individual countries studied in this report, the piracy rate dropped in sixty-seven countries from 2006 to 2007 and increased in only eight countries. However, the weighted impact of high market growth in emerging markets was again felt worldwide. Because the worldwide

As part of a child pornography investigation, FBI agents and Arkansas State Police officers raided evangelist Tony Alamo's headquarters in Fouke, Arkansas, in September 2008.

TABLE 11.5 Pornography Time Statistics

Every second: $3,075.64 is being spent on pornography.

Every second: 28,258 Internet users are viewing pornography.

Every second: 372 Internet users are typing adult search terms into search engines.

Every 39 minutes: A new pornographic video is being created in the United States.

SOURCE: http://www.internet-filter-review.toptenreviews.com/internet-pornography-statistics.html. © 2003–2007 TopTenREVIEWS, Inc.

PC market grew much faster in higher-piracy countries and regions, the worldwide PC software piracy rate increased three percentage points to 38% from 2006 to 2007. PC shipments in Brazil, Russia, India, and China—commonly referred to as the BRIC countries—grew 26% last year, compared to 13% in North America, Western Europe, and Japan. The combined BRIC countries are now as large a PC market as the United States. At the same time, because the size of the market grew significantly in 2007 and the value of the US dollar dropped nearly 7% against other currencies, losses from piracy rose by $8 billion to nearly $48 billion worldwide. In fact, real losses did not grow as fast as the overall PC software market, which grew faster than 15% last year. While the worldwide weighted average piracy rate is 38%, the median piracy rate in 2007 is 61%, down one percentage point from last year despite the addition of six new countries to this report. This means that half of the countries studied have a piracy rate of 61% or higher. In more than one-quarter of the countries studied, the piracy rate is 80% or higher. Among the larger emerging economies, Russia's piracy rate dropped a remarkable seven percentage points to 73% from 2006 to 2007. The reduction in the piracy rate is the result of legalization programs by vendors, enforcement and education by the government and anti-piracy groups, agreements between vendors and local distributors to bundle legal software with hard-

ware, and, of course, an oil economy that helped drive a 22% increase in personal disposable income in 2007 and lower consumers' propensity to use pirated software. . . .

So, piracy remains an issue for the software industry. In 2007, for every two dollars spent on legitimate software purchases, one dollar's worth of software was obtained illegally. In the highest piracy countries—those with 75% piracy or higher—for every one dollar spent on PC hardware, less than seven cents was spent on legitimate software. In developed markets, that ratio is eight times higher. . . .

By the end of 2007, there were more than one billion PCs installed around the world; nearly half have pirated software on them. With more PCs being shipped into emerging markets, lowering that percentage will be a long-term challenge.

Pornography Online

Online pornography is, by any and all estimates, a large and often profitable business. Reliable and valid sources of data are, once again, difficult to obtain. The most frequently cited data are far less than ideal but still provide a reasonable picture of the extent of the phenomenon even if one assumes under- and overestimation. The most recent compilation of pornography data is summarized in Figures 11.5 and 11.6 and Tables 11.5, 11.6, and 11.7. The data are notable for a host of reasons,

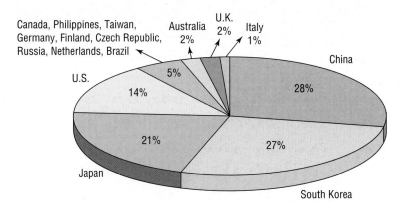

Country	Revenue (billlions)	Per Capita	Notes
China	$27.40	$27.41	1
South Korea	$25.73	$526.76	
Japan	$19.98	$156.75	
United States	$13.33	$44.67	
Australia	$2.00	$98.70	
United Kingdom	$1.97	$31.84	
Italy	$1.40	$24.08	
Canada	$1.00	$30.21	
Philippines	$1.00	$11.18	
Taiwan	$1.00	$43.41	1
Germany	$.64	$7.77	1
Finland	$.60	$114.70	1
Czech Republic	$.46	$44.94	1
Russia	$.25	$1.76	1
Netherlands	$.20	$12.13	
Brazil	$.10	$53.17	1
Other 212	Unavailable		2
	$97.06 Billion		

Notes: 1 = Incomplete, 2 = Unavailable data

FIGURE 11.5 Worldwide pornography revenues, 2006. The pornography industry is larger than the combined revenues of the top technology companies: Microsoft, Google, Amazon, eBay, Yahoo!, Apple, Netflix, and EarthLink.

Source: http://www.internet-filter-review.toptenreviews.com/internet-pornography-statistics.html. © 2003–2007 TopTenREVIEWS, Inc.

TABLE 11.6 Internet Pornography Statistics

	Number/Percent
Pornographic websites	4.2 million (12% of total websites)
Pornographic pages	420 million
Daily pornographic search engine requests	68 million (25% of total search engine requests)
Daily pornographic e-mails	2.5 billion (8% of total e-mails)
Internet users who view porn	42.7%
Received unwanted exposure to sexual material	34%
Average daily pornographic e-mails/user	4.5 per Internet user
Monthly pornographic downloads (peer-to-peer)	1.5 billion (35% of all downloads)
Daily Gnutella "child pornography" requests	116,000
Websites offering illegal child pornography	100,000
Sexual solicitations of youth made in chat rooms	89%
Youths who received sexual solicitation	1 in 7 (down from 2003 statistic of 1 in 3)
Worldwide visitors to pornographic websites	72 million monthly
Internet pornography sales	$4.9 billion

SOURCE: http://www.internet-filter-review.toptenreviews.com/internet-pornography.statistics.html. © 2003–2007 TopTenREVIEWS, Inc.

TABLE 11.7 2006 Top Adult Search Requests

					Demographics						
Search Term	2006 Search Requests	2006 % Change	2005 % Change	Web Pages Containing Keyword (Millions)	Male	Female	<18	18–24	25–34	35–49	50+
Sex	75,608,612	7%	40%	414.00	50%	50%	20%	20%	20%	20%	20%
Adult dating	30,288,325	622%	80%	1.40	36%	64%	20%	20%	21%	20%	19%
Adult DVD	13,684,718	53%	21%	1.82	58%	42%	20%	19%	23%	21%	17%
Porn	23,629,211	−3%	29%	88.80	96%	4%	23%	14%	10%	36%	17%
Sex toys	15,955,566	4%	1%	2.65	58%	42%	20%	16%	19%	19%	26%
Teen sex	13,982,729	36%	25%	2.10	44%	56%	22%	19%	19%	22%	18%
Free sex	13,484,769	0%	20%	2.42	44%	56%	22%	19%	19%	22%	18%
Adult sex	13,362,995	301%	51%	1.58	36%	64%	19%	21%	21%	20%	19%
Sex ads	13,230,137	382%	40%	0.28	50%	50%	20%	20%	19%	20%	21%
Group sex	12,964,651	88%	33%	2.07	50%	50%	20%	20%	20%	20%	20%
Free porn	12,964,651	−10%	54%	2.74	97%	3%	22%	14%	10%	35%	19%
XXX	12,065,000	25%	14%	181.00	50%	50%	20%	20%	20%	20%	20%
Sex chat	11,861,035	97%	36%	2.21	50%	50%	20%	20%	20%	20%	20%
Anal sex	9,960,074	76%	21%	2.95	67%	33%	19%	19%	16%	28%	19%
Cyber sex	8,502,524	−20%	3%	1.24	41%	59%	23%	25%	14%	30%	8%
XXX videos	7,411,220	71%	40%	1.44	64%	37%	17%	19%	26%	27%	11%
Playboy	6,641,209	−6%	24%	43.20	86%	14%	10%	33%	25%	25%	7%
Teen porn	6,130,065	7%	38%	1.97	82%	18%	23%	17%	14%	28%	18%
Nude	5,487,925	−26%	14%	71.30	77%	23%	33%	14%	10%	17%	26%
Sexy	4,344,924	21%	33%	198.00	50%	50%	20%	20%	20%	20%	20%

SOURCE: http://www.internet-filter-review.toptenreviews.com/internet-pornography-statistics.html. © 2003–2007 TopTenREVIEWS, Inc.

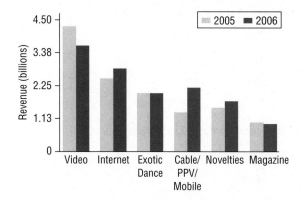

FIGURE 11.6 Pornography industry revenue statistics, 2006 and 2005. Pornography revenue in the United States exceeds the combined revenues of ABC, CBS, and NBC.

Source: http://www.internet-filter-review.toptenreviews.com/internet-pornography-statistics.html. © 2003–2007 TopTenREVIEWS, Inc.

even discounting the many concerns that criminologists have about their accuracy.

Mail Bombings

Computers can be used to steal money and information. They can also be used for more aggressive purposes. Like the bully told to rough up the new kid in the school yard, computers can be instructed to attack other machines. A common method is that of mail bombings. Mail bombs are the products of computer programs that instruct a computer to literally bombard another computer with information, often irrelevant electronic mail (e-mail). Mail bombs are capable of shutting down computers, and even entire networks, if the amount of incoming information is too large for the receiving computer to digest.

◼ *Child pornography is easy to find on the Internet if you know where to go—for example, newsgroups, chat rooms, and bulletin boards. Popular search engines are highly suggestive but rarely bring you to illegal images. Most "legal" sites are self-regulated, requiring an adult content alert and some form of registration.*

Google Brand Features are trademarks or distinctive brand features of Google Inc.

Password Sniffers

Entry into a computer system often requires a password or some other form of user identification to protect the information it contains. Password sniffers are programs that carefully record the names and passwords of network users as they log in. With such confidential information, unauthorized users are able to gain unlawful access to the computer and the information it contains. Passwords can also be sold to other users for illegal purposes.

Credit Card Fraud

Computers and the Internet are used more and more to conduct business. There are now more than 1.4 billion users. Remarkably, nearly three out of every four households in the United States have access to the Internet. It has become commonplace to order merchandise, make payments, and conduct personal banking online. This use of credit cards is very appealing to people involved in credit card fraud. Computers can facilitate credit card fraud in two ways. First, a conventionally stolen credit card can be used to order merchandise online, and, because no time is wasted going from store to store, a perpetrator can maximize his or her gain before the card is inactivated. Detection is also reduced because there is no physical contact with sales staff who might alert authorities should they suspect fraud. Second, credit card numbers can be stolen from the Internet

as customers are making legitimate purchases. Programs similar to those designed to steal passwords from unsuspecting users are often used for this purpose. Another way of stealing credit card numbers is for offenders to access computers located in credit bureaus or financial institutions. The FBI estimates that credit card fraud costs exceed $50 billion per year.[66]

Characteristics of the High-Tech Criminal

While all the crimes and deviant acts discussed so far rely heavily on technology, there are still human offenders behind them. Do these people, resemble other property criminals, or do they have distinct characteristics? While it is true that modern technology is so widespread that virtually anyone is capable of high-tech crime, it also remains a fact that most high-tech offenders, especially computer hackers, fit a rather unique profile. These individuals usually are young (14 to 19 years old) white males from middle-class backgrounds. They often possess superior levels of intelligence (IQ over 120), but on a social level they tend to be withdrawn and to associate mainly with peers who share their fascination for electronic gadgets and computer-related activities. Some youths also believe that they are part of a counterculture, fighting censorship, liberating information, and challenging big business and major

corporations.[67] In a way, they perceive themselves as modern-day Robin Hoods.

The Criminal Justice Problem

High-tech crimes pose a special problem to law enforcement agencies, for two reasons. First, these crimes are not easily detected because the offenders can quietly commit them from any computer terminal, usually in the comfort of their own homes. Second, while a few organizations have mobilized to attack high-tech crime, most law enforcement agencies are not equipped to deal with the phenomenon: "Technology changes at an astounding rate while law enforcement techniques, which traditionally are reactionary, do not."[68] It is clear that the police forces of the future need to address this problem by concentrating on detection and by arming themselves with the technological tools necessary to deal with it. By necessity, computer and/or Internet classes should find their way into police academies.

BURGLARY

A "burg," in Anglo-Saxon terminology, was a secure place for the protection of oneself, one's family, and one's property. If the burg protects a person from larceny and assault, what protects the burg? The burghers, perhaps. But there had to be a law behind the burghers. And that was the law of burglary, which made it a crime to break and enter the dwelling of another person at night with the intention of committing a crime therein. (Of course it had to be at night, for during the day the inhabitants could defend themselves, or so it was thought.) The common law defined **burglary** as:

> The breaking
> And entering
> Of the dwelling house
> Of another person
> At night
> With the intention to commit a felony or larceny inside

By "breaking," the law meant any trespass (unauthorized entry), but usually one accompanied by a forceful act, such as cracking the lock, breaking a windowpane, or scaling the roof and entering through the chimney. The "entering" was complete as soon as the perpetrator extended any part of his or her body into the house in pursuit of the objective of committing a crime in the house. The house had to be a "dwelling," but that definition was extended to cover the "curtilage," the attached servants' quarters, carriage houses, and barns. The dwelling also had to be that of "another." And, as we mentioned, the event had to occur at "night," between sundown and sunup.

The most troublesome element has always been the "intention to commit a felony or larceny" (even a petty or misdemeanor larceny) inside the premises. How can we know what a burglar intends to do? The best evidence of intent is what the burglar actually does inside the premises: Steal jewelry? Commit a rape? Set the house afire? Any crime the burglar commits inside is considered evidence of criminal intention at the moment the burglar broke and entered the dwelling.[69]

Today burglary is no longer limited to night attacks, although by statute the crime may be considered more serious if it is committed at night. Statutes have also added buildings other than dwellings to the definition. The UCR defines burglary simply as the unlawful entry into a structure (criminal trespass) to commit a felony or theft. The use of force to gain entry is not a required element of burglary under the UCR.

Burglary rates have consistently declined over the past decade. Even so, in 2007, almost 2.2 million burglaries were reported to the police, with an average loss of $1,991 per burglary. These crimes account for nearly a fifth of all Index offenses. Most burglaries are not cleared by arrests.[70]

Criminologists ask questions about the characteristics of offenders who commit burglaries and of the places that are burglarized. Neal Shover described the "good burglar" as one having competence, personal integrity, a specialty in burglary, financial success, and an ability to avoid prison.[71] Another study demonstrated that burglars are versatile, committing a wide range of offenses, but that they do specialize in burglary for short periods of time. Compared with male burglars, female burglars begin offending at a later age, more often commit burglaries with others, and have fewer contacts with the criminal justice system.[72]

Recent research on burglary asks questions not only about who is likely to commit a burglary or what distinguishes one burglar from another. In addition, as we note in Chapter 9, criminologists are looking, for instance, at the process that leads to the burglary of a particular house in a specific neighborhood—that is, how a burglar discriminates between individual areas and targets when there are so many alternatives—and at ways to make the process of burglary more difficult for any burglar.

FENCING: RECEIVING STOLEN PROPERTY

We are treating burglary as a property crime. An occasional burglar enters with the intention of committing rape, arson, or some other felony inside the building. But most burglars are thieves; they are looking for cash and for other property that can be turned into cash. Burglars and thieves depend on a network of fences to turn stolen property into cash.

Jonathan Wild controlled the London underworld from about 1714 until his hanging in 1725. For over 2½ centuries, he has captured the imagination of historians, social scientists, and writers. Henry Fielding wrote *The Life of Mr. Jonathan Wild, the Great,* and Mack the Knife in John Gay's *Beggar's Opera* was modeled on Wild. Wild was known as a "thief-taker." Thief-takers made an occupation of capturing thieves and claiming the rewards offered for their arrest. By law, thief-takers were allowed to keep the possessions of the thieves they caught, except objects that had been stolen, which were returned to their owners.

Wild added a devious twist to his trade: He bought stolen goods from thieves and sold them back to their rightful owners. The owners paid much more than the thief could get from the usual fences, so both Wild and the thief made a considerable profit. To thieves, he was a fellow thief; to honest people, he was a legitimate citizen helping them get back their property. Playing both roles well, he ran competing fencing operations out of business, employed about 7,000 thieves, and became the most famous fence of all time.[73]

A **fence** is a person who buys stolen property, on a regular basis, for resale. Fences, or dealers in stolen property, operate much like legitimate businesses: They buy and sell for profit. Their activity thrives on an understanding of the law governing the receiving of stolen property, on cooperation with the law when necessary, and on networking. The difference between a legitimate business and a fencing operation is that the channeling of stolen goods takes place in a clandestine environment (created by law enforcement and deviant associates) with high risks and with a need to justify one's activities in the eyes of conventional society.

Carl Klockars's *Professional Fence* and Darrell Steffensmeier's *Fence,* each focusing on the life of a particular fence, present us with fascinating accounts of this criminal business. The proprietors of such businesses deal in almost any commodity. "Oh, I done lots of business with him," said Klockars's fence, Vincent Swazzi. "One time I got teeth, maybe five thousand teeth in one action. You know, the kind they use for making false teeth—you see, you never know what a thief's gonna come up with." And many fences are quite proud of their positions in the community. Said Swazzi, "The way I look at it, this is actually my street. I mean I am the mayor. I walk down the street an' people come out the doors to say hello."[74]

Until recently, it was believed that professional thieves and fences were totally interdependent and that their respective illegal activities were mutually reinforcing. Recent research, however, demonstrates a change in the market for stolen goods. D'Aunn Webster Avery, Paul F. Cromwell, and James N. Olson conducted extensive interviews with 38 active burglars, shoplifters, and their fences and concluded that it is no longer the professional fence who takes care of stolen goods but, rather, occasional receivers—otherwise honest citizens—who buy from thieves directly or at flea markets.[75] This willingness to

THEORY CONNECTS

Burglary

Rational-choice theories, when first imported to criminology, were used to explain residential burglary. What insights can you bring from rational-choice theory to the practical effort of crime prevention?

buy merchandise that the buyers must at least suspect has been stolen may indicate that the general public is more tolerant of stealing than previous generations were.

ARSON

The crimes against property that we have discussed so far involve the illegitimate transfer of possession. The property in question is "personal property" rather than real property, or real estate. Only two types of property crime are concerned with real property. Burglary is one; the other is arson.

The common law defined **arson** as the malicious burning of or setting fire to the dwelling of another person. Modern statutes have distinguished degrees of severity of the offense and have increased its scope to include other structures and even personal property, such as automobiles. The most severe punishments are reserved for arson of dwellings, because of the likelihood that persons in the building may be injured or die.

Arson has always been viewed as a more violent crime than burglary. In comparison with burglary, however, arson is a fairly infrequent offense. A total of 64,332 arson offenses were reported in 2007.[76] A national survey of fire departments, however, indicates that the actual number of arson incidents is likely to be far higher than the reported figure.[77]

Buildings were the most frequent targets (42.9 percent); 27.9 percent of the targets were mobile property (motor vehicles, trailers, and the like); and crops and timber constituted 29.2 percent.[78] The annual estimated property loss is well over $2 billion.[79]

The seriousness of this crime is demonstrated by a series of spectacular fires set in resort hotels in such cities as San Juan, Puerto Rico (in conjunction with a labor dispute), and Las Vegas, Nevada. Although these fires were not set with the intent to kill any of the people in the buildings, many lives were lost. The inferno created by arsonists in the Du Pont Plaza Hotel in San Juan in 1987 killed 97 people. The arson at the Las Vegas Hilton caused no deaths but did result in $14 million in damages, not including the loss of business.

While insurance fraudsters and organized-crime figures may be responsible for some of the more spectacular arsons, it is juveniles who account for the single most significant share. Why do children set fires?[80] Some research suggests that the motive may be psychological pain, anger, revenge, need for attention, malicious mischief, or excitement.[81] Juvenile fire setters have been classified in three groups: the playing-with-matches fire setter, the crying-for-help fire setter, and the severely disturbed fire setter.[82] Many juvenile fire setters are in urgent need of help. In response to their needs,

juvenile arson intervention programs have been established.[83]

An interesting English study found that while arsonists were in many respects comparable to offenders classified as violent, they had a lower incidence of interpersonal aggression and rated themselves as less assertive than did violent offenders—perhaps because, as the study showed, arsonists were taken into care at an earlier age.[84] The motives of adult arsonists are somewhat different from those of juveniles, though here, too, we find disturbed offenders (pyromaniacs) and people who set fires out of spite. We are also much more likely to encounter insurance fraudsters, as well as organized-crime figures who force compliance or impose revenge by burning establishments (the "torches").[85] One classification of fire setters by motive includes:

- Revenge, jealousy, and hatred

- Financial gain (mostly insurance fraud)

- Intimidation and/or extortion (often involving organized crime)

- Need for attention

- Social protest

- Arson to conceal other crimes

- Arson to facilitate other crimes

- Vandalism and accidental fire setting[86]

As arson continues to be a serious national problem, policy makers have been developing two distinct approaches for dealing with it. The offender-specific approach focuses on educational outreach in schools and the early identification of troubled children, for purposes of counseling and other assistance.[87] The offense-specific (geographic) approach focuses on places. It seeks to identify areas with a high potential for arson. The aim is to deploy arson specialists to correct problems and to stabilize endangered buildings and neighborhoods.[88]

COMPARATIVE CRIME RATES

The rates of property crime are much higher than those of the violent crime discussed in Chapter 10. It is interesting to compare these rates for various regions of the world. If we compare the property-owning, consumer-oriented countries of the industrialized Western world with the still largely agricultural but rapidly urbanizing countries of the Third World, we note a significant discrepancy: In 1990, the rate of thefts per 100,000 population in the developed countries was 4,200, while the rate in developing countries was 600.[89]

Recall the Coca-Cola bottle that disrupted the lives of the bushmen in *The Gods Must Be Crazy*. We just may have discovered the secret of that bottle: If there is no Coke bottle, no one is going to steal it. The more property people have, especially portable property, the greater opportunity other people have to make off with it. Europeans have an old saying: "Opportunity makes thieves." The foremost opportunity for theft may simply be an abundance of property.

REVIEW

Not all crimes against property are aimed at acquiring the property. A burglar invades a dwelling or other structure usually—but not necessarily—to commit a larceny inside. An arsonist endangers the existence of the structure and its occupants. Both amateurs and professionals commit property crimes of all sorts. Each new form of legitimate trade, such as the development of credit card use and computers, offers criminals new opportunities to exploit the situation for gain. It is evident that most high-tech offenders are quite sophisticated and, given the vastness of technological wonders such as the Internet, a new challenge lies ahead for social scientists and criminal justice professionals alike.

Some property-oriented crimes, as we will see in Chapter 12, depend not on the cunning and daring of the perpetrator who targets a lone victim, but on the normal business operations of legitimate enterprises.

CRIMINOLOGY & PUBLIC POLICY

In the mid-1990s, fear of violent crime hit California voters with a vengeance. Reeling from the vicious crimes of repeat offenders like Richard Allen Davis, Californians lobbied their state representatives for legislative change. Davis, a twice-convicted kidnapper, abducted 12-year-old Polly Klass, murdering her soon thereafter. In 1994, the year following Klass's killing, the state legislature passed a "Three Strikes" law, requiring prison terms of 25 years to life for any offender convicted of a third felony after two prior ones. The United States Supreme Court reviewed the California law, considering whether the law should be applied if the third strike is for a lesser offense—a misdemeanor. (SOURCE: Adapted from http://www.sentencingproject.org/pubs/3strikes.pdf.)

Questions for Discussion Do you think it is fair to sentence a person to prison for life for petty theft or shoplifting after he or she has had two prior felony convictions? Would you change your mind if the intent of three strikes laws is to deter felonies (serious crimes)?

YOU BE THE CRIMINOLOGIST

Computers are now part of our everyday lives at work, in school, or at home as vehicles to pay bills, shop online, or simply surf the Internet. With the growing use of computers in all facets of our lives, the potential for misuse increases as well. This chapter has discussed some of the most pressing issues at the heart of computer crimes, including online credit card fraud, the use of the Internet in promoting child pornography, viruses and worms that invade the hard drives of computers, and software piracy. Select at least two forms of computer crime. What, in your opinion, are the causes of and the motivations for committing such crimes? What specifically does the offender stand to gain? Describe ways to counteract the problem. What can be done to prevent this emerging type of property crime?

KEY TERMS

The numbers next to the terms refer to the pages on which the terms are defined.

arson (294)
burglary (292)
check forging (280)
confidence game (280)
false pretenses, obtaining property by (277)
fence (293)
fraud (277)
high-tech crime (284)
larceny (268)
proprietary economic information (286)
shoplifting (270)

12

White-Collar and Corporate Crime

Defining White-Collar Crime
Crimes Committed by Individuals
Types of White-Collar Crimes
Corporate Crime
Frequency and Problems of Definition
Phases of Corporate Criminal Law
Theories of Corporate Liability
Models of Corporate Culpability
Governmental Control of Corporations
Investigating Corporate Crime
Environmental Crimes
Curbing Corporate Crime
The Future of White-Collar and Corporate Crime
Review
Criminology & Public Policy
You Be the Criminologist
Key Terms

■ *In the aftermath of the recent credit crisis, which included the recent bankruptcy of investment bank Lehman Brothers in September 2008, many were left wondering who should be held responsible. Were crimes committed? If not, should any of the actions that led to the crisis be made criminal?*

BROCADE COMMUNICATIONS SYSTEMS, INC. (San Francisco): Brocade Communications Systems, Inc. (Brocade), a technology company based in San Jose, California, routinely used stock options to compensate its employees. In July 2006, former Chief Executive Officer (CEO) Gregory L. Reyes and former Vice-President of Human Resources Stephanie Jensen were charged in connection with a scheme to backdate stock option grants. The two executives made fraudulent entries into Brocade's financial books and records, made false statements to auditors, and filed false financial statements with the SEC in furtherance of the scheme. After internal auditors restated earnings for the years 1999 through 2004, it was estimated that the cost to Brocade exceeded $400 million. On August 7, 2007, a jury convicted Reyes of ten counts of conspiracy and securities fraud. Reyes was the first person to be tried on charges related to stock options backdating and was sentenced to 21 months in prison. On December 5, 2007, a jury convicted Jensen of conspiracy to commit securities fraud and falsifying corporate records. Jensen is currently awaiting sentencing.

QWEST COMMUNICATIONS (Denver): Qwest Communications (Qwest) is a Fortune 500 company and one of the largest providers of telecommunications services in the U.S. In 2000 and 2001, the company reported sales revenues of $16 billion and $19 billion, respectively, in its published financial statements. In 2002, Qwest issued a press release that acknowledged the company had improperly recorded $1.1 billion in revenue since 1999, and the FBI opened a criminal investigation. Five executives were indicted and either pled guilty or were convicted of securities fraud or insider trading. This included the former CEO Joseph Nacchio, who was convicted of insider trading on April 19, 2007. He was sentenced to six years in prison, ordered to forfeit $52 million gained as a result of his illegal stock sales, and fined $19 million.

HOLLINGER INTERNATIONAL, INC. (Chicago): Hollinger International (Hollinger) is an international newspaper holding company and owner of the *Chicago Sun Times* and *The Daily Telegraph* newspapers. This case was initiated based on allegations that $32 million in non-competition payments were made to CEO and Chairman of the Board Conrad Black and three other corporate executives in conjunction with newspaper sales without proper authority. It was also alleged that newspaper circulation numbers were overstated for the purpose of misleading advertising companies and causing them to pay more in advertising fees. In November 2005, Black and three others were indicted on 15 counts of

racketeering, mail and wire fraud, money laundering, obstruction of justice, and tax fraud. On July 13, 2007, Black and the three other co-defendants were convicted after a four-month jury trial. On December 10, 2007, Black was sentenced to 78 months imprisonment.

BRITISH PETROLEUM, INC. (Anchorage): On October 25, 2007, British Petroleum (BP) and several of its subsidiaries agreed to pay $373 million in fines and restitution for environmental violations stemming from a fatal explosion at a Texas refinery that occurred in March 2005 and from leaks of crude oil from pipelines in Alaska in March 2006, as well as for conspiring to manipulate the price of propane.

MERCURY FINANCE, INC. (Chicago): Mercury Finance Company (Mercury) was a subprime lender whose corporate officers intentionally misstated the company's financial records. Mercury executives falsely reported a 1996 profit of more than $120 million instead of a loss of $30 million. Executives provided materially false financial statements to more than 20 financial institutions, enabling Mercury to obtain more than $1.5 billion in loan commitments and lines of credit. When the fraud was discovered, Mercury's stock price dropped significantly, costing shareholders nearly $2 billion in market value. In addition, lenders lost over $40 million in loans extended to the company. Lawrence Borowiak, former Accounting Manager, was sentenced to 12 months in prison and ordered to pay $585,000 in restitution after pleading guilty to insider trading charges. Former Treasurer Bradley Vallem pled guilty to wire and bank fraud and was sentenced to 20 months in prison. In October 2006, former Chief Executive Officer John Brincat, Sr., pled guilty to wire fraud and making a false statement to a bank. On May 23, 2007, Brincat was sentenced to 10 years imprisonment.

XUJIA WANG, VICE PRESIDENT OF FINANCE—MORGAN STANLEY (New York): This investigation was initiated on the basis of regulatory reporting related to suspicious options trading activity in Genesis Healthcare Corporation (GHC) immediately preceding the acquisition of GHC by private equity firms. Through her employment as Vice President of Finance for Morgan Stanley, Xujia Wang obtained material non-public information on GHC and other acquisitions, which she and her husband, Ruopian Chen, used to execute illicit trades in an account held in the name of a family member. On September 5, 2007, Wang and Chen [pled] guilty to charges of securities fraud and conspiracy to commit securities fraud for their roles in this insider trading scheme that resulted in illicit trading profits in excess of $600,000. On December 4, 2007, Wang and Chen were each sentenced to 18 months imprisonment and required to forfeit $611,248.[1]

What do these crimes have in common? All involve business enterprises.[2] It is the use of a legitimate or an illegitimate business enterprise for illegal profit that distinguishes organizational crimes from other types of offenses. Organizational offenses are also different in another important respect. Unlike violent crimes and property offenses, which the Model Penal Code classifies quite neatly, organizational offenses are a heterogeneous mix of crimes, ranging from homicide, fraud, and conspiracy to racketeering and the violation of a host of federal environmental statutes.

DEFINING WHITE-COLLAR CRIME

With a daily barrage of media reports on the latest corporate scandal—from allegations of fraud for selling subprime mortgages to evidence of widespread corruption in some of the most respected and admired multinational corporations—it is only natural to think that we are in the midst of an unprecedented wave of white-collar and corporate crime. Anecdotal evidence aside, there is no empirical evidence that much, if anything, has changed.

Not surprisingly, politicians seized the opportunity to call for corporate reforms in light of almost daily accusations of illegalities. With little reflection, President Bush signed the Sarbanes-Oxley Act of 2002 to quell public concerns over the legitimacy and integrity of the markets. This act adopts tough provisions to deter and punish corporate and accounting fraud and corruption.

According to a press release from the White House, the act "ensures justice for wrongdoers, and protects the interests of workers and shareholders. This bill improves the quality and transparency of financial reporting, independent audits, and accounting services for public companies."

To its credit, the Sarbanes-Oxley Act of 2002 does the following:

- Creates a public company accounting oversight board to enforce professional standards, ethics, and competence for the accounting profession

- Acts to strengthen the independence of firms that audit public companies

- Increases corporate responsibility and the usefulness of corporate financial disclosure

- Increases penalties for corporate wrongdoing

■ Martha Stewart, an icon of good homemaking, was accused of selling thousands of shares of ImClone Systems, Inc., stock just prior to the company's announcement that it failed to receive Food and Drug Administration approval for an anticancer drug. Was this insider trading? Did she trade on material, nonpublic information?

■ *Bernard ("Bernie") Madoff, former chairman of the NASDAQ stock exchange and a large securities firm, has been convicted of carrying out the largest Ponzi scheme in U.S. history—perhaps world history—with losses to investors that might exceed $100 billion. He is serving a 150-year sentence in prison.*

- Protects the objectivity and independence of securities analysts
- Increases Securities and Exchange Commission resources

Perhaps most noteworthy, CEOs and chief financial officers must personally vouch for the truth and fairness of their company's disclosures.

Prosecutors, regulators, and legislators are carefully considering the consequences of the most recent credit crisis and the resulting recession. They are asking: Were crimes committed by large and small financial firms? In what ways did regulators and regulations fail? What role should the criminal law play in policing the very behaviors that resulted in one of the worst series of economic failures in our nation's history?

For those who think that the problem of white-collar and corporate crime is young, consider that in ancient Greece, public officials reportedly violated the law by purchasing land slated for government acquisition. Much of what we today define as white-collar crime, however, is the result of laws passed within the last century. For example, the Sherman Antitrust Act, passed by Congress in 1890, authorized the criminal prosecution of corporations engaged in monopolistic practices.[3] Federal laws regulating the issuance and sale of stocks and other securities were passed in 1933 and 1934. In 1940, Edwin H. Sutherland provided criminologists with the first scholarly account of

white-collar crime. He defined it as crime "committed by a person of respectability and high social status in the course of his occupation."[4]

The 2002 conviction of Arthur Andersen, LLP, for obstruction of justice (overturned in 2005 by the U.S. Supreme Court) demonstrates that Sutherland's definition is not entirely satisfactory: White-collar crime can be committed by a corporation as well as by an individual. As Gilbert Geis has noted, Sutherland's work is limited by his own definition. He has a "striking inability to differentiate between the corporations themselves and their executive management personnel."[5] Other criminologists have suggested that the term "white-collar crime" not be used at all; we should speak instead of "corporate crime" and "occupational crime."[6] Generally, however, **white-collar crime** is defined as a violation of the law committed by a person or group of persons in the course of an otherwise respected and legitimate occupation or business enterprise[7] (Table 12.1).

Just as white-collar and corporate offenses include a heterogeneous mix of corporate and individual crimes, from fraud, deception, and corruption to pollution of the environment, victims of white-collar crime range from the savvy investor to the unsuspecting consumer. No one person or group is immune[8] (Table 12.2). The Vatican lost millions of dollars in a fraudulent stock scheme; fraudulent charities have swindled fortunes from unsuspecting investors; and many banks have been forced into bankruptcy by losses due to deception and fraud.[9] Perhaps just as important, public perceptions of the legitimacy of financial institutions and markets have been undermined, at least in part, by allegations of corporate abuses.

Crimes Committed by Individuals

As we have noted, white-collar crime occurs during the course of a legitimate occupation or business enterprise. Over time, socioeconomic developments have increasingly changed the dimensions of such crimes.[10] Once, people needed only a few business relationships to make their way through life. They dealt with an employer or with employees. They dealt on a basis of trust and confidence with the local shoemaker and grocer. They had virtually no dealings with government.

This way of life has changed significantly and very rapidly during the past decades. People have become dependent on large bureaucratic structures; they are manipulated by agents and officials with whom they have no personal relationship. This situation creates a basis for potential abuses in four sets of relations:

- Employees of large entities may abuse their authority for private gain by making their services to members of the public contingent on a

THEORY CONNECTS

Crimes Committed by Individuals (White-Collar Crime)

To what extent does Robert Merton's strain theory (page 105) offer an explanation for white-collar crimes such as embezzlement and tax fraud?

TABLE 12.1 The NIBRS Classifications of White-Collar Offenses

Criminal Behavior

Academic crime	Influence peddling
Adulterated food, drugs, or cosmetics	Insider trading
Antitrust violations	Insufficient funds checks
ATM fraud	Insurance fraud
Bad checks	Investment scams
Bribery	Jury tampering
Check kiting	Kickback
Combinations in restraint of trade	Land sale frauds
Computer crime	Mail fraud
Confidence game	Managerial fraud
Contract fraud	Misappropriation
Corrupt conduct by juror	Monopoly in restraint of trade
Counterfeiting	Ponzi schemes
Defense contract fraud	Procurement fraud
Ecology law violations	Racketeering Influenced and Corrupt Organizations (RICO)
Election law violations	
Embezzlement	Religious fraud
Employment agency and education-related scams	Sports bribery
Environmental law violations	Strategic bankruptcy
False advertising and misrepresentation of products	Subornation or perjury
	Swindle
False and fraudulent actions on loans, debts, and credits	Tax law violations
	Telemarketing or boiler room scams
False pretenses	Telephone fraud
False report/statement	Travel scams
Forgery	Unauthorized use of a motor vehicle [lawful access but the entrusted vehicle is misappropriated]
Fraudulent checks	
Health and safety laws	Uttering
Health care providers fraud	Uttering bad checks
Home improvement frauds	Welfare fraud
Impersonation	Wire fraud

SOURCE: Cynthia Barnett, *The Measurement of White-Collar Crime Using Uniform Crime Reporting (UCR) Data* (Washington, D.C.: Department of Justice, 2000).

TABLE 12.2 Victims of White-Collar Crime (NIBRS)

	Total	Property	Fraud	Bribery	Counterfeiting	Embezzlement
Total victims	5,886,566	4,069,324	103,993	198	110,545	21,356
Individual	3,998,310	2,621,843	47,826	143	45,270	3,006
Business	934,469	934,469	47,907	16	55,676	17,627
Financial institution	11,378	11,378	2,989	0	5,310	182
Government	73,623	73,623	3,844	36	2,949	260
Religious organization	10,794	10,794	70	0	104	35
Society or other	857,992	417,217	1,357	3	1,236	246

SOURCE: Cynthia Barnett, *The Measurement of White-Collar Crime Using Uniform Crime Reporting (UCR) Data* (Washington, D.C.: Department of Justice, 2000).

bribe, a kickback, or some other favor. A corrupt employee of an insurance company, for example, may write a favorable claim assessment in exchange for half of the insurance payment.

• Taking advantage of the complexity and anonymity of a large organization, such as a corporation, employees may abuse the systems available to them or the power they hold within the structure for purposes of unlawful gain, as by embezzlement.

■ *Ricky Churchwell, a former chancery clerk from Lucedale, Mississippi, was indicted on 15 counts of embezzlement in July 2002. Churchwell is the fourth clerk in 4 years to be indicted in Mississippi.*

• Members of the public who have to deal with a large organization do not have the faith and trust they had when they dealt with individual merchants. If they see an opportunity to defraud a large organization, they may seize it in the belief that the organization can easily absorb the loss and nobody will be hurt.

• Because the relation of buyer to seller (or of service provider to client) has become increasingly less personal in an age of medical group practice, HMOs, large law firms, and drugstore chains, opportunities for **occupational crimes**—crimes committed by individuals for themselves in the course of rendering a service—have correspondingly increased. Medicare fraud, misuse of clients' funds by lawyers and brokers, substitution of inferior goods—all such offenses are occupational crimes.[11]

Types of White-Collar Crimes

White-collar crimes are as difficult to detect as they are easy to commit.[12] The detection mechanisms on which police and government traditionally rely seem singularly inadequate for this vast new body of crimes. Moreover, though people have learned through the ages to be wary of strangers on the street, they have not yet learned to protect themselves against vast enterprises. Much more scientific study has to be undertaken on the causes, extent, and characteristics of white-collar crimes before we can develop workable prevention strategies (Figure 12.1).[13]

Eight categories of white-collar offenses committed by individuals can be identified:

• Securities-related crimes

• Bankruptcy fraud

FIGURE 12.1 Criminal white-collar crime prosecutions over the last 5 years.

When monthly 2008 prosecutions are compared with those of the same period in the previous year, the number of filings was down (−2.9 percent). Prosecutions over the past year are still much lower than they were 5 years ago. Overall, the data show that prosecutions of this type are down 19.5 percent from levels reported in 2003. The vertical bars represent the number of white-collar crime prosecutions of this type recorded on a month-to-month basis. The superimposed line on the bars plots the 6-month moving average so that natural fluctuations are smoothed out.

Source: Figure 1 and two paragraphs from *White Collar Crime Prosecutions for August 2008.* Transactional Records Access Clearinghouse (TRAC) at Syracuse University. (http://trac.syr.edu). © 2008, TRAC Reports, Inc. Reprinted with permission.

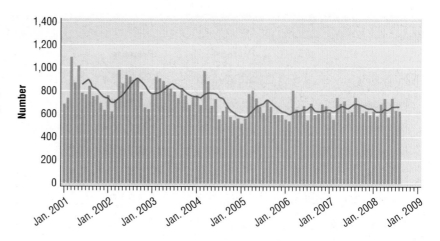

- Fraud against the government
- Consumer fraud
- Insurance fraud
- Tax fraud
- Bribery, corruption, and political fraud
- Insider-related fraud[14]

Let us briefly examine each type of crime.

Securities-Related Crimes

State and federal securities laws seek to regulate both the registration and issuance of a security and the employment practices of personnel in the securities industries. After the stock market crash on October 26, 1929, the federal government enacted a series of regulatory laws, including the Securities Act of 1933 and the Securities Exchange Act of 1934, aimed at prohibiting manipulation and deceptive practices. The 1934 act provided for the establishment of the Securities and Exchange Commission (SEC), an organization with broad regulatory and enforcement powers. The SEC is empowered to initiate civil suits and administrative actions and to refer criminal cases to the U.S. Department of Justice.

Crime in the securities field remains common. The problem of securities fraud was made more apparent in recent years with some notable cases. The significance of the problem, however, is highlighted by the sheer size of the equities market.

Four kinds of offenses are prevalent: churning, trading on insider information, stock manipulation, and boiler-room operations.

Churning is the practice of trading a client's shares of stock frequently in order to generate large commissions. A broker earns a commission on every trade, so whether the stock traded increases or decreases in value, the broker makes money. Churning is difficult to prove, because brokers typically are allowed some discretion. Therefore, unless the client has given the broker specific instructions in writing, a claim of churning often amounts to no more than the client's word against the broker's.

Insider trading is the use of material, non-public financial information to obtain an unfair advantage in trading securities.[15] A person who has access to confidential corporate information may make significant profits by buying or selling stock on the strength of that information. The prototype case of insider trading was that against Dennis Levine. Levine, a 34-year-old managing director of the securities firm formerly known as Drexel Burnham Lambert, used insider information to purchase stock for himself and others in corporations such as International Telephone and Telegraph, Sperry Corporation, Coastal Corporation, American National Resources, and McGraw Edison. After the SEC found out, Levine implicated other Wall Street executives—including Ivan Boesky, who had made millions of dollars in illegal profits.

◾ *Dr. Samuel Waksal, former chief executive officer, ImClone Systems, Inc., testifies before the U.S. House Energy and Commerce Subcommittee on Oversight and Investigations hearing on "An Inquiry into the ImClone Cancer-Drug Story" in Washington on June 13, 2002. On June 10, 2003, he was sentenced to over 7 years in jail and ordered to pay $4 million in back taxes and fines.*

Stock manipulation is common in the "pink sheets" over-the-counter market, in which some stocks are traded at very low prices, but it is by no means limited to such stocks. Brokers who have a stake in a particular security may make misleading or even false statements to clients to give the impression that the price of the stock is about to rise and thus to create an artificial demand for it.

Boiler rooms are operations run by stock manipulators who, through deception and misleading sales techniques, seduce unsuspecting and uninformed individuals into buying stocks in obscure and often poorly financed corporations. Significant federal and state legislation has been passed (Penny Stock Reform Act of 1990) to curtail these operations, but the manipulation continues. The problem is particularly significant in Florida, where the state has warned the public.

Bankruptcy Fraud

The filing of a bankruptcy petition results in proceedings in which the property and financial obligations of an insolvent person or corporation are disposed of. Bankruptcy proceedings are governed by laws enacted to protect insolvent debtors. Unscrupulous persons have devised numerous means to commit **bankruptcy fraud**—any scam designed to take advantage of loopholes in the bankruptcy laws. The most common are the "similar-name" scam, the "old-company" scam, the "new-company" technique, and the "successful-business" scam.

The similar-name scam involves the creation of a corporation that has a name similar to that of an established firm. The objective is to create the impression that this new company is actually the older one. If the trick is successful, the swindlers place large orders with established suppliers and quickly resell any merchandise they receive, often to fences. At the same time the swindlers remove all the money and assets of the corporation and either file for bankruptcy or wait until creditors sue. Then they leave the jurisdiction or adeptly erase their tracks.

The old-company scam involves employees of an already established firm who, motivated by a desire for quick profits, bilk the company of its money and assets and file for bankruptcy. Such a scam typically is used when the company is losing money or has lost its hold on a market.

The new-company scam is much like the similar-name scam: A new corporation is formed, credit is obtained, and orders are placed. Once merchandise is received, it is converted into cash with the assistance of a fence. By the time the company is forced into bankruptcy, the architects of the scheme have liquidated the corporation's assets.

The successful-business scam involves a profitable corporation that is well positioned in a market but experiences a change in ownership. After the new owners have bilked the corporation of all its money and assets, the firm is forced into bankruptcy.

The Federal Bureau of Investigation estimates that 10 percent of all bankruptcy filings involve fraud. On average, this suggests that, in recent years, approximately 250 fraudulent bankruptcies were filed every day. Two-thirds of these cases involve some form of hidden assets.

The FBI launched a series of joint undercover investigations with multiple field offices—for example, Remington Raider and Total Disclosure.

Al Qaeda's Battle Is Economic, Not Military

Many of the post-9/11 reforms involved passage or modification of laws affecting white-collar crimes, for example, money laundering and federal fraud statutes. After all, terrorist acts need financing, and funds supporting terrorist groups make their way to and from the United States through legitimate and illegitimate means.

There is, however, another connection between our economy and terrorism that is both obvious and overlooked by criminologists. One stated objective of certain terrorist groups is the compromise of our economy to the point of "exhaustion," thereby diminishing our ability to resist their inevitable domination. To the extent that Al Qaeda's battle is economic, what kinds of crimes by terrorist groups should criminologists examine?

To place this economic motive in context, the following Al Qaeda communiqué outlines, with accompanying rhetoric, the group's true intention.

Abu Mus `ab al-Najadi
The Islamic nation has entered through al-Qaeda's war with America a new period that is different from all the other periods experienced by Muslims against their enemies. This period is based on the economic war due to the peculiar nature of the adversary in this ferocious battle. Usually, wars are based on military strength and victory belongs to those who are military superior on the battle field.

But our war with America is fundamentally different for the first priority is defeating her economically. For that, anything that negatively affects their economy is considered for us a step in the right direction in the path to victory. Military defeats do not greatly effect how we measure total victory, but these defeats indirectly affect the economy which can be demonstrated with breaching the confidence of capitalists and investors in this nation's ability to safeguard their various trade and dealings. As for the infrastructure or machinery that is effected in the battlefield it does signify anything for two reasons:

1. It is relatively affordable for the world's largest economy [U.S.].
2. America did not enter this war alone; rather it is supported by many nations such as Japan and Germany or the traitors [Arab Gulf nations].

In light of this matter, the difficulty and ease of the task becomes apparent. In addition, it becomes apparent why additional al-Qaeda strikes inside the United States have been delayed. When thinking about military strikes, it is not difficult to carry out an attack that would kill a good number of American civilians, but in my opinion this is a waste of resources without much benefit. However directing these resources against economic targets is more effective and can get us many steps closer toward victory. An attack that kills a large number of Americans can not achieve a tenth of this effectiveness. This reveals the importance of the blessed September 11th attacks, which is not that it killed large number of infidels, but what is more important, is the economic effect that this strike achieved.

I will not be exaggerating if I said that striking the Pentagon was purely symbolic and had no noticeable effect on the course of the battle. It is symbolic for it shows the Americans that their foremost military facility can be destroyed by handful of individuals, which is a blow to their morale and a point of pride for the Islamic peoples who have been drowning in defeat for many years.

The ease of our battle is that few strikes are sufficient to exhaust the American budget, leading to its downturn and eventual fall. For that, all who are concerned with our battle with America should comprehend this strategy well. By doing so, with god's permission, we can reduce the length of the battle by directing all our power and resources on economic targets which unfortunately many see as insignificant, while directing a small part of these resources at other targets that serve a symbolic purpose in the battle.

When looking at the battlefronts that al-Qaeda is involved in we can divide them into two:

—**First,** battlefronts aimed at *indirectly* exhausting the enemy economically. Many will be surprised by this uncommon categorization. These battlefronts serve as the beginning, not for the direct

---

Operation Total Disclosure alone resulted in the arrest of 110 bankruptcy fraud subjects.

Fraud against the Government

Governments at all levels are victims of a vast amount of fraud, which includes collusion in bidding, payoffs and kickbacks to government officials, expenditures by a government official that exceed the budget, the filing of false claims, the hiring of friends or associates formerly employed by the government, and offers of inducements to government officials.

Consider, for example, the fall of Wedtech—a military contractor with annual sales in excess of $100 million. At one time the Wedtech Corporation was hailed as the first major employer of blacks and Hispanics in New York City's blighted South Bronx. Before its fall from grace, Wedtech was a highflier on the New York Stock Exchange. What fueled the company? As a minority-controlled business, it won defense contracts without the need to bid. But in early 1986, Wedtech lost its status as a minority business, and by the end of that year the company was in ruins.

exhaustion of the enemy, but for informing the public, which serves the economic target indirectly. For example, the battle in Saudi Arabia and all operations carried out previously are more directed at exposing and revealing to the people the extent of the collaboration of the ruling regime, and the treason of the religious clerics that serve under this regime, who are silent about the regime's crimes toward the Mujahideen. This leads to the Saudi people living the climate of the battle, and donating their sons as fuel to this battle which is what is really occurring in the Saudi Arabia and Iraq. By doing so, we have invested in this battle for our benefit; for what the enemy does not realize is that we were able to awaken a considerable number of Saudi youth who will carry the battle as indicated by sheikh Usama [Bin Laden] 'may god save him,' "by entering the battle with the sons al-Haramayn [two holy sites, i.e., Saudi Arabia], America will forget the hell of Vietnam."

We can say that the blessed Madrid operations were not aimed at exhausting the enemy, rather to motivate the Spanish people to break ranks with the American thieves, which serves the economic interest indirectly by isolating America on the battlefield. As for the attack on England, it was aimed at punishing the United Kingdom for their aid to the American thieves, to embarrass their security services, and rub their noses in the dirt in front of the European nations, because they turned down the cease-fire offered by sheikh Usama.

—**Second,** battlefronts aimed at *directly* exhausting the enemy economically.

We can categorize the battle in Iraq as part of the economic exhaustion front of the enemy, because the Mujahideen with god's glory prevented America from controlling a large segment of the Iraqi oil which they hoped would compensate for their economic losses in September 11th. While currently they control the oil in Saudi Arabia which amounts to two thirds of the pie, they hoped to control the whole pie after they controlled Iraq.

Any operation targeting a field of infrastructure in a new country that does not have a history of countering these operations is considered as bleeding to the greater enemy America and the targeted nation itself. It is so because these nations will be required to protect all similar potential targets which results in economic exhaustion. More so, the effect will be on America when the target nation is incapable of doing so, they will turn over the mission to the Americans who will need to personally defend their interests. This is what is occurring in a number of countries like some of the African nations. For example if a hotel that caters to western tourists in Indonesia is targeted, the enemy will be required to protect all hotels that cater to western tourists in all countries which may become a target of similar attacks. You can say the same thing about residential buildings, economic establishments, embassies and other.

I conclude by taking a look at future operations of al-Qaeda which I can predict based on their communiqués and past operations. I predict they will concentrate on the oil infrastructure in

one of the following three nations (Kuwait—Venezuela—Saudi Arabia). In addition, there is a possibility that al-Qaeda will, one way or another target the Wall Street stock exchange which signifies the nerve of domestic American economy. Finally, continuing to prevent the American thieves from benefiting from Iraqi oil by concentrating a large effort on the following, with the possibility of partial American withdrawal from Iraq.

Warning:
When I indicated that the battle with the U.S. and others is economic I do not mean that it is for the sake of the economy itself; rather, because they use the economy to control the Muslims and destroy them. This is first and foremost a religious war in all its forms.

Source
Abu Mus`ab al-Najadi, "Al-Qaeda's Battle Is Economic not Military," Oct. 3, 2005.

Questions for Discussion

1. To what extent can the United States harden economic targets so that they are protected from terrorist attack?

2. What kinds of crimes can we expect from terrorist groups seeking to further compromise our economic strength?

Wedtech officials had used fraudulent accounting methods, issued false financial reports, and counted profits before they were received. Caught in the cross fire of charges was Congressman Mario Biaggi, who was later convicted of soliciting bribes in order to obtain special government support for Wedtech. Other company and government officials either pled guilty or were convicted.[16]

Is the Wedtech scandal an isolated case? Clearly not. From 1986 through 1994, the Department of Defense reported that 138 defense contractors made 325 voluntary disclosures of potential procurement

fraud. Recoveries from these disclosures amounted to $290 million.[17]

An important step to curb government contract fraud was taken with the passage of the Major Fraud Act (1988), creating a separate offense of government contract fraud in excess of $1 million. What kinds of activities does this act cover? Federal prosecutors seek indictments against contractors who engage in deceptive pricing or overcharging by submitting inaccurate cost and pricing data; mischarging by billing the government for improper or nonallowable charges; collusion in bidding (a conspiracy between presumed competitors to inflate bids); product substitution or the delivery of inferior, nonconforming, or untested goods; or the use of bribes, gratuities, conflicts of interest, and a whole range of other techniques designed to influence procurement officials.

Clearly there is more to government-related fraud than the manipulation of contractors and consultants.[18] The Inspector General's Office in the Department of Health and Human Services reported that an estimated $20 billion may be lost annually to fraud in the Medicare program alone.[19]

Consumer Fraud

Consumer fraud is the act of causing a consumer to surrender money through deceit or a misrepresentation of a material fact. These offenses range from health care fraud to Internet auction fraud (Table 12.3). Consumer frauds often appear as confidence games and may take some of the following forms:

• *Home-improvement fraud.* Consumers have been defrauded through the promise of low-cost home renovation. The home owners give sizable down payments to the contractors, who have no plans to complete the job. In fact, contractors often leave the jurisdiction or declare bankruptcy.

• *Deceptive advertising.* Consumers are often lured into a store by an announcement that a product is priced low for a limited period of time. Once in the store, the customer is told that the product is sold out, and he or she is offered a substitute, typically of inferior quality or at a much higher price. Such schemes are known as "bait-and-switch advertising."

• *Telemarketing fraud.* You are no doubt familiar with the old adage "If a deal sounds too good to be true, it probably is!" Each day, countless phone calls are made to homes around the United States with a very familiar opening script: "Congratulations! You are a grand prize winner." "Please donate money to _____ fund or _____ charity." Telemarketers lure consumers by making attractive offers (e.g., vacations, prizes, discounts on household items) that are nothing more than scams. Once you pay, your name is often added to a "sucker list" that may be sold to other scam telemarketers.

Of course, not all telemarketing is fraudulent. The New York State Attorney General, for example, estimates that approximately 10 percent of over 140,000 New York businesses using telemarketing to sell their products are frauds. (See Table 12.4.)

• *Land fraud.* Consumers are easy prey for land fraud swindlers. Here the pitch is that a certain piece of vacation or retirement property is a worthy investment, many improvements to

TABLE 12.3 The Top 10 Categories of Consumer Fraud Complaints in 2002
• Internet auctions
• Internet services and computer complaints
• Advance fee loans and credit protection
• Shop-at-home/catalog sales
• Foreign money offers
• Prizes/sweepstakes and lotteries
• Business opportunity and work-at-home plans
• Telephone services
• Health care
• Magazines and buyers clubs

the property will be made, and many facilities will be made available in the area. Consumers often make purchases of worthless or overvalued land.

• *Business opportunity fraud.* The objective of business opportunity fraud is to persuade a consumer to invest money in a business concern through misrepresentation of its actual worth. Work-at-home frauds are common: Victims are told they can make big money by addressing envelopes at home or performing some other simple task. Consumers lose large sums of money investing in such ventures.

Insurance Fraud

There are many varieties of insurance fraud: Policyholders defraud insurers, insurers defraud the public, management defrauds the public, and third parties defraud insurers. Policyholder fraud is most often accomplished by the filing of false claims for life, fire, marine, or casualty insurance. Sometimes an employee of the insurance company is part of the fraud and assists in the preparation of the claim. The fraud may be simple—a false death claim—or it may become complex when multiple policies are involved.

A different type of insurance fraud is committed when a small group of people create a "shell" insurance firm without true assets. Policies are sold with no intent to pay legitimate claims. In fact, when large claims are presented to shell insurance companies, the firms disband, leaving a trail of policyholder victims. In yet another form of insurance fraud, middle- and upper-level managers of an insurance company loot the firm's

TABLE 12.4 Common telemarketing scams

ADVANCE-FEE LOAN OR CREDIT SCHEMES

Telemarketers seek out people with bad credit and offer them loans or credit cards in exchange for fees. Victims offered loans never receive them. Victims offered credit cards usually only get a standard application form or generic information on how to apply.

FOREIGN LOTTERY SCHEMES

Telemarketers offer victims the opportunity to "invest" in tickets in well-known foreign lotteries (e.g., Canada or Australia), or give them a "one in six" chance of winning a substantial prize. This is a common cross-border offense since it plays upon the ignorance of victims of the rules (or even the existence) of foreign lotteries. If offenders purport to sell real lottery chances but deceive victims about their chances of winning, it may be both a gambling offense and fraud. If real chances are sold without deception, it may still be a gambling offense.

INVESTMENT SCHEMES

Victims are sold "investments" in a wide range of merchandise or securities that appear to offer high profit margins. The fraud lies in misrepresenting the true value (or actual existence) of what is being sold, and/or the true extent of the risk in buying it. Common "opportunities" have involved stocks or securities, investment-grade gemstones, precious or strategic metals or minerals, and business opportunities such as oil and gas ventures, pizza ovens, and ostrich farms. These schemes commonly defraud victims more than once (see "reloading" schemes). Once funds have been committed, the victim can be induced to make additional payments to increase the value of the "investment" or avoid its loss (e.g., "margin calls"). Since legitimate investments normally tie up assets for extended periods, victims often do not realize for some time that they have been defrauded.

PRIZE PROMOTION

Telemarketers "guarantee" that the victims have won valuable prizes or gifts, such as vacations or automobiles, but require victims to submit one or more payments for non-existent shipping, taxes, customs or bonding fees, or anything else the offender thinks plausible. Some schemes never provide their victims with any prize or gift, while others provide inexpensive items, often called "gimme gifts" by U.S. telemarketers and "cheap gifts" by Canadian telemarketers.

TELEFUNDING SCHEMES

These prey on the charity of victims by soliciting donations for worthy causes such as antidrug programs or victims of natural disasters. The pitch may simply ask for donations or it may include other inducements, such as donor eligibility for valuable prizes, which never materialize (see "prize promotion" schemes). Charitable donors do not usually expect something in return for their contribution and thus may never become aware that they have been defrauded.

TRAVEL-RELATED SCHEMES

Fraudulent telemarketers purporting to be travel agencies offer substantial travel packages at comparatively low cost. The use of travel as a commodity makes the long-distance nature of the transaction plausible. The fraud usually involves lies, misrepresentations, or non-disclosure of information about the true value of travel and accommodations, limitations or restrictions on when or where purchasers may go, or what awaits them at the destination. In some cases, the travel proves to be a complete fabrication or has so many terms and conditions as to be completely unusable.

RELOADING AND RECOVERY ROOM SCHEMES

These target the same victims again and again. Persons victimized once are most likely to be deceived repeatedly. Unfortunately, victims' understandable desires to recover their original losses make them more vulnerable to further schemes. This is known as "reloading" or "loading." Those who "invest" money are "reloaded" for more to protect or increase their investment, those asked for customs or shipping fees are "reloaded" for additional charges, and those who give to a spurious "worthy cause" are often "reloaded" for further donations.

Recovery room schemes exploit the victim's desire to recover losses from previous frauds. Offenders, often from the same organization which defrauded the victim in the first place, call with inside knowledge of the fraud and a promise to recover the losses if "taxes" or "fees" are paid. A common tactic of callers is to represent themselves as law enforcement or other government or professional employees (e.g., bank or stock-exchange officials), using inside knowledge of the victim and the fraud to establish credibility. Recovery room operations frequently deprive victims of their last remaining funds.

SOURCE: http://www.fbi.gov.

assets by removing funds and debiting them as payments of claims to legitimate or bogus policyholders.[20]

Criminologists Paul Tracy and James Fox conducted a field experiment to find out how many auto-body repair shops in Massachusetts inflate repair estimates to insurance companies, and by how much. These researchers rented two Buick Skylarks with moderate damage, a Volvo 740 GLE with superficial damage, and a Ford Tempo with substantial damage. They then obtained 191 repair estimates, some with a clear understanding that the car was insured, others with the understanding that there was no insurance coverage. The results were unequivocal: Repair estimates for insured vehicles were significantly higher than those for noncovered cars. This finding is highly suggestive of fraud.[21]

Tax Fraud

The Internal Revenue Code makes willful failure to file a tax return a misdemeanor. An attempt to evade or defeat a tax, nonpayment of a tax, or willful filing of a fraudulent tax return is a felony. What must the government prove? In order to sustain a conviction, the government must present evidence of income tax due and owing, willful avoidance of payment, and an affirmative act toward tax evasion.[22] How are tax frauds accomplished? Consider the following techniques:

- *Keeping two sets of books.* A person may keep one set of books reflecting actual profits and losses and another set for the purpose of misleading the Internal Revenue Service.

- *Shifting funds.* In order to avoid detection, tax evaders often shift funds continually from account to account, from bank to bank.

- *Faking forms.* Tax evaders often use faked invoices, create fictitious expenses, conceal assets, and destroy books and records.

The IRS lacks the resources to investigate all suspicious tax forms. When the difficulty of distinguishing between careless mistakes and willful evasion is taken into account, the taxes that go uncollected each year are estimated to exceed $100 billion.[23]

Bribery, Corruption, and Political Fraud

Judges who fix traffic tickets in exchange for political favors, municipal employees who speculate with city funds, businesspeople who bribe local politicians to obtain favorable treatment— all are part of the corruption in our municipal, state, and federal governments. The objectives of such offenses vary—favors, special privileges, services, business. The actors include officers of corporations as well as of government; they may even belong to the police or the courts.

Bribery and other forms of corruption are ingrained in the political machinery of local and state governments. Examples abound: Mayors of large cities attempt to obtain favors through bribes; manufacturers pay off political figures for favors; municipal officials demand kickbacks from contractors.[24] In response to the seriousness of political corruption and bribery, Congress established two crimes: It is now a felony to accept a bribe or to provide a bribe.[25] Of course, political bribery and other forms of corruption do not stop at the nation's borders. Kickbacks to foreign officials are common practice, and countries develop reputations for both facilitating and tolerating corruption.[26] Business sectors develop reputations for corruption as well.

Corruption can also be found in private industry. One firm pays another to induce it to use a product or service; a firm pays its own board of directors or officers to dispense special favors; two or more firms, presumably competitors, secretly agree to charge the same prices for their products or services.

Insider-Related Fraud

Insider-related fraud involves the use and misuse of one's position for pecuniary gain or privilege. This category of offenses includes embezzlement, employee-related theft, and sale of confidential information.

Embezzlement is the conversion (misappropriation) of property or money with which one is entrusted or for which one has a fiduciary responsibility. Yearly losses attributable to embezzlement are estimated at over $1 billion.[27]

Employee-related thefts of company property are responsible for a significant share of industry losses. Estimates place such losses between $4 billion and $13 billion each year. Criminologists John Clark and Richard Hollinger have estimated that the 35 percent rate of employee pilferage in some corporations results primarily from vocational dissatisfaction and a perception of exploitation.[28] And not only goods and services are taken; time and money are at risk as well. Phony payrolls, fictitious overtime charges, false claims for business-related travel, and the like are common.

Finally, in a free marketplace where a premium is placed on competition, corporations must guard against the *sale of confidential information* and trade secrets. The best insurance policy is employee loyalty. Where there is no loyalty, or where loyalty is compromised, abuse of confidential information is possible. The purchase of confidential information from employees willing to commit industrial espionage is estimated to be a multimillion-dollar business.[29]

CORPORATE CRIME

The idea of white-collar crime is straightforward. Employees in a business step over the line by pocketing corporate funds. Tax avoiders become tax evaders. Home owners file fraudulent insurance claims. The crimes of white-collar criminals make fascinating television and movie scripts, from complex insider trading scandals to smoke-filled, boiler-room stock frauds. There are, however, other kinds of crimes that take place in the course of a respected and legitimate business enterprise. For the balance of this chapter, we will consider crimes by one or more employees of a corporation that are attributed to the organization itself—corporate crimes. The concept of **corporate crime** may be familiar if you have heard or read about the fall of Arthur Andersen and other companies that have been convicted—as corporations—of a host of criminal law violations. In fact, the concept of a "corporate" crime is more than a century old.

Frequency and Problems of Definition

There is no central repository for data on the number of cases of corporate crime in either state or federal courts. The best source of data, the United States Sentencing Commission, is less than ideal. The commission compiles information on cases of corporations that have been convicted of a federal crime.

On average, between 200 and 350 corporations are convicted each year in federal courts for offenses ranging from tax law violations to environmental crimes. The vast majority of these companies are small- to medium-size privately held corporations. In fact, between November 1, 1996, and June 30, 2005, nearly 92 percent of all corporations convicted had fewer than 50 employees. Less than 5 percent of all convicted corporations had more than 500 employees.

One problem with corporate crime is defining it. In 1989, the supertanker *Exxon Valdez* ran aground in Prince William Sound, Alaska, spilling 250,000 barrels of oil. The spill became North America's largest ecological disaster. Prosecutors were interested in determining the liability of the captain, his officers, and his crew. But there were additional and far-reaching questions. Was the Exxon Corporation liable? If so, was this a corporate crime? The same problem presented itself with the filing of criminal charges against Arthur Andersen. Should the firm bear the brunt of the crimes of its employees?

During the Great Depression, thousands of unemployed people heard that there was work to be had in the little West Virginia town of Hawk's Nest, where a huge tunnel was to be dug. Thousands of people came to work for a pittance. The company set the men up in crude camps and put them to work drilling rock for the tunnel project—without masks or other safety equipment. The workers breathed in the silicon dust that filled the air. Many contracted silicosis, a chronic lung disease that leads to certain death. They died by the dozens. Security guards dragged the bodies away and buried them secretly. No one was to know. The work went on. The deaths multiplied. Who was to blame? The corporation?[30]

Phases of Corporate Criminal Law

Corporate criminal law has moved through five distinct phases over the past century (Figure 12.2, page 312). In the first phase, courts wrestled with the idea that a corporation may be a "person" who is criminally liable. But can a corporation have a soul? Judges concluded that the idea that a corporation, without a soul, intended harm was too much of a fiction. Between 1850 and 1910, however, rising concerns over the possibility of corporate abuses captured the public's attention. Corporate criminal liability, no matter how illusory or illogical, became increasingly appealing as a hedge against the abuses considered inevitable with the rise of corporate power.

In the second phase, initiated by the decision of *New York Central Railroad* (1909), courts reviewed a wide variety of criminal cases against corporations.[31] Corporate regulation in this new world of interstate commerce required a more powerful and formal social control. This was all the more true as the first wave of mergers ended and large corporations increasingly spun off divisions—decentralizing. Centralized functions were now specialized and complex. In the years leading up to *New York Central Railroad*, concerns emerged that as corporations grew large, managerial oversight and control of employees would diminish.[32] Holding management responsible, through vicarious corporate criminal liability, soon became the rule of law in all federal courts.

Perceptions that this rule was unduly harsh prompted pleas by firms that they should be given a break for attempting compliance with laws.[33] Within 4 years of *New York Central Railroad*, corporations were telling courts that they were doing everything possible to comply with the law—even if they sometimes failed.

The third phase of the corporate criminal law saw a significant rise in the power of government regulators and, not surprisingly, the reach of regulatory law. Getting companies to comply with laws replaced punishment as the preferred sanction. Literally hundreds of thousands of criminal provisions were found in a wide range of federal statutory laws.[34] Marshall Clinard and his colleagues captured a glimpse of the effects of

THEORY CONNECTS

Corporate Crime

What would social control theorists (p. 155) say about the power of fines against corporations? Would they propose other sanctions that might be more effective? If so, what would those punishments look like?

How Much Corporate Power Is Too Much?

In a report on the rise of power in the world's top 200 corporations, it was noted that corporations are larger (in gross domestic product [GDP] terms) than many sizable countries (see 2005 revenue/GDP data in the following list). For example, the report stated that "General Motors is now bigger than Denmark; DaimlerChrysler is bigger than Poland; Royal Dutch/Shell is bigger than Venezuela; IBM is bigger than Singapore; and Sony is bigger than Pakistan."

Country/Corporation	GDP/Sales ($ million)	Country/Corporation	GDP/Sales ($ million)
1. United States	11,667,510.00	40. General Electric	134,187.00
2. Japan	4,623,398.00	41. Malaysia	117,775.80
3. Germany	2,714,418.00	42. Israel	117,548.40
4. United Kingdom	2,140,898.00	43. ChevronTexaco	112,937.00
5. France	2,002,582.00	44. Venezuela, RB	109,321.90
6. Italy	1,672,302.00	45. Czech Republic	107,046.80
7. China	1,649,329.00	46. Singapore	106,818.30
8. Spain	991,441.60	47. Hungary	99,712.02
9. Canada	979,764.20	48. New Zealand	99,686.83
10. India	691,876.30	49. ConocoPhillips	99,468.00
11. Korea, Rep.	679,674.30	50. Colombia	97,383.93
12. Mexico	676,497.30	51. Pakistan	96,114.84
13. Australia	631,255.80	52. Citigroup	94,713.00
14. Brazil	604,855.10	53. Chile	94,104.94
15. Russian Federation	582,395.00	54. Intl. Business Machines	89,131.00
16. Netherlands	577,259.60	55. Philippines	86,428.60
17. Switzerland	359,465.30	56. Algeria	84,649.01
18. Belgium	349,829.80	57. American Intl. Group	81,300.00
19. Sweden	346,404.10	58. Egypt, Arab Rep.	75,147.83
20. Turkey	301,949.80	59. Romania	73,166.83
21. Austria	290,109.50	60. Hewlett-Packard	73,061.00
22. Wal-Mart Stores	258,681.00	61. Nigeria	72,105.84
23. Indonesia	257,641.50	62. Peru	68,394.96
24. Saudi Arabia	250,557.30	63. Verizon Communications	67,752.00
25. Norway	250,168.00	64. Ukraine	65,149.34
26. Denmark	243,043.30	65. Home Depot	64,816.00
27. Poland	241,832.50	66. Berkshire Hathaway	63,859.00
28. Exxon Mobil	213,199.00	67. Altria Group	60,704.00
29. South Africa	212,777.30	68. McKesson	57,129.20
30. Greece	203,401.00	69. Bangladesh	56,844.49
31. General Motors	195,645.20	70. Cardinal Health	56,829.50
32. Finland	186,597.00	71. State Farm Insurance Co.	56,064.60
33. Ireland	183,559.60	72. Kroger	53,790.80
34. Portugal	168,281.40	73. Fannie Mae	53,766.90
35. Ford Motor	164,496.00	74. Boeing	50,485.00
36. Thailand	163,491.50	75. Morocco	50,054.92
37. Hong Kong, China	163,004.70	76. Amerisource Bergen	49,657.30
38. Iran, Islamic Rep.	162,709.30	77. Target	48,163.00
39. Argentina	151,501.20		

Country/Corporation	GDP/Sales ($ million)	Country/Corporation	GDP/Sales ($ million)
78. Bank of America Corp.	48,065.00	90. Kazakhstan	40,743.19
79. Pfizer	45,950.00	91. Valero Energy	37,968.60
80. Vietnam	45,210.45	92. Marathon Oil	37,137.00
81. J. P. Morgan Chase & Co.	44,363.00	93. MetLife	36,261.00
82. Time Warner	43,877.00	94. Safeway	35,552.70
83. Procter & Gamble	43,377.00	95. Albertson's	35,436.00
84. Costco Wholesale	42,545.60	96. Morgan Stanley	34,933.00
85. Johnson & Johnson	41,862.00	97. AT&T	34,629.00
86. Dell	41,444.00	98. Medco Health Solutions	34,264.50
87. Sears Roebuck	41,124.00	99. Croatia	34,199.98
88. Slovak Republic	41,091.85		
89. SBC Communications	40,843.00	100. United Parcel Service	33,485.00

SOURCE: Ranking based on corporation revenue data from *Fortune*, October 1, 2005, and GDP data from *World Bank World Development Indicators (WDI)* Report, 2005.

With a near unprecedented recession, many of the companies listed have lost significant revenue. There have also been losses in the gross domestic product of countries around the world. That the estimates of both are ever-changing with the volatility of global markets is less important than the fact that corporations as well as countries have much power. If you accept the notion that GDP and sales are comparable measures of "power," some companies have as much power as many countries—perhaps even more. Consider the authors' conclusions:

1. Of the 100 largest economies in the world, 51 are corporations; only 49 are countries (based on a comparison of corporate sales and country GDPs).
2. The top 200 corporations' sales are growing at a faster rate than overall global economic activity. Between 1983 and 1999, their combined sales grew from the equivalent of 25 percent to 27.5 percent of world GDP.
3. The top 200 corporations' combined sales are bigger than the combined economies of all countries minus the biggest 10.
4. The top 200s' combined sales are 18 times the size of the combined annual income of the 1.2 billion people

(24 percent of the total world population) living in "severe" poverty.
5. While the sales of the top 200 are the equivalent of 27.5 percent of world economic activity, they employ only 0.78 percent of the world's workforce.
6. Between 1983 and 1999, the profits of the top 200 firms grew 362.4 percent, while the number of people they employ grew by only 14.4 percent.
7. A full 5 percent of the top 200s' combined workforce is employed by Wal-Mart, a company notorious for union-busting and widespread use of part-time workers to avoid paying benefits. The discount retail giant is the top private employer in the world, with 1,140,000 workers—more than twice as many as number two, DaimlerChrysler, which employs 466,938.
8. U.S. corporations dominate the top 200, with 82 slots (41 percent of the total). Japanese firms are second, with only 41 slots.
9. Of the U.S. corporations on the list, 44 did not pay the full standard 35 percent federal corporate tax rate during the 1996–1998 period. Seven of the firms actually paid less than zero in federal income taxes in 1998 (because of rebates). These include Texaco, Chevron, PepsiCo,

Enron, WorldCom, McKesson, and the world's biggest corporation—General Motors.
10. Between 1983 and 1999, the share of total sales of the top 200 made up by service sector corporations increased from 33.8 percent to 46.7 percent. Gains were particularly evident in financial services and telecommunications sectors, in which most countries have pursued deregulation.

Activists often refer to these data in arguing that the grant of corporate personhood—pretending that corporations are persons—poses many risks and a distinct danger. The risks are that corporate persons will be given too many rights and achieve too great a share of power. With this power, some argue, comes the danger that corporations will victimize their stakeholders.

Questions for Discussion

1. What are these risks and what is this danger?
2. How can the evils of personhood be accommodated?
3. How does the combination of economic influence and political power pose a near-insurmountable challenge for the regulation of large multinational corporations?

FIGURE 12.2 The five phases of the corporate criminal law, 1850–present.

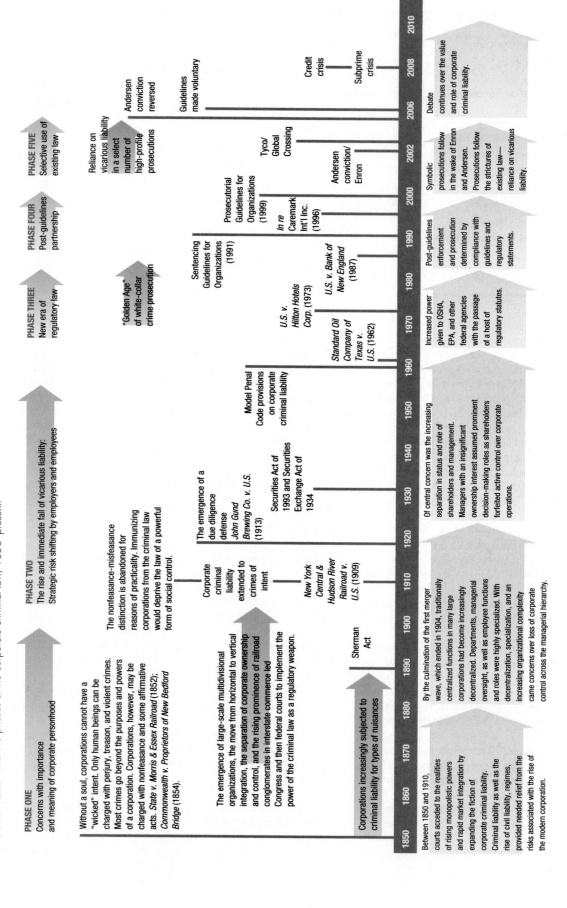

In Tyler, Texas, Jim and Kathy Taylor hold a photo of their daughter Jessica, a cheerleader who died in a tire blowout crash on her way to a game. In the background, their lawyer, Randell Roberts, holds a Firestone tire from the SUV. Subsequently, Firestone recalled 6.5 million of its most widely used product.

In February 2009, chief executives from major banks and other financial institutions that received federal money in the wake of the economic crisis that began in 2008 testified before the House Financial Services Committee in Washington. Companies represented at the hearing included, among others, Goldman Sachs, Bank of America, and Morgan Stanley.

this new regulatory state on large corporations in their influential work *Illegal Corporate Behavior*.[35]

In the fourth phase, defined by the passage of the Sentencing Guidelines for Organizations, corporations joined with the government in routing out crime (Figure 12.3). Following significant lobbying from business associations, a congressionally appointed body—the United States Sentencing Commission—announced guidelines that govern the sentencing of corporations in federal courts. Drafters of the sentencing guidelines wanted corporations to face the threat of significant punishment and, at the same time, the possibility of mitigation, leniency, and amnesty (Table 12.5). This was the incentive for corporations to help ferret out crime.

The sentencing guidelines require judges to consider a fine multiplied by a score reflecting factors that make the corporation more or less blameworthy. A corporation's willingness to accept responsibility, cooperate with authorities, and implement a compliance reveals corporate due diligence and mitigates a sanction. To help companies understand how to best position themselves relative to prosecutors and regulators, consultants for a new and emerging industry—the corporate compliance industry—offered their skills.

The compliance industry markets the story that evidence of **organizational due diligence** (cooperating with authorities, creating an ethics code, hiring ethics officers, etc.) likely forestalls a criminal investigation, minimizes the likelihood of a

FIGURE 12.3 The development of the corporate criminal law, pre-guidelines–present.

Pre-Guidelines

Post-Guidelines I: "A practical partnership" between government and business. New age of government-corporate cooperation characterized by a shift away from command and control strategies of corporate regulation to negotiated compliance, coerced cooperation, and regulatory persuasion. Concerns: gaming, moral hazards, and flipping.

Post-Guidelines
A period of "Corporate Accountability" emerged with the appearance of widespread corporate deviance. Strategic call for corporate investigation, prosecution, and law reform are designed to calm investor fears and return confidence to the markets.

Rise of "reverse whistle-blowing"

U.S. Sentencing Commission, Sentencing of Organizations (Discussion Draft 1988)

United States Sentencing Commission, Sentencing of Organizations (Preliminary Draft 1989)

United States Sentencing Commission, Sentencing of Organizations (Proposed Guidelines 1990)

U.S. Sentencing Commission, Guidelines for Organizations (1991)

Antitrust Division, Corporate Amnesty Policy, Antitrust Division, DOJ, 1993

Sequa Corp. plea agreement

Prudential plea agreement

DOJ, Factors in Decisions on Criminal Prosecutions for Environmental Violations in the Context of Significant Voluntary Compliance or Disclosure Efforts by the Violator (1994); Memorandum Regarding Exercise of Investigative Discretion, Office of Criminal Enforcement, EPS (1994)

Voluntary Disclosure Program Guidelines, Office of the Inspector General, Department of Health and Human Services (1995); Incentives for Self-Policing: Discovery, Disclosure, Correction and Prevention of Violations, United States Environmental Protection Agency (EPA) (1995)

In re Caremark Int'l Inc. (1996)

Reputation management and compliance risk management practices join the business ethics cottage industry in counseling corporations

Prosecutorial Guidelines for Organizations (1999)

Enron & Andersen

Tyco/ Global Crossing

Andersen conviction reversed

Guidelines made voluntary

Subprime crisis

Bank failures

| 1988 | 1989 | 1990 | 1991 | 1992 | 1993 | 1994 | 1995 | 1996 | 1997 | 1998 | 1999 | 2000 | 2001 | 2002 | 2006 | 2008 | 2010 |

Debate over optimal penalty theory and the possible role, if any, of mitigating circumstances in the drafts of the sentencing guidelines for organizations. Heavy lobbying from industry groups and big business to include some recognition of organizational due diligence.

In this phase of "Post-Guidelines" cases, corporate compliance for large, decentralized multinationals is bought and sold as cost-effective risk management in a marketplace of experts from "business integrity" consulting, insurance, and accounting firms. Evidence of organizational due diligence may forestall an investigation, minimize the chance of a criminal indictment, and possibly lead to a grant of governmental amnesty.

Prosecutors are increasingly likely to decline cases involving organizations with compliance programs modeled after Guidelines' prescriptive steps. This is especially true in complex white-collar and corporate crime cases (e.g., antitrust and securities fraud) that require significant investigative and prosecutorial resources. Declinations reward firms for their proactive and reactive efforts, focusing scarce resources on the most-abusive firms.

The Prosecutorial and Sentencing Guidelines provide reciprocal promises—organizational cooperation and acceptance of responsibility in exchange for mitigation, exculpation, or absolution.

Symbolic prosecution follows in the wake of Enron and Andersen. Prosecution follows the strictures of existing reliance on vicarious liability.

Debate continues on the role of the corporate criminal law.

TABLE 12.5 United States Sentencing Guidelines for Organizational Defendants (1991)

Factors to Be Considered in Sentencing Organizations	Organizational Factors to Be Considered in Sentencing
1. The organization must have established compliance standards and procedures to be followed by its employees and other agents that are reasonably capable of reducing the prospect of criminal conduct.	Firm size is considered in the assessment of organizational culpability.
2. Specific individual(s) within high-level personnel of the organization must have been assigned overall responsibility to oversee compliance with such standards and procedures.	If by custom or convention it is more likely that deviance will occur in a particular business, business sector, or market, an organization is more culpable if it failed to put in place and enforce policies to prevent such deviance from occurring.
3. The organization must have used due care not to delegate substantial discretionary authority to individuals whom the organization knew, or should have known through the exercise of due diligence, had a propensity to engage in illegal activities.	The criminal history of an organization will affect the assessment of culpability.
4. The organization must have taken steps to communicate effectively its standards and procedures to all employees and other agents.	Corporate compliance programs that are perceived to be effective decrease culpability.
5. The organization must have taken reasonable steps to achieve compliance with its standards, e.g., by utilizing monitoring and auditing systems reasonably.	Organizational obstruction of justice increases culpability.
6. The standards must have been consistently enforced through appropriate disciplinary mechanisms, including, as appropriate, discipline of individuals responsible for the failure to detect an offense.	Organizational cooperation, admission of guilt, and acceptance of responsibility reduce culpability.
7. After an offense has been detected, the organization must have taken all reasonable steps to respond appropriately to the offense and to prevent further similar offenses—including any necessary modifications to its program to prevent and detect violations of law.	Closely held organizations may be alter egos of management.

criminal indictment, and regularly leads to a grant of governmental leniency, if not amnesty. Regulators and prosecutors decline cases involving corporations that demonstrate a commitment to compliance and actively cooperative with authorities. Declinations reward firms for their proactive, reactive, and cooperative efforts, reserving resources for the most abusive firms.

The result is a new enforcement landscape—one of substantial assistance, mitigation credits, and voluntary disclosure. In theory, the substantive corporate criminal law is unchanged since *New York Central & Hudson River Railroad.* In practice, negotiated compliance has all but replaced the substantive law. Corporate cooperation that facilitates the flow of evidence to authorities is the critical feature of this regulatory strategy.

In the final phase, law enforcement, regulators, and prosecutors have joined academics in debating the fair and just reaction to the subprime crisis and the fraudulent misrepresentations of some of the most respected financial institutions.

Theories of Corporate Liability

A "corporation" is an artificial person created by state charter. The charter provides such an entity with the right to engage in certain activities—to buy and sell certain goods or to run a railroad, for instance. The charter limits the liability of the persons who own the corporation (the shareholders) to the extent of the value of their investment (their shares). The corporation thus is an entity separate from the people who own or manage it. This convenient form of pooling resources for commercial purposes, with a view toward profiting from one's investment, has had a significant impact on the development of the United States as a commercial and industrial power. Moreover, millions of wage earners whose savings or union funds

■ Sotheby's auction house head Alfred Taubman leaves federal court April 22, 2002, in New York City. A federal judge sentenced Taubman to a year in prison and ordered him to pay a $7.5 million fine for price-fixing.

Crime Surfing WWW

www.herring.com/
Home/10179

Corporate crime poses serious law enforcement investigatory problems. How much more difficult is the investigation of corporate crime in high-tech industries?

are invested in corporate stocks and bonds reap dividends from such investments in the form of income or retirement benefits.

But what if a senior official of a corporation engages in unlawful activity? Can we say that the corporation committed the crime? If so, what can be done about it?[36] Initially, corporations were considered incapable of committing crimes. After all, crimes require mens rea, an awareness of wrongdoing. Since corporations are bodies without souls, they were deemed to be incapable of forming the requisite sense of wrongdoing. Nor could a corporation be imprisoned for its crimes. Further, corporations were not authorized to commit crimes; they were authorized only to engage in the business for which they had been chartered. So how should the "blameworthiness" or "culpability" of a corporation be conceived?

Models of Corporate Culpability

Over the past several decades, scholars have revisited the allegiance of courts to **vicarious liability**. Should courts consider the reactions of a corporation to the discovery of illegal behavior? Should courts focus on corporate cultures that encourage crime commission or corporate policies that tolerate, if not promote, law violation? Nearly a century after the criminal law was first applied to corporations, there is increasing interest in proactive, reactive, culture-based, and corporate policy models of culpability.

Proactive corporate fault (PCF) assumes that a corporation is to blame where practices and procedures are inadequate to prevent the commission of a crime. Corporations are culpable when they fail to take reasonable steps to implement policies and practices that reduce the likelihood of crime commission.

Reactive corporate fault (RCF) considers the corporate reaction to the discovery of a criminal act. Evidence of how well a company reacts to the discovery of an offense is the basis for finding blame. Failure to undertake reasonable corrective or remedial measures in reaction to an offense is evidence of fault.

Where an organization's ethos or personality encourages agents to commit criminal acts there is liability under a theory of **corporate ethos** (CE). Such a corporate ethos is determined by the corporate hierarchy, corporate goals and policies, efforts to ensure compliance with ethics codes and legal regulations, and the indemnification of guilty employees. Questions relating to the role of the board of directors and to how the corporation has reacted to past violations, if any, will be asked as well.

Finally, commentators have argued that corporate actions and intention may be found in decisions and choices that are communicated through **corporate policy** (CP). It has been argued, for example, that the components of the corporation's internal decision structure, consisting of the corporation's flowchart and procedures, define corporate intentionality. A summary of all four models appears in Table 12.6.

An additional model of corporate blame has been proposed—**constructive corporate culpability** (CCC). Here the concern is with whether corporations may be said to have a culpable "mental state." Of course, corporations do not actually have mental states. That is precisely why this is a "constructive" theory. Constructive corporate culpability asks such questions as: Did the corporation act "purposely"? Did the corporation act "knowingly"? Did the corporation act "recklessly"? Did the corporation act "negligently"? Evidence of corporate mental states may be gleaned from asking these questions in relation to what an average corporation would have intended. Courts would, therefore, ask whether a corporation, given the circumstances, exhibits an awareness of the illegality. Did it appear to disregard risks that are associated with the crimes alleged? Should the company have known of the illegalities? These questions turn on the reasonableness of attributions of fault.

TABLE 12.6 Summary of Models

Model	Postulates	Constructs	Hypotheses
PCF	Culpability is a function of the reasonableness of steps taken to prevent an offense.	Proactive corporate fault; proactive due diligence; proactive duty	An entity is more or less blameworthy if it engages or fails to engage in proactive efforts. Proactive safeguards (e.g., internal audits) are effective in inhibiting law violation.
RCF	Culpability is a function of the reasonableness of steps taken in reaction to the discovery of an offense.	Reactive corporate fault; reactive due diligence; reactive duty	An entity is more or less blameworthy if it engages or fails to engage in reactive or remedial efforts. Reactive programs and remedial efforts are effective in controlling corporate deviance.
CE	Culpability derives from the corporate ethos, culture, or personality.	Corporate ethos; corporate personality; corporate culture	Corporate ethos is strongly associated with or causes corporate deviance. A distinct corporate culture and personality may be determined from organizational attributes.
CP	Corporate intentionality is found in decisions and choices that are communicated through corporate policy.	Corporate internal decision structure (CID); corporate policy	Corporate policies, goals, and objectives reflect corporate rather than individual intentionality.
CCC	Corporate fault is found in the reasonableness of judgments.	Corporate purpose; corporate knowledge; corporate recklessness; corporate negligence	Corporate fault is a function of reasonable attributed blame.

Governmental Control of Corporations

Corporate misconduct is covered by a broad range of federal and state statutes, including the federal conspiracy laws; the Racketeer Influenced and Corrupt Organizations (RICO) Act; federal securities laws; mail-fraud statutes; the Federal Corrupt Practices Act; the Federal Election Campaign Act; legislation on lobbying, bribery, and corruption; the Internal Revenue Code (especially regarding major tax crimes, slush funds, and improper payments); the Bank Secrecy Act; and federal provisions on obstruction of justice, perjury, and false statements.

The underlying theory is that if the brain of the artificial person (usually the board of directors of the corporation) authorizes or condones the act in question, the body (the corporation) must suffer criminal penalty. That seems fair enough, except for the fact that if the corporation gets punished—usually by the laying of a substantial fine—the penalty falls on the shareholders, most of whom had no say in the corporate decision. And the financial loss resulting from the fine may be passed on to the consumer. The counterargument, of course, is that shareholders often benefit from the illegal actions of the corporation. Thus, in fairness, they should suffer some detriment or loss when and if the corporation is apprehended and convicted.

Reliance on Civil Penalties

Beginning in the nineteenth century, corporations were suspected of wielding monopolistic power to the detriment of consumers. The theory behind monopoly is simple: If you buy out all your competitors or drive them out of business, then you are the only one from whom people can buy the product you sell. So you can set the price, and you set it very high, for your profit and to the detriment of the consumers. The Sugar Trust was one such monopoly. A few powerful businessmen eliminated all competitors and then drove up the price of sugar, to the detriment of the public. Theodore Roosevelt fought and broke up the Sugar Trust.

In 1890, Congress passed the **Sherman Antitrust Act**, which effectively limited the exercise of monopolies.[37] The act prohibited any contract, conspiracy, or combination of business interests in restraint of foreign or interstate trade. This legislation was followed by the Clayton Antitrust Act (1914), which further curbed the ability of corporations to enrich their shareholders at the expense of the public, by prohibiting acts such as price-fixing.[38] But the remedies this act provided consisted largely of splitting up monopolistic enterprises or imposing damages—sometimes triple damages—for the harm caused. In a strict sense, this was not a use of the criminal law to govern corporate misconduct.

> **THEORY CONNECTS**
>
> **Corporate Crime**
>
> In what ways may subcultural theories of crime (Chapter 6) help explain white-collar and organizational offenses?

In March 2009, President Barack Obama, shown here with National Economic Council Chairman Lawrence Summers, spoke outside the White House about his desire to put new corporate regulations into place.

Criminal Liability

A movement away from exclusive reliance on civil remedies was apparent in the 1960s, when it was discovered that corporate mismanagement or negligence on the part of officers or employees could inflict vast harm on identifiable groups of victims. Negligent management at a nuclear power plant can result in the release of radiation and injury to thousands or millions of people. The marketing of an unsafe drug can cause crippling deformities in tens of thousands of bodies.[39] Violation of environmental standards can cause injury and suffering to generations of people who will be exposed to unsafe drinking water, harmful air, or eroded soil. The manufacture of hazardous products can result in multiple deaths.[40]

The problem of corporate criminal liability since the 1960s, then, goes far beyond an individual death or injury. Ultimately, it concerns the health and even the survival of humankind. Nor is the problem confined to the United States. It is a global problem. It thus becomes necessary to look at the variety of activities attributable to corporations that in recent years have been recognized as particularly harmful to society.

When it comes to proving corporate criminal liability, prosecutors face formidable challenges: Day-to-day corporate activity has a low level of visibility. Regulatory agencies that monitor corporate conduct have different and uncoordinated recording systems. Offending corporations operate in a multitude of jurisdictions, some of which regard a given activity as criminal while others do not. Frequently, the facts of a case are not adjudicated at a trial; the parties may simply agree on a settlement approved by the court. Those corporations that are convicted tend to be first offenders without effective compliance programs.

Investigating Corporate Crime

We know very little about the extent of economic criminality in the United States. There is no national database for the assessment of corporate criminality, and corporations are not likely to release information about their own wrongdoing. The situation is worse in other countries, especially in the developing countries of Africa south of the Sahara, where few national crime statistics are kept and where corporations are least subject to governmental control. Yet the evidence in regard to corporate crime is gradually coming in.[41]

As we noted earlier, the first American criminologist who was alert to the potential for harm in corporate conduct was Edwin Sutherland, who described the criminal behavior of 70 of the 200 largest production corporations in his 1946 book *White Collar Crime*.[42] An even more ambitious study was completed by Marshall B. Clinard and Peter C. Yeager, who investigated corporations within the jurisdiction of 25 federal agencies during 1975 and 1976. Of 477 major American corporations whose conduct was regulated by these agencies, 60 percent had violated the law. Of the 300 violating corporations, 38 (or 13 percent) accounted for 52 percent of all violations charged in 1975 and 1976, an average of 23.5 violations per firm.[43] Large corporations were found to be the chief violators, and a few particular industries (pharmaceutical, automotive) were the most likely to violate the law.

According to Clinard and Yeager, what makes it so difficult to curb corporate crime is the enormous political power corporations wield in the shaping and administration of the laws that govern their conduct. This is particularly the case in regard to multinational corporations that wish to operate in developing countries. The promise of jobs and development by a giant corporation is a temptation too great for the governments of many developing countries to resist. They would rather have employment opportunities that pollute air and water than unemployment in a clean environment. Government officials in some Third World countries can be bribed to create or maintain a legal climate favorable to the business interests of the corporation, even though doing so may be detrimental to the people of the host country.

The work of Sutherland, Clinard, and Yeager and other traditional scholars, as well as that of a group of radical criminologists;[44] hearings on white-collar and corporate crime held by the Subcommittee on Crime of the House Judiciary Committee, under the leadership of Congressman John Conyers Jr. in 1978; the consumer protection movement, spearheaded by Ralph Nader; and investigative reporting by the press have all contributed to public awareness of large corporations' power to inflict harm on large population groups.

In 1975, James Q. Wilson still considered such crime to be insignificant,[45] but more recent studies show that the public considers corporate criminality at least as serious as, if not more serious than, street crime. Marvin Wolfgang and his associates found in a national survey that Americans regard illegal retail price-fixing (the artificial setting of prices at a high level, without regard for the demand for the product) as a more serious crime than robbery committed with a lead pipe.[46] Within the sphere of corporate criminality, perhaps no other group of offenses has had as great an impact on public consciousness as crimes against the environment. As we shall see, however, enforcement of major environmental statutes has been weak in the past. There is some evidence that this is changing.

Environmental Crimes

The world's legal systems include few effective laws and mechanisms to curb destruction of the environment. The emission of noxious fumes into the air and the discharge of pollutants into the water have until recently been regarded as common law nuisances at the level of misdemeanors, usually commanding no more than a small fine. Industrial polluters could easily absorb such a fine and tended to regard it as a kind of business tax. In 1969, Congress passed the National Environmental Policy Act (NEPA). Among other things, the act created the Environmental Pro-tection Agency (EPA). It requires environmental impact studies so that any new development that would significantly affect the environment can be prevented or controlled.

The EPA is charged with enforcing federal statutes and assisting in the enforcement of state laws enacted to protect the environment. The agency monitors plant discharges all over the country and may take action against private industry or municipal governments. Yet during the first 5 years of its existence, the EPA referred only 130 cases to the U.S. Department of Justice for criminal prosecution, and only 6 of those involved major corporate offenders.[47] The government actually charged only one of the corporations, Allied Chemical, which admitted responsibility for 940 misdemeanor counts of discharging toxic chemicals into the Charles River in Virginia, thereby causing 80 people to become ill.[48]

A 1979 report of the General Accounting Office stated that the EPA inadequately monitored, inaccurately reported, and ineffectively enforced the nation's basic law on air pollution, although the agency's chief at that time contended that corrective action had been taken during the previous year.[49] The situation improved during the 1990s, but the environment is far from safe. Catastrophic releases of toxic and even nuclear substances, usually attributable to inadequate safeguards and human negligence, pose a particularly grave hazard, as the disasters at Bhopal in India and at Chernobyl in the former Soviet Union have demonstrated.

The effects of environmental crimes touch more than the environment. Employees in "culpable" companies may be victims as well. Consider, for example, the criminal investigation and prosecution of Darling International, Inc., a meat and meat-processing company located in Minnesota, for violations of the Clean Water Act.[50] The case of *United States v. Darling* is often thought of as representing a trend of management to exchange or trade culpable employees for corporate leniency.[51]

In 1989, Darling International bought a rendering plant in Blue Earth, Minnesota. Under significant pressure to increase production to meet sales objectives, its wastewater system soon became overloaded. Beginning in 1991, employees sought to remedy this situation by illegally dumping millions of gallons of ammonia and blood-contaminated water into the Blue Earth River, causing significant environmental damage. Soon thereafter, on orders of the plant manager and with the knowledge of the vice president of environmental affairs, employees attempted to hide the illegal dumping by diluting and tampering with at least nine wastewater samples sent to state pollution control authorities. The government had evidence that employees also fabricated and submitted discharge-monitoring reports and related documents that were later sent to state regulators.

The federal government's investigation into these environmental crimes stalled until Darling's board required retained counsel to cooperate with authorities and provide evidence of any criminal acts by its employees. With newly offered evidence, prosecutors obtained criminal convictions of four employees, all of whom had

Corporate Fraud

The most recent Financial Crimes Report from the Federal Bureau of Investigation details the federal effort to respond to crimes by both individuals and corporations within and outside the financial markets. It is notable for the breadth of cases and for the focus on individual liability.

I. GENERAL OVERVIEW

As the lead agency investigating corporate fraud, the FBI has focused its efforts on cases that involve accounting schemes, self-dealing by corporate executives, and obstruction of justice. The majority of corporate fraud cases pursued by the FBI involve accounting schemes designed to deceive investors, auditors, and analysts about the true financial condition of a corporation. Through the manipulation of financial data, the share price of a corporation remains artificially inflated based on fictitious performance indicators provided to the investing public. In addition to significant financial losses to investors, corporate fraud has the potential to cause immeasurable damage to the U.S. economy and investor confidence.

While the number of cases involving the falsification of financial information remains relatively stable, the FBI has recently observed a spike in the number of corporate fraud cases involving subprime mortgage lending companies. A subprime lender is a business that lends to borrowers who do not qualify for loans from mainstream lenders. The subprime market has grown from 2 percent of mortgages in 1998 to 20 percent of mortgages in 2006. Currently, the total value of subprime loans outstanding is estimated at $1.3 trillion, while total mortgage loans outstanding is $4.5 trillion.

As the housing market declines, subprime lenders have been forced to buy back a number of non-performing loans. Many of these subprime lenders have relied on a continuous increase in real estate values to allow the borrowers to refinance or sell their properties before going into default. However, based on the sales slowdown in the housing market, loan defaults have increased, and the secondary market for subprime loans has dwindled. As a result, subprime lenders' publicly traded stocks have dramatically decreased in value, resulting in financial difficulties and bankruptcies.

As publicly traded subprime lenders have suffered financial difficulties due to rising defaults, analyses of company financials have identified instances of false accounting entries, and fraudulently inflated assets and revenues. Investigations have determined that many of these bankrupt subprime lenders manipulated their reported loan portfolio risks and used various accounting schemes to inflate their financial reports. In addition, before these subprime lenders' stocks rapidly declined in value, executives with insider information sold their equity positions and profited illegally. The FBI is working with the U.S. Department of Justice (DOJ), the U.S. Securities and Exchange Commission (SEC), and other U.S. regulatory agencies to identify possible subprime lenders engaged in corporate fraud and insider trading.

In addition to the subprime mortgage issue, corporate fraud matters involving the backdating of executive stock options continue to be an issue of concern. Stock options are corporate incentives that allow the holder to purchase stock at a fixed "strike" price sometime in the future, regardless of the prevailing market price. Generally, the strike price is the cost of the stock on the date the options were granted. The benefit to the options holder is the difference between the strike price and the later sales price. When stock options are backdated, however, the date of the options is set to a time in the past when the price of the stock was lower than on the date the options were actually issued. Backdating stock options inflates their value to the holder at the expense of regular shareholders. Some corporate executives have also changed their stock options exercise date (the date the option can be converted to stock) to avoid paying income tax. As of the end of Fiscal Year 2007, the FBI was investigating over 70 cases involving the manipulation of executive stock options.

Corporate fraud remains the highest priority of the Financial Crimes Section, and the FBI is committed to dealing with this significant crime problem. As of the end of Fiscal Year 2007, 529 corporate fraud cases were being pursued by FBI field offices throughout the U.S., several of which involve losses to public investors that individually exceed $1 billion.

---

been fired by Darling after fully cooperating with counsel retained by the company and federal prosecutors. Darling entered into a plea agreement, and prosecutors recognized the company's cooperation by recommending a significantly mitigated fine—one quarter of the originally recommended fine. The company promptly implemented an environmental compliance program, adopted a code of business conduct, and created a corporate ombudsman's position to "encourage employees to report suspected problems even when they are reluctant to go directly to their supervisors, legal counsel, or someone else in management."[52]

Darling is notable for many reasons: the complicity and knowledge of management, the distance between the employees held responsible and those cooperating with authorities, the absence of compliance initiatives or programs, and a culture that permitted scapegoating and the deception that can and often does accompany it. Simply put, existing principles and practices of corporate

CORPORATE FRAUD INVESTIGATIONS INVOLVE THE FOLLOWING ACTIVITIES:

1. Falsification of financial information, including:
   a. False accounting entries;
   b. Bogus trades designed to inflate profit or hide losses; and,
   c. False transactions designed to evade regulatory oversight.
2. Self-dealing by corporate insiders, including:
   a. Insider trading;
   b. Kickbacks;
   c. Backdating of executive stock options;
   d. Misuse of corporate property for personal gain; and,
   e. Individual tax violations related to self-dealing.
3. Obstruction of justice designed to conceal any of the above-noted types of criminal conduct, particularly when the obstruction impedes the inquiries of the SEC, other regulatory agencies, and/or law en-forcement agencies.

The FBI has formed partnerships with numerous agencies to capitalize on their expertise in specific areas such as Securities, Tax, Pensions, Energy, and Commodities. The FBI has placed greater emphasis on investigating allegations of these frauds by working closely with the SEC, Financial Industry Regulation Authority, Internal Revenue Service (IRS), Department of Labor, Federal Energy Regulatory Commission, Commodity Futures Trading Commission, and U.S. Postal Inspection Service (USPIS). As reflected in the statistical accomplishments of the President's Corporate Fraud Task Force, founded in 2002, which includes the above-mentioned agencies, the cooperative and multi-agency investigative approach has resulted in highly successful prosecutions.

The FBI has also worked with numerous organizations in private industry to increase public awareness about combating corporate fraud, to include: Public Company Accounting Oversight Board, American Institute of Certified Public Accountants, and the North American Securities Administrator's Association, Inc. These organizations have been able to provide referrals for expert witnesses and other technical assistance regarding accounting and securities issues. In addition, the Financial Crimes Enforcement Network (FinCEN) and Dun & Bradstreet have been able to provide significant background information on subject individuals and/or subject companies to further investigative efforts.

II. OVERALL ACCOMPLISHMENTS

Through FY [fiscal year] 2007, cases pursued by the FBI resulted in 183 indictments and 173 convictions of corporate criminals. Numerous cases are pending plea agreements and trials. During Fiscal Year 2007, the FBI secured $12.6 billion in restitution orders and $38.6 million in fines from corporate criminals. The chart reflects corporate fraud pending cases from Fiscal Year 2003 through Fiscal Year 2007 as follows: Fiscal Year 2003—279 cases; Fiscal Year 2004—

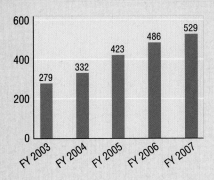

332; Fiscal Year 2005—423; Fiscal Year 2006—486; and Fiscal Year 2007—529 cases.

Source:

Federal Bureau of Investigation, Financial Crimes Report to the Public, Fiscal Year 2007 (October 1, 2006—September 30, 2007). Available at http://www.fbi.gov/publications/financial/fcs_report2007/financial_crime_2007.htm.

Questions for Discussion

1. To what extent should the government continue to focus on individual liability in cases of corporate fraud?
2. Should the focus remain with the criminal law, or should it shift to regulatory agencies for a more "cooperative" approach?
3. Is sufficient priority given to corporate fraud cases relative to violent and property offenses? How serious are corporate crimes relative to street crimes?

criminal law offer a less-than-optimal solution and remedy.

Enforcing Legislation

The difficulties of enforcing legislation designed to protect the environment are enormous. Consider the 250,000 barrels of oil spilled by the *Exxon Valdez* in 1989. What legislation could have prevented the disaster? Developing effective laws to protect the environment is a complex problem. It is far easier to define the crimes of murder and theft than to define acts of pollution, which are infinitely varied. A particular challenge is the separation of harmful activities from socially useful ones. Moreover, pollution is hard to quantify. How much of a chemical must be discharged into water before the discharge is considered noxious and subjects the polluter to punishment? Discharge of a gallon by one polluter may not warrant punishment, and a small quantity may not even be detectable. But what do we do with a hundred polluters, each of whom discharges a gallon?

A catastrophic explosion at the Union Carbide plant in Bhopal, India, on December 2, 1984, spewed clouds of deadly gas, causing nearly 6,500 fatalities and more than 20,000 injuries.

Many other issues must be addressed as well. For instance, should accidental pollution warrant the same punishment as intentional or negligent pollution? Since many polluters are corporations, what are the implications of penalties that force a company to install costly antipollution devices? To cover the costs, the corporation may have to increase the price of its product, so the consumer pays. Should the company be allowed to lower plant workers' wages instead? Should the plant be forced or permitted to shut down, thereby increasing unemployment in the community? The company may choose to move its plant to another state or country that is more hospitable.

Addressing Sensitive Issues

Fines imposed on intentional polluters have been increased so that they can no longer be shrugged off as an ordinary cost of doing business. General Electric Company was fined $7 million and Allied Chemical Corporation $13.2 million for pollution offenses. Fines of such magnitude are powerful incentives to corporations to limit pollution. But because many of the enterprises that are likely to pollute are in the public sector, or produce for the public sector, the public ultimately will have to pay the fine in the form of increased gas or electricity bills.[53]

In the Third World, the problems of punishing and preventing pollution are enormous. Industries preparing to locate there have the power to influence governments and officials, surreptitiously and officially, into passing legislation favorable to the industry. The desire to industrialize outweighs the desire to preserve the environment. Some countries find ways to address the problem, only

to relinquish controls when they prove irksome. While Japan was trying to establish its industrial dominance, for example, it observed a constitutional provision stating, "The conservation of life environment shall be balanced against the needs of economic development."[54] This provision was deleted in 1970, when Japan had achieved economic strength.

Developing Effective Legislation

U.S. legislators have several options in developing legislation to protect the environment:

• *The independent use of the criminal sanction: direct prohibition of polluting activities.* This is the way American legislators have typically tried to cope with the problem in the past. They simply made it a criminal offense to maintain a "nuisance," that is, an ongoing activity that pollutes the water, the soil, or the air.

• *The dependent-direct use of the criminal sanction: prohibition of certain polluting activities that exceed specified limits.* This is a more sophisticated legislative method. If pollution is to be kept at a low level, no one person or company can be allowed to emit more than an insignificant amount of noxious waste into the environment. This amount is fixed by administrative regulation. Anyone who exceeds the limit commits a criminal offense.

• *The dependent-indirect approach: criminal sanction reserved for firms that fail to comply with specific rulings rendered by administrative organs against violators of standards.* Under this option, polluters have already been identified by regulatory agencies, and they are now under order to comply with the agencies' requirements. If they violate these orders, a criminal punishment can be imposed.

- *The preventive use of the criminal sanction: penalties imposed for failure to install or maintain prescribed antipollution equipment.* This is the newest and most sophisticated means of regulating polluting industries. The law determines what preventive and protective measures must be taken (to filter industrial wastewater, to put chemical screens on smokestacks, and so on). Any firm that fails to take the prescribed measures is guilty of a violation.[55]

In the past, legal systems relied primarily on the independent use of the criminal sanction. More recent legislation has concentrated on administrative orders and technological prevention.

Curbing Corporate Crime

Laws and regulations prescribing criminal sanctions have been passed and continue to be passed to guard the public against the dangers rooted in the power of corporate enterprise. As we noted, Congress passed sentencing guidelines that significantly increased corporate sanctions but at the same time allowed for reductions in fines where there was evidence of organizational due diligence—that is, implementation of effective ethics **corporate compliance programs**.[56] While such laws, regulations, and guidelines may provide some disincentives for illegal acts, many governments recognize that criminal justice systems are not well prepared to deal with economic crimes, in terms of either strategy or resources.[57] They also recognize the importance of attacking this problem at the international level, perhaps by designing strategies, standards, and guidelines that may be helpful to all governments.[58]

A disturbing thought remains: Is imposing criminal liability on the corporations themselves for their conduct really the best way to curb corporate misconduct? If corporations act on the decisions of their principal officers or agents, might it not be appropriate to restrict the reach of the law to these corporate actors rather than to subject the innocent and uninformed shareholders to financial loss? Why not rely more on administrative and civil proceedings? Both can and often do contain penalties that exceed those of the criminal law.

The recent spate of corporate scandals has brought about new legislation to combat corporate crime. Of particular note is the Sarbanes-Oxley Act of 2002. At the center of this act are provisions that mandate auditor independence and increased penalties for securities fraud.

Curbing corporate crime is as much a matter of politics as of careful law reform. As the effects of new legislation take place, we will see whether critics are right that these first few steps are not enough.

■ *Mary Shapiro, appointed by President Barack Obama, was sworn in on January 27, 2009 as the 29th chairman of the Securities and Exchange Commission.*

The Future of White-Collar and Corporate Crime

Some of the most respected names on Wall Street are under investigation or indictment or lie in ruins, bankrupt. Others have been criminally convicted and are desperately reinventing themselves. From WorldCom to Lehman Brothers, the very companies that made billions for investors in the 1990s are both perpetrators and victims of fraud, mismanagement, and conflicts of interest. And repercussions from the scandals continue in an economy that brings back memories of the Great Depression.

The icon of this wave of corporate scandals is a company that now lies in ruin. Its property was put up for auction. Its employees desperately searched for jobs. If you go on eBay, you can buy a copy of the company's ethics code put up for sale by former employees looking to make a couple of dollars and prove the point that what companies say they are doing and what they actually do are often two very different things. In 2000, this company had worldwide assets of more than $65 billion and revenue of $101 billion. As of 2000, *Fortune* magazine called it "the Most Innovative Company in America." That year, the same magazine ranked it 22nd of the "100 Best Companies to Work for in America."

One cannot imagine working for a more ethical and socially minded company. In its 2000 Corporate Responsibility Annual Report, the chairman and CEO of this company, Kenneth Lay, articulated four of its guiding principles:

Respect: We will work to foster mutual respect with communities and stakeholders who are affected by our operations; we will treat others as we would like to be treated ourselves.

Integrity: We will examine the impacts, positive and negative, of our business on the environment and on society, and will integrate human health, social, and environmental considerations into our internal management and value system.

Communication: We will strive to foster understanding and support with our stakeholders and communities, as well as measure and communicate our performance.

Excellence: We will continue to improve our performance and will encourage our business partners and suppliers to adhere to the same standards.

The name of this company, in case you have not yet guessed it, is Enron Corporation. Enron was created in 1985 following a merger of Houston Natural Gas and InterNorth, a natural gas company with headquarters in Omaha, Nebraska. Both companies were in the business of transporting and selling natural gas, and their merger created a network of more than 37,000 miles of gas pipeline. Soon after the merger, however, deregulation of the nation's energy markets, including the natural gas market, posed a significant challenge for Enron's business model. With the help of the large and prestigious consulting firm of McKinsey & Co., Enron diversified, going into the business of creating its own natural gas market, that is, buying and selling gas through contracts while controlling costs and prices.

Jeff Skilling, the young McKinsey consultant who brought the idea of Enron's creating its own energy market, was hired as chairman and CEO of Enron Finance Corporation, later becoming president and chief operating officer of Enron. The rest is history—a very sad page of business history. The history of Enron is marked by a single employee corporate **whistle-blower,** Sherron Watkins, who sent a one-page anonymous letter to Ken Lay (then chief executive officer) immediately after Jeff Skilling unexpectedly resigned. Portions of it read:

> Has Enron become a risky place to work? For those of us who didn't get rich over the last few years, can we afford to stay? . . . The spotlight will be on us, the market just can't accept that Skilling is leaving his dream job. I think that the valuation issues can be fixed and reported with other good will write-downs to occur in 2002. How do we fix the Raptor and Condor deals? They unwind in 2002 and 2003, we will have to pony up Enron stock and that won't go unnoticed.
>
> To the layman on the street, it will look like we recognized funds flow of $800 million from merchant asset sales in 1999 by selling to a vehicle (Condor) that we capitalized with a

promise of Enron stock in later years. Is that really funds flow or is it cash from equity issuance?

> We have recognized over $550 million of fair value gains on stocks via our swaps with Raptor. Much of that stock has declined significantly—Avici by 98 percent from $178 million, to $5 million; the New Power Company by 80 percent from $40 a share, to $6 a share. The value in the swaps won't be there for Raptor, so once again Enron will issue stock to offset these losses. Raptor is an LJM entity. It sure looks to the layman on the street that we are hiding losses in a related company and will compensate that company with Enron stock in the future.
>
> I am incredibly nervous that we will implode in a wave of accounting scandals. My eight years of Enron work history will be worth nothing on my résumé, the business world will consider the past successes as nothing but an elaborate accounting hoax. Skilling is resigning now for "personal reasons" but I would think he wasn't having fun, looked down the road and knew this stuff was unfixable and would rather abandon ship now than resign in shame in two years.

You need not understand the accounting alchemy that Enron used to defraud investors—for example, special-purpose entities like Raptor or Condor and "related party transactions and disclosures." Many accountants still find these technicalities difficult to explain. Suffice it to say, Enron was built on an accounting house of cards. When that house tumbled down, a host of victims emerged, from the thousands of loyal and hard-working Enron employees to countless investors whose pensions and retirement plans dramatically lost value. Once nearly a $90-per-share stock, Enron stock certificates trade on eBay as collectors' items. The accounting firm that offered advice and counsel to Enron, Arthur Andersen, LLP, was indicted and convicted of obstruction of justice for shredding thousands of documents related to Enron audits. They, too, suffered corporate death. Tens of thousands of Andersen employees sought employment elsewhere as the accounting world watched in horror. It was common to refer to Andersen as one of the top five accounting firms. Now there are four.

Most important, Enron and the fall of Arthur Andersen sent a strong signal that Wall Street had a problem with corporate governance, that is, the way in which a corporation is managed and overseen. Principles of corporate governance require that both senior management and the board of directors participate in the affairs of the company. But they do so differently. Senior managers run the day-to-day operations of the company. The board of directors has the special function of providing an independent oversight of senior management—an independent check on managers. This is accomplished through governance and nominating committees, audit committees, finance committees, and compensation committees that tirelessly review the health of the company. In recent years, boards have been called upon to see that systems of internal controls are implemented and monitored.

What happened to the systems of control and governance structures of Enron? Why and how did all of the gatekeepers (accountants, lawyers, credit-rating agencies) fail? Answers are difficult to find, particularly because Enron followed many of the "best practices" of corporate governance, including an independent board of directors of competent outsiders. Enron had all the trappings of an ethical, Fortune 500 company with a bright future. Enron hired the best accountants and lawyers. Until answers to the many questions about Enron emerge, it is only fair to ask, How significant is the problem of corporate misgovernance in the United States? To this question the only answer is that the future of Wall Street and its perceived legitimacy hang in the balance.

Organizational crimes are characterized by the use of a legitimate or illegitimate business enterprise for illegal profit. As American corporations grew in the nineteenth and twentieth centuries, they amassed much of the nation's wealth. Many corporations abused their economic power. Government stepped in to curb such abuses by legislation.

Edwin Sutherland, who provided the first scholarly insight into the wrongdoing of corporations, originated the concept of white-collar crime. Subsequent scholars have distinguished white-collar crime, committed by individuals, from corporate crime, committed by business organizations. Corporate or individual white-collar offenses include securities-related crimes, such as misrepresentation and churning; bankruptcy fraud of various kinds; fraud against the government, in particular contract and procurement fraud; consumer fraud; insurance fraud; tax fraud; bribery and political fraud; and insider-related fraud. In the twentieth century, corporations have been subjected to criminal liability for an increasing number of offenses, including common law crimes and environmental as well as other statutory offenses.

The phases of the corporate criminal law include a transition from a period when concerns over personhood predominated to a time when corporations used creative strategies to avoid criminal liability. In recent years—after a series of compliance and governance failures and multiple scandals—legislators, regulators, judges, and academics are raising questions about extant law. Models of corporate culpability that focus on proactive fault, reactive fault, corporate culture, constructive concepts of organizations, and corporate policy extend current law. With new allegations of fraud stemming from the credit crisis and the recent recession, it is clear that the future of organizational criminality and the legitimacy of Wall Street are inextricably connected.

"Sutherland challenged the traditional image of criminals and the predominant etiological theories of crime of his day. The white-collar criminals he identified were middle-aged men of respectability and high-social status. They lived in affluent neighborhoods, and they were well respected in the community. Sutherland was not the first to draw attention to such criminals. In earlier decades, scholars such as W. A. Bonger (1916) and E. A. Ross (1907) and popular writers such as Upton Sinclair (1906) and Lincoln Steffens (1903) pointed out a variety of misdeeds by businessmen and elites. However, such people were seldom considered by those who wrote about or studied crime and were not a major concern of the public or policy makers when addressing the crime problem." (SOURCE: David Weisburd and Elin Waring, *White-Collar Crime and Criminal Careers* [Cambridge: Cambridge University Press, 2001], p. 8.)

Questions for Discussion Professors Weisburd and Waring make the point, in the introduction to their book *White-Collar Crime and Criminal Careers*, that much of the conventional wisdom of white-collar offenders is untrue. These researchers previously established that white-collar offenders are not "elite" offenders as Sutherland conceived. White-collar criminals generally come from the middle class and have multiple contacts with the criminal justice system. White-collar offenders have criminal careers as well! What can you conclude from the similarity between and among white-collar and street criminals? Should criminologists expect meaningful differences in the life course of offenders? Should policy makers ensure different or similar treatment in the criminal process?

CHAPTER 12

YOU BE THE CRIMINOLOGIST

For obvious reasons, the extent of corporate crime is difficult to assess and measure. But criminologists do not shy away from significant challenges.

How would you approach the problem of assessing and measuring crimes committed by corporations?

KEY TERMS

The numbers next to the terms refer to the pages on which the terms are defined.

bankruptcy fraud (303)
boiler rooms (303)
churning (302)
constructive corporate culpability (316)
consumer fraud (306)
corporate compliance programs (323)
corporate crime (309)
corporate ethos (316)
corporate policy (316)
embezzlement (308)
insider trading (302)
occupational crimes (301)
organizational due diligence (313)
proactive corporate fault (316)
reactive corporate fault (316)
Sherman Antitrust Act (317)
stock manipulation (303)
vicarious liability (316)
whistle-blower (324)
white-collar crime (299)

Public Order Crimes

13

Drug Abuse and Crime
The History of Drug Abuse
The Extent of Drug Abuse
Patterns of Drug Abuse
Crime-Related Activities
Drug Control
Alcohol and Crime
The History of Legalization
Crime-Related Activities
Sexual Morality Offenses
Deviate Sexual Intercourse by Force or
  Imposition
Prostitution
Pornography
Review
Criminology & Public Policy
You Be the Criminologist
Key Terms

■ Strip clubs and other adult entertainment shops tend to be concentrated in seedy parts of town, where public order crimes are also frequently committed.

In cities across the country and around the world, people buying and selling illicit goods and services congregate in certain areas easily identifiable by storefronts that boldly advertise live sex shows. Shops feature everything from the latest DVD pornography to sex toys of every sort. Prostitutes openly solicit; drunks propped up in doorways clutch brown bags; drug addicts deal small amounts of whatever they can sell to support their habit. The friendly locals will deliver virtually any service to visitors at any price.

Cities across the country and around the world also are home to an under-ground market—on the Internet, in informal "shadow" markets in developing nations, and in the living rooms and bedrooms of suburban America—where people buying and selling illicit goods and services seek to avoid the scrutiny of law enforcement, exploit lax enforcement of laws, and avoid detection or apprehension because of the sheer number of law violators. From prostitution to the purchase of child pornography, from "recreational" drug use to the transport of cocaine or heroin across international borders, the crimes are varied. They are generally increasing in rate, entail vastly

different degrees of harm and extent of
victimization, and are as global as any
form of commerce. As we shall see, to call
these offenses "public order crimes" does
not capture their breadth, scale, or
complexity.

DRUG ABUSE AND CRIME

An 82-year-old woman from Bogota who struggled economically to care for her mentally retarded son was convinced by narco-traffickers
that one trip to New York as a "drug mule" would
supply her with enough money for her son's
future. But her dream ended when a pellet full of
narcotics ruptured in her stomach as she got into
a cab at John F. Kennedy Airport in New York.
She died before the cab could reach a hospital.[1] In
New York City, a heroin addict admits that "the
only livin' thing that counts is the fix . . . : Like I
would steal off anybody—anybody, at all, my
own mother gladly included."[2] In Chicago, crack
cocaine has transformed some of the country's
toughest gangs into ghetto-based drug-trafficking
organizations that guard their turf with automatic
weapons and assault rifles.[3]

On a college campus in the northeast, a crowd
sits in the basement of a fraternity house drinking
beer and smoking pot through the night. At a
beachfront house in Miami, three young professional couples gather for a barbecue. After dinner
they sit down at a card table in the playroom. On
a mirror, someone lines up a white powdery substance into rows about 1/8 inch wide and 1 inch
long. Through rolled-up paper they breathe the
powder into their nostrils and await the "rush" of
the coke. In a quiet suburban home, two middle-
school students inhale paint thinner after school.

These incidents demonstrate that when we
speak of the "drug problem," we are talking about
a wide variety of conditions that stretch beyond
our borders, that involve all social classes, that in
one way or another touch most people's lives,
and that cost society significant sums of money
(Figure 13.1). The drug scene includes manufacturers, importers, primary distributors (for large
geographical areas), smugglers (who transport
large quantities of drugs from their place of origin), dealers (who sell drugs on the street and in
crack houses), corrupt criminal justice officials,
and users who endanger other people's lives
through negligence (train engineers, pilots, physicians) (Table 13.1).

The drug problem is further complicated by
the wide diversity of substances abused, their varying effects on the mind and body, and the kinds of
dependencies users develop. There is also the much-
debated issue of the connection between drug use

and crime—an issue infinitely more complex than
the stereotype of maddened addicts committing
heinous acts because they either are under the
influence of drugs or need to get the money to
support a habit. Many of the crimes we have discussed in earlier chapters are part of what has
been called the nation's (or the world's) drug
problem. Let us examine this problem in detail.

The History of Drug Abuse

The use of chemical substances that alter physiological and psychological functioning dates back
to the Old Stone Age.[4] Egyptian relics from 3500
B.C. depict the use of opium in religious rituals. By
1600 B.C., an Egyptian reference work listed opium
as an analgesic, or painkiller. The Incas of South
America are known to have used cocaine at least
5,000 years ago. Cannabis, the hemp plant from
which marijuana and hashish are derived, also
has a 5,000-year history.[5]

Since antiquity, people have cultivated a variety of drugs for religious, medicinal, and social
purposes. The modern era of drug abuse in the
United States began with the use of drugs for
medicinal purposes. By the nineteenth century,
the two components of opium, which is derived
from the sap of the opium poppy, were identified
and given the names "morphine" and "codeine."
Ignorant of the addictive properties of these
drugs, physicians used them to treat a wide variety of human illnesses. So great was their popularity that they found their way into almost all
patent medicines used for pain relief and were
even incorporated into soothing syrups for babies
(Mother Barley's Quieting Syrup and Mumm's
Elixir were very popular).

During the Civil War, the use of injectable morphine to ease the pain of battle casualties was so
extensive that morphine addiction among veterans came to be known as the "soldier's disease."[6]
By the time the medical profession and the public
recognized just how addictive morphine was, its
use had reached epidemic proportions. Then, in
1898, the Bayer Company in Germany introduced
a new opiate, supposedly a nonaddictive substitute for morphine and codeine. It came out under
the trade name Heroin; it proved to be even more
addictive than morphine.[7]

When cocaine, which was isolated from the
coca leaf in 1860, appeared on the national drug
scene, it, too, was used for medicinal purposes.
(Its use to unblock the sinuses initiated the "snort-
ing" of cocaine into the nostrils.) Its popularity
spread, and soon it was used in other products:
Peruvian Wine of Coca ($1 a bottle in the Sears,
Roebuck catalog); a variety of tonics; and, the
most famous of all, Coca-Cola, which was made
with coca until 1903.[8]

As the consumption of opium products (narcotics) and cocaine spread, states passed a variety

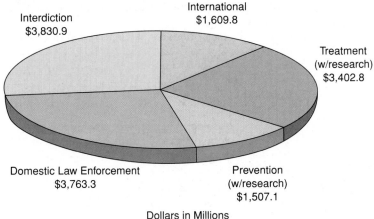

Federal Drug Control Spending by Function, FY2009*

Interdiction
$3,830.9

International
$1,609.8

Treatment
(w/research)
$3,402.8

Prevention
(w/research)
$1,507.1

Domestic Law Enforcement
$3,763.3

Dollars in Millions
*Total President's Request = $14.1 Billion

FIGURE 13.1 National spending for drug control.

Sources: (top) *National Drug Control Strategy, 2008 Annual Report* (Washington, D.C.: The White House, 2008), p. 5; (bottom) Office of National Drug Control Policy, *Fact Sheet: Drug Data Summary* (Washington, D.C.: U.S. Government Printing Office, April 1999), updated to 2002.

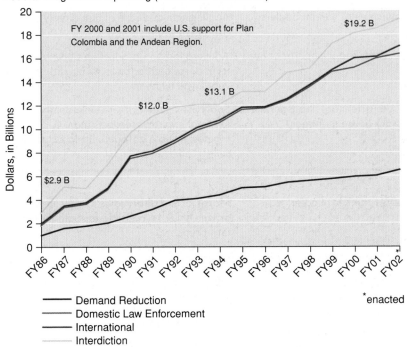

Demand Reduction and Domestic Law Enforcement Account for the Bulk of Federal Drug Control Spending (Fiscal Year 1986–2001)

FY 2000 and 2001 include U.S. support for Plan Colombia and the Andean Region.

$19.2 B

$13.1 B

$12.0 B

$2.9 B

Dollars, in Billions

FY86 FY87 FY88 FY89 FY90 FY91 FY92 FY93 FY94 FY95 FY96 FY97 FY98 FY99 FY00 FY01 FY02*

*enacted

— Demand Reduction
— Domestic Law Enforcement
— International
— Interdiction

of laws to restrict the sale of these substances. Federal authorities estimated that there were 200,000 addicts in the early 1900s. Growing concern over the increase in addiction led in 1914 to the passage of the Harrison Act, designed to regulate the domestic use, sale, and transfer of opium and coca products. Though this legislation decreased the number of addicts, it was a double-edged sword: By restricting the importation and distribution of drugs, it paved the way for the drug smuggling and black-market operations that are so deeply entrenched today.

It was not until the 1930s that the abuse of marijuana began to arouse public concern. Because marijuana use was associated with groups outside the social mainstream—petty criminals, jazz musicians, bohemians, and, in the Southwest, Mexicans—a public outcry for its regulation arose.[9] Congress responded with the Marijuana Tax Act of 1937, which placed a prohibitive tax of $100 an ounce on the drug. With the passage of the Boggs Act in 1951, penalties for possession of and trafficking in marijuana (and other controlled substances) increased. Despite all the legislation, the popularity of marijuana continued.

As the drugs being used proliferated to include glue, tranquilizers (such as Valium and Librium), LSD, and many other substances, the public became increasingly aware of the dangers of drug abuse. In 1970, another major drug law, the

TABLE 13.1 Roles and Functions in the Drug Distribution Business Compared with Those in Legitimate Industry

Approximate Role Equivalents in Legal Markets	Roles by Common Names at Various Stages of the Drug Distribution Business	Major Functions Accomplished at This Level
PROVIDERS		
Grower producer	Coca farmer, opium farmer, marijuana grower	Grow coca, opium, marijuana—the raw materials
Manufacturer	Collector, transporter, elaborator, chemist, drug lord	All stages for preparation of heroin, cocaine, marijuana as commonly sold
TRAFFICKERS		
Importer	Multikilo importer, mule, airplane pilot, smuggler, trafficker, money launderer	Smuggling of large quantities of substances into the United States
Wholesale distributor	Major distributor, investor, "kilo connection"	Transportation and redistribution of multi-kilograms and single kilograms
DEALERS		
Regional distributor	Pound and ounce men, weight dealers	Adulteration and sale of moderately expensive products
Retail store owner	House connections, suppliers, crack-house supplier	Adulteration and production of retail-level dosage units (bags, vials, grams) in very large numbers
Assistant manager, security chief, or accountant	"Lieutenant," "muscle man," transporter, crew boss, crack-house manager/proprietor	Supervises three or more sellers, enforces informal contracts, collects money, distributes multiple dosage units to actual sellers
SELLERS		
Store clerk, salesmen (door-to-door and phone)	Street drug seller, runner, juggler	Makes actual direct sales to consumer; private seller responsible for both money and drugs
LOW-LEVEL DISTRIBUTORS		
Advertiser, security guard, leaflet distributor	Steerer, tout, cop man, lookout, holder runner, help friend, guard, go-between	Assists in making sales, advertises, protects seller from police and criminals, solicits customers; handles drugs or money but not both
Servant, temporary employee	Run shooting gallery, injector (of drugs), freebaser, taster, apartment cleaner, drug bagger, fence, money launderer	Provides short-term services to drug users or sellers for money or drugs; not responsible for money or drugs

SOURCE: From Bruce D. Johnson, Terry Williams, Kojo A. Dir, and Harry Sanabria, "Drug Abuse in the Inner City: Impact on Hard-Drug Users and the Community," in *Drugs and Crime*, vol. 13: *Crime and Justice*, eds. Michael Tonry and James Q. Wilson (Chicago: University of Chicago Press, 1990), p. 19. Copyright © 1990 by the University of Chicago. All rights reserved. Reprinted by permission of the University of Chicago Press.

Comprehensive Drug Abuse Prevention and Control Act (the Controlled Substances Act), updated all federal drug laws since the Harrison Act.[10] This act placed marijuana in the category of the most serious substances. The 1970 federal legislation made it necessary to bring state legislation into conformity with federal law. The Uniform Controlled Substances Act was drafted and now is the law in 48 states, the District of Columbia, Puerto Rico, the Virgin Islands, and Guam.

Most of the basic federal antidrug legislation has been drawn together in Title 21 of the United States Code, the collection of all federal laws. It includes many amendments passed since 1970, especially the Anti-Drug Abuse Act of 1988, which states, "It is the declared policy of the United

States Government to create a drug-free America by 1995."[11]

Title 21, as amended, has elaborate provisions for the funding of national and international drug programs; establishes the Office of National Drug Control Policy, headed by a so-called drug czar; and provides stiff penalties for drug offenses. The manufacture, distribution, and dispensing of listed substances in stated (large) quantities are each subject to a prison sentence of 10 years to life and a fine (for individuals) of $4 million to $10 million. Even simple possession now carries a punishment of up to 1 year in prison and a $100,000 fine. Title 21, along with other recent crime-control legislation, defines many other drug crimes as well and provides for the forfeiture of any property constituting or derived from the proceeds of drug trading.

The Extent of Drug Abuse

The National Survey on Drug Use and Health (NSDUH) provides some of the best estimates of drug use and drug use trends for the United States.[12] According to the 2007 NSDUH survey, an estimated 19.9 million Americans (8.3 percent) age 12 and older are current users, and 6.9 million Americans 12 or older abuse illicit drugs or have a dependence on illicit drugs (Figure 13.2). The 2007 NSDUH survey revealed a near across-the-board decline in drug use. Consider the decrease in the use of marijuana, cocaine, and LSD shown in Table 13.2. Estimates of marijuana use or dependence among youths 12 to 17 declined from 8.2 percent in 2002 to 6.7 percent in 2007. (See Table 13.3 for more survey findings.)

Patterns of Drug Abuse

New and more potent varieties of illicit substances, as well as increasing levels of violent crime associ-

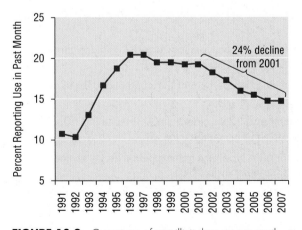

FIGURE 13.2 Current use of any illicit drug among youth.

Source: National Drug Control Strategy 2008 Annual Report (Washington, D.C.: The White House, 2008), p. 1; available at http://www.whitehouse.gov/news/releases/2008/03/national _drug_control_strategy_2008.pdf.

ated with drug abuse, have led researchers to ask many questions about the phenomenon. Is drug abuse a symptom of an underlying mental or psychological disorder that makes some people more vulnerable than others? Some investigators argue that the addict is characterized by strong dependency needs, feelings of inadequacy, a need for immediate gratification, and lack of internal controls.[13] Or is it possible that addicts lack certain body chemicals and that drugs make them feel better by compensating for that deficit?

Perhaps the causes are environmental. Is drug abuse a norm in deteriorated inner cities, where youngsters are learning how to behave from older addicted role models? Do people escape from the realities of slum life by retreating into drug abuse?[14] If so, how do we explain drug abuse among the upper classes?

Just as there are many causes of drug abuse, there are many addict lifestyles—and the lifestyles may be linked to the use of particular substances. During the 1950s, heroin abuse began to increase markedly in the inner cities, particularly among young black and Hispanic males.[15] In fact, it was their drug of choice throughout the 1960s and early 1970s. Heroin addicts spend their days buying heroin; finding a safe place to shoot the substance into a vein with a needle attached to a hypodermic syringe; waiting for the euphoric feeling, or rush, that follows the injection; and ultimately reaching a feeling of overall well-being known as "a high," which lasts about 4 hours.[16] The heroin abuser's lifestyle is typically characterized by poor health, crime, arrest, imprisonment, and temporary stays in drug treatment programs.[17] Today AIDS, which is spread, among other ways, by the shared use of needles, has become the most serious health problem among heroin addicts.

During the 1960s, marijuana became one of the major drugs of choice in the United States, particularly among white, middle-class young people who identified themselves as antiestablishment. Their lifestyles were distinct from those of the inner-city heroin addicts. What began as a hippie drug culture in the Haight-Ashbury area of San Francisco spread quickly through the country's college campuses.[18] In fact, a Harvard psychologist, Timothy Leary, traveled across the country in the 1960s telling students to "turn on, tune in, and drop out." Young marijuana users tended to live for the moment. Disillusioned by what they perceived as a rigid and hypocritical society, they challenged its norms through deviant behavior. Drugs—first marijuana, then hallucinogens (principally LSD), amphetamines, and barbiturates— came to symbolize the counterculture.[19]

In the 1960s and 1970s, attitudes toward recreational drug use became quite lax, perhaps as a result of the wide acceptance of marijuana.[20]

TABLE 13.2 Percent Reporting Past Month Use

	2001	2007	Change as a % of 2001
Any Illicit Drug	**19.4%**	**14.8%**	**−224***
Marijuana	16.6%	12.4%	−25*
MDMA (Ecstasy)	2.4%	1.1%	−54*
LSD	1.5%	0.6%	−60*
Amphetamines	4.7%	3.2%	−32*
Inhalants	2.8%	2.6%	−7
Methamphetamine	1.4%	0.5%	−64*
Steroids	0.9%	0.6%	−33*
Cocaine	1.5%	1.4%	−7
Heroin	0.4%	0.4%	0
Alcohol	35.5%	30.1%	−15*
Cigarettes	20.2%	13.6%	−33*

*Denotes statistically significant change from 2001.

Note: Past month use, 8th, 10th, and 12th grade combined; percent change calculated from figures having more precision than shown.

SOURCE: 2007 Monitoring the Future (MTF) study. special tabulations for combined 8th, 10th, and 12th graders (December 2007). National Drug Control Strategy 2008 Annual Report (Washington, D.C.: The White House, 2008), p. 1; available at http://www.whitehouse.gov/releases/2008/03/national_drug_control_strategy_2008.pdf.

TABLE 13.3 2007 National Survey on Drug Use and Health Statistics: Illicit Drug Use and Alcohol Use

- In 2007, an estimated 19.9 million Americans age 12 or older were current (past month) illicit drug users, meaning they had used an illicit drug during the month prior to the survey interview. This estimate represents 8.0 percent of the population age 12 years old or older. Illicit drugs include marijuana/hashish, cocaine (including crack), heroin, hallucinogens, inhalants, or prescription-type psychotherapeutics used nonmedically.

- The rate of current illicit drug use among persons age 12 or older in 2007 (8.0 percent) was similar to the rate in 2006 (8.3 percent).

- Marijuana was the most commonly used illicit drug (14.4 million past month users). Among persons age 12 or older, the rate of past month marijuana use in 2007 (5.8 percent) was similar to the rate in 2006 (6.0 percent).

- In 2007, there were 2.1 million current cocaine users age 12 or older, comprising 0.8 percent of the population. These estimates were similar to the number and rate in 2006 (2.4 million or 1.0 percent).

- Hallucinogens were used in the past month by 1.0 million persons (0.4 percent) age 12 or older in 2007, including 503,000 (0.2 percent) who had used Ecstasy. These estimates were similar to the corresponding estimates for 2006.

- There were 6.9 million (2.8 percent) persons age 12 or older who used prescription-type psychotherapeutic drugs nonmedically in the past month. Of these, 5.2 million used pain relievers, the same as the number in 2006.

- In 2007, there were an estimated 529,000 current users of methamphetamine age 12 or older (0.2 percent of the population). These estimates were not significantly different from the estimates for 2006 (731,000 or 0.3 percent).

- Among youths ages 12 to 17, the current illicit drug use rate remained stable from 2006 (9.8 percent) to 2007 (9.5 percent). Between 2002 and 2007, youth rates declined significantly for illicit drugs in general (from 11.6 to 9.5 percent) and for marijuana, cocaine, hallucinogens, LSD, Ecstasy, prescription-type drugs used nonmedically, pain relievers, stimulants, methamphetamine, and illicit drugs other than marijuana.

- The rate of current marijuana use among youths ages 12 to 17 declined from 8.2 percent in 2002 to 6.7 percent in 2007. The rate decreased for both males (from 9.1 to 7.5 percent) and females (from 7.2 to 5.8 percent). *(continues)*

- Among young adults ages 18 to 25, there were decreases from 2006 to 2007 in the rate of current use of several drugs, including cocaine (from 2.2 to 1.7 percent), Ecstasy (from 1.0 to 0.7 percent), stimulants (from 1.4 to 1.1 percent), methamphetamine (from 0.6 to 0.4 percent), and illicit drugs other than marijuana (from 8.9 to 8.1 percent).

- From 2002 to 2007, there was an increase among young adults ages 18 to 25 in the rate of current use of prescription pain relievers, from 4.1 to 4.6 percent. There were decreases in the use of hallucinogens (from 1.9 to 1.5 percent), Ecstasy (from 1.1 to 0.7 percent), and methamphetamine (from 0.6 to 0.4 percent).

- Among those ages 50 to 54, the rate of past month illicit drug use increased from 3.4 percent in 2002 to 5.7 percent in 2007. Among those ages 55 to 59, current illicit drug use showed an increase from 1.9 percent in 2002 to 4.1 percent in 2007. These trends may partially reflect the aging into these age groups of the baby boom cohort, whose lifetime rates of illicit drug use are higher than those of older cohorts.

- Among persons age 12 or older who used pain relievers nonmedically in the past 12 months, 56.5 percent reported that the source of the drug the most recent time they used was from a friend or relative for free. Another 18.1 percent reported they got the drug from just one doctor. Only 4.1 percent got the pain relievers from a drug dealer or other stranger, and 0.5 percent reported buying the drug on the Internet. Among those who reported getting the pain reliever from a friend or relative for free, 81.0 percent reported in a follow-up question that the friend or relative had obtained the drugs from just one doctor.

- Among unemployed adults age 18 or older in 2007, 18.3 percent were current illicit drug users, which was higher than the 8.4 percent of those employed full time and 10.1 percent of those employed part time. However, most illicit drug users were employed. Of the 17.4 million current illicit drug users age 18 or older in 2007, 13.1 million (75.3 percent) were employed either full or part time.

- In 2007, there were 9.9 million persons age 12 or older who reported driving under the influence of illicit drugs during the past year. This corresponds to 4.0 percent of the population age 12 or older, similar to the rate in 2006 (4.2 percent), but lower than the rate in 2002 (4.7 percent). In 2007, the rate was highest among young adults ages 18 to 25 (12.5 percent).

- Slightly more than half of Americans age 12 or older reported being current drinkers of alcohol in the 2007 survey (51.1 percent). This translates to an estimated 126.8 million people, which was similar to the 2006 estimate of 125.3 million people (50.9 percent).

- More than one-fifth (23.3 percent) of persons age 12 or older participated in binge drinking (having five or more drinks on the same occasion on at least 1 day in the 30 days prior to the survey) in 2007. This translates to about 57.8 million people, similar to the estimate in 2006.

- In 2007, heavy drinking was reported by 6.9 percent of the population age 12 or older, or 17.0 million people. This rate was the same as the rate of heavy drinking in 2006. Heavy drinking is defined as binge drinking on at least 5 days in the past 30 days.

- In 2007, among young adults ages 18 to 25, the rate of binge drinking was 41.8 percent, and the rate of heavy drinking was 14.7 percent. These rates were similar to the rates in 2006.

- The rate of current alcohol use among youths ages 12 to 17 was 15.9 percent in 2007. Youth binge and heavy drinking rates were 9.7 and 2.3 percent, respectively. These rates were essentially the same as the 2006 rates.

- Past month and binge drinking rates among underage persons (ages 12 to 20) have remained essentially unchanged since 2002. In 2007, about 10.7 million persons ages 12 to 20 (27.9 percent of this age group) reported drinking alcohol in the past month. Approximately 7.2 million (18.6 percent) were binge drinkers, and 2.3 million (6.0 percent) were heavy drinkers.

- Among persons ages 12 to 20, past month alcohol use rates in 2007 were 16.8 percent among Asians, 18.3 percent among blacks, 24.7 percent among Hispanics, 26.2 percent among those reporting two or more races, 28.3 percent among American Indians or Alaska Natives, and 32.0 percent among whites.

- In 2007, 56.3 percent of current drinkers ages 12 to 20 reported that their last use of alcohol in the past month occurred in someone else's home, and 29.4 percent reported that it had occurred in their own home. About one-third (30.2 percent) paid for the alcohol the last time they drank, including 8.2 percent who purchased the alcohol themselves and 21.8 percent who gave money to someone else to purchase it. Among those who did not pay for the alcohol they last drank, 37.2 percent got it from an unrelated person age 21 or older, 20.7 percent from another person under 21 years of age, and 19.5 percent from a parent, guardian, or other adult family member.

- In 2007, an estimated 12.7 percent of persons age 12 or older drove under the influence of alcohol at least once in the past year. This percentage has decreased since 2002, when it was 14.2 percent. From 2006 to 2007, the rate of driving under the influence of alcohol among persons ages 18 to 25 decreased from 24.4 to 22.8 percent.

SOURCE: *2007 National Survey on Drug Use and Health: National Findings* (Washington, D.C.: Department of Health and Human Services, 2007), pp. 1–3.

The countercultural Woodstock Music and Art Fair in 1969 drew over 450,000 people to open fields in New York State. The rock concert, where drugs and "free love" flowed, lasted for 4 days.

Actor Robert Downey Jr. in a Malibu, California, courtroom just prior to being sentenced to 6 months in jail for violating parole on a prior drug conviction. Subsequently, in 2002, he was once again in trouble when authorities allegedly found drugs in his Palm Springs hotel room.

By the 1980s, cocaine, once associated only with deviants, had become the drug of choice among the privileged, who watched (and copied) the well-publicized drug-oriented lifestyles of some celebrities and athletes. Typical cocaine users were well-educated, prosperous, upwardly mobile professionals in their twenties and thirties. They were lawyers and architects, editors and stockbrokers. They earned enough money to spend at least $100 an evening on their illegal recreational activities. By and large they were otherwise law-abiding, even though they knew their behavior was against the law.

The popularity of cocaine waned toward the end of the 1980s. The same is not true for crack, however, which spread to the inner-city population that had abused heroin in the latter part of the 1980s.[21] Crack is cheaper than powdered cocaine, fast-acting, and powerful. Though individual doses are inexpensive, once a person is hooked on crack, a daily supply can run between $100 and $250. The price of cocaine continues to rise (Figure 13.3).

Drug addicts continually search for new ways to extend their highs. In 1989, a mixture of crack and heroin, called "crank," began to be used. Crank is smoked in a pipe.[22] It is potentially very dangerous—first, because it prolongs the brief high of crack alone and, second, because it appeals to younger drug addicts who are concerned about the link between AIDS and the sharing of hypodermic needles. The history of drug abuse is evolutionary. "Crank" is now the name of methamphetamine—also known as "ice," "crystal," "chalk," and "speed."

Crime-Related Activities

Many researchers have examined the criminal implications of addiction to heroin and, more recently, cocaine. James Inciardi found that 356 addicts in Miami, according to self-reports, committed 118,134 offenses (27,464 Index crimes) over a 1-year period.[23] A national program, Drug Use Forecasting, found that in 1996, 49 to 82 percent of arrestees in 24 major U.S. cities had used drugs.[24] Official statistics on drug-related offenses make it quite clear that street crime is significantly related to drug abuse.

The nature of the drug–crime relationship, however, is less clear. Is the addict typically an adolescent who never committed a crime before he or she became hooked, but who thereafter was forced to commit crimes to get money to support the drug habit? In other words, does drug abuse lead to crime?[25] Or does criminal behavior precede drug abuse? Another possibility is that both drug abuse and criminal behavior stem from the same factors (biological, psychological, or sociological).[26] The debate continues, and many questions are still unanswered. But on one point most researchers agree: Whatever the temporal or causal sequence of drug abuse and crime, the frequency and seriousness of criminality increase as addiction increases. Drug abuse may not "cause" criminal behavior, but it does enhance it.[27]

Until the late 1970s, most investigators of the drug–crime relationship reported that drug abusers were arrested primarily for property offenses. Recent scholarly literature, however, presents a

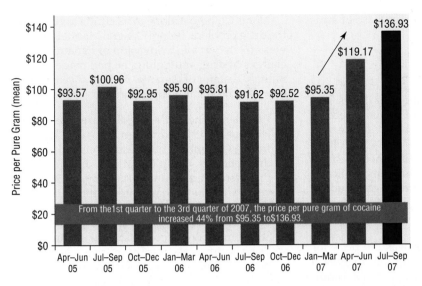

FIGURE 13.3 United States cocaine purchase prices: April 2005–September 2007.

Source: 2007 National Survey on Drug Use and Health: National Findings (Washington, D.C.: Department of Health and Human Services, 2007), p. 36.

different perspective. There appears to be an increasing amount of violence associated with drugs, and it may be attributable largely to the appearance of crack. Beginning in the 1980s and continuing to today, drug wars became more frequent. Cities across the country have been divided into distinct turfs. Rival drug dealers settle disputes with guns, power struggles within a single drug enterprise lead to assaults and homicides, one dealer robs another, informers are killed, their associates retaliate, and bystanders, some of them children, get caught in the cross fire.[28]

Money Laundering

The illegal drug economy is vast. Annual sales are estimated to be between $300 billion and $500 billion. The American drug economy alone generates $40 billion to $50 billion in sales. Profits are enormous, and no taxes are paid on them. Because the profits are "dirty money," they must undergo **money laundering.** Typically, the cash obtained from drug sales in the United States is physically smuggled out of the country because it cannot be legally exported without disclosure (Table 13.4).

Smuggling cash is not easy—$1 million in $20 bills weighs 100 pounds—yet billions of dollars are exported, in false-bottomed suitcases and smugglers' vests, to countries that allow numbered bank accounts without identification of names.

New methods of laundering drug profits that do not involve physical transfer of cash have recently been devised, such as fake real estate transactions; purchase of gold, antiques, and art; and cybercurrency (microchip-based electronic money), which utilizes the Internet. Such transactions permit electronic transfer of drug funds worldwide with minimal chance of detection. Once deposited in foreign accounts, the funds are "clean" and can be returned to legitimate businesses and investments. They may also be used

TABLE 13.4 A Typical Money-Laundering Scheme

La Mina, the Mine, reportedly laundered $1.2 billion for the Colombian cartels over a 2-year period.

Currency from selling cocaine was packed in boxes labeled "jewelry" and sent by armored car to Ropex, a jewelry maker in Los Angeles.

↓

The cash was counted and deposited in banks, but few suspicions were raised because the gold business is based on cash.

↓

Ropex then wire-transferred the money to New York banks in payment for fictitious gold purchased from Ronel, allegedly a gold bullion business.

↓

Ronel shipped Ropex bars of lead painted gold to complete the fake transaction. Ropex used the alleged sale of this gold to other jewelry businesses to cover further currency conversions.

↓

Ronel then transferred the funds from American banks to South American banks where the Colombian cartel could gain access to them.

SOURCE: Adapted from "Getting Banks to Just Say 'No,'" *Business Week*, Apr. 17, 1989, p. 17; and Maggie Mahar, "Dirty Money: It Triggers a Bold New Attack in the War on Drugs," *Barron's*, **69** (June, 1989): 6–38, at p. 7. From the U.S. Department of Justice, *Drugs, Crime and the Justice System* (Washington, D.C.: U.S. Government Printing Office, 1992).

for illegal purposes, such as the purchase of arms for export to terrorist groups.

The Political Impact

The political impact of the drug trade on producer countries is devastating. In the late 1970s and early 1980s, the government of Bolivia became completely corrupt. The minister of justice was referred to as the "minister of cocaine." In Colombia, drug lords and terrorists combined their resources to wrest power from the democratically elected government. Thirteen supreme court judges and 167 police officers were killed; the minister of justice and the ambassador to Hungary were assassinated.

The message was that death was the price for refusal to succumb to drug corruption. In 1989, a highly respected Colombian presidential candidate who had come out against the cocaine cartel was assassinated. The government remained fragile and the situation precarious. Over the years, the scandal aroused by liaisons between notorious drug lords and high-ranking government officials has endured. One of the scandals, perhaps most injurious to diplomatic relations with the United States, was that involving Colombia's former president Ernesto Samper. Samper received $6 million toward his 1994 campaign fund from the renowned Cali cartel—the leader in cocaine trafficking. Despite his exoneration by Colombia's House of Representatives, the United States government sent an unequivocal message to President Samper by revoking his U.S. visa and decertifying Colombia (the United States "certifies" countries considered as allies in the drug war).

Nor is Colombia alone in its efforts to cope with the drug problem. Before General Manuel Noriega was arrested in a U.S. invasion of Panama to face charges of drug smuggling, he had made himself military dictator of Panama. By 1996 (7 years later), however, little had really changed:

> President Ernesto Perez Balladares has admitted that his 1994 campaign received $51,000 from a Colombian businessman later jailed on drug charges. Other donations to the President are also under scrutiny. . . . Seven years after the military intervention, Panama's banking system once again is a conduit for drug traffickers laundering their profits. Secret numbered accounts, legal in Panama, prevent prosecutors from putting a name to a number. Lawyers create shell corporations with little more than a stroke of a pen and about $1,000. Those behind the companies remain a mystery. The collapse earlier this year of a Panamanian bank, under investigation in the US for money laundering, with links to two senior aides of the president underscored, for many, the pervasiveness of the problem.[29]

Corruption and crime rule in all drug-producing countries. Government instability is the necessary consequence. Coups replace elections. Nor are the populations of these countries immune to addiction themselves. Several South American countries, including Colombia, Bolivia, and Peru, are now experiencing major addiction problems; Peru alone has some 60,000 addicts. The Asian narcotics-producing countries, which thought

■ A Lahu hill tribe girl in Myanmar holds opium poppies as she assists her tribe in eradicating illegal poppies.

themselves immune to the addiction problem, also became victims of their own production. Pakistan, for example, now counts about 200,000 addicts.[30]

One of the more remarkable aspects of the expansion of the drug trade has been the spread of addiction and the drug economy to the Third World and to the former socialist countries. Of all political problems, however, the most vicious is the alliance that drug dealers have forged with terrorist groups in the Near East, in Latin America, and in Europe.[31]

Drug Control

In September 1989, then-president George Bush unveiled his antidrug strategy. On the international level, the president sought modest funding for the United Nations effort to combat the international narcotics drug traffic. He also called for far greater expenditures for bilateral cooperation with other countries to deal with producers and traffickers. This effort extends to crop eradication programs.[32] He singled out Colombia, Bolivia, and Peru for such efforts and immediately sent U.S. Army assistance, including helicopters and crews, to Colombia for use in that country's very difficult battle with the Medellín cartel.

On the national level, the strategy focused on federal aid to state and local police for street-level attacks on drug users and small dealers, for whom alternative punishments such as house arrest (confinement in one's home rather than in a jail cell) and boot camps (short but harsh incarceration with military drill) were started. It also called for rigorous enforcement of forfeiture laws, under which money is confiscated from offenders if it can be established that it came from the drug trade; property purchased with such money also is forfeited.[33] The Bush war on drugs followed a host of federal drug-control initiatives. All of them, like the Bush administration initiatives, have been at best only slightly effective.[34]

The Bush plan continued the American emphasis on law enforcement options for drug control (Table 13.5). Treatment and prevention received only a fraction of the money allocated to traditional law enforcement efforts throughout the 1980s and early 1990s. The Clinton administration's approach, unveiled on February 9, 1994, earmarked $13 billion for a national strategy that emphasized antidrug education as well as treatment programs. His 1995 strategy, which targeted four major initiatives, was advanced by the drug czar, Barry McCaffrey. McCaffrey placed a decided emphasis on treatment, prevention, domestic law enforcement, interdiction, and international control. The White House has proposed a budget of more than $14 billion for the 2009 drug-control strategy, which continues to focus on law enforcement, education, and treatment, as well as on reducing the supply of drugs coming into the country.

Treatment

The treatment approach to drug control is not new. During the late 1960s and into the 1970s, hope for the country's drug problem centered on treatment programs. These programs took a variety of forms, depending on the setting and modality—for example, self-help groups (Narcotics Anonymous, Cocaine Anonymous), psychotherapy, detoxification ("drying out" in a hospital), "rap" houses (neighborhood centers where addicts can come for group therapy sessions), various community social-action efforts (addicts clean up neighborhoods, plant trees, and so on), and the two most popular, residential therapeutic communities and methadone maintenance programs.[35]

The therapeutic community is a 24-hour, total-care facility where former addicts and professionals work together to help addicts become drug-free. In methadone maintenance programs, addicts are given a synthetic narcotic, methadone, that prevents withdrawal symptoms (physical and psychological pain associated with giving up drugs) while addicts reduce their drug intake slowly over a period of time. Throughout the program, addicts receive counseling designed to help them return to a normal life.

It is difficult to assess the success of most treatment programs. Even if individuals appear to be drug-free within a program, it is hard to find out what happens to them once they leave it (or even during a week when they do not show up). In addition, it may well be that the addicts who succeed in drug treatment programs are those who have already resolved to stop abusing drugs before they voluntarily come in for treatment; the real hard-core users may not even make an effort to become drug-free.

A program to divert drug offenders (users and purchasers) from criminal careers is the drug court, in which the judge has the option to divert nonviolent drug offenders to a counseling program in lieu of incarceration. Since the first drug court was established in Dade County, Florida, in 1989, more than 2,100 similar courts have been established in counties throughout the country (see Figure 13.4). The S.T.O.P. program in Portland, Oregon, diverted 944 cases within an 18-month period and has a rearrest rate of 6 percent for the first year following completion of the program. Other drug courts enjoy similar success rates.[36]

Education

While drug treatment deals with the problem of addiction after the fact, education tries to prevent people from taking illegal drugs in the first place. The idea behind educational programs is straightforward: People who have information about the

Crime Surfing

www.unodc.org

Find out what the United Nations has been doing to combat drugs and violence.

TABLE 13.5 Drug Control Funding* by Agency, FY 2007–FY 2009

	FY 2007 Final	FY 2008 Enacted	FY 2009 Request
Department of Defense	**1,329.8**	**1,177.4**	**1,060.5**
Department of Education	**495.0**	**431.6**	**218.1**
Department of Health and Human Services			
Centers for Medicare & Medicaid Services	–	45.0	265.0
Indian Health Service	148.2	173.2	162.0
National Institute on Drug Abuse	1,000.0	1,000.7	1,001.7
Substance Abuse and Mental Health Services Administration	2,443.2	2,445.8	2,370.6
Total HHS	**3,591.4**	**3,664.8**	**3,799.3**
Department of Homeland Security			
Office of Counternarcotics Enforcement	2.5	2.7	4.0
Customs and Border Protection	1,968.5	2,130.9	2,191.9
Immigration and Customs Enforcement	422.8	412.3	428.9
U.S. Coast Guard	1,080.9	1,004.3	1,071.0
Total DHS	**3,474.8**	**3,550.1**	**3,695.8**
Department of the Interior			
Bureau of Indian Affairs	2.6	6.3	6.3
Total DOI	**2.6**	**6.3**	**6.3**
Department of Justice			
Bureau of Prisons	65.1	67.2	69.2
Drug Enforcement Administration	1,969.1	2,105.3	2,181.0
Interagency Crime and Drug Enforcement	497.9	497.9	531.6
Office of Justice Programs	245.5	222.8	114.2
Total DOJ	**2,777.7**	**2,893.2**	**2,896.0**
Office of National Drug Control Policy			
Counterdrug Technology Assessment Center	20.0	1.0	5.0
High Intensity Drug Trafficking Area Program	224.7	230.0	200.0
Other Federal Drug Control Programs	193.0	164.3	189.7
Drug-Free Communities (non-add.)	*79.2*	*90.0*	*80.0*
National Youth Anti-Drug Media Campaign (non-add.)	*99.0*	*60.0*	*100.0*
Salaries and Expenses	26.8	26.4	26.8
Total ONDCP	**464.4**	**421.7**	**421.5**
Small Business Administration	**1.0**	**1.0**	**1.0**
Department of State			
Bureau of International Narcotics and Law Enforcement Affairs	1,055.7	640.8	1,173.2
United States Agency International Development	239.0	361.4	315.8
Total State	**1,294.7**	**1,002.2**	**1,489.0**
Department of Transportation			
National Highway Traffic Safety Administration	**2.9**	**2.7**	**2.7**
Department of Treasury			
Internal Revenue Service	**55.6**	**57.3**	**59.2**
Department of Veterans Affairs			
Veterans Health Administration	**354.1**	**447.2**	**465.0**
Total	**$13,844.0**	**$13,655.4**	**$14,114.4**

*In millions of dollars.

Note: Detail may not add due to rounding.

In addition to the resources displayed in the table above, the Administration requests $385.1 million in FY 2008 supplemental funding for counternarcotics support to Mexico and Central America.

SOURCE: *National Drug Control Strategy 2008 Annual Report* (Washington, D.C.: The White House, 2008), p. 71.

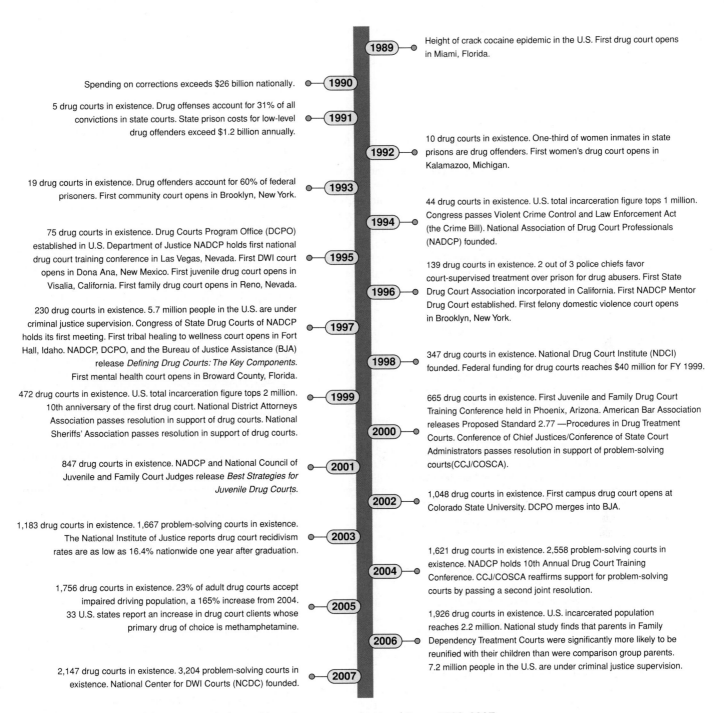

1989 — Height of crack cocaine epidemic in the U.S. First drug court opens in Miami, Florida.

1990 — Spending on corrections exceeds $26 billion nationally.

1991 — 5 drug courts in existence. Drug offenses account for 31% of all convictions in state courts. State prison costs for low-level drug offenders exceed $1.2 billion annually.

1992 — 10 drug courts in existence. One-third of women inmates in state prisons are drug offenders. First women's drug court opens in Kalamazoo, Michigan.

1993 — 19 drug courts in existence. Drug offenders account for 60% of federal prisoners. First community court opens in Brooklyn, New York.

1994 — 44 drug courts in existence. U.S. total incarceration figure tops 1 million. Congress passes Violent Crime Control and Law Enforcement Act (the Crime Bill). National Association of Drug Court Professionals (NADCP) founded.

1995 — 75 drug courts in existence. Drug Courts Program Office (DCPO) established in U.S. Department of Justice NADCP holds first national drug court training conference in Las Vegas, Nevada. First DWI court opens in Dona Ana, New Mexico. First juvenile drug court opens in Visalia, California. First family drug court opens in Reno, Nevada.

1996 — 139 drug courts in existence. 2 out of 3 police chiefs favor court-supervised treatment over prison for drug abusers. First State Drug Court Association incorporated in California. First NADCP Mentor Drug Court established. First felony domestic violence court opens in Brooklyn, New York.

1997 — 230 drug courts in existence. 5.7 million people in the U.S. are under criminal justice supervision. Congress of State Drug Courts of NADCP holds its first meeting. First tribal healing to wellness court opens in Fort Hall, Idaho. NADCP, DCPO, and the Bureau of Justice Assistance (BJA) release *Defining Drug Courts: The Key Components.* First mental health court opens in Broward County, Florida.

1998 — 347 drug courts in existence. National Drug Court Institute (NDCI) founded. Federal funding for drug courts reaches $40 million for FY 1999.

1999 — 472 drug courts in existence. U.S. total incarceration figure tops 2 million. 10th anniversary of the first drug court. National District Attorneys Association passes resolution in support of drug courts. National Sheriffs' Association passes resolution in support of drug courts.

2000 — 665 drug courts in existence. First Juvenile and Family Drug Court Training Conference held in Phoenix, Arizona. American Bar Association releases Proposed Standard 2.77 —Procedures in Drug Treatment Courts. Conference of Chief Justices/Conference of State Court Administrators passes resolution in support of problem-solving courts(CCJ/COSCA).

2001 — 847 drug courts in existence. NADCP and National Council of Juvenile and Family Court Judges release *Best Strategies for Juvenile Drug Courts.*

2002 — 1,048 drug courts in existence. First campus drug court opens at Colorado State University. DCPO merges into BJA.

2003 — 1,183 drug courts in existence. 1,667 problem-solving courts in existence. The National Institute of Justice reports drug court recidivism rates are as low as 16.4% nationwide one year after graduation.

2004 — 1,621 drug courts in existence. 2,558 problem-solving courts in existence. NADCP holds 10th Annual Drug Court Training Conference. CCJ/COSCA reaffirms support for problem-solving courts by passing a second joint resolution.

2005 — 1,756 drug courts in existence. 23% of adult drug courts accept impaired driving population, a 165% increase from 2004. 33 U.S. states report an increase in drug court clients whose primary drug of choice is methamphetamine.

2006 — 1,926 drug courts in existence. U.S. incarcerated population reaches 2.2 million. National study finds that parents in Family Dependency Treatment Courts were significantly more likely to be reunified with their children than were comparison group parents. 7.2 million people in the U.S. are under criminal justice supervision.

2007 — 2,147 drug courts in existence. 3,204 problem-solving courts in existence. National Center for DWI Courts (NCDC) founded.

FIGURE 13.4 Timeline of drug courts and other problem-solving courts in the United States, 1989–2007.

Source: Figure 1 from C. West Huddleston III, Douglas B. Marlowe, J.D., Ph.D., and Rachel Casebolt, *Painting the Current Picture: A National Report Card on Drug Courts and Other Problem-Solving Court Programs in the United States,* Volume II, Number 1, May 2008. Washington, D.C.: National Drug Court Institute, p. 1. Copyright © 2008 National Drug Court Institute. Reprinted with permission.

harmful effects of illegal drugs are likely to stay away from them. Sometimes the presentation of the facts has been coupled with scare tactics. Some well-known athletes and entertainers have joined the crusade with public-service messages ("a questionable approach," says Howard Abadinsky, "given the level of substance abuse reported in these groups").[37]

The educational approach has several drawbacks. Critics maintain that most addicts are quite knowledgeable about the potential consequences of taking drugs but think of them as just a part of the "game."[38] Most people who begin to use drugs believe they will never become addicted, even when they have information about addiction.[39] Inner-city youngsters do not lack information about the harmful effects of drugs. They learn about the dangers from daily exposure to addicts desperately searching for drugs, sleeping on the streets, going through withdrawal, and stealing family belongings to get money.[40]

Legalization

Despite increases in government funding for an expanded war on drugs, the goal of a drug-free society in the 1990s was not achieved and is hardly likely to be achieved within the next decade. There is much evidence that all the approaches, even the "new" ones, have been tried before with little or no effect. Some experts are beginning to advocate a very different approach—legalization. Their reasoning is that because the drug problem seems to elude all control efforts, why not deal with heroin and cocaine the same way we deal with alcohol and tobacco? In other words, why not subject these drugs to some government control and restrictions but make them freely available to all adults?[41]

They argue that current drug-control policies impose tremendous costs on taxpayers without demonstrating effective results. In addition to spending less money on crime control, the government would make money on tax revenue from the sale of legalized drugs. This is, of course, a hotly debated issue. Given the dangers of drug abuse and the moral issues at stake, legalization surely offers no easy solution and has had little public support. However, the surgeon general of the United States, in 1994, mentioned the option of legalization—only to be rebuffed by the president.

ALCOHOL AND CRIME

Alcohol is another substance that contributes to social problems. One of the major differences between alcohol and the other drugs we have been discussing is that the sale and purchase of alcohol are legal in most jurisdictions of the United States. The average annual consumption of alcoholic beverages by each individual 14 years of age and over is equivalent to 591 cans of beer, or 115 bottles of wine, or 35 fifths of liquor; this is more than the average individual consumption of coffee and milk.[42] Alcohol is consumed at recreational events, business meetings, lunches and dinners at home, and celebrations; in short, drinking alcohol has become the expected behavior in many social situations.

Drinking is widespread among young people. While the rate of use has been fairly steady since 1994, the percentage of drinkers in 2007 was 50.9 percent of the population above 12 years old. Recent research demonstrates that 15.9 percent of current drinkers were 12 to 17 years old. Of this group, 9.3 percent were binge drinkers, and 2.3

percent were classified as heavy drinkers.[43] (See Table 13.3.)

The History of Legalization

Alcohol consumption is not new to our culture; in colonial days alcohol was considered safer and healthier than water. Still, the history of alcohol consumption is filled with controversy. Many people through the centuries have viewed it as wicked and degenerate. By the turn of the twentieth century, social reformers linked liquor to prostitution, poverty, the immigrant culture, and corrupt politics.

Various lobbying groups, such as the Women's Christian Temperance Union and the American Anti-Saloon League, bombarded politicians with demands for the prohibition of alcohol.[44] On January 16, 1920, the Eighteenth Amendment to the Constitution went into force, prohibiting the manufacture, sale, and transportation of alcoholic beverages. The Volstead Act of 1919 had already defined as "intoxicating liquor" any beverage that contained more than ½ of 1 percent alcohol.

Historians generally agree that no law in America has ever been more widely violated or more unpopular. Vast numbers of people continued to consume alcohol. It was easy to manufacture and to import. The illegal business brought tremendous profits to suppliers, and it could not be controlled by enforcement officers, who were too inefficient, too few, or too corrupt. The unlawful sale of alcohol was called "bootlegging." The term originated in the early practice of concealing liquor in one's boot to avoid payment of liquor taxes.

Bootlegging created empires for gangsters such as Al Capone and Dutch Schultz, as we saw in Chapter 10. Private saloons, or "speakeasies," prospered. Unpopular and unenforceable, the Eighteenth Amendment was repealed 13 years after its birth—on December 5, 1933. Except for a few places, the manufacture and sale of alcohol have been legal in the United States since that time.

Crime-Related Activities

Two alcohol-related activities that have become serious social problems are violent crime and drunk driving.

Violence

The only national survey of inmates in jails and prisons and substance abuse shows the following:

- About 40 percent of the convicted offenders incarcerated for violent crimes used alcohol immediately before the crimes.

- About 40 percent of prison inmates engaged in binge drinking in the past.

- Over one-third of prison inmates have gotten into a physical fight while drinking or directly afterward.

- About one-third of state inmates convicted of violent crimes described themselves as daily drinkers.[45]

For many decades, criminologists have probed the relationship between alcohol and violence. Marvin Wolfgang, in a study of 588 homicides in Philadelphia, found that alcohol was present in two-thirds of all homicide cases (both victim and offender, 44 percent; victim only, 9 percent; offender only, 11 percent).[46] Similar findings were reported from northern Sweden: Two-thirds of the offenders who committed homicide between 1970 and 1981 and almost half of their victims were intoxicated when the crime was committed.[47]

Many other offenses show a significant relationship between alcohol and violence. In the United States, 58 percent of those convicted for assault and 64 percent of offenders who assaulted police officers had been drinking.[48] In about one-third of rapes, the offender, the victim, or both had been drinking immediately before the attack.[49] The role of alcohol in violent family disputes has been increasingly recognized. Among 2,413 American couples, the rate of severe violence by the husband was 2.10 per 100 couples in homes where the husbands were never drunk and 30.89 per 100 couples in homes where the husbands were drunk "very often."[50]

Many explanations have been offered for the relationship between alcohol and violence.[51] Some studies focus on the individual. When people are provoked, for example, alcohol can reduce restraints on aggression.[52] Alcohol also escalates aggression by reducing awareness of consequences.[53] Other studies analyze the social situation in which drinking takes place. Experts argue that in some situations aggressive behavior is considered appropriate or is even expected when people drink together.[54]

Drunk Driving

The effect of alcohol on driving is causing continuing concern. The incidence of drunk driving, referred to in statutes as "driving under the influence" and "driving while intoxicated" (depending on the level of alcohol found in the blood), has been steadily rising. Statistics indicate the extent of the problem:

- Between 2003 and 2007 the number of arrests for driving under the influence increased 1.6 percent.

- Before arrest for driving while intoxicated (DWI), the majority of convicted offenders drink at least 4 ounces of pure alcohol within 4 hours.

- About 45 percent of prison inmates have driven while intoxicated.

- In 2006, there were an estimated 13,470 alcohol-related traffic fatalities (32 percent of all traffic fatalities for that year).

- The annual cost of drunk driving (property damage, medical bills, and so on) is estimated at $24 billion.

- There were 888,660 arrests for driving under the influence in 2007.[55]

Cari Lightner, age 13, was killed in May 1980 by a drunk driver while she was walking on a sidewalk.[56] The driver had been arrested only a few days before on a DUI charge. The victim's mother, Candy, took action almost immediately to push for new legislation that would mandate

THEORY CONNECTS

Alcohol and Crime

Criminologists have identified many associations between illegal drug/alcohol use and strain (Chapter 5), cultural deviance (Chapter 5), and social control theories (Chapter 7). But these casual influences are both contingent and probabilistic (i.e., drugs and alcohol may contribute to crime, and crime may contribute to drug and alcohol use). Criminologists are still uncovering all of the variables that contribute to the substance abuse–crime connection. What do you think?

■ *Alcohol and driving don't mix. Drunk drivers (there are almost 1.5 million arrests per year for driving under the influence) cause thousands of fatal accidents every year. Remarkably, evidence reveals that cell phone texting is even more dangerous than driving while under the influence. States are aggressively passing legislation prohibiting texting while driving.*

much stiffer penalties for drunk driving. It was difficult at first to get government to respond, but she did get the attention of journalists. By the end of the year in which Cari died, Mrs. Lightner had organized the Governor's Task Force on Drinking and Driving in California.

Also, her own advocacy group, Mothers Against Drunk Driving (MADD), was in the national spotlight. MADD's members were people who themselves had been injured or whose family members had been injured or killed in an accident involving an intoxicated driver. The organization has grown to more than 300 chapters.[57] Remove Intoxicated Drivers (RID) and Students Against Drunk Drivers (SADD) have joined the campaign.

The citizens' groups called public attention to a major health and social problem, demanded action, and got it. Congress proclaimed one week each December to be Drunk and Drugged Awareness Week, and the Presidential Commission on Drunk Driving was formed. Candy Lightner was appointed a commissioner. The federal government attached the distribution of state highway funds to various anti-drunk-driving measures, thereby pressuring the states to put recommendations into action. Old laws have been changed, and new laws have been passed.

After the ratification in 1971 of the Twenty-Sixth Amendment to the U.S. Constitution, which lowered the voting age to 18 years, many states lowered their minimum-age requirement for the purchase and sale of alcoholic beverages. By 1983, 33 states had done so, but by 1987 all but one state had raised the minimum drinking age back to 21. Under New York's Civil Forfeiture Law, the government can take any car involved in a felony drunk-driving case, sell it, and give the money to the victims. Texas has a similar law.[58] Tuscarawas County in Ohio once placed brightly colored orange plates on cars of drivers whose licenses had been suspended for drunk driving.[59]

Other objectives of legislation have been to limit the "happy hours" during which bars serve drinks at reduced prices, to shorten hours when alcoholic beverages can be sold, to make hosts and bartenders liable for damages if their guests or patrons drink too much and become involved in an accident, to limit advertisements, and to put health warnings on bottles. Most states have increased their penalties for drunk driving to include automatic license suspension, higher minimum fines, and even mandatory jail sentences.

Thus far, the results of such legislation are mixed. A study carried out in Seattle, Minneapolis, and Cincinnati found that such measures did indeed lower the number of traffic deaths, while other investigations did not show positive results.[60] Nevertheless, drunk driving has achieved national attention, and modern technology is being used in the effort to find solutions: Japanese and American technicians have developed a device that locks the ignition system and can be unlocked only when the attached Breathalyzer (which registers alcohol in the blood) indicates that the driver is sober.[61] California, Washington, Texas, Michigan, and Oregon have passed legislation authorizing its use.

SEXUAL MORALITY OFFENSES

All societies endeavor to regulate sexual behavior, although what specifically is considered not permissible has varied from society to society and from time to time. The legal regulation of sexual conduct in Anglo-American law has been greatly influenced by both the Old and the New Testaments. In the Middle Ages, the enforcement of laws pertaining to sexual morality was the province of church courts. Today, to the extent that immorality is still illegal, it is the regular criminal courts that enforce such laws.

Morality laws have always been controversial, whether they seek to prevent alcohol abuse or to prohibit certain forms of sexual behavior or its public display or depiction. Sexual activity other than intercourse between spouses for the purpose of procreation has been severely penalized in many societies and until only recently in the United States. Sexual intercourse between unmarried persons ("lewd cohabitation"), seduction of a female by promise of marriage, and all forms of "unnatural" sexual relations were serious crimes—some carrying capital sentences—as late as the nineteenth century. In 1962, the Model Penal Code proposed some important changes. Fornication and lewd cohabitation were dropped from the list of offenses, as was homosexual intercourse between consenting adults.

The idea behind these changes is that the sexual relations of consenting adults should be beyond the control of the law, not only because throughout history such legal efforts have proved ineffective but also because the harm to society, if any, is too slight to warrant the condemnation of law. "The state's power to regulate sexual conduct ought to stop at the bedroom door or at the barn door," said sex researcher Alfred Kinsey four decades ago.[62]

Although the Model Penal Code (MPC) has removed or limited sanctions for conduct among consenting adults, the code retains strong prohibitions against sexual activities involving children. Penalties are severe for **statutory rape** (illegal sexual activity between two people when it would otherwise be legal if not for their age), deviate sexual intercourse with a child, corruption of a minor, sexual assault, and endangering the welfare of a child. Of course, the recommendations of the American Law Institute are not always accepted by state legislatures.

Let us take a close look at three existing offenses involving sexual morality: deviate sexual intercourse by force or imposition, prostitution, and pornography.

Deviate Sexual Intercourse by Force or Imposition

The Model Penal Code defines "deviate sexual intercourse" as "sexual intercourse per os or per anum [by mouth or by anus] between human beings who are not husband and wife, and any form of sexual intercourse with an animal" [sec. 213.2(1)]. The common law called such sexual acts **sodomy,** after the biblical city of Sodom, which the Lord destroyed for its wickedness, presumably because its citizens had engaged in such acts. The common law dealt harshly with sodomy, making it a capital offense and referring to it as *crimen innominatum*—a crime not to be mentioned by name.

Yet other cultures, including ancient Greece, did not frown on homosexual activities. And Alfred Kinsey reminded us that homosexual (from the Greek word *homos,* meaning "same") relations are common among all mammals, of which humans are but one species.[63] The MPC subjects "deviate sexual intercourse" between two human beings to punishment only if it is accomplished by severe compulsion or if the other person is incapable of granting consent or is a child less than 10 years old. To conservative lawmakers, this model legislation is far too liberal; to liberals, it does not go far enough. Generally, liberal thinkers prefer the law not to interfere with the sexual practices of consenting adults at all.

The gay and lesbian rights movement has done much to destigmatize consensual, private adult sexual relationships for the lesbian, gay, bisexual, and transgender (LGBT) community. Legislatures have been slow to respond, and the U.S. Supreme Court has taken a conservative stance as well. Laws on same-sex relationships and marriage are being debated in state legislatures, however, and are changing. New laws with respect to "marriage equality" and "civil unions" have been passed in several states, including Massachusetts, Connecticut, Maine, Iowa, and Vermont. Many other states, such as California, are in the midst of a long and protracted debate over the constitutionality of same-sex marriage.

Prostitution

Not so long ago it was a crime to be a prostitute.[64] The law punished women for a status acquired on the basis of sexual intercourse with more than one man. Under some statutes it was not even necessary to prove that money was paid for the sexual act. The Supreme Court ruled in 1962—in a case involving the status of being a drug addict—that criminal liability can be based only on conduct, that is, on doing something in violation of law.[65] This decision would seem to apply to prostitution as well. Therefore, one can no longer be penalized for being a prostitute. But soliciting for sex is an act, not a status, and nearly all states make solicitation of sex for money the misdemeanor of **prostitution.**

■ At a gay rights rally on November 15, 2008, at the state capitol in Sacramento, California, Kimberly and Jennifer Coleman and their family protest the passage of Proposition 8, which amended the state constitution to define marriage as between a man and a woman, effectively banning same-sex marriage.

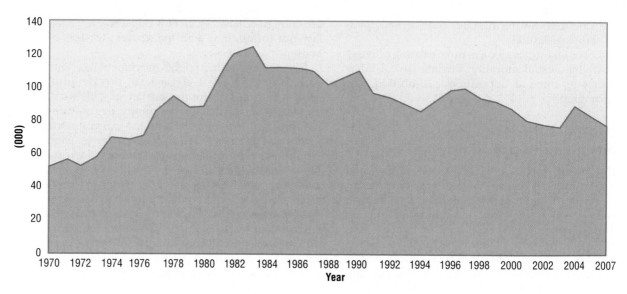

FIGURE 13.6 Estimated number of prostitution arrests in the United States, 1970–2007.

Source: Uniform Crime Reports, 1970–2008.

The Uniform Crime Reports recorded 90,231 arrests for prostitution and commercialized vice during 2004 (Figure 13.6).[66] The number would be extremely high if we were to include all acts of sexual favor granted in return for some gratuity. Even if the number were limited to straightforward cash transactions (including, nowadays, credit card transactions), there is no way of arriving at a figure. Many persons may act as prostitutes for a while and then return to legitimate lifestyles. There are part-time and full-time prostitutes, male and female prostitutes, itinerant and resident prostitutes, street hookers and high-priced escorts who do not consider themselves prostitutes.[67]

Many law enforcement agencies do not relish the task of suppressing prostitution. In some jurisdictions, the police have little time to spend on vice control, given the extent of violent and property crimes. Thus, when prostitutes are arrested, it is likely to be in response to demands by community groups, business establishments, or church leaders to "clean up the neighborhood." Occasionally, the police find it expedient to arrest prostitutes because they may divulge information about unsolved crimes, such as narcotics distribution, theft, receiving stolen property, or organized crime.

Prostitution encompasses a variety of both acts and actors. The prostitute, female or male, is not alone in the business of prostitution. A **pimp** provides access to prostitutes and protects and exploits them, living off their proceeds. There are still madams who maintain houses of prostitution. And, finally, there are the patrons of prostitutes, popularly called "johns." Ordinarily, it is not a criminal offense to patronize a prostitute, yet the framers of the MPC proposed to criminalize this act. The section was hotly debated before the American Law Institute. A final vote of the members rejected criminalization.

Researchers have found that many prostitutes come from broken homes and poor neighborhoods and are school dropouts. Yet all social classes contribute to the prostitution hierarchy. High-priced call girls, many of them well-educated women, may operate singly or out of agencies. The television "blue channels" that broadcast after midnight in most metropolitan areas carry commercials advertising the availability of call girls, their phone numbers, and sometimes their specialties. At the next lower level of the prostitution hierarchy are the massage-parlor prostitutes. When Shirley, a masseuse, was asked, "Do you consider yourself a prostitute?" she answered: "Yes, as well as a masseuse, and a healer, and a couple of other things."[68] One rung lower on the prostitution ladder are the "inmates" (a term used by the MPC) of the houses of prostitution, locally called "bordellos," "whorehouses," "cathouses," or "red-light houses."

According to people "in the life" (prostitution), the streetwalkers are the least-respected class in the hierarchy. They are the "working girls" or "hookers." They are found clustered on their accustomed street corners, on thoroughfares, or in truck and bus depots, dressed in bright attire, ready to negotiate a price with any passerby. Sexual services are performed in vehicles or in nearby "hot-sheet" hotel rooms. Life for these prostitutes—some of whom are transvestite males—is dangerous and grim. Self-reports suggest that many are drug addicts and have been exposed to HIV.[69] Other varieties of prostitution range from the legal houses that a few

For years, the Mustang Ranch, near Reno, was one of the many legal brothels in Nevada. The Ranch property was forfeited to the federal government in 1999 after guilty verdicts were obtained against the ranch's owner in a fraud and racketeering trial. The, furnishings were auctioned off, and the buildings sold on eBay to a bordello owner who moved them five miles away and reopened the ranch under a different name.

counties permit to operate in Nevada to troupes of prostitutes who travel from one place of opportunity to another (work projects, farm labor camps, construction sites) and bar ("B") girls who entertain customers in cocktail lounges and make themselves available for sexual activities for a price.

Popular, political, and scientific opinions on prostitution have changed, no doubt largely because prostitution has changed. Around the turn of the century, it probably was true that a large number of prostitutes had been forced into the occupation by unscrupulous men. Indeed, it was this pattern that led to the enactment of the White Slave Traffic Act (called the Mann Act, after the senator who proposed the bill), prohibiting the interstate transportation of females for purposes of prostitution. There is some evidence that today the need for money, together with limited legitimate opportunities to obtain it, prompts many young women and men to become prostitutes.

Sex researcher Paul Gebhard found in 1969 that only 4 percent of U.S. prostitutes were forced into prostitution. More recently, Jennifer James found that the majority entered the life because of its financial rewards.[70] Whatever view we take of adult prostitutes as victims of a supposedly victimless criminal activity, one subgroup clearly is a victimized class: children, female and male, who are enticed and sometimes forced into prostitution, especially in large cities. Some are runaways, picked up by procurers at bus depots; some are simply "street children"; and others have been abused and molested by the adults in their lives.[71]

Pornography

Physical sexual contact is a basic component of both sodomy and prostitution. **Pornography** requires no contact at all; it simply portrays sexually explicit material. Statutes in all states make it a criminal offense to produce, offer for sale, sell, distribute, or exhibit certain kinds of pornographic (sometimes called "obscene," "lewd," or "lascivious") material. Federal law prohibits the transportation of illegal material in interstate commerce and outlaws the use of the mails, the Internet, the telephone, radio, and television for the dissemination of pornographic material.[72]

The Problem of Definition

The term "pornographic" is derived from the Greek *pornographos* ("writing of harlots," or descriptions of the acts of harlots). The term "obscene" comes from the Latin *ob* ("against," "before") plus *caenum* ("filth"), or possibly from *obscena* ("offstage"). In Roman theatrical performances, disgusting and offensive parts of plays took place offstage, out of sight but not out of hearing of the audience.[73] Courts and legislators have used the two terms interchangeably, but nearly all statutes and decisions deal with pornography (with the implication of sexual arousal) rather than with obscenity (with its implication of filth).[74]

Scholars generally agree that the statutes in existence appear to be addressed primarily to pornographic materials.[75] What, then, is the contemporary meaning of "pornography"? The Model Penal Code (1962) says that a publication is pornographic (obscene or indecent) "if, considered as a whole, its predominant appeal is to prurient interests" and if, "in addition, it goes substantially beyond customary limits in describing or representing such matters" (sec. 251.4). This definition, which is full of ambiguities, was to play a major role in several Supreme Court decisions.

Two presidential commissions were no more successful in defining the term. The Commission

Global Sexual Slavery: Women and Children

"I thought I was going to work as a waitress," a young Dominican, transported to Greece, told BBC television, her eyes welling with tears. "Then they said if I didn't have sex, I'd be sent back to Santo Domingo without a penny. I was beaten, burned with cigarettes. I knew nobody. I was a virgin. I held out for five days, crying, with no food. [Eventually] I lost my honor and my virginity for $25."(1)

This woman's story is a common one. While some women in foreign countries become prostitutes by choice, many are forced into it. The growing sex trade around the world needs a constant supply of bodies, and it is getting them however it can (see map, below). The statistics are horrifying: For the brothels of Bombay, some 7,000 adolescents from Nepal's Himalayan hill villages are sold to slave traders each year. In Brazil, the number of girls forced into prostitution in mining camps is estimated at 25,000. Japan's bars feature approximately 70,000 Thai "hostesses" working as sex slaves. Some 200,000 Bangladeshi women have been kidnapped into prostitution in Pakistan.(1)

The numbers of underage prostitutes are equally shocking, whether the children were sold into slavery or are trying to survive in a harsh world by selling their bodies: 800,000 in Thailand; 400,000 in India; 250,000 in Brazil; and 60,000 in the Philippines. Child prostitution has increased in Russian and East European cities, with an estimated 1,000 youngsters working in Moscow alone.(2) In Vietnam, fathers may act as pimps for their daughters to get money for the family to survive:

Dr. Hoa, [a] pediatrician from Vietnam, said she asked the fathers of her young patients why they sold their daughters' services. "One father came with his 12-year-old daughter," Dr. Hoa recalled. "She was bleeding from her wounds and as torn as if she had given birth. He told me, 'We've earned $300, so it's enough. She can stop now.'"(3)

The physical wounds suffered by underage prostitutes are part of the terrible irony of the growing market for sex with children. Customers request children under the mistaken belief that they are less likely to be infected with the virus that causes AIDS. In fact, because children are so likely to incur injuries in intercourse, they are more vulnerable to infection.(2)

Experts at a 1993 conference on the sex trade and human rights cited the global AIDS epidemic, pornography, peep shows, and "sex tours" as factors responsible for the increasing demand for child prostitutes.(3) Organized sex tours form a large part of the market for bodies of any age; Taiwan, South Korea, the Philippines, and Thailand have been favorite destinations for sex tourists, and many other places are gaining in popularity.

Criminologists who are drawn to the problem of trafficking face a difficult obstacle that is, in itself, an important research question: Just how widespread is the problem of sexual slavery? In the introduction to UNESCO's website for its Trafficking Statistics Project, the problem is posed:

When it comes to statistics, trafficking of girls and women is one of several highly emotive issues which seem to overwhelm critical faculties. Numbers take on a life of their own, gaining acceptance through repetition, often with little inquiry into their derivations. Journalists, bowing to the pressures of editors, demand numbers, any number. Organizations feel compelled to supply them, lending false precisions and spurious authority to many reports.(4)

The bar graph illustrates the range of estimates by government organizations and non-governmental organizations (NGOs).

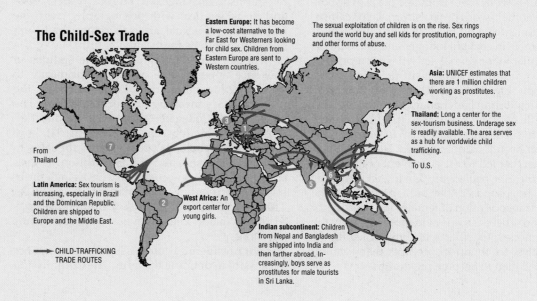

The Child-Sex Trade

Eastern Europe: It has become a low-cost alternative to the Far East for Westerners looking for child sex. Children from Eastern Europe are sent to Western countries.

The sexual exploitation of children is on the rise. Sex rings around the world buy and sell kids for prostitution, pornography and other forms of abuse.

Asia: UNICEF estimates that there are 1 million children working as prostitutes.

Thailand: Long a center for the sex-tourism business. Underage sex is readily available. The area serves as a hub for worldwide child trafficking.

To U.S.

From Thailand

Latin America: Sex tourism is increasing, especially in Brazil and the Dominican Republic. Children are shipped to Europe and the Middle East.

West Africa: An export center for young girls.

Indian subcontinent: Children from Nepal and Bangladesh are shipped into India and then farther abroad. Increasingly, boys serve as prostitutes for male tourists in Sri Lanka.

→ CHILD-TRAFFICKING TRADE ROUTES

Richard Berk, in discussing the challenges of estimating forced agricultural workers, for example, opines that counting the actual number of such "workers in a given area will be difficult under the best of circumstances. Under the worst of circumstances, it may be impossible. It is important, therefore, not to promise better figures than are likely to be obtained." Berk also noted, however, that "one must be careful not to let the perfect become the enemy of the good. Given how little is known about the problem, even rough, first approximation numbers can be useful."(5)

Sources

1. Margot Hornblower, "The Skin Trade," *Time,* June 21, 1993, pp. 45–51.
2. Michael S. Serrill, "Defiling the Children," *Time,* June 21, 1993, pp. 53–55.
3. Marlise Simons, "The Sex Market: Scourge on the World's Children," *New York Times,* Apr. 9, 1993, p. A3.
4. http://www.unescobkk.org/index.php?id=1022).
5. Richard Berk, "Some Thoughts on Estimating the Size of Hidden Populations: The Special Case of Forced Labor," unpublished paper, University of Pennsylvania, July 31, 2007, p. 15; Available at http://www.crim.upenn.edu/faculty/papers.html).

Questions for Discussion

1. How would you begin to fight the exploitation of women and children in the sex market?
2. What are some of the forces at work that would make such a fight difficult?

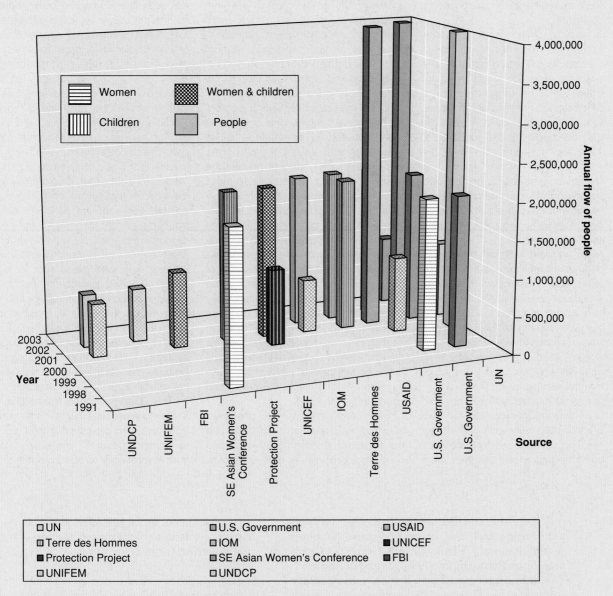

Worldwide trafficking estimates by organizations. Figures cited by or attributed to various organizations regarding the annual flow of trafficked people worldwide (data compiled on September 2004).

Data: Comparison Sheet #1: Worldwide Trafficking Estimates by Organizations. © Copyright UNESCO 2003.

Cyberporn: Where Do We (Should We) Draw the Line?

- The dean of the Harvard Divinity School resigned his post after a computer tech discovered an extensive collection of hard-core pornography on his Harvard-owned computer. This Lutheran minister, divinity school dean, scholar, and father of two committed no crime, but his actions violated the school's ban on having materials that are "inappropriate, obscene, bigoted or abusive" on school computers.(1) The case received widespread media coverage.

- A deputy sheriff from Palmdale, California, was indicted on federal charges for child pornography. The evidence was found on his hard drive. Also, he allegedly tried to solicit sex via the Internet from a person he thought was a 13-year-old girl. The deputy sheriff faced up to 15 years in prison if convicted.(2)

- A Cub Scout leader from Long Island was arrested for having child pornography on his computer, which he downloaded from the Internet and reportedly swapped with other porn peddlers.(3)

- A 23-year-old woman started her own porn website as a hobby. She expected to make about $50,000 a week on the site in the first year. This money would allow her to cut back on making movies and dancing at clubs. She is one of many women in the porn industry who have set up their own websites as alternative businesses.(4)

- Some men find themselves "addicted" to cyberporn, spending as much as 80 hours per week online. Their real sex lives and relationships are damaged as online sex becomes more important and fulfilling than the real thing, leading some marriages to end in divorce.(5)

The Internet provides an ever-increasing number of avenues for the distribution of pornography. For entrepreneurs setting up porn sites, the Internet is proving quite lucrative. However, some of those who use it find themselves in legal trouble when they go beyond legal pornography to child pornography or use sex chat rooms to solicit sex with children. Even those who stick to legal porn may face problems related to their jobs or their personal relationships. It is unlikely that pornography—both legal and illegal—on the Internet will decrease in the years to come.

Of all the issues regarding pornography on the Internet, one of the most hotly debated is censorship. While some programs exist that limit access to porn sites, they do not prevent the exploitation of children or keep those who wish to access the sites from doing so. Child pornographers are creative and adaptable, shying away from explicit child pornography. Many frequent preteen and teen nudism news groups and sites, where thousands of photographs of nude children await them in an apparently "constitutionally protected" cyberspace. The question remains as to what can be done to limit children's access to pornographic sites as well as to prevent their exploitation on the Internet while still protecting freedom of speech. Where should courts draw the line?

Few criminologists have attempted to answer this question or to delve into the world of pornography—including child pornography—in spite of the complex and important issues associated with it. Perhaps the best-known and most competent work in this area has been done by Philip Jenkins. In his work *Beyond Tolerance: Child Pornography on the Internet*, Jenkins raises and wrestles with the more significant issues facing the regulation of this phenomenon. In his own words:

Child pornography is a substantial presence on the Internet, and its potential audience is likely to grow rapidly as Internet usage expands. Given this fact, what, if anything, can be done? Is it possible to suggest solutions or responses that would not sabotage many of the positive aspects of the Internet? In other words, is there a cure that is not worse than the disease? Trafficking in Internet child porn may be so securely protected that total eradication could be achieved only by means that could not fail to damage many innocent users. Deciding which means are too severe or intrusive to combat this problem produces some troubling ethical debates. Briefly, do civil liberties and privacy rights end when one accesses the Internet? Some citizens may well place such a high value on child protection that they would accede to granting police or government the right to observe all Web traffic, to read all mail at random. Most of us, however, would be appalled by such an idea. So what is the proper balance between given technologies being both effective and tolerable?

This is not a simple transaction, a straightforward equation of "how many rights are you prepared to give up to safeguard children?" Repressive new laws theoretically directed against child

on Obscenity and Pornography (1970) avoided a definition and used instead the term "explicit sexual material."[76] The Attorney General's Commission on Pornography (1986) gave no definition.[77] The definition created by a British parliamentary committee in 1979 seems to describe pornography best:

A pornographic representation combines two features: It has a certain function or intention, to arouse its audience sexually, and also a certain content, explicit representation of sexual materials (organs, postures, activity, etc.).[78]

This definition indicates nothing about any danger inherent in pornography. The law will step in only when pornography is exhibited or distributed in a manner calculated to produce harm.

porn might well cause injustice and inconvenience without having the slightest impact on that traffic. Recognizing a serious problem is one thing: using it as an excuse to implement dangerously bad laws is quite another. The answer to child porn is not to be found by adding ever more legal weapons to an already bulging police arsenal but rather in the proper deployment of existing powers and technologies.

From the outset, we have to realize what goals are achievable, and the total elimination of electronic child porn simply may not be within the bounds of possibility. That does not mean that we have to learn to accept or live with the problem, and we might well achieve a massive reduction of production and availability, on the lines of what was accomplished in the 1980s. The great majority of child porn users are rational enough to be deterred, if the proper methods are applied. If we could achieve, say, a 90 or 95 percent reduction of availability, that would be a massive victory in its own right. The fact that some residual trade will continue indefinitely should not provide grounds for ever-increasing encroachments on the liberties of law-abiding Netizens.

To illustrate just how intractable the child porn problem is, let us imagine a means by which this material could be removed or destroyed entirely. Purely as a fantasy, let us suggest that the Internet should simply be prohibited, along with private communication over computer networks. Such a desperate solution was briefly discussed in Mike Cane's Computer Phone Book in the mid-1980s, when he reacted angrily to sysops who "resent having the government come into their domain because of systems for child molesters." Cane argued simply, "If there's a choice between most BBS's existing or protecting innocent children, I'll be the first to throw away my modem. How about you?" Nobody was suggesting such a scheme seriously, and that was long before the Internet came to occupy its present hegemonic position in the U.S. economy. Put bluntly, the vast majority of citizens would not be prepared to throw away their modems in the quest for child protection, even if such a scheme were vaguely conceivable. And if a hypothetical government did prohibit computer networks, it still would not eliminate child porn. Such a ban could be enforced only by computers in the hands of police or security forces, and many precedents indicate that these government employees would surreptitiously be sharing pornographic images. If there are computers, there will be computerized child pornography.

To take a marginally less outrageous solution, consider the experience of China, which, like many authoritarian nations, faces a fundamental paradox in its attitudes toward Internet technology. The Chinese want the massive economic benefits of the Net and also realize the military implications of having a computer-literate populace. The ongoing cold war between the People's Republic of China (PRC) and Taiwan is increasingly fought in the form of hacker attacks on each other's electronic installations. At the same time, the PRC's rulers are nervous about the democratic implications of the Internet, the ability of ordinary citizens to form political or cultural groupings online and to circulate information critical of the state. In response to this dilemma, the Chinese government has ordained that all Internet traffic must pass through two portals, both run by the state. The authorities strictly limit what sites can be accessed and keep detailed records of who is visiting what site. All ISPs and Internet users have to register with authorities. Under present arrangements, "Chinese in the People's Republic can now log onto the China Wide Web and find links with the Chinese version of Yahoo, but without the freedom to connect with sites the government does not wish them to see." Even stricter laws have been proposed: under a recent measure, "the use of e-mail to transmit what might be regarded as secret information is expressly forbidden. The regulations also put operators of chat rooms on notice that they will be held liable for their content. And Internet sites are required to submit to 'examination and approval by the appropriate secrecy work offices,' although the rules do not specify what that process involves. . . . A basic principle of the new regulations is that 'whoever puts it on the Internet assumes responsibility.'"

Anyone using encryption technology is required to notify a government agency of that fact. Other countries with comparably strict laws are Singapore, Saudi Arabia, and Vietnam, and one state has taken the principle of control to its logical extent: "Burma [Myanmar] has taken the strongest measures by outlawing the use of the Internet and making ownership of an unregistered computer with networking capabilities illegal."

With such a model, much child pornography could indeed be kept off the Internet and its aficionados rounded up or terrorized into inactivity. The difficulty is that a Western nation would find such a solution unacceptable from a myriad [of] different perspectives, not least because it would hamstring the whole Internet and introduce controls

(continued)

Historically, that harm has been seen as a negative effect on public morals, especially those of children. That was the stance taken by many national and local societies devoted to the preservation of public morality in the nineteenth century. More recently, the emphasis has shifted to the question of whether the availability and use of pornography produce actual, especially violent, victimization of women, children, or, for that matter, men.

Pornography and Violence

The National Commission on Obscenity and Pornography in 1970 and the Attorney General's Commission on Pornography in 1986 reviewed the evidence of an association between pornography, on one hand, and violence and crime, on the other. The National Commission provided funding for more than 80 studies to examine public attitudes toward pornography, experiences that most members of a democratic society would regard as utterly intolerable. But would it even work? China has an age-old tradition of technological innovation, while successive generations of Chinese dissidents over long centuries have devised ever more imaginative means of outwitting repressive governments and distributing their own propaganda. Not surprisingly, the latest restrictions do not appear too burdensome in practice. Chinese computer users access forbidden sites by means of proxy servers, of which there are far too many to permit concerted government action against them. Users also make extensive use of Internet cafés rather than private machines, so even if authorities note that an unregulated site has been accessed, the odds of detecting a specific individual are slight. The Chinese experience neatly illustrates the remark of Internet pioneer John Gilmore that "the Internet interprets censorship as damage and routes around it." As Ian Buruma notes after describing a recent harsh crackdown on Internet dissidents, "these are desperate measures which cannot stop thousands of others from surfing in forbidden areas." Once again, too, we face the issue of "who guards the guards?" We may wonder what frivolous, decadent, and obscene Web sites are regularly frequented by the guardians of electronic morality in socialist China.

While a Chinese (or Burmese) solution is inconceivable in the West, it is scarcely less Orwellian than some of the ideas that have been floated, however speculatively. Given the nature of the child porn trade, the only policies that might conceivably attempt eradication would involve wide-ranging surveillance of Web traffic by official agencies. This effort might be carried out in a directed way under the approval of court warrants or randomly through general fishing expeditions undertaken against the sort of people thought likely to offend in this particular way. The British example of GTAC and the extravagant powers granted to MI5 indicate that something like this may not be too far away. Yet, as the Chinese example indicates, even such an intolerable set of burdens probably would not eliminate the underlying problem.(6)

Sources

1. Trent Gegax, "An Odd Fall from Grace: Computer Porn Undoes a Divinity-School Dean," *Newsweek*, May 31, 1999, p. 70.
2. "Deputy in Custody Allegedly Tried to Solicit Sex in Internet Chat Room," *City News Service*, Oct. 22, 1999.
3. "Scout Leader Accused of Child Pornography," *New York Times*, Oct. 22, 1999, p. B14.
4. John Leland, "More Bang for the Buck: How Sex on the Internet Has Transformed the Business of Pornography," *Newsweek*, Oct. 11, 1999, p. 73.
5. Greg Gutfield, "The Sex Drive: Web Pornography Has Turned Computers into Sex Objects, and Men, by the Millions, Are Hooking Up, Should You?" *Men's Health*, Oct. 1, 1999, p. 116.
6. From Philip Jenkins, *Beyond Tolerance: Child Pornography on the Internet*, pp. 204–208. Copyright © 2001 by New York University. Reprinted by permission of New York University Press.

Questions for Discussion

1. Why do you think seemingly normal individuals procure child pornography on the Internet or become "addicted" to cyberporn?
2. What can society do to limit the damage done to children by child pornographers who use the Internet as a means of distribution? What should be done with those who are caught?

Psychologists have long studied the deleterious effect on children of violence on television (Chapter 4). Does cyber pornography pose similar threats to children? To what extent does violent pornography, freely available on the Internet, legitimize violence against girls and women?

with pornography, the association between the availability of pornography and crime rates, the experience of sex offenders with pornography, and the relation between pornography and behavior. The commission concluded:

> [E]mpirical research designed to clarify the question has found no evidence to date that exposure to explicit sexual materials plays a significant role in the causations of delinquent or criminal behavior among youth or adults. The Commission cannot conclude that exposure to erotic materials is a factor in the causation of sex crimes or sex delinquency.[79]

Between 1970 (when the National Commission reported its findings) and 1986 (when the Attorney General's Commission issued its report), hundreds of studies have been conducted on this question. For example:

• Researchers reported in 1977 that when male students were exposed to erotic stimuli, those stimuli neither inhibited nor had any effect on levels of aggression. When the same research team worked with female students, they found that mild erotic stimuli inhibited aggression and that stronger erotic stimuli increased it.[80]

• Researchers who exposed students to sexually explicit films during six consecutive weekly sessions in 1984 concluded that exposure to increasingly explicit erotic stimuli led to a decrease in both arousal responses and aggressive behavior. In short, these subjects became habituated to the pornography.[81]

After analyzing such studies, the Attorney General's Commission concluded that nonviolent and nondegrading pornography is not significantly associated with crime and aggression. It did conclude, however, that exposure to pornographic materials

Preventing Child Pornography

In late November about 3,500 people from some 170 governments and from international and nongovernmental organizations attended the third World Congress Against Sexual Exploitation of Children and Adolescents in Rio de Janeiro. The conference declared that accessing, downloading, storing or viewing child pornography on the Internet is a crime. It urged governments to legally prohibit such acts.

Justice and home affairs ministers of the Group of Eight nations declared in June: "We strongly condemn and denounce all forms of sexual exploitation of children, including the practice of persons travelling abroad and engaging in sexual conduct with children, as well as the alarming flood of images of sexual abuse of children—so-called child pornography—on the Internet."

In Japan and Russia, the possession of child porn is not punishable if it is not for sale or offering. The international community accuses Japan of being a major child porn exporter. Around the time of the Rio de Janeiro conference, there was reportedly heavy access from abroad and home after file-swapping software used in Japan allowed child porn to be placed on the Net.

In June the ruling bloc submitted a bill to the Diet that would call for the imprisonment of up to one year or a fine of up to ¥1 million [1 million yen] if a person possesses child pornography to satisfy his or her sexual curiosity. It also calls on Internet providers to cooperate with the police and take steps to prevent the spread of child porn.

The Democratic Party of Japan submitted its own bill, thinking that the ruling bloc's bill could lead to arbitrary investigations. Under the DPJ bill, a person could be imprisoned for up to three years or fined up to ¥3 million [3 million yen] if he or she buys child porn or obtains it repeatedly. Both bills are to revise a 1999 law that protects children under 18 against sexual exploitation.

Although the Rio de Janeiro declaration is not legally binding, it is an international call for Japan to strengthen regulations against child pornography. The ruling bloc and the DPJ should act quickly to find a common ground for effective regulation.

Questions for Discussion

1. How did the Rio de Janeiro conference affect the laws about child pornography in Japan?
2. What role should the global community take in policing child pornography?

SOURCE: Editorial, "Preventing Child Pornography," *The Japan Times*, December 25, 2008. Reprinted by permission of The Japan Times.

---

(1) leads to a greater acceptance of rape myths and violence against women; (2) results in pronounced effects when the victim is shown enjoying the use of force or violence; (3) is arousing for rapists and for some males in the general population; and (4) has resulted in sexual aggression against women in the laboratory.[82]

The Feminist View: Victimization

To feminists, these conclusions supported the call for greater restrictions on the manufacture and dissemination of pornographic material. Historian Joan Hoff has coined the term "pornerotic," meaning

> any representation of persons that sexually objectifies them and is accompanied by actual or implied violence in ways designed to encourage readers or viewers that such sexual subordination of women (or children or men) is acceptable behavior or an innocuous form of sex education.[83]

Hoff's definition also suggests that pornography, obscenity, and erotica may do far more than offend sensitivities. Such material may victimize not only the people who are depicted but all women (or men or children, if they are the people shown). Pornographers have been accused of promoting the exploitation, objectification, and degradation of women. Many people who call for the abolition of violent pornography argue that it also promotes violence toward women. Future state and federal legislation is likely to focus on violent and violence-producing pornography, not on pornography in general.

The Legal View: Supreme Court Rulings

Ultimately, defining pornographic acts subject to legal prohibition is a task for the U.S. Supreme Court. The First Amendment to the Constitution guarantees freedom of the press. In a series of decisions culminating in *Miller v. California* (1973), however, the Supreme Court articulated the view that obscenity, really meaning pornography, is outside the protection of the Constitution. Following the lead of the Model Penal Code and reinterpreting its own earlier decisions, the Court announced the following standard for judging a representation as obscene or pornographic:

- The average person, applying contemporary community standards, would find that the work, taken as a whole, appeals to prurient interests.

- The work depicts or describes, in a patently offensive way, sexual conduct specifically defined by the applicable state law.

- The work, taken as a whole, lacks serious literary, artistic, political, or scientific value.[84]

While this proposed standard is flexible enough to be expanded or contracted as standards change over time and from place to place, its terms are so vague that they give little guidance to local law enforcement officers or to federal and state courts. In 1987, the Supreme Court addressed this problem and modified the Miller decision. In *Pope v. Illinois,* the Court ruled that the third aspect of Miller (that the work has "no value") may be judged by an objective test rather than by local community standards. Justice Byron White wrote for the majority:

> The proper inquiry is not whether an ordinary person of any given community will find serious literary, artistic, political, or scientific value in the allegedly obscene material, but whether a reasonable person would find such value in the material, taken as a whole.[85]

Crime Surfing WWW

http://internet-filter
-review
.toptenreviews.com/
internet-pornography
-statistics.html

Check out these statistics on Internet pornography.

Whether this test makes juries' tasks easier when they must decide whether a film or magazine is pornographic or obscene is still not clear.

Pornography and the Internet

Any child with basic knowledge of a computer and a minimal amount of curiosity can, with a few clicks of a mouse, open a doorway to the world of cyberporn: pictures of adults having sexual intercourse, adults having intercourse with animals, video clips of adults having sex with children, and guides to bordellos, massage parlors, and various pleasure districts—both local and international.[86]

Censorship of the Internet has been a heavily debated issue in recent times. Almost everyone agrees that access of minors to pornographic material over the Internet should be restricted, but the primary point of contention remains: Who should be responsible for policing access to such material? Parents? Educators? The government? Responding to a nationwide outcry, Congress passed the Communications Decency Act (CDA) on February 8, 1996. This portion of the Telecommunications Decency Act of 1996 made it a felony to "knowingly use a telecommunications device or interactive computer to send an indecent communication to a child or to use a computer to display indecent material in a manner accessible to a child." Violations of this act are punishable by up to 2 years' imprisonment and a fine of $250,000.

Four months after the passage of this law, however, a federal court in Philadelphia ruled that it is in conflict with the constitutional right to free speech. According to the court, blocking enforcement of the CDA was justified because (1) the term "indecent" was found to be impermissibly vague and (2) while the CDA could restrict Americans from disseminating "indecent" material, it had no jurisdiction over communications originating outside the United States and would thus be ineffective. Existing federal and state laws, however, still ban the sale and possession of child pornography.

One of the biggest issues surrounding government regulation of pornography on the Internet is the lack of global cooperation. The recent conviction of the head of the German division of the American online service CompuServe for the spread of child pornography on the Internet highlights this fact. Legislation on pornography varies around the world, and thus means that pornography can be easily sent across borders. Strategies are currently being developed by several international agencies to increase communication, provide hotlines for users to report illegal material, make laws more unified, and prevent the exploitation of children on a global scale.

Another significant issue is the fine line between what some call eroticism and others call child pornography. Perhaps the most famous photographer of young girls—David Hamilton—prides himself on belonging to an elite group of art photographers. His books—which no doubt appeal to child pornographers—are carried by most large chain bookstores and are "on" the Internet. But is this art or child pornography? Is it constitutionally protected, or should it be criminally prosecuted? These two questions will be at the forefront of a debate about pornography on and off the Web.

In the wake of the continued controversy over "cybersmut," several computer programs have been developed to assist parents and educators in regulating children's access to the Internet. Programs such as Net Nanny, CyberPatrol, and Web Watcher are designed to block access to sites deemed inappropriate for children.

These programs, however, are far from effective. The software must be continually updated to keep up with the new sites added on a daily basis. If activated by certain keywords, access may also be limited to potentially educational sites (such as those related to sexual harassment). Also, the cost of implementing such programs in a particular school district could run into tens of thousands of dollars.

■ Anyone with a computer and a modem can access cyber pornography, even children. The FBI, U.S. Customs Service, Department of Justice, and U.S. Postal Service have committed significant resources to investigate and prosecute distributors and consumers of child pornography.

The Gap between Behavior and Law

When we examine sexual morality offenses, we note an enormous gap between the goals of law and actual behavior. As long ago as the late 1940s and early 1950s, the pioneering Kinsey reports brought us evidence about this gap. According to these studies, of the total white male population in the United States:

- 69 percent had had some experience with prostitutes.

- Between 23 and 37 percent had had extramarital intercourse.

- 37 percent had had at least one homosexual experience.[87]

Among women:

- 26 percent could be expected to have extramarital intercourse by age 40.

- 19 percent had had some physical contact with other females that was deliberately and consciously, at least on the part of one of the partners, intended to be sexual.[88]

Morton Hunt noted that the frequency with which Americans were breaking legally imposed moral standards had increased significantly by the 1970s, yet far fewer American men were buying sex from prostitutes than had done so in the 1940s.[89] This finding raised the question of whether the sexual revolution of the 1960s and 1970s made access to sexual partners more freely available.

REVIEW

Intoxicating substances have been used for religious, medicinal, and recreational purposes throughout history. Lifestyles of people who use them are as varied as the drugs they favor.

Governments have repeatedly tried to prevent the abuse of these substances. The drug problem today is massive, and it grows more serious every year. Heroin and cocaine in particular are associated with many crimes. A vast international criminal empire has been organized to promote the production and distribution of drugs. Efforts of law enforcement and health agencies to control the drug problem take the forms of international cooperation in stemming drug trafficking, treating addicts, educating the public, and arresting and incarcerating offenders. Some observers, comparing the drug problem with the wide evasion of the Prohibition amendment and the consequent rise in crime, believe that drugs should be legalized.

Legalization of alcoholic beverages, however, has not solved all problems related to alcohol. The abuse of alcohol has been reliably linked to violence, and the incidence of drunk driving has increased so alarmingly that citizen groups have formed to combat the problem.

The legal regulation of sexual conduct has undergone striking changes in recent decades. Many sexual "offenses" once categorized as capital crimes no longer concern society or government. In this sphere, research has done much to influence public opinion and, consequently, legislation. Pornography, however, remains a hotly debated issue.

"Child pornography law presents the opportunity for a case study of how censorship law responds to and shapes a cultural crisis. We have two corresponding events. On the one hand, we have the 'discovery' in the late 1970s of the twin problems of child sexual abuse and child pornography, and the continuation of the problems to the point where they have reached the level of an ongoing, 'ever-widening' crisis. On the other hand, we have child pornography law. Born in the same period, created to solve the problem of child sexual abuse, child pornography law too has grown dramatically in the past two decades, expanding and proliferating along with the underlying problem that it targets. Yet, curiously, the law's expansion has not solved the problem, but only presided over its escalation. As child pornography law has expanded since the late 1970s, so has a 'culture of child abuse,' a growing 'panic' about the threat to children.

"What, if any, is the relationship between these two concurrent phenomena—the expansion of child pornography law and the growing problem of child sexual abuse, including child pornography? Does their correlative temporal connection allow us to draw any conclusions about a possible causal relationship?

"There is a standard, conventional explanation for this correlation. This account casts law in a reactive stance: As the sexual exploitation of children, or at least our awareness of the problem, has risen, legislatures and courts have responded by passing and upholding tougher child pornography laws. As the crisis has surged, so has the law. In this view, cultural horror drives law to play a game of catch-up. Law is always a step behind the problem, racing to keep pace with a burgeoning social crisis.

"I am sure that is at least part of what is going on. But in this Article, I propose two alternative readings—readings that do not exclude the conventional account described above, but supplement it. In the first reading, I explore the possibility that certain sexual prohibitions invite their own violation by increasing the sexual allure of what they forbid. I suggest that child pornography law and the eroticization of children exist in a dialectic of transgression and taboo: The dramatic expansion of child pornography law may have unwittingly heightened pedophilic desire.

"I then turn to a second reading, which reveals the previous one to be an only partially satisfactory account. In the second reading, I view law and the culture it regulates not as dialectical opposites, but as intermingled. Child pornography law may represent only another symptom of and not a solution to the problem of child abuse or the cultural fascination with sexual children. The cross purposes of law and culture that I describe above (law as prohibition, which both halts and incites desire) may mask a deeper harmony between them: The legal discourse on prohibiting child pornography may represent yet another way in which our culture drenches itself in sexualized children.

"Child pornography law explicitly requires us to take on the gaze of the pedophile in order to root out pictures of children that harbor secret pedophilic appeal. The growth of child pornography law has opened up a whole arena for the elaborate exploration of children as sexual creatures. Cases require courts to engage in long, detailed analyses of the 'sexual coyness' or playfulness of children, and of their potential to arouse. Courts have undertaken Talmudic discussions of the meaning of 'pubic area' and 'discernibility' of a child's genitals in a picture at issue. But even when a child is pictured as a sexual victim rather than a sexual siren, the child is still pictured as sexual. Child pornography law becomes in this view a vast realm of discourse in which the image of the child as sexual is preserved and multiplied.

"The point of this Article is that laws regulating child pornography may produce perverse, unintended consequences and that the legal battle we are waging may have unrecognized costs. I do not doubt, however, that child pornography law has substantial social benefits. In fact, I do not doubt that these benefits might outweigh the costs detailed. I nonetheless focus on these costs as a means to unsettle the confident assumption of most courts, legislators, and academics that the current approach to child pornography law is unequivocally sound. I question their conviction that the more regulation we impose the more harm we avert. Ultimately, I raise questions about the nature of censorship itself." (SOURCE: From Amy Adler, "The Perverse Law of Child Pornography," *Columbia Law Review*, Vol. 101 (2001): 209. Copyright 2001 by Columbia Law Review Association, Inc. Reproduced with permission of Columbia Law Review Association, Inc., in the format Textbook via Copyright Clearance Center.)

Questions for Discussion What do you think of Professor Adler's thesis? Is it possible that child pornography laws further the very victimization that they are designed to inhibit?

YOU BE THE
CRIMINOLOGIST

Significant debate continues over how to reduce drug use and what to do with users and dealers. If you were to make a recommendation to the president on how to design the next drug-control strategy, what would you recommend? On what evidence would you base your recommendations?

The numbers next to the terms refer to the pages on which the terms are defined.

money laundering (335)

pimp (344)

pornography (345)

prostitution (343)

sodomy (343)

statutory rape (342)

14

International and Comparative Criminology

■ Child prostitution has become a problem worldwide. In St. Petersburg, Russia's second largest city, some 16,000 street kids, like Anastasia, Natasha, and Masha, are involved in prostitution and drugs.

What Is Comparative Criminology?
The Definition of Comparative Criminology
The History of Comparative Criminology
The Goals of Comparative Research
Engaging in Comparative Criminological Research
Comparative Research
Comparative Research Tools and Resources
The Special Problems of Empirical Research
Theory Testing
Validation of Major Theories
The Socioeconomic Development Perspective
Practical Goals
Learning from Others' Experiences
Developing International Strategies
Globalization versus Ethnic Fragmentation
Review
Criminology & Public Policy
You Be the Criminologist
Key Terms

The sexual exploitation of children, once thought to occur only in third-world countries, has recently permeated the United States. A recent study conducted by the University of Pennsylvania found that as many as 300,000 children in the United States are at risk of becoming victims of commercial sexual exploitation, while other organizations argue that as many as 800,000 children may be in danger.[1] In response to the growing problem of child trafficking, the FBI joined forces with the Department of Justice's Child Exploitation and Obscenity section and

the National Center for Missing and Exploited Children (NCMEC), and in June 2003 a national initiative named Innocence Lost was implemented to address the sexual exploitation of children in the United States.

Child prostitution has grown to epidemic proportions both in the United States and abroad. "Trafficking of children links all countries and regions in a web of international crime," generating more than $4 billion worldwide.[2] According to UNICEF, 1.2 million children are trafficked annually, and 2 million children are forced into the commercial sex industry, 60 percent of whom are under age 16.[3] Children as young as 1 year are bought and sold daily in cities across America. Child sex tourism is the practice of traveling from one's home country to another country to engage in sexual activity with children enslaved in the commercial sex industry.[4] U.S. citizens account for one-quarter of child sex tourists around the world.[5]

Child trafficking has gained considerable global attention in recent years, and countries around the world continue to take steps to combat the sexual exploitation of children. Human trafficking, including the trafficking of children, represents the second-largest organized crime in the world.

Child sex tourism is not a new phenomenon. What is new is the way countries are handling the detection, prosecution, and punishment of individuals involved in the sexual exploitation of children in a country other than their own. Cambodia, Thailand, and Costa Rica at one time were the leading destinations for child sex tourism. However, what was once confined to a handful of countries is now a widespread problem plaguing nearly every country. Rapid globalization, less restrictive borders, and affordable airfare have contributed to the influx of sexually enslaved children in developed countries.

Sociocultural factors such as limited education, extreme poverty, poor law enforcement, government corruption, and discrimination against females have exacerbated an already disturbing trend. Technological advancements have further compounded the problem. The Internet has offered predators, pimps, and child traffickers an easy and, until recently, untraceable underground communication network. Online activities including chat rooms, Internet sharing sites, and promotional websites have played a tremendous role in transforming the sexual exploitation of children to a crime that knows no boundaries.

How do these underground networks evolve? What mechanisms allow them to thrive? Do these mechanisms differ regionally and across borders? How does the exploitation of children in Penang, Malaysia, differ from exploitation in San Diego, California? Are the underlying frameworks the same from country to country? Are the sociological theories used to explain this type of offense the same in Western countries as they are in developing nations? Do the preventive strategies and laws in place in one region have any contributory value for countries facing similar issues?

We begin this chapter with a description of comparative criminology. We then consider the historical evolution of comparative criminology and the purpose (relevance), goals, and objectives of this type of criminological study. We address the challenges globalization poses. Finally, we discuss the contribution—past and present—of comparative research and offer insight into the future of comparative analyses of crime.

WHAT IS COMPARATIVE CRIMINOLOGY?

Comparison is something all human beings do every day. In choosing a home, for example, we compare elements such as square footage and price; location; access to transportation, shopping, and recreation; age of the structure; and so on. Done in a systematic manner, these comparisons become a science. And so it is with comparative criminology.[6]

The Definition of Comparative Criminology

Comparative criminology—or the historical and cross-cultural study of crime and crime control—examines criminality and the social response across regions, cultures, countries, and historical periods.[7] Comparative criminologists study crime as a social phenomenon determined by the legal norms and customs of each society. Comparative research provides a framework with which to study crime trends and criminal justice systems at both the micro and macro levels. (Micro-level criminology explores offending behaviors from an individualistic perspective, while macro-level criminology considers the offending behaviors in a certain group, neighborhood, or culture.)

Comparative criminology requires a comparison across cultures or nations. For example, a comparative study of victimization rates between Montana and Mississippi is not comparative criminology, because the two states are part of one nation and of one basic culture. But if we were to compare the role of alcohol in the escalation of violence among the Cheyenne nation, in Montana or Wyoming, with that among the people of the rest of the state, we might well have a cross-cultural comparison, because the Cheyenne have a distinct legal system and a culture of their own.

The History of Comparative Criminology

Comparative criminology is not new. When the Romans had a crime problem in the fifth century B.C., they sent a delegation to the more advanced nation of Greece to learn better techniques for dealing with crime, such as the publication of laws. In the late Middle Ages and during the Renaissance (fourteenth to sixteenth centuries), all of continental Europe became a vast comparative laboratory as laws that had developed in the various principalities and cities were compared against the rediscovered laws of the old Roman Empire.

During this era crime control methods became increasingly brutal. The situation did not change until the eighteenth century, when—again through comparison, cooperation, and transfer—the work of the classical school (see Chapter 3) began to introduce rationality and humanitarian principles into crime control in Europe and America.

■ Luther and Johnny Htoo, 12-year-old twin Myanmar messianic guerrilla leaders. Luther prepares to fire an M-16 rifle.

In the nineteenth century, as communications improved, policy makers and scholars of criminology compared approaches and introduced into one another's systems what seemed to work. Ideas such as the juvenile court, the penitentiary, the reformatory, probation, and parole gained worldwide acceptance as a result of comparison. Yet the comparisons of the nineteenth and early twentieth centuries lacked scientific rigor; they were impressionistic and often emotional. For example, the juvenile court, first established in Chicago in 1899, seemed such a good idea that it gained acceptance in many parts of the world. But as later experience showed, it did not necessarily work everywhere.

The founders of criminology, including those of American criminology, were, for the most part, comparatists. They would gather at international meetings and share ideas; they would visit each other and stimulate criminological thought. Comparatists were regarded as dreamers, and the comparative approach was viewed as impractical and idealistic. Truly comparative studies, measuring up to scholarly standards, could not be done until criminology itself became a science. Throughout the first half of the twentieth century, internationalism met resistance due to isolationism.

The Global Village: Advantages

Circumstances have changed drastically. Comparative criminologists have become a necessity, simply because the world has become a "global village." Consider these figures from the U.S. Department of Commerce: In 1960, U.S. exports amounted to $19,659 million. By 2004, that figure had increased to $800 billion. Similarly, in 1960, imports amounted to $15,073 million. By 2004 that figure had increased to $1.5 trillion. And that is only part of the global trade picture.

World economies have become totally integrated and interdependent. Japanese cars are often manufactured in the United States and likely have parts made in more than 30 countries. Similarly, many American-based clothing companies manufacture their items in other countries capable of producing the items at a fraction of the cost of producing them in the United States.

Communications likewise have become global. Communicating via the Internet and by cell phone is now commonplace, allowing for instant personal and business communications. Transportation advances, especially since the introduction of jumbo jets, together with the opening of frontiers, have made it possible for millions of people to move across oceans within hours. Air-traffic volume increased from 33.4 billion passenger miles in 1960 to close to 5 trillion by the end of 2003.

Europe is feeling the effects of globalization even more intensely than the rest of the world. The collapse of Communist dictatorships in central and eastern Europe[8] and the virtual abolition of frontiers within Europe[9] have brought crime problems. Consequently, national criminology has been transformed to reflect international influences, resulting in a globalized criminology.[10]

The Global Village: Disadvantages

While many aspects of the global village are beneficial, others have brought serious problems. Instant communication not only promotes the spread of benefits, in goods, lifestyles, and useful knowledge but also provides a forum for the dissemination of illegal materials and aids in the planning and orchestrating of international child trafficking. Economic globalization, as much as it promotes useful commerce, also aids organized crime and fosters the global spread of frauds that were once confined to smaller localities or single countries.

Jet planes transport not just legitimate travelers but also illegal aliens, criminal entrepreneurs, drug dealers, money launderers, and terrorists. Airlines themselves have become the targets and tools of international criminals. Moreover, the industrialization of the world brings not just economic benefits but threats to the world ecology so severe that, unless checked, they could compromise the food, water, and clean air supply for all people. It is little wonder, then, that criminologists must look across borders to study crime and crime-control efforts, and to search for internationally acceptable solutions to common problems.

The Goals of Comparative Research

Before the 1970s, there was very little literature on comparative research in criminology. Since then, however, it has been growing rapidly, a fact attrib-

utable to (1) a realization that we will learn more about crime if we test our theories under diverse cultural conditions and (2) renewed interest in trying to discover what we can learn from the experience of other nations.[11]

Comparative criminology, then, has both theoretical and practical goals. It helps us better understand crime causation and find successful means of crime control. Global collaboration helps ensure that no nation need repeat costly mistakes made elsewhere. Presently, a large number of UN and affiliated organizations are engaged in the task of establishing international measures to deal with dangers that threaten people of all cultures (Table 14.1.)

Before we discuss the implementation of comparative research, we must look at the methods used by comparative criminologists.

ENGAGING IN COMPARATIVE CRIMINOLOGICAL RESEARCH

Comparative research requires special preparatory work to ensure that research data and information are in fact comparable. Researchers must become familiar with the country's history, politics, economy, and social structure. They must have a working knowledge of the laws of the country and of the cultural norms to which the comparison extends. Because there is always a gap between the laws on the books and the law in action, the comparatist must consult the criminal justice research literature. Contemporary cross-cultural texts and treatises are available and contain descriptions of developments in criminology and criminal justice for over 50 countries.[12]

Some countries do not yet have the resources needed to systematically collect information on

■ A group of seated Afghani men gathers for Shura (or elders meeting) near Kandahar, Afghanistan.

Center for International Crime Prevention, in the Office for Drug Control and Crime Prevention (of the UN Secretariat at Vienna, Austria): Reports to the UN Commission on Crime Prevention and Criminal Justice and conducts the quinquennial UN Congress on the Prevention of Crime and the Treatment of Offenders; provides extensive reports, research, documentation, and technical assistance; is responsible for UN standards and guidelines in criminal justice; conducts worldwide statistical surveys.

UNICRI—United Nations Interregional Crime and Justice Research Institute (located in Turin, Italy): Research arm of the UN Secretariat in crime prevention and criminal justice; is responsible for extensive research and publications.

UNAFEI—United Nations Asia and Far East Institute for the Prevention of Crime and the Treatment of Offenders (Fuchu, Japan): Services the region with training, technical assistance, research, and publications.

ILANUD—United Nations Latin American Institute for the Prevention of Crime and the Treatment of Offenders (San José, Costa Rica): Services the region with training, technical assistance, research, and publications.

UNAFRI—United Nations African Regional Institute for the Prevention of Crime and the Treatment of Offenders (Kampala, Uganda): Services the region with training and technical assistance.

HEUNI—Helsinki European Institute for Crime Prevention and Control; affiliated with the United Nations (Helsinki, Finland): Provides extensive research, training, research publications, and technical assistance services on behalf of European countries for both developed and developing countries.

AIC—Australian Institute of Criminology (Canberra, Australia): Under agreement with the UN, provides research, publication, training, and technical assistance services for Oceania, including Australia and New Zealand.

Arab Security Studies and Training Centre (Riyadh, Saudi Arabia): In close cooperation with the UN, provides extensive educational and training services, research, publications, and development and technical assistance to Arab countries.

International Centre for Criminal Law Reform and Criminal Justice Policy (Vancouver, B.C., Canada): Newly established, by agreement with the UN, to provide services within its sphere of expertise.

ISPAC—International Scientific and Professional Advisory Council of the United Nations Crime Prevention and Criminal Justice Programme (Milan, Italy): By agreement with the UN, provides advisory services to the UN with respect to data and information, both in general and on specific subjects falling within the mandate of the UN.

UNCJIN—United Nations Crime and Justice Information Network (Albany, N.Y.): In close cooperation with *WCJLN*—World Criminal Justice Library Network (Newark, N. J.)—assembles, integrates, and disseminates criminal justice information and data worldwide, with a view to complete electronic accessibility.

NIJ—The National Institute of Justice, of the U.S. Department of Justice: By an agreement with the United Nations signed in 1995, joined the Network of UN-affiliated institutes to make the services of the National Criminal Justice Reference Service—especially its UNOJUST computer services—available to the UN community through its International Center.

NGOs—Nongovernmental organizations in consultative status with the United Nations Economic and Social Council: International organizations whose expertise is made available to the UN. They include many major scientific, professional, and advocacy groups, such as:

- International Association of Penal Law
- International Penal and Penitentiary Foundation (special status)
- International Society of Criminology
- International Society of Social Defense
- Institute of Higher Studies in Criminal Sciences
- Centro Nazionale di Prevenzione e Difesa Sociale
- International Association of Chiefs of Police
- International Prisoners Aid Association
- Amnesty International

NGO Alliances in Crime Prevention and Criminal Justice (New York, N.Y., and Vienna, Austria): Made up of the headquarters' representatives of NGOs; provide coordination and research services to the UN.

UN agencies: Concerned with various aspects of crime and justice. The agencies include:

- Centre for Human Rights (Geneva, Switzerland)
- UNICEF—United Nations Children's Fund (New York, N.Y.)

The United Nations Centre for International Drug Control: Concerned with various aspects of international drug control and drug abuse prevention. The programs include:

- Division on Narcotic Drugs
- International Narcotic Drug Control Board
- UN Fund for Drug Abuse Control

Regional intergovernmental organizations: Have organizational units and/or conduct programs concerned with crime prevention and criminal justice. Examples include:

- Council of Europe
- European Union (EU)
- Organization of American States
- Organization of African Unity
- North Atlantic Treaty Organization

their crime problems;[13] however, the great majority send statistics to the International Criminal Police Organization (Interpol), which publishes the data biannually,[14] or participate in the United Nations Surveys of Crime Trends, Operation of Criminal Justice Systems, and Crime Prevention Strategies. The UN surveys, published periodically, began with data for the year 1970 and by now include statistics from well over a hundred countries on the prevalence of crime and the operation of criminal systems.[15]

Several other international databases are available to the researcher, including the homicide statistics of the World Health Organization;[16] the private initiative Comparative Crime Data File, which covers 110 sovereignties (published in 1984);[17] and the Correlates of Crime (published in 1989).[18] International (or nation-by-nation) crime statistics suffer from the same problems as American Uniform Crime Reports statistics, only magnified several times.[19]

Two additional statistical instruments are available to assist researchers in developing an accurate picture:

1. The International Crime Victims Survey (ICVS): Beginning in 1989 and working through 1997, a conglomeration of international researchers conducted three victimization surveys in numerous developed (industrialized) and developing countries; 130,000 people were interviewed around the world, in 40 languages.[20]

2. A 1992 self-report study measured delinquency among 14- to 21-year-old subjects in 12 countries, extending to property, violence, and drug criminality. This survey did not include developing countries.[21]

A comparison between the "official" crime rates of the UN surveys and the victimization rates reported shows that the two are reasonably related, although victimization studies usually show higher crime rates and tend to fluctuate over the years more than do the UN survey rates. One may cautiously conclude that the UN survey rates provide a fairly accurate account of crime rates for most countries.

Comparative Research

Up to this point we have reviewed the general approach to doing comparative criminological research: studying foreign law, criminal justice systems, cultures, and available data. Comparative criminological research begins only after this groundwork has been done. It is at this point that the comparatist sets sail for uncharted seas. The comparatist meets two problems right at the outset: the interdependence of all crime and criminal justice phenomena, and culture specificity.

Interdependent Phenomena

Think of an elaborately assembled mobile hanging from the ceiling. All the parts are in perfect balance. If you remove a single part, the whole mobile will shift out of balance. It is the same with problems of crime and justice in any society: The existence of each is related to all the others and is explainable by reference to the others. Bicycle thefts may exist in countries like China, Denmark, and the Netherlands—all of which rely heavily on bicycle transportation—as well as in the United States or Mexico. But such theft plays a different role in the various countries, generates different responses, and leads to different consequences.

Is the bicycle theft problem comparable around the world? What could be learned from a comparison, and what factors must be considered? Would it be more useful to compare the Chinese bicycle theft problem with the Italian automobile theft problem? How do these problems fit in their countries' respective crime and justice mobiles?

Culture-Specific Phenomena

The task of a comparative criminologist is like that of a surgeon about to transplant a heart or a liver. The surgeon studies a great variety of factors to be sure the donor's organ is compatible with the recipient's body. If we want to compare Japan's low crime rates with the high crime rates in the United States, we must consider many factors, such as the role of shame in Japanese society. Misconduct brings shame not only on individual Japanese wrongdoers but also on their families, schools, and companies. Could shaming, as a sanction, play a role in American criminal justice, or is it too culture-specific? It is easier to ask such questions than it is to answer them, as research experience in comparative criminology is still limited.

Comparative Research Tools and Resources

The first book titled *Comparative Criminology* appeared as recently as 1965. Its author, the late German-English scholar Hermann Mannheim, relied on his vast cross-cultural experience in criminology but offered no guide to the comparative method.[22] Researchers and teachers of the field now have at their disposal a variety of reference works,[23] textbooks,[24] scholarly books,[25] and book-length informative coverage of United Nations activities in the field, of which the *Global Report on Crime and Justice* is the most significant.[26]

The Special Problems of Empirical Research

Criminologists who cannot find or rely upon comparative data must generate their own, usually by parallel field investigations proceeding

Crime Surfing

www.ncjrs.org

For the most extensive references to the field of international and comparative criminology and criminal justice, check the website of the National Criminal Justice Reference Service.

■ *The preferred means of transportation during rush hour in the streets of Beijing, China.*

more or less simultaneously. They confront three problems: first, the identification of comparable problems; second, the identification of sources of information; third, the selection of a research method compatible in the countries under comparison.

Identification of Comparable Problems

Researchers of New York University's Comparative Criminal Law Project, in the 1960s, compared the prevalence of delinquency in several cultures. To their surprise, they learned that Egypt had a high rate of delinquency for railroad offenses. Only local assistance could provide a plausible answer: The long railroad line running parallel to the Nile River is a favored haunt for local youths. Their delinquent acts were recorded as railroad offenses, rather than as delinquency.[27] These "railroad offenses" had to be made comparable to nonrailroad delinquencies in both Egypt and the other countries under comparison.

Identification of Sources of Information

The social groups of one society may not be comparable to those of another. American junior high school students may represent American youngsters of that age range as a whole, but Haitian junior high school students would not. What groups are comparable to such favorite research subjects as American college students, blue-collar workers, and self-employed small-business-people? What is a fair cross section of any country's population?

Police records may be highly reliable in Belgium, but are they in Mali and Malawi or in Armenia? And if they are not, what comparable substitutes can the comparatist find? Such problems challenge the researcher's ingenuity.

Selection of Compatible Research Methods

Criminologist James Finckenauer, studying attitudes toward legal and other values among American and Russian youngsters, was at first confronted with the reluctance of Russian administrators to ask youngsters to report (even anonymously) their own delinquencies. The Soviet culture had blocked any such initiative. The problem was overcome only by indirect questions to the youngsters, such as "How wrong would it be (to do this, that, or the other)?" This was followed by further semidirect questions, such as "Do your peers (parents, and so on) view you as a good kid, bad kid, or something in between?" It was only after the end of communism in 1992 that Finckenauer could administer a self-report delinquency questionnaire in Russia.

Certain research methods simply are unknown in many other countries or, if known, are frowned upon. In a study of perceptions of police power in four cultures, for example, the commanding officer of a foreign police department was asked to have some questionnaires distributed to his officers. At first the officer responded, "You don't seem to understand our police! It is we who ask the questions!" Finally, he agreed and distributed the questionnaires. After the results were analyzed, the researchers were astonished to find that all the answers were identical. Apparently, all the questionnaires had been reviewed and "corrected" by an attorney to make sure they were "accurate."[28]

THEORY TESTING

As we noted earlier, the cross-cultural testing of criminological theories has become one of the major goals of comparative criminology. Recent

The proliferation of supermarkets, like this one in Moscow, Russia, is a phenomenon of socioeconomic development that brings about an increase in crime.

studies have extended to several of the crime-causation theories discussed in this book. Yet cross-cultural theory testing requires the utmost caution.[29]

Validation of Major Theories

After Sheldon and Eleanor Glueck had completed *Unraveling Juvenile Delinquency* (1950),[30] their work was criticized as too culture-specific because it was based on a sample of American children. In response, scholars replicated the Glueck research in different cultural settings—Puerto Rico, Germany, and Japan. As the Gluecks themselves put it, "all these [studies] . . . have provided the most definite of all proofs, that of applicability to other samples by other researchers."[31] These cross-cultural validations of the Gluecks' delinquency-prediction system are some of the earliest empirical comparative criminological studies.

Criminologist Obi Ebbe reviewed the Gluecks' studies and found their theories applicable to juvenile delinquents in Nigeria.[32] He also examined the cross-cultural validity of other American theories, such as differential association, social control, and culture conflict. Other scholars have tested opportunity theory,[33] situational characteristics of crime,[34] routine-activity theory,[35] differential opportunity theory,[36] social control and strain theory,[37] the synnomie explanation of low crime rates,[38] and Durkheim's anomie theory.[39] Most of these studies have shown the theories to have moderate to significant validity.[40]

The Socioeconomic Development Perspective

Cross-cultural researchers have devoted particular attention to the hypothesis that modernization and urbanization lead to increases in crime[41] as well as to the general question of whether socioeconomic development necessarily brings an increase in crime.[42] Several have noted a connection between rapid development and an increase in certain types of crime, especially property crime.[43] Other research has demonstrated that sudden urbanization and industrialization have not led to increased crime in some countries,[44] but that unguided socioeconomic and political changes, such as the current transformation from a socialist to a market economy in central and eastern Europe, do produce an increase in crime.[45] The complexity of the relation between development and crime has prompted some comparative criminologists to warn that, as yet, there is no universal theoretical framework linking crime and development.[46]

PRACTICAL GOALS

Learning from Others' Experiences

With increasing globalization, the similarity of crime problems increases as well. It is natural that criminologists would look at the experiences of other countries in their search for solutions, especially the experiences of countries that seem to have found workable solutions.[47] For the worldwide drunk-driving problem, for example, comparative research has been done in Australia, Norway, and the United States.[48] As for gun control, one study investigated the situation in 7 nations,[49] another in 26.[50] Insurance fraud researchers have looked at the situation in 8 countries,[51] insider-trading researchers in 3.[52]

A 1992 symposium compared differential methods of dealing with ecological crime in the United States, Germany, Austria, Japan, and Taiwan.[53] Comparative criminological research has also been done on violent crime, such as homicides of children,[54] spousal homicides,[55] homicides among young males,[56] and urban violence.[57] For the past 35 years, much attention has been

THEORY CONNECTS

Theory Testing

Some strain theorists focus on the "American Dream" and the frustration that sets in when achievement is limited by opportunities (Chapter 5). To what extent is the American Dream a cross-culturally valid explanation of crime? Would it explain crime in China? In Switzerland? In Cameroon?

The Motives and Intentions of Terrorist Organizations

When new agents are trained at the FBI Academy in Quantico, Virginia, the course on counterterrorism includes original communiqués from the leadership of Al Qaeda. One such writing, part of the standard new agent curriculum, is from the Abu Hafez al-Masri Brigade—Al Qaeda in Europe.

Increasingly, criminologists are asked to comment on the motives and intentions of terrorist organizations. Their ability to do so with authority and accuracy depends on an understanding of the history, culture, and background of the terrorist author. As you consider the generalizability of criminological findings to other cultures and the value of cross-cultural and comparative research, think about what criminologists have to offer those committed to thwarting the next significant attack on U.S. soil.

The New York and Manhattan operation [September 11, 2001] was the onset of an Islamic intifada against the crimes of the crusaders toward the Muslim nation. Yes, Islam is a religion of peace toward those at peace with Islam; but toward those who are hostile to Islam, it is an unrelenting religion of war.

The Benefits of This Operation:
a. *Exposing the new world order and revealing its true face.*
b. *Exposing the lie of democracy, individual rights and human rights. Guantanamo, Abu Ghraib and the prisons of thousands of Muslims without trials in the United States,*

Britain and Europe are the biggest proof. Look at Kuwait which the United States entered in the name of freedom and democracy; is it still not ruled by a tyrant and a dictatorship which are protected by America? Who defends these bloody rulers except for America and Europe? As is also the case in Saudi Arabia, Tunisia, Algeria, Morocco, and Iraq when the tyrant Saddam was on their side.
c. *Exposing the [true nature] of Arab and Muslim rulers.*
d. *Destroying the American economy. Up until this day, America is still suffering economically from trade deficits and inflation.*
e. *Destroying the image of an invincible America.*
f. *Revival of the spirit of Jihad and rise of the victorious sect [members of Al Qaeda].*
g. *Drawing a line [in the sand] and dividing the people into two camps.*
h. *Collapsing the secular and national forces that are represented in the government and artificial opposition.*
i. *Exposing and bankrupting the loyalist Islamic movements that are aligned with the apostate governments who adhere to a curriculum of humiliation.*
j. *That a small group can combat and destroy a large group.*
k. *Converting many to Islam as the enemy admits. An example is what was published in Times Magazine on November 29, 2003, that roughly 10,000 European citizens*

converted to Islam in the past 18 months.
l. *Raising the general awareness [of the Muslim public], when even common people discuss matters such as the Caliphate, treason of leaders, and loyalty, which in the past they did not know of.*

Our Goals in the Next Period:
1. *Increasing the scope of the conflict by spreading operations all around the world. Dragging America into a third quagmire in addition to Iraq and Afghanistan; let it be Yemen god willing. We have mentioned this in our communiqué on March 11, 2004: "we tell the company of Abu Ali al-Harithi, the leadership has decided that Yemen will be the third quagmire for the hegemon of our era, America. More so, to discipline the collaborating infidel government that is second only to Musharaf."*
2. *Shaking the confidence of investors in the American economy.*
3. *Exposing the Crusader-Jewish project.*
4. *Scattering and bleeding [exhausting] the enemy.*

Following these steps comes the awaited strike that will break the will of America, which will abandon its collaborators and agents, so we can settle our scores with them. Then we launch the caravan to Jerusalem with god's permission.

What Is Required of the Brothers, Members of the Victorious Party [Al Qaeda]:
1. *Devotion to God almighty and patience knowing that victory is*

---

devoted to the comparative study of the problem of juvenile delinquency.[58]

By now there is also a considerable body of cross-cultural research on various aspects of crime-control policy. One of the earliest studies in this area examined the perception of police power among divergent population groups in four countries.[59] The perception of law was studied in six cultures,[60] and teenagers' perception of crime and criminal justice was the subject of a more recent two-country study.[61]

Issues in policing[62] as well as sanctions[63] occupy the attention of comparatists in their search for "what works." Victimologists have been particularly active in cross-cultural study.[64]

Developing International Strategies

Comparative criminology reveals that problems of crime and deviance are not unique to a single country. So we are challenged to develop strategies around the corner and god protects those who serve him.

2. Establishing small groups under various different names such as al-Tawhid wal-Jihad and Abu Hafez al-Masri Brigades . . . etc. This makes it difficult for the enemy to expose and track down these groups. In addition, this thins out the pressure of the security services [i.e., overwhelms intelligence services with many leads and many names of groups].

3. Jihadi education including doctrinal teaching, loyalty, purity and work according to these teachings.

4. Military and physical training and spreading this among sons and members of the clans (for the battle may be protracted).

5. Learning modern skills like computers and the Internet and all that can be beneficial to the Mujahideen and Muslims.

6. Igniting a psychological war against the enemy.

What Is Required of the Muslim Nation:

1. Learning the doctrine . . . especially loyalty and purity.

2. Sincere repentance for neglecting Jihad.

3. Wishing for the Mujahideen and providing them with financial and moral support.

4. Setting up small cells inside and outside the cities.

5. Sheltering and protecting the Mujahideen.

6. Defending their honor.

7. Joining their ranks.

8. Advising them.

What We Want From the Crusaders:

These operations will not stop until [President] Bush and his collaborators among the Arabs, Persians and Jews review their policies toward Islam and Muslims, which can be summed up in the following:

1. To release our prisoners in American prisons especially the Guantanamo prisoners and Sheikh Omar Abed al-Rahman. In addition, all those in prisons of American agents among Arabs, Persians and Jews.

2. To cease their global war on Islam and Muslims under the banner of fighting terrorism.

3. Purifying all Muslim lands from the filth of Jews, Americans and Hindus including Jerusalem and Kashmir.

4. That America and its allies not interfere in the political, economic, cultural, and educational matters of Muslims; and not conspire against the rise of a Muslim state.

5. That the Crusader west not interfere between the Muslims and their apostate rulers.

Our Strategy with the Enemy Is:

The enemy may be patient, but it can not endure. As for us with our doctrine, belief and love for meeting god, we can endure until the enemy crumbles. If this takes decades or centuries, we are committed to fighting them come victory or martyrdom.

He Who Gives a Prior Warning Is Excused [does not bare responsibility]:

1. To the European people. . . . You only have few more days to accept

a ceasefire or else you have but yourself to blame.

2. To Muslims who live in the west. . . . Those of you who can immigrate to Muslim lands should do so, those who can not should be careful and live in Muslim neighborhoods. They should gather a month worth of food, and should acquire the means to defend themselves and their family. They should keep in the house enough money for a month or so. To increase their warship, and rely on god.

3. For those who preach for dialogue among civilizations. . . . This is your day, only [a] few days remain for sheikh Usama's promise to come to fruition. Now you are in a race against time as the European governments has refused to stop their aggression against Muslims. You should not blame us for what is about to occur, we apologize in advance if you are among the dead.

Source

Abu Hafez al-Masri Brigade—Al Qaeda in Europe, "A Communiqué," July 1, 2004.

Questions for Discussion

1. What did you learn about Al Qaeda's motives from reading this communiqué?

2. How can studying and understanding Al Qaeda's views help criminologists and others combat terrorism?

jointly with other countries in order to establish crime-prevention and crime-control programs to benefit all. This is particularly necessary for those crime problems that have international implications. For the sake of convenience, we can group crime problems reaching beyond national borders into three categories:

- Internationally induced local crime problems

- Transnational crime

- International crime

Internationally Induced Local Crime Problems

The skinhead phenomenon is a prime example of the simultaneous appearance of a similar type of crime in various parts of the world.[65] As yet, little is known about what causes such simultaneous appearances, although instantaneous reporting in the mass media may aid the process,[66] and some international organizational connections also may play a role. Recently, the Internet has come to play a role in connecting people pursuing common criminal goals. (Yet none of these factors was

What Should Be Done to Prevent International Corporate Fraud?

"Massive fraud," "World's biggest banking crash," and "Financial deception of 'epic proportions.'" Journalists had a field day characterizing the magnitude of the collapse of the Bank of Credit and Commerce International (BCCI), which failed in July 1991. But let's talk numbers instead of adjectives:

- Founded in Pakistan, the international financial institution owed some $2 billion when it folded.
- A senior official admitted to playing a major role in frauds totaling $1.242 billion.
- Thousands of creditors, both businesses and individuals, lost every penny of the money they had deposited.
- In 1991, BCCI agreed to forfeit $550 million to begin compensating depositors worldwide and to salvage institutions the corporation owned secretly in the United States.
- The U.S. investigation that preceded the prosecution of a single person

accused of participating in the scandal cost a whopping $20 million.
- In England alone, BCCI had a staff of 1,200 and 45,000 customers—personnel who lost their jobs and customers who lost their life savings when the bank failed.

Those are big numbers. What are the crimes that led to this scandal of "epic proportions"? In the United States, BCCI pleaded guilty to federal and state charges of racketeering, fraud, and money laundering. Individuals were charged with withholding information in a scheme to defraud federal and state bank regulators and depositors. In Britain, charges against bank officials include false accounting, furnishing false information, and conspiracy to defraud.

HOW IT WORKED

A picture of the corporation's operations has unfolded since the crash:

BCCI's reported profits had been "falsely inflated" by $614 million

between January 1983 and December 1985. The misuse of clients' funds by the bank amounted to another $627 million by the end of 1985. . . . By the early 1980s the bank needed to demonstrate its profitability and a healthy balance sheet to maintain the confidence of banking regulators and current and potential investors. In desperation, the bank's founder and his senior officers turned to the trading of commodities as a likely source of funds and began a series of high-risk speculations trading in futures. Most of these were in options on large-scale purchases of silver, which went badly wrong when the price of the metal turned sharply downwards. As money was lost upon money, the frauds became more widespread. The methods involved to maintain the pretense of solidity included filing accounts in which commissions on silver-trading deals that had never taken place were recorded as profits. . . .

present in another simultaneous occurrence of a crime problem—namely, piracy in several widely separated waterways of the world in the mid-1970s, perpetrated in large part by rootless young offenders.[67]) The skinheads are part of the broader problem of crimes of discrimination against minorities, which itself is fueled by vastly increased intracontinental and intercontinental migrations. The appearance of new ethnic minorities within heretofore monoethnic communities often results in the victimization of minorities. These population migrations have also resulted in the migration of crime perpetrated by migrants—often against their fellow migrants, but also against the indigenous population. Consequently, criminologists have had to look for new ways to deal with these new forms and dimensions of crime.[68]

Internationally induced local crime problems can be far greater than hate crimes or other forms of crime associated with culture conflict and migration. Consider that drugs produced abroad and distributed locally create a vast problem of crime: Not only is drug dealing illegal, but a considerable portion of street crime is associated with

narcotics. Ultimately, it could be said that there are very few crime problems that are not associated with persons and events abroad over which we have no direct control. Although the problem is a vast, largely uncharted territory, a number of criminal activities with foreign connections have recently been identified and given the title "transnational crime."

Transnational Crime

Criminologists use the term **transnational crime** to refer to criminal activities, transactions, or schemes that violate the laws of more than one country or have a direct impact on a foreign country. Neither individually, nor by type, nor collectively by category do transnational crimes conform to the definitions and categorizations found in penal codes.

In a recent questionnaire sent to all the world's national governments and a subsequent report on the results, the United Nations, for the first time in history, demonstrated the existence and prevalence of transnational crime.[69] Eighteen categories of transnational criminality emerged. While it

Accounts were falsified and large sums of customers' money diverted using a financial labyrinth to fool auditors into thinking the bank was solvent when it was actually hugely in deficit.(1)

A HARD LESSON

While the settlement in the United States provided funds for the compensation of some depositors, many more will never see their money again. Some consider this a "school of hard knocks" lesson about the inability of the criminal justice system to deal effectively with international fraud. Gathering the documents needed to provide evidence ranges from difficult to impossible. After one trial in the United States, a *Chicago Tribune* editorial commented, "International financial transactions can be made so complex as to effectively conceal what is really going on; key officials can always flee the jurisdiction and take vital evidence with them."(2) One lawyer summed up his observation of the outcomes of big international cases succinctly: "No one gets caught but huge sums of money disappear."(3)

More recently, the Daewoo Group in Korea imploded in a 22.9 trillion won ($22.57 billion) accounting fraud

scandal—the largest in history. The fraud, resulting in countless victims across a wide range of stake-holders, highlights the inadequacy of effective governance structures and controls, not to mention the abject failure of the gatekeepers (e.g., accountants, lawyers, etc.).

Most recently, the largest international Ponzi scheme ever was uncovered, committed by a well-respected former chairman of the NASDAQ—one of the largest stock exchanges in the world.(4) Bernard Madoff, it seems, defrauded investors around the world of more than $50 billion (possibly as much as $100 billion), with losses stretching from Austria to Italy, from Switzerland to Kuwait. His arrest and prosecution raise many questions, perhaps the most significant of which is, How did regulators both here and abroad miss this ongoing fraud for so many years?

What should be done to prevent international corporate fraud? This question remains the subject of lively debate. How should liability and culpability be assessed? What kinds of punishments ensure just deserts and deter future offenses? What international bodies must be created to investigate, prosecute, and punish corporate

offenders? These are the debatable issues.

Sources

1. Ben Fenton and Sonia Purnell, "Bank Official Admits $750m Fraud, 'Financial Juggler' Was at the Heart of BCCI Scandal," *Daily Telegraph*, Sept. 28, 1993, p.1.
2. "BCCI Still a Mystery," *Chicago Tribune*, Aug. 27, 1993, p. 23.
3. Peter Blackman, "The BCCI Problem; System's Flaws Stymie Probes of Foreign Banks," *New York Law Journal*, Aug. 26, 1993, p. 5.
4. See, e.g., Diana B. Henriques, "Madoff Scheme Kept Rippling Outward, Across Borders," *New York Times*, Dec. 20, 2008; available at http://www.nytimes.com/2008/12/20/business/20madoff.html?_r=1&scp=2&sq=madoff&st=cse.

Questions for Discussion

1. How could depositors be protected from losing their money in international scams like BCCI?
2. Would an international criminal court be better able to deal with massive international fraud?

---

is conceivable that all these activities could be committed within a single jurisdiction and/or by individual perpetrators, it is the hallmark of all that they are typically perpetrated by means of transnational activities and by organized groups of perpetrators.[70]

1. *Money laundering.* This category ranks number one on the list because of its massive impact on the global economy. Money laundering is an activity aimed at making illegally obtained funds seem legitimate so that such funds can be spent or invested in the legitimate economy without arousing suspicion. Consider that a substantial part of the financial gain of the world's citizens is ill-gotten—for example, by bribery, by corruption, by black-market activities and transactions outside the tax laws, and, especially, by dealing in contraband.

The drug barons and others who have illegitimate income have devised many schemes to launder dirty money, including bogus real estate transactions, purchases of gold (many times consisting of lead bars with a coating of gold), and

sales (real or fictitious) of art and antiques. But the standard method remains the physical transfer of cash out of the country (by planes or ships or by trucks and trailers with false bottoms) and the deposit of such cash abroad, followed by a series of international (electronic) transfers at the end of which the source is untraceable and the money seems clean and legitimately invested in the economy (Figure 14.1).

The true dimensions of money laundering are largely unknown. Estimates range from as low as $500 billion to as high as $1 trillion annually.[71] Nevertheless, policy research (especially the Financial Transactions Task Force of the Group of Seven [highly industrialized countries]) has resulted in some remedies.

2. *Terrorist activities.* Americans had been largely unaware of the international scope of terrorist activities, primarily because their homeland had been relatively unaffected. This naiveté changed with the growing awareness that Americans, and American interests and installations abroad, have become targets of international

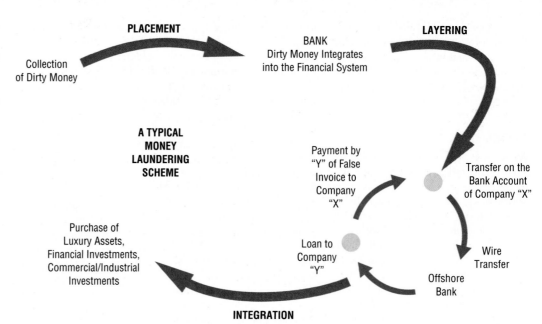

FIGURE 14.1 The operational principles of money laundering are as follows: First, move the funds from direct association with the crime; second, disguise the trail to foil pursuit; third, make the money available to the criminal once again with its origins hidden.

Source: United Nations Office for Drug Control and Crime Prevention, *United Nations Global Programme against Money Laundering* (New York: United Nations, 1998), pp. 18–19.

PLACEMENT

Collection of Dirty Money

BANK
Dirty Money Integrates into the Financial System

LAYERING

A TYPICAL MONEY LAUNDERING SCHEME

Payment by "Y" of False Invoice to Company "X"

Transfer on the Bank Account of Company "X"

Purchase of Luxury Assets, Financial Investments, Commercial/Industrial Investments

Loan to Company "Y"

Wire Transfer

Offshore Bank

INTEGRATION

terrorists. But only the bombing of the World Trade Center in New York City in February 1993 by an organized group of Middle Eastern terrorists alerted Americans to the vulnerability of their own country. Similarly, Russians were shocked when Chechen rebels took 800 people hostage in a Moscow theater in October 2002. Rescue efforts killed 41 terrorists and 123 hostages. Of course, the victimization of air transport to and from America is a continuing reminder of terrorists' capability to harm American interests. The most horrific demonstration of air terrorism was the use of four hijacked jets by Al Qaeda terrorists to completely destroy the World Trade Center towers and damage the Pentagon on September 11, 2001, with a loss of thousands of lives (see Chapter 10).[72]

Much scholarly inquiry has been directed at understanding and explaining international terrorism.[73] And there have been legislative responses. As a matter of fact, a network of international conventions is in place to deal with international terrorism. International judicial collaboration and police cooperation have been vastly improved. Yet there is no international machinery in operation to ensure the arrest or adjudication of international terrorists, and criminologists have yet to arrive at theoretically sound explanations that would help nations deal with a problem that knows no boundaries.

3. *Theft of art and cultural objects.* This category ranked third because of its potential for robbing entire cultures and nations of their cultural heritage. Tombs and monuments have been plundered since the time of the pharaohs. But with the development of modern tools and the high demand for cultural objects, as well as the ease

of transport, international thieves have developed systems that can strip an entire region or country of its heritage—as well as the work of contemporary artists. Every country has been victimized. An estimated $4.5 billion worth of fine art is stolen every year for sale on the international market. A database lists 45,000 stolen art objects, with 2,000 items added each month.[74] With few exceptions,[75] criminologists have paid scant attention to this phenomenon, though the art industry has endeavored to come up with some practical solutions.[76]

4. *Theft of intellectual property.* Theft of intellectual property includes the unauthorized use of the rights of authors and performers and of copyrights and trademarks. There is obviously a great temptation to reproduce works of protected originators at a fraction of franchise (or similar) costs, especially in countries with relatively unregulated economies. Yet the destructive impact on the economies of producing or originating countries is immediately apparent. Intellectual property theft costs American corporations $250 billion every year. In 2004, the Motion Picture Association of America (MPAA) estimated that the movie industry lost $3.5 billion, the Recording Industry Association of America (RIAA) estimated losses in the music industry of roughly $12.5 billion; and the U.S. Software Publishers Association estimated losses of $7.5 billion. Intellectual theft also includes counterfeit versions of pharmaceuticals, automotive parts, and electrical equipment, which pose significant health and safety issues in addition to economic losses.[77] Despite international agreements, this transnational crime category remains a problem without a solution.

5. *Illicit traffic in arms.* Local, regional, or national armed conflicts, which today plague every part of the globe, would be unimaginable without an international network of weapons producers and suppliers. This is a shadowy world beyond the reach of statistical assessment. Criminological information on the illegal arms trade is also lacking. Yet the largest portion of the world's homicides potentially is traceable to the illegal traffic in arms.

The most lethal part of the world's illegal arms trade involves the transfer of nuclear materials. It has become clear that several relatively small quantities of nuclear material, including pure plutonium, have been diverted from nuclear facilities in former Soviet republics and offered for sale in Germany and other countries west of Russia.

First indications are that the diversions of nuclear material that have occurred so far were carried out by small groups of individuals, rather than organized crime, for motives of individual gain (or possibly to assist in financing underfunded former Soviet laboratories and scientists). Most of the efforts were amateurish, and none of the material apparently reached a viable buyer. Indeed, most ended up in sting operations. However, the quantities of nuclear material seized by authorities are not insubstantial. In September 1999, Georgian authorities seized 2.2 pounds of uranium 235 at the Georgian-Turkish border.[78] In several cases, the thieves, transporters, and the public have been exposed to radiation hazards—in itself a substantial danger.[79] Criminologists have been caught by surprise. As yet, there have been few criminological responses.[80] At this point, governments have cooperated to control nuclear materials at the source.

6. *Aircraft hijacking.* The system for curbing and responding to the illegal interception of aircraft is in place and has proved somewhat effective. The number of hijackings has declined significantly, yet incidents still occur with regularity, as the events of September 11, 2001, have horribly demonstrated.

The airline industry had been plagued by aircraft hijackings in the 1970s and into the 1980s. While a few such incidents were attributable to individuals who demanded ransom, most were political statements with typical terrorist characteristics, aimed at demonstrating the ability of the terrorist organization to strike at vulnerable targets almost anywhere in the world.

Because the entire world community was affected—especially diplomats and politicians, whose mobility depends on air travel—the reaction to the flood of hijackings was swift. The industry itself reacted by increasing security measures.

The criminological literature on this phenomenon is considerable, centering on the profiles of hijackers, causes, regions, carriers involved, and the like, all of which has led to the improvement of controls.

7. *Sea piracy.* Virtually forgotten until the mid-1970s, sea piracy has resurfaced:

• Illegal narcotics drug smuggling from South and Central America into the United States initially relied heavily on yachts and fishing vessels captured at sea or in port, after owners and crews were killed. Several thousand vessels were victimized. As the drug trade became prosperous, smugglers began to rely on purchased or illegally chartered vessels.

• At the roadstead of Lagos, Nigeria, and the narrow shipping channel of the Malacca Straits—as well as in several comparable sea lanes—the opportunity of deriving some benefit by attacking commercial vessels at anchor or slow speed attracted thousands of marginalized young men in Africa, Southeast Asia, and Latin America. Such piracies (often not piracies in the international law sense, since they occurred in the territorial waters of states) reached a high level of frequency (one a day in the 1980s) but are now on the decline, thanks largely to the research and policy activities of the International Maritime Bureau (London) of the International Chamber of Commerce (Paris), the International Maritime Organization (UN), and a number of criminologists.[81] (See "Debatable Issues," Chapter 11.)

• There has been a major increase in piracy off the Somali coast. An estimated 230 foreign sailors were being held hostage for ransom in ships off the coast of Somalia as of June 2009. More than a dozen warships from navies around the world have joined in the hunt. Prudent shipping lines order "piracy watches" on their vessels in affected waters. National and regional maritime law enforcement agencies maintain closer watch, and the International Maritime Bureau maintains a special branch office in Kuala Lumpur, Malaysia, to monitor developments. Worldwide attention to the problem of piracy was heightened in April 2009 with the daring high seas rescue of Captain Richard Phillips. Phillips was held hostage for four days after pirates boarded his container ship.

8. *Land hijacking.* The inclusion of land hijacking in the list of transnational crimes was a surprise. At the national level, hijacking of trucks had been well documented as a form of robbery or theft. But the world economy shifted. Long-distance trucking from eastern to western Europe or from the central Asian republics to the Baltic States now is a reality and involves a high percentage of goods transported transnationally. The opportunity to divert such cargos has increased proportionately.

It is telling that only four countries responded to this item on the UN questionnaire. At this point, the evidence is entirely episodic but seems to point to the involvement of organized groups. Predictably, the problem will increase as a result of the openness of borders, the growth of organized crime (especially in eastern Europe), and the lack of data and criminological analysis.

9. *Insurance fraud.* The insurance industry is internationally linked, especially through reinsurance and other methods of spreading risks and benefits. Thus, local insurance fraud ultimately affects all insurers, and all insured, worldwide. The global dimensions of the problem have not been calculated, but for the United States alone, the loss likely amounts to $100 billion annually.[82]

10. *Computer crime.* The Internet serves legitimate commerce, governments, and researchers. But the global Internet also presents a host of opportunities for criminals, including exploitation, criminal schemes, and wide use by organized crime. Current estimates of losses through computer crime range up to $8 billion annually.[83] Unfortunately, we lack information on this issue, though criminologists are taking an increasing interest in the development of legal and other protections.

11. *Environmental crime.* Well into the middle of the twentieth century, harming the environment was regarded as a matter to be controlled by local authorities. It was not until the United Nations Congress on the Environment (Stockholm, 1972) that the global dimensions of environmental destruction, and thus the need for its control, were recognized. In the more than three decades since Stockholm, much has been achieved in recognizing environmental dangers, quantifying them, and devising control mechanisms (by treaties, legislation, and, ultimately, technology) in order to avert the dangers. Criminological research has contributed a great deal in this regard.[84]

12. *Trafficking in persons.* Original forms of trafficking in persons included the slave trade and the white slave trade (traffic in women). While the slave trade may be largely a matter of the past, the traffic in persons is on the increase, including

• the transport of illegal immigrants, often resulting in involuntary servitude;

• the transport of women and young children for purposes of prostitution;

• the transport of migratory laborers to work under slavelike conditions;

• the transport of household workers from developing countries;

• the transfer of children for adoptions not sanctioned by law.

For the most part, laws are in place to prevent the illegal trafficking in persons. Their enforcement is another matter. The problem is bound to increase as the populations of a stagnant Third World press to emigrate to the relatively prosperous countries.

Much of the illegal population flow is controlled by organized crime.[85] The newcomers in the industrialized countries, being largely unemployable, are forming a new marginalized class, likely to be exploited but also contributing to crime and unrest.

13. *Trade in human body parts.* The first kidney transplant was performed in 1954, the first lung transplant in 1963, and the first heart transplant in 1967. Transplant surgery has become a highly specialized branch of medicine, and the supply of transplantable organs has spawned a very large industry. In the United States, more than 200 agencies and programs have been established, and federal and state laws seek to control their activities.

Yet, at any given moment, tens of thousands of people are waiting for a transplant (and the number increases by 14 percent annually); thus, the demand far outstrips the supply. (The number of potential donors in the United States is estimated at about 12,000.) An illegitimate industry has sprung up to satisfy the demand. Recipients are flown to a country where organs can be procured virtually on demand. "Donors" may in fact have been murdered for their organs or may be children of poor parents sold for their organs at extremely low prices.

14. *Illicit drug trafficking.* Illicit traffic in narcotic drugs is entirely controlled by organized-crime networks, loosely related to each other geographically as well as at the various levels of production and marketing and by type of narcotic drugs.[86] The criminological literature exploring this phenomenon from every angle is vast but by no means clear in terms of policy implications.[87] With the Single Convention on Narcotic Drugs (1961), the Convention on Psychotropic Substances (1971), and the United Nations Convention against Illicit Traffic in Narcotic Drugs and Psychotropic Substances (1988), a theoretically perfect international legal structure to control this traffic is in place. Yet its application and enforcement suffer from several shortcomings:

- The UN structure to oversee this treaty scheme is inadequate, primarily due to underfunding.

- Similarly underfunded are comparable national and regional programs.

- Nations differ vastly in their emphases (interdiction versus repression and control versus tolerance versus treatment approaches).

- Some of the most important countries of origin suffer from corruption at all levels—due to the vast income base of the trade—thus affecting enforcement.

- Corruption similarly affects law enforcement in many countries receiving the drugs.

- Most developing and newly democratic countries lack the legal and technical infrastructure necessary to implement the treaties.

No other form of transnational and organized crime is as costly in terms of human suffering and national financial burden as the illicit trade in narcotic drugs.

15. *Fraudulent bankruptcy.* The internationalization of commerce has turned fraudulent bankruptcy into a transnational crime. The dimensions of the phenomenon are largely unknown. Evidence is anecdotal but includes information that organized crime, after acquiring an enterprise, may subject it to bankruptcy when the gains from bankruptcy exceed the expectations of profit. There is a need to strengthen national enforcement efforts and to coordinate these efforts internationally.

16. *Infiltration of legal business.* This is the logical and temporal sequence of money laundering, the principal objective of which is seemingly legitimate investment. At this point, the information available permits no quantitative or qualitative assessment of the phenomenon, but it must be considered that the drug trade alone has between $200 billion and $500 billion to invest in the market. At this rate we could theoretically predict a time when the world's economy would be controlled by organized crime.[88]

17. *Corruption and bribery of public officials, party officials, and elected representatives.* While in several countries bribery of party officials is not punishable, all other forms of bribery encompassed by this title are prohibited by penal codes. The problem lies with the enforceability of such laws, in developed and developing countries alike, particularly with respect to international investments and trade. Disguised as "commissions," "consultancies," and agency or attorneys' fees, bribes have become a necessary cost of doing business worldwide. Nor is the practice universally condemned. Traders and investors have often proclaimed that it cannot be their business to improve the business or political ethics in countries with which they have commercial relations.[89] A highly regarded international organization, Transparency International (Berlin), has undertaken the formidable task of investigating international business ethics. Among its accomplishments are

- publishing a country-by-country bribery index;

- pressing for national legislation abolishing the tax deductibility of bribes;

- seeking international governmental cooperation in criminalizing the bribing of officials;

- strengthening international cooperation among nongovernmental organizations, such as the International Chamber of Commerce;

- creating independent watchdog mechanisms.

18. *Other offenses committed by organized criminal groups.* This catchall category permitted governments to report problems that could not be easily included in the 17 other categories. For example, both North America and western Europe are experiencing large-scale automobile theft, with the stolen vehicles being transported abroad. These activities are controlled by international organized criminal groups. They affect not just individual owners, but the insurance industry of each country.

This review of the 18 categories of transnational criminality demonstrates the vast impact these criminal activities have on individuals, various

Crime Surfing WWW

http://www.unodc .org/unodc/en/data -and-analysis/United -Nations-Surveys-on -Crime-Trends-and -the-Operations-of -Criminal-Justice -Systems.html

How does the United States' crime rate compare with that of the world as a whole? You will find this information in the UN Survey of Crime Trends and Operations of Criminal Justice Systems.

Crime Surfing

www.interpol.com

If you want to find out how the International Criminal Police Organization (ICPO— Interpol) helps in the fight against transnational crime (or anything else you ever wanted to know about Interpol), access the organization's website.

branches of the economy, and the world economy itself. Individuals and individual commercial enterprises can do relatively little to protect themselves from these dangers, and increased international cooperation among nations has been recognized as absolutely necessary. But international action must be preceded by research. Thus, comparative criminological research will increasingly focus on transnational crime.[90]

International Crime

International crimes are the major criminal offenses so designated by the community of nations for the protection of interests common to all humankind. They may be found in precedent (much like the Anglo-American common law of crimes) or in written form in international conventions. They can be tried in the courts of countries that recognize them or by international courts. The war crimes tribunals that tried German and Japanese war criminals after World War II were such courts. In 1993, the UN Security Council ordered the establishment of an international tribunal to sit in the Netherlands for war crimes committed on the territory of the former Yugoslavia; a court for the trial of persons charged with genocide in Rwanda was added. These courts have issued several hundred indictments—the exact number is unknown because the indictments are sealed. Several trials have been held, leading to convictions as well as acquittals. Among those in custody was General Momir Talic, the chief of staff of the Bosnian Serb army, who spent three years in jail (released on grounds of health). Some other powerful indicted war criminals are still in hiding, but they cannot leave the small territories under their control for fear of being taken into custody under outstanding international arrest warrants. The former President of Yugoslavia, Slobodan Milosevic, was on trial for war crimes at the Amsterdam Tribunal of the United Nations when he died of a heart attack in the war criminal prison located in the Hague.

In May 2002, a long-standing dream of establishing a permanent **international criminal court** became a reality after more than 60 nations ratified the treaty. The court, which tries only cases involving the most heinous crimes, became effective on July 1, 2002. The ICC is a court of last resort—it will only try future cases that other countries cannot or will not handle. The jurisdiction of the new court extends only to the most serious international crimes, such as crimes against humanity, genocide, and war crimes. While such an agreement was impossible during the era of the cold war, the governments of the world, meeting in Rome in 1998, agreed by a vast majority vote to establish the Permanent International Criminal Court. Under the Clinton Administration, the United States signed the treaty in 2000 but has yet to ratify it. The handful of other nations that have not yet approved the treaty are Pakistan, China, India, and a few small—so-called rogue—countries. Many fear that the power of the court will be greatly weakened without the support of these countries. Except for the few major international crimes over which the international court has jurisdiction, all other crimes are triable only before national criminal courts.

Which crimes are listed as international crimes? The Draft Code of Crimes lists the following as crimes against the peace and security of humanity:

- Crimes against humanity

- Aggression (by one state against another)

- Threat of aggression

- Intervention (in the internal or external affairs of another state)

- Colonial domination and other forms of alien domination

- Genocide (destroying a national, ethnic, racial, or religious group)

- Apartheid (suppression of a racial or an ethnic group)

- Systematic or mass violations of human rights

- Exceptionally serious war crimes

- Recruitment, use, financing, and training of mercenaries (soldiers of fortune)

- International terrorism

- Illicit traffic in narcotic drugs

- Willful and severe damage to the environment[91]

The commission of these crimes takes many forms. For example, "systematic or mass violations of human rights" may be organized, large-scale rapes of women in occupied territories, as occurred in Bosnia in 1992 and 1993.[92]

In addition to the listed international crimes, many others are recognized by convention; these include the cutting of undersea cables, the transportation of women for purposes of prostitution ("white slavery"), and fisheries offenses. There is now a considerable body of research and scholarship on international crimes.[93]

Globalization versus Ethnic Fragmentation

We have entered the twenty-first century. Comparative criminologists view the new millennium with some uneasiness. Globalization raises great hopes for a better future for all human beings, yet it brings with it grave dangers in terms of the

Crime Surfing

www.iccnow.org

For the latest developments on the establishment of the permanent International Criminal Court, check their website.

DID YOU KNOW?

. . . that the United Nations started in 1945 with 51 Member States? By fall 1999, there were 188 Member States, united "to achieve international cooperation in solving economic, social, cultural and humanitarian problems," including the prevention of crime. By 2003, the number of Member States stood at 191, its current number.

■ Civil war in the Darfur region of Sudan has forced tens of thousands of refugees, like these arriving at a camp in the northern part of the region, to flee from their homes. The Sudanese government has been accused of covering up and even taking part in the Darfur violence. The International Criminal Court has issued an arrest warrant for Sudan's president on charges of murder and crimes against humanity.

internationalization of crime. Comparative criminology has a significant role to play in the investigation of new forms of transnational crime. Researchers can apply the methods used when such crimes were strictly local or national, but benefit from the sophistication of the science of comparative criminology.

The new millennium presents additional hazards arising from the trend toward balkanization. "Balkanization," the opposite of globalization, is the breakup of nation-states into ethnic entities. Many ethnic groups are striving for the independence and sovereignty denied them when they were incorporated in larger nation-states, as in the former Soviet Union or Yugoslavia; or when they were joined arbitrarily with other groups in colonial times, as in Africa; or when other accidents of history included them within empires, as in western Europe. Frequently, such ethnic groups had to abide by laws and customs that were not of their own choosing and had to suppress their own languages and cultures. Now they are searching for identities, territories, and criminal justice systems of their own. Unfortunately, the struggle has brought with it human rights violations, war crimes, and genocide on a massive scale. This is the latest challenge for criminologists and criminal justice specialists working on the international level.

REVIEW

Comparative criminology, despite its historical antecedents, is a young science, a subspecialty of criminology. In view of the globalization brought about by recent technological advances and the enormous increase in international commerce—both legal and illegal—comparative studies in criminology have become a necessity. Comparatists are called upon to assist governments in devising strategies to deal with a wide variety of international and transnational crimes.

In this chapter, we traced the history of comparative criminology, sought to define it, and attempted to identify its goals. These goals may be theoretical, like the cross-cultural testing of prominent theories of crime. They can also be very practical, like the search for transplantable crime-fighting strategies or for techniques to deal with specific transnational and international crimes.

There are a number of requirements for successful comparative research: studying foreign law, understanding foreign criminal justice systems, learning about a foreign culture, collecting reliable data, engaging in comparative research, and, when needed, doing cross-cultural empirical research.

We paid special attention to three dimensions that pose special challenges to comparative criminology: internationally induced local crime, transnational crime, and international crime. There is much research to be conducted before progress can be expected in these three areas.

The accomplishments of criminologists who have engaged in comparative studies form the foundation for further research. The tools of comparative criminology should prove useful in helping both individual nations and the United Nations solve some of their common crime problems. The United Nations and its agencies continue to do very practical work to help nations deal with crime on a worldwide basis.

CHAPTER 14

CRIMINOLOGY & PUBLIC POLICY

Why is it that criminologists rarely if ever study genocide? Have we forgotten the systematic decimation of 1½ million Armenians by the Young Turks during World War I; the planned killing of 6 million Jews; and the extermination of another 5 million untermenschen, including Gypsies, political opponents, mentally ill, retarded, and other "inferior" peoples between 1941 and 1945? How could criminology have neglected an examination of the crimes against humanity that resulted in an estimated 7 to 16 million deaths over the past 60 years since World War II?

Some of the more obvious and yet unacceptable reasons are offered here.

1. Genocide is a political act reflecting the will of sovereignty.

2. Genocide is a breach of international norms and international law.

3. Genocide is committed by the state.

4. The magnitude of victimization in genocide defies belief.

5. Criminology has little to offer the study of genocide.

6. There are problems in denying or in admitting atrocity.

Consider how the criminology of genocide would add to our knowledge of victimization, homicide, aggression, and violence. Consider, as well, how research on genocide might support the theoretical work of critical and Marxist scholars in their efforts to explain a different conception of the state in relation to crime. Most important, reflect on the contribution that criminologists could make to further our understanding as to how genocide may be prevented. Nowhere are matters of prevention more important than with the crime of genocide.

It is all too easy to say that criminology's neglect of genocide suggests a disciplinary denial; that our failure to recognize genocide implicitly contributes to the evil of revisionism; and that we should know better than to have the boundaries of our field permanently fixed by the criminal law—especially where extant law is so frail and uncertain. It is all too easy to say these things, because they are true. (Source: William S. Laufer, "The Forgotten Criminology of Genocide," *The Criminology of Criminal Law: Advances in Criminological Theory*, **8**, 1999).

Questions for Discussion   Why do you suppose the field of criminology neglects the study of genocide? Is it justifiable if genocide is the most serious form of homicide?

YOU BE THE CRIMINOLOGIST

What advice would you give to the U.S. Congress regarding how to alleviate the global crime problem as it affects U.S. citizens? Should the United States go it alone? Enter into bilateral arrangements? Attempt to find global solutions? Explain your recommendations.

KEY TERMS

The numbers next to the terms refer to the pages on which the terms are defined.

comparative criminology (357)

international crimes (372)

international criminal court (372)

transnational crime (366)

Notes

CHAPTER 1

1. Gerhard O. W. Mueller and Freda Adler, "The Criminology of Disasters," in *Criminology on the Threshold of the 21st Century: Essays in Honor of Hans Joachim Schneider,* eds. H. Dieterschwind et al. (Berlin: Walter deGruyter, 1998), pp. 161–181.
2. Robert Chapman et al., *Local Law Enforcement Responds to Terrorism* (Washington, D.C.: Police Foundation, 2002).
3. *Patterns of Global Terrorism 1999* (Washington, D.C.: U.S. State Department, April 2000).
4. Robert Spear and Philip Shenou, "Customs Switches Priority from Drugs to Terrorism," *New York Times,* Oct. 10, 2001, www.crimelynx.com/custswitch.html; Jerry Seper, "Mexicans, Russian Mob New Partners in Crime," *Washington Times,* Sept. 14, 2002, www.rusnet.nl/info/cis-today/archive/01-05/28wnl.shtm.
5. Secret bank account transfers are not the only method of laundering money. Other methods are Market Peso Exchange, cash smuggling, gold transfers, and many others.
6. Steven Erlanger, "Hamburg Police Raid 2 Import-Export Firms," www.nytimes.com/2002/09/11/international/11GERM.html; "3 Former Executives Indicted in Fraud," *New York Times,* Sept. 6, 2002, Sec. C, p. 4; Leif Pagrotsky and Joseph Stiglitz, "Blocking the Terrorists' Funds: The Global Financial System Provides Hiding Places for Dirty Money," *Financial Times,* Dec. 7, 2001; Daniel Williams, "Swiss Probe Illustrates Difficulties in Tracking Al Qaeda's Cash," *Washington Post,* Nov. 12, 2001.
7. P. K. Semler, "Rich Linked to Money Laundering," *Washington Times,* June 21, 2002, www.washtimes.com/world/20020621-417508.htm. The reference is to the American fugitive financier Mark Rich, who defrauded clients of millions of dollars, found safe haven (and business opportunities) in Zug, Switzerland, and was ultimately pardoned by President Clinton.
8. R. Mark Bortner, "Cyberlaundering; Anonymous Digital Cash and Money Laundering," www.law.miami.edu/~fro@mkin/seminar/papers/bortner.htm (1996).
9. Jim Wolf, "Cyber Attack Fears Stir Security Offices," http://story.news.yahoo.com/news?tmplstory2@cid-ncid-564@e-11@u-lnm/2002.
10. Barton Gellman, "Cyber-Attacks by Al Qaeda Feared," www.crime-research.org/eng/library/Barton.htm (2002).
11. For example, Associated Press, International News, "Italian Police Arrest 15 Alleged Islamic Extremists," Sept. 16, 2002.
12. For example, see Ross Sorkin, "2 Top Tyco Executives Charged with $600 Million Fraud Scheme," *New York Times,* Sept. 13, 2002, pp. 1, C3.
13. "The Mariner Group—Oil Spill History," www.marinergroup.com/oil-spill-history.htm; CNN.com/world, "Chinese Oil Tanker Explodes at Sea," www.cnn.com/2002/WORLD/asiapcf/east/09/11/china.tanker.reut/index.html; Toby Reynolds, "South Africa Blocks Oil Spill from Wetlands," www.swissinfo.org/sen/Swissinfo.html.Environmental; Timeline, www.mapreport.com/subtopics/d/l.html; Incident News, www.incidentnews.gov/, National Ocean Service, National Oceanic and Atmospheric Administration, Apr. 11, 2002.
14. Raffaele Garofalo, *Criminologia* (Naples, 1885), published in English as *Criminology,* trans. Robert W. Millar (Boston: Little, Brown, 1914; rpt., Montclair, N.J.: Patterson Smith, 1968).
15. Paul Topinard, "L'Anthropologie criminelle," *Revue d'anthropologie,* **2** (1887).
16. Edwin H. Sutherland, *Principles of Criminology,* 2d ed. (Philadelphia: Lippincott, 1934), originally published as *Criminology,* 1924.
17. Some legal scholars argue that criminologists should study only lawbreaking. See Note 1.
18. Jack D. Douglas and Frances C. Waksler, *The Sociology of Deviance* (Boston: Little, Brown, 1982).
19. Garofalo, *Criminologia,* p. 5.
20. Émile Durkheim, *Rules of Sociological Method,* trans. S. A. Solaway and J. H. Mueller (Glencoe, Ill.: Free Press, 1958), p. 64.
21. Freda Adler, "Our American Society of Criminology, the World, and the State of the Art—The American Society of Criminology 1995 Presidential Address," *Criminology,* **34** (1995): 1–9.
22. *Critical Criminal Justice Issues: Task Force Reports to Attorney General Janet Reno* (Washington, D.C.: National Institute of Justice/American Society of Criminology, 1995).

CHAPTER 2

1. James Finckenauer, *Scared Straight: The Panacea Phenomena* (Englewood Cliffs, N.J.: Prentice Hall, 1982).
2. Anthony Petrosino et al., "Scared Straight and Other Juvenile Awareness Programs for Preventing Juvenile Delinquency: A Systematic Review of Randomized Experimental Evidence," *Annals,* **589** (Sept. 2003).
3. The Anglo-American concept of crime was developed by a long line of distinguished legal scholars, as discussed in G. O. W. Mueller, *Crime, Law, and the Scholars* (London: Heinemann; Seattle: University of Washington Press, 1969).
4. Jerome Hall, *General Principles of Criminal Law,* 2d ed. (Indianapolis: Bobbs-Merrill, 1960).
5. American Law Institute, Model Penal Code, sec. 2.01(1). The American Law Institute, dedicated to law reform, is an association of some of the most prestigious American lawyers. Between 1954 and 1962 this group sought to codify the best features of the penal codes of the various states. The resultant Model Penal Code (MPC) has had considerable influence on law reform in many states, and has been adopted nearly in full by New Jersey and Pennsylvania. We shall have frequent occasion to refer to the MPC as "typical" American criminal law. See also Gerhard O. W. Mueller, "The Public Law of Wrongs—Its Concepts in the World of Reality," *Journal of Public Law,* **10** (1961): 203–260; and Michael Moore, *Act and Crime—The Philosophy of Action and Its Implications for Criminal Law* (Oxford: Clarendon Press, 1993).
6. Nanci Adler, *The Gulag Survivor: Beyond the Soviet System* (New Brunswick, N.J.: Transaction Publishers, 2002).
7. *Robinson v. California,* 370 U.S. 660 (1962).

8. *State v. Palendrano,* 120 N.J. Super 336, 293 A. 2d 747 (1972).

9. Ibid.

10. G. O. W. Mueller, "Causing Criminal Harm," in *Essays in Criminal Science,* ed. Mueller (South Hackensack, N.J.: Fred B. Rothman, 1961), pp. 167–214.

11. *Lambert v. California,* 355 U.S. 225 (1957). This decision must be approached with care. It does not stand for the proposition that ignorance of the law is an excuse. The Supreme Court was very careful to limit the scope of its decision to offenses by omission of adherence to regulations not commonly known, when the defendant in fact did not know—and had no means of knowing—of the prohibition.

12. G. O. W. Mueller, "On Common Law Mens Rea," *Minnesota Law Review,* **42** (1958): 1043–1104, at p. 1060.

13. For a recent look at the insanity defense, and its many challenges, see Richard Moran, *Knowing Right from Wrong: The Insanity Defense of Daniel McNaughtan* (New York: Free Press, 2000).

14. David Weisburd, Lorraine Mazerolle, and Anthony Petrosino, "The Academy of Experimental Criminology: Advancing Randomized Trials in Crime and Justice," (unpublished paper), available at http://www.crim.upenn.edu/aec/.

15. Coalition for Evidence-Based Research, "Which Study Designs Can Produce Rigorous Evidence of Program Effectiveness? A Brief Overview" (working paper, Coalition for Evidence-Based Policy, January 2006).

16. Karen L. Sees et al., "Methadone Maintenance vs. 180-Day Psychosocially Enriched Detoxification for Treatment of Opioid Dependence: A Randomized Controlled Trial," *Journal of the American Medical Association,* **283(10)** (March 8, 2000): 1303–1310, http://jama.ama-assn.org/cgi/content/abstract/283/10/1303; Frances A. Campbell et al., "Early Childhood Education: Young Adult Outcomes from the Abecedarian Project," *Applied Developmental Science,* **6(1)** (2002): 42–57, http://www.leaonline.com/doi/abs/10.1207/S1532480X ADS0601_05. See also Lawrence J. Schweinhart, H. V. Barnes, and David P. Weikart, *Significant Benefits: The High/Scope Perry Preschool Study through Age 27* (High/Scope Press, 1993), http://www.highscope.org/Research/PerryProject/perryfact.htp; Gilbert J. Botvin et al., "Long-Term Follow-up Results of a Randomized Drug Abuse Prevention Trial in a White, Middle-class Population," *Journal of the American Medical Association,* **273(14)** (April 12, 1995): 1106–1112, http://jama.ama-assn.org/cgi/content/abstract/273/14/1106; Anthony A. Braga et al., "Problem-Oriented Policing in Violent Crime Places: A Randomized Controlled Experiment," *Criminology,* **37(3)** (August 1999): 541–580, http://www.ncjrs.org/rr/vol1_1/37.html; Denise C. Gottfredson, Stacy S. Najaka, and Brook Kearley, "Effectiveness of Drug Treatment Courts: Evidence from a Randomized Trial," *Criminology and Public Policy,* **2(2)** (March 2003): 171–196, http://www.criminologyandpublicpolicy.com/search/abstrGottfredson03.php; Harry K. Wexler et al., "Three-Year Reincarceration Outcomes for Amity In-Prison Therapeutic Community and Aftercare in California," The *Prison Journal,* **79(3)** (Sept. 1999): 321–336, http://www.amityfoundation.com/lib/libarch/99wexler_3yroutcom.pdf; Lawrence W. Sherman, Edward Poole, and Christopher S. Koper, "Preliminary Report to the Pennsylvania Department of Revenue on the 'Fair Share' Project," Jerry Lee Center of Criminology, Fels Institute of Government, University of Pennsylvania, 2004.

17. Coalition, for Evidence-Based Research, "Which Study Designs?"

18. Ibid.

19. J. McGuire, C. A. L. Bilby, R. M. Hatcher et al., "Evaluation of Structured Cognitive-Behavioural Treatment Programmes in Reducing Criminal Recidivism," *Journal of Experimental Criminology* **4**(2008):21–40.

20. D. P. Farrington, M. Gill, S. J. Waples, and J. Argomaniz, "The Effects of Closed-Circuit Television on Crime: Meta-Analysis of an English National Quasi-Experimental Multi-site Evaluation," *Journal of Experimental Criminology* **3**(2007):21–38.

21. E. Blais and J.-L. Bacher, "Situational Deterrence and Claim Padding: Results from a Randomized Field Experiment," *Journal of Experimental Criminology* **3**(2007):337–352.

22. D. L. MacKenzie, D. Bierie and O. Mitchell, "An Experimental Study of a Therapeutic Boot Camp: Impact on Impulses, Attitudes and Recidivism," *Journal of Experimental Criminology* **3**(2007):221–246.

23. Personal communication from Anne Campbell. Based on Campbell, *The Girls in the Gang: A Report from New York City* (New York: Basil Blackwell, 1984).

24. Edwin H. Sutherland, *The Professional Thief* (Chicago: University of Chicago Press, 1937).

25. Marvin E. Wolfgang, "Ethics and Research," in *Ethics, Public Policy, and Criminal Justice,* ed. A. F. Ellison and N. Bowie (Cambridge, Mass.: Oelgeschlager, Gunn & Hain, 1982).

26. "Draft of ASC Code of Ethics," *Criminologist,* **24** (July–August 1999): 13–21.

27. Seth A. Bloomberg and Leslie Wilkins, "Ethics of Research Involving Human Subjects in Criminal Justice," *Crime and Delinquency,* **23** (1977): 435–444.

28. Lawrence Sherman and Barry Glick, "The Quality of Arrest Statistics," *Police Foundation Reports,* **2** (1984): 1–8.

29. Michael Couzens, "Getting the Crime Rate Down: Political Pressure and Crime Reporting," *Law and Society Review,* **8** (1974): 457–493.

30. President's Commission on Law Enforcement and Administration of Justice, *The Challenge of Crime in a Free Society* (Washington, D.C.: U.S. Government Printing Office, 1967), p. 25.

31. Patrick Jackson, "Assessing the Validity of Official Data on Arson," *Criminology,* **26** (1988): 181–195.

32. Patrick G. Jackson, "Sources of Data," in *Measurement Issues in Criminology,* ed. Kimberly L. Kempf (New York: Springer-Verlag, 1990), p. 42. For a comparison of the NCVS, UCR, and NIBRS, with a particular emphasis on what can be learned from incident-based police data that cannot be learned from other sources, see Michael G. Maxfield, "The National Incident-Based Reporting System: Research and Policy Applications," *Journal of Quantitative Criminology,* **15** (1999): 119–149.

33. For a comparison of victimization data with official police data, see Alfred Blumstein, Jacqueline Cohen, and Richard Rosenfeld, "Trend and Deviation in Crime Rates: A Comparison of UCR and NCS Data for Burglary and Robbery," *Criminology,* **29** (1991): 237–263.

34. James Levine, "The Potential for Crime Over-reporting in Criminal Victimization Surveys," *Criminology,* **14** (1976): 307–330.

35. James S. Wallerstein and Clement J. Wyle, "Our Law-Abiding Law-Breakers," *Probation,* **25** (March–April 1947): 107–112.

36. Martin Gold, "Undetected Delinquent Behavior," *Journal of Research in Crime and Delinquency,* **3** (1966): 27–46.

37. D. Wayne Osgood, Lloyd Johnston, Patrick O'Malley, and Jerald Bachman, "The Generality of Deviance in

Late Adolescence and Early Adulthood," *American Sociological Review,* **53** (1988): 81–93.

38. Franklin Dunford and Delbert Elliott, "Identifying Career Offenders Using Self-Reported Data," *Journal of Research in Crime and Delinquency,* **21** (1983): 57–86.

39. Josine Junger-Tas, Gert-Jan Terlouw, and Malcolm W. Klein, eds., *Delinquent Behavior among Young People in the Western World* (Amsterdam: Kugler, 1994).

40. Michael Hindelang, Travis Hirschi, and Joseph Weis, *Measuring Delinquency* (Beverly Hills, Calif.: Sage, 1981).

41. Tom Squitieri, "Soaring Murder Rate 'Tears Apart' Charlotte," *USA Today,* Jan. 31, 1992, p. 6A.

42. U.S. Department of Justice, Federal Bureau of Investigation, *Crime in the United States, 1992* (hereafter cited as Uniform Crime Reports, available at http://www.fbi.gov/ucr/ucr.htm) (Washington, D.C.: U.S. Government Printing Office, 1993), p. 140; Uniform Crime Reports, 1986, p. 94; Uniform Crime Reports, 1997, p. 147; Uniform Crime Reports, 2001, p. 142; Uniform Crime Reports, 2004, p. 102.

43. United States Department of Justice, Uniform Crime Reports, 2007 (released Sept. 2008), available at http://www.fbi.gov/ucr/cius2007/offenses/property_crime/index.html.

44. U.S. Department of Justice, Bureau of Justice Statistics, *Criminal Victimization, 2004* (Washington, D.C.: U.S. Government Printing Office, September 2005), p. 1.

45. See http://www.ojp.usdoj.gov/bjs/cvict.htm.

46. *Criminal Victimization, 2004,* p. 1.

47. Bureau of Justice Statistics, *Crime and Victim Statistics,* found at http://www.ojp.usdoj.gov/bjs/cvict_c.htm #place, Feb. 20, 2006.

48. H. Snyder and M. Sickmund, *Juvenile Offenders and Victims: 2006 National Report* (Washington, D.C.: Office of Juvenile Justice and Delinquency Prevention, 2006), ch. 3. Retrieved June 4, 2008 from *OJJDP Statistical Briefing Book,* available at http://ojjdp.ncjrs.gov/ojstatbb/offenders/qa03304.asp?qaDate=2001.

49. Derral Cheatwood, "The Effects of Weather on Homicide," *Journal of Quantitative Criminology,* **11** (1995): 51–70.

50. U.S. Department of Justice, "The Severity of Crime, Bureau of Justice Statistics Bulletin" (Washington, D.C.: U.S. Government Printing Office, Jan. 1984).

51. U.S. Department of Justice, Federal Bureau of Investigation, *Crime in the United States, 2006.* Retrieved June 5, 2008, from http://www.fbi.gov/ucr/cius2006/data/table_29.html.

52. James C. McKinley Jr., "Six Armed Men, Aged 40–72, Held in Bungled Robbery of a Club," *New York Times,* Apr. 20, 1989, p. D6.

53. *New York Times,* Nov. 6, 1994, p. 24.

54. U.S. Department of Justice, Federal Bureau of Investigation, *Crime in the United States, 2006,* "Overview," chart 38 (released Sept. 2007). Retrieved June 6, 2008, from http://www.fbi.gov/ucr/cius2006/data/table_38.html.

55. U.S. Census Bureau, Population Division. *National Population Estimates—Characteristics.* Retrieved June 9, 2008, from http://www.census.gov/popest/national/asrh/NC-EST2006-sa.html.

56. Michael Gottfredson and Travis Hirschi, "The True Value of Lambda Would Appear to Be Zero: An Essay on Career Criminals, Criminal Careers, Selective Incapacitation, Cohort Studies, and Related Topics," *Criminology,* **24** (1986): 213–234.

57. Michael Gottfredson and Travis Hirschi, "Science, Public Policy, and the Career Paradigm," *Criminology,* **26** (1988): 37–55. For a test of those contentions, see

Sung Joon Jang and Marvin D. Krohn, "Developmental Patterns of Sex Differences in Delinquency among African American Adolescents: A Test of the Sex-Invariance Hypothesis," *Journal of Quantitative Criminology,* **11** (1995): 195–222.

58. James Q. Wilson and Richard Herrnstein, *Crime and Human Nature* (New York: Simon & Schuster, 1985), pp. 126–147.

59. Alfred Blumstein, Jacqueline Cohen, and David Farrington, "Criminal Career Research: Its Value for Criminology," *Criminology,* **26** (1988): 1–35.

60. Dawn R. Jeglum Bartusch, Donald R. Lynum, Terrie E. Moffitt, and Phil A. Silva, "Is Age Important? Testing a General versus a Developmental Theory of Antisocial Behavior," *Criminology,* **35** (1997): 13–48.

61. Alfred Blumstein, Jacqueline Cohen, Jeffrey Roth, and Christy Visher, *Criminal Careers and "Career Criminals"* (Washington, D.C.: National Academy Press, 1986). On the relationship between crime and age, see Robert J. Sampson and John H. Laub, *Crime in the Making: Pathways and Turning Points through Life* (Cambridge, Mass.: Harvard University Press, 1993); Neal Shover and Carol Y. Thompson, "Age, Differential Expectations, and Crime Desistance," *Criminology,* **30** (1992): 89–104; David F. Greenberg, "The Historical Variability of the Age-Crime Relationship," *Journal of Quantitative Criminology,* **10** (1994): 361–373; Daniel S. Nagin, David P. Farrington, and Terrie E. Moffitt, "Life-Course Trajectories of Different Types of Offenders," *Criminology,* **33** (1995): 111–139; and Julie Horney, Wayne Osgood, and Ineke Haen Marshall, "Criminal Careers in the Short-Term: Intra-individual Variability in Crime and Its Relation to Local Life Circumstances," *American Sociological Review,* **60** (1995): 655–673.

62. Marvin Wolfgang, Robert Figlio, and Thorsten Sellin, *Delinquency in a Birth Cohort* (Chicago: University of Chicago Press, 1972). For a discussion of how each delinquent act was weighted for seriousness, see Thorsten Sellin and Marvin Wolfgang, *The Measurement of Delinquency* (New York: Wiley, 1964). See also Douglas A. Smith, Christy A. Visher, and G. Roger Jarjoura, "Dimensions of Delinquency: Exploring the Correlates of Participation, Frequency, and Persistence of Delinquent Behavior," *Journal of Research in Crime and Delinquency,* **28** (1990): 6–32.

63. Marvin E. Wolfgang, Terence Thornberry, and Robert Figlio, *From Boy to Man, from Delinquency to Crime* (Chicago: University of Chicago Press, 1987).

64. Paul E. Tracy, Marvin E. Wolfgang, and Robert M. Figlio, *Delinquency Careers in Two Birth Cohorts* (New York: Plenum, 1990), pp. 275–280.

65. Terence P. Thornberry, "What's Working and What's Not Working in Safeguarding Our Children and Preventing Violence," Safeguarding Our Youth: Violence Prevention for Our Nation's Children, speech presented at Department of Education, Washington, D.C., July 20, 1993.

66. Uniform Crime Reports, 2007, http://www.fbi.gov/ucr/cius2007/data/table_33.html.

67. *Criminal Victimization in the United States, 2000,* p. 51.

68. Howard N. Snyder, *Juvenile Arrests 2006* (Washington, D.C.: Office of Juvenile Justice and Delinquency Prevention, 2008), p. 8.

69. Delbert Elliott and Suzanne Ageton, "Reconciling Race and Class Differences in Self-Reported and Official Estimates of Delinquency," *American Sociological Review,* **45** (1980): 95–110; Roy L. Austin, "Recent Trends in Official Male and Female Crime Rates: The

Convergence Controversy," *Journal of Criminal Justice,* **21** (1993): 447–466.

70. John Hagan, John Simpson, and A. R. Gillis, "Class in the Household: A Power Control Theory of Gender and Delinquency," *American Journal of Sociology,* **92** (1987): 788–816. See also Gary F. Jensen, John Hagan, and A. R. Gillis, "Power-Control vs. Social Control Theories of Common Delinquency: A Comparative Analysis," in *New Directions in Criminological Theory,* eds. Freda Adler and William S. Laufer (New Brunswick, N.J.: Transaction, 1993), pp. 363–398.

71. Merry Morash and Meda Chesney-Lind, "A Reformulation and Partial Test of the Power Control Theory of Delinquency," *Justice Quarterly,* **8** (1991): 347–377. For an examination of sexual abuse of girls and how it leads to later delinquency, as well as a discussion of how the double standard influences female criminality, see Meda Chesney-Lind, *The Female Offender: Girls, Women, and Crime* (Thousand Oaks, Calif.: Sage, 1997). For a discussion about the role family controls have on female delinquency, see Karen Keimer and Stacy De Coster, "The Gendering of Violent Delinquency," *Criminology,* **37** (1999): 277–318. For an application of strain theory to female crime, see Lisa Broidy and Robert Agnew, "Gender and Crime: A General Strain Theory Perspective," *Journal of Research in Crime and Delinquency,* **34** (1997): 275–306. For a discussion of the implications of the feminization of poverty and welfare on property crime and assault, see Anne Campbell, Steven Muncer, and Daniel Bibel, "Female–Female Criminal Assault: An Evolutionary Perspective," *Journal of Research in Crime and Delinquency,* **35** (1998): 413–428; and Lance Hannon and James DeFronzo, "Welfare and Property Crime," *Justice Quarterly,* **15** (1998): 273–288.

72. Cesare Lombroso and William Ferrero, *The Female Offender* (London: T. Fisher Unwin, 1895).

73. Sheldon Glueck and Eleanor T. Glueck, *Five Hundred Delinquent Women* (New York: Knopf, 1934).

74. Otto Pollack, *The Criminality of Women* (Philadelphia: University of Pennsylvania Press, 1950).

75. Freda Adler, *Sisters in Crime* (New York: McGraw-Hill, 1975), pp. 6–7.

76. Rita Simon, *The Contemporary Woman and Crime* (Rockville, Md.: National Institute of Mental Health, 1975).

77. Meda Chesney-Lind, "Female Offenders: Paternalism Reexamined," in *Women, the Courts, and Equality,* eds. Laura Crites and Winifred Hepperle (Newbury Park, Calif.: Sage, 1987).

78. Darrell J. Steffensmeier, "Crime and the Contemporary Woman: An Analysis of Changing Levels of Female Property Crimes, 1960–1975," *Social Forces,* **57** (1978): 566–584; Lee H. Bowker, *Women, Crime, and the Criminal Justice System* (Lexington, Mass.: Heath, 1978). For a description of the typical female offender, see Nancy T. Wolfe, Francis T. Cullen, and John B. Cullen, "Describing the Female Offender: A Note on the Demographics of Arrests," *Journal of Criminal Justice,* **12** (1984): 483–492.

79. Mary E. Gilfus, "From Victims to Survivors to Offenders: Women's Routes of Entry and Immersion into Street Crime," *Women and Criminal Justice,* **4** (1992): 63–89; Sally S. Simpson and Lori Ellis, "Doing Gender: Sorting Out the Caste and Crime Conundrum," *Criminology,* **33** (1995): 47–81. For a discussion of the internalization of gender roles by female prisoners, see Edna Erez, "The Myth of the New Female Offender: Some Evidence from Attitudes toward Law and Justice," *Journal of Criminal Justice,* **16** (1988): 499–509.

80. Nanci Koser Wilson, "The Masculinity of Violent Crime—Some Second Thoughts," *Journal of Criminal Justice,* **9** (1981): 111–123; Ronald L. Simons, Martin G. Miller, and Stephen M. Aigner, "Contemporary Theories of Deviance and Female Delinquency: An Empirical Test," *Journal of Research in Crime and Delinquency,* **17** (1980): 42–57.

81. For a discussion of a unisex theory of crime, see Coramae Richey Mann, *Female Crime and Delinquency* (Tuscaloosa: University of Alabama Press, 1984). For an analysis of the relation of both gender and race to crime, see Vernetta D. Young, "Women, Race, and Crime," *Criminology,* **18** (1980): 26–34; Gary D. Hill and Elizabeth M. Crawford, "Women, Race, and Crime," *Criminology,* **28** (1990): 601–626; and Sally S. Simpson, "Caste, Class, and Violent Crime: Explaining Differences in Female Offending," *Criminology,* **29** (1991): 115–136. For a discussion of female crime in countries around the world, see Freda Adler, ed., *The Incidence of Female Criminality in the Contemporary World* (New York: New York University Press, 1984). See also Freda Adler and Rita James Simon, eds., *The Criminology of Deviant Women* (Boston: Houghton Mifflin, 1979). For other sources on the subject of female crime, see Victoria E. Brewster and M. Dwayne Smith, "Gender Inequality and Rates of Female Homicide Victimization across U.S. Cities," *Journal of Research in Crime and Delinquency,* **32** (1995): 175–190; R. Barri Flowers, *Female Crime, Criminals and Cellmates: An Exploration of Female Criminality and Delinquency* (Jefferson, N.C.: McFarland & Company, 1995); R. Emerson Dobash, Russell P. Dobash, and Lesley Noaks, eds., *Gender and Crime* (Cardiff: University of Wales Press, 1995); and Ruth Triplett and Laura B. Myers, "Evaluating Contextual Patterns of Delinquency: Gender-Based Differences," *Justice Quarterly,* **12** (1995): 59–84. For an examination of women who commit murder, see Coramae Richey Mann, *When Women Kill* (Albany, N.Y.: SUNY Press, 1996).

82. Charles Tittle, Wayne Villemez, and Douglas Smith, "The Myth of Social Class and Criminality: An Empirical Assessment of the Empirical Evidence," *American Sociological Review,* **43** (1978): 643–656; Charles R. Tittle and Robert F. Meier, "Specifying the SES/Delinquency Relationship," *Criminology,* **28** (1990): 271–299. For a discussion of the relationship between crime and aspects of social class that influence juveniles' personality and behavior, see G. Roger Jarjoura and Ruth A. Triplett, "Delinquency and Class: A Test of the Proximity Principle," *Justice Quarterly,* **14** (1997): 763–792. For an elaboration on the relationship between socioeconomic status (SES) and delinquency, see Bradley R. Entner Wright, Avshalom Caspi, Terrie E. Moffitt, Richard A. Miech, and Phil A. Silva, "Reconsidering the Relationship between SES and Delinquency: Causation but Not Correlation," *Criminology,* **37** (1999): 175–194.

83. Elliott and Ageton, "Reconciling Race and Class Differences."

84. Delbert Elliott and David Huizinga, "Social Class and Delinquent Behavior in a National Youth Panel: 1976–1980," *Criminology,* **21** (1983): 149–177.

85. The data on socioeconomic factors come from U.S. Department of Justice, *Report to the Nation on Crime and Justice,* pp. 48–49.

86. U.S. Department of Justice, Bureau of Justice Statistics, *Annual Report, Fiscal 1986* (Washington, D.C.: U.S. Government Printing Office, April 1987), p. 39.

87. Uniform Crime Reports, 1997, p. 240. See also Gary LaFree, Kriss A. Drass, and Patrick O'Day, "Race and Crime in Postwar America: Determinants of African-American and White Rates, 1957–1988," *Criminology,* **30** (1992): 157–188.

88. Joan Petersilia, "Racial Disparities in the Criminal Justice System: A Summary," *Crime and Delinquency,* **31** (1985): 15–34.

89. *Criminal Victimization, 2004,* p. 8.

90. Delbert Elliott and Harwin Voss, *Delinquency and Dropout* (Lexington, Mass.: Lexington Books, 1974).

CHAPTER 3

1. Quote: attributed to Socrates by Plato, wording unconfirmed by researchers; see *Respectfully Quoted,* ed. Suzy Platt (Washington, D.C.: Library of Congress, 1989), p. 42.

2. Leon Radzinowicz, *Ideology and Crime* (New York: Columbia University Press, 1966), p. 2; Marc Ancel, *Introduction to the French Penal Code,* ed. G. O. W. Mueller (South Hackensack, N.J.: Fred B. Rothman, 1960), pp. 1–2.

3. Thorsten Sellin, *Slavery and the Penal System* (New York: Elsevier, 1976); Thorsten Eriksson, *The Reformers: An Historical Survey of Pioneer Experiments in the Treatment of Criminals* (New York: Elsevier, 1976).

4. Marcello T. Maestro, *Cesare Beccaria and the Origins of Penal Reform* (Philadelphia: Temple University Press, 1973), p. 16.

5. George Rude, *The Crowd in the French Revolution* (New York: Oxford University Press, 1959), appendix.

6. Harry Elmer Barnes, *The Story of Punishment: A Record of Man's Inhumanity to Man,* 2d ed. (Montclair, N.J.: Patterson Smith, 1972), p. 99.

7. Cesare Beccaria, *On Crimes and Punishment,* 2d ed., trans. Edward D. Ingraham (Philadelphia: Philip H. Nicklin, 1819), pp. 15, 20, 22–23, 30–32, 60, 74–75, 80, 97–98, 149, 156. For a debate on the contribution of Beccaria to modern criminology, see G. O. W. Mueller, "Whose Prophet Is Cesare Beccaria? An Essay on the Origins of Criminological Theory," *Advances in Criminological Theory,* **2** (1990): 1–14; Graeme Newman and Pietro Marongiu, "Penological Reform and the Myth of Beccaria," *Criminology,* **28** (1990): 325–346; and Piers Beirne, "Inventing Criminology: The 'Science of Man,' in Cesare Beccaria's *Dei delitti e delle pene,*" *Criminology,* **29** (1991): 777–820.

8. Marcello T. Maestro, *Voltaire and Beccaria as Reformers of Criminal Law* (New York: Columbia University Press, 1942), p. 73.

9. Jeremy Bentham, *A Fragment on Government and an Introduction to the Principles of Morals and Legislation,* ed. Wilfred Harrison (Oxford: Basil Blackwell, 1967), p. 21.

10. Barnes, *The Story of Punishment,* p. 102.

11. Quoted in Leon Radzinowicz, *A History of English Criminal Law and Its Administration from 1750,* vol. 1 (New York: Macmillan, 1948), p. 330.

12. Charles Darwin, *Origin of Species* (1854; Cambridge, Mass.: Harvard University Press, 1859); Charles Darwin, *The Descent of Man and Selection in Relation to Sex* (1871; New York: A. L. Burt, 1874).

13. Havelock Ellis, *The Criminal,* 2d ed. (New York: Scribner, 1900), p. 27.

14. Christopher Hibbert, *The Roots of Evil* (Boston: Little, Brown, 1963), p. 187.

15. Arthur E. Fink, *The Causes of Crime: Biological Theories in the United States, 1800–1915* (Philadelphia: University of Pennsylvania Press, 1938), p. 1.

16. Hermann Mannheim, *Comparative Criminology* (Boston: Houghton Mifflin, 1965), p. 213.

17. George B. Vold, *Theoretical Criminology* (New York: Oxford University Press, 1958), pp. 44–49.

18. Gina Lombroso Ferrero, *Criminal Man: According to the Classification of Cesare Lombroso,* with an Introduction by Cesare Lombroso (1911; Montclair, N.J.: Patterson Smith, 1972), pp. xxiv–xxv.

19. Cesare Lombroso and William Ferrero, *The Female Offender* (New York: Appleton, 1895), pp. 151–152.

20. Cesare Lombroso, *Crime, Its Causes and Remedies* (Boston: Little, Brown, 1918).

21. Marvin Wolfgang, "Cesare Lombroso," in *Pioneers in Criminology,* ed. Hermann Mannheim (London: Stevens, 1960), p. 168.

22. Thorsten Sellin, "The Lombrosian Myth in Criminology," *American Journal of Sociology,* **42** (1937): 898–899. For Lombroso's impact on American anthropological criminology, see Nicole Hahn Rafter, "Criminal Anthropology in the United States," *Criminology,* **30** (1992): 525–545.

23. Wolfgang, "Cesare Lombroso."

24. Thorsten Sellin, "Enrico Ferri: Pioneer in Criminology, 1856–1929," in *The Positive School of Criminology: Three Lectures by Enrico Ferri,* ed. Stanley E. Grupp (Pittsburgh: University of Pittsburgh Press, 1968), p. 13.

25. Raffaele Garofalo, *Criminology,* trans. Robert Wyness Millar (Montclair, N.J.: Patterson Smith, 1968), pp. 4–5.

26. Marc Ancel, *Social Defense: The Future of Penal Reform* (Littleton, Colo.: Fred B. Rothman, 1987).

27. Charles B. Goring, *The English Convict: A Statistical Study* (London: His Majesty's Stationery Office, 1913), p. 145. For a critique of Goring's work, see Piers Beirne, "Heredity versus Environment," *British Journal of Criminology,* **28** (1988): 315–339.

28. E. A. Hooten, *The American Criminal* (Cambridge, Mass.: Harvard University Press, 1939), p. 308.

29. E. A. Hooten, *Crime and the Man* (Cambridge, Mass.: Harvard University Press, 1939), p. 13.

30. Ernst Kretschmer, *Physique and Character* (New York: Harcourt Brace, 1926).

31. William H. Sheldon, *Varieties of Delinquent Youth: An Introduction to Constitutional Psychiatry* (New York: Harper, 1949). See also Emil M. Hartl, Edward P. Monnelly, and Ronald D. Elderkin, *Physique and Delinquent Behavior: A Thirty-Year Follow-Up of William H. Sheldon's Varieties of Delinquent Youth* (New York: Academic Press, 1982).

32. Eleanor Glueck and Sheldon Glueck, *Unraveling Juvenile Delinquency* (Cambridge, Mass.: Harvard University Press, 1950). See also Sheldon Glueck and Eleanor Glueck, *Of Delinquency and Crime* (Springfield, Ill.: Charles C Thomas, 1974), p. 2. For a recent reanalysis of the Gluecks' data, see John H. Laub and Robert J. Sampson, "Unravelling Families and Delinquency: A Reanalysis of the Gluecks' Data," *Criminology,* **26** (1988): 355–380. For the life and work of Eleanor Touroff Glueck, see John H. Laub and Jinney S. Smith, "Eleanor Touroff Glueck: An Unsung Pioneer in Criminology," *Women in Criminal Justice,* **6** (1995): 1–22.

33. S. L. Washburn, book review, "Varieties of Delinquent Youth, An Introduction to Constitutional Psychiatry," *American Anthropologist,* **53** (1951): 561–563.

34. Richard L. Dugdale, *The Jukes: A Study in Crime, Pauperism, Disease, and Heredity,* 5th ed. (New York: Putnam, 1895), p. 8.

35. Henry H. Goddard, *The Kallikak Family: A Study in the Heredity of Feeble-Mindedness* (New York: Macmillan, 1912), p. 50.

36. *Buck v. Bell,* 274 U.S. 200, 207 (1927).

37. Isaac Ray, *The Medical Jurisprudence of Insanity* (Boston: Little, Brown, 1838).

38. Philippe Pinel, *A Treatise on Insanity* (1806; New York: Hafner, 1962).

39. Peter Scott, "Henry Maudsley," *Journal of Criminal Law, Criminology, and Police Science,* 46 (March–April 1956): 753–769.

40. Henry H. Goddard, *The Criminal Imbecile* (New York: Macmillan, 1915), pp. 106–107.

41. Adolphe Quételet, *A Treatise on Man,* facs. ed. of 1842 ed., trans. Salomon Diamond (1835; Gainesville, Fla.: Scholars Facsimiles and Reprints, 1969), p. 97.

42. Quételet, *A Treatise on Man,* p. 103. For Quételet's influence on modern scholars, see Derral Cheatwood, "Is There a Season for Homicide?" *Criminology,* 26 (1988): 287–306.

43. Gabriel Tarde, *Penal Philosophy,* trans. R. Howell (Boston: Little, Brown, 1912), p. 252.

44. Gabriel Tarde, *Social Laws: An Outline of Sociology* (New York: Macmillan, 1907).

45. Émile Durkheim, *The Rules of Sociological Method,* ed. George E. G. Catlin (Chicago: University of Chicago Press, 1938), p. 71.

46. T. S. Kuhn, *The Structure of Scientific Revolutions* (Chicago: Chicago University Press, 1962), p. 10

47. Gary LaFree, "Expanding Criminology's Domain: The American Society of Criminology 2006 Presidential Address," *Criminology,* 45 (2007): 1–31.

CHAPTER 4

1. http://www.cnn.com/2005/LAW/06/27/btk/index.html.

2. http://www.cnn.com/2005/LAW/06/28/victims.son/index.html.

3. See Ronald Blackburn, *The Psychology of Criminal Conduct: Theory, Research, and Practice* (Chichester, England: Wiley, 1993); and Hans Toch, *Violent Men: An Inquiry into the Psychology of Violence,* rev. ed. (Washington, D.C.: American Psychological Association, 1992).

4. See, e.g., Cathy Spatz Widom, "Cycle of Violence," *Science,* 244 (1989): 160–165; and Nathaniel J. Pallone and J. J. Hennessy, *Criminal Behavior: A Process Psychology Analysis* (New Brunswick, N.J.: Transaction, 1992).

5. See, generally, A. J. Reiss Jr., K. A. Klaus, and J. A. Roth, eds., *Biobehavioral Influences:* vol. 2, *Understanding and Preventing Violence* (Washington, D.C.: National Academy Press, 1994); M. Hillbrand and N. J. Pallone, "The Psychobiology of Aggression: Engines, Measurement, Control," *Journal of Offender Rehabilitation,* 21 (1994): 1–243; and J. T. Tedeschi and R. B. Felson, *Violence, Aggression, and Coercive Actions* (Washington, D.C.: American Psychological Association, 1994).

6. J. Puig-Antich, "Biological Factors in Prepubertal Major Depression," *Pediatric Annals,* 12 (1986): 867–878.

7. See, e.g., Guenther Knoblich and Roy King, "Biological Correlates of Criminal Behavior," in *Facts, Frameworks, and Forecasts: Advances in Criminological Theory,* vol. 3, ed. J. McCord (New Brunswick, N.J.: Transaction, 1992); Diana H. Fishbein, "Biological Perspectives in Criminology," *Criminology,* 28 (1990): 17–40; David Magnusson, Britt af Klinteberg, and Hakan Stattin, "Autonomic Activity/ Reactivity, Behavior, and Crime in a Longitudinal Perspective," in McCord, *Facts, Frameworks, and Forecasts;* Frank A. Elliott, "Violence: The Neurologic Contribution: An Overview," *Archives of Neurology,* 49 (1992): 595–603; L. French, "Neuropsychology of Violence," *Corrective and Social Psychiatry and Journal of Behavior Technology Methods and Therapy,* 37 (1991): 12–17; and Elizabeth Kandel and Sarnoff A. Mednick, "Perinatal Complications Predict Violent Offending," *Criminology,* 29 (1991): 519–530.

8. Edward O. Wilson, *Sociobiology: The New Synthesis* (Cambridge, Mass.: Harvard University Press, 1975).

9. C. Ray Jeffery, *Biology and Crime* (Beverly Hills, Calif.: Sage, 1979).

10. P. A. Brennan and S. A. Mednick, "Genetic Perspectives on Crime," *Acta Psychiatria Scandinavia,* 370 (1993): 19–26.

11. See Sarnoff A. Mednick, Terrie E. Moffitt, and Susan A. Stack, *The Causes of Crime: New Biological Approaches* (New York: Cambridge University Press, 1987).

12. A. A. Sandberg, G. F. Koepf, and T. Ishihara, "An XYY Human Male," *Lancet* (August 1961): 488–489.

13. Herman A. Witkin et al., "Criminality, Aggression, and Intelligence among XYY and XXY Men," in *Biosocial Bases of Criminal Behavior,* eds. Sarnoff A. Mednick and Karl O. Christiansen (New York: Wiley, 1977).

14. Johannes Lange, *Verbrechen als Schicksal* (Leipzig: Georg Thieme, 1929).

15. Cf. Gregory Carey, "Twin Imitation for Antisocial Behavior: Implications for Genetic Environment Research," *Journal of Abnormal Psychology,* 101 (1992): 18–25.

16. See Karl O. Christiansen, "A Preliminary Study of Criminality among Twins," in Mednick and Christiansen, *Biosocial Bases of Criminal Behavior.*

17. David C. Rowe and D. Wayne Osgood, "Heredity and Sociological Theories of Delinquency: A Reconsideration," *American Sociological Review,* 49 (1986): 526–540; David C. Rowe, "Genetic and Environmental Components of Antisocial Behavior: A Study of 256 Twin Pairs," *Criminology,* 24 (1986): 513–532.

18. Sarnoff A. Mednick, William Gabrielli, and Barry Hutchings, "Genetic Influences in Criminal Behavior: Evidence from an Adoption Court," in *Prospective Studies of Crime and Delinquency,* ed. K. Teilmann et al. (Boston: Kluwer-Nijhoff, 1983).

19. These and other studies are reviewed in Mednick et al., *The Causes of Crime.*

20. Hannah Bloch and Dick Thompson, "Seeking the Roots of Violence," *Time,* Apr. 19, 1993, pp. 52–53.

21. Daniel Goleman, "New Storm Brews on Whether Crime Has Roots in Genes," *New York Times,* Sept. 15, 1992, p. C1.

22. Bloch and Thompson, "Seeking the Roots of Violence."

23. Study Group on Serious and Violent Juvenile Offenders, Office of Juvenile Justice and Delinquency Prevention (Washington, D.C.: NIJ, 1998); Fox Butterfield, "Study Cites Biology's Role in Violent Behavior," *New York Times,* Nov. 13, 1992, p. A7.

24. Goleman, "New Storm Brews on Whether Crime Has Roots in Genes."

25. Ibid.

26. Hugo Munsterberg, *On the Witness Stand* (New York: Doubleday, 1908); Henry H. Goddard, *Feeble-Mindedness: Its Causes and Consequences* (New York: Macmillan, 1914).

27. Edwin H. Sutherland, "Mental Deficiency and Crime," in *Social Attitudes,* ed. K. Young (New York: Henry Holt, 1931).

28. Robert H. Gault, "Highlights of Forty Years in the Correctional Field—and Looking Ahead," *Federal Probation,* 17 (1953): 3–4.

29. Arthur Jensen, *Bias in Mental Testing* (New York: Free Press, 1979).

30. Ibid.; Richard J. Herrnstein, *IQ in the Meritocracy* (Boston: Atlantic–Little, Brown, 1973).

31. Travis Hirschi and Michael J. Hindelang, "Intelligence and Delinquency: A Revisionist Review," *American Sociological Review,* 42 (1977): 571–586.

32. Travis Hirschi, *Causes of Delinquency* (Berkeley: University of California Press, 1969).

33. Marvin E. Wolfgang, Robert F. Figlio, and Thorsten Sellin, *Delinquency in a Birth Cohort* (Chicago: University of Chicago Press, 1972).

34. Albert J. Reiss and Albert L. Rhodes, "The Distribution of Juvenile Delinquency in the Social Class Structure," *American Sociological Review,* 26 (1961): 720–732.

35. See M. Rutter, T. E. Moffitt, and A. Caspi, "Gene-Environment Interplay and Psychopathology: Multiple Varieties but Real Effects." *Journal of Child Psychology and Psychiatry,* 47 (2006): 226–261; T. E. Moffitt, A. Caspi, and M. Rutter, "Measured Gene-Environment Interactions in Psychopathology: Concepts, Research Strategies, and Implications for Research, Intervention, and Public Understanding of Genetics," *Perspectives on Psychological Science,* 1 (2006): 5–27. See also James Q. Wilson and Richard Herrnstein, *Crime and Human Nature* (New York: Simon & Schuster, 1985); Deborah W. Denno, "Sociological and Human Developmental Explanations of Crime: Conflict or Consensus?" *Criminology,* 23 (1985): 711–740; and Deborah W. Denno, "Victim, Offender, and Situational Characteristics of Violent Crime," *Journal of Criminal Law and Criminology,* 77 (1986): 1142–1158.

36. "Taking the Chitling Test," *Newsweek,* July 15, 1968.

37. Sandra Scarr and Richard Weinberg, "I.Q. Test Performance of Black Children Adopted by White Families," *American Psychologist,* 31 (1976): 726–739.

38. See Doris J. Rapp, *Allergies and the Hyperactive Child* (New York: Simon & Schuster, 1981).

39. Diana H. Fishbein and Susan Pease, "The Effects of Diet on Behavior: Implications for Criminology and Corrections," *Research on Corrections,* 1 (1988): 1–45.

40. Stephen Schoenthaler, "Diet and Crime: An Empirical Examination of the Value of Nutrition in the Control and Treatment of Incarcerated Juvenile Offenders," *International Journal of Biosocial Research,* 4 (1982): 25–39.

41. Heather M. Little, "Food May Be Causing Kids' Problems," *Chicago Tribune,* Oct. 29, 1995, p. 1; Abram Hoffer, "The Relation of Crime to Nutrition," *Humanist in Canada,* 8 (1975): 2–9.

42. Benjamin F. Feingold, *Why Is Your Child Hyperactive?* (New York: Random House, 1975).

43. James W. Swanson and Marcel Kinsbourne, "Food Dyes Impair Performance of Hyperactive Children on a Laboratory Test," *Science,* 207 (1980): 1485–1487.

44. Anthony R. Mawson and K. W. Jacobs, "Corn Consumption, Tryptophan, and Cross-National Homicide Rates," *Journal of Orthomolecular Psychiatry,* 7 (1978): 227–230.

45. "Toddler Dies after Being Thrown in Lake by Dad in Diabetic Seizure," *Chicago Tribune,* July 10, 1995, p. 9.

46. Matti Virkkunen, "Insulin Secretion during the Glucose Tolerance Test among Habitually Violent and Impulsive Offenders," *Aggressive Behavior,* 12 (1986): 303–310.

47. E. A. Beeman, "The Effect of Male Hormones on Aggressive Behavior in Mice," *Physiological Zoology,* 20 (1947): 373–405.

48. D. A. Hamburg and D. T. Lunde, "Sex Hormones in the Development of Sex Differences," in *The Development of Sex Differences,* ed. Eleanor E. Maccoby (Stanford, Calif.: Stanford University Press, 1966).

49. A. Booth and D. W. Osgood, "The Influence of Testosterone on Deviance in Adulthood: Assessing and Explaining the Relationship," *Criminology,* 31 (1993): 93–117; L. E. Kreuz and R. M. Rose, "Assessment of Aggressive Behavior and Plasma Testosterone of a Young Criminal Population," *Psychosomatic Medicine,* 34 (1972): 321–332; R. T. Rada, D. R. Laws, and R. Kellner, "Plasma Testosterone Levels in the Rapist," *Psychosomatic Medicine,* 38 (1976): 257–268.

50. Katharina Dalton, *The Premenstrual Syndrome* (Springfield, Ill.: Charles C Thomas, 1971).

51. Julie Horney, "Menstrual Cycles and Criminal Responsibility," *Law and Human Behavior,* 2 (1978): 25–36.

52. *Regina v. Charlson,* 1 A11. E. R. 859 (1955).

53. L. P. Chesterman et al., "Multiple Measures of Cerebral State in Dangerous Mentally Disordered Inpatients," *Criminal Behavior and Mental Health,* 4 (1994): 228–239; Lee Ellis, "Monoamine Oxidase and Criminality: Identifying an Apparent Biological Marker for Antisocial Behavior," *Journal of Research in Crime and Delinquency,* 28 (1991): 227–251.

54. A. Raine, M. S. Buchsbaum, and L. LaCasse, "Brain Abnormalities in Murderers Indicated by Positron Emission Tomography," *Biological Psychiatry,* 42 (1997): 496–508.

55. A. Raine, J. R. Meloy, S. Bihrle, J. Stoddard, L. LaCasse, and M. S. Buchsbaum, "Reduced Prefrontal and Increased Subcortical Brain Functioning Assessed Using Positron Emission Tomography in Predatory and Affective Murderers," *Behavioral Sciences and the Law,* 16 (1998): 319–332.

56. A. Raine, T. Lencz, S. Bihrle, L. LaCasse, and P. Colletti, "Reduced Prefrontal Gray Matter Volume and Reduced Autonomic Activity in Antisocial Personality Disorder," *Archives of General Psychiatry,* 57 (2000): 119–127.

57. Raine, Buchsbaum, and LaCasse, "Brain Abnormalities in Murderers."

58. A. Raine and Y. Yang, "The Neuroanatomical Bases of Psychopathy: A Review of Brain Imaging Findings," in *Handbook of Psychopathy,* ed. C. J. Patrick (New York: Guilford Press, 2006), pp. 278–295.

59. H. Forssman and T. S. Frey, "Electroencephalograms of Boys with Behavior Disorders," *Acta Psychologica et Neurologia Scandinavica,* 28 (1953): 61–73; H. de Baudouin et al., "Study of a Population of 97 Confined Murderers," *Annales Medico-Psychologique,* 119 (1961): 625–686.

60. Sarnoff A. Mednick, Jan Volavka, William F. Gabrielli, and Turan M. Itil, "EEG as a Predictor of Antisocial Behavior," *Criminology,* 19 (1981): 219–229.

61. Jan Volavka, "Electroencephalogram among Criminals," in Mednick et al., *The Causes of Crime.* See also J. Volavka, *Neurobiology of Violence* (Washington, D.C.: American Psychiatric Press, 1995); Adrian Raine, Monte Buchsbaum, and Lori LaCasse, "Brain Abnormalities in Murderers Indicated by Positron Emission Tomography," *Biological Psychiatry,* 42 (1997): 495–508; and Adrian Raine, J. Reid Meloy, Susan Bihrle, Jackie Stoddard, Lori LaCasse, and Monte S. Buchsbaum, "Reduced Prefrontal and Increased Subcortical Brain Functioning Assessed Using Positron Emission Tomography in Predatory and Affective

Murderers," *Behavioral Sciences and the Law,* **16** (1998): 319–332.

62. DSM III-R, 314.01. See also Michael Rutter, "Syndromes Attributed to 'Minimal Brain Dysfunction' in Children," *American Journal of Psychiatry,* **139** (1980): 21–33.

63. Lorne T. Yeudall, D. Fromm-Auch, and P. Davies, "Neuropsychological Impairment of Persistent Delinquency," *Journal of Nervous and Mental Disorders,* **170** (1982): 257–265; R. D. Robin et al., "Adolescents Who Attempt Suicide," *Journal of Pediatrics,* **90** (1977): 636–638.

64. Edward Sagarin, "Taboo Subjects and Taboo Viewpoints in Criminology," in *Taboos in Criminology,* ed. Sagarin (Beverly Hills, Calif.: Sage, 1980), pp. 8–9.

65. Diana H. Fishbein, "Biological Perspectives in Criminology," *Criminology,* **28** (1990): 27–40.

66. See, e.g., Sigmund Freud, *A General Introduction to Psychoanalysis* (New York: Liveright, 1920); and Sigmund Freud, *The Ego and the Id* (London: Hogarth, 1927).

67. August Aichhorn, *Wayward Youth* (New York: Viking, 1935).

68. Kate Friedlander, *The Psycho-Analytic Approach to Juvenile Delinquency* (New York: International Universities Press, 1947).

69. See Hans Eysenck, *The Rise and Fall of the Freudian Empire* (New York: Plenum, 1987).

70. Lawrence Kohlberg, "The Development of Modes of Moral Thinking and Choice in the Years Ten to Sixteen," Ph.D. dissertation, University of Chicago, 1958.

71. Lawrence Kohlberg, "Stage and Sequence: The Cognitive-Developmental Approach to Socialization," in *Handbook of Socialization Theory and Research,* ed. David A. Goslin (Chicago: Rand McNally, 1969).

72. Carol Gilligan has studied moral development in women—extending Kohlberg's role-taking theory of moral development. She found that moral reasoning differed in women. Women, according to Gilligan, see morality as the responsibility to take the view of others and to ensure their well-being. See Carol Gilligan, *In a Different Voice: Psychological Theory and Women's Development* (Cambridge, Mass.: Harvard University Press, 1982).

73. G. L. Little, "Meta-analysis of MRT Recidivism Research on Post-incarceration Adult Felony Offenders," *Cognitive-Behavioral Treatment Review,* **10** (2001): 4–6; William S. Jennings, Robert Kilkenny, and Lawrence Kohlberg, "Moral Development Theory and Practice for Youthful Offenders," in *Personality Theory, Moral Development, and Criminal Behavior,* eds. William S. Laufer and James M. Day (Lexington, Mass.: Lexington Books, 1983). See also Daniel D. Macphail, "The Moral Education Approach in Treating Adult Inmates," *Criminal Justice and Behavior,* **15** (1989): 81–97; Jack Arbuthnot and Donald A. Gordon, "Crime and Cognition: Community Applications of Sociomoral Reasoning Development," *Criminal Justice and Behavior,* **15** (1988): 379–393; and J. E. LeCapitaine, "The Relationships between Emotional Development and Moral Development and the Differential Impact of Three Psychological Interventions on Children," *Psychology in the Schools,* **15** (1987): 379–393.

74. John Bowlby, *Attachment and Loss,* 2 vols. (New York: Basic Books, 1969, 1973). See also Bowlby's "Forty-Four Juvenile Thieves: Their Characteristics and Home Life," *International Journal of Psychoanalysis,* **25** (1944): 19–52.

75. John Bowlby, *The Making and Breaking of Affectional Bonds* (London: Tavistock, 1979). See also Michael Rutter, *Maternal Deprivation Reassessed* (Harmondsworth, Engl.: Penguin, 1971).

76. Michael Lewis, Candice Feiring, Carolyn McGuffog, and John Jaskir, "Predicting Psychopathology in Six-Year-Olds from Early Social Relations," *Child Development,* **55** (1984): 123–136.

77. L. Sroufe, "Infant Caregiver Attachment and Patterns of Adaptation in Preschool: The Roots of Maladaption and Competence," in *Minnesota Symposium on Child Psychology,* vol. 16, ed. Marion Perlmutter (Hillsdale, N.J.: Erlbaum, 1982).

78. Alicia F. Lieberman, "Preschoolers' Competence with a Peer: Influence of Attachment and Social Experience," *Child Development,* **48** (1977): 1277–1287.

79. Heather Juby and David P. Farrington, "Disentangling the Link between Disrupted Families and Delinquency: Sociodemography, Ethnicity and Risk Behaviours," *British Journal of Criminology,* **41** (2001): 22–40; Joan McCord, "Some Child-Rearing Antecedents of Criminal Behavior," *Journal of Personality and Social Psychology,* **37** (1979): 1477–1486; Joan McCord, "A Longitudinal View of the Relationship between Paternal Absence and Crime," in *Abnormal Offenders, Delinquency, and the Criminal Justice System,* eds. John Gunn and David P. Farrington (London: Wiley, 1982). See also Scott W. Henggeler, Cindy L. Hanson, Charles M. Borduin, Sylvia M. Watson, and Molly A. Brunk, "Mother-Son Relationships of Juvenile Felons," *Journal of Consulting and Clinical Psychology,* **53** (1985): 942–943; and Francis I. Nye, *Family Relationships and Delinquent Behavior* (New York: Wiley, 1958).

80. Sheldon Glueck and Eleanor T. Glueck, *Unraveling Juvenile Delinquency* (New York: Commonwealth Fund, 1950); Lee N. Robins, "Aetiological Implications in Studies of Childhood Histories Relating to Antisocial Personality," in *Psychopathic Behaviour,* eds. Robert D. Hare and Daisy Schalling (Chichester, Engl.: Wiley, 1970); Lee N. Robins, *Deviant Children Grow Up* (Baltimore: Williams & Wilkins, 1966).

81. Joan McCord, "Instigation and Insulation: How Families Affect Antisocial Aggression," in *Development of Antisocial and Prosocial Behavior: Research Theories and Issues,* eds. Dan Olweus, Jack Block, and M. Radke-Yarrow (London: Academic Press, 1986).

82. Albert Bandura, *Aggression: A Social Learning Analysis* (Englewood Cliffs, N.J.: Prentice-Hall, 1973); Albert Bandura, "The Social Learning Perspective: Mechanism of Aggression," in *Psychology of Crime and Criminal Justice,* ed. Hans Toch (New York: Holt, Rinehart & Winston, 1979).

83. Leonard D. Eron and L. Rowell Huesmann, "Parent-Child Interaction, Television Violence, and Aggression of Children," *American Psychologist,* **37** (1982): 197–211; Russell G. Geen, "Aggression and Television Violence," in *Aggression: Theoretical and Empirical Reviews,* vol. 2, eds. Russell G. Geen and Edward I. Donnerstein (New York: Academic Press, 1983).

84. Leonard D. Eron and L. Rowell Huesmann, "The Control of Aggressive Behavior by Changes in Attitudes, Values, and the Conditions of Learning," in *Advances in the Study of Aggression,* vol. 1, eds. Robert J. Blanchard and D. Caroline Blanchard (Orlando, Fla.: Academic Press, 1984).

85. *National Television Violence Study: Executive Summary 1994–1995* (Studio City, Calif.: Mediascope, 1996);

O. Wiegman, M. Kuttschreuter, and B. Baarda, "A Longitudinal Study of the Effects of Television Viewing on Aggressive and Prosocial Behaviors," *British Journal of Social Psychology,* **31** (1992): 147–164; B. S. Centerwall, "Television and Violence: The Scale of the Problem and Where to Go from Here," *Journal of the American Medical Association,* **267** (1992): 3059–3063; J. E. Ledingham, C. A. Ledingham, and John E. Richardson, *The Effects of Media Violence on Children* (Ottawa, Canada: National Clearinghouse on Family Violence, Health and Welfare, 1993); M. I. Tulloch, M. L. Prendergast, and M. D. Anglin, "Evaluating Aggression: School Students' Responses to Television Portrayals of Institutionalized Violence," *Journal of Youth and Adolescence,* **24** (1995): 95–115.

86. See Caroline Schulenburg, "Dying to Entertain: Violence on Prime Time Broadcast Television" (executive summary), available at http://www.parentstv .org/PTC/publications/reports/violencestudy/ exsummary.asp.

87. See Gerald R. Patterson, R. A. Littman, and W. Brickler, *Assertive Behavior in Children: A Step toward a Theory of Aggression,* monograph of the Society for Research in Child Development, no. 32 (1976).

88. Bandura, *Aggression.*

89. C. Ray Jeffery, "Criminal Behavior and Learning Theory," *Journal of Criminal Law, Criminology and Police Science,* **56** (1965): 294–300.

90. Ernest L. Burgess and Ronald L. Akers, "A Differential Association-Reinforcement Theory of Criminal Behavior," *Social Problems,* **14** (1966): 128–147. See also Reed Adams, "Differential Association and Learning Principles Revisited," *Social Problems,* **20** (1973): 458–470.

91. See D. W. Andrews and J. Stephen Wormith, "Personality and Crime: Knowledge Destruction and Construction in Criminology," *Justice Quarterly,* **6** (1989): 149–160.

92. William S. Laufer, Dagna K. Skoog, and James M. Day, "Personality and Criminality: A Review of the California Psychological Inventory," *Journal of Clinical Psychology,* **38** (1982): 562–573.

93. Richard E. Tremblay, "The Prediction of Delinquent Behavior from Childhood Behavior: Personality Theory Revisited," in McCord, *Facts, Frameworks, and Forecasts.*

94. Michael L. Gearing, "The MMPI as a Primary Differentiator and Predictor of Behavior in Prison: A Methodological Critique and Review of the Recent Literature," *Psychological Bulletin,* **36** (1979): 929–963.

95. Edwin I. Megargee and Martin J. Bohn, *Classifying Criminal Offenders* (Beverly Hills, Calif.: Sage, 1979); William S. Laufer, John A. Johnson, and Robert Hogan, "Ego Control and Criminal Behavior," *Journal of Personality and Social Psychology,* **41** (1981): 179–184; Edwin I. Megargee, "Psychological Determinants and Correlates of Criminal Violence," in *Criminal Violence,* eds. Marvin E. Wolfgang and Neil A. Weiner (Beverly Hills, Calif.: Sage, 1982); Edwin I. Megargee, "The Role of Inhibition in the Assessment and Understanding of Violence," in *Current Topics in Clinical and Community Psychology,* ed. Charles Donald Spielberger (New York: Academic Press, 1971); Edwin I. Megargee, "Undercontrol and Overcontrol in Assaultive and Homicidal Adolescents," Ph.D. dissertation, University of California, Berkeley, 1964; Edwin I. Megargee, "Undercontrolled and Overcontrolled Personality

Types in Extreme Antisocial Aggression," *Psychological Monographs,* **80** (1966); Edwin I. Megargee and Gerald A. Mendelsohn, "A Cross-Validation of Twelve MMPI Indices of Hostility and Control," *Journal of Abnormal and Social Psychology,* **65** (1962): 431–438.

96. See, e.g., William S. Laufer and James M. Day, eds., *Personality Theory, Moral Development, and Criminal Behavior* (Lexington, Mass.: Lexington Books, 1983).

97. Milton Metfessel and Constance Lovell, "Recent Literature on Individual Correlates of Crime," *Psychological Bulletin,* **39** (1942): 133–164.

98. Karl E. Schuessler and Donald R. Cressey, "Personality Characteristics of Criminals," *American Journal of Sociology,* **55** (1950): 476–484.

99. Daniel J. Tennenbaum, "Personality and Criminality: A Summary and Implications of the Literature," *Journal of Criminal Justice,* **5** (1977): 225–235. See also G. P. Waldo and Simon Dinitz, "Personality Attributes of the Criminal: An Analysis of Research Studies, 1950–1965," *Journal of Research in Crime and Delinquency,* **4** (1967): 185–202; and R. D. Martin and D. G. Fischer, "Personality Factors in Juvenile Delinquency: A Review of the Literature," *Catalog of Selected Documents in Psychology,* vol. 8 (1978), ms. 1759.

100. Samuel Yochelson and Stanton Samenow, *The Criminal Personality* (New York: Jason Aronson, 1976).

101. Laufer et al., "Personality and Criminality"; Harrison G. Gough and Pamela Bradley, "Delinquent and Criminal Behavior as Assessed by the Revised California Psychological Inventory," *Journal of Clinical Psychology,* **48** (1991): 298–308.

102. See Anne Campbell and John J. Gibbs, eds., *Violent Transactions: The Limits of Personality* (Oxford: Basil Blackwell, 1986); Lawrence A. Pervin, "Personality: Current Controversies, Issues, and Direction," *Annual Review of Psychology,* **36** (1985): 83–114; and Lawrence A. Pervin, "Persons, Situations, Interactions: Perspectives on a Recurrent Issue," in Campbell and Gibbs, *Violent Transactions.*

103. See Hans J. Eysenck, *Crime and Personality* (London: Routledge & Kegan Paul, 1977); H. J. Eysenck, "Personality and Crime: Where Do We Stand?" *Psychology, Crime and Law,* **2** (1996): 143–152; Hans J. Eysenck, "Personality, Conditioning, and Antisocial Behavior," in Laufer and Day, *Personality Theory;* Hans J. Eysenck, "Personality and Criminality: A Dispositional Analysis," in *Advances in Criminological Theory,* vol. 1, eds. William S. Laufer and Freda Adler (New Brunswick, N.J.: Transaction, 1989); and Hans J. Eysenck and Gisli H. Gudjonnson, *The Causes and Cures of Crime* (New York: Plenum, 1990).

104. Seymour L. Halleck, *Psychiatry and the Dilemmas of Crime* (New York: Harper & Row, 1967); Nicholas N. Kittrie, *The Right to Be Different: Deviance and Enforced Therapy* (Baltimore, Md.: Johns Hopkins Press, 1971).

105. Karl Menninger, *The Crime of Punishment* (New York: Viking, 1968).

106. See Daniel L. Davis et al., "Prevalence of Emotional Disorders in a Juvenile Justice Institutional Population," *American Journal of Forensic Psychology,* **9** (1991): 5–17.

107. Hervey Cleckley, *The Mask of Sanity,* 5th ed. (St. Louis: Mosby, 1976), pp. 271–272. Copyright 1976, 1988. Published by Emily S. Cleckley, 3024 Fox Spring Road, Augusta, GA 30909.

108. Ibid., p. 57; Robert D. Hare, *Psychopathy: Theory and Research* (New York: Wiley, 1970); M. Philip Feldman,

Criminal Behavior: A Psychological Analysis (New York: Wiley, 1978); William McCord and Joan McCord, *Psychopathy and Delinquency* (New York: Wiley, 1956).

109. *The American Psychiatric Association's Diagnostic and Statistical Manual of Mental Disorders,* 3d rev. ed. (DSM III-R) (Washington, D.C., 1987), classifies psychopathy as "antisocial personality." See Benjamin Karpman, "On the Need of Separating Psychopathy into Two Distinct Clinical Types: The Symptomatic and the Idiopathic," *Journal of Criminal Psychopathology,* **3** (1941): 112–137.

110. Eysenck and Gudjonnson, *The Causes and Cures of Crime.* See also Robert D. Hare, "Research Scale for the Assessment of Psychopathology in Criminal Populations," *Personality and Individual Differences,* **1** (1980): 111–119.

111. Anastasia Toufexis, "Dancing with Devils: Forensic Psychiatrist Park Dietz Tracks America's Serial Killers, Bombers and Mass Murderers," *Psychology Today,* **32**(3) (May 1999): 54. Reprinted with permission from *Psychology Today* magazine. Copyright © 1999 Sussex Publishers, Inc.

112. Wilson and Herrnstein, *Crime and Human Nature.* Infants develop attachment to mothers, or mother substitutes, for comfort, security, and warmth.

CHAPTER 5

1. Roger Ebert, November 11, 2008, available at http://rogerebert.suntimes.com/apps/pbcs.dll/article?AID=/20081111/REVIEWS/811110297/1001.

2. Ysabel Rennie, *The Search for Criminal Man* (Lexington, Mass.: Lexington Books, 1978), p. 125.

3. James T. Carey, *Sociology and Public Affairs: The Chicago School* (Beverly Hills, Calif.: Sage, 1975), pp. 19–20.

4. See the discussion of sociological theory in Frank P. Williams III and Marilyn D. McShane, *Criminological Theory* (Englewood Cliffs, N.J.: Prentice-Hall, 1988).

5. Émile Durkheim, *The Division of Labor in Society* (New York: Free Press, 1964).

6. Émile Durkheim, *Rules of Sociological Method* (New York: Free Press, 1966).

7. Émile Durkheim, *Suicide* (Glencoe, Ill.: Free Press, 1951), pp. 241–276.

8. Ibid., p. 247.

9. Robert K. Merton, "Social Structure and Anomie," *American Sociological Review,* **3** (1938): 672–682. For a complete history of the social structure and anomie paradigm, see recent reflections of Merton in Robert K. Merton, "Opportunity Structure: The Emergence, Diffusion, and Differentiation of a Sociological Concept, 1930s–1950s," in *Advances in Criminological Theory: The Legacy of Anomie,* vol. 6, eds. Freda Adler and William S. Laufer (New Brunswick, N.J.: Transaction, 1994), pp. 3–78. Several measures of anomie have been developed. Probably the best-known indicator of anomie at the social level was formulated by Bernard Lander in a study of 8,464 cases of juvenile delinquency in Baltimore between 1939 and 1942. Lander devised a measure that included the rate of delinquency, the percentage of nonwhite population in a given area, and the percentage of owner-occupied homes. According to Lander, those factors were indicative of the amount of normlessness (anomie) in a community. See Bernard Lander, *Towards an Understanding of Juvenile Delinquency* (New York: Columbia University Press, 1954), p. 65.

10. Carmen DeNavas-Walt, Bernadette D. Proctor, and Jessica Smith, "Income, Poverty, and Health Insurance Coverage in the United States: 2006," United States Census Bureau.

11. Oscar Lewis, "The Culture of Poverty," *Scientific American,* **215** (1966): 19–25.

12. Gunnar Myrdal, *The Challenge of World Poverty* (New York: Vintage, 1990).

13. William Julius Wilson, *The Truly Disadvantaged* (Chicago: University of Chicago Press, 1987).

14. Robert K. Merton, *Social Theory and the Social Structure* (New York: Free Press, 1957), p. 187.

15. Albert J. Reiss Jr. and Albert L. Rhodes, "The Distribution of Juvenile Delinquency in the Social Class Structure," *American Sociological Review,* **26** (1961): 720–732. For the relationship between economic changes and crime, see Pamela Irving Jackson, "Crime, Youth Gangs, and Urban Transition: The Social Dislocations of Postindustrial Economic Development," *Justice Quarterly,* **8** (1991): 380–397.

16. F. Ivan Nye, James F. Short, and Virgil J. Olson, "Socioeconomic Status and Delinquent Behavior," *American Journal of Sociology,* **63** (1958): 381–389.

17. Charles R. Tittle, Wayne J. Villemez, and Douglas A. Smith, "The Myth of Social Class and Criminality: An Empirical Assessment of the Empirical Evidence," *American Sociological Review,* **43** (1978): 652; Charles R. Tittle and Robert F. Meier, "Specifying the SES/Delinquency Relationship by Social Characteristics of Contexts," *Journal of Research in Crime and Delinquency,* 28 (1991): 430–455.

18. Gary F. Jensen and Kevin Thompson, "What's Class Got to Do with It? A Further Examination of Power-Control Theory," *American Journal of Sociology,* **95** (1990): 1009–1023.

19. John Braithwaite, "The Myth of Social Class and Criminality Reconsidered," *American Sociological Review,* **46** (1981): 41. See also Delbert S. Elliott and Suzanne S. Ageton, "Reconciling Race and Class Differences in Self-Reported and Official Estimates of Delinquency," *American Sociological Review,* **45** (1980): 95–110; Michael W. Neustrom and William M. Norton, "Economic Dislocation and Property Crime," *Journal of Criminal Justice,* **23** (1995): 29–39; and James De Fronzo, "Welfare and Homicide," *Journal of Research in Crime and Delinquency,* **34** (1997): 395–406.

20. Nikos Passas, "Anomie, Reference Groups, and Relative Deprivation," in *The Future of Anomie Theory,* eds. Nikos Passas and Robert Ignew (Boston: Northeastern Press, 1997), pp. 64–65.

21. Terence P. Thornberry and Margaret Farnsworth, "Social Correlates of Criminal Involvement: Further Evidence on the Relationship between Social Status and Criminal Behavior," *American Sociological Review,* **47** (1982): 505–518; Thomas J. Bernard, "Control Criticisms of Strain Theories: An Assessment of Theoretical and Empirical Adequacy," *Journal of Research in Crime and Delinquency,* **21** (1984): 353–372; Delbert S. Elliott and David Huizinga, "Social Class and Delinquent Behavior in a National Youth Panel," *Criminology,* **21** (1983): 149–177.

22. See, e.g., Shaun L. Gabbidon and Helen Taylor Greene, *Race and Crime* (Thousand Oaks, Calif.: Sage, 2005).

23. Bradley R. Entner Wright, Avshalom Caspi, Terrie E. Moffitt, Richard A. Miech, and Phil A. Silva, "Reconsidering the Relationship between SES and Delinquency Causation but Not Correlation," *Criminology,* **37** (1999): 175–194.

24. Tomislav V. Kovandzic, Lynne M. Vieraitis, and Mark R. Yeisley, "The Structural Covariates of Urban Homicide: Reassessing the Impact of Income Inequality and Poverty in the Post-Reagan Era," *Criminology,* **36** (1998): 569–600.

25. William R. Avison and Pamela L. Loring, "Population Diversity and Cross-National Homicide: The Effects of Inequality and Heterogeneity," *Criminology,* **24** (1986): 733–749; Harvey Krahn, Timothy F. Hartnagel, and John W. Gartrell, "Income Inequality and Homicide Rates: Cross-National Data and Criminological Theories," *Criminology,* **24** (1986): 269–295; Richard Fowles and Mary Merva, "Wage Inequity and Criminal Activity: An Extreme Bounds Analysis for the United States, 1975–1990," *Criminology,* **34** (1996): 163–182.

26. Krahn et al., "Income Inequality," p. 288.

27. David Brownfield, "Social Class and Violent Behavior," *Criminology,* **24** (1986): 421–438.

28. David Matza, "The Disreputable Poor," in *Class, Status, and Power,* eds. Reinhard Bendix and Seymour M. Lipset (New York: Free Press, 1966). See also William S. Laufer, "Vocational Interests of Homeless, Unemployed Men," *Journal of Vocational Behavior,* **18** (1981): 196–201; and Chris Hale, "Unemployment and Crime: Differencing Is No Substitute for Modeling," *Journal of Research in Crime and Delinquency,* **28** (1991): 426–429.

29. John Hagan, "The Social Embeddedness of Crime and Unemployment," *Criminology,* **31** (1993): 465–492.

30. Judith R. Blau and Peter M. Blau, "The Cost of Inequality: Metropolitan Structure and Violent Crime," *American Sociological Review,* **47** (1982): 114–129. For a discussion of the relationship of job accessibility and racial inequality to crime rates within racial groups, see Karen F. Parker and Patricia L. McCall, "Structural Conditions and Racial Homicide Patterns: A Look at the Multiple Disadvantages in Urban Areas," *Criminology,* **37** (1999): 447–478. See also Steven F. Messner and Reid M. Golden, "Racial Inequality and Racially Disaggregated Homicide Rates: An Assessment of Alternative Theoretical Explanations," *Criminology,* **30** (1992): 421–446; and James A. Chambers, *Blacks and Crime: A Function of Class* (Westport, Conn.: Praeger, 1995).

31. John Braithwaite, *Inequality, Crime, and Public Policy* (London: Routledge & Kegan Paul, 1979), p. 219.

32. Thomas J. Bernard, "Merton versus Hirschi: Who Is Faithful to Durkheim's Heritage?" in *Advances in Criminological Theory,* vol. 4, pp. 81–91; Nikos Passas, "Continuities in the Anomie Tradition," in *Advances in Criminological Theory,* vol. 4, pp. 91–112; Scott Menard, "A Developmental Test of Mertonian Anomie Theory," *Journal of Research in Crime and Delinquency,* **32** (1995): 136–174.

33. Gary F. Jensen, "Salvaging Structure through Strain: A Theoretical and Empirical Critique," in *Advances in Criminological Theory,* vol. 4, pp. 139–158; Velmer S. Burton Jr., Francis T. Cullen, T. David Evans, and R. Gregory Dunaway, "Reconsidering Strain Theory: Operationalization, Rival Theories, and Adult Criminality," *Journal of Quantitative Criminology,* **10** (1994): 213–239.

34. Ian Taylor, Paul Walton, and Jock Young, *The New Criminology* (New York: Harper & Row, 1973), p. 107.

35. Freda Adler, *Nations Not Obsessed with Crime* (Littleton, Colo.: Fred B. Rothman, 1983).

36. Steven F. Messner and Richard Rosenfeld, *Crime and the American Dream* (Belmont, Calif.: Wadsworth, 1994).

37. Mitchell B. Chamlin and John K. Cochran, "Assessing Messner and Rosenfeld's Institutional Anomie Theory: A Partial Test," *Criminology,* **33** (1995): 411–429.

38. Freda Adler, "Synnomie to Anomie: A Macrosociological Formulation," in *Advances in Criminological Theory,* vol. 4, pp. 271–283.

39. Robert Agnew, "Foundations for a General Strain Theory of Crime and Delinquency," *Criminology,* **30** (1992): 47–87.

40. Robert Agnew, "The Contribution of Social-Psychological Strain Theory to the Explanation of Crime and Delinquency," in *Advances in Criminological Theory,* vol. 6, pp. 113–137. See also John P. Hoffman and Alan S. Miller, "A Latent Variable Analysis of General Strain Theory," *Journal of Quantitative Criminology,* **14** (1998): 83–110.

41. Raymond Paternoster and Paul Mazerolle, "General Strain Theory and Delinquency: A Replication and Extension," *Journal of Research in Crime and Delinquency,* **31** (1994): 235–263. See also Robert Agnew, Timothy Brezina, John Paul Wright, and Francis T. Cullen, "Strain, Personality Traits, and Delinquency: Extending General Strain Theory," *Criminology,* **40** (2002): 43–71; Paul Mazerolle and Jeff Maahs, "General Strain and Delinquency: An Alternative Examination of Conditioning Influences," *Justice Quarterly,* **17** (2000): 753–773; Timothy Brezina, "Adapting to Strain: An Examination of Delinquent Coping Responses," *Criminology,* **34** (1996): 39–60; and Robert Agnew and Helene Raskin White, "An Empirical Test of General Strain Theory," *Criminology,* **30** (1992): 475–499. For an examination of gender and delinquent behavior from a general strain theory perspective, see Paul Mazerolle, "Gender, General Strain and Delinquency: An Empirical Examination," *Justice Quarterly,* **15** (1998): 65–91.

42. "Head Start Impact Study First Year Findings: Executive Summary June 2005," available at www.acf .hhs.gov/programs/opre/hs/impact_study/reports/ first_yr_execsum/first_yr_execsum.pdf.

43. John R. Berrueta-Clement, Lawrence J. Schweinhart, W. Steven Barnett, Ann S. Epstein, and David P. Weekart, *Changed Lives: The Effects of the Perry Preschool Program on Youths through Age 19* (Ypsilanti, Mich.: High/Scope, 1984).

44. Jane Gross, "A Remnant of the War on Poverty, the Job Corps Is a Quiet Success," *New York Times,* Feb. 17, 1992, pp. 1, 14.

45. Tammy Joyner, "Atlanta Job Corps Exec Wins Award," *Atlanta Journal and Constitution,* June 8, 1999, p. 2F.

46. Lawrence W. Sherman, Denise Gottfredson, Doris McKenzie, John Eck, Peter Reuter, and Sharon Bushway, *Preventing Crime: What Works, What Doesn't, What's Promising,* U.S. Department of Justice, Office of Justice Programs, February 1997, chap. 6, p. 40.

47. W. I. Thomas and Florian Znaniecki, *The Polish Peasant in Europe and America* (Boston: Gorham, 1920).

48. Robert E. Park, "Human Ecology," *American Journal of Sociology,* **42** (1936): 1–15.

49. Clifford R. Shaw, Frederick M. Forbaugh, Henry D. McKay, and Leonard S. Cottrell, *Delinquency Areas* (Chicago: University of Chicago Press, 1929).

50. Clifford R. Shaw and Henry D. McKay, *Juvenile Delinquency and Urban Areas* (Chicago: University of Chicago Press, 1942); see also the revised and updated edition: Clifford R. Shaw and Henry D. McKay, *Juvenile Delinquency and Urban Areas: A Study of Delinquency in Relation to Differential Characteristics of Local Communities*

in American Cities (Chicago: University of Chicago Press, 1969). See also Frederick M. Thrasher, *The Gang* (Chicago: University of Chicago Press, 1927).

51. Ralph B. Taylor, "The Impact of Crime on Communities," *The Annals of the American Academy,* **539** (1995): 28–45.

52. Ralph B. Taylor, Steve D. Gottfredson, and Sidney Brower, "Attachments to Place: Discriminant Validity and Impacts of Disorder and Diversity," *American Journal of Community Psychology,* **13** (1985): 525–542.

53. Michael Marriott, "Living in 'Lockdown,' " *Newsweek,* Jan. 23, 1995, p. 57.

54. Lynn Newhart Smith and Gary D. Hill, "Victimization and Fear of Crime," *Criminal Justice and Behavior,* **18** (1991): 217–239. See also Fred E. Markowitz, Paul E. Bellair, Allen E. Liska, and Jianhong Liu, "Extending Social Disorganization Theory: Modeling the Relationships between Cohesion, Disorder, and Fear," *Criminology,* **39** (2001): 293–319; and Randy L. LaGrange, Kenneth F. Ferraro, and Michael Supancic, "Perceived Risk of Fear of Crime: Role of Social and Physical Incivilities," *Journal of Research in Crime and Delinquency,* **29** (1992): 311–334. For research that measures safety and perceived safety resources in the context of other environmental concerns (as an alternative to measuring fear of crime), see John J. Gibbs and Kathleen J. Hanrahan, "Safety Demand and Supply: An Alternative to Fear of Crime," *Justice Quarterly,* **10** (1993): 369–394.

55. Ralph Taylor and Jeanette Covington, "Community Structural Change and Fear of Crime," *Social Problems,* **40** (1993): 374–392.

56. Douglas A. Smith, "The Neighborhood Context of Police Behavior," in *Communities and Crime,* eds. Albert J. Reiss and Michael Tonry (Chicago: University of Chicago Press, 1986), pp. 313–341; Terance D. Miethe, Michael Hughes, and David McDowall, "Social Change in Crime Rates: An Evaluation of Alternative Theoretical Approaches," *Social Forces,* **70** (1991): 165–185; E. Britt Paterson, "Poverty, Income Inequality, and Community Crime Rates," *Criminology,* **29** (1991): 755–776; Josefina Figueira-McDonough, "Community Structure and Delinquency: A Typology," *Social Service Review,* **65** (1991): 65–91; Denise C. Gottfredson, Richard J. McNeil, and Gary D. Gottfredson, "Social Area Influence on Delinquency: A Multilevel Analysis," *Journal of Research in Crime and Delinquency,* **28** (1991): 197–226.

57. Dina R. Rose and Todd R. Clear, "Incarceration, Social Capital, and Crime: Implications for Social Disorganization Theory," *Criminology,* **36** (1998): 441–479.

58. Robert J. Sampson and Dawn Jeglum Bartusch, *Attitudes toward Crime, Police, and the Law: Individual and Neighborhood Differences,* National Institute of Justice Research Preview, June 1999.

59. Steve J. South and Gary D. Deane, "Race and Residential Mobility: Individual Determinants and Structural Constraints," *Social Forces,* **72** (1993): 147–167.

60. See Faith Peeples and Rolf Loeber, "Do Individual Factors and Neighborhood Context Explain Ethnic Differences in Juvenile Delinquency?" *Journal of Quantitative Criminology,* **10** (1994): 141–157; and Thomas A. Petee, Gregory S. Kowlaski, and Don W. Duffield, "Crime, Social Disorganization, and Social Structure: A Research Note on the Use of Interurban Ecological Models," *American Journal of Criminal Justice,*

19 (1994): 117–132. For generalizability of social disorganization theory to nonurban areas, see D. Wayne Osgood and Jeff M. Chambers, "Social Disorganization Outside the Metropolis: An Analysis of Rural Youth Violence," *Criminology,* **38** (2000): 81–115.

61. Taylor, "The Impact of Crime on Communities," p. 36.

62. Andrew J. Buck, Simon Hakim, and Ulrich Spiegel, "Casinos, Crime, and Real Estate Values: Do They Relate?" *Journal of Research in Crime and Delinquency,* **28** (1991): 288–303.

63. Robert J. Bursik and Harold G. Grosmick, *Neighborhoods and Crime* (New York: Lexington Books, 1993).

64. Anthony Sorrentino and David Whittaker, "The Chicago Area Project—Addressing the Gang Problem," *FBI Law Enforcement Bulletin,* **63** (1994): 8–12; "Philadelphia Settles with Estates of MOVE Members," *Jet,* Feb. 17, 1997, p. 40; Steven Schlossman, Goul Zellman, and Richard Shavelson, "Delinquency Prevention in South Chicago: A Fifty-Year Assessment of the Chicago Area Project," report prepared for the National Institute of Education by the Rand Corporation, May 1984, p. 1; Solomon Kobrin, "The Chicago Area Project: 25 Years of Assessment," *Annals of the American Academy of Political and Social Science,* **332** (1959): 20–29.

65. Terence Dunworth and Gregory Mills, *National Evaluation of Weed and Seed,* NIJ Research in Brief, June 1999.

66. M. Isolina Ferre, "Prevention and Control of Violence through Community Revitalization, Individual Dignity, and Personal Self-Confidence," *Annals of the American Academy of Political and Social Science,* **494** (1987): 27–36.

67. Edwin H. Sutherland, *Principles of Criminology,* 3d ed. (Philadelphia: Lippincott, 1939).

68. William Chambliss, *Boxmen* (New York: Harper & Row, 1972).

69. James F. Short, "Differential Association as a Hypothesis: Problems of Empirical Testing," *Social Problems,* **8** (1960): 14–15.

70. Travis Hirschi, *Causes of Delinquency* (Berkeley: University of California Press, 1969), p. 95.

71. Beth Bjerregaard and Carolyn Smith, "Patterns of Male and Female Gang Membership," working paper no. 13, Rochester Youth Development Study (Albany, N.Y.: Hindelang Criminal Justice Research Center, 1992), p. 20. For contradictory findings, see Mark D. Reed and Pamela Wilcox Roundtree, "Peer Pressure and Adolescent Substance Abuse," *Journal of Quantitative Criminology,* **13** (1997), 143–180. For the relationship of delinquents to their delinquent siblings, see Janet L. Lauritsen, "Sibling Resemblance in Juvenile Delinquency: Findings from the National Youth Survey," *Criminology,* **31** (1993): 387–409.

72. Mark Warr, "Age, Peers, and Delinquency," *Criminology,* **31** (1993): 17–40.

73. Charles Tittle, *Sanctions and Social Deviance* (New York: Praeger, 1980).

74. Clayton A. Hartjen, *Crime and Criminalization* (New York: Praeger, 1974), p. 51.

75. Ross L. Matsueda, "The Current State of Differential Association," *Crime and Delinquency,* **34** (1988): 277–306; Craig Reinarman and Jeffrey Fagan, "Social Organization and Differential Association: A Research Note from a Longitudinal Study of Violent Juvenile Offenders," *Crime and Delinquency,* **34** (1988): 307–327.

76. Susan Chira, "A Program That Works for Teen-Age Mothers," *New York Times,* Apr. 28, 1993, p. A12.

77. Fox Butterfield, "Programs Seek to Stop Trouble before It Starts," *New York Times,* Dec. 30, 1994, A25.

78. Thorsten Sellin, *Culture Conflict and Crime,* Bulletin 41 (New York: Social Science Research Council, 1938); Avison and Loring, "Population Diversity and Cross-National Homicide"; Mark R. Pogrebin and Eric D. Poole, "Culture Conflict and Crime in the Korean-American Community," *Criminal Justice Policy Review,* **4** (1990): 69–78; Ira Sommers, Jeffrey Fagan, and Deborah Baskin, "The Influences of Acculturation and Familism on Puerto Rican Delinquency," *Justice Quarterly,* **11** (1994): 207–228.

CHAPTER 6

1. Federal Bureau of Investigation, "The MS-13 Threat: A National Assessment" available at www.fbi.gov/page2/jan08/ms13_011408.html.

2. Excerpts from *2005 National Gang Threat Assessment* (Washington, D.C.: Bureau of Justice Assistance, 2006), p. vi; available at www.nagia.org/PDFs/2005_national_gang_threat_assessment.pdf.

3. Albert K. Cohen, *Delinquent Boys: The Culture of the Gang* (Glencoe, Ill.: Free Press, 1955).

4. For example, James F. Short Jr. and Fred L. Strodtbeck, *Group Process and Gang Delinquency* (Chicago: University of Chicago Press, 1965).

5. Kenneth Polk and Walter B. Schafer, eds., *School and Delinquency* (Englewood Cliffs, N.J.: Prentice-Hall, 1972); Alexander Liazos, "School, Alienation, and Delinquency," *Crime and Delinquency,* **24** (1978): 355–370.

6. Travis Hirschi, *Causes of Delinquency* (Berkeley: University of California Press, 1969).

7. Delbert S. Elliott and Harwin L. Voss, *Delinquency and Dropout* (Lexington, Mass.: Lexington Books, 1974).

8. G. Roger Jarjoura, "Dropping Out of School Enhances Delinquent Involvement? Results from a Large-Scale National Probability Sample," *Criminology,* **31** (1993): 149–172.

9. Albert J. Reiss and Albert L. Rhodes, "Deprivation and Delinquent Behavior," *Sociological Quarterly,* **4** (1963): 135–149.

10. Marvin Krohn, R. L. Akers, M. J. Radosevich, and L. Lanza-Kaduce, "Social Status and Deviance," *Criminology,* **18** (1980): 303–318.

11. Mark Warr, "Organization and Instigation in Delinquent Groups," *Criminology,* **34** (1996): 11–37.

12. David F. Greenberg, "Delinquency and the Age Structure of Society," *Contemporary Crisis,* **1** (1977): 189–223.

13. John I. Kitsuse and David C. Dietrick, "Delinquent Boys: A Critique," *American Sociological Review,* **24** (1959): 208–215.

14. David J. Bordua, "Delinquent Subcultures: Sociological Interpretations of Gang Delinquency," *Annals of the American Academy of Political and Social Science,* **338** (1961): 119–136.

15. Albert K. Cohen and James F. Short Jr., "Research in Delinquent Subcultures," *Journal of Social Issues,* **14** (1958): 20–37.

16. Richard A. Cloward and Lloyd E. Ohlin, *Delinquency and Opportunity* (Glencoe, Ill.: Free Press, 1960).

17. Clifford R. Shaw, *The Jack-Roller* (Chicago: University of Chicago Press, 1930), p. 54.

18. James R. David, *Street Gangs* (Dubuque, Iowa: Kendall/Hunt, 1982).

19. Hirschi, *Causes of Delinquency,* p. 227.

20. John M. Hagedorn, "Homeboys, Dope Fiends, Legits, and New Jacks," *Criminology,* **32** (1994): 197–219.

21. James Short, Ramon Rivera, and Ray Tennyson, "Perceived Opportunities, Gang Membership, and Delinquency," *American Sociological Review,* **30** (1965): 56–57.

22. Lecture by Ko-lin Chin, Rutgers University, Nov. 22, 1993. See also K. Chin, *Chinese Subculture and Criminality: Nontraditional Crime Groups in America,* Criminology and Penology Series, vol. 29 (Westport, Conn.: Greenwood, 1990); Mark Warr, "Organization and Instigation in Delinquent Groups," *Criminology,* **34** (1996): 11–37; and Kevin M. Thompson, David Brownfield, and Ann Marie Sorenson, "Specialization Patterns of Gang and Nongang Offending: A Latent Structure Analysis," *Journal of Gang Research,* **3** (1996): 25–35.

23. Finn-Aage Esbensen and David Huizinga, "Gangs, Drugs, and Delinquency in a Survey of Urban Youth," *Criminology,* **31** (1993): 565–587; Terence P. Thornberry, Marvin D. Krohn, Alan J. Lizotte, and Deborah Chard-Wierschem, "The Role of Juvenile Gangs in Facilitating Delinquent Behavior," *Journal of Research in Crime and Delinquency,* **30** (1993): 55–87; Malcolm Klein, Cheryl L. Maxson, and Lea C. Cunningham, " 'Crack,' Street Gangs, and Violence," *Criminology,* **29** (1991): 623–650.

24. K. Chin and J. Fagan, "Social Order and Gang Formation in Chinatown," in *Advances in Criminological Theory,* vol. 6, eds. Freda Adler and William S. Laufer (New Brunswick, N.J.: Transaction, 1994).

25. George W. Knop, Edward D. Tromanhauser, James G. Houston, et al., *The Economics of Gang Life: A Task Force Report of the National Gang Crime Research Center* (Chicago: National Crime Research Center, 1995).

26. Ibid., p. ii.

27. John P. Hoffman and Timothy Ireland, "Cloward and Ohlin's Strain Theory Reexamined: An Elaborated Theoretical Model," in *Advances in Criminological Theory,* vol. 6.

28. Marvin E. Wolfgang and Franco Ferracuti, *The Subculture of Violence* (London: Tavistock, 1967).

29. Elijah Anderson, *Code of the Street* (New York: W. W. Norton & Company, 1999); T. Brezina, Robert Agnew, and F. T. Cullen, "The Code of the Street: A Quantitative Assessment of Elijah Anderson's Subculture of Violence Thesis and Its Contribution to Youth Violence Research," *Youth Violence and Juvenile Justice,* **2(4)** (2004): 303–328; Liqun Cao, Anthony Adams, and Vickie J. Jensen, "A Test of the Black Subculture of Violence Thesis: A Research Note," *Criminology,* **35(2)** (1997): 367–379; Lance Hannon, "Race, Victim-Precipitated Homicide, and the Subculture of Violence Thesis," *Social Science Journal,* **41** (2004): 115–121; Howard S. Erlanger, "The Empirical Status of the Subcultures of Violence Thesis," *Social Problems,* **22** (1974): 280–292. For the relationship of the thesis to routine activities, see Leslie W. Kennedy and Stephen W. Baron, "Routine Activities and a Subculture of Violence: A Study on the Street," *Journal of Research in Crime and Delinquency,* **30** (1993): 88–112. For a look at regional differences in punitiveness, see Marian J. Borg, "The Southern Subculture of Punitiveness? Regional Variation in Support for Capital Punishment," *Journal of Research in Crime and Delinquency,* **34** (1997): 25–45.

30. William G. Doerner, "A Regional Analysis of Homicide Rates in the United States," *Criminology,* **13** (1975): 90–101.

31. Jo Dixon and Alan J. Lizotte, "Gun Ownership and the Southern Subculture of Violence," *American Journal of Sociology,* **93** (1987): 383–405.

32. Colin Loftin and Robert Hill, "Regional Subculture of Violence: An Examination of the Gastril-Hackney Thesis," *American Sociological Review,* **39** (1974): 714–724. See also Colin Loftin and David McDowall, "Regional Culture and Patterns of Homicide," *Homicide Studies,* **7(4)** (2003): 353–367.

33. Judith Blau and Peter Blau, "Metropolitan Structure and Violent Crime," *American Sociological Review,* **47** (1982): 114–129. For a study that examines the subculture of violence thesis as it relates to three groups—blacks, Hispanics, and American Indians— see Donald J. Shoemaker and J. Sherwood Williams, "The Subculture of Violence and Ethnicity," *Journal of Criminal Justice,* **15** (1987): 461–472.

34. Wolfgang and Ferracuti, *The Subculture of Violence,* pp. 258–265. See also Marvin E. Wolfgang, *Patterns in Criminal Homicide* (Philadelphia: University of Pennsylvania Press, 1958).

35. Marvin E. Wolfgang, Robert M. Figlio, and Thorsten Sellin, *Delinquency in a Birth Cohort* (Chicago: University of Chicago Press, 1972); Simon I. Singer, "Victims of Serious Violence and Their Criminal Behavior: Subcultural Theory and Beyond," *Violence and Victims,* **1** (1986): 61–70. See also Neil Alan Weiner and Marvin E. Wolfgang, "The Extent and Character of Violent Crime in America, 1969–1982," in *American Violence and Public Policy,* ed. Lynn Curtis (New Haven, Conn.: Yale University Press, 1985), pp. 17–39.

36. Steven Messner, "Regional and Racial Effects on the Urban Homicide Rate: The Subculture of Violence Revisited," *American Journal of Sociology,* **88** (1983): 997–1007.

37. Scott H. Decker, "Collective and Normative Features of Gang Violence," *Justice Quarterly,* **13** (1996): 243–264.

38. Jeffrey Fagan, "The Social Organization of Drug Use and Drug Dealing among Urban Gangs," *Criminology,* **27** (1989): 633–666.

39. Joseph B. Treaster, "Jamaica's Gangs Take Root in U.S.," *New York Times,* Nov. 13, 1988, p. 15.

40. Walter B. Miller, "Lower-Class Culture as a Generating Milieu of Gang Delinquency," *Journal of Social Issues,* **14** (1958): 5–19.

41. Claude Brown, *Manchild in the Promised Land: A Modern Classic of the Black Experience* (New York: New American Library, 1965), p. 22.

42. Ibid., p. 129.

43. Miller, "Lower-Class Culture."

44. Stephen A. Cernovich, "Value Orientations and Delinquency Involvement," *Criminology,* **15** (1978): 443–458.

45. Gresham Sykes and David Matza, "Techniques of Neutralization: A Theory of Delinquency," *American Sociological Review,* **22** (1957): 664–673.

46. Barbara Kantrowitz, "Wild in the Streets," *Newsweek,* Aug. 2, 1993, p. 46.

47. Eugene O'Neill, *Long Day's Journey into Night,* in *Great Scenes from the World Theater,* ed. James L. Steffenson Jr. (New York: Avon, 1965), p. 199.

48. Dorothea Lange, *A Photographer's Life* (Syracuse, N.Y.: Syracuse University Press, 2000).

49. Jean Merl, "Sentencing and Elegy for Slain Boy Court: Emotional Statements by Victim's Family Have Many in Tears. Three Gang Members Receive Lengthy Terms," *Los Angeles Times,* Sept. 16, 1999, p. B1.

50. Michael Cooper, "17-Year-Old Is Arrested in Boy's Death: Slaying of Bystander Is Linked to Gangs," *New York Times,* Aug. 22, 1999, p. 37.

51. Bill Miller, "Guilty Plea in Slaying of D.C. Boy, 12; Teen Was Triggerman in Gang-Related Case," *Washington Post,* Feb. 21, 1998, p. D01.

52. Rene Sanchez, "Placid Santa Monica Roiled by 5 Gang War Deaths in 2 Weeks," *Washington Post,* Oct. 31, 1998, p. A02.

53. S. Hollandsworth, "Girl, Interrupted," *Texas Monthly,* 2008. Retrieved July 1, 2008, from www.texasmonthly.com/2008-05-01/letterfromhouston.php.

54. *National Gang Threat Assessment 2005* (Washington, D.C.: U.S. Department of Justice and National Alliance of Gang Investigators Associations, 2005.) Retrieved July 1, 2008, from www.ojp.usdoj.gov/BJA/what/2005_threat_assesment.pdf.

55. *National Drug Threat Assessment 2006* (Washington, D.C.: National Drugs Intelligence Center, U.S. Department of Justice (2006). Retrieved July 1, 2008, from www.usdoj.gov/ndic/pubs11/18862/index.htm#Contents.

56. *Youth Gang Drug Trafficking* (Washington, D.C.: Office of Juvenile Justice and Delinquency Prevention, U.S. Department of Justice, December 1999).

57. Beth Bjerregaard and Alan J. Lizotte, "Gun Ownership and Gang Membership," *Journal of Criminal Law and Criminology,* **86** (1995): 37–58; Alan J. Lizotte, James M. Tesoriero, Terence P. Thornberry, and Marvin D. Krohn, "Patterns of Adolescent Firearms Ownership and Use," *Justice Quarterly,* **11** (1994): 51–74. On the extent of gang organizations, see Scott H. Decker, Tim Bynum, and Deborah Weisel, "A Tale of Two Cities: Gangs as Organized Crime Groups," *Justice Quarterly,* **15** (1998): 395–425.

58. Office of Juvenile Justice and Delinquency Prevention, *Juvenile Offenders and Victims: 1999 National Report* (Washington, D.C.: Office of Juvenile Justice and Delinquency Prevention, 1999); U.S. Department of Justice, Federal Bureau of Investigation, *Uniform Crime Report 1985–1995* (Washington, D.C.: Federal Bureau of Investigation, 1999). See also Alfred Blumstein, "Youth, Violence, Guns and the Illicit Gun Industry," *Journal of Criminal Law and Criminology,* **86** (1995): 10–36; and Howard N. Snyder, "Juvenile Arrests 2003," U.S. Department of Justice, Office of Juvenile Justice and Delinquency Prevention, Juvenile Justice Bulletin, August 2005 (www.ncjrs.gov/pdffiles1/ojjdp/209735.pdf).

59. John P. Sullivan and Martin E. Silverstein, "The Disaster within Us: Urban Conflict and Street Gang Violence in Los Angeles," *Journal of Gang Research,* **2** (1995): 11–30 (at p. 28).

60. Cohen and Short, "Research in Delinquent Subcultures."

61. Anne Campbell, *The Girls in the Gang* (New York: Basil Blackwell, 1984), p. 267.

62. Jill Leslie Rosenbaum, "A Violent Few: Gang Girls in the California Youth Authority," *Journal of Gang Research,* **3** (1996): 17–23. For reasons girls join gangs, see Finn-Aage Esbensen and Elizabeth Piper Deschenes, "A Multisite Examination of Youth Gang Membership: Does Gender Matter?" *Criminology,* **36** (1998): 799–828.

63. M. Eghigian and K. Kirby, "Girls in Gangs: On the Rise in America," *Corrections Today,* **68(2):** 48–50.

64. Seth Mydans, "Life in Girls' Gang: Colors and Bloody Noses," *New York Times,* Jan. 29, 1990, pp. 1, 20.

65. David Lauderback, Joy Hansen, and Dan Waldorf, "'Sisters Are Doin' It for Themselves': A Black Female Gang in San Francisco," *Gang Journal,* **1** (1992): 57–72.

66. Ibid., p. 67.

67. Beth Bjerregaard and Carolyn Smith, *Rochester Youth Development Study: Patterns of Male and Female Gang Membership,* working paper no. 13 (Albany, N.Y.: Hindelang Criminal Justice Research Center, 1992).

68. Seth Mydans, "Not Just the Inner City: Well-to-Do Join Gangs," *New York Times,* Apr. 10, 1990, p. A10.

69. C. Ronald Huff, ed., *Gangs in America* (Newbury Park, Calif.: Sage, 1990).

70. Mydans, "Not Just the Inner City."

71. Dan Korem, *Suburban Gangs: Affluent Rebels* (Richardson, Tex.: International Focus, 1994).

72. As quoted in Mydans, "Not Just the Inner City."

73. Korem, *Suburban Gangs.*

74. Anti-Defamation League, "ADL Reports Resurgence of Racist Skinheads in U.S. and Launches New Online Racist Skinhead Project," press release (2006). Retrieved July 4, 2008, from www.adl.org/PresRele/NeoSk_82/4860_82.htm.

75. *Hate-Crime Statistics, 2006,* U.S. Department of Justice, Federal Bureau of Investigation. Retrieved July 4, 2008, from www.fbi.gov/ucr/hc2006/abouthcs.htm.

76. "Hate Crime Statistics 2003," Federal Bureau of Investigation report, U.S. Department of Justice, November 2004.

77. "L.A. Style: A Street Gang Manual of the Los Angeles County Sheriff's Department," in *The Modern Gang Reader,* eds. Malcolm W. Klein, Cheryl L. Maxson, and Jody Miller (Los Angeles: Roxbury, 1995).

78. Albert K. Cohen, "Middle-Class Delinquency and the Social Structure," in *Middle-Class Delinquency,* ed. E. W. Vaz (New York: Harper & Row, 1967), pp. 207–221.

79. S. Preski and D. Shelton, "The Role of Contextual, Child, and Parental Factors in Predicting Criminal Outcomes in Adolescence," *Issues in Mental Health Nursing,* **22:** 197–205.

80. Irving A. Spergel, Kwai Ming Wa, and Rolando V. Sosa, "Evaluation of the Bloomington-Normal Comprehensive Gang Program," U.S. Department of Justice, Office of Juvenile Justice and Delinquency Prevention (National Institute of Justice, October 2001); Irving A. Spergel, Kwai Ming Wa, and Rolando V. Sosa, "Evaluation of the Mesa Gang Intervention Program (MGIP)," U.S. Department of Justice, Office of Juvenile Justice and Delinquency Prevention (National Institute of Justice, October 2002); Irving A. Spergel, Kwai Ming Wa, and Rolando V. Sosa, "Evaluation of the Riverside Comprehensive Community-Wide Approach to Gang Prevention, Intervention, and Suppression Program," U.S. Department of Justice, Office of Juvenile Justice and Delinquency Prevention (National Institute of Justice, October 2003); Irving A. Spergel, Kwai Ming Wa, and Rolando V. Sosa, "Evaluation of the San Antonio Comprehensive Community-Wide Approach to Gang Prevention, Intervention, and Suppression Program," U.S. Department of Justice, Office of Juvenile Justice and Delinquency Prevention (National Institute of Justice, June 2004); Irving A. Spergel, Kwai Ming Wa, and Rolando V. Sosa, "Evaluation of the Tucson Comprehensive Community-Wide Approach to Gang Prevention, Intervention, and Suppression Program," U.S. Department of Justice, Office of Juvenile Justice and Delinquency Prevention (National Institute of Justice, October 2004).

81. Lynn A. Curtis, Preface to "Policies to Prevent Crime: Neighborhood, Family, and Employment Strategies," *Annals of the American Academy of Political and Social Science,* **494** (1987).

82. Robert Reinhold, "In the Middle of L.A.'s Gang Warfare," *New York Times Magazine,* May 22, 1988, p. 31.

83. Ibid., p. 70.

84. Second Chance Grace, *Tattoo Removal Program* (2008). Retrieved July 4, 2008, from http://2ndchancegrace.org/home/index.php?option=com_content&task=view&id=27&Itemid=33.

85. Jon D. Hull, "No Way Out," *Time,* Aug. 17, 1992, p. 40.

86. R. S. Mueller, "Federal Bureau of Investigation: Major Executive Speeches" (2007). Retrieved July 9, 2008, from www.fbi.gov/pressrel/speeches/mueller011807.htm.

87. U.S. Department of Justice, "Attorney General's Report to Congress on the Growth of Violent Street Gangs in Suburban America." Retrieved July 9, 2008, from www.justice.gov/ndic/pubs27/27612/dept.htm#start.

88. Ibid. Retrieved July 9, 2008 from http://www.justice.gov/ndic/pubs27/27612/dojgangs.htm#Top.

CHAPTER 7

1. William Golding, *Lord of the Flies* (New York: Coward-McCann, 1954), p. 31.

2. Jack P. Gibbs, "Social Control, Deterrence, and Perspectives on Social Order," *Social Forces,* **56** (1977): 408–423. See also Freda Adler, *Nations Not Obsessed with Crime* (Littleton, Colo.: Fred B. Rothman, 1983).

3. Travis Hirschi, *Causes of Delinquency* (Berkeley: University of California Press, 1969).

4. Donald J. Black, *The Behavior of Law* (New York: Academic Press, 1976), p. 105. See Allan V. Horwitz, *The Logic of Social Control* (New York: Plenum, 1990), for an exceptional evaluation of Black's work.

5. American Nonsmokers Rights Foundation, "100% Smoke-Free Correctional Facilities (2008). Retrieved July 14, 2008, from http://www.no-smoke.org/pdf/100smokefreeprisons.pdf.

6. Nanette J. Davis and Bo Anderson, *Social Control: The Production of Deviance in the Modern State* (New York: Irvington, 1983); S. Cohen and A. Scull, eds., *Social Control and the State* (New York: St. Martin's Press, 1983).

7. Jackson Toby, "Social Disorganization and Stake in Conformity: Complementary Factors in the Predatory Behavior of Hoodlums," *Journal of Criminal Law, Criminology, and Police Science,* **48** (1957): 12–17.

8. Scott Briar and Irving Piliavin, "Delinquency, Situational Inducements, and Commitment to Conformity," *Social Problems,* **13** (1965): 41.

9. Ibid, p. 36.

10. Hirschi, *Causes of Delinquency.*

11. See John Bowlby, *Attachment and Loss,* 2 vols. (New York: Basic Books, 1969, 1973); John Bowlby, "Forty-Four Juvenile Thieves: Their Characteristics and Home Life," *International Journal of Psychoanalysis,* **25** (1944): 19–25; and John Bowlby, *The Making and Breaking of Affectional Bonds* (London: Tavistock, 1979).

12. Hirschi, *Causes of Delinquency.*

13. Ibid., p. 145.

14. The National Youth Violence Prevention Resource Center, "After-School Programs Fact Sheet" (2007). Retrieved July 12, 2008, from http://www.safeyouth.org/scripts/facts/afterschool.asp.

15. After School Matters, "Frequently Asked Questions" (2007). Retrieved July 14, 2008 from http://www.afterschoolmatters.org/faqs/#A1.

16. Hirschi, *Causes of Delinquency.*

17. http://www.phillyasap.org/.

18. Jeff Lofvers, "I Don't Understand Why Teens Get Such a Bad Rap," *Orlando Sentinel,* June 5, 1996, p. A13.

19. Michael J. Hindelang, "Causes of Delinquency: A Partial Replication and Extension," *Social Problems,* **20** (1973): 471–487.

20. Marvin D. Krohn and James L. Massey, "Social Control and Delinquent Behavior: An Examination of the Elements of the Social Bond," *Sociological Quarterly,* **21** (1980): 529–544.

21. Michael D. Wiatrowski, David Griswold, and Mary K. Roberts, "Social Control Theory and Delinquency," *American Sociological Review,* **46** (1985): 525–541.

22. Robert Agnew, "Social Control Theory and Delinquency: A Longitudinal Test," *Criminology,* **23** (1985): 47–61. See also Scott Menard, "Demographic and Theoretical Variables in the Age-Period-Cohort Analysis of Illegal Behavior," *Journal of Research in Crime and Delinquency,* **29** (1992): 178–199; Stephen A. Cernovich and Peggy C. Giordano, "School Bonding, Age, Race, and Delinquency," *Criminology,* **30** (1992): 261–291; Kimberly L. Kempf, "The Empirical Status of Social Control Theory," in *New Directions in Criminological Theory,* eds. Freda Adler and William S. Laufer (New Brunswick, N.J.: Transaction, 1993), pp. 143–185; Marc LeBlanc and Aaron Caplan, "Theoretical Formalization, a Necessity: The Example of Hirschi's Bonding Theory," in *New Directions in Criminological Theory,* pp. 237–336; and Orlando Rodriguez and David Weisburd, "The Integrated Social Control Model and Ethnicity: The Case of Puerto Rican American Delinquency," *Criminal Justice and Behavior,* **18** (1991): 464–479.

23. David F. Greenberg, "The Weak Strength of Social Control Theory," *Crime and Delinquency,* **45** (1999): 66–81.

24. Kimberly K. Leonard and S. H. Decker, "The Theory of Social Control: Does It Apply to the Very Young?" *Journal of Criminal Justice,* **22** (1994): 89–105; Karen S. Rook, "Promoting Social Bonding: Strategies for Helping the Lonely and Socially Isolated," *American Psychologist,* **39** (1984): 1389–1407.

25. Milton Rokeach, *The Nature of Human Values* (New York: Free Press, 1973).

26. See Donald J. Shoemaker, *Theories of Delinquency: An Examination of Explanations of Delinquent Behavior,* 2d ed. (New York: Oxford University Press, 1990), pp. 172–207, for an evaluation of social control theory.

27. Terence P. Thornberry, "Toward an Interactional Theory of Delinquency," *Criminology,* **25** (1987): 863–891.

28. David Matza, *Delinquency and Drift* (New York: Wiley, 1964), p. 21.

29. Gresham Sykes and David Matza, "Techniques of Neutralization: A Theory of Delinquency," *American Sociological Review,* **22** (1957): 664–670. For a more recent look at techniques of neutralization, see John Hamlin, "The Misplaced Role of Rational Choice in Neutralization Theory," *Criminology,* **26** (1988): 425–438.

30. Richard A. Ball, "An Empirical Exploration of Neutralization Theory," *Criminologica,* **4** (1966): 103–120. See also N. William Minor, "The Neutralization of Criminal Offense," *Criminology,* **18** (1980): 103–120.

31. Robert Gordon, James F. Short Jr., D. Cartwright, and Fred L. Strodtbeck, "Values and Gang Delinquency: A Study of Street Corner Groups," *American Journal of Sociology,* **69** (1963): 109–128.

32. Albert J. Reiss, "Delinquency as the Failure of Personal and Social Controls," *American Sociological Review,* **16** (1951): 206.

33. Toby, "Social Disorganization," p. 137.

34. Walter C. Reckless, "A New Theory of Delinquency and Crime," *Federal Probation,* **25** (1961): 42–46; Walter C. Reckless, Simon Dinitz, and E. Murray, "Self-Concept as an Insulator against Delinquency," *American Sociological Review,* **21** (1956): 744–746; Frank R. Scarpitti, Ellen Murray, Simon Dinitz, and Walter C. Reckless, "The Good Boy in a High Delinquency Area: Four Years Later," *American Sociological Review,* **25** (1960): 555–558. See also K. Heimer and R. L. Matsueda, "Role-Taking, Role Commitment, and Delinquency: A Theory of Differential Social Control," *American Sociological Review,* **59** (1994): 365–390.

35. Walter C. Reckless, "A Non-causal Explanation: Containment Theory," *Excerpta Criminologia,* **2** (1962): 131–132.

36. Francis Ivan Nye, *Family Relationships and Delinquent Behavior* (New York: Wiley, 1958).

37. L. Edward Wells and Joseph H. Rankin, "Broken Homes and Juvenile Delinquency: An Empirical Review," *Criminal Justice Abstracts,* **17** (1985): 249–272.

38. Mary Reige, "Parental Affection and Juvenile Delinquency in Girls," *British Journal of Criminology,* **12** (1972): 55–73; Lawrence Rosen, "Family and Delinquency: Structure or Function?" *Criminology,* **23** (1985): 553–573.

39. Stephen Demuth and Susan L. Brown, "Family Structure, Family Processes, and Adolescent Delinquency: The Significance of Parental Absence Versus Parental Gender," *Journal of Research in Crime and Delinquency,* **41(1)** (2004): 58–81; L. Edward Wells and Joseph H. Rankin, "Direct Parental Controls and Delinquency," *Criminology,* **26(2)** (1988): 263–285; Ruth Seydlitz, "Complexity in the Relationships among Direct and Indirect Parental Controls and Delinquency," *Youth & Society,* **24(3)** (1993): 243–275. L. Edward Wells and Joseph H. Rankin, "Direct Parental Controls and Delinquency," *Criminology,* **26** (1988): 263–285. See also Douglas Smith and Raymond Paternoster, "The Gender Gap in Theories of Deviance: Issues and Evidence," *Journal of Research in Crime and Delinquency,* **24** (1987): 140–172; John Hagan, A. R. Gillis, and John Simpson, "The Class Structure of Gender and Delinquency: Toward a Power-Control Theory of Common Delinquent Behavior," *American Journal of Sociology,* **90** (1985): 1151–1178; and Joan McCord, "Some Child-Rearing Antecedents of Criminal Behavior in Adult Men," *Journal of Personality and Social Psychology,* **36** (1979): 1477–1486. For an examination of the family backgrounds of female offenders, see Jill Leslie Rosenbaum, "Family Dysfunction and Female Delinquency," *Crime and Delinquency,* **35** (1989): 31–44.

40. Betti Jane Levine, "Tender Mercies: They Traded Their Humanity for a Life in Crime," *Los Angeles Times,* June 21, 1996, p. 1.

41. Reckless et al., "Self-Concept as an Insulator"; Scarpitti et al., "The Good Boy in a High Delinquency Area."

42. Gary F. Jensen, "Delinquency and Adolescent Self-Conceptions: A Study of the Personal Relevance of Infraction," *Social Problems,* **20** (1972): 84–103.

43. Clarence Schrag, *Crime and Justice American Style* (Washington, D.C.: U.S. Government Printing Office, 1971), pp. 82–89.

44. Allen Liska, Marvin D. Krohn, and Steven F. Messner, "Strategies and Requisites for Theoretical Integration in the Study of Crime and Deviance," in *Theoretical Integration in the Study of Deviance and Crime: Problems and Prospects,* eds. S. F. Lessner, M. D. Krohn, and A. Liska (New York: SUNYA, 1989), p. 4. See also R. J. Hepburn, "Testing Alternative Models of Delinquency

Causation," *Journal of Criminal Law and Criminology*, **67** (1977): 450–460; T. Ross Matsueda, "Testing Control Theory and Differential Association: A Causal Modeling Approach," *American Sociological Review*, **47** (1982): 489–497; Frank S. Pearson and Neil A. Weiner, "Toward an Integration of Criminological Theories," *Journal of Criminal Law and Criminology*, **76** (1985): 116–150; Terrie E. Moffitt, "Adolescence-Limited and Life-Course-Persistent Antisocial Behavior: A Developmental Taxonomy," *Psychological Review*, **100** (1993): 674–701; Terrie E. Moffitt et al., "Childhood-Onset versus Adolescent-Onset Antisocial Conduct Problems in Males: Natural History from Ages 3 to 18 Years," *Development and Psychopathology*, **8** (1996): 399–424; and Terrie E. Moffitt, "Adolescence-Limited and Life-Course-Persistent Offending: A Complementary Pair of Developmental Theories," in T. P. Thornberry, ed., *Developmental Theories of Crime and Delinquency: Advances in Criminological Theory*, **7** (1997).

45. See Alfred Blumstein et al., "Introduction: Studying Criminal Careers," in A. Blumstein et al., eds., *Criminal Careers and Career Criminals* (Washington, D.C.: National Academy Press), p. 12.

46. Sheldon Glueck and Eleanor Glueck, *Unraveling Juvenile Delinquency* (New York: Commonwealth Fund, 1950).

47. Sheldon Glueck and Eleanor Glueck, *Delinquents and Non-Delinquents in Perspective* (Cambridge, Mass.: Harvard University Press, 1968).

48. Robert J. Sampson and John H. Laub, *Crime in the Making: Pathways and Turning Points through Life* (Cambridge, Mass.: Harvard University Press, 1993).

49. Ibid.

50. Ibid.

51. Sampson and Laub, *Crime in the Making*; R. J. Sampson and J. H. Laub, "Understanding Variability in Lives through Time: Contributions of Life-Course Criminology," *Studies on Crime and Crime Prevention*, **4** (1995): 143–158.

52. Terence P. Thornberry, A. J. Lizotte, and M. D. Krohn, "Delinquent Peers, Beliefs, and Delinquent Behavior: A Longitudinal Test of Interactional Theory," *Criminology*, **32** (1994): 47–83; Terence P. Thornberry, Alan J. Lizotte, Marvin D. Krohn, Margaret Farnsworth, and Sung Joun Jung, "Testing Interactional Theory: An Examination of Reciprocal Causal Relationships among Family, School, and Delinquency," *Journal of Criminal Law and Criminology*, **82** (1991): 3–35. See also Madeline G. Aultman and Charles F. Wellford, "Toward an Integrated Model of Delinquency Causation: An Empirical Analysis," *Sociology and Social Research*, **63** (1979): 316–317; and Thornberry, *Developmental Theories of Crime and Delinquency*.

53. D. S. Nagin and D. P. Farrington, "The Onset and Persistence of Offending," *Criminology*, **30** (1992): 501–524; D. S. Nagin and D. P. Farrington, "The Stability of Criminal Potential from Childhood to Adulthood," *Criminology*, **30** (1992): 235–260; D. P. Farrington, "Explaining the Beginning, Progress, and Ending of Antisocial Behavior from Birth to Adulthood," *Advances in Criminological Theory*, **3** (1992): 253–286.

54. Delbert S. Elliott, Suzanne S. Ageton, and R. J. Canter, "An Integrated Theoretical Perspective on Delinquent Behavior," *Journal of Research in Crime and Delinquency*, **16** (1979): 3–27; S. Menard and Delbert S. Elliott, "Delinquent Bonding, Moral Beliefs, and Illegal Behavior: A Three Wave Panel Model," *Justice Quarterly*, **11** (1994): 173–188.

55. David J. Hawkins and Joseph G. Weis, "The Social Development Model: An Integrated Approach to Delinquency Prevention," *Journal of Primary Prevention*, **6** (1985): 73–97.

56. Michael R. Gottfredson and Travis Hirschi, *A General Theory of Crime* (Stanford, Calif.: Stanford University Press, 1990); Michael Gottfredson and Travis Hirschi, "A Propensity-Event Theory of Crime," in *Advances in Criminological Theory*, vol. 1, eds. W. Laufer and F. Adler (New Brunswick, N.J.: Transaction, 1989); B. J. Arneklev, H. G. Grasmick, and C. R. Tittle, "Low Self-Control and Imprudent Behavior," *Journal of Quantitative Criminology*, **9** (1993): 225–247; D. Brownfield and A. M. Sorenson, "Self Control and Juvenile Delinquency: Theoretical Issues and an Empirical Assessment of Selected Elements of a General Theory of Crime," *Deviant Behavior*, **14** (1993): 243–264; T. Hirschi and M. Gottfredson, "Commentary: Testing the General Theory of Crime," *Journal of Research in Crime and Delinquency*, **30** (1993): 47–54.

57. Travis Hirschi and Michael Gottfredson, "The Significance of White-Collar Crime for a General Theory of Crime," *Criminology*, **27** (1989): 359–371; Darrell Steffensmeier, "On the Causes of 'White Collar' Crime: An Assessment of Hirschi and Gottfredson's Claim," *Criminology*, **27** (1989): 345–358.

58. Alex R. Piquero, John MacDonald, Adam Dobrin, Leah E. Daigle, and Frances T. Cullen, "Self-Control, Violent Offending, and Homicide Victimization: Assessing the General Theory of Crime," *Journal of Quantitative Criminology*, **21(1)** (2005): 55–71; Alexander T. Vazsonyi and Jennifer M. Crosswhite, "Test of Gottfredson and Hirschi's General Theory of Crime in African-American Adolescents," *Research in Crime and Delinquency*, **41(4)** (2004): 407–432; Alexander T. Vazsonyi, Janice E. Clifford Wittekind, Lara M. Belliston, and Timothy D. Van Loh, "Extending the General Theory of Crime to 'The East:' Low Self-Control in Japanese Late Adolescents," *Journal of Quantitative Criminology*, **23(3)** (2004): 189–216.

59. Dina Perrone, Christopher J. Sullivan, Travis C. Pratt, and Satenik Margaryan, "Parental Efficacy, Self-Control, and Delinquency: A Test of a General Theory of Crime on a Nationally Representative Sample of Youth," *International Journal of Offender Therapy and Comparative Criminology*, **48(3)** (2004): 298–312.

60. Robert Agnew, *Why Do Criminals Offend? A General Theory of Crime and Delinquency* (Los Angeles, CA: Roxbury, 2004).

61. See W. Timothy Austin, "Crime and Custom in an Orderly Society: The Singapore Prototype," *Criminology*, **25** (1987): 279–294; J. M. Day and William S. Laufer, eds., *Crime, Values, and Religion* (Norwood, N.J.: Ablex, 1987); and Freda Adler and William S. Laufer, "Social Control and the Workplace," in *US-USSR Approaches to Urban Crime Prevention*, ed. James Finckenauer and Alexander Yakovlev (Moscow: Soviet Academy of State and Law, 1987).

62. David J. Hawkins, Richard F. Catalano, Gwen Jones, and David Fine, "Delinquency Prevention through Parent-Training: Results and Issues from Work in Progress," in *From Children to Citizens*: vol. 3, *Families, Schools, and Delinquency Prevention*, eds. James Q. Wilson and Glenn C. Loury (New York: Springer Verlag, 1987), pp. 186–204.

63. Denise C. Gottfredson, "An Empirical Test of School-Based Environmental and Individual Interventions to

Reduce the Risk of Delinquent Behavior," *Criminology,* **24** (1986): 705–731.

64. Jeffrey Fagan, "Neighborhood Education, Mobilization, and Organization for Juvenile Crime Prevention," *Annals of the American Academy for the Advancement of Political and Social Sciences,* **494** (1987): 54–70.

65. For an examination of community social control, see David Weisburd, "Vigilantism as Community Social Control: Developing a Quantitative Criminological Model," *Journal of Quantitative Criminology,* **4** (1988): 137–153.

66. "Fostering the Family: An Intensive Effort to Keep Kids with Parents," *Newsweek,* June 22, 1992, p. 64.

67. Ibid.

68. George Judson, "Fighting Temptations of Summer: Bridgeport Puts Teenagers to Work Helping Other Youths," *New York Times,* Aug. 22, 1992, p. B1.

69. Susan Chira, "A 'Learnfare' Program Offers No Easy Lessons," *New York Times,* Apr. 28, 1993, p. A12.

CHAPTER 8

1. Howard S. Becker, *Outsiders: Studies in the Sociology of Deviance* (New York: Macmillan, 1963), p. 9.

2. For an excellent discussion of how society controls deviance, see Nicholas N. Kittrie, *The Right to Be Different* (Baltimore: Johns Hopkins University Press, 1972).

3. William I. Thomas, *The Unadjusted Girl* (1923; New York: Harper & Row, 1967).

4. George Herbert Mead, "The Psychology of Punitive Justice," *American Journal of Sociology,* **23** (1918): 577–602. See also Charles Horton Cooley, "The Roots of Social Knowledge," *American Journal of Sociology,* **32** (1926): 59–79.

5. Herbert Blumer, "Sociological Implications of the Thought of George Herbert Mead," in *Symbolic Interactionism,* ed. Blumer (Englewood Cliffs, N.J.: Prentice-Hall, 1969), pp. 62, 65, 66.

6. Frank Tannenbaum, *Crime and the Community* (Boston: Ginn, 1938), p. 27.

7. Edwin M. Lemert, *Social Pathology* (New York: McGraw-Hill, 1951).

8. Edwin M. Lemert, *Human Deviance, Social Problems, and Social Control* (Englewood Cliffs, N.J.: Prentice-Hall, 1967), chap. 3.

9. Lemert, *Social Pathology,* pp. 75–76.

10. Lemert, *Human Deviance,* p. 46. See also Albert K. Cohen, *Deviance and Control* (Englewood Cliffs, N.J.: Prentice-Hall, 1966), pp. 24–25.

11. Erving Goffman, *Stigma: Notes on the Management of Spoiled Identity* (Englewood Cliffs, N.J.: Prentice-Hall, 1963).

12. Gerhard O. W. Mueller, "Resocialization of the Young Adult Offender in Switzerland," *Journal of Criminal Law and Criminology,* **43** (1953): 578–591, at p. 584.

13. Kai T. Erickson, "Notes on the Sociology of Deviance," in *The Other Side: Perspectives on Deviance,* ed. Howard S. Becker (New York: Free Press, 1964), p. 11.

14. Edwin Schur, *Labeling Deviant Behavior* (New York: Harper & Row, 1971), p. 21.

15. Edwin M. Schur, *Crimes without Victims* (Englewood Cliffs, N.J.: Prentice-Hall, 1965).

16. M. Ray, "The Cycle of Abstinence and Relapse among Heroin Addicts," *Social Problems,* **9** (1961): 132–140.

17. David Matza, *Becoming Deviant* (Englewood Cliffs, N.J.: Prentice-Hall, 1969), pp. 44–53.

18. Becker, *Outsiders,* pp. 18, 20.

19. C. J. Chivers and W. K. Rashbaum, "Army Lets a Felon Join Up, but N.Y.P.D. Will Not," *New York Times* online, Jan. 6, 2008. Retrieved July 13, 2008 from http://www.nytimes.com/2008/01/06/nyregion/06soldier.html?_r=1&fta=y&pagewanted=all.

20. D. L. Rosenhan, "On Being Sane in Insane Places," *Science,* **179** (1973): 250–258. See also Bruce G. Link, "Understanding Labeling Effects in the Area of Mental Disorders: An Assessment of the Effects of Expectations of Rejection," *American Sociological Review,* **52** (1987): 96–112; and Anthony Walsh, "Twice Labeled: The Effect of Psychiatric Labeling on the Sentencing of Sex Offenders," *Social Problems,* **37** (1990): 375–389.

21. Carol Warren and John Johnson, "A Critique of Labeling Theory from the Phenomenological Perspective," in *Theoretical Perspectives on Deviance,* eds. J. D. Douglas and R. Scott (New York: Basic Books, 1973), p. 77; James P. Spradley, *You Owe Yourself a Drunk: An Ethnography of Urban Nomads* (Boston: Little, Brown, 1979), p. 254.

22. Richard D. Schwartz and Jerome H. Skolnick, "Two Studies of Legal Stigma," *Social Problems,* **10** (1962): 133–138.

23. Anthony Platt, *The Child Savers* (Chicago: University of Chicago Press, 1969). For a further discussion of the effects of stigmatization by the criminal justice system, see Charles W. Thomas and Donna M. Bishop, "The Effect of Formal and Informal Sanctions on Delinquency: A Longitudinal Comparison of Labeling and Deterrence Theories," *Journal of Criminal Law and Criminology,* **75** (1984): 1222–1245.

24. William J. Chambliss, "The Saints and the Roughnecks," *Society,* **11** (1973): 24–31.

25. Walter R. Gove, "Deviant Behavior, Social Intervention, and Labeling Theory," in *The Uses of Controversy in Sociology,* eds. Lewis A. Coser and Otto N. Larsen (New York: Free Press, 1976), pp. 219–227; Ross L. Matsueda, "Reflected Appraisals, Parental Labeling, and Delinquency: Specifying a Symbolic Interactionist Theory," *American Journal of Sociology,* **97** (1992): 1577–1611.

26. Ronald L. Akers, "Problems in the Sociology of Deviance," *Social Forces,* **46** (1968): 455–465.

27. Ronald L. Akers, *Deviant Behavior: A Social Learning Approach,* 2d ed. (Belmont, Calif.: Wadsworth, 1977); David Ward and Charles R. Tittle, "Deterrence or Labeling: The Effects of Informal Sanctions," *Deviant Behavior,* **14** (1993): 43–64.

28. Jack P. Gibbs, "Conceptions of Deviant Behavior: The Old and the New," *Pacific Sociological Review,* **9** (Spring 1966): 9–14.

29. Charles Wellford, "Labeling Theory and Criminology: An Assessment," *Social Problems,* **22** (1975): 343; Charles F. Wellford and Ruth A. Triplett, "The Future of Labeling Theory: Foundations and Promises," in *Advances in Criminological Theory,* vol. 4, eds. Freda Adler and William S. Laufer (New Brunswick, N.J.: Transaction, 1993).

30. Alexander Liazos, "The Poverty of the Sociology of Deviance: Nuts, Sluts, and Perverts," *Social Problems,* **20** (1972): 103–120.

31. Howard S. Becker, "Labelling Theory Reconsidered," in *Outsiders: Studies in the Sociology of Deviance,* rev. ed., ed. Becker (New York: Free Press, 1973), pp. 177–208. See also Schur, *Labeling Deviant Behavior,* for an excellent review of labeling theory.

32. Robert J. Sampson and John H. Laub, "A Life-Course Theory of Cumulative Disadvantage and Stability of

Delinquency," in T. Thornberry, ed., *Developmental Theories of Crime and Delinquency: Advances in Criminology Theory,* 7 (1997).

33. Compare this perspective with the emerging notion of criminology as peacemaking; see Harold E. Pepinsky and Richard Quinney, eds., *Criminology as Peace-Making* (Bloomington: Indiana University Press, 1991).

34. Émile Durkheim, *The Division of Labor in Society* (New York: Free Press, 1947), p. 80.

35. Ibid., p. 102.

36. Roscoe Pound, *An Introduction to the Philosophy of Law* (Boston: Little, Brown, 1922), p. 98.

37. Richard Quinney, *Crime and Justice in Society* (Boston: Little, Brown, 1969), pp. 26–30.

38. William Chambliss, "The State, the Law, and the Definition of Behavior as Criminal or Delinquent," in *Handbook of Criminology,* ed. Daniel Glaser (Chicago: Rand McNally, 1974), pp. 7–44.

39. Austin Turk, "Law as a Weapon in Social Conflict," *Social Problems,* 23 (1976): 276–291.

40. George Vold, *Theoretical Criminology* (New York: Oxford University Press, 1958), pp. 204, 209.

41. Ralf Dahrendorf, *Class and Class Conflict in Industrial Society* (Stanford, Calif.: Stanford University Press, 1959). See also Ralf Dahrendorf, "Out of Utopia: Toward a Reorientation of Sociological Analysis," *American Journal of Sociology,* 64 (1958): 127.

42. Austin Turk, *Criminality and Legal Order* (Chicago: Rand McNally, 1969), pp. 25, 33, 41–42, 48. See also Thomas O'Reilly-Fleming et al., "Issues in Social Order and Social Control," *Journal of Human Justice,* 2 (1990): 55–74.

43. Austin Turk, *Political Criminality: The Defiance and Defense of Authority* (Beverly Hills, Calif.: Sage, 1982), p. 15.

44. Turk, "Law as a Weapon."

45. William J. Chambliss, "A Sociological Analysis of the Law of Vagrancy," *Social Problems,* 12 (1966): 67–77. For an opposing view on the historical development of criminal law, see Jeffrey S. Adler, "A Historical Analysis of the Law of Vagrancy," *Criminology,* 27 (1989): 209–229; and a rejoinder to Adler: William J. Chambliss, "On Trashing Criminology," ibid., pp. 231–238.

46. Alan Lizotte, "Extra-Legal Factors in Chicago's Criminal Courts: Testing the Conflict Model of Criminal Justice," *Social Problems,* 25 (1978): 564–580. See also Kathleen Daly, "Neither Conflict nor Labeling nor Paternalism Will Suffice: Intersections of Race, Ethnicity, Gender, and Family in Criminal Court Decisions," *Crime and Delinquency,* 35 (1989): 136–168; and Elizabeth Comack, ed., "Race, Class, Gender and Justice," *Journal of Human Justice,* 2 (1990): 1–124.

47. Freda Adler, "Socioeconomic Variables Influencing Jury Verdicts," *New York University Review of Law on Social Change,* 3 (1973): 16–36. See also Martha A. Myers, "Social Background and the Sentencing Behavior of Judges," *Criminology,* 26 (1988): 649–675.

48. Celesta A. Albonetti, Robert M. Hauser, John Hagan, and Ilene H. Nagel, "Criminal Justice Decision-Making as a Stratification Process: The Role of Race and Stratification Resources in Pretrial Release," *Journal of Quantitative Criminology,* 5 (1989): 57–82.

49. Austin Turk, "Law, Conflict, and Order: From Theorizing toward Theories," *Canadian Review of Sociology and Anthropology,* 13 (1976): 282–294.

50. Georg Rusche and Otto Kirchheimer, *Punishment and Social Structure* (New York: Columbia University Press, 1939), p. 93.

51. Friedrich Engels, "To the Working Class of Great Britain," Introduction to *The Condition of the Working Class in England (1845),* in Karl Marx and Friedrich Engels, *Collected Works,* vol. 4 (New York: International Publishers, 1974), pp. 213–214, 298.

52. Karl Marx and Friedrich Engels, *The Communist Manifesto* (1848; New York: International Publishers, 1979), p. 9.

53. Willem Adriaan Bonger, *Criminality and Economic Conditions,* trans. Henry P. Horton (Boston: Little, Brown, 1916).

54. Ibid., p. 669.

55. J. M. Van Bemmelen, "Willem Adriaan Bonger," in *Pioneers in Criminology,* ed. Hermann Mannheim (London: Stevens, 1960), p. 361.

56. Ian Taylor, Paul Walton, and Jock Young, *The New Criminology: For a Social Theory of Deviance* (London: Routledge & Kegan Paul, 1973), pp. 264, 281. See also Jock Young, "Radical Criminology in Britain: The Emergence of a Competing Paradigm," *British Journal of Criminology,* 28 (1988): 159–183.

57. Gresham Sykes, "The Rise of Critical Criminology," *Journal of Criminal Law and Criminology,* 65 (1974): 206–213.

58. Richard Quinney, "Crime Control in Capitalist Society: A Critical Philosophy of Legal Order," *Issues in Criminology,* 8 (1973): 75–95; Richard Quinney, "There's a Lot of Us Folks Grateful to the Lone Ranger: Some Notes on the Rise and Fall of American Criminology," *Insurgent Sociologist,* 4 (1973): 56–64.

59. Richard Quinney, "Crime Control in Capitalist Society," in *Critical Criminology,* ed. Ian Taylor, Paul Walton, and Jock Young (London: Routledge & Kegan Paul, 1975), p. 199.

60. Richard Quinney, *Class, State, and Crime: On the Theory and Practice of Criminal Justice,* 2d ed. (New York: David McKay, 1977), p. 10.

61. Richard Quinney, *Critique of Legal Order: Crime Control in a Capitalist Society* (Boston: Little, Brown, 1974), pp. 11–13.

62. William Chambliss and Robert Seidman, *Law, Order, and Power* (Reading, Mass.: Addison-Wesley, 1971), p. 503.

63. Ibid., p. 504.

64. Barry Krisberg, *Crime and Privilege: Toward a New Criminology* (Englewood Cliffs, N.J.: Prentice-Hall, 1975).

65. Herman Schwendinger and Julia Schwendinger, "Delinquency and Social Reform: A Radical Perspective," in *Juvenile Justice,* ed. Lamar Empey (Charlottesville: University of Virginia Press, 1979), pp. 246–290.

66. Elliot Currie, "A Dialogue with Anthony M. Platt," *Issues in Criminology,* 8 (1973): 28.

67. Steven F. Messner and Marvin D. Krohn, "Class, Compliance Structures, and Delinquency: Assessing Integrated Structural-Marxist Theory," *American Journal of Sociology,* 96 (1990): 300–328.

68. Lance H. Selva and Robert M. Bohm, "A Critical Examination of the Informalism Experiment in the Administration of Justice," *Crime and Social Justice,* 29 (1987): 43–57; Timothy Carter and Donald Clelland, "A Neo-Marxian Critique, Formulation, and Test of Juvenile Dispositions as a Function of Social Class," *Social Problems,* 27 (1979): 96–108; David Greenberg and Drew Humphries, "The Co-optation of Fixed Sentencing Reform," *Crime and Delinquency,* 26 (1980): 216–225.

69. Jackson Toby, "The New Criminology Is the Old Sentimentality," *Criminology*, **16** (1979): 516–526; Jim Thomas and Aogan O'Maolchatha, "Reassessing the Critical Metaphor: An Optimistic Revisionist View," *Justice Quarterly*, **6** (1989): 143–171; David Brown and Russell Hogg, "Essentialism, Radical Criminology and Left Realism," *Australian and New Zealand Journal of Criminology*, **25** (1992): 195–230.

70. Carl B. Klockars, "The Contemporary Crises of Marxist Criminology," *Criminology*, **16** (1979): 477–515.

71. Ibid.

72. Richard F. Sparks, "A Critique of Marxist Criminology," in *Crime and Justice: An Annual Review of Research*, ed. Norval Morris and Michael Tonry (Chicago: University of Chicago Press, 1980), p. 159.

73. Milton Mankoff, "On the Responsibility of Marxist Criminology: A Reply to Quinney," *Contemporary Crisis*, **2** (1978): 293–301.

74. Austin T. Turk, "Analyzing Official Deviance: For Nonpartisan Conflict Analysis in Criminology," in *Radical Criminology: The Coming Crisis*, ed. James A. Inciardi (Beverly Hills, Calif.: Sage, 1980), pp. 78–91. See also Sykes, "The Rise of Critical Criminology," p. 212.

75. Philip L. Reichel and Andrzej Rzeplinski, "Student Views of Crime and Criminal Justice in Poland and the United States," *International Journal of Comparative and Applied Criminal Justice*, **13** (1989): 65–81.

76. Quinney, *Class, State, and Crime*, p. 40.

77. R. Weitzer, "Flawed Theory and Method in Studies of Prostitution," *Violence against Women*, **11(7)** (2005): 934–949.

78. J. Raphael and D. Shapiro, "Violence in Indoor Prostitution Venues," *Violence against Women*, **10** (2004): 126–139.

79. M. Farley, "Prostitution: Factsheet on Human Rights Violations," (San Francisco: Prostitution Research and Education, 2000).

80. M. Farley, "Bad for the Body, Bad for the Heart: Prostitution Harms Women Even if Legalized or Decriminalized," *Violence against Women*, **10** (2004): 1087–1125.

81. R. Weitzer, "Flawed Theory and Method in Studies of Prostitution," *Violence against Women*, **11(7)** (2005): 934–949.

82. K. Martin, L. M. Vieraitis and S. Britto, "Gender Equality and Women's Absolute Status: A Test of the Feminist Models of Rape," *Violence against Women*, **12(4)** (2006): 321–339.

83. Martin D. Schwartz and Walter S. DeKeseredy, "Left Realist Criminology: Strengths, Weaknesses and the Feminist Critique," *Crime, Law and Social Change*, **15** (1991): 51–72; John Lowman and Brian D. MacLean, eds., *Realist Criminology: Crime Control and Policing in the 1990s* (Ontario: University of Toronto Press, 1990); Walter S. DeKeseredy and Martin D. Schwartz, "British and U.S. Left Realism: A Critical Comparison," *International Journal of Offender Therapy and Comparative Criminology*, **35** (1991): 248–262.

84. Jock Young, "Ten Points of Realism," in *Rethinking Criminology: The Realist Debate*, ed. J. Young and R. Matthews (London: Sage, 1992), pp. 24–28.

85. Pepinsky and Quinney, eds., *Criminology as Peace-Making*; Richard Quinney, "Socialist Humanism and the Problem of Crime," *Crime, Law and Social Change*, **23** (1995): 147–156; Robert Elias et al., Special Issue, "Declaring Peace on Crime," *Peace Review: A Transnational Quarterly*, **6** (1994): 131–254.

86. B. A. Arrigo and Y. Takahashi, "Recommunalization of the Disenfranchised: A Theoretical and Critical Criminological Inquiry," *Theoretical Criminology*, **10(3)** (2006): 307–336.

CHAPTER 9

1. Bruce Golding, "Jeweler Held in Botched Heist," *New York Post*, December 9, 2008, p. 7.

2. Richard Winton, "Car-to-Car Shooting Leaves Woman Dead," *Los Angeles Times*, December 9, 2008, p. B2.

3. Theodore Decker, "Rapist Blamed for 7th Attack: Nov. 2 Crime Took Place Near Site of Oct. 5 Assault," *Columbus Dispatch*, November 12, 2008.

4. Paul J. Brantingham and Patricia L. Brantingham, "Introduction: The Dimensions of Crime," in *Environmental Criminology*, ed. Brantingham and Brantingham (Prospect Heights, Ill.: Waveland, 1991), p. 8. For a discussion on the application of environmental criminology to urban planning, see Paul J. Brantingham and Patricia L. Brantingham, "Environmental Criminology: From Theory to Urban Planning Practice," *Studies on Crime and Crime Prevention*, **7** (1998): 31–60.

5. André M. Guerry, *Essai sur la Statistique Morale de la France* (Paris: Crochard, 1833).

6. Adolphe Quételet, *A Treatise on Man* (Edinburgh: Chambers, 1842), reprinted excerpt Adolphe Quételet, "Of the Development of the Propensity to Crime," in *Criminological Perspectives: A Reader*, ed. John Muncie, Eugene McLaughlin, and Mary Langan (Thousand Oaks, Calif.: Sage, 1996), p. 19.

7. Ronald Clarke and Derek Cornish, "Modeling Offenders' Decisions: A Framework for Research and Policy," in *Crime and Justice*, vol. 6, ed. Michael Tonry and Norval Morris (Chicago: University of Chicago Press, 1985), pp. 147–185; Derek B. Cornish and Ronald V. Clarke, eds., *The Reasoning Criminal* (New York: Springer Verlag, 1986).

8. Jeremy Bentham, *On the Principles and Morals of Legislation* (New York: Kegan Paul, 1789) [reprinted 1948]; Gary S. Becker, "Crime and Punishment: An Economic Approach," *Journal of Political Economy*, **76** (1968): 169–217.

9. David Weisburd, Tomer Enat, and Matt Kowalski, "The Miracle of the Cells: An Experimental Study of Interventions to Increase Payment of Court-Ordered Financial Obligations," *Criminology & Public Policy*, **7(1)** (2008): 5–8.

10. Bradley R. E. Wright, Avshalom Caspi, Terrie E. Moffitt, and Raymond Paternoster, "Does the Perceived Risk of Punishment Deter Criminally-Prone Individuals? Rational Choice, Self-Control, and Crime," *Journal of Research in Crime and Delinquency*, **41** (2004): 180–213.

11. Daniel S. Nagin, "Thoughts on the Broader Implications of the Miracle of the Cells," *Criminology & Public Policy*, **7(1)** (2008): 37–42.

12. Lawrence E. Cohen and Marcus Felson, "Social Change and Crime Rate Trends: A Routine Activity Approach," *American Sociological Review*, **44** (1979): 588–608; Marcus Felson, "Linking Criminal Choices, Routine Activities, Informal Control, and Criminal Outcomes," in *The Reasoning Criminal: Rational Choice Perspectives on Offending*, ed. Derek B. Cornish and Ronald V. Clarke (New York: Springer-Verlag, 1986), pp. 119–128.

13. Marcus Felson, *Crime and Everyday Life: Insights and Implications for Society* (Thousand Oaks, Calif.: Pine Forge Press, 1994), pp. 20–21, 35.

14. Mangai Natarajan, "Telephones as Facilitators of Drug Dealing," paper presented at the Fourth International Seminar on Environmental Criminology and Crime Analysis, July 1995, Cambridge, England; Mangai Natarajan, Ronald V. Clarke and Mathieu Belanger, "Drug Dealing and Pay Phones: The Scope for Intervention," *Security Journal,* 7 (1996): pp. 245–251.

15. Lawrence W. Sherman, Patrick R. Gartin, and Michael E. Buerger, "Hot Spots of Predatory Crime: Routine Activities and the Criminology of Place," *Criminology,* 27 (1989): 27–55; Ronald V. Clarke and Patricia M. Harris, "A Rational Choice Perspective on the Targets of Automobile Theft," *Criminal Behaviour and Mental Health,* 2 (1992): 25–42. See also the following articles in Ronald V. Clarke and Marcus Felson, eds., *Routine Activity and Rational Choice, Advances in Criminological Theory,* vol. 5 (New Brunswick, N.J.: Transaction, 1993): Raymond Paternoster and Sally Simpson, "A Rational Choice Theory of Corporate Crime," pp. 37–58; Richard W. Harding, "Gun Use in Crime, Rational Choice, and Social Learning Theory," pp. 85–102; Richard B. Felson, "Predatory and Dispute-Related Violence: A Social Interactionist Approach," pp. 103–125; Nathaniel J. Pallone and James J. Hennessy, "Tinderbox Criminal Violence: Neurogenic Impulsivity, Risk-Taking, and the Phenomenology of Rational Choice," pp. 127–157; Max Taylor, "Rational Choice, Behavior Analysis, and Political Violence," pp. 159–178; Pietro Marongiu and Ronald V. Clarke, "Ransom Kidnapping in Sardinia, Subcultural Theory and Rational Choice," pp. 179–199; Bruce D. Johnson, Mangai Natarajan, and Harry Sanabria, "'Successful' Criminal Careers: Toward an Ethnography within the Rational Choice Perspective," pp. 201–221.

16. George Rengert and John Wasilchick, *Suburban Burglary: A Time and a Place for Everything* (Springfield, Ill.: Charles C Thomas, 1985).

17. Paul F. Cromwell, James N. Olson, and D'Aunn Webster Avary, *Breaking and Entering: An Ethnographic Analysis of Burglary* (Newbury Park, Calif.: Sage, 1991), pp. 45–46.

18. Clarke and Felson, *Routine Activity and Rational Choice;* Richard T. Wright and Scott H. Decker, *Burglars on the Job: Streetlife and Residential Break-Ins* (Boston: Northeastern University Press, 1994), pp. 63–68; Alex Piquero and George F. Rengert, "Studying Deterrence with Active Residential Burglars: A Research Note," *Justice Quarterly,* 16 (1999): 451–472.

19. Richard T. Wright and Scott Decker, *Armed Robbers in Action: Stickups and Street Culture* (Boston: Northeastern University Press, 1994). For a feminist analysis of Wright and Decker's ethnographic work on street robbers, see Jody Miller, "Up It Up: Gender and the Accomplishment of Street Robbery," *Criminology,* 36 (1998): 37–66.

20. Philip J. Cook, *Robbery in the United States: An Analysis of Recent Trends and Patterns,* U.S. Department of Justice (Washington, D.C.: U.S. Government Printing Office, 1983).

21. Wayland Clifton Jr., *Convenience Store Robbery in Gainesville, Florida* (Gainesville, Fla.: Gainesville Police Department, 1987), p. 15.

22. Cohen and Felson, "Social Change and Crime Rate Trends."

23. Ronald V. Clarke, *Hot Products: Understanding, Anticipating and Reducing Demand for Stolen Goods,* Policing and Reducing Crime Unit, Police Research Series Paper 112 (London: Home Office, 1999). For discussions of what drives shoplifters, see Read Hayes, "Shop Theft: An Analysis of Shoplifter Perceptions and Situational Factors," *Security Journal,* 12 (1999): 7–18; and David P. Farrington, "Measuring, Explaining, and Preventing Shoplifting: A Review of British Research," *Security Journal,* 12 (1999): 9–28. For details on measuring and preventing crime against retail business, see a special issue of *Security Journal,* 7 (1996): 1–75.

24. Bonnie S. Fisher, John J. Sloan, Francis T. Cullen, and Chunmeng Lu, "Crime in the Ivory Tower: The Level and Sources of Student Victimization," *Criminology,* 36 (1998): 671–710. For additional research supporting the routine-activity approach, see also Verna A. Henson and William E. Stone, "Campus Crime: A Victimization Study," *Journal of Criminal Justice,* 27 (1999): 295–308.

25. Hans von Hentig, "Remarks on the Interaction of Perpetrator and Victim," *Journal of Criminal Law and Criminology,* 31 (1941): 303–309.

26. Hans von Hentig, *The Criminal and His Victim* (New Haven, Conn.: Yale University, 1948).

27. See Beniamin Mendelsohn, "The Origin of the Doctrine of Victimology," in *Victimology,* ed. Israel Drapkin and Emilio Viano (Lexington, Mass.: Lexington Books, 1974), pp. 3–4.

28. Frederic Wertham, *The Show of Violence* (Garden City, N.Y.: Country Life Press, 1948), p. 259.

29. Ezzat A. Fattah, "Victims and Victimology: The Facts and the Rhetoric," *International Review of Victimology,* 1 (1989): 44–66, at p. 44.

30. Ezzat A. Fattah, "The Rational Choice/Opportunity Perspective as a Vehicle for Integrating Criminological and Victimological Theories," in Clarke and Felson, *Routine Activity and Rational Choice,* pp. 230–231. For an examination of the relationship between lifestyle factors and the victimization of prostitutes, see Charisse Coston and Lee Ross, "Criminal Victimization of Prostitutes: Empirical Support for the Lifestyle/Exposure Model," *Journal of Crime and Justice,* 21 (1998): 53–70.

31. Fattah, "Victims and Victimology," p. 54.

32. Michael J. Hindelang, Michael R. Gottfredson, and James Garofalo, *Victims of Personal Crime: An Empirical Foundation for a Theory of Personal Victimization* (Cambridge, Mass.: Ballinger, 1978), p. 245.

33. Ibid., pp. 251–265.

34. Marvin E. Wolfgang, *Patterns in Criminal Homicide* (Philadelphia: University of Pennsylvania Press, 1958), p. 253.

35. James T. Tedeschi and Richard B. Felson, *Violence, Aggression, and Coercive Actions* (Washington, D.C.: American Psychological Association, 1994).

36. Richard B. Felson, "Big People Hit Little People: Sex Differences in Physical Power and Interpersonal Violence," *Criminology,* 34 (1996): 433–452.

37. Dan Olweus, "Aggressors and Their Victims: Bullying at School," in *Disruptive Behaviors in Schools,* ed. N. Frude and H. Gault (New York: Wiley, 1984), pp. 57–76.

38. Alan Trickett, Dan Ellingworth, Tim Hope, and Ken Pease, "Crime Victimization in the Eighties: Changes in Area and Regional Inequality," *British Journal of Criminology,* 35 (1995): 343–359; Graham Farrell, "Preventing Repeat Victimization," in *Building a Safer Society: Strategic Approaches to Crime Prevention, Crime and Justice,* vol. 19, ed. Michael Tonry and David P. Farrington (Chicago: University of Chicago Press, 1995), pp. 469–534.

39. Dan Ellingworth, Graham Farrell, and Ken Pease, "A Victim Is a Victim Is a Victim? Chronic Victimization in Four Sweeps of the British Crime Survey," *British Journal of Criminology*, **35** (1995): 360–365.

40. William Spelman, "Once Bitten, Then What? Cross-Sectional and Time-Course Explanations of Repeat Victimization," *British Journal of Criminology*, **35** (1995): 366–383.

41. Natalie Polvi, Terah Looman, Charlie Humphries, and Ken Pease, "The Time-Course of Repeat Burglary Victimization," *British Journal of Criminology*, **31** (1991): 411–414.

42. Graham Farrell, Coretta Phillips, and Ken Pease, "Like Taking Candy: Why Does Repeat Victimization Occur?" *British Journal of Criminology*, **35** (1995): 384–399.

43. James P. Lynch, Michael L. Berbaum, and Mike Planty, *Investigating Repeated Victimization with the NCVS* (Washington, D.C.: National Institute of Justice, 1998).

44. Lawrence W. Sherman, Patrick R. Gartin, and Michael E. Buerger, "Hot Spots of Predatory Crime: Routine Activities and the Criminology of Place," *Criminology*, **27** (1989): 27–55.

45. See, e.g., Kate J. Bowers, Shane D. Johnson, and Ken Pease, "Prospective Hot-Spotting: The Future of Crime Mapping?" *British Journal of Criminology*, **44** (2004): 641–658.

46. Dennis W. Roncek and Donald Faggiani, "High Schools and Crime: A Replication," *Sociological Quarterly*, **26** (1985): 491–505.

47. Dennis W. Roncek and Pamela A. Maier, "Bars, Blocks, and Crimes Revisited: Linking the Theory of Routine Activities to the Empiricism of 'Hot Spots,' " *Criminology*, **29** (1991): 725–753.

48. Richard L. Block and Carolyn R. Block, "Space, Place and Crime: Hot Spot Areas and Hot Places of Liquor-Related Crime," in *Crime and Place: Crime Prevention Studies*, vol. 4, ed. John E. Eck and David Weisburd (Monsey, N.Y.: Criminal Justice Press; Washington, D.C.: The Police Executive Research Forum, 1995), pp. 145–183.

49. Per-Olof Wikström, "Preventing City-Center Street Crimes," in Tonry and Farrington, *Building a Safer Society*, vol. 19, pp. 429–468.

50. William Spelman, "Abandoned Buildings: Magnets for Crime?" *Journal of Criminal Justice*, **21** (1993): 481–495.

51. Dennis W. Roncek and Ralph Bell, "Bars, Blocks, and Crimes," *Journal of Environmental Systems*, **11** (1981): 35–47; Roncek and Faggiani, "High Schools and Crime."

52. Jeffrey Peck, G. O. W. Mueller, and Freda Adler, "The Vulnerability of Ports and Marinas to Vessel and Equipment Theft," *Security Journal*, **5** (1994): 146–153.

53. David Weisburd and Lorraine Green with Frank Gajewski and Charles Bellucci, Jersey City Police Department, "Defining the Street Level Drug Market," in *Drugs and Crime: Evaluating Public Policy Initiatives*, ed. Doris Layton MacKenzie and Craig Uchida (Newbury Park, Calif.: Sage, 1994), pp. 61–76. For a discussion of the role of place managers in controlling drug and disorder problems, see Lorraine Green Mazerolle, Colleen Kadleck, and Jan Roehl, "Controlling Drug and Disorder Problems: The Role of Place Managers," *Criminology*, **36** (1998): 371–404. For an analysis of problem-oriented policing in troubled areas, see Anthony A. Braga, David L. Weisburd, Elin J. Waring, Lorraine Green Mazerolle, William Spelman, and Francis Gajewski, "Problem-Oriented Policing in Violent Crime Places: A Randomized Controlled Experiment," *Criminology*, **37** (1999): 541–580.

54. Lawrence W. Sherman, "Hot Spots of Crime and Criminal Careers of Places," in Eck and Weisburd, *Crime and Place*, vol. 4, pp. 35–52.

55. See Fattah, "The Rational Choice/Opportunity Perspective," in Clarke and Felson, *Routine Activity and Rational Choice*, pp. 225–258.

56. James R. Lasley, "Drinking Routines/Lifestyles and Predatory Victimization: A Causal Analysis," *Justice Quarterly*, **6** (1989): 529–542.

57. Martin D. Schwartz and Victoria L. Pitts, "Exploring a Feminist Routine Activities Approach to Explaining Sexual Assault," *Justice Quarterly*, **12** (1995): 9–31.

58. Robert F. Meier and Terance D. Miethe, "Understanding Theories of Criminal Victimization," in *Crime and Justice: A Review of Research*, vol. 17, ed. Michael Tonry (Chicago: University of Chicago Press, 1993), pp. 459–499; Richard Titus, "Bringing Crime Victims Back into Routine Activities Theory/Research," paper presented at Fourth International Seminar on Environmental Criminology and Crime Analysis, July 1995, Cambridge, England.

59. C. Ray Jeffery, *Crime Prevention through Environmental Design* (Beverly Hills, Calif.: Sage, 1971).

60. Oscar Newman, *Defensible Space: Crime Prevention through Urban Design* (New York: Macmillan, 1972).

61. Ronald V. Clarke, "Introduction," in *Situational Crime Prevention: Successful Case Studies*, ed. Ronald V. Clarke (New York: Harrow and Heston, 1992), pp. 3–36.

62. Ronald V. Clarke and Ross Homel, "A Revised Classification of Situational Crime Prevention Techniques," in *Crime Prevention at a Crossroads*, ed. Steven P. Lab (Cincinnati: Anderson, 1997). For a discussion of precipitating factors and opportunity, see Richard Wortley, "A Two-Stage Model of Situational Crime Prevention," *Studies on Crime and Crime Prevention*, **7** (1998): 173–188.

63. See Gresham M. Sykes and David Matza, "Techniques of Neutralization: A Theory of Delinquency," *American Sociological Review*, **22** (1957): 664–670; Harold G. Grasmick and Robert J. Bursik, "Conscience, Significant Others, and Rational Choice," *Law and Society Review*, **34** (1990): 837–861; and John Braithwaite, *Crime, Shame and Reintegration* (Cambridge: Cambridge University, 1989).

64. Clifford D. Shearing and Phillip C. Stenning, "From the Panopticon to Disney World: The Development of Discipline," in *Perspectives in Criminal Law: Essays in Honour of John L. J. Edwards*, ed. Anthony N. Doob and Edward L. Greenspan (Aurora: Canada Law Book, 1984), pp. 335–349.

65. Kim Hazelbaker, "Insurance Industry Analyses and the Prevention of Motor Vehicle Theft," paper presented at the Business and Crime Prevention Conference, an International Seminar Sponsored by the National Institute of Justice and Rutgers, State University of New Jersey, New Brunswick, N.J., 1996.

66. Ronald D. Hunter and C. Ray Jeffery, "Preventing Convenience Store Robbery through Environmental Design," in Clarke, *Situational Crime Prevention*, pp. 194–204. See also Lisa C. Bellamy, "Situational Crime Prevention and Convenience Store Robbery," *Security Journal*, **7** (1996): 41–52.

67. All information for this section abstracted from Mary S. Smith, *Crime Prevention through Environmental Design in Parking Facilities*, Research in Brief, for National Institute of Justice (Washington, D.C.: U.S. Government Printing Office, 1996).

68. Ronald V. Clarke, "Situational Prevention, Criminology and Social Values," in *Ethical and Social Perspectives on Situational Crime Prevention*, eds. A. von Hirsch, D. Garland, and A. Wakefield (Portland, Ore.: Hart Publishing, 2000).

69. R. A. Duff and S. E. Marshall, "Benefits, Burdens and Responsibilities: Some Ethical Dimensions of Situational Crime Prevention," in von Hirsch et al., *Ethical and Social Perspectives.*

70. Clarke, "Situational Prevention, Criminology and Social Values."

71. Ibid.; Richard Wortley, "Reconsidering the Role of Opportunity in Situational Crime Prevention," in *Rational Choice and Situational Crime Prevention*, eds. G. Newman, R. V. Clarke, and S. G. Shoham (Aldershot, U.K.: Dartmouth, 1997).

72. Ibid.

73. Clarke, "Situational Prevention, Criminology and Social Values."

74. Marcus Felson and Ronald V. Clarke, "The Ethics of Situational Crime Prevention," in Newman et al., *Rational Choice and Situational Crime Prevention.*

75. Clarke, "Situational Prevention, Criminology and Social Values."

76. Felson and Clarke, "The Ethics of Situational Crime Prevention."

77. Duff and Marshall, "Benefits, Burdens and Responsibilities."

78. Felson and Clarke, "The Ethics of Situational Crime Prevention"; Graeme Newman, "Introduction: Towards a Theory of Situational Crime Prevention," in Newman et al., *Rational Choice and Situational Crime Prevention.*

79. David J. Smith, "Changing Situations and Changing People," in von Hirsch et al., *Ethical and Social Perspectives.*

80. Felson and Clarke, "The Ethics of Situational Crime Prevention."

81. David Weisburd et al., *Does Crime Just Move around the Corner? A Study of Displacement and Diffusion in Jersey City, NJ* (Washington, D.C.: National Institute of Justice, 2005).

82. M. Felson and R. V. Clarke, *Opportunity Makes the Thief: Practical Theory for Crime Prevention.* Police Research Series paper 98. (London: Home Office, 1998).

83. Home Office, *A Practical Guide to Crime Prevention for Local Partnerships.* (London: Home Office, 1993).

CHAPTER 10

1. *Crimes of Violence: A Staff Report Submitted to the National Commission on the Causes and Prevention of Violence* (Washington, D.C.: U.S. Government Printing Office, December 1969), vol. 12, p. xxvii; vol. 11, p. 4.

2. G. O. W. Mueller, "Where Murder Begins," *New Hampshire Bar Journal,* **2** (1960): 214–224; G. O. W. Mueller, "On Common Law Mens Rea," *Minnesota Law Review,* **42** (1958): 1043–1104.

3. Wayne R. LaFave and Austin W. Scott, *Handbook on Criminal Law* (St. Paul, Minn.: West, 1972), pp. 572–577.

4. *Commonwealth v. Welansky,* 316 Mass. 383, N.E. 2d 902 (1944), at pp. 906–907. See G. O. W. Mueller, "The Devil May Care—Or Should We? A Reexamination of Criminal Negligence," *Kentucky Law Journal,* **55** (1966–1967): 29–49.

5. Uniform Crime Reports, 2007, http://www.fbi.gov/ucr/cius2007/offenses/violent_crime/index.html.

6. Ibid., http://www.fbi.gov/ucr/cius2007/offenses/violent_crime/murder_homicide.html.

7. Ibid., http://www.fbi.gov/ucr/cius2007/offenses/expanded_information/homicide.html.

8. Ibid., http://www.fbi.gov/ucr/cius2007/offenses/expanded_information/homicide.html.

9. James Alan Fox and Alex R. Piquero, "Deadly Demographics: Population Characteristics and Forecasting Homicide Trends," *Crime and Delinquency,* July 2003; Steven D. Levitt, "Understanding Why Crime Fell in the 1990s: Four Factors That Explain the Decline and Six That Do Not," *Journal of Economic Perspectives,* **18** (2004): 163–190. See also James Alan Fox, "Demographics and U.S. Homicide," in *The Crime Drop in America,* ed. A. Blumstein and J. Wallman (Cambridge: Cambridge University Press, 2000), pp. 288–317; Steven D. Levitt, "The Limited Role of Changing Age Structure in Explaining Aggregate Crime Rates," *Criminology,* **37(3)** (1999): 581–597; and Roland Chilton, "Twenty Years of Homicide and Robbery in Chicago: The Impact of the City's Changing Racial and Age Composition," *Journal of Quantitative Criminology,* **3(3)** (1987): 195–214.

10. William Julius Wilson, "Work," *New York Times Magazine,* Aug. 18, 1996, pp. 27, 28.

11. William B. Harvey, "Homicide among Young Black Adults: Life in the Subculture of Exasperation," in *Homicide among Black Americans,* ed. Darnell F. Hawkins (Lanham, Md.: University Press of America, 1986), pp. 153–171. See also Robert L. Hampton, "Family Violence and Homicide in the Black Community: Are They Linked?" in *Violence in the Black Family,* ed. Hampton (Lexington, Mass.: Lexington Books, 1987), pp. 135–156.

12. Coramae Richey Mann, "Black Women Who Kill," in *Homicide among Black Americans,* pp. 157–186.

13. Hans von Hentig, *The Criminal and His Victim* (New Haven, Conn.: Yale University Press, 1948).

14. Marvin E. Wolfgang, *Patterns in Criminal Homicide* (Philadelphia: University of Pennsylvania Press, 1958), p. 253. See also Marvin E. Wolfgang, "A Sociological Analysis of Criminal Homicide," in *Studies in Homicide,* ed. Wolfgang (New York: Harper & Row, 1967), pp. 15–28.

15. Richard B. Felson and Steven F. Messner, "Disentangling the Effects of Gender and Intimacy on Victim Precipitation in Homicide," *Criminology,* **36** (1998): 405–423.

16. Robert A. Silverman and Leslie W. Kennedy, "Relational Distance and Homicide: The Role of the Stranger," *Journal of Criminal Law and Criminology,* **78** (1987): 272–308. See also Nanci Koser Wilson, "Gendered Interaction in Criminal Homicide," in *Homicide: The Victim/Offender Connection,* ed. Anna Victoria Wilson (Cincinnati: Anderson, 1993), pp. 43–62.

17. Margaret A. Zahn and Philip C. Sagi, "Stranger Homicides in Nine American Cities," *Journal of Criminal Law and Criminology,* **78** (1987): 377–397.

18. Uniform Crime Reports, 2007, http://www.fbi.gov/ucr/cius2007/offenses/expanded_information/data/shrtable_09.html.

19. Marc Riedel, "Stranger Violence: Perspectives, Issues, and Problems," *Journal of Criminal Law and Criminology,* **78** (1987): 223–258.

20. Kenneth Polk, "Observations on Stranger Homicide," *Journal of Criminal Justice,* **21** (1993): 573–582.

21. Coramae Richey Mann, *When Women Kill* (Albany: State University of New York Press, 1996).

22. See, e.g., Colin Loftin, Karen Kindley, Sandra L. Norris, and Brian Wiersema, "An Attribute Approach to Relationships between Offenders and Victims in

Homicide," *Journal of Criminal Law and Criminology,* **78** (1987): 259–271.

23. Angela Browne, "Assault and Homicide at Home: When Battered Women Kill," *Advances in Applied Social Psychology,* **3** (1986): 57–79.

24. Martin Daly and Margo Wilson, *Homicide* (New York: Aldine–De Gruyter, 1988), pp. 294–295.

25. Coramae Richey Mann, "Getting Even?: Women Who Kill in Domestic Encounters," *Justice Quarterly,* **5** (1988): 33–51.

26. Martha Smithey, "Infant Homicide: Victim/Offender Relationship and Causes of Death," *Journal of Family Violence,* **13** (1998): 285–297.

27. Ibid.

28. Lawrence A. Greenfeld, *Child Victimizers: Violent Offenders and Their Victims* (Washington, D.C.: Bureau of Justice Statistics, 1996), p. 3.

29. Etienne G. Krug, James A. Mercy, Linda Dahlberg, and Kenneth Powell, "Firearm- and Non-Firearm-Related Homicide among Children: An International Comparison," *Homicide Studies,* **2** (1998): 83–95.

30. Uniform Crime Reports, 2007, http://www.fbi.gov/ucr/cius2007/offenses/expanded_information/homicide.html.

31. William R. Holcomb and Anasseril E. Daniel, "Homicide without an Apparent Motive," *Behavioral Sciences and the Law,* **6** (1988): 429–439.

32. See Michael Newton, *Mass Murder: An Annotated Bibliography* (New York: Garland, 1988).

33. N. R. Kleinfield, "Cruelty of Strangers: 3 Men Evoke a Fearsome Trend," *New York Times,* June 23, 1996, p. 27.

34. See http://www.mayhem.net/crime/serial.html.

35. Daniel Klaidman, "The End of the Line," *Newsweek,* July 26, 1999, p. 71.

36. Michael D. Kelleher and C. L. Kelleher, *Murder Most Rare: The Female Serial Killer* (Westport, Conn.: Praeger, 1998).

37. Daniel Pedersen, "Death in Dunblane," *Newsweek,* Mar. 25, 1996, pp. 24–29.

38. *Sourcebook of Criminal Justice Statistics,* 2003, pp. 314–315.

39. Susan Faludi, "Rage of the American Male," *Newsweek,* Aug. 16, 1999, p. 31. See also http://www.cnn.com/US/9908/31/atlanta.shooting.03/.

40. See Dawn N. Castillo and E. Lynn Jenkins, "Industries and Occupations at High Risk for Work-Related Homicide," *Journal of Occupational Medicine,* **36** (1994): 125–132.

41. David Abrahamsen, *The Murdering Mind* (New York: Harper & Row, 1973).

42. Mel Heimer, *The Cannibal: The Case of Albert Fish* (New York: Lyle Stuart, 1971).

43. Margaret Cheney, *The Co-ed Killer* (New York: Walker, 1976).

44. Jack Levin and James Alan Fox, *Mass Murder: America's Growing Menace* (New York: Plenum, 1985). See also Ronald M. Holmes and Stephen T. Holmes, "Understanding Mass Murder: A Starting Point," *Federal Probation,* **56** (1992): 53–61.

45. James Fox and Jack Levin, "Multiple Homicide: Patterns of Serial and Mass Murder," in *Crime and Justice: A Review of Research,* ed. Michael Tonry (Chicago: University of Chicago Press, 1998), pp. 407–455.

46. James Alan Fox and Jack Levin, *Overkill: Mass Murder and Serial Killing Exposed* (New York: Plenum, 1994); Philip

47. Jenkins, "African-Americans and Serial Homicide," *American Journal of Criminal Justice,* **17** (1993): 47–60.

47. Ronald M. Holmes and James de Burger, *Serial Murder* (Newbury Park, Calif.: Sage, 1988), p. 155.

48. Cheryl L. Maxson, Margaret A. Gordon, and Malcolm W. Klein, "Differences between Gang and Nongang Homicides," *Criminology,* **23** (1985): 209–222.

49. G. David Curry and Irving A. Spergel, "Gang Homicide, Delinquency, and Community," *Criminology,* **26** (1988): 381–405.

50. Range Hutson, Deirdre Anglin, and Marc Eckstein, "Drive-by-Shootings by Violent Street Gangs in Los Angeles: A Five-Year Review from 1989 to 1993," *Academic Emergency Medicine,* **3** (1996): 300–303.

51. Sam Howe Verhovek, "Houston Knows Murder, but This . . .," *New York Times,* July 9, 1993, p. A8.

52. Graeme Newman, ed., *Global Report on Crime and Justice* (New York: United Nations; Oxford University Press, 1999), p. 50.

53. Uniform Crime Reports, 2001.

54. U.S. Department of Justice, Office of Juvenile Justice and Delinquency Prevention, *Juvenile Offenders and Victims, 1999 National Report* (Washington, D.C.: U.S. Department of Justice, OJJDP, 1999), p. 17. See also Krug et al., "Firearm- and Non-Firearm-Related Homicide among Children."

55. Harvey Krahn, Timothy F. Hartnagel, and John W. Gartrell, "Income Inequality and Homicide Rates: Cross-National Data and Criminological Theories," *Criminology,* **24** (1986): 269–295.

56. Glenn D. Deane, "Cross-National Comparison of Homicide: Age/Sex-Adjusted Rates Using the 1980 U.S. Homicide Experience as a Standard," *Journal of Quantitative Criminology,* **3** (1987): 215–227.

57. Dane Archer and Rosemary Gartner, *Violence and Crime in Cross-National Perspective* (New Haven, Conn.: Yale University Press, 1984).

58. Candice Nelsen, Jay Corzine, and Lin Corzine-Huff, "The Violent West Reexamined; A Research Note on Regional Homicide Rates," *Criminology,* **32** (1994): 149–161.

59. See Scott H. Decker, "Exploring Victim-Offender Relationships in Homicide: The Role of Individual and Event Characteristics," *Justice Quarterly,* **10** (1993): 585–612. See also Scott H. Decker, "Reconstructing Homicide Events: The Role of Witnesses in Fatal Encounters," *Journal of Criminal Justice,* **23** (1995): 439–450.

60. David F. Luckenbill, "Criminal Homicide as a Situated Transaction," *Social Problems,* **25** (1977): 176–186. Although Luckenbill focused on homicides, the stages he identified are identical in assaults.

61. For a comprehensive, multidisciplinary review of the literature on violence, see James T. Tedeschi and Richard B. Felson, *Violence, Aggression, and Coercive Actions* (Washington, D.C.: American Psychological Association, 1994). See also Barry R. Ruback and Neil Alan Weiner, eds., *Interpersonal Violent Behaviors: Social and Cultural Aspects* (New York: Springer, 1994).

62. See Michael R. Rand, *Criminal Victimization, 2007* (Washington, D.C.: BJS, 2008), p. 1.

63. C. H. Kempe, F. N. Silverman, B. F. Steele, W. Droegemueller, and H. K. Silver, "The Battered-Child Syndrome," *Journal of the American Medical Association,* **181** (1962): 17–24.

64. Elizabeth Pleck, "Criminal Approaches to Family Violence, 1640–1980," in *Family Violence,* ed. Lloyd

Ohlin and Michael Tonry, vol. 2 (Chicago: University of Chicago Press, 1989), pp. 19–57.

65. For a special journal issue on the subject of family violence, see Richard J. Gelles, ed., "Family Violence," *Journal of Comparative Family Studies,* 25 (1994): 1–142.

66. Lyn Nell Hancock, "Why Batterers So Often Go Free," *Newsweek,* Oct. 16, 1995, pp. 61–62.

67. Murray A. Straus and Richard J. Gelles, "How Violent Are American Families?: Estimates from the National Family Violence Resurvey and Other Studies," in *Family Abuse and Its Consequences,* ed. Gerald T. Hotaling, David Finkelhor, John T. Kirkpatrick, and Murray A. Straus (Newbury Park, Calif.: Sage, 1988). See also Ann Goetting, *Homicide in Families and Other Special Populations* (New York: Springer, 1995); and Ronet Bachman, *Violence against Women: A National Crime Victimization Survey Report* (Washington, D.C.: U.S. Bureau of Justice Statistics, 1994).

68. Richard B. Felson, "Big People Hit Little People: Sex Differences in Physical Power and Interpersonal Violence," *Criminology,* 34 (1996): 433–452.

69. Straus and Gelles, "How Violent Are American Families?" p. 17.

70. Terrie E. Moffitt and Avshalom Caspi, *National Institute of Justice, Research in Brief, Findings about Partner Violence from the Dunedin Multidisciplinary Health and Development Study* (Washington, D.C.: U.S. Department of Justice, Office of Justice Programs, National Institute of Justice, July 1999).

71. Patrick A. Langan and Christopher A. Innes, *Preventing Domestic Violence against Women,* for U.S. Department of Justice, Bureau of Justice Statistics (Washington, D.C.: U.S. Government Printing Office, 1986).

72. Marvin E. Wolfgang and Franco Ferracuti, *The Subculture of Violence: Toward an Integrated Theory in Criminology* (London: Tavistock, 1967).

73. Joan McCord, "Parental Aggressiveness and Physical Punishment in Long-Term Perspective," in *Family Abuse and Its Consequences,* pp. 91–98.

74. Margery A. Cassidy, "Power-Control Theory: Its Potential Application to Woman Battering," *Journal of Crime and Justice,* 18 (1995): 1–15.

75. Donald G. Dutton, *The Domestic Assault of Women* (Boston: Allyn and Bacon, 1988), p. 15.

76. Lenore E. Walker, *The Battered Woman Syndrome* (New York: Springer Verlag, 1984); Brenda A. Miller, Thomas H. Nochajski, Kenneth E. Leonard, Howard T. Blane, Dawn M. Gondoli, and Patricia M. Bowers, "Spousal Violence and Alcohol/Drug Problems among Parolees and Their Spouses," *Women and Criminal Justice,* 1 (1990): 55–72.

77. Study conducted by Mohammed Ayat, Atiqui Abdelaziz, Najat Kfita, and El Khazouni Zineb, at the request of UNESCO and the Union of Arab Lawyers, Fez, Morocco, 1989.

78. David Levinson, *Family Violence in Cross-Cultural Perspective* (Newbury Park, Calif.: Sage, 1989).

79. Carolyn F. Swift, "Surviving: Women's Strength through Connections," in *Abuse and Victimization across the Life Span,* ed. Martha Straus (Baltimore: Johns Hopkins University Press, 1988), pp. 153–169.

80. See Christine Rasche, "Early Models for Contemporary Thought on Domestic Violence and Women Who Kill Their Mates: A Review of the Literature from 1895 to 1970," *Women and Criminal Justice,* 1 (1990): 31–53.

81. *Thurman v. Torrington,* 596 F. Supp. 1521 (1985).

82. Matthew R. Durose et al., *Bureau of Justice Statistics, Family Violence Statistics: Including Statistics on Strangers and Acquaintances,* (U.S. Department of Justice, 2005), available at http://www.ojp.usdoj.gov/bjs/pub/pdf/fvs.pdf.

83. Jeffrey Fagan, *The Criminalization of Domestic Violence: Promises and Limits* (Washington, D.C.: U.S. National Institute of Justice, 1996).

84. Lawrence W. Sherman and Richard A. Berk, "The Minneapolis Domestic Violence Experiment," *Police Foundation Reports,* 1 (1984): 1–8. See also J. David Hirschel, Ira W. Hutchinson, Charles W. Dean, and Anne-Marie Mills, "Review Essay on the Law Enforcement Response to Spouse Abuse: Past, Present and Future," *Justice Quarterly,* 9 (1992): 247–283; Cynthia Grant Bowman, "The Arrest Experiments: A Feminist Critique," *Journal of Criminal Law and Criminology,* 83 (1992): 201–208; Albert R. Roberts, "Psychosocial Characteristics of Batterers: A Study of 234 Men Charged with Domestic Violence Offenses," *Journal of Family Violence,* 2 (1987): 81–93; Donald G. Dutton and Susan K. Golant, *The Batterer: A Psychological Profile* (New York: Basic Books, 1995); Lisa A. Frisch, "Research That Succeeds, Policies That Fail," *Journal of Criminal Law and Criminology,* 83 (1992): 209–216; David B. Mitchell, "Contemporary Police Practices in Domestic Violence Cases: Arresting the Abuser: Is It Enough?" *Journal of Criminal Law and Criminology,* 83 (1992): 241–249; and Lawrence W. Sherman, Janell D. Schmidt, Dennis P. Rogan, Patrick R. Gartin, Ellen G. Cohn, Dean J. Collins, and Anthony R. Bacich, "From Initial Deterrence to Long-Term Escalation: Short Custody Arrest for Poverty Ghetto Domestic Violence," *Criminology,* 29 (1991): 821–850.

85. Lawrence W. Sherman, Janell D. Schmidt, Dennis P. Rogan, Douglas A. Smith, Patrick R. Gartin, Ellen G. Cohn, Dean J. Collins, and Anthony R. Bacich, "The Variable Effects of Arrest on Criminal Careers: The Milwaukee Domestic Violence Experiment," *Journal of Criminal Law and Criminology,* 83 (1992): 137–169. See also J. David Hirschel and Ira W. Hutchinson III, "Female Spouse Abuse and the Police Response: The Charlotte, North Carolina, Experiment," *Journal of Criminal Law and Criminology,* 83 (1992): 73–119.

86. Joan Zorza, "The Criminal Law of Misdemeanor Domestic Violence, 1970–1990," *Journal of Criminal Law and Criminology,* 83 (1992): 46–72. See also Candace Kruttschnitt and Maude Dornfeld, "Will They Tell? Assessing Preadolescents' Reports of Family Violence," *Journal of Research in Crime and Delinquency,* 29 (1992): 136–147.

87. See http://www.americanhumane.org/about-us/newsroom/fact-sheets/child-physical-abuse.html.

88. Ibid.

89. See http://www.acf.hhs.gov/programs/cb/index.htm.

90. Cathy Spatz Widom and M. Ashley Ames, "Criminal Consequences of Childhood Sexual Victimization," *Child Abuse and Neglect,* 18 (1994): 303–318; Carolyn Smith and Terence P. Thornberry, "The Relationship between Childhood Maltreatment and Adolescent Involvement in Delinquency," *Criminology,* 33 (1995): 451–481.

91. U.S. Department of Justice, OJJDP, *Juvenile Offenders and Victims, 1999 National Report,* p. 41.

92. Ibid.

93. Kathleen Brewer, Daryl Rowe, and Devon Brewer, "Factors Related to Prosecution of Child Sexual Abuse Cases," *Journal of Child Sexual Abuse,* 6 (1997): 91–111.

94. Deborah Daro, "Half Full and Half Empty: The Evaluation of Results of Nineteen Clinical Research and Demonstration Projects," *Summary of Nineteen Clinical Demonstration Projects Funded by the National Center on Child Abuse and Neglect, 1978–81* (Berkeley: University of California, School of Social Welfare, 1986).

95. See Candace Kruttschnitt and Maude Dornfeld, "Childhood Victimization, Race, and Violent Crime," *Criminal Justice and Behavior,* **18** (1991): 448–463.

96. See "The Basics: What Is Elder Abuse?" at www.gwja pan.com/NCEA/basic/index.html (accessed online Sept. 19, 1999).

97. See http://www.census.gov/population/www/pop -profile/elderpop.html.

98. Mildred Daley Pagelow, "The Incidence and Prevalence of Criminal Abuse of Other Family Members," in Ohlin and Tonry, *Family Violence,* p. 267.

99. Jordan I. Kosberg and Juanita L. Garcia, eds., "Elder Abuse: International and Cross-Cultural Perspectives," *Journal of Elder Abuse and Neglect,* **6** (1995): 1–197.

100. See Mark Whatley, "For Better or Worse: The Case of Marital Rape," *Violence and Victims,* 8 (1993): 29–39.

101. Susan Brownmiller, *Against Our Will: Men, Women, and Rape* (New York: Simon & Schuster, 1975), pp. 1–9.

102. Duncan Chappell, "Sexual Criminal Violence," in *Pathways to Criminal Violence,* ed. Neil Alan Weiner and Marvin E. Wolfgang (Newbury Park, Calif.: Sage, 1989), pp. 68–108.

103. Uniform Crime Reports, 2007, http://www.fbi.gov/ucr/cius2007/offenses/violent_crime/forcible_rape.html.

104. Ibid.

105. Whatley, "For Better or Worse."

106. Menachem Amir, *Patterns in Forcible Rape* (Chicago: University of Chicago Press, 1977), pp. 233–234.

107. U.S. Department of Justice, Bureau of Justice Statistics, *Highlights from 20 Years of Surveying Crime Victims* (Washington, D.C.: U.S. Government Printing Office, 1993), p. 24.

108. Ida Johnson and Robert Sigler, *Forced Sexual Intercourse in Intimate Relationships* (Brookfield, Vt.: Ashgate, 1997).

109. Clark Staten, "Roofies, The New Date Rape Drug of Choice," Jan. 6, 1996 (see http://www.emergency.com/roofies.htm).

110. M. P. Koss, C. A. Gidycz, and N. Wisniewski, "The Scope of Rape: Incidence and Prevalence of Sexual Aggression and Victimization in a National Sample of Higher Education Students," *Journal of Consulting and Clinical Psychology,* 55 (1987): 162–170.

111. Uniform Crime Reports, 2007, http://www.fbi.gov/ucr/cius2007/offenses/clearances/index.html.

112. James L. LeBeau, "Patterns of Stranger and Serial Rape Offending: Factors Distinguishing Apprehended and At Large Offenders," *Journal of Criminal Law and Criminology,* **78** (1987): 309–326.

113. J. Marolla and D. Scully, *Attitudes toward Women, Violence, and Rape: A Comparison of Convicted Rapists and Other Felons* (Rockville, Md.: National Institute of Mental Health, 1982).

114. Christine Alder, "An Exploration of Self-Reported Sexually Aggressive Behavior," *Crime and Delinquency,* **31** (1985): 306–331; P. R. Sanday, "The Socio-Cultural Context of Rape: A Cross-Cultural Study," *Journal of Social Issues,* 37 (1981): 5–27.

115. Julia R. Schwendinger and Herman Schwendinger, *Rape and Inequality* (Beverly Hills, Calif.: Sage, 1983), p. 220.

116. M. Dwayne Smith and Nathan Bennett, "Poverty, Inequality, and Theories of Forcible Rape," *Crime and Delinquency,* 31 (1985): 295–305.

117. Ruth D. Peterson and William C. Bailey, "Forcible Rape, Poverty, and Economic Inequality in U.S. Metropolitan Communities," *Journal of Quantitative Criminology,* 4 (1988): 99–119.

118. Matthew Hale, *History of the Pleas of the Crown,* vol. 1 (London, 1736), p. 635.

119. Martin D. Schwartz and Todd R. Clear, "Toward a New Law on Rape," *Crime and Delinquency,* 26 (1980): 129–151.

120. Patricia Frazier and Beth Haney, "Sexual Assault Cases in the Legal System: Police, Prosecutor, and Victim Perspectives," *Law and Human Behavior,* **20** (1996): 607–628.

121. Christian Berthelsen, "Women Are Speaking Out to Heal Trauma of Rape," *New York Times,* Apr. 4, 1999, p. 19, Section 1.

122. Cassia C. Spohn and Julie Horney, "The Impact of Rape Law Reform on the Processing of Simple and Aggravated Cases," *Journal of Criminal Law and Criminology,* 86 (1996): 861–884; Gilbert Geis, "Rape-in-Marriage: Law and Law Reform in England, the United States, and Sweden," *Adelaide Law Review,* 6 (1978): 284–303; Joel Epstein and Stacia Langenbahn, *The Criminal Justice and Community Response to Rape* (Washington, D.C.: U.S. National Institute of Justice, 1994).

123. Janet Gornick, Martha R. Burt, and Karen J. Pittman, "Structures and Activities of Rape Crisis Centers in the Early 1980's," *Crime and Delinquency,* 31 (1985): 247–268.

124. Alexis Chiu, "Dad Pleads Guilty to Kidnapping," May 28, 1999 (see http://more.abcnews.go.com/sections/us/DailyNews/father990527.html).

125. Uniform Crime Reports, 2004, p. 31.

126. Uniform Crime Reports, http://www.fbi.gov/ucr/cius2007/offenses/violent_crime/robbery.html.

127. U.S. Department of Justice, Bureau of Justice Statistics, *Criminal Victimization in the United States,* 2003 (Washington, D.C.: U.S. Government Printing Office, 2004).

128. John Conklin, *Robbery and the Criminal Justice System* (Philadelphia: Lippincott, 1972), pp. 59–78.

129. Uniform Crime Reports, 2007, http://www.fbi.gov/ucr/cius2007/offenses/violent_crime/robbery.html.

130. Terry L. Baumer and Michael D. Carrington, *The Robbery of Financial Institutions,* for U.S. Department of Justice (Washington, D.C.: U.S. Government Printing Office, 1986).

131. Uniform Crime Reports, 2007, http://www.fbi.gov/ucr/cius2007/data/table_23.html.

132. Philip J. Cook, "Is Robbery Becoming More Violent?: An Analysis of Robbery Murder Trends since 1968," *Journal of Criminal Law and Criminology,* 76 (1985): 480–489.

133. John Lehmann and Al Guart, "Ciao: Gotti Gang Gone," *New York Post,* June 21, 2002, p. 5. Reprinted with permission from *The New York Post,* 2002, copyright © NYP Holdings, Inc.

134. William Balsamo and George Carpozi Jr., *Under the Clock: The Inside Story of the Mafia's First 100 Years* (Far Hills, N.J.: New Horizon Press, 1988). Some legal historians trace the appearance of organized crime in the United States to the early 1860s; see Humbert S. Nelli, "A Brief History of American Syndicate Crime," in *Organized Crime in America: Concepts and Controversies*, ed. Timothy S. Bynum (Monsey, N.Y.: Criminal Justice Press, 1987). See also Richard Gambino, *Blood of My Blood: The Dilemma of the Italian American* (Garden City, N.Y.: Doubleday, 1974), p. 3; Luigi Barzini, "Italians in New York: The Way We Were in 1929," *New York Magazine*, Apr. 4, 1977, p. 36; and Howard Abadinsky, *Organized Crime*, 2d ed. (Chicago: Nelson Hall, 1985).

135. Abadinsky, *Organized Crime*, pp. 43–53.

136. Ibid., p. 91. For a description of some of the more colorful characters of the Prohibition era, see David E. Ruth, *Inventing the Public Enemy* (Chicago: University of Chicago Press, 1996); Joseph McNamara, "Dapper Bootlegger," *New York Daily News*, Oct. 15, 1995, p. 42; Charles Rappleye and Ed Becker, *All American Mafioso: The Johnny Roselli Story* (New York: Barricade Books, 1995); Mary M. Stolberg, *Fighting Organized Crime: Politics, Justice, and the Legacy of Thomas E. Dewey* (Boston: Northeastern University Press, 1995); Colin Wilson, Ian Schott, Ed Shedd, et al., *World Famous Crimes* (New York: Carroll & Graf, 1995); Jay Robert Nash, *World Encyclopedia of Organized Crime* (New York: Paragon House, 1992); Robert J. Schoenberg, *Mr. Capone: The Real and Complete Story of Al Capone* (New York: William Morrow, 1992); and Robert Lacey, *Little Man: Meyer Lansky and the Gangster Life* (Boston: Little, Brown, 1991).

137. James Inciardi, *Careers in Crime* (Chicago: Rand McNally, 1975), p. 113; Norman Lewis, *The Honored Society: A Searching Look at the Mafia* (New York: Putnam, 1964), p. 25.

138. For a European perspective on the harms generated by the Sicilian Mafia, see John Follain, *A Dishonoured Society: Sicilian Mafia's Threat to Europe* (London: Little, Brown, 1995); and Brian Freemantle, *The Octopus: Europe in the Grip of Organized Crime* (London: Orion Books, 1995). For a description of the Sicilian Mafia's reach into the former Soviet Union, see Werner Raith, *Das Neue Mafia-Kartell: Wie de Syndikate den Osten Erober* (The New Mafia Cartel: How the Syndicates Conquer the East) (Berlin: Rowohlt, 1994). For a global perspective, see Phil Williams and Ernesto U. Savona, "Problems and Dangers Posed by Organized Transnational Crime in the Various Regions of the World," *Transnational Organized Crime*, **1** (1995): 1–42; Louise I. Shelley, "Transnational Organized Crime: An Imminent Threat to the Nation-State?" *Journal of International Affairs*, **48** (1995): 463–489; Raimondo Catanzaro, *Men of Respect: A Social History of the Sicilian Mafia* (New York: Free Press, 1992); and Pino Arlacchi, *Men of Dishonor: Inside the Sicilian Mafia* (New York: William Morrow, 1992). For a description of how the Sicilian Mafia attempted to join forces with the Colombian cocaine cartels, see William Gately and Yvette Fernandez, *Dead Ringer: An Insider's Account of the Mob's Colombian Connection* (New York: Donald I. Fine, 1994); and Abadinsky, *Organized Crime*, pp. 56–62.

139. Ronald Goldfarb, *Perfect Villains, Imperfect Heros: Robert F. Kennedy's War against Organized Crime* (New York: Random House, 1995); Annelise Graebner Anderson, *The Business of Organized Crime: A Cosa Nostra Family* (Stanford, Calif.: Hoover Institution Press, 1979); Peter Maas, *The Valachi Papers* (New York: Putnam, 1968); U.S. Senate Committee on Governmental Affairs, Subcommittee on Investigations, *Organized Crime: 25 Years after Valachi* (Washington, D.C.: U.S. Government Printing Office, 1990).

140. Jay Albanese, *Organized Crime in America* (Cincinnati: Anderson, 1985), p. 25. See also Francis A. J. Ianni, *A Family Business: Kinship and Social Control in Organized Crime* (New York: Russell Sage, 1972); Joseph Albini, *The American Mafia: Genesis of a Legend* (New York: Irvington, 1971); and Merry Morash, "Organized Crime," in *Major Forms of Crime*, ed. Robert F. Meier (Beverly Hills, Calif.: Sage, 1984), pp. 191–220. For a response, see Claire Sterling, *Octopus: The Long Reach of the International Sicilian Mafia* (New York: W. W. Norton, 1990); and Ralph Blumenthal, *Last Days of the Sicilians: At War with the Mafia* (New York: Pocket Books, 1994). See also Shana Alexander, *The Pizza Connection* (New York: Weidenfeld & Nicolson, 1988).

141. For a perceptive analysis of the changing focus of the two most recent commission reports listed, see Jay S. Albanese, "Government Perceptions of Organized Crime: The Presidential Commissions, 1967 and 1987," *Federal Probation*, **52** (1988): 58–63.

142. For a popular account of how a Sicilian Mafia associate infiltrated and almost destroyed one of the largest movie studios in Hollywood, see "The Predator: How an Italian Thug Looted MGM, Brought Credit Lyonnais to Its Knees, and Made the Pope Cry," *Fortune*, July 8, 1996, p. 128. Despite the denial of generations of Italian and Sicilian organized-crime figures concerning the trafficking of illegal narcotics, criminologists have discussed the involvement of all major American syndicates; see Peter A. Lupsha, "La Cosa Nostra in Drug Trafficking," in Bynum, *Organized Crime in America*. See also Dwight Smith, *The Mafia Mystique* (New York: Basic Books, 1975).

143. P. Beseler, Wayne Brewer, and Julienne Salzano, "Focus on Environmental Crimes," *FBI Law Enforcement Bulletin*, **64** (1995): 1–26; Joel Epstein, Theodore M. Hammett, and Laura Collins, *Law Enforcement Response to Environmental Crime* (Washington, D.C.: U.S. National Institute of Justice, 1995). For a global perspective on environmental stability, see Norman Myers, *Ultimate Security: The Environmental Basis of Political Stability* (New York: W. W. Norton & Company, 1993). For a uniquely Italian organized-crime perspective on the illegal disposal of toxic wastes throughout the United States, see Frank R. Scarpitti and Alan A. Block, "America's Toxic Waste Racket: Dimensions of the Environmental Crisis," in Bynum, *Organized Crime in America*. For a discussion of predicting which legitimate businesses will be infiltrated by organized crime, see Jay S. Albanese, "Predicting the Incidence of Organized Crime: A Preliminary Model," in Bynum, *Organized Crime in America*, pp. 103–114.

144. Past efforts to develop civil and criminal causes of action against corporations are found in RICO legislation. See Racketeer Influenced and Corrupt Organizations (RICO) Provisions of the Organized Crime Control Act of 1970 [Act of Oct. 15, 1970, Public Law 91-452, Section 901(a), 84 Stat. 941, 18 U.S.C. §§ 1961 through 1968, effective Oct. 15, 1970, as amended Nov. 2, 1978, Public Law 95-575, Sec. 3(c), 92 Stat.

2465, and Nov. 6, 1978, Public Law 95-598, Sec. 314(g), 92 Stat. 2677]. For a discussion of the pros and cons of RICO, see Donald J. Rebovich, "Use and Avoidance of RICO at the Local Level: The Implementation of Organized Crime Laws," in *Contemporary Issues in Organized Crime,* ed. Jay Albanese (Monsey, N.Y.: Criminal Justice Press, 1995).

145. See http://www.usmarshals.gov/witsec/index.html.

146. For a description of the contemporary leadership of New York's five Italian-American organized-crime families, see Jeffrey Goldberg, "The Mafia's Morality Crisis," *New York Magazine,* Jan. 9, 1995, p. 22. See also Donald Cressey, *Theft of the Nation* (New York: Harper & Row, 1969).

147. Abadinsky, *Organized Crime,* pp. 8–23; Donald Cressey, in President's Commission, *Task Force Report,* pp. 7–8; Gay Talese, *Honor Thy Father* (New York: World, 1971).

148. For a discussion of "Commission" membership, mores, and dispute resolution, see William F. Roemer Jr., *Accardo: The Genuine Godfather* (New York: Donald I. Fine, 1995); Sidney Zion, *Loyalty and Betrayal: The Story of the American Mob* (San Francisco: Collins, 1994); John H. Davis, *Mafia Dynasty: The Rise and Fall of the Gambino Crime Family* (New York: HarperCollins, 1993); Sam Giancana and Chuck Giancana, *Double Cross: The Explosive, Inside Story of the Mobster Who Controlled America* (New York: Warner Books, 1992); and John Cummings and Ernest Volkman, *Goombata: The Improbable Rise and Fall of John Gotti and His Gang* (Boston: Little, Brown, 1990).

149. *United States v. Bonanno,* 180 F. Supp. 71 (S.D.N.Y. 1960), upholding the Apalachin roundup as constitutional; *United States v. Bonanno,* 177 F. Supp. 106 (S.D.N.Y. 1959), sustaining the validity of the conspiracy indictment; *United States v. Bufalino,* 285 F. 2d 408 (2d Cir. 1960), reversing the conspiracy conviction.

150. James Walston, "Mafia in the Eighties," *Violence, Aggression, and Terrorism,* 1 (1987): 13–39. For a look into organized crime's once mighty and still lingering hand on gambling in the United States, see Jay Albanese, "Casino Gambling and Organized Crime: More Than Reshuffling the Deck," in Albanese, *Contemporary Issues in Organized Crime;* Ronald A. Farrelland and Carole Case, *The Black Book and the Mob: The Untold Story of the Control of Nevada's Casinos* (Madison: University of Wisconsin Press, 1995); Nicholas Pileggi, *Casino: Love and Honor in Las Vegas* (New York: Simon & Schuster, 1995); and David Johnston, *Temples of Chance: How America Inc. Bought Out Murder Inc. to Win Control of the Casino Business* (New York: Doubleday, 1992).

151. Organized-crime activities are certainly not limited to local communities. Rather, an ever-evolving organized-crime syndicate feeds off ever-increasing global opportunities; see Petrus van Duyne and Alan A. Block, "Organized Cross-Atlantic Crime: Racketeering in Fuels," *Crime, Law and Social Change,* 22 (1995): 127–147; and Umberto Santino, "The Financial Mafia: The Illegal Accumulation of Wealth and the Financial-Industrial Complex," *Contemporary Crises,* 12 (1988): 203–243.

152. For a description of the damage inflicted on society by contemporary Russian organized-crime figures, see New York State Organized Crime Task Force, New York State Commission of Investigation, New Jersey State Commission of Investigation, *An Analysis of Russian-Émigré Crime in the Tri-State Region* (White Plains, N.Y.: New York State Organized Crime Task Force, June 1996); and Dennis J. Kenny and James O. Finckenauer, *Organized Crime in America* (Belmont, Calif.: Wadsworth, 1995).

153. Robert J. Kelly and Rufus Schatzberg, "Galvanizing Indiscriminate Political Violence: Mind-Sets and Some Ideological Constructs in Terrorism," *International Journal of Comparative and Applied Criminal Justice,* 16 (1992): 15–41; Jeffrey D. Simon, *The Terrorist Trap: America's Experience with Terrorism* (Bloomington: Indiana University Press, 1993); Brent L. Smith and Gregory P. Orvis, "America's Response to Terrorism: An Empirical Analysis of Federal Intervention Strategies during the 1980s," *Justice Quarterly,* 10 (1993): 661–681.

154. Cindy Combs, *Terrorism in the Twenty-First Century* (Upper Saddle River, N.J.: Prentice-Hall, 1997).

155. See http://www.usmarshals.gov/witsec/index.html.

156. See "Blast in Moscow Mall Wounds 33," Aug. 31, 1999 (http://www.cnn.com/wysiwgy://partner/55/http://cnn. . .europe/9908/31/moscow.blast.08/).

157. http://www.cnn.com/2005/WORLD/europe/07/29/london.tube/; http://www.cnn.com/2005/WORLD/europe/07/14/homegrown.terror/; http://www.cnn.com/SPECIALS/2005/london.bombing/.

158. Harvey J. Iglarsh, "Terrorism and Corporate Costs," *Terrorism,* 10 (1987): 227–230.

159. United States Department of State Publication, Office of the Coordinator for Counterterrorism, *Country Reports on Terrorism 2007* (Washington D.C.: U.S. Government Printing Office, 2008).

160. "A Cloud of Terror and Suspicion," *Newsweek,* Apr. 3, 1995, pp. 36–41. See also Stewart A. Wright, ed., *Armageddon in Waco: Critical Perspectives on the Branch Davidian Conflict* (Chicago: University of Illinois Press, 1995).

161. James Brooke, "Wyoming City Braces for Gay Murder Trial," *New York Times,* Apr. 4, 1999, p. 14.

162. Sylvester Monroe, "A Burning in Alabama," *Time,* Mar. 15, 1999, p. 47.

163. Frank Gibney Jr., "The Kids Got in the Way," *Time,* Aug. 23, 1999, p. 22.

164. See http://www.fbi.gov/hq/cid/civilrights/hate.htm.

165. Active Hate Groups in the United States, 2007: Southern Poverty Law Center Intelligence Project, available at http://www.splcenter.org/intel/map/hate.jsp.

166. Rebecca Leung, "Hate Crimes in America: Texas Killing Spotlights Nation's Racial Divide," June 17, 1999 (see http://abcnews.go.com/sections/us/DailyNews/hatecrimes980611.html).

167. For discussions of recent events that have shaped the philosophy of militias, see Alan W. Bock, *Ambush at Ruby Ridge: How Government Agents Set Randy Weaver Up and Took His Family Down* (Irvine, Calif.: Dickens Press, 1995).

168. Morris Dees and James Corcoran, *Gathering Storm: America's Militia Threat* (New York: Harper Collins, 1996).

169. Michael Winerip, "Ohio Case Typifies the Tensions between Militia Groups and the Law," *New York Times,* June 23, 1996, p. 1.

170. "The View from the Far Right," *Newsweek,* May 1, 1995, pp. 36–39.

171. Ibid.

172. Gordon Crew and Reid Countes, *The Evolution of School Disturbance in America: Colonial Times to Modern Day* (Westport, Conn.: Praeger, 1997).

173. T. Trent Gegax, Jerry Adler, and Daniel Pedarion, "The Boys behind the Ambush," *Newsweek,* Apr. 6, 1998, pp. 20–24; Geoffrey Cowley, "Why Children Turn Violent," *Newsweek,* Apr. 6, 1998, pp. 24–26; Nadya Lobi, "The Hunter and the Choirboy," *Time,* Apr. 6, 1998, pp. 28–37; Richard Lacayo, "Toward the Root of the Evil," *Time,* Apr. 6, 1998, pp. 38–39.

174. Sam Howe Verhovek, "Sounds from a Massacre: 'Oh God, Kids, Stay Down,' " *New York Times,* Apr. 24, 1999, p. 1.

175. Tammerlin Drummond, "Battling the Columbine Copycats," *Time,* May 10, 1999, p. 29.

176. See NSSC Review of School Safety Research, School Safety Statistics January 2006, available at: http://www.schoolsafety.us/pubfiles/school_crime_and_violence_statistics.pdf. Vincent Schiraldi, "Hype Aside, School Violence Is Declining." This report appeared in *Newsday, The Washington Post,* and other media, Sept. 30, 1998.

177. See http://nces.ed.gov/programs/crimeindicators/crimeindicators2008/.

178. Mary Jo Nolin, Elizabeth Davies, and Kathryn Chandler, "Student Victimization at School," *Journal of School Health,* **66** (1996): 216.

179. Samuel Walker, *Sense and Nonsense about Crime and Drugs: A Policy Guide,* 4th ed. (Belmont, Calif.: West/Wadsworth, 1998).

180. Richard Woodbury, "Taking Back the School," *Time,* Aug. 16, 1999, pp. 32–33.

181. Claudia Kalb, "Schools on the Alert," *Newsweek,* Aug. 23, 1999, pp. 42–44.

182. John Cloud, "What Can the Schools Do?" *Time,* May 3, 1999, pp. 38–40.

183. U.S. Department of Justice, Office of Justice Programs, *Promising Strategies to Reduce Gun Violence* (Washington, D.C.: Office of Juvenile Justice and Delinquency Prevention, February 1999).

184. Matt Bai, "Caught in the Cross-Fire," *Newsweek,* June 28, 1999, pp. 31–32.

185. Sam Howe Verhovek, "2 Youths Wanted to 'Destroy the School,' Sheriff Says," *New York Times,* Apr. 23, 1999, p. 1.

186. Roger Rosenblatt, "Get Rid of the Damned Things," *Time,* Aug. 9, 1999, pp. 38–39.

187. Marianne W. Zawitz, *Guns Used in Crime* (Washington, D.C.: Bureau of Justice Statistics, 1995), p. 2.

188. Walker, *Sense and Nonsense about Crime and Drugs.*

189. See http://www.ojp.gov/bjs/guns.htm.

190. Marianne W. Zawitz, *Firearm Injury from Crime* (Washington, D.C.: Bureau of Justice Statistics, 1996), p. 4; www.cdc.gov/mmwr/preview/mmwrhtml/mm4845a1.htm.

191. Robert D. McFadden, "On a Bus in Queens, Three Bandits Stage a Frontier Robbery," *New York Times,* July 31, 1993, p. 1.

192. Alan J. Lizotte, James M. Tesoriero, Terence P. Thornberry, et al., "Patterns of Adolescent Firearms Ownership and Use," *Justice Quarterly,* **11** (1994): 51–74.

193. *Juvenile Offenders and Victims, 1999 National Report,* p. 69.

194. Joseph F. Sheley, "Drugs and Guns among Inner-City High School Students," *Journal of Drug Education,* **24** (1994): 303–321.

195. M. Dwayne Smith and Joseph F. Sheley, "The Possession and Carrying of Firearms among a Sample of Inner-City High School Females," *Journal of Crime and Justice,* **18** (1995): 109–128.

196. Jon D. Hull, "A Boy and His Gun," *Time,* Aug. 2, 1993.

197. Alan J. Lizotte, James M. Tesoriero, Terence P. Thornberry, et al., "Patterns of Adolescent Firearms Ownership and Use." See also Joseph F. Sheley and James D. Wright, *In the Line of Fire: Youth, Guns, and Violence in Urban America* (Hawthorne, N.Y.: Aldine de Gruyter, 1995); and Joseph F. Sheley and Victoria E. Brewer, "Possession and Carrying of Firearms among Suburban Youth," *Public Health Reports,* **110** (1995): 18–26.

198. James B. Jacobs and Kimberly A. Potter, "Comprehensive Handgun Licensing and Registration: An Analysis and Critique of Brady II, Gun Control's Next (and Last?) Step," *Journal of Criminal Law and Criminology,* **89** (1998): 81–110.

199. U.S. Department of Justice, OJJDP, *Juvenile Offenders and Victims, 1999 National Report,* p. 69.

200. Glenn L. Pierce and William J. Bowers, "The Bartley-Fox Gun Law's Short-Term Impact on Crime in Boston," *Annals of the American Academy of Political and Social Science,* **455** (1981): 120–137.

201. Patrick W. O'Carroll, Colin Loftin, John B. Waller Jr., David McDowall, Allen Bukoff, Richard O. Scott, James A. Mercy, and Brian Wiersema, "Preventing Homicide: An Evaluation of the Efficacy of a Detroit Gun Ordinance," *American Journal of Public Health,* **81** (1991): 576–581.

202. Lawrence W. Sherman, James W. Shaw, and Dennis P. Rogan, *The Kansas City Gun Experiment* (Washington, D.C.: U.S. National Institute of Justice, 1995).

203. James A. Beha II, "And Nobody Can Get You Out: The Impact of a Mandatory Prison Sentence for the Illegal Carrying of a Firearm on the Administration of Criminal Justice in Boston," *Boston University Law Review,* **57** (1977): 96–146, 289–333.

204. Colin Loftin, Milton Heumann, and David McDowall, "Mandatory Sentencing and Firearms Violence: Evaluating an Alternative to Gun Control," *Law and Society Review,* **17** (1983): 288–318.

205. Michael Janofsky, "Fighting Crime by Making Federal Case about Guns," *New York Times,* Feb. 10, 1999, p. A12.

206. Elaine Shannon, "Have Gun? Will Travel," *Time,* Aug. 16, 1999, p. 30.

207. Janofsky, "Fighting Crime by Making Federal Case about Guns."

208. Colin Loftin, David McDowall, Brian Wiersema, and Talbert J. Cottey, "Effects of Restrictive Licensing of Handguns on Homicide and Suicide in the District of Columbia," *New England Journal of Medicine,* **325** (1991): 1615–1620.

209. U.S. Department of the Treasury, Bureau of Alcohol, Tobacco and Firearms, *Implementation of the Brady Law* (Washington, D.C.: U.S. Government Printing Office, September 1999).

210. U.S. Department of Justice, Bureau of Justice Statistics, *Presale Handgun Checks, the Brady Interim Period, 1994–1998* (Washington, D.C.: U.S. Government Printing Office, June 1999).

211. David McDowall and Alan Lizotte, "Gun Control," in *Introduction to Social Problems,* ed. Craig Calhoun and George Ritzer (New York: Primis Database, McGraw-Hill, 1993).

212. Marjolijn Bijlefeld, ed., *The Gun Control Debate: A Documentary History* (Westport, Conn.: Greenwood Press, 1997).

213. John A. Arthur, "Criminal Victimization, Fear of Crime, and Handgun Ownership among Blacks: Evidence from National Survey Data," *American Journal of Criminal Justice,* **16** (1992): 121–141; Gary S. Green, "Citizen Gun Ownership and Criminal Deterrence: Theory, Research, and Policy," *Criminology,* **25** (1987): 63–81; John A. Arthur, "Gun Ownership among Women Living in One-Adult Households," *International Journal of Comparative and Applied Criminal Justice,* **18** (1994): 249–263; Wilbur Edel, *Gun Control: Threat to Liberty or Defense against Anarchy?* (Westport, Conn.: Praeger, 1995).

214. *Concealed Carry: The Criminal's Companion. Florida's Concealed Weapons Law—A Model for the Nation?* (Washington, D.C.: Violence Policy Center, 1995).

215. Fox Butterfield, "America under the Gun," *New York Times,* Sept. 16, 1999 (see http://www.nytimes.com/library/national/091699guns-overview.html).

CHAPTER 11

1. J. W. Cecil Turner, *Kenny's Outlines of Criminal Law,* 2d ed. (Cambridge, Mass.: Cambridge University Press, 1958), p. 238.

2. Jerome Hall, *Theft, Law, and Society* (Indianapolis: Bobbs-Merrill, 1935).

3. Uniform Crime Reports, 2007, http://www.fbi.gov/ucr/cius2007/offenses/property_crime/larceny-theft.html.

4. U.S. Department of Justice, Bureau of Justice Statistics, *Criminal Victimization 2003* (Washington, D.C.: U.S. Government Printing Office, 2004), p. 2.

5. Uniform Crime Reports, 2007, http://www.fbi.gov/ucr/cius2007/offenses/property_crime/larceny-theft.html.

6. See Abraham S. Blumberg, "Typologies of Criminal Behavior," in *Current Perspectives on Criminal Behavior,* 2d ed., ed. Blumberg (New York: Knopf, 1981).

7. See John Hepburn, "Occasional Criminals," in *Major Forms of Crime,* ed. Robert Meier (Beverly Hills, Calif.: Sage, 1984), pp. 73–94; and John Gibbs and Peggy Shelly, "Life in the Fast Lane: A Retrospective View by Commercial Thieves," *Journal of Research in Crime and Delinquency,* **19** (1982): 299–330, at p. 327.

8. James Inciardi, "Professional Thief," in Meier, *Major Forms of Crime,* p. 224. See also Harry King and William Chambliss, *Box Man—A Professional Thief's Journal* (New York: Harper & Row, 1972).

9. *The Professional Thief,* annotated and interpreted by Edwin H. Sutherland (Chicago: University of Chicago Press, 1937).

10. Jo-Ann Ray, "Every Twelfth Shopper: Who Shoplifts and Why?" *Social Casework,* **68** (1987): 234–239. For a discussion of who gets caught and what kinds of treatment programs exist, see Gail A. Caputo, "A Program of Treatment for Adult Shoplifters," *Journal of Offender Rehabilitation,* **27** (1998): 123–137.

11. Abigail Buckle and David P. Farrington, "An Observational Study of Shoplifting," *British Journal of Criminology,* **24** (1984): 63–73.

12. Donald Hartmann, Donna Gelfand, Brent Page, and Patrice Walder, "Rates of Bystander Observation and Reporting of Contrived Shoplifting Incidents," *Criminology,* **10** (1972): 247–267.

13. *1998–1999 Retail Theft Trends Report: Executive Summary* (Winter Park, Fla.: Loss Prevention Specialists, 1999).

14. P. James Carolin Jr., "Survey of Shoplifters," *Security Management,* **36** (1992): 11–12.

15. From "Theft surveys," http://www.hayesinternational.com/thft_srvys.html.

16. Mary Owen Cameron, *The Booster and the Snitch* (New York: Free Press, 1964). See also John Rosecrance, "The Stooper: A Professional Thief in the Sutherland Manner," *Criminology,* **24** (1986): 29–40.

17. Richard Moore, "Shoplifting in Middle America: Patterns and Motivational Correlates," *International Journal of Offender Therapy and Comparative Criminology,* **28** (1984): 53–64. See also Charles A. Sennewald and John H. Christman, *Shoplifting* (Boston: Butterworth-Heinemann, 1992).

18. Trevor N. Gibbens, C. Palmer, and Joyce Prince, "Mental Health Aspects of Shoplifting," *British Medical Journal,* **3** (1971): 612–615.

19. *1998–1999 Retail Theft Trends Report.*

20. Ibid.

21. Barry Poyner and Ruth Woodall, *Preventing Shoplifting: A Study in Oxford Street* (London: Police Foundation, 1987).

22. John Carroll and Frances Weaver, "Shoplifters' Perceptions of Crime Opportunities: A Process-Tracing Study," in *The Reasoning Criminal,* ed. Derek Cornish and Ronald V. Clarke (New York: Springer Verlag, 1986), pp. 19–38.

23. Joshua Bamfield, "Retail Civil Recovery: Filling a Deficit in the Criminal Justice System?" *International Journal of Risk Security and Crime Prevention,* **3** (1998): 257–267.

24. Truc-Nhu Ho, "Prevention of Art Theft at Commercial Art Galleries," *Studies on Crime and Crime Prevention,* **7** (1998): 213–219. See also "FBI—Major Investigations—National Stolen Art File" (http://www.fbi.gov/majcases/arttheft/art.htm).

25. See Truc-Nhu Ho, *Art Theft in New York City: An Exploratory Study in Crime Specificity,* Ph.D. dissertation, Rutgers University, 1992; and Christopher Dickey, "Missing Masterpieces," *Newsweek,* May 29, 1989, pp. 65–68.

26. Truc-Nhu Ho, "Prevention of Art Theft at Commercial Galleries."

27. Winnie Hu, "11 Arrested in Video Piracy Crackdown," *New York Times,* Aug. 21, 1999, p. B3.

28. Truc-Nhu Ho, "Prevention of Art Theft at Commercial Art Galleries."

29. Uniform Crime Reports, 2007, http://www.fbi.gov/ucr/cius2007/offenses/property_crime/motor_vehicle_theft.html.

30. Ibid.

31. Ibid.

32. See Charles McCaghy, Peggy Giordano, and Trudy Knicely Henson, "Auto Theft," *Criminology,* **15** (1977): 367–385.

33. See http://www.lojack.com/theft.htm.

34. National Insurance Crime Bureau, "Vehicle Theft Booming in Port and Border Communities; People Should Be More Vigilant Than Ever, Warns NICB," press release, Apr. 30, 2002 (http://www.nicb.org/services/notspotsrelease.html).

35. Kevin Blake, "What You Should Know about Car Theft," *Consumer's Research* (October 1995): 26–28.

36. See http://www.ojp.usdoj.gov/bjs/abstract/c02.htm.

37. Eric Peters, "Anti–Car Theft System Starts in Virginia: D.C., Maryland Next," *Washington Times*, Aug. 13, 1993, p. G2.

38. Lawman Armor Corporation, *New BRAKEthrough Anti-Theft Device from Lawman Armor Corporation Puts the Brakes on Auto Theft*, press release, Sept. 16, 1999 (http://www.biz.yahoo.com/prnews/990917/pa_lawman_1.html).

39. See "The Silent Scorpion" (http://www.carjacking.com).

40. See "The Watch Your Car Program" (http://www.ojp.usdoj.gov/BJA/html/wycfaq.htm).

41. Ronald V. Clarke, "Situational Crime Prevention: Theoretical Basis and Practical Scope," in *Crime and Justice: An Annual Review of Research*, vol. 4, ed. Michael Tonry and Norval Morris (Chicago: University of Chicago Press, 1983).

42. Jeffrey Peck, G. O. W. Mueller, and Freda Adler, "The Vulnerability of Ports and Marinas to Vessel and Equipment Theft," *Security Journal*, 5 (1994): 146–153.

43. Edwin Lemert, "An Isolation and Closure Theory of Naive Check Forgery," *Journal of Criminal Law, Criminology, and Police Science*, 44 (1953–1954): 296–307.

44. Johannes Knutsson and Eckart Kuhlhorn, "Macro Measures against Crime: The Example of Check Forgeries," in *Situational Crime Prevention: Successful Case Studies*, 2d ed., ed. Ronald V. Clarke (Albany, N.Y.: Harrow and Heston, 1997).

45. W. A. Watts, "Credit Card Fraud: Policing Plastic," *Journal of Financial Crime*, 7 (1999): 67–69.

46. See http://www.ic3.gov/media/annualreports.aspx.

47. Michael Levi and Jim Handley, *A Research and Statistics Directorate Report: The Prevention of Plastic and Cheque Fraud Revisited* (London: Home Office, 1998).

48. Ibid.

49. Leonard Sloane, "Rising Fraud Worrying Car Insurers," *New York Times*, Nov. 16, 1991, p. 48.

50. Michael Clarke, "The Control of Insurance Fraud," *British Journal of Criminology*, 30 (1990): 1–23.

51. Sloane, "Rising Fraud Worrying Car Insurers."

52. Edmund J. Pankan and Frank E. Krzeszowski, "Putting a Claim on Insurance Fraud," *Security Management*, 37 (1993): 91–94.

53. P. Jesilow, H. N. Pontell, and G. Geis, "Physician Immunity from Prosecution and Punishment for Medical Program Fraud," in *Punishment and Privilege*, ed. W. B. Groves and G. R. Newman (New York: N.Y. Harrow and Heston, 1987), p. 8.

54. H. N. Pontell, P. Jesilow, and G. Geis, "Policing Physicians: Practitioner Fraud and Abuse in a Government Medical Program," *Social Problems*, 30 (1982): 117–125.

55. See Yahoo! News, Sept. 15, 1999 (http://www.dailynews.yahoo.com).

56. Larry E. Coutorie, "The Future of High-Technology Crime: A Parallel Delphi Study," *Journal of Criminal Justice*, 23 (1995): 13–27.

57. "Survey Finds Computer Crime Widespread in Corporate America," *The News and Observer*, Raleigh, N.C., Oct. 25, 1995.

58. Natalie D. Voss, "Crime on the Internet," *Jones Telecommunications and Multimedia Encyclopedia*, Drive D:\Studios, Jones Digital Century (1996). (Found on the Internet at http://www.digitalcentury.com/encyclo/update/crime.html.)

59. Marc Goodman, "Why the Police Don't Care about Computer Crime," *Harvard Journal of Law and Technology*, 10 (1997): 465–494.

60. Richard Overill, "Denial of Service Attacks: Threats and Methodologies," *Journal of Financial Crime*, 6 (1999): 351–353.

61. See http://www.ic3.gov/media/annualreports.aspx.

62. 18 U.S.C. § 1831–1839) (2008).

63. 18 U.S.C. Sec. 1832 (2008).

64. See Yahoo! News, "Employer Beware . . . National Survey Cites Employees as Significant Contributors to Software Piracy in the Workplace," Sept. 16, 1999 (http://www.biz.yahoo.com/bw/990916/dc_bsa_1.html).

65. From Fifth Annual BSA and IDC Global Software Piracy Study. Washington, D.C.: Business Software Alliance, 2007, pp. 2, 3. Reprinted with permission.

66. Federal Bureau of Investigation.

67. Robert W. Taylor, "Computer Crime," in *Criminal Investigation*, ed. C. R. Swanson, N. C. Chamelin, and L. Tersito (New York: Random House, 1991).

68. Coutorie, "The Future of High-Technology Crime."

69. Kenneth C. Sears and Henry Weihofen, *May's Law of Crimes*, 4th ed. (Boston: Little, Brown, 1948), pp. 307–317.

70. See http://www.fbi.gov/ucr/cius2007/offenses/property_crime/burglary.html.

71. Neal Shover, "Structures and Careers in Burglary," *Journal of Criminal Law and Criminology*, 63 (1972): 540–549.

72. Scott Decker, Richard Wright, Allison Redfern, and Dietrich Smith, "A Woman's Place Is in the Home: Females and Residential Burglary," *Justice Quarterly*, 10 (1993): 143–162.

73. Darrell Steffensmeier, *The Fence: In the Shadow of Two Worlds* (Totowa, N.J.: Rowman & Littlefield, 1986), p. 7.

74. Carl Klockars, *The Professional Fence* (New York: Free Press, 1976), pp. 110, 113.

75. D'Aunn Webster Avary, Paul F. Cromwell, and James N. Olson, "Marketing Stolen Property: Burglars and Their Fences," paper presented at the 1988 Annual Meeting of the American Society of Criminology, Reno, Nev.

76. Uniform Crime Reports, 2004, p. 62.

77. Patrick G. Jackson, "Assessing the Validity of Official Data on Arson," *Criminology*, 26 (1988): 181–195.

78. Uniform Crime Reports, 2004, p. 62.

79. See Crime in the United States 2007 (Washington, D.C.: Department of Justice, 2008), available at http://www.fbi.gov/ucr/07cius.htm.

80. Irving Kaufman and Lora W. Heims, "A Reevaluation of the Dynamics of Firesetting," *American Journal of Orthopsychiatry*, 31 (1961): 123–136.

81. Rebecca K. Hersch, *A Look at Juvenile Firesetter Programs*, for U.S. Department of Justice, Office of Justice Programs, Office of Juvenile Justice and Delinquency Prevention (Washington, D.C.: U.S. Government Printing Office, May 1989).

82. Wayne S. Wooden and Martha Lou Berkey, *Children and Arson* (New York: Plenum, 1984), p. 3.

83. See Jessica Gaynor and Chris Hatcher, *The Psychology of Child Firesetting* (New York: Brunner/Mazel, 1987).

84. Howard F. Jackson, Susan Hope, and Clive Glass, "Why Are Arsonists Not Violent Offenders?" *International Journal of Offender Therapy and Comparative Criminology*, 31 (1987): 143–151.

85. See Wayne W. Bennett and Karen Matison Hess, *Investigating Arson* (Springfield, Ill.: Charles C Thomas, 1984), pp. 34–38.

86. John M. Macdonald, *Bombers and Firesetters* (Springfield, Ill.: Charles C Thomas, 1977), pp. 198–204.

87. See Federal Emergency Management Agency, U.S. Fire Administration, *Interviewing and Counseling Juvenile Firesetters* (Washington, D.C.: U.S. Government Printing Office, 1979).

88. Clifford L. Karchmer, *Preventing Arson Epidemics: The Role of Early Warning Strategies,* Aetna Arson Prevention Series (Hartford, Conn.: Aetna Life & Casualty, 1981).

89. "Third United Nations Survey of Crime Trends, Operations of Criminal Justice Systems and Crime Prevention Strategies," A/CONF. 144/6, July 27, 1990.

CHAPTER 12

1. Federal Bureau of Investigation, *Financial Crimes Report to the Public, Fiscal Year 2007;* available at http://www.fbi.gov/publications/financial/fcs_report2007/financial_crime_2007.htm.

2. Marshall B. Clinard and Peter C. Yeager, *Corporate Crime* (New York: Free Press, 1980), pp. 59–60.

3. Sally S. Simpson, "Strategy, Structure, and Corporate Crime: The Historical Context of Anticompetitive Behavior," in *Advances in Criminological Theory,* vol. 4, ed. Freda Adler and William S. Laufer (New Brunswick, N.J.: Transaction, 1993), pp. 71–93. See also Melissa Baucus and Terry Moorehead-Dworkin, "What Is Corporate Crime? It Is Not Illegal Corporate Behavior," *Law and Policy,* 13 (1991): 231–244; and Ron Boostrom, *Enduring Issues in Criminology* (San Diego, Calif.: Greenhaven Press, 1995).

4. Edwin H. Sutherland, "White Collar Criminality," *American Sociological Review,* 5 (1940): 1–20.

5. Gilbert Geis, *On White Collar Crime* (Lexington, Mass.: Lexington Books, 1982), p. 9.

6. Marshall B. Clinard and Richard Quinney, *Criminal Behavior Systems,* 2d ed. (New York: Holt, Rinehart & Winston, 1982); Marshall B. Clinard, *Corporate Corruption: The Abuse of Power* (Westport, Conn.: Praeger, 1990); Gilbert Geis and Paul Jesilow, eds., "White-Collar Crime," *Annals of the American Academy of Political and Social Science,* 525 (1993): 8–169; David Weisburd, Stanton Wheeler, and Elin Waring, *Crimes of the Middle Classes: White-Collar Offenders in the Federal Courts* (New Haven, Conn.: Yale University Press, 1991); John Braithwaite, "Poverty, Power, White-Collar Crime and the Paradoxes of Criminological Theory," *Australian and New Zealand Journal of Criminology,* 24 (1991): 40–48; Frank Pearce and Laureen Snider, eds., "Crimes of the Powerful," *Journal of Human Justice,* 3 (1992): 1–124; Hazel Croall, *White Collar Crime: Criminal Justice and Criminology* (Buckingham, England: Open University Press, 1991); Stephen J. Rackmill, "Understanding and Sanctioning the White Collar Offender," *Federal Probation,* 56 (1992): 26–33; Brent Fisse, Michael Bersten, and Peter Grabosky, "White Collar and Corporate Crime," *University of New South Wales Law Journal,* 13 (1990): 1–171; Susan P. Shapiro, "Collaring the Crime Not the Criminal: Reconsidering the Concept of White-Collar Crime," *American Sociological Review,* 55 (1990): 346–365; Kip Schlegel and David Weisburd, eds., *White-Collar Crime Reconsidered* (Boston: Northeastern University Press, 1992); David Weisburd, Ellen F. Chayet, and Elin J. Waring, "White-Collar Crime and Criminal Careers: Some Preliminary Findings," *Crime and Delinquency,* 36 (1990): 342–355; David Weisburd, Elin Waring, and Stanton Wheeler, "Class, Status, and the Punishment of White-Collar Criminals," *Law and Social Inquiry,* 15 (1990): 223–243; Lisa Maher and Elin J. Waring, "Beyond Simple Differences: White Collar Crime, Gender and Workforce Position," *Phoebe,* 2 (1990): 44–54; John Hagan and Fiona Kay, "Gender and Delinquency in White-Collar Families: A Power-Control Perspective," *Crime and Delinquency,* 36 (1990): 391–407.

7. See James W. Coleman, *The Criminal Elite: The Sociological White-Collar Crime,* 2d ed. (New York: St. Martin's Press, 1989); and Michael L. Benson and Elizabeth Moore, "Are White-Collar and Common Offenders the Same? An Empirical and Theoretical Critique of a Recently Proposed General Theory of Crime," *Journal of Research in Crime and Delinquency,* 29 (1992): 251–272. See also Lori A. Elis and Sally S. Simpson, "Informal Sanction Threats and Corporate Crime: Additive versus Multiplicative Models," *Journal of Research in Crime and Delinquency,* 32 (1995): 399–424. For a view of white-collar offending in which the risks and rewards are considered by potential offenders, see David Weisburd, Elin Waring, and Ellen Chayet, "Specific Deterrence in a Sample of Offenders Convicted of White-Collar Crimes," *Criminology,* 33 (1995): 587–605.

8. Not only are governments at all levels victimized by corporate crimes, governments of all nations are also victimized; see Karlhans Liebl, "Developing Trends in Economic Crime in the Federal Republic of Germany," *Police Studies,* 8 (1985): 149–162. See also Jurg Gerber and Susan L. Weeks, "Women as Victims of Corporate Crime: A Call for Research on a Neglected Topic," *Deviant Behavior,* 13 (1992): 325–347; and Elizabeth Moore and Michael Mills, "The Neglected Victims and Unexamined Costs of White-Collar Crime," *Crime and Delinquency,* 36 (1990): 408–418.

9. August Bequai, *White Collar Crime: A 20th-Century Crisis* (Lexington, Mass.: Lexington Books, 1978), p. 3; Linda Ganzini, Bentson McFarland, and Joseph Bloom, "Victims of Fraud: Comparing Victims of White Collar and Violent Crime," *Bulletin of the American Academy of Psychiatry and the Law,* 18 (1990): 55–63.

10. For the relationship between patterns of crimes in the savings and loan industry and those in organized crime, see Kitty Calavita and Henry N. Pontell, "Savings and Loan Fraud as Organized Crime: Toward a Conceptual Typology of Corporate Illegality," *Criminology,* 31 (1993): 519–548.

11. For an international perspective on consumer fraud, see U.S. Senate Committee on Governmental Affairs, *International Consumer Fraud: Can Consumers Be Protected?* (Washington, D.C.: U.S. Government Printing Office, 1994); Gilbert Geis, Henry N. Pontell, and Paul Jesilow, "Medicaid Fraud," in *Controversial Issues in Criminology and Criminal Justice,* ed. Joseph E. Scott and Travis Hirschi (Beverly Hills, Calif.: Sage, 1987); and Maria S. Boss and Barbara Crutchfield George, "Challenging Conventional Views of White Collar Crime: Should the Criminal Justice System Be Refocused?" *Criminal Law Bulletin,* 28 (1992): 32–58. See also Richard M. Titus, Fred Heinzelmann, and John M. Boyle, "Victimization of Persons by Fraud," *Crime and Delinquency,* 41 (1995): 54–72. For a description of fraud in an organizational setting presented from the perspective of the perpetrator, fellow employees, and the organization itself, see Steve W. Albrecht, Gerald W. Wernz, and Timothy L. Williams, *Fraud: Bringing Light to the Dark Side of Business* (Burr Ridge, Ill.: Irwin Professional Publishing, 1995).

12. For an outline of a general theory of crime causation applicable to both street crime and white-collar crime,

see Travis Hirschi and Michael Gottfredson, "Causes of White-Collar Crime," *Criminology,* **25** (1987): 949–974; James W. Coleman, "Toward an Integrated Theory of White Collar Crime," *American Journal of Sociology,* **93** (1987): 406–439; and James R. Lasley, "Toward a Control Theory of White Collar Offending," *Journal of Quantitative Criminology,* **4** (1988): 347–362.

13. Donald R. Cressey, "The Poverty of Theory in Corporate Crime Research," in *Advances in Criminological Theory,* vol. 1, ed. William Laufer and Freda Adler (New Brunswick, N.J.: Transaction, 1989); for a response, see John Braithwaite and Brent Fisse, "On the Plausibility of Corporate Crime Theory," in *Advances in Criminological Theory,* vol. 2, ed. William Laufer and Freda Adler (New Brunswick, N.J.: Transaction, 1990). See also Travis Hirschi and Michael Gottfredson, "The Significance of White-Collar Crime for a General Theory of Crime," *Criminology,* **27** (1989): 359–371; and Darrell Steffensmeier, "On the Causes of 'White Collar' Crime: An Assessment of Hirschi and Gottfredson's Claims," *Criminology,* **27** (1989): 345–358.

14. Bequai, *White Collar Crime.* Bequai also includes antitrust and environmental offenses, which are corporate crimes, discussed in the next section.

15. Kenneth Polk and William Weston, "Insider Trading as an Aspect of White Collar Crime," *Australian and New Zealand Journal of Criminology,* **23** (1990): 24–38. In a report before Congress, insider trading scandals were said to have cost the securities industry nearly half a billion dollars in the early 1970s; see U.S. Congress House Select Committee on Crime, *Conversion of Worthless Securities into Cash* (Washington, D.C.: U.S. Government Printing Office, 1973). For a review of the insider trading that persists on Wall Street, see Gene G. Marcial, *Secrets of the Street: The Dark Side of Making Money* (New York: McGraw-Hill, 1995); Martin Mayer, *Nightmare on Wall Street: Salomon Brothers and the Corruption of the Marketplace* (New York: Simon & Schuster, 1993); Nancy Reichman, "Insider Trading," in *Beyond the Law: Crime in Complex Organizations,* eds. Michael Tonry and Albert J. Reiss Jr. (Chicago: University of Chicago Press, 1993).

16. For a more extensive review of the Wedtech debacle, see Mark S. Hamm, "From Wedtech and Iran-Contra to the Riots at Oakdale and Atlanta: On the Ethics and Public Performance of Edwin Meese III," *Journal of Crime and Justice,* **14** (1991): 123–147; Marilyn W. Thompson, *Feeding the Beast: How Wedtech Became the Most Corrupt Little Company in America* (New York: Charles Scribner's Sons, 1990); and William Power, "New York Rep. Biaggi and Six Others Indicted as Wedtech Scandal Greatly Expands," *The Wall Street Journal,* June 4, 1987, p. 9.

17. See http://www.fas.org/man/gao/gao9621.htm.

18. For a discussion of the many ways in which a person may be defrauded, see Phil Berger and Craig Jacob, *Twisted Genius: Confessions of a $10 Million Scam Man* (New York: Four Walls Eight Windows, 1995). For an Australian perspective of fraud, see M. Kapardis and A. Kapardis, "Co-regulation of Fraud Detection and Reporting by Auditors in Australia: Criminology's Lessons for Non-compliance," *Australian and New Zealand Journal of Criminology,* **28** (1995): 193–212.

19. Bequai, *White Collar Crime,* pp. 70–71.

20. For a European perspective on insurance fraud, with a particular focus on the enforcement activities in France and Belgium, see Andre Lemaitre, Rolf Lemaitre, Rolf Arnold, and Roger Litton, "Insurance and Crime," *European Journal on Criminal Policy,* **3** (1995): 7–92. For a description of insurance fraud prevalent in the American insurance industry, see Kenneth D. Myers, *False Security: Greed & Deception in America's Multibillion-Dollar Insurance Industry* (Amherst, N.Y.: Prometheus Books, 1995); and Andrew Tobias, *The Invisible Banker* (New York: Washington Square Press, 1982).

21. Paul E. Tracy and James A. Fox, "A Field Experiment on Insurance Fraud in Auto Body Repair," *Criminology,* **27** (1989): 589–603.

22. Kathleen F. Brickey, *Corporate Criminal Liability,* 2 vols. (Wilmette, Ill.: Callaghan, 1984). See also Thomas Gabor, *Everybody Does It! Crime by the Public* (Toronto: University of Toronto Press, 1994). For a uniquely British perspective, see Doreen McBarnet, "Whiter Than White Collar Crime: Tax, Fraud, Insurance and the Management of Stigma," *British Journal of Sociology,* **42** (1991): 323–344.

23. Alan Murray, "IRS Is Losing Battle against Tax Evaders Despite Its New Gain," *The Wall Street Journal,* Apr. 10, 1984, p. 1.

24. Ralph Salerno and John S. Tompkins, "Protecting Organized Crime," in *Theft of the City,* ed. John A. Gardiner and David Olson (Bloomington: Indiana University Press, 1984); Edwin Sutherland, *The Professional Thief* (Chicago: University of Chicago Press, 1937).

25. 18 U.S.C. § 166(b) and (c).

26. Bequai, *White Collar Crime,* p. 45.

27. Ibid., p. 87. See Virginia Department of Social Services, *Report of the Financial Exploitation of Older Adults and Disabled Younger Adults in the Commonwealth* (Richmond, Va.: Senate Document no. 37, 1994). For steps to take to avoid being a victim of embezzlement, see Russell B. Bintliff, *Complete Manual of White Collar Crime Detection and Prevention* (Englewood Cliffs, N.J.: Prentice Hall, 1993). For a historic account of embezzlement in the United Kingdom from 1845 to 1929, see George Robb, *White Collar Crime in Modern England: Financial Fraud and Business Morality, 1845–1929* (Cambridge: Cambridge University Press, 1992).

28. John Clark and Richard Hollinger, *Theft by Employees in Work Organization* (Washington, D.C.: U.S. Government Printing Office, 1983).

29. Bequai, *White Collar Crime,* p. 89.

30. M. David Ermann and Richard J. Lundman, "Corporate and Governmental Deviance: Origins, Patterns, and Reactions," in *Corporate and Governmental Deviance: Problems of Organizational Behavior in Contemporary Society,* 3d ed., ed. M. David Ermann and Richard J. Lundman (New York: Oxford University Press, 1996). A school of thought holds that corporations, unlike people, have no personality, no conscience, and no shame. See, for example, Thomas Donaldson, *Corporations and Morality* (Englewood Cliffs, N.J.: Prentice-Hall, 1982); Donald R. Cressey, "The Poverty of Theory in Corporate Crime Research," in *Advances in Criminological Theory,* vol 1. Over 100 years ago a New York court in *Darlington v. The Mayor,* 31 N.Y. 164 (1865), observed: "A corporation, as such, has no human wants to be supplied. It cannot eat, drink, or wear clothing, or live in houses." Steven Walt and William S. Laufer, "Corporate Criminal Liability and the Comparative Mix of Sanctions," in *White-Collar Crime Reconsidered,* ed. Kip Schlegel and David

Weisburd (Boston: Northeastern University Press, 1992), describe corporations as being given a life and a moral personhood that clouds the distinction between crimes attributable to individuals (hourly employees, line managers, corporate officers, etc.) and those attributable to the corporate entity. See also John Braithwaite and Brent Fisse, "On the Plausibility of Corporate Crime Theory," in *Advances in Criminological Theory,* vol. 2.

31. William S. Laufer, "Corporate Bodies and Guilty Minds," *Emory Law Journal,* **43** (1994): 647, 651–58 (discusses origins of corporate criminal liability).

32. See generally Richard S. Gruner, *Corporate Crime and Sentencing* (Charlottesville, Va.: Michie, 1994).

33. William S. Laufer, "Corporate Liability, Risk Shifting, and the Paradox of Compliance," *Vanderbilt Law Review,* **52** (1999): 1343.

34. William S. Laufer, "Culpability and the Sentencing of Corporations," *Nebraska Law Review,* **71** (1992): 1049.

35. Marshall Clinard, Peter C. Yeager, Jeanne Brissette, David Petrashek, and Elizabeth Harries, *Illegal Corporate Behavior* (Washington, D.C.: U.S. Government Printing Office, 1979).

36. Nearly a century ago, D. R. Richberg asked the question, "Should it not be the effort of all legislation dealing with corporations, to place them as nearly as possible on a plane of equal responsibility with individuals?" D. R. Richberg, "The Imprisonment of the Corporation," *Case and Comment,* **18** (1912): 512–529. Saul M. Pilchen discovered that although notions of corporate criminal culpability have been broadened over the years, initial prosecutions under the federal sentencing guidelines for organizations generally have been limited in scope. Saul M. Pilchen, "When Corporations Commit Crimes: Sentencing under the Federal Organizational Guidelines," *Judicature,* **78** (1995): 202–206. See Daniel R. Fischel and Alan O. Sykes, "Corporate Crime," *Journal of Legal Studies,* **xxv** (1996): 319–349. Ronald L. Dixon believes, "No corporation should be unaware of these statutes or of the theories upon which criminal liability can be established. Corporations must realize that no one is immune from criminal liability, and corporate practices must reflect this fact." Ronald L. Dixon, "Corporate Criminal Liability," in *Corporate Misconduct: The Legal, Societal, and Management Issues,* ed. Margaret P. Spencer and Ronald R. Sims (Westport, Conn.: Quorum Books, 1995). For a British perspective on corporate liability, see "Great Britain, The Law Commission," in *Criminal Law: Involuntary Manslaughter: A Consultation Paper,* no. 135 (London: Her Majesty's Stationery Office, 1994). For a general overview of the corporate crime problem, see Francis T. Cullen, William J. Maakestad, and Gray Cavender, *Corporate Crime under Attack: The Ford Pinto Case and Beyond* (Cincinnati: Anderson, 1987), pp. 37–99.

37. Sherman Antitrust Act, Act of July 2, 1890, c. 647, 26 Stat. 209, 15 U.S.C. §§ 1–7 (1976).

38. Clayton Antitrust Act, Act of Oct. 15, 1914, c. 322, 38 Stat. 730, 15 U.S.C. §§ 12–27 (1976); Robinson-Patman Act, Act of June 19, 1936, c. 592, § 1, 49 Stat. 1526, 15 U.S.C. § 13(a) (1973). See also Brickey, *Corporate Criminal Liability.*

39. Phillip Knightly, Harold Evans, Elaine Potter, and Marjorie Wallace, *Suffer the Children: The Story of Thalidomide* (New York: Viking, 1979).

40. The Ford Pinto case is fully described in Cullen et al., *Corporate Crime under Attack.* For more information

on crimes against consumer safety, see Raymond J. Michalowski, *Order, Law, and Crime* (New York: Random House, 1985), pp. 334–340. For a description of corporate greed in its most vile form, see James S. Kunen, *Reckless Disregard: Corporate Greed, Government Indifference, and the Kentucky School Bus Crash* (New York: Simon & Schuster, 1994).

41. For an examination of corporate criminality in the United States and the response of the criminal justice system of America, see Spencer and Sims, *Corporate Misconduct.* See also Russell Mokhiber, *Corporate Crime and Violence: Big Business Power and the Abuse of the Public Trust* (San Francisco: Sierra Club, 1988); Susan P. Shapiro, *Wayward Capitalists: Target of the Securities and Exchange Commission* (New Haven, Conn.: Yale University Press, 1984); M. David Ermann and Richard J. Lundman, *Corporate and Governmental Deviance: Problems of Organizational Behavior in Contemporary Society,* 2d ed. (New York: Oxford University Press, 1982); Cullen et al., *Corporate Crime under Attack;* Knightly et al., *Suffer the Children;* and W. Byron Groves and Graeme Newman, *Punishment and Privilege* (New York: Harrow & Heston, 1986).

42. See Edwin Sutherland, *White Collar Crime* (New York: Dryden, 1949). Sutherland had earlier published articles on the topic, including "White Collar Criminality" and "Is White Collar Crime 'Crime'?" *American Sociological Review,* **10** (1945): 132–139.

43. See Gary E. Reed and Peter Cleary Yeager, "Organizational Offending and Neoclassical Criminology: Challenging the Reach of a General Theory of Crime," *Criminology,* **34** (1996): 357–382; and Clinard and Yeager, *Corporate Crime,* p. 116. See also Peter C. Yeager, "Analysing Corporate Offences: Progress and Prospects," *Research in Corporate Social Performance and Policy,* **8** (1986): 93–120. For similar findings in Canada, see Colin H. Goff and Charles E. Reasons, *Corporate Crime in Canada* (Scarborough, Ontario: Prentice-Hall, 1978).

44. Richard Quinney, *Critique of Legal Order: Crime Control in Capitalist Society* (Boston: Little, Brown, 1974); Richard Quinney, *Class, State, and Crime: On the Theory and Practice of Criminal Justice* (New York: David McKay, 1977); Ian Taylor, Paul Walton, and Jock Young, *The New Criminology: For a Social Theory of Deviance* (London: Routledge & Kegan Paul, 1973); William Chambliss and Robert Seidman, *Law, Order, and Power,* 2d ed. (Reading, Mass.: Addison-Wesley, 1982).

45. James Q. Wilson, *Thinking about Crime* (New York: Basic Books, 1975). For a competing school of thought, see Gilbert Geis, "Criminal Penalties for Corporate Criminals," *Criminal Law Bulletin,* **8** (1972): 377–392; Chamber of Commerce of the United States, *White Collar Crime* (Washington, D.C.: U.S. Government Printing Office, 1974); John Collins Coffee Jr., "Beyond the Shut-Eyed Sentry: Toward a Theoretical View of Corporate Misconduct and an Effective Legal Response," *Virginia Law Review,* **63** (1977): 1099–1278; Gilbert Geis and Robert F. Meier, *White-Collar Crime: Offenses in Business, Politics, and the Professions* (New York: Free Press, 1977); Marshall B. Clinard, *Illegal Corporate Behavior* (Washington, D.C.: U.S. Government Printing Office, 1979); Miriam S. Saxon, *White-Collar Crime: The Problem and the Federal Response* (Report no. 80-84 EPW, Library of Congress, Congressional Research Service, Washington, D.C., Apr. 14, 1980); and Laura S. Schrager and James F. Short Jr., "How Serious a Crime?

Perceptions of Organizational and Common Crimes," in *White-Collar Crime: Theory and Research*, ed. Gilbert Geis and Ezra Stotland (Beverly Hills, Calif.: Sage, 1980). More recent works include James W. Coleman, *The Criminal Elite: The Sociology of White-Collar Crime* (New York: St. Martin's Press, 1989); Laureen Snider, "The Regulatory Dance: Understanding Reform Processes in Corporate Crime," *International Journal of the Sociology of Law*, **19** (1991): 209–236; Kip Schlegel and David Weisburd, *White-Collar Crime: The Parallax View* (Boston: Northeastern University Press, 1993); Michael Tonry and Albert J. Reiss, *Beyond the Law: Crime in Complex Organizations* (Chicago: University of Chicago Press, 1993); and Robert Tillman and Henry Pontell, "Organizations and Fraud in the Savings and Loan Industry," *Social Forces*, **73** (1995): 1439–1463.

46. Patsy Klaus and Carol Kalish, *The Severity of Crime*, Bureau of Justice Statistics Bulletin NCJ-92326 (Washington, D.C.: U.S. Government Printing Office, 1984). See also Schrager and Short, "How Serious a Crime?"; Francis Cullen, B. Link, and C. Polanzi, "The Seriousness of Crime Revisited," *Criminology*, **20** (1982): 83–102; Francis Cullen, R. Mathers, G. Clark, and J. Cullen, "Public Support for Punishing White Collar Crime: Blaming the Victim Revisited," *Journal of Criminal Justice*, **11** (1983): 481–493; and Richard Sparks, Hazel G. Genn, and David Dodd, *Surveying Victims* (New York: Wiley, 1977).

47. Mark A. Cohen, "Environmental Crime and Punishment: Legal/Economic Theory and Empirical Evidence on Enforcement of Federal Environmental Statutes," *Journal of Criminal Law and Criminology*, **82** (1992): 1054–1108. See, for an early treatment, Timothy R. Young, "Criminal Liability under the Refuse Act of 1899 and the Refuse Act Permit Program," *Journal of Criminal Law, Criminology and Police Science*, **63** (1972): 366–376. For a global perspective on the prevention of environmental crimes, see Boon Khoo Hui, Prathan Watanavanich, Edgar Aglipay, et al., *Effective Countermeasures against Crimes Related to Urbanization and Industrialization: Urban Crime, Juvenile Delinquency and Environmental Crime* (Tokyo: Report for 1993 and Resource Material Series no. 45, UNAFEI, 1994).

48. Clinard and Yeager, *Corporate Crime*, p. 92, citing *New York Times* survey of July 15, 1979.

49. Gerhard O. W. Mueller, "Offenses against the Environment and Their Prevention: An International Appraisal," *Annals of the American Academy of Political and Social Science*, **444** (1979): 56–66.

50. 33 U.S.C. § 1251 (2001).

51. *United States v. Darling Int'l Inc.*, No. CR 4-96-162 (D. Minn. July 10, 1997) (factual basis statement, plea agreement, and sentencing stipulations on file with author); see also Barry Shanoff, "Company Incriminates Employees: Darling International." *World Wastes* **40** (1997): 64, 65 ("The Darling case is part of a pattern throughout the country. Companies under scrutiny are winning leniency for themselves by 'giving up' their employees."); Tom Meersman, "Company Fined $4 Million for Polluting," *Star Tribune*, Dec. 17, 1996, p. 1B ("[S]ome of the most serious charges resulted from the company 'blowing the whistle on itself.'"); and Dean Starkman, "Pollution Case Highlights Trend to Let Employees Take the Rap," *The Wall Street Journal*, Oct. 9, 1997, p. B10 ("What happened in the Darling case is being repeated across the country. Corporations under

government investigation are increasingly turning on their employees to win leniency for themselves.")

52. Defendant's Sentencing Memorandum, at 8–9 (on file with author).

53. Mueller, "Offenses against the Environment," p. 60.

54. Ryuichi Hirano, "The Criminal Law Protection of Environment: General Report," Tenth International Congress of Comparative Law, Budapest, 1978. For a discussion of the problems of multinational corporations operating in developing countries, see Richard Schaffer, Beverly Earle, and Filiberto Agusti, *International Business Law and Its Environment*, 2d ed. (St. Paul, Minn.: West, 1993). For a discussion of corporate crime in Japan, see Harold R. Kerbo and Mariko Inoue, "Japanese Social Structure and White Collar Crime: Recruit Cosmos and Beyond," *Deviant Behavior*, **11** (1990): 139–154.

55. Kerbo and Inoue, "Japanese Social Structure and White Collar Crime."

56. John Braithwaite, "Challenging Just Deserts: Punishing White-Collar Criminals," *Journal of Criminal Law and Criminology*, **73** (1982): 723–763; Stanton Wheeler, David Weisburd, and Nancy Boden, "Sentencing the White-Collar Offender," *American Sociological Review*, **47** (1982): 641–659. For a thoughtful analysis of corporate illegality, see Nancy Frank and Michael Lombness, *Corporate Illegality and Regulatory Justice* (Cincinnati: Anderson, 1988); Kip Schlegel, *Just Deserts for Corporate Criminals* (Boston: Northeastern University Press, 1990); and John C. Coffee Jr., Mark A. Cohen, Jonathan R. Macey, et al., "A National Conference on Sentencing of the Corporation," *Boston University Law Review*, **71** (1991): 189–453.

57. Sally S. Simpson and Christopher S. Koper, "Deterring Corporate Crime," *Criminology*, **30** (1992): 347–375; Genevra Richardson, *Policing Pollution: A Study of Regulation and Enforcement* (Oxford: Clarendon, 1982); Albert J. Reiss and Albert D. Biderman, *Data Sources on White-Collar Law-Breaking* (Washington, D.C.: National Institute of Justice, 1980); Susan Shapiro, "Detecting Illegalities: A Perspective on the Control of Securities Violations," Ph.D. dissertation, Yale University (University Microfilms), 1980. See also Brian Widlake, *Serious Fraud Office* (London: Little, Brown, 1995).

58. Dan Magnuson, ed., *Economic Crime: Programs for Future Research* (Stockholm: National Council for Crime Prevention, 1985); Michael L. Benson, Francis T. Cullen, and William A. Maakestad, *Local Prosecutors and Corporate Crime: Final Report* (Washington, D.C.: National Institute of Justice, 1991); Michael L. Benson, Francis T. Cullen, and William J. Maakestad, "Local Prosecutors and Corporate Crime," *Crime and Delinquency*, **36** (1990): 356–372.

CHAPTER 13

1. Carmen Sesin, "Caring for 'drug mules' who perish on the job," MSNBC, May 25, 2004; available at http://www.msnbc.msn.com/id/5050399/.

2. Arthur Santana, "For Liz, a Heroin User, Time Is Running Out—Health Officials Estimate 15,000 Addicts in King County," *Seattle Times*, July 12, 1999, p. B1.

3. David Heinzmann, "Violence No Stranger Where Boy Shot; 4-Year-Old Victim of Gun Battle in Good Condition," *Chicago Tribune*, Oct. 9, 1999, p. 5. See also Robert C. Davis and Arthur J. Lurigio, *Fighting Back: Neighborhood Antidrug Strategies* (Thousand Oaks, Calif.: Sage, 1996); Bureau of Justice Statistics, *Guns Used in*

Crime (Washington, D.C.: U.S. Department of Justice, 1995); and Susan J. Popkin, Lynn M. Olson, Arthur J. Lurigio, et al., "Sweeping Out Drugs and Crime: Residents' Views of the Chicago Housing Authority's Public Housing Drug Elimination Program," *Journal of Research in Crime and Delinquency,* **41** (1995): 73–99.

4. Mark D. Merlin, *On the Trail of the Ancient Opium Poppy* (Rutherford, N.J.: Fairleigh Dickinson University Press, 1984). For a historic account of alcohol consumption, see Harvey A. Siegal and James A. Inciardi, "A Brief History of Alcohol," in *The American Drug Scene: An Anthology,* ed. James A. Inciardi and Karen McElrath (Los Angeles: Roxbury, 1995).

5. Howard Abadinsky, *Drug Abuse: An Introduction* (Chicago: Nelson Hall, 1989), pp. 30–31, 54. For the medicinal benefits of marijuana, see Lester Grinspoon and James Bakalar, "Marijuana: The Forbidden Medicine," in Inciardi and McElrath, *The American Drug Scene.*

6. Michael D. Lyman, *Narcotics and Crime Control* (Springfield, Ill.: Charles C Thomas, 1987), p. 8. See also F. E. Oliver, "The Use and Abuse of Opium," in *Yesterday's Addicts: American Society and Drug Abuse, 1865–1920,* ed. H. Wayne Morgan (Norman: University of Oklahoma Press, 1974).

7. W. Z. Guggenheim, "Heroin: History and Pharmacology," *International Journal of the Addictions,* **2** (1967): 328. For a history of heroin use in New York City, from just after the turn of the twentieth century into the late 1960s, see Edward Preble and John J. Casey, "Taking Care of Business: The Heroin Addict's Life on the Street," *International Journal of the Addictions,* **4** (1969): 1–24.

8. Abadinsky, *Drug Abuse,* p. 52.

9. Ibid., p. 56.

10. Lyman, *Narcotics and Crime Control,* p. 10.

11. Public Law 100-690, of Nov. 18, 1988, 102 Stat. 4187.

12. *2007 National Survey on Drug Use and Health: National Findings* (Washington, D.C.: Department of Health and Human Services, 2007).

13. Lisa Maher, Eloise Dunlap, Bruce D. Johnson, and Ansley Hamid, "Gender, Power, and Alternative Living Arrangements in the Inner-City Crack Culture," *Journal of Research in Crime and Delinquency,* **33** (1996): 181–205; H. Virginia McCoy, Christine Miles, and James A. Inciardi, "Survival Sex: Inner-City Women and Crack-Cocaine," in Inciardi and McElrath, *The American Drug Scene;* Jody Miller, "Gender and Power on the Streets: Street Prostitution in the Era of Crack Cocaine," *Journal of Contemporary Ethnography,* **23** (1995): 427–452; Ann Sorenson and David Brownfield, "Adolescent Drug Use and a General Theory of Crime: An Analysis of a Theoretical Integration," *Canadian Journal of Criminology,* **37** (1995): 19–37. For a summary of psychiatric approaches, see Marie Nyswander, *The Drug Addict as a Patient* (New York: Grune & Stratton, 1956), chap. 4.

14. Richard Cloward and Lloyd Ohlin, *Delinquency and Opportunity* (New York: Free Press, 1960), pp. 178–186. See also Jeffrey A. Fagan, "The Social Organization of Drug Use and Drug Dealing among Urban Gangs," *Criminology,* **27** (1989): 633–669. See also Marcia R. Chaiken, *Identifying and Responding to New Forms of Drug Abuse: Lessons Learned from "Crack" and "Ice"* (Washington, D.C.: National Institute of Justice, 1993).

15. D. F. Musto, "The History of Legislative Control over Opium, Cocaine, and Their Derivatives," in *Dealing with Drugs,* ed. Ronald Hamowy (Lexington, Mass.: Lexington Books, 1987), pp. 37–73.

16. Marsha Rosenbaum, *Women on Heroin* (New Brunswick, N.J.: Rutgers University Press, 1981), pp. 14–15; Jeannette Covington, "Theoretical Explanations of Race Differences in Heroin Use," in *Advances in Criminological Theory,* vol. 2, ed. William S. Laufer and Freda Adler (New Brunswick, N.J.: Transaction). See also U.S. Senate Judiciary Committee, Subcommittee to Investigate Juvenile Delinquency, *The Global Connection: Heroin Entrepreneurs. Hearings, July 28 and August 5, 1976* (Washington, D.C.: U.S. Government Printing Office, 1976).

17. Freda Adler, Arthur D. Moffett, Frederick G. Glaser, John C. Ball, and Diana Horwitz, *A Systems Approach to Drug Treatment* (Philadelphia: Dorrance, 1974).

18. Erich Goode, *Drugs in American Society* (New York: Basic Books, 1972). See also Ned Polsky, *Hustlers, Beats, and Others* (Chicago: Aldine, 1967).

19. Norman E. Zinberg, "The Use and Misuse of Intoxicants: Factors in the Development of Controlled Abuse," in Hamowy, *Dealing with Drugs,* p. 262.

20. Abadinsky, *Drug Abuse,* p. 53. See also, as an early treatment, Hope R. Victor, Jan Carl Grossman, and Russell Eisenman, "Openness to Experience and Marijuana Use in High School Students," *Journal of Consulting and Clinical Psychology,* **41** (1973): 78–85; U.S. Narcotics and Dangerous Drugs Bureau, *Marijuana: An Analysis of Use, Distribution and Control* (Washington, D.C.: U.S. Government Printing Office, 1971); California Department of Public Health and Welfare, Research and Statistics Section, *Five Mind-Altering Drugs: The Use of Alcoholic Beverages, Amphetamines, LSD, Marijuana, and Tobacco, Reported by High School and Junior High School Students, San Mateo County, California, Two Comparable Surveys, 1968 and 1969* (San Mateo: California Department of Public Health, 1969); Erich Goode, "Multiple Drug Use among Marijuana Smokers," *Social Problems,* **17** (1969): 48–64.

21. Bruce A. Jacobs, "Crack Dealers' Apprehension Avoidance Techniques: A Case of Restrictive Deterrence," *Justice Quarterly,* **13** (1996): 359–381; Bruce A. Jacobs, "Crack Dealers and Restrictive Deterrences: Identifying Narcs," *Criminology,* **34** (1996): 409–431; Bruce D. Johnson, Andrew Golub, and Jeffrey Fagan, "Careers in Crack, Drug Use, Drug Distribution, and Nondrug Criminality," *Journal of Crime and Delinquency,* **41** (1995): 275–295; Abadinsky, *Drug Abuse,* p. 83. See also Jeffrey A. Fagan, "Initiation into Crack and Powdered Cocaine: A Tale of Two Epidemics," *Contemporary Drug Problems,* **16** (1989): 579–618; Jeffrey A. Fagan, Joseph G. Weis, and Y. T. Cheng, "Drug Use and Delinquency among Inner City Youth," *Journal of Drug Issues,* **20** (1990): 349–400; James A. Inciardi et al., "The Crack Epidemic Revisited," *Journal of Psychoactive Drugs,* **24** (1992): 305–416; and B. D. Johnson, M. Natarajan, E. Dunlap, and E. Elmoghazy, "Crack Abusers and Noncrack Abusers: A Comparison of Drug Use, Drug Sales, and Nondrug Criminality," *Journal of Drug Issues,* **24** (1994): 117–141. Smoking crack is certainly not limited to the inner cities of America. For a description of crack use in the tropical paradise of Hawaii, see Gordon James Knowles, "Dealing Crack Cocaine: A View from the Streets of Honolulu," *The FBI Law Enforcement Bulletin,* July 1996, pp. 1–7.

22. Michael Marriott, "Potent Crack Blend on the Streets Lures a New Generation to Heroin," *New York Times,* July 13, 1989, pp. A1, B3.

23. James Inciardi, "Heroin Use and Street Crime," *Crime and Delinquency,* **25** (1979): 335–346; Bruce D. Johnson, Paul J. Goldstein, Edward Preble, James Schmeidler, Douglas S. Lyston, Barry Spunt, and Thomas Miller, *Taking Care of Business: The Economics of Crime by Heroin Abusers* (Lexington, Mass.: Heath, 1985); James Inciardi, *The War on Drugs: Heroin, Cocaine, Crime, and Public Policy* (Palo Alto, Calif.: Mayfield, 1986); Eric Wish and Bruce Johnson, "The Impact of Substance Abuse on Criminal Careers," in *Criminal Careers and Career Criminals,* ed. Alfred Blumstein, Jacqueline Cohen, Jeffrey A. Roth, and Christy A. Visher (Washington, D.C.: National Academy Press, 1986), pp. 52–58.

24. Office of National Drug Control Policy, "Drug Facts. Marijuana, 2002" (www.whitehousedrugpolicy.gov/drugfact/marijuana/index.html).

25. For a determination of the causal link between drug use and crime, see Bruce L. Benson and David W. Rasmussen, *Illicit Drugs and Crimes* (Oakland, Calif.: The Independent Institute, 1996); James A. Inciardi, Duane C. McBride, and James E. Rivers, *Drug Control and the Courts* (Thousand Oaks, Calif.: Sage, 1996); Inciardi and McElrath, *The American Drug Scene*; and Sybille M. Guy, Gene M. Smith, and P. M. Bentler, "The Influence of Adolescent Substance Use and Socialization on Deviant Behavior in Young Adulthood," *Criminal Justice and Behavior,* **21** (1994): 236–255.

26. George Speckart and M. Douglas Anglin found that criminal records preceded drug use; see their "Narcotics Use and Crime: An Overview of Recent Research Advances," *Contemporary Drug Problems,* **13** (1986): 741–769, and "Narcotics and Crime: A Causal Modeling Approach," *Journal of Quantitative Criminology,* **2** (1986): 3–28. See also Cheryl Carpenter, Barry Glassner, Bruce D. Johnson, and Julia Loughlin, *Kids, Drugs, and Crime* (Lexington, Mass.: Heath, 1988); and Louise L. Biron, Serge Brochu, and Lyne Desjardins, "The Issue of Drugs and Crime among a Sample of Incarcerated Women," *Deviant Behavior,* **16** (1995): 25–43.

27. James A. Inciardi and Anne E. Pottieger, "Kids, Crack, and Crime," *Journal of Drug Issues,* **21** (1991): 257–270; David N. Nurco, Thomas E. Hanlon, Timothy W. Kinlock, and Karen R. Duszynski, "Differential Criminal Patterns of Narcotics Addicts over an Addiction Career," *Criminology,* **26** (1988): 407–423; M. Douglas Anglin and George Speckart, "Narcotics Use and Crime: A Multisample, Multimethod Analysis," *Criminology,* **26** (1988): 197–233; M. Douglas Anglin and Yining Hser, "Addicted Women and Crime," *Criminology,* **25** (1987): 359–397.

28. Paul Goldstein, "Drugs and Violent Crime," in *Pathways to Criminal Violence,* ed. Neil Alan Weiner and Marvin E. Wolfgang (Newbury Park, Calif.: Sage, 1989), pp. 16–48.

29. Colin McMahon, "Panama's Future Uncertain as Ever; Corruption Persists in Post-Noriega Era," *Chicago Tribune,* Aug. 25, 1996, p. 17.

30. United Nations, "Commission on Narcotic Drugs, Comprehensive Review of the Activities of the United Nations Fund for Drug Abuse Control in 1985," E/CN.7/1986/ CRP.4, Feb. 4, 1986. See also Elaine Sciolino, "U.N. Report Links Drugs, Arms, and Terror," *New York Times,* Jan. 12, 1987.

31. John Warner, "Terrorism and Drug Trafficking: A Lethal Partnership," *Security Management,* **28** (1984): 44–46. See, as an early treatment, U.S. Congress, House Public Health and Environment Subcommittee, *Production and Abuse of Opiates in the Far East* (Washington, D.C.: U.S. Government Printing Office, 1971).

32. For a review of drug enforcement policies aimed directly at the users of illicit narcotics, see Richard Lawrence Miller, *Drug Warriors and Their Prey: From Police Power to Police State* (Westport, Conn.: Praeger, 1996). For a comprehensive guide to state agencies that address drug abuse concerns, see Bureau of Justice Statistics, *State Drug Resources: 1994 National Directory* (Washington, D.C.: U.S. Department of Justice, 1994).

33. James A. Inciardi, *The War on Drugs II: The Continuing Epidemic of Heroin, Cocaine, Crack, Crime, AIDS, and Public Policy* (Mountain View, Calif.: Mayfield, 1992).

34. Even before President Bush's drug initiatives, government agencies recognized the ineffectiveness of narcotic countermeasures during the 1970s; see U.S. Comptroller General, *Gains Made in Controlling Illegal Drugs, Yet the Drug Trade Flourishes* (Washington, D.C.: U.S. Government Printing Office, 1979).

35. See Rae Sibbitt, *The Ilps Methadone Prescribing Project* (London: Home Office, 1996); Paul J. Turnbull, Russell Webster, and Gary Stillwell, *Get It While You Can: An Evaluation of an Early Intervention Project for Arrestees with Alcohol and Drug Problems* (London: Home Office, 1996); Ira Sommers, Deborah R. Baskin, and Jeffrey Fagan, "Getting out of the Life: Crime Desistance by Female Street Offenders," *Deviant Behavior,* **15** (1994): 125–149; and Sandra L. Tunis, *The State of the Art in Jail Drug Treatment Programs* (San Francisco: National Council on Crime and Delinquency, 1994).

36. See Peter Finn and Andrea K. Newlyn, *Miami's "Drug Court,"* National Institute of Justice (Washington, D.C.: U.S. Government Printing Office, 1993), for Dade County; see Christopher S. Wren, "Arizona Finds Cost Savings in Treating Drug Offenders," *New York Times,* Apr. 21, 1999, for Arizona; see also Bureau of Justice Assistance, *Two Special Drug Court Models: Dedicated Drug Treatment vs. Speedy Trial and Differentiated Case Management (DCM)—The Program Concept* (Washington, D.C.: U.S. Government Printing Office, 1998); and Jonathan Alter, "The Buzz on Drugs," *Newsweek,* September 6, 1999, pp. 25–28.

37. Abadinsky, *Drug Abuse,* p. 171.

38. David N. Nurco, Norma Wegner, Philip Stephenson, Abraham Makofsky, and John W. Shaffer, *Ex-Addicts' Self-Help Groups: Potentials and Pitfalls* (New York: Praeger, 1983); Harold I. Hendler and Richard C. Stephens, "The Addict Odyssey: From Experimentation to Addiction," *International Journal of the Addictions,* **12** (1977): pp. 25–42.

39. For a perspective on how corporate America educates employees on the risks of drug abuse, see Mark A. de Bernardo, *What Every Employee Should Know about Drug Abuse* (Washington, D.C.: Institute for a Drug-Free Workplace, 1993); see also Troy Duster, *The Legislation of Morality: Law, Drugs, and Moral Judgment* (New York: Free Press, 1970), p. 192.

40. Dan Waldorf, "Natural Recovery from Opiate Addiction," *Journal of Drug Issues,* **13** (1983): 237–280.

41. See James A. Inciardi, Duane C. McBride, Clyde B. McCoy, et al., "Violence, Street Crime and the Drug Legalization Debate: A Perspective and Commentary on the U.S. Experience," *Studies on Crime and Crime Prevention,* **4** (1995): 105–118; Steven Foy Luper, Curtis Brown, et al., *Drugs, Morality, and the Law* (New York: Garland, 1994); Robert J. MacCoun, James P. Kahan,

and James Gillespie, "A Content Analysis of the Drug Legalization Debate," *Journal of Drug Issues,* **23** (1993): 615–629; and Arnold S. Trebach and James A. Inciardi, *Legalize It? Debating American Drug Policy* (Washington, D.C.: American University Press, 1993).

42. James B. Jacobs, *Drunk Driving: An American Dilemma* (Chicago: University of Chicago Press, 1989), p. xiii.

43. *2007 National Survey on Drug Use and Health: National Findings* (Washington, D.C.: Department of Health and Human Services, 2007), pp. 1–3.

44. James Inciardi, *Reflections on Crime* (New York: Holt, Rinehart & Winston, 1978), pp. 8–10. For an even earlier perspective, see Herbert Berger and Andrew A. Eggston, "Should We Legalize Narcotics?" *Coronet,* **38** (June 1995): 30–34.

45. Lawrence A. Greenfield, *Alcohol and Crime: An Analysis of National Data on the Prevalence of Alcohol Involvement in Crime* (Washington, D.C.: U.S. Government Printing Office, 1998); Christopher J. Mumola, *Substance Abuse and Treatment, State and Federal Prisoners, 1997* (Washington, D.C.: U.S. Government Printing Office, January 1999).

46. Marvin E. Wolfgang, *Patterns in Criminal Homicide* (New York: Wiley, 1966).

47. P. Linquist, "Criminal Homicides in Northern Sweden, 1970–81: Alcohol Intoxication, Alcohol Abuse, and Mental Disease," *International Journal of Law and Psychiatry,* **8** (1986): 19–37. See also Roland Gustafson, "Is It Possible to Link Alcohol Intoxication Causally to Aggression and Violence? A Summary of the Swedish Experimental Approach," *Studies on Crime and Crime Prevention,* **4** (1995): 22–42.

48. D. Mayfield, "Alcoholism, Alcohol Intoxification, and Assaultive Behavior," *Diseases of the Nervous System,* **37** (1976): 288–291; C. K. Meyer, T. Magedanz, B. C. Kieselhorst, and S. G. Chapman, *A Social-Psychological Analysis of Police Assaults* (Norman: Bureau of Government Research, University of Oklahoma, April 1978).

49. For the role of alcohol consumption in violent episodes against intimates and women, see Christine A. Scronce and Kevin J. Corcoran, "The Influence of the Victim's Consumption of Alcohol on Perceptions of Stranger and Acquaintance Rape," *Violence against Women,* **1** (1995): 241–253; Bureau of Justice Statistics, *Violence between Intimates* (Washington, D.C.: U.S. Department of Justice, 1994); Bureau of Justice Statistics, *Violence against Women: A National Crime Victimization Survey Report* (Washington, D.C.: U.S. Department of Justice, 1994); S. D. Johnson, L. Gibson, and R. Linden, "Alcohol and Rape in Winnipeg, 1966–1975," *Journal of Studies on Alcohol,* **39** (1987): 1877–1894; and Menachem Amir, *Patterns of Forcible Rape* (Chicago: University of Chicago Press, 1971), p. 99.

50. D. H. Coleman and M. A. Straus, "Alcohol Abuse and Family Violence," in *Alcohol, Drug Abuse, and Aggression,* ed. E. Gottheil, K. A. Druley, T. E. Skoloda, and H. M. Waxman (Springfield, Ill.: Charles C Thomas, 1983).

51. See Maggie Sumner and Howard Parker, *Law in Alcohol: A Review of International Research into Alcohol's Role in Crime Causation* (Manchester, U.K.: Department of Social Policy and Social Work, University of Manchester, 1995); Klaus A. Miczek et al., "Alcohol, Drugs of Abuse, Aggression, and Violence," in *Understanding and Preventing Violence,* ed. Albert J. Reiss Jr. and Jeffrey A. Roth (Washington, D.C.: National Academy Press, 1993).

52. K. E. Leonard, "Alcohol and Human Physical Aggression," *Aggression,* **2** (1983): 77–101. See also Matthew W. Lewis, Jon F. Merz, Ron D. Hays, et al., "Perceptions of Intoxication and Impairment at Arrest among Adults Convicted of Driving under the Influence of Alcohol," *Journal of Drug Issues,* **25** (1995): 141–160.

53. C. M. Steele and L. Southwick, "Alcohol and Social Behavior: I. The Psychology of Drunken Excess," *Journal of Personality and Social Psychology,* **48** (1985): 18–34. See also Peter B. Wood, John K. Cochran, Betty Pfefferbaum, et al., "Sensation-Seeking and Delinquent Substance Use: An Extension of Learning Theory," *Journal of Drug Issues,* **25** (1995): 173–193.

54. S. Ahlstrom-Laakso, "European Drinking Habits: A Review of Research and Time Suggestions for Conceptual Integration of Findings," in *Cross-Cultural Approaches to the Study of Alcohol,* ed. M. W. Everett, J. O. Waddell, and D. Heath (The Hague: Mouton, 1976).

55. *2007 National Survey on Drug Use and Health: National Findings* (Washington, D.C.: Department of Health and Human Services, 2007), pp. 1–3; Lawrence A. Greenfeld, *Drunk Driving,* for Bureau of Justice Statistics (Washington, D.C.: U.S. Government Printing Office, February 1988), p. 1; See also Gwen W. Bramlet, "DUI Offenders, Drug Users, and Criminals: A Comparison," *Journal of Crime and Justice,* **18** (1995): 59–78; Greenfield, *Alcohol and Crime;* and Mumola, *Substance Abuse and Treatment.*

56. Joseph R. Gusfield, "The Control of Drinking-Driving in the United States: A Period of Transition," in *Social Control of the Drinking Driver,* ed. Michael D. Lawrence, John R. Snortum, and Franklin E. Zimring (Chicago: University of Chicago Press, 1988).

57. Jacobs, *Drunk Driving,* p. xvi.

58. Faye Silas, "Gimme the Keys," *American Bar Association Journal,* **71** (1985): 36.

59. Atic Press, "The Menace on the Roads," *Newsweek,* Dec. 21, 1987, p. 42.

60. Brandon K. Applegate, Francis T. Cullen, Bruce G. Link, Pamela J. Richards, and Lonn Lanza-Kaduce, "Determinants of Public Punitiveness toward Drunk Driving: A Factorial Survey Approach," *Justice Quarterly,* **13** (1996): 57–79; Stephen D. Mastrofski and R. Richard Ritti, "Police Training and the Effects of Organization on Drunk Driving Enforcement," *Justice Quarterly,* **13** (1996): 291–320.

61. *The Effectiveness of the Ignition Interlock Device in Reducing Recidivism among Driving under the Influence Cases* (Honolulu: Criminal Justice Commission, 1987).

62. Personal communication, 1951. See, as additional early treatments, Dr. Eustace Chesser, *Strange Loves: The Human Aspects of Sexual Deviation* (New York: William Morrow, 1971); and David Reuben, *Everything You Always Wanted to Know about Sex: But Were Afraid to Ask* (New York: David McKay, 1969). Contemporary works include Samuel S. Janus and Cynthia L. Janus, *The Janus Report on Sexual Behavior: The First Broad-Scale Scientific National Survey since Kinsey* (New York: Wiley, 1993).

63. Alfred C. Kinsey, Wardel B. Pomeroy, and Clyde E. Martin, *Sexual Behavior in the Human Male* (Philadelphia: Saunders, 1948), p. 613. See also Judith A. Reisman and Edward W. Eichel, *Kinsey, Sex and Fraud: The Indoctrination of a People* (Lafayette, La.: Huntington House, 1990).

64. Nickie Roberts, *Whores in History: Prostitution in Western Society* (London: HarperCollins, 1992).

65. *Robinson v. California,* 370 U.S. 660 (1962).

66. Uniform Crime Reports, 2004, p. 280.

67. See Cudore L. Snell, *Young Men in the Street: Help-Seeking Behavior of Young Male Prostitutes* (Westport, Conn.: Praeger, 1995); Sari van der Poel, "Solidarity as Boomerang: The Fiasco of the Prostitutes' Rights Movement in the Netherlands," *Crime, Law and Social Change,* **23** (1995): 41–65; Barbara Sherman Heyl, "The Madam as Teacher: The Training of House Prostitutes," in *Deviant Behavior,* ed. Delos H. Kelly (New York: St. Martin's Press, 1993); Sari van der Poel, "Professional Male Prostitution: A Neglected Phenomenon," *Crime, Law, and Social Change,* **18** (1992): 259–275; and David F. Luckenbill, "Deviant Career Mobility: The Case of Male Prostitutes," *Social Problems,* **33** (1986): 283–296.

68. Jeremiah Lowney, Robert W. Winslow, and Virginia Winslow, *Deviant Reality—Alternative World Views,* 2d ed. (Boston: Allyn and Bacon, 1981), p. 156. For a law enforcement perspective on countering prostitution in New York City, where female undercover police officers are used to seek out the patrons of prostitutes, see Dean Chang, "Dear John, It's a Bust: Cops Target Sex Clients," *New York Daily News,* June 26, 1994, p. 10.

69. Bureau of Justice Statistics, *HIV in Prisons 1994* (Washington, D.C.: U.S. Department of Justice, 1996); Bureau of Justice Statistics, *HIV in Prisons and Jails, 1993* (Washington, D.C.: U.S. Department of Justice, 1995); James A. Inciardi, Anne E. Pottieger, Mary Ann Forney, et al., "Prostitution, IV Drug Use, and Sex-for-Crack Exchanges among Serious Delinquents: Risks for HIV Infection," *Criminology,* **29** (1991): 221–236; Joseph B. Kuhns III and Kathleen M. Heide, "AIDS-Related Issues among Female Prostitutes and Female Arrestees," *International Journal of Offender Therapy and Comparative Criminology,* **36** (1992): 231–245; David J. Bellis, "Reduction of AIDS Risk among 41 Heroin Addicted Female Street Prostitutes: Effects of Free Methadone Maintenance," *Journal of Addictive Diseases,* **12** (1993): 7–23; L. Maher and R. Curtis, "Women on the Edge of Crime: Crack Cocaine and the Changing Contexts of Street-Level Sex Work in New York City," *Crime, Law, and Social Change,* **18** (1992): 221–258; Edward V. Morse, Patricia M. Simon, Stephanie A. Baus, et al., "Cofactors of Substance Use among Male Street Prostitutes," *Journal of Drug Issues,* **22** (1992): 977–994.

70. Paul Gebhard, "Misconceptions about Female Prostitution," *Medical Aspects of Human Sexuality,* **3** (1969): 28–30; Jennifer James, "Prostitutes and Prostitution," in *Deviants: Voluntary Action in a Hostile World,* ed. Edward Sagarin and F. Montanino (Glenview, Ill.: Scott, Foresman, 1977), p. 384.

71. R. Karl Hanson, Heather Scott, and Richard A. Steffy, "A Comparison of Child Molesters and Nonsexual Criminals: Risk Predictors and Long-Term Recidivism," *Journal of Research in Crime and Delinquency,* **32** (1995): 325–337; Dennis Howitt, *Paedophiles and Sexual Offences against Children* (Chichester, U.K.: Wiley, 1995); Human Rights Watch: Asia, *Rape for Profit: Trafficking of Nepali Girls and Women to India's Brothels* (New York: Human Rights Watch, 1995).

72. See Gerhard O. W. Mueller, *Legal Regulation of Sexual Conduct* (New York: Oceana, 1961), pp. 139–147, tables 9A, 9B. Note, however, that some states have amended their statutes since these data were collected.

73. Edward Donnerstein et al., *The Question of Pornography: Final Report of the Attorney General's Commission on Pornography* (Nashville, Tenn.: Rutledge Hill Press, 1986), p. 147.

74. For the now famous Justice Potter Stewart comment on pornography, where he couldn't truly define obscenity, but stated he knew it when he saw it, see *Jacobellis v. Ohio,* 378 U.S. 184 (1964). See also Joel Feinberg, "Pornography and Criminal Law," in *Pornography and Censorship,* ed. D. Copp and S. Wendell (New York: Prometheus, 1979).

75. See Susan M. Easton, *The Problem of Pornography: Regulation and the Right to Free Speech* (London: Routledge, 1994); Donald A. Downs, *The New Politics of Pornography* (Chicago: University of Chicago Press, 1989). See also Donnerstein et al., *The Question of Pornography,* chap. 7; and Gordon Hawkins and Franklin E. Zimring, *Pornography in a Free Society* (New York: Cambridge University Press, 1988), p. 26.

76. *The Report of the Commission on Obscenity and Pornography* (Washington, D.C.: U.S. Government Printing Office, 1970).

77. U.S. Department of Justice, *Attorney General's Commission on Pornography, Final Report,* vols. 1 and 2 (Washington, D.C.: U.S. Government Printing Office, 1986). For comments on the scientific underpinnings of this report, see Edward Donnerstein, "The Pornography Commission Report: Do Findings Fit Conclusions?" *Sexual Coercion and Assault Issues and Perspectives,* **1** (1986): 185–188.

78. Home Office, *Report of the Committee on Obscenity and Film Censorship* (London: Her Majesty's Stationery Office, 1979), p. 103. See also Dennis Howitt and Guy Cumberbatch, *Pornography: Impacts and Influences: A Review of Available Research Evidence on the Effects of Pornography* (London: Research and Planning Unit, U.K. Home Office, 1990).

79. *The Report of the Commission on Obscenity and Pornography.*

80. R. A. Barron and P. A. Bell, "Sexual Arousal and Aggression by Males: Effects of Type of Erotic Stimuli and Prior Provocation," *Journal of Personality and Social Psychology,* **35** (1977): 79–87. For a more current study, see Scot B. Boeringer, "Pornography and Sexual Aggression: Associations of Violent and Nonviolent Depictions with Rape and Rape Proclivity," *Deviant Behavior,* **15** (1994): 289–304.

81. Dolf Zillman and Jennings Bryant, "Pornography, Sexual Callousness, and the Trivialization of Rape," *Journal of Communication,* **32** (1984): 10–21. See also Berl Kutchinsky, "Evidence Proves That Pornography Does Not Promote Rape," in the Current Controversies series, *Violence against Women,* ed. Karin L. Swisher, Carol Wekesser, and William Barbour (San Diego: Greenhaven Press, 1994); and Cynthia S. Gentry, "Pornography and Rape: An Empirical Analysis," *Deviant Behavior,* **12** (1991): 277–288.

82. Donnerstein et al., *The Question of Pornography,* esp. pp. 38–47. See also Swisher, Wekesser, and Barbour, *Violence against Women;* Myriam Miedzian, "How Rape Is Encouraged in American Boys and What We Can Do to Stop It," in *Transforming a Rape Culture,* ed. Emilie Buchwald, Pamela R. Fletcher, and Martha Roth (Minneapolis: Milkweed Editions, 1993); and Judith A. Reisman, *Images of Children, Crime and Violence in Playboy, Penthouse and Hustler* (Washington, D.C.: Office of Juvenile Justice and Delinquency Prevention, Office of Justice Assistance, Research and Statistics, U.S. Department of Justice, 1990).

83. Joan Hoff, "Why Is There No History of Pornography?" in *For Adult Users Only: The Dilemma of Violent Pornography,* ed. Susan Gubar and Joan Hoff

(Bloomington: Indiana University Press, 1989), p. 18. See also Franklin Mark Osanka and Sara Lee Johann, "Pornography Contributes to Violence against Women," in Swisher, Wekesser, and Barbour, *Violence against Women*.

84. *Miller v. California*, 413 U.S. 15 (1973). See also Laura Lederer, Richard Delgado, et al., *The Price We Pay: The Case against Racist Speech, Hate Propaganda, and Pornography* (New York: Hill and Wang, 1995).

85. *Pope v. Illinois*, 481 U.S. 497 (1987). See also Adele M. Stan et al., *Debating Sexual Correctness: Pornography, Sexual Harassment, Date Rape, and the Politics of Sexual Equality* (New York: Dell, 1995); Bill Thompson, *Soft Core: Moral Crusades against Pornography in Britain and America* (London: Cassell, 1994); and Catherine Itzen et al., *Pornography: Women, Violence and Civil Liberties* (Oxford: Oxford University Press, 1993).

86. Laura Davis, Marilyn D. McShane, and Frank P. Williams III, "Controlling Computer Access to Pornography: Special Conditions for Sex Offenders," *Federal Probation*, **59** (1995): 43–48; Marty Rimm, "Marketing Pornography on the Information Superhighway: A Survey of 917,410 Images, Descriptions, Short Stories and Animations Downloaded 8.5 Million Times by Consumers in Over 2,000 Cities in Forty Countries, Provinces, and Territories," *Georgetown Law Journal*, **83** (1995): 1849–2008; Great Britain House of Commons, *Computer Pornography* (London: Her Majesty's Stationery Office, 1994). For a perspective on the government's plan to police the Internet's superhighway, see James Aley, "How Not to Help High Tech," *Fortune Magazine*, May 16, 1994, p. 100.

87. Kinsey et al., *Sexual Behavior in the Human Male*.

88. Alfred C. Kinsey, Wardel B. Pomeroy, Clyde E. Martin, and Paul H. Gebhard, *Sexual Behavior in the Human Female* (Philadelphia: Saunders, 1953), p. 453.

89. Morton M. Hunt, *Profiles of Social Research: The Scientific Study of Human Interactions* (New York: Russell Sage Foundation, 1985).

CHAPTER 14

1. R. J. Estes and N. A. Weiner, *The Commercial Sexual Exploitation of Children in the U.S., Canada, and Mexico.* (Philadelphia: University of Pennsylvania, School of Social Work, Center for the Study of Youth Policy, 2002), available at http://www.sp2.upenn.edu/~restes/CSEC_Files/Complete_CSEC_020220.pdf (retrieved June 20, 2008).

2. UNICEF, *Combating Child Trafficking: Handbook for Parliamentarians* (Inter-Parliamentary Union & UNICEF, 2005).

3. Ibid.

4. U. S. Department of State, "The Facts about Child Sex Tourism" (2005), available at http://www.state.gov/documents/organization/51459.pdf (retrieved June 25, 2008).

5. UNICEF, *Combating Child Trafficking*.

6. Piers Beirne and David Nelken, eds., *Issues in Comparative Criminology* (Aldershot, U.K.: Dartmouth, 1997), is a useful anthology of scientific issues in comparative criminology.

7. The term "comparative criminology" appears to have been coined by Sheldon Glueck. See Sheldon Glueck, "Wanted: A Comparative Criminology," in *Ventures in Criminology*, ed. Sheldon Glueck and Eleanor Glueck (London: Tavistock, 1964), pp. 304–322.

8. James O. Finckenauer, *Russian Youth: Law, Deviance and the Pursuit of Freedom* (New Brunswick, N.J.: Transaction, 1995); Nanci Adler, "Planned Economy and Unplanned Criminality: The Soviet Experience," *International Journal of Comparative and Applied Criminal Justice*, **17** (1993): 189–201; Wojciech Cebulak, "White-Collar Crime in Socialism: Myth or Reality?" *International Journal of Comparative and Applied Criminal Justice*, **15** (1991): 109–120; Klaus Sessar, "Crime Rate Trends before and after the End of the German Democratic Republic—Impressions and First Analyses," in *Fear of Crime and Criminal Victimization*, ed. Wolfgang Bilsky, Christian Pfeiffer, and Peter Wetzels (Stuttgart, Germany: Ferdinand Enke Verlag, 1993), pp. 231–244; Louise I. Shelley et al., "East Meets West in Crime," *European Journal on Criminal Policy and Research*, **3** (1995): 7–107. As China is undergoing a transformation, mostly economic, changes in that country are noteworthy. See Yue Ma, "Crime in China: Characteristics, Causes and Control Strategies," *Journal of Comparative and Applied Criminal Justice*, **34** (1994): 54–68.

9. Martin Killias et al., "Cross-Border Crime," *European Journal on Criminal Policy and Research*, **1** (1993): 7–134.

10. William F. McDonald, "The Globalization of Criminology: The New Frontier Is the Frontier," *Transnational Organized Crime*, **1** (1995): 1–12.

11. Piers Beirne and Joan Hill, *Comparative Criminology—An Annotated Bibliography* (New York: Greenwood, 1991), pp. vii–viii.

12. Dae H. Chang, *Criminology: A Cross-Cultural Perspective*, 2 vols. (Durham, N.C.: Carolina Academic Press, 1976); George F. Cole, Stanislaw J. Frankowski, and Marc G. Gertz, *Major Criminal Justice Systems—A Comparative Survey*, 2d ed. (Newbury Park, Calif.: Sage, 1987); Richard J. Terrill, *World Criminal Justice Systems*, 2d ed. (Cincinnati: Anderson, 1985); Robert Heiner, ed., *Criminology—A Cross-Cultural Perspective* (Minneapolis/St. Paul: West, 1996); Obi N. I. Ebbe, ed., *Comparative and International Criminal Justice Systems* (Boston: Butterworth-Heinemann, 1996); Charles B. Fields and Richter H. Moore, eds., *Comparative Criminal Justice: Traditional and Non-traditional Systems of Law and Control* (Prospect Heights, Ill.: Waveland Press, 1996).

13. G. O. W. Mueller, *World Survey on the Availability of Criminal Justice Statistics*, Internet-UNCJIN-ftp238.33.18WSAYL. See also G. O. W. Mueller, "International Criminal Justice: Harnessing the Information Explosion—Coasting down the Electronic Superhighway," *Journal of Criminal Justice Education* **7**(2) (Fall 1996): 253–261.

14. Interpol, located in Lyons, France, has published the crime statistics supplied to it by member states since 1951.

15. First survey: 1970–1975, A/32/199; second survey: 1975–1980, A/Conf. 121/18; third survey: 1980–1986, A/Conf. 144/6; fourth survey: 1986–1990, A/Conf. 169/15 and Add. 1; fifth survey (see United Nations, Office on Drugs and Crime, *Global Report on Crime and Justice*, ed. Graeme Newman (New York: Oxford University Press, 1999).

16. World Health Organization, "Homicide Statistics," in *World Health Statistics* (Geneva: World Health Organization, annually).

17. Dane Archer and Rosemary Gartner, *Violence and Crime in Cross-National Perspective* (New Haven, Conn.: Yale University Press, 1984).

18. Richard R. Bennett, *Correlates of Crime: A Study of Nations, 1960–1984* (Ann Arbor, Mich.: Inter-University Consortium for Political and Social Research, 1989).

19. Richard R. Bennett and James P. Lynch, "Does a Difference Make a Difference?" *Criminology*, **28** (1990): 155–182; Carol B. Kalish, *International Crime Rates* (Washington, D.C.: Bureau of Justice Statistics, 1988).

20. Jan J. M. Van Dijk, Pat Mayhew, and Martin Killias, *Experiences of Crime across the World: Key Findings from the 1989 International Crime Survey* (Deventer, Netherlands: Kluwer, 1990); Richard R. Bennett and R. Bruce Wiegand, "Observations on Crime Reporting in a Developing Nation," *Criminology*, **32** (1994): 135–148; Ugljesa Zvekic and Anna Albazzi del Frate, eds., *Criminal Victimization in the Developing World* (Rome: United Nations Interregional Crime and Justice Research Institute, 1995); Gail Travis et al., "The International Crime Surveys: Some Methodological Concerns," *Current Issues in Criminal Justice*, **6** (1995): 346–361; Van Dijk, Box 0.9 in United Nations, *Global Report on Crime and Justice*, p. 9.

21. Josine Junger-Tas, Gert-Jan Terlouw, and Malcolm W. Klein, *Delinquent Behavior among People in the Western World* (Amsterdam: RDC Ministry of Justice, Kugler Publ., 1994); Junger-Tas, Box 0.10 in United Nations, *Global Report on Crime and Justice*, p. 16.

22. Hermann Mannheim, *Comparative Criminology* (Boston: Houghton Mifflin, 1965).

23. See Jerome L. Neapolitan, *Cross-National Crime—A Research Review and Sourcebook* (Westport, Conn.: Greenwald Press, 1997); Dennis Benamati, Phyllis Schultze, Adam Bouloukos, and Graeme Newman, *Criminal Justice Information: How to Find It, How to Use It* (Phoenix, Ariz.: Onyx Press, 1997); Harry R. Dammer and Philip L. Reichel, eds., *Teaching about Comparative/International Criminal Justice—A Resource Manual* (Highland Heights, N.Y.: Academy of Criminal Justice Sciences, 1997).

24. Elmer H. Johnson, ed., *International Handbook of Contemporary Developments in Criminology*, 2 vols. (Westport, Conn.: Greenwood Press, 1983); George F. Cole, Stanislaw J. Frankowski, and Marc G. Gertz, *Major Criminal Justice Systems—A Comparative Survey*, 2d ed. (Newbury Park, Calif.: Sage, 1987); Richard J. Terrill, *World Criminal Justice Systems: A Survey* (Cincinnati: Anderson, 1984); Obi N. Ignatius Ebbe, *Comparative and International Criminal Justice Systems* (Boston: Butterworth, 1996); Philip L. Reichel, *Comparative Criminal Justice Systems: A Topical Approach* (Upper Saddle River, N.J.: Prentice Hall, 1994); Brunon Holyst, *Comparative Criminology* (Lexington, Mass.: Lexington Books, 1979); Louise I. Shelley, ed., *Readings in Comparative Criminology* (Carbondale: Southern Illinois University Press, 1981).

25. United Nations, *The United Nations Crime Prevention and Criminal Justice Program: Formulation of Standards and Efforts at Their Implementation* (Philadelphia: University of Pennsylvania, 1994); Benedict Alper and Jerry F. Boren, *Crime: International Agenda* (Lexington, Mass.: Lexington Books, 1972); Ethan N. Nadelman, *Cops across Borders* (University Park: Penn State Press, 1993); André Bossard, *Transnational Crime and Criminal Law* (Chicago: Office of International Criminal Justice, 1990).

26. United Nations, *Global Report on Crime and Justice*. See also *The United Nations and Crime Prevention: Seeking Security and Justice for All* (New York: UNDPI, 1996);

and *The United Nations and Criminal Justice, 1946–1996: Resolutions, Reports, Documents and Publications*, International Review of Criminal Policy, Issue 47–48 (Vienna: United Nations, 1996/97).

27. G. O. W. Mueller, Michael Gage, and Lenore R. Kupperstein, *The Legal Norms of Delinquency: A Comparative Study*, Criminal Law Education and Research Center Monograph Series, vol. 1 (South Hackensack, N.J.: Fred B. Rothman, 1969).

28. Anastassios Mylonas, *Perception of Police Power: A Study in Four Cities*, Comparative Criminal Law Project Monograph Series, vol. 8 (South Hackensack, N.J.: Fred B. Rothman, 1973).

29. Setsuo Miyazawa, "The Enigma of Japan as a Testing Ground for Cross-Cultural Criminological Studies," *Annales Internationales de Criminologie*, **32** (1994): 81–103; B. Hebenton and J. Spencer, "The Contribution and Limitations of Anglo-American Criminology to Understanding Crime in Central-Eastern Europe," *European Journal of Crime, Criminal Law and Criminal Justice*, **2** (1994): 50–61.

30. Sheldon Glueck and Eleanor Glueck, *Unraveling Juvenile Delinquency* (New York: The Commonwealth Fund; Cambridge, Mass.: Harvard University Press, 1950).

31. Sheldon Glueck and Eleanor Glueck, *Of Delinquency and Crime—A Panorama of Years of Search and Research*, Publications of the Criminal Law Education and Research Center, vol. 8 (Springfield, Ill.: Charles C Thomas, 1974), p. 332.

32. Obi N. I. Ebbe, "Juvenile Delinquency in Nigeria: The Problem of Application of Western Theories," *International Journal of Comparative and Applied Criminal Justice*, **16** (1992): 353–370.

33. Rosemary Gartner, "The Victims of Homicide: A Temporal and Cross-National Comparison," *American Sociological Review*, **55** (1990): 92–106.

34. Gary LaFree and Christopher Birkbeck, "The Neglected Situation: A Cross-National Study of the Situational Characteristics of Crime," *Criminology*, **29** (1991): 73–98.

35. Richard R. Bennett, "Routine Activities: A Cross-National Assessment of a Criminological Perspective," *Social Forces*, **70** (1991): 147–163.

36. Richard R. Bennett and P. Peter Basiotis, "Structural Correlates of Juvenile Property Crime: A Cross-National, Time-Series Analysis," *Journal of Research in Crime and Delinquency*, **28** (1991): 262–287.

37. Sam S. Souryal, "Juvenile Delinquency in the Cross-Cultural Context: The Egyptian Experience," *International Journal of Comparative and Applied Criminal Justice*, **16** (1992): 329–352.

38. Adel Helal and Charisse T. M. Coston, "Low Crime Rates in Bahrain: Islamic Social Control—Testing the Theory of Synnomie," *International Journal of Comparative and Applied Criminal Justice*, **15** (1991): 125–144.

39. Gregory C. Leavitt, "General Evaluation and Durkheim's Hypothesis of Crime Frequency: A Cross-Cultural Test," *Sociological Quarterly*, **33** (1992): 241–263; Suzanne T. Ortega, Jay Corzine, and Cathleen Burnett, "Modernization, Age Structure, and Regional Context: A Cross-National Study of Crime," *Sociological Spectrum*, **12** (1992): 257–277.

40. Christopher Birkbeck, "Against Ethnocentrism: A Cross-Cultural Perspective on Criminal Justice

Theories and Policies," *Journal of Criminal Justice Education,* **4** (1993): 307–323.

41. Louise I. Shelley, *Crime and Modernization: The Impact of Industrialization and Urbanization on Crime* (Carbondale: Southern Illinois University Press, 1981).

42. David Shichor, "Crime Patterns and Socio-Economic Development: A Cross-National Analysis," *Criminal Justice Review,* **15** (1990): 64–78; John Arthur, "Development and Crime in Africa: A Test of Modernization Theory," *Journal of Criminal Justice,* **19** (1991): 499–513.

43. "New Perspectives in Crime Prevention and Criminal Justice and Development: The Role of International Cooperation," working paper prepared by the Secretariat, United Nations, 1980, A/Conf. 87/10.

44. Freda Adler, *Nations Not Obsessed with Crime,* Comparative Criminal Law Project Publications Series, vol. 15 (Littleton, Colo.: Fred B. Rothman, 1983).

45. See Note 8.

46. See Ugljesa Zvekic, ed., *Essays on Crime and Development* (Rome: UN Interregional Crime and Justice Research Institute, 1990).

47. V. Lee Hamilton and Joseph Sanders, *Everyday Justice: Responsibility and the Individual in Japan and the United States* (New Haven, Conn.: Yale University Press, 1992); Hans Joachim Schneider, "Crime and Its Control in Japan and in the Federal Republic of Germany, a Comparative Study," *International Journal of Offender Therapy and Comparative Criminology,* **36** (1992): 47–63.

48. Dale E. Berger et al., "Deterrence and Prevention of Alcohol-Impaired Driving in Australia, the United States, and Norway," *Justice Quarterly,* **7** (1990): 453–465.

49. David B. Kopel, *The Samurai, the Mountie, and the Cowboy: Should America Adopt the Gun Controls of Other Democracies?* (Buffalo, N.Y.: Prometheus, 1992).

50. Robert L. Nay, *Firearms Regulations in Various Foreign Countries* (Washington, D.C.: Law Library of Congress, 1990).

51. Michael Clarke, "The Control of Insurance Fraud: A Comparative View," *British Journal of Criminology,* **30** (1990): 1–23.

52. Kenneth Polk and William Weston, "Insider Trading as an Aspect of White Collar Crime," *Australian and New Zealand Journal of Criminology,* **23** (1990): 24–38.

53. Yü-Hsiu Hsü, ed., *International Conference on Environmental Criminal Law* (Taipei: Taiwan/ROC Chapter of the International Association of Penal Law, 1992).

54. Rosemary Gartner, "Family Structure, Welfare Spending, and Child Homicide in Developed Democracies," *Journal of Marriage and the Family,* **53** (1991): 231–240.

55. Margo I. Wilson and Martin Daly, "Who Kills Whom in Spouse Killings? On the Exceptional Sex Ratio of Spousal Homicides in the United States," *Criminology,* **30** (1992): 189–215.

56. Lois A. Fingerhut and Joel C. Kleinman, "International and Interstate Comparisons of Homicide among Young Males," *Journal of the American Medical Association,* **263** (1990): 3292–3295.

57. F. H. McClintock and Per-Olof H. Wikstrom, "The Comparative Study of Urban Violence—Criminal Violence in Edinburgh and Stockholm," *British Journal of Criminology,* **32** (1992): 505–520.

58. Dae H. Chang and Galan M. Janeksela, eds., "Special Issue on Comparative Juvenile Delinquency," *International Journal of Comparative and Applied Criminal Justice,* **16** (1992): 135–170, with contributions by Gaban M. Janeksela, David P. Farrington, Alison Hatch and Curt T. Griffiths, Günther Kaiser, Josine Junger-Tas, Paul C. Friday, James O. Finckenauer and Linda Kelly, Hualing Fu, Michael S. Vaughn and Frank F. Y. Huang, Byung In Cho and Richard J. Chang, Clayton A. Hartjen and Sesharajani Kethineni, Sam S. Souryal, and Obi N. I. Ebbe.

59. Mylonas, *Perception of Police Power.*

60. Graeme Newman, *Comparative Deviance: Perception and Law in Six Cultures* (New York: Elsevier Scientific, 1976).

61. Russel P. Dobash, R. Emerson Dobash, Scott Balliofyne, Karl Schuman, Reiner Kaulitzki, and Hans-Werner Guth, "Ignorance and Suspicion: Young People and Criminal Justice in Scotland and Germany," *British Journal of Criminology,* **30** (1990): 306–320.

62. Ronald D. Hunter, "Three Models of Policing," *Police Studies,* **13** (1990): 118–124; R. I. I. Mawby, *Comparable Policing Issues: The British and American Experience in International Perspective* (London: Unwin Hyman, 1990).

63. Leslie T. Wilkins, *Punishment, Crime and Market Forces* (Aldershot, England: Dartmouth, 1991); Dennis Wiechman, Jerry Kendall, and Ronald Bae, "International Use of the Death Penalty," *International Journal of Comparative and Applied Criminal Justice,* **14** (1990): 239–259.

64. See Gunther Kaiser, Helmut Kury, and Hans-Jorg Albrecht, eds., *Victims and Criminal Justice,* 3 vols. (Freiburg, Germany: Max Planck Institut, 1991); Emilio C. Viano, ed., *Critical Issues in Victimology—International Perspectives* (New York: Springer Verlag, 1992).

65. Jack Levin and Jack McDevitt, *Hate Crimes—The Rising Tide of Bigotry and Bloodshed* (New York: Plenum, 1993).

66. See Hans-Dieter Schwind et al., "Causes, Prevention and Control of Violence," *Revue Internationale de Criminologie et de Police Technique,* **43** (1990): 395–520.

67. Gerhard O. W. Mueller and Freda Adler, *Outlaws of the Ocean: The Complete Book of Contemporary Crime on the High Seas* (New York: Hearst Marine Books, 1985); Gerhard O. W. Mueller and Freda Adler, "A New Wave of Crime at Sea," *The World and I* (February 1986): 96–103.

68. Mike King, *Towards Federalism: Policing the Borders of a "New" Europe* (Leicester, United Kingdom: University of Leicester, 1993); H. Lensing, "The Federalization of Europe: Towards a Federal System of Criminal Justice," *European Journal of Crime, Criminal Law and Criminal Justice,* **1** (1993): 212–229; Ethan A. Nadelman, *Cops across Borders: The Internationalization of U.S. Criminal Law Enforcement* (University Park: Penn State University Press, 1994).

69. See fourth U.N. Survey, 1986–1990, A/Conf.169/15 and Add. 1.

70. See, for example, Jonathan Reuvid, ed., *The Regulation and Prevention of Economic Crime Internationally* (London: Kogan Page, 1995).

71. See Financial Action Task Force on Money Laundering, *Report on Money Laundering Typologies, 2003–2004* (Paris: FATF, 2005). See also Global Programme Against Money Laundering, http://www.unodc.org/unodc/en/money_laundering.html.

72. Laurence Zuckerman and John Sullivan, "An FAA Study Shows Few Gains in Improving Security at Airports," *New York Times,* Nov. 5, 1999, p. 30.

73. Several journals are devoted entirely to terrorism. See *Terrorism* (New York); *Studies in Conflict and Terrorism* (London); and *Violence, Aggression, Terrorism* (Danbury, Conn.).

74. Reuters "High-Tech Art Sleuths Snare Thieves," *C. J. International*, **9** (1993): 4–6.

75. Truc-Nhu Ho, *Art Theft in New York City: An Explanatory Study in Crime Specificity*, Ph.D. dissertation, Rutgers University, 1992.

76. Ralph Blumenthal, "Museums Getting Together to Track Stolen Art," *New York Times*, July 16, 1996, pp. C13, C15.

77. Department of Justice, *Progress Report of the Department of Justice's Task Force on Intellectual Property* (Office of the United States Trade Representative, 2006), available at http://www.usdoj.gov/opa/documents/ipreport61906.pdf (retrieved June 20, 2008).

78. Michael R. Gordon, "Stolen Uranium Intercepted by Georgia in the Caucasus," *New York Times*, Sept. 24, 1999, p. 6.

79. "For Sale—Nukes: Deadly Plutonium from Russia's Vast Nuclear Network Is Turning Up on the European Market. Who Is Buying—and Can They Be Stopped?" *Newsweek*, Aug. 29, 1994, pp. 30–31; Bruce W. Nolan, "Formula for Terror," *Time*, Aug. 29, 1994.

80. Les Johnston, "Policing Plutonium: Issues in the Provision of Policing Services at Nuclear Facilities and for Related Materials in Transit," *Policing and Society*, **4** (1994): 53–72; Phil Williams and Paul H. Woessnar, *Nuclear Material Trafficking: An Interim Assessment* (Pittsburgh: Ridgway Center for International Security Studies, 1995).

81. Eric Ellen, "The Dimensions of International Maritime Crime," in *Issues in Maritime Crime: Mayhem at Sea*, ed. Martin Gill (Leicester, United Kingdom: Perpetuity Press, 1995), pp. 4–11; Martin Gill, *Crime at Sea: A Forgotten Issue in Police Co-operation* (Leicester, United Kingdom: Centre for the Study of Public Order, 1995); Gerhard O. W. Mueller and Freda Adler, "Piraterie: le 'Jolly Roger' flotte à nouveau les Corsaires des Caribes," *Revue Internationale de Criminologie et de Police Technique*, **4** (1992): 408–424.

82. National Insurance Crime Bureau, fax of July 29, 1996.

83. British Banking Association estimate. See Larry E. Coutorie, "The Future of High-Technology Crime: A Parallel Delphi Study," *Journal of Criminal Justice*, **23** (1995): 13–27.

84. E.g., Sally M. Edwards, Terry D. Edwards, and Charles B. Fields, eds., *Environmental Crime and Criminality* (New York: Garland, 1996).

85. Ko-lin Chin, *Chinese Subculture and Criminality: Non-traditional Crime Groups in America* (Westport, Conn.: Greenwood, 1990); Alex P. Schmid, ed., *Migration and Crime* (Milan, Italy: International Scientific and Professional Advisory Council of the United Nations Crime Prevention and Criminal Justice Programme, 1998).

86. Michael Woodiwiss, "Crime's Global Reach," in *Global Crime Connections*, ed. Frank Pearce and Michael Woodiwiss (Houndmills, United Kingdom: Macmillan, 1993), pp. 1–31.

87. Raphael F. Perl, ed., *Drugs and Foreign Policy: A Critical Review* (Boulder, Colo.: Westview Press, 1994); Günther Kaiser, "International Experiences with Different Strategies of Drug Policy," *EuroCriminology*, **7** (1994): 3–29.

88. See Frederick T. Martens, "Transnational Enterprise Crime and the Elimination of Frontiers," *International Journal of Comparative and Applied Criminal Justice*, **15** (1991): 99–107; and Wojciech Cebulak, "The Antitrust Doctrine: How It Was Internationalized," *International Journal of Comparative and Applied Criminal Justice*, **14** (1990): 261–267.

89. See "Crime Prevention and Criminal Justice in the Context of Development: Realities and Perspectives of International Cooperation," *International Review of Criminal Policy*, **41/42** (1993): 1–19.

90. Gerhard O. W. Mueller, "Transnational Crime: An Experience in Uncertainties," in *Organized Crime: Uncertainties and Dilemmas*, ed. S. Einstein and M. Amir (Chicago: Office of International Criminal Justice, 1999), pp. 3–18.

91. Draft Articles of the Draft Code of Crimes against the Peace and Security of Mankind, adopted by the International Law Commission on First Reading, United Nations, New York, 1991. For a complete listing, see M. Cherif Bassiouni, *International Criminal Law—A Draft International Criminal Code* (Alphen an den Rijn, Netherlands: Sijthoff & Noordhoff, 1980).

92. Shana Swiss and Joan E. Giller, "Rape as a Crime of War," *Journal of the American Medical Association*, **270** (1993): 612–615.

93. For an analysis of all international crimes, see M. Cherif Bassiouni, ed., *International Criminal Law*: vol. 1, *Crimes*, 2d ed. (Ardsley, N.Y.: Transnational, 1999); M. Cherif Bassiouni, *A Draft International Criminal Code and Draft Statute for an International Criminal Tribunal* (Dordrecht, Netherlands: Martinus Nijhoff, 1987); Farhad Malekian, *International Criminal Law*, 2 vols. (Motala, Sweden: Borgstroms Trycker, 1991); and Gerhard O. W. Mueller and Edward M. Wise, *International Criminal Law*, Comparative Criminal Law Project, Publications Series, vol. 2 (South Hackensack, N.J.: Fred B. Rothman, 1965).

Glossary

Accommodate In regard to achieving the American dream, to adjust noneconomic needs so that they are secondary to and supportive of economic ones.

Accomplice A person who helps another commit a crime.

Aggravated assault An attack on another person in which the perpetrator inflicts serious harm on the victim or uses a deadly weapon.

Aging-out phenomenon A concept that holds that offenders commit less crime as they get older because they have less strength, initiative, stamina, and mobility.

Anomie A societal state marked by normlessness, in which disintegration and chaos have replaced social cohesion.

Arraignment First stage of the trial process, at which the indictment or information is read in open court and the defendant is requested to respond.

Arson At common law, the malicious burning of the dwelling house of another. This definition has been broadened by state statutes and criminal codes to cover the burning of other structures or even personal property.

Assault At common law, an unlawful offer or attempt with force or violence to do a corporal hurt to another or to frighten another.

Atavistic stigmata Physical features of a human being at an earlier stage of development, which—according to Cesare Lombroso—distinguish a born criminal from the general population.

Attachment The bond between a parent and child or between individuals and their family, friends, and school.

Bankruptcy fraud A scam in which an individual falsely attempts to claim bankruptcy (and thereby erase financial debts) by taking advantage of existing laws.

Battery A common law crime consisting of the intentional touching of or inflicting of hurt on another.

Behavioral modeling Learning how to behave by fashioning one's behavior after that of others.

Belief The extent to which an individual subscribes to society's values.

Biocriminology The subdiscipline of criminology that investigates biological and genetic factors and their relation to criminal behavior.

Birth cohort A group consisting of all individuals born in the same year.

Boiler rooms Operations run by one or more stock manipulators who, through deception and misleading sales techniques, seduce the unsuspecting and uninformed public into buying stocks in obscure and often poorly financed corporations.

Born criminal According to Lombroso, a person born with features resembling an earlier, more primitive form of human life, destined to become a criminal.

Burglary A common law felony; the nighttime breaking and entering of the dwelling house of another, with the intention to commit a crime (felony or larceny) therein.

Case study An analysis of all pertinent aspects of one unit of study.

Certiorari, writ of A writ issued by a higher court directing a lower court to prepare the record of a case and send it to the higher court for review.

Challenges for cause Challenges to remove a potential juror because of his or her inability to render a fair and impartial decision in a case. *See also* Peremptory challenges; Voir dire.

Check forging The criminal offense of making or altering a check with intent to defraud.

Chromosomes Basic cellular structures containing genes, i.e., biological material that creates individuality.

Churning Frequent trading, by a broker, of a client's shares of stock for the sole purpose of generating large commissions.

Classical school A criminological perspective suggesting that (1) people have free will to choose criminal or conventional behavior, (2) people choose to commit crime for reasons of greed or personal need, and (3) crime can be controlled by criminal sanctions, which should be proportionate to the guilt of the perpetrator.

Commitment A person's support of and participation in a program, cause, or social activity, which ties the individual to the moral or ethical codes of society.

Community policing A strategy that relies on public confidence and citizen cooperation to help prevent crime and make the residents of a community feel more secure.

Comparative criminology The study of crime in two or more cultures in an effort to gain broader information for theory construction and crime-control modeling.

Conditioning The process of developing a behavior pattern through a series of repeated experiences.

Conduct norms Norms that regulate the daily lives of people and that reflect the attitudes of the groups to which they belong.

Confidence game A deceptive means of obtaining money or property from a victim who is led to trust the perpetrator.

Conflict model A model of crime in which the criminal justice system is seen as being used by the ruling class to control the lower class. Criminological investigation of the conflicts within society is emphasized.

Conflict theory A theory that holds that the people who possess the power work to keep the powerless at a disadvantage.

Conformity Correspondence of an individual's behavior to society's patterns, norms, or standards.

Conjugal visits A program that permits prisoners to have contact with their spouses or significant others in order to maintain positive relationships.

Consensus model A model of criminal lawmaking that assumes that members of society agree on what is right and wrong and that law is the codification of agreed-upon social values.

Constable An officer, established by the Statute of Winchester in 1285, who was responsible for suppressing riots and violent crimes in each county; later, a local law enforcement officer, lowest rank in some police hierarchies.

Constructive corporate culpability Corporate fault is found in the reasonableness of judgments, as a function of reasonable attributed blame.

Consumer fraud An act that causes a consumer to surrender money through deceit or a misrepresentation of a material fact.

Containment theory A theory positing that every person possesses a containing external structure and a protective internal structure, both of which provide defense, protection, or insulation against delinquency.

Corporate compliance programs Corporate codes and training programs designed to prevent crimes and ethical violations.

Corporate crime A crime attributed to a corporation but perpetrated by or on the authority of an officer or high managerial agent.

Corporate ethos Corporate culture or character and its effect on the actions of an organization.

Corporate policy Standards and decisions of a corporation that produce policies resulting in law abidance or law violation.

Corrections Implementation and execution of sentences imposed by the courts; also, the system that administers those sentences.

Cortical arousal Activation of the cerebral cortex, a structure of the brain that is responsible for higher intellectual functioning, information processing, and decision making.

Crime An act in violation of law that causes harm, is identified by law, is committed with criminal intent, and is subject to punishment.

Crimes against property Crimes involving the illegal acquisition or destruction of property. *See* Crime.

Crimes against the person Crimes violative of life or physical integrity. *See* Crime.

Criminal attempt An act or omission constituting a substantial step in a course of conduct planned to culminate in the commission of a crime.

Criminal careers A concept that describes the onset of criminal activity, the types and amount of crime committed, and the termination of such activity.

Criminal justice system The interdependent and interactive components of police, courts, and corrections that form a unified whole (a system).

Criminologists Persons who collect information on crime and criminals for study and analysis in accordance with the research methods of modern science.

Criminology The body of knowledge regarding crime as a social phenomenon. It includes within its scope the process of making laws, of breaking laws, and of reacting toward the breaking of laws (Sutherland). Thus, criminology is an empirical, social-behavioral science that investigates crime, criminals, and criminal justice.

Cultural deviance theories Theories positing that crime results from cultural values that permit, or even demand, behavior in violation of the law.

Cultural transmission A theory that views delinquency as a socially learned behavior transmitted from one generation to the next in disorganized urban areas.

Culture conflict theory A theory positing that two groups may clash when their conduct norms differ, resulting in criminal activity.

Data Collected facts, observations, and other pertinent information from which conclusions can be drawn.

Defense counsel A lawyer retained by an individual accused of a crime, or assigned by the court if the individual is unable to pay.

Deterrence The theory of punishment which envisages that potential offenders will refrain from committing crimes out of fear of punishment (sometimes called "general prevention").

Deviance A broad concept encompassing both illegal behavior and behavior that departs from the social norm.

Differential association-reinforcement A theory of criminality based on the incorporation of psychological learning theory and differential association with social learning theory. Criminal behavior, the theory claims, is learned through associations and is contained or discontinued as a result of positive or negative reinforcements.

Differential association theory A theory of criminality based on the principle that an individual becomes delinquent because of an excess of definitions learned that are favorable to violation of law over definitions learned that are unfavorable to violation of law.

Differential opportunity theory A theory that attempts to join the concept of anomie and differential association by analyzing both legitimate and illegitimate opportunity structures available to individuals. It posits that illegitimate opportunities, like legitimate opportunities, are unequally distributed.

Direct control An external control that depends on rules, restrictions, and punishments.

Directed verdict A verdict of acquittal pronounced by the judge when the evidence against the accused is so poor that acquittal is the only possible verdict.

Direct file Prosecutor's power to try juveniles directly in adult criminal court.

Displacement In the event that a crime has been prevented, the commission of a quantitatively similar crime at a different time or place.

Dizygotic (DZ) twins Fraternal twins, who develop from two separate eggs fertilized at the same time. *See also* Monozygotic twins.

Drift According to David Matza, a state of limbo in which youths move in and out of delinquency and in which their lifestyles can embrace both conventional and deviant values.

Due process According to the Fourteenth Amendment of the U.S. Constitution, a fundamental mandate that a person should not be deprived of life, liberty, or property without reasonable and lawful procedures.

Ego The part of the psyche that, according to psychoanalytic theory, governs rational behavior; the moderator between the superego and the id.

Embezzlement The crime of withholding or withdrawing (conversion or misappropriation), without consent, funds entrusted to an agent (e.g., a bank teller or officer).

Employment prisons Prisons for low-risk offenders. Prisoners work at jobs outside the prison during the day but return to prison after work.

Environmental criminology An approach to crime that examines the location of a specific crime and the context in which it occurred in order to understand and explain crime patterns.

Equal protection A clause of the Fourteenth Amendment to the U.S. Constitution that guarantees equal protection of the law to everyone, without regard to race, origin, economic class, gender, or religion.

Eugenics A science, based on the principle of heredity, that has for its purpose the improvement of the race.

Exclusionary rule A rule prohibiting use of illegally obtained or otherwise inadmissible evidence in a court of law.

Experiment A research technique in which an investigator introduces a change into a process in order to make measurements or observations that evaluate the effects of the change.

Extroversion According to Hans Eysenck, a dimension of the human personality; describes individuals who are sensation-seeking, dominant, and assertive.

False pretenses, obtaining property by Leading a victim to part with property on a voluntary basis through trickery, deceit, or misrepresentation.

Federal Witness Protection Program A program, established under the Organized Crime Control Act of 1970, designed to protect witnesses who testify in court by relocating them and assigning to them new identities.

Fee system A system, used in some rural areas, in which the county government pays a modest amount of money for each prisoner per day as an operating budget.

Felonies Severe crimes, subject to punishment of 1 year or more in prison or to capital punishment.

Felony murder The imposition of criminal liability for murder upon one who participates in the commission of a felony that is dangerous to life and that causes the death of another.

Fence A receiver of stolen property who resells the goods for profit.

Field experiment An experiment conducted in a real-world setting, as opposed to one conducted in a laboratory.

Frankpledge An ancient system whereby members of a tithing, an association of 10 families, were bound together by a mutual pledge to keep the peace. Every male over age 12 was part of the system.

Fraud An act of trickery or deceit, especially involving misrepresentation.

Fundamental psycholegal error An error in thinking or mistaken belief that occurs when we identify a cause for criminal behavior and then assume that it naturally follows that any behavior resulting from that "cause" must be excused by law.

General strain theory A criminological theory positing that criminal behavior can result from strain caused by failure to achieve positively valued goals, stress caused by the removal of positively valued stimuli from the individual, or strain caused by the presentation of negative stimuli.

Genetic fingerprinting Forensic method that employs DNA technology to evaluate blood, semen, and tissue samples taken from crime scenes. The DNA from these samples is used to search for an evidentiary match.

Good-time system A system under which time is deducted from a prison sentence for good behavior within the institution.

Habeas corpus A writ requesting that a person or an institution that is detaining a named prisoner bring him or her before a judicial officer and give reasons for the prisoner's capture and detention so that the lawfulness of the imprisonment may be determined.

High-tech crime The pursuit of illegal activities through the use of advanced electronic media.

Homicide The killing of one person by another.

Hypoglycemia A condition that may occur in susceptible individuals when the level of blood sugar falls below an acceptable range, causing anxiety, headaches, confusion, fatigue, and aggressive behavior.

Hypothesis A proposition set forth as an explanation for some specified phenomenon.

Id The part of the personality that, according to psychoanalytic theory, contains powerful urges and drives for gratification and satisfaction.

Index crimes The eight major crimes included in Part I of the Uniform Crime Reports: criminal homicide, forcible rape, robbery, aggravated assault, burglary, larceny-theft, auto theft, and arson.

Indictment Accusation against a criminal defendant rendered by a grand jury on the basis of evidence constituting a prima facie case.

Indirect control A behavioral influence that arises from an individual's identification with noncriminals and his or her desire to conform to societal norms.

Information Accusation against a defendant prepared by a prosecuting attorney.

Inmate code An informal set of rules that reflects the values of the prison society.

Insider trading The use of material nonpublic financial information to obtain an unfair advantage in trading securities.

Intensive-supervision probation (ISP) An alternative to prison for convicted nonviolent offenders who do not qualify for routine probation.

Internalized control Self-regulation of behavior and conformity to societal norms as a result of guilt feelings arising in the conscience.

International crimes The major criminal offenses so designated by the community of nations for the protection of interests common to all humankind.

International criminal court The United Nations Court with jurisdiction over the most heinous international crimes.

Involuntary manslaughter Homicide in which the perpetrator unintentionally but recklessly causes the death of another person by consciously taking a grave risk that endangers the person's life.

Involvement An individual's participation in conventional activities.

Just deserts A philosophy of justice which asserts that the punishment should fit the crime and culpability of the offender. *See also* Retribution.

Justices of the peace Originally (established in 1326), untrained men, usually of the lower nobility, who were assigned to investigate and try minor cases; presently, judges of a lower local or municipal court with limited jurisdiction.

Justifiable homicide A homicide, permitted by law, in defense of a legal right or mandate.

Kidnapping A felony consisting of the seizure and abduction of a person by force or threat of force and against the victim's will. Under federal law, the victim of a kidnapping is one who has been taken across state lines and held for ransom.

Labeling theory A theory that explains deviance in terms of the process by which a person acquires a negative identity, such as "addict" or "ex-con," and is forced to suffer the consequences of outcast status.

Larceny The trespassory (unconsented) taking and carrying away of personal property belonging to another with the intent to deprive the owner of the property permanently.

Laws of imitation An explanation of crime as learned behavior. Individuals are thought to emulate behavior patterns of others with whom they have contact.

Longitudinal studies Analyses that focus on studies of a particular group conducted repeatedly over a period of time.

Macrosociological studies The study of overall social arrangements, their structures, and their long-term effects.

Mafia The entirety of those Sicilian families which, in both the United States and Sicily, are loosely associated with one another in operating organized crime.

Malice aforethought The mens rea requirement for murder, consisting of the intention to kill with the awareness that there is no right to kill. *See also* Mens rea.

Mandatory sentence A sentence that is specified by law and that a judge has no power to alter.

Manslaughter Criminal homicide without malice, committed intentionally after provocation (voluntary manslaughter) or recklessly (involuntary manslaughter).

Mass murder The killing of several persons, in one act or transaction, by one perpetrator or a group of perpetrators.

Mens rea (Latin, "guilty mind") Awareness of wrongdoing; the intention to commit a criminal act or behave recklessly.

Microsociological studies The study of everyday patterns of behavior and personal interactions.

Minimal brain dysfunction (MBD) An attention-deficit disorder that may produce such asocial behavior as impulsivity, hyperactivity, and aggressiveness.

Miranda warning A warning that explains the rights of an arrestee. An arresting officer is required by law to recite the warning at the time of the arrest.

Misdemeanors Crimes less serious than a felony and subject to a maximum sentence of 1 year in jail or a fine.

Money laundering The process by which money derived from illegal activities (especially drug sales) is unlawfully taken out of the country, placed in a numbered account abroad, and then transferred as funds no longer "dirty."

Monozygotic (MZ) twins Identical twins, who develop from a single fertilized egg that divides into two embryos. *See also* Dizygotic twins.

Motions Oral or written requests to a judge that ask the court to make a specified ruling, finding, decision, or order. May be presented at any appropriate moment from arrest until the end of the trial.

Motion to dismiss A request by the defense that the trial proceedings be terminated.

Murder The unlawful (usually intentional) killing of a human being with malice aforethought.

Negligent homicide A homicide designation used by some states to differentiate between involuntary manslaughter and situations in which the offender assumed a lesser risk.

Neuroticism A personality condition marked by low self-esteem, excessive anxiety, and wide mood swings (Eysenck).

Night watchmen Originally, thirteenth-century untrained citizens who patrolled at night on the lookout for disturbances.

Nonparticipant observation A study in which investigators observe closely but do not become participants.

Occupational crimes Crimes committed by an individual for his or her own benefit, in the course of performing a profession.

Organizational due diligence Implementation of effective ethics corporate compliance programs, which may include cooperating with authorities, creating an ethics code, and hiring ethics officers.

Parens patriae (Latin, "father of the fatherland") Assumption by the state of the role of guardian over children whose parents are deemed incapable or unworthy.

Parole Supervised conditional release of a convicted prisoner before expiration of the sentence of imprisonment.

Participant observation Collection of information through involvement in the social life of the group a researcher is studying.

Penitentiary A prison or place of confinement and correction for persons convicted of felonies; originally, a place where convicts did penance.

Penologists Social scientists who study and apply the theory and methods of punishment for crime.

Peremptory challenges Challenges (limited in number) by which a potential juror may be dismissed by either the prosecution or the defense without assignment of reason. *See also* Challenges for cause; Voir dire.

Phrenology A nineteenth-century theory based on the hypothesis that human behavior is localized in certain specific brain and skull areas. According to this theory, criminal behavior can be determined by the bumps on the head.

Physiognomy The study of facial features and their relation to human behavior.

Pimp A procurer or manager of prostitutes who provides access to prostitutes and protects and exploits them, living off their proceeds.

Plea bargaining Making an agreement between defense and prosecution for certain leniencies in return for a guilty plea.

Plead To respond to a criminal charge. Forms of pleas are guilty, not guilty, and nolo contendere.

Police subculture The result of socialization and bonding among police officers due to the stress and anxiety produced on the job.

Population A large group of persons in a study.

Pornography The portrayal, by whatever means, of lewd or obscene (sexually explicit) material prohibited by law.

Positivist school A criminological perspective that uses the scientific methods of the natural sciences and suggests that human behavior is a product of social, biological, psychological, or economic forces.

Preliminary hearing A preview of a trial held in court before a judge, in which the prosecution must produce sufficient evidence of guilt for the case to be bound over for the grand jury or to proceed to trial.

Presumptive sentence A sentence whose length is specified by law but that may be modified by a judge under limited circumstances.

Prima facie case A case in which there is as much evidence as would warrant the conviction of the defendant if properly proved in court, unless contradicted; a case that meets evidentiary requirements for grand-jury indictment.

Primary data Facts and observations that researchers gather by conducting their own measurements for a study.

Prisonization A socialization process in which new prisoners learn the ways of prison society, including rules, hierarchy, customs, and culture.

Proactive corporate fault The failure of a corporation to prevent ethical or legal violations.

Probable cause A set of facts that would induce a reasonable person to believe that an accused person committed the offense in question; the minimum evidence requirement for an arrest, according to the Fourth Amendment to the U.S. Constitution.

Probation An alternative to imprisonment, allowing a person found guilty of an offense to stay in the community, under conditions and with supervision.

Problem-oriented policing A strategy to enhance community relations and to improve crime prevention whereby police work with citizens to identify and respond to problems in a given community.

Proprietary economic information Any information, whether tangible or intangible, that a corporation has made reasonable efforts to keep confidential.

Prosecutor An attorney and government official who represents the people in proceedings against persons accused of criminal acts.

Prostitution The practice of engaging in sexual activities for hire.

Psychoanalytic theory In criminology, a theory of criminality that attributes delinquent and criminal behavior to a conscience that is either so overbearing that it arouses excessive feelings of guilt or so weak that it cannot control the individual's impulses.

Psychopathy A condition in which a person appears to be psychologically normal but in reality has no sense of responsibility, shows disregard for truth, is insincere, and feels no sense of shame, guilt, or humiliation (also called "sociopathy").

Psychosis A mental illness characterized by a loss of contact with reality.

Psychoticism A dimension of the human personality describing individuals who are aggressive, egocentric, and impulsive (Eysenck).

Racketeer Influenced and Corrupt Organizations (RICO) Act A federal statute that provides for forfeiture of assets derived from a criminal enterprise.

Radical criminology A criminological perspective that studies the relationships between economic disparity and crime, avers that crime is the result of a struggle between owners of capital and workers for the distribution of power and resources, and posits that crime will disappear only when capitalism is abolished.

Random sample A sample chosen in such a way as to ensure that each person in the population to be studied has an equal chance of being selected. *See also* Sample.

Rape At common law, a felony consisting of the carnal knowledge (intercourse), by force and violence, by a man of a woman (not his wife) against her will. The stipulation that the woman not be the man's wife is omitted in modern statutes. Many states now call rape "sexual assault."

Rational choice A theory stating that crime is the result of a decision-making process in which the offender weighs the potential penalties and rewards of committing a crime.

Reaction formation An individual response to anxiety in which the person reacts to a stimulus with abnormal intensity or inappropriate conduct.

Reactive corporate fault The failure of a corporation to respond responsibly to the discovery of an ethical or legal violation.

Reasonable suspicion Warranted suspicion (short of probable cause) that a person may be engaged in the commission of a crime.

Rehabilitation A punishment philosophy that asserts that through proper correctional intervention, a criminal can be reformed into a law-abiding citizen.

Restorative justice An approach to sentencing that seeks both to restore those who have suffered from a crime to their original sense of well-being and to make it clear that justice itself is being restored.

Retribution An "eye for an eye" philosophy of justice. *See also* Just deserts.

Robbery The taking of the property of another, or out of his or her presence, by means of force and violence or the threat thereof.

Routine activity A theory stating that an increase or decrease in crime rates can be explained by changes in the daily habits of potential victims; based on the expectation that crimes will occur where there is a suitable target unprotected by guardians.

Sample A selected subset of a population to be studied. *See also* Random sample.

Secondary data Facts and observations that were previously collected for a different study.

Selective incapacitation The targeting of high-risk and recidivistic offenders for rigorous prosecution and incarceration.

Self-report surveys Surveys in which respondents answer in a confidential interview or, most often, by completing an anonymous questionnaire.

Sentencing commissions Independent agencies authorized by a legislature to create sentencing guidelines.

Serial murder The killing of several victims over a period of time by the same perpetrator(s).

Sheriff The principal law enforcement officer of a county.

Sherman Antitrust Act An act (1890) of Congress prohibiting any contract, conspiracy, or combination of business interests in restraint of foreign or interstate trade.

Shock incarceration (SI) Short-term, high-intensity confinement intended to shock convicts into disciplined lifestyles.

Shoplifting Stealing goods from stores or markets.

Simple assault An attack that inflicts little or no physical harm on the victim.

Social control theory An explanation of criminal behavior that focuses on control mechanisms, techniques, and strategies for regulating human behavior, leading to conformity or obedience to society's rules, and which posits that deviance results when social controls are weakened or break down, so that individuals are not motivated to conform to them.

Social disorganization theory A theory of criminality in which the breakdown of effective social bonds, primary-group associations, and social controls in neighborhoods and communities is held to result in development of high-crime areas.

Social interactionists Scholars who view the human self as formed through a process of social interaction.

Social learning theory A theory of criminality that maintains that delinquent behavior is learned through the same psychological processes as nondelinquent behavior, e.g., through reinforcement.

Social norms Perceived standards of acceptable behavior prevalent among members of a society.

Sociopaths Persons who have no sense of responsibility; show disregard for truth; are insincere; and feel no sense of shame, guilt, or humiliation.

Sodomy Sexual intercourse by mouth or anus; a felony at common law.

Somatotype school A criminological perspective that relates body build to behavioral tendencies, temperament, susceptibility to disease, and life expectancy.

Statutory rape Sexual intercourse with a person incapable of giving legally relevant consent, because of immaturity (below age) or mental or physical condition.

Sting operation An undercover operation in which police officers attract likely perpetrators by posing as criminals.

Stock manipulation An illegal practice of brokers in which clients are led to believe that the price of a particular stock will rise, thus creating an artificial demand for it.

Strain theory A criminological theory positing that a gap between culturally approved goals and legitimate means of achieving them causes frustration that leads to criminal behavior.

Stranger homicide Criminal homicide committed by a person unknown and unrelated to the victim.

Strict liability Liability for a crime or violation imposed without regard to the actor's guilt; criminal liability without mens rea. *See also* Mens rea.

Subculture A subdivision within the dominant culture that has its own norms, beliefs, and values.

Subcultures of violence Subcultures with values that demand the overt use of violence in certain social situations.

Superego In psychoanalytic theory, the conscience, or those aspects of the personality that threaten the person or impose a sense of guilt or psychic suffering and thus restrain the id.

Survey The systematic collection of information by asking questions in questionnaires or interviews.

Synnomie A societal state, the opposite of anomie, marked by social cohesion achieved through the sharing of values.

Target hardening A crime-prevention technique that seeks to make it more difficult to commit a given offense, by better protecting the threatened object or person.

Team policing A strategy for improving contacts between citizens and police, whereby a team of officers is responsible for a specific neighborhood on a 24-hour basis.

Terrorism The use of violence against a target to create fear, alarm, dread, or coercion for the purpose of obtaining concessions or rewards or commanding public attention for a political cause.

Theories of victimization Theories that explain the role that victims play in the crimes that happen to them.

Theory A coherent group of propositions used as principles in explaining or accounting for known facts or phenomena.

Tithing In Anglo-Saxon law, an association of 10 families bound together by a frankpledge, for purposes of crime control. *See also* Frankpledge.

Torts Injuries or wrongs committed against another, subject to compensation; infringements of the rights of an individual that are not founded on either contract or criminal law prohibition.

Transnational crime A criminal act or transaction violating the laws of more than one country or having an impact on a foreign country.

Utilitarianism A criminological perspective positing that crime prevention and criminal justice must serve the end of providing the greatest good for the greatest number;

based on the rationality of lawgivers, law enforcers, and the public at large.

Variables Changeable factors.

Vicarious liability The imputation of liability from an agent to a principal, e.g., from an employee to an employer.

Victim precipitation Opening oneself up, by either direct or subliminal means, to a criminal response.

Victimization surveys Surveys that measure the extent of crime by interviewing individuals about their experiences as victims.

Vindication Condemnation of the commission of offenses.

Violations Minor criminal offenses, usually under a city ordinance, commonly subject only to a fine.

Voir dire A process in which lawyers and a judge question potential jurors in order to select those who are acceptable, that is, those who are unbiased and objective in relation to the particular trial. *See also* Challenges for cause; Peremptory challenges.

Voluntary manslaughter Homicide in which the perpetrator intentionally, but without malice, causes the death of another person, as in the heat of passion, in response to strong provocation, or possibly under severe intoxication.

Whistle-blower An employee, or interested party, who reports corporate illegalities to authorities.

White-collar crime A sociological concept encompassing any violation of the law committed by a person or group of persons in the course of an otherwise respected and legitimate occupation or business enterprise.

Credits

TEXT AND ILLUSTRATION CREDITS

CHAPTER 1
Page 16: © 2009 by Charles Montaldo (http://crime.about
.com/od/famousdiduno/ig/celebrity_mugshots/).
Used with permission of About, Inc., which can be
found online at www.about.com. All rights reserved.

CHAPTER 2
Page 44: From van Dijk, J. J. M., Manchin, R., van
Kesteren, J. N., and Hideg, G. (2007). *The Burden of
Crime in the EU. Research Report: A Comparative Analysis
of the European Crime and Safety Survey (EU ICS) 2005*.
Brussels: Gallup Europe, p. 19. Reprinted by permission
of The Gallup Organisation Europe, s.a.

CHAPTER 4
Pages 91–93: From Caroline Schulenburg, *Dying to
Entertain: Violence on Prime Time Broadcast Television
1998–2006* (Executive Summary). Reprinted with
permission from the Parents Television Council.

Page 97: From Hervey Cleckley, *The Mask of Sanity*,
5th edition, pp. 271–272. Copyright 1976, 1988.
Reprinted by permission of Emily S. Cleckley.

Pages 98–99: From Anastasia Toufexis, "Dancing with
Devils: Forensic Psychiatrist Park Dietz Tracks America's
Serial Killers, Bombers and Mass Murderers," *Psychology
Today*, vol. 32, no. 3 (May/June 1999), p. 54. Reprinted
with permission from *Psychology Today* Magazine,
(Copyright © 1999 Sussex Publishers, LLC.).

CHAPTER 5
Figure 5.2: From Baumer, E. P. & Gustafson, R. (2007).
Social organization and instrumental crime: Assessing
the empirical validity of classic and contemporary
anomie theories. *Criminology*, 45(3): 617–663, Figure 1
(p. 620). Reprinted by permission of the American
Society of Criminology.

Figure 5.6: Reprinted by permission of Chicago Area
Project.

CHAPTER 6
Pages 129–130: Excerpts from *2005 National Gang Threat
Assessment*. National Alliance of Gang Investigators
Association, p. vi. Reprinted by permission of the
National Alliance of Gang Investigators Association.

Table 6.1: *2005 National Gang Threat Assessment*. National
Alliance of Gang Investigators Association, Table 2
(p. 1). Reprinted by permission of the National Alliance
of Gang Investigators Association.

Table 6.3: *2005 National Gang Threat Assessment*. National
Alliance of Gang Investigators Association, Table 1
(p. 1). Reprinted by permission of the National Alliance
of Gang Investigators Association.

Table 6.4: *2005 National Gang Threat Assessment*. National
Alliance of Gang Investigators Association, Table 20
(p. 33). Reprinted by permission of the National
Alliance of Gang Investigators Association.

CHAPTER 8
Pages 178–179: From Bernard E. Harcourt, *Muslim
Profiles Post 9/11: Is Racial Profiling an Effective
Counterterrorist Measure and Does It Violate the Right
to be Free from Discrimination?* Paper presented at the
Oxford Colloquium on Security and Human Rights at
Oxford University, March 17, 2006, p. 1. Reprinted by
permission of Bernard E. Harcourt.

CHAPTER 9
Page 194: From Bruce Golding, "Jeweler Held in Botched
Heist," *New York Post*, December 9, 2008, p. 7. Reprinted
with permission from *The New York Post*, 2002,
Copyright, NYP Holdings, Inc.

Pages 194–195: From Richard Winton, "Car-to-Car
Shooting Leaves Woman Dead," *Los Angeles Times*,
December 9, 2008, p. B2. © 2008 by The Los Angeles
Times. All rights reserved. Reprinted with permission.

Page 195: From Theodore Decker, "Rapist Blamed for
7th Attack: Nov. 2 Crime Took Place Near Site of Oct.
5 Assault," *The Columbus Dispatch*, November 12, 2008.
Reprinted by permission of The Columbus Dispatch.

CHAPTER 10
Page 240: John Lehmann and Al Guart, "Ciao: Gotti Gang
Gone," *New York Post*, June 21, 2002, p. 5. Reprinted
with permission from *The New York Post*, 2002,
Copyright, NYP Holdings, Inc.

CHAPTER 11
Table 11.1: From "Theft Surveys." http://www
.hayesinternational.com/thft_srvys.html. © 2008 Jack L.
Hayes International. Reprinted with permission.

Pages 287–288: From *Fifth Annual BSA and IDC Global
Software Piracy Study*. Washington, DC: Business
Software Alliance, 2007, pp. 2, 3. Reprinted with
permission.

PHOTO CREDITS

Page 3: © AP Photo/Eric Gay; 6: © Brand X Pictures/
PunchStock; 8: © Michael Smith/Getty; 9 (top): © Paula
Bronstein/Getty Images; 9 (bottom): © EFE/SIPA; 12:
© SAJJAD HUSSAIN/AFP/Getty Images; 13: © AP
Graphic; 14: © Giraudon/Art Resource; 17 (left to right,
top to bottom): Photo by Los Angeles County Sheriff's
Department via Getty Images; Photo by Jonathan Ernst/
Getty Images; Photo by the Aiken County Sheriff's
Office via Getty Images; Photo by Glendale City Police
Department via Getty Images; Photo by Los Angeles
County Sheriff's Department via Getty Images; © AP
Photo/Los Angeles Police Department; Photo by Dade
County Jail/Getty Images; 18: © A. Ramey/Stock.Boston;
21: © Haviv/Corbis Saba; 24: © Kent Knudson/
PhotoLink; 27: © Al Grillo/AP/Wide World; 28: ©
Mike Derer/AP/Wide World Photos; 42: © Andrew
Lichtenstein/The Image Works; 48: © Associated

Press; **52:** © Pushkin Museum of Fine Arts, Moscow, Scala/Art Resource; **53:** © PhotoEdit; **54:** © REUTERS/ Werner Nosko/File Photo/Corbis; **56:** © Granger Collection; **58:** © AP/Wide World Photos; **59:** "Book Cover," copyright © 2009 by Random House, Inc. from *The Life You Can Save: Acting Now to End World Poverty* by Peter Singer. Used by permission of Random House, Inc.; **61:** "How to Read Character. A New Illustrated Hand-Book of Physiology, Phrenology and Physiognomy for Students and Examiners," by Samuel Wells, Fowler & Wells Co., NY, 1890; **62:** © Topham/The Image Works; **64:** Arthur Estabrook Papers, M. E. Grenander Department of Special Collections and Archives, University at Albany; **67:** © Corbis; **72:** © Handout/Sedgwick County Sheriff's Office/Reuters/Corbis; **73:** © Joel Gordon; **79:** © Jose Azel/Aurora Photos; **80:** © Richard Carson/ Reuters/Landov; **81:** © Adrian Raine, Departments of Criminology, Psychiatry, and Psychology, University of Pennsylvania; **88:** © Martin Rodgers/Stock.Boston; **94:** © Steve Senne/Reuters/Landov; **95:** © Gretchen Ertl/AP/ Wide World Photos; **98 (left):** © George Widman/AP/ Wide World Photos; **98 (right):** © SIPA; **102:** SLUMDOG MILLIONAIRE, Ayush Mahesh Khedekar, 2008. © Fox Searchlight/courtesy Everett Collection; **107:** © Collart Herve/Corbis Sygma; **108:** © Elaine Thompson/AP/ Wide World Photos; **110:** © A. Ramey/Stock.Boston; **116:** © Greg Smith/Corbis Saba; **121:** © Lisa Terry/Getty Images; **123:** © Mary D'Anella/Corbis Sygma; **125:** © Sankei Shimbun/Corbis Sygma; **128:** © YURI CORTEZ/ AFP/Getty Images; **132:** © PhotoLink/Getty Images; **133:** © Mark Peterson/Corbis/Saba; **135:** © Rick Hunter/SA Express News/Corbis Sygma; **138:** © Jim Cooper/AP/ Wide World Photos; **142:** Library of Congress; **144:** © Greg Mellis; **146:** © A. Ramey/PhotoEdit; **148:** © Steven Rubin/ The Image Works; **153:** © Frederick J. Brown/AFP/Getty Images; **154:** © AP/Wide World Photos; **157:** © Creatas Images/Jupiter Images; **162:** © AP Photo; **165:** © Joel Gordon; **167:** © Richard Steinwald/AP/Wide World; **168:** © Fujiphotos/The Image Works; **173:** © Mike Nelson/ AFP/Getty Images; **176:** © John Paul Filo/Getty Images; **182:** © Rick Reinhard; **183:** © Micah Walter/Reuters/ Corbis; **190:** © Greuorgui Pinkhassov/Magnum; **191:** © Rick Reinhard; **194:** © Monika Graff/UPI/Landov; **196:** © Mark Peterson/Corbis Saba; **199:** © Creasource/ Corbis; **200:** © Oscar Abolafia; **201:** © Mike Siluk/The Image Works; **205:** © Rudi Von Briel/PhotoEdit; **209:** © Joel Gordon; **211:** © David Butow/Corbis Saba; **219:** © Ceneta Manuel/Gamma Presse; **220:** © Paul Samuka/ AP/Wide World Photos; **223:** © Taylor/Montgomery Journal/Gamma Presse; **226 (top):** © Norman Y. Lono/ The New York Times; **226 (bottom):** © Scott Dalton/AP/ Wide World Photos; **230:** © Jim West/PhotoEdit; **232:** © Charles Drupa/AP/Wide World Photos; **242:** Library of Congress; **243:** © AP Photo/Edouard H.R. Gluck; **245:** © AP Photo/John Marshall Mantel; **249:** © Shannon Stapleton/Reuters/Landov; **250:** FBI, from http://www .fbi.gov/wanted/terrorists/fugitives.htm; **254:** © Pam Francis/www.pamfrancis.com; **255:** © Max Whittaker/ Corbis; **261:** © Rick Reinhard; **265:** © JESSICA RINALDI/ Reuters/Landov; **267:** © 20th Century Fox/Everett Collection; **271:** © Los Angeles County Courts/Getty Images; **275:** © George Widman/AP/Wide World Photos; **277:** © Courtesy Freda Adler; **280:** © Mark Terrill/AP/ Wide World Photos; **282:** © AP Photo/Steven Senne; **288:** © AP Photo/Mike Wintroath; **292:** © Daniel Hulshizer/ AP/Wide World Photos; **296:** © The McGraw-Hill Companies, Inc./Lars A. Niki; **298:** © William Miller/

SIPA; **299:** © Stephen Chernin/Getty Images; **301:** © Jason Straziuso/AP/Wide World Photos; **302:** © 8383/ Gamma Presse; **303:** © Kenneth Lambert/AP/Wide World Photos; **313 (top):** © Bob Shaw; **313 (bottom):** © EPA/Matthew Cavanaugh/Corbis; **316:** © Getty Images; **318:** © EPA/Matthew Cavanaugh/Corbis; **322:** © Photo by Sandro Tucci/Liaison/Getty; **323:** © Jay Mallin/ Bloomberg News/Landov; **327:** © Michael Schmelling/ AP/Wide World Photos; **334 (top left):** © Tom Miner/ The Image Works; **334 (top right):** © Nick Ut/AP/Wide World Photos; **336:** © Apichart Weerawong/AP/Wide World Photos; **341:** © Tomi/PhotoLink/Getty Images; **343:** © Autumn Cruz/MCT/Landov; **345:** © Jim Wilson/ Woodfin Camp & Associates; **353:** © Jim Wilson/Woodfin Camp & Associates; **356:** © Scott Peterson/Getty Images; **358:** © Apichart Weerawong/AP/Wide World Photos; **359:** © Mia Foster/PhotoEdit; **362:** © David C. Johnson; **363:** © Peter Blakely/Redux Pictures; **369:** © Vladimir Sichov/SIPA; **373:** © AP Photo/Sarah El Deeb

"DID YOU KNOW?" SOURCES

Page 12: T. F. T. Plucknett, *A Concise History of The Common Law,* 5th edition (London: Butterworth and Co., 1956), pp. 15, 156, 323, 355; **32, 39, 45:** *Juvenile Offenders and Victims: 1999 National Report,* Office of Juvenile Justice and Delinquency Prevention, September 1999; **55:** http://www.utm.edu/research/rep/b/beccarea .htm; **62:** http://www.epub.orgbr/cm/m01/frenolog/ frenmod.htm; **74:** Former FBI Agent Jack Douglas, quoted in Kevia Johnson, "Several Serial Killers Said to Be At Large," *USA Today,* July 1, 1999, p. 12A; **75:** "Cholesterol and Violence: Is There a Connection?" *Annals of Internal Medicine,* 128 (1998): 478–487; **106:** http://www.irp.wisc.edu/irp/faqs/faq3.htm; **121:** *Juvenile Offenders and Victims: 1999 National Report,* Office of Juvenile Justice and Delinquency Prevention, September, 1999; **146:** http://www.clasp.org/Pubs/ DMS/Documents/1012503181.48/teen_pregnancy_a _key_strategy.pdf; **155:** American Nonsmokers Rights Foundation, "100% Smoke-Free Correctional Facilities" (2008). Retrieved July 14, 2008, from http://www .no-smoke.org/pdf/100smokefreeprisons.pdf; **165:** Anthony Walsh and Lee Ellis, "Political Ideology and American Criminologists' Explanations for Criminal Behavior," *Criminologist,* 24 (1999): 1; **198:** Marcus Felson and Ronald V. Clarke, "Routine Precautions, Criminology, and Crime Prevention," in *Crime and Public Policy: Putting Theory to Work,* ed. Hugh D. Barlow, Boulder, Colo.: Westview Press, 1995; **212:** Ronald V. Clarke, *Hot Products: Understanding, Anticipating and Reducing Demand for Stolen Goods,* Policing and Reducing Crime Unit, Police Research Series Paper 112 (London: Home Office, 1999); John Burrow and D. Cooper, *Theft and Loss from UK Libraries,* Police Research Group Crime Prevention Unit Series Paper 37 (London: Home Office, 1992); **224:** *Juvenile Offenders and Victims: 1999 National Report,* Office of Juvenile Justice and Delinquency Prevention, 1999, p. 16; **230:** *Juvenile Offenders and Victims: 1999 National Report,* Office of Juvenile Justice and Delinquency Prevention, 1999, p. 17; **286:** "1998 Internet Fraud Statistics" (http:// www.fraud.org/internet/9923stat.htm); **318:** U.S. Sentencing Commission, Organizational Datafile, FY2003; **340:** Anti–Drug Abuse Act of 1986, 21 USC 801.

Name Index

Citations in italics refer to figures and tables

A

Abadinsky, Howard, 241, 339, N-28, N-29, N-38, N-39, N-40
Abde-laziz, Atiqui, N-26
Abraham, Nathaniel, 167
Abrahamsen, David, N-24
Adams, Anthony, N-14
Adams, Reed, N-9
Adler, Freda, 46, 48, 55, 111, 168, 169, 184, 276, N-1, N-4, N-9, N-10, N-11, N-13, N-15, N-16, N-17, N-18, N-19, N-22, N-31, N-32, N-33, N-36, N-42, N-43
Adler, Jeffrey S., N-19
Adler, Jerry, N-29
Adler, Nanci, N-1
Africa, John, 125
Ageton, Suzanne S., 49, N-3, N-4, N-10, N-17
Aglipay, Edgar, N-35
Agnew, Robert, 111, 158, 166, 170, N-4, N-11, N-13, N-16, N-17
Agusti, Filiberto, N-35
Ahlstrom-Laakso, S., N-38
Aichhorn, August, N-8
Aigner, Stephen M., N-4
Akers, Ronald L., 94, 180, N-9, N-13, N-19
Albanese, Jay, 242, N-27, N-28
Albazzi del Frate, Anna, N-41
Albini, Joseph, N-27
Albonetti, Celesta A., N-19
Albrecht, Hans-Jorg, N-42
Albrecht, Steve W., N-32
Alder, Christine, N-26
Alexander, Shana, N-27
Aley, James, N-40
Alper, Benedict, N-41
Amaechi, Rotimi, 151
Ames, M. Ashley, N-25
Amir, Menachem, 236, N-26, N-38, N-43
Anastasia, Albert, 244
Ancel, Marc, N-5
Anderson, Annelise Graebner, N-27
Anderson, Bo, N-15
Anderson, Elijah, N-13
Anderson, Pamela, 232
Andrews, D. W., N-9
Andrienko, Yuri, 141
Anglin, Deirdre, N-24

Anglin, M. Douglas, N-9, N-37
Applegate, Brandon K., N-38
Applewhite, Marshall, 124
Arbuthnot, Jack, N-8
Archer, Dane, N-24, N-40
Argomaniz, J., N-2
Aristotle, 185
Arlacchi, Pino, N-27
Arneklev, B. J., N-17
Arnold, Rolf, N-33
Arrigo, Bruce, 190, N-20
Arthur, John A., N-30, N-42
Asahara, Shoko, 254
Atkins, Daryl, 66
Aultman, Madeline G., N-17
Austin, James, 171
Austin, Roy L., N-3
Austin, W. Timothy, N-17
Avary, D'Aunn Webster, 293, N-21, N-31
Avison, William R., N-11, N-13
Ayat, Mohammed, 233, N-25

B

Baarda, B., N-9
Bacher, J.-L., 29, N-2
Bachman, Jerald, N-2
Bachman, Ronet, N-25
Bacich, Anthony R., N-25
Bae, Ronald, N-42
Bai, Matt, N-29
Bailey, William C., N-26
Bakalar, James, N-36
Baker, Rodger, 247
Ball, John C., N-36
Ball, Richard A., N-16
Balladares, Ernesto Perez, 336
Balliofyne, Scott, N-42
Balsamo, William, N-27
Bamfield, Joshua, N-30
Bandura, Albert, 90, 94, N-8, N-9
Barbara, Joseph M., 244, 245
Barbour, William, N-39, N-40
Barclay, Gordon, 141
Barnes, H. V., N-2
Barnes, Harry Elmer, 55, N-5
Barnett, Cynthia, 300
Barnett, W. Steven, N-11
Baron, Stephen W., N-13
Barovick, Harriet, 162
Barron, R. A., N-39
Barton, Mark O., 228
Bartusch, Dawn Jeglum, N-3, N-12

Barzini, Luigi, N-27
Bashir, Omar Hassan Ahmed, 188, 189
Basiotis, P. Peter, N-41
Baskin, Deborah, N-13, N-37
Bassiouni, M. Cherif, N-43
Baucus, Melissa, N-32
Baum, K., 209
Baumer, Eric P., 112
Baumer, Terry L., N-26
Baus, Stephanie A., N-39
Beccaria, Cesare, 1, 52, 53, 55–57, 65, 69, 185, N-5
Becker, Ed, N-27
Becker, Gary S., N-20
Becker, Howard S., 175, 177, 181, N-18
Bedenbaugh, Edward III, 40–41
Beeman, E. A., N-7
Beha, James, A., II, N-29
Beirne, Piers, N-5, N-40
Belanger, Mathieu, N-21
Bell, P. A., N-39
Bell, Ralph, N-22
Bellair, Paul E., N-12
Bellis, David J., N-39
Belliston Lara M., N-17
Bellucci, Charles, N-22
Benamati, Dennis, N-41
Bendix, Reinhard, N-11
Bennett, Nathan, N-26
Bennett, Richard R., N-41
Bennett, Wayne W., N-31
Bennett, William C., 50
Benson, Bruce L., N-37
Benson, Michael L., N-32, N-35
Bentham, Jeremy, 53, 57, 58, 59, 69, 185, N-5, N-20
Bentler, P. M., N-37
Bequai, August, N-32, N-33
Berbaum, Michael L., N-22
Berger, Dale E., N-42
Berger, Herbert, N-38
Berger, Phil, N-33
Berk, Richard A., 347, N-25
Berkey, Martha Lou, N-31
Berkowitz, David "Son of Sam," 225
Bernard, Thomas J., N-10, N-11
Berrueta-Clement, John R., N-11
Bersten, Michael, N-32
Berthelsen, Christian, N-26
Berube, A., 141
Beseler, P., N-27
Biaggi, Mario, 305

Bibel, Daniel, N-4
Biderman, Albert D., N-35
Bierie, D., N-2
Bihrle, Susan, N-7
Bijlefeld, Marjolijn, N-30
Bilby, C. A. L., N-2
Binet, Alfred, 78
Bin Laden, Osama, 251
Bintliff, Russell B., N-33
Birkbeck, Christopher, N-41
Biron, Louise L., N-37
Bishop, Donna M., N-18
Bjerregaard, Beth, N-12, N-14, N-15
Black, Conrad, 297
Black, Donald J., 154, N-15
Blackburn, Ronald, N-6
Blackman, Peter, 367
Blackstone, William, 238
Blais, E., 29, N-2
Blake, Kevin, N-30
Blanchard, D. Caroline, N-8
Blane, Howard T., N-25
Blau, Judith R., 110, N-11, N-14
Blau, Peter M., 110, N-11, N-14
Bloch, Hannah, N-6
Block, Alan A., N-27, N-28
Block, Carolyn R., N-22
Block, Jack, N-8
Block, Richard L., N-22
Bloom, Joseph, N-32
Bloomberg, Seth, 31, N-2
Blum, Alfred, N-15
Blumberg, Abraham S., N-30
Blumenthal, Ralph, N-27, N-43
Blumer, Herbert, N-18
Blumstein, Alfred, 45, N-2, N-3, N-14, N-17, N-23, N-37
Bock, Alan W., N-28
Boden, Nancy, N-35
Boeringer, Scot B., N-39
Boesky, Ivan, 302
Bohm, Robert M., N-19
Bohn, Martin J., N-9
Bonanno, Joe, 244
Bonger, Willem Adriaan, 185, 325, N-19
Booth, A., N-7
Bordua, David J., N-13
Borduin, Charles M., N-8
Boren, Jerry F., N-41
Borg, Marian J., N-13
Borowiak, Lawrence, 297
Bortner, R. Mark, N-1
Boss, Maria S., N-32
Bossard, André, N-41
Botvin, Gilbert J., N-2
Bouloukos, Adam, N-41
Bowers, Kate J., N-22
Bowers, Patricia M., N-25
Bowers, William J., N-29

Bowie, N., N-2
Bowker, Lee H., N-4
Bowlby, John, 89, N-8, N-15
Bowman, Cynthia Grant, N-25
Boyle, Danny, 102, 103
Boyle, John M., N-32
Bracton, Henry de, 268
Bradley, Pamela, N-9
Brady, James, 262–263
Brady, Sarah, 262, 263
Braga, Anthony A., N-2, N-22
Braithwaite, John, 110, 191, N-10, N-11, N-22, N-32, N-33, N-34, N-35
Brame, Robert, 163
Bramlet, Gwen W., N-38
Brantingham, Patricia L., 214, N-20
Brantingham, Paul J., 214, N-20
Brennan, P. A., N-6
Brewer, Devon, N-26
Brewer, Kathleen, N-26
Brewer, Victoria E., N-29
Brewer, Wayne, N-27
Brewster, Victoria E., N-4
Brezina, Timothy, N-11, N-13
Briar, Scott, 155, N-15
Brickey, Kathleen F., N-33
Brickler, W., N-9
Brincat, John, Sr., 297
Brissette, Jeanne, N-34
Britto, Sarah, 190, N-20
Brochu, Serge, N-37
Broidy, Lisa, N-4
Brooke, James, N-28
Brosnan, Pierce, 200
Brower, Sidney, N-12
Brown, Claude, N-14
Brown, Curtis, N-37
Brown, David, N-20
Brown, James, 16, 17
Brown, Susan L., 163, N-16
Browne, Angela, N-24
Brownfield, David, 110, N-11, N-13, N-17, N-36
Brownmiller, Susan, N-26
Brunk, Molly A., N-8
Bryant, Jennings, N-39
Buchsbaum, Monte, 82, 83, N-7
Buchwald, Emilie, N-39
Buck, Andrew J., N-12
Buckle, Abigail, N-30
Buerger, Michael E., 204, N-21, N-22
Bukoff, Allen, N-29
Bundy, Theodore "Ted," 225
Burgess, Ernest, 94, 117, 118, N-9
Burnett, Cathleen, N-41
Bursik, Robert J., N-12, N-22
Burt, Martha R., N-26
Burton, Velmer S., Jr., N-11

Buruma, Ian, 350
Bush, George H. W., 337, N-37
Bush, George W., 151, 178, 249, 298
Bushway, Sharon, N-11
Butler, Charles, 254
Butterfield, Fox, 263, N-6, N-13, N-30
Bynum, Timothy S., N-14, N-27
Byrd, James, 254

C
Calavita, Kitty, N-32
Calder, Paul, 228
Caldwell, Charles, 60, 69
Cameron, Mary Owen, 270, N-30
Campbell, Anne, 30, 144, 146, 147, N-2, N-4, N-9, N-14
Campbell, Frances A., N-2
Cane, Mike, 349
Canter, R. J., N-17
Cao, Liqun, N-13
Caplan, Aaron, N-16
Capone, Al, 241, 242, 340
Caputo, Gail A., N-30
Carey, Gregory, N-6
Carey, James T., N-10
Carneiro, Robert L., 55, 107
Carolin, P. James, Jr., N-30
Carpenter, Cheryl, N-37
Carpozi, George Jr., N-27
Carrington, Michael D., N-26
Carroll, John, N-30
Carter, Timothy, N-19
Cartwright, D., N-16
Case, Carole, N-28
Casey, John J., N-36
Cash, David, 220
Caspi, Avshalom, N-4, N-7, N-10, N-20, N-25
Cassidy, Margery A., N-25
Castellano, Paul, 244
Castiglia, Francesco, 244
Castillo, Dawn N., N-24
Catalano, Richard F., N-17
Catanzaro, Raimondo, N-27
Cavender, Gray, N-34
Cebulak, Wojciech, N-43
Centerwall, B. S., N-9
Cernovich, Stephen A., 140, N-14, N-16
Chaiken, Marcia R., N-36
Chambers, James, A., N-11
Chambers, Jeff M., N-12
Chambliss, William J., 178–179, 186, N-12, N-18, N-19, N-30, N-34
Chamelin, N. C., N-31
Chamlin, Mitchell B., N-11
Chandler, Kathryn, N-29

Chang, Dae H., N-40, N-42
Chang, Dean, N-39
Chang, Richard J., N-42
Chapman, Robert, N-1
Chapman, S. G., N-38
Chapman, Steve, 209
Chappell, Duncan, N-26
Chard-Wierschem, Deborah, N-13
Chayet, Ellen F., N-32
Cheatwood, Derral, N-3, N-6
Chen, Hui, 94
Chen, Ruopian, 298
Cheney, Margaret, N-24
Cheng, Y. T., N-36
Chernoff, David, 107
Chesney-Lind, Meda, 46, N-4
Chesser, Eustace, N-38
Chesterman, L. P., N-7
Chilton, Roland, 223, N-23
Chin, Ko-lin, 135, N-13, N-43
Chira, Susan, N-12, N-18
Chiu, Alexis, N-26
Chivers, C. J., N-18
Cho, Byung In, N-42
Christiansen, Karl O., 76, N-6
Christman, John H., N-30
Churchwell, Ricky, 301
Clark, Douglas "Sunset Strip Killer," 225
Clark, G., N-35
Clark, John, 172, 308, N-33
Clarke, Michael, N-31, N-42
Clarke, Ronald V., 196, 197, 201, 209, 214, 215, N-20, N-21, N-22, N-23, N-30, N-31
Clear, Todd R., 119, 237, 238, N-12, N-26
Cleckley, Hervey, 97, N-9
Clelland, Donald, N-19
Clifton, Wayland, Jr, N-21
Clinard, Marshall B., 169, 309, 313, 318, 319, N-32, N-34, N-35
Clinton, William Jefferson, 262, 337, 372
Cloud, John, N-30
Cloward, Richard A., 130, 133, 134, 135, 136, 156, N-13, N-36
Cochran, John K., N-11, N-38
Coffee, John Collins, Jr., N-34, N-35
Cohen, Albert K., 130–133, 134, 136, 144, 148, 156, N-13, N-14, N-15, N-18
Cohen, Jacqueline, N-2, N-3, N-37
Cohen, Lawrence E., 198, 201, N-20, N-21
Cohen, Mark A., N-35

Cohen, S., N-15
Cohn, Ellen G., N-25
Colburn, James Blake, 66
Cole, George F., N-40, N-41
Coleman, D. H., N-38
Coleman, James W., N-32, N-33, N-35
Coleman, Jennifer, 343
Coleman, Kimberly, 343
Coll, Vincent "Mad Dog," 241
Colletti, P., N-7
Collins, Dean J., N-25
Collins, Jennifer M., 92–93
Collins, Laura, N-27
Comack, Elizabeth, N-19
Combs, Cindy, N-28
Comey, Jim, 240
Comte, Auguste, 58, 60, 69
Conklin, John, 239, N-26
Conyers, John, Jr., 319
Cook, Philip J., N-21, N-26
Cooley, Charles Horton, 175
Cooper, Darryl L., 279
Cooper, Michael, N-14
Copp, D., N-39
Corcoran, James, N-28
Corcoran, Kevin J., N-38
Cordero, Wilfredo, 232
Cornish, Derek B., 197, N-20, N-30
Corozzo, Nicolas, 243
Corzine, Jay, N-24, N-41
Corzine-Huff, Lin, N-24
Coser, Lewis A., N-18
Costanzo, Raymond Joseph, 279
Costello, Frank, 241, 244, 245
Costin, Michael, 95
Coston, Charisse T. M., N-21, N-41
Cottey, Talbert J., N-29
Cottrell, Leonard S., N-11
Countes, Reid, N-29
Coutorie, Larry E., N-31, N-43
Couzens, Michael, N-2
Covington, Jeanette, N-12, N-36
Cowley, Geoffrey, N-29
Craig, Christopher, 280
Crawford, Elizabeth M., N-4
Cressey, Donald R., 95, N-9, N-28, N-33
Crew, Gordon, N-29
Crites, Laura, N-4
Croall, Hazel, N-32
Cromwell, Paul F., 293, N-21, N-31
Crook, Shirley, 84
Crosswhite, Jennifer M., N-17
Croswell, Edgar, 244
Cullen, Francis T., N-4, N-11, N-13, N-17, N-21, N-34, N-35, N-38

Cullen, John B., N-4, N-35
Cummings, John, N-28
Cunningham, Lea C., N-13
Currie, Elliott, N-19
Curry, G. David, N-24
Curtis, Lynn A., N-14, N-15
Curtis, R., N-39

D

Dahlberg, Linda, N-24
Dahmer, Jeffrey, 98, 99, 225
Dahrendorf, Ralf, 183, 186, N-19
Daigle, Leah E., N-17
Dalton, Katharina, 81, N-7
Daly, Kathleen, N-19
Daly, Martin, N-24, N-42
Damiens, Robert-François, 54
Dammer, Harry R., N-41
Daniel, Anasseril E., N-24
Daro, Deborah, N-26
D'Arpa-Calandra, Angela, 141
Darwin, Charles, 58–59, 60, 69, N-5
David, James, R., N-13
Davies, Elizabeth, N-28
Davies, P., N-8
Davis, Daniel L., N-9
Davis, Dolores, 73–74
Davis, Jeff, 73–74
Davis, John H., N-28
Davis, Latia, 41
Davis, Laura, N-40
Davis, Nanette J., N-15
Davis, Richard Allen, 295
Davis, Robert C., N-35
Day, James M., N-8, N-9, N-17
Dean, Charles W., 163, N-25
Deane, Gary D., N-12
Deane, Glenn D., N-24
De Baudouin, H. N-7
De Bernardo, Mark A., N-37
De Burger, James, N-24
Decker, Scott H., 200, N-14, N-16, N-21, N-24, N-31
De Coster, Stacy, N-4
Dees, Morris, N-28
De Fronzo, James, N-4, N-10
DeKeseredy, Walter S., N-20
Demuth, Stephen, 163, N-16
DeNavas-Watt, Carmen, N-10
Denno, Deborah W., 70, 78, N-7
Deschenes, Elizabeth Piper, N-14
Desjardins, Lyne, N-37
DeVoe, J. F., 209
Dickey, Christopher, N-30
Dieterschwind, H., N-1
Dietrick, David C., N-13
Dietz, Park, 98
DiLeonardo, Michael, 240
Dinitz, Simon, N-9, N-16

Dionne, E. J., 125
Dixon, Jo, N-13
Dixon, Ronald L., N-34
Dobash, R. Emerson, N-4, N-42
Dobash, Russell P., N-4, N-42
Dobrin, Adam, N-17
Dodd, David, N-35
Doerner, William G., N-13
Donaldson, Thomas, N-33
Donnerstein, Edward, N-8, N-39
Donovan, Kevin, 240
Doob, Anthony N., N-22
Dornfeld, Maude, N-25, N-26
Doto, Guiseppe "Joe Adonis,"
    241
Douglas, Jack D., 12, N-1, N-18
Douglas, Rosemary, 150–151
Downey, Robert, Jr., 334
Downs, Donald A., N-39
Drapkin, Israel, N-21
Drass, Kriss A., N-4
Droegemueller, W., N-24
Druley, K. A., N-38
Drummond, Tammerlin, N-29
Duff, R. A., N-23
Duffield, Don W., N-12
Dugdale, Richard L., 64, 69, N-5
Dunaway, R. Gregory, N-11
Duncan, David, 303
Duncan, Ross, 265
Dunford, Franklin, N-3
Dunlap, Eloise, N-36
Dunworth, Terence, N-12
Dupont, John, 99
Durkheim, Émile, 14, 67–68, 69,
    104–105, N-1, N-6, N-10,
    N-19
Durose, Matthew R., N-25
Duster, Troy, N-37
Duszynski, Karen R., N-37
Dutton, Donald G., N-25
Dzerzhinsky, Felix, 190

E
Earle, Beverly, N-35
Easton, Susan M., N-39
Ebbe, Obi N. I., 363, N-40, N-41,
    N-42
Ebert, Roger, N-10
Eck, John E., N-11, N-22
Eckstein, Marc, N-24
Edel, Wilbur, N-31
Edwards, Sally M., N-43
Edwards, Terry D., N-43
Eggston, Andrew A., N-38
Eghigian, M., N-14
Eichel, Edward W., N-38
Eisenman, Russell, N-36
Elderkin, Ronald D., N-5
Elias, Robert, N-20
Elis, Lori A., N-32

Ellen, Eric, N-43
Ellingworth, Dan, N-22
Elliott, Delbert S., 49, 132, 166,
    N-3, N-4, N-5, N-10, N-11,
    N-13, N-14, N-17, N-18
Elliott, Frank A., 166
Ellis, Havelock, N-5
Ellis, Lee, N-7
Ellis, Lori, N-4
Ellison, A. F., N-2
Elmoghazy, E., N-36
Empey, Lamar, N-19
Enat, Tomer, N-20
Engels, Friedrich, 185, N-19
Epstein, Ann S., N-11
Epstein, Joel, N-26, N-27
Erez, Edna, N-4
Erickson, Kai T., 178, N-18
Eriksson, Thorsten, N-5
Erlanger, Howard S., 137, N-13
Erlanger, Steven, N-1
Ermann, M. David, N-33, N-34
Eron, Leonard D., 90, N-8
Esbensen, Finn-Aage, N-13,
    N-14
Estes, R. J., N-40
Evans, Harold, N-34
Evans, T. David, N-11
Everett, M. W., N-38
Eysenck, Hans J., 96, 97, N-8,
    N-9, N-10

F
Fagan, Jeffrey, 138, N-12, N-13,
    N-14, N-18, N-25, N-36,
    N-37
Fagan, Stephen, 238
Faggiani, Donald, N-22
Faludi, Susan, N-24
Farley, Margaret, 190, N-20
Farnsworth, Margaret, 109,
    N-10, N-17
Farrell, Graham, N-21
Farrelland, Ronald A., N-28
Farrington, David P., 29, 90, 166,
    167, N-2, N-3, N-8, N-17,
    N-21, N-22, N-30, N-42
Fattah, Ezzat A., 149, 202, N-21
Favre, Brett, 162
Feingold, Benjamin F., 80, N-7
Feiring, Candice, N-8
Felson, Marcus, 196, 198, 201,
    203, 214, 215, 224, N-17,
    N-20, N-21, N-22, N-23
Felson, Richard B., 231, N-6,
    N-8, N-21, N-23, N-24
Fenton, Ben, 367
Ferguson, Colin, 226
Fernandez, Yvette, N-27
Ferracuti, Franco, 130, 136, 137,
    N-13, N-25

Ferraro, Kenneth F., N-12
Ferre, M. Isolina, 121, N-12
Ferrero, Gina Lombroso, 97, N-5
Ferrero, William, 46, N-4, N-5
Ferri, Enrico, 1, 60, 62, 63, 69,
    N-5
Ferri, Gian Luigi, 228
Fielding, Henry, 293
Fields, Charles B., N-40, N-43
Fields, Gary, 41
50 Cent, *138*
Figlio, Robert, 42, 45, N-3, N-7,
    N-14
Figueira-McDonough, Josefina,
    N-12
Finckenauer, James, O., 22, 362,
    N-17, N-28, N-42
Fine, David, N-17
Fingerhut, Lois A., N-42
Fink, Arthur E., N-5
Finkelhor, David, N-25
Finn, Peter, N-37
Fischer, D. G., N-9
Fish, Albert, 228
Fishbein, Diana H., 83, N-6, N-7,
    N-8
Fisher, Bonnie S., N-21
Fisse, Brent, N-32, N-33, N-34
Flegenheimer, Arthur "Dutch
    Schultz," 241
Fleming, Zachary, 214
Fletcher, Pamela R., N-39
Flowers, Barri, N-4
Follain, John, N-27
Forbaugh, Frederick M., N-11
Ford, Richard, 35
Forney, Mary Ann, N-39
Forssman, H., N-7
Foucault, Michel, 70
Fowles, Richard, N-10
Fox, James Alan, 223, 228, N-23,
    N-33
Frank, Nancy, N-35
Frankowski, Stanislaw J., N-40,
    N-41
Frazier, Patricia, N-26
Freemantle, Brian, N-27
French, L., N-6
Freud, Sigmund, 68, 86, N-8
Frey, T. S., N-7
Friday, Paul C., N-42
Friedlander, Kate, N-8
Frisch, Lisa A., N-25
Fromm-Auch, D., N-8
Frude, N., N-21
Fu, Hualing, N-42
Furrow, Buford O., 254

G
Gabbidon, Shaun L., N-10
Gabor, Thomas, N-33

Gabrielli, William F., N-6, N-7
Gage, Michael, N-41
Gaither, Billy Jack, 254
Gajewski, Frank, N-22
Galea, John, 30
Gall, Franz Joseph, 60, 69
Gambino, Carlo, 244, 245
Gambino, Richard, N-27
Ganzini, Linda, N-32
Garcia, Juanita L., N-26
Gardiner, John A., N-33
Garofalo, James, 202, N-21
Garofalo, Raffaele, 1, 10, 14, 60, 62–63, 69, N-1, N-5
Gartin, Patrick R., 204, N-21, N-22, N-25
Gartner, Rosemary, N-24, N-40, N-41, N-42
Gartrell, John W., N-11, N-24
Gass, Otto, 241
Gately, William, N-27
Gault, Gerald Francis, 78
Gault, H., N-6
Gault, Robert H., N-6
Gay, John, 293
Gaynor, Jessica, N-31
Gearing, Michael L., N-9
Gebhard, Paul H., 345, N-39
Geen, Russell G., N-8
Gegax, Trent, 350, N-29
Geis, Gilbert, 299, N-26, N-31, N-32, N-34, N-35
Gelfand, Donna, N-30
Gelles, Richard J., 232, N-25
Gellman, Barton, N-1
Genn, Hazel G., N-35
Genovese, Vito, 241, 244, 245
Gentry, Cynthia S., N-39
George, Barbara Crutchfield, N-32
George, Soboma, 150
Gerber, Jurg, N-32
Gertz, Marc G., N-40, N-41
Giancana, Chuck, N-28
Giancana, Sam, 244, N-28
Gibbens, Trevor N., N-32
Gibbs, Jack P., N-16, N-19
Gibbs, John J., N-8, N-12, N-31
Gibney, Frank, Jr., N-29
Gibson, L., N-38
Gibson, Mel, 16, 17
Gidycz, C. A., N-26
Gigante, Vincent "The Chin," 244
Gilfus, Mary E., N-4
Gill, Martin, N-2, N-43
Giller, Joan E., N-43
Gillespie, Darlene, 280
Gillespie, James, N-38
Gilligan, Carol, N-8
Gillis, A. R., N-4, N-16

Gilmore, John, 350
Giordano, Peggy C., N-16, N-30
Giuffra, Robert, 303
Glaser, Daniel, N-19
Glaser, Frederick G., N-36
Glass, Clive, N-31
Glasser, Ira, 50
Glassner, Barry, N-37
Glick, Barry, 33, N-2
Glueck, Eleanor T., 46, 64, 69, 90, 166, 363, N-4, N-5, N-8, N-17, N-40, N-41
Glueck, Sheldon, 46, 64, 69, 166, 363, N-4, N-5, N-8, N-17, N-40, N-41
Goddard, Henry H., 64, 65, 69, 78, N-5, N-6
Goetting, Ann, N-25
Goff, Colin H., N-34
Goffman, Erving, N-18
Golant, Susan K., N-25
Gold, Martin, N-2
Goldberg, Jeffrey, N-28
Golden, Andrew, 256
Golden, Reid M., N-11
Goldfarb, Ronald, N-27
Golding, Bruce, N-20
Golding, William, 153, N-15
Goldman, Ronald, 16, 232
Goldstein, Paul J., N-37
Goleman, Daniel, N-6
Golub, Andrew, N-36
Gondoli, Dawn M., N-25
Good, Kenneth, 107
Goode, Erich, N-36
Goodman, Marc, N-31
Gordon, Donald A., N-8
Gordon, Margaret A., N-24
Gordon, Michael R., N-43
Gordon, Robert, N-16
Gordon, Waxey, 241
Goring, Charles Buckman, 63, 69, 74, N-5
Gornick, Janet, N-26
Goslin, David A., N-8
Gottfredson, Denise C., N-2, N-11, N-17
Gottfredson, Gary D., N-12
Gottfredson, Michael R., 42, 166, 169–170, 202, N-3, N-17, N-21, N-33
Gottfredson, Steve D., N-12
Gottheil, E., N-38
Gotti, John, Jr., 240
Gotti, Peter, 240
Gough, Harrison G., N-9
Gove, Walter R., N-18
Grabosky, Peter, N-32
Grasmick, Harold G., N-22
Green, Gary S., N-30
Green, Lorraine, N-22

Greenberg, David F., N-3, N-13, N-16, N-19
Greene, Helen Taylor, N-10
Greenfeld, Lawrence A., N-24, N-38
Greenhouse, Linda, 66
Greenspan, Edward L., N-22
Greenwald, Brian, 194
Grieve, Dominic, 35
Griffiths, Curt T., N-42
Grinspoon, Lester, N-36
Griswold, David, N-16
Grosmick, Harold G., N-12
Gross, Jane, N-11
Grossman, Jan Carl, N-36
Groves, W. Byron, N-31, N-34
Gruner, Richard S., N-34
Grupp, Stanley E., N-5
Guart, Al, N-26
Gudjonsson, Gisli H., N-9, N-10
Guerry, André Michel, 65, 66, 69, 196, N-20
Guggenheim, W. Z., N-36
Gunn, John, N-8
Gusfield, Joseph R., N-38
Gustafson, Regan, 112
Gutfield, Greg, 350
Guth, Hans-Werner, N-42
Guy, Sybille M., N-37
Gwynne, S. C., 209

H

Hagan, John, 46, 110, N-4, N-11, N-16, N-19, N-32
Hagedorn, John M., 135, 147, 152, N-13
Hakim, Simon, 211, N-12
Hale, Chris, N-11
Hale, Matthew, 237, N-26
Hall, Jerome, N-1, N-30
Halleck, Seymour L., 97, N-9
Hamburg, D. A., N-7
Hamid, Ansley, N-36
Hamilton, David, 352
Hamilton, Thomas, 226
Hamilton, V. Lee, N-42
Hamlin, John, N-16
Hamm, Mark S., N-33
Hammett, Theodore M., N-27
Hampton, Robert L., N-23
Hancock, Lyn Nell, N-25
Hand, David, 35
Handley, Jim, N-31
Haney, Beth, N-26
Hanlon, Thomas, E., N-37
Hannon, Lance, N-4, N-13
Hanrahan, Kathleen J., N-12
Hansen, Joy, N-14
Hanson, Cindy L., N-8
Hanson, R. Karl, N-39
Harcourt, Bernard E., 178–179

Harding, Richard W., N-21
Hare, Robert D., N-8, N-9, N-10
Harries, Elizabeth, N-34
Harris, Eric, 256
Harris, Patricia M., N-21
Harrison, Wilfred, N-5
Hartjen, Clayton A., N-12, N-42
Hartl, Emil M., N-5
Hartmann, Donald, N-30
Hartnagel, Timothy F., N-11, N-24
Harvey, William B., N-23
Hatch, Alison, N-42
Hatch, Orrin, 114
Hatcher, Chris, N-31
Hatcher, R. M., N-2
Hauser, Robert M., N-19
Hawkins, Darnell F., N-23
Hawkins, David J., N-17
Hawkins, Gordon, N-39
Hayes, Read, N-21
Hays, Ron D., N-38
Hazelbaker, Kim, N-22
Heath, D., N-38
Hebenton, B., N-41
Heide, Kathleen M., N-39
Heimer, K., N-16
Heimer, M., N-24
Heims, Lora W., N-31
Heinzelmann, Fred, N-32
Heinzmann, David, N-35
Helal, Adel, N-41
Helmke, Paul, 262
Helvétius, Claude Adrien, 55
Henderson, Russell, 254
Hendler, Harold I., N-37
Henggeler, Scott W., N-8
Hennessy, James, J., N-6, N-21
Henry, D. Alan, 172
Henson, Trudy Knicely, N-30
Henson, Verna A., N-21
Hepburn, John, N-30
Hepburn, R. J., N-16
Hepperle, Winifred, N-4
Hernandez, Osvaldo, 177
Hernriques, Diana B., 367
Herring, Albert, 41
Herrnstein, Richard J., 42, 78, 99, N-3, N-7, N-10
Hersch, Rebecca K., N-31
Hess, Karen Matison, N-31
Heumann, Milton, N-29
Heyl, Barbara Sherman, N-39
Heymann, Philip, 216
Heywood, Jeremy, 34
Hibbert, Christopher, N-5
Hickey, Joseph, 89
Hideg, G., 44
Hill, Gary D., N-4, N-12
Hill, James Brian, 92

Hill, Joan, N-40
Hill, Robert, 137, N-14
Hillbrand, M., N-6
Hinckley, John W., Jr., 24, 84, 262
Hindelang, Michael J., 37, 78, 157, 202, N-3, N-7, N-16, N-21
Hirano, Ryuichi, N-35
Hirschel, J. David, N-25
Hirschi, Travis, 37, 42, 78, 122, 131–171, 132, 135, 155–160, 161, 163, 165, 166, 169–170, N-3, N-7, N-12, N-13, N-15, N-17, N-32, N-33
Hitler, Adolf, 8, 185
Ho, Truc-Nhu, N-30, N-43
Hobbs, Sylvester III, 92
Hoff, Joan, 351
Hoffer, Abram, N-7
Hoffman, John, N-11, N-13
Hogan, Robert, N-9
Hogg, Russell, N-20
Holcomb, William R., N-24
Hollandsworth, S., N-14
Hollinger, Richard C., 308, N-33
Holmes, Oliver Wendell, Jr., 58–59, 64
Holmes, Ronald M., N-24
Holmes, Stephen T., N-24
Holt, Joe, 80
Holyst, Brunon, N-41
Homel, Ross, 209, N-22
Honeywood, Wesley "Pop," 41
Hooten, Ernest, 63, 69, 74, N-5
Hope, Tim, N-21
Hope, Susan, N-31
Horace, 185
Hornblower, Margot, 347
Horney, Julie, N-3, N-7, N-26
Horowitz, Irving Louis, 189
Horton, Henry P., N-19
Horwitz, Allan V., N-15
Horwitz, Diana, N-36
Hotaling, Gerald T., N-25
Houston, James, G., N-13
Howitt, Dennis, N-39
Hser, Yining, N-37
Hsü, Yü-Hsiu, N-42
Htoo, Johnny, 358
Htoo, Luther, 358
Hu, Winnie, N-30
Huang, Frank F. Y., N-42
Huberty, James, 225
Huesmann, L. Rowell, N-8
Huff, C. Ronald, N-15
Hughes, Michael, N-12
Hui, Boon Khoo, N-35
Huizinga, David, N-4, N-10, N-13
Hull, Jon D., N-15, N-29
Hume, David, 55

Humphries, Charlie, N-22
Humphries, Drew, N-19
Hunt, Morton, 353, N-40
Hunter, Ronald D., N-22, N-42
Hutchings, Barry, N-6
Hutchinson, Ira W., III, N-25
Hutson, Range, N-24

I

Ianni, Francis A. J., N-27
Iavares, Cynthia, 141
Iglarsh, Harvey J., N-28
Ileto, Joseph, 254
Inciardi, James A., 334, N-20, N-27, N-30, N-36, N-37, N-38, N-39
Innes, Christopher A., N-25
Inoue, Mariko, N-35
Ireland, Timothy, N-13
Ishihara, T., N-6
Itil, Turan M., N-7
Iverson, Sherrice, 220

J

Jackson, Howard F., N-31
Jackson, Pamela Irving, N-10
Jackson, Patrick G., N-2, N-31
Jacob, Craig, N-33
Jacobs, Bruce A., N-36
Jacobs, James, B., N-29, N-38
Jacobs, K. W., 80, N-7
James, Frank, 125
James, Jennifer, 345, N-39
Janeksela, Galan M., N-42
Jang, Sung Joon, N-3
Janofsky, Michael, N-29
Janus, Cynthia L., N-38
Janus, Samuel S., N-38
Jargowsky, Paul, 141
Jarjoura, G. Roger, 132, N-3, N-4, N-13
Jaskir, John, N-8
Jeffery, C. Ray, 75, 94, 207, N-6, N-9, N-22
Jenkins, E. Lynn, N-24
Jenkins, Philip, 348, 350, N-24
Jennings, William S., 89, N-8
Jensen, Arthur, 78, N-7
Jensen, Gary F., 109, N-4, N-10, N-11, N-16
Jensen, Stephanie, 296, 297
Jensen, Vickie J., N-13
Jesilow, Paul, N-31, N-32
Johnson, Bruce D., N-21, N-36, N-37
Johnson, Elmer H., N-41
Johnson, Harold, 27
Johnson, Ida, N-26
Johnson, John, N-9, N-18
Johnson, Keyshawn, 162

Johnson, Lyndon B., 113, 114, 149, 242, 263
Johnson, Shane D., N-22, N-38
Johnston, David, N-28
Johnston, Les, N-43
Johnston, Lloyd, N-2
Jones, Gwen, N-17
Jones, Jim, 125
Jones, Richard Lezin, 179
Jordan, James, 261
Jordan, Michael, 106, 261
Jouret, Luc, 124
Joyner, Tammy, N-11
Juby, Heather, 90, N-8
Judge, Mychal, *249*
Judson, George, N-18
Jukes, Ada, 64
Jung, Sung Juon, N-17
Junger-Tas, Josine, N-3, N-41, N-42
Junta, Thomas, 95

K

Kadleck, Colleen, N-22
Kagan, Jerome, 77
Kahan, James P., N-37
Kaiser, Günther, N-42, N-43
Kalb, Claudia, N-29
Kalish, Carol, N-35, N-41
Kallikak, Martin, 64
Kandel, Elizabeth, N-6
Kantrowitz, Barbara, N-14
Kapardis, A., N-33
Kapardis, M., N-33
Karchmer, Clifford L., N-32
Karpman, Benjamin, N-10
Kaufman, Irving, N-31
Kaulitzki, Reiner, N-42
Kay, Fiona, N-32
Kearley, Brook, N-2
Keimer, Karen, N-4
Kelleher, C. L., N-24
Kelleher, Michael D., N-24
Kelley, R., 16, 17, 179
Kellner, R., N-7
Kelly, Delos H., N-39
Kelly, Linda, N-42
Kelly, Mary, 269
Kelly, Robert J., N-28
Kempe, C. H., N-24
Kemper, Edmund, 228
Kempf, Kimberly L., N-2, N-16
Kendall, Jerry, N-42
Kennedy, David, 40
Kennedy, John F., 149, 184
Kennedy, Leslie W., 224, N-13, N-23
Kennedy, Robert F., 184
Kenny, Dennis J., N-28
Kerbo, Harold R., N-35
Kethineni, Sesharajani, N-42

Kfita, Najat, N-25
Kieselhorst, B. C., N-38
Kilkenny, Robert, N-8
Killias, Martin, N-40, N-41
Kindley, Karen, N-23
King, Harry, N-30
King, John William, 254
King, Martin Luther, Jr., 184
King, Mike, N-42
King, Roy, N-6
Kinlock, Timothy W., N-37
Kinsbourne, Marcel, N-7
Kinsey, Alfred C., 343, 353, N-38, N-40
Kirby, K., N-14
Kirchheimer, Otto, 185–186, N-19
Kirkpatrick, John T., N-25
Kitsuse, John I., N-13
Kittrie, Nicholas N., N-9, N-18
Klaidman, Daniel, N-24
Klass, Polly, 295
Klaus, K. A., N-6
Klaus, Patsy, N-35
Klebold, Dylan, 256
Klein, Malcolm W., N-3, N-13, N-15, N-24, N-41
Kleinfield, N. R., N-24
Kleinman, Joel C., N-42
Klinteberg, Britt af, N-6
Klockars, Carl B., 187, 293, N-20, N-31
Knightly, Phillip, N-34
Knoblich, Guenther, N-6
Knop, George W., N-13
Knowles, Gordon James, N-36
Knutsson, Johannes, N-31
Kobrin, Solomon, N-12
Koepf, G. F., N-6
Kohlberg, Lawrence, 87, *88*, N-8
Kopel, David B., N-42
Koper, Christopher S., N-2, N-35
Korem, Dan, N-15
Koresh, David, 254
Kosberg, Jordan I., N-26
Koss, M. P., N-26
Kovandzic, Thomislav V., N-11
Kowalski, Matt, N-20
Kowlaski, Gregory S., N-12
Krahn, Harvey, N-11, N-24
Kretschmer, Ernst, 63, 69, N-5
Kreuz, L. E., N-7
Krisberg, Barry, N-19
Kroc, Ray, 106
Krohn, Marvin D., 132, N-3, N-13, N-14, N-16, N-17, N-19
Krug, Etienne G., N-24
Kruttschnitt, Candace, N-25, N-26
Krzeszowski, Frank E., N-31

Kuhlhorn, Eckart, N-31
Kuhn, T. S., N-6
Kuhns Joseph B., III, N-39
Kuklinski, Richard, *226*
Kupperstein, Lenore R., N-41
Kurth, Barbara, 238
Kury, Helmut, N-42
Kutchinsky, Berl, N-39
Kuttschreuter, M., N-9

L

Labelle, Huguette, 181
LaCasse, Lori, 82, 83, N-7
Lacayo, Richard, N-29
Lacey, Robert, N-27
LaFave, Wayne R., N-23
LaFree, Gary, 68, N-4, N-6, N-41
LaGrange, Randy L., N-12
Lander, Bernard, N-10
Langan, Mary, N-20
Langan, Patrick A., N-25
Lange, Dorothea, 142, N-14
Lange, Johannes, 76, N-6
Langenbahn, Stacia, N-26
Langer, Lawrence L., 188
Lanza-Kaduce, L., N-13, N-38
Larsen, Otto N., N-18
Lasley, James, R., N-22, N-33
Laub, John H., 165, 166, 181, N-3, N-5, N-17, N-18
Lauderback, David, N-14
Laufer, William S., N-4, N-8, N-9, N-10, N-11, N-13, N-16, N-17, N-18, N-32, N-33, N-34, N-36
Lauritsen, Janet L., N-12
Lavater, Johann Kaspar, 60, 69
Lawrence, Michael D., N-38
Laws, D. R., N-7
Lay, Kenneth, 323, 324
Leavitt, Gregory C., N-41
LeBeau, James, L., N-26
LeBlanc, Marc, 166, 167, N-16
LeCapitaine, J. E., N-8
Ledingham, C. A., N-9
Ledingham, J. E., N-9
Lee, Tommy, 232
Lehmann, John, N-26
Leland, John, 350
Lemaitre, Andre, N-33
Lemaitre, Rolf, N-33
Lemert, Edwin M., 175, 176, 177, 280–281, N-18, N-31
Lencz, T., N-7
Lenin, V., 8
Lensing, H., N-42
Leonard, Kenneth E., N-25, N-38
Leonard, Kimberly K., N-16
Lepse, Kerry, 108
Lepse, Sammy, 108

Lessner, S. F., N-16
Leung, Rebecca, N-28
Levi, Michael, N-31
Levin, Jack, 41, 228, N-24, N-42
Levine, Betti Jane, N-16
Levine, Dennis, 302
Levine, James, N-2
Levinson, David, N-25
Levitt, Steven, 223, N-23
Levung, Shirley, 125
Lewis, Matthew W., N-38
Lewis, Michael, N-8
Lewis, Norman, N-27
Lewis, Oscar, 106, N-10
Liazos, Alexander, N-13, N-18
Lieberman, Alicia F., N-8
Liebl, Karlhans, N-32
Lightner, Candy, 341–342
Lightner, Cari, 341
Lindbergh, Charles, 238
Linden, R., N-38
Link, Bruce G., N-18, N-35, N-38
Linquist, P., N-38
Lipset, Seymour M., N-11
Lipstadt, Deborah, 188, 189
Liska, Alan, N-12, N-16
Little, G. L., N-8
Little, Heather M., N-7
Littman, R. A., N-9
Litton, Roger, N-33
Liu, Jianhong, N-12
Lizotte, Alan J., 184, 264, N-13,
    N-14, N-17, N-19, N-29,
    N-30
Lobi, Nadya, N-29
Locke, John, 55
Loeber, Rolf, N-12
Loftin, Colin, 137, N-14, N-23,
    N-29
Lofvers, Jeff, 157, N-15
Logan, John, 275
Lohan, Lindsay, 16, 17
Lombness, Michael, N-35
Lombroso, Cesare, 1, 11, 46,
    60–62, 63, 69, 74, N-4, N-5
Looman, Terah, N-22
Lopez, Pedro Alonso, 225
Loring, Pamela L., N-11, N-13
Loughlin, Julia, N-37
Loury, Glenn C., N-17
Lovell, Constance, 95, N-9
Lowman, John, N-20
Lowney, Jeremiah, N-39
Lu, Chunmeng, N-21
Luciana, Salvatore "Lucky
    Luciano," 241, 245
Luckenbill, David F., N-24, N-39
Lunde, D. T., N-7
Lundman, Richard J., N-33,
    N-34
Luper, Steven Foy, N-37

Lupsha, Peter A., N-27
Lurigio, Arthur J., N-35, N-36
Lyman, Michael D., N-36
Lynch, James P., N-22, N-41
Lynum, Donald R., N-3
Lyston, Douglas S., N-37

M
Maahs, Jeff, N-11
Maakestad, William J., N-34,
    N-35
Maas, Peter, N-27
MacCoun, Robert J., N-37
MacDonald, John M., N-17,
    N-31
Macey, Jonathan R., N-35
Mackenzie, D. L., N-2, N-22
MacLean, Brian D., N-20
Macphail, Daniel D., N-8
Madden, Owney, 241
Madoff, Bernard, 299, 367
Maestro, Marcello T., N-5
Magaddino, Stefano, 244
Magedanz, T., N-38
Magnuson, Dan, N-35
Magnusson, David, N-6
Maher, Lisa, N-32, N-36, N-39
Maier, Pamela A., N-22
Makofsky, Abraham, N-37
Malekian, N-43
Malle, Louis, 102
Malvo, John Lee, 226
Manchin, R., 44
Mankoff, Milton, N-20
Mann, Coramae Richey, 223,
    N-4, N-23, N-24
Mannheim, Hermann, N-5,
    N-19, N-41
Manson, Charles, 124
Manuel, Yolanda, *220*
Marcial, Gene G., N-33
Margaryan, Satenik, N-17
Markowitz, Fred E., N-12
Marolla, J., N-26
Marongiu, Pietro, N-5, N-21
Marriott, Michael, N-12, N-36
Marshall, Ineke Haen, N-3
Marshall, S. E., N-23
Martens, Frederick T., N-43
Martin, Clyde E., N-38, N-40
Martin, Kimberly, 190, N-20
Martin, R. D., N-9
Martins, Jens, 141
Martone, Mark, 92
Marx, Karl, 185, N-19
Massey, James, L., N-16
Mastrofski, Stephen D., N-38
Mathers, R., N-35
Matsueda, Ross L., N-12, N-16,
    N-17, N-18
Matthews, R., N-20

Matza, David, 110, 160, 161,
    N-11, N-14, N-16, N-18,
    N-22
Maudsley, Henry, 65, 69
Mawby, R. I. I., N-42
Mawson, Anthony R., 80, N-7
Maxson, Cheryl L., N-13, N-15,
    N-24
Maxfield, Michael G., N-2
Mayer, Martin, N-33
Mayfield, D., N-38
Mayhew, Pat, N-41
Mazerolle, Lorraine, N-2, N-22
Mazerolle, Paul, 163, N-11
McBarnet, Doreen, N-33
McBride, Duane C., N-37
McCaffrey, Barry, 337
McCaghy, Charles, N-30
McCall, Patricia L., N-11
McClelland, Kenneth J., 178
McClintock, F. H., N-42
McConathy, Hunter, 265
McCord, Frank A., N-8, N-17
McCord, Joan, 90, N-6, N-8, N-9,
    N-10, N-16, N-25
McCord, William, N-10
McCoy, Clyde B., N-37
McCoy, H. Virginia, N-36
McDevitt, Jack, N-42
McDonald, Mark, 276
McDonald, William F., N-40
McDowall, David, 264, N-12,
    N-14, N-29, N-30
McElrath, Karen, N-36, N-37
McFadden, Robert D., N-29
McFarland, Bentson, N-32
McGuffog, Carolyn, N-8
McGuire, J., 29, N-2
McKay, Henry D., 117, 119, 120,
    121, N-11
McKenzie, Doris, N-11
McKenzie, R. D., 118
McKinley, James C., Jr., N-3
McKinney, Aaron, 254
McLaughlin, Eugene, N-20
McMahon, Colin, N-37
McNamara, Joseph, N-27
McNeil, Richard J., N-12
McShane, Marilyn D., N-10,
    N-40
McVeigh, Timothy, 255
Mead, George Herbert, 175,
    N-18
Mednick, Sarnoff A., 76, 77, 83,
    N-6, N-7
Mee, James, 16
Meersman, Tom, N-35
Megargee, Edwin I., N-9
Meier, Robert F., N-4, N-10,
    N-22, N-27, N-30, N-34
Meloy J. Reid, N-7

Menard, Scott, N-11, N-16, N-17
Mendelsohn, Beniamin, 202, N-21
Mendelsohn, Gerald A., N-9
Meng, Xiaodong Sheldon, 287
Menninger, Karl, 97, N-9
Mercy, James, A., N-24, N-29
Merl, Jean, N-14
Merlin, Mark D., N-36
Merton, Robert K., 105–109, 112, 131, 133, 163, 299, N-10
Merva, Mary, N-11
Merz, Jon F., N-38
Messner, Steven F., 111, 112, 126, N-11, N-14, N-16, N-19, N-23
Metfessel, Milton, 95, N-9
Meyer, C. K., N-38
Michalowski, Raymond J., N-34
Miczek, Klaus A., N-38
Miech, Richard A., N-4, N-10
Miedzian, Myriam, N-39
Miethe, Terance D., N-12, N-22
Miles, Christine, N-36
Milk, Harvey, 79
Millar, Robert Wyness, N-5
Miller, A. S., N-11
Miller, Bill, N-14
Miller, Brenda A., N-25
Miller, Jody, N-15, N-21, N-36
Miller, Martin G., N-4
Miller, Nelson, 279
Miller, Richard Lawrence, N-37
Miller, Thomas, N-37
Miller, Walter B., 130–131, 138–142, N-14
Mills, Anne-Marie, N-25
Mills, Gregory, N-12
Mills, Michael, N-32
Ming Wa, Kwai, N-15
Minor, N. William, N-16
Mitchell, David B., N-25
Mitchell, O., N-2
Miyazawa, Setsuo, N-41
Moffett, Arthur D., N-36
Moffitt, Terrie E., 166, N-3, N-4, N-6, N-7, N-10, N-17, N-20, N-25
Mokhiber, Russell, N-34
Monnelly, Edward P., N-5
Monroe, Sylvester, N-28
Montanino, Fred, N-39
Montesquieu, 55
Moore, Elizabeth, N-32
Moore, Joan, 152
Moore, Michael, N-1
Moore, Richard, N-30
Moore, Richter H., N-40
Moorehead-Dworkin, Terry, N-32
Moran, Richard, N-2

Moran, Thomas Bartholomew, 269
Morash, Merry, 46, N-4, N-27
More, Thomas, 185
Moreno-Ocampo, Luis, 188, 189
Morgan, H. Wayne, N-36
Morka, Ghandi Ben, 279
Morris, Norval, N-20, N-31
Morse, Edward V., N-39
Morse, Stephen J., 84, 98, 100
Moscone, George, 79
Mueller, Gerhard O. W., 55, 276, N-1, N-2, N-5, N-18, N-22, N-23, N-31, N-35, N-39, N-40, N-41, N-42, N-43
Mueller, J. H., N-1
Mueller, R. S., N-15
Muhammed, John, 226
Mukasey, Michael, 282
Mullins, Steven, 254
Mumola, Christopher J., N-38
Muncer, Steven, N-4
Muncie, John, N-20
Munsterberg, Hugo, 78, N-6
Murray, Alan, N-33
Murray, Ellen, N-16
Mustaine, E. E., 163
Musto, D. F., N-36
Mydans, Seth, N-14, N-15
Myers, Kenneth D., N-33
Myers, Laura B., N-4
Myers, Martha A., N-19
Myers, Norman, N-27
Mylonas, Anastassios, N-41, N-42
Myrdal, Gunnar, 106, N-10

Nacchio, Joseph, 297
Nadelman, Ethan N., N-41, N-42
Nader, Ralph, 319
Nagel, Ilene H., N-19
Nagin, Daniel S., 198, N-3, N-17, N-20
Nahmias, David E., 279
Najadi, Abu Mus 'ab al-, 304–305
Najaka, Stacy S., N-2
Nash, Jay Robert, N-27
Natarajan, Mangai, N-21, N-36
Nay, Robert L., N-42
Neapolitan, Jerome L., N-41
Nelken, David, N-40
Nelli, Humbert S., N-27
Nelsen, Candice, N-24
Neustrom, Michael W., N-10
Newlyn, Andrea K., N-37
Newman, Graeme, N-5, N-17, N-23, N-24, N-31, N-34, N-40, N-41, N-42

Newman, Oscar, 207, N-22
Newton, Michael, N-24
Noaks, Lesley, N-4
Nochajski, Thomas, H., N-25
Nolan, Bruce W., N-43
Nolen, John T. "Legs Diamond," 241
Nolin, Mary Jo, N-29
Noonan, M., 209
Noriega, Manuel, 336
Norris, Sandra L., N-23
Norton, William M., N-10
Nowak, Lisa Marie, 48
Nsirimovu, Anyakwee, 150
Nurco, David N., N-37
Nye, Francis Ivan, N-8, N-10, N-16
Nyswander, Marie, N-36

O
Obama, Barack, *318*, 323
O'Brien, Margaret, 147
O'Carroll, Patrick W., N-29
O'Day, Patrick, N-4
Oefelein, William, 48
Oetzi, 54–55
Ogan, George, 151
Ohlin, Lloyd E., 130, 133, 134, 135, 136, 156, N-13, N-25, N-26, N-36
Oliver, F. E., N-36
Olson, David, N-33
Olson, James N., 293, N-21, N-31
Olson, Lynn M., N-36
Olson, Virgil J., N-10
Olson, Walter, 209
Olweus, Dan, N-8, N-21
O'Malley, Patrick M., N-2
O'Maolchatha, Aogan, N-20
Omehia, Celestine, 151
O'Neill, Eugene, 142, N-14
O'Reilly-Fleming, Thomas, N-19
Ortega, Suzanne T., N-41
Orvis, Gregory P., N-28
Osgood, D. Wayne, 76, N-2, N-3, N-6, N-7, N-12
Overill, Richard, N-31
Owens, O'dell, 40
Owens, Terrell, 162

P
Page, Brent, N-30
Pagelow, Mildred Daley, N-26
Pagrotsky, Leif, N-1
Palendrano, Marion, 23
Pallone, Nathaniel J., N-6, N-21
Palmer, C., N-30
Pankan, Edmund J., N-31
Park, Robert E., 117, 118, N-11
Parker, Howard, N-38

Parker, Karen F., N-11
Pasco, James, 41
Passas, Nikos, 109, N-10, N-11
Patel, Dev, 103
Paternoster, Raymond, 163, N-11, N-16, N-20, N-21
Paterson, E. Britt, N-12
Patrick, C. J., N-7
Patterson, Gerald R., 93, N-9
Pearce, Frank, N-32, N-43
Pearson, Karl, 63
Pease, Ken, N-21, N-22
Pease, Susan, N-7
Peck, Jeffrey, N-22, N-31
Pedarion, Daniel, N-29
Pedersen, Daniel, N-24
Peeples, Faith, N-12
Pepinsky, Harold E., N-19, N-20
Perl, Raphael F., N-43
Perlmutter, Marion, N-8
Perrone, Dina, N-17
Pervin, Lawrence A., N-9
Petee, Thomas, A., N-12
Peter, K., 209
Peters, Eric, N-31
Petersilia, Joan, N-5
Peterson, Ruth D., N-26
Petrashek, David, N-34
Petrosino, Anthony, N-1, N-2
Pfefferbaum, Betty, N-38
Philip, Diana, 209
Phillips, Coretta, N-22
Pierce, Glenn L., N-29
Pilchen, Saul M., N-34
Pileggi, Nicholas, N-28
Piliavin, Irving, 155, N-15
Pinel, Philippe, 65, 97, N-6
Piquero, Alex R., 163, N-17, N-21, N-23
Pittman, Karen J., N-26
Pitts, Victoria L., N-22
Planty, Mike, N-22
Plato, 185, N-5
Platt, Anthony M., 178, 186, N-18
Platt, Suzy, N-5
Pleck, Elizabeth, N-24
Pogrebin, Mark R., N-13
Poindexter, John, 266
Polanzi C., N-35
Polgreen, Lydia, 151
Polk, Kenneth, N-13, N-23, N-33, N-42
Pollack, Otto, 46, N-4
Polsky, Ned, N-36
Polvi, Natalie, N-22
Pomeroy, Wardel B., N-38, N-40
Pontell, Henry N., N-31, N-32, N-35
Poole, Edward, N-2

Poole, Eric D., N-13
Popkin, Susan J., N-36
Porta, Giambattista della, 60, 69
Potter, Elaine, N-34
Potter, Kimberly A., N-29
Pottieger, Anne E., N-37, N-39
Pound, Roscoe, N-19
Powell, Kenneth, N-24
Power, William, N-33
Poyner, Barry, N-30
Pratt, Travis C., N-17
Preble, Edward, N-36, N-37
Prendergast, M. L., N-9
Preski, S., N-15
Prichard, James C., 97
Prince, Joyce, N-30
Proctor, Bernadette D., N-10
Puig-Antich, J., N-6
Purnell, Sonia, 367

Q
Quételet, Adolphe, 65–66, 69, 185, 196, N-6, N-20
Quinney, Richard, 186, 190, N-19, N-20, N-32, N-34

R
Rackmill, Stephen J., N-32
Rader, Dennis Lynn, 73, 226
Radke-Yarrow, M., N-8
Radosevich, M. J., N-13
Radzinowicz, Leon, N-5
Rafter, Nicole Hahn, N-5
Raine, Adrian, 81, 82, 83, N-7
Raith, Werner, N-27
Rand, Michael R., N-24
Rankin, Joseph H., N-16
Raphael, J., N-20
Rapp, Doris J., N-7
Rappleye, Charles, N-27
Rasche, Christine, N-25
Rashbaum, W. K., N-18
Rasmussen, David W., N-37
Ray, Isaac, 65, 69, N-6
Ray, Jo-Ann, N-30
Ray, M., N-18
Reagan, Ronald, 24, 84, 242, 266
Reasons, Charles E., N-34
Rebovich, Donald J., N-28
Reckless, Walter C., 161–165, 171, N-16
Redfern, Allison, N-31
Reed, Gary E., N-34
Reed, Mark D., N-12
Reichel, Philip L., N-20, N-41
Reichman, Nancy, N-33
Reige, Mary, N-16
Reinarman, Craig, N-12
Reinhold, Robert, N-15
Reisman, Judith A., N-38, N-39

Reiss, Albert J., Jr., 78, 132, 161, 171, N-6, N-7, N-10, N-12, N-13, N-16, N-33, N-35, N-38
Rengert, George F., 199, 200, N-21
Rennie, Ysabel, N-10
Resendez, Angel Leonicio Reyes Maturino, 225
Reuben, David, N-38
Reuter, Peter, N-11
Reuvid, Joanthan, N-42
Reyes, Gregory L., 296, 297
Reynolds, Toby, N-1
Rhodes, Albert L., 78, 132, N-7, N-10, N-13
Rich, Mark, N-1
Richards, Pamela J., N-38
Richardson, Genevra, N-35
Richardson, John E., N-9
Richberg, D. R., N-34
Ricker, Robert A., 261
Riedel, Marc, 224, N-23
Rifkin, Joel, 225
Ritti, R. Richard, N-38
Rivera, Ramon, N-13
Rivers, James, E., N-37
Robb, George, N-33
Roberts, Albert R., N-25
Roberts, Mary K., N-16
Roberts, Nickie, N-38
Roberts, Randell, 313
Robin, R. D., N-8
Robins, Lee N., 90, N-8
Rochefoucauld, François de la, 59
Rock, Joe, 241
Rodriguez, Orlando, N-16
Roehl, Jan, N-22
Roemer, William F., Jr., N-28
Rogan, Dennis P., N-25, N-29
Rokeach, Milton, N-16
Romilly, Samuel, 57
Roncek, Dennis W., N-22
Rook, Karen S., N-16
Rose, Dina R., 119, N-12
Rose, R. M., N-7
Rosecrance, John, N-30
Rosen, Lawrence, N-16
Rosenbaum, Jill Leslie, N-14, N-16
Rosenbaum, Marsha, N-36
Rosenblatt, Roger, N-29
Rosenfeld, Richard, 111, 112, 126, N-2, N-11
Rosenhan, D. L., N-18
Ross, E. A., 325
Ross, Lee, N-21
Roth, Jeffrey A., N-3, N-6, N-37, N-38

Roth, Martha, N-39
Rothstein, Arnold, 241
Roundtree, Pamela Wilcox, N-12
Rousseau, Jean-Jacques, 55
Rowe, Daryl, N-26
Rowe, David C., 76, N-6
Ruback, Barry R., N-24
Rude, George, N-5
Rudovsky, David, 51
Rusche, Georg, 185–186, N-19
Ruth, David E., N-27
Rutter, Michael, N-7, N-8
Ryder, Winona, *271*
Rzeplinski, Andrzej, N-20

S

Sagarin, Edward, 83, N-8, N-39
Sagi, Philip, 224, N-23
Salama, Sammy, 207
Salerno, Ralph, N-33
Salzano, Julienne, N-27
Samenow, Stanton, 95, N-9
Samper, Ernesto, 336
Sampson, Robert J., 165, 166, 181, N-3, N-5, N-12, N-17, N-18
Sanabria Harry, N-21
Sanchez, Rene, N-14
Sanday, P. R., N-26
Sandberg, A. A., N-6
Sanders, Joseph, N-42
Santana, Arthur, N-35
Santino, Umberto, N-28
Savona, Ernesto U., N-27
Saxon, Miriam S., N-34
Scarpitti, Frank R., N-16, N-27
Scarr, Sandra, 78, N-7
Scatchard, Dave, 96
Schafer, Walter B., N-13
Schaffer, Richard, N-35
Schalling, Daisy, N-8
Schatzberg, Rufus, N-28
Scheffer, David, 188, 189
Schiraldi, Vincent, N-29
Schlegel, Kip, N-32, N-33, N-35
Schlossman, Steven, N-12
Schmeidler, James, N-37
Schmid, Alex P., N-43
Schmidt, Janell D., N-25
Schneider, Hans Joachim, N-42
Schneider, Paul Schäfer, 124
Schoenberg, Robert J., N-27
Schoenthaler, Stephen, 79, N-7
Scholar, Michael, 34
Schott, Ian, N-27
Schrag, Clarence, 165, N-16
Schrager, Laura S., N-34, N-35
Schuessler, Karl E., 95, N-9
Schulenburg, Caroline, N-9

Schultz, Dutch, 340
Schultze, Phyllis, N-41
Schuman, Karl, N-42
Schur, Edwin M., 177, N-18
Schwartz, Martin D., 237, 238, N-20, N-22, N-26
Schwartz, Richard D., 178, N-18
Schweinhart, Lawrence J., N-2, N-11
Schwendinger, Herman, 186, 237, N-19, N-26
Schwendinger, Julia R., 186, 237, N-19, N-26
Schwind, Hans-Dieter, N-42
Sciandra, Carmine, 240
Sciandra, Margaret, 240
Sciandra, Mildred, 240
Sciandra, Salvatore, 240
Sciolino, Elaine, N-37
Scott, Austin W., N-23
Scott, Heather, N-39
Scott, Joseph E., N-32
Scott, Peter, N-6
Scott, R., N-18
Scott, Richard O., N-29
Scronce, Christine A., N-38
Scull, A., N-15
Scully, D., N-26
Sears, Kenneth C., N-31
Seda, Heriberto, 225
Sees, Karen L., N-2
Seidman, Robert, 186, N-19, N-34
Sellin, Thorsten, 45, 62, 123, 125, 126, N-3, N-5, N-7, N-13, N-14
Selva, Lance H., N-19
Semler, P. K., N-1
Sennewald, Charles A., N-30
Seper, Jerry, N-1
Serrill, Michael S., 347
Sesin, Carmen, N-35
Shaban, Sami, 178
Shachmurove, Yochanan, 211
Shaffer, John W., N-37
Shakespeare, William, 60
Shannon, Elaine, N-29
Shanoff, Barry, N-35
Shapiro, D., N-20
Shapiro, Mary, *323*
Shapiro, Susan P., N-32, N-34, N-35
Shavelson, Richard, N-12
Shaw, Bud, 162
Shaw, Clifford R., 117, 119, 120, 121, N-11, N-13
Shaw, James W., N-29
Shearing, Clifford D., N-22
Shedd, Ed, N-27
Sheldon, William, 63–64, 69, N-5

Sheley, Joseph F., N-29
Shelley, Louise I., N-27, N-40, N-41, N-42
Shelly, Peggy, N-30
Shelton, D., N-15
Shenou, Philip, N-1
Shepard, Matthew, 254
Sherman, Lawrence W., 29, 33, 204, N-2, N-11, N-21, N-22, N-25, N-29
Shichor, David, N-42
Shipman, Colleen, 48
Shoemaker, Donald J., 117, 132, 134, N-14, N-16
Shoham, S. G., N-23
Short, James F., 122, 144, N-10, N-12, N-13, N-14, N-16, N-34, N-35
Shover, Neal, 293, N-3, N-31
Shree Rajneesh, Bhagwan, 124
Sibbitt, Rae, N-37
Sickmund, M., N-3
Siegal, Harvey A., N-36
Siegel, Steven, 178
Sigler, Robert, N-26
Silas, Faye, N-38
Silva, Phil A., N-3, N-4, N-10
Silver, H. K., N-24
Silverman, F. N., N-24
Silverman, Robert, 224, N-23
Silverstein, Martin E., N-14
Simmons, Christopher, 84
Simon, Jeffrey D., N-28
Simon, Patricia M., N-39
Simon, Rita, 46, 48, N-4
Simons, Marlise, 347
Simons, Ronald L., N-4
Simpson, John, N-4, N-16
Simpson, Nicole Brown, 16, 232
Simpson, O. J., 16, 17, 232
Simpson, Sally S., N-4, N-21, N-32, N-35
Sims, Ronald R., N-34
Sinclair, Upton, 325
Singer, Peter, 58–59
Singer, Simon I., 42, N-14
Skilling, Jeff, 324
Skolnick, Jerome H., 178, N-18
Skoloda, T. E., N-38
Skoog, Dagna K., N-9
Sloan, John J., N-21
Sloane, Leonard, N-31
Smith, Akili, 162, N-3
Smith, Brent L., N-28
Smith, Carolyn, N-12, N-15, N-25
Smith, David J., N-23
Smith, David L., 292
Smith, Dietrich, N-31

Smith, Douglas A., 49, 119, N-3, N-4, N-10, N-12, N-16, N-25
Smith, Dwight, N-27
Smith, Gene M., N-37
Smith, Jacqui, 35
Smith, Jessica, N-10
Smith, Jinney S., N-5
Smith, Lynn Newhart, N-12
Smith, M. Dwayne, N-4, N-26, N-29
Smith, Mary S., N-22
Smithey, Martha, N-24
Snell, Cudore L., N-39
Snider, Laureen, N-32, N-35
Snortum, John R., N-38
Snyder, Howard N., N-3, N-14
Snyder, I. D., 209
Socrates, 52, 60, N-5
Solaway, A., N-1
Sommers, Ira, N-13, N-37
Sorenson, Ann Marie, N-13, N-17, N-36
Sorkin, Ross, N-1
Sorrentino, Anthony, N-12
Sosa, Rolando V., N-15
Sosa, Sammy, 106, 108
Souryal, Claire, N-45
Souryal, Sam S., N-41, N-42
South, Steve J., N-12
Southwick, L., N-38
Sparks, Richard F., 187, N-20, N-35
Spear, Robert, N-1
Speck, Richard, 76
Speckart, George, N-37
Spelman, William, N-22
Spencer, J., N-41
Spencer, Margaret P., N-34
Spergel, Irving A., N-15, N-24
Spiegel, Ulrich, N-12
Spielberger, Charles Donald, N-9
Spohn, Cassia C., N-26
Spradley, James, P., N-18
Spunt, Barry, N-37
Spurzheim, Johann Kaspar, 60, 69
Squitieri, Tom, N-3
Sroufe, L., N-8
Stack, Susan A., N-6
Stalin, J., 23
Stamatel, Janet, 169
Starkman, Dean, N-35
Staten, Clark, N-26
Stattin, Hakan, N-6
Steele, B. F., N-24
Steele, C. M., N-38
Steffens, Lincoln, 325
Steffensmeier, Darrell, 293, N-4, N-17, N-31, N-33

Steffenson James, L. Jr., N-14
Steffy, Richard A., N-39
Steinbeck, John, 142
Steinberg, Jacques, 209
Stenning, Phillip C., N-22
Stephens, Richard C., N-37
Stephenson, Philip, N-37
Sterling, Claire, N-27
Stevens, Larry, 225
Stevens, William K., N-38
Stewart, Martha, 49, 298
Stewart, Potter, N-39
Stiglitz, Joseph, N-1
Stillwell, Gary, N-37
Stoddard, J., N-7
Stolberg, Mary M., N-27
Stone, William E., N-21
Straus, Martha, N-25
Straus, Murray A., 232, N-25, N-38, N-41
Strodtbeck, Fred L., N-13, N-16
Strohmeyer, Jeremy, 220
Sullivan, Chrisopher J., N-17
Sullivan, John, N-42
Sullivan, John P., N-14
Sullivan, Mark, 282
Summers, Lawrence, *318*
Sumner, Maggie, N-38
Supancic, Michael, N-12
Sutherland, Edwin H., 10, 11, 30, 67, 78, 94, 121–122, 131, 269, 299, 318, 319, 325, N-1, N-2, N-6, N-12, N-30, N-32, N-33, N-34
Sutherland, Kiefer, 16
Swanson, C. R., N-31
Swanson, James W., N-7
Swazzi, Vincent, 293
Swift, Carolyn F., N-25
Swisher, Karin L., N-39, N-40
Swiss, Shana, N-43
Sykes, Alan O., N-34
Sykes, Gresham M., N-14, N-16, N-19, N-20, N-22

T
Takagi, Paul, 186
Takahashi, Toshiko, 190
Takahashi, Y., N-20
Talese, Gay, N-28
Tannenbaum, Frank, 175, N-18
Tarde, Gabriel, 66–67, 69, 185, N-6
Tata, Ratan, 13
Taubman, Alfred, 316
Taylor, Ian, 186, N-11, N-19, N-34
Taylor, Jessica, 313
Taylor, Jim, 313
Taylor, Kathy, 313

Taylor, Max, N-21
Taylor, Ralph B., 118, N-12
Taylor, Robert W., N-31
Teague, Jeffrey Allen, 279
Tedeschi, James, T., 203, 231, N-6, N-21, N-24
Tennenbaum, Daniel J., 95, N-9
Tennyson, Ray, N-13
Teresa, Mother, 102
Terlouw, Gert-Jan, N-3, N-41
Terrill, Richard J., N-40, N-41
Tersito, L., N-31
Tesoriero, James M., N-14, N-29
Tewksbury, R., 163
Thomas, Charles W., N-18
Thomas, Jim, N-20
Thomas, William I., 116, 175, N-11, N-18
Thompson, Bill, N-40
Thompson, Carol Y., N-3
Thompson, Dick, N-6
Thompson, Kevin M., 109, N-10, N-13
Thompson, Marilyn W., N-33
Thornberry, Terence P., 45, 109, 166, 167, N-3, N-10, N-13, N-14, N-16, N-17, N-19, N-25, N-29
Thornton, Joe, 96
Thurman, Tracey, 233
Tillman, Robert, N-35
Tittle, Charles R., 49, 109, N-4, N-10, N-12, N-17, N-18
Titus, Richard M., N-22, N-32
Toby, Jackson, 155, 161, 171–172, N-15, N-16, N-20
Toch, Hans, N-6, N-8
Tompkins, John S., N-33
Tonry, Michael, N-12, N-20, N-21, N-22, N-24, N-25, N-26, N-31, N-33, N-35
Topinard, Paul, 10, N-1
Torrio, Johnny, 241
Toufexis, Anastasia, N-10
Tracy, Paul E., 42, 45, N-3, N-33
Trafficante, Santo, Jr., 244
Travis, Gail, N-41
Treaster, Joseph B., N-14
Trebach, Arnold S., N-38
Tremblay, Richard E., N-9
Trickett, Alan, N-21
Triplett, Ruth, N-4, N-18
Tromanhauser, Edward D., N-13
Tulloch, M. I., N-9
Tunis, Sandra L., N-37
Turk, Austin T., 183, 184, N-19, N-20
Turnbull, Paul J., N-37
Turner, Carlton Akee, Jr., 92
Turner, J. W. Cecil, N-30

U

Uchida, Craig, N-22

V

Valachi, Joseph, 242, 243
Vallario, Louis "Big Louie," 240
Vallem, Bradley, 297
Van Bemmelen, J. M., N-19
Van Der Poel, Sari, N-39
Van Dijk, Jan J. M., 44, N-41
Van Duyne, Petrus, N-28
Van Kesteren, J. N., 44
Van Loh, Timothy D., N-17
Vaughn, Michael S., N-42
Vaz, E. W., N-15
Vazsonyi, Alexander T., N-17
Verhovek, Sam Howe, N-24, N-29
Verrett, Mary Nell, 254
Verri, Pietro, 55
Viano, Emilio C., N-21, N-42
Vick, Michael, 16, 17
Victor, Hope R., N-36
Vieraitis, Lynne M., 190, N-11, N-20
Villemez, Wayne J., 49, N-4, N-10
Virgil, 185
Virkkunen, Matti, 81, N-7, N-9
Visher, Christy A., N-3, N-37
Volavka, Jan, 83, N-7
Vold, George B., 183, 186, N-5, N-19
Volkman, Ernest, N-28
Voltaire, 55, 57
Von Hentig, Hans, 201, 224, N-21, N-23
Voss, Harwin L., 132, N-5, N-13
Voss, Natalie D., N-31

W

Waddell, J. O., N-38
Waksal, Samuel, 302
Waksler, Frances C., 12, N-1
Walder, Patrice, N-30
Waldo, G. P., N-9
Waldorf, Dan, N-14, N-37
Walker, Lenore E., N-25
Walker, Samuel, N-29
Wallace, Marjorie, N-34
Waller, John B., Jr., N-29
Wallerstein, James, S., 36, N-2
Wallis, Lynne, 107
Wallman, J., N-23
Walsh, Anthony, N-18
Walston, James, N-28
Walt, Steven, N-33
Walton, Paul, 186, N-11, N-19, N-34
Waples, S. J., N-2

Ward, David, N-18
Waring, Elin J., 325, N-22, N-32
Warner, John, N-37
Warr, Mark, 122, N-12, N-13
Warren, Carol, N-18
Washburn, S. L., N-5
Wasilchick, John, 199, 200, N-21
Watanavanich, Prathan, N-35
Watkins, Curtis, 41
Watkins, Sherron, 324
Watson, Sylvia M., N-8
Watters, Ricky, 162
Watts, W. A., N-31
Waxman, H. M., N-38
Weaver, Frances, N-30
Webster, Russell, N-37
Weekart, David P., N-11
Weeks, Susan L., N-32
Wegner, Norma, N-37
Weihofen, Henry, N-31
Weikart, David P., N-2
Weinberg, Bo, 241
Weinberg, George, 241
Weinberg, Richard, 78, N-7
Weiner, Neil Alan, N-9, N-14, N-17, N-24, N-26, N-37, N-40
Weis, Joseph G., 37, 166, N-3, N-17, N-36
Weisburd, David, 28, 197, 325, N-2, N-16, N-18, N-20, N-22, N-23, N-32, N-34, N-35
Weisel, Deborah, N-14
Weitzer, R., N-20
Wekesser, Carol, N-39, N-40
Wellford, Charles F., 180, N-17, N-18
Wells, L. Edward, N-16
Wendell, S., N-39
Wernz, Gerald W., N-32
Wertham, Frederic, 202, N-21
Weston, William, N-33, N-42
Wexler, Harry K., N-2
Whatley, Mark, N-26
Wheeler, David, 207
Wheeler, Stanton, N-32, N-35
White, Dan, 79–80
White, Helen Raskin, N-11
White, Jacqueline, N-26
Whittaker, David, N-12
Wiatrowski, Michael D., N-16
Widlake, Brian, N-35
Widom, Cathy Spatz, N-6, N-25
Wiechman, Dennis, N-42
Wiegand, R. Bruce, N-41
Wiegman, O., N-9
Wiersema, Brian, N-23, N-29
Wikström, Per-Olof H., N-22, N-42

Wild, Jonathan, 293
Wilkins, Leslie T., 31, N-2, N-42
Williams, Daniel, N-1
Williams, Frank P., III, N-10, N-40
Williams, J. Sherwood, N-14
Williams, Phil, N-27, N-43
Williams, Timothy L., N-32
Wilson, Anna Victoria, N-23
Wilson, Colin, N-27
Wilson, Edward O., N-6
Wilson, James, Q., 42, 78, 99, 264, 319, N-3, N-7, N-10, N-17, N-34
Wilson, Margo, N-24, N-42
Wilson, Nanci Koser, N-4, N-23
Wilson, William Julius, 106, 223, N-10, N-23
Winerip, Michael, N-28
Winslow, Robert W., N-39
Winslow, Virginia, N-39
Wintemute, Garen, 262
Winton, Richard, N-20
Wise, Edward M., N-43
Wish, Eric, N-37
Wisniewski, N., N-26
Witkin, Herman A., N-6
Wittekind, Janice E. Clifford, N-17
Wolf, Jim, N-1
Wolfe, Nancy T., N-4
Wolfgang, Marvin E., 40, 42, 45, 62, 78, 136, 137, 203, 224, 319, 341, N-2, N-3, N-5, N-7, N-9, N-13, N-14, N-21, N-23, N-25, N-26, N-37, N-38
Wood, Peter B., N-38
Woodall, Ruth, N-30
Woodbury, Richard, N-29
Wooden, Wayne S., N-31
Woodiwiss, Michael, N-43
Woods, Ickey, 162
Wormith, J. Stephen, N-9
Wortley, Richard, N-22, N-23
Wren, Christopher S., N-37
Wright, Bradley R., 197–198, N-4, N-10, N-20
Wright, James D., N-29
Wright, John Paul, N-11
Wright, Richard, 200, N-21, N-31
Wright, Stewart A., N-28
Wyle, Clement J., 36, N-2

Y

Yakovlev, Alexander, N-17
Yang, Y., 82, N-7
Yardley, Jim, 66
Yates, Andrea, 81

Yates, Michael, 141
Yeager, Peter C., 318, 319, N-32, N-34, N-35
Yeisley, Mark R., N-11
Yeudall, Lorne T., N-8
Yochelson, Samuel, 95, N-9
Young, Jock, 186, 190, N-11, N-19, N-34
Young, K., N-6

Young, Timothy R., N-35
Young, Vernetta D., N-4

Z
Zahn, Margaret A., 224, N-23
Zawitz, Marianne W., N-29
Zellman, Goul, N-12
Zerilli, Joe, 244
Zhang Xinfeng, 94

Zillman, Dolf, N-39
Zimring, Franklin E., N-38, N-39
Zinberg, Norman E., N-36
Zineb, El Khazouni, N-25
Zion, Sidney, N-28
Znaniecki, Florian, 116, N-11
Zorza, Joan, N-25
Zuckerman, Laurence, N-42
Zvekic, Ugljesa, N-41, N-42

Subject Index

Citations in italics refer to figures and illustrations

A

abolitionist criminology, 191
abortion, conflict theory and, 183
Academy of Experimental Criminology (AEC), 28
Academy of Fists, 55
access control, *210*
accommodation, 111
achievement orientation, 126
acquaintance homicides, *224–225*
acting-out joyriders, *214*
act requirement, 22–23
   act versus status, 23
   failure to act, 23
actus reus, and insanity defense, 25
adaptation modes
   conformity, 106, 107–108
   innovation, 106, 108
   rebellion, 106, 108
   retreatism, 106, 108
   ritualism, 106, 108
addict robbers, 240
Adelphia scandal, 8
Admitting the Holocaust (Langer), 188
adolescents
   parracide offenders, 92–93
   See also juvenile crime
adoptions, illegal, 370
adoption studies, 76–77, 100
advance-fee loan schemes, 307
advertising, deceptive, *133*
Afghanistan
   Buddas of, destruction, 8, *9*
   and Operation Enduring Freedom, 249, 251
   opium production, 5
   Shura, *359*
   Taliban, 5
   terrorist training camps in, 251
African Americans
   and crime, 49
   and due process and equal protection, 174
   and subculture of violence theory, 137
After School Activities Partnerships, 157
After School Matters (ASM), 156
age
   and crime, 38, 41–45

violent crime Index arrests by, *45*
   See also juvenile crime
aggravated assault, 231
aggression
   and alcohol, 341
   as instrumental behavior, 231
   See also violence
aging-out phenomenon, 43
AIDS. *See* HIV/AIDS
aircraft hijacking, 359, 369
alcohol
   and aggression, 341
   and crime, 26
   and drunk driving, 341–342
   and family violence, 233, 341
   history of legalization, 340
   and homicide, 341
   National Survey on Drug Use and Health Statistics, 2007, *332–333*
   and victimization, 204–205
   and violence, 340–341
   See also drugs; drunk driving
alcoholic robbers, 240
Algeria, 169
Alien Tort Claims Act, 188
Allied Chemical, 319, 322
Al Qaeda
   Abu Hafez al-Masri Brigade, 364–365
   and cybercrime, 7
   economic battle, 304–305
   and September 11, 6–7, 206–207, 251, 364–365, 368
   target selection calculus, 206–207
amateur thieves, 269
American Anti-Saloon League, 340
American Association for the Advancement of Science, 77
American Bar Association (ABA), 32
American Civil Liberties Union, on racial profiling, 50–51, 177
American dream, 111
American Indian gangs, 130
American Institute of Criminal Law and Criminology, 185
American Me, 142
American Shooting Sports Council, 261

American Society of Criminology, 68
Amish culture, 116
Amnesty International, 66
amphetamines, 331
anarchist criminology, 191
anger, 112
anomie
   Durkheim on, 68, 104–105
   Merton on, 105–111, *112*, 163
   Messner and Rosenfeld on, 111, *112*
   and suicide, 105
Anti-Defamation League, 148
Anti-Drug Abuse Act of 1988, 330
anti-drug education, 337, 339–340
antisocial personality, as mental illness, 97
antitrust legislation, 317
anxious attachment, 89, 90
Apalachin convention, 244–245
Argus program, 149
Armenian genocide, 188, 374
arms trafficking, 7, 369
arson
   juvenile fire setters, 294
   pyromaniacs, 294
Arthur Andersen, LLP, 9, 299, 309, 324
art theft, 269, 272
   top ten crimes, *273*
   as transnational crime, 368
Aryan Nation, 254
Asia, addiction issues in, 337
assassination, 221
assault, 230–231
   defined, 230
   stages of, 231
asthenic physique, 63
atavistic stigmata, 61, 62
athletics physique, 63
attachment
   and biology, 89
   family atmosphere and delinquency, 90
   and social control, 155–156, 157–158, 163, 171
   studies of, 89–90
attention deficit hyperactivity disorder (ADHD), 83
Attorney General's Commission on Pornography, 348, 349, 350

Aum Shinrikyo cult, 124, 125, 254
auto-body repair shops, 308
automatism defense, 98
automobile insurance fraud. *See* motor vehicle insurance fraud
automobile theft. *See* motor vehicle theft
autonomy, focal concern, 138, 139
aversive instigators, 94

B

baby-boom generation, 38
Baby Boy, 142
Babylonian Code of Hammurabi, 14
Balkanization, 373
Balkans, 189
Bandidos, the, 245
Bank of America, 313
Bank of Credit and Commerce International (BCCI) scandal, 366–367
bankruptcy fraud, 303–304
   as transnational crime, 371
Bank Secrecy Act, 317
bar ("B") girls, 345
barbiturates, 331
battered child syndrome, 92, 231
battered wife syndrome, 231
battered women's shelters, 233
battery, 231
Bay Area Women Against Rape, 238
Bayer Company, 328
Beggar's Opera, The (Gay), 293
behavioral factors, and modeling, 90
Beirut, Lebanon, bombing of U.S. embassy, 251
belief, as social bond, 157, 158, 163, 171
Belly, 142
"Beltway" snipers, 225, 226
Bentham Society, 59
Beyond Tolerance: Child Pornography on the Internet (Jenkins), 348
Bhagwan Shree Rajneesh communities, 124
Bhopal disaster, 319
Big Brother/Big Sister programs, 121
binge drinking, 340
biochemical factors, 79–83
   diet, 79–80
   food allergies, 79
   hormones, 81
   hypoglycemia, 80–81

biocriminology, 75, 99
   adoption studies, 76–77
   criticisms of, 83, 86
   racist undertones, 83
   and sexual predators
   twin studies, 76
biological determinism, 59–60, 63–64, 68
   challenges to, 63
   chronology of, 69
   inherited criminality, 64–65
   return to, 63–64
   somatotype school, 63–64
   timeline for
biology and criminality, 68
   biochemical factors, 79–83
   biocriminology, 75–77, 83, 86
   genetics and criminality, 75–77
   IQ debate, 78–79
   violence and genes, controversy over, 77–78
birth cohort, 45
Black Thursday, 105
blaming the victim, 187
Bloods, middle class members, 146, 147
boat theft, 204, 276–277
Boggs Act, 329
boiler rooms, 303
Bolivia
   addiction problems, 336
   cocaine and marijuana from, 245
   political impact of drug trade, 336
bonds. *See* stocks and bonds
boot camps, 30, 337
born criminals, 60, 61–62
Born Into Brothels, 102
Bosnia-Herzegovina, 188, 189, 372
Boston violence-prevention programs, 170, 171
Brady Act, 262–264
Brady Background Checks: 15 Years of Saving Lives, 262
Brady Center to Prevent Gun Violence, 262–263
brain
   abnormal functioning of murderers, 83
   differences in volume, 82
   imaging, 81
   prefrontal volumes, and antisocial behavior, 82
brain overclaim syndrome, 84–85
Branch Davidian cult, FBI (Federal Bureau of Investigation) and, 124, 254

Breathalyzers, 342
bribery
   of public officials, 371
   white-collar crime, 308
BRIC countries (Brazil, Russia, India, and China), PC shipments to, 288
British Petroleum, Inc., 297
Brocade Communications Systems, Inc., 296
BTK killer, the, 73–74, 226
Buck v. Bell, 58
Bulgaria, 169
Bureau of Alcohol, Tobacco and Firearms, Youth Crime Gun Interdiction Initiative, 261
Bureau of Justice Statistics (BJS), 27, 34
Bureau of the Census. *See* Census Bureau
burglary, 292–293
   crime day of burglar, 200
   defined, 292
   factors contributing to, 211
   hot products, 201
   by professional thieves, 269
   repeat, 204
   and situational theories, 199–200
businesses
   infiltration of legal, 6–7, 371
   See also corporate crime; white-collar crime
business opportunity fraud, 306
Business Software Association, 287
buy-back programs, for handguns, 263

C

Calcutta, 102
Cali Cartel, 336
California Psychological Inventory (CPI), 95
Cambodia, child sex tourism, 357
Cambridge Study of Delinquent Development, 90, 167
Canada, gun control, 264
capitalism, 185, 187
capital punishment, 183
   Garofolo on, 63
   and homicide rates, 230
   and mental illness, 66
   methods of execution, 70
Cargo cults, 124
carjacking, 275
case studies, 27, 30
causation requirement, 24
causation theory, 26
Causes of Delinquency (Hirschi), 155

celebrities, and crime, 16–17
cellular telephone crimes. *See* high-tech crimes
censorship
   and child pornography, 348
   of Internet, 352
Census Bureau
   crime victimization surveys, 34
   taking census, 27
   use of data in research, 31
Challenge of Crime in a Free Society, The, 17
Charlotte, North Carolina
   arrest trends, 39
   homicides, 37
cheating, 277, 279
Chechen terrorism, 368, *369*
check forgery, 280–281
Chernobyl disaster, 319
Chevron Texaco, 8
Cheyenne culture, 358
Chicago, immigration to, 104
Chicago Area Project (CAP), *120*
child abuse
   battered child syndrome, 92, 231
   emotional abuse, 234
   extent of, 234
   nature of, 234–235
   neglect, 234
   sexual abuse, 92, 190, 234
   and subculture of violence, 234
   See also child pornography; children
child pornography
   and censorship, 348
   and FBI, 288
   on Internet, 288, *291*, 348–349, 350
   laws, 354
   prevention, 351
Child Protective Services (CPS), 234
children
   child sex tourism, 357
   and guns, 259, 261
   as homicide victims, 225
   illegal transfer for adoption, 370
   percentage of living in poverty or with no working parent, *138*
   prostitution, 356
   regulation of access to Internet, 352
   sexual exploitation of, *346*, 356–357
   See also child abuse

China
   and the Internet, 349–350
   and Internet porn, 94
   software piracy, 287–288
Chinese gangs, 135, 245, *248*
choice structuring properties, 197
cholesterol levels, and violence, 75
chop shops, 274
chromosomes, 75–76
churning, 302
cigarettes. *See* smoking
civil penalties. *See* fines and penalties
civil recovery, 272
class. *See* social class
classical criminology, 1, 52–58
   evaluation of, 57–58
Clayton Antitrust Act, 317
Clean Water Act, 319
Coalition Against Insurance Fraud (CAIF), 283
Coalition for Evidence-Based Policy, 29
cocaine
   historical use of, 328
   U.S. purchase prices, *335*
   user lifestyle, 331, 334
Cocaine Anonymous (CA), 337
Coconut Grove disaster, 222
codeine, 328
Code of Hammurabi, 14
Code of the Street (Anderson), 137
coercive actions, 203
"college boys," 131
college campus crime, 201
   sexual assault against women, 206
Colombia
   addiction issues, 336
   Cali Cartel, 336
   cocoa trade, 5
   crime families, 245
   drug cartels, 335
   FARC, 247
   political impact of drug trade, 336
Colors (film), 142
Columbine High School shootings, 226, 256, 258
Commission on Obscenity and Pornography, 345, 347
commitment, and social bond, 156–157, 158, 163, 171
Committee on Mercenary Crimes, 242
common law, 268
Communications Decency Act (CDA), 352

Communist Manifesto (Marx), 185
community life cycles, 119
Community Tolerance Study, 110
Community Youth Gang Service, 149–150
Comparative Crime Data File, 361
comparative criminological research, 359–362
   comparative research tools and resources, 361
   culture-specific phenomena, 361
   identification of comparable problems, 362
   identification of sources of information, 362
   interdependent phenomena, 361
   selection of comparable methods, 362
comparative criminology
   defined, 357–358
   development of international strategies, 364–372
   global village, 358–359
   goals of, 359
   history of, 358–359
   internationally induced local crime problems, 365–366
   learning from others' experiences, 363–364
   socioeconomic development perspective, 363
   theory testing, 362–363
   transnational crime, 366–372
   validation of theories, 363
Comprehensive Drug Abuse Prevention and Control Act (Controlled Substances Act), 330
COMPSTAT, 21, *196*
CompuServe, 352
computer crime. *See* high-tech crimes
computer network break-ins, 286
Computer Phone Book (Cane), 349
computer vandalism, 286
computer viruses, 286
concentrated poverty, 140, *141*
concurrence requirement, 25
"conditioned free will," 83
conditioning theory, 96–97
Condition of the Working Class in England, The (Engels), 185
conduct norms, 124
confidence games, 269, 280
confidential information, sale of, 308

conflict resolution, 123
conflict theory, 181–184, 186, 192
    conflict model, 19, 182–183
    consensus model, 182, 183
    and criminology, 183–184
conformity
    as adaptation, 106
    social control and, 161
Congo, 189
conscience, and social control, 163, 171
consensus model, 14, 19, 182
constructive corporate culpability, 316
consumer fraud, top categories of, 306
containment theory, 161–165
    empirical tests of, 164–165
    evaluation of, 165
Controlled Substances Act, 330
control mechanisms, failure of, 161
control theory, at level of criminality, 167
convenience stores, and crime, 212–213
conventional morality, 87, 88
copycat crimes, 228
    school shootings, 256
corner boys, 131, 134
corporate compliance programs, 323
corporate crime, 26, 299, 309–325
    and corporate power, 310–311
    criminal liability, 309, 318
    curbing, 323
    definition problems, 309
    environmental crimes, 319–323
    fraud, 320
    frequency of, 309
    future of, 323–325
    insurance-related, 283
    international, preventing, 366–367
    investigation of, 318–319
    liability theories, 315–316
    models of, 316–317
    phases of criminal law, 309, 312, 313, 314, 315
    and Sarbanes-Oxley Act, 298–299, 323
    See also white-collar crime
corporate ethos theory, 316
corporate policy model, 316
corporations
    government control of, 317–318
    power of, 310–311

Correlates of Crime, 361
corruption and bribery of public officials, as transnational crime, 371
Corruption Perceptions Index (CPI), 180
cortical arousal, 97
Costa Rica, 169
    child sex tourism, 357
counterterrorism measures, 178–179, 246
Countrywide Home Loans, 279
Course in Positive Philosophy (Cours de philosophie positive) (Comte), 58
courts
    International Criminal Court (ICC), 188, 189, 372, 373
    juvenile courts, 187, 358
    Supreme Court, 351–352
    war crimes tribunals, 189, 372
crack cocaine, 328, 334
crank, 334
CRAVED (consumer goods that are attractive), 201
Crazy Crew, 142
credit card fraud, 281–282, 291
    and Internet, 282
    and professional thieves, 269
credit crisis, 296, 299
crime
    characteristics of, 37–40
    concept of, 12, 13
    degrees of severity, 25
    elements of, 191
    Index crimes, 32
    ingredients of, 22–25
    locations and times of criminal acts, 38–39
    nature and extent of, 32–37
    persons, crimes against, 32
    process of bringing to attention of police, 32
    property, crimes against, 32
    rates, computation of, 32–33
    severity, public ranking of, 42
    severity of, 40
    typologies of, 26
    vulnerability to political pressure, 34–35
    See also crime statistics; criminals
crime and place research, 204
Crime and the American Dream (Messner & Rosenfeld), 111
"Crime Control in Capitalist Society" (Quinney), 186
crime-prevention programs, 38

crime statistics
    abuse of in UK, 34–35
    comparative crime rates, 294–295
    comparative property crime rates, 294–295
    crime trends, 37–38
    murders, robberies, and aggravated assaults using firearms, 1973–2006, 260
    nations with low rates, 168–169
    police statistics, 32–34
    self-report surveys, 35–37
    victimization surveys, 34–35
crime surfing
    Annual Report on School Safety and Indicators of School Crime and Safety, 259
    Beccaria, 57
    British Home Office crime-prevention guide, 214
    Bureau of Alcohol, Tobacco and Firearms, 261
    chat room, 15
    computer crimes, 284
    corporate crime, 316
    critical criminology and death penalty, 185
    Durkheim, Émile, and religion, 67
    gangs and street crimes, 116, 142, 144
    insanity defense, 96
    international and comparative criminology, 361
    International Criminal Court (ICC), 372
    Internet pornography, 352
    Interpol, 371
    Justice Research and Statistics Association (JRSA), 31
    making of laws, 11
    maternal deprivation, 90
    National Incident Based Reporting System (NIBRS) data, 33
    Omega Boys Club, 157
    situational crime prevention, 210
    "Sourcebook of Criminal Justice Statistics," 17, 38
    Southern Poverty Law Center, 255
    United Nations anti-drug efforts, 337
    United Nations Office on Drugs and Crime (UNODC), 41

United Nations Survey of Crime Trends and Operations of Criminal Justice Systems, 371
victimization and neighborhoods, 119
"Watch Your Car" program, 275
crime type displacement, 215
Criminal and His Victim, The (Von Hentig), 202
criminal gangs, 133–134
criminal homicide, 220
Criminality and Economic Conditions (Bonger), 185
criminal justice, focus of, 18
criminal justice specialists, 17
criminal justice system
and criminology, 17–18
discrimination in, 184
Criminal Man, The (L'uomo delinquente) (Lombroso), 60, 65
Criminal Personality, The (Yochelson & Samenow), 95
criminal psychology, pioneers in, 65
criminals
age of, 41–45
careers, 45
characteristics of, 40–50
gender, 46–48
psychological studies of, 65
race, 49–50
social class, 48–49
criminal sexual conduct, 237–238
criminal status, 184
criminal stock, 63
criminology
biological theories
changing boundaries of, 4–10
and conflict theory, 183–184
and criminal justice system, 17–18
definition of, 1, 10–11, 19
empirical research, 11
experimental, 22
focus of, 18
four perspectives, *174*
reach of, 8–10
schools of, 1
time line of historical and contemporary, 68, *69*
Criminology, 188
criminoloids, 62
Crips, 135, 142
middle class in, 147
cross-cultural research. *See* comparative criminology

crossfire homicides, 228
cross-sectional studies, 28
cults
defined, 125
doomsday, 253–254
cultural deviance theories, 126
nature of cultural deviance, 115–116
social disorganization theory, 115, 116–118
and subcultural theory, 130
cultural disorientation defense, 98
cultural objects, theft of, 368
cultural property, destruction of, 8
cultural transmission, 118
culture conflict theory, 115, 123–126, 126
subculture of violence and, 136
See also differential association theory; social disorganization theory
culture of poverty, 106
cyberattacks, 7
CyberPatrol, 352
cyberporn, *288, 289, 290,* 348–350, 352, 353
cyber spies, 286
cyber vandals, 286

D
Daewoo Group, 367
Darfur, genocide, 188, 189, 373
Darling International case, 319–321
data collection methods, 26, 27–31
case studies, 30
participant and nonparticipant observation, 30
surveys, 27–28
date rape, 236
death penalty. *See* capital punishment
Debam, 151
deceptive advertising, 306
defense contractors, and procurement fraud, 305
defenses, 25
defensible space, 207
deflection of offenders, *210*
delinquency. *See* juvenile crime
"delinquent boys," 131
delusional instigators, 94
demography, and crime trends, 41
denial-of-service attacks, 286

Denver Youth Survey, 135
Denying the Holocaust (Lipstadt), 188
depression, biocriminology and, 75
detoxification programs, 337
developmental/life course theory, 165–168, *166*
deviance, 11–12
defined, 116
funnel of, *13*
modes of, *109*
probability of as indicated by inner and outer containment, *164*
society's reaction to, 16–19
See also cultural deviance theories
deviant sexual intercourse, 343
Dewell, 151
diet and criminality, 79–80
differential association reinforcement, 94
differential association theory, 67, 115, 121–123, 126, 130
evaluation of, 122–123
policy and, 123
Sutherland's theory, 121–122
tests of, 122
differential opportunity theory
and delinquency, 133–136
evaluation of, 136
tests of, 135–136
direct control, 164
direct experience learning, 93–94
disasters, types of crimes during, 3–4
disenfranchisement, of convicted felons, 192
Disney World, crime prevention in, 210–212
displacement
and gun control, 264
and situational crime prevention, 213, 214–215
Division of Social Labor (Durkheim), 67
dizygotic (DZ) twins, 76
Doctors Without Borders, 151
dogs, curbing of, 11
domestic elder abuse, 235
domestic violence. *See* family-related crimes; family violence
doomsday cults, 253–254
Down syndrome, 58
Draft Code of Crimes, 372
Drexel Burnham Lambert scandal, 302

drift, and social control theories, 160–161
drive-by shootings, 143–144, 145, 146, 228
driving while intoxicated (DWI). *See* drunk driving
dropout-delinquency relationship, 132
drug control
    drug courts and other problem-solving courts, 337, *339*
    education, 337, 339–340
    funding by agency, 2007–2009, *338*
    legalization, 340
    national spending for, *329*
    Title 21 provisions, 330–331
    treatment, 337
    See also drugs; drug trafficking
drug czar, 330
Drug Enforcement Agency statistics, 31
drugs
    addict lifestyles, 331
    and crime, 26, 331, 334–337
    decline in use, 2001 to 2007, *332*
    extent of abuse, 330
    and family violence, 233
    history of, 328–331
    and HIV/AIDS, 331, 334
    patterns of abuse, 330–334
    2007 survey of use, *332–333*
    use among youth, *331*
    See also alcohol; *specific types of drugs*
drug trafficking
    and gangs, 142, 328
    and money laundering, *335–336*
    "mules," 328
    organizations (DTOs), 142
    political impact of, 336–337
    roles and functions of business compared with legitimate industry, *330*
    by sea, 276, 369
    and terrorism, 5
    as transnational crime, 371
Drug Use Forecasting, 334
drunk driving, 341–342
due process, 174
Dunedin, New Zealand, study, 198
duration of attachment, 89
dynamic explanations of criminality, 167

E
East Jersey State Prison (formerly Rahway State Prison), 28
ecocide, 10
ecological analysis, 117
economic choice theory, and rational-choice perspective, 197
economic factors
    and class conflicts, 186
    and crime trends, 41
economic norms, penetration of, 111
ectomorphs, 63
education
    devaluation of, 111
    drug control, 337, 339–340
    middle-class measuring rod, 131, 133, 140, 152
EEG abnormalities, 83
ego, 86, 163
Eighteenth Amendment, 241, 340
Eighth Amendment, 23, 66
Eight Trey Gangster Crips, 142
elderly persons
    abuse of, 235
    in prisons, *42*
embezzlement, as white-collar crime, 308
emotion, engagement of, 89
emotional abuse, of children, 234
employer and employee
    insider-related fraud, 308
    occupational crimes, 301
    See also white-collar crime
encryption technology, 349
endomorphs, 63
engagement of emotion, 89
enhancement of sentence. *See* sentence enhancements
Enron Corporation, 8, 324–325
environmental crime, 319–323
    effective legislation, 322–323
    enforcement of legislation, 321–322
    sensitive issues, 322
    as transnational crime, 370
environmental criminology, 196, 204
    and victimization theory, 204
EPA (Environmental Protection Agency), 319
equal protection, 174
equal rights, 174
equity skimming, 278
Estelle Prison, Huntsville, Texas, elderly inmates, *42*

ethics
    for criminology and criminal justice fields, 31
    and research, 31
ethnic cleansing, 188
ethnic gangs, 129–130, 130, 135
ethnicity
    ethnic profiling, 50
    fragmentation, 372–373
    and organized crime, 245, 248
eugenics, 64
event model, burglary in middle-class suburb, *197*
evidence-based crime and justice policy, importance of, 29–30
evolution theory, 58–59
exceptional means, percent of crimes cleared by arrest of, *236*
excitement, focal concern, 138, 139
executions. *See* capital punishment
experimental criminology, 22
experimental school-based parent-training programs, 171
experimental studies, 27, 68
    data collection methods, 28–30
    human experimentation review committees, 31
extroversion, 96, 97
Exxon Valdez disaster, 9, 309
Eysenck Personality Questionnaire (EPQ), 96

F
facilitators, controlling, *210*
failure to act, 23
fame, and crime, 16–17
Families First program, 171
family
    atmosphere, and delinquency, 90
    See also children; family-related crimes; family violence
"family ganging" health insurance fraud, 284
family-related crimes, 231–235
    and alcohol, 233, 341
    battered child syndrome, 92, 231
    battered wife syndrome, 231
    child abuse, 92, 190, 234–235
    elder abuse, 235

family-based crime prevention, by ecological context, *91*
spousal abuse, 232–234
spousal rape, 231
family violence
  and drugs, 233
  effects on children, 90
  and radical feminist theory, 190
FBI (Federal Bureau of Investigation)
  and bankruptcy fraud, 303–304
  Financial Crimes Report, 320–321
  and insurance fraud, 283
  list of most wanted terrorists, *250,* 251
  MS-13 National Joint Task Force, 129
  National Stolen Art File, 272
  Stolen Boat File, 276
  Suspicious Activity Reports (SARS), 278–279
  See also Uniform Crime Reports (UCR)
fear of crime, and media, 19
Federal Bureau of Prisons statistics, 31, 32
Federal Election Campaign Act, 317
Federal Witness Protection Program, 243
felicific calculus, 57
felon disenfranchisement, 192
felonies, 25, 26
  and felon disenfranchisement, 192
  felony murder, 221
female delinquent subcultures, 133, 144–147, 152
Female Offender, The (Lombroso and Ferrero), 4646
feminist view
  and battered wives, 231
  radical feminist theory, 190
  and rape, 237
Fence (Steffensmeier), 293
fencing, 293–294
  and CRAVED goods, 201
field experiments, 28
Fifth Amendment, variation in rights with crime, 20
FinCEN (Financial Crimes Enforcement Network), 279
fines and penalties, for corporate crime, 317
firearms
  extent of firearm-related

crimes, 259
and gangs, 143–144
murders, robberies, and aggravated assaults using firearms, 1973–2006, *260*
youth and guns, 259, 261
See also gun control; weapons
First Amendment, 228, 351
first degree murder, 221
Five Percent Nation, 144
Florida Convenience Store Security Act, 213
food allergies/additives, and criminality, 79
forcible rape. *See* rape
foreign lottery schemes, 307
Foreign Terrorist Organizations (FTOs), 252
Forfeiture Law, 342
Fourth Amendment, variation in rights with crime, 20
Frankfurt, progressive school of, 185
fraud, 277–284
  check forgery, 280–281
  confidence games, 269, 280
  credit card fraud, 269, 281–282
  employee fraud, 308
  against the government, 304–306
  health insurance fraud, 284
  insurance fraud, 275, 282–284
  in marine shipping industry, 276
  mortgage fraud, 278–279
  obtaining property by, 277, 279
  and professional thieves, 269
  tax fraud, 297
  See also white-collar crime
freedom fighters, 253
Freemen of Montana, 256
free speech, 352
free will doctrine, 60, 62, 65
  chronology of, *69*
functional magnetic resonance imaging (fMRI), 81
fundamental psycholegal error, 98
funnel of deviance, *13*
Fur ethnic group, 189

G
gallows, 16
Gambino crime family, 240, 243, 244
gangs, 128–130

American Indian gangs, 130
Chinese gangs, 135
conflict gangs, 134
criminal gangs, 133–134
demographic profile of members, 1995, *145*
and differential association theory, 133–134
drug-trafficking, *138,* 142, *143,* 328
in early twenty-first century, 142
factors leading to development of, *134*
female gangs, 130, 144–147, 152
getting out of, 150–151
and guns, 143–144
Hispanic gangs, 129–130
initiation rites, 136, 145
law enforcement agencies reporting problems with, *148*
legal and illegal income sources, 136
middle-class gangs, 133
movies about, 142
murder, 228
Nigerian, 150–151
outlaw motorcycle gangs (OMGs), 130
retreatist, 134
satanic, 148
and social control theories, *159–160*
tattoo removal, 151
Gangster Disciples, 142
gays. *See* homosexuality; lesbian, gay, bisexual, and transgender (LGBT) community
gender and crime, 46–48
  battered wife syndrome, 231
  female gangs, 130, 144–147, 152
  female serial killers, 225
  juvenile female arrests, 1980–2006, *47*
  See also rape
General Electric Company, 322
general strain theory, 111–113, 126
general theories of crime, examples of, *166*
Genesis Healthcare Corporation, 298
genetics and criminality, 75–77
  adoption studies, 76–77
  twin studies, 76
  and violence, 77–78
  XYY Syndrome, 75–76

genocide
    Armenian, 188, 374
    Darfur, 188, 189, 373
    ethnic cleansing, 188
    and international trials, 189, 372
    and Jews, 188, 374
    and mentally retarded persons, 188, 374
    neglect in study of, 188, 374
    rape as, 188–189
    Rwandan, 188, 372
Genovese crime family, 242
geographical displacement, 215
geography of crime, 204
Gini index of income inequality, 140
Girls in the Gang, The (Campbell), 146
globalization
    and approach to breaking laws, 18–19
    economic, 18
    and ethnic fragmentation, 372–373
    and organized crime, 359
    and sexual slavery, 356–357
Global Software Piracy Study, 287
global village, 358–359
glue sniffing, 329
Gods Must Be Crazy, The, 267, 295
Goldman Sachs, 313
Good Samaritan laws, 23
government
    control of corporations, 317–318
    fraud against, 304–306
Grapes of Wrath, The (Steinbeck), 142
Great Depression, 105, 142, 309
"Green River Killer," 225
"Ground Zero," 249
guillotine, 53
guilt or shame, techniques to induce, 210
guilty mind, 24–25
Gulf cartel, 247
gun control
    criminal background checks, 262–263
    debate, 264–265
    handgun control, 261–264
    and violence, 259–265
Gun Control Act of 1968, 263
Gun Free Schools Act, 257
guns. *See* firearms; weapons
Gypsies, 188, 374

H

hacking, 286, 291, 349
Hale-Bopp comet, 124
Hale Doctrine, 235
"Half Full and Half Empty," 235
hallucinogens, 331
Hammurabi's Code. *See* Code of Hammurabi
handgun control, 261–264
    buy-back programs, 263
Handgun Control (organization), 264
happy hours, 342
Harlem Little League team, 154
harm requirement, 23–24
Harrison Act, 329, 330
hashish, 328
hate crimes
    explosion of, 254
    Ku Klux Klan and, 116, 254
hate groups
    active U.S., *255*
    deviant, 116
    middle-class gangs, 147–148
Hayes International Retail Theft Survey, 270
Head Start program, 113–114, 123
health insurance fraud, 284
Heaven's Gate cult, 124
Hell's Angels, 116
heroin
    addict lifestyle, 331
    introduction of, 328
high-tech crimes, 284–292
    and cell phones, 198
    characteristics of, 285, 291–292
    computer network break-ins, 286
    credit card fraud, 291
    criminal justice problem, 292
    industrial espionage, 286–287
    mail bombings, 290
    online pornography, *288–290*
    password sniffers, 291
    software piracy, 287–288
    and terrorism, 7
    top ten Internet crime complaints, *286*
    as transnational crime, 370
hijacking
    aircraft, 359
    land, 370
Hirschi-Gottfredson self-control model, *169–170*
Hispanic gangs, 129–130
HIV/AIDS
    and demand for child prostitutes, 346

and drug use, 331, 334
and prostitution, 344
Hollinger International, Inc., 297
Holocaust, 188, 374
homeboys, 145
Homebuilders program, 171
home-improvement fraud, 306
homeless, recommunalizing of, 191
homicide, 220–230
    and alcohol, 341
    child victims, 225
    criminal, 220
    current rates in the U.S., 222–223
    extent of, 222–223
    gang murder, 228
    as intraracial crime, 223
    justifiable, 220
    manslaughter, 221–222
    murder, 220–221
    nature of, 224–228
    parricide, 92–93
    rates in the U.S. over time, 223
    by relatives and acquaintances, *224–225*
    serial and mass murders, 225–228
    social class and, 109–110
    stranger homicides, 224
    victim precipitation, 224
    without apparent motive, 225
    workplace, 226, *227,* 228
    young and old perpetrators, 225
homicide rates, 228–230, *229*
    and capital punishment, 230
    cross-national comparison, 228–230
    and economic factors, 137
    and income inequality, 230
    in the South, 137
    in South Africa, 140
    and youth population, 230
homosexuality, 343
    and hate crimes, 354
    See also lesbian, gay, bisexual, and transgender (LGBT) community
homosexual rape, 238
hormones and aggression, 81
hot products, 201
hot spots
    evidence, theory, and causes, *205*
    and victimization theory, 204, 216
House Financial Services Committee hearings, *313*
household crimes, times of, 39

House of Umoja program, 149
houses of prostitution, 344
How to Read Character: A New Illustrated Hand-Book of Physiology, Phrenology and Physiognomy for Students and Examiners, 61
human body parts, trade in, 370–371
human experimentation review committees, 31
human nature, and crime
  criticisms of biocriminology, 83, 86
  and social control theory, 163
Human Rights Watch, 150
human trafficking, 247, 357
  as transnational crime, 7–8, 370
  See also sexual slavery
Hurricane Katrina, 3–4
  and insurance fraud, 283, 284
hypoglycemia, 80–81
hypothesis, 26, 28

I

id, 86, 87
Illegal Corporate Behavior (Clinard), 313
illegal migrants, smuggling of, 7–8, 370
ImClone Systems scandal, 298, 302
immediate gratification, 86, 87
immigration, social disorganization theory and, 116
incentive instigators, 94
Index crimes, 32
India, 102–103
  Bhopal disaster, 319
  software piracy, 287–288
Indicators of School Safety Report, 257
indirect control, 164
industrial espionage, 286–287
Industrial Espionage Act, 287
Industrial Revolution, 185
industry insider fraud, 278
infancy defense, 25
infanticide, 58, 189
infiltration of legal business, 371
informed consent, 31
inherited criminality, 64–65
initiation rites, of gangs, 136
inner-city neighborhoods, and joblessness, 223
inner containment, 163, *164*
Innocence Lost, 356
innovation, 106
insane criminals, 62

insanity defense, 25, 68
insider-related fraud, 308
insider trading, 297, 302
instigators, 94
Institute for Juvenile Research, Chicago, 120
institutional anomie theory, 111, *112*
institutional elder abuse, 235
instructional instigators, 94
instrumental offenders, *214*
insurance fraud, 282–284, 306, 308
  corporate fraud, 283
  health insurance fraud, 284
  and Hurricane Katrina, 283, 284
  and motor vehicles, 275, 282, 308
  premium diversion/ unauthorized entities, 283
  as transnational crime, 370
  viatical settlement fraud, 283
  Workers Compensation Fraud, 283–284
integrated theory of criminology, examples of, *166*, 168–169
intellectual property theft, 368
intelligence quotient (IQ), 65, 68
  debate over genetics or environment, 78–79
  and delinquency, 100
intelligence tests, 65
interest groups, 187
Intergovernmental Panel on Climate Change, 19
intermittent explosive disorder, 83
internalized control, 164
Internal Revenue Code, 317
International Association of Chiefs of Police (IACP), 32, 34
International Association of Insurance Fraud Agencies, 283
international crime, 18, 372. *See also* international issues
International Crime Victim Survey (ICVS), *44*, 361
International Criminal Court (ICC), 188, 189, 372, 373
International Criminal Police Organization (Interpol), 361
international issues
  comparative crime rates, 294–295
  internationally induced local crime problems, 365–366

low-crime-rate nations, 168–169
  oil spill disasters, 9–10
  pollution of oceans, 9–10
  sea crime, 276, 366
  sexual slavery, *346–347*, 356–357
  See also comparative criminology; transnational crime
International Monetary Fund (IMF), 181, 182
International Self-Report Delinquency (ISRD) study, 37
Internet
  cafés, 350
  and censorship, 352
  and consumer fraud, *306*
  cyberporn, *288, 289, 290,* 348–350, 352, 353
  and globalization of crime, 18
  regulation of children's access to, 352
  and sexual exploitation of children, 18
Internet crime. *See* high-tech crimes
Internet Crime Complaint Center (IC3), 286
Interpol (International Criminal Police Organization)
investment schemes, 307
involuntary manslaughter, 222
involuntary servitude, 370
involvement, as social bond, 157, 158, 163, 171
IQ. *See* intelligence quotient
Iraq war, 7
Irish Republican Army (IRA), 251
Islamic Jihad, 206–207
Israel, 264
Israeli Mafia, 245
Italian Mafia. *See* Mafia
Italian School. *See* positivist criminology

J

Jamaica
  cocaine and marijuana from, 245
  posses from, 138
"*Janjaweed* babies," 189
Japan
  child pornography, 351
  crime rates, 169
  environmental protection, 322
  random murders, 221
  Yakuza, 245

Job Corps, 114–115
    performance and results, 2004–2006, *115*
    profile of members, 114
joblessness, 223
"johns," 344
Journal of Criminal Law and Criminology, 188
joyriding, *214,* 274
junk food defense, 80
jury trials, nonlegal factors in jury decision making, 184
just-community intervention approach, 89
Justice Department, Child Exploitation and Obscenity section, 356
Justice Research and Statistics Association (JRSA), 31
justifiable homicide, 220
Justitia, 24
Juvenile Awareness Program (formerly Scared Straight), 28
juvenile courts
    establishment, 358
    and social class, 187
juvenile crime
    arson, 294
    and culture conflict theory, 130
    and differential opportunity theory, 133–136
    drug use, *331*
    family atmosphere and, 90
    and guns, 143–144, 259, 261
    and labeling theory, 175–176, 178–179
    male and female arrests, 1980–2006, *47*
    Miller's theory of focal concerns, 138–142
    motor vehicle theft, *274*
    race and, 49
    rates of, 41–43
    and reaction formation, *131*
    and school, 131–132
    self-report data, 36–37
    and social class, 49
    and strain theory, 111
    violence, behavior precursors to, 77
    violent crime with injury, by time of day, *39*
juvenile justice system
    detention costs, 114
    establishment of, 178
    inherent discrimination in, 179

K

Kefauver crime committee, 242
Kent State University killings, *176*

kickbacks, 308
kidnapping, 238
Knapp Commission
Ku Klux Klan, and hate crimes, 116, 254

L

labeling, of countries as "corrupt," 180
labeling theory, 15, 174–181, 192
    in action, 177
    basic assumptions of, 175–176
    empirical evidence for, 177–180
    evaluation of, 180–181
    origins of, 175
    in the 1960s, 176–177
Labor Department statistics, 31
La Cosa Nostra, 240, 242, 243
La Mina, 335
land fraud, 306
land hijacking, 370
larceny, 268–277
    amateur thieves, 269
    art theft, 272–273
    boat theft, 276–277
    distribution of crimes, 2007, *269*
    elements of, 268
    extent of, 268–269
    motor vehicle theft, 274–275
    professional thieves, 269–270
    shoplifting, 270–272
Latin America
    Yanomamö tribe, 107
    See also specific countries
Latin Kings, 121, 142
laundering money. *See* money laundering
Law, Order, and Power (Chambliss & Seidman), 186
laws
    antitrust legislation, 317
    breaking of, 15–16, 19
    child pornography, 354
    common law, 268
    conflict model of, 14
    consensus model of, 14
    environmental, 321–323
    global approach to breaking of, 18–19
    Hammurabi's Code, 14
    handgun control, 262–264
    making of, 11–14
    as mechanism of control, 183
    and rape, 237–238
    three-strikes laws, 172, 295
laws of imitation, 67
LEAP (learning, earning, and parenting) project, 123

Learnfare program, 171
learning
    aggression and violence, 90–94
    and attachment, 89
left realism, 190–191
legality requirement, 23, 25
legislation. *See* laws
Lehman Brothers, 296, 323
lesbian, gay, bisexual, and transgender (LGBT) community, 343
lettres de cachet, 54
Librium, 329
life course/developmental theory, 165–168, *166*
life-course perspective, 42–43, 44
Life of Mr. Jonathan Wild, the Great, The (Fielding), 293
lifestyle theories, of victimization, 202–203, 204
Life You Can Save, The: Acting Now to End World Poverty (Singer), 59
Lindbergh Act, 238
L.L.C., 9
locations for crime, 39
"lockdown" strategy, 118–119
Long Day's Journey into Night (O'Neill), 142
looting, 4
Lord of the Flies (Golding), 153
lower-class families
    and child abuse, 234
    and cultural deviance theory, 115
    focal concerns, and juvenile delinquency, 138–142, *139,* 152
    and middle-class measuring rod, 131
    and social disorganization theory, 118–119
    See also social class
LSD, 331
luck, focal concern, 138, 139

M

macrosociological studies, 171
Mafia
    organization chart for, *244*
    origin of term, 242
mail bombings, 290
mail-fraud statutes, 317
Major Fraud Act, 305–306
Malacca Straits, 369–370
malice aforethought, 220–221
Manchild in the Promised Land (Brown), 139
mandatory sentencing, 38

Mangano crime family, 244
Manhattan Bail Project
manie sans délire, 97
Mann Act, 345
manslaughter, 221–222
Mara Salvatrucha (MS-13),
    128–129, 142, 152
Marie Antoinette, 53
marijuana
    historical use of, 328
    regulation, 329, 330
    user lifestyle, 331
Marijuana Tax Act, 329
marine shipping industry, fraud
    in, 276
marital rape. *See* spousal abuse,
    rape
Marxist criminological theory
    class interests versus interest
        groups, 187
    collapse of economic order,
        187, 190
    evaluation of, 187, 190
    intellectual heritage of,
        184–185
    and rape, 237
massage-parlor prostitutes,
    344
Massalit ethnic group, 189
mass murder, 188, 225–228
McClellan Committee, 242
McDonald's, 106
McKinsey & Co., 324
"Measure of Social Control"
    (Hirschi), *156*
measuring crime, 26–31
Medellín cartel, 337
media
    and copycat crimes, 228
    and fear of crime, 19
*Medical Jurisprudence of Insanity,
    The* (Ray), 65
medieval penal practices, 53–55
Melissa virus, 292
mens rea, 24–25, 316
mental illness
    capital punishment and, 66
    continuum of, 97
    and crime, 97–99
    insane criminals, 62
    and insanity defense, 25, 68
    integrated theory, 99
    psychological causation,
        98–99
mentally retarded persons, and
    genocide, 188, 374
Mercury Finance, Inc., 297
mesomorphs, 63, 64
methadone maintenance
    programs, 337
methamphetamines, 334

Mexican drug cartels, 246–247
Mexican Mafia, 246–247
Michigan Militia Corps,
    255–256
microsociological studies, 171
middle-class gangs, 133, 136,
    146–149
    delinquent gangs, 147
    explanations for, 148–149
    hate gangs, 147–148
    satanic gangs, 148
middle-class measuring rod,
    131, 133, 140, 152
militias, 254–255
Miller v. California, 351, 352
minimal brain dysfunction
    (MBD), 83
Minneapolis Domestic Violence
    Experiment, 233
Minnesota Multiphasic
    Personality Inventory
    (MMPI), 95
Minuteman Project, *255*
misdemeanors, 25, 26
mistake of fact defense, 25
MOBY (Mobilization for Youth),
    149
modeling instigators, 94
Model Penal Code
    and meaning of
        "pornography," 345, 351
    and robbery, 238
    and sexual morality offenses,
        342, 343
    typology of crimes, 26
money laundering, 297
    and cyberspace, 7
    and drug economy,
        335–336
    infiltration of legal
        businesses, 6–7
    operational principles
        diagram, *368*
    and terrorism, 5–6
    as transnational crime, 367
monozygotic (MZ) twins, 76
"Monster of the Andes," 226
moral anomalies, 62–63
moral development, 87–89
moral entrepreneurs, 177
moral insanity, 65, 97
morality offenses. *See* sexual
    morality offenses
Moral Reconation Therapy, 89
Morgan Stanley, 298, 313
morphine, 328
mortgage fraud, 278–279
Mothers Against Drunk Driving
    (MADD), 342
Motion Picture Association of
    America, 368

motorcycle gangs, 116
motor vehicle theft, 274–275,
    277
    and insurance fraud, 275
    juvenile arrest rates for, *274*
    in Pakistan, 212
    prevention of, 212, 275
    and professional thieves, 269
    times of, 39
    top ten auto-theft cities, *213,
        274*
    top ten most stolen autos, *213*
    transnational, 371
    typologies of thieves, *214*
Motor Vehicle Theft Prevention
    Act of 1994, 275
MOVE group, 123, 124–125
M/S Nautica, 276
multiple personality defense, 98
multiple victimization theory,
    203–204
murder, 220–221
    assassination, 221
    felony murder, 221
    first degree, 221
    and malice aforethought,
        220–221
    second degree, 221
    serial and mass murders,
        73–74, 225–228
    spikes in rates, 40–41
    victims, 223
Muslims, and racial profiling,
    178–179
Mustang Ranch, 345
Myanmar, *336*, 349
    messianic guerrilla leaders,
        358

N

narco-terrorists, 246
Narcotics Anonymous (NA), 337
National Academy of Science
    (NAS), 77
National Advisory Commission
    on Civil Disorders, 49
National Association of
    Insurance Commissioners,
    283
National Automobile Theft
    Bureau, 282
National Center for Missing and
    Exploited Children, 356
National Center for the
    Prevention and Control of
    Rape (NCPCR), 235
National Commission
    on Obscenity and
    Pornography, 349, 350
National Council against Health
    Fraud, 80

National Crime Victimization Survey (NCVS), 32, 34–35
and assaults, 231
comparison of reported crimes on firearm incidents
comparison to Uniform Crime Reports (UCR), 36
and domestic assault, 232–233
National Deviancy Conference (NDC), 186
National Environmental Policy Act (NEPA), 319
National Football League (NFL), 162
National Gang Threat Assessment, 129
National Incident-Based Reporting System (NIBRS), 31, 34
National Instant Criminal Background Check System, 264
National Institute of Justice (NIJ)
and juvenile gun ownership, 261
and partner violence, 232
National Insurance Crime Bureau (NICB), 283
National Rifle Association (NRA), 259, 262, 263, 264
National School Safety Center, 257
National Sheriffs' Association, 34
National Stolen Art File, 272
National Survey of Crime Severity, 40
National Survey on Drug Use and Health (NSDUH), 331
National Television Violence Study, 91
natural crimes, 63
natural urban areas, 117, 118
Nazis, 62, 185
neglect, child, 234
negligence, of corporations, 318
negligent homicide, 222
Neighborhood Anticrime Self-Help programs, 149
neighborhoods
neighborhood-based organizations, 171
social disorganization and personal control, 161
Neighborhood Watch groups, 38
Nepal, 169
Net Nanny, 352
neurocriminology, 68, 81–83
EEG abnormalities, 83
minimal brain dysfunction, 83
See also brain

neuroticism, 96
"New Bio-Psycho-Social Horizons: Victimology" (Mendelsohn), 202
new-company scam, 303
New Criminology, The (Taylor Walton & Young), 186
New York Central & Hudson River Railroad v. United States, 309, 315
New York City firefighters, and September 11, 249
New York Stock Exchange, 194
New York University Criminal Law Education and Research Center, 362
Nigerian gangs, 150–151
nonconformist communities, 116
noneconomic functions, devaluation of, 111
nonparticipant observation, 27, 30
North Korean Communist Party, 153
nuclear material, transfer of, 369

O

observational learning, 90–93
obstruction of justice, 297
occupational crimes, 301
Ocean Mafia, 276
oceans
crime on, 276, 366
pollution of, 9–10
offense specialization, 163
Office of Juvenile Justice and Delinquency Prevention (OJJDP)
Comprehensive Gang Model, 149
Study Group on Serious and Violent Juvenile Offenders, 77
Office of National Drug Control Policy, 331
oil spill disasters, 9–10
Oklahoma City bombings, 256
old-company scam, 303
Omega Boys Club, 157
On Crimes and Punishment (Dei delitti e delle pene) (Beccaria), 55–57, 65
online pornography, 288–290
ontogeny and attachment, 89
Operation Atalanta, 276
Operation Enduring Freedom, 249
Operation Weed and Seed, 120–121

opium
historical use of, 328
production, 5
opportunity
and crime, 15, 196
opportunistic robbers, 239
organizational due diligence, 313
organization and attachment, 89
organized crime, 240–248
in Chicago, 104
and economic globalization, 359
as geopolitical crime, 247
history of, 241–242
in Mexico, 246–247
new ethnic diversity in, 245, 248
and Prohibition, 104, 340
structure and impact of, 242–245
"the Commission," 243
See also Mafia
Organized Crime Control Act of 1970, 243
Origin of Species (Darwin), 59
outer containment, 161, 163, 164
outlaw motorcycle gangs (OMGs), 130, 245
outlaws, 55
Outlaws, the, 245
outsiders, 175
oversocialization, and shoplifting, 212
overutilization, 284

P

Pagans, the, 245
Pakistan
addiction issues in, 337
automobile theft in, 212
Panama, political impact of drug trade, 336
panel studies, 28
parental control, 164
Parents Anonymous, 234
Parents Television Council, 91–93
parking facilities, situational crime prevention, 213
parricide, 92–93
Parrot Middle School program, 157
participant observation, 27, 30
password sniffers, 291
PATHE (Positive Action Through Holistic Education), 171
peacemaking criminology, 191–192

peers. *See* gangs
peine forte et dure, 54
penalties. *See* fines and penalties
penologists, 186
Pentagon, attack on. *See*
    September 11th attacks
Pentagon, "Total Information
    Awareness," 265–266
People's Temple cult, 125
perception of crime, 210
Pereira, Colombia, mass
    murder, 226
Perry Preschool Project, 114, 123
personal control. *See* self-control
personality
    and criminality, 95–97
    Eysenck's conditioning
        theory, 96–97
    Freud's theory of, 68
personal thefts, times of, 39
persons, trafficking in. *See*
    human trafficking
Peru
    addiction problems, 336
    cocaine and marijuana from,
        245
    crime rates, 169
phrenology, 60, 64
physiognomy, 60
pickpocketing, 269
Pico Rivera Gang, *146*
pimps, 344
Ping-Ponging health insurance
    fraud, 284
pink sheets, 303
piracy. *See* sea piracy
Pleas of the Crown (Hale), 237
police
    late nineteenth-century, 187
    private police, 187
    racial profiling, 50–51
police statistics, 32–34
*Polish Peasant in Europe and
    America, The* (Thomas &
    Znaniecki), 116
political fraud, 308
politics
    and crime, 34–35
    and drug trafficking, 336–337
pollution. *See* environmental
    crime
Ponce Plaza project, 121
pooper-scooper requirement, 24
Pope v. Illinois, 352
Popular Revolutionary Army,
    247
population for surveys, 27
pornography
    definition problem, 345, 347,
        348
    feminist view of, 351

industry revenue statistics,
    290
online, *288, 289, 290,* 348–350
and rape, 237
Supreme Court rulings on,
    351–352
and violence, 349–351
worldwide revenues from,
    289
See also child pornography
positivist criminology, 1, 53,
    58–59, 60–64, 68, 105
positron emission tomography
    (PET) imaging, 81, 83
postconventional morality, 87, 88
postpartum psychosis/
    depression, 81
Potrero Hill Posse (PHP), 145
poverty
    children living in, *138*
    concentrated poverty, 140, *141*
    culture of, 106
    and violence, 110
power, 187
    corporate, *310–311*
preconventional morality, 87, 88
predatory rape, 236
pre-menstrual syndrome (PMS)
    defense, 81, 98
premium diversion/
    unauthorized entities, 283
preschool programs
    Head Start program, 113–114,
        123
    Perry Preschool Project, 114
Presidential Commission on
    Drunk Driving, 342
President's Commission on
    Law Enforcement and the
    Administration of Justice,
    *The Challenge of Crime in a
    Free Society,* 17
President's Commission on
    Organized Crime, 242
President's Commission on the
    Causes and Prevention of
    Violence, 137
President's Corporate Fraud
    Task Force, 321
prevention of crime, 38
    Boston violence-prevention
        programs, *170,* 171
    Brady Center to Prevent Gun
        Violence, 262–263
    child pornography, 351
    corporate crime, 366–367
    Disney World, 210–212
    family-based crime
        prevention, *91*
    motor vehicle theft, 212, 275
    school violence, 209, 259

and strain theory, 113–115
    See also situational crime
        prevention
primary conflicts, 126
primary data, 27
primary deviations, 175
Principles of Criminology
    (Sutherland), 121
prison culture, migration of to
    communities, 40
prison gangs, 129
prison reform movements, 187
private police, 187
prize promotions, 307
proactive corporate fault (PCF),
    316
procurement fraud, 305
Professional Fence (Klockars), 293
professional robber, 239
Professional Thief, The
    (Sutherland), 30
Prohibition, 104, 340
Project Exile, 262
Project Follow Through, 113
Project Freedom, 151
property crimes, 26
    comparative crime rates,
        294–295
    and fraud, 277, 279
property flipping, 278
Proposition 8, California, 343
proprietary economic
    information, 286–287
prostitution, 183, 343–345
    pimps and johns, 344
    and radical feminist theory, 190
    sexual slavery, *346–347,*
        356–357
    Uniform Crime Reports
        (UCR) reports, *344*
psychoanalytic theory, of
    criminology, 86–87
psychological causation, 98–99
psychological determinism
    chronology of, *69*
    pioneers in criminal
        psychology, 65
    psychological studies of
        criminals, 65
psychological development,
    86–87
psychology and criminality,
    86–97
    learning aggression and
        violence, 90–94
    maternal deprivation and
        attachment theory, 89–90
    moral development, 87–89
    personality, 95–97
    psychological development,
        86–87

psychosis, 97
psychoticism, 96
public housing, and defensible space, 207
public punishment, 53, 54
Puerto Rico, Ponce Plaza project, 121
Punishment and the Social Structure (Rusche & Kirchheimer), 186
punishment requirement, 25
punishments, public, 53, 54
pyknic physique, 63
pyromaniacs, 294

Q

Qwest Communications, 297

R

race
    and biocriminology, 83
    and crime, 49–50, 110
    and juvenile crime, 49
    racial profiling, 50–51
    See also hate crimes
racial profiling, 50–51
Racketeer Influenced and Corrupt Organizations (RICO) Act, 243, 317
racketeering
    and organized crime, 243
    and white-collar criminals, 297
radical feminist theory, 190
radical idealists, 190
radical theory, 15, 111, 184–192
    abolitionist and anarchist criminology, 191
    emerging explanations, 190–192
    Engels and Marx, 185, 186
    evaluation of Marxist criminology, 187, 190
    Georg Rusche and Otto Kirchheimer, 185–186
    intellectual heritage of Marxist criminology, 184–185
    left realism, 190–191
    peacemaking criminology, 191–192
    radical feminist theory, 190
    and rape, 237
    since the 1970s, 186–187
    and white-collar crime, 319
    Willem Adriaan Bonger, 185
Raëlians, 124
Rahwau maximum-security prison, New Jersey, Scared Straight Program, 21–22
"railway killer," 226

randomized controlled trials (RCT), 28–29, 68
random samples, 27
rape
    characteristics of event, 236
    community response, 238
    defined, 235
    difficulties of prosecution, 237
    as genocide, 188–189, 372
    and guilt, 187
    homosexual, 238
    and legal system, 237–238
    legislative changes, 237–238
    myths, 351
    psychological factors, 236–237
    sociocultural factors, 237
    spousal, 231
    and women's absolute status, 190
rape shield laws, 238
rap houses, 337
rational-choice perspective, 15, 17, 197–198, 204
    and guilt or shame, 210
    and offender's perception of crime opportunity, 210
    and utilitarianism, 197
    and victimization theory, 204
reaction formation, 131, 133
reactive corporate fault (RCF), 316
Reasoning and Rehabilitation, 89
rebellion, adaptation by, 106
receiving stolen property. *See* fencing
Recording Industry Association of America, 368
recovery room schemes, 307
red hair, 60
relative and acquaintance homicides, *224–225*
reloading schemes, 307
Remove Intoxicated Drivers (RID), 342
repeat burglary, 204
repeat victimization, 203–204, 216
research
    case studies, 27, 30
    crime and place research, 204
    cross-sectional studies, 28
    empirical research, 11
    ethics, 31
    experimental studies, 27, 28–30, 31, 68
    panel studies, 28
    population for surveys, 27
    samples, 27
    self-report surveys, 35–37
    studies using available data, 31

See also comparative criminological research
residential therapeutic communities, 337
responsibility, and containment theory, 161, 164, 171
restorative justice model, 191
retail price-fixing, 319
retreatism, 106
retreatist gangs, 134
revolution, 185
Revolutionary Armed Forces of Colombia (FARC), 247
Richmond Youth Study, 110
ritualism, adaptation by, 106, 108
robber barons, 241
robbery, 238–240
    carjacking, 275
    characteristics of robbers, 239–240
    college campus crime, 201
    consequences of, 240
    and hot products, 201
    location, *239*
    and situational theories, 200–201
    types of weapons used, *239*
Robin Hood myth, 292
Robinson v. California, 23
Rochester Youth Development Study, 145–146, 158
Rohypnol, 236
Roman law, categorization of crime of the Twelve Tables, 14
Ronel, 335
Roper v. Simmons, 84
Ropex, 335
routine-activity approach, 15, 17, *198*, 203
    and "suitable target," 198, 206, 210
    and target-hardening techniques, 210
    and victimization theory, 204
rule of law, 56, 190
Russia
    Chechen terrorism, 368, *369*
    Chernobyl disaster, 319
    PC shipments to, 288
    Russian-Jewish Mafia, 245
    socioeconomic development, 363
    software piracy, 288
Rwandan genocide, 188
    international tribunal for, 372

S

Sacred Straight, 21–22, 28
safe havens, 126, 233
same-sex marriage, 343

samples, 27
sanctions. *See* sentencing and sanctions
Sandman Ladies, 144
Sarbanes-Oxley Act, 298–299, 323
satanic gangs, 148
Saudia Arabia, 169, 349
schizophrenia study, 177–178
School Crime and Safety report, 208
schools
    and delinquency, 131–132
    and middle-class measuring rod, 131, 133, 140, 152
school violence, 208–209, 256–259
    nonfatal crimes against students by location and year, *258*
    nonfatal crimes against students by type of crime and location, *208, 257*
    prevention, 209, 259
"scissors job" automobile theft, 274
sea piracy, 276, 366, 369–370
seasons, and crime, 39, 195, 200
Second Amendment
    and gun control, 264
    and militias, 255
secondary conflicts, 126
secondary data, 27, 31
secondary deviations, 175, 176, 177
secondary elaboration, 177
Second Chance Grace, 151
second degree murder, 221
Securities Act of 1933, 302
Securities and Exchange Commission (SEC), 34, 302
Securities Exchange Act of 1934, 302
securities fraud, 297
securities-related crimes, 302–303
self-abuse, elderly persons, 235
self-concept
    and labeling theory, 175
    social control and, 163, 164, 165, 171
self-control theory
    and containment theory, 163–164
    and failure of control mechanisms, 161
    and Hirschi-Gottfredson model, 169–170
    and policy, 170–171
    and social control, 161, 171
    and stake in conformity, 161

self-defense, parricide and, 92
self-help groups, 337
self-neglect, elderly persons, 235
self-regulation, 164
self-report surveys, 35–37
sentence enhancements
    statutes, 262
    three-strikes laws, 172, 295
sentencing and sanctions
    guidelines, 323
    inequalities, 184
    reform, 187
Sentencing Guidelines for Organizations, 313
September 11th attacks, 4, 8, 20, 226, 248–251, 368, 369
    and al-Qaeda, 6–7, 206–207, 251, 364–365, 368
    and ethnic profiling, 50, 178–179
    "Ground Zero," 249
    motives and intentions of terrorists, 364–365
serial and mass murders, 225–228
    female serial killers, 225
    serial killers, 73–74
serial rape, 236
severity of crime, 40
    public ranking of, *41*
sex chat rooms, 348
Sex Girls, 144
sex tours, 346
sexual assault. *See* child abuse; rape
sexual harassment, 352
sexual morality offenses, 26, 342–353
    deviant sexual intercourse, 343
    gap between behavior and law, 353
    prostitution, 343–345
    sodomy, 343
    statutory rape, 342
sexual predators, and civil commitment, 100
sexual slavery
    global, 356–357
    as transnational crime, *346–347*, 370
shanghaiing, 238
Sherman Antitrust Act, 299, 317
shoplifting, 199, 270–272
    apprehensions survey, *270*
    frequently shoplifted items, *202, 271*
    and oversocialization, 212
    by professional thieves, 269
Sicily, organized crime and, 241
Sierra Leone, 189

"Silent Scorpion," 275
similar-name scam, 303
simple assault, 231
Singapore, 349
single-room-occupancy (SRO) units, 191
Sinolas cartel, 247
Sirius Star, 276
situational crime prevention (SCP), 207–216, 210–212
    auto theft, 212
    convenience stores, 212–213
    parking facilities, 213
    phantom crime prevention at Disney World, 210–212
    pros and cons, 213–214
    in schools, 208
    sixteen techniques of, *210*
    target-hardening techniques, 209, 210
situational theories, 196–201
    environmental criminology, 196, 204, 216
    interrelatedness of, 204–205
    and policy, 215
    practical applications of, 199–200
    rational-choice perspective, 197–198, 204, 216
    routine-activity approach, 198–199, 204, 216
Sixth Amendment and juveniles and Miranda warnings
skinheads, 147–148
    internationally induced local crime, 365–366
slave trade, 370
sleepwalking defense, 98
Slumdog Millionaire, 102–103
smartness, focal concern, 138, 139
smoking, social control and, 154–155
smuggling. *See* drug trafficking
social bonds, 155–157, 171
    attachment, 155–156
    belief, 157
    commitment, 156–157
    involvement, 157
social class
    and conflict, 105
    and crime, 48–49, 109–110
    and income disparities, 106
    and intelligence, 78–79
    and interest groups, 187
    and juvenile crime, 49, 131
    and strain theory, 112, 115
    See also lower-class families; middle-class gangs; middle-class measuring rod; social disorganization theory

social contract, 56
social control, 54, 126
   and attachment, 155–156,
     157–158, 163, 171
   defined, 154–155
   defying, 162
   and Stone Age crime, 54
   See also social control theories
social control theories, 118,
    154–155
   developmental/life course
    theory, 165–168
   and drift, 160–161
   evaluation of theory, 158–160
   general theories, 169–170
   Hirschi-Gottfredson self-
    control model, *169–170*
   macrosociological studies,
    155
   microsociological studies,
    Hirschi, 155–160
   and personal control, 161
   in relation to risk factors for
    gang membership, *159–160*
   and social bonds, 155–157
   test of theory, 157–158
   theoretical explorations,
    165–171
social definition, 175
social disorder, 204
social disorganization, 126
   behavioral effects, 119
   economic effects, 119
   and high incarceration rates,
    119
   psychological and social
    effects, 118–119
social disorganization theory,
    115, *117*, 130
   evaluation of, 119–120
   Park and Burgess model, 117,
    118
   policy formulation and,
    120–121
   Shaw and McKay model,
    117–118
   tests of, 118–119
social ecologists, 118
social interactionists, 175
social learning theory
   differential reinforcement, 94
   direct experience, 93–94
   observational learning,
    90–93
social norms, 11
socioeconomic development
    perspective, 363
sociological determinism,
    65–68
   chronology of, *69*

sociological theories, of
    criminology, 53, 74
   cultural deviance theory, 104,
    115–118
   interconnectedness of, 104
   social control theory, 104,
    154–170
   strain theory, 104, 105–114
sociopaths, 97, 228
sodomy, 343
software
   piracy, 287–288, 368
   regulating children's access to
    Internet, 352
Software-Publishers
    Association, 287, 368
Solar Temple cult, 124, 125
Somalia, and piracy, 276, 370
somatotype school of
    criminology, 63–64
"Son of Sam," 226
Sons of Silence, 245
"Sourcebook of Criminal Justice
    Statistics," 17, 38
South America. *See* Latin
    America
South Bay Family gang, 146
Southeast Asian immigrant
    children, 126
Southern Poverty Law Center,
    255
   on hate crimes, 254
Soviet Union, collapse of
    Marxist economic order,
    187, 190
specificity of attachment, 89
sports. *See* athletics
spousal abuse, 232–234
   extent of, 232–233
   nature of, 233–234
   rape, 231, 236
square of crime, 191
St. Valentine's Day massacre, *242*
static explanations of
    criminality, 167
status crimes, 23
status deprivation, 131, 133
statutory rape, 342
steering, 284
sterilization, 63
sterilization laws, 64
stock market crash of 1929, 105,
    302
stocks and bonds
   manipulation, 303
   stock options, backdating,
    297, 320
stocks and pillories, 16
Stone Age crime, 54
S.T.O.P. program, 337

strain theory, 105–114, 126, 130,
    133, 154
   and crime prevention
    strategies, 113–115
   evaluation of Merton's theory,
    110–111
   general strain theory, 111–113
   institutional imbalance and
    crime, 111, 112
   and Merton's theory of
    anomie, 105–106
   modes of adaptation, 106–109
   race and crime, 110
   social class and crime,
    109–110
   and subcultural theory, 130
   tests of Merton's theory,
    109–110
stranger homicides, 224
stranger rape, 236
streetwalkers, 344
strict liability, 25
strip and run automobile theft,
    274
structural-functionalist
    perspective, 105
student protest movement, 176
Students Against Drunk Drivers
    (SADD), 342
subcultural theories of
    delinquency and crime, 15
   Cohen's theory of, 131–133
   Cohen *vs.* Miller, 140–141
   and middle-class measuring
    rod, 131, 140
   Miller's theory of lower-class
    focal concerns, 138–142
   and policy, 149–150
   subcultures of violence, 130,
    136–138, 234
subcultures
   of aggressiveness, 90
   and class differentials, 131
   defined, 130
   delinquent subcultures, 130,
    131
   of exasperation, 223
   value systems, 111
   of violence, 130, 136–138, 234
subprime mortgage lending
    crisis, 8–9, 297, 315, 320
successful-business scam, 303
Sudan, genocide in, 189
sugar, criminality and, 79–80
Sugar Trust, 317
suicide, and anomie, 105
"Sunset Strip killer," 226
superego, 86
Supreme Court, rulings on
    pornography, 351–352

surveys, 27–28
Denver Youth Survey, 135
Hayes International Retail Theft Survey, 270
International Crime Victim Survey (ICVS), *44*
National Crime Victimization Survey (NCVS), 32, 34–35, 36, 231, 232–233
National Survey of Crime Severity, 40
National Survey on Drug Use and Health (NSDUH), 331
self-report surveys, 35–37
Survey of Crime Trends and Operations of Criminal Justice Systems, 361, 371
victimization surveys, 34–35
World Crime Survey, 168, 228
S.W.E.A.T. Team program, 171
Sweden, 341
Switzerland, 169, 264
synnomie, 169

T

Tacoma Skinhead Movement, 147
tactical displacement, 215
Taiwan, 349
Taj Mahal Palace & Tower, Mumbai, 12–13, 251
Taliban, 5, 8
Tallahassee Convenience Store Study, 212
target hardening techniques, 209, 210
and credit card fraud, 282
and motor vehicle theft, 275
Task Force on Firearms, 259
Task Force on Organized Crime, 242, 243
Tata Group, 13
Tatari Design, 6
Tatex Trading GmbH, 6
Tattooed Men, 245
tax fraud, 297, 308
and Internal Revenue Code, 317
technology. *See* high-tech crimes
Telecommunications Decency Act of 1996, 352
telefunding schemes, 307
telemarketing fraud, 306
common scams, *307*
television
and intoxication defense, 98
observational learning and, 90–91
temporal displacement, 215
terrorism, 248–254

and arms trafficking, 7
blood-feud, 251
Chechen, 368, *369*
and computer crime, 7
counterterrorism measures, 178–179, 246
criminal justice system and
and cultural property destruction, 8
defined, 4–5, 251
extent of, 251–*252*
FBI list of most wanted terrorists, *250*, 251
Foreign Terrorist Organizations (FTOs), *252*
and Human Rights Watch, 150
and illicit drug trafficking, 5
and infiltration of legal business, 6–7
international efforts against, 251, 253–254
and London transportation system, 251
and money laundering, 5–6
motives and intentions of organizations, 364–365
narco-terrorists, 246
new crimes related to, 4
persons, trafficking in, 7–8
and public policy, 216
seven-spoke wheel of, *5–8*
Taj Mahal Palace & Tower, Mumbai, 12–13, 251
terrorist training camps, 251
as transnational crime, 367–368
U.S. embassy bombings, 251
USS *Cole,* attack on, 251
war against, 5, 246
See also Al Qaeda; September 11th attacks
testosterone, 81
Thailand, child sex tourism, 357
theft. *See* larceny
theory, 26
therapeutic communities, 337
"There's a Lot of Us Folks Grateful to the Lone Ranger" (Quinney), 186
Thomas Crowne Affair, 200
three-strikes laws, 172, 295
thrill-seekers, *214*
Thurman v. Torrington, 233
time of day, and crime, 39
Tiny Diablas, 145
tobacco. *See* smoking
torts, 25
torture, in medieval Europe, 54

"Total Information Awareness," 265–266
toughness, focal concern, 138, 139
trade secrets, sale of, 308
tranquilizers, 329
transnational crime, 366–372
aircraft hijacking, 369
arms trafficking, 369
art theft, 368
corruption and bribery of public officials, 371
cultural objects, theft of, 368
fraudulent bankruptcy, 371
growth in, 18
human body parts, trade in, 370–371
human trafficking, 370
illicit drug trafficking, 371
infiltration of legal business, 371
insurance fraud, 370
intellectual property, theft of, 368
land hijacking, 370
money laundering, 367
organized crime group offenses, 371
sea piracy, 369–370
sexual slavery, *346–347*, 370
terrorist activities, 367–368
Transparency International (TI), 180
Transparency International (TI), 8, 371
transplant, trade in body parts for, 370–371
travel-related schemes, 307
treason, 14
Treasury Department statistics, 31
trends in crime, 37–38
trouble, focal concern, 138–139
tryptophan deficiencies, 80
Tutsis, 188
Twenty-Sixth Amendment, 342
Twinkie defense, 80, 98
twin studies, 76, 100
Tyco scandal, 8
typologies
of crime, 26
of thieves, *214*

U

Uganda, 189
Unbreakable Autolock, 275
underclass, 186
UNESCO, Trafficking Statistics Project, 346

UNICEF, on global sexual slavery, 356–357
Uniform Controlled Substances Act, 330
Uniform Crime Reports (UCR), 361
  comparison to National Crime Victimization Survey, *36*
  counting crime in, *33*
  crime rates, 32–33
  crime trends, 37–38
  forcible rapes, 236
  hate crimes, 254
  Index crimes, 37, *38, 39*
  limitations of, 33–34
  motor vehicle theft, 274
  number of offenses cleared by arrest, 33
  omissions, 34
  Part II offenses, 32, 35
  Part I offenses, 32, 34
  prostitution, 344
  use of data in research, 31, 32
Union Carbide plant, Bhopal, *322*
United Nations
  and international terrorism, 251
  organizations and affiliates for solving worldwide crime, *360*
  Security Council, 189
  Survey of Crime Trends and Operations of Criminal Justice Systems, 361, 371
United States Coast Guard law enforcement team, 277
United States Postal Service, workplace homicides, 228
United States Sentencing Commission, 309, 313
United States Sentencing Guidelines for Organizational Defendants, *315*
United States v. Darling, 319
University of Chicago sociology program, 104
Unraveling Juvenile Delinquency (Glueck & Glueck), 363
untermenschen, 374
upgrading health insurance fraud, 284
uranium, 369
U.S.-Iraq war, 7
U.S.A. PATRIOT Act
utilitarianism, 57
  abuses of, 58–59
  and rational-choice perspective, 197

V
valet automobile theft, 275
Valium, 329
value systems, of subcultures, 111
variables, 28
viatical settlement fraud, 283
vicarious liability, 316
Vice Lords, 142
victimization surveys, 34–35
victimless crimes, 183
victimology, 202
victims and victimization
  and geography of crime, 204
  and hot spots of crime, 204, 216
  lifestyle theories, 202–203, 204
  offender-victim interaction, 203
  rape victims, 237
  repeat victimization, 203–204
  theories of, 201–206, 216
  victim precipitation, 203
video piracy, 272
Vietnam War, 176
Villa Baviera, 124
violations, 25, 26
violence
  and alcohol, 340–341
  Boston violence-prevention programs, *170, 171*
  and cholesterol, 75
  and conflict gangs, 134
  criminal, defined, 220
  and genetics, 77–78
  and gun control, 259–265
  juvenile crime, *39,* 77
  learning, 90–94
  subculture of, 136, 137, 234
  See also family violence; school violence; terrorism; violent crime
violent crime, 26
  common locations for, 39
  defined, 220
  by state, *222*
  times of, 39
  violent crime Index arrests by age, *45*
Violent Juvenile Offender Research and Development programs, 149
vitamin deficiencies, 80
Volstead Act, 340
voluntary manslaughter, 222

W
Wal-Mart, 311
war against terrorism, 5, 246
war crimes tribunals, 189, 372
war on drugs, 5

Washington D.C. snipers, 223
weapons
  arms trafficking, 7, 369
  See also firearms; gun control
Web Watcher, 352
Wedtech Corporation, 304–305
whistleblowers, in Enron scandal, 324
white-collar crime, 298–308
  bankruptcy fraud, 303–304
  bribery, 308
  churning, 302
  consumer fraud, *306*
  corruption, 308
  defined, 299
  future of, 323–325
  against the government, 304–306
  individuals committing, 299, 301
  insider-related fraud, 308
  insider trading, 302
  insurance fraud, 282–284, 306, 308
  NIBRS classifications of, *300*
  occupational crimes, 301
  political fraud, 308
  prosecutions over last five years, *302*
  securities-related crimes, 302–303
  stock options backdating, 297
  tax fraud, 297, 308
  types of, 301–308
  victims of, *301*
  See also corporate crime
White Collar Crime (Sutherland), 318
white slave trade, 370
White Slave Traffic Act, 345
white supremacy, 255
wife beating. *See* spousal abuse
wilderness camps, 165
Witness for Peace, 191
women. *See* feminist view; gender
Women's Christian Temperance Union, 340
Woodstock Music and Art Fair, *334*
Wood Street Commons project, 191
Workers Compensation Fraud, 283–284
workplace homicide, 226, *227,* 228
"Work" (Wilson), 223
World Bank, 181
WorldCom scandal, 8, 323

World Congress Against Sexual Exploitation of Children and Adolescents, 351
world crime rates, 168–169
World Crime Survey, 168, 228
World Health Organization (WHO) homicide statistics, 361
World Ministerial Conference on Organized Crime
World Trade Center attacks. *See* September 11th attacks

World Trade Organization, protests against, 173

X

XYY syndrome defense, 75–76, 98, 100

Y

Yamaguchi-Gumi family, 245, 248
Yanomami tribe, 107
Young Turks, 188, 374

youth, and guns, 143–144, 259, 261
Youth Crime Gun Interdiction Initiative, 261
Yugoslavia, international tribunal for, 372
yuppie gangs, 147

Z

Zaghawa ethnic group, 189
Zapatista National Liberation Army, 247
Zodiac Killer, 225